DISCARD

HANDBOOK OF RESEARCH ON
SOCIAL STUDIES TEACHING AND LEARNING

EDITOR
  James P. Shaver

EDITORIAL ADVISORY BOARD
Appointed by the National Council for the Social Studies
  Beverly J. Armento
  Catherine Cornbleth
  Jean Fair
  Thomas S. Popkewitz
  Stephen J. Thornton
  William W. Wilen

HANDBOOK OF RESEARCH ON SOCIAL STUDIES TEACHING AND LEARNING

A Project of the National Council for the Social Studies

James P. Shaver

EDITOR

MACMILLAN PUBLISHING COMPANY
New York

Collier Macmillan Canada
Toronto

Maxwell Macmillan International
New York   Oxford   Singapore   Sydney

Copyright © 1991 by National Council for the Social Studies

Macmillan Publishing Company
866 Third Avenue, New York, N.Y. 10022

Collier Macmillan Canada, Inc.
1200 Eglinton Avenue East, Suite 200
Don Mills, Ontario, M3C 3N1

Library of Congress Catalog Card Number: 90-38751

Printed in the United States of America

printing number
1 2 3 4 5 6 7 8 9 10

Library of Congress Cataloging-in-Publication Data

Handbook of research on social studies teaching and learning / James
    P. Shaver, editor.
        p.   cm.
    "A project of the National Council for the Social Studies."
    Includes bibliographical references and index.
    ISBN 0-02-895790-3
    1. Social sciences—Study and teaching—United States.
I. Shaver, James P. II. National Council for the Social Studies.
LB1584.H275   1991
300'.7'073—dc20   90-38751
                                        CIP

CONTENTS

Section II

THE STUDENT IN SOCIAL STUDIES EDUCATION   107

Section III

TEACHERS IN SOCIAL STUDIES EDUCATION   183

Section IV

CONTEXTS OF SOCIAL STUDIES EDUCATION   263

Section
V

TEACHING FOR AND LEARNING SOCIAL STUDIES OUTCOMES   343

Section
VI

COMPONENTS OF INSTRUCTION   481

Section
VII

INTERRELATIONS BETWEEN SOCIAL STUDIES AND OTHER CURRICULUM AREAS 549

Section
VIII

INTERNATIONAL PERSPECTIVES ON RESEARCH ON SOCIAL STUDIES 589

PREFACE

As the first research handbook on social studies education, this volume has presented a unique opportunity to provide a comprehensive view and analysis of research in the field. The synthesis of past research and the identification of needed future efforts were, as might be expected, major goals for the *Handbook*. A third goal, stemming from the recurrent criticisms of the quality and contributions of research on social studies education, was to raise issues of epistemology and methodology for the consideration of those interested in increasing the fruitfulness of future research efforts. The chapters in the first section of the *Handbook* are directed specifically at such issues and the authors of the other chapters were asked to discuss approaches to research as deemed appropriate to advancing research on their topic.

ternal to formal instruction could not be ignored. Nevertheless, it was necessary to delineate some boundaries, for the *Handbook* could not be about life in general.

The common conception of *social studies* as having to do with curriculum and instruction in the school setting was adopted as the focus for the *Handbook*, with other factors in learning treated from that perspective. Authors were asked to keep in mind that social studies is often defined with citizenship education as a central aim. Nevertheless, the purpose was not to substitute "citizenship" in the chapters for "social studies" in the *Handbook* title, and the authors have varied in their orientations. Authors were also encouraged to include research not done specifically on social studies if pertinent to their topic.

AUDIENCE

The *Handbook* was produced first of all for practicing and prospective researchers. It is intended to be used by people in a variety of roles—including university professors and graduate students and persons in local, state, regional, and national agencies that conduct and support research—as they seek to identify research problems and plan investigations on social studies education. The *Handbook* could be a basic reference in seminars for the graduate students who do a good share of the research on social studies.

Although translating research findings into recommendations for practice was not the primary concern, a secondary audience was in mind: curriculum developers, instructional leaders, and school policy-makers interested in using research information in addressing their questions and tasks. Teachers, too, will find much of value in the *Handbook*. As important as they are to the scheme of education, however, *Handbook* authors were not asked to aim their chapters directly at teachers' immediate classroom interests.

SCOPE

The title for the *Handbook,* which was developed by the NCSS Publications Committee, is rather long. It does, however, signify an important dual, complementary emphasis: on teaching *and* learning. From that orientation, the role of factors ex-

STRUCTURE

The structure of the *Handbook* flowed from the purposes and scope laid out above. The first set of chapters reflects the primary concern with research quality and productiveness. Rejecting any notion of research orthodoxy and seeking to encourage reflection about the conduct of research, authors were invited to write about historiography and critical theory, philosophy and theory development, qualitative and quantitative approaches to research, the quantitative reviewing of research literature, and program evaluation. They were asked to make connections to research on social studies, while not ignoring foundational work in other fields.

A major consideration in planning the *Handbook* was the conception of the elements of teaching and learning that should guide the selection and organization of the chapters that constitute the bulk of the volume—those on social studies as a curricular area. Six ingredients were identified, each serving as an organizing rubric for a group of chapters:

- Two immediately obvious components of social studies education are *students* and *teachers,* and a section is devoted to each. Conceptions of teaching as well as of teachers themselves were of concern, as was the diversity in students at different grade levels and in the same classroom. (Some readers will be struck by the lack of a chapter on gender and social studies. Authors were encouraged to treat gender issues as pertinent to their topics, and many did.)

- Adequate understanding of social studies education depends on attention to *context,* the setting factors that affect what happens in classrooms as well as directly influence the outcomes sought by social studies educators. Chapter topics ranging from the home to the school to the mass media are intended to deflect researchers from their tendency to focus exclusively on the classroom.

- Instructional *outcomes* are an essential aspect of an curricular area, and how to achieve them raises important research questions. Social studies educators address outcomes in a variety of ways: from the perspective of citizenship education (e.g., political participation, multicultural understanding), from the point of view of educational psychology (e.g., concept development), and in terms of content (e.g., history, geography, economics). The titles of the chapters in the section on outcomes reflect these varying perspectives.

- The means used to effect learning by students—i.e., the *components of instruction*—are another crucial element in social studies education. Classroom discourse, textbooks, and technology are among the topics treated in this set of chapters.

- Often overlooked in conceptions of social studies, and yet a potentially fruitful area for research, are the *interrelations between social studies and other curriculum areas*—art, science, reading, and writing. Chapters are included on each.

Finally, with social studies educators from the United States and other countries increasingly interacting with one another on professional issues, a section on *international perspectives on social studies* was deemed important. A chapter on cross-national research is accompanied by chapters on research in Eastern Europe, England, and Africa. Unfortunately, a chapter on Asia was not completed in time to be included.

THE DEVELOPMENT OF THE HANDBOOK

From my perspective as editor, the development of the *Handbook* began with a phone call from David Naylor, Chairman of the NCSS Publications Committee, on September 15, 1987. He invited me to serve as handbook editor and we talked at some length about the importance and possible nature of the volume. I also talked with Fran Haley, Executive Director of NCSS, and within a couple of days decided to take on the challenge.

An Editorial Advisory Board had been nominated by the Publications Committee for my review and approval. When contacted, those able to serve were Beverly Armento, Catherine Cornbleth, Jean Fair, Thomas Popkewitz, Stephen Thornton, and, as a representative of the Publications Committee, William Wilen. We met in Washington, D.C., in January of 1988, for an evening and a day to formulate a plan for the *Handbook* and develop a list of potential authors. Prior to the meeting, I prepared and shared with the Editorial Advisory Board a memo outlining much of the perspective and many of the ideas for structure and content sketched out above, including a proposed Table of Contents (with brief sketches of possible content for each chapter) and a list of potential authors. During a frank and productive exchange, modifications were suggested. I returned

to Utah State University to do some rewriting, to which the Board reacted by mail and telephone.

I then began the task of contacting potential authors by telephone and letter. Also, the Editorial Advisory Board had concurred with me that I should try to obtain two reviewers to critique each chapter, and I began to identify and contact those important individuals.

Editorial Aims

My perspective as editor of the *Handbook* included some goals for the actual writing of chapters, which I wanted to serve as models of research writing for doctoral students and other reporters of research. I sought clear, direct writing, both to be sure authors were clear about what they were saying and to aid readers in discerning their intent. My assumption was that if I had difficulty understanding a manuscript, others would too. I put my editor's pencil to obtuse words and phrases and to complex, obscure sentences, and sometimes pushed authors to make their conceptual structure clearer. I went after reifications and anthropomorphisms with zeal, because I believe they obscure thinking and diffuse responsibility. (If "the study reported" or "the analysis found," where is the responsible human?) Some remain because I missed them, because they were used metaphorically, or because the authors insisted they were a common form of expression in their area of research.

I also urged authors not to rely exclusively on statistical significance as the indicator of the magnitude and importance of research findings. I advocated the use of effect sizes—metrics of magnitude of result not dependent on sample size or scale of measurement. That this suggestion was foreign to many authors and that those who tried could find few effect sizes reported in the literature is apt commentary on the continued dominance of inferential statistics in the training and thinking of educational researchers.

In most cases, I did not edit for redundancy between chapters. To do so would have left gaps in some chapters. Moreover, the differing perspectives from which authors dealt with the same material minimized conceptual redundancy. In any event, readers cannot assume that all that is said about a topic is in the chapter by that title; concept development, for example, is also treated in the chapters on teaching geography and on reading, as well as in others.

ACKNOWLEDGMENTS

I am not a timid editor and my intensive involvement in the manuscripts undoubtedly surprised and even shocked some authors. All recognized, I think, that my intent was to help them develop the best possible piece of work; certainly, that is the way that all responded. I was heartened by their reactions. The authors are, of course, the sine qua non of such a venture, and the first and most abundant thanks must go to them.

Although to those uninitiated as editors it may sound like a trifling matter, I especially appreciate those authors who were prompt about deadlines. In an endeavor of this scale, having to follow-up with authors to obtain overdue manuscripts can (and did) consume inordinate amounts of time and energy and be very frustrating. Such matters rarely get mentioned, but to that approximately 60% who got their outline, first draft, and final manuscript to me within a month of each deadline, hearty and heartfelt thanks!

I obtained at least one reviewer for each chapter. Each was asked to critique a preliminary chapter outline prepared by the author(s) and an initial draft of the manuscript. Most reviewers completed their tasks, and the reviews were often comprehensive and insightful. Reviewers are acknowledged at the beginning of each chapter. Here, I want to give them a collective "thank you."

Although I had not intended to ask anyone to be both an author and a reviewer or to be a reviewer for more than one chapter, I did so in a few cases. I especially appreciated the responses of Catherine Cornbleth, Jean Fair, Richard Knight, and Stephen Thornton. In several cases, authors obtained their own reviewers. When identified to me, they, too, are recognized at the beginning of each chapter. Also, I appreciate the efforts of Eugene Gillion and JoAnn Sweeney who reviewed the author's outline for the chapter on research in Asia that did not materialize and Jane Bernard-Powers and Gerald Ponder who did the same for a chapter on the history of teacher education.

The Editorial Advisory Board provided me with essential assistance in conceptualizing the *Handbook,* suggesting authors, reacting to manuscripts, and providing me with other advice when I requested it during the course of the project. It was, nevertheless, their moral support that I appreciated most.

Special thanks go to Oral L. Ballam, Dean of the College of Education at Utah State University, for his general support of scholarly activities and, specifically, for recognizing that I needed some slack in carrying out my role as Associate Dean if I was to find the time necessary for the *Handbook.* The College and the University were generous with other support, including secretarial assistance.

The task of organizing a system for keeping track of the many contacts with authors and reviewers and of handling the mass of initial correspondence fell on Kay McCuller, and she handled it with her usual skill and aplomb. Her ability to keep track of myriad details made my work manageable during the most demanding stages of the *Handbook.* Linda Hill stepped into the middle of the process and her assistance in completing the *Handbook* is also gratefully acknowledged. Ken Bell's willing, careful, and imaginative library detective work added much to the completeness and accuracy of citations in the volume.

The patient, seasoned, and good-humored counsel of Lloyd Chilton, Executive Editor at Macmillan, helped me to maintain perspective throughout the nearly three years during which the *Handbook* was the center of my professional life. Lori Stambaugh, of York Production Services, an exceptionally congenial and effective production coordinator, made our interchanges about editorial details a pleasure. Finally, my family understood the extraordinary demands of the *Handbook* and bore with the late evenings and lost weekends with considerable patience, or life could have been quite unbearable. I am grateful!

James P. Shaver
Logan, Utah

ABOUT THE CONTRIBUTORS

Susan A. Adler is Assistant Professor of Teacher Education and of Curriculum and Instruction at the University of Missouri, Kansas City. She is a member of the Board of Directors of the National Council for the Social Studies, served on the Executive Committee of the College and University Faculty Association of NCSS, and was a member of the Publication and Advisory Board of the Association of Teacher Educators. Her research interests include the curriculum of teacher education and the development of the perspectives of preservice teachers.

Janet Elaine Alleman is Professor of Teacher Education at Michigan State University. She is a member of the National Council for Social Studies Task Force for Advanced Certification, a member of the Editorial Board for the Elementary Section in *Social Education* and past Chair of the NCSS Testing Committee. She is coauthor of *Teaching Social Studies in the Elementary and Middle School.* Her current research is focused on student activities.

Ted T. Aoki is Professor Emeritus of the University of Alberta, Edmonton. He served as a social studies teacher and vice-principal in public schools in Alberta for 19 years. For 20 years, until retiring in 1985, he was social studies teacher education and curriculum theorist and Chair, Department of Secondary Education, University of Alberta. Between 1975 and 1978, he was Director of the Centre for the Study of Curriculum and Instruction at the University of British Columbia. His interests have been focused on phenomenology, hermeneutics, and critical social theory, and recently on questioning the limits of Western metaphysical tradition.

Beverly J. Armento is Professor of Social Studies and Director of the Center for Economic Education at Georgia State University, Atlanta. Her research areas include concept learning in social studies, teacher knowledge and pedagogical skills, and economic education. She has served as President of the National Association of Economic Educators. Her chapter on "Research on Teaching Social Studies" appeared in the third edition of the *Handbook of Research on Teaching.*

James A. Banks is Professor of Education and former Chairman of Curriculum and Instruction at the University of Washington, Seattle. He has been President of the National Council for the Social Studies and has held fellowships from the National Academy of Education, the Kellogg Foundation, and the Rockefeller Foundation. Known internationally for his work in social studies and multicultural education, he was named a Distinguished Scholar/Researcher on Minority Education by the American Educational Research Association. His books include *Teaching Strategies for Ethnic Studies, Teaching Strategies for the Social Studies,* and (with Cherry A. McGee Banks) *Multicultural Education: Issues and Perspectives.*

Isabel L. Beck is Professor of Education in the School of Education and Senior Scientist at the Learning Research and Development Center at the University of Pittsburgh. Her research interests are the cognitive and instructional processes underlying reading and learning from text. Among the issues she has investigated are requisite background knowledge, text coherence and structure, and the development of concepts. She has authored and coauthored numerous journal articles and book chapters for both professional and scholarly audiences. In 1988 she received the Oscar S. Causey award for outstanding reading research from the National Reading Conference.

Rodger W. Bybee is Associate Director of the Biological Sciences Curriculum Study (BSCS), Colorado College, Colorado Springs. Dr. Bybee is principal investigator for two new National Science Foundation (NSF) programs, an elementary school program entitled *Science for Life and Living: Integrating Science, Technology, and Health* and a middle school program entitled *Science and Technology: Investigating Human Dimensions.* He received his Ph.D. degree in science education and psychology from New York University. Throughout his career, Dr. Bybee has written widely, publishing in both education and psychology. He is coauthor of a leading textbook entitled *Becoming a Secondary School Science Teacher.*

Kay Camperell is Associate Professor in the Department of Secondary Education at Utah State University, Logan. A reading specialist, she focuses on methods of teaching reading in content area classes. She is coeditor of the *Yearbook of the American Reading Forum* and has published in a variety of books and journals.

Cleo H. Cherryholmes is Professor of Political Science at Michigan State University. His research areas include social science research methodology and curriculum. He is interested in philosophy of social science, literary theory and criticism, and how power influences texts and social practices. He has published in the *American Journal of Education, Journal of Curriculum Studies, Curriculum Inquiry, Theory and Research in Social Education* (of which he was the founding editor), and *Social Education*. His latest book is *Power and Criticism: Poststructural Investigations in Education*.

Ambrose A. Clegg, Jr. is Professor of Education and Director of the Center for Educational Research at Kent State University in Ohio. His research studies on teacher education, the social studies, and use of microcomputers in classroom learning have appeared in numerous journals and monographs. He is currently involved in developing programs for microcomputers that involve the use of artificial intelligence and expert systems related to learning and organizing information for problem solving. He is coauthor (with James A. Banks) of *Teaching Strategies for the Social Studies*.

Dan Conrad is a social studies teacher at Hopkins High School (Minnetonka, MN) and member of the faculty at the Center For Youth Development and Research at the University of Minnesota. A primary focus of his work, both as researcher and practitioner, has been on experience-based learning programs for youth. He is the author, often with his wife, Diane Hedin, of numerous publications on this topic, including *Youth Participation and Experiential Education* and *Youth Service: A Guidebook for Developing and Operating Effective Programs*.

Catherine Cornbleth is Professor and Director, Buffalo Research Institute on Education for Teaching (BRIET), Graduate School of Education, State University of New York at Buffalo. Her research interests are in the areas of curriculum studies and teacher education, particularly questions of practice and reform. She has edited *An Invitation to Research in Social Education* and authored *Curriculum in Context*.

Larry Cuban is Professor of Education at Stanford University, teaching history of education, administration, and policy analysis courses, and he heads the Stanford Schools Collaborative. He has taught high school social studies in inner-city schools for 14 years, administered teacher-training programs at school sites, and served as a district superintendent. His books include: *Teachers and Machines: The Use of Classroom Technology Since 1920, How Teachers Taught, 1890–1980, Urban School Chiefs Under Fire*, and *To Make a Difference: Teaching in the Inner City*.

Charles K. Curtis is Associate Professor of Social and Educational Studies in the Faculty of Education, The University of British Columbia, Vancouver. His research interests include social studies for slow-learning and at-risk students. He has extensive experience in teaching rights to advocacy groups of persons with mental retardation. Most recently his publications have been focused on research on modifying attitudes towards persons with disabilities.

Philip A. Cusick is Professor of Educational Administration at Michigan State University. His research interests include organizational theory and field studies of school groups. He is the author of *Inside High School, The Egalitarian Ideal and The American High School*, and coauthor of *Selling Students*

Short. He is presently completing *School Organization and the Social System*.

James R. Delisle is Associate Professor of Special Education at Kent State University in Ohio, where he coordinates the undergraduate and graduate programs in gifted-child education. He is President of *The Association for the Gifted* (TAG), a Division within *The Council for Exceptional Children*. He is the author of four books related to the social and emotional development of gifted students and more than 75 articles about gifted children which have appeared in various journals and magazines.

Matthew T. Downey is Director of the Clio Project in History-Social Studies Education, Graduate School of Education, University of California, Berkeley. The Clio Project undertakes curriculum development projects, inservice teacher training programs, and research on the teaching and learning of history, K–12. Downey has written extensively on the teaching of history. He was editor of "Teaching the History of Childhood," a special section in the April/May 1986 issue of *Social Education*. He was formerly a Professor of History at the University of Colorado, Boulder.

Lee H. Ehman is Professor of Education and Director of Education Technology Services at Indiana University, Bloomington. He has conducted research on schooling's influence on the political socialization of youth. More recently, he has studied the use and impact of technology in teaching and learning in social education and has published a monograph on that topic, with Allen Glenn, *Computer-Based Education in the Social Studies*. He was editor of *Theory and Research in Social Education*.

Elliot W. Eisner is Professor of Education and Art at Stanford University. His major interests are on the uses of the arts in the development of cognition and in their application to the study of educational practice. In his forthcoming book, *The Enlightened Eye: Qualitative Inquiry and the Enhancement of Educational Practice,* he explores those topics.

Elizabeth Farquhar is a Policy Analyst at the U.S. Department of Education where she specializes in studies of early education and care. She also works with contracts concerning drug prevention, education of disadvantaged children, and school reform. Previously she has directed federal activities in law-related education, citizen education, ethnic studies, Indian education, and international studies.

Patrick Ferguson is Professor of Secondary Education and Program Coordinator for Curriculum and Instruction at The University of Alabama. He is a comparative educator with research interests in teacher cognition, political socialization, and teacher education. He is the author of several chapters in NCSS publications and has published articles in *Theory and Research In Social Education, Social Studies,* and *Social Education*.

Jack R. Fraenkel is Professor of Interdisciplinary Studies in Education and Director of the Research and Development Center, School of Education, San Francisco State University. His current research interests center around the critical analysis and improvement of social studies research. He is the author of several books, including *Helping Students Think and Value, How to Teach About Values,* and *How to Design and Evaluate Research in Education.* In 1989, he was the recipient (with Norman E. Wallen) of the Annual Award for Outstanding Research in Social Studies Education from the National Council for the Social Studies.

Robert K. Fullinwider is Senior Research Associate at the Institute for Philosophy and Public Policy, University of Maryland, College Park, where he has directed research programs on military manpower policies and civil rights law. His current work is focused on moral and civic education. He is the author of *The Reverse Discrimination Controversy* (1980) and the editor of *Conscripts and Volunteers* (1983) and *The Moral Foundations of Civil Rights* (1986). Each spring he teaches a course on ethics and politics at the Graduate School of Political Management in New York City.

Geneva Gay is Professor of Curriculum and Multicultural Education at Purdue University, West Lafayette, Indiana. In addition to teaching courses in these areas, she has written over 80 articles and book chapters, and consults nationally and internationally on issues related to curriculum development, instructional strategies, and staff development for multicultural education. She is coeditor of *Expressively Black: The Cultural Basis of Ethnic Identity.*

James R. Giese is Executive Director of the Social Science Education Consortium. He has been involved in social studies program planning, research in program implementation and classroom practice, and a variety of curriculum development and teacher training activities. He has been principal investigator and director of numerous projects in social studies education sponsored by such agencies as the National Endowment for the Humanities, the U.S. Department of Education, the Office of Juvenile Justice and Delinquency Prevention, and the National Science Foundation, including two projects focused on implementing Science/Technology/Society in precollegiate science and social studies programs.

Robert L. Gilstrap is Professor of Education at George Mason University in Fairfax, Virginia, where he coordinates programs in middle education, serves as Associate Director of the Northern Virginia Writing Project, and teaches courses in social studies and language arts methods. For the past 12 years, his major area of study has been writing across the curriculum. His most recent book on this topic is *Writing in Elementary School Social Studies,* coedited with Barry K. Beyer. He is past President of the Association for Childhood Education International.

Allen D. Glenn is Dean of the College of Education and Professor of Curriculum and Instruction at the University of Washington, Seattle. His areas of research and teaching include social studies education and technology. He has conducted research on problem solving, the use of data bases in social studies classrooms, and the technology of skills of teachers.

Carole L. Hahn is Professor of Social Studies Education and Director of the Division of Educational Studies at Emory University, Atlanta, Georgia. She is past President of the National Council for the Social Studies (NCSS) and former Chair of the College and University Faculty Assembly of NCSS. She has conducted research on the diffusion and implementation of social studies innovations and gender and social studies learning. Her recent work includes a cross-national study of political socialization and case studies of classroom climate with particular attention to controversial issues discussions.

John D. Hoge is Assistant Professor of Social Science Education at the University of Georgia. He received his Ph.D. from Florida State University and has held faculty appointments at the Social Science Education Consortium/University of Colorado, Boise State University, and the Social Studies Development Center at Indiana University. His current research interests center on the development of critical thinking skills in citizenship and law-related education and the role of historical time knowledge in the development of historical understanding.

William W. Joyce is Professor of Education and Interim Director of the Canadian Studies Center at Michigan State University. His research interests include the political socialization of high school students and the use of computer simulations in teaching Canadian-American relations in U.S. and Canadian schools. Former Chair of the College and University Faculty Assembly of the National Council for the Social Studies and cofounder of the *Michigan Social Studies Journal,* he has authored professional books in social studies education, elementary and middle school social studies textbooks, and standardized achievement tests.

Richard S. Knight is Associate Professor in the Department of Secondary Education at Utah State University, Logan. He teaches social studies curriculum and instruction, values education, and foundations of teaching and learning. He has written articles and books about social studies and values education.

Dana G. Kurfman is K–12 Social Studies Supervisor for the Prince George's County Public Schools, Maryland. A major interest and responsibility has been the development of social studies criterion-referenced tests, as well as procedures for curriculum evaluation. He has written numerous articles on testing and evaluation, edited yearbooks for the National Council for Geographic Education and the National Council for the Social Studies, and served on several NAEP social studies committees, the most recent being the Geography Assessment Committee.

Margaret Diane LeCompte is Associate Professor of Sociology of Education at the University of Colorado, Boulder. Her research includes studies of dropouts, school and community organization, classroom interaction and socialization, and qualitative methods of research and evaluation. Her books include *Ethnography and Qualitative Design in Educational Research,* with Judith Goetz; *The Way Schools Work: A Sociological Analysis of Education,* with Kathleen Bennett; and *Giving Up In School: Teacher Burnout and Student Dropout in America,* with A. Gary Dworkin (in press). She is active in AERA and has been President of the Council on

Anthropology and Education of the American Anthropological Association.

James S. Leming is Professor of Curriculum and Instruction at Southern Illinois University, Carbondale. His research interests center on approaches to moral and values education and the influences of cultural and educational environments on the development of the political and moral values of youth. He is the author of *Contemporary Approaches to Moral Education: An Annotated Bibliography* and *Foundations of Moral Education: An Annotated Bibliography.*

Linda S. Levstik is Associate Professor of Social Studies Education at the University of Kentucky, Lexington. Her research interests and publications center on the development of historical understanding in elementary and middle-school-aged children, and on the connections between narrative and historical understanding. She has served as Chairperson of the Early Childhood/Elementary Special Interest Group of the National Council for the Social Studies and on the NCSS Task Force on Early Childhood/Elementary Social Studies. Her most recent publications include working on the 1990 NAEP *The U.S. History Report Card* and coauthoring *An Integrated Language Perspective in the Elementary School.*

Ian Lister is Professor of Education and Head of the Education Department at the University of York, England. With Bernard Crick he was Codirector of the British National Programme for Political Education in the 1970s. He is past President of the British Association for the Teaching of the Social Sciences. He has lectured on Political Education in many countries, including West Germany, India, Australia, and the United States.

Timothy H. Little is Professor of Social Studies Education at Michigan State University, East Lansing. He has served as the Chairman of the NCSS Citizenship and Technology Committees and is currently President of the NCSS Microcomputer Special Interest Group. He is coauthor of four textbooks and a regular columnist for two periodicals. His research and teaching specialties include the uses of educational technology in social studies instruction and law-related education. He is the founder of the Michigan State University Summer Law-Related Education Seminar, of which the 20th consecutive session will take place in the summer of 1990.

Michael Bruce Lybarger is Professor of History at Edgewood College of the Sacred Heart in Madison, Wisconsin; he also teaches social studies methods courses and supervises student teachers. His work has been published in the *History of Education Quarterly* and *Theory and Research in Social Education.* He is the author of "Need as Ideology: Social Workers, Social Settlements, and the Social Studies," a chapter in *The Formation of The School Subjects: The Struggle for Creating an American Institution,* and is completing a book, *The Origins and Development of the Social Studies: An Essay in the History and Archeology of Ideas.*

James A. Mackey is Professor of Curriculum and Instruction at the University of Minnesota, Minneapolis. He has conducted research on adolescent alienation, adolescent attitudes toward the police, and concept learning in adolescents. He has

published articles on adolescents in education journals and in the popular press. He is the coauthor of a recent general curriculum textbook, *School Curriculum.*

Peter H. Martorella is Professor of Social Studies Education at North Carolina State University, Raleigh. He has served as Chair of both the Research in Social Studies Special Interest Group of AERA and the College and University Faculty Assembly of NCSS. The author of several books, including two on concept learning, his most recent publication is *Teaching Social Studies in Middle and Secondary Schools.* He also serves as editor of the State University of New York Press series, Theory, Research, and Practice in Social Education.

Byron G. Massialas is Professor of Education and Multicultural Studies at Florida State University, Tallahassee. He has served as Executive Editor of *The Social Studies.* He is the author or coauthor of several books and monographs including *Inquiry in Social Studies, Education and the Political System, Social Issues Through Inquiry, Social Studies in a New Era: The School as Laboratory, Teaching Creatively,* and *Arab Education in Transition.*

Margaret G. McKeown is Research Scientist at the Learning Research and Development Center at the University of Pittsburgh. Her research interests include vocabulary development during school years and learner and text effects on learning in verbal domains. She received a Spencer Fellowship from the National Academy of Education in 1988. Her work in the areas of learning from text and vocabulary development, done in collaboration with Isabel Beck, has been published in such journals as *Reading Research Quarterly, Journal of Educational Psychology,* and *Cognition and Instruction.*

Merry M. Merryfield is Assistant Professor of Social Studies and Global Education at The Ohio State University. Her research interests are global perspectives in education, social studies in Africa, and cross-cultural inquiry. Her most recent publications include "Lessons From Africa," "Naturalistic Inquiry and Cross-Cultural Research," and "STS: Thinking Globally and Acting Locally."

Peter Muyanda-Mutebi is the Executive Director of the African Social Studies Programme, based at the regional headquarters of the organization in Nairobi, Kenya. Formerly a Senior Lecturer in the Faculties of Education at Makerere University in Kampala, Uganda, and Kenyatta University of Kenya. Dr. Muyanda-Mutebi is currently a consultant for UNESCO, UNICEF, and UNEP in the areas of textbook writing, primary health care, global development education, and environmental social studies for sustainable development. He was educated at Makerere University, Columbia University, and the University of California, Los Angeles.

Jack L. Nelson is Professor of Education and Director of the Center for Social Education at Rutgers University. His research interests are the social contexts of schooling, teacher professional socialization, and academic freedom. He was editor of *Theory and Research in Social Education* and *Social Science Record,* and has published 15 books, the most recent of which is *Critical Issues in Education.* He was the founding Chair of the College and University Faculty Assembly of the National Council for Social Studies and on Committee A (Academic Freedom and Tenure) of the American Association of University Professors.

Murry R. Nelson is Professor of Education at The Pennsylvania State University. He is past President of the Pennsylvania Council for the Social Studies and of the Society for the Study of Curriculum History. His areas of research interest include curriculum history, law-related education, and conflict resolution. He has authored over 60 articles and chapters, as well as *Children and Social Studies*. He has been a Senior Fulbright Lecturer at the University of Iceland and for the Ministry of Education of Norway.

Lynn Parisi is a senior staff associate at the Social Science Education Consortium. She has coordinated several Science/Technology/Society projects focusing on teacher training, curriculum development, and program implementation, including Building Support Networks for Improved Science/Technology/Society Education and Science-Related Social Issues: Computer-Based Decision-Making Exercises. She currently codirects Interpreting the History and Nature of Science in School Science and Social Studies Programs. Her publications include *Creative Role Playing Exercises in Science and Technology* and *Global Issues in the Elementary Classroom*.

Walter C. Parker is Associate Professor of Education and Director, Center for the Study of Civic Intelligence, at the University of Washington, Seattle. His inquiries on civic reasoning and the social studies curriculum have appeared in numerous books and journals, and he writes the social studies trends column for *Educational Leadership*. He most recently is author of *Renewing the Social Studies Curriculum*.

John J. Patrick is Professor of Education at Indiana University, Bloomington, where he is also Director of the Social Studies Development Center and of the ERIC Clearinghouse for Social Studies/Social Science Education. He is the author or coauthor of many publications on social studies education and civic education. He has also been the director of several projects on civic education, funded by public and private foundations or agencies.

Thomas S. Popkewitz is Professor of Curriculum and Instruction at the University of Wisconsin—Madison and a Faculty Associate at the Wisconsin Center for Education Research. He has studied educational reform and research in the United States and Europe and coauthored a book on issues of educational reform, *The Myth of Educational Reform*, edited books on issues in the study of change, and written about the sociology of educational research in the United States and the Soviet Union in *Paradigm and Ideology in Educational Research*. In *A Political Sociology of Educational Reform*, he examines educational research efforts to explain school change.

Judith Preissle-Goetz is Professor of Social Science Education at the University of Georgia where she teaches graduate courses in the qualitative and ethnographic research program she designed for the College of Education. Her articles have appeared in *Anthropology of Education Quarterly, Review of Educational Research, The Elementary School Journal*, and other research journals and anthologies. From 1977 to 1980 she served as Secretary Treasurer of the Council on Anthropology and Education. She is coauthor, with Margaret D. LeCompte, of *Ethnography and Qualitative Design in Educational Research*, now being revised for a second edition.

Cheryl L. Rosaen is Assistant Professor in the Department of Teacher Education, Michigan State University, and Senior Researcher for the Center for the Teaching and Learning of Elementary Subjects. She coordinates and teaches in the Academic Learning Teacher Education Program and has done extensive work in establishing and participating in a professional-development school. Her research interests are in learning to teach and writing to learn subject matter. Recent publications include "Writing in the Content Areas: Reaching its Potential in the Learning Process" in *Advances in Research on Teaching*.

Mark C. Schug is Professor of Curriculum and Instruction at the University of Wisconsin—Milwaukee and Executive Director of Educational Programs for the Wisconsin Economic Education Council. He taught for eight years in two public school districts, and has written and spoken widely about economic education in the United States and in England. Author of over 70 publications, his most recent book is *Teaching Social Studies in the Elementary School*. Currently, he is editor of *The Senior Economist*, published by the Joint Council on Economic Education.

Kathryn P. Scott is Professor of Education at Florida State University, Tallahassee, specializing in social studies and elementary education. She coauthored *Active Learning in Social Studies: Promoting Cognitive and Social Growth* and has published her research in numerous journals including *American Educational Research Journal, Journal of Educational Psychology, Theory Into Practice, Elementary School Journal, Social Education*, and *Theory and Research in Social Education*. She is currently Research Editor for *Social Education*.

James P. Shaver is Professor of Secondary Education, member of the Research and Evaluation Program faculty, Associate Dean for Research, College of Education, and Acting Dean of the School of Graduate Studies, Utah State University, Logan. He has been President of the National Council for the Social Studies and has received NCSS's Citation for Exemplary Research. His numerous books and articles include materials for students, research reports, and discussions of research philosophy, rationale-building, and rationales for social studies.

John E. Splaine is Associate Professor of Education Policy and Social Foundations at the University of Maryland, College Park. His work on viewing critically the media and politics has been published in numerous journals. He has served as Research Editor of the *Media Management Journal*, published by the Division of Educational Media Management of the Association for Educational Communications and Technology. He is the coauthor of the high school text, *Critical Viewing: Stimulant to Critical Thinking.*

Henry St. Maurice is Director of Field Experiences and Assistant Professor at the University of Wisconsin—Stevens Point. He has taught in a variety of settings including elementary, secondary, and rehabilitation programs. His research interests involve rhetorical, philosophical, and historical studies of teacher education.

Robert J. Stahl is Associate Professor of Secondary Education, Division of Curriculum and Instruction, Arizona State University. He is a member of the NCSS Research Committee and the NCSS Psychology Special Interest Group, and a former member of the NCSS Board of Directors. In addition to extensive research and writing in the area of precollege psychology, he has conducted teacher workshops and consulted with publishers on textbooks in this area. His articles on values education, cognitive psychology, and effective teaching methods have appeared in several journals including *Social Education, Educational Leadership,* and *Theory and Research in Social Education.*

William B. Stanley is Professor of Social Studies/Curriculum and Chair of the Department of Educational Development at the University of Delaware. His research interests include the foundations of social education, curriculum theory, and concept formation. He was editor of *Research in Social Studies:1976–1983.* His other publications have appeared in various journals including *Journal of Experimental Psychology, The Quarterly Journal of Experimental Psychology, Educational Theory, Theory and Research in Social Education,* and *The Journal of Thought.*

Joseph P. Stoltman is Professor of Geography and University Distinguished Faculty Scholar at Western Michigan University, Kalamazoo. His research areas include the development of geographic education within the American educational system, international comparative studies on spatial learning, and student learning styles in geography. He has served as President of the Commission on Geographical Education of the International Geographical Union and as Secretary to the Committee on Teaching Science of the International Council of Scientific Unions.

Cynthia Szymanski Sunal is an Associate Professor of Curriculum and Instruction at the University of Alabama, Tuscaloosa. Her research interests include school-family communication, teacher decision-making, and international education, and she has conducted studies in several countries, including Nigeria and Thailand. She authored *Early Childhood Social Studies* and has been published in journals including *Theory and Research in Social Education* and *Journal of Research in Childhood Education.* She has served as Chair of the Early Childhood Advisory Committee of the National Council for the Social Studies and as a member of the board of the NCSS College and University Faculty Assembly.

Péter Szebenyi is Senior Researcher in the National Institute for Education, Budapest, Hungary. He is Secretary of the national committee that awards research degrees in pedagogy for the Hungarian Academy of Sciences, General Editor of the 1978 national curriculum for elementary schools, and a member of the International Society for History Didactics. His research areas include the teaching of history, social science education, and curriculum theory. His books include *Objectives, Methods and Means: A Look at the Past of Hungarian History Teaching, Development of Historical Concepts of Learners, Toward the Improvement of History Teaching,* and *History Teaching in Great Britain.*

Stephen J. Thornton, previously Associate Professor of Education at the University of Delaware, Newark, is now Associate Professor of Education at Teachers College, Columbia University. He is a member of the editorial board of *Theory and Research in Social Education.* In 1988–1989, he was Chair of the College and University Faculty Assembly of the National Council for the Social Studies. His work on the relationships between curriculum theory and practice in social studies has appeared in numerous journals.

Judith Torney-Purta is Professor of Human Development, University of Maryland, College Park. She is a member of the Board on International Comparative Studies in Education of the National Academy of Sciences. She has served as Chair of the Committee on International Relations of AERA and received an award for her research from NCSS. Her research areas are political socialization and assessment of the outcomes of social studies from the perspective of cognitive psychology. She has published three books, including *Civic Education in Ten Countries: An Empirical Study,* and numerous chapters and articles.

Norman E. Wallen is Professor of Interdisciplinary Studies in Education at San Francisco State University. His research includes evaluation of social studies curricula and process/product studies of teaching. He was director of the Taba Curriculum Development Project in Social Studies. His most recent book is (with Jack R. Fraenkel) *How to Design and Evaluate Research in Education.*

William B. Walstad is Distinguished Professor of Economics at the University of Nebraska, Lincoln where he directs the Center for Economic Education and the National Center for Research in Economic Education. He has written many journal articles on economic education and serves on the editorial board of the *Journal of Economic Education.* He is coeditor of three books, including *Econometric Modeling in Economic Education Research,* and coauthor of three national achievement tests in economics. He has also served as President of the National Association of Economic Educators.

Jane J. White is Associate Professor of Education and Elementary Education Coordinator at the University of Maryland, Baltimore County. She is Chair of the American Anthropological Association Task Force on Teaching Anthropology, Secretary-Treasurer of the Council on Anthropology and Education, and Book Review Editor of *Theory and Research in Social Education.* Her research studies based on discourse analysis of classroom interaction have been published in *Anthropology and Education Quarterly, Journal of Curriculum and Supervision, Journal of Teacher Education,* and *Childhood Education.*

William W. Wilen is Professor of Education, Department of Teacher Development and Curriculum Studies, Kent State University. He is on the Executive Committee of the College and University Faculty Assembly, National Council for the Social Studies and serves on the NCSS Research Committee. He is past President of the Ohio Council for the Social Studies. He has authored *Questioning Skills, for Teachers,* coauthored *Dynamics of Effective Teaching,* and edited *Questions, Questioning Techniques, and Effective Teaching* and *Teaching and Learning Through Discussion.* His work on questioning, interaction, and social studies instruction has appeared in numerous journals.

Nancy E. Winitzky is Assistant Professor of Educational Studies at the University of Utah, Salt Lake City. She is actively involved in synthesizing and translating the knowledge base on teaching for preservice and inservice teachers. Her scholarly interests center on the application of theories of cognitive psychology to research and practice in teacher education.

Stanley P. Wronski is Professor Emeritus of Education and Social Science at Michigan State University. Past President of the National Council for the Social Studies, he organized the first session on social studies research presented at an annual meeting of the NCSS. He is coauthor (with the late Edgar B. Wesley) of *Teaching Secondary School Social Studies in a World Society,* and coeditor (with Donald H. Bragaw) of *The Social Studies and the Social Sciences: A Fifty-Year Perspective.* He has taught courses for teachers in international schools in Japan, Okinawa, the Philippines, the Netherlands, Belgium, Egypt, and Central America.

Nancy B. Wyner is Associate Professor in the Leadership and Schooling doctoral program and Director, International Studies Resource Center, College of Education, University of Lowell, Massachusetts. A past President of the Massachusetts Council for the Social Studies, her research areas include managing change, school culture, and collaboration as a teaching model in leadership education. Her articles include "Educating Linguistic Minorities: Public Education and the Search for Unity," and "Spoiled Child Syndrome in China." Her chapter, "Membership and Myth in Cultures of Teaching," is in the forthcoming book, *Current Perspectives in School Cultures,* which she edited.

HANDBOOK OF RESEARCH ON
SOCIAL STUDIES TEACHING AND LEARNING

ISSUES OF EPISTEMOLOGY
AND METHODOLOGY

THE HISTORIOGRAPHY OF SOCIAL STUDIES:
RETROSPECT, CIRCUMSPECT, AND PROSPECT

Michael Bruce Lybarger
EDGEWOOD COLLEGE

The dating of events in intellectual history is often arbitrary and almost always problematic. Nonetheless, it may be said with some certainty that the publication of *The Social Studies in Secondary Education* (Dunn, 1916), the final report of the Committee on Social Studies of the Commission on the Reorganization of Secondary Education, marked the formal introduction of social studies into the secondary school curriculum. The recommendations of the committee established the scope and sequence of the social studies curriculum, which remained basically unchanged until the mid-1970s (Gross, 1976, p. 196).

However, social studies had a history antedating its incorporation into *The Social Studies in Secondary Education*. In this chapter, historical accounts of the origins and development of the social studies curriculum are examined, the present state of scholarly inquiry into the history of social studies is assessed, and possible directions for further historical work in the field are ventured.

EDUCATIONAL HISTORY

Since the birth of western civilization, education, especially instruction in what is today called history and social studies, has been expected to foster habits of good citizenship. According to Aristotle, "that which contributes most of the permanence of constitutions is the adaptation of education to the form of government. The best laws will be of no avail unless the young are trained by habit and example in the spirit of the constitution" (1943, pp. 249–250).

Celebratory History

The first historian, Herodotus, wrote his *History of the Persian Wars* to "celebrate the great and wonderful deeds of the Greeks and the Barbarians." Herodotus's approach to history is called *celebratory*. Most often, celebratory historians produce an account of the present as the happy result of past struggles. Sometimes celebratory histories glorify a past hero or a golden age. Not infrequently, celebratory histories are created to legitimate some new institution, idea, or practice. In American history, the work of George Bancroft (1834–1874) is celebratory. In the historiography of American education, Elwood P. Cubberly's *Public Education in the United States* (1919) is celebratory history. In the historiography of the curriculum, Mary Louise Seguel's *The Curriculum Field: Its Formative Years* (1965) is celebratory. In the history of the social studies curriculum, the

Reviewers were James Akenson, Tennessee Technological University; George L. Mehaffy, San Diego State University.

Historians of the social studies owe Hazel Hertzberg a great debt. No researcher should ignore her *Historical Parallels for the Sixties and the Seventies: Primary Sources and Core Curriculum Revisited* (1971) and *Social Studies Reform: 1880–1980* (1981). Historians should be grateful for her work with the Bradley Commission. Hazel Hertzberg was a scholar to her fingertips, and this chapter is dedicated to her with respect and affection.

In this chapter, the reader must keep the work of two commissions in mind. In 1912, the National Education Association (NEA) constituted a Commission on the Reorganization of Secondary Education. The commission established 16 committees, each dealing with some aspect of the curriculum or administration of secondary education. The Committee on Social Studies is considered one of the most successful. In 1929, the American Historical Association created a Commission on the Social Studies. The commission produced a 16-volume report, which is the most definitive account of the development of the social studies available today. In this chapter, the full name of the Committee on Social Studies or of the Commission on the Social Studies is given upon the first mention in a paragraph. In subsequent uses in the same paragraph, the word *commission* or *committee* is used. The Commission on the Reorganization of Secondary Education is often referred to as the CRSE.

works of Henry Johnson (1932), Rolla Tryon (1929, 1934), and Edgar Wesley (1937) are celebratory accounts.

Revisionist History

Another approach to history is often called *revisionist*. Like the celebratory historian, the revisionist chronicles conflict, usually between the progressive few and the conservative or indolent many, but the outcome is not always certain. Revisionist historians seek to address the question "Who or what prevailed and why?" Perhaps the most famous example of a revisionist history is Charles A. Beard's *An Economic Interpretation of the Constitution of the United States* (1912). Beard was concerned about understanding the ratification of the Constitution in terms of the economic interests of its supporters. In the history of education, Lawrence Cremin's *The Transformation of the School* (1964) and Bernard Bailyn's *Education in the Forming of American Society* (1960) are revisionist accounts. Herbert Kliebard's *The Struggle for the American Curriculum: 1893–1958* (1986) is a revisionist account of curricular history.

Robinson (1980) suggested a revisionist approach to the history of social studies in which its emergence is viewed as part of a societal endeavor to ease the tensions and strains brought on by the rapid development of an urban industrial society. In this model, which draws heavily upon the work of Robert Wiebe, especially *The Search for Order* (1967), the emergence of social studies is interpreted as one manifestation of a nationwide "search for order." The search was a consequence of the public's lack of certainty concerning appropriate values for a changing society, and it was part of an effort to "validate a cultural unanimity which had lost its coherence" (Robinson, 1977, p. 4).

Radical History

A third school of history is called *radical*. The radical historian, as the name implies, seeks the "roots" of the issues being studied. Usually these roots are viewed as consequences of social and/or economic factors. The radical's account is the story of conflict between social and economic classes. History is a weapon in that struggle and is expected to contribute significantly to the quick resolution of the problems of contemporary social and educational reform. Clarence Karier (Karier, Violas, & Spring, 1973), for example, charged that the work of Cremin and his followers was "short of meaningful criticism, and long on apology" (p. 5). David Tyack (1974) asserted that "the public schools have rarely taught the children of the poor effectively—and this failure has been systemic, not idiosyncratic" (p. 12).

Karier, Tyack, and their colleagues have sought to understand the history of American education by examining the ways in which schooling has served to legitimate the selective and unequal distribution of social, economic, and political power. Michael Katz (1975) has gone further:

American society and all its institutions including educational ones need restructuring. At this point in history any reform worthy of the name must begin with a redistribution of power and resources. That is

the only way in which to make education and other social institutions, as well, serve new purposes. (p. xi)

The work of the radical historians of education has not been without its critics. Tyack (1974) warned against presentism, contending that "disillusionment with institutionalized education, and discouragement with the results of schooling in the present . . . may prompt historians to tell a tale of woe as one sided as the previous story of the public school triumphant" (pp. 29–30). Carl Kaestle (1976) suggested that some of the work of the radicals "may have reduced the complexity of history unduly" (p. 391).

There are no radical historians of the social studies curriculum. Paul Robinson (1980) suggested that historians of the social studies look to the radical historians of education: Karier, Katz, Hogan, Bowles, and Gintis. A radical history of social studies would be an endeavor to understand the development of social studies as one aspect of a societywide effort to legitimate inequality. From this viewpoint, the emergence of social studies would be seen as part of the school's function of maintaining social order through the imposition of upper- and middle-class values. The development of social studies would be situated in the context of an effort to have have schoolteachers and their charges view social problems, not as institutional failures, but as consequences of individual inadequacies.

Robinson's (1980) suggestions of categories of history have merit, but they are not without their difficulties. In the first place, the enumeration of possible models for the interpretation of the history of the social studies presupposes a historiography illustrative of those models. Schools of history usually emerge from a body of historical writings. Conflicting interpretations of historical events, persons, or movements emerge from a consideration of the documents, literature, and sources about those events. Although the past decade has seen the emergence of a modest body of historical literature about the development of social studies, it can be argued that the historians of social studies have not as yet developed a sufficiently diverse range of writings.

CURRICULAR HISTORY

This brief survey of the historiography of American education discloses three different traditions: the celebratory history of Cubberley and his followers; the revisionist history of Cremin, Bailyn, and their school; and the radical histories of Katz, Karier, and their followers. The historiography of the curriculum is poorer than that of education. Nonetheless, an account of some of these efforts can be instructive.

For almost 20 years, Mary Louise Seguel's *The Curriculum Field: Its Formative Years* (1965) was the only historical account of the development of curriculum as a field of study. Seguel's account celebrated how that which had begun as the speculations of laymen in the 1890s had by 1938 become a university subject with a set of practicing professionals, an organization, and several respected journals. Seguel's account closed with the appointment in 1938 of Hollis Caswell to the first university department of curriculum at Teachers College, Columbia University. From 1938 to 1965, Seguel concluded, there had been "remarkably little change in the field. The forms with which it was established continue to endure. The work of the shapers of the field seems in most respects still timely" (p. 155).

The year 1986 saw the publication of the first book-length treatments of curricular history since the publication of Seguel's work: Herbert Kliebard's *The Struggle for the American Curriculum: 1893–1958* and Barry Franklin's *Building the American Community: The School Curriculum and the Search for Social Control*. The books warrant consideration here because each illuminates an aspect of the history of the social studies curriculum.

In *The Struggle for the American Curriculum,* (1986) Kliebard viewed the history of the school curriculum as the account of the struggle of five interest groups for control of its content. The first of these groups, which Kliebard called "humanists," was represented by men like Charles W. Eliot and William Torrey Harris. A second group, which Kliebard called "social efficiency" educators, was represented by men like Franklin Bobbitt and David Snedden. A third group Kliebard called "child development" educators, and it was represented by men like G. Stanley Hall and William Heard Kilpatrick. A fourth group, called "social reconstructionist" educators, included social reformers like Harold Rugg and George Counts. The beliefs of a fifth group, life adjustment educators, included elements of social efficiency, social reform, and child development. At any particular time, one or two of these groups may have been dominant but not to the extent of submerging the other groups (p. 270).

Barry Franklin's *Building the American Community* (1986) offered a different perspective on the history of the curriculum. Franklin's narrative goes something like this. Between 1890 and 1910, urbanization, immigration, and industralization opened a gap between the new society and the liberal democratic ideals upon which this nation was founded. In response to this situation, a new middle class of professionals and intellectuals sought to create "within the urban, industrialized society the kind of like-mindedness and cooperation which they believed to have existed in the rural town" (p. 8). According to Franklin, "social control referred to the diverse efforts of social groups to bring the attitudes and behavior of their members into line with accepted and customary social expectations" (p. 10).

Kliebard's and Franklin's books are complementary. Kliebard's account of the role of conflict in the development of the cirriculum places him in the revisionist camp, whereas Franklin's discussion of the idea of social control makes his account the more radical. Both accounts permit historians of social studies to explore the origins of leading ideas and locate these in their social, political, and intellectual contexts.

Summary

This brief survey of educational and curricular history is meant to suggest that historical studies are less numerous and diverse as the field of study is narrowed. The historiography of general education afforded us four traditions, and historical work in the curriculum field was, until very recently, represented by a single book-length celebratory account (Seguel, 1965). In recent years, two book-length accounts of the history of the curriculum have been published, Kliebard's (1986) revisionist account and Barry Franklin's (1986) more radical view. The implications of both for the historiography of the social studies are explored later.

HISTORY OF THE HISTORY OF SOCIAL STUDIES

Historical accounts of the development of the social studies curriculum are less numerous than curriculum histories. Nevertheless, the social studies field does have a past, and that past is far from dead.

The past of the social studies lives not as written history but as a kind of academic folklore; people acquire a sense of development from their own experience and from hearing the tales of their elders. It is thus possible for major movements to run their course and disappear from current consciousness, continuing to affect present behavior while the records and artifacts of such movements are largely forgotten. (Hertzberg, 1971, p. 12)

The 1916 Report: Immediate Reception

Any effort to make a history out of the past of the social studies curriculum must begin with the report of the Committee on Social Studies of the Commission on the Reorganization of Secondary Education, *The Social Studies in Secondary Education* (Dunn, 1916). At least four elements of the modern social studies curriculum can be traced to the recommendations of the committee: first, the courses in vocational civics and community civics in the seventh and eighth grades; second, the high school course in Problems of American Democracy; third, the high school courses in European and American history; fourth, the popular use of thte term *social studies* to refer collectively to economics, history, political science, sociology, and civics (Tryon, 1934, pp. 21–22).

Charles Judd (1918) made one of the first efforts to understand the development of the recommendations found in *The Social Studies in Secondary Education*. He asserted that Arthur W. Dunn, the secretary of the Committee on Social Studies, and John Dewey were the pedagogical parents of the "New Civics." Judd contended that the committee's curricular recommendations were shaped by three factors. The first was the emergence of the new social sciences in the 1880s and 1890s. The second was the work of William Graham Sumner, which popularized a view of society based on the work of Herbert Spencer and Charles Darwin. The third was the increasing numbers of poor and newly arrived immigrants whose presence in city schools created a demand "for something which will teach children in American schools what society really is." Whatever that "something" might be, Judd (1918) was convinced that it did not include history: "The social studies include sociology, economics, ethics, vocational guidance, and civics, not history" (p. 517).

Judd was not the only educator to define the social studies in terms of specific social sciences. The years immediately following the publication of *The Social Studies in Secondary Edu-*

cation saw the efforts of professional associations of sociologists, political scientists, and economists to establish a social studies curriculum, each placing its own discipline at the center and each claiming that it addressed the claims of the other social sciences. According to Hazel Hertzberg (1981), "it seemed that the newly named 'social studies' were 'up for grabs' " (pp. 34–35).

The 1920s

One consequence of the curricular ferment just recounted was the organization of the National Council for the Social Studies (NCSS) in 1921. The purpose was to "bring about the association and cooperation of teachers of education and others interested in obtaining the maximum results in education for citizenship through social studies" (*"A National Council,"* 1921, p. 144).

The organization of the NCSS reflected a growing awareness on the part of teachers and curriculum developers that history alone was not an adequate preparation for citizenship in an increasingly complex, urban, industrial society. As early as 1915, the historian and methods book author, Henry Johnson noted that "The demand is for social studies of direct and immediate concern to individual communities, [and] there is a growing tendency to ask of history primarily and chiefly that it contribute to an understanding of these problems" (pp. 159–160). Eight years later Harold Rugg (1923) noted that "It is to the curriculum of the social studies that we must look to bring our millions of growing youth into contact with the insistent problems of today" (pp. 2–3). Three years later, Rugg (1926) contended that

a gap between the curriculum and the concrete discussion of industrial, political, and cultural forces and institutions in America has been perpetuated [and] . . . we have today almost no objectively ascertained facts and principles for determination of content or for its grade placement and organization. (p. 113)

The 1920s also witnessed the efforts of historians to determine and come to grips with the role of history in the social studies curriculum and "to take the social studies seriously" (Hertzberg, 1981, p. 43). In 1925, the American Historical Association (AHA) formed another committee on the teaching of history and the social studies. In reporting to the AHA in 1927, the committee presented a plan for a detailed study of history and social studies education. In January 1929 the committee secured a grant from the Carnegie Foundation and renamed itself the Commission on the Social Studies. This group turned out to be the "most elaborate and comprehensive commission in the history of the social studies" (Hertzberg, 1981, p. 44); it produced several books that remain critical for anyone seeking to understand the history of the social studies.

Rolla M. Tryon

One member of the Commission on the Social Studies was Rolla M. Tryon, Professor of the Teaching of History at the University of Chicago, who wrote *The Social Sciences as School Sub-*

jects (1934) to describe what "has been and is in the realm of the social sciences as school subjects" (p. ix). According to Tryon, "what has been and is" was the result of the combined efforts of learned societies, professional organizations, civic and fraternal groups, and educational associations.

Tyron devoted the first part of his book to a consideration of the "Efforts of National Organizations in Behalf of the Social Sciences as School Subjects." Here he listed and discussed at length the influence on the development of social studies of groups like the American Historical Association, the American Bar Association, the National Municipal League, the National Security League, and the National Education Association. The recommendations of all of these groups, Tryon contended, were incorporated into the social studies curriculum through the combined efforts of college professors, elementary and secondary teachers, and administrators.

The remainder of *The Social Sciences as School Subjects* consists of historical accounts of the development of history, economics, political science, and sociology as school subjects. Tryon discussed each subject under the following categories: the values claimed for it, its incorporation into the curriculum, its development as part of the curriculum, and, finally, the changes in the subject wrought by the exigencies of the 20th century.

To Tryon, the publication of *The Social Studies in Secondary Education* (Dunn, 1916), marked the establishment of the social sciences as school subjects: "It is within the bounds of truth to say that the history of the social sciences other than history and civics as subjects of study in the elementary and secondary schools begins about 1916" (p. 334). The divisions of *The Social Sciences as School Subjects* reflected this view. In the chapter on history as a subject of study, 102 pages out of 148 dealt with the period between 1900 and 1915. In the case of political science, 52 out of 74 pages dealt with the period between 1897 and 1915.

Tryon's account of the development of the social sciences in the curriculum goes something like this: In 1916, the Committee on Social Studies of the Commission on the Reorganization of Secondary Education published *The Social Studies in Secondary Education* in response to the recommendations of professional social scientists, educators, interested laymen, and the "spirit of the times." As part of this effort, economists, political scientists, sociologists, and historians put aside the interests of their particular disciplines and helped create a social studies curriculum characterized by intellectual honesty and rigor, as well as by responsiveness to the needs of the students of a modern school system in a modern society.

Tryon was not sure of the content or limits of the social studies curriculum. His book went through three changes of title before it was published. In 1932, the title was announced as *Materials and Instruction in the Social Science Programs*. (A list of forthcoming titles was printed in the back of each of the 16 volumes of the report of the Commission on Social Studies.) In 1934, the title was announced as *The Social Studies as School Subjects*. The book was published in 1934 as *The Social Sciences as School Subjects*. The changes in title may reflect ambiguity about the nature of and relationship among social studies, the social sciences, and history and the role each ought to play in the education of citizens. This ambiguity was "born with the field" and may explain the difficulty that contemporaries have in defining social studies. Ambiguity certainly characterizes the contemporary view of the relationship among, as well as the nature of, history, social studies, and the social sciences.

Henry Johnson

The work of one of Tryon's colleagues on the Commission on the Social Studies affords a different perspective. Henry Johnson, professor of history at Teachers College, Columbia University, in *An Introduction to the History of the Social Sciences in Schools* (1932), tried to identify the remote antecedents of some of the recommendations esteemed as "new and most important" by members of the Committee on Social Studies in 1916. Johnson credited Jacob Wimpheling, a German teacher in the 18th century, with being the first educator to advocate teaching the history of a particular nation to stimulate children's patriotism. He noted that Christian Wise in *Der Kluge Hoff-Meister* first argued that history and geography ought to be taught together. In Johnson's account, Rousseau emerged as the first advocate of tailoring instruction to the present needs of children (pp. 15–16).

As early as 1915, Johnson had disagreed with the recommendation of the Committee on Social Studies that history instruction ought to be sequenced according to the "interests and needs" of the students. According to Johnson (1915), the committee's recommendations "subjected history as history to severe questioning" (pp. 360–361). Johnson warned about another possible misuse of history by the committee.

To seek the easiest and shortest route to the use of the past in explaining the present is natural and proper. But any road that really reaches the desired end must make the past which it traverses intelligible and must, therefore, lead to what mattered then on the way to what matters now. (p. 136)

Edgar Wesley

Although on the staff of the Commission on the Social Studies, Edgar Wesley did not write any part of its report. However, his view of the history of the social studies was incorporated in his methods text, *Teaching the Social Studies* (1937), which went through six editions and probably reached more teachers than either Tryon's or Johnson's books (Robinson, 1980, p. 66). One reviewer indicated that "the background and present status of the social studies are then, effectively presented. [Dr. Wesley] ... has very effectively surveyed and synthesized the very numerous and scattered writings on the social studies" (quoted in Robinson, 1980, p. 68).

Tryon, Johnson, and Wesley

Tryon, Johnson, and Wesley displayed important similarities in their works. All agreed that the social studies curriculum, whose history they wrote, was largely the result of the work of the Committee on Social Studies. They also agreed that work in

social studies had as its object the cultivation of citizenship. All three used a chronological framework, with each of the social sciences treated separately. All three drew most of their data from government or scholarly sources. The analysis of all three was "in house," with little reference made to any broader historical or intellectual context. All three (but Johnson the least) understood educational progress as being marked by growing systematization and rationalization of the curriculum and ongoing professionalization of the teaching staff.

Tryon and Wesley knew that instruction in history promoted good citizenship, but neither knew how or why. In considering the development of history as a school subject, Tryon (1934) pointed out that the claim that the study of history produced good citizenship,

greatly enhanced its prospects as a school subject at a time when it needed vigorous support to make substantial headway. While no one seemed to be able to specify the qualities of a good citizen, it was felt in some unexplainable way that history had large value in the making of something of which no one knew the chief characteristics. (pp. 83–84)

Because social studies promoted good citizenship, Wesley (1937) accorded society a great role in determining the content of the social studies curriculum: "Society decides what *shall* be taught. Public education implies a public investment for a public good. We too must adapt ourselves, willy-nilly, to changing ideals and purposes" (pp. 163–165).

Neither Johnson, Tryon, nor Wesley made much of an effort to consider the social and political context of schooling or of the activities of the national subject-matter committees. Johnson was able to carry the notion of fitting history instruction to "the needs of present growth" to ruinously logical conclusions. But the contemporary reader will search *An Introduction to the History of the Social Sciences in the Schools* in vain for an account of why it happened that American educators and layfolk around the turn of the century thought it necessary to claim that history instruction ought to serve "the needs of present growth." Moreover, it is difficult to determine what Johnson and his colleagues meant by those words.

Johnson's, Tryon's, and Wesley's histories of social studies were celebratory accounts. According to Robinson (1980), these histories were intended to "help create a collective sense of the past, a reigning ideology, which social studies educators believed necessary to assist stabilizing a curriculum area which they perceived as frequently distended, chaotic, and insecure." For all three men, the history of the social studies was marked by an "expanding curriculum, growing professionalism, increasingly scientific adjustment to the needs of both student and society, and acceptance as a 'mainline' subject" (p. 69).

The 1940s and 1950s

The 1940s were dominated by World War II. Until very recently, historians have shown little interest in the impact of the war on the social studies curriculum. In a brief survey of this impact, Nelson (1986) concluded that social studies professionals' reaction to the war was "calm and judicious." He demonstrated that, in some areas of the social studies curriculum (notably in the development of texts dealing with air power and travel), change took place rather quickly and well-thought-out materials were developed and introduced in little time (p. 264).

The 1950s were not favorable for the development of a history of the social studies. Johnson and Tryon had laid a solid foundation, but it was not built upon or extended. The dominant historiography of the 1950s was called "consensus" history. Such a view of history constrained historians to look to a past marked by the American people's success in resolving their differences without conflict.

Arthur Bestor, a historian, was the most widely read critic of education in the 1950s. (Ironically, Bestor's early education took place at the Lincoln School, Teachers College, Columbia, where Harold Rugg's social studies curriculum was called "social stew" by many of the students and teachers [Hertzberg, 1981, p. 89]). In *Educational Wastelands: The Retreat from Learning in Our Public Schools,* Bestor (1953) centered his attack on the history and philosophy of education courses for teachers, characterizing them as "warping the great intellectual disciplines to serve the narrow purposes of indoctrination and vocationalism" (p. 144). Social studies, Bestor asserted, ought to be abolished because most social science courses were history courses anyway. Echoing Henry Johnson, Bestor contended that the term "social studies" was neither necessary nor clear, led to educational "faddism," and trivialized the study of history (p. 134).

Parts of Bestor's critique were well founded. In considering social studies, however, he stopped with the publication of *The Social Studies in Secondary Education,* which he scorned as the work of "educationists." According to Hertzberg (1980), "Bestor's historical clock stopped with the [the publication of] the 1916 report" (p. 90).

When professionals find themselves under attack, they sometimes look to their past for the resources to resist the attack. By the early 1950s, however, social studies professionals had few historical resources to draw upon.

The history of the social studies was not pursued by teacher-educators in the Tryon/Johnson mold [and] there was little new work. Thus the social studies were fast losing their own past, which existed in dimming memories and which was unrefreshed by the vigorous new investigations and interpretations needed in a living historiography. (Hertzberg, 1980, p. 102)

Social Sciences and the Social Studies

Lacking historical resources, professionals sometimes look for support from colleagues in related fields. So it was in 1958 that the National Council for the Social Studies and the American Council of Learned Societies announced a joint venture that resulted in the publication in 1962 of *The Social Sciences and the Social Studies,* edited by Bernard Berelson.

Most of the contributors to *The Social Sciences and the Social Studies* were ignorant of the history of the issues they discussed. There were a few allusions to *The Social Studies in Secondary Education,* which was called "outdated" by Berelson and by Lewis Paul Todd, the editor of *Social Education.* The

work of the AHA Commission on the Social Studies was forgotten. The work of educational historians from Cubberley on was ignored (Hertzberg, 1980, p. 103).

The New Social Studies

After the success of Sputnik, most levels and aspects of American education came under scrutiny and criticism. Federal and private monies became available, first in mathematics and science curricula, and then in the humanities and the social studies. Social studies subject-matter professionals in universities, colleges, and schools of education, and a few secondary school administrators and classroom teachers, developed and tried to implement social studies programs that they hoped would address some of the pedagogical and methodological shortcomings identified by Bestor and reflect the most recent and best scholarship in each social studies discipline. Included in the "New Social Studies" were the "inquiry method" and the "structure of the disciplines" approach, as embodied in projects such as Man: a Course of Study, Sociological Resources for the Social Studies, Social Science Laboratory Units, and the Amherst Project. All of these reforms flourished and disappeared from view. Hertzberg contended that "never was such a major reform cut off from its roots" (1980, p. 103).

In 1976, James P. Shaver, in his presidential address to the National Council for the Social Studies, asserted that "the 'structure of the discipline approach' that dominated most of the curriculum development projects which masqueraded as social studies projects in the 1960s was a fad that exemplified our long standing and unthinking subservience to professors in the academic disciplines" (Shaver, 1977, p. 305). By 1982, Shaver contended that "there would have been little discernable effect on educational practice if most of the studies reported in educational journals had never been conducted" (Shaver, 1982, p. 2).

Shaver's remarks indicated a high level of intellectual fragmentation in the social studies curriculum. By the middle 1970s, this intellectual fragmentation had bred curricular fragmentation. History, as central to the social studies, suffered most. Under presure from students, radical teachers, community activists, liberal reformers, university professors, and assorted cranks, the social studies curriculum incorporated African-American and ethnic studies, family history, survival and law education, future studies, values clarification, family science, sex education, environmental education, death and dying, and women's studies, to name only a few. Thus, more than 60 years after its entry into the curriculum, the social studies continued to be a pursuit of "all manner of efforts to promote human betterment" (Jones, 1913, p. 13).

HISTORIOGRAPHY OF SOCIAL STUDIES: PROSPECTS AND OPPORTUNITIES

Recent years have seen a revival of interest in the history of social studies. The reasons for this renewed interest are not now clear, but one or more of the following offer evidence of its onset. Since 1975, every meeting of the NCSS has had at least one session devoted to the history of the social studies. In 1977 the NCSS recognized a special interest group dealing with the historical and philosophical foundations of the social studies. James Barth became the group's first president, and Murry Nelson was chosen president elect. The Fall, 1980, edition of *Theory and Research in Social Education,* the journal of the College and University Faculty Assembly of NCSS, was given over to history of the social studies. The *Indiana Social Studies Quarterly,* now *The International Journal of Social Education,* devoted an issue to the founders of the social studies, and historical work of the first quality is quite often published there. At the University of Texas, Austin, O. L. Davis is assembling an oral history of social studies that may help preserve unwritten sources of the history of social studies.

What Is Social Studies?

One of the most remarkable aspects of the history of the social studies has been the ongoing debates over the nature, scope, and definition of the field. These debates were well chronicled by Alberta Macke Dougan (1985). They began with the emergence of the field and give no evidence of abating. The debates may be understood in two ways by the historian of social studies: as a manifestation of intellectual vitality or as a consequence of the inability of social studies professionals to understand the nature of their field.

Robert Barr, James Barth, and S. Samuel Shermis's (1978) work, which has been a rich source of controversy about the foundations of social studies, is a recent effort to define the social studies. They claimed to have identified three distinct traditions within the field: first, "the social studies taught as citizenship transmission"; second, "the social studies taught as social science"; and third, "the social studies taught as reflective inquiry." They contended that these traditions are inadequately, if at all, understood today. Consequently, social studies teachers don't know what to do because they don't know what they are or have been doing.

Although Barr, Barth, and Shermis have drawn attention to the past of social studies, *The Nature of the Social Studies* (1978) is not without limitations. First, the authors do not make the case for their three traditions. It is by no means clear that there might not be more or less than three traditions. For example, might not "the social studies taught as social science" or "the social studies taught as reflective inquiry" also serve the ends of "citizenship transmission"? Moreover, it is not clear how these three traditions ought to be understood today. For example, can modern ideas about the teaching of citizenship be subsumed under the rubric of "citizenship transmission"?

Sources of Social Studies Ideas

Historians of the social studies have not used the insights from other social sciences to understand how it happened that, out of a plurality of ideas and visions about social studies, people at a particular time and place chose one set and rejected others. To pursue that question, historians need to go beyond the who, what, when, where, why, and how of the origins of social studies and raise other questions about its past. Michael Young (1971) argued "that there exists a dialectical relationship between access to power and the opportunity to legitimate certain dominant categories, and the process by which the availability of such categories to some groups enables them to assert power and control over others" (p. 7).

If Young's argument is anywhere near the mark, the historian of social studies needs to attend to other questions about the past of social studies. Among these questions might be ones like: What view of society did the early social studies curriculum embody? Whose view was this? What counted as social studies knowledge? Whose knowledge was this? What forms of social actions did this knowledge legitimate and what forms did it proscribe?

These are not new questions for social studies educators. More than 50 years ago, Charles A. Beard (1934) reminded social studies teachers that

The social sciences also bring one conclusion of fundamental and inescapable significance which must preface the beginning of the operation [of thinking about and formulating objectives]: Every human brought up in society inevitably has in mind a frame of social knowledge, ideas and ideals—a more or less definite pattern of things deemed *necessary,* things deemed *possible* and things deemed *desirable* [italics in original]; and to this frame or pattern, his thought and action will be more or less consciously referred. (p. 181)

A potentially significant effort to address the issues articulated by Beard flows from efforts to apply insights from Marxist scholarship to the history of education. An often used (and misused) Marxist concept is ideology. Carl Kaestle (1982) rescued ideology from polemicists by using the term *social outlook,* which he defined as "a set of compatible propositions about human nature and society that help an individual to interpret complex human problems and take action that the individual believes is in his or her best interests and the best interest of society as a whole" (p. 125). According to Kaestle, the "social outlook" of mid-nineteenth-century school reformers centered on republicanism, Protestantism, and capitalism and had the following major propositions:

1. the sacredness and fragility of the republican polity;
2. the importance of individual character in fostering social morality;
3. the central role of personal industry in defining rectitude and merit;
4. the delineation of a highly respected but limited domestic role for women;
5. the importance for character building of familial and social environment;
6. the sanctity and social virtues of property;
7. the equality and abundance of economic opportunity in the United States;
8. the superiority of American Protestant culture;
9. the grandeur of America's destiny;
10. the urgent necessity of a determined public effort to unify America's polygot population, chiefly through education. (pp. 129–130)

Each of the ideas found in *The Social Studies in Secondary Education* had a history and rationale antedating its incorporation into the report. Each recommendation existed as part or whole of an earlier perspective in an earlier context where it was called *social study* or *social studies*. Out of the work of the American Social Science Association came a conception of social studies as information about social welfare, which the Committee on Social Studies in 1916 called "the methods of human betterment" or the "elements of welfare" (Lybarger, 1981, pp. 41–89). Out of the work of the early American sociologists, especially Albion W. Small and Franklin A. Giddings, came the idea of a science of society that would justify existing conditions while making more certain the pursuit of individual and social welfare described earlier (Lybarger, 1981, pp. 88–123). Out of the civic education work of the National Municipal League, came a view of politics in which the public interest was understood to be best served by the extension of efficient, economic, and expert government, ratified, but not shaped, by the voters (pp. 190–240). Out of the work of charity organization societies and social settlements came a vision of need and interest that educators hoped would allow them to help the children of immigrants as the social settlement had helped their parents. This vision shaped an emphasis on the duties, rather than the rights, of citizenship and reflected an unduly narrow conception of citizenship (pp. 245–285).

The Community and Social Studies

Some years ago Bernard Bailyn (1960) pointed out that schools were only one source of education in society, and he suggested that historians of education examine the educational efforts of churches, workplaces, and newspapers. In a more recent work, Kaestle (1988) looked to educational institutions other than schools. In studying the history of literacy in the United States from the 1880s to the 1980s, Kaestle claimed that from 1880 to 1900 the public press offered readers diverse fare. From 1880 to 1910 the number of foreign language newspapers increased each year. By 1912, there were more than 300 socialist publications, which included 13 daily newspapers (pp. 528–530). From 1910 to 1920 (when social studies was developing) this diversity was replaced by standardization as mass-circulation newspapers and popular magazines increased their numbers at the expense of smaller publications. In the history of social studies, the period from 1900 to 1920 saw the introduction of courses in current events, community civics, and problems of American democracy. The Committee on Social Studies suggested that social studies teachers look to the popular press and newspapers for material for class consideration at the time when that press was becoming less diverse and more standardized.

Historians of social studies ought to examine other forms of social education that took place outside of schools. Settlement houses, charity workers, neighborhood social and political organizations, immigrant aid associations, reform groups, and churches and synagogues did educational work, much of it with adults. Moreover, this work was similar in content and end to that found in the recommendations of the Committee on Social Studies (Lybarger, 1987, p. 187).

The Struggle to Control Social Education

Herbert Kliebard's work suggests further research in a related area. In "Bureaucracy and Curriculum Theory" Kliebard (1976) contended that the curriculum field has been characterized by a rigid technological perspective and a persistent ameliorative urge since its inception. The origins of the perspective lay in scientific management in industry, from which it entered curricular thought through the work of Franklin Bobbitt. The technological perspective has wed curricular thought to a single metaphor, the school as factory, and the ameliorative urge has resulted in curriculum workers' lack of "toleration of the kind of long range research that has little immediate value, but which may, in the long run, contribute significantly to our basic knowledge and understanding" (p. 180). Research on the interest that many members of the Committee on Social Studies had in charity organization and settlement house work (Lybarger, 1987) confirms Kliebard's findings and affords historians another perspective on the sources of the committee's recommendations.

In *The Struggle for the American Curriculum*, Kliebard (1986) viewed curricular history as an account of the struggle of five groups for control of its content. Might a similar account be written of the history of the social studies curriculum? Certainly the material for conflict is there: between the historians and the social scientists in the 1920s; between the social reconstructionists and their opponents in the 1930s, 1940s, and the 1950s; between the program developers and the classroom teachers in the 1960s and early 1970s; and now the struggle between the traditionalists and the advocates of a "more relevant," but more diffuse, social studies curriculum.

New Labels, Old Courses

Barry Franklin's *Building the American Community* (1986) affords the historians of social studies further insight into the development of their field. In his last chapter, "Curriculum Thought to School Practice," Franklin examined the impact of one curricular change in the schools of Minneapolis. After World War II, the school system instituted a "Common Learnings" program the centerpiece of which was a 2-hour combined class in English and social studies. Two teachers told Franklin that their Common Learning classes were not different from the regular English and history classes they taught. Franklin concluded that often curriculum change "was merely putting new labels on old courses" (p. 142).

There are few case studies of what happened to the New Social Studies reforms of the 1950s and 1960s, but there is one that lends support to Franklin's conclusions about curricular change. In a historical study of what happened to the Sociological Resources for the Social Studies (SRSS) program, David Smith (1985) contended that it was a failure for three reasons. *First,* the major reason the program was developed was that federal money was available. Smith could find no demand for the reform from classroom teachers. *Second,* there was little classroom teacher involvement in development of the materials and, as a result, the materials did not reflect the realities of classroom teaching. For example, the materials did not lend themselves to use in large classes. Moreover, to work well, nearly perfect attendance was necessary. Perfect attendance and small class sizes did not exist in most schools in the 1970s. *Third*, SRSS was positivist in its orientation and did not address the social studies teachers' concern for the teaching of citizenship (pp. 19–23). Case studies of the introduction, development, and demise of some of the more widely used programs of the New Social Studies would certainly be useful.

Old Masters

One of the most promising approaches to the history of the social studies today is the development of the idea of the "Old Masters" of the social studies. The earliest use of the idea was in a paper, "The Earliest Master: Henry Johnson," presented by Paul Robinson at the 1981 meeting of the National Council of the Social Studies.

James Barth and Samuel Shermis (1985) have articulated a set of questions that might help in understanding the work of an Old Master. Some of these questions are: "What was the particular person like?" "What do various Old Masters have in common?" "In what ways are they different?" "What can we learn about their social background from examining their writing, teaching, and organizing activities?" "What can be learned about the ways in which a relatively few individuals succeeded in shaping the way people *think* [italics in original] about the field and therefore the way the field is shaped" (p. 7).

Their examination of the lives and work of important Old Masters led Barth and Shermis to ask questions very similar to those raised earlier in the discussion of Michael Young's work.

Why did the social studies evolve from a collection of separate courses into one field? With what purposes did the social studies begin? Whose purposes were these? What unrecognized and implicit assumptions were important? What are the meanings of the critical terms of the field, e.g., *citizenship, decision-making, problem-solving, integration, democracy,* and *discipline?* (pp. 5–8, italics in original)

As a focus for research, the idea of Old Masters demonstrates that it would be possible to learn a great deal about members of the Committee on Social Studies, as about other important figures in the history of the social studies, by trying to reconstruct what they read, learned, and taught. It is possible to secure the college transcripts of many committee members, and it is sometimes possible to determine the textbooks they used. There is ample material available about the interests and careers of many members of the committee. It is not too difficult to determine club membership, church affiliation, and participation in political and social organizations. *Who's Who* is a good place to begin.

For example, there is abundant material available by and about Thomas Jesse Jones, the chairman of the Committee on Social Studies. Jones's transcripts, along with his master's essay (1897) and doctoral dissertation (1905), are available from Columbia University. In both, Jones discussed at length the connection between the study of sociology and the study of education. It is possible to examine the syllabi for courses Jones took under Franklin Henry Giddings, his major professor. The Ar-

chives at Hampton Institute contain syllabi and reading lists for the courses Jones taught there, along with some of the sermons he delivered as Associate Chaplain.

Arthur W. Dunn is another old master whose career and work warrant further study. One of the authors of *The Teaching of Community Civics* (Barnard, Carrier, Dunn, & Kingsley, 1915) and the compiler of *The Social Studies in Secondary Education* (1916), Dunn's attention was drawn to the educational implications of sociology by Albion W. Small (1896), an early American sociologist who had given much thought to the subject. Dunn claimed the intellectual warrant of Small's sociology for his *The Community and the Citizen* (1907), the first textbook in community civics. Dunn was also the chairman of the National Municipal League's Committee on Civic Education, and the League paid his salary while he was serving as the Specialist in Civic Education at the United States Bureau of Education (Lybarger, 1980, p. 37). In addition to Dunn, at least 10 members of the committee were members of the National Municipal League, a turn-of-the-century municipal reform organization, and some of the recommendations found in *The Social Studies in Secondary Education* reflect that interest (Lybarger, 1981, p. 39).

Old Masters sometimes attained their status by writing textbooks, and those written by members of the Committee on Social Studies repay examination. Henry Reed Burch was the most prolific writer on the committee, writing one textbook and co-authoring two others. *American Social Problems: An Introduction to the Study of Society* (Burch & Patterson, 1937) was intended to meet the demand for "socialized history," a term used by committee members to describe the approach to history they advocated. Burch described his second book, *American Economic Life in its Civic and Social Aspects* (1921) as dealing with "concrete problems from the civic and social standpoint." Those words were also used to describe the content of the Problems of American Democracy course recommended by the committee. A third book by Burch and S. Howard Patterson was called *Problems of American Democracy: Political, Economic, Social* (1918). The title came from the course recommended in *The Social Studies in Secondary Education* for the senior year. According to the authors, the publication of this book marked "the advent of a new movement in secondary education" (p. 4).

Three other members of the Committee on Social Studies wrote books that they claimed addressed the new courses recommended in *The Social Studies in Secondary Education.* James Lynn Barnard and Jesse C. Evans wrote a vocational civics text, *Getting a Living* (1919), and a community civics text, *Citizenship in Philadelphia* (1918). In *Getting a Living* the authors identified the "civic virtues" with "business ethics" (p. vi). Finally, Samuel Burnett Howe wrote *Actual Democracy* (1921), which he intended to be a textbook for the Problems of American Democracy course recommended in the committee's report (p. 2). A reading of some of the textbooks discussed here with the elements of Kaestle's idea of "social outlook" in mind might make clear what members of the committee meant by terms like "civic virtues," "need," "interest," and "social education."

The Old Masters approach could be applied to some of the

teachers of members of the Committee on Social Studies. For example, many of the sociological ideas found in *The Social Studies in Secondary Education* came from Franklin Henry Giddings of Columbia University (Thomas Jesse Jones's major professor) and, to a significantly lesser extent, Albion W. Small of the University of Chicago. The social world created by Giddings and Small was one to which both sociologists counseled "adjustment" or "adaptation." It was a world to which human beings were expected to conform and one in which the role of human choice in shaping that world was strictly limited by Small and of almost no account in the work of Giddings (Lybarger, 1981, pp. 143–178). Moreover, the kind of sociology that entered social studies through Giddings did not for the most part represent the popularization of American sociological thought that, as early as 1900, was being shaped by historians and sociologists trained in Germany whose interest and orientation were historical and institutional. Giddings was a self-taught sociologist whose work owed a greater intellectual debt to the classical economists such as Smith, Malthus, and Ricardo. To the extent that Giddings's work was formative of the recommendations found in *The Social Studies in Secondary Education,* that work was, by 1916, an intellectual fossil, a relic from an earlier view of sociology (Lybarger, 1981, p. 307).

Harold Rugg is perhaps the oldest Old Master. Any study of Rugg's life and work must begin with his autobiography, *That Men May Understand: An American in the Long Armistice* (1941). Aspects of Rugg's life and work have been the subject of two fine doctoral dissertations (Nelson, 1975; Winters, 1968). Nelson has also assembled an exhaustive bibliography of Rugg's work that will be indispensable for later students.

Social Reconstruction

It would be shallow to write about Rugg without a consideration of the social studies textbook series he developed and the curricula in which they were used. These textbooks reflected a pro–New Deal liberal bias and sold well during the Great Depression. In the late 1930s, the series came under attack from business and patriotic groups. In some school districts the series was dropped; in others, the curriculum's supporters were successful (Bagenstos, 1979).

As World War II approached, Rugg's criticisms of World War I made the series unpopular (Kliebard & Wegner, 1987, pp. 284–285). During and immediately after World War II, the series was quietly dropped, even by school boards that had earlier retained it despite pressure. By the end of the 1940s, social reconstruction had all but disappeared from the schools.

Rugg's social studies curriculum deserves the historian's attention for two reasons. *First,* the materials represented the only sustained effort to fashion a social studies curriculum with a view to fostering social change. *Second,* Rugg had to face and respond to the charge of indoctrination. His response was inadequate. According to Rugg, students were already indoctrinated by the business culture and its institutions; the schools were only serving as a vital counterweight. Rugg also contended that, in the best intellectual and artistic circles, a consensus over what was the good society was developing to which the citizen

could and should give informed consent (Bagenstos, 1979, p. 24).

Any effort to understand social reconstruction must begin with two articles written by William Stanley (1981a, 1981b) that appeared in *Theory and Research in Social Education.* In the first article, "The Radical Reconstructionist Rationale for Social Education," Stanley articulated and analyzed the basic tenets of the reconstructionist rationale for social education as found in the work of George Counts and Theodore Brameld. In the subsequent article, "Toward a Reconstruction of Social Education," Stanley dealt with the extent to which the ideas of radical reconstruction are reflected in five contemporary rationales for social education: Oliver and Shaver's jurisprudential rationale, Wesley and Wronski's history and the social science disciplines rationale, Goldmark and Brubaker's inquiry as a rationale, Hunt and Metcalf's social education as inquiry into selected social problems, and Newmann's citizen action as a rationale (Stanley, 1981b, pp. 67–89).

Although not specifically historical, Stanley's articles call the historian's attention to important social and educational issues. *First,* social studies educators need a philosophy of education that embodies a theory of social criticism. *Second,* social studies educators need to see the importance of an interdisciplinary analysis of social issues. *Third,* social studies educators need "to define the purpose and role of social education as it relates to the need for cultural transformation" (1981a, p. 76). *Finally,* social studies educators need to deal directly with the issues of teacher neutrality and ideological imposition. Many of Stanley's points are not new; the fact that they need repetition may indicate the lack of a critical sense of history on the part of social studies educators.

Some historian should give attention to the persistence of the social reconstructionist perspective on social education. R. Freeman Butts (1988) contended that the "moral imperative" for the schools is to "inflame the civic temper" of youth. Millard Clements (1989) articulated a social reconstructionist position for students, teachers, and university and college educators.

Progressive Education and the Progressive Movement

It is difficult to detach the development of social studies from progressive education, and it is difficult to detach progressive education from the progressive movement. At the risk of oversimplifying an exceedingly complex and interesting historiographical controversy, it can be asserted that progressivism had four aspects: one liberal, humane, and democratic (Lubove, 1965; Scott, 1959); another, defensive and conservative (Hofstader, 1955); a third, oppressive and reactionary (Kolko, 1967; Weinstein, 1968); and a fourth, lying somewhere between the first two (White, 1976).

What aspect of progressivism is represented by the work of the Committee on Social Studies? According to Lawrence Cremin (1965), progressive education reflected "the radical faith that culture could be democratized without becoming vulgarized" (p. 15). What aspects of social, political, and intellectual culture did committee members seek to democratize? There is no ready answer to that question.

Some historian of social studies is going to have to come to grips with the influence of John Dewey on its origins and development. Dewey has been quoted in support of or opposition to almost every curriculum reform measure from his day to ours. According to Kieran Egan (1980), most, if not all, of the problems of contemporary social studies may be traced to Dewey's inadequate pedagogy, psychology, and sense of history. Egan recommended that social studies be abolished and children be taught history. Stephen Thorton (1984), on the other hand, contended that Egan did not understand Dewey. Kliebard (1986) presented Dewey as rising above many of the competing interest groups contending for a segment of the curriculum. According to David Labaree (1987), "Dewey's complex and sweeping vision never took hold in the American curriculum as powerfully as did the slogans and simplistic slogans offered in his name by the competing curriculum factions" (p. 485).

Educational psychology also emerged with progressive education. Historians ought to pay attention to the influence of the early educational psychologists upon the development of social studies. Edward Lynn Thorndike's work is one example. Thorndike taught at Teachers College, Columbia, while two future members of the Committee on Social Studies were in attendance (Lybarger, 1981). Moreover, Thorndike's view of what constituted good citizenship was nearly identical with that found in *The Social Studies in Secondary Education* (Thorndike, 1916). The developmental psychologist G. Stanley Hall told the National Educational Association that curricular reformers should look to the curriculum of Hampton Institute as a model worthy of emulation (Hall, 1902, pp. 260–268). In regard to the shape of the Problems of American Democracy course, the committee gave social studies teachers the same advice (Dunn, 1916, p. 52).

CONCLUSIONS: THE PAST IN THE PRESENT

At this point someone might ask, What is to be gained by establishing that particular aspects of the social studies curriculum are older than we thought and have origins of which we have been unaware? What is the difference so long as social studies is well taught and meets the needs of students?

Jacques Barzun (1978) claimed that historical study is a useful antidote against "self-centering." We have seen that social studies professionals and other curriculum workers have inherited a strong disposition to do good and a short historical memory. These qualities have often led them to assume, usually implicitly, that things have always been as they are now and that they will continue thus. For such persons, Barzun held, some form of study is needed that demonstrates that many taken-for-granted parts of their intellectual universe had a beginning. In short, there was a time when "what is" could have been otherwise. Recreating such times and studying the dominant issues should sensitize social studies educators to assuming that behind modern ideas and practices lies some grand scheme of historical necessity, sanctioning and giving meaning to them.

Social studies educators need to be reminded that very little of what they consider new is indeed novel. More than 40 years ago, Henry Johnson (1943) observed:

In my own lifetime I have seen the rise and fall of most of the educational ideas which I find in the literature of education from Plato to John Dewey. Of some of those ideas I have myself been the original discoverer and have felt that because the ideas were new to me that they must be new to the rest of the world until I had the misfortune to stumble on the same ideas in writings published before I was born. One of the things history can do is to take the joy out of original discovery. (pp. 238–239)

The knowledge that men and women more than 70 years ago struggled with questions of social education remarkably similar to those encountered today, and arrived at answers much like modern ones, should help us understand our tendency to overvalue the importance of our thoughts and activities. That understanding is history's unique contribution to education. To secure it we should restore historical study to its rightful place at the center of the social studies curriculum, whether at the university or in the elementary school. Given the past and present of the social studies curriculum, that would represent an advance of some importance.

References

Aristotle. (1943). *Politics* (B. Jowett, Trans.). New York: Walter J. Black.

Bagenstos, N. T. (1979). Social reconstruction: The controversy over the textbooks of Harold Rugg. *Theory and Research in Social Education, 4,* 22–39.

Bailyn, B. (1960). *Education in the forming of American society: Needs and opportunities for study.* Chapel Hill, NC: University of North Carolina Press.

Bancroft, G. (1834–1874) *History of the United States.* New York: Appleton.

Barnard, J. L., & Evans, J. C. (1918). *Citizenship in Philadelphia.* New York: Lippincott.

Barnard, J. L., & Evans, J. C. (1919). *Getting a living.* New York: Lippincott.

Barnard, J. L., Carrier, F. W., Dunn, A., & Kingsley, C. (1915). *The teaching of community civics* (Bulletin No. 23). Washington, DC: U.S. Bureau of Education.

Barr, R., Barth, J., & S. S. Shermis. (1978). *The nature of the social studies.* Palm Springs, CA: ETC Publications.

Barth, J. L., & Shermis, S. S. (1981). Defining social problems. *Theory and Research in Social Education, 7,* 22–34.

Barth, J. L., & Shermis, S. S. (1985). Founders of the social studies: Who are they and how do we know them? *Indiana Social Studies Quarterly, 7,* 7–11.

Barzun, J. (1978). *Clio and the doctors.* New York: Macmillan.

Beard, C. A. (1912). *An economic interpretation of the constitution of the United States.* New York: Charles Scribner's Sons.

Beard, C. A. (1934). *The nature of the social sciences in relation to objectives of instruction.* New York: Charles Scribner's Sons.

Berelson, B. (Ed.). (1962). *The Social Sciences and the Social Studies.* New York: Harcourt, Brace & World.

Bestor, A. E. (1953). *Educational wastelands: The retreat from learning in our public schools.* Urbana, IL: University of Illinois Press.

Burch, H. R. (1921). *American economic life in its civic and social aspects*. New York: Macmillan.

Burch, H. R., & S. Howard Patterson (1918). *Problems of American democracy: Political, economic, social*. New York: Macmillan.

Burch, H. R., & S. H. Patterson. (1937). *American social problems: An introduction to the study of society*. New York: Macmillan.

Butts, R. F. (1988). The moral imperative for American schools: ". . . inflame the civic temper." *American Journal of Education, 97*, 162–191.

Clements, M. (1989). A note from the editor. *Theory and Research in Social Education, 17*, 170–174.

Cremin, L. (1964). *The transformation of the school: Progressivism in American education*. New York: Random House, Vintage.

Cremin, L. (1965). *The wonderful world of Elwood Patterson Cubberley: An essay on the historiography of American education*. New York: Columbia University Press.

Cubberley, E. P. (1919). *Public education in the United States*. Boston: Houghton Mifflin.

Dougan, A. M. (1985). The search for a definition of the social studies: A historical overview. *Indiana Journal of Social Education, 3*, 13–35.

Dunn, A. W. (Compiler). (1916). *The social studies in secondary education* (Bulletin No. 28). Washington, DC: United States Bureau of Education.

Egan, K. (1980). John Dewey and the social studies curriculum. *Theory and research in social education 8*, 37–53.

Franklin, B. M. (1986). *Building the American community: The school curriculum and the search for social control*. Philadelphia: Falmer Press.

Gross, R. E. (1976). The status of the social studies in the public schools of the United States: Facts and impressions of a national survey. *Social Education, 40*, 194–196.

Hall, G. S. (1902). The high school as the people's college. *Addresses and Proceedings National Educational Association, 38*, 260–268.

Hertzberg, H. (1971). *Historical parallels for the sixties and the seventies: Primary sources and core curriculum revisited*. Boulder, CO: ERIC Clearinghouse for Social Studies/Social Science Education.

Hertzberg, H. (1981). *Social studies reform: 1880–1980*. Boulder, CO: Social Sciences Educational Consortium.

Hofstadter, R. (1955). *The age of reform*. New York: Random House, Vintage.

Howe, S. B. (1921). *Actual democracy*. New York: D. C. Heath.

Johnson, H. (1915). *Teaching of history in elementary and secondary schools*. New York: Macmillan.

Johnson, H. (1932). *An introduction to the history of the social sciences in the schools*. New York: Charles Scribner's Sons.

Johnson, H. (1943). *The other side of main street: A history teacher from Sauk Centre*. New York: Columbia University Press.

Jones, T. J. (1897). *Social education in the elementary school*. Unpublished master's thesis, Columbia University, New York.

Jones, T. J. (1905). *Sociology of a city block*. New York: Columbia University Press.

Jones, T. J. (1913). Statement of the chairman of the committee on social studies. *Preliminary statements by chairmen of committees of the commission on the reorganization of secondary education* (Bureau of Education Bulletin No. 41). Washington DC: United States Bureau of Education.

Judd, C. H., (1918). The teaching of civics. *School Review, 26*, 511–532.

Kaestle, C. (1976). Conflict and consensus revisited: Notes toward a reinterpretation of educational history. *Harvard Educational Review, 46*, 390–396.

Kaestle, C. (1982). Ideology and American educational history. *History of Education Quarterly, 22*, 123–137.

Kaestle, C. (1988). Literacy and diversity: Themes from a social history of the American reading public. *History of Education Quarterly, 28*, 122–156.

Karier, C., Violas, P., & Spring, J. (1973). *Roots of crisis: American education in the twentieth century*. Chicago: Rand McNally.

Katz, M. (1971). *Class, bureaucracy and schools: The illusion of educational change in America*. New York: Praeger.

Kliebard, H. (1976). Bureaucracy and curriculum theory. In V. Haubrick (Ed.), *Class, bureaucracy, and schooling* (pp. 75–89). Washington, DC: Association for Supervision and Curriculum Development.

Kliebard, H. (1986). *The struggle for the American curriculum: 1893–1958*. Boston: Routledge and Kegan Paul.

Kliebard, H., & Wegner, G. (1987). Harold Rugg and the reconstruction of the social studies curriculum: The treatment of the "great war" in his textbook series. In T. S. Popkewitz (Eds.), *The formation of the school subjects: The struggle for creating an American institution* (pp. 268–287). Philadelphia: Falmer Press.

Kolko, G. (1967). *The triumph of conservatism: A reinterpretation of American history, 1900–1916*. Chicago: Quadrangle.

Labaree, D. (1987). Politics, markets, and the compromised curriculum. *Harvard Educational Review, 57*, 483–493.

Lubove, R. (1965). *The professional altruist: The emergence of social work as a career*. Cambridge, MA: Harvard University Press.

Lybarger, M. B. (1980). The political context of the social studies: Creating a constituency for political reform. *Theory and Research in Social Education, 8*(3), 43–64.

Lybarger, M. B. (1981). *The origins of the social studies: 1865–1916*. Unpublished doctoral dissertation, University of Wisconsin, Madison.

Lybarger, M. B. (1987). Need as ideology: Social workers, social settlements and the social studies. In T. S. Popkewitz (Eds.), *The formation of the school subjects: The struggle for creating an American institution* (pp. 176–180). New York: Falmer Press.

A National Council for the Social Studies. (1921, April). *The Historical Outlook, 12*, 144.

Nelson, M. R. (1975). *Building a science of society: The social studies and Harold Rugg*. Unpublished doctoral dissertation, Stanford University, Stanford.

Nelson, M. R. (1986). The social studies in World War Two. *Theory and Research in Social Education 14*, 255–267.

Robinson, P. (1977, November). *Re-interpreting the history of the social studies*. Paper presented to the College and University Faculty Assembly of the National Council for the Social Studies, Cincinnati.

Robinson, P. (1980). The conventional historians of the social studies. *Theory and Research in Social Education, 8*(3), 65–88.

Robinson, P. (1981, November). *The earliest master: Henry Johnson*. Paper presented at the annual meeting of the National Council of the Social Studies, Detroit.

Rugg, H. (1923). Do social studies prepare pupils adequately for life activities? In H. Rugg (Ed.), The social studies in the elementary and secondary school 22nd Yearbook of the National Society for the Study of Education Part II, pp. 1–19. Bloomington, IL.: Public School Publishing Company.

Rugg, H. (1926). A century of curriculum-construction in American schools. In G. M. Whipple (Ed.), *The foundations of curriculum-making*. 26th Yearbook of the National Society for the Study of Education (Part I, pp. 3–119). Bloomington, IL: Public School Publishing Company.

Rugg, H. (1941). *That men may understand: An American in the long armistice*. New York: Doubleday Doran.

Scott, A. (1959). The progressive era in perspective. *Journal of Politics 21*, 685–701.

Seguel, M. L. (1965). *The curriculum field: Its formative years*. New York: Columbia University Press.

Shaver, J. P. (1977). A critical view of the social studies profession. *Social Education, 40*, 300–307.

Shaver, J. P. (1982). Reappraising the theoretical goals of research in social studies education. *Theory and Research in Social Education, 9*, 1–16.

Small, A. W. (1986). The demands of sociology upon pedagogy. *Proceedings of the Annual Meeting of the National Educational Association*. Washington, DC.

Smith, D. (1985). What went wrong with the social studies reform movement? *Theory and Research in Social Education, 7(4)*, 35–57.

Stanley, W. B. (1981a). The radical reconstructionist rationale for social education. *Theory and Research in Social Education, 8(4)*, 55–79.

Stanley, W. B. (1981b). Toward a reconstruction of social education. *Theory and Research in Social Education, 9(1)*, 67–89.

Thorndike, E. L. (1916). Education for initiative and originality. *Teachers College Record 18*, 405–416.

Thornton, S. J. (1984). Social studies misunderstood: A reply to Kieran Egan. *Theory and Research in Social Education 12*, 43–47.

Tryon, R. (1929). Thirteen years of problems of American democracy in the senior high school. *Historical Outlook, 12*, 81–83.

Tryon, R. (1934). *The social sciences as school subjects*. New York: Charles Scribner's Sons.

Tyack, D. (1974). *The one best system: A history of American urban education*. Cambridge, MA: Harvard University Press.

Weinstein, J. (1968). *The corporate ideal in the liberal state*. Boston: Beacon Press.

Wesley, E. B. (1937). *Teaching the social studies*. Boston: D. C. Heath.

White, M. (1976). *Social thought in America: The revolt against formalism*. London: Oxford University Press.

Wiebe, R. (1967). *The search for order: 1877–1920*. New York: Hill and Wang.

Winters, E. (1968). *Harold Rugg and education for social reconstruction*. Unpublished doctoral dissertation, University of Wisconsin, Madison.

Young, M. (1971). *Knowledge and control*. London: Collier-Macmillan.

2

PHILOSOPHICAL INQUIRY AND SOCIAL STUDIES

Robert K. Fullinwider

UNIVERSITY OF MARYLAND AT COLLEGE PARK

The question, "What can philosophical inquiry contribute to research about, or the teaching of, social studies?" asked without further qualification, is too indefinite to answer. Too many kinds of activity, too many levels of inquiry, too many sorts of aims fit under the umbrella-word *philosophy*. Whom shall we take as our model: Socrates, who was unsystematic, a talker not a writer, more interested in creating and exploring perplexities than in answering them, unconcerned about the world around him, and for whom philosophizing was a personal, divinely ordained mission? Or how about Plato, who wanted the answers, systematically worked them out, made blueprints for social life on their basis, and, while running a school to propagate his doctrines, promoted his plans to receptive rulers? What subject matter, method, or ambition unites Abelard and Aurelius, Descartes and Dewey, Emerson and Engels, Hobbes and Husserl, Kant and Kierkegaard, Locke and Lucretius, Santayana and Sartre, Wittgenstein and Whitehead?

Perhaps one way to characterize philosophers is to say that they ask basic questions, they look for fundamental grounds. However, questions are never just basic or fundamental, they are always *basic to* or *fundamental for* some task, problem, puzzle, or aim. It is useful, for example, to notice that a particular social studies curriculum presupposes (a) that students will not read extensively after leaving school, (b) that young people should be active voters as soon as they reach voting age, or (c) that making negative judgments about other cultures is ethnocentric. Getting such assumptions out in the open makes it easier to challenge or defend the curriculum. For example, (a) is a dubious empirical assumption; it can be put to the test of observation. Assumption (b) expresses an ideal almost always taken for granted; bringing it to light may cause second thoughts. And (c) involves a conceptual leap that ought to be questioned.

It makes sense to say that basic to this social studies curriculum is some model of a life of learning, some ideal of civic participation, or some view about ineluctable bias in judgment. How much deeper must inquiry go? If the curriculum presupposes an ideal of the active voter, then it presupposes the legitimacy of democratic elections. Need its proponents articulate a conception and defense of democracy? Possibly. Different conceptions of democracy may put the voting ideal in a different light. Whether it is worth moving to this deeper level depends on the understanding the analysis would bring to the higher level—is it understanding that makes a difference?

What about deeper yet? The assumption about bias in judgment that underlies the curriculum may rest in turn on some unstated distinction between facts and values. Its defenders may take facts to be public in a way that values are not; or think that factual disagreements can be settled rationally, but that value disagreements cannot; or assign facts exclusively to the cognitive domain, values to the affective. Probing these assumptions about facts and values may clarify much about the curriculum's particular features and weaken (or strengthen) the support for them, or it may show that the curriculum is consistent with several different views about facts and values.

Questions about fact and value can themselves be put at different levels. Need the curriculum designer show more than that the proposed curriculum rests on widely shared views of the fact-value distinction, or that the assumed distinction is sufficiently general not to prejudice particular policy choices? Need the distinction be secured in some *metaphysics,* buttressed by an *ontology?* Wouldn't that be going too deep? Metaphysical views are indeed basic or fundamental to some inquiries, but not to understanding the curriculum proposal, are they?

There are many who think otherwise. They think that the goals and techniques of our educational practices rest on meta-

Reviewers were Bonnie Kent, University of Maryland at College Park; Richard S. Knight, Utah State University; Donald W. Oliver, Harvard University; Lynda Stone, University of Hawaii; Robert Wachbroit, University of Maryland at College Park.

This chapter was written during a period of work on moral and civic education supported by the Spencer Foundation.

physical premises and stand or fall on the quality of their metaphysical commitments. Cherryholmes (1980, p. 128), for example, offered overworked and harried social educators some bad news: that if, say, they wanted to push Shirley Engle's idea of citizenship education as education in decision making (Engle, 1968), they had better be prepared to defend Alfred Tarski's theory of truth (Tarski, 1956). This is daunting news, indeed, since Tarski's definition of truth cannot even be fully stated without the use of mathematical set theory. An educator who is discouraged by this and turns instead to a recent treatise on test validation with the hope of perhaps getting a clearer idea of whether a set of tests is measuring critical thinking ability may be dismayed to be told that he or she must adjudicate the quarrel between logical positivists and scientific realists (Norris, 1983).

Think back to the descending levels of questions that the social studies educator might ask about a proposed curriculum. Are questions at any level philosophical, or only those asked at the deeper levels? Do we hit the philosophical level only when we get to the questions where I introduced the words *metaphysics* and *ontology? That* surely is a philosophical level. That is the level on which we confront questions of the greatest generality and abstraction. How do I know that other minds exist? How can I reconcile my freedom with universal causation? What is the nature of the "me" that is thinking these thoughts? When does change alter identity? Can I know anything at all with certainty? What is truth? What is reality? These have been the perennial puzzles of what I will call *first philosophy*.

Need the social studies educator, whether theorist or practitioner, grapple with these questions and the answers that philosophers have given them? (Can it really be the case that citizenship-education-as-decision-making stands or falls with Tarski's semantic definition of truth?) If so, this is a particularly confusing time to join the philosophical discussion. Philosophy itself—the academic discipline—is in marvelous disarray. Wildly competing approaches, terminologies, and research programs abound, along with confusion and self-doubt about philosophy's history, utility, and future prospects.

THE FEMINIST CHALLENGE AND OTHER BATTLEGROUNDS

According to Putnam (1987), for example, 20th-century philosophy has been led into a blind alley by a "disastrous picture of the world" inherited from the 17th century (pp. 8, 16). Rorty (1982) counseled that rather than seek philosophy's way out of the blind alley, we should give up philosophy (with a capital *P*) altogether (pp. xiii–xliii). Perhaps that isn't a bad idea anyway, because, if the feminists are right, the entire tradition is rotten to the core, founded on a distinctly masculinist penchant for dichotomizing (e.g., mind-body, subject-object, self-other, appearance-reality, reason-emotion, will-nature) "linked to an invidious male-female dichotomy" that posits woman "as the other to be mastered and suppressed" (Fraser, 1985, p. 181). However, its complicity in that particularly invidious dichotomy means we cannot just turn away from philosophy, we have to *exorcise* it. Those fundamental dichotomies are more than intellectual errors!

According to a variety of poststructuralists, post-Marxists, and postmodernists, our social arrangements, political practices, and educational institutions reflect the urge toward hierarchy and domination characteristic of philosophical thought itself, whose effort to represent a fluid and ever-various world by imposing concepts on it spawns the desire in those very concepts to negate or annihilate "the other" that escapes their grasp (Lyotard, 1983). Conceptual schemes—"discourses"—are "a violence we do to things" (Foucault, 1972, p. 229), a violence that carries into the social and political arrangements organized around those schemes. The possibility of a social life not oriented around the instrumental domination of nature and people begins with abandoning the philosophical quest to represent reality. There are big stakes in the metaphysical wars!

These depth charges being set off in the murky seas of metaphysics may leave their intended victim, "first philosophy," intact, but so roil the cultural surface that any number of creaky, barnacle-encrusted social, political, and educational traditions floating there are put in peril of sinking. The wide-ranging feminist critiques alone show how much of that surface needs rehabilitation, how much of our "common sense" about politics, education, science, sports, military service, business, finance, religion, and art needs rethinking. This rethinking, and the "unthinking" that must precede it, need not involve plumbing the depths for metaphysical doctrines, but they do require that we "think behind appearances," that is, that we bring to awareness beliefs and methods we more or less have taken for granted and have never much thought about, at least from the point of view of gender. Making gender a central category changes everything. What we thought was adequate, complete, impartial, neutral, objective, and comprehensive often looks, through the prism of gender, to be partial, one-sided, incomplete, loaded, selective, and biased.

The broad-scale rethinking occasioned by feminism can certainly count as philosophical even if it does not, or need not, plumb the briny deep. The central questions raised by feminism have to do with perspective and judgment. What would an ungendered point of view look like? How can we correct for bias, partial vision, limited perspective? Now, we can force these questions all the way down to the bottom level. We can argue about whether complete aperspectivity is possible and quarrel about what the very idea of objectivity means. These quarrels and arguments will involve us in the deepest epistemological conundrums. But we can also raise these questions about perspective at much higher levels, with quite practical matters in mind.

Are the objectivity and completeness of current biological research undermined, for example, by the absence of women biologists in universities and laboratories (Harding, 1986, pp. 83–110)? Must female judges be added to the bench in substantial numbers before women lawyers can represent their clients effectively (Czapanskiy, 1988)? These are not just empirical questions, resolved by detecting a differential success rate among male and female attorneys or noting different research projects among male and female biologists. They are also questions about the very meaning of good science, the very meaning of justice in the courtroom. They make us think, for example, about what the aims of science are—our science, here and now—and how those aims might be differently understood, how they are given a specific form by the institutional organization of scientific research, and whether those forms are defensible as maximally truth finding and problem solving. Practices have to be measured against ideals and the ideals rethought at the same time.

PHILOSOPHICAL METHOD? PHILOSOPHICAL SUBJECTS?

I have been using the idea of levels to get at what philosophy is and does, suggesting that philosophical questions are general, deeper-level ones. The idea is only partly helpful, however, because there are deep-level investigations that are not philosophical. They are about technical or theoretical problems in, say, mathematics, cell biology, or the syntax of languages. Perhaps another approach to characterizing philosophy is through method or subject matter. Is there a particular way to answer philosophical questions? Are such questions about a particular subject?

Michael Scriven (1988, p. 132) has emphasized to educators the importance of skills for *conceputal analysis,* skills that can be learned from the practice of philosophers. Indeed, philosophers during this century have often put a premium on clarity and precision of expression, and much of their work has been focused on the very ideas of meaning and reference. They have dwelt on issues of definition, speaker's intention, logical form, and truth conditions. Their best work is technically and conceptually sophisticated.

This so-called analytic philosophy would seem well grounded in precedent: All of the Socratic dialogues involve searches for definition. However, the Socratic precedent won't support the identification of philosophy with the practice of a certain form of analysis.

Socrates was, indeed, always after definitions, but his search for meanings was not promiscuous. He confined himself to a handful of notions—justice, persuasion and truth, piety, love—that are central to any quest for knowledge or worth, notions that supply the regulative ideals of the most enduring human practices. These are the concepts that inhabit those perennial questions of first philosophy.

Not only did Socrates confine his questions to these basic concepts, he also had a particular aim. Scriven (1988, pp 144–45) in discussing the various procedures for conceptual analysis, recommended the "method of examples and contrasts," the method of clarifying a notion by giving examples of it rather than by giving an explicit definition. For ordinary arguments and discussions, this is practical advice. But it is exactly the opposite of what Socrates aimed for. In each of the dialogues, the characters initially respond to Socrates' requests for definition by giving an example, and each time Socrates replies that he was not asking for an *instance* of the concept in question but its *meaning.* Knowing instances and examples can aid us in using a concept correctly—and for most purposes that is enough—but that is different from understanding it in the philosophical sense, understanding its essence. At least so thought Socrates, and his entire philosophical mission centered on a quest for the real, timeless, unchanging meanings of the central concepts of existence and value. In the Socratic conception, then, philosophy has a certain subject matter. Philosophers do not analyze just any concepts and they do not clarify meanings just for the sake of clarification.

Nor is there a particular method all philosophers follow. Socrates' technique of question-and-response is often emulated, but for him it typically led to acknowledgement of ignorance rather than final illumination. Plato in *The Republic* pictured a long process of education and training that eventually would bring the philosopher to intuit directly the deepest truths. The stategies and devices used by philosophers in this century to get themselves in contact with those deepest truths have included common sense (Moore, 1959), logical reconstruction (Carnap, 1947), phenomenology (Husserl, 1960; Merleau-Ponty, 1962), hermeneutics (Gadamer, 1975), cultural "archeology" (Foucault, 1972), immanent critique (Adorno, 1973), and deconstruction (Derrida, 1976). Whatever the chosen method, it must help philosophers think both *clearly* and *deeply* about philosophical subjects.

BASIC QUESTIONS

First philosophy involves the most general and abstract questions we can ask, about the handful of ideas underlying all human practices, with the aim to understanding their essential or real meaning—that is how we can define the project Socrates began and Rorty (1979, 1982) thinks it is time to abandon. Other questions and projects can be philosophical, too, philosophical with a small *p,* but they must be fairly general and focused on the grounding for some practice, activity, institution, or profession—that is to say, focused on the regulative ideals that set the goals and rationale for the activity and on the concepts that make the activity what it is (*law* for lawyering and judging, *education* for teaching and certifying, *health* for doctoring and medicating, and so on).

For example, the questions above that emerge out of feminist challenges to the practice of science are quite general, abstracting from the particularities and peculiarities of geology, botany, and chemistry. But they are still about *our* (dated and located) idea and practice of science. They are far from the most general questions we could ask. The deepest levels of generality may be irrelevant to us, however, if they abstract from the very social forms or cultural features in which we are interested. The basic questions that will most reward pursuit are those focused on the temporally and culturally specific practices that directly concern us.

There are many such basic questions about the direction, procedures, and worth of the social studies, to which educators and researchers return time and again. For example, one commonly stated aim of social studies is to prepare students to be citizens. What conception of citizenship do social studies educators work from? How do they picture the civic virtues? Where do they place the political in a person's complete system of ends? Do they possess a general, guiding ideal of the educated life? (See, e.g., Butts. 1988, 1989.)

Social studies curricula often deal with personal and social values. What understanding of values and valuing underlies them? What distinctions, if any, are drawn between facts and values, emotion and cognition, thinking and acting? Is the social studies classroom the proper arena for inculcating values? Which values? How are value-charged controversies to be dealt with in the school? How can teachers distinguish between indoctrinating and teaching, manipulating and correcting, proselytizing and clarifying? Do social studies approaches encourage or discourage moral relativism? (See, e.g., Coles, 1986, 1989; Kohlberg, 1981; Purpel & Ryan, 1976; Shaver & Strong, 1982; Snook, 1972.)

A common goal for social studies is to teach critical thinking. What is critical thinking, and how is it improved? Can skills be learned apart from content, or is this even a tenable distinction? Is the aim to teach children to be rational or to be reasonable? What is the difference? What conception of rationality do social studies professionals work from? Do emphases on problem solving and inquiry give short shrift to reflection, meditation, and thoughtfulness? (See Siegel, 1988, including references.)

The core discipline of social studies is history. What, if any, intellectual and moral virtues does history teach? Is history properly a social science, or is it a humanistic discipline? Should it be studied only for the light it sheds on present problems and concerns? Of what value are temporal chronicles and narratives? What constitutes historical literacy, and is it more or less important than scientific, economic, or mathematical literacy? (See, e.g., Bradley Commission, 1988; *Education for Democracy*, 1987; Fitzgerald, 1979; Gagnon, 1989; Krug, 1967; Ravitch & Finn, 1987; *The Social Studies*, 1983.)

These questions have been argued since social studies emerged at the beginning of this century as a school subject. They are still contested today, with efforts to answer them often hobbled by tangles of assumptions and conceptual habits. In the following sections, I want to focus in more detail on a few questions that arise from the efforts of theorists and educators to identify the distinctive goals and methods of social studies. I hope to throw into relief tensions and strains that are not always confronted directly and to point toward philosophical resources that might contribute to the ongoing conversation among social educators about the very nature of their enterprise. The problems discussed have to do with values and the social sciences and with the ideal of political participation.

SOCIAL STUDIES, SOCIAL SCIENCE, AND VALUES

I begin with the newly issued report of the National Commission on Social Studies in the Schools (1989), *Charting a Course: Social Studies for the 21st Century*. The Commission, a joint project of the American Historical Association, the Carnegie Foundation for the Advancement of Teaching, the National Council for the Social Studies, and the Organization of American Historians, was chartered to restate the "goals and vision" of social studies (National Commission, 1989, p. v). The restatement sets out a K–12 curriculum and offers perspectives from the constituent social sciences—anthropology, psychology, economics, geography, history, political science, and sociology. Advocates from each discipline urge that students be acquainted with its leading concepts and theories. The study of anthropological concepts, for example, is supposed to help students with their concerns about love, marriage, parents, death, and gender (White, 1989, pp. 34–35). Students should know the "core con-

cepts and theories" of psychology so that they can apply them to their own lives (Baum & Cohen, 1989, p. 66). The sociological perspective offers students a "conceptual framework for understanding" their social environment (Gray, 1989, p. 74). The political scientist's theoretical understanding of politics is the vehicle for producing "socially effective and democratically oriented citizens" (Brody, 1989, p. 62).

Papered over in *Charting a Course's* "goals and vision" are several deep fissures in the history of social studies about the relation of social studies to the social sciences. Is social studies "the social sciences simplified for pedagogical purposes" (Wesley & Wronski, 1964, p. 3) or something quite different? This much-quoted phrase is often used by scholars to identify one of the "traditions" in social studies. Barth and Shermis (1970), for example, distinguished three traditions: the citizenship transmission tradition, the social science tradition, and the reflective inquiry tradition. Each is supposed to be an alternative way of conceiving of the aim and content of social studies. Other scholars argue about the Barth-Shermis scheme and classify differently the contests over the nature of social studies (see Stanley, 1985, pp. 311–327).

Whether these classifications are useful depends, in part, upon how the social sciences are understood. Wesley and Wronski, in fact, took a quite catholic and inclusive approach, defining the social sciences as "scholarly materials about human beings and their interrelations." Moreover, their description of the kinds of inquiry needed for understanding contemporary society includes philosophy, literature, history, and natural science, as well as economics and sociology (Wesley & Wronski, pp. 3, 56–58). Such an embracing view of social inquiry allows one to accommodate almost any of the various aims and contents proposed for social studies education and call the result "simplified social science." Likewise, if such a generous construction of social science were to underlie *Charting a Course*, the easy assumption throughout the document about the central role of social science concepts in social studies education would be uncontroversial.

The Nature of the Social Sciences

More restrictive conceptions of the social sciences create a genuine debate about the place of social science concepts and principles in social studies education. These narrower conceptions, in fact, generate important debates about the very nature of the social sciences themselves. One way to frame these debates is in terms of the kind of understanding social scientists aim for.

In our commonsense picture of the social world, we describe people and their works in a special language, the language of belief and desire, hope and fear, purpose and intention. We talk, correct, and guide each other in this language and explain the present and the past: "I am working harder because I want a raise"; "students need to feel self-esteem"; "you should show more respect for your elders"; "Of course she's crushed by his inattention, she's in love"; "it was Longstreet's unhappiness with Lee's plan to attack the flank of the Union Army that led him to be dilatory in moving his division"; "people dread dishonor more than poverty." Are the descriptions and explanations we thus make real knowledge? Are they the elements of a "social science"?

Most modern social scientists eschew this type of language. They substitute a technical vocabulary of stimulus-response, power relationships, input/output systems, revealed preferences, or class struggle. Or, they retain elements of our commonsense language but redefine them in behavioral or operational terms. For example, values and purposes are turned into observable and quantifiable data—into "values" and "purposes," in quotation marks, that refer to subjective states of persons reflected in and measurable by their responses on attitude surveys (sociology), their "willingness to pay" (economics), or their voting behavior (political science). Consider the following:

The study of politics brings into clear focus the central role that "purposes," "ends," and "values" play in human affairs. One cannot understand the political processes that yield public policy unless one understands that ends are being sought . . . "values" are indispensable political "facts." (Brody, 1989, p. 61; see also Baum & Cohen, 1989, p. 67)

This kind of social science is modeled on the natural sciences and aimed at the same predictive success. Researchers seek to provide causal theories of underlying mechanisms—whether of economic exchange, personality development, status relations, or cycles of electoral domination—as the groundwork for increasingly reliable predictions of social phenomena. Consequently, they are driven toward the same precision of measurement characteristic of natural science; their technical vocabulary is no mere perversity but the way of identifying and categorizing data to allow measurement.

This mainstream conception of social science has always had its detractors and its problems. Its practitioners must either treat our commonsense language of beliefs and desires as mere superstition or find some way to translate the language into the new scientific vocabularies. The latter project has never met with real success, and the former alternative founders on the fact that we do not seem to be able to dispense with talking about "beliefs" and "values" the way we could dispense with "phlogiston" (Stich, 1983, pp. 1–4, 14–28).

Indeed, a long tradition going back to Dilthey in the 19th century (see Dilthey, 1976) has been critical of social scientists' ambitions to be like natural scientists. This form of criticism has become especially forceful and effective in the last 30 years. Its proponents insist that social science is radically misconceived if modeled on the natural sciences and their aim of predictive success (see Dallmayr & McCarthy, 1977; Rabinow & Sullivan, 1979; Winch, 1958). The aim of social science must be quite different because the social world is different from the natural world: it is a world constituted out of meanings, not just comprised of events.

The kind of understanding social scientists can hope to achieve is interpretive rather than predictive. Social science renders the social world understandable by making it intelligible, that is, by showing its intersubjective meaning and significance (Rosenberg, 1988, pp. 8–18). This task escapes the grasp of mainstream social scientists who always attempt to turn *intersubjective* meaning into *subjective* meaning. Charles Taylor (1979) put it this way:

It is not just that the people in . . . society all or most have a given set of ideas in their heads and subscribe to a given set of goals. The

meanings and norms implicit in . . . [their] practices are not just in the minds of the actors but are out there in the practices themselves, practices which cannot be conceived as a set of individual actions, but which are essentially modes of social relation, of mutual action. (p. 48)

What Taylor means is this: Political scientists or sociologists purport to take values into account in their descriptions of political or social reality. However, something odd happens when they do so. Suppose, for example, the issue is abortion. In our lived world, someone's claim that abortion is murder is an invitation to the rest of us to consider the claim's validity against the backdrop of religious, legal, and moral practices that embody and express our collective idea of human dignity and respect for persons. It invites each of us to reexamine our ideas of murder, death, killing, self-defense, vulnerable and innocent life, personhood, autonomy, self-determination, and responsibility to others; and in light of the reexamination to dispute the claim that abortion is murder or to reorient our attitudes and behavior toward legislative and judicial limitations on abortion, protest of abortion clinics, and moral suasion of potential aborters. In supporting or contesting the truth of the claim, we and the claimant jointly contribute to shaping the social, moral, and political meaning of abortion.

The political scientist or sociologist, however, takes the claim about abortion not as a value or belief, not, that is, as the invitation just described, but as a "value" or "belief," *as a fact about the claimant, not a fact about the world*. That is what Taylor meant by saying that social science turns the intersubjective into the subjective. As a fact about the claimant, the "value" can be verified (through survey answers or voting behavior) and can be correlated with other facts about him or her (party affiliation, religious denomination, age, gender, race) and about larger social and political events (the election of Ronald Reagan, the growth of evangelism, the defeat of the ERA). But whatever the interest and importance of the social scientist's findings here, something has been dropped out: the invitation—implicit in the claim that abortion is murder—jointly to discover and add to the meaning of abortion. The scientist has changed the subject from "the truth about abortion" to "the truth about the seeker-after-the-truth about abortion." According to Taylor, to understand the social world properly, one can't leave out what mainstream, predictive social scientists leave out when they change the subject.

The debate between the "predictivists" and the "interpretivists" turns, in part, on what gets counted as scientific understanding and scientific explanation. To the extent that we want lawlike generalizations about human and social behavior, we are likely to be driven in the direction of mainstream, "predictive" social science. Interpretivists can point out that users of commonsense language meet with predictive success, too: they have the ability to "navigate successfully in a society of other human beings" (Rosenberg, 1988, p. 15). But this is to settle for something far short of general laws of human and social behavior. Whether our commonsense language can contend as the best predictive language for social phenomena, and whether there are genuine explanations that are not ultimately rooted in general laws, are still questions much in debate. The reader who wishes to pursue such issues further can find much of interest in Phillips (1987), Rabinow and Sullivan (1979), Rosenberg (1988), and Ryan (1970).

Common Language and Citizenship

However that debate goes, for our purposes here it is important to note that our commonsense language serves for us not only the role of prediction and explanation but other crucial roles as well. It is in terms of this language that we *evaluate, criticize, appreciate,* and *justify.* Whether or not these are crucial dimensions that must be captured by scientific understanding, they are central dimensions to ordinary life. This fact has important implications for general education no matter how the debate about the nature of social science turns out.

A general education is education in the languages of appreciation, justification, and criticism. This is especially true for that part of general education that is training for citizenship. A citizen appropriately treats political claims made by legislators, political officers, and other citizens as invitations to affirm or contest their truth. A desirable civic education helps a young person to become adept at political criticism and justification. An education in which the subject is always changed just as a student is ready to engage a political claim cannot support or strengthen his or her ability to play a proper civic role. In fact, it impedes it. The theoretical understanding of the political scientist, for example, does not produce "socially effective and democratically oriented citizens," as *Charting a Course* supposes (Brody, 1989, p. 62), unless it is embedded in a wider educational practice in which students confront political values *as* values, not just as "values."

The Place of Values

This point needs to be emphasized. Nearly all the various "traditions" of social studies acknowledge the central place of values. To prepare students for the civic and social roles they will assume as adults, schools must train them to deal intelligently with political and moral conflict. But it is also very common for social studies educators to treat values as subjective, just in the way that Taylor (1979) described.

Consider this composite picture of a social studies orientation toward students and public controversy. In learning to confront controversies, students need the methods of inquiry and critical thinking. They need to learn how to pose questions, gather and classify data, make generalizations, test hypotheses, and reach conclusions (see, e.g., Fenton, 1967, p. 11; London, 1989, pp. xii, 14, 29, 33; Baum & Cohen, 1989, p. 67). They need to learn how to avoid logical fallacies, distinguish fact from opinion, recognize appeals to emotion, and master the forms of proof (Dawson, 1989, p. 142). Where conflict cannot be resolved through the careful and patient application of inquiry and critical thinking, they need to learn tolerance and respect for difference.

Where do values come in? In this composite picture they are starting points. They are what move students and put them into conflict. A student's position in a controversy can be represented as an equation in which a value premise plus factual premises lead to a conclusion. Failures in the position may stem from the inadequate grasp of facts (further inquiry can help here) or errors in reasoning (critical thinking can help here). The value premise is not itself immune from discussion, but exploration of it turns back into one of the previous two modes of investigation. That is, a student can clarify his values by tracing out the factual consequences of holding them (Engle, 1968, p. 346) or by understanding their sources (an understanding supplied by sociology, political science, and psychology; see National Commission, 1989).

In the approach pictured, values are treated as "subjective." One reason is because the social educator cannot fathom any other way to treat them honestly. The alternative to helping students see the factual consequences and historical/cultural sources of their value positions seems to be indoctrination, which is how Barth and Shermis characterize the "citizenship transmission" alternative in their "three traditions" (Stanley, 1985, p. 312). However, the alternative to understanding values subjectively, according to Taylor (1979), is not indoctrination but understanding them intersubjectively. What does Taylor mean by *intersubjectivity?* What is he getting at when he locates meanings "out there" in social practices themselves?

Taylor's point is that we learn values through acquiring and mastering social vocabularies of value. For Americans, the meanings of liberty and equality, for example, are not some contentless abstractions that philosophers might draw from the pure concepts themselves, nor mere idiosyncratic subjectivities, but the historically specific acts embodied in the Declaration of Independence, the Constitution, Washington's Farewell Address, the struggle over the extension of slavery, Lincoln's Second Inaugural Address, the vast westward migration and the myth of the cowboy, the Pullman Car strike, Martin Luther King's "I Have a Dream," and the Civil Rights Act of 1964. Their meaning is constituted out of the canonical texts of American history and the emblematic acts of resistance, struggle, and progress toward human dignity, social harmony, economic justice, and racial accord. This collective cultural possession supplies a vocabulary of criticism and justification that students can make their own and become adept at in the same way they become fluent and skilled in their native language. The vocabulary does not yield a *method* for resolving our disagreements except as it provides a ground for mutual understanding of our differences and a field for imaginative exploration of common texts and examples, model deeds and cautionary tales, historical hopes and national achievements.

Learning and using this vocabulary is not the same as learning how to be logical, to use the scientific method, or learning about the causal and generative sources of value beliefs. Consequently, it is most effectively achieved not by approaches that "change the subject," but by approaches like the "jurisprudential" approach (Newmann, 1970; Oliver & Shaver, 1966/1974) and law-related education, and those that draw strongly from the humanities and history. As Engle (1989) proposed:

Because questions of what is morally good or evil are involved in most or all kinds of [social] problems . . . and because models for thinking about questions of good and evil are more likely to be found in the humanities than in the social sciences, selections from literature, art, music, religion, philosophy, and journalism would be used alongside, and on a par with, selections from the social sciences and history. . . . (pp. 187–188)

In these approaches, the political language and texts of American history are taken at face value and on their own terms, without trying to turn them into something else. Students are asked to take the political claims of other citizens and public officers as truth claims, to be contested or defended in terms of the very historically embedded ideals they invoke; and to take constitutional and legal rules and findings as authoritative norms, to be applied in terms of the background ideals of justice and security they presuppose. The students are to act as fledgling judges, advocates, and legislators (not fledgling sociologists and political scientists), speaking the political and legal language from those points of view. Those points of view do not exclude social scientific knowledge, but frame its utility and significance in the context of vocabularies of value.

This somewhat schematic discussion of social science and the subjective versus intersubjective treatment of value captures some older and continuing divisions in social studies theory and bears quite directly on the emerging debate occasioned by the growing movement to restore history—especially American history—to the center of social studies education (see, e.g., Bradley Commission, 1988; *History-Social Science Framework,* 1987). The place and utility of history in social studies is perhaps the oldest ongoing debate in the field. The debate is often posed as between those who want chronological, narrative history "as a means of assuring adequate cultural knowledge among our youth" and those who want to borrow from history only in so far as "historical data [can] be brought to bear directly on the larger questions facing our nation" (Evans, 1989, p. 85). However, the choice between history as mere cultural deposit and history as providing lessons for present policy choices is a false one in the Taylor (1979) conception of value and meaning. History as a story of our past bears on the present, not by providing guidelines for present policy choices, but by grounding students in our culturally rooted language of political criticism and value.

This theme extracted from Taylor (1979) is developed at greatest length in the works of Alasdair MacIntyre (1981, 1988). MacIntyre sees our entire Western culture over the past 200 years as embracing an essentially skeptical, distancing, even nihilistic outlook on value, foreshadowing the triumph of the social scientific "managerial" and "therapeutic" outlooks. This decline MacIntyre attributes largely to the failed Enlightenment ambition to base social life on a purely rational foundation. In contrast, he argues, human lives can only be understood as narratives unfolding within and given meaning by larger narratives (MacIntyre, 1981, pp. 190–209). MacIntyre's and Taylor's arguments about the nature of social understanding (and self-understanding in relation to social understanding) can enrich the argument (likely to be central in the next decade) about the place of history in civic education.

PARTICIPATION

I turn now to the ideal of political participation. *Charting a Course* is typical in its assumption that the social studies curriculum should enable students to become active, participating citizens (National Commission, p. 6). Social studies educators commonly avow that education for citizenship should produce a sophisticated knowledge of our political system, a desire to engage in political activity, and possession of the skills to do so effectively (see, e.g., Remy, 1980). However, between these aspirations and the actual political behavior of students and adults there is, and always has been, a considerable gap. Decades of research have failed to detect much positive effect of the social studies curriculum on subsequent political attitudes and participation (see Washburn, 1986). One scholar, Leming (1986), has recently drawn from his review of the research the conclusion that social studies educators should adopt more modest goals (p. 149).

Indeed, that the avowed purpose of social studies is to produce "an entire population of rational/activist citizens" (Leming, 1986, p. 148) is a bit of an overstatement, but not by much. Educators occasionally acknowledge that the goals of social education often won't be achieved until well into adult life, if at all (Wesley & Wronski, 1964, p. 78). Far more common, however, is the belief that low political participation among adults reflects somehow on the adequacy and success of civic education in the schools. What assumptions about political interest and behavior propel the hard-to-shake vision of the social studies classroom as a place in which civic zeal and participant ability should be incubated? Or, to turn the question around: Would a reasonable picture of the etiology of political interest and commitment make the vision more or less credible?

Consider the usual course of a person's lifespan. The years of adolescence and early adulthood are dominated by the often painful struggle to forge a sense of self and to deal with intense social and sexual pressures. This struggle might find an outlet in political enthusiasm but there is no particular reason why it should, in competition as it is with the preoccupations adolescents more typically exhibit—dating, being accepted by the right crowd, earning money for clothes and cars, getting into the right college, trying out drugs and alcohol—in short, the rites of passage that drive parents to despair and teachers to distraction. The college years are given over to more of the same with a strong vocational orientation added on.

Politics excites some students and leaves others indifferent. Youthful political enthusiasms tend toward large causes, uncompromising ideals, and great abstractions. How could it be otherwise? At this point in one's life, politics is largely notional.

Soon, however, the young adult gets a job, marries, has children, buys a house. Regardless of whether an individual was concerned about politics before, newly acquired desires and responsibilities lead to quite real and substantial interests in the quality of local schools, the amount of community crime and vandalism, the stability of property taxes, the rate of inflation, and the level of unemployment. These interests give adults reasons to join the PTA, support the local boys' and girls' clubs, stay abreast of school-board elections, complain to the alderman about slow garbage pickups, shovel the sidewalk when it snows, and keep an eye out for the neighbors' children.

From these interests other interests grow outward, encompassing a larger world, and the small habits of attention and participation get wedded to larger projects and activities. After a decade or more out of school, our hypothetical citizen may start to fit the image of activist-participant that underlies the social studies curriculum—or perhaps not. Whether our citizen does or not may well be more a function of the availability of institutions of adult political education and action than of the quality of the social studies classes taken in school. The feature that is typically different about nations in which there is high participation is not the civic education in the schools, but the strong system of political parties, unions, churches, and public-interest groups that capitalize on the emerging interests of young adults, mobilize their energies, and educate them about policies and options (on civic education in European schools, see Torney-Purta & Hahn, 1988). The absence or ineffectiveness of such a system may reduce our hypothetical citizen to apathy and political alienation.

If a typical lifespan is like this, then Leming (1986) may be right that the aim of schools should be modest. If adult political education is pivotal, schools should aim to prepare students to be able to continue learning from other institutions of society. If schools produce graduates who love to read, who are inquisitive, and who have a rudimentary understanding of history and science, then the natural evolution of the graduates' lives, in combination with supporting systems of adult political tutelage, will lead many, if not most, toward living out the ideal of the informed, participating citizen. To the extent that the schools can augment these goals with instruction in our nation's political structure and constitutional history, so much the better. However, if the foregoing account of a typical lifespan is valid, social studies educators should hardly imagine that the schools can be expected to send forth graduates possessing a high level of political and cultural sophistication, charged with a passion to participate, and skilled at the arts of persuasion and communication.

What Is Participation?

Not only is it important for social educators to have some explicit conception of political evolution in a typical life as a backdrop for thinking about civic education, it is also important to focus more sharply on the meaning of participation itself. Is being an "informed, participating citizen" something instrumentally important or intrinsically valuable? Is the main reason for attempting to inculcate in young people this civic character the need for high levels of participation to keep democracy healthy, or is there another reason as well, namely, as Aristotle proposed, the centrality of political participation to a full human life (Barnes, 1984, vol. II, pp. 1986ff.)? Different answers to these questions might imply different emphases, purposes, and content in a civic education curriculum.

The last two decades have been unusually fertile for political theory. John Rawls's *A Theory of Justice* (1971) began a renewal of political liberalism that is still active and fruitful, and that has stimulated in response a growing literature reviving the tradition of civic republicanism. There has also been an active rethinking of libertarianism and Marxism, neither of which I touch on here (see Cohen, 1978; Elster, 1985; Nozick, 1974).

What is at issue in the liberal and civic republican traditions is the nature of the state and its relation to the moral lives of its citizens. The traditions provide frameworks for answering questions about how individual citizens should conceive of themselves and their roles. Two themes in particular should interest social educators, neutrality and individualism, and I will touch briefly on them here.

Neutrality. The defining characteristic of the liberal state, according to Dworkin (1985), is its neutrality. Liberalism, he argues, is based on the belief that "government must be neutral on what might be called the question of the good life" (p. 191). People have a diversity of answers to that question—religiously, philosophically, and morally based views about what makes a human life valuable and what persons should dedicate themselves to. A liberal state is organized in a way that does not presuppose the truth of a particular view and that accords protections to individuals to live as they desire, compatible with the like liberty of others.

The liberal state, then, embodies no substantive ideal itself, and will be characterized by (a) fair procedures by which citizens can contest for power and (b) protection, through legal rights, of the zones of freedom necessary for people to live their lives by their own ideals. The public sphere of government operates to protect the private spheres, where people find their fulfillment. The participation of citizens in a liberal democratic state is, at the first level, justified instrumentally. It serves to maintain the system that allows individuals and groups to follow their diverse, self-defined interests.

In contrast, the civic republican criticism of liberalism rejects the possibility or desirability of the state remaining morally neutral. In Aristotle's words, a state "is not a mere society, having a common place, established for the prevention of mutual crime and for the sake of exchange. . . . [P]olitical society exists for the sake of noble actions, and not of living together" (Barnes, 1984, pp. 2032–2033). The civic republican vision pictures citizens participating together "in the selection of the values that ought to control public and private life" (Michelman, 1986, p. 19; and see references). The participation of citizens is not just instrumentally useful, but a component of their virtue as persons. Through the activity of jointly deliberating about and creating the values embodied in their collective life, citizens find their own highest realization. Their fulfillment comes through their public involvement, not their private activities.

Individualism. Related to the civic republican criticism of state neutrality is its criticism of individualism. Liberalism rests on a false idea of individuals, according to many civic republican critics, and encourages an unhealthy, even "cancerous," individualism in modern society (Bellah et al., 1985, p. viii). It views individuals as "atomistic," joined together in a state to secure the resources and protections to pursue their independently derived aims (Taylor, 1985, pp. 187–210). To the contrary, according to civic republicans, individuals are by their nature social creatures who get their purposes from the societies in which they live.

Liberals, however, need not deny the social nature of persons. Rawls (1971, pp. 522–525), for example, developed his theory from this very starting point. Precisely because peoples' conceptions of value and meaning are supplied by the societies in which they live, if we want to ask about the justice of the basic institutions of our society, we need to take up some standpoint altogether outside it. Otherwise, we would be assessing the institutions, not against values that are independent of them, but against standards these very institutions create in us.

The need to take a standpoint outside our society in order to assess it is what accounts for the complex and peculiar structure of Rawls's (1971) account of justice. His theory supposes an imaginary contract among rational individuals behind a "veil of ignorance" that precludes their knowing anything about themselves or about their own ends except that they want to maximize their primary goods (goods like freedom and self-respect that are generically basic to having any other goods at all) (pp. 90ff, 118–150). Given this assumption, the independent contractors choose principles of justice for distributing liberty, opportunity, and wealth, which are to govern the design of basic institutions of any society in which they might live (pp. 60–90).

These principles, according to Rawls (1971), give us ideal standards by which we can assess and criticize the political and economic arrangements of our society independently of the desires, values, intentions, hopes, and fears those very arrangements form in us. In a society that ideally expressed the principles, individuals would see that its institutions were fair to them and reflected their status as free and equal beings, and they would come to value those arrangements not just as instrumentally necessary, but as good in themselves (pp. 453–510). Citizens would see their participation not merely as prudent, but also as intrinsically valuable.

Liberalism thus need not presume that people are naturally selfish or that they come to their desires and goals independently of society. As the Dworkin (1985) formulation indicates, the framework of liberalism can as easily be described in relation to groups (who have their own religious or moral conception of the good life) as to individuals. And as Rawls's theory shows, liberalism makes room for persons to come to view their political structure as valuable in itself, independently of its instrumental usefulness.

Even so, some critics suggest that the liberal project, though it can come a far way toward accommodating the social nature of persons, still rests on an imperfect representation of that nature. Sandel (1982, 1984), in particular, has argued that Rawls, by abstracting from all of the self's specifically social ends as it chooses behind the veil of ignorance, creates choosers radically unrepresentative of us as real persons and, thus, creatures whose choices cannot represent *our* conception of justice. More generally, Sandel aligns himself with MacIntyre, Taylor, and others who claim, following Aristotle, "that we cannot justify political arrangements without reference to common purposes and ends, and that we cannot conceive of our personhood without reference to our role as citizens, and as participants in a common life" (Sandel, 1984, p. 5).

The Tie to Social Studies. Although the argument between Rawls and Sandel often involves metaphysical and epistemological issues that a social educator may not want to pursue, the importance of understanding their general views should be evident. Political participation as an aim of social studies cannot be fully developed or articulated without exploring, as do Rawls and Sandel, how participation might be tied to the purposes of political institutions and to the self-realization of citizens.

This brief sketch of the ongoing discussion in political theory about neutrality and individualism neglects the many other writers and dimensions that make the area an extremely rich one for social studies educators to explore. In addition to Rawls and Sandel, Ackerman (1980), Dworkin, (1977, 1985, 1986), Fried (1978), Galston (1980), Gutmann (1980, 1987), Larmore (1987), Lomasky (1987), MacIntyre (1981, 1988), Okin (1989), Posner (1973), Rosenblum (1989), and Walzer (1983, 1987) among others, provide striking, powerful, and often competing frameworks for raising and answering fundamental questions about state and society, law and liberty, equality and rationality, the individual and the community. What they have to say about the circumstances of justice, the ends of the state, the moral standing of persons, and the modes of social reason and public rationality can provide new languages in which social studies educators can debate the goals of civic education. The influence of this stream of political philosophy is already apparent in such recent works as Battistoni (1985), Butts (1988), and Pratte (1988).

Citizenship, as the core concept around which social studies is formed, and *participation,* as the key idea for understanding citizenship, invite the social educator—whether researcher or teacher, theorist or practitioner—on a quest after the basic meaning of individuals living in union with others. That is a journey properly philosophical, and one whose path has been much illumined recently. The path can be traversed without engaging all the deepest problems in first philosophy, but not without seriously thinking behind appearances and even unthinking many of our dearly held habits of seeing things. To meditate on the idea of citizenship in general and American citizenship in particular links us across the ages to Socrates, whose impassioned defense before the Athenian jury of his life and conduct as a citizen of his city, and whose thoughtful defense to his friends of his obedience to that jury's verdict, remain to this day our most inspiring models of philosophical inquiry.

References

Ackerman, B. (1980). *Social justice in the liberal state.* New Haven, CT: Yale University Press.

Adorno, T. W. (1973). *Negative dialectics.* New York: Continuum Press.

Barnes, J. (Ed.). (1984). *The complete works of Aristotle.* Princeton, NJ: Princeton University Press.

Barth, J. L., & Shermis, S. S. (1970). Defining the social studies: An exploration of three traditions. *Social Education, 34,* 745–751.

Battistoni, R. (1985). *Public schooling and the education of democratic citizens.* Jackson, MS: University Press of Mississippi.

Baum, C. G., & Cohen, I. S. (1989). Psychology and the social science curriculum. In National Commission on Social Studies in the Schools, *Charting a course: Social studies for the 21st century—A report of the Task Force on Curriculum* (pp. 65–69). Washington, DC: Author

Bellah, R. N., Madsen, R., Sullivan, W. M., Swidler, A., & Tipton, S. M. (1985). *Habits of the heart: Individualism and commitment in American life.* Berkeley, CA: University of California Press.

Bradley Commission on History in the Schools (1988). *Building a cur-*

riculum: Guidelines for teaching history in the schools. Washington, DC: Educational Excellence Network.

Brody, R. A. (1989). Why study politics? In National Commission on Social Studies in Schools, *Charting a course: Social studies for the 21st century—A report of the Task Force on Curriculum* (pp. 59–63). Washington, DC: Author.

Butts, R. F. (1988). *The morality of democratic citizenship: Goals for civic education in the republic's third century.* Calabasas, CA: Center for Civic Education.

Butts, R. F. (1989). *The civic mission of educational reform: Perspectives for the public and the profession.* Stanford, CA: Hoover Institution Press.

Carnap, R. (1947). *Meaning and necessity.* Chicago: University of Chicago Press.

Cherryholmes, C. (1980). Social knowledge and citizenship education: Two views of truth and criticism. *Curriculum Inquiry, 10,* 115–141.

Cohen, G. A. (1978). *Karl Marx's theory of history.* Princeton, NJ: Princeton University Press.

Coles, R. (1986). *The moral life of children.* Boston: Houghton Mifflin.

Coles, R. (1989). *The call of stories: Teaching and the moral imagination.* Boston: Houghton Mifflin.

Czapanskiy, K. (1988). *Gender bias in the courts.* Baltimore: Court of Appeals of Maryland and Maryland State Bar Association.

Dallmayr, F., & McCarthy, T. (1977). *Understanding and social inquiry.* Notre Dame, IN: University of Notre Dame Press.

Dawson, G. (1989). Teaching government. In H. I. London (Ed.), *Social science theory: Structure and application* (pp. 122–149). New Brunswick, NJ: Transaction Press.

Derrida, J. (1976). *On grammatology.* Baltimore: Johns Hopkins University Press.

Dilthey, W. (1976). *Selected writings.* Cambridge: Cambridge University Press.

Dworkin, R. (1977). *Taking rights seriously.* Cambridge, MA: Harvard University Press.

Dworkin, R. (1985). *A matter of principle.* Cambridge, MA: Harvard University Press.

Dworkin, R. (1986). *Law's empire.* Cambridge, MA: Harvard University Press.

Education for democracy (1987). Washington, DC: American Federation of Teachers.

Elster, J. (1985). *Making sense of Marx.* Cambridge: Cambridge University Press.

Engle, S. (1968). Decision making: The heart of social studies instruction. In J. P. Shaver & H. Berlak (Eds.), *Democracy, pluralism, and the social studies* (pp. 342–348). Boston: Houghton Mifflin.

Engle, S. (1989). Proposals for a typical issue-centered curriculum. *The Social Studies, 80,* 187–181.

Evans, R. W. (1989). Diane Ravitch and the revival of history: A critique. *The Social Studies, 80,* 85–91.

Fenton, E. (1967). *The new social studies.* New York: Holt, Rinehart & Winston.

Fitzgerald, F. (1979). *America revised: History schoolbooks in the twentieth century.* Boston: Little, Brown.

Foucault, M. (1972). *The archeology of knowledge.* New York: Pantheon Books.

Fraser, N. (1985). Michel Foucault: A "Young Conservative?" *Ethics, 96,* 165–184.

Fried, C. (1978). *Right and wrong.* Cambridge, MA: Harvard University Press.

Gadamer, H-G. (1975). *Truth and method.* New York: Seabury Press.

Gagnon, P. (Ed.). (1989). *Historical literacy: The case for history in American education.* New York: Macmillan.

Galston, W. (1980). *Justice and the human good.* Chicago: University of Chicago Press.

Gary, P. S. (1989). Sociology. In National Commission on Social Studies in the Schools, *Charting a course: Social studies for the 21st century—A report of the Task Force on Curriculum* (pp. 71–75). Washington, DC: Author.

Gutmann, A. (1980). *Liberal equality.* Cambridge: Cambridge University Press.

Gutmann, A. (1987). *Democratic education.* Princeton, NJ: Princeton University Press.

Harding, S. (1986). *The science question in feminism.* Ithaca, NY: Cornell University Press.

History-social science framework (1987). Scaramento, CA: California State Department of Education.

Husserl, E. (1960). *Cartesian meditations.* The Hague, Neth.: Martinus Nijhoff.

Kohlberg, L. (1981). *Essays on moral development: The philosophy of moral development.* New York: Harper and Row.

Krug, M. (1967). *History and the social sciences: New approaches to the teaching of social studies.* Waltham, MA: Blaisdell.

Larmore, C. (1987). *Patterns of moral complexity.* Cambridge: Cambridge University Press.

Leming, J. (1986). Rethinking social studies research and the goals of social education. *Theory and Research in Social Education, 14,* 139–152.

Lomasky, L. (1987). *Persons, rights, and the moral community.* New York: Oxford University Press.

London, H. I. (Ed.). (1989). *Social science theory: Structure and application.* New Brunswick, NJ: Transaction Press.

Lyotard, J-F. (1983). Presentations. In A. Montefiore (Ed.), *Philosophy in France today* (pp. 116–135). Cambridge: Cambridge University Press.

MacIntyre, A. (1981). *After virtue.* Notre Dame, IN: University of Notre Dame Press.

MacIntyre, A. (1988). *Whose justice? Which rationality?* Notre Dame, IN: University of Notre Dame Press.

Merleau-Ponty, M. (1962). *Phenomenology of perception.* London: Routledge & Kegan Paul.

Michelman, F. (1986). Traces of self-government. *Harvard Law Review, 12,* 4–77.

Moore, G. E. (1959). *Philosophical papers.* London: George Allen and Unwin.

National Commission on Social Studies in the Schools. (1989). *Charting a course: Social studies for the 21st century—A report of the Task Force on Curriculum.* Washington, DC: Author.

Newmann, F. M. (1970). *Clarifying public controversy: An approach to teaching social studies.* Boston: Little, Brown.

Norris, S. P. (1983). The inconsistencies at the foundations of construct validation theory. In Ernest P. House (Ed.), *Philosophy of evaluation* (pp. 53–74). San Francisco: Jossey-Bass.

Nozick, R. (1974). *Anarchy, state, and utopia.* New York: Basic Books.

Okin, S. M. (1989). *Justice, gender, and the family.* New York: Basic Books.

Oliver, D. W., & Shaver, J. P. (1974). *Teaching public issues in the high school.* Logan, UT: Utah State University Press. (original work published 1966)

Phillips, D. C. (1987). *Philosophy, science, and social inquiry.* New York: Pergamon Press.

Posner, R. (1973). *Economic analysis of law.* Boston: Little, Brown.

Pratte, R. (1988). *The civic imperative: Examining the need for civic education.* New York: Teachers College Press.

Purpel, D., & Ryan, K. (1976). *Moral education . . . It comes with the territory.* Berkeley, CA: McCutchan.

Putnam, H. (1987). *The many faces of realism.* Lasalle, IL: Open Court.

Rabinow, P., & Sullivan, W. (1979). *Interpretive social science: A reader.* Berkeley, CA: University of California Press.

Ravitch, D., & Finn, C. (1987). *What do our 17-year-olds know?* New York: Harper & Row.

Rawls, J. (1971). *A theory of justice.* Cambridge, MA: Harvard University Press.

Remy, R. (1980). *Handbook of basic citizenship competencies.* Alexandria, VA: Association for Supervision and Curriculum.

Rorty, R. (1979). *Philosophy and the mirror of nature.* Princeton, NJ: Princeton University Press.

Rorty, R. (1982). *Consequences of pragmatism.* Minneapolis: University of Minnesota Press.

Rosenberg, A. (1988). *Philosophy of social science.* Boulder, CO: Westview Press.

Rosenblum, N. (Ed.). (1989). *Liberalism and the moral life.* Cambridge, MA: Harvard University Press.

Ryan, A. (1970). *The philosophy of the social sciences.* New York: Pantheon Books.

Sandel, M. (1982). *Liberalism and the limits of justice.* Cambridge: Cambridge University Press.

Sandel, M. (Ed.). (1984). *Liberalism and its critics.* New York: New York University Press.

Scriven, M. (1988). Philosophical inquiry methods in education. In R. M. Jaeger (Ed.), *Complementary methods for research in education* (pp. 129–148). Washington, DC : American Educational Research Association.

Shaver, J., & Strong, W. (1982). *Facing value decisions: Rationale-building for teachers.* New York: Teachers College Press.

Siegel, H. (1988). *Educating reason: Rationality, critical thinking, and education.* New York: Routledge.

Snook, I. A. (1972). *Indoctrination and education.* London: Routledge & Kegan Paul.

The Social Studies (1983). Special issue on teaching history, *74,* 4–45.

Stanley, W. (1985). Recent research in the foundations of social education: 1976–1983. In W. Stanley (Ed.), *Review of research in social studies education: 1976–1983* (pp. 309–399). Washington, DC: National Council for Social Studies.

Stich, S. (1983). *From folk psychology to cognitive science: The case against belief.* Cambridge, MA: MIT Press.

Tarski, A. (1956). *Logic, semantics, metamathematics.* Oxford: Clarendon Press.

Taylor, C. (1979). Interpretation and the sciences of man. In P. Rabinow & W. Sullivan (Eds.), *Interpretive social science: A reader* (pp. 25–71). Berkeley, CA: University of California Press.

Taylor, C. (1985). *Philosophy and the human sciences: Vol. 2. Philosophical papers.* Cambridge: Cambridge University Press.

Torney-Purta, J., & Hahn, C. (1988). Values education in the Western European tradition. In W. Cummings & S. Gopinathan (Eds.), *The revival of values education in Asia and the West* (pp. 31–57). New York: Pergamon Press.

Walzer, M. (1983). *Spheres of justice: A defense of pluralism and equality.* New York: Basic Books.

Walzer, M. (1987). *Interpretation and social criticism.* Cambridge, MA: Harvard University Press.

Washburn, P. (1986). The political role of the American school. *Theory and Research in Social Education, 14,* 51–65.

Wesley, E. B., & Wronski, S. P. (1964). *Teaching social studies in the classroom* (5th ed.). Boston: D. C. Heath.

White, J. J. (1989). Anthropology. In National Commission on Social Studies in the Schools, *Charting a course: Social studies for the 21st century—A report of the Curriculum Task Force* (pp. 31–36). Washington, DC: Author.

Winch, P. (1958). *The idea of a social science.* London: Routledge & Kegan Paul.

3

SOCIAL STUDIES EDUCATION AND THEORY: SCIENCE, KNOWLEDGE, AND HISTORY

Thomas S. Popkewitz
UNIVERSITY OF WISCONSIN—MADISON

Henry St. Maurice
UNIVERSITY OF WISCONSIN—STEVENS POINT

Theory is typically considered to be broadly explanatory statements about reality. For years, the progress of theory in science was portrayed in an accumulative model in which one researcher was said to build on the work of another. Recent studies in the history, philosophy, and sociology of science, including the work of Thomas Kuhn (1970), suggest that scientific theories are formed by a process of conflict among ideas. In this model of theory, researchers operating within different paradigms clash over the kinds of explanations that are acceptable, and theories and knowledge are said to change in a revolutionary, rather than in an incremental, way. The limitation of both models is that theories and knowledge are idealized and taken out of the social contexts in which they are formed and changed. The purpose in this chapter is to take the perspective of social epistemology, that is, to consider the social and historical contexts in which various forms of knowledge are articulated.

Social epistemology is a way of coming to grips with the multiple dimensions of assumptions, values, and cognition that interweave in the construction of theory. On one hand, there are statements of research that describe, interpret, and explain the phenomena of schooling. Any such statement is a form of language and thereby contains, at the same time, distinctions and categorizations that organize *both* perception and ways of acting upon the world. Theory, then, always has the multiple dimensions of describing, interpreting, and explaining, whether it be behavioral, phenomenological, or critical/Marxian. The conventional concept of theory as explanation is insufficient, because it does not take into account the complexities of language. On the other hand, a different dimension of theory is the *social* one that encompasses the philosophical assumptions and social/historical context in which theories are produced. Theories that are used as the basis for research about social education are developed in accordance with socially constructed rules and conventions. These social formations shape the theory and direct theorists' interpretations. Social epistemology is a way to consider the interrelation of social and historical contexts with rules and standards for organizing statements about social education (Manicas, 1987; Popkewitz, in press; Tiles, 1984).

Social epistemology is based on the assumption that various ways of knowing are overlapping and continuously reconstructed through the interactions of researchers with their colleagues, their sponsors, and their audiences. This approach to theory is in the philosophical tradition of pragmatism, in that metaphysical questions about knowledge are set aside in order to explore the immediate contexts in which knowledge claims are made. Pragmatism, which West (1989) called the "evasion of epistemology-centered philosophy," entails skepticism about the possibility of absolutely true knowledge and criticism of the social and linguistic conventions by which any knowledge is defined.

Reviewers were Patricia G. Avery, University of Minnesota; Fazal A. Rizvi, Deakin University, Australia; Lee S. Shulman, Stanford University; and Lynda Stone, University of Hawaii. The authors' Wednesday Seminar Group also made helpful comments, Ahmad Sultan provided thoughtful help with the section on Habermas, and Paula Bozoian provided editorial assistance.

This chapter consists of three parts. *First,* an example of theoretical statements about teacher thinking is given to illustrate how epistemological and social assumptions become interwoven into the construction of knowledge about social studies education. *Second,* the historical development of social and psychological theory is explored to show how social and institutional transformations are continually involved in the production of reasonable statements about social studies and schooling. *Third,* the question is asked, What are different ways in which educational theory can be understood and what should educators expect from theory? To rethink the notion of theory in relation to the current debates over the nature and purposes of scientific methods in educational research, an exemplar is offered.

In the history of social studies research, educational and social sciences (including psychology) are interrelated. There are no histories of the epistemology of research practices in social studies, but there are such histories in social science that do point out directions that theory constructions have followed within social studies. A review of *Theory and Research in Social Education,* the central American journal in the field, reveals distinct topics and concerns that relate to social studies, but these arguments are always placed in relation to general theories and methodological practices from other disciplines. For example, one would find that theoretical orientations to social studies research are provided by G. Almond and S. Verba in political socialization, C. Geertz in anthropology, and H. Gadamer in phenomenology, to name a few.

In constructing this chapter, we have not looked at curriculum theory. This *Handbook* is concerned with educational research, rather than with curriculum deliberation and implementation. Although curriculum theorists do provide symbolic canopies for the construction of research programs, it is the concepts and methods in the cognitive and behavioral psychologies, political socialization, sociology, and anthropology that give impetus to the study of social studies education. The focus of this chapter is on theories that are directly involved in the practice of research.

THEORY IN THE PRESENT CONTEXT: STATEMENTS AS MULTIPLE ASSUMPTIONS

To examine the formation of theory in social studies education, this section is focused on ways that scientific knowledge is socially constructed and institutionally grounded. This entails asking how contemporary educational researchers build upon particular assumptions. How are concepts, variables, and methods chosen to interpret school phenomena? These processes are evident in a recent example, a review of research on teacher thinking (Clark & Peterson, 1986). Research on teacher thinking holds a prominent position in current efforts to improve social studies teaching and teacher education, efforts supported by federal and philanthropic agencies interested in educational reform (see Wilson & Wineberg, 1988). This research program also exemplifies the matrix of assumptions and presuppositions prevalent in most U.S. psychology, a network of ideas that have long been important in theories about social studies teaching and learning.

Clark and Peterson assembled a variety of research findings in an extensive work that can be read at two different levels of analysis. First, it is an organized topical summary and interpretation that draws together different strands of research. These strands include studies of teachers' theories, beliefs, attributes, and perspectives on their roles, as well as investigations of relations among teachers' implicit theories and those of curriculum developers. Clark and Peterson's collection of diverse research findings may be summarized as follows: (a) Thinking plays an important part in teaching and it is varied and rich; (b) teachers' thought processes constitute "a more or less adaptive array of responses to perceived task demands of the profession"; (c) if teachers' implicit beliefs are different from those held by curriculum designers, they will be "unlikely to bring the innovation alive with great enthusiasm, thoroughness and persistence"; (d) and the "maturing professional" is one who makes explicit his or her implicit beliefs (p. 292). According to Clark and Peterson, these summarized descriptions of teacher thinking are said to provide "potential sources of hypotheses about and explanation of some of the implementation research" (p. 292). Clearly, their chapter is meant to provide credible explanations of teaching and curriculum implementation.

At another level, Clark and Peterson's chapter about teacher thinking can be read as the implementation of specialized discourse in conformance with implicit and explicit rules for constructing knowledge. Research findings are considered reasonable in relation to philosophical assumptions within social and cultural environments. These "rules of the game" can be described as two intertwined patterns: a formal style of scientific presentation joined with equally formal presuppositions about human affairs.

The style of writing in Clark and Peterson's chapter follows rules codified in the American Psychological Association's (APA) *Publication Manual.* These canons have been adopted by a community of scholars (including the writers of this chapter) to make their texts conform with a way of truth telling accepted by modern U.S. psychological science. For instance, authors are required to use citations so that preceding texts are positioned prominently in the structure of their own. Precedents are cited so as to give an appearance of durable and generally accepted knowledge. Also, the tone of the chapter is restrained, approximating that of an impartial arbiter of testimony from many sources about an exactly defined phenomenon.

This style of presentation contrasts with those found in such disciplines as philosophy, literary criticism, and variants of sociology, fields of study far older than psychology that are more tolerant of idiosyncratic approaches to citing precedents and surveying the fields of study. The construction of reports in contemporary educational research also contrasts sharply with the structure of early modern scientific texts such as those written in the 18th century by Isaac Newton in which he appealed for a science that would identify God's laws on earth (Manuel, 1974). As recently as the turn of the 20th century, this explicit purpose was prevalent in scientific discourse; for example, the founder of the American Economics Association, Richard Ely, overtly stated his intent to justify Christian ethics through his social research (Silva & Slaughter, 1984).

Although prevailing rules and standards of scientific discourse provide boundaries within which theoretical positions are considered acceptable, those boundaries are continuously redrawn as conventions change. Many historians suggest that the circumstances that affect the rules of discourse are neither predictable nor systematic (Braudel, 1980; Foucault, 1970; Ortega Y Gasset, 1964). The rules for making theories at any one time or place may have little bearing on their successors. Scientific discourse, whether that of physics, economics, or the psychology of teachers' cognition, is less like a chain of interchangeable links than like a tapestry woven of distinctive threads into various patterns.

The epistemological rules followed in Clark and Peterson's chapter were developed in the 19th century as advocates of modern psychology strove for roles in making and implementing policy (Bazerman, 1987; Gould, 1981; O'Donnell, 1985; Silva & Slaughter, 1984). Their summary of scientific knowledge about teacher thinking therefore reflects a distinctive institutional tradition in which particular standards of presentation for psychological literature have been derived from programs of research and development concentrated upon the mental structures of individuals. This research emphasized the functions of individual lives, with little or no attention to the cultural and social processes through which individual lives are formed (Mills, 1959). It is typical of this tradition that Clark and Peterson did not discuss the historical and social contexts of school curricula in their review of research on teachers' thinking.

In Clark and Peterson's review of research, as in most contemporary educational research, concrete data about particular actions are given central importance. This epistemological position that gives primacy to immediate contexts and phenomena has long been associated with science, particularly the physical sciences. Metaphorically, this epistemology resembles paying attention to the colors of thread in a tapestry instead of making references to the patterns into which they are woven or references to the times and places in which the tapestries were made. Although now rejected by many contemporary philosophers of science (Cronbach, 1986; Manicas, 1987; Nelson, Megill, & McCloskey, 1987; Phillips 1987; Udehn, 1987), certain aspects of this position are residually maintained in theoretical statements and methodological practices in social studies research (see Shaver, 1982; L. Smith, 1986; Trigg, 1985; Wittrock & Elzinga, 1985). To examine how these residues affect social studies theory and research, four widespread assumptions will be discussed in the following sections as follows. *First,* there is still notable evidence of belief in an essential underlying truth to be obtained through an identification of facts. *Second,* a separation between descriptive and interpretive research is often postulated. *Third,* a distinction is assumed between contexts of justification and those of discovery. *Fourth,* scientific writing is still evaluated in terms of standards based upon these assumptions.

Essential Truths

It would be difficult to find a social studies researcher who would publicly declare that research identifies essential laws about teaching or learning. The language of theory in educa-

tional research, however, seems to support such a belief. For instance, Kerlinger (1973, p. 3), in discussing theory, said that data can represent objective reality without mediation or interpretation through language. This assumption that rigorous collection of data produces true statements is a belief implicit in a variety of research reports in social studies, in the ways through which findings and procedures are presented.

Studies of curriculum reforms, for example, contain statements that assume that science identifies essential qualities and that prescribe fixed values to subject matter (Hall, Loucks, Rutherford, & Newlove, 1975; also see Napier & Grant, 1986). Carter and Hacker (1988), in reporting about curriculum innovation, discussed the mediations that produce a lack of congruence between reform goals and classroom practices. The authors' methodological strategy was to assess the organizing categories held by social studies teachers to explain variations in the use of curricular materials. Psychometrics were employed to locate the "essential features" of teacher behaviors that influence reforms (p. 53). This entailed constructing a typological framework concerned with "identifying and characterizing regularities" (p. 55). Carter and Hacker identified a scheme of 13 "generic categories of teacher behavior ... which encapsulate intellectual abilities, derived from the organizing elements of social studies" (p. 55). An argument for the validity of these categories, according to formulations of construct validity, must depend upon a belief that, in the case of social studies, such distinctions have an essential nature from which the constructs of intellectual aptitude can be derived (see Cherryholmes, 1988; Cook & Campbell, 1979). By stipulating generic qualities (i.e., specific behaviors for a specified number of forms and functions of classroom activities), Carter and Hacker appear to assume that operational definitions can capture all of the qualities of curriculum use. In their stance, Carter and Hacker, ironically, take subjectivism to an extreme by assuming that their categories and observations are real, without requiring any more justification than the specifications of their procedures for data collection.

In some social studies research, such essentialist assumptions are manifest in discussions of experimental designs. In many reports of research in which constructs are operationally defined and tested through experimental procedures, assertions are not distinguished from the phenomena they are meant to describe and are judged solely through their logical consequences or logical relations to experimental results. For example, drawing upon Tennyson's (1973) research on concept acquisition with nonexamples, McKinney, Gilmore, Peddicord, and McCallum (1987) constructed an experimental design with treatment and control groups. Precedent scientific theories and procedures for data collection were said to ensure that the constructs were operationalized (i.e., precise data could be obtained through procedures that reduced or eliminated human values and bias). The role of the construct of "non-example" in learning concepts was thereby tested according to whether the treatment group made fewer errors on measures of concept acquisition. It was overtly assumed that knowledge, or "concept acquisition," had an essential quality that could be measured on tests and that test errors were directly equivalent to incorrect knowledge. The tacit epistemological assumption underlying this study was that a principle applicable to all learning in any context could be identified through controlling and manipulating a limited set of learning environments. In this epistemology, according to Kerlinger (1973), science is distinguished from common sense: "The scientist . . . systematically builds his theoretical structures, tests them for internal consistency and subjects aspects of them to empirical tests" (p. 3). Presumably, essential truths can be discovered in ways inaccessible to teachers and students through their everyday experiences.

Similar instances of essentialism can be found in ethnographic research aimed at producing results far different from those of experimental methods. Goetz (1981), for instance, claimed that she aimed her ethnographic research on sex-role socialization at the generation of "empirically grounded hypotheses rather than rigorous testing of *a priori* explanations" (p. 33). Although the study does provide important insights into classroom interactions, the report also contains assertions that ethnography involves hypothesis testing. Hypothesis testing is based on inductive logic, an epistemological position in which knowledge is said to conform to expected regularities. These assumptions pose dilemmas for ethnographic researchers, who claim that their theoretical formulations are grounded in data and interpretation. By assuming an inductive logic, these researchers have already presumed expected regularities.

Atheoretical Descriptions

A different traditional epistemological residue can be found in works called *descriptive research,* often referred to as "atheoretical" (see Larkins & McKinney, 1980, for philosophical discussion; Toulmin, 1972; Udehn, 1987). It is frequently assumed that certain methods can provide direct access to social phenomena, allowing the researcher to display them transparently without bias. For example, educational researchers using survey methods (e.g., D. Smith, 1986) produce data that can be grouped in various combinations of multiple variables. In clustering these data, researchers refer to "cross-sections" that are said to depict such complex and fleeting phenomena as classroom life. Research in which data are aggregated with no explicit theoretical statements can be called "dustbowl" empiricism, in that the researchers seem to assume that all possible combinations can be swept together through large-scale statistical techniques. In recent variants, some qualitative or naturalistic case studies are given legitimacy as providing more accurate pictures of educational phenomena than survey research; the field-data studies are seen as records of the naturally occurring speech and actions of people.

Although all research involves data collection, the epistemological position is taken in much descriptive research that the collection of data can somehow be separate from processes of theoretical speculation. For example, in a survey of social studies teachers, Shermis and Washburn (1986) collected data about teachers' backgrounds, career patterns, political opinions, professional perspectives, and beliefs about social studies curricular material. Shermis and Washburn called their study descriptive and nontheoretical, yet the categories chosen (e.g., career

patterns, definitions of reading as a school skill) and the terms used (e.g., "decision making," "empowerment," "cognition"), are imposed categories, theoretical constructs with distinctive historical and philosophical characteristics.

Supposedly atheoretical data are products of the structures, norms, and standards particular to the researchers' intellectual traditions and social circumstances. For example, a data set that might be considered simply descriptive (e.g., numbers of students completing a course) entails general presuppositions and assumptions that are theoretical in import. Course completion appears to be a generally concrete and incontrovertible form of data. As recent large-scale studies have shown, however, curriculum differentiation and placement policies can directly affect the composition of course rosters and whether students finish courses (see Mehan, Hertwick, & Meihls, 1986; Oakes, 1985). Although hundreds of decisions go into the curricular and instructional aspects of a course, and the theoretical assumptions of decision making have been long debated in sociology and political science (see Bachrach & Baratz, 1963), the construct of course completion is nevertheless presented as atheoretical. From the standpoint of social epistemology, any statement of fact also contains the presenter's embedded beliefs and the language's structural implications. Facts, however plentiful in number and pedestrian at first glance, are never isolated monoliths but always confluences of interpretations. Large congeries of data are not exempt from this rule; indeed, dynamic and reciprocal relations between theory and data are correspondingly multiplied as the data set grows.

Justification and Discovery

In social science and educational research, the terms *justification* and *discovery* are often used interchangeably to describe methodological procedures; however, a distinction between two kinds of knowledge can be associated with these terms. As Kaplan (1964) pointed out, the procedures of justification differ from those of discovery. Both can be considered as "logic-in-use" or treated as "reconstructed logic" (p. 14). Justification, Kaplan argued, involves identifying analytic terms and relations as a basis for judging whether the researcher's conclusions are warranted. Processes of discovery, in contrast, are those by which a person or group comes to pursue an area of research and to select the methods for that pursuit. In other words, justification procedures are used to specify how the researcher determines what is true, whereas discovery procedures involve the process by which findings and theory emerge.

Justification procedures involve attending to the logic of argument and the formal rules for data collection and interpretation. In stating their theories and reporting their research programs, most contemporary researchers give high priority to these procedures. In most currently published theory and research in social studies, as with Carter and Hacker (1988), data obtained through efficient and reliable methods are equated with truthful statements about the real world. Reality, in this conceptualization, can be captured by methods that assure a great quantity of correct details. Theoretical truth is defined as the sum of many truthful facts, a version of empiricism succinctly summarized a century ago by Dilthey as "loving absorption in the individuality of the historical event" (in Lepenies, 1988, p. 236). This empiricism is concentrated on atomistic events detached from networks of historical and interpretive relations, including this researcher's own beliefs, personal experience, or social context.

In contrast with justification procedures, those of discovery are aimed at contextual issues through psychological and historical studies of research programs or through epistemological criticism. Apart from works in subdisciplines such as history or sociology of science, most social education researchers do not emphasize discovery processes. However, Campbell (1986), in recommending "an epistemologically relevant sociology of science," suggested that a central goal for social scientists is to "establish and maintain a disputatious scholarly community for each problem area" (p. 129). Granting central importance to the contexts of discovery in the work of these communities, he concluded,

There are social, psychological, and ecological requirements for being scientific that are shared by successful physical sciences and unsuccessful social sciences. The relative lack of success of the social sciences, as well as possibilities for improvement, are understandable in terms of these requirements. (p. 131)

Although many researchers now claim to abjure preoccupation with justification at the expense of discovery, evidence of the persistence of this tendency may be readily found in graduate social science curricula at practically all U.S. research universities, where seminars on history, philosophy, and theory are conducted separately (often as electives) from required courses in methods such as statistics or ethnography.

The "Scholarly Style"

A fourth epistemological residue lies in the discourse of research reports. Theoretical statements are published in formats in which interpretation, explanation, and description are separated. As demonstrated earlier in this chapter, many layers of meaning reside in texts of research reports. Presentations of social studies research customarily emphasize the logical organization of argumentation; theoretical statements are treated as standing apart from the procedures, findings, and interpretation. Recent studies of scholarly prose suggest that such written communication in social and educational sciences has been shaped by particular assumptions about objectivity and neutrality (Nelson et al., 1987). As Bazerman (1987) said in reviewing the rhetoric of the APA *Publication Manual,*

Though many practicing social scientists wish to embrace a single, correct, absolute way of writing science, any model of scientific writing embeds rhetorical assumptions. The explicit examination of these embedded assumptions reasserts our control of choices now determined by tradition, stereotype, and ideology. (p. 125)

Although most researchers would not explicitly claim that their observations and discussions provide objective knowledge about the world, the stylistic mandates they follow in their research reports do imply that claim. For example, as has been noted earlier, the APA. *Manual* requires that citations of precedent or substantiating works be made with parenthetical references in the body of the text. Bazerman pointed out that these rules "help bring the references into the flow of the discussion as items for conscious attention. Both the dates and the names of the authors serve as facts in the argument" (p. 129). Even when authors assert, as we do here, that facts are social constructions subject to continuous processes of interpretation, their citations must be given in authoritative-seeming asides within the text. In disciplines in which styles of citation permit the extensive use of footnotes, a rhetorical predilection for factual buttresses within the text is set aside in favor of dialogues among diverse interpretive texts.

Especially in discussions of matters deemed theoretical, the language of scholarly argument has accrued within it residues of traditional assumptions about the existence of universal properties of matter, thought, and action. These assumptions have been discarded by most contemporary philosophers of science, but they retain their currency within the details dictated by editorial standards for published theoretical statements and research findings. Certain elements of contemporary theory and research in social education thereby uphold epistemological traditions canonized in 19th century natural science.

To conduct this social epistemology further, we turn now to a more specific examination of the development of epistemological assumptions in educational research in the United States over the past century. It is our aim to show that research programs in social studies have taken complex shape through continuous processes of deliberation and change. As do many contemporary scholars (e.g., Bourdieu, 1975; Foucault, 1970; Habermas, 1966/1988; Toulmin, 1972), we contend that theorists and researchers have incessantly reconstructed their theories and practices as their social environments have changed. Especially as pertains to social science and schooling, theories are predicated upon assumptions that shift along with social norms and institutional practices.

THEORY IN AN HISTORICAL CONTEXT

In debates and struggles about social science knowledge that occurred as the disciplines developed, particular assumptions and presuppositions embedded in theoretical statements were socially constructed in response to certain institutional developments. Whether a theoretical statement is accepted as reasonable depends largely upon the conditions under which social groups struggle over the parameters of legitimate thought and reason. To pursue this argument, we focus upon the history of the social sciences, because, at this time, no history of educational and social studies research is available. However, links are made throughout.

Logic as a Social Construction

In this section we examine the provenance of rules that underlie contemporary approaches to research and teaching in social studies. We focus upon the ways that statements are made plausible in socially and materially changing worlds. To emphasize the social context in which general rules and standards of theoretical reasoning are presumed, the term *logic* is used as a social–historical category. We do this both to underscore the method of social epistemology that we use in this chapter and to focus upon the condensed view of logic taken in most 20th century empiricist methodologies; that is, logic is usually strictly and exclusively defined as the formal organization and internal consistency of statements.

In 15th–century European universities, the scholarly study of logic encompassed the discovery of universal, god-given laws in the microcosmic forms of human grammar, rhetoric, music, and poetry (Durkheim, 1938/1977). Today, after the triumph of modern natural science, the study of logic is undertaken for the very different purpose of explicating systematic relations among propositions about empirical phenomena. Religious purposes, although not necessarily excluded from logical analysis, are no longer the sole ends of scientific and technological analyses.

Changes in the definitions and purposes of logic entail important social and epistemological consequences. For example, by the 18th century, scientific researchers studying physical medicine were articulating relations among language and the human body that made it possible for physicians to speak and act about sickness and health without invoking divine intervention. As Foucault (1973) argued, the historical situation in which the human body began to be studied by means of modern medicine emerged, not from a sudden awareness of the body as providing empirical data, but from an epistemological change through which people began to see the body in new ways. In this sense, the creation of the new system of logic about life and death was a precondition for the invention of modern notions of health, illness, and medical research.

In such examples of social studies research as concept acquisition and curriculum innovation, results are customarily said to be derived from standardized rules about empirical evidence, independent of the social status or spiritual beliefs of the scholar (Gouldner, 1979). Contemporary social scientists assume that the logical structure of their language has cross-contextual validity, with rules for presenting knowledge that transcend particular circumstances and individual idiosyncrasies. Approached as social epistemology, the logic of modern scientific theory entails the continuous maintenance of norms of validity, even as the norms shift following changes in the values upheld by communities of scientists, their sponsors, and the general society.

For example, research in the education of social studies teachers has been based on assumptions about professionalism (e.g., Russel & Morrow, 1986). The values that give definition to professionalism have been historically defined in changing social and institutional conditions (see Popkewitz, 1987). The term has undergone shifts in meaning that have become part of social and educational research in the United States during the past 2 centuries. In the early 19th century, professionalism was closely linked to the notion of a clerical elite who "professed" Christian sincerity (McLoughlin, 1978). By the turn of the century, this meaning was succeeded by that of an economic

transaction in which scarce expertise was exchanged for status and compensation (Larson, 1979). Today, professionalism is associated with rational organization, technical knowledge, altruism, and cultural authority. In addition, professionalism in teaching social studies has historically come to mean that differentiated roles are used to organize the occupation. On the one hand, there are the responsibilities, semiautonomy, and obligation of those who administer schools and who teach in universities. And then there are the responsibilities, obligations, and semi-autonomy of those who teach in public schools, with the latter largely in a feminized work situation since the mid-19th century. The patterns of relations and meanings subsumed in the term *professionalism* are not the same across these two strata of occupational life, and they produce different approaches to study. The particular meanings of professionalism in contemporary research are, therefore, related to changing institutional settings.

The changeable and institutional character of theories is, however, neglected in contemporary scientific discussions, which often focus on individuals as innovators, creators, and sometime geniuses who add to the corpus of knowledge. Thus, biographical or intellectual histories of social studies educators are written to illustrate the growth of the field. Although individual scientists' and practitioners' intentions play significant roles in processes of change, their knowledge is nonetheless socially constructed. Statements by the individual scholars or professionals exist in historical context. The rules of language and logic that govern scientific inquiry are contingent upon the values of particular communities in specific circumstances. Epistemological assumptions, such as those pointed out in the earlier discussion of research on teacher thinking, are not entirely the products of researchers' conscious decisions but are also manifestations of implicit social rules about research practice and communication. Those practices can be challenged and do change, but all researchers' thinking and communication, including our own, retain, in residual forms, unquestioned and untested elements.

Progressive Reforms and Theoretical Commitments

Social studies research takes place among intersecting institutional developments. Most importantly, the dispositions and assumptions that undergird social studies research are directly related to the implementation of mass schooling. Public schooling was a major reform program of modern state governments, and its rapid expansion precipitated demands to administer and evaluate large numbers of personnel. A comprehensive history of social studies research has yet to be written, but histories of social science and psychology indicate that theories in these related fields underwent large epistemological shifts during the second half of the 19th century (Bazerman, 1987; Haskell, 1977; Koch & Leary, 1985; Napoli, 1981; O'Donnell, 1985; Silva & Slaughter, 1984). Prior to this time, the tradition of thought from which social science came was the "concern of men and women of affairs debating the practical problems of government and education and of gentlemen scholars and clergymen discussing history, morals, philosophy and natural history—the larger humanistic traditions from which these subjects branched" (Ross, 1979, p. 107). Usually, social or psychological phenomena were studied systematically in advanced courses of moral or mental philosophy within the religious curricula that dominated higher education in the new republic. By the mid-19th century, however, those engaged in the pursuit of higher learning in the United States increasingly accepted natural science as the most effective model for all studies, including those of social institutions (Bruce, 1986). The epistemology of social theories was closely related to that of the natural sciences, sharing assumptions about evolution, equilibrium, and functionalism (Gould, 1981). The interplay between social and natural sciences was effected by new institutions that formed as the economy, culture, society, and political agencies changed (for general discussion, see Hamilton, 1989).

The epistemological assumptions underlying social and educational sciences developed in the 19th century in western Europe and the United States, amidst rapid social change and intensified pressures on community resources. In response, the central state emerged as a major force in governing change and promoting progress. Many reformers in the Progressive Era (1880–1920) declared that only state agencies could provide the large-scale initiatives needed to ensure material progress while maintaining stability among competing groups (Hofstadter, 1955). These reformers, settlement house workers, and educators influenced the emergence of "social studies" as part of the effort to direct resources toward social amelioration (Lybarger, 1987).

As state agencies grew and became more involved in regulating major segments of society during the Progressive Era, public schooling was expanded to promote progress and harmony. Public schooling was the major area of reform as the modern nation-state formed and assumed responsibility for the administration of large sectors of the economy and the society.

As disciplinary academic fields were fashioned within newly enfranchised research universities, the study of educational topics gained impetus. From a variety of approaches, academicians generally proposed that their knowledge and theories about the world would be of practical benefit in pursuing social and material progress through schooling. These aims maintained long-standing religious missionary purposes oriented toward reform through the social and psychological sciences (Haskell, 1977; Furner, 1975; O'Donnell, 1985). Theories of "need" for example, were introduced to emphasize that social welfare institutions could mitigate the unfortunate circumstances of immigrants. Theories of need were eventually transformed into psychological concepts that were used to shape progressive social studies curricula (Franklin, 1987; Lybarger, 1987).

In these processes, a particularly American amalgamation of positivism, empiricism, and pragmatism became the dominant philosophical position (Lears, 1981). Progressive reformers and researchers proclaimed that schools were institutions that could diminish class distinctions by promoting success according to objective criteria of merit. This amalgamation, however, had different strands as research strategies were constructed. Some, such as G. Stanley Hall, offered a theory of development that defined growth among children as a natural progression

that was to be recapitulated in schools. E. L. Thorndike likewise concentrated on human growth but formulated a behavioral theory of networks of connections. In each case, theoretical knowledge was focused upon aggregates of individuals to determine how they could function effectively in society.

Wide debates about the nature and purpose of social and educational theories occurred during the Progressive Era as the disciplines took organizational shape. There was intense conflict among social scientists about what knowledge was of greatest worth (Silva & Slaughter, 1984). Some wanted to tie the social sciences to an activist role in reforming society. Others sought to develop postures of objectivity that would enable researchers to work with different governmental agencies, independent of party politics or legislative agenda. By the end of the Progressive Era, the latter groups had won control of the professional organizations. Concentrating upon strictly functional analyses in their theoretical statements, these social and educational scientists claimed to make their work free of partisanship.

One programatic purpose of these professional reformers was to ensure access to resources needed for institutional development of their disciplines. Many of the early psychologists, for example, held positions in normal schools and university pedagogical faculties, as mass schooling rapidly expanded. During the Progressive Era, the pages of newly founded professional publications were filled with statements assuring that social scientists' work in schools was value-neutral and that their professional interventions were unencumbered by political interests. So-called positivist philosophy was not a precursor to the construction of progressive social scientific theories, as recent studies show, commitments to objectivity, functional statements, and separation of the logics of justification and discovery occurred decades before the arrival of positivistic philosophies of science (O'Donnell, 1985; L. Smith, 1986). Theories were adapted to the politics of the Gilded Age by social scientists who pragmatically highlighted their procedures and formally eschewed ideological commitment.

The politics and epistemologies of progressivism supported the continuing expansion of universities and, in turn, were supported by university administrators who were consolidating authority over scientific research and development (Franklin, 1986; Powell, 1980; Silva & Slaughter, 1984). Academic leaders sought to make their services indispensable to various segments of government, agriculture, business, and cultural affairs. To promote these broad agendas, administrators rejected those social scientists who overtly combined scientific methods with partisan agitation for reform in the name of the poor or working-class clients. The presidents feared that the governing boards who oversaw the budgets of their institutions, and who heavily represented clergy and business interests, would object to overtly political actions and withdraw support for the growth of their institutions. Pressures for broadly nonpartisan research programs also came from within professional organizations as social scientists sought to widen their markets.

Theory making in social studies education was directly, albeit subtly, related to the development of norms for social science research. As particular commitments to objectivity that separated logics of discovery from those of justification were incorporated into the methodological and administrative mechanisms of disciplined research, the struggles and conflicts about purposes from which these commitments arose were downplayed in conventional institutional historiography. The styles of writing and reporting were also canonized in such forms as the APA *Publications Manual* discussed earlier.

Although we have not directly addressed curriculum theory in this chapter, it is important to recognize that generally held epistemological assumptions have had great influence upon the deliberation over and the implementation of curriculum. In such general cases, epistemological assumptions are not derived from science alone but are confluences of scientific conceptions and cultural or institutional predispositions. For example, research programs in the social studies were closely integrated with the practical demands of schooling, as in the case of the expanding-environments organization of elementary social studies. This curriculum strategy strongly persists at all levels of contemporary curriculum planning and can be traced back to Herbartian recapitulation theory from the late 19th century (Akenson, 1987; Kliebard, 1986). As Akenson argued, the development of this theory was related to cultural and social changes, as well as to scientific theories advanced within the discipline of psychology.

Belief in working with the interests and experiences of children, belief in developmental stages of children's mental growth, belief in unification and correlation, belief in citizenship education, and belief in moving from the simple and concrete to the abstract all worked nicely with the evolving conception of social studies. (p. 168)

The conception of expanding environments had longevity largely because it shares epistemological assumptions with continuing theories in developmental psychology. By assuming that all development must have equilibrium, psychologists, in Akenson's (1987) phrase, collectively "draw the artificially happy and conflict free picture of society, and the manner in which the social world presents itself to children"(p. 169). Theories of knowledge and cognitive development are said to explain individual children's cognition. Many progressive social theorists claimed that such research-based knowledge could be used to guarantee that children could be made into productive citizens. In these specific ways, theories in educational science were integrated with the politics of American curriculum development at the outset of the Progressive Era.

Theoretical statements incorporate epistemological assumptions that affect research, practice, and policy alike. Beliefs in psychological individualism and cognitive equilibrium permeate current social studies research programs in areas of study such as higher-order thinking, citizenship education, and teacher effectiveness. As Shaver (1979) said, it is an error to base educational policy on empirical data from such research. Any claim that such data can be used to justify policy is at risk of being a circular argument, because theoretical statements, research findings, and political agendas are based on similar epistemological assumptions. Nevertheless, scientists have frequently claimed that their works could provide impartial guidance for politicians and practitioners, as is discussed next in a brief look at the history of American psychology, a major disciplinary framework for theoretical approaches to social studies research.

Psychology and Pragmatic Problems of Institutional Development

Psychology had long been a part of philosophy before growing to prominence in Progressive Era reforms as the first social science discipline to develop solely within the university (Gould, 1981; Koch & Leary, 1985; Silva & Slaughter, 1984). University presidents, especially from eastern and private institutions with religious origins, embraced psychology as a way of reconciling "faith, reason, Christian belief and Enlightenment empiricism" (O'Donnell, 1985, p. 58). Psychology was originally promoted in the college curriculum to help maintain the theological dualism of matter and spirit that was being challenged by the acceptance of theories of evolution. Psychological researchers set out to relate material conditions to the functions of the mind in ways that were consistent with theological dicta about the soul. Hall (1885) was one such visionary who called psychology the great interpreter of the Bible, saying, "Deeper psychologic insights are to effect a complete atonement between modern culture and religious sentiments and verities" (p. 134).

Behavioral methodologies imported from Germany were found to be well-suited to the religious and political purposes of the new psychologists in the United States, many of whom visited newly organized laboratories of physiological psychology, particularly Wilhelm Wundt's in Leipzig. Leading American academicians learned a pragmatic and experimental approach to mental phenomena in his labs, but Wundt's theories were often changed in transit (Koch & Leary, 1985). Even though he pioneered the many empirical methods later linked with strictly behaviorist theories, Wundt insisted that the human mind was an active form of consciousness that was constructed within social–historical contexts. United States psychologists adapted Wundt's methods to fit their theories of individualism, redefining cognitive processes as mental functions that could be assessed individually but meaningfully interpreted in reference to statistical distributions. The most famous of these assessments were the early intelligence quotient (IQ) tests by Yerkes (Gould, 1981). Unlike Wundt's intention to study the group processes by which social and cultural groups are defined, the aim of U.S. psychologists was to construct assessments of specific capacities, or "skills," to be used to help individuals adjust successfully to their social environments. Central in the forming of these methodological commitments was a growing awareness of the problems of administering the newly formed mass school systems in the United States (O'Donnell, 1985).

As Tolman argued (in L. Smith, 1986), American psychological theory has been based on the assumption of individual agents coping with their immediate environments and struggling for survival. Tolman considered psychological theories to be a scientific means of helping individuals deal with ambiguities and changing environments. The theories of many of the early psychologists were pragmatic in the sense that their purpose was to apply research methods to immediate social conditions. As William James (1892) said,

What every educator, every jail-warden, every clergyman, ever asylum-superintendent, asks of psychology is practical rule. Such men care little or nothing about the ultimate philosophic grounds of mental phenomena, but they do care immensely about improving the ideas, dispositions, and conduct of the particular individuals in their charge. (p. 148)

In this statement, James expressed the mind-set of most of the first American "new" psychologists. In this disciplinary context, knowledge and action were defined primarily in terms of individual agents whose knowledge was evaluated against the political and economic needs of particular social-interest groups.

In brief, the social history of psychological research programs raises questions about how the possibilities and limits of theoretical knowledge are constructed. Contemporary theories of social studies teaching and learning have grown out of many complex and contentious struggles among social scientists over the ways that valid knowledge is constructed. Through the lens of social epistemology, social research may be seen as interrelated with developments and struggles in institutions and societies that theorists and researchers occupy. At this point, it is fair to ask what suggestions this approach can offer to those who are currently making theoretical statements and conducting research on social studies education. In reply, an exemplar is provided to demonstrate how contemporary theoretical work can deal with the dilemmas posed by epistemological uncertainties surrounding standards of truth and method in social science.

AN EXEMPLAR: INTERESTS, RECONSTRUCTION, AND COMMUNICATION

In this section, an approach to theory is presented by which researchers may view questions about social studies teaching and learning as problems in social epistemology. Current ideas about valid scientific knowledge in contemporary social contexts are explicated in this exemplar, which suggests ways of portraying specific theoretical statements in relation to both general rules of validity and practical situations. As an exemplar of theory representing processes of social knowledge construction, we have selected a theory of interests developed by Jurgen Habermas. In his work, Habermas proposes to think about rationality as multidimensional processes in continuous interplay. These processes are said to be directed toward specific purposes, which he calls "interests." Rationality, he claims, involves interests that may initially be classified as cognitive interests that shape the form of thoughts, or communicative interests that guide the actions through which thoughts are shaped into linguistic terms and social relations. These two types of interest are not always distinct, however, especially in works of scholarship and theory.

Habermas proposes that scientific rationality must be defined in broader terms than individual consciousness, because socially constructed codes provide the frameworks upon which canons of validity are built. Although complex social systems may seem to be organized through disorderly processes incomparable to the precision and rigor that are hallmarks of reason, Habermas nevertheless maintains that social patterns and processes can be examined as rational interactions based on cognitive and communicative interests.

Habermas classifies cognitive and communicative interests as *technical-instrumental, interpretive-hermeneutic,* and *emancipatory-critical,* distinguishing among interests related to work, symbolic interaction, and power. Instances of technical-instrumental interests in social science theory can be found in works that focus upon such concepts as the functionality and validity of knowledge and communication (e.g., Fiske & Shweder, 1986). Instrumental interest are also evident in research such as the example given earlier in which models of teacher thinking were developed as strategies for teacher education reform (Clark & Peterson, 1986). In these instances, thinking and communication are concentrated upon concrete phenomena; researchers seek empirical results that show what is going on in a reality external to the research program. The cognitive interests in these research programs are communicated through specialized discourses about what works or might work in teaching.

Cognitive and communicative interests that Habermas would classify as interpretive-hermeneutic attend to the meanings given to statements, not only as preconditions to the validity of knowledge and communication, but also as processes that shape credibility and utility. In interpretive research, reality is not considered to be external to the research program but constructed within it. Interpretive researchers claim that "thick" descriptions and inductive generalizations can be used to describe interactions among engaged participants in a culture and detached observers of that culture. The cognitive and communicative interests involved in these processes of cultural construction and interpretation are epitomized in ethnographic texts produced by "participant-observers" whose reports are said to contain both insiders' knowledge and outsiders' reflections (e.g., White, 1986). In theories that are used to pursue interpretive-hermeneutic interests, it is recognized that knowledge and communication are results of interactions among various points of view. Social constructions such as "meanings" and "awareness" are therefore given priority in these theories and research programs.

Emancipatory-critical cognitive and communicative interests are focused upon conceptions of power, subordinating interests in functionality and meaning to those involved in social action. For example, Stanley (1986) has called for social studies research based on ethical principles and political agendas, in which the teacher is viewed as emancipating students. In pursuit of these interests, concepts of emancipation are applied in reflective knowledge and deliberate action, in response to questions about why things are as they are and what is to be done (see Fay, 1987).

At a rudimentary level, Habermas's classification of knowledge and communication into three types of interest can be used to label theoretical statement as *instrumental, interpretive,* or *critical-emancipatory.* Such a rigid scheme of classification is misleading, however, because any social science theory or research program involves many ways of understanding and interpreting social phenomena (Tabachnick, 1981). It is more pertinent to ask to what extent these ways of knowing and communicating reflect the social circumstances under which they occur. Referring to this question in terms of traditional and critical approaches to theory, Habermas (1966/1988) stated

The traditional idea of theory is abstracted from scientific activity as it is carried on within the division of labor at a particular stage of the latter's development. It corresponds to the activity of the scholar which takes place alongside all other activities of a society, but in no immediately clear connection with them. In this view of theory, therefore, the real function of science is not made manifest; it conveys not what theory means in human life, but only what it means in the isolated sphere, in which, for historical reasons, it comes into existence. As opposed to this, critical theory is to become conscious of its calling; it knows that in and through the very act of knowing it belongs to the objective context of life that it strives to grasp. The context of its emergence does not remain external to the theory; rather the theory takes this reflectively up into itself. . . . (p. 401)

To Habermas, theories are highly charged acts of communication in specific settings, as researchers raise competing questions about possibilities for instituting techniques, mediating meanings, and making changes. According to this approach, consensus over what constitutes valid knowledge must not be assumed, but canons of validity must be decided upon deliberately in acts of "reconstruction" in which political or cultural consequences of theoretical statements are articulated and critiqued.

Habermas argues that reconstructive theories merge cognitive and communicative interests. This combination of reflection and action is said to most closely correspond with critical and interpretive approaches to theory. Especially in the realm of science, the cognitive and communicative interests of researchers must be evaluated for more than admissibility according to prevailing standards within each discipline, but also for their relations with other disciplines and abutting realms of everyday discourse and practice. In Habermas's works, theoretical statements are not considered to be the products of detached contemplation but are instead the outcomes of practical action in particular settings. Theoretical statements do not depict natural laws, nor are theories derived solely from researchers' interpretations of natural and social phenomena. Rather, according to Habermas, theories are interpretive statements about nature and society that reconstruct specific epistemological traditions. Diverse ideas about true knowledge are present in theoretical statements, often in competition without resolution. Researchers build theories upon precedents and often clash over their terminology, but their works are neither cumulative nor revolutionary so much as cyclical. Habermas (1979) said:

Reconstruction means that one takes a theory apart and puts it back together in a new form in order to better achieve that goal which it set for itself. [This] is the normal . . . way of dealing with a theory that requires revision in many respects, but whose potential for stimulation has not yet been exhausted. (pp. 97–98)

Habermas uses the term *rational reconstructive science* to denote the continuous recycling of epistemological ideas and theoretical statements. To illustrate rational reconstruction, he analyzed Marx's materialist theory, originally anchored in terms of labor and production, to show that it can be reconstructed in terms of communicative actions that are submerged in economic transactions (1979).

According to Habermas, the social sciences are necessarily different from the natural sciences in that social science researchers are trying to comprehend a more symbolically structured reality. Natural sciences are predominantly empirical, in that scientists of nature primarily make theoretical statements that "develop nomological hypotheses about domains of observable events" (1979, p. 9). These theories are continuously tested and reconstructed, but Habermas points out that, in their theoretical statements, social scientists place much higher priority on drawing a distinction between *observation* and *understanding,* the former being a characteristic of nomological hypothesis testing and the latter more typical of reconstructive science. In effect, hypotheses are about expected variations or consistencies in phenomena, but reconstructions involve unexpected new dimensions that emerge as ideas are woven into new patterns in different social contexts.

When theories are used to pose hypotheses about natural or social phenomena and are tested in laboratory or field settings by experimental or correlational methods, research questions are thereby limited to asking whether the conclusions bear out the premises of inquiry. In contrast, a rationally reconstructive theory is constructed as one part of a long series of inquiries about a set of research questions within specific epistemological traditions and social–institutional circumstances. To Habermas, an important quality of reconstructive science is that scientists must treat apparently incongruent theories and practices as likely material for critical analysis. Scientific questions are not raised as a means of finding out about nature or society, but as a means of posing improved questions.

One implication of Habermas's ideas about scientists' cognitive and communicative interests is that researchers must recognize that their work requires continuous and complex symbolic transactions. To him, theories are especially tentative acts of communication reconstructed in various contexts and for various reasons. Educational research, conceptualized as communicative acts aimed at understanding communicative action, especially involves acts of reconstruction. For researchers to examine what they say about practitioners' speech and acts and the contexts in which they and the practitioners speak is not incidental to their purposes, but cardinal. Habermas asserts that knowledge and truth are problematic in every social situation.

Habermas provides many examples of rational reconstructions, not the least of which are of his own ideas and actions. For our purposes here, his critique of Kohlberg's theory of moral development provides a useful example, because the theory has had widespread influence in social studies education. According to Habermas (1983), Kohlberg's concept of moral development has not been tested empirically, so much as interpreted in a self-referential process akin to a hermeneutic circle. As Habermas says, this "empirical theory presupposes the normative validity of the reconstruction by which it is informed, yet this validity becomes doubtful as soon as the reconstruction does not 'work empirically' " (p. 269). Kohlberg's arguments assume what he set out to prove, that is, that stages of moral development occur in human beings. Under rational reconstruction, this recursivity serves a communicative interest, specifically linked to interpretive ways of knowing and communicating. As Habermas said, in setting forth a moral philosophy,

Both the psychologist's subjects and the moral philosopher adopt the same performative attitude of a participant in practical discourse. In both cases, the outcome of moral reasoning, whether it is an expression of the layperson's moral intuition or the expert's reconstruction of it, is evaluated in the light of claims to normative rightness. (pp. 265–266)

In this conceptualization of the interests involved in Kohlberg's theory Habermas links the cognitive and communicative interests of expert with those of laypersons. In effect, theories under reconstruction are forms of communication in which knowledge claims are articulated and tested. The first priority of researchers, therefore, would be to establish clear communication among the various parties inhabiting the context of the research program. Unlike traditional approaches to theory, in which the first priorities are the clarification and examination of hypotheses, a reconstructive approach is based on the assumption that the work of making theoretical knowledge and communication is attached to their practical situations. According to Habermas and other neopragmatists (Rorty, 1982; West, 1989), theories such as Kohlberg's are provisional forms of knowledge and communication that are continually contingent upon their circumstances.

In short, distinctions between cognition and communication, as well as among technical, interpretive, and critical kinds of interests, are more like links than boundaries. Differing ways of knowing, communicating, and acting may be logically distinct but interact in specific ways within particular social fields. The technical-analytic interests involved in a theory of moral development are joined to interpretive-hermeneutic interests as hypotheses are clarified, then reconstructed in accordance with critical-emancipatory interests as researchers, subjects, and their audiences (both lay and expert) communicate. The treatment of theory in social education research would therefore resemble that of a text undergoing analysis and interpretation, much as a literary work or historical document is continually reinterpreted by new generations of responsive readers. Shakespeare's *Othello* and the U.S. Constitution's Bill of Rights, as two examples, have been reconstructed by audiences newly sensitized to the enduring significance of race in human affairs.

Proponents of moral-stage theories in social studies usually begin their communicative interactions by asking, "What do these theories say about moral development?" From a reconstructive approach, according to Habermas, they would, in contrast, start out by asking, "What are the conditions in which particular representations of moral deliberation are possible?" It is not as if the names Kohlberg (or Habermas) evoke entities with a single presence, regardless of the listener's perspective. These are names given to concepts and discourses that involve variegated cognitive and communicative interests.

There are many theorists whose works provide further exemplars of reflective and reconstructive communicative inter-

ests, under such headings as *poststructuralist* (Cherryholmes, 1988) and *neopragmatist*. It is especially significant that many reconstructions emerge from traditions either outside dominant and non-Western tradition (Said, 1988; West, 1989) or from other previously marginalized social groups: for example, feminist social theorists have made trenchant critiques of theories such as Kohlberg's that presume that certain phenomena are universal or free gender differentiation (Benhabib & Cornell, 1987; Fraser, 1989; Gilligan, 1982; Irigaray, 1984; Lather, 1986). Weedon (1987), a feminist theorist, asked, for example,

why we need a theory of the relationship between experience, social power, and resistance, and what sort of theory will serve us best. For a theoretical perspective to be politically useful to feminists, it should be able to recognize the importance of the subjective in constituting the meaning of women's lived reality. (p. 8)

Linking differing personal and political realms of thought and action, many feminist scholars ground their theoretical statements in practical and subjective experiences. Their theoretical works, including those critical of Habermas's theories, provide specific examples of his method of rational reconstructionism.

Critical and reconstructive approaches are as old as the concept of theory, dating back to the first written records of philosophical and religious discussion; in the 19th century, there were many notable critiques of the dominance of naturalistic social science (e.g., those of Nietzsche and Weber). The work of Habermas provides but one example of contemporary theory that is actively aimed at a broad range of issues and that draws upon a large variety of traditions and methods. Through continuous reconstruction, such theoretical work can enrich a disciplinary tradition while raising questions about its epistemological and methodological assumptions.

CONCLUSION

If theoreticians' primary purpose in making theory is to decide what kinds of knowledge are to be considered valid, and cognitive and communicative interests are reconstructed as social conditions change in space and time, then social epistemology is an ongoing process, one of continuous inquiry into the past and present possibilities of science and education. The aim in this chapter has been to show the necessity of such continuous inquiry, especially into the historical backgrounds and social circumstances that contribute to the processes of making theoretical statements and conducting research programs.

Truth and inquiry are always qualified by social relations. Theory, informed by social epistemology and reconstructed according to various interests, becomes a matter of asking whose truth, and what are the means and purpose of inquiry? Theories are statements about the world, but they are also technologies for creating and maintaining social relations, regulating human life by incorporating norms of possibility and admissibility. As Foucault said,

Truth is a thing of this world: it is produced only by multiple forms of constraint. And it induces regular effects of power. Each society has its regime of truth, its "general politics" of truth: that is, the types of discourse which it accepts and makes function as true; the mechanisms and instances which enable one to distinguish true and false statements, the means by which each is sanctioned; the techniques and procedures accorded value in the acquisition of truth; the status of those who are charged with saying what counts as true. (in Gordon, 1982, p. 131)

Social epistemology is a way of asking about the mechanisms by which valid theories are produced and the social conditions within which validity is defined.

Today, those engaged in producing theories and conducting research on social education have inherited structures and traditions that were formed in the 19th century during the Progressive Era of reforms and social engineering. The histories of educational institutions and professions from that era provide analogies to the processes now taking place and affecting the conduct of disciplined research about schooling. Despite the gigantic scale attained by educational institutions and profes-

sions that have grown out of progressive reforms aimed at achieving a stable and productive social order, long-promised social harmony and civil justice remain elusive goals. Educators in coming years will have to grapple with ethical and moral problems, as did their predecessors, in a world that is evidently less safe than the environments in which progressive reformers first made their optimistic claims.

Pessimism, however, is not a proper antidote to the conventional wisdom that has predominated and impoverished educational research. Nor need criticism always imply cynicism; it can entail a cautious skepticism that can guide and inform thoughts, words, and deeds. Knowing that there are limits to discourse and action need not thwart human purposes but can intensify them. No matter how unattainable truth may be, and however tentative the efforts to define it, there is still no better alternative way to safety and justice than inquiry about nature, mind, and society. Admittedly, searching *for* the best answers is an endless task, but the process of searching might *be* the best answer.

References

Akenson, J. (1987). Historical factors in the development of elementary social studies. *Theory and Research in Social Education, 15*(3), 155–172.

Bachrach, P., & Baratz, M. (1963). Decisions and non-decisions: An analytical framework. *American Political Science Review, 57,* 632–642.

Bazerman, C. (1987). Codifying the scientific style. In J. Nelson, A. Megill & D. McCloskey (Eds.), *The rhetoric of the human sciences* (pp 125–144). Madison, WI: University of Wisconsin Press.

Benhabib, S., & Cornell, D. (1987). *Feminism as critique: On the politics of gender.* Minneapolis: University of Minnesota Press.

Bourdieu, P. (1975). The specificity of the scientific field and the social conditions of the progress of reason. *Social Science Information, 14*(6), 19–47.

Braudel, F. (1980). *On history.* Chicago: University of Chicago Press.

Bruce, R. (1986). *The launching of modern American science, 1848–1896.* Cambridge, MA: Harvard University Press.

Campbell, D. T. (1986). Science's social system of validity-enhancing collective belief change and the problems of the social sciences. In D. Fiske & R. Shwerder (Eds.), *Metatheory in social science* (pp. 108–135). Chicago: University of Chicago Press.

Carter, D., & Hacker, R. (1988). A typology of social studies teaching process. *Theory and Research in Social Education, 16*(1), 51–64.

Cherryholmes, C. (1988). *Power and criticism: Poststructural investigations in education.* New York: Teachers College Press.

Clark, C., & Peterson, P. (1986). Teachers' thought processes. In M. Wittrock (Ed.), *Handbook of research on teaching* (3rd ed., pp. 225–296). New York: Macmillan.

Cook, T. D., & Campbell, D. T. (1979). *Quasi-experimentation: Design & analysis issues for field settings.* Chicago: Rand McNally.

Cornbleth, C. (1986). The invitation. In C. Cornbleth (Ed.), *An invitation to research in social education,* (Bulletin 77, pp. 1–9). Washington, DC: National Council for the Social Studies.

Cronbach, L. (1975). Five decades of public controversy over mental testing. *American Psychologist, 30,* 1–14.

Cronbach, L. (1986). Social inquiry by and for earthlings. In D. Fiske & R. Shweder (Eds.), *Metatheory in social science* (pp. 83–107). Chicago: University of Chicago Press.

Durkheim, E. (1977). *The evolution of educational thought: Lectures on the formation and development of secondary education in France* (P. Collins Trans.). London: Routledge and Kegan Paul. (Original work published 1938)

Fay, B. (1987). *Critical social science: Liberation and its limits.* Ithaca, NY: Cornell University Press.

Fiske, D., & Shweder, R. (Eds.). (1986). *Metatheory in social science: Pluralisms and subjectivities.* Chicago: University of Chicago Press.

Foucault, M. (1970). *The order of things: An archeology of the human sciences.* New York: Random House, Vintage Books.

Foucault, M. (1973). *The birth of the clinic: An archeology of medical perception.* New York: Random House, Vintage Books.

Franklin, B. (1986). *Building the American community: The school curriculum and the search for social control.* London: Falmer Press.

Franklin, B. (1987). The first crusade for learning disabilities: The movement for the education of backward children. In T. S. Popkewitz (Ed.), *The formation of school subjects: The struggle for creating an American institution* (pp. 190–209). New York: Falmer Press.

Fraser, N. (1989). *Unruly practices: Power, discourse and gender in contempory social theory.* Minneapolis: University of Minnesota Press.

Gilligan, C. (1982). *In a different voice: Psychological theory and women's development.* Cambridge, MA: Harvard University Press.

Goetz, J. (1981). Children's sex-role knowledge and behavior: An ethnographic study of first grades in the rural south. *Theory and Research in Social Education, 8*(4), 31–54.

Gordon, C. (Ed.). (1982). *Power/knowledge: Selected interviews & other writings by Michel Foucault.* New York: Pantheon.

Gould, S. (1981). *The mismeasure of man.* New York: W. W. Norton.

Gouldner, A. (1979). *The future of the intellectual and the rise of the new class.* New York: Seabury Press.

Habermas, J. (1979). *Communication and the evolution of society.* Boston: Beacon Press.

Habermas, J. (1983). Interpretive social science vs. hermeneuticism. In N. Haan (Ed.), *Social science as moral inquiry* (pp. 251–269). New York: Columbia University Press.

Habermas, J. (1988). *On the logic of the social sciences.* (S. W. Nicholson & J. Stark, Trans.). Cambridge, MA: MIT Press. (Original work published 1966)

Hall, G. S. (1885). The new psychology. *Andover Review, 3,* 130–140.

Hall, G., Loucks, S., Rutherford, H., & Newlove, B. (1975). Level of use of innovation: A framework for analyzing innovation adaptation. *Journal of Teacher Education, 26*(1), 52–56.

Hamilton, D. (1989). *Toward a theory of schooling.* London: Falmer Press.

Haskell, T. (1977). *The emergence of professional social science: The American Social Science Association and the nineteenth-century crisis of authority.* Urbana, IL: University of Illinois Press.

Hofstadter, R. (1955). *The age of reform, from Bryan to FDR.* New York: Vintage.

Irigaray, L. (1984). Sexual difference. In T. Moi (Ed.), *French feminist thought* (pp. 118–130). Oxford: Basil Blackwell.

James, W. (1892). A plea for psychology as a 'natural science.' *Philosophical Review, 1,* 140–150.

Kaplan, A. (1964). *The conduct of inquiry: Methodology for behavioral sciences.* Scranton, PA: Chandler Publishing.

Kerlinger, F. (1973). *Foundations of behavioral research* (2nd ed.) New York: Holt, Rinehart & Winston.

Kliebard, H. (1986). *The struggle for the American curriculum.* London: Routledge and Kegan Paul.

Koch, S., & Leary, D. (1985). *A century of psychology as science.* New York: McGraw-Hill.

Kuhn, T. (1970). *The structure of scientific revolutions* (2nd ed.). Chicago: University of Chicago Press.

Larkins, A. G., & McKinney, C. W. (1980). Four types of theory: Implications for research in social education. *Theory and Research in Social Education, 8*(1), 9–17.

Larson, M. (1979). *The rise of professionalism: A sociological analysis.* Berkeley, CA: University of California Press.

Lather, P. (1986). Research as praxis. *Harvard Educational Review, 56*(3), 257–275.

Learned, W. (1927). *The quality of the educational process in the United States and in Europe.* (Carnegie Commission on Higher Education). Boston: Merrymount Press.

Lears, J. (1981). *No place of grace: Antimodernism, and the transformation of American culture, 1880–1920.* New York: Pantheon.

Lepenies, W. (1988). *Between literature and science: The rise of sociology.* New York: Cambridge University Press.

Lybarger, M. (1987). Need as ideology: Social workers, social settlements and social studies. In T. S. Popkewitz (Ed.), *The formation of school subjects: The struggle for creating an American institution* (pp. 176–190). London: Falmer Press.

Manicas, P. (1987). *A history and philosophy of the social sciences.* Oxford: Basil Blackwell.

Manuel, F. (1974). *The religion of Isaac Newton, The Fremantle Lectures, 1973.* Oxford: Clarendon Press.

McKinney, C. W., Gilmore, A. C., Peddicord, H. Q., & McCallum, R. S. (1987). Effects of a best example and critical attributes on prototype formation in the acquisition of a concept. *Theory and Research in Social Education, 15*(3), 189–201.

McLoughlin, W. G. (1978). *Revivals, awakenings, and reform: An essay on religion and social change in America, 1607–1977.* Chicago: University of Chicago Press.

Mehan, H., Hertweck, A., & Meihls, J. (1986). *Handicapping the handicapped: Decision making in student's educational careers.* Stanford, CA: Stanford University Press.

Mills, C. W. (1959). *The sociological imagination.* New York: Oxford University Press.

Napier, J., & Grant, F. (1986). Evaluation of a second generation dissemination of a local improvement project: Implications for theory and procedures. *Theory and Research in Social Education, 14*(1), 67–90.

Napoli, D. (1981). *Architects of adjustment: The history of the psychological profession in the United States.* Port Washington, NY: Kennikat Press.

Nelson, J., Megill, A., & McCloskey, D. (Eds.). (1987). *Rhetoric of the human sciences: Language and argument in scholarship and public affairs.* Madison, WI: University of Wisconsin Press.

Nelson, J., & Shaver, J. P. (1985). On research in social education. In W. Stanley (Ed.), *Review of research in social education: 1976–1983,* (Bulletin 75, pp. 401–433). Washington, DC: National Council for the Social Studies.

Oakes, J. (1985). *Keeping track: How schools structure inequality.* New Haven, CT: Yale University Press.

O'Donnell, J. (1985). *The origins of behaviorism: American psychology, 1876–1920.* New York: New York University Press.

Ortega y Gasset, J. (1964). *History as a system and other essays towards a philosophy of history.* New York: W. W. Norton.

Phillips, D. (1987). *Philosophy, science, and social inquiry: Contemporary methodological controversies in social science and related applied fields of research.* Elmsford, NY: Pergamon Press.

Popkewitz, T. (Ed.). (1987). *The formation of school subjects: The struggle for creating an American institution.* London: Falmer Press.

Popkewitz, T. (in press). *A political sociology of educational reform.* New York: Teachers College Press.

Powell, A. (1980). *The uncertain profession: Harvard and the search for educational authority.* Cambridge, MA: Harvard University Press.

Rorty, R. (1982). *Consequences of pragmatism.* Minneapolis: University of Minnesota Press.

Ross, D. (1979). The development of social science. In A. Oleson & S. Voss (Eds.), *The organization of knowledge in modern America, 1860–1920* (pp. 107–138). Baltimore: Johns Hopkins University Press.

Russel, T., & Morrow, J. (1986). Reform in teacher education: Perceptions of secondary social studies teachers. *Theory and Research in Social Education. 14*(4), pp. 325–330.

Said, E. (1988). Representing the colonized: Anthropology and its interlocuters. *Critical Inquiry, 15*(2), 205–225.

Shaver, J. P. (1979). The usefulness of educational research in curricular/instructional decision-making in social studies. *Theory and Research in Social Education, 7*(3), pp. 21–46.

Shaver, J. P. (1982). Reappraising the theoretical goals of research in social education. *Theory and Research in Social Education, 9*(4), 1–16.

Shermis, S., & Washburn, D. (1986). Social studies educators and their beliefs: Preliminary data from Indiana colleges and universities. *Theory and Research in Social Education, 14*(4), 331–340.

Silva, E., & Slaughter, S. (1984). *Serving power: The making of the academic social science expert.* Westport, CT: Greenwood Press.

Smith, D. (1986). Survey research. In C. Cornbleth (Ed.), *An invitation to research in social education* (Bulletin 77, pp. 28–39). Washington, DC: National Council for the Social Studies.

Smith, L. (1986). *Behaviorism and logical positivism: A reassessment of the alliance.* Stanford, CA: Stanford University Press.

Stanley, W. (1986). Critical research. In C. Cornbleth (Ed.). *An invitation to research in social education* (Bulletin 77, pp. 78–90). Washington, DC: National Council for the Social Studies.

Tabachnick, B. R. (1981). Teacher education as a set of dynamic social events. In B. R. Tabachnick, T. Popkewitz, & C. Szekeley (Eds.), *Studying teaching and learning: Trends in Soviet and American research* (pp. 76–86). New York: Praeger.

Tennyson, R. (1973). Effects of negative instances in concept acquisition using a verbal-learning task. *Journal of Educational Psychology, 46,* 247–260.

Tiles, M. (1984). *Bachelard: Science and objectivity.* Cambridge, England: Cambridge University Press.

Toulmin, S. (1972). *Human understanding: The collective uses and evolution of concepts.* Princeton, NJ: Princeton University Press.

Trigg, R. (1985). *Understanding social science*. New York: Basil Blackwell.

Udehn, L. (1987). *Methodological individualism: A critical appraisal*. Uppsala, Sweden: Uppsala Universitet, Sociologiska Institutionen.

Weedon, C. (1987). *Feminist practice and poststructuralism*. London: Basil Blackwell.

West, C. (1989). *The American evasion of philosophy: A genealogy of pragmatism*. Madison, WI: University of Wisconsin Press.

White, J. (1986). An ethnographic approach. In C. Cornbleth (Ed.), *An invitation to research in social education* (Bulletin 77, pp. 51–77). Washington, DC: National Council for the Social Studies.

Wilson, S. M., & Wineburg, S. W. (1988). Peering at history through different lenses: The role of disciplinary perspectives in teaching history. *Teachers College Record, 89*(4), 525–539.

Wittrock, B., & Elzinga, A. (Eds.). (1985). *The university research system: The public policies of the home of scientists*. Stockholm: Almquist and Wiksell International.

Wittrock, B., & Wagner, P. (1988, August). *Social science and state developments: The structuration of discourse in the social sciences*. Paper presented at the meeting of the XIVth World Congress of the International Political Science Association, Washington, D.C.

4

CRITICAL RESEARCH AND SOCIAL STUDIES EDUCATION

Cleo H. Cherryholmes

MICHIGAN STATE UNIVERSITY

research: *n* [MF *recerche,* fr. *recerchier* to investigate thoroughly, fr. OF, fr. *re-* + *cerchier* to search—more at SEARCH] (1577) **1:** careful or diligent search **2:** studious inquiry or examination; *esp*: investigation or experimentation aimed at the discovery and interpretation of facts, revision of accepted theories or laws in the light of new facts, or practical application of such new or revised theories or laws **3:** the collecting of information about a particular subject

critical: adj (1590) **1 a:** inclined to criticize severely and unfavorably **b:** consisting of or involving criticism . . .; *also*: of or relating to the judgment of critics . . . **c:** exercising or involving careful judgment or judicious evaluation **d:** including variant readings and scholarly emendations . . . **2 a:** of, relating to, or being a turning point or specially important juncture . . . **b:** CRUCIAL, DECISIVE . . . **c:** INDISPENSABLE, VITAL . . . **d:** being in or approaching a state of crisis . . . **3:** characterized by risk or uncertainty . . . CRITICAL may also imply an effort to see a thing clearly and truly in order to judge it fairly. (*Webster's Ninth New Collegiate Dictionary,* 1983, pp. 1002, 307)

It is somewhat odd to have a separate chapter on critical research in a handbook on research. All research, presumably, is critical. That some research is critical and other research is noncritical will surely come as a surprise to many practicing researchers, even to students who have only completed an introductory course in research design or data analysis. If textbooks on social research are valid indicators, however, criticism is often aimed only at research techniques. Criticism in any boarder sense is either excluded outright or marginalized. This requires comment.

One consequence of the Norman (French) victory over the Saxons (English) at the Battle of Hastings in 1066 continues to be reflected in our everyday life: The English language has since been enriched by an infusion of French words. The word *research* derives from the French *recerche,* as noted in the epigraph. Like many other English words of French ancestry such as *gourmet, gourmand, flamboyant,* and *gaffe,* it is thoroughly integrated into the English language as we find and employ it.

Meanings change. Research (*recerche*) initially meant either to investigate thoroughly or a careful and diligent search. It means something quite different in contemporary educational research, making it possible to identify some research as critical and some as noncritical. Note the meanings that the *Webster* lexicographers assign to critical, "exercising or involving care-

Reviewers were Jere Brophy, Michigan State University; Henry Giroux, Miami University; James A. (Tony) Whitson, Louisiana State University.

ful judgment or judicious evaluation," "variant readings and scholarly emendations," "turning point or specially important juncture," "in or approaching a state of crisis," and "critical may also imply an effort to see a thing clearly and truly in order to judge it fairly" (*Webster's Ninth New Collegiate Dictionary,* 1983, p. 307).

These meanings of *research* and *critical* can be traced to the 16th century. Given this, it is instructive to consider a view of research advanced in one of the most, if not *the* most, influential textbooks on educational research, Kerlinger's *Foundations of Behavioral Research* (1973). This book, he wrote,

is a treatise on scientific research; it is limited to what is generally accepted as the scientific approach. It does not discuss historical research, legal research, library research, philosophical inquiry, and so on. It emphasizes, in short, understanding scientific research problem solution. (p. viii)

A bit later he elaborated, *"Scientific research is systematic, controlled, empirical, and critical investigation of hypothetical propositions about the presumed relations among natural phenomena"* (p. 11).

It is always possible to take exception to a brief characterization of something as complex as scientific research; one exception will be mentioned before proceeding. Educational research does not deal with naturally occurring phenomena; physicists deal with natural phenomena when they study things called quarks and black holes and gravity and time and light, but educational researchers study *socially constructed* phenomena when they study classroom interaction or school academic climate or student test performance.

Kerlinger added the following and little else about critical investigation, "The scientist must always subject his notions to the court of empirical inquiry and test. He is hypercritical of the results of his own and others' research results" (p. 11). Criticism, in this view, occurs when researchers check each other for mistakes. Tracing the etymology of words (where this chapter began with *research* and *critical*) is not allowed because it is historical, or literary, or philosophical, or all three. In his effort to distinguish scientific from nonscientific research, however, Kerlinger ran into a problem that he failed to recognize, address, or solve. The problem is that research procedures, practices, and results must be interpreted (judgments must be made about validity, generalizability, and applicability); yet the scientific status of interpretation remains unclear because interpretation involves, at one time or another, historical, linguistic, library, literary, and philosophical research.

To draw out the point, first, all research occurs in historical context. Theoretical constructs, hypotheses to be tested, and theories to be evaluated are objects of that historical context. Surely, the "scientific" aspirations of Kerlinger (as quoted before) are not that our hypotheses and theories transcend time in some ethereal fashion. Second, the attempts to establish a firm boundary between scientific research and philosophy lack plausibility. This is easily demonstrated. Theories, by most empiricist standards, are required to be internally consistent and not contradictory. Decisions about consistency and contradictoriness are made by reference to logic. Logic is a branch of philosophy. Another example: Scientists are concerned about the

meaning of their theoretical terms, such guidance is provided by yet other areas of philosophy: semantics, philosophy of language, philosophy of science, and epistemology. Kerlinger's depiction of educational research excludes earlier meanings of *research/recerche* as thorough investigation or careful and diligent inquiry, because some kinds of inquiry necessary for understanding and evaluating scientific research are excluded. Kerlinger's view of empirical research, and it may represent the beliefs of many, if not most, educational researchers, is a radical departure, restructuring, and restriction of its historical meaning. Its newer scientific meaning, however, remains unclear.

Criticism involves the exercise of careful judgment or judicious evaluation that often includes variant readings and scholarly emendations. It also has a negative side, however, that is sometimes overemphasized. Bernstein (1983) put it like this:

"The expression "critical" and its cognates 'critic' and "critique" have been sadly abused in recent times. There is a vulgar sense of "critical" where it means little more than "scoring negative points" ... There is always a moment of negativity or distancing in critique, but a critique demands that one seeks to understand what is being criticized. (p. x)

Criticism that celebrates and privileges only negativity is vulgar. It can also be mean spirited, demeaning, and sarcastic. It misses nuances of reading and interpretation that contribute to the productive and constructive effects of criticism and the subtleties and complexities that produce critical insights.

In this vein, it is useful to distinguish being critical from being judgmental. *Judgment,* again from *Webster's Ninth New Collegiate Dictionary,* is "a formal utterance of an authoritative opinion," or "the process of forming an opinion or evaluation by discerning and comparing," or "an opinion or estimate so formed" (1983, p. 653). In judging, one forms an opinion or estimate by applying criteria and standards. To employ judgment is one aspect of criticism and is captured by *Webster's* first definition of critical, "exercising or involving careful judgment or judicious evaluation." Criticism that moves beyond judgment and *Webster's* first definition involves "relating to, or being a turning point or specially important juncture," or "CRUCIAL, DECISIVE," or "being in or approaching a state of crisis," or "characterized by risk or uncertainty" (1983, p. 307). Judgments are based upon comparisons with standards; criticism involves questioning those standards themselves as problematic.

Now I will extend the second part of *Webster's* definition to criticism in educational research. Criticism also consists of, "being alert to the implications, to the historical sedimentation of the language we use" (Derrida, 1972, p. 271). Critics assume that conventional standards are historically sedimented, or incorporated into language and social practices and institutions, in the present case those of social studies education. *But* they find no compelling reason to accept those standards simply because they are present and in force. Critics inquire into texts, institutions, practices, uses of language, and actions, in order to clarify their meanings, constitution, and justification.

Criticism is neither simple nor straightforward, because it is also characterized by paradox and contradiction. Criticism depends, in the first instance, upon attempts to *understand* the object of interest; in the second, it involves *distancing* oneself from the object of criticism, whether the object is degree of social and political tolerance, factual recall, or the changing role of women in the United States and around the world. The paradox is that one must (a) be close to something in order to understand it before (b) distancing oneself in order to be critical of it, give it variant readings, and make judgments about it, thereby (c) enabling one to understand it more fully. Closeness *and* distance are required.

Critical, most of the time in the following review, is used as "decisive," "crucial," and in terms of the "historical sedimentation of the language we use." All of the research on social studies education that, conceivably, can be called critical is not summarized in this chapter, although much of it is cited. Instead, an introduction is provided to a number of approaches to social studies research that are self-consciously critical in one way or another, exemplary pieces of social studies research are discussed, and research questions that remain to be investigated are proposed.

Social studies research patterned after research in the natural sciences is discussed first. Because this approach to educational research, often referred to simply as quantitative research, is widely known, it provides a background against which alternatives can be contrasted. These include structuralism; critical theory; phenomenology (ethnography), hermeneutics, and reader response theory; and two forms of poststructural criticism, interpretive analytics and deconstruction. These alternatives are *neither* exhaustive *nor* mutually exclusive. For example, feminist criticism and theory and critical legal studies are not discussed. Furthermore, these approaches overlap in various ways, and sometimes a single study represents ideas from more than one of them.

QUANTITATIVE RESEARCH

Alternative approaches to criticism in educational research can usefully be seen as counterpositions to what is called quantitative research because it is modeled after research in the natural sciences. (See Kerlinger, 1973, and Borg & Gall, 1983, for general introductions to what I call *quantitative research;* elsewhere it is called *empirical* or *mainstream research* or some combination of these.) In the quantitative case, researchers question or observe subjects or units of analysis that are "objectively" defined by variable attributes, for example, age, gender, measured academic ability, recall of information, number and type of classroom interactions. An important characteristic of this approach to research is that the subjective perceptions and beliefs of researchers, that is, their opinions and attitudes and those reported in the research literature, determine what is studied and how it is studied; those who are studied are treated as objects, that is, they are "objectively" defined. Correlations, causal inferences perhaps, are sought among these variables and among the constructs they measure. In the next two sections, the search for structures in social studies teaching and learning is identified and, sometimes, criticized.

STRUCTURALISM

Structural analysis is based on the assumption that underlying structures exist to be exposed and analyzed. *Webster's Ninth*

New Collegiate Dictionary defines the noun *structure* as "something arranged in a definite pattern of organization," and, "organization of parts as dominated by the general character of the whole" (1983, p. 1169). Structural analysis can be applied to social studies education, to cultures, to literature, to political systems, or to standardized achievement tests. There are several elements to structuralism. (For extended discussions of structuralism see Hawkes, 1977; Lane, 1970. See Cherryholmes, 1988b, chap. 2, for an introduction to structuralism in education.) To begin, a structure is constituted and defined by relationships among its parts and the parts only have meaning in relation to the whole. Structural analysis is ahistorical and produces what might be called slice-of-time (synchronic) analysis. Additionally, structural analysis is purported to be value free, even though its findings can be used for ideological and political purposes. Structural analysts identify the organization of what is studied by locating the binary oppositions or distinctions it supports or promotes. The following are examples of such oppositions or distinctions in contemporary educational practices: Cognitive/affective, high achieving/low achieving, attentive/nonattentive, time on task/time off task, academic learning/nonacademic learning, conceptual understanding/nonconceptual understanding, higher order thinking/lower order thinking, excellence in education/nonexcellence in education, intelligent/unintelligent, interested/disinterested, fact/value, and conceptual/factual. The category that is valued in the structure is listed first and the disvalued, second. For example, many educators argue that the first category in the examples listed is, or should be, valued over the second. Other educational structures and practices could be premised on the inversion of some or all of these oppositions and distinctions. Additionally, the organization of a structure is maintained and changed by sets of regulative and transformative rules.

Almost all of contemporary educational research is designed to uncover underlying structures, processes, and products. Rorty (1985) expressed the general idea like this: "Much of the rhetoric of contemporary intellectual life takes for granted that the goal of scientific inquiry into man is to understand 'underlying structures,' or 'culturally invariant factors,' or 'biologically determined patterns' " (p. 5). Consistent with structural analysis, many educational researchers attempt to free themselves of values and ideology and report just the facts; this characterizes both quantitative and ethnographic research, for example. On the other hand, it is arguable that almost all of contemporary educational practice, including social studies education, is premised on *desired* structural outcomes and principles (Cherryholmes, 1988b, chap. 2). Value-free structural analysis is quite distinct, it should be noted, from the promotion of desired structural outcomes. Furthermore, thinking along structural lines in either educational research or practice remains largely unacknowledged.

Critical theory and research, treated in the next section, shares important assumptions with structuralism, even though the value-free assumption is dropped, history is added to the analysis, and a neo-Marxist empirical and normative analysis of culture and society is provided. Phenomenological and ethnographic researchers also look for, if not essences of phenomena, structures by which people make sense of and understand their everyday lives and social practices as they consume and produce understandings about themselves and their world. Quantitative research is also based on the presumption of a structure to the world to be discovered. Instrumental knowledge is produced that policy-makers, for example social studies educators, utilize in developing or modifying social programs and policies (see Fay, 1977 chaps. 1, 2).

Anyon's analysis of social studies textbooks illustrates how structural analysis can be used to promote structures counter to those in place. In 1978, Anyon published the first in a series of articles in which she analyzed relationships among social class, school knowledge, legitimation of existing social institutions, and support of widely accepted ideological positions. In her analysis of four leading elementary textbook series she found that, for the most part, political criticism was either omitted or actively denigrated. With respect to economic systems and institutions, attention was selectively drawn to capitalism. The textbooks consistently displayed an idealized view of American society, and any mismatch between these idealizations and objective social conditions or limitations to their realization were ignored. Anyon concluded that these books, while giving the appearance of being apolitical and ideologically neutral, were, in fact, highly politicized.

Shaver (1979) initiated an exchange with Anyon that illuminates the structural approach. He agreed with Anyon that elementary and secondary social studies textbooks are slanted to promote a positive view of American society and that many elementary and secondary teachers use them for that purpose. He objected, however, to Anyon's use of "mindlessness," a term that she appropriated from his 1977 National Council for the Social Studies presidential address. Shaver contended that mindlessness, "the thoughtless use of method and/or content without examination of the underlying assumptions and the potential outcomes that may impact the achievement of one's purposes" (1979, p. 44), was a matter of process, not outcome. Anyon, he claimed, had confused the matter by suggesting that the use of biased textbooks was mindless, without attending to whether there was a rational justification for the use.

Anyon's (1979a) response is structural to the core. Her emphasis on structure dramatized the break between structural analysis, in its various forms, and liberal humanistic approaches to education that focus on the individual. She wrote,

The concept [mindlessness], by focusing on individuals, trivializes the constraints and sanctions that impinge on educators as social actors; it mystifies the contributions of history, and of society and culture to schooling. Educational institutions are thus reified, appearing both timeless and eternal, and yet *changeable* by mere individual cogitation. (p. 52)

Anyon's point is that mindlessness avoids questions of social structure; material, social, and economic inequalities; and unequal distributions of social opportunities. These questions, she argued, are systematically and consistently avoided in the social studies literature. Liberal social theorists and humanistic educators, among others, put individuals at the center of the social stage. Individuals have beliefs, make plans, choose courses of action, and act. Structuralists emphasize that social arrangements, power structures, cultural beliefs, and the material distri-

bution of resources place severe limitations on what individuals can think and do. The Anyon–Shaver exchange highlights a subjective-structural distinction that is often not far below the surface of social studies discourse (see Parker, 1986, for a discussion of this issue).

Anyon (1979b) continued her pursuit of structuralist themes in a study of the ideological content of United States history textbooks. Beginning with the unremarkable but widely ignored idea that, "Textbooks are social products that can be examined in the context of their time, place, and function" (p. 361), she studied 17 top-selling high school United States history textbooks. Her investigation was limited to their treatment of economic and labor union developments during the period of industrialization between the end of the Civil War and the beginning of World War I, from 1865–1917.

Anyon assumed that school knowledge is also social knowledge and reveals much about the society that produced it. School knowledge reveals which groups have power and displays how their interests and views are legitimized in the school curriculum. Also, the *silences* of school knowledge reveal who is at the margins of society and whose views are disvalued in the curriculum. She concluded

The present analysis suggests that the United States working class is one such group [that is not empowered in our society].... Omissions, stereotypes, and distortions that remain in "updated" social studies textbook accounts of Native Americans, Blacks, and women reflect the powerlessness of these groups. (p. 382)

The textbooks promoted the following: There is no working class, we are all middle class, and those who are impoverished deserve their poverty. An additional finding was that the textbooks varied little from publisher to publisher or year to year (p. 364).

An analysis of school textbooks that was more explicitly structural was conducted by Gilbert (1984a, 1984b; see Whitson, 1986, for a review of 1984a). He studied the images of society and the disciplinary knowledge and perspectives presented in 180 British textbooks published after 1969. Among other things, he found that the social scientific disciplines do not present images of society that are consistent with each other, for example, economic texts emphasize market and social equilibrium and geography texts, progress. Progress, of course, is often destabilizing. Some of Gilbert's conclusions reinforce Anyon's findings; for example, inequalities in wealth and power are largely overlooked, and the absence of a discussion of inequalities creates the impression that social equality exists (Gilbert, 1984b, pp. 222–223).

Structural analysis per se has been little utilized in social studies research. Many structural questions remain to be investigated. They range widely and include: Are structures of social scientific and humanities knowledge promoted in social studies education? If so, what are they? Do cognitive beliefs and values about society and social processes have identifiable structures? Are there competing structural orientations to social studies education? Do the identifiable structures in materials such as social studies textbooks, social studies methods textbooks, standardized achievement tests, school district curricula guidelines, and state department of education requirements reinforce or contradict each other? Put another way, what is (are) the aesthetic, cognitive, and affective structural configuration(s) of social studies education?

CRITICAL THEORY AND RESEARCH

Although critical theorists and researchers do not dispute the existence of underlying structures, they break with structuralism in several ways. Critical theorists are not value neutral, ahistorical in their analyses, or uninterested in producing social structural changes and, at least in the case of Habermas (see later), they are concerned with universal theories of speech and communication (universal pragmatics) that will prevent the systematic distortion of communication in the service of domination and oppression.

Critical theory is the name given to the work of members of the Frankfurt Institute of Social Research and their followers, the Frankfurt School (see Jay, 1973, for a history of their work from 1923–1950). Prominent members were Max Horkheimer, Herbert Marcuse, Theodor Adorno, Walter Benjamin, and their prominent current theorist, Jurgen Habermas. They were heavily influenced by the writings of Karl Marx, but not dogmatically so. Horkheimer (Foreword in Jay, 1973) described the origins of the school and its connection with Marx like this

Already near the end of the twenties, certainly by the beginning of the thirties, we were convinced of the probability of a National Socialist victory [in Germany], as well as of the fact that it could be met only through revolutionary actions. That it needed a world war we did not yet envisage at that time. We thought of an uprising in our own country and because of that, Marxism won its decisive meaning for our thought. After our emigration to America via Geneva, the Marxist interpretation of social events remained, to be sure, dominant, *which did not mean in any way, however, that a dogmatic materialism had become the decisive theme of our position* [italics added]. Reflecting on political systems taught us rather that it was necessary, as Adorno has expressed it, "not to think of claims to the Absolute as certain and yet, not to deduct anything from the appeal to the emphatic concept of the truth." (pp. xi–xii)

Two points are worth noting. *First,* Marx's thought had a particular historical appeal to these German theorists, but they were not bound to it in a deterministic way. *Second,* an epistemological point, they were ambivalent with respect to truth; they appear to have been simultaneously searching for truth and denying its existence. Both elements are important in understanding their work.

In Marx's sophisticated analysis of the rise and development of capitalism through the 19th century, he claimed to have discovered, not only structures of capitalism, but also a structure in the history of capitalism and its projected decline as well. Twentieth-century critical theorists and researchers, such as members of the Frankfurt School, have subjected classical Marxism to searching analyses and have rejected many of its basic tenets while reformulating those retained and articulating new views on social research and theory, social domination, and possibilities for emancipation from oppressive social relation-

ships (see McCarthy, 1978, for a sympathetic yet critical introduction to the work of Habermas that includes many of these elements).

Critical theorists propose that symbolic and material structures of various types unjustifiably privilege some individuals and groups and deprive others. Critical theorists are in the business of exposing such social inequalities and injustices—for example, racial and gender discrimination, exploitation of unskilled laborers, inadequate provision of universal health care for all, and failure to provide information upon which both the socially oppressed and oppressors can act to ameliorate such conditions. Even though critical theory is concerned with structures and counterstructures, it is obvious from Horkheimer's Foreword (Jay, 1973) that critical theorists break with structural analysts on several points. They hope to anticipate and defeat, for example, the rise of neo-Fascist and neo-Nazi movements. In doing this, they are concerned with social and political structures but are equivocal about the nature and possibility of truth.

Apple (1971) may have been the first to introduce these arguments into social studies education in, "The Hidden Curriculum and the Nature of Conflict." Jackson (1968) had labeled the hidden curriculum as that which implicitly teaches norms and values that are usually not talked about, for example, how students learn to cope with crowds, praise, and power in classrooms. Apple revealed that social studies, along with science, the second curricular area he examined, made important contributions to the hidden curriculum by not mentioning, analyzing, recognizing, or reflecting upon social conflict.

The comparison with science is apt. Whereas science can be portrayed as a "history of competing research programs" (Lakatos, 1970, p. 155), science as a school subject does not show students "how critical interpersonal and intergroup argumentation and conflict have been for the progress of science" (Apple, 1971, p. 32). Social studies curricula also tend to be silent on criticism and conflict, and point

to an acceptance of society as basically a cooperative system.... The orientation stems in large part from the (perhaps necessarily unconscious) basic assumption that conflict, and especially social conflict, is *not an essential* feature of the network of social relations we call society (Apple, 1971, p. 33).

Apple identified 1960s social studies materials that repeatedly emphasized adjustment to social rules, cooperation, social stability, peaceful interaction, and that rewards come to those who obey the rules and punishment to those who break the rules. "The functions of social conflict" to borrow from Lewis Coser (1956), were excluded from these social studies materials. Conflict, a crucial and inescapable part of social life, is marginalized in social studies education not unlike the way criticism is marginalized in educational research. Oliver (1957) was one of the few social studies educators who argued that conflict was an essential element of our society and should be included in social studies teaching and learning. This was particularly insightful given the social quietude of the 1950s. He continued this line of argument into the 1960s (Oliver & Shaver, 1966/1974, chap. 1).

Popkewitz added similar criticism in 1977 when he reported

that social studies textbooks promote social consensus and functional stability and avoided discussing conflict and its social functions. The textbooks he examined advanced the ideas that few in the United States are disadvantaged and that those who are can press their claims in elections and through other formal means of political participation. Textbooks repeatedly claimed, Popkewitz found, that the existing social structure was fair and equitable, but they provided little or no supporting evidence or arguments. The textbooks represented curriculum reform efforts of the 1960s and emphasized social science content and disciplinary "structure."

The effects of emphasizing social scientific knowledge include, Popkewitz argued, detachment from everyday affairs, legitimation of social scientific knowledge, and representation of social scientists as an expert elite. Popkewitz identified contradictions between the rhetorical claims (*rhetorical* refers here to what the textbooks asserted or claimed to do) in these textbooks and their supporting logical arguments (*logical* refers here to the propositional content of what the textbooks asserted). Even though he did not use the term, this is known as *deconstructive criticism* and is discussed in a later section. Popkewitz showed that the textbooks *rhetorically* appealed to an open-ended notion of citizenship while *logically* focusing on closed-ended learning of specific concepts and generalizations that portray only one version of political participation. Popkewitz wrote, "Because all social theory arises from our everyday knowledge and commitments, no theory can be neutral. Thus, any curriculum disposes a student toward social action" (p. 54). Presenting social scientific information as definitive social knowledge, then, hides the underlying interests, ideology, and power that produced it. As Popkewitz (1977) wrote,

Understanding social inquiry as social invention can enable the modes of social analysis to enlarge our perception of the whole and our relationship to social structures, challenging in the process the very presuppositions and prescriptions by which we act. To reify inquiry, in contrast, is to create new forms of mystification which make the social world seem mechanistic and predeterministic. (p. 58)

Popkewitz (1978) followed his analysis of textbooks with an article entitled "Educational Research: Values and Visions of Social Order." He contended that the language of social science, including its theories and explanations, is metaphorical and rhetorical and, therefore, incapable of use for a purely scientific and truthful "representation" of the world. These metaphors and their rhetorical expression contain social visions inextricably intertwined with claims of objective knowledge. Knowledge is produced, in part, from the subjective perceptions and beliefs of researchers who are part of and responsive to their social world; knowledge is socially constructed. Because it is socially constructed, value commitments and ideological positions are embedded in it. This aspect of knowledge has long been, and continues to be, ignored in social studies education.

Criticism begets criticism. By 1980 political leftist writing in social studies education (such as that of Anyon, Apple, and Popkewitz), even though it comprised a very small literature, began to generate critical responses, sometimes of a different political persuasion. Proefriedt (1980) criticized and then built upon their ideas. He rejected the more despairing analyses, such as those of Bowles and Gintis (1976) who saw schools as appendages of a capitalist system where even successful school reform might leave major social inequalities and injustices untouched. Proefriedt wrote,

The genius of the socialist criticism is to have worked through the Marxist understanding of the influence of production relations on other aspects of society and to have spelled out specifically how school policies and practices mirror those production relations. At the same time, however, the critics have become imprisoned in their own paradigm. (p. 473)

The strategies he described to bypass this imprisonment were throwing off a positivist epistemology that includes value neutrality and that rules out critical inquiry, using ideology as a basis for criticism of educational thought and practice, adopting a Deweyan view of critical thinking to avoid subtle indoctrination, being critical of one's own definitions and data, and articulating the unarticulated assumptions underlying one's concepts and terms.

Giroux has produced, perhaps, the largest body of work bringing critical theory to bear on contemporary education, including the social studies. In 1980, he followed Bernstein (1976) by relating three modes of rationality to citizenship education: technical, hermeneutic or interpretative, and emancipatory. Technical rationality refers to *instrumentalism,* means–ends analysis, and utilitarianism that prizes efficiency. Hermeneutic rationality refers to *interpretation* of the categories and assumptions that we employ in the practice of our everyday life. Emancipatory rationality refers to *criticism* of oppressive social relations and structures in our lives and social practices.

Giroux (1983) advocated a form of radical criticism in citizenship education and criticized the radical educational thought of the 1960s and 1970s. As with Proefriedt, Giroux noted that reproduction theorists, who develop theories of schooling based on the assumption and conclusion that schools are an ideological state apparatus concerned largely with reproducing existing social structures and relations (for example, Bowles & Gintis, 1976), overemphasize the idea of class domination and fail to provide teachers, students, or administrators with a basis for action in the correction of social injustice and inequity. He found analyses of economic reproduction, cultural reproduction, and hegemonic-state reproduction wanting. As a result he began working toward a theory of resistance that would take advantage of the contradictions in relations of gender, race, and class and turn overt acts of student rebellion from self-destructive displays into the development of productive social relations. Giroux (1983) argued that "the concept of resistance must have a revealing function that contains a critique of domination and provides theoretical opportunities for self-reflection and struggle in the interest of social and self emancipation" (p. 290). In the critique one must "unravel the ideological interests embedded in the various message systems of the schools ..., point to the ideology underlying the hegemonic curriculum ..., suggest that radical educators must develop a critical rather than a pragmatic relationship with students" (pp. 292–293).

Along the same tack was the systematic exploration (Cherryholmes, 1980) of three interpretations of citizenship education as decision making: one from a position of logical positivism-empiricism, one from the perspective of Karl Popper's (1976) critical rationalism, and one from the viewpoint of Jurgen Habermas's (1979) critical theory. Citizenship education as decision making from a logical positivism-empiricism stance assumes such things as the following: Language is description and not action (this has been called the *descriptivist fallacy*); factual statements do not contain valuations (overlooking that values lead one to choose which facts are worth stating in the first place); scientific knowledge is grounded in a given reality (even though objects and events can be perceived from an indefinite number of vantage points); scientific knowledge is produced by inductive processes (ignoring that conceptions precede observation statements); and description precedes explanation (although descriptions rely upon explanations that tell us what constitutes valid descriptions). I rejected these positivist-empiricist assumptions along with the particular view of citizenship education as decision making to which they lead.

Then I analyzed citizenship education as decision making in terms of Popper's (1976) view of science and criticism that elaborates and defends classically liberal views of scientific research and knowledge (Cherryholmes, 1980). Popper's assumptions for scientific research include impartiality, egalitarianism, freedom of criticism, freedom of thought, and clarity of communication (classic interpretations of First Amendment freedoms). Finally, citizenship education was discussed in terms of Habermas's (1979) critical theoretical view of scientific research and knowledge. These assumptions include the following: Facts and theories are linguistic, speech is action and value laden, truth is the product of unconstrained consensus in an ideal speech situation where anyone, in principle, can participate and raise any question or make any comment.

This argument was later expanded with the contention that social studies educators generally operate on the basis of the correspondence theory of truth, that is, a statement is true if and only if it is satisfied by all objects (Cherryholmes, 1982). Philosophers well know that what constitutes correspondence is problematic, to say the least. I then posed as an alternative Habermas's consensus theory of truth and the ideal speech situation: where everyone may speak, no strategic behavior such as voting or debating or agenda setting is allowed, and any comment, including those that introduce meta-ethical and meta-theoretical issues, may be made. What would classroom discourse be like, I asked, if it were patterned on Habermas's ideal speech situation? *First,* teachers would have to understand and be committed to critical discourse. *Second,* characteristics of critical discourse would have to be communicated to students, even though not all classroom interactions could be critically discursive in this sense. *Third,* teachers would advance authoritative knowledge, but openings for critical discussion and analysis would be provided, in order that authoritative knowledge claims and interpretations could be challenged. *Fourth,* still following Habermas, only the best arguments would be pursued. This requires that students be taught some elementary logic to assist them in separating better from worse arguments, at least in a formal sense, and in learning to evaluate the evidence upon which such arguments are premised. Apart from the characteristics of ideal speech outlined by Habermas, it was hypothesized that a socially heterogeneous classroom contributes to critical

discourse by ensuring that different perspectives are represented.

Moving in a different direction, Wood (1985) compared citizenship education for a protectionist democracy to that for a participatory democracy. One argument has it that, in a protectionist democracy, voting rates are acceptable even if only a fraction of the population participates in elections, because an electorate that is fully participatory may act more like a mob. He argued that the social studies work of Remy (1980), Shaver (1977), and Newmann (1975) supported such an interpretation. The latter authors emphasized, Wood argued, an acceptance of leadership elites and formal participation patterns that do not include widespread mass participation. Wood also cited a *Newsweek* column in which George Will (1983) asserted that, if nonparticipants were not satisfied with their society, they would mobilize politically. On the other hand, feelings of alienation and powerlessness could lead to such political withdrawal. Shaver (1977) maintained, consistent with some interpretations by political analysts, that, even if mass participation is normatively desirable, its empirical effect might be to destabilize our political institutions. Given the declining electoral turnout of registered voters, the destabilization hypothesis is unlikely to be put to the test in the near future.

In 1985, at least a decade after critical theoretical ideas began appearing in the social studies literature, Kickbusch (1985) observed that critical discourse had not had a major role in social studies education. On the basis of classroom observations, he found that discussions about Civil War draft riots in New York, for example, focused on who the rioters were and how many were injured. These typical empirical questions are not without value, but little attention was given to the perceived injustices that precipitated the riots.

Then in 1987, Kickbusch merged the work of Foucault (see later) with critical theory and posed questions about the types of discourse that preservice teachers are taught. On the basis of observing student teachers, he found that the central concerns in their classroom discourse were with management and control and citizenship transmission. University education and teacher training, he concluded, may not be a liberating force but, instead, may be a powerful conservative influence on schools as we find them.

Structuralism provides one formalization, as it were, of the goals of quantitative research. Critical theory capitalizes, after a fashion, on structuralism, in order to criticize quantitative research. In one sense, then, naturalism, structuralism, and critical theory can be grouped together even though they oppose each other in various ways, sometimes quite vigorously. In other approaches to criticism, however, quite different, sometimes radically different, arguments are made about social research and social studies education.

INTERPRETATIVE RESEARCH: PHENOMENOLOGY, HERMENEUTICS, AND READER RESPONSE THEORY

Phenomenology, hermeneutics, and reader response theory are loosely, but only loosely, related. Phenomenological researchers attempt to adopt a posture of radical freedom that permits the phenomenon under investigation to reveal itself as it is. Hermeneutical researchers attempt to determine the original meaning of texts as intended by their authors. Reader response researchers investigate how readers experience and realize texts as they are read.

If one compares the writing of one of the first phenomenologists, Edmund Husserl (translated in 1970), with contemporary views on reader response theory, sometimes referred to as *reception theory*, there may be a temptation to deny any contiguity or relationship between them. This is the connection: Husserl, writing around the turn of the century, objected to "the surreptitious substitution of the mathematically substructed world of idealities for the only real world, the one that is actually given through perception, that is ever experienced and experienceable—our everyday life-world" (1962/1970, p. 48). Husserl was interested in underlying structures and "essences." To discover them, he argued, a new conception of science was needed. In order that the world could reveal itself, one had to free and open oneself, undergoing a personal transformation not unlike a religious conversion, thereby transcending one's time and place in order to *see* the world as *it is.*

Phenomenologically oriented researchers in social studies education and educational research generally have never seriously entertained the idea of transcending one's time, place, and subjectivity. They have, however, retained the idea of psychologically and cognitively "freeing" and "opening" themselves to students and to teaching by listening, observing, describing, reporting, and watching.

Hermeneutic research descended from an older tradition of studying scriptures. Hermeneutical and phenomenological researchers share the problem of how to interpret words on a page and their observations. At present, the issues of interpretation have shifted to focus on the responses of readers to texts, including social texts of the world. How do readers "realize" or "produce" a text? Reader response researchers are concerned with the latter question and others like it. By the time we get to reader response theory in contemporary literary criticism, the transcendental project of discovering underlying essences, Husserl's original project, has long been abandoned.

Text, textuality, and *intertextuality* are words often used in this and related research and descriptions of it. The following discussion follows Lewis and Simon's (1986) use of the word *text:*

"Text" refers to a particular concrete manifestation of practices organized within a particular discourse. In everyday life, meaning-making does not exist in isolation, but forms complexes that are organized contingently through time and space. Examples of text include written passages, oral communication, nonverbal communication accomplished through body movement and expression, and visual forms of representation such as paintings, photographs, and sculpture. (p. 458)

Their usage of *text* goes far beyond words on a page to include the practices by which meanings are constructed, maintained, and conveyed.

The Influence of Phenomenology

Those who follow phenomenological guidelines in their research criticize important assumptions that quantitative researchers take for granted. Those who are phenomenologically oriented advocate that researchers free themselves from the commonsense and theoretical ways of seeing to which they have been socialized by their society, culture, and research literature, so that what *is* before them can reveal itself *as it is.* They do not assume that the quantitative research literature identifies legitimate, appropriate and essential phenomena. (See Ihde, 1979, for an introduction to phenomenology and Jacob, 1987, for a review of interpretative and qualitative research in education.) As noted, phenomenology as a body of philosophical thought was first formulated by Husserl (1962/1970), whose work spanned the late 19th century and the early 20th century. He proposed an approach in which the researcher refuses to accept mere appearance as reality, an approach to research that he argued would be fundamentally objective.

In doing phenomenological research, researchers adopt an approach to viewing the world that is radically different from that of quantitative researchers. Phenomenology requires that researchers perform, or at least attempt, a philosophical act of pure reflection in their research that Husserl called *epoché.* This requires researchers to free themselves, as much as possible, from their past experiences, culture, history, and beliefs and values. Imagine the contrary. If researchers are not *free* of these and other factors that have shaped them as individuals and subjects, then, when they report their observations and descriptions, they are reporting on themselves and their times as much as on the phenomena they have observed. Martin Heidegger (1949), a student of Husserl's, held that truth depends upon freedom. He described the link between freedom and truth like this: *"The essence of truth is freedom* ... In order to be able to turn an action and thus the action of a representative statement and indeed that of agreeing or not agreeing, into a 'truth,' the agent of course must be free" (pp. 330–331).

The effect of these and other phenomenological arguments has been to focus attention on interpretations that are offered by those who are being studied, the subjects of the research, and away from interpretations offered by researchers, the subjects conducting the research. One consequence of the influence of phenomenology has been to shift from researchers to the subjects of the research the power to define what is going on and what is important about it. I broadly refer to these approaches to social research that have been more or less directly influenced by phenomenology as *interpretative research.* Included in this group are ethnography, hermeneutics, and reader-response research.

Van Manen (1975a) first introduced phenomenological ideas into the social studies literature in his response to the Shaver and Larkins (1973) chapter on social studies research in the *Second Handbook of Research on Teaching* (also see van Manen, 1982a, 1982b). Van Manen argued that social studies research could benefit from "a metatheoretical view [that] permits one to make explicit how the source ideas for doing research unwittingly animate the perceptions and formulations of the relevant problems in the theory and practice of social studies curriculum and instruction to which the investigator applies his research" (p. 23). *Metatheory* refers to theory about theory, and van Manen's comment underscores the lack of methodological self-consciousness among quantitative researchers that phenomenologists highlight in their criticisms of such mainstream research traditions. He argued for bringing social context and criticism into social studies research, in order to move away from naive empiricism or naive realism.

Criticism, again, evoked more criticism. Larkins (1975) agreed with van Manen that social studies education could benefit by drawing upon a wider range of research methodologies. He suggested that empirical-analytic, interpretative, and critical research might triangulate, to use a term from Webb, Campbell, Swartz, and Sechrest (1969), on social studies phenomena. Larkins noted, however, several problems in van Manen's argument about the relationship between oppression and emancipation in social studies education and research.

Van Manen's (1975b) rebuttal joined the issue more on critical theoretical than phenomenological grounds. Critical theorists pursue criticism to lessen individual and social oppression and emancipate individuals from distorted and mistaken beliefs. Larkins had posed the problem of a devout Christian being liberated from oppressive religious beliefs: Is the "emancipated" individual more or less liberated in the state of self-doubt and crisis that follows? Van Manen answered with a counterexample: "This would be like arguing, as some do, that a freed but frustrated slave is less 'emancipated' than the slave in chains, who is not 'oppressed' by the newly created anxieties of his personal freedom" (p. 40).

The burden of knowledge that interpretation and criticism bring with them is not a simple matter. The van Manen exchange with Larkins illustrates the complexity that criticism adds to the standard problems of interpretation and utilization of research findings as the boundaries of criticism become more ill-defined and inclusive new critical standards are introduced into the discourses of research. Criticism now includes ethical, political, and ideological matters, in addition to more standard questions of measurement, sampling, data analysis, and validity. This additional complexity may partially explain the paucity of ethnographic research, one form of interpretative research, in social studies education.

Palonsky (1987) suggested other reasons that social studies educators have not made greater use of ethnographic research. Among the reasons he found most plausible were that the research questions to be addressed are too narrow, the findings have little generalizability to other settings (lack of external validity), the costs of extended field studies are high, and it is often difficult to observe a wide range of teacher behaviors. Furthermore, he noted, maintaining the anonymity of participating teachers and students is difficult. It remains to be seen whether these issues will continue to inhibit ethnographic research in social studies.

Because of these and, presumably, other factors, only a limited number of interpretative studies have been reported in social studies education. Goodman and Adler (1985) studied how 16 preservice social studies teachers interpreted and made sense of social studies education. In an in-depth interpretative study of preservice teachers' conceptions of social studies education, Adler (1984) found such conceptions to be related more closely to general dimensions of teaching and learning than to anything specific about social studies education.

Because interpretive research has only recently been pursued in social studies education there are many opportunities for innovative research. The influence of gender, ethnicity, race,

and class on social studies education has yet to be explored in substantial detail. Gender and mathematics education has been a subject of concern for some time, but little attention has been paid to gender in social studies education. We know little about social studies education from the perspectives of students and teachers; teacher-thinking research points in this direction in only the broadest terms. A range of issues remains to be researched that would map, as it were, the complex of meanings, interpretations, and sense-making processes and products by which individuals negotiate their way through social studies education.

Hermeneutics and Reader Response Theory

Hermeneutics is concerned with interpretation and, from this approach, the researcher "attempts to preserve meaning by locating it in the social practices and literary texts which man produces" (Dreyfus & Rabinow, 1983, p. xix). Reader response theory is concerned with how texts are "realized" when they are read. (see Suleiman & Crosman, 1980, or Tompkins, 1980, for a general introduction). Hermeneutics is different from, albeit related to, reader response theory; the focus here is on reader response theory.

Eagleton (1983) described the intellectual origins of hermeneutics (textual interpretation) and the subsequent turn to the response of the reader: "The word 'hermeneutics' was originally confined to the interpretation of the sacred scripture; but during the nineteenth century it broadened its scope to encompass the problem of textual interpretation as a whole" (p. 66). The questions that hermeneuticists confront were influenced in important ways by the work of Hans Gadamer (1975). They include, as Eagleton summarized, "What is the meaning of a literary text? How relevant to this meaning is the author's intention? Can we hope to understand works which are culturally and historically alien to us? Is 'objective' understanding possible, or is all understanding relative to our own historical situation?" (p. 66).

Reader response theorists assume that the meaning of a work is problematic. This is at variance with certain contemporary theories of criticism, such as that advanced by E. D. Hirsch, Jr. (1976), who claimed that the meaning of a work is something willed by the author that remains fixed. Readers, according to Hirsch, may find different "significances" in a work depending upon their purpose, culture, ethnicity, class, or historical situation, but its *meaning* remains the same. A reader response theorist would take exception to this and argue, for example, that it is not likely that original affirmations in the Bill of Rights could have anticipated current extensions of First Amendment rights to African-Americans and, neo-Nazis, homosexuals, even though Supreme Court decisions have found such significance. Continuing, the reader response theorist might ask, How does one separate original meanings from the significances we encounter as we read? Or, put differently, How would one *know* if she or he were to stumble upon the original meaning of the Bill of Rights?

Reader response theory is a relatively recent development in textual interpretation. How do readers receive and respond to a text? Criticism, in this vein, involves attention to textual gaps and silences. The text is realized, it is produced, as readers fill in its gaps and silences. Eagleton (1983) described it like this:

The work [e. g., a social studies textbook or an assessment test] is full of "indeterminacies," elements which depend for their effect upon the reader's interpretation, and which can be interpreted in a number of different, perhaps mutually conflicting ways. The paradox of this is that the more information the work provides, the more indeterminate it becomes. (p. 76)

There are no brute facts, there are only facts *about* brute and socially constructed phenomena.

Research along the lines of reader response theory and textual interpretation has rarely been pursued in social studies education. An exception is a study by Levstik (1986) of sixth graders' responses to the use of narratives in teaching history. Even though the report is not couched in reader response terms, Levstik's purpose was to explore the use of "the connected discourse of literature" in studying history. She focused on reader interpretations but attended to academic learning as an outcome and did not pursue more open-ended types of reader responses.

To the extent that social studies researchers have explicitly thought of social studies teaching and learning as textual consumption or analysis, they seem to have implicitly rejected a number of reader response assumptions. *First,* social studies researchers seem to assume that textbooks and other materials are univocal—they have one message and one truth to convey. *Second,* perceived gaps or silences in a work often seem to be viewed as structural flaws or political statements or both and not as parts of the text itself. For example, if women and minorities are excluded from American history textbooks, it can be attributed to a patriarchal view of American history or to incompetence by the author or to patriarchal incompetence. But whether or not these perceived shortcomings are flaws or biases, per se, they are also the text. *Third,* teaching and learning in the social studies, it is arguable, is based on the value of convergence on "truth," and divergent readings are disvalued. To the extent that social studies teaching and learning is responsive to standardized achievement tests, there is overt pressure to arrive at the "correct" reading and response.

Reader response theory is a recent, though not necessarily the most influential, development in modern literary criticism. Eagleton (1983) argued that "Indeed one might very roughly periodize the history of modern literary theory in three stages: a preoccupation with the author (Romanticism and the nineteenth century); an exclusive concern with the text (New Criticism); and a marked shift of attention to the reader over recent years" (p. 74). Social studies education and research seem to be caught in a version of the second period, an exclusive concern with the text, although some usage of original historical documents in teaching is related to the first period. A preoccupation with text has produced two concerns. How are we to produce proper, adequate, correct, and true (small *t*) texts, for example, social studies textbooks, tests, and curriculum guidelines? How are we to produce proper, adequate, correct, and true (small *t*) readings by teachers, coordinators, and students? This is not to say that social studies researchers have not on occasion looked quite closely at texts. They have not, however, researched reader responses to them, in part because the importance of reader response has been denied.

A variety of research questions are suggested for social studies researchers by reader response theory. How do readers constitute social studies texts, from the text of the textbook to that of classroom organization? How do students or whoever make sense and produce texts upon social studies texts? What is read as a textual gap and silence? How do teachers, students, and others fill in those gaps and silences? What new texts are produced, if any, to counter the structure of texts that are authoritatively thrust upon them? What texts do students, teachers, coordinators produce about their social world? (The last question is quite different, it should be noted, from questions asked in conventional political socialization research.) What narratives, even metanarratives, are produced? What linguistic devices are employed, for example, metaphor, theme, image, analogy? In what ways do the texts produced upon the texts of social studies education and society converge and diverge?

Reader response research would fill in some of the existing gaps and silences in research on social studies teaching and learning. Recall the epigraph, research is, according to *Webster's,* "**1**: careful or diligent search **2**: studious inquiry or examination; *esp:* investigation or experimentation aimed at the discovery and interpretation of facts, revision of accepted theories or laws in the light of new facts, or practical application of such new or revised theories or laws" (1983, p. 1002). The response of the reader, writ large, is a silence in contemporary social studies research. By attending to readers and their responses to texts, as well as to their textual responses, it may be possible to provide new interpretations of old facts, as well as to generate new facts.

POSTSTRUCTURAL CRITICISM

Research that is focused on interpretation and reader response moves away from the structures sought by quantitative researchers, structuralists, and ethnographers. Poststructural thought sometimes this term is used interchangeably with *postmodern* or *postanalytic thought;* see Cherryholmes, 1988b, pp. 9–13) breaks dramatically with the search for structures or their promotion. (A caveat: Strictly speaking, poststructural analysis and criticism is an analysis and commentary on structures that *simultaneously* affirms and undermines those structures; postmodernist thought, however, is not bound to, or dependent upon, structures one way or another.) Two important versions of poststructuralism are the interpretive analytics of Michel Foucault, who denies the existence of underlying, natural substructures of social phenomena, and the deconstruction of Jacques Derrida, who denies the existence of structures in texts. Criticism and critical research along these lines are new to social studies education.

Foucault's Interpretive Analytics

Foucault (1972) was interested in the discursive practices of modern social institutions, the conditions for their existence, and the practical fields in which they are deployed. He acknowledged that the discursive practices he studied, such as modern prisons (1975/1979), mental institutions (1973), hospitals (1975), and sexuality (1980), were organized and run in an orderly manner, but he denied that they were governed by natural or objective laws that would be revealed by deep structural analysis. He rejected the structuralist label with some vehemence.

When Foucault began his professional career, structuralism was the dominant intellectual orientation in France. It should be understood that structuralism is not only a social scientific approach and methodology, but also has ideological overtones. The structural characteristics of modern bureaucracies are a case in point. Bannet (1989) wrote,

"Bureaucracy" . . . classifies, it orders, it programmes; it endeavours to control and determine every aspect of life, leaving no place for innovation, creativity and non-conformity. Its technocrats presuppose that society is a rational system and, through their planning, they endeavour to make it one. Structuralist systems with their rational coherence and transparent cohesion . . . are a technocratic ideal. If Foucault . . . protested that he was not a structuralist . . . his point was that he was not a supporter of the technocrats, that he was not trying to extend the System or to increase its domination and its constraints. (p. 4)

Foucault's interpretive analytics, not unlike the structuralism he opposed, constituted an ideological position as well as an approach to social and historical analysis.

Foucault argued that knowledge and what passes for truth are products of history, power, and social interests. Whereas critical theorists are concerned about the effects of ideology and power in the distortion of communication and knowledge, Foucault avoided the term *ideology* because it presumed an opposite, that is, absolute truth or some other escape from "false" ideology to "true" ideology that cannot be confirmed. Social discourse and practice, then, are both the effects of and exercise of power. What we do and say, for example, in social studies education, are effects of power whose traces can be found in history.

Foucault's analysis points to a tension, if not a contradiction, in quantitative research. Often, quantitative researchers search for deep structures and objective laws concerning issues such as how students learn, what they learn, and what they do with what they learn, but then they invoke educational strategies and decisions based on liberal and humanist assumptions that suggest we can act to modify such deep structures. Fay (1977) put it like this: "Explanations . . . lay the foundation for the instrumental control of phenomena by providing the sort of information which would enable one to . . . bring about a certain state of affairs or prevent its occurrence" (p. 37). Foucault *denied* both the existence of deep structures *and* the individual autonomy that liberals and humanists presume.

The influence of Foucault's work is starting to be seen in a variety of fields, for example, history, literary theory and criticism, sociology, social theory, political philosophy, and educational research. Lesko (1988b), for example, employed Foucault's concept of bio-power in a study of high school cheerleading (for a more fully detailed account of this work see Lesko, 1988a). Her investigations also demonstrated how one piece of research can span several approaches to critical research by combining Foucault's interpretive analytics, critical theory, and feminist criticism. She reported that national cheerleading organizations promote themselves by advertising and encouraging cheerleading as a means of increasing status and skill development.

Cheerleaders, Lesko found, are selected on the basis of "rational" criteria and skill-based standards. The result is that because (a) rational standards lead to cheerleader selection, (b) schools lose control over the selection of their own cheerleaders, and (c), moreover, the standards produce a highly stylized display with clipped body movements executed with speed and precision that resemble military drill displays. Foucault (1975/1979) developed the concept of bio-power to identify how power invades and disciplines the body. In this instance, Lesko interpreted effects of the external control of cheerleading as an example of patriarchy operating in the school through the extracurricular activity of cheerleading. The activities of young women are trivialized (because they are organized by a group external to the school) while they are controlled (by external standards that are "rationally" determined).

In an analysis of the effects of power on social studies rationales and textbooks I argued that social studies education is pushed and pulled by social and economic forces external to professional education, whereas the discourse of social studies education is conceptualized by its practitioners as if it were an autonomous enterprise (Cherryholmes, 1983). In 1987, I traced the effects of power that shaped and propelled the "structure of the disciplines" movement in the 1960s. That movement was, I argued, shaped by a confluence of the perceived threat to the national security of the United States posed by the Soviet space program, movements to make curriculum and instruction more rational (i.e., the Bloom, 1956, *Taxonomy of Educational Objectives* and the Tyler, 1949, rationale for curriculum development), and a push, largely by noneducators and nonphilosophers, to make disciplinary "structure" the center of public school instruction (Bruner, 1960). These efforts subsequently proved to be technically infeasible and philosophically unjustifiable.

Social studies research in a Foucauldian agenda might address such questions as the following. What is the history of present theory and practice in social studies education? What practical effects, in broad and narrow terms, are produced by social studies education? What social and political conditions constitute social studies education? What qualifies social studies experts to speak? What are the silences in social studies discourse? How does power operate to enforce and produce these silences? How can students, teachers, social studies coordinators, principals, and others inquire into the history of the social studies discourses they are expected to learn and master? How can we inquire into the effects and exercise of power in our educational, social, and political lives?

Derrida's Deconstruction

Deconstruction is quite different from critical theory and Foucault's interpretive analytics, each of which argues for forms of criticism based on particular interpretations of social texts, institutions, and interactions. Deconstruction is based on certain logical or nonlogical properties, as the case happens to be, of language and texts. One way to understand deconstruction is as a development in modern logic of natural language arguments and texts (a natural language is one that "naturally" occurs, e.g., English, French, Russian, Chinese, in contrast to formally constructed or artificial languages, e.g., computer languages or those of symbolic logic or mathematics).

Quine (1953) showed that it is not possible to know whether the truth of the premises of an argument is preserved through to its conclusions when the argument is made in a natural language, even though truth preservation is a stipulated characteristic of a valid deductive argument. This is because a clear characterization of the meaning of synonyms (synonymy) is not available. Arguments in a natural language require the substitution of one word for another, and it is not possible to know if an assertion in which one word is used means the same thing as an assertion in which a second word is substituted for the first. A Quinian skeptic might ask at the outset, If two words are different, how can they be identical in meaning?

Here is an example of this problem. A key concept in Durkheim's famous study of suicide is *social cohesion* (cited from Merton's, 1968, reformulation). He was interested in whether variations in social cohesion are related to differences in suicide rates. The abstract term *social cohesion* is used in the generalization, "Catholics have greater social cohesion than Protestants." The latter generalization is tested by observing Catholic and Protestant communities. But the generalization, what counts as a Catholic or Protestant community, and what one observes are different. How would we know if the meaning of social cohesion is retained from its abstract usage through to a specific observation? (See Cherryholmes, 1988a, for an extended discussion of this and related issues.)

A second example follows. Imagine that we wish to determine the meaning of the word *criticism,* a main theme of this chapter. This is *Webster's* (1983) third definition (a definition, it should be remembered, is a group of words purported to be synonymous with one word) of *criticism:* "the scientific investigation of literary documents (as the Bible) in regard to such matters as origin, text, composition, or history" (p. 308). *Scientific* is used broadly in this definition and in a way that Kerlinger (cited earlier), for one, did not sanction. To clear up potential ambiguity it is always possible to appeal to the definition of scientific: "of, relating to, or exhibiting the methods or principles of science" (p. 1051), or of science: "knowledge covering general truths or the operation of general laws esp. as obtained through the scientific method" (p. 1051). If the quest for clarity and certainty were to proceed, we would search out the meaning of "truth" or "general laws" or "method." But the meaning of *criticism* could also have been traced from *Webster's* second definition that points in a quite different direction: "the art of evaluating or analyzing works of art or literature" (p. 308). Or, the meaning of criticism could have been pursued through other words that share its roots: *crisis, criterion, critique,* or *critic.*

The case that Derrida and others made for deconstruction, although not argued on the basis of developments in logic and analytic philosophy (e.g., Quine, 1953), has a number of important implications for social studies education and research. Be-

cause the meaning of words and concepts cannot be definitively fixed, even though we commonly use and continually invoke definitions and synonyms in everyday conversation, there is no way to know if one word means the same thing as another word to different persons or to the same person at different points in time. The deconstructive point of *differance,* a new word introduced by Derrida, is that meanings are constantly and continually dispersed throughout texts and deferred in time. Put differently, if we cannot clearly characterize a synonym, then meanings are floating, shifting, ambiguous, and equivocal. (See Cherryholmes, 1988b, chap. 4, for a discussion of meaning in Derridean terms in the context of textbooks and teaching.)

Deconstructive criticism focuses on this characteristic of language and text, that the meaning of a word is provided by other words whose meanings are traced to and through yet other words and so on indefinitely. This instability of meanings produces ambiguities, contradictions, and uncertainties. Gasche' (1986) noted that this nonlogical property of language (that is, it is not possible to treat meaning as an identity as in an algebraic equation) produces three kinds of problems in textual interpretation—and social studies education is concerned, among other things, with the consumption and production of social texts:

1. There are problems with conceptual distinctions that do not hold up when analyzed, for example, cognitive/affective, theory/practice, subject-centered learning/student-centered learning, and concept/fact. (See Cherryhomles, 1988b, chap. 7, for an analysis of these binary distinctions that turn out not to be categorically independent of each other but instead dependent on each other.)
2. There are problems generated by differences between the rhetorical claims of a text (what it is claimed to be doing) and its logical arguments (what it does). See Cherryholmes, 1988b, chap. 3, for an analysis of Tyler's (1949) rationale for curriculum development and Schwab's (1983) "The practical 4: Something for curriculum professors to do" for analyses along these lines.)
3. There are problems with other textual inconsistencies, for example, the same word is used differently from place to place (see *Webster's* definition earlier of the "art" of evaluating a work of "art"; 1983, p. 308), or a common theme is used at cross-purposes.

Deconstructive criticism does not account for such inconsistencies by providing a new foundation or acting as a final authority. Deconstructive criticism provides insights into the textual and intertextual play of words and arguments. Texts never contain only one story, nor does a story have only one interpretation, nor can stories and interpretations be criticized from only one vantage point (see Scholes, 1985; Cherryholmes, 1988b, chap. 8). Texts always have subtexts and the meaning of texts and their subtexts are, to some degree, undecidable. Whether particular ambiguities are significant or important for the reader's purposes always remains to be determined.

Parker's (1986) investigation of the concept of social justice illustrates Gasche's first point about conceptual distinctions that cannot be sustained. Parker contrasted the subjective conception of social justice in the cognitive developmental literature with the structural conception in the literature of historical materialism. He observed that each is reductionist, the former reducing justice to subjective considerations of one's situation and the latter ignoring such individual considerations and focusing instead on social structural differences and inequalities. The writers in each literature presume a subjective/structural distinction or opposition. Parker deconstructed, although this term and literature is not cited, this categorical separation by showing that the conceptions of subjective and structural depend upon each other. Parker made the point quite clearly, "To reject the either/or approach is to reject the passivity of dichotomous classifying for the activity of theorizing" (p. 291).

Maxcy (1986) illustrated the dispersal and deferral of meanings of the term *problem* in social studies discourse. His argument is compelling, insightful, and in a deconstructive spirit. Problems are problematic. They are not objectively given in a situation nor can they be reduced entirely to subjective opinion or belief. The constitution of problems is constrained by objective conditions and is formed within specific contexts. Different social contexts generate different problems, thereby providing for the dispersal and deferral of social problems through the texts that are projected onto the world.

Because deconstruction is based upon the nonlogical properties of language and texts, it breaks radically with previous approaches to social criticism and research. Deconstruction cannot be dismissed on the basis of one's social preferences and values, as one might dismiss critical theory because of disagreements with the importance critical theorists attach to social equality and emancipation from oppressive social conditions or Foucault's interpretive analytic approach to history and social institutions because its argument is so skeptical about social reform. Deconstructive readings and criticism, simply put, are here to stay unless or until a way is discovered to fix, once and for all, textual meanings.

Deconstructive criticism has only begun to surface in social studies education, and it offers a powerful methodology for analyzing and criticizing texts and the textual interpretations that we project on the world around us. Deconstruction promises a glimpse of deeper textual meanings and infrastructures as rhetorical assertions that often pass as authoritative are challenged. A number of research opportunities await social studies researchers who choose to avail themselves of its powerfulness: What central binary distinctions are assumed in contemporary social studies education, for example, cognitive/affective, higher-order thinking/lower-order thinking, conceptual understanding/nonconceptual understanding, knowledge of generalizations/knowledge of specifics? How does each category in these distinctions depend for its existence upon the other, for example, how does cognitive knowledge depend upon affective preferences? (These two questions demonstrate how deconstructive criticism depends upon structural analysis.) If the categorical distinctions upon which social studies education is organized are unstable, what purpose(s) is (are) served by retaining them? What steps are involved in teaching students, teachers, student teachers, and others to read deconstructively? How does deconstructive criticism alter classroom interactions and the way textbooks are employed? Can deconstructive readings by students decrease their alienation and apathy? How can deconstructive analysis help a student to find his or her "voice" as he or she analyzes history, culture, society, and social institutions and interactions? What are the possible deconstructive readings of alternative approaches to social studies teaching and learning?

CONCLUSION

In the space available for this chapter, justice could not be done to the critical literature in social studies education nor to critical research possibilities. Neither feminist theory and criticism nor the critical legal studies movement, to mention but two examples, have been discussed. (See Alcoff, 1988, for an incisive view of feminist theory and poststructuralism and Unger, 1986, for a lucid account of the critical legal studies movement.) Feminist theory holds promise for the reconceptualization of major aspects of social studies education, from classroom interactions (Lewis & Simon, 1986) to interpretion and criticism of the role of women in society (Alcoff, 1988). The critical legal studies movement has infused law school education with critical theory and poststructural criticism and analysis at such prestigious law schools as those at Harvard University, University of Wisconsion, Stanford University, and the University of Pennsylvania. Implications of critical legal studies for law-related education have yet to be developed.

The word *research*, when it entered the English language, indicated a "careful or diligent search" or "studious inquiry or examination." The means for conducting such searches, inquiries, or examinations currently outdistance the way social studies research and educational research in general are conducted. Whatever their reasons, many educational researchers believe that "serious" research must be quantitative. Educational researchers also seem to suffer a shared amnesia as they promote research patterned after the natural sciences. They seem to have collectively forgotten one of the most elementary lessons in research design and methodology: *numbers require interpretation* and *interpretations are problematic*. Most quantitative researchers, ironically, would agree. But this problematic has been ignored; thus, some research is called critical and some is not.

This chapter has dealt broadly with the interpretation and critical analysis of social studies teaching and learning. Such results shed light, it is hoped, on how people make sense of their social worlds and how we continually construct and reconstruct our social worlds anew. Critical theory and interpretive analytics instruct social studies educators to look to history, to the effects and exercise of power, and to search for distorted beliefs and communications in trying to understand what has gone on and is going on in their world. Reader-response theory inserts readers (students, teachers, student teachers, social studies educators) into the texts of their world by making them producers as well as consumers of texts. No longer need students be simply parasitic on what is authoritatively presented to them. Deconstruction points out that our texts are not as authoritative and foundational as we have previously been led to believe. Encouraging students themselves to engage in criticism may be simultaneously a step away from social studies instruction and a step toward social studies education.

References

Adler, S. (1984). A field study of selected student teacher perspectives toward social studies. *Theory and Research in Social Education, 12*(1), 13–32.

Alcoff, L. (1988). Cultural feminism versus poststructuralism. *Signs: Journal of Women in Culture and Society, 13,* 405–436.

Anyon, J. (1978). Elementary social studies textbooks and legitimating knowledge. *Theory and Research in Social Education, 6*(3), 40–55.

Anyon, J. (1979a). Education, social "structure" and the power of individuals. *Theory and Research in Social Education, 7*(1), 49–59.

Anyon, J. (1979b). Ideology and United States history textbooks. *Harvard Educational Review, 49,* 361–386.

Apple, M. (1971). The hidden curriculum and the nature of conflict. *Interchange, 2*(4), 27–40.

Bannet, E. T. (1989). *Structuralism and the logic of dissent.* Champaign: University of Illinois Press.

Bernstein, R. J. (1976). *The reconstruction of social and political theory.* Philadelphia: University of Pennsylvania Press.

Bernstein, R. J. (1983). *Beyond objectivism and relativism: science, hermeneutics, and praxis.* Philadelphia: University of Pennsylvania Press.

Bloom, B. S. (1956). *Taxonomy of educational objectives: Cognitive domain.* New York: David McKay.

Borg, W. R., & Gall, M. D. (1983). *Educational research: an introduction* (4th ed.). New York: Longman, Inc.

Bowles, S., & Gintis, H. (1976). *Schooling in capitalist America.* New York: Basic Books.

Bruner, J. (1960). *The process of education.* Cambridge, MA: Harvard University Press.

Cherryholmes, C. H. (1980). Social knowledge and citizenship education: Two views of truth and criticism. *Curriculum Inquiry, 10,* 115–141.

Cherryholmes, C. H. (1982). Discourse and criticism in the social studies classroom. *Theory and Research in Social Education, 9*(4), 57–73.

Cherryholmes, C. H. (1983). Knowledge, power, and discourse in social studies education. *Journal of Education, 165*(3), 341–358.

Cherryholmes, C. H. (1987). A social project for curriculum: Post-structural perspectives. *Journal of Curriculum Studies, 19,* 295–316.

Cherryholmes, C. H. (1988a). Construct validity and the discourses of research. *American Journal of Education, 96,* 421–457.

Cherryholmes, C. H. (1988b). *Power and criticism: Poststructural investigations in education.* New York: Teachers College Press.

Coser, L. (1956). *The functions of social conflict.* New York: Free Press.

Derrida, J. (1972). Discussion: Structure, sign and play in the discourse of the human sciences. In R. Macksey & E. Donato (Eds.), *The structuralist controversy* (pp. 247–272). Baltimore: Johns Hopkins University Press.

Dreyfus, H. L., & Rabinow, P. (1983). *Michel Foucault: Beyond structuralism and hermeneutics.* Chicago: University of Chicago Press.

Eagleton, T. (1983). *Literary theory: An introduction.* Minneapolis: University of Minnesota Press.

Fay, B. (1977). *Social theory and political practice.* London: George Allen and Unwin.

Foucault, M. (1972). *The archaeology of knowledge.* New York: Harper & Row.

Foucault, M. (1973). *Madness and civilization: A history of insanity in the age of reason.* New York: Random House, Vintage Books.

Foucault, M. (1975). *The birth of the clinic: An archaeology of medical perception.* New York: Random House, Vintage Books.

Foucault, M. (1979). *Discipline and punish: A birth of the prison.* (A. Sheridan, Trans.) New York: Random House, Vintage (Original work published 1975).

Foucault, M. (1980). *The history of sexuality* (Vol. 1). New York: Pantheon.

Gadamer, H. (1975). *Truth and method.* London: Sheed and Ward.

Gasche', R. (1986). *The tain of the mirror.* Cambridge, MA: Harvard University Press.

Gilbert, R. (1984a). Images of society in the analysis of ideologies in the school subjects. *Theory and Research in Social Education, 22*(3), 1–15.

Gilbert, R. (1984b). *The impotent image: Reflections of ideology in the secondary school curriculum.* London: Falmer Press.

Giroux, H. A. (1980). Critical theory and rationality in citizenship education. *Curriculum Inquiry, 10,* 329–366.

Giroux, H. A. (1983). Theories of reproduction and resistance in the new sociology of education: A critical analysis. *Harvard Educational Review, 53,* 257–293.

Goodman, J., & Adler, S. (1985). Becoming an elementary social studies teacher: A study in perspectives. *Theory and Research in Social Education, 13*(2), 1–20.

Habermas, J. (1979). *Communication and the evolution of society.* Boston: Beacon Press.

Hawkes, T. (1977). *Structuralism and semiotics.* Berkeley, CA: University of California Press.

Heiddeger, M. (1949). *Existence and being.* Chicago: Henry Regnery.

Hirsch, E. D., Jr. (1976). *Validity in interpretation.* New Haven, CN: Yale University Press.

Horkheimer, M. (1973). Foreword. In M. Jay, *The dialectical imagination: A history of the Frankfurt school and the Institute of Social Research, 1923–1950* (pp. xi–xii). Boston: Little, Brown.

Husserl, E. (1970). *The crises of European sciences and transcendental phenomenology.* (David Carr, Trans.). Evanston, IL: Northwestern University Press. (Original work published 1962)

Ihde, D. (1979). *Experimental phenomenology.* New York: Paragon Books.

Jacob, E. (1987). Qualitative research traditions: A review. *Review of Educational Research, 57*(1), 1–50.

Jay, M. (1973). *The dialectical imagination: A history of the Frankfurt school and the institute of social research, 1923–1950.* Boston: Little Brown.

Jackson, P. (1968). *Life in classrooms.* New York: Holt, Rinehart & Winston.

Kerlinger, F. (1973). *Foundations of behavioral research.* New York: Holt, Rinehart & Winston.

Kickbusch, K. W. (1985). Ideological innocence and dialogue: A critical perspective on discourse in the social studies. *Theory and Research in Social Education, 13*(3), 45–56.

Kickbusch, K. W. (1987). Civic education and preservice educators: Extending the boundaries of the discourse. *Theory and Research in Social Education, 15*(3), 173–188.

Lakatos, I. (1970). Falsification and the methodology of scientific research programmes. In I. Lakatos & A. Musgrave (Eds.), *Criticism and the growth of knowledge* (pp. 91–195). New York: Oxford University Press.

Lane, M. (Ed.). (1970). *Structuralism: A reader.* London: Jonathan Cape.

Larkins, A. G. (1975). Critique of alternative research orientations. *Theory and Research in Social Education, 3*(1), 29–35.

Lesko, N. (1988a). *Symbolizing society: Stories, rites and structure in a Catholic high school.* London: Falmer Press.

Lesko, N. (1988b). We're leading America: The changing organization and form of high school cheerleading. *Theory and Research in Social Education, 16*(4), 263–278.

Levstik, L. S. (1986). The relationship between historical response and narrative in a sixth-grade classroom. *Theory and Research in Social Education, 14*(1), 1–19.

Lewis, M., & Simon, R. J. (1986). A discourse not intended for her: Learning and teaching within patriarchy. *Harvard Educational Review, 56*(4), 457–472.

Maxcy, S. J. (1986). The conception of problem and the role of inquiry in education. *Theory and Research in Social Education, 14*(4), 295–306.

McCarthy, T. (1978). *The critical theory of Jurgen Habermas.* Cambridge, MA: MIT Press.

Merton, R. K. (1968). *Social theory and social structure.* Glencoe, IL: Free Press.

Newmann, F. (1975). *Education for citizen action.* Berkeley, CA: McCutchan.

Oliver, D. W. (1957). The selection of content in social studies. *Harvard Educational Review, 28,* 271–300.

Oliver, D., & Shaver, J. P. (1974). *Teaching public issues in the high school.* Logan, UT: Utah State University Press. (Original work published 1966)

Palonsky, S. (1987). Ethnographic scholarship and social education. *Theory and Research in Social Education, 15*(2), 77–87.

Parker, W. C. (1986). Justice, social studies, and the subjectivity/structure problem. *Theory and Research in Social Studies Education, 14*(4) 277–295.

Popkewitz, T. S. (1977). The latent values of the discipline-centered curriculum. *Theory and Research in Social Education, 5*(1), 41–60.

Popkewitz, T. S. (1978). Educational research: Values and visions of social order. *Theory and Research in Social Education, 6*(4), 20–39.

Popkewitz, T. S. (1980). Global education as a slogan system. *Curriculum Inquiry, 10*(3), 303–316.

Popper, K. (1976). The logic of the social sciences. In T. Adorno (Ed.), *The positivist dispute in German sociology* (pp. 87–105). New York: Harper & Row.

Proefriedt, W. A. (1980). Socialist criticisms of education in the United States: Problems and possibilities. *Harvard Educational Review, 50*(4), 467–480.

Quine, W. V. O. (1953). *From a logical point of view.* Cambridge, MA: Harvard University Press.

Remy, R. (1980). *Handbook of basic citizenship competencies.* Alexandria, VA. Association for Supervision and Curriculum Development.

Rorty, R. (1985). Solidarity or objectivity? In J. Rajchman & C. West (Eds.), *Post Analytic Philosophy* (pp. 3–19). New York: Columbia University Press.

Scholes R. (1985). *Textual power.* New Haven, CT: Yale University Press.

Schwab, J. (1983). The practical 4: Something for curriculum professors to do. *Curriculum Inquiry, 13,* 239–266.

Shaver, J. P. (Ed.). (1977). *Building rationales for citizenship education.* Arlington, VA: National Council for the Social Studies.

Shaver, J. P. (1979). Political and economic socialization in elementary school social studies textbooks: A reaction. *Theory and Research in Social Education, 7*(1), 43–48.

Shaver, J. P., & Larkins, A. G. (1973). Research on teaching social studies. In R. M. Travers (Ed.), *Second handbook of research on teaching* (pp. 1243–1262). Chicago: Rand McNally.

Suleiman, S. R., & Crosman, I. (Eds.). (1980). *The reader in the text: Essays on audience and interpretation.* Princeton, NJ: Princeton University Press.

Tompkins, J. P. (Ed.). *Reader-response criticism.* Baltimore: Johns Hopkins University Press.

Tyler, R. W. (1949). *Basic principles of curriculum and instruction.* Chicago: the University of Chicago Press.

Unger, R. M. (1986) *The critical legal studies movement.* Cambridge, MA: Harvard University Press.

Van Manen, M. (1975a). An exploration of alternative research orientations in social education. *Theory and Research in Social Education, 3*(1), 1–28.

Van Manen, M. (1975b). Rebuttal to Larkins' critique. *Theory and Research in Social Education. 3*(1), 37–42.

Van Manen, M. (1982a). Edifying theory: Serving the good. *Theory Into Practice, 21*(1), 44–49.

Van Manen, M. (1982b). Phenomenological pedagogy. *Curriculum Inquiry, 12*(3), 283–299.

Webb, E. J., Campbell, D. J., Swartz, R. D., & Sechrest, L. (1969). *Unobstrusive measures.* Chicago: Rand McNally.

Webster's Ninth New Collegiate Dictionary. (1983). Springfield, MA: Merriam-Webster.

Whitson, J. A. (1986). [Review of Rod Gilbert 1984]. *Educational Studies, 17*(2), 290–291.

Will, G. (1983, October 10). In defense of nonvoting. *Newsweek,* p. 73.

Wood, G. (1985). Education for democratic participation: Democratic values and the nuclear freeze campaign. *Theory and Research in Social Education, 12*(4), 39–56.

· 5 ·

QUALITATIVE RESEARCH IN SOCIAL STUDIES EDUCATION

Judith Preissle-Goetz

UNIVERSITY OF GEORGIA

Margaret Diane LeCompte

UNIVERSITY OF COLORADO, BOULDER

In 1970, one of us, then a classroom teacher not yet dreaming she would become an educational researcher, struggled with the problem of how to design a study investigating children's reactions to the value clarification lessons she was using. For guidance, her advisor handed her a copy of Campbell and Stanley's *Experimental and Quasi-Experimental Designs for Research* (1963). She used a pretest-posttest control group design to produce a mediocre investigation with ambiguous results. This enabled her to finish a master's degree, but left both her and her thesis committee members with nagging questions about what had happened and why. Fortunately, the days of such rigidity of design in educational research have ended.

Introductory research textbooks once discussed only experimental, quasi-experimental, and survey designs. Now such books include simulation research, standardized observation, historical research, case study investigation, conceptual research, ethnography, and other permutations of qualitative design (e.g., Borg & Gall, 1989). In the past 20 years, approaches to research design have diversified. Scholars who once felt compelled to use conventional quantitative designs now use as criteria for choice of design their own research purposes and questions. More scholars have pursued years-long investigations in various substantive areas; in so doing, they have raised new questions and concerns.

Our goal is to examine how one variety of research design—popularly referred to as qualitative investigation—is being and can be applied to social studies education. What is qualitative research? How is qualitative research different from and similar to quantitative research? What is involved in applying qualitative research to social studies teaching and learning? We intend our discussion to illustrate how qualitative design modes offer a fruitful perspective on the significant issues and problems raised in social studies education.

WHAT IS QUALITATIVE RESEARCH?

Qualitative research is a loosely defined category of research designs or models (Goetz & LeCompte, 1984), all of which elicit verbal, visual, tactile, olfactory, and gustatory data. These data take the form of descriptive narratives like field notes, recordings or other transcriptions from audio- and videotapes, and other written records, as well as pictures or films. Qualitative researchers also may collect artifacts—products or things people use—such as objects people make and records of what they do, say, produce, or write.

Qualitative research is based on and grounded in descriptions of observations. These descriptions address the question, "What is happening here?" Most qualitative research designs are intended to address this question. It can be asked about anything—ordinary occurrences, extraordinary events, or circumstances puzzling to an investigator.

Some methodologists object to the name *qualitative research*. They believe it to be imprecise, misleading, and implying a lack of concern with quantity. Among the synonyms used are *interpretive research* (Erickson, 1986), *naturalistic research*

Reviewers were Robert Bogdan, Syracuse University; David Lancy, University of Toledo; George Noblit, University of North Carolina, Chapel Hill.

(Lincoln & Guba, 1985), *phenomenological research* (Wilson, 1977), and *descriptive research* (Wolcott, 1980).

Each of these labels emphasizes a characteristic of much qualitative research. Erickson's preference for the term *interpretive* focuses investigation on meaning, highlighting the premise that human activity can only be understood when the meaning of the action to the actor is taken into account. Lincoln and Guba use the term *naturalistic* because it indicates a concern for studying human life as it proceeds unaffected by the scientists interested in studying it. Like Erickson, Lincoln and Guba are interested in understanding human phenomena from the perspective of the human participants who produce them.

The same quality is conveyed by the label *phenomenological research,* a philosophical stance whose adherents assert that knowledge, reality, and value can only be known through human experience (Giorgi, 1971). They focus on the concrete and specific characteristics of phenomena as experienced by the human observer. Adequately representing the phenomena requires that they be faithfully described just as they were experienced.

Because of its preoccupation with complete, detailed, and concrete depictions, some people call qualitative research *descriptive research.* This label is more inclusive than the preceding terms, but it is used less often than the others. Many researchers find it unsatisfactory because the term *descriptive* is also a label for some statistical designs. In addition, the results of qualitative research may vary from highly descriptive to highly inferential.

Qualitative designs differ according to their own history and their links to human science and inquiry (Jacob, 1987). The designs most frequently considered to be qualitative are ethnographies, field studies, community studies, case studies, biographical or life history investigations, and document analyses.

Ethnographies are reconstructions of the culture of a human group or the cultures encapsulated in some human scene. They are almost uniformly qualitative, although they may include quantitative data. They are distinguished from other qualitative designs by their focus on culture and on human groups. Developed throughout the 20th century by anthropologists studying face-to-face groups, ethnographic research design has been adopted by sociologists and by researchers across a range of professional areas.

In its broadest sense, a field study is exactly what it implies. It is research conducted in the field—an environment natural to whatever inhabits it or occurs within it. The field may be immense—the universe is the field within which stars are viewed. It may be minute—drops of water constitute the field of some microorganisms. Investigators from across disciplines and professions have used field studies: biologists, geologists, sociologists, astronomers, geographers, journalists, historians, anthropologists, and ecological psychologists (Fink, 1978). The field study tradition most influential on research in education is sociological (Schatzman & Strauss, 1973).

This tradition also is the source of a category of field study, the community study (Stein, 1960). This investigation of a human community is customarily geographically bounded or defined—a neighborhood, a hamlet or small town, even a city. Communities may also be bounded by common interests, common work, or common play. Examples of these are the tennis circuit in athletics, the American Medical Association in professions, and the International Wizard of Oz Club in voluntary associations. Although sociologists see the community study as their special purview, historians, economists, political scientists, journalists, and other researchers also have used this design.

Like the field study, the case study design is an approach to research used throughout the natural and social sciences, as well as in the humanities. Merriam (1988, pp. 9–11) defined case study as the investigation of any phenomenon clearly separable from other phenomena. The examples of phenomena she designated are programs, events, persons, processes, institutions, and groups. She emphasized that the selected phenomenon must be an instance of some category of phenomena. Case study research can be traced to the beginnings of human record keeping.

Unlike ethnography—which always consists of a core of qualitative data that may or may not be supplemented by quantitative data—field studies, community studies, and case studies vary in the extent to which they are qualitative research. Some are composed entirely of qualitative data. Others are a mix of qualitative and quantitative data and analyses. Some are not qualitative at all because the data collected—based on a priori abstractions and in enumerative formats—are analyzed statistically. The extent to which these three designs are qualitative must be assessed study by study.

Like ethnography, life history and biographical designs always consist of a core of qualitative data. These data come from narrative accounts about the individual being investigated. Enumerative data are rarely used in these designs, except for background, context, or comparison.

Document and content analyses vary in much the same ways as field, community, and case study designs. They may be entirely quantitative, entirely qualitative, or they may involve a mix of such data. What they have in common is that the data originate from written texts. Some analyses depend on statistical manipulations of frequency counts. What are counted are events or items sorted into categories conceptualized in advance of data collection. Other analyses are highly interpretive renderings of the content of texts or of the processes assumed to have been used in creating the texts.

Two kinds of research designs often assumed by educational researchers to be quantitative are surveys and observational studies. This is usually a legitimate assumption, but there are exceptions. In many classroom observational studies, standardized protocols (e.g., Rosenshine & Furst, 1973) are used to record how frequently something such as teacher questioning occurs or how well a quality such as teacher enthusiasm is expressed. However, observational researchers may compile data bases partially or entirely consisting of qualitative data. Likewise, most survey designs use precoded responses, but many surveys include open-ended questions, and some are composed entirely of open-ended requests and tasks. Hence, those survey and observational studies based on sensory data recorded in narrative form are qualitative.

Quantitative data can be integrated into qualitative studies, just as studies once thought to be preeminently quantitative now include a variety of qualitative data-collection strategies.

Research design, then, has become the development and evolution of a way to ask particular questions regarding particular phenomena, framed by particular philosophical assumptions and theoretical orientations. Consequently, all research models function as scholarly conventions to guide, not dictate, creative research.

The diversity of qualitative research designs provides an indication of the range of sources from which this approach has developed. The models we have discussed have long been used in such scholarly disciplines as social and cultural anthropology, qualitative sociology, and history. Other disciplines such as clinical, developmental, and cognitive psychology, and those disciplines with case study traditions—political science, economics, law, and business—also have used qualitative designs. Journalism, especially investigative reporting, has influenced qualitative design since the 19th century (Bogdan & Biklen, 1982), and some variants, like the field study design discussed previously, are shared with the natural sciences. Even the humanities provide a variety of scholarly models, conceptual frameworks, and heuristics for qualitative research design (Clifford & Marcus, 1986). Discussions about development and evaluation of qualitative designs are permeated with references to ideas from philosophy, literature, art, and other areas.

Students of educational research, especially those not trained in disciplines with qualitative traditions, often believe that these research designs are new. However, investigators have used variations of such designs to examine educational questions since the 1920s and 1930s (e.g., Monroe, 1932). The advent of computers after World War II and the developing sophistication in quantitative design and instrumentation that accompanied it, as well as the popularity of testing and measurement practices in education, placed qualitative approaches at a disadvantage in many disciplines. From the late 1940s to the end of the 1960s, qualitative designs were often discussed only as examples of shoddy research. However, as investigators began to discover the limitations of experimental designs in laboratory settings, they began to use more diverse approaches to research. What followed might be considered a renaissance of alternative approaches to educational research, including revitalization of qualitative design.

Beginning in the late 1960s and continuing through the 1970s a number of landmark qualitative studies were published. Among those from the 1960s are Jackson's (1968) and Smith and Geoffrey's (1968) studies of classroom interactions and Leacock's (1969) comparative analysis of four elementary classrooms. These were followed in the 1970s by such research as Rist's (1973) study of the consignment of poor African-American children to failure before they even finish the primary grades, and Carew and Lightfoot's (1979) examination of teachers' interactions with their students.

ETHNOGRAPHY AS A SPECIAL FORM OF QUALITATIVE RESEARCH

Many of these researchers were trained in cultural anthropology and presented what they were doing as ethnography. They saw their task as describing and analyzing the everyday life of people in groups so as to depict the underlying culture of that life. This underlying culture is represented in shared meanings and symbols, beliefs, practices, artifacts, folk knowledge, and behaviors. It is also revealed by polarities of themes, oppositional values that pose dilemmas for people living in a group. Spindler and Spindler (1987) see these dilemmas as enacted in ongoing dialogues on the issues never really settled by the members of a group. Geertz (1973) sees them as patterns—the body of knowledge specifying how to live life as a member of a particular group. Although cultural anthropologists may disagree about the definition of culture, what they do agree on is that ethnography is a label for a research design intended to reveal aspects of a group's culture. Whatever else may be examined in an ethnography, it is culture that is the focus.

As more qualitative studies have been published and as more educational researchers have developed qualitative designs, however, the label *ethnography* has often come to be used as a synonym for qualitative research itself. In Britain, for example, scholars have virtually dropped the association between ethnography and cultural reconstruction; any qualitative design is likely to be called an ethnography (e.g., Burgess, 1984).

We agree with many of our U. S. colleagues that the distinction between qualitative research generally and ethnography particularly is useful and should be defended. It is part of communicating what scholars are up to—or are not up to. This use of ethnography is one way to keep clear the distinction between cultural patterns indigenous to groups—the patterns of central concern to ethnographers—and those imposed, a priori, by outside observers. Ignoring this distinction can result in major distortions in scholarship.

We would like to see the term *ethnography* used to denote an ideal type of qualitative research, one associated with cultural anthropology. Consequently, we advocate the restricted and judicious use of the term *ethnographic* as a label for research whose purpose is cultural reconstruction. The designs for such research vary, of course, in the degree to which they are cultural analyses, in the kind of cultural analysis, and even in what is and is not considered cultural. However, the convention of associating culture with ethnography is useful and illuminating, and it fosters a precision in terms that supports clearer scholarship.

QUALITATIVE AND QUANTITATIVE DESIGNS

The revitalization of qualitative design has been accompanied by efforts to develop, refine, systematize, and conventionalize practice. As a result, debate over terms, definitions, and appropriate conventions for all levels of qualitative research, as well as applications of data collection and analysis methods, are not only to be expected, but to be encouraged. They are especially inevitable in an area that, as Peshkin and Eisner (1990) said, "grew-like-Topsy."

How is qualitative research different from quantitative research? For some methodologists (e.g., Bogdan & Biklen, 1982; Filstead, 1979), the two areas comprise two competing, mutually exclusive paradigms. *Paradigm* here denotes a scientific worldview, including assumptions about reality, knowledge, and value, assertions about theory and conceptual frameworks, and claims for methods, procedures, and perspectives (Kuhn, 1962).

These writers characterize the quantitative paradigm as wedded to experimental and quasi-experimental research, surveys, simulations, and standardized observation. It is based on the assumptions that reality is fixed and absolutely knowable, that knowledge consists of explanations and predictions proven to be completely certain, and that research designs and results can be unaffected by the values of researcher and subject.

In contrast, the qualitative paradigm involves the use of designs such as ethnography, field study, case study, and document analysis. It is characterized as based on the assumptions that reality is ever changing and only incompletely knowable, that knowledge consists of always tentatively held understandings, and that research designs and results are inevitably permeated by values—those of the researcher, the research participants, and the research audience.

For many years the notion that qualitative and quantitative approaches to research constituted competing paradigms has dominated discussion of alternative methodologies in educational research and the related human sciences. That distinctiveness is discussed in the social sciences (e.g., Bruyn, 1966) and advocated in education and other professional areas (e.g., Kuzel, 1986; Rist, 1982).

Those who believe that incompatible paradigms divide the human sciences vary along a number of dimensions. Some claim that the paradigms are antithetical and that methods from the two ought not to be mixed (e.g., Bogdan & Biklen, 1982). Others believe that research informed by different paradigms can be complementary; methods from different paradigms can be used judiciously in a single study (e.g., Patton, 1980).

Complicating matters are those who see more than two competing paradigms in human research (Guba, 1988). For example, van Manen (1975) proposed three: interpretive, corresponding to what others have called qualitative; empirical-analytical, corresponding to the quantitative approach; and critical, deriving from such theorists as Marx and currently represented in educational thought by such scholars as Apple (1979). Finally, there are those methodologists who question the value of thinking of inquiry as paradigmatically divided (e.g., Howe, 1988).

Methodologists have complained that the paradigmatic view fails along two dimensions. First, research studies do not divide neatly among paradigmatic types, whether there are two, three, or more. Most research studies combine characteristics shared among paradigms (Reichardt & Cook, 1979). Thus, classification of research by paradigms is unsatisfactory. Second, the paradigmatic view is prescriptively restrictive; it may limit creativity if consistent adherence to a designated paradigm results in new orthodoxies. Having understood that the quantitative paradigm became a kind of doctrine through the middle decades of this century, scholars are reluctant to substitute multiple dogmas for the single one. Furthermore, some of the research most highly valued in the human sciences combines characteristics across so-called paradigms.

Notwithstanding these criticisms, conceptualizing the hu-

man sciences as divided into paradigmatic traditions is helpful pedagogically. Presenting provocative alternatives is one way to assist students to rethink their preconceptions. Guba (1986), for example, referred to the everyday scientific world as one dominated by quantitative stereotypes that "All of us ... grew up with literally from our mother's knee on" (p. 6); it therefore is normally difficult for Westerners to think about science in any other way.

Presenting research design in paradigmatic clusters helps students understand alternatives; it also can be a useful heuristic for methodologists. First, treating paradigms as only heuristic devices avoids some of the problems listed previously in this section. Second, it helps locate similarities and differences among research philosophies, assumptions, perspectives, theories and conceptual frames, and methods and procedures. By comparing and contrasting their research with others, investigators can use the literature cited thus far in this chapter as a resource for examining their goals, the unintended consequences of their actions, and the broader social and political implications of their work, as well as a host of underlying assumptions about the world they study. The paradigmatic view is thus a valuable conceptual tool.

In general, however, we prefer to think of the research process as multidimensional rather than multiparadigmatic. This facilitates the study of similarities and differences among research efforts in the human sciences and permits assembling several dimensions into patterns or ideal types that resemble what some writers are calling paradigms.

In the remainder of this section, we discuss six dimensions of research commonly—but not uniformly—shared among qualitative research studies: philosophical underpinnings, purposes of research, methods of gathering information, modes of analysis, the relationship of researchers to those studied, and characteristics and uses of evidence. Some of these dimensions highlight sharp differences between qualitative and quantitative approaches; others are merely differences in degree.

Philosophical Underpinnings

Searching for the philosophical frameworks underlying research approaches requires attention to history. One complication of locating the philosophical framework for qualitative research is that, as an accepted label for a group of approaches to research, its usage dates to only the middle of this century. This means that its philosophy must be traced through its individual components, like ethnography and life history, and the work of practitioners who identified themselves as qualitative researchers as well as those who used other labels.

Some methodologists link the duality in research paradigms to differing philosophical underpinnings. The quantitative paradigm in the social sciences is seen to be based on the philosophical premises of positivism, sometimes called logical positivism, which Bogdan and Taylor (1975) trace to the thinking of Comte and Durkheim. They characterize positivism as based on the premise that there are externally verifiable factors that determine human behavior. By contrast, qualitative research is seen as guided by the philosophy of phenomenology, which, according to Bogdan and Taylor, Weber introduced into the social sciences. As previously noted, the term *phenomenological* often is given as an alternative label for qualitative research.

A central argument in discussions of qualitative philosophical frames versus quantitative philosophical frames has been whether work informed by the two can be complementary (e.g., Firestone, 1987), can even be synthesized, or cannot be put together at all. Smith and Heshusius (1986) posited a basic incompatibility of the frames and traced the antagonism to irreconcilable differences between the realism of positivism and the idealism of phenomenology.

Other scholars see qualitative design as informed by constructivism (Magoon, 1977). Related to phenomenology and studies in cognition, constructivism is based on the assumption that because humans are thinkers who know things, any actions they undertake are shaped by this knowing.

Especially in Britain (e.g., Willis, 1977), qualitative research is influenced by a philosophy variously named materialism, critical theory, or neo-Marxism. It is an expression of a concern for how power and various resources are differentially distributed among groups—even the small, face-to-face groups studied by qualitative researchers—and how this asymmetry affects what happens in these groups. Finally, scholars like Roman and Apple (1990) have explored how feminism may serve as a philosophical frame for qualitative study.

The preceding philosophical frameworks are only some of the major influences on qualitative work and the human sciences generally (Polkinghorne, 1983). Our own position is that qualitative research is informed by many frames. For example, much ethnography of the first half of this century was clearly positivistic, and much of it continues to be influenced by that framework. Van Maanen (1988) even demonstrates how different frames can be used to produce different views of the same data base. What is most important is that scholars be aware of their frames and that their assumptions and premises be made clear.

Purposes

The formal goals or purposes of research fall into three broad areas: descriptive, analytical, and theoretical. These in turn are linked to the kind of question addressed in any given study. The purposes and kind of question affect the type of research design chosen.

Descriptive purposes, the underlying framework for much qualitative research, address the question introduced previously in this chapter, "What is happening here?" Researchers especially ask this question when studying unfamiliar settings and people, those unlike the investigators' normal experiences and cultures. Researchers whose purposes are analytical address the question, "What does it mean?" Based on detailed, longitudinal investigation, these researchers build analytical accounts of processes and interconnected phenomena. Researchers whose purpose is theoretical address the question, "How can it be explained and understood?" These researchers apply their findings to the generation, refinement, and verification of generalizations about some area of human experience. Qualita-

tive investigators are usually more concerned with generating theory than with confirming already established explanations. As a result, qualitative research is more often inductive than is quantitative research.

Qualitative investigators do, however, draw on established social science theories in many ways (Goetz & LeCompte, 1984), often to help frame questions and guide initial data collection. Many of these theories are, in turn, related to the philosophical frames discussed in the preceding section. Examples of theories used by qualitative researchers are plentiful: symbolic interactionism, related to phenomenology; structural functionalism, related to logical positivism; and systems theory, related to the organicism derived from Hegelian philosophy. Some human science theories, such as behaviorism, also related to logical positivism, are rarely used by qualitative researchers.

Sometimes a theory will underlie a study from beginning to end. But a theory may be discarded if the data gathered indicate it is not useful. Or, a theory may be sought well into data collection or analysis, after the researcher discovers what is relevant. What the researcher makes of the data and finds in the material gathered is the key. This also makes qualitative research more discovery-oriented. Investigators are usually more concerned with finding out something than with verifying something they already believe. Qualitative researchers thrive on surprises. This is directly connected to the emphasis on description.

Methods of Gathering Information

A major contrast between qualitative and quantitative designs is how information is gathered. The core of data collection in qualitative design consists of results garnered from apparently simple behaviors—watching, listening, asking questions, and collecting things. Campbell (1979) commented that these behaviors are the foundation of all inquiry, qualitative and quantitative. The revitalization of qualitative research traditions emphasizes that all researchers watch, listen, smell, touch, and taste. They ask questions and collect things. However, the principal instrument in qualitative research is the researcher, working face to face with those studied (Wolcott, 1975). In contrast, the quantitative researcher is usually distanced from research participants, often by paper-and-pencil instruments, administered by interchangeable research assistants.

Qualitative researchers record their observations, manually or mechanically. Audio- and videotape recorders, still and motion cameras, laptop computers, and wireless microphones are among the mechanical devices used. Nearly all qualitative researchers also produce field notes. These typically consist of records of observations and a commentary on what was observed, how it was observed, and what it might mean. Qualitative researchers typically spend as much as 9 to 24 months onsite to wait out the initial reactivity of their presence, to ascertain which data are stable and which data change, and to pursue and verify evolving interpretations and explanations.

Participant and nonparticipant observation are two ways qualitative researchers frequently collect data; they differ principally in the extent to which interaction with research participants is involved. Interviews, qualitative surveys, and collection of artifacts such as children's drawings, letters, and diaries, as well as documents and demographic information also are commonly used. Many different kinds of data-collection methods are used to pursue questions and confirm answers. In its multimodality (Wolcott, 1988), qualitative research contrasts starkly with quantitative approaches, where investigations often rely on a single method of gathering data. When quantitative researchers do use multiple instruments, they often are variations of the same thing—a collection of attitude surveys, for example, or several different psychometric measures.

Modes of Analysis

Sharp contrasts also exist between qualitative and quantitative modes of data analysis. Although analysis of quantitative data often occurs after the data are collected, qualitative analysis can begin as soon as information is gathered about the questions posed. Often this analysis proceeds throughout data collection, into an initial interpretation of the material, and sometimes beyond into many years as the data base is viewed, reviewed, and reinterpreted.

Although investigators have some analytic approaches in mind as they begin, each analysis is developed to fit its accumulating data base. Consequently, qualitative analysis possesses a flexible, evolving character that contrasts with the fixed and linear approaches of much quantitative research. Rather than a one-shot process at the end of data collection, qualitative analysis is ongoing and recursive—the investigator reviews and re-analyzes previous material as new material is developed. The process is similar to that used by writers, in which each new section of text is viewed in the context of previous text.

A special problem in qualitative work is that the copious data must be stored, organized, retrieved, and analyzed. Storage, organization, and retrieval have been expedited by word-processing and software programs for coding, sorting, and matching (Tesch, 1989). However, some material may always have to be handled manually and stored in places like file cabinets.

What computers cannot provide is the thinking and decision making required for data analysis. Regardless of the approach taken, all qualitative analysis methods require that the records be literally or figuratively pulled apart, divided into chunks, and grouped. From these groups, categories are developed. Once categories exist, researchers can look for temporal, causal, correlational, and other connections among them. These are very time-consuming processes. Wolcott (1975) recommended that as much time be devoted to analysis as to collection.

Relationship of Researcher to Those Studied

The distinction qualitative researchers make between objective and subjective data is more ambiguous, context-dependent, and relative than that often found in discussions of traditional quantitative research. Whereas quantitative researchers often view the subjective as a source of bias in need of control, qualitative researchers actively seek out subjective data and stances as well as objective ones. Subjectivity is confronted at least

twice. Qualitative researchers address how the world is experienced from the perspective of those studied—their perceptions, conceptions, feelings, beliefs, and values. Second, the subjective reactions of the researcher constitute an integral part of the qualitative data base. Researchers keep diaries of what they have thought, felt, believed, said, and done. These data become both part of the evidence and part of its assessment.

Qualitative research is sometimes seen as less reactive than much quantitative work, because participants are studied during the course of normal behavior in their natural settings. The researcher becomes a customary fixture in the setting, treatments are not administered, and people are studied over a length of time sufficient to ascertain behavioral and cultural patterns. Respondents can become accustomed to the researcher who fades into the woodwork after a time. Nevertheless, the investigator is present and interacts to varying degrees with participants. In that sense, the setting is disturbed. Possible reactivity is handled by tracking the researcher's impact; such methods include paying attention to participant interaction with the researcher, independent records kept by participants of their reactions to the investigator, and review of data by independent analysts.

Characteristics and Uses of Evidence for Claims

Like all scientists, qualitative researchers make claims about the truth or warrantability of what they have observed. Data are offered as evidence in support of the claims. Data analysis constitutes construction of evidence to substantiate conclusions. Evidence can vary in degree of abstraction and in how confidently claims made on its basis are held. Some evidence is merely a narrative of what happened; that is, the narratives provide empirical support for claims that the events were rendered accurately and authentically. Other claims are about the existence of categories of phenomena—concepts—discovered, sought, or substantiated in the data.

More sophisticated are claims about linkages among categories. Such connections are variously labeled as hypotheses, generalizations, or empirical statements. As the investigator works through the analysis, building claims about the nature and content of the data, the search for evidence to support the claims proceeds simultaneously. The initial evidence for a claim is a pattern in the data. Because generalization in qualitative research is grounded in thick, descriptive accounts of what goes on, there may be plentiful examples of these patterns.

Qualitative researchers generally study fewer people than do quantitative researchers, but they study those few more intensively. As a consequence, they are often able to pursue patterns in the behavior, belief, and knowledge of individuals across settings, circumstances, time, and other variations. Investigators can substantiate hunches, collect multiple points of view, and establish ranges for discerned patterns.

Among the strategies used to confirm patterns are cross-checking information and inferences with data from several individuals, looking at a given phenomenon with data obtained in different ways, enlisting as a confederate another researcher or an informed participant, and soliciting from participants reactions and interpretations of patterns developed by the researcher. All of these are means of triangulation (Denzin, 1978). Most qualitative investigators triangulate with data-collection methods and sources: They use two or more different kinds of data or data sources to get differing perspectives on the same phenomena. However, other elements such as conceptual frameworks and data-analysis methods can also be triangulated.

APPLYING QUALITATIVE RESEARCH TO ISSUES IN SOCIAL STUDIES EDUCATION

Applying qualitative research to social studies education involves many of the same issues of concern in any area of education or human endeavor. Among these are setting boundaries for what is to be examined, establishing whether a qualitative approach is appropriate for the questions posed, and assessing the applicability of the results of qualitative research to social studies teaching and learning.

Bounding the Research Effort

Using qualitative research to examine social studies education poses two issues of boundary. First, social studies education is not clearly defined. Is it formal instruction in the social sciences? Is it citizenship education? Is it decision making? Is it social inquiry? Is it social education, broadly conceived? If the last, then nearly all the qualitative research done in schools in the past two decades could be considered social studies research, especially the research done from sociocultural perspectives.

At its narrowest, research in social studies education is the formal study of teaching and learning about something occurring in school classrooms that people believe to be social studies. This includes social studies curricula and what people do to develop, disseminate, and adopt such curricula, as well as the preparation of individuals to teach them. This perspective precludes the study of social education—the informal socialization, enculturation, and acculturation occurring in schools—but the boundaries are clearly defined.

Such a limited definition might work well at the upper grades, but it is not a very satisfactory resolution for research in social studies education in elementary schools. In the elementary classrooms we have studied (e.g., Goetz & Breneman, 1988; LeCompte, 1978), social studies instruction is erratic, ephemeral, and above all informal. Although present in most classrooms, it often is disguised; social studies material permeates the reading, language arts, mathematics, and science programs. Furthermore, exercises in citizenship, decision making, social competency, and many other forms of sociocultural learning occur throughout the elementary school day.

The vagueness with which social studies education is defined makes it difficult to identify research—quantitative or qualitative—directed to social studies education. It is more difficult to identify and locate in the literature at the elementary level than at the secondary level. The even greater paucity of qualitative research in social studies education may be a conse-quence of the relative recency of its acceptability in educational research circles. Additionally, not only are the research reports scattered widely across such sources as professional journals, but what might be considered the social studies component of much research is embedded in material on other aspects of the curriculum and in information about factors other than social studies.

Our consideration of research studies in social studies education is bounded, as much as possible, by the literature itself. We have selected research for this chapter by assessing each piece of research, study by study, for characteristics that classify it as both qualitative research and social studies research. For example, an unquestionably qualitative study like King's (1982) observational examination of the function of play in socializing kindergarteners to becoming students qualifies as social studies research in the social education sense. That judgment is supported by the fact that the article was published in the premier journal for social studies research.

Advantages and Disadvantages of Qualitative Research

The use of qualitative research in social studies education has been advocated for decades. In Metcalf's (1963) review of research on social studies teaching, a combination, quantitative-qualitative investigation (Bayles, 1956) was cited as an example of noteworthy scholarship. The revitalization of qualitative research in education that began in the late 1960s was not ignored by social studies researchers. In 1973, Shaver and Larkins called for elaborating research in social education. The Shaver and Larkins piece was followed by the previously cited article by van Manen (1975), advocating research thrusts in three areas.

The advocacy has continued with each major reassessment of the state of social studies research (e.g., Armento, 1986; Cornbleth, 1986; Herman, 1980; Popkewitz, 1986). These scholars see multiple benefits of qualitative research for social studies education. Qualitative researchers attend to context, a significant factor in social education (Cornbleth, 1982; Giroux & Penna, 1979). Qualitative researchers build system and rigor into ways to observe classrooms, lessons, and teacher-student interactions—an invaluable tool for revealing what occurs there. A major emphasis is placed on the perspective of the participants involved. What are they making of what is going on, and how are their understandings affecting what they and others know and do—especially knowledge of and action in the social world? This is basic to the descriptive mandate of most qualitative research: "What is happening here?"

Qualitative researchers attempt to construct holistic views of events, permitting analysis of the complex relationships among such factors as students, teachers, classrooms, and curricula. This holism typically extends beyond the borders of the school itself, taking into account communities and their subgroups and the general sociocultural context within which they are embedded (Newmann, 1985). These perspectives allow qualitative researchers to address the question, "What does what is happening here mean?" This is the analytic purpose discussed previously.

Third, much qualitative research is devoted to the generation, refinement, and examination of theory (Gilbert, 1984; Larkins & McKinney, 1980; Popkewitz, 1978), a component of significant research lacking in many conventional studies in social studies education ("Theory and Research," 1982). Qualitative analysis is inductive and recursive, allowing investigators to trace through what actually does happen to something like a social studies innovation, rather than merely reporting the degree to which what was expected occurred or failed to occur. These analytic strategies allow researchers to address the question, "How can what has happened be understood and explained?"

Finally, because qualitative researchers are on site for long periods of time, they may be better able to assist educators with ongoing and formative evaluations than other kinds of researchers. Because they can establish a special rapport and trust, they may be better able than others to provide feedback in a way the participants find productive and encouraging (cf. e.g., Leming, 1986; Noblit, 1981, 1984; Shaver, 1979).

Given these benefits, why is qualitative design not more plentiful in social studies research? The reasons are inherent to the limitations of all qualitative investigation. It requires enormous resources of time, money, personnel, information, and energy. Its success depends on cooperation and commitment from participants, from whom researchers require much and to whom little may be returned. Finding a study site requires a persistence often difficult to maintain.

Finally, people who do qualitative research know that there are no right answers to the questions they ask. Qualitative research calls into question the existence of correct, absolute solutions to human problems and treats knowledge in tentative, skeptical, and relative ways. For educators whose lives and research have been devoted to improving the human condition, using qualitative approaches means settling for the possibility that there are no quick fixes.

The Content of Qualitative Research in Social Studies Education

Palonsky (1987) has taken the community of social studies ethnographers to task for publishing more about how to do the work than actually doing it. His astute observations about the state of ethnography in social studies education have informed our thinking about this chapter; they also contribute to the improvement of research. We do, however, take issue with his central contention that there is little research currently from the qualitative or ethnographic tradition in social studies education. As noted above, how much exists depends on what is defined as qualitative research in social studies education.

We see a ferment of activity. Some remains in fugitive sources like dissertations, theses, and paper presentations; but much is readily available now, and the activity has increased over time. When Shaver and Norton (1980) reviewed the research studies published in *Theory and Research in Social Education (TRSE)* and in the Research Department of *Social Education* through 1978, they labeled the category that would include qualitative research as *other,* meaning "other than the custom-

ary quantitative designs." Studies in that category constituted 2% of the total—a dismal total indeed. Later, Hepburn and Dahler (1985) classified social studies dissertations conducted from 1977 to 1982. They reported that 3% of the studies were ethnographies. However, another 45% were grouped as descriptive and 7% as developmental. In some of these, qualitative research methods were used.

In recent years, the news has become more positive. Wallen and Fraenkel (1988) reported astounding increases in qualitative work. Although their data base was limited to *TRSE,* it covered the 8 years from 1979 to 1986. Of the research studies published during this period, 20% were classified as ethnographic and 13% were presumed to be qualitative interviews. As was the case for the other two reviews, no attention was given to designs that combined qualitative and quantitative methods.

This information establishes that an increase in the amount of qualitative work in social studies education is under way. What is this work? Who is doing it? What topics are being addressed? What designs are being and have been developed?

White's (1985) review provides a useful compilation of the range of ethnographic studies from many disciplines that are relevant to social studies education. Focusing on the social education of young children, Bloch (1986) examined a series of qualitative research studies. More reviews like these are needed to draw scholars' attention to the work that has been done.

Much qualitative research is focused on social studies teachers (e.g., Boag & Massey, 1981; McCutcheon, 1981; Milburn, 1985; Palonsky, 1986; Parker, 1987; Peterson & Nett, 1982). Because preparation for teaching is considered so vital and, of course, because participants are so handy to social studies researchers, some of this work has been centered on preservice teachers (e.g., Adler, 1984; Goodman & Adler, 1985; Palonsky & Nelson, 1980; Ross, 1987).

Rarer are studies of students (e.g., Bennett, 1984; Diem, 1986; Lesko, 1988; Schug & Birkey, 1985). Given the holistic, contextual orientation of much qualitative research, it may not be surprising that research on children has often been conducted from the perspective of their interaction with teachers (e.g., Evans, 1988; Larkins & Oldham, 1976; McNeil, 1986; White, 1986).

Social studies researchers using qualitative designs also have examined the work and roles of those in higher education (e.g., Kingston & Bennett, 1986; Shermis & Barth, 1978; Shermis & Wasburn, 1986), as well as the curricula and texts produced for social studies classrooms at this level. These latter may be content analyses (e.g., Anyon, 1983; Clements, 1979; Taxel, 1983; White, 1988) or examinations of a curriculum in action as it is played out in precollegiate classrooms (e.g., Levstik, 1986).

Other researchers have taken a broader perspective and addressed issues of program and school community (e.g., Hamilton, 1981; Marker, 1980; Popkewitz, Tabachnick, & Wehlage, 1982). Although most of the preceding research topics stray from what some consider the proper boundaries of social studies research, it is at this programmatic, community level that such straying may be most inevitable. Of course, the same boundary wandering can be found in quantitative research in social studies education, as well as in studies combining qualitative and quantitative approaches (e.g., LeSourd, 1984; Siegel, 1977).

CONCLUSION

The goals for this chapter have been to review what scholars in the human sciences consider qualitative research to be and to discuss how the diverse perspectives informing these designs can be applied to problems in social studies education. To be understood, qualitative work must be seen in the broader context of the community of human scholarship. We believe that the recent revitalization of qualitative research is part of a redirection or renaissance of human efforts to understand human environments, beliefs, and behavior—an endeavor of particular importance for educators.

Most educators are, of course, concerned with society and culture and the people who create them. Social studies educators and researchers, however, have a special interest in society and culture because they are charged with teaching the young

about the human world. The qualitative approaches discussed in this chapter are an effective way to study this kind of instruction. Qualitative approaches also can increase the level of understanding of the inside world of students, teachers, administrators, parents, and others involved in education.

The qualitative social studies research cited here indicates the wide diversity of topics, issues, and questions this perspective can illuminate. In a 1971 assessment of the contribution of anthropology to understanding education, Wax and Wax pleaded for a refocusing of research to address the question, "What is happening [in schools] to our children as human beings" (p. 16)? Since that time, researchers also have asked what is happening to teachers and the many others who contribute to education in any society. Those questions are not yet answered, but remarkable progress has been made toward understanding both what needs to be asked and what dimensions will be forthcoming in the answers.

References

Adler, S. (1984). A field study of selected student teacher perspectives toward social studies. *Theory and Research in Social Education, 12*(1), 13–30.

Anyon, J. (1983). Workers, labor and economic history, and textbook content. In M. W., Apple & L. Weis (Eds.), *Ideology and practice in schooling* (pp. 37–60). Philadelphia: Temple University Press.

Apple, M. W. (1979). *Ideology and curriculum.* Boston: Routledge & Kegan Paul.

Armento, B. J. (1986). Research on teaching social studies. In M. C. Wittrock (Ed.), *Handbook of research on teaching* (3rd ed., pp. 942–951). New York: Macmillan.

Bayles, E. E. (1956). Experiments with reflective teaching. *Kansas Studies in Education, 6*(3), 1–32.

Bennett, C. (1984). Interracial contact experience and attrition among black undergraduates at a predominantly white university. *Theory and Research in Social Education, 12*(2), 19–47.

Bloch, M. N. (1986). Social education of young children. In C. Cornbleth (Ed.), *An invitation to research in social education* (pp. 91–108). Washington, DC: National Council for the Social Studies.

Boag, N., & Massey, D. (1981). Teacher perspectives on program change. *Theory and Research in Social Education, 9*(3), 37–59.

Bogdan, R. C., & Biklen, S. K. (1982). *Qualitative research for education: An introduction to theory and methods.* Boston: Allyn & Bacon.

Bogdan, R. C., & Taylor, S. J. (1975). *Introduction to qualitative research methods: A phenomenological approach to the social sciences.* New York: Wiley.

Borg, W. R., & Gall, M. D. (1989). *Educational research: An introduction* (5th ed.). New York: Longman.

Bruyn, S. T. (1966). *The human perspective in sociology: The methodology of participant observation.* Englewood Cliffs, NJ: Prentice-Hall.

Burgess, R. G. (1984). *In the field: An introduction to field research.* London: Allen & Unwin.

Campbell, D. T. (1979). "Degrees of freedom" and the case study. In T. D. Cook & C. S. Reichardt (Eds.), *Qualitative and quantitative methods in evaluation research* (pp. 49–67). Beverly Hills, CA: Sage.

Campbell, D. T., & Stanley, J. C. (1963). *Experimental and quasi-experimental designs for research.* Chicago: Rand McNally.

Carew, J. V., & Lightfoot, S. L. (1979). *Beyond bias: Perspectives on classrooms.* Cambridge, MA: Harvard University Press.

Clements, M. (1979). The taxonomy of educational objectives: An ethnographic perspective on an occupational culture. *Theory and Research in Social Education, 7*(3), 47–63.

Clifford, J., & Marcus, G. E. (Eds.). (1986). *Writing culture: The poetics and politics of ethnography.* Berkeley: University of California Press.

Cornbleth, C. (1982). On the social study of social studies. *Theory and Research in Social Education, 10*(4), 1–16.

Cornbleth, C. (1986). Social studies research reconsidered. In C. Cornbleth (Ed.), *An invitation to research in social education* (pp. 127–137). Washington, DC: National Council for the Social Studies.

Denzin, N. K. (1978). *The research act: A theoretical introduction to sociological methods* (2nd ed.). New York: McGraw-Hill.

Diem, R. A. (1986). Computers in a school environment: Preliminary report of the social consequences. *Theory and Research in Social Education, 14,* 163–170.

Erickson, F. (1986). Qualitative methods in research on teaching. In M. C. Wittrock (Ed.), *Handbook of research on teaching* (3rd ed., pp. 119–161). New York: Macmillan.

Evans, R. E. (1988). Lessons from history: Teacher and student conceptions of the meaning of history. *Theory and Research in Social Education, 16,* 203–225.

Filstead, W. J. (1979). Qualitative methods: A needed perspective in evaluation research. In T. D. Cook & C. S. Reichardt (Eds.), *Qualitative and quantitative methods in evaluation research* (pp. 33–48). Beverly Hills, CA: Sage.

Fink, L. D. (1978). *Field work as an investigative device.* Unpublished manuscript, University of Chicago, Department of Geography, Chicago.

Firestone, W. A. (1987). Meaning in method: The rhetoric of quantitative and qualitative research. *Educational Researcher, 16*(7), 16–21.

Geertz, C. (1973). *The interpretation of cultures: Selected essays.* New York: Basic Books.

Gilbert, R. (1984). Images of society and the analysis of ideologies in the social subjects. *Theory and Research in Social Education, 12*(3), 1–15.

Giorgi, A. (1971). Phenomenology and experimental psychology: I. In A. Giorgi, W. F. Fischer, & R. Von Eckartsberg (Eds.), *Duquesne studies in phenomenological psychology (Vol. I,* pp. 6–16). Pittsburgh, PA: Duquesne University Press.

Giroux, H. A., & Penna, A. N. (1979). Social education in the classroom: The dynamics of the hidden curriculum. *Theory and Research in Social Education, 7*(1), 21–42.

Goetz, J. P., & Breneman, E. A. R. (1988). Desegregation and black students' experiences in two rural southern elementary schools. *The Elementary School Journal, 88,* 489–502.

Goetz, J. P., & LeCompte, M. D. (1984). *Ethnography and qualitative design in educational research.* New York: Academic Press.

Goodman, J., & Adler, S. (1985). Becoming an elementary social studies teacher: A study of perspectives. *Theory and Research in Social Education, 13*(2), 1–20.

Guba, E. G. (1986, April). *The development of parallel criteria for trustworthiness.* Paper presented at the meeting of the American Educational Research Association, San Francisco.

Guba, E. G. (1988). Special conference explores alternative models for research. *News, Notes, and Quotes: Newsletter of Phi Delta Kappa, 33*(1), 24.

Hamilton, S. F. (1981). Adolescents in community settings: What is to be learned? *Theory and Research in Social Education, 9*(2), 23–38.

Hepburn, M. A., & Dahler, A. (1985). An overview of social studies dissertations, 1977–1982. *Theory and Research in Social Education, 13*(2), 73–82.

Herman, W. L., Jr. (1980). Toward a more adequate research base in social studies education. *Journal of Research and Development in Education, 13*(2), 24–35.

Howe, K. R. (1988). Against the quantitative-qualitative incompatibility thesis or dogmas die hard. *Educational Researcher, 17*(8), 10–16.

Jackson, P. W. (1968). *Life in classrooms.* New York: Holt, Rinehart & Winston.

Jacob, E. (1987). Qualitative research traditions: A review. *Review of Educational Research, 57,* 1–50.

King, N. R. (1982). School uses of materials traditionally associated with children's play. *Theory and Research in Social Education, 10*(3), 17–27.

Kingston, P. W., & Bennett, C. T. (1986). Improving high school social studies: Advice from the colleges. *Theory and Research in Social Education, 14,* 35–49.

Kuhn, T. S. (1962). *The structure of scientific revolutions* (2nd ed.). Chicago: University of Chicago Press.

Kuzel, A. J. (1986). Naturalistic inquiry: An appropriate model for family medicine. *Family Medicine, 18,* 369–374.

Larkins, A. G., & McKinney, C. W. (1980). Four types of theory: Implications for research in social education. *Theory and Research in Social Education, 8*(1), 9–17.

Larkins, A. G., & Oldham, S. E. (1976). Patterns of racial separation in a desegregated high school. *Theory and Research in Social Education, 4*(2), 23–38.

Leacock, E. B. (1969). *Teaching and learning in city schools: A comparative study.* New York: Basic Books.

LeCompte, M. D. (1978). Learning to work: The hidden curriculum of the classroom. *Anthropology and Education Quarterly, 9,* 22–37.

Leming, J. S. (1986). Rethinking social studies research and the goals of social education. *Theory and Research in Social Education, 14,* 139–152.

Lesko, N. (1988). "We're leading America": The changing organization and form of high school cheerleading. *Theory and Research in Social Education, 16,* 263–278.

LeSourd, S. J. (1984). An exploratory comparison of two methods of assessing teacher attitude toward instructional strategies. *Theory and Research in Social Education, 12*(1), 31–41.

Levstik, L. S. (1986). The relationship between historical response and narrative in a sixth-grade classroom. *Theory and Research in Social Education, 14,* 1–19.

Lincoln, Y. S., & Guba, E. G. (1985). *Naturalistic inquiry.* Beverly Hills, CA: Sage.

Magoon, A. J. (1977). Constructivist approaches in educational research. *Review of Educational Research, 47,* 651–693.

Marker, G. W. (1980). Why schools abandon "New Social Studies" materials. *Theory and Research in Social Education, 7*(4), 35–57.

McCutcheon, G. (1981). Elementary school teachers' planning for social studies and other subjects. *Theory and Research in Social Education, 9*(1), 45–66.

McNeil, L. M. (1986). *Contradictions of control: School structure and school knowledge.* Philadelphia: Metheun.

Merriam, S. B. (1988). *Case study research in education: A qualitative approach.* San Francisco: Jossey-Bass.

Metcalf, L. E. (1963). Research on teaching the social studies. In N. L. Gage (Ed.), *Handbook of research on teaching* (pp.929–965). Chicago: Rand McNally.

Milburn, G. (1985). Deciphering a code or unraveling a riddle: A case study in the application of a humanistic metaphor to the reporting of social studies teaching. *Theory and Research in Social Education, 13*(3), 21–44.

Monroe, M. (1932). *Children who cannot read.* Chicago: University of Chicago Press.

Newmann, F. M. (1985). The radical perspective on social studies: A synthesis and critique. *Theory and Research in Social Education, 13,* 1–18.

Noblit, G. W. (1981). The holistic alternative in policy research. *The High School Journal, 65,* 43–49.

Noblit, G. W. (1984). The prospects of an applied ethnography for education: A sociology of knowledge interpretation. *Educational Evaluation and Policy Analysis, 6,* 95–101.

Palonsky, S. B. (1986). *900 shows a year: A look at teaching from a teacher's side of the desk.* New York: Random House.

Palonsky, S. B. (1987). Ethnographic scholarship and social education. *Theory and Research in Social Education, 15,* 77–87.

Palonsky, S. B., & Nelson, J. (1980). Political restraint in the socialization of student teachers. *Theory and Research in Social Education, 7*(4), 19–34.

Parker, W. C. (1987). Teachers' mediation in social studies. *Theory and Research in Social Education, 15,* 1–22.

Patton, M. Q. (1980). Making methods choices. *Evaluation and Program Planning, 3,* 219–228.

Peshkin, A., & Eisner, E. W. (1990). Introduction. In E. W. Eisner & A. Peshkin (Eds.), *Qualitative inquiry in education: The continuing debate* (pp. 1–14). New York: Teachers College Press.

Peterson, E. L., & Nett, E. M. (1982). Sexuality in the classrooms of teachers with various sex role orientations. *Theory and Research in Social Education, 10*(3), 29–40.

Polkinghorne, D. (1983). *Methodology for the human sciences: Systems of inquiry.* Albany: State University of New York Press.

Popkewitz, T. S. (1978). Educational research: Values and visions of social order. *Theory and Research in Social Education, 6*(4), 20–39.

Popkewitz, T. S. (1986). Paradigm and purpose. In C. Cornbleth (Ed.), *An invitation to research in social education* (pp. 10–27). Washington, DC: National Council for the Social Studies.

Popkewitz, T. S., Tabachnick, B., & Wehlage, G. (1982). *The myth of educational reform.* Madison: University of Wisconsin Press.

Reichardt, C. S., & Cook, T. D. (1979). Beyond qualitative versus quantitative methods. In T. D. Cook & C. S. Reichardt (Eds.), *Qualitative and quantitative methods in evaluation research* (pp. 7–32). Beverly Hills, CA: Sage.

Rist, R. C. (1973). *The urban school: A factory for failure—A study of education in American society.* Cambridge, MA: MIT Press.

Rist, R. C. (1982). On the application of ethnographic inquiry to education: Procedures and possibilities. *Journal of Research in Science Teaching, 19,* 439–450.

Roman, L. G., & Apple, M. W. (1990). Is naturalism a move away from positivism? Materialist and feminist approaches to subjectivity in ethnographic research. In E. W. Eisner & A. Peshkin (Eds.), *Qualitative inquiry in education: The continuing debate* (pp. 38–73). New York: Teachers College Press.

Rosenshine, B., & Furst, N. (1973). The use of direct observation to study teaching. In R. M. W. Travers (Ed.), *Second handbook of research on teaching* (pp. 122–183). Chicago: Rand McNally.

Ross, E. W. (1987). Teacher perspective development: A study of preservice social studies teachers. *Theory and Research in Social Education, 15,* 225–243.

Schatzman, L., & Strauss, A. L. (1973). *Field research: Strategies for a natural sociology.* Englewood Cliffs, NJ: Prentice-Hall.

Schug, M. C., & Birkey, C. J. (1985). The development of children's economic reasoning. *Theory and Research in Social Education, 13,* 31–42.

Shaver, J. P. (1979). The usefulness of educational research in curricular/instructional decision-making in social studies. *Theory and Research in Social Education, 7*(3), 21–46.

Shaver, J. P., & Larkins, A. G. (1973). Research on teaching social studies. In R. M. W. Travers (Ed.), *Second handbook of research on teaching* (pp. 1243–1262). Chicago: Rand McNally.

Shaver, J. P., & Norton, R. S. (1980). Populations, samples, randomness, and replication in two social studies journals. *Theory and Research in Social Education, 8*(2), 1–10.

Shermis, S. S., & Barth, J. L. (1978). Social studies and the problem of knowledge: A re-examination of Edgar Bruce Wesley's classic definition of the social studies. *Theory and Research in Social Education, 6*(1), 31–43.

Shermis, S. S., & Wasburn, P. C. (1986). Social studies educators and their beliefs: Preliminary data from Indiana colleges and universities. *Theory and Research in Social Education, 14,* 331–340.

Siegel, M. E. (1977). Citizenship education in five Massachusetts high schools. *Theory and Research in Social Education, 5*(2), 31–55.

Smith, J. K., & Heshusius, L. (1986). Closing down the conversation: The end of the quantitative-qualitative debate among educational inquirers. *Educational Researcher, 15*(1), 4–12.

Smith, L. M., & Geoffrey, W. (1968). *The complexities of an urban classroom: An analysis toward a general theory of teaching.* New York: Holt, Rinehart & Winston.

Spindler, G. D., & Spindler, L. (1987). Ethnography: An anthropological view. In G. D. Spindler (Ed.), *Education and cultural process: An*thropological approaches (2nd ed., pp. 151–156). Prospect Heights, IL: Waveland Press.

Stein, M. R. (1960). *The eclipse of community: An interpretation of American studies.* Princeton, NJ: Princeton University Press.

Taxel, J. (1983). The American Revolution in children's fiction: An analysis of literary content, form, and ideology. In M. W. Apple & L. Weis (Eds.), *Ideology and practice in schooling* (pp. 61–88). Philadelphia: Temple University Press.

Tesch, R. (1989). *Qualitative research: Analysis types and software tools.* London: Falmer Press.

Theory and Research in Social Education. (1982). [Special issue]. *9*(4).

Van Maanen, J. (1988). *Tales of the field: On writing ethnography.* Chicago: University of Chicago Press.

van Manen, M. J. M. (1975). An exploration of alternative research orientations in social education. *Theory and Research in Social Education, 3*(1), 1–28.

Wallen, N. E., & Fraenkel, J. R. (1988). An analysis of social studies research over an eight year period. *Theory and Researh in Social Education, 16,* 1–22.

Wax, M. L., & Wax, R. H. (1971). Great tradition, little tradition, and formal education. In M. L. Wax, S. Diamond, & F. O. Gearing (Eds.), *Anthropological perspectives on education* (pp. 3–18). New York: Basic Books.

White, J. J. (1985). What works for teachers: A review of ethnographic research studies as they inform issues of social studies curriculum and instruction. In W. B. Stanley (Ed.), *Review of research in social studies education: 1976–1983* (pp. 215–307). Washington, DC: National Council for the Social Studies.

White, J. J. (1986). An ethnographic approach. In C. Cornbleth (Ed.), *An invitation to research in social education* (pp. 51–77). Washington, DC: National Council for the Social Studies.

White, J. J. (1988). Searching for substantial knowledge in social studies texts. *Theory and Research in Social Education, 16,* 115–140.

Willis, P. E. (1977). *Learning to labour: How working class kids get working class jobs.* Farnborough, Eng.: Saxon House.

Wilson, S. (1977). The use of ethnographic techniques in educational research. *Review of Educational Research, 47,* 245–265.

Wolcott, H. F. (1975). Criteria for an ethnographic approach to research in schools. *Human Organization, 34,* 111–127.

Wolcott, H. F. (1980). How to look like an anthropologist without really being one. *Practicing Anthropology, 3*(1), 6–17, 56–59.

Wolcott, H. F. (1988). Ethnographic research in education. In R. M. Jaeger (Ed.), *Complementary methods for research in education* (pp. 187–206). Washington, DC: American Educational Research Association.

6

QUANTITATIVE RESEARCH IN SOCIAL STUDIES EDUCATION

Jack R. Fraenkel and Norman E. Wallen
SAN FRANCISCO STATE UNIVERSITY

The word *quantitative,* as used in this chapter, refers to a particular orientation that a number of research methodologies have in common. Borg and Gall (1983, pp. 32–33) have identified six desirable, or ideal, characteristics of quantitative research:

Precise measurement of variables using instruments that yield reliable and valid scores.
Generalizability to a population of results obtained from a limited set of observations.
Control of extraneous factors that might account for observed effects.
Statistical analysis of data to illuminate phenomena.
Clarity of constructs, thus allowing for replicability of studies.
A positivistic orientation toward knowledge.

In addition, quantitative researchers, almost always, are more specific than other types of researchers about the details of the research process itself. That is, they try to specify *ahead of time* exactly what it is they are after, what they will do, what they expect to find, and what will count as evidence that they have found it.

By way of contrast, researchers who do not adopt a quantitative orientation (e.g., qualitative and critical researchers) argue that too much attention to these features can obscure the essential nature of the phenomena being investigated. The result, they argue, is a fragmented view of phenomena that in actuality are extremely complex.

Quantitative researchers try to control their subjectivity. Accordingly, the procedures they employ are designed to help them minimize the impact of their personal views, biases, or orientations on the phenomena they are trying to study. Advocates of other methodologies (e.g., historiographies, ethno-graphies, case studies) are much less concerned with trying to minimize the subjective framework of the investigator; indeed, some view it as a pivotal ingredient in the research endeavor.

Quantitative research methodologies are frequently compared and contrasted with another set of research methodologies summarily referred to as qualitative research. The pros and cons of each, and their usefulness to educators, are frequently debated in the literature (e.g., see Firestone, 1987; Howe, 1985; J. K. Smith, 1983; Smith & Heshusius, 1986; Soltis, 1984). As a further attempt to clarify the orientation of quantitative research, the two approaches are compared along a number of dimensions in Table 6–1.

METHODOLOGIES USED IN QUANTITATIVE RESEARCH

Several methodologies are typically used in quantitative research. Those most commonly mentioned include true experiments, quasi-experiments, correlational studies, causal-comparative investigations, questionnaire-type or interview-type surveys, and content analyses. The discussion in this chapter is restricted to these types of research. A brief description of each type follows.

True Experiments. Two or more groups of subjects that receive different treatments are compared in some way. Subjects are randomly assigned to treatment and control groups. Administration of the treatment is controlled by the researcher. (See Kleg, Karabinus, & Carter, 1986; Maddocks & Smith, 1986; McKinney, Burts, Ford, & Gilmore, 1987; Yoho, 1986, for examples of experimental research in social studies education.)

Reviewers were Wayne L. Herman, Jr., and William D. Schafer, University of Maryland; Ronald VanSickle, University of Georgia.

TABLE 6–1. Quantitative vs. Qualitative Research

Quantitative Methodologies	Qualitative Methodologies
Preference for precise hypotheses stated at the outset	Preference for hypotheses that emerge as study develops
Preference for precise definitions stated at the outset	Preference for definitions in context or as study progresses
Data reduced to numerical scores	Preference for narrative description
Much attention to assessing and improving reliability of scores obtained from instruments	Preference for assuming that reliability of inferences is adequate
Assessment of validity through a variety of procedures with reliance on statistical indices	Assessment of validity through cross-checking sources of information (triangulation)
Preference for random techniques for obtaining meaningful samples	Preference for expert informant (purposive) samples
Preference for precise descriptions of procedures	Preference for narrative/literary descriptions of procedures
Preference for design or statistical control of extraneous variables	Preference for logical analysis in controlling or accounting for extraneous variables
Preference for specific design control for procedural bias	Primary reliance on researcher to deal with procedural bias
Preference for statistical summary of results	Preference for narrative summary of results
Preference for breaking down of complex phenomena into specific parts for analysis	Preference for holistic description of complex phenomena
Willingness to manipulate aspects, situations, or conditions in studying complex phenomena	Unwillingness to tamper with naturally occurring phenomena

Quasi-Experiments. Two or more groups of subjects are compared in some way. Subjects are not randomly assigned to treatment and control groups. Administration of the treatment variable may or may not be controlled by the researcher. (See Barnes & Curlette, 1985; Beem & Brugman, 1986; Hahn & Avery, 1985; Mckenzie & Sawyer, 1986, for examples of quasi-experimental research in social studies education.)

Correlational Studies. The scores of a single group of subjects on two or more different measures are correlated. There is no manipulation or intervention on the part of the researcher other than that required to administer the instrument(s) necessary to collect the data. Complex analyses, such as multiple regression or path analysis, may be performed. (See Curtis, 1983; Guyton, 1988; Haladyna, Shaughnessy & Redsun, 1982a; B. D. Smith, 1983, for examples of correlational research in social studies education.)

Causal-Comparative Studies. Two or more groups differing in known ways are compared on one or more variables. As in correlational research, the variables involved are not manipulated. Only two examples of this type of methodology (Fouts, 1987; Napier & Grant, 1984) could be located in reviewing the social studies research literature published since 1979.

Surveys. Two types of surveys are conducted by social studies researchers. (a) In *questionnaire-type survey studies,* a written questionnaire is administered, either by mail or in person, to one or more groups of subjects. No treatment is involved. The responses of the subjects to the questions are then reported. (b) In *interview-type survey studies,* an interview schedule is prepared and administered orally to one or more groups of subjects. No treatment is involved. The subjects' responses to the questions are then reported. (See Bennett, 1984; Farmer, 1983; Jantz, Weaver, Cirrincione, & Farrell, 1985; LeSourd, 1984; Schug & Birkey, 1985, for examples of questionnaire- or interview-type survey research in social studies education.)

Content Analysis. The contents of one or more documents are analyzed to determine the occurrence of various words, statements, concepts, pictures, images, etc. Frequency of occurrence of the variables of interest are reported. (See Evans, 1988; Miller & Rose, 1983; Romanish, 1983; Stanley, 1984; Wallen & Fraenkel, 1988; White, 1988, for examples of content analysis in social studies education.)

Methodologies Not Discussed. Excluded from the discussion in this chapter are those methodologies categorized as primarily qualitative research (e.g., ethnographies, naturalistic observations, case studies), or as relating to the foundations of social education (e.g., philosophical analyses, historiographies, critical and phenomenological approaches). These methodologies are discussed in other chapters in this handbook. For the same reason, little will be said, except in passing, about content analysis studies.

PURPOSE OF THIS CHAPTER

Our intent in this chapter is to examine the nature of quantitative research in social studies over the last 10 years (1979–1988), and to draw some conclusions about how well—or how poorly—various aspects of the quantitative approach have been applied by social studies educators. The data upon which our conclusions are based were obtained from a detailed search of the professional literature in which most of the reports of social studies research are published. Thus all of the quantitative research reports published from the beginning of 1979 until the end of 1988 in *Theory and Research in Social Education (TRSE), The Journal of Social Studies Research (JSSR),* the research section of *Social Education (SE),* the *American Educational Research Journal (AERJ),* and the *Journal of Educational Research (JER)* were reviewed. In addition, various reviews of research published during these years were consulted, including the *Review of Educational Research (RER),* and the *Reviews of Research in Social Studies Education: 1970–1975* (Hunkins, Ehman, Hahn, Martorella, & Tucker, 1977) and *1976–1983* (Stanley, 1985b), as well as chapters dealing with social studies research in the first, second, and third *Handbook of Research on Teaching,* the Yearbook of the National Society for the Study of Education (NSSE), and the *Encyclopedia of Educational Research* (Armento, 1986; Cornbleth, 1982; Ehman & Hahn, 1981; Metcalf, 1963; Ponder & Davis, 1982; Shaver & Larkins, 1973). No individual doctoral dissertations were reviewed, although two general reviews of them were examined (Hepburn & Dahler, 1985; Larkins & Mckinney, 1983).

The search for studies to be reviewed was guided by various terms commonly used in social studies education, including *social studies, social science, citizenship education, global education,* and *geographic (economic,* etc.) *education,* as mentioned in the most recent revision of the NCSS social studies curriculum guidelines (Osborne, 1979). The selection of a specific study for review was based on two criteria: (a) the researchers utilized one of the five quantitative methodologies described above; and (b) the study took place in a social studies classroom with students, or it involved social studies teachers, teachers-in-training, supervisors, or other professionals.

A total of 205 reports of social studies research published between 1979 and 1988 were located. Over three fourths of these (176) involved some type of quantitative methodology. A somewhat different analysis of some of these studies (118 published between 1979 and 1986) was reported previously (Fraenkel & Wallen, 1988). The present chapter extends and elaborates on the previous work, but also offers additional analysis and commentary.

DOMINANCE OF QUANTITATIVE RESEARCH

Quantitative research continues to be the most common type of research conducted by social studies educators. Out of a total of 87 empirical studies published in *TRSE* during the 10 years from 1979 to 1988, 62 (71%) were quantitative in nature. Even larger percentages were found for this same period in the two other journals in which most social studies research is reported: 62 of a total of 65 empirical studies (95%) published in the *JSSR,* and 31 of 31 (100%) of such studies published in *SE* were quantitative. Similar percentages hold for reports of social studies research published in more general education journals during this period. In eight of eight (100%) empirical studies dealing with social studies topics or issues published in *AERJ* and in 13 of 13 (100%) empirical studies published in the *JER,* quantitative methodologies were utilized.

In sum, of a total of 205 published reports of empirical social studies research located for the 10-year period 1979–1988, 176 (86%) involved some type of quantitative methodology. By way of contrast, there were only 29 studies (14%) in which the authors utilized some type of qualitative methodology. Other reviewers of social studies research have also reported that quantitative methodologies dominate the efforts of researchers in social studies education (Armento, 1986; Shaver & Norton, 1980), and such dominance is not a new phenomenon (Hunkins et al., 1977; Shaver & Larkins, 1973).

Quantitative methodologies are also the methodologies most commonly used by social studies education graduate students who conduct empirical studies for their doctoral disserta-

tions. Based on a review of the abstracts of 394 doctoral dissertations in 1983, Hepburn and Dahler (1985) found that descriptive methodologies (which included content analyses and surveys) comprised 177 (45%) of the total, while experimental methodologies (which included both true and quasi-experiments) constituted 105 (27%) of the total. The two together totaled 282, or 72% of the total number of dissertations reviewed. Similarly, of the 40 selected dissertations published in the year 1980 that Larkins and McKinney (1983) reviewed, 31 (78%) were quantitative studies of one type or another.

THE NATURE OF QUANTITATIVE RESEARCH IN SOCIAL STUDIES

Many commentators have critically described much of the quantitative research in social studies education as flawed in both conception and execution, and as being essentially atheoretical. Some of the most common criticisms follow. Too many research questions are trivial. Treatments are often vaguely defined, briefly administered, and/or weakly implemented. Threats to internal validity are not controlled. Aptitude-by-treatment interactions are almost always ignored. Evidence of reliability and validity with regard to instrumentation is lacking. The durability of effects is rarely assessed. Replication of studies is more the exception that the rule. Statistical procedures are inappropriate. External validity is virtually nonexistent. (See Jantz & Klawitter, 1985; Leming, 1985; Martorella, 1977; Metcalf, 1963; Nelson & Shaver, 1985; Shaver & Larkins, 1973; Shaver & Norton, 1980; Wallen, 1983.) Unfortunately, these criticisms still apply. In the remainder of the chapter, we discuss some of the most prevalent characteristics of current social studies research and, in doing so, illustrate many of the flaws mentioned above. We shall also provide some examples of studies that, in the main, were well done.

Lack of Theory

The lack of theoretical development continues to characterize most of the research in social studies education. Metcalf (1963), writing in the first *Handbook of Research on Teaching* some 25 years ago, noted that summaries of social studies research revealed that it had not been guided by "a framework or theory that would make possible a distinction between basic and trivial investigations" (p. 933). Similar observations have been made by more recent reviewers (Armento, 1986; Fraenkel & Wallen, 1988; Shaver & Larkins, 1973).

A theory is a set of interrelated propositions that specify relationships among variables, and thus helps to explain or predict phenomena. As has been the case in the past, most current social studies research is atheoretical. Few social studies researchers attempt to connect their work to some underlying theory, although a few exceptions to this general trend can be found (see Bennett, 1984; Eyler, 1982; Haladyna et al., 1982a, 1982b).

Partly this is due to the nature of the field itself, it being an example of applied rather than pure science. Social studies researchers are not only concerned with understanding particular phenomena, but also primarily with influencing, developing, and promoting certain behaviors. This emphasis is reflected in the research. Experimental and quasi-experimental research in social studies is usually done not to test theory, but rather to assess the effectiveness of particular methods. Survey research is usually done not to understand better particular variables (such as the attitudes of students toward different kinds of content and methodology), but rather to describe the characteristics, attitudes, or opinions of teachers, supervisors, professors, and/or other social studies professionals. Most correlational research is done not to identify and better understand the relationships among particular phenomena, but to predict (in a purely utilitarian sense).

The field is further complicated by a lack of agreed-upon and clearly defined variables to investigate. Research in reading, science, mathematics, and other content areas has proven profitable, despite the same absence of theory as in social studies. The reason is that researchers in these other fields are in far more agreement as to the critical variables to be studied. One can usefully study variables related to competence in solving arithmetic story problems, for example, without a theory about how such competence develops. Unfortunately, social studies researchers are not in agreement as to what competencies are most worthwhile to develop.

Greater attention to theoretical underpinnings would provide more direction and focus for the field, and help to ensure significance for individual studies. It would help individual researchers to identify important questions and relationships to investigate in order to obtain answers to questions of more than trivial import. It would enable researchers to design studies (often utilizing different methodologies) with a common purpose, studies that could be replicated with different samples, in different settings, and under different conditions, in order to verify the findings of individual studies. This would be a start toward building a knowledge base of research findings that the profession still does not have.

Methodology

Experimental research (including both true and quasi-experiments) is the methodology most commonly utilized by social studies researchers, followed closely by survey research. When broken down by type and listed in order of frequency, of the 176 studies reviewed for this chapter, 71 (40%) were either true or quasi-experiments. Of these, 42 (24%) were quasi-experiments, whereas 29 (16%) were true experiments. Sixty-three (36%) were either questionnaire- or interview-type surveys. Of these, 50 (28%) utilized written questionnaires, while 13 (7%) involved interviews. Twenty-five (14%) were content analyses and 15 (9%) were correlational studies. Only two studies (1%) that were causal-comparative investigations could be located.

Research Design

The concept of research design applies most directly to experimental studies. Those researchers who conduct quasi-ex-

periments almost always utilize a nonequivalent control group design (Campbell & Stanley, 1963). Intact groups (usually classrooms) are compared, although the groups rarely, if ever, have known preexperimental equivalence. Accordingly, both the experimental and the control groups are given a pretest and a posttest. The assignment of the treatment to one group or the other, however, is frequently made randomly, and some effort is made to adjust initial inequivalence of the groups through matching or analysis of covariance (ANCOVA). In one study in which the authors investigated the effects of value analysis discussions and of reading controversial news articles on students' political attitudes and reading comprehension, for example, the sample consisted of 15 intact secondary United States history classes from a metropolitan county school district (Hahn & Avery, 1985). The authors employed a pretest-posttest design, and then used ANCOVA, with the pretest as the covariate, to control differences with regard to reading ability.

Other quasi-experimental designs, such as equivalent time samples, equivalent materials, or counterbalanced designs do not appear to be used by social studies researchers, even though these designs control well for most threats to internal validity (Campbell & Stanley, 1963). Factorial designs also are almost never employed in social studies research, even though their usefulness was demonstrated almost 25 years ago (see Oliver & Shaver, 1966/1974).

Although there are far more quasi- than true experiments conducted by social studies researchers, those who conduct true experiments utilize either a posttest-only control group or a pretest-posttest control group design (Campbell & Stanley, 1963). The use of the Solomon four-group design (Solomon, 1949) is notable by its absence, probably due (at least in part) to the difficulty involved in getting a large enough sample to divide into four groups. Surprisingly, despite the well-known defects of preexperimental designs, examples of one-shot case studies and single group, pre-post designs can still be found in the recent social studies literature (Barth & Sommersdorf, 1981; Beck, 1979; Ferguson, 1986; Kirman, 1984; Powell & Powell, 1984).

Survey research in social studies education primarily involves the use of mailed questionnaires, although on occasion one finds a questionnaire administered directly to a group. Interview-type surveys are comparatively infrequent (see Kingston & Bennett, 1986; Marker, 1980; Nelson & Palonsky, 1980; Palonsky & Nelson, 1980; Schug & Birkey, 1985).

Correlational research in social studies, although comparatively infrequent compared to experimental and survey research, ranges in sophistication from fairly straightforward cross-sectional descriptive studies (e.g., Haladyna et al., 1982a; B. D. Smith, 1983) to quite sophisticated factor analysis and multiple regression (Daily, 1983) and path analysis (Eyler, 1982; Guyton, 1988; Jackstadt & Brennan, 1983) studies.

Hypotheses

An hypothesis is generally taken to be a specific prediction concerning the expected outcomes of a study. Some critics have argued that hypotheses are unnecessarily limiting because they may cause investigators to miss other relationships that emerge as a study progresses. Although this may be true in some instances, it hardly seems a necessary result. To the contrary, the formulation of hypotheses can help a researcher specify his or her research question more precisely and thus clarify the particular variables to be investigated. Furthermore, the formulation of hypotheses encourages the development of a body of knowledge. Many studies designed to investigate the same general hypothesis, yet involving different moderator variables, might contribute to the building of the knowledge base that is currently lacking in social studies education. Researchers who conduct experimental, correlational, and causal-comparative studies obviously expect to find relationships. These should be stated at the outset in the interest of clarity. In less than half of the research reports reviewed for this chapter did the researchers present a clearly stated hypothesis.

Definition of Important Variables

Closely related to the matter of stating hypotheses is that of clarity concerning the variables being investigated. Clarity of meaning with regard to variables varies widely in social studies research. Although in many studies key variables are clearly defined (e.g., see Guyton, 1988; Hahn & Avery, 1985; Levstik, 1986), in many others they are not defined at all. In one survey study, for example, a questionnaire on inquiry teaching was mailed to two groups of respondents—classroom teachers and college/university faculty. The questionnaire sought to determine the perceptions of both groups concerning what had happened to inquiry teaching in recent years, as well as their perceptions as to possible factors that might have influenced the implementation of inquiry as a curriculum innovation. Nowhere in the author's report of the results of the survey, however, does one find a definition of the term "inquiry" (Jantz et al., 1985). In another, otherwise well-designed, experimental study, the authors compared the effectiveness of two approaches to teaching concepts, yet failed to define the term "concept" (McKinney, Burts, Ford, & Gilmore, 1987). In one quasi-experimental study, the authors investigated the effects of three levels (knowledge, comprehension, application) of behavioral objectives on the achievement and retention of students of differing ability (as measured by GPA), yet did not define what they meant by the term "behavioral objectives" (Ahlawat, Saadeh, Bader, & Khalifeh, 1988). In a fourth study, the author argued persuasively for the use of "visual diagrams" as an aid to help students assimilate knowledge in eighth-grade social studies classes, yet never defined what such a diagram would look like (Blankenship, 1983).

Sometimes definitions are provided, but the definitions themselves are not clear. The authors of one study, for example, attempted to synthesize current definitions in order to arrive at a concensus concerning the meaning of "multicultural education" (Bennett, Burbach, & Cruz, 1984). Unfortunately, the definitions they selected are themselves vague and ambiguous.

The failure of some researchers to define important terms precisely, or even to define them at all, has serious consequences for subsequent research. It suggests to neophyte social studies researchers that it is not important to provide precise definitions. It subtly encourages even experienced researchers to make less than a concerted effort to clarify the terms they use in their research. It furthers the use of vague terms in oral and written discourse by social studies educators, thereby contributing to a lack of precision in much of the language used by the profession.

Verification of Independent Variables

Almost 20 years ago Shaver and Larkins (1973), in the *Second Handbook of Research on Teaching,* pointed out that the lack of consistent and cumulative findings in social studies research might be due largely to the failure of researchers to confirm that the independent variable actually occurred as they intended. Recent social studies research shows such lack of confirmation to be, in the main, no longer the case.

Although a few researchers still fail to verify the occurrence of the independent variable (e.g., Ahlawat et al., 1988; Shepard & Svasti, 1988; B. D. Smith, 1983), more and more investigators are now taking pains to ensure that the independent variable occurs as they intend. This is especially the case where the independent variable involves some variation of instructional method. In several such studies, observations of instruction or analysis of teaching plans were performed by the researchers to check on the implementation of the independent variable (e.g., Alvermann, Boothby, & Wolfe, 1984; Betres, Zajano, & Gumieniak, 1984; Blankenship, 1983; Burts, McKinney, & Burts, 1985; Hahn & Avery, 1985; McKinney, Burts, Ford, & Gilmore, 1987; O'Brien, Meszaros, & Pulliam, 1985; Randall, Carr, Gerofsy, & Biggers, 1987).

In one quasi-experimental study, for example, the researchers utilized an observation instrument, for which evidence of reliability and interobserver agreement had been obtained in previous studies, to verify that the independent variable was implemented as intended (Larkins & McKinney, 1982). In another study, the treatment involved structured discussions of controversial issues one day a week for 10 weeks. Each of the classes in the experimental group was observed twice during this 10-week period, and each teacher kept a log of instructional methods (Hahn & Avery, 1985). Control group teachers were interviewed at the conclusion of the study to verify that they did not use the experimental method (value analysis during classroom discussions). This kind of double checking—using both observation and documentation—to ensure that the treatment occurred as intended, plus checking also to ensure that the control group did *not* use the treatment, is to be commended.

Unfortunately, this kind of detail is not always reported. Many authors state only that an observer was present to verify that the treatment was followed (e.g., Betres et al., 1984; Blankenship, 1983; Gilmore & McKinney, 1986; McKinney, Larkins, & Burts, 1984; McKinney, Burts, Ford, & Gilmore, 1987). Discussion of what the observers did to verify the independent variable (i.e., what instruments or procedures they used) would provide readers with assurance that treatments in intervention studies were actually implemented as intended. Some researchers used only a check on lesson plans as a method of verification (Randall et al., 1987). Relying on lesson plans as the sole check on the implementation of the independent variable is a weak form of verification, and needs to be corroborated by observations of actual classroom behavior.

Sometimes the nature of the independent variable itself is not described, and hence exactly what the treatment was cannot be determined. This occurs particularly in studies in which the independent variable involves some aspect of teacher training. One researcher, for example, analyzed the impact of teacher training workshops in economics on both teacher and student opinions and achievement (Schober, 1984). What happened in the workshops, however, was not described. The authors of another study required students in a graduate course in "Global Understanding" to read "a wide variety of periodicals and literature produced by educational groups," yet did not describe the nature of this literature (Barnes & Curlette, 1985). Although the authors stated in a footnote that a description of the treatment was available, such information should have been provided in the report itself. Such failure to describe the nature of the treatment is a serious omission, for it leaves the reader with no idea as to what happened in the experiment, and hence no way to judge the applicability of reported results to other settings or groups, or to replicate the study. A thorough description of the treatment would seem to be an absolute necessity for all intervention studies (see Shaver, 1979, 1983).

Dependent Variables

A recurring problem for social studies researchers is that many of the dependent variables they seek to observe are extremely difficult to measure (Shaver & Larkins, 1973). This difficulty of measurement is due to a number of factors. Many social studies objectives (e.g., "good citizenship") are long-term, aimed at adult citizen behavior, and the achievement of such lasting accomplishment is difficult, if not impossible, to determine on a short-term basis. Some objectives are attitudinal in nature (e.g., tolerance, courtesy), and accomplishment can only be inferred, not observed directly. Still others (e.g., critical thinking) are difficult to define satisfactorily so as to embrace the underlying concept in its entirety. Accordingly, much of the measurement of objectives in social studies research falls back on that which is the easiest to measure—knowledge of information per se. Partly this is due to a lack of instruments that permit reliable and valid inferences about more complex performances.

Whatever the reasons, the dependent variable in much social studies research involves either knowledge of some kind of social studies content or the ability to use some kind of social studies skill (as evidenced by most experimental, quasi-experimental, or correlational studies), or opinions about some aspects of the social studies curriculum (as evidenced by most surveys). With a few exceptions (see Beem & Brugman, 1986; Curtis, 1983; McKinney et al., 1984), in almost all of the studies reviewed for this chapter some kind of pencil-and-paper test or questionnaire was utilized solely as the measurement device. Other forms of measurement, such as observational category systems, anecdotal records, performance rating scales, perfor-

mance checklists, sociometric devices, and participation flow charts (see Sawin, 1969), as well as unobtrusive measures (Webb, Campbell, Schwartz, & Sechrest, 1966) need to be used (or used more frequently), however, if we are to measure adequately and comprehensively the vast array of social studies objectives.

Reliability and Validity of Inferences Drawn From Instruments

In every standard textbook on educational research, a fair amount of space is devoted to a discussion of the concepts of reliability and validity with regard to the instrumentation process (e.g., Borg & Gall, 1983; Gay, 1987; Kerlinger, 1986; Tuckman, 1988; Wiersma, 1986). Unfortunately, many of the authors still talk about reliability and validity as though the instruments used in research investigations *themselves* had reliability and/or validity (the Wiersma text is an exception). We thus find discussions of *instrument* reliability and content (or predictive, or concurrent, or construct) validity *of tests*. Borg and Gall (1983), for example, define reliability as "the level of internal consistency or stability of the measuring *device* over time" (p. 281, italics added). Gay (1987) defines content validity as "the degree to which a test measures an intended content area" (p. 129).

It is more accurate, however, to view the concept of reliability as referring to the consistency of test *scores*—how consistent the scores are from one measurement to another. The same test may yield scores with widely varying reliability, depending on the conditions of administration or the population tested. Similarly, the concept of validity refers to the "appropriateness, meaningfulness, and usefulness" of the specific *inferences* made from test scores (American Psychological Association, 1985). The process of instrument validation is now viewed as the accumulation of evidence to support these inferences. The older, traditional view that there were several different "types" of validity (e.g., content, concurrent, construct) has now been replaced by the view that validity is a single concept that is based on different types of evidence. Thus, it is more appropriate to speak of "content-related evidence" for validity rather than content validity per se or, similarly, "criterion-related evidence" and "construct-related evidence" (Gronlund, 1988). Whether very many social studies researchers understand the above distinctions appears at present, however, somewhat moot, for few reports could be found wherein the authors included a discussion of either topic.

Reliability. In two thirds of the reports of recent social studies research, regardless of the type of instrument used, the authors made no check on the reliability of scores. Even when a reliability check was made, very few authors reported stability data, which in most studies is more important than internal consistency. Particularly in intervention studies, a posttest score that is stable over some significant time period is essential to the meaningful interpretation of results. While it is inconvenient and occasionally impossible to check stability, there is no excuse for failure to check internal consistency since the necessary data are typically available.

Many authors seem to take it for granted that the instruments they use will yield reliable scores if a high reliability coefficient is attained once. They appear to forget that an instrument may yield reliable scores in one setting or with one population but not another. This is why researchers should accept previous data (as in test manuals) as a sufficient basis for assuming that the scores from a particular test will be reliable only if repeated coefficients are available with populations and settings like those for the study to be conducted. The failure to obtain important treatment outcome differences (in intervention studies) or correlations in much social studies research may well be due to the use of instruments that produce scores of low reliability. It is for this reason that it is especially important to check on the reliability of scores and to report one's findings.

Validity. Many of the outcomes measured in social studies research involve variables for which there is little agreement as to meaning. There are few instruments used by social studies researchers for which a strong case can be made that the scores represent a valid indicator of that which is being measured. Partly this is due to the fact that, as mentioned above, many of the variables of interest to social studies researchers are highly abstract and rarely defined precisely. Attempts at such definition find little agreement within the profession. Even when variables are precisely defined, use of the instrument with a new population casts doubt on prior evidence. It is probably unrealistic to except researchers to conduct an extensive validation of the instrumentation process as a part of every study; nevertheless, some attention should be paid in particular to ensuring that the variables that the instrument is purported to measure are precisely defined.

In less than one fourth of the reports located of social studies research conducted during the last 10 years was any evidence whatsoever presented concerning the validity of scores obtained by using various instruments. When validity checks are conducted, the most common check is that of agreement among judges, although the qualifications of the judges are seldom described. The use of an additional instrument to check validity is rare. In only five (less than 3%) of the studies reviewed for this chapter did the authors utilize an additional instrument to check validity (Bennett, 1984; Betres et. al, 1984; Hahn & Avery, 1985; Kennedy, 1983; and Marker, 1980).

The lack of evidence as to the validity of scores obtained from instruments used continues to be, regrettably, a characteristic of most social studies research. This is especially distressing because the need to check on the validity of scores has been a recurring theme in the literature over the last several years (Shaver & Larkins, 1973; Shaver & Norton, 1980; VanSickle, 1986).

Internal Validity

The concept of internal validity refers primarily to the soundness of a conclusion as to whether the experimental treatment(s) made a difference—that is, actually produced an effect—in a particular study, as opposed to one or more extraneous variables confounding the effect (Campbell & Stanley, 1963,

p. 175). Although the concept of internal validity is particularly applicable to experimental studies, it also applies, with some modification, to other types of quantitative research. When one or more relationships are found to exist among variables, the fundamental question of interest (regardless of the type of study) is whether the relationships are genuine or are an artifact of something else—either other variables or procedural defects in the study.

Campbell and Stanley (1963) list eight different classes of extraneous variables that pose a threat to the internal validity of an experiment if they are not controlled. These are history, differential selection, maturation, testing, instrumentation, statistical regression, mortality, and selection-maturation or other interactions (p. 175). Whereas maturation and regression threats rarely appear in social studies research, the other threats remain a concern as they do not appear to be taken into account and controlled for by many social studies researchers. A few words about each of these threats, therefore, follow.

History. History refers to the possibility of an extraneous event occurring in addition to the experimental variable that possibly affects the outcomes of a study. Some extraneous events are frequently assumed to be unrelated to the outcomes studied—although this assumption is always questionable. Knowledge of the specific nature of an event provides a basis for considering its possible effects. Exposure of only one treatment group to a political speech, for example, might be expected to influence certain attitudes but probably can be dismissed if achievement is the dependent variable.

History is the most difficult of all threats to internal validity to control in social studies research. This is especially true for intrasession history (see Campbell & Stanley, 1963, p. 184). Even random assignment of subjects cannot ensure the same subsequent experience for all groups. Probably the best a researcher can do in experimental studies is to keep a systematic log of known events and perhaps ask subjects to do the same. No discussion of the possibility of a history threat was found in any of the social studies research reports reviewed for this chapter.

Testing. Testing refers to the effect of taking a test upon the scores of subjects on a second testing. Thus, posttest scores may differ from pretest scores as a result of the pretesting (e.g., if subjects develop a test-taking strategy, reflect on ideas or attitudes, look up answers, discuss questions), rather than because of the treatment. A meta-analysis of outcomes from 32 studies, for example, revealed a general elevating effect of pretests on posttests (Willson & Putnam, 1982). There is also the possibility that the treatment may become more (or less) effective as a result of subjects being sensitized by the pretest (i.e., a pretest-treatment interaction). There is some evidence, however, that pretest and sensitization effects are not serious problems when the treatment occurs in normal classrooms and when test taking is part of the daily routine (e.g., see Welch & Walberg, 1970).

Instrumentation. Instrumentation refers to changes in the nature of the instrument, or changes in the data collectors, observers, or scorers. When tests, inventories, or other instruments are used repeatedly, they may be changed (e.g., in the directions given to respondents), and this can affect subsequent responses. This is frequently referred to as instrument *decay*.

A more serious threat in most studies is that resulting from the *characteristics* of the data collectors. There can be little question that the personal attributes of those who administer tests, questionnaires, or interviews can influence the responses of subjects. This is almost never discussed in social studies research reports. Perhaps the reason is that the same data collectors are used for all groups—in which case the danger is avoided—but this should be made clear. Even with one data collector, an interaction between administrator and group is still possible, as when the ethnicity or gender of the administrator matches one group better than the other(s). There also may be an effect on the overall validity of the data, as when a dour administrator depresses the performance of all groups.

Another potential problem with regard to instrumentation is that of data collection and scoring *bias*. In most social studies research, it appears that the researchers themselves collected and/or scored the data. We assume that researchers do not deliberately alter their procedures in order to substantiate hypotheses or establish relationships (if they do, the only protection afforded methodologically is that of replication by other researchers). But unintentional, unconscious bias is a concern. There are many ways in which bias may be introduced in comparison-group studies so as to produce biased results. Directions can be changed; the amount of task clarification can vary; time limits can be varied for different groups; more encouragement can be given to one group than another; the scoring system (if it requires judgment about responses) can be applied to favor certain groups.

One solution to the problem of unintentional bias is to standardize materials and procedures, including the training of data collectors and scorers when necessary. A better solution is *planned ignorance*. Data collectors and scorers should, if possible, be kept ignorant of any information that would bias the results of a study, such as the purpose or hypothesis, and which treatment (or control) groups they are testing, observing, or scoring.

In some studies, the data collectors may become aware of such details if they are deeply involved. This can be avoided by having different data collectors for different treatment groups or for different instruments, by carefully training data collectors to maximize standardization of administration, and by checking on actual administration. Such measures as these complicate research logistics and may not be necessary in a particular study. However, the lack of discussion of these threats in almost all social studies research reports suggests that the researchers may have failed to consider them.

Differential Selection of Experimental and Comparison Groups.
In experimental research, it is essential that the groups to receive differing treatments be identical in all other ways if outcome differences are to be validly ascribed to the treatments. The preferred method of equating groups is generally held to be random assignment of subjects to experimental and comparison groups. Unfortunately, in much social studies research, even when random assignment is used, the groups that are formed are still likely to differ initially because of the sampling error with small *n*'s. When random assignment is not feasible or is questionable due to small *n*'s, two alternatives are possible: (a) the use of a counterbalanced design; and (b) matching on other subject variables or equating groups statistically using ANCOVA. Although less satisfactory than random assignment (because the adequacy of measurement of pertinent variables may be questionable and all relevant variables may not be controlled), it seems that greater efforts could be made by social studies researchers to establish the equivalence of their groups. For a detailed discussion of alternative ways to design studies to control for the possibility of selection bias, see Linn (1984).

Mortality.
Mortality refers to differential loss of subjects from the comparison groups. In experimental research, loss of subjects may bias the results if the loss is not proportional, number-wise or characteristic-wise, for all treatments. Replacement of subjects does not solve the problem, even if done randomly, because those lost may be lost for some reason that makes them different on the dependent variable from those who remain and those who replace them. When loss occurs, it is sometimes possible to argue that no bias is introduced—by showing, for example, that those lost were very similar to those remaining on certain indices (e.g., pretest scores). If very similar numbers of subjects are lost in all treatment groups for similar reasons (e.g., a band field trip), the argument that no systematic bias was introduced is much stronger.

The same problem essentially exists in causal-comparative studies in that the groups compared may, with disproportionate loss of subjects, no longer differ only in the ways the researcher intends. A comparison of the attitude toward school of males and females, for example, could be confounded with such attributes as rebelliousness and respect for authority if more subjects were lost from one group than the other. Loss of subjects also can affect correlational studies since the loss of certain subjects (e.g., very intelligent ones) can affect the nature of the relationship found. When differential loss of subjects occurs in social studies research, this should be pointed out and the possibility of bias discussed.

Interaction Effects.
In an experimental study, there is always the possibility that pretest-posttest differences between the experimental and control groups can be explained away by an interaction effect between such various extraneous factors as history, maturation, or testing and any specific selection differences between the experimental and control groups. This is particularly true when intact classes are used (as is almost always the case in school-based experimental research) and the classes differ initially in various ways (e.g., age, prior experience, physical or mental ability). The possibility of such interaction effects in experimental studies has not, to date, been given attention by social studies researchers.

In addition to the threats to internal validity discussed above, there are four additional factors that social studies researchers need to attend to more regularly. They are the setting in which a study takes place, the attitude of the subjects involved in the study, the characteristics and/or behavior of the implementers of the treatment, and the characteristics of the subjects in correlational and causal-comparative studies.

Setting. The setting in which treatments are given or in which data are collected might also, at times, provide an alternative explanation for the outcomes of a study. By *setting* is meant the environment—in its entirety. The only way to ensure against this problem is to make sure that the setting is the same for all treatments or data collections. A standardized setting is seldom the case in social studies research, although it might become more common if greater attention were paid to the problem. When it is not the case, variations in setting should at least be examined for differences that could affect results. In experimental studies, for example, treatments are often presented in different classrooms or schools. These may differ in terms of physical characteristics (e.g., sound, lighting, space allocation) and/or in terms of available resources (personnel, supplies, outside-of-school resources). In a study in which performance on different tasks is to be correlated, some subjects may be tested under optimum conditions and others under difficult conditions, thereby creating poor performance on the tasks for the latter group of subjects.

Attitude of Subjects. Subject attitude pertains to the way in which subjects may change during an experimental study simply because they are (or are not) part of a special activity—the research study. The famous Hawthorne effect refers to the tendency of subjects to perform better or in accordance with expectations after being identified as "special," presumably because of the extra attention or status accorded them. Likewise, the John Henry effect refers to the fact that the control group may perform better because they realize they are *not* part of the study and want to do as well as the experimental-group subjects. Or, to the contrary, a control group may experience a demoralization effect upon learning that they are not receiving the experimental treatment. One solution for these threats is to provide a placebo treatment for the control group (see Borg, 1984). Another possibility is to keep the control and experimental groups unaware that there is an experiment going on, although this is usually difficult to do.

Implementer Characteristics and/or Behavior. Whenever treatments are administered by different persons, there is the possibility that the implementers rather than, or in addition to, the treatments are responsible for differential results. Although it is possible to control this threat by randomly assigning implementers to treatments, the number of implementers (and groups) needed renders this solution generally unacceptable. Where feasible, counterbalancing implementers is probably the best control, although in some cases this may not be possible—if, for example, teachers are unwilling or unable to use both methods. Social studies researchers should give careful thought to the method of implementation of the experimental treatment, and train implementers to administer treatments carefully according to predetermined specifications. Checking by the use of observers or other means to ensure that the treatment is implemented as intended seems essential.

Subject Characteristics in Correlational Studies. Social studies researchers who do correlational research also should consider and, if possible, control for other variables that might account for observed relationships. A researcher investigating the relationship between educational level and political attitude, for example, should be expected to control for parental economic status, because it is a probable cause of each. Such control might involve, for example, the measurement of extraneous variable(s) for each subject for use in partial correlation.

Information. Many of the threats to internal validity that were identified by Campbell and Stanley (1963; also see Cook and Campbell, 1979) are frequently present in social studies research. It is difficult to say with certainty, however, because so little information is provided in this regard in most reports. The lack of details concerning conditions (e.g., settings, data-collection procedures, time) in many studies, however, makes the likelihood of one or more of these threats probable. To their credit, a few authors discussed in their reports the likelihood of particular threats—a data collection or scoring bias (Burts et al., 1985; Hahn & Avery, 1985; VanSickle & Ehman, 1981); a Hawthorne effect (Grant & Napier, 1981); or an implementation threat (VanSickle & Ehman, 1981). Perhaps a desirable requirement in all reports of social studies research in the future would be for the investigator to indicate what alternative explanations for findings have been considered, and which have been rejected and why, as was done by Larkins and McKinney (1982).

External Validity

External validity refers to the question of generalizability. To what populations, settings, treatments, and/or outcomes can a particular effect be generalized (Campbell & Stanley, 1963)? Many things can limit external validity. The characteristics or behavior of the experimenter, the novelty of the treatment, the particular instruments used, the time of measurement, the administration of more than one treatment, the subjects' perception of the treatment(s), the use of a pretest, all can have an effect (Bracht & Glass, 1968). Historically, however, the most attention has been paid to the population of subjects to which results are generalizable. In less than 10% of the studies reviewed for this chapter, generalizations were made to appropriate target populations of subjects. In 35%, the authors generalized to indefensible target populations. In 30%, there was no mention of the intended target population. On the positive side, some 25% did include appropriate cautions on population generalizability.

The nature of the subject samples used in social studies research places serious limitations on any attempt to generalize research findings. In the main, social studies researchers collect data from one of four kinds of samples: (1) students in social studies classes (e.g., Glenn & Ellis, 1982; McKenzie & Sawyer, 1986; Yoho, 1986); (2) teachers in schools (e.g., Farmer, 1983; Ochoa, 1981; Passe, 1988; Tixier & Dick, 1987); (3) social studies supervisors, social studies methods professors, or other social studies professionals (e.g., Jantz et al., 1985; Tiou & Bennett, 1982; Turner, 1982); and (4) textbooks (e.g., Hahn & Blankenship, 1983; Stanley, 1984; White, 1988). Convenience samples, to which tests of statistical significance cannot justifiably be applied for population inferences, remain the norm, with truly random samples being almost never found. Less than 5% of all studies reviewed for this chapter involved the use of random samples. Two of these were indeed random, but from trivial accessible populations—students in two high schools in the midwest (Schug, Todd, & Beery 1984) and students in two high schools in the northeast (Long, 1980). Three were survey studies in which the sample was randomly selected, but the return rates destroyed the claim of randomness for the actual sample (Farmer, 1983; Hahn, 1985; Nelson, 1984). The random sample utilized in a seventh study consisted of only six classrooms in a particular school district (Curtis, 1983). Admittedly, random samples are difficult, and often costly, to obtain. In most studies, the realities of school life, of response failure, or of data collection make true random selection virtually impossible.

One way to help the profession determine the applicability of findings from a particular study to other populations, therefore, would be for researchers to describe the nature of the sample in greater detail. The difficulty with this suggestion lies in deciding which variables to describe. There is no consensus within the profession that certain demographics (e.g., age, gender, ethnicity, ability level, years of experience, philosophical orientation, teaching style) should always be reported. In addition, data on some variables (e.g., socioeconomic status) are notoriously difficult to obtain. One possibility, however, would be for researchers to describe those characteristics that (based on previous research, logic, or prior experience) appear to be related to the variables of interest in the study, and then provide comparison data on these variables for their sample(s) and the appropriate population(s) to which they think the results would apply.

The description of the sample in almost all reports of social studies research leaves much to be desired. Descriptions are frequently couched in overly general, often vague terms. Specificity is more the exception than the rule. In one survey study, for example, questionnaires were obtained from 74 social studies teachers in two Southeastern states. No information whatsoever (e.g., age, experience, subjects taught, ability level of classes) was given on these teachers. We are told only that they were "secondary teachers, grade 8 through 12, [and] represented thirteen schools and seven different school divisions" (Ball, Doss, & Dewalt, 1986). Similar overly general descriptions of samples can be found in many other surveys by social studies researchers (e.g., Blaga & Nielsen, 1983; Hahn, 1985; Masters, 1984; Russell & Morrow, 1986).

When descriptions of the samples in a study are provided, usually no more than one or two characteristics (most often gender and grade level) of the subjects are provided. This is an unfortunate omission because information about other variables relevant to the outcomes of a particular study (e.g., age, ethnicity, ability level, size of school, IQ) is often not difficult to obtain and is helpful in determining external validity. There are many characteristics, of course, that are irrelevant to a particular study (i.e., unlikely to have an effect on the outcomes), and hence need not be reported; but many others can shed considerable light about the nature of the sample and help interested others gauge the applicability of the results of the study to their situations.

Furthermore, descriptors frequently are not defined. In one study, for example, students in the sample were described as coming from "upper-lower to lower-middle-class" families without any definition by the researchers as to what was meant by those terms (Ford & McKinney, 1986). In another, the subjects were students in three average-level United States history classes, yet the term *average* was never defined (Eddinger, 1985). The use of vague, overly general descriptors and the provision of only a limited number of sample characteristics are common occurrences in social studies research and make the applicability of specific results to other populations and settings difficult, if not impossible, to determine.

Examples of reports in which the researchers provided a greater-than-usual number of sample descriptors, however, can be found in Haladyna et al. (1982a, 1982b) and Kleg et al. (1986). In the former, the authors provided a breakdown of the sample by grade level, gender, family ethnicity, family mobility, socioeconomic status, average amount of TV viewing, and self-reported school absence, each of which was related to the hypothesis of the study. In the latter, the authors provided a breakdown by age, sex, race, religion, mean IQ scores, and mean SAT percentiles in order to show the comparability of the experimental and control groups.

Equally important to the issue of population generalizability is that of ecological generalizability. This refers to generalization to settings (environments) other than those found in the study (e.g., to different subject matters, materials, physical conditions). Some authors, for example, generalized inappropriately to other subject areas or content (Barnes & Curlette, 1985; Glenn & Ellis, 1982; Marker, 1980; McKenzie & Sawyer, 1986; Stahl, 1981). Of these, two implied that a method was generally effective, despite the fact that only one teacher implemented the method being studied (Barnes & Curlette, 1985; Glenn & Ellis, 1982). In another report, the author generalized to innovations in general, although only social studies innovations were studied (Marker, 1980).

Several authors, however, are to be commended for suggesting caution in generalizing beyond the ecological boundaries of their study. Various researchers cautioned specifically against generalizing to other implementers or researchers (Blankenship, 1983; Burts et al., 1985; Grant & Napier, 1981; Hahn & Avery, 1985, McKinney, Larkins & Burts, 1984); to other content areas (Grant & Napier, 1981; Stanley, Charlesworth, & Ringuest, 1985; Tyo, 1980); to different instructional time periods (Blankenship, 1983; Burts et al., 1985; Hahn & Avery, 1985); to different settings (Burts et al., 1985; Stanley et al., 1985); to other methods of instruction (McGowan, 1984; McKinney, Larkins, & Burts, 1984); and to other times of the year (Grant & Napier, 1981).

The vast majority of current social studies research reports, however, contain no reference whatsoever to ecological characteristics or generalizability. The importance of this matter seems not to have yet been fully appreciated by the social studies research community.

Although both internal and external validity are important, increasing the one may often result in jeopardizing the other.

Internal validity, however, is an absolute prerequisite to external validity. Campbell and Stanley (1963) call it the sine qua non (p. 175). A study that lacks internal validity cannot have external validity! A study that is internally valid, however, may still not be externally valid. The design of research strong in both types of validity, of course, is the ideal.

Analysis of Data

The statistical analysis of data is one of the hallmarks of the quantitative approach. Generally speaking, descriptive statistics are used appropriately by social studies researchers, although their interpretation is occasionally suspect—as in one study where the authors made much of the fact that the addition of a third predictor variable increased predicted variance from 42% to 43%—a 1% gain (O'Brien et al., 1985)! Unfortunately, the use of inferential statistics is often inappropriate or even incorrect, as in the interpretation of statistical significance. This remains one of the most serious areas of weakness in much social studies research.

Many social studies researchers appear to be confused about the meaning of statistical significance. A finding of statistical significance, as reflected in the reporting of a p value (such as $p = .05$), simply means statistical *rareness* (Carver, 1978). A p value only tells us the proportion of the time that we could be expect to find a difference (or a relationship) that large or larger from random samples of the same size taken from the same population, assuming no difference (or relationship) exists within that population. It does not tell us the probability that the null hypothesis is true, that the research hypothesis is true, or that the results of a particular study will replicate (Carver, 1978).

When a result is found to be statistically significant, this only means that it is unlikely that such a result would occur due to sampling error. When a test of statistical significance reveals that an obtained correlation, for example, is statistically significant, this means it is unlikely that such a correlation would occur when no correlation exists in the population from which the random sample of scores to be correlated was selected. It does not mean that such a correlation is educationally or practically important (see Hays, 1981). Similar logic applies to the finding of a statistically significant difference between the means of two samples. Such a finding tells us only that such a difference is unlikely, given random samples of a particular size and no difference between the means of the two populations from which the samples were selected. Yet many researchers continue to imply that statistically significant results are important in their own right.

The author of one correlational study, for example, reported an r of .14 between historical understanding scores and information processing capacity scores (Kennedy, 1983). He then went on to suggest that the latter is a factor influencing the former, a highly questionable assumption in any event, but especially on the basis of a correlation of this size. A correlation of .14 yields a coefficient of determination (r^2) of only .02, indicating that the scores on these two variables have only two percent of their variance in common! In another study, the author reported a correlation coefficient of .22 between "positive interracial contact" and "satisfaction with university life" for African-American female students (Bennett, 1984). Shared variance here is only .05! In both cases, the authors made note of these small correlations because they were statistically significant. While a case can sometimes be made for the importance of correlations of this magnitude in testing theory, in most cases they are not very important. In any case, the authors of these studies did not discuss the (possible) educational (as opposed to statistical) importance of these correlations.

Far more important than whether or not a result is statistically significant is the *size* (i.e., the magnitude) of the result (i.e., the effect size). A result that is actually quite small may be statistically significant, whereas a fairly large result can be statistically nonsignificant, depending on the size of the sample involved. If a sample is large enough, even miniscule results can show up as statistically significant.

In a recent quasi-experimental study, for example, the authors concluded that a single term of economics instruction had a statistically significant effect on certain economic attitudes of ninth-grade students. Using ANCOVA, the researchers found that students exposed to such a course (the experimental group) were more supportive of the American economic system, showed more trust in business, expressed more emphatic rejection of alienation items, were more likely to feel that the treatment of workers is fair, and were less likely to be critical of the distributive status quo (Ingels & O'Brien, 1988). The actual difference between experimental and control groups on each of these items (on a scale of 1 to 7, with 1 = strongly disagreeing with, and 7 = strongly agreeing with, scale values), however, was only .27, .16, .14, .16, and .15 of a point, respectively. Although the authors admitted that these differences are not large in absolute magnitude, they went on to say that they "seem impressive as outcomes of a single term of instruction" (p. 285).

By way of contrast, the authors of another quasi-experimental study concluded, on the basis of nonsignificant tests, that the independent variable (being exposed to the curriculum, Man: A Course of Study) had no effect on the attitudes of fourth-grade students, even though the students in the experimental group became slightly more tolerant of certain kinds of activities than did the control group (Barnes, Stallings, & Rivner, 1981). Although the obtained result was not statistically significant, the *absolute* difference in means between the experimental and control groups was actually quite large. Estimation of the standard deviation of change scores for the comparison group suggested a standardized mean difference of .6 to .7, an impressive difference that should have been discussed.

What counts as a large result, of course, is a matter of judgment. Cohen (1988) has described a large effect size as one that is "grossly perceptible" (p. 27) and presents as an example the difference in mean IQ between Ph.D. holders and typical college freshmen. A medium effect size is one that is large enough to be "visible to the naked eye in the course of normal experience" (p. 26). An example of a medium effect size would be the average IQ difference between clerical and semi-skilled workers. A small effect size is one that is not likely to be observable without high-quality measurement and research strategies.

An example of a small effect size would be the difference in mean IQ between twins and nontwins.

Although Cohen's definitions are still somewhat vague, they do provide some idea of how to go about differentiating important from unimportant results. Of greater help, perhaps, would be comparisons of the magnitude of an obtained result with the magnitude of results obtained on the same dependent variable by other groups (especially extreme groups) known to the researcher or reported in the literature. For example, if an experimental group of 11th-grade U.S. history students achieves a mean posttest score (on a test of historical understanding) similar to that of college sophomores majoring in history, whereas a comparison group's mean posttest score is similar to that of 11th-grade U.S. history students in general, this could constitute grounds for concluding that the difference between the experimental and control groups is an important one.

In all of the experimental, quasi-experimental, and correlational studies that were reviewed for this chapter, and in slightly more than half of the survey studies, the authors utilized one or more tests of statistical significance (a t test, an F test, or a chi-square test), despite violation of the fundamental assumption of random sampling. In almost all of these instances, at least some statistically significant results were reported. Most of the time, however, the researchers who conducted experimental or quasi-experimental studies did not present any data on the magnitude of the obtained result, nor discuss its importance in any practical or educational sense, although there were some notable exceptions (e.g., see Barnes & Curlette, 1985; Curtis & Shaver, 1980; 1981; Gilmore & McKinney, 1986; LeSourd, 1985; McKinney, Peddicord, Davis, Richmond, & McKinney, 1987; Powell & Powell, 1984).

In addition to (or perhaps in place of) the reporting of a statistically significant finding (as an indication of important differences) more social studies researchers might consider reporting the magnitude of the obtained result. There are various ways to measure and report an effect sizes, including absolute differences, eta^2, omega^2, Cohen's d, Glass's Δ, and Hedges g (see Cohen, 1988; Cooper, 1984; Glass, McGaw, & Smith, 1981; Rosenthal, 1984). The educational significance of obtained results could then be discussed by comparing the magnitude of any obtained results with similar results obtained by known groups, or against some other standard of importance.

In studies in which the results are found to be statistically nonsignificant, the possibility remains that there actually was an important outcome, but the tests used did not possess sufficient power to detect that result. The term *statistical power* refers to the probability that application of a statistical test will correctly lead to rejection of a false null hypothesis, and is expressed in the form of a decimal fraction (1 minus the probability of a Type II error). Cohen (1988) has recommended that studies be designed to have at least a .80 level of statistical power. Van-Sickle (1983) analyzed a total of 33 instances of social studies research in terms of statistical power and found that none of them had sufficient power (using Cohen's criterion of .80) to detect a small effect size (d = .20) and only 42% had sufficient power to detect a medium effect size (d = .50). As VanSickle (1983) suggested, this is an important consideration, since large effect sizes are rarely observed in social studies research.

When a test of statistical significance is appropriate, the actual probability of the obtained result might be reported (see Stallings, 1985) because it makes little sense, for example, to treat p = .04 as importantly different from p = .06. Furthermore, the power of the statistical test (the probability of rejecting a false null hypothesis), as well as the effect size and the sample size necessary to achieve a desired level of power, should be reported. Finally, the number of times a study has been replicated (see below) and how many times the same or larger result has been obtained, should also be reported.

Replication of Studies

The replication of previous or related work, so common in the natural sciences, has never become widespread among social studies researchers. Examples of replicated studies remain few in the social studies literature, as many observers have noted (Jantz & Klawitter, 1985; Leming, 1985; Shaver & Norton, 1980; Wallen & Fraenkel, 1988).

One reason for this failing, undoubtedly, is the greater difficulty of data collection in social studies research. Another may be a lesser tendency for researchers to define for themselves a definite research focus. Third, there may be a (probably justifiable) fear that positive results will not be replicated.

Several commentators have noted that social studies researchers do not build upon previous work (Leming, 1985; Shaver & Norton, 1980; Stanley, 1985a). For whatever reason, most of the authors of currently published social studies research appear to have conducted only a single study, or if they have conducted more than one, to have conducted them on a variety of unrelated topics. Similar, or related, work of others often seems to be ignored (Stanley, 1985a). There are a few notable exceptions, however, as can be seen in certain experimental studies on concept attainment (Gilmore & McKinney, 1986; McKinney, 1985; McKinney, Burts, Ford, & Gilmore, 1987; McKinney, Gilmore, Peddicord, & McCallum, 1987; McKinney, Larkins, Ford, & Davis, 1983; McKinney, Larkins, Peddicord, & Ford, 1984; McKinney, Peddicord, Davis, Richmond, & McKinney, 1987; Park, 1984; Yoho, 1986); on teacher enthusiasm (Larkins & McKinney, 1982; McKinney & Larkins, 1982; McKinney, Larkins, & Burts, 1984); on aptitude-treatment interactions in teaching analysis of public issues (Oliver & Shaver, 1966/1974; Shaver, 1985) and in a few correlational and survey investigations of the relationships between classroom environment and student attitudes toward social studies (Haladyna, et al., 1982a, 1982b; McGowan, 1984; Schug et al., 1984).

Serious consideration should be given to a requirement that studies (not necessarily results) be replicated at least once before publication. As Bauernfeind (1968) pointed out over 20 years ago, an investigator in the natural sciences may repeat an experiment 10 or 20 times, cross-comparing results, before he or she publishes any findings (p. 126).

Replication is even more important in social studies research than it is in the physical sciences. It is more difficult to control threats to internal and external validity in social studies research than in research in the physical or biological sciences. The necessity for replication of studies under systematically altered and described conditions is further supported by the increasing recognition that it is impossible to sample randomly across all of the possible variations of conditions that are important (Cook & Campbell, 1979).

A Few Comments About Surveys

Survey studies dealing with some aspect of social studies education deserve a few special words of comment, if for no other reason than that they are one of the more common types of research. As mentioned earlier, most surveys involve mailed questionnaires to either social studies supervisors, teacher educators, or classroom teachers. Rarely are students surveyed (but see Schug et al., 1984). Surveys are exempt from some, but not all, of the criticisms discussed above.

Perhaps the most common weakness in survey research in social studies is that the authors frequently have specified a target sample much larger than the sample actually obtained. Return rates in many surveys were sufficiently low so as to destroy any claim of randomness that the authors might make. As a result, external validity was often far more limited than the authors, seemingly, were willing to admit, as evidenced by the misleading claims such as that the results showed that "teachers agreed" or "supervisors believed." More justified statements, limited to the nature of the data-producing sample, in many cases are strikingly absent. One study, for example, to describe differences in interest in the social science disciplines between males and females, was based on a sample from only one area in the South (McTeer, 1979). Another, involving a description of opinions regarding effects of policies on research with human subjects, was based on a volunteer sample of "interested" faculty members (Turner, 1982). Yet a third report of teacher perceptions concerning the nature of discipline problems was based on teachers in only one school in a low-income neigh-

borhood where discipline was considered a major problem (Tlou & Bennett, 1983). And for still a fourth, to describe the social action activities of social studies educators, a sample of volunteer respondents was used (Nelson, 1984). In each of these studies, the nature of the sample virtually required the researchers to limit their conclusions to only the individuals surveyed rather than implying that the findings transcended the particular samples involved.

CONCLUSION

The quality of quantitative research in social studies education continues to be, regrettably, less than what one might hope for. Many of the weaknesses identified in the past by other reviewers persist today. Although considerable progress has been made by individual researchers in replicating work, verifying independent variables, exercising care in generalizing only to appropriate populations, and acknowledging limitations, there is still much room for improvement. Too many important questions remain unpursued. Too many variables continue to be vaguely defined. Too seldom are reliability and validity checks performed. Too seldom are threats to internal validity checked. Too often are statistical inference tests used inappropriately or incorrectly. Too rarely are individual studies replicated in different settings, with different samples, and under different conditions.

On the bright side, some studies are quite well done, with the authors investigating important topics, using sophisticated research designs, and providing meaningful and insightful discussions of results. Nevertheless, too many researchers still continue to conduct studies that could be markedly improved with a little more thought and effort beforehand. Much work remains if the profession is to improve the quality of the quantitative research its members conduct.

References

Ahlawat, K. S., Saadeh, J. A., Bader, Q. H., & Khalifeh, G. (1988). An investigation of the use of behavioral objectives in Jordanian social studies classrooms. *Theory and Research in Social Education, 16*(3), 227–243.

Alvermann, D. E., Boothby, P. R., & Wolfe, J. (1984). The effect of graphic organizer instruction on fourth graders' comprehension of social studies text. *Journal of Social Studies Research, 8*(1), 13–221.

American Psychological Association. (1985) *Standards for educational and psychological testing.* Washington, DC: Author.

Armento, B. J. (1986). Research on teaching social studies. In M. C. Wittrock (Ed.), *Handbook of research on teaching* (3rd ed., pp. 942–951). New York: Macmillan.

Ball, D. W., Doss, A. R., & Dewalt, M. W. (1986). Level of teacher objectives and their classroom tests: Match or mismatch. *Journal of Social Studies Research, 10*(2), 27–30.

Barnes, B. R., & Curlette, W. L. (1985). Effects of instruction on teachers' global-mindedness and patriotism. *Theory and Research in Social Education, 13*(1), 43–49.

Barnes, B., Stallings, W., & Rivner, R. (1981). Are the critics right about MACOS? *Theory and Research in Social Education, 9*(1), 35–44.

Barth, J. L., & Sommersdorf, D. L. (1981). A study of preservice teachers' change in attitude measured by Barth/Shermis social studies preference scale. *Journal of Social Studies Research, 5*(2), 64–68.

Bauernfeind, R. H. (1968). The need for replication in educational research. *Phi Delta Kappan, 50*(2), 126–128.

Beck, W. W. (1979). Utilizing an interdisciplinary "teacher centered" model in developing individual social studies materials. *Journal of Social Studies Research, 3*(1), 1–7.

Beem, A. L., & Brugman, D. (1986). The effects of values development lessons on pupils' well-being, pleasure in school, mutual relationships, and on pupils' valuational behavior during classroom dialogues. *Theory and Research in Social Education, 14*(2), 97–112.

Bennett, C. (1984). Interracial contact experience and attrition among black undergraduates at a predominantly white university. *Theory and Research in Social Education, 12*(2), 19–48.

Bennett, C. T., Burbach, H. J., & Cruz, J. (1984). A conceptual framework for selecting and evaluating multicultural educational materials. *Journal of Social Studies Research, 8*(2), 39–52.

Betres, J, Zajano, M., & Gumieniak, P. (1984). Cognitive style, teacher methods, and concept attainment in social studies. *Theory and Research in Social Education, 12*(2), 1–18.

Blaga, J. L., & Nielsen, L. E. (1983). The status of state history instruction. *Journal of Social Studies Research, 7*(1), 45–57.

Blankenship, G., Jr. (1983). The use of visual diagrams with eighth grade social studies students at four ability levels. *Journal of Social Studies Research, 7*(1), 23–44.

Borg, W. R. (1984). Dealing with threats to internal validity that randomization does not rule out. *Educational Researcher, 12,* 11–14.

Borg, W. R., & Gall, M. D. (1983). *Educational research: An introduction.* New York: Longman.

Bracht, G. H., & Glass, G. V. (1968). The external validity of experiments. *American Educational Research Journal, 5*(4), 437–474.

Burts, D. C., McKinney, C. W., & Burts, B. L. (1985). Effects of teacher enthusiasm on three- and four-year-old children's acquisition of four concepts. *Theory and Research in Social Education, 13*(1), 19–30.

Campbell, D. T., & Stanley, J. C. (1963). Experimental and quasi-experimental designs for research on teaching. In N. L. Gage (Ed.). *Handbook of research on teaching* (pp. 171–246). Chicago: Rand McNally.

Carver, R. P. (1978). The case against statistical significance testing. *Harvard educational review, 48*(3), 378–399.

Cohen, J. (1988). *Statistical power analysis for the behavioral sciences* (2nd ed.). Hillsdale, NJ: Lawrence Erlbaum Associates.

Cook, T. D., & Campbell, D. T. (1979). *Quasi-experimentation: Design and analysis issues for field settings.* Boston: Houghton-Mifflin.

Cooper, H. M. (1984). *The integrative research review: A systematic approach.* Beverly Hills, CA: Sage.

Cornbleth, C. (1982). Citizenship education. In H. E. Mitzel, (Ed.). *Encyclopedia of educational research* (5th ed., pp. 259–265). New York: Macmillan.

Curtis, C. K. (1983). Relationships among certain citizenship variables. *Journal of Social Studies Research, 7*(2), 18–28.

Curtis, C. K., & Shaver, J. P. (1980). Slow learners and the study of contemporary problems. *Social Education, 44*(4), 302–309.

Curtis, C. K., & Shaver, J. P. (1981). Improving slow learners' self-esteem in secondary social studies classes. *Journal of Educational Research, 74*(4), 216–223.

Daily, A. R. (1983). Educational attainment and political attitudes: An effect of schools or schooling? *Theory and Research in Social Education, 11*(2), 35–52.

Eddinger, S. S. (1985). The effect of different questioning sequences on achievement in high school social studies. *Journal of Social Studies Research, 9*(1), 17–29.

Ehman, L. H., & Hahn, C. L. (1981). Contributions of research to social studies education. In H. D. Mehlinger & O. L. Davis, Jr. (eds.). *The social studies. Eightieth yearbook of the National Society for the Study of Education,* (Part II, pp. 60–81). Chicago: National Society for the Study of Education.

Evans, R. W. (1988). Lessons from history: Teacher and student conceptions of the meaning of history. *Theory and Research in Social Education, 16*(3), 203–226.

Eyler, J. (1982). A test of a model relating political attitudes to participation in high school activities. *Theory and Research in Social Education, 10*(1), 43–62.

Farmer, R. (1983). Elementary social studies teacher education: Some points to ponder. *Journal of Social Studies Research, 7*(2), 29–36.

Ferguson, P. (1986). The effects of teaching microcomputer programming skills to social studies teachers. *Journal of Social Studies Research, 10*(1), 53–56.

Firestone, W. A. (1987). Meaning in method: The rhetoric of quantitative and qualitative research. *Educational Researcher, 16*(7), 16–21.

Ford, M. J., & McKinney, C. W. (1986). The effects of recycling and response on the acquisition of social studies concepts. *Theory and Research in Social Education, 14*(1), 21–34.

Fouts, J. T. (1987). High school social studies classroom environments and attitudes: A cluster analysis approach. *Theory and Research in Social Education, 15*(2), 105–114.

Fraenkel, J. R., & Wallen, N. E. (1988). *Toward improving research in social studies education.* Monograph #1. Boulder, CO: Social Science Education Consortium.

Gay, L. R. (1987). *Educational research: Competencies for analysis and application* (3rd ed.). Columbus, OH: Merrill.

Gilmore, A. G., & McKinney, C. W. (1986). The effects of student questions and teacher questions on concept acquisition. *Theory and Research in Social Education, 14,*(3), 225–244.

Glass, G., McGraw, B., & Smith, M. (1981). *Meta-analysis in social research.* Beverly Hills, CA: Sage.

Glenn, A. D., & Ellis, A. K. (1982). Direct and indirect methods of teaching problem solving to elementary school children. *Social Education 46,*(2), 134–136.

Grant, E. T., & Napier, J. D. (1981). Comparing an aesthetic and a political approach to teaching world history. *Social Education, 45*(5), 372–375.

Gronlund, N. E. (1988). *How to construct achievement tests* (4th ed.). Englewood Cliffs, NJ: Prentice-Hall.

Guskey, T. R. (1981). The relationship of affect toward teaching and teaching self-concept to responsibility for student achievement. *Journal of Social Studies Research, 5*(2), 69–74.

Guyton, E. M. (1988). Critical thinking and political participation: Development and assessment of a causal model. *Theory and Research in Social Education, 16*(1), 23–49.

Hahn, C. L. (1985). The diffusion of an innovation: A case study of one social studies program. *Journal of Social Studies Research, 9*(2), 26–39.

Hahn, C. L., & Avery, P. G. (1985). Effect of value analysis discussions on students' political attitudes and reading comprehension. *Theory and Research in Social Education, 13*(2), 47–60.

Hahn, C. L., & Blankenship, G. (1983). Women and economic textbooks. *Theory and Research in Social Education, 11*(3), 67–76.

Haladyna, T., Shaughnessy, J., & Redsun, A. (1982a). Correlates of attitude toward the social studies. *Theory and Research in Social Education, 10*(1), 1–26.

Haladyna, T., Shaughnessy, J., & Redsun, A. (1982b). Relations of student, teacher, and learning environment variables to attitudes toward social studies. *Journal of Social Studies Research, 6*(2), 36–44.

Hays, W. L. (1981). *Statistics* (3rd ed.). New York: CBS College Publishing.

Hepburn, M. A., & Dahler, A. (1985). An overview of social studies dissertations, 1977–1982. *Theory and Research in Social Education, 13*(2), 73–82.

Howe, K. R. (1985). Two dogmas of educational research. *Educational Researcher, 14*(8), 10–18.

Hunkins, F. P., Ehman, L. H., Hahn, C. L., Martorella, P. H., & Tucker, J. L. (1977). *Review of research in social studies education: 1970–1975.* Washington, DC: National Council for the Social Studies.

Ingels, S. J., & O'Brien, M. U. (1988). The effects of economics instruction in early adolescence. *Theory and Research in Social Education, 16*(4), 279–294.

Jackstadt, S. L., & Brennan, J. M. (1983). Economic knowledge and high school student attitudes toward the american economic system, business, and labor unions. *Theory and Research in Social Education, 11*(3), 1–16.

Jantz, R. K., & Klawitter, K. (1985). Early childhood/elementary social studies: A review of recent research. In W. B. Stanley (Ed.)., *Review of research in social studies education: 1976–1983* (pp. 65–122). Washington, DC: National Council for the Social Studies.

Jantz, R. K., Weaver, V. P., Cirrincione, J. M., & Farrell, R. T. (1985). Inquiry and curriculum change: Perceptions of school and college/university faculty. *Theory and Research in Social Education, 13,*(2), 61–72.

Kennedy, K. J. (1983). Assessing the relationship between information processing capacity and historical understanding. *Theory and Research in Social Education, 11*(2), 1–22.

Kerlinger, F. N. (1986). *Foundations of behavioral research* (4th ed.). New York: Holt, Rinehart & Winston.

Kingston, P. W., & Bennett, C. T. (1986). Improving high school social studies: Advice from the colleges. *Theory and Research in Social Education, 14*(1), 35–50.

Kirman, J. M. (1984). A new elementary level map skill: Landsat "Band 5" satellite images. *Social Education, 48*(3), 191–194.

Kleg, M., Karabinus, R., & Carter, T. (1986). Direct concept instruction in U.S. History. *Journal of Social Studies Research, 10*(2), 1–12.

Larkins, A. G., & McKinney, C. W. (1982). Two studies of the effects of teacher enthusiasm on the social studies achievement of seventh grade students. *Theory and Research in Social Education, 10*(1), 27–41.

Larkins, A. G., & McKinney, C. W. (1983). Reviews of dissertations in social studies: 1980. *Journal of Social Studies Research Monographs* (1).

Leming, J. S. (1985). Research on social studies curriculum and instruction; Iinterventions and outcomes in the socio-moral domain. In W. B. Stanley (Ed.)., *Review of research in social studies education: 1976–1983* (pp. 123–213). Washington, DC: National Council for the Social Studies.

LeSourd, S. J. (1984). An exploratory comparison of two methods for assessing teacher attitudes toward instructional strategies. *Theory and Research in Social Education, 12*(1), 31–41.

LeSourd, S. J. (1985). Using text structure to improve social science concept attainment. *Journal of Social Studies Research, 9*(2), 1–14.

Levstik, L. (1986). The relationship between historical response and narrative in a sixth-grade classroom. *Theory and Research in Social Education, 14*(1), 1–20.

Linn, R. L. (1986). Quantitative methods in research on teaching. In M. C. Wittrock (Ed.), *Handbook of Research on Teaching* (3rd ed., pp. 92–118). New York: Macmillan.

Long, S. (1980). Urban adolescents and the political system: Dimensions of disaffection. *Theory and Research in Social Education, 8*(1), 31–44.

Maddocks, W. H., & Smith, L. R. (1986). The effects of student IQ and programmed instruction frame length on social studies achievement. *Journal of Social Studies Research, 10*(1), 40–51.

Marker, G. W. (1980). Why schools abandon "new social studies" materials. *Theory and Research in Social Education, 7*(4), 35–57.

Martorella, P. H. (1977). Research on social studies learning and instruction: Cognition. *Review of research in social studies education: 1970–1975* (pp. 15–54). Washington, DC: National Council for the Social Studies.

Masters, P. E., Jr., (1984). Political socialization in an international city: The case of Atlanta. *Journal of Social Studies Research, 8*(2), 17–38.

McGowan, T. M. (1984). Does methodology make a difference? A comparison of instructional practices of teacher and student attitudes toward social studies. *Journal of Social Studies Research, 8*(1), 22–39.

McKenzie, G. R., & Sawyer, J. (1986). Effects of test-like practice and mnemonics on learning geographic facts. *Theory and Research in Social Education, 14*(3), 201–210.

McKinney, C. W. (1985). A comparison of the effects of a definition, examples and nonexamples on student acquisition of the concept of "transfer propaganda." *Social Education, 49*(1), 66–70.

McKinney, C. W., Burts, D. C., Ford, M. J., & Gilmore, A. C. (1987). The effects of ordinary and coordinate concept nonexamples on first-grade students' acquisition of three coordinate concepts. *Theory and Research in Social Education, 15*(1), 45–50

McKinney, C. W., Gilmore, A. C., Peddicord, H. Q., & McCallum, R. S. (1987). Effects of a best example and critical attributes on prototype formation in the acquistion of a concept. *Theory and Research in Social Education, 15*(3), 189–201.

McKinney, C. W., & Larkins, A. G. (1982). Effects of high, normal, and low teacher enthusiasm on secondary social studies achievement. *Social Education, 46*(4), 290–292.

McKinney, C. W., Larkins, A. G., and Burts, D. C. (1984). Effects of overt teacher enthusiasm on first-graders acquisition of three concepts. *Theory and Research in Social Education, 11*(4), 15–24.

McKinney, C. W., Larkins, A. G., Ford, M. J., & Davis, J. C. (1983). The effectiveness of three methods of teaching social studies concepts to fourth-grade students: An aptitude-treatment interaction study. *American Educational Research Journal, 20,* 663–670.

McKinney, C. W., Larkins, A. G., Peddicord, H. Q., & Ford, M. J. (1984). The effectiveness of three methods of teaching social studies concepts to sixth-grade students. *Journal of Educational Research, 78,* 35–39.

McKinney, C. W., Peddicord, H. Q., Davis, J. C., Richmond, M. G., & McKinney, K. C. (1987). Effects of best examples, critical attributes, definitions, and practice on concept acquisition and prototype formation. *Journal of Social Studies Research, 11*(2), 1–14.

McTeer, J. H. (1979). Sex differences in students' interest in certain discipline areas of the social studies. *Journal of Social Studies Research, 3*(2), 58–64.

Metcalf, L. E. (1963). Research on teaching the social studies. In N. L. Gage (Ed.), *Handbook of research on teaching* (pp. 929–965). Chicago: Rand McNally.

Miller, S. L., & Rose, S. A. (1983). The great depression: A textbook case of problems with American history textbooks. *Theory and Research in Social Education, 11*(1), 25–40.

Napier, J. D., & Grant, E. T. (1984). Delimiting the problem of generalizability of research results: An example from a trend study of a citizenship education project. *Theory and Research in Social Education, 12*(3), 17–34.

Nelson, J. L., & Palonsky, S. (1980). Preservice teacher perceptions of social education. *Journal of Social Studies Research, 4*(1), 5–12.

Nelson, J. L., & Shaver, J. P. (1985). On research in social education. In W. B. Stanley (Ed.)., *Review of research in social studies education: 1976–1983* (pp. 401–433). Washington, DC: National Council for the Social Studies.

Nelson, M. R. (1984). Social educators and social action. *Journal of Social Studies Research, 8*(1), 54–63.

O'Brien, L. M., Meszaros, B., & Pulliam, W. E. (1985). Effects of teachers' use of objectives on student achievement in social studies. *Theory and Research in Social Education, 13*(3), 57–65.

Ochoa, A. (Ed.). (1981). A profile of social studies teachers. *Social Education, 45*(6), 401–421.

Oliver, D. W., & Shaver, J. P. (1974). *Teaching public issues in the high school.* Logan, UT: Utah State University Press. (original work published 1966)

Osborne, R. (1979). Revision of the NCSS social studies curriculum guidelines. *Social Education, 43*(4), 261–278.

Palonsky, S., & Nelson, J. L. (1980). Political restraint in the socialization of student teachers. *Theory and Research in Social Education, 7*(4), 19–34.

Park, O. C. (1984). Example comparison strategy versus attribute identification strategy in concept learning. *American Educational Research Journal, 21,* 145–162.

Passe, J. (1988). The role of internal factors in the teaching of current events. *Theory and Research in Social Education, 16*(1), 83–89.

Ponder, G., & Davis, O. L., Jr. (1982) Social Studies education. In H. E. Mitzel (Ed.). *Encyclopedia of educational research* (5th ed., pp. 1723–1732). New York: Macmillan.

Powell, P. M., & Powell, J. V. (1984). An investigation of political apathy among selected high school students. *Journal of Social Studies Research, 8*(2), 53–66.

Randall, C. S., Carr, G. D., Gerofsky, R., & Biggers, W. (1987). An experimental study to evaluate the give and take instructional materials. *Journal of Social Studies Research, 11*(1), 15–21.

Romanish, B. A. (1983). Modern secondary economics textbooks and ideological bias. *Theory and Research in Social Education, 11*(1), 1–24.

Rosenthal, R. (1984). *Meta-analytic procedures for social science research.* Beverly Hills, CA: Sage.

Russell, T. E., & Morrow, J. E. (1986). Reform in teacher education: Perceptions of secondary social studies teachers. *Theory and Research in Social Education, 14*(4), 325–330.

Sawin, E. I. (1969). *Evaluation and the work of the teacher.* Belmont, CA: Wadsworth.

Schober, H. (1984). An analysis of the impact of teacher training in economics. *Theory and Research in Social Education, 12*(1), 1–12.

Schug, M C., & Birkey, C. J. (1985). The development of children's economic reasoning. *Theory and Research in Social Education, 13*(1), 31–42.

Schug, M. C., Todd, R. J., & Beery, R. (1984). Why kids don't like social studies. *Social Education, 47*(5), 382–387.

Shaver, J. P. (1979). The usefulness of educational research in curricular/instructional decision-making in social studies. *Theory and Research in Social Education, 7*(3), 21–42.

Shaver, J. P. (1983). The verification of independent variables in teaching methods research. *Educational Researcher, 12*(8), 3–9.

Shaver, J. P. (1985). The lack of aptitude-treatment interactions in teaching students to discuss public issues. *Contemporary Social Psychology, 11*(3), 19.

Shaver, J. P., & Larkins, A. G. (1973). Research on teaching social studies. In R. M. W. Travers (Ed.), *Second handbook of research on teaching* (pp. 1243–1262). Chicago: Rand McNally.

Shaver, J. P., & Norton, R. S. (1980). Populations, samples, randomness, and replication in two social studies journals. *Theory and Research in Social Education, 8*(2), 1–10.

Shepherd, T. R., & Svasti, S. (1987). Improved sixth grade social studies test scores via instruction in listening. *Journal of Social Studies Research, 11*(2), 20–23.

Smith, B. D. (1983). Instructional planning: Attitudes, decisions, and preparation time among secondary social studies teachers. *Journal of Social Studies Research, 7*(1), 1–22.

Smith, J. K. (1983). Quantitative versus qualitative research; An attempt to clarify the issue. *Educational Researcher, 12*(3), 6–13.

Smith, J. K., & Heshusius, L. (1986). Closing down the conversation: The end of the quantitative-qualitative debate. *Educational Researcher, 15*(1), 4–12.

Solomon, R. F. (1949). On extension of control group design. *Psychological Bulletin, 46,* 137–150.

Soltis, J. F. (1984). On the nature of educational research. *Educational Researcher, 13*(10), 5–9.

Stahl, R. J. (1981). Achieving values and content objectives simultaneously within subject matter-oriented social studies classrooms. *Social Education, 45*(7), 580–585.

Stallings, W. M. (1985). Mind your *p*'s and Alphas. *Educational Researcher, 14*(9), 19–20.

Stanley, W. B. (1984). Approaches to teaching concepts and conceptualizing: An analysis of social studies textbooks. *Theory and Research in Social Education, 11*(4), 1–14.

Stanley, W. B. (1985a). Recent research in the foundations of social education: 1976–1983. In W. B. Stanley (Ed.), *Review of research in social studies education: 1976–1983* (pp. 309–400). Washington, DC: National Council for the Social Studies.

Stanley, W. B. (Ed.). (1985b). *Review of research in social studies education: 1976–1983.* Washington, DC: National Council for the Social Studies.

Stanley, W. B., Charlesworth, R., & Ringuest, J. L. (1985). Kindergarten and first grade children's social concept development. *Journal of Social Studies Research, 9*(1), 11–16.

Tixier, Y. V., & Dick, J. (1987). Attitudes toward and perceived use of textbook reading strategies among junior and senior high school social studies teachers. *Theory and Research in Social Education, 15*(1), 51–59.

Tlou, J. S. & Bennett, C. T. (1982). Social Studies educators' attitudes toward censorship in public schools in the Commonwealth of Virginia. *Journal of Social Studies Research, 6*(2), 48–52.

Tlou, J. S., & Bennett, C. T. (1983). Teacher perceptions of discipline problems in a central Virginia middle school. *Journal of Social Studies Research, 7*(2), 37–59.

Tuckman, B. W. (1988). *Conducting educational research* (3rd ed.). San Diego, CA: Harcourt.

Turner, T. N. (1982). Controlling research with human subjects and its effects on educational research: Report of a survey of what teacher educators think. *Journal of Social Studies Research, 6*(1), 29–31.

Tyo, J. (1980). An alternative for poor readers in social science. *Social Education, 44,* 309–310.

VanSickle, R. L. (1983). Statistical power and effect size in social education research. *Journal of Social Studies Research, 7*(2), 1–17.

VanSickle, R. L. (1986). Toward more adequate quantitative instructional research. *Theory and Research in Social Education, 14*(2), 171–186.

VanSickle, R. L., & Ehman, L. H. (1981). Developing and evaluating teacher training materials: A case study. *Journal of Social Studies Research, 5,* 52–63.

Wallen, N. E. (1983, November). *Research in social studies: What is needed?* Paper presented at the annual meeting of the National Council for the Social Studies, San Francisco. ERIC Document Reproduction Service No. 240009.

Wallen, N. E., & Fraenkel, J. R. (1988). An analysis of social studies research over an eight year period. *Theory and Research in Social Education, 16*(1), 1–22.

Webb, E. J., Campbell, D. T., Schwartz, & Sechrest, L. (1966). *Unobtrusive measures: Nonreactive research in the social sciences.* Chicago: Rand McNally.

Welch, W. W., & Walberg, H. J. (1970). Pretest and sensitization effects in curriculum evaluation. *American Educational Research Journal, 7*(4), 605–614.

White, J. J. (1988). Searching for substantial knowledge in social studies texts. *Theory and Research in Social Education, 16*(2) 115–140.

Wiersma, W. (1986). *Research methods in education: An introduction* (4th ed.). Boston: Allyn and Bacon.

Willson, V. L., & Putnam, R. R. (1982). A meta-analysis of pretest sensitization effects in experimental design. *American Educational Research Journal, 19*(2), 249–258.

Yoho, R. F. (1986). Effectiveness of four concept teaching strategies on social studies concept acquisition and retention. *Theory and Research in Social Education, 14*(3), 211–224.

7

QUANTITATIVE REVIEWING OF RESEARCH

James P. Shaver

UTAH STATE UNIVERSITY

The era of the quantitative review of research in education and psychology was inaugurated by Gene Glass in his presidential address to the American Educational Research Association (AERA) in 1976. In that speech, Glass introduced the term *meta-analysis* to refer to the quantification and statistical analysis of the characteristics and findings of primary research studies as a method of literature review. Meta-analysis caught the imagination of the educational research community. The numbers of meta-analyses reported in the succeeding years have, according to some observers, been "staggering" (Pillemer, 1984, p. 34). Bangert-Drowns (1986) cited an estimate of 300 such reports by 1984. Slavin (1986) referred to "scores of meta-analyses", and estimated a 100% increase in meta-analysis articles from 1979 to 1983 (p. 5). Hedges and Olkin (1982) suggested that the growth was exponential, with "indiscriminate overpopularity" approaching "faddish proportions" (p. 160). Interestingly, few meta-analyses directly pertinent to social studies have been published (e.g., Schlaefli, Rest, & Thoma, 1985; VanSickle, 1986).

Along with the reports of meta-analyses, a methodological literature has developed rapidly. Published discussions of methods for literature reviews were rare prior to 1976 (Jackson, 1980, p. 439). Now, however, articles and chapters (e.g., Cooper, 1982; Glass, 1977; Green & Hall, 1984; Hedges, 1986; Kulik & Kulik, 1989; McGaw, 1988) and books (Cooper, 1989; Glass, McGaw, & Smith, 1981; Hedges & Olkin, 1985; Hunter & Schmidt, 1990; Hunter, Schmidt, & Jackson, 1982; Rosenthal, 1980, 1984; Wolf, 1986) on meta-analysis methodology are available. Computer programs for meta-analytic procedures (Mullen & Rosenthal, 1985; also see McDaniel, 1986) are also beginning to appear. The meta-analytic conceptual frame has been applied to reviewing qualitative research (Noblit & Hare, 1988) and to the quantitative synthesis of single-subject research (Center, Skiba, & Casey, 1985–1986; Scruggs, Mastropieri, & Casto,

1987), although not without controversy (Salzberg, Strain, & Baer, 1987; O. R. White, 1987).

In short, the research review has been accepted as a respectable research activity—as Glass (1976), and Feldman (1971) before him, argued it should be. Even reviews of prior reviews, a major step in laying the groundwork for a review of the research literature (Jackson, 1978, 1980), are being published (e.g., Curtis & Shaver, 1987; Jackson, 1980; Waxman & Walberg, 1982; White, Bush, & Casto, 1985–1986).

WHAT IS META-ANALYSIS?

Concern with methodology for quantitatively summarizing and synthesizing research results was not new in 1976 (see, e.g., Bangert-Drowns, 1986; Hedges & Olkin, 1982; Kulik & Kulik, 1989). As Glass (1976; Glass et al., 1981, pp 24–25) acknowledged, prior reviewers had analyzed quantitative information from primary research reports. However, the emphasis had been primarily on combining probability levels, rather than descriptive statistics, from different studies. And none of the prior efforts to combine numerical estimates of study results or to use quantitative information systematically in literature reviews approached the methodological complexity of meta-analysis as developed by Glass (1977; Glass et al., 1981) and others, especially Rosenthal (1984), Cooper (1989), and Hunter et al. (1982).

In his seminal AERA address, Glass (1976) defined meta-analysis as "the statistical analysis of a large collection of analysis results from individual studies for the purpose of integrating the findings" (p. 3). Later, he and his associates (Glass et al., 1981) referred to meta-analysis as "the attitude of data analysis applied to quantitative summaries of individual experiments". Meta-analysis, they asserted, "is not a technique; rather, it is a

Reviewers were Robert L. Bangert-Drowns, State University of New York, Albany; Joseph Jesunathadas, California State College, San Bernadino; James A. Kulik, University of Michigan; David B. Pillemer, Wesley College; Robert E. Slavin, The Johns Hopkins University; Carol J. Strong, Utah State University; Karl R. White, Utah State University.

perspective that uses [sic] many techniques of measurement and statistical analysis" (p. 21). In a chapter published in 1977 and in the first book on meta-analysis (Glass et al., 1981), Glass elaborated what has been called *Glassian meta-analysis* (Bangert-Drowns, 1986). The emphasis is on coding and analyzing the characteristics, including methodological attributes and the outcomes, of all available studies in order to come to general conclusions about the nature of research and the research-based knowledge in the area under review.

Meta-analysis has not developed as a unitary construct. There are differences among the primary methodologists in purpose and method. Bangert-Drowns (1986) and the Kuliks (1989) have provided thorough discussions of those differences, including disagreements over the application of the term *meta-analysis*.

Among the divergent views, Glass defined meta-analysis as an approach to integrating results from a large number of studies, but others consider the quantitative analysis of even a few studies to be meta-analysis. Glass may include in a meta-analysis all studies on the topic for which reports can be located; others argue that studies that don't meet minimal methodological standards should never be included. Glass has based analyses on individual findings, often more than one per study; others insist that the study must be the unit of analysis. Glassian meta-analyses are intended to describe a body of literature—not only the knowledge to be gained about study outcomes, but the modes of inquiry themselves, especially as they are related to outcomes; other meta-analyses may be conducted only to determine what can be gleaned from the research literature about a substantive topic, such as the effectiveness of a treatment. Some meta-analysts only combine and analyze descriptive statistics, others combine probability levels across studies. Some meta-analysts only summarize available findings, others estimate population parameters using the techniques of inferential statistics. It is important, then, in discussing meta-analysis, to keep in mind the diversity in the approaches to which that label may be applied (Bangert-Drowns, 1986; Kulik & Kulik, 1989).

PROBLEMS WITH TRADITIONAL NARRATIVE REVIEWS

What was the methodological context for the impact of Glass's (1976) enunciation of meta-analysis? The typical research review then, as is often the case today, was a narrative in which the reviewer discussed the characteristics of a few studies, including their strengths and weaknesses, and the outcomes—usually in terms of statistical significance—and then drew conclusions based on an often discursive analysis. Studies were commonly selected for the review either because they represented a topic that had been rather narrowly defined or because they met rigorous design-quality criteria. The purpose of selection was frequently to make the review manageable.

As Glass (1976) pointed out, with the large and growing research literature there can be hundreds of studies on any topic. For example, he located some 475 studies of the effects of psychotherapy, whereas one prior reviewer had included only 19 studies in his synthesis (Kulik & Kulik, 1989). To ignore large

bodies of evidence, Glass maintained, was dysfunctional; yet to construct a meaningful summary of such large numbers of studies in a traditional narrative review would be as impossible a task as trying to make sense out of hundreds of test scores without methods for organizing and analyzing data. He rejected the approach of finding design or analysis deficiencies by which to exclude all but a few studies and then presenting "verbal synopses of studies . . . strung out in dizzying lists" (p. 4).

Light and Pillemer (1982, 1984) also criticized the traditional, unsystematic, narrative review in which studies are discussed serially with informal, selective attention to their strengths and weakness (1984, p. 3). They noted three common criticisms of such reviews.

Narrative reviews have been criticized as overly subjective because the reviewers typically do not formalize rules for such decisions as which studies to include. Narrative reviewers have also been faulted for relying too often on a statistically unsound *vote count* approach to summarizing outcomes (Light & Smith, 1971, p. 433). With this procedure, studies are categorized according to whether they yielded statistically significant positive results, statistically significant negative results, or statistically nonsignificant results (see, e.g., Leming, 1981; Wade, 1983). If one category of results has more studies in it than the others, that is assumed to be the best estimate of the independent-dependent variable relationship. However, as Glass (1977) observed:

Suppose that nine small-sample studies yield not quite [statistically] significant results, and the tenth large-sample result is [statistically] significant. The vote is one "for" and nine "against", a conclusion quite at odds with one's best instincts. (p. 358)

A related problem is that frequencies of statistically significant and nonsignificant results provide little information about the magnitude of a relationship or its importance. As Glass (1977) noted: "To know that televised instruction beats traditional classroom instruction in 25 of 30 studies—if, in fact, it does—is not to know whether TV wins by a nose or in a walkaway" (p. 359). And, of course, tallies of statistical significance tell the reviewer nothing about the relationship of design characteristics to outcomes.

The third deficiency in narrative reviews mentioned by Light and Pillemer (1982, 1984) was alluded to above in referring to Glass's concerns with traditional efforts to integrate the research literature: the difficulty in extracting and analyzing information, especially if a large number of studies, say 50 or more, is being reviewed and multiple relationships are of interest. As Cook and Leviton (1980) noted, there can be considerable "cognitive overload" for those who attempt such reviews.

The quality of traditional reviews was systematically investigated by Jackson (1978, 1980). He selected a random sample of 36 review articles from journals in education, psychology, and sociology for the years 1974 to 1976. As a basis for an instrument to code the reviews, Jackson conceptualized integrative reviews as involving a set of tasks analogous to those of primary research (i.e., studies in which data are collected on individual subjects). The tasks are basically (a) the selection and definition of a topic or problem; (b) the review of prior reviews in the area and the formulation of questions or hypotheses; (c) selection of the studies to be reviewed; (d) the coding of study findings and pertinent study characteristics; (e) data analysis; (f) interpretation of results; and (g) preparation of a report.

Among the weaknesses that Jackson found in most of the reviews were failure to examine prior reviews critically; lack of reporting of the process for identifying and selecting research reports; analysis of only a subset, usually not randomly selected, of the available studies; inadequate representations of study findings; lack of systematic analyses of relationships between outcomes and study characteristics; and too little information reported on the review procedures to allow either reasoned judgments about the validity of the conclusions or replication of the review. Jackson (1980) concluded: "It seems likely that some of the confusion that surrounds many topics in the social sciences is partly a result of nonrigorous reviews of research . . ." (p. 459). He commended Glass's meta-analytic approach as a major source of ideas for improving on the methods being used for research reviews.

IS META-ANALYSIS A PANACEA?

Despite the remarkable enthusiasm with which meta-analysis has been applied to the task of reviewing the research literature, the methodology has not been without criticism. Glass's AERA address and his first report of a meta-analysis, on the outcomes of psychotherapy (Glass, 1976; Smith & Glass, 1977), engendered sharp reactions. Questions were raised about the methods of data analysis (Gallo, 1978), the lumping together of variables (Presby, 1978), the aggregation of different dependent measures (Gallo, 1978), and the inclusion of studies with poor designs (Eysenck, 1978; Mansfield & Busse, 1977).

Continuing criticism has been focused on the meta-analytic conceptual frame (e.g., Biddle & Anderson, 1986; Chipman, 1988; Eysenck, 1984; Guskin, 1984; Shaver, 1979a, 1979b, 1986; Slavin, 1986; Strube, Gardner, & Hartmann, 1985; Wilson & Rachman, 1983) and on problems in conducting meta-analyses (e.g., Abrami, Cohen, & d'Apollonia, 1988; Bryant & Wortman, 1985; Oliver & Spokane, 1983; Orwin & Cordray, 1985), as well as on the improper application of the approach (Slavin, 1984a; also see Carlberg et al., 1984). Even the promise that the objectivity and full reporting of quantitative reviews would make them replicable (e.g., Fiske, 1983) and avoid the conflicting conclusions of narrative reviews (see, e.g., Light & Pillemer, 1984, p.5) has not been fulfilled (e.g., Abrami et al., 1988; Bryant & Wortman, 1985; Bullock & Svyantek, 1985; Sampson, Stryowski, Weinstein, & Walberg, 1987; Scruggs, White, & Bennion, 1986; see Shapiro & Shapiro, 1982, for a success). The reasons include inadequate reporting of search procedures and inclusion criteria, as well as inadequate reporting of and ambiguity in schemata for coding study characteristics. Quantification alone is not a control for human subjectivity.

Clearly, meta-analysis is not a panacea for the ills of qualitative literature reviews. However, that does not deny the potential importance of quantitative methods for reviewing large bodies of research, but suggests that qualitative and quantitative review methods might not be as distinctly dichotomous as early

meta-analysis advocates discerned them to be. In fact, a literature is growing around the idea that adequate reviews will have qualitative and quantitative elements (Cook & Leviton, 1980; Guskin, 1984; Light & Pillemer, 1982, 1984), paralleling the rejection in the general research methodology literature of sharp distinctions between quantitative and qualitative approaches or of marked advantages for one over the other.

As Slavin (1986) pointed out, only reporting the quantitatively coded features of the studies reviewed is not sufficient; a research synthesis should include the "critical, intelligent examination of the literature" (p. 10). The best quantitative reviews have included such discussions (see, e.g., White & Greenspan, 1987). According to Light and Pillemer (1984): "The growth of quantitative procedures . . . has not banished subjectivity, turned all investigators into good ones, or eliminated poor analyses. There is still a role for careful description, process analysis, insight, and creativity" (p. 105).

Hedges (1986), too, has called for greater use of qualitative and quantitative methods in combination, suggesting that qualitative information and analyses should be used to set the context for and guide the use of quantitative review methods. Qualitative review approaches are particularly important in theory construction and, in particular, the development and challenging of constructs (Cook & Leviton, 1980). In fact, in reviews aimed at bringing the research in one area (such as cognitive process research) to bear on conventional views in another area (such as myths that interfere with social studies educators' thinking about critical thinking) (Cornbleth, 1985), the qualitative elements take precedence, and quantitative review methodology may have little relevance.

Ironically, in the type of circumstance most frequently tabbed as particularly advantageous for application of meta-analysis—i.e., when large numbers of studies are to be reviewed—the sheer volume of studies and quantitative information may preclude the qualitative discussion of individual studies that can add so much to understanding and interpretation. That was a frustration during a quantitative review of some 273 reports of research on modifying attitudes toward persons with disabilities (Shaver, Curtis, Jesunathadas, & Strong, 1987). The constraints of space, even in a 577-page final report, and even more so in a journal article (Shaver, Curtis, Jesunathadas, & Strong, 1989), did not allow the exploration of the conceptual and methodological issues in individual studies.

In part to counter the numbers problem, Slavin (1986, 1987) has proposed that once a reviewer has located all available reports on a topic, he or she should use substantive and methodological criteria to select a *best evidence* set of studies. Then, journal space would be allocated to the discussion of critical issues in the context of individual studies, rather than the presentation of statistical analyses of "a literature that is too large and diverse for the reviewer to describe or for the reader to comprehend" (1987, p. 16).

The usefulness of quantitative information in conjunction with qualitative analysis does not depend on the number of studies, however. With small sets of studies, the complex coding and data analyses usually associated with meta-analyses may not be appropriate (Cook & Leviton, 1980). Nevertheless, a thorough, fully reported literature search, the quantitative reporting of study outcomes, and the quantitative summaries of the treatment, sample, design, and setting characteristics of studies can provide valuable information about the status of research in the area under review, as has been demonstrated in two recent dissertations (Friedman, 1985; Strong, 1989). The challenge is how to use quantitative procedures appropriately, whether in meta-analyses or as augmentation to qualitative narrative reviews.

ISSUES IN APPLYING THE QUANTITATIVE PERSPECTIVE

Glass's (1976) advocacy of meta-analysis focused attention on review methodology. As Hedges (1986) observed:

The most significant contribution is not that meta-analysis has led to more applications of quantitative methods in research reviews, but rather that it has helped to focus attention on the issue of methodological *rigor* in research reviewing ... [and] has led to serious examination of methodological standards. (p. 354; also see Strube et al., 1985)

The rest of this chapter is focused on issues in regard to quantitative review methodology and standards.

The Literature Search

The problem of bias in the sample of studies, as Strube et al. (1985) pointed out, must be faced with all reviews, qualitative or quantitative. Jackson (1980) emphasized the importance of full reporting of search procedures, including the indexes searched and the criteria for including or excluding studies. Full documentation of the studies included in a review is crucial not only for readers to evaluate the adequacy of the search and judge bias, but for any effort to replicate the literature review. Altough the reporting of search procedures is not intrinsic to meta-analysis, the emphasis on initially locating all available studies has made such reporting a frequent element of quantitative reviews.

One important methodological consideration has been raised by the increased use of computers for literature searches. A thorough literature search to ensure that all relevant studies are located is a crucial basis for a sound review (Glass et al., 1981). Reliance on computer searches of data bases such as ERIC, *Psychological Abstracts,* and *Dissertation Abstracts* may, however, result in inadequate sets of studies. White (1985–1986), for example, reported that computer searches of eight data bases, using more than 200 key works and combinations of key words, yielded less than 15% of the 326 studies identified for a meta-analysis of research on the efficacy of early intervention with disadvantaged and handicapped children. We (Shaver et al., 1987, 1989) had the same experience. Bracey (1986) reported the frustration of a researcher whose ERIC search identified only 46% of the research reports on reading comprehension that he *knew* existed. He doubted that incorrect keywords were the problem. I have had the same experience with the social studies literature. In addition, older, important reports may not be in the computer data bases. For these reasons, hand searches of indexes should not be abandoned. Moreover, the

reference lists of prior reviews and of the reports of studies are likely to be rich sources of studies not identified in searches of computer databases.

Quantifying Outcomes

How to represent the outcomes of quantitative research studies is no trifling matter. Educational researchers have relied heavily on statistical significance as the indicator of the magnitude of results. For most educational research, however, the commonly used tests of statistical significance answer a trivial question: Would the result be a likely *chance occurrence* (at the specified α level) *under H_o* (i.e., assuming the null hypothesis to be true) with *randomization* and samples of *this size?* (See, e.g., Carver, 1978; Morrison & Henkel, 1970a; Shaver, 1985a, 1985b.)

The test of statistical significance is particularly deficient as a measure of the magnitude of a research outcome because the probability level for a result is a function of sample size. Trivial as well as important results may be statistically significant (see Cohen & Hyman, 1979, for examples). The dramatic impact of sample size is obvious if one considers that with a standard deviation of 10 and $N = 20$, a difference between independent means must be 9.4 to be statistically significant at the .05 level in a nondirectional test, but a difference of only 4.0 is required with $N = 100$, or 1.2 with $N = 1,000$. Knowing only that a result was statistically significant, then, tells a researcher very little about its magnitude (see, e.g., Royall, 1986; also see Chow, 1988, on statistical significance in theory testing). At the same time, the size of differences between means is dependent upon the scale of measurement, and so mean differences are not adequate indicators of the magnitude of results from different dependent measures.

The Standardized Mean Difference (SMD). One of Glass's (1976) major contributions was calling attention to the standardized mean difference (SMD) as a metric for quantifying outcomes in research reviews that is independent of sample size and scale of measurement. The SMD was not Glass's creation (Glass, 1977, pp. 356–357; Kulik & Kulik, 1989). For example, Cohen (1988) had, in the 1969 edition of his book, advocated the SMD as an index of effect size for use in statistical power analysis. Nor was Glass the first to use the SMD in research syntheses (see, e.g., Rosenthal, 1976). Glass, however, popularized the SMD as a solution to the difficulties posed for reviewers by scale of measurement and sample size differences across studies.

Choices in Obtaining SMDs. The choice of a standard deviation (SD) in computing the SMD is not a trivial matter (Glass et al., 1981, pp. 106, 116). Glass is often cited as defining SMD as a difference between means divided by the control group standard deviation (e.g., Light & Pillemer, 1984, p. 55; McGaw, 1988, p. 679; Rosenthal, 1984, p. 22). In his AERA presidential address, however, referring to the SMD only as the "effect size", Glass (1976) defined it as "the mean difference on the outcome variable between treated and untreated subjects divided by the within-group standard deviation [the square root of the within group variance estimate in a one-way analysis of variance]" (p. 6). In 1977, Glass used ES as the symbol for the SMD, defined as in 1976. In 1981, Glass et al. used Δ (Delta) as the symbol. The SMD was defined with the within-group standard deviation in the denominator for comparisons not involving treatment and control groups (p. 38), but with the control group standard deviation in the denominator for treatment-control comparisons (p. 29). Cohen (1988), who uses d as the symbol for the SMD, has suggested that either the treatment or control group standard deviation can be used in the denominator, because in the use of typical tests of significance, the groups are assumed to come from populations with homogeneous standard deviations (p. 20). By extension, Cohen used the within-group standard deviation in computational examples (p. 21), as did Hedges (1986), who labeled the SMD as g.

One issue, then, is whether the control group SD or a pooled estimate, the within-group SD, should be used in computing an SMD (Glass et al., 1981, pp. 106–111). Of course, in some studies no group is identifiable as a standard control group. Moreover, the within-group SD, with its greater number of cases, will be a more stable estimate of population variability. However, if the magnitude of results relative to the dispersion of scores in an untreated population is of interest, it is relevant that variability in the treatment group might be affected by the treatment. Heterogeneity in variances that is not large enough to be of concern in applying an inferential test could have a significant impact on an SMD. For that reason, the SD of the control group may be preferred (Kulik & Kulik, 1989, p. 39; McGaw & Glass, 1980; Rosenthal, 1984, p. 22). To increase the stability of the estimate of variability in the untreated population, the SDs for the pretest scores of the control and experimental groups and the posttest scores of the control group can be pooled (Shaver et al., 1987, 1989).

Unfortunately, underlying many discussions of computing SMDs is the tacit assumption that data come only from a simple posttest-only design (Kulik & Kulik, 1989). The choice of an SD can be particularly critical when the results come from an analysis of covariance, are based on gain or residual scores, or come from a factorial analysis of variance (Glass et al., pp. 116–126; Kulik & Kulik, 1989). If the SD is based on scores from which sources of variability have been removed by regression analysis or blocking, the SMD will be an overestimate of the magnitude of the result, as compared with standardization using a raw score SD. In order for SMDs to be interpretable across studies, unadjusted SDs should typically be used so that that size of the SMD is not a function of the study design (Glass et al., 1981; Kulik & Kulik, 1989). If group means, rather than individual scores, are the unit of analysis in a study, overestimation of the SMD will also occur; the SD of a set of means will be less than that of the scores on which they are based, as Becker and Hedges (1984) and Scruggs et al. (1986) noted in their analyses of extreme SMD values from a prior review.

When raw score SDs are not reported, they can be estimated from adjusted standard deviations. If neither means nor SDs are reported, SMDs can be estimated from information such as t- or F-ratios (e.g., Glass et al., 1981; Holmes, 1984; McGaw & Glass, 1980). Holmes (1984, p. 109) indicated that the approxi-

mations of SMDs will be conservative estimates. That was not our experience (Shaver et al., 1987, pp. 166–167), however. SMDs computed using estimates of the raw score SD and SMDs estimated from tests of significance yielded higher SMDs on the average than did SMDs computed from raw data. However, type of SMD might have been confounded with other study characteristics. In another study, Taylor and White (1990) found little difference between computed and estimated SMDs for the same 778 research results. Whether estimated effect sizes are accurate indicators of outcomes is an important area for continued investigation.

The choice of means for an SMD is also an issue. Glass and his associates (Glass et al., 1981, pp. 114–116; McGaw & Glass, 1980) have argued for the use of final-status raw score means in computing SMDs. As compared to gain score, residual, and covariance-adjusted means, raw score means are more readily interpretable. When posttest comparisons are biased due to pretreatment differences, gain score means may be preferable to residual and covariance-adjusted means as adjustments for pretest differences because they are on the same scale of measurement as posttest scores, unless pretest assessment was on a different scale than the final-status measure. Then residuals and covariance adjusted means are preferable. The reviewer may not be able to make a choice of means; for example, only covariance adjusted means may be available. In that case, coding the type of mean in order to later analyze whether the results are divergent is important.

In short, "although effect size [i.e., the standardized mean difference] is a simple concept, its definition can be clouded and its derivation complicated" (McGaw & Glass, 1980, p. 337). Careful formulation of decisions about the computation and extimation of SMDs, whether for a meta-analysis, data to augment a qualitative review, or a report of primary research, is critical.

Other Indices. The definition of effect size (ES) as synonymous with the standardized mean difference (SMD) is unfortunate, as it tends to preclude the consideration of other indices of the magnitude of results. Hedges and Olkin (1985, p. xvi), recognizing that the narrow use of *effect size* was well established, introduced the term *effect magnitude* as a more general term, and some variation of that label has been used on occasion (e.g., Murray & Dosser, 1987; Strube, 1988); but the continuing use of effect size as synonymous with standardized mean difference is more common.

Effect size is better defined as *a metric of the magnitude of a result that is independent of scale of measurement and sample size.* The SMD is one such metric. Correlation coefficients are as well. For example, in White's (1982) meta-analysis of prior research on the relationship between socioeconomic status and academic achievement, rs were the outcome of interest. Testing the difference between means in an experimental design can also be conceptualized in correlational terms: that is, the extent to which scores on the dependent measure are associated with group membership. As the difference between the means increases relative to the size of the SD, so does the degree of relationship. The magnitude of the result can be described with the SMD or, with two groups, by the point biserial correlation (r_p). With two or more groups, Eta^2 (E^2) is an appropriate correlation (with $k = 2$, $r_p^2 = E^2$). Cohen (1988, chap. 2) has provided formulae as well as a table by which r_p can be estimated from d, and vice versa.

Proportions are also effect sizes by the above definition, as is the ratio of variances (Light & Pillemer, 1984, pp. 56–57). Kulik and Kulik (1989) referred to a difference between percentages of correct final exam answers as an effect size; Shaver et al. (1987) divided the posttest variance of the experimental group by that of the control group as a metric of variability in posttest attitude scores. Cohen (1988) has discussed other effect sizes.

Interpreting the SMD

The SMD is an intuitively attractive indicator of the magnitude of results. Its computation is visually obvious, involving familiar statistics, and the SMD is conceptually related to the familiar z score and Z-ratio (or critical ratio) so interpretation seems to be straightforward. Differences between means expressed in standard deviation units appear readily comparable. Moreover, most educational researchers are accustomed to interpreting z scores and Z-ratios in terms of the proportion of the area of the normal curve that lies below or above a particular point. The interpretation of SMDs in terms of the overlap between distributions (Cohen, 1988) is based on that familiar concept. A statement, for example, that an SMD of 1 indicates that 84% of the control group subjects' scores fall at or below the mean of the experimental group or, conversely, that 84% of the experimental groups' scores fall at or above the control group mean, is a graphic representation of a result.

Reviewers often overlook, however, that the overlap-of-distributions interpretation is based on the assumption that the underlying distributions are normal (Cohen, 1988, p. 21; Glass et al., 1981, pp. 104–106). That assumption depends on the further assumption that any experimental effects were distributed across all subjects equally and were not the result of atypical responses by a small minority of subjects (Kraemer & Andrews, 1982).

Negative Changes. Other cautions to be kept in mind in interpreting SMDs include the potential for fallacious conclusions when only the magnitude and direction of differences are reported. For example, in a move rarely reported in quantitative reviews, Shaver et al. (1987) coded whether the treatment group's pre-posttest change was positive or negative. For 12% of the SMDs, the treatment group's change was negative, indicating that with treatments intended to improve attitudes toward persons with disabilities, attitudes became more negative on the average.

Causality. The word *effect,* frequently used to refer to a statistical comparison (e.g., a main effect), has an implicit connotation of causality in the rhetoric of quantitative research (Davis & Hersh, 1987). The choice of the term *effect size* to refer to magnitude-of-results metrics was unfortunate. Despite the conventional disavowal of casual implications (e.g., Cohen, 1988, p. 9),

the term can avert attention from threats to internal validity and lead to misinterpretation in reviews as well as in primary research. For example, although VanSickle (1986) was generally cautious in reporting his review of simulation gaming research, he did refer to positive and negative effects, rather than effect sizes (p. 252); and, based on a comparisons of SMDs, he concluded that "overall, simulation gaming produced greater cognitive learning to a small degree . . . [than did] other instructional techniques" (p. 249). Similarly, Schlaefli et al. (1985) referred to the effect size as "an indicator of the power of the treatment effect, relative to within-group variance" (p. 337) and commented, for example, that:

> The effect sizes . . . indicate that the Dilemma Discussion programs have on the average the greatest impact, followed by Personality Development programs. . . . The Academic Course and Short Term programs, on the average, do not have an effect on normal judgement development. (p. 343)

As with a test of statistical significance, an effect size does not address per se the cause of a result. Casuality is a matter of internal validity. Even in a randomized experiment, an effect size may reflect chance or the impact of one or more other threats to internal validity, such as selection or history, rather than the influence of the treatment. Unfortunately, even sophisticated statistics textbooks contain misleading statements such as that $Omega^2$ indicates the "percent of the variance [that] is due to treatment effects" (Winer, 1971, p. 430). For these reasons, a term used to refer to the magnitude of findings should not be one that predisposes the researcher, reviewer, or reader to conclusions about causality. *Result size* (RS) would meet that condition better than effect size; but because of the difficulty in changing conventional usage and to avoid confusion, effect size is used throughout this chapter.

Accuracy. An important question is whether a reported ES (i.e., RS) is an accurate representation of the outcome. Miscalculations of effect sizes do occur (Stock, Okun, Haring, Miller, & Ceurvorst, 1982). For example, Slack and Larkins (1982) reported partial Eta^2 coefficients of .62 and .85 (p. 15). However, computations from the data that they thoughtfully provided in their analysis of covariance tables yielded partial Eta^2 s of .43 and .21, respectively.

In addition, unreliable assessment of the dependent variable will attenuate SMDs as well as correlation coefficients (O'Grady, 1982). Hunter et al. (1982, p. 111) presented a correction for attenuation in an SMD that is analogous to that for a correlation coefficient (e.g., Ferguson & Takane, 1989, p. 474). An estimate of the SMD or r for true scores will not often be of interest, because actual results, not those from "theoretically perfect measures", are what seem most pertinent (Cohen, 1988, pp. 337; Kulik & Kulik, 1989). However, that errors of measurement attenuate the magnitude of result sizes should always be kept in mind as an interpretive consideration.

Study Design. Another factor to be taken into account in evaluating the magnitude of a result size is study design. For example, Cooper (1981) suggested that tightly controlled laboratory studies should yield larger results than studies carried out in natural settings. O'Grady (1982) has argued that several aspects of design will affect the ESs obtained: Larger ESs would be excepted (a) if the study is correlational rather than a true experiment, (b) if a within-subjects (repeated measures) rather than a between-subjects design is used, (c) as the number of levels in a fixed factor design is increased, and (d) with increased variability in the sample of subjects.

In their review of research on the effects of teacher questions, Sampson et al. (1987) found that "more carefully designed" studies produced lower ESs on the average (p. 293). Shaver et al. (1987) found that quasi-experimental designs produced a lower mean SMD (.35) than did single-group, pre-post-test comparisons (.50). Studies rated as having medium internal validity had a slightly lower mean SMD (.32) than that for low internal validity studies ($\bar{X}$ = .38), but studies rated high on internal validity yielded the highest mean SMD (.89). However, there were only 15 SMDs from high validity studies, as contrasted with 211 from medium and 418 from low validity studies. (See Slavin, 1987, for an example of the effects of design in research on mastery learning.)

Eysenck (1984) also noted that whether the comparison subjects are in a placebo group (the "proper *control*" [p. 50], he argued) or a no-treatment control group can be an important consideration. Consistent with the placebo effect Eysenck identified for studies of psychotherapy, Shaver et al. (1987) reported a slightly lower mean SMD for placebo as contrasted with control group comparisons (.29 and .36, respectively). To sum up, design factors can be an important factor in the magnitude of results, but generalizations about the effects of design should be drawn cautiously.

Perceptions of Magnitude. Hedges and Olkin (1986) pointed out that "how large an effect [*sic*] is perceived to be depends a great deal on the way [it] is expressed" (p. 21; also see, Cooper, 1981, pp. 1014–1015). As noted above, when differences between groups are of interest, there is a choice between an SMD or a measure of correlation, such as the r_p, r_p^2, or *Eta²*. An alternative to differences in proportions or percentages is r_{phi}, the phi coefficient.

Although the proportion of the variance on the dependent measure that is associated with treatment-control group membership, as indicated by r_p^2 or *Eta²*, is a powerful concept to some, concern has been expressed (e.g., Hedges & Olkin, 1985, p. 77; Rosenthal, 1984) that use of correlation coefficients as effect sizes will lead to underappraisal of the magnitude of results. Inspection of the table that Cohen (1988, p. 22) provided for transforming SMD to r_p and vice versa indicates the basis for the apprehension. For the same mean difference, the r_p will be considerably less than the SMD. For example, if SMD = 2.0, r_p = .71; if SMD = 1, r_p = .45; if SMD = .5, r_p = .24. Squaring r_p to obtain the proportion of variance associated with group membership yields even smaller coefficients of determination: for the above example, .50, .20, .06, respectively. Investigators or readers may be more likely to perceive an ES as small, even trivial, if expressed as a correlation coefficient rather than an SMD. This discrepancy is not, however, a problem with a difference between proportions and r_{phi}; they will correspond closely (Cohen, 1988, pp. 184–185). (See Murray & Dosser, 1987; O'Grady, 1982; Strube, 1988, for cautions in intrepreting *Eta²*.)

A corrective for the tendency of researchers to underestimate the magnitude of possible treatment effects in interpreting r_p and r_p^2 was proposed by Rosenthal and Rubin (1982)—the display of data in a 2 × 2 table (i.e., the binomial effect size display, or BESD), categorized according to treatment-control group membership and success-failure on the dependent variable (also see Rosenthal, 1984). With r_{phi} = .32 and equal marginal *n*s, the difference in success rate for the treatment and control groups is 32%. That is, r_{phi} for the 2 × 2 table equals the difference in success rates. That, Rosenthal and Rubin argued, is a more impressive index than r_{phi}^2, which they interpret as 10% variance in scores associated with treatment-control group membership. (Their interpretation of r_{phi}^2 is problematic; with dichotomous variables, variance and, consequently, r_{phi}^2 have little meaning. Also, it is important to be cautious about interpreting a difference in success rate as "attributable" to the treatment, as Rosenthal & Rubin, 1982, did.)

Others (e.g., Cohen, 1988; Hedges & Olkin, 1985; Light & Pillemer, 1984) have applauded the BESD as a valuable contribution to interpreting the magnitude of results. However, caution is needed. As Preece (1983) has noted, Rosenthal and Rubin's estimate of difference in success rates is based on equal numbers of total successes and failures (i.e., a median split for continuous data). If the overall success rate is less than .50, the difference in success rates for the treatment and control group will be less than r_{phi}. For example, if r_{phi} = .32 and the overall success rate is .10 rather than .50, the difference in success rates for the treatment and control groups is lowered to .19. That is an important consideration in research, such as in social studies education, where the success rate cannot be controlled at 50%.

Perhaps the most important consideration for social studies researchers, however, is the success-failure construct. Rosenthal and Rubin used life-death rate following medical treatment as the success-failure dichotomy. Few would argue with the life-death success criterion. Such definitive success criteria have not, however, been identified for the dependent measures typically used in social science research or research on social studies education (see, e.g., Bracey, 1985; Chipman, 1988; Gallo, 1978; O'Grady, 1982). Certainly, being above or below the median on such measures is not an inherent indicator of success or failure. That consideration poses a particularly knotty question in the interpretation of research results in social studies: Given a result of a particular magnitude, how does the reseacher or report reader determine if it represents an *educationally* significant outcome?

Educational Significance. Evaluating the magnitude of a result in terms of educational importance presents a formidable challenge, in primary research as well as in reviews of research. Unfortunately, the criteria for small, medium, and large effect sizes proposed by Cohen (1988) are often used unthinkingly as indicators of educational significance.

Cohen's discussion of the magnitude of ESs stems from an

essential step in power analysis—the stipulation of the magnitude of result (ES) that the researcher wants to detect at the specified level of probability (α). One approach has been to identify typical magnitudes of results in an area of research as the basis for the predesignated ES (see, e.g., Cohen & Hyman, 1979, 1981; Haase, Waechter, & Solomon, 1982). Cohen (1988, pp. 24–27) presented a careful rationale for specifying small, medium, and large ESs (for the SMD, .2, .5, and .8, respectively), based on typical findings in behavioral research and on the perceptibility of results. He cautioned, however (p. 12), that his magnitude-of-ES criteria, like all conventions, are arbitrary, even if based on reason. They may not be valid for other areas of research. Above all, they should not be given the sanctification of the ritualized .05 level of significance. Glass et al. (1981) went even further:

There is no wisdom whatsoever in attempting to associate regions of the effect-size metric with descriptive adjectives such as "small", "moderate", "large", and the like. Dissociated from a context of decision and comparative value, there is no inherent value to an effect size. (p. 104)

It is especially important to note the crucial distinction between findings that are *usual* or *perceptible* and those that have *educational value.* The latter judgment calls for analyses of costs and benefits—that is, value judgments about the importance of an outcome. For example, given similar instructional costs, an SMD = .20 that indicated a program resulted in a 10% reduction in inter–ethnic violence in a school would likely be deemed more important than an SMD = .80 that indicated a 10% increase in recall of facts from a textbook (see, e.g., Gallo, 1978; Shaver, 1985b).

Despite the strong caveats, Cohen's (1988) conventions are often applied without attention to context and relative value. Schlaefli et al. (1985, p. 341), for example, adopted the Cohen criteria for small, medium, and large SMDs with no acknowledgement of their arbitrary nature, no discussion of the applicability of the conventions to moral education, and no consideration of the costs and benefits of differing scores on the dependent variable. VanSickle (1986, p. 248) acknowledged the arbitrariness of Cohen's criteria, but then accepted them without discussion. Shaver et al. (1987) accepted the criteria by default after contemplating the quandaries involved, especially the lack of evidence for the consequences of differences in attitude assessment scores. They remarked: "In the absence of empirically based answers to such questions [about the benefits indicated by different dependent measure values], establishing. . . effect size [criteria]. . . is, at best, a loosely bounded guessing game, albeit a necessary one" (p. 124).

The empirical base for evaluating the importance of different outcomes is lacking in social studies education. What is the benefit of a mean SMD of .43 for simulation experimental Ss versus *untreated* control group Ss on immediate recall of knowledge, or of a mean SMD of .80 for "attitude toward social phenomena" (VanSickle, 1986, p. 249)? A major challenge is the development of conceptual and empirical frameworks for judging the importance of research results in terms of the benefits indicated by the findings, especially in the context of the overarching goal of citizenship education.

The benefits associated with results are a matter of assessment validity (with validity issues compounded by the admixture of different measures in a quantitative review), not of correspondence to Cohen's (1988) criteria. Can a difference of .43 or .80 standard deviations be translated into meaningful differences in valued performance? (See Sternberg & Taylor, 1982, for an analysis of an SMD = .39 on a test of psycholinguistic ability.) The same question, of course, can be raised in regard to Schlaefli et al.'s (1985) finding of an overall mean SMD of .28 on the Defining Issues Test (DIT), or their SMDs for types of treatments that included, for example, a .41 mean SMD for dilemma discussions. Although there are validity data on the DIT (Schaefli et al., 1985), there is a notable absence of data on the relationships of DIT scores with actual moral decision-making or with moral behavior.

Messick (1989) has argued vociferously that "the key issues of test validity are the meaning, relevance, and utility of scores, the import or value implications of scores as a basis for action, and the functional worth of scores in terms of the social consequences of their use" (p. 5). As he noted, "validity judgements *are* value judgements" (p. 10). Until social studies researchers accumulate evidence on the relationships of assessment scores to desired adult citizenship behavior (which may shift as the societal context changes [Cooper, 1981]), meaningful judgments cannot be made about the educational importance of effect sizes in the context of that central goal of social studies education. Other interpretive issues pale in the face of the assessment validity issues to be confronted in judging the educational significance of research results in social studies.

External Validity. Whether the treatment is germane to the classroom is an essential question of external validity to be considered in judging the importance of results in social studies research. The outcomes of a treatment that requires materials that are not likely to be available to classroom teachers, makes unrealistic demands of them, or, as Slavin (1986, 1987) pointed out, was tested over an unrealistically short duration, lack the contextual relevance to be judged educationally significant.

Given contextual relevance, whether a result can be reproduced in the ongoing educational setting is pertinent to its importance. For example, is enough known about the experimental treatment to reproduce its essential elements? Was the treatment construct (independent variable) defined and implementation verified (e.g., Ladas, 1980; Shapiro & Shapiro, 1983; Shaver, 1983)? Assuming fidelity of implementation, was there treatment validity in the sense that other attributes of the treatment or the Ss' reactions to the treatment (e.g., the Hawthorne, novelty, or John Henry effects) did not invalidate the construct (Shaver et al., 1987), making practical reproduction of treatment and results unlikely?

Another crucial issue in external validity is whether the reliability and generalizability of treatment effects have been established through replication. Some authors (e.g., Bangert-Drowns, 1986, p. 398; Carlberg & Miller, 1984, pp. 9, 10; Fiske, 1983, p. 67; Hedges & Olkin, 1985, p. 3; Hunter & Schmidt, 1990, p. 37; Jackson, 1980, p. 445; Rosnow & Rosenthal, 1989, pp. 1280–1281) imply that meta-analysis is equivalent to replication. In Glass's (1977; Glass et al., 1981) conception of meta-analysis, a major purpose for a research review should be to gain understanding of the conditions under which a treatment can be duplicated and similar results produced. As important as the integration of research findings is, however, reviewers must be cautious about assuming that the post hoc assembly of studies that have few, if any, planned connections and unknown differences among them is an adequate substitute for purposely designed replications (Eysenck, 1984).

Interpreting Combined Effect Sizes

The obvious purpose of a review of literature is to draw conclusions based on the findings from a body of research. Especially when the number of studies is large, the quantification of outcomes provides a basis for the use of descriptive statistics to summarize and analyze results. A number of issues should be considered in combining and interpreting effect sizes in a review.

One issue to be confronted is how to handle multiple outcomes from individual studies. One approach is to treat the ES for each finding, regardless of the number in individual studies, as the unit of analysis to allow for analyses of the relationships of study characteristics to outcomes (McGaw, 1988, p. 683). Others argue that each study should contribute only one ES to an analysis, or one ES per type of outcome if separate analyses are conducted (Bangert-Drowns, 1986). For example, a median ES might be obtained for each study or each type of outcome (Hedges, 1986; Rosenthal, 1984). The concern with multiple ESs from individual studies is twofold: ESs from one study are not independent, and a study with multiple ESs may contribute disproportionately to the data set. To get around the latter problem, some reviewers include all ESs, but weight each, inversely proportional to the number of ESs from the study (Raudenbush, Becker, & Kalaian, 1988).

Light and Pillemer (1984) proposed that the data be summarized and reported in terms of ESs for both findings and studies. When that was done by Shapiro and Shapiro (1982) and by Shaver et al. (1987), the results were similar—mean SMDs of .93 and .98, and of .37 and .42, respectively. Shaver et al. did note problems in computing a median effect size for each study, because of both the loss of information and the confounding of important categories (e.g., immediate versus delayed posttests, different grade levels, scores for males and females). (See Scruggs et al., 1986, pp. 72–73 for another example of difficulties in obtaining study ESs.)

Interpretation of Mean ESs. Quantification can be applied fruitfully to small samples of studies without computing descriptive statistics for the ESs (e.g., Friedman, 1985; Strong, 1989). However, representing study findings in summary form is essential to a meta-analysis. As in primary research, the mean is typically the summary descriptive statistic of choice for reviews. Occasionally (e.g., Shavelson, Webb, & Burstein, 1986), quantitative researchers are reminded that they have become overly dependent on a one-number representation, typically the mean, of performance in a group, and that, as a consequence, insights into potentially important within-group vari-

ability are obscured. Focusing exclusively on a measure of central tendency is dysfunctional in literature reviews as well. For example, both VanSickle (1986) and Schlaefli et al. (1985) reported mean ESs but no measure of variability. Thus, VanSickle reported that "four studies detected a .80 mean effect [*sic*] . . . for attitude toward social phenomena" (p. 249), even though perusal of his tables indicated that the five SMDs from the four studies ranged from .15 to 1.76. His reporting of the knowledge outcomes from studies that compared simulation gaming against other instructional techniques is even more susceptible to misinterpretation. He reported a mean SMD of .12 for immediate recall of knowledge and a mean SMD of .28 for retention. The overall mean SMD for immediate knowledge recall and retention was .18, which he referred to as "a small positive effect using Cohen's conventions" (p. 249). He then concluded: "Overall, simulation gaming produced greater cognitive learning to a small degree when compared with other instructional techniques" (p. 249). Yet, 6 out of the 15 SMDs were negative (with one -.43 and another -.34). Inspection of the tables for the meta-analysis reported by Schaefli et al. (1985) also indicated that the mean SMD was an inadequate summation of findings. For example, for an overall mean of .28, the SMDs ranged from −.37 to 1.72.

As Guskin (1984) noted in a similar situation, the most reasonable conclusion would be that the "findings are ambiguous and conflicting" (p. 77). Clearly, with such variation, the studies grouped together for purposes of a review must have differed in important respects (Fiske, 1983). Reporting measures of variability makes such differences more evident. For example, a standard deviation of .61 for treatment SMDs was viewed in one review as "a reminder that the effects of each [attitude modification] technique were not homogeneous . . . [with] considerable overlap among the distributions of *D*s" (Shaver et al., 1989, p. 43).

Investigating Variability. Light and his associates (Light, 1979; Light & Pillemer, 1984; Light & Smith, 1971) have emphasized that variation in outcomes should not be treated as distracting noise, but as a signal that further analysis is needed to determine the circumstances for treatment effectiveness. Their stance and that of Cook and Leviton (1980) that more attention should be paid to interactions between treatments and study characteristics are consistent with Glass's emphasis on the examination of potential moderator variables as an essential element in a meta-analysis (e.g., Glass et al., 1981).

Although investigating variability is a potentially important step in a review, two difficulties can thwart efforts at such analyses. One is missing information (Orwin & Cordray, 1985). Obviously, if pertinent study characteristics are not reported, they cannot be analyzed. Second, the lack of adequate *n*s in cells when the data are broken down for such analyses can result in the confounding of treatments and characteristics (Shaver et al., 1987; Strube, 1988). That is an important way in which quantitative reviews are not an adequate substitute for planned replications.

A significant aspect of the analysis of study characteristic-by-treatment interactions is study quality. Of course, in a Glassian meta-analysis in which all studies are included initially, those interactions should be the subject of early analysis to determine if low-quality studies produced different results and so should be dropped from the data set. Here, missing information can be a serious problem (Bullock & Svyantek, 1985, p. 111). In our meta-analysis (Shaver et al., 1987), we found that it was particularly difficult to ferret out whether some threats to internal validity had been present in studies. We included in our coding instrument a *can't tell* option. Can't tell was coded for history and maturation as threats to internal validity for 71% and 51%, respectively, of the SMDs. In contrast, can't tell was coded for only 4% of the SMDs for statistical regression, 5% for instrumentation, and 8% for selection (p. 170).

Another difficulty can be lack of the variability in study characteristics needed to determine if study quality is associated with outcomes. For example, we (Shaver et al., 1987, p. 177) found that only 4 out of 644 SMDs came from studies coded as having excellent treatment validity (245 came from studies coded fair and 395 from studies coded poor), only 9 SMDs came from studies in which the validity of scores on the dependent measure was coded as high (520 were coded moderate and 115 low), and only 15 SMDs came from studies coded as high in internal validity (211 were coded medium and 418 low). Although the Eta^2s for study quality ratings and SMDs were low—.01, .02, and .02, respectively—they may be more indicative of a lack of variability in study quality than a lack of association between quality and outcome.

A number of authors (e.g., Cook & Leviton, 1980; Guskin, 1984; Shaver, 1979a; Slavin, 1984a) have pointed out a related difficulty with quality-outcome checks: the possibility of a pervasive threat of which the primary researchers are not aware or that they do not report (see Cook, 1987; Eysenck, 1984, p. 43), or that the reviewer does not detect. Among the pervasive threats mentioned have been the reliance on achievement tests as dependent measures (Guskin, 1984), the gender of the experimenter (Eagly & Carli, 1981), inappropriate matching and test reactivity (Slavin, 1984a), biased samples due to research convenience (Chipman, 1988), and the Hawthorne effect (Borg & Gall, 1989, p. 174). Of these, the inappropriateness of dependent measures is perhaps the most extensive threat to valid conclusions from research reviews in social studies education.

Reporting, Publishing Bias. A related issue of interpretability stems from reporting and publishing bias. The well-known tendency for authors to submit and editors to favor the publication of manuscripts in which statistically significant findings are reported creates a potentially biased population of reports (Kupfersmid, 1988). Rosenthal's (1979) application of his statistical estimate of the "file drawer problem" (the reports left in authors' file drawers because the results are not statistically significant) indicates that the bias may not be severe. However, a consistent finding is that when published and unpublished reports are included in a quantitative analysis, the published reports yield higher average SMDs (e.g., Glass et al., 1981). The conclusions in reviews based only on published reports are likely, then, to be overly optimistic.

A related type of bias is threatened by the lack of adequate reporting of the information needed to quantify outcomes. Although the use of ESs in quantitative literature reviews has be-

come commonplace, the reporting of ESs in primary research reports has not. I perused the 1981 to 1988 issues of *Theory and Research in Social Education* (TRSE) and found only 1 report, of 19 reports of analyses of mean differences, in which the SMD, although undefined, was utilized (Gilmore & McKinney, 1986). Omega^2 was reported as the ES in another article (Beem & Brugman, 1986). The means and standard deviations to compute SMDs are also often not reported, most typically when results are not statistically significant (Hedges & Olkin, 1985, p. 286). Moreover, efforts to obtain such information from authors yield a consistently low rate of return—about 12% (Shaver et al., 1987, pp. 84–85).

Hedges and Olkin (1985, p. 286) and Stanley (1987) have raised concerns about the bias introduced when such missing-information studies are excluded from a review. Slavin (1986) recommended that if information of at least statistical significance is available, such studies should be included in the review. VanSickle (1986) did compare the results from a vote count of statistical significance for all of his 42 studies against the results for the 22 studies for which SMDs could be computed. He found slight differences in the conclusions that could be drawn from the two sets of studies. Shaver et al. (1987) found minor differences in the characteristics and outcomes of their missing-ES-information and ES-available studies. For example, missing-information studies were rated slightly lower in internal validity (Cramer's V = .11) and had a slightly lower percentage of statistically significant results (35% vs. 45%).

Inferential Statistics in Reviews. Particularly troublesome are recommendations that the data in quantitative reviews of the literature be analyzed with inferential statistics, that population ESs be estimated, and that standard errors be computed for establishing confidence intervals (e.g., Hedges & Olkin, 1985; Rosenthal, 1984; Wolf, 1986). (See Schaefli et al., 1985, for such use.) The use of inferential statistics is especially problematic if the reviewer, as is typical in a meta-analysis, has done an exhaustive search and included all of the relevant available studies—that is, the accessible population—in the review. When data for a population are at hand, parameters can be computed directly, not inferred. In fact, inferential statistics are nonsensical. Moreover, unless a sample of studies has been randomly selected, the statistical theory, which rests on randomly generated data, is not applicable (see, e.g., Cohen & Hyman, 1981; Glass & Hopkins, 1984. p. 177; Morrison & Henkel, 1970b). Paradoxically, Glass and his associates (1981, pp. 197–199) recognized the inapplicability of inferential statistics in a meta-analysis, but then acceded to their use based on social convention (the "appetites" of some readers for inferential results) and went on to discuss applications.

Equally vexing is the advocacy of combining the probabilities from various studies as a quantitative methodology (e.g., Rosenthal, 1978, 1984). As noted above, the statistical significance levels for individual studies are relatively meaningless, and combining them to obtain an overall probability estimate will not add meaning.

Unfortunately, a number of those who write about meta-analysis convey misunderstandings of inferential statistics. For example, Carlberg and Miller (1984, p. 10) and Carlberg and

Walberg (1984, p. 25) asserted faith in the operation of the central limit theorem in meta-analyses, even though random sampling or assignment is integral to the theorem. Abrami et al. (1988, p. 162), in ruing the lack of statistical tests for the homogeneity of effect sizes, referred to sampling error as if that concept were applicable to results from nonrandom samples of studies.

The limited question about a chance occurrence under H_o that is addressed with a test of statistical significance has often been overlooked as well. Cooper (1981), for example, claimed that "rejecting the null, though a crude level of description, tells us that an effect size of zero has ... been effectively ruled out" (p. 1017). Strube and Hartmann (1983) suggested that the use of inferential statistics "aids the meta-analyst in his or her quest for precise delineation of effects" (p. 22) and claimed erroneously that a test of statistical significance tells the researcher "whether a particular result occurred due to chance" and that "the combination of probabilities across studies allows the reviewer to determine whether a set of results could have arisen by chance" (p. 15; also see Strube, 1988). Strube et al. (1985) stated that in combining results, a sign test "would provide an indication of whether an overall hypothesis of no effect of treatment is plausible" (pp. 72–73). Statistical significance was also confused with causality by Carlberg and Walberg (1984), who stated that inferential techniques "permit inferences about such matters as the overall [and differential] effectiveness of treatments" (1984, p. 15) and by Sampson et al. (1987), who stated that "one-way analysis of variance ... allows ... for comparison among variables to see which are significantly affected by the experimental treatment" (p. 292). Tests of statistical significance haunt quantitative reviews as they have the primary research enterprise.

Study-Subject Populations. An important distinction in interpreting review results is that between the *population of studies* and the *population* or *populations of subjects* represented by the samples in the studies (Hedges, 1986). Generalizations to the latter should be drawn cautiously. Even if a reviewer were to sample randomly from a population of studies, the population of subjects of interest might not be represented in the sample, because of sampling error or because the population was not present in the primary studies.

In any event, generalizations from study means may not hold for individual Ss. Light and Pillemer (1984, pp. 41–42) gave an example in which a negative relationship between hours of job training and post-training income across studies might not hold for individuals, because the most training was obtained in neighborhoods with the poorest employment opportunities. Erroneous study-to-individual generalization may also occur due to Simpson's paradox (Glass, 1977): With unbalanced experimental designs in the primary studies, the accumulation of ESs can indicate an overall result contradictory to that which would be obtained if the data for individual Ss were aggregated from the studies.

Coding Instruments. Ultimately, all interpretations in quantitative reviews depend on the validity of coding. The development of instruments to code studies should be approached with the same concern for reliability and validity as is called for with dependent measures in primary research (Bullock & Svyantek, 1985; Shaver, 1986). In addition, the categories and scoring conventions must be communicated clearly in reports if the reviewer's findings are to be meaningful to others, the conclusions critiqued adequately by readers, and/or the review replicated (Bullock & Svyantek, 1985; Stock et al., 1982). The reliability and validity of their coding were not addressed by Schaefli et al. (1985) or VanSickle (1986) in their reviews of social studies research.

Our experience (Shaver et al., 1987) is that coders tend to develop a common frame of reference which allows them to code independently with high agreement, but which is difficult to describe totally for others. A desirable, although costly, procedure would be to, first, develop the coding instrument until the coding team can reach adequate agreement on the application of individual categories. Then, before final coding begins, bring one or more nonproject persons in to determine if an outsider to the project can produce scores consistent with those of the staff. Only when the coding instrument can be used reliably at that level of independence would coding for the review be started.

The development of a scoring instrument that yields adequately reliable and valid scores is no easy task (Abrami et al., 1988). Shaver et al. (1987) spent three months in instrument development, even though they built on prior instrumentation by White and others (White, 1985–1986). Included were conceptual development (see Strube & Hartmann, 1983), innumerable revisions as the categories were tried out, and checks on both intercoder and intracoder agreement (Stock et al., 1982). It takes intimate knowledge of a field to develop a coding system that will reflect adequately the research and the interests of scholars and practitioners (Hedges, 1986). Even then the nuances that arise during coding suggest that the optimally valid coding instrument might be developed only after all of the studies have been read and preliminarily coded. Finally, coding is too important a task to be left to research assistants (Rosnow & Rosenthal, 1989; Wachter, 1988) if the project leader is to evaluate the adequacy of the coding instrument and adequately grasp the meaning of the findings.

The Danger of Numbers

Traditional narrative reviews have been soundly criticized for lack of precision and for subjectivity. The use of quantitative methods for reviews can provide a greater measure of objectivity and, especially, the capacity to review systematically large bodies of literature that might overwhelm a narrative reviewer. Clearly, however, issues of subjectivity, interpretability, and replicability remain.

While traditional reviews obviously may suffer from subjectivity, with quantitative reviews a danger in the misplaced precision of numbers has concerned a number of authors. For example, Cook and Leviton (1980) observed that "the [seemingly] descriptive accuracy of a point estimate in meta-analysis can have mischievous consequences because of its apparent 'objectivity', 'precision', and 'scientism' " (p. 445). Strube and Hartman (1983) warned the meta-analyst "not [to] be seduced by the quantitative nature of the approach" (p. 25) and, similarly, Carlberg and Walberg (1984) cautioned that "the logic that underlies quantitative research synthesis is simple, compelling, and elegant. It is also, therefore, seductive" (p. 25). Wilson and Rachman (1983) pointed out that meta-analysis cannot "make acceptable poor quality data" and noted the "danger that sophisticated techniques could lend themselves to misuse and may serve as smoke screens that obscure damaging flaws in the evidence" (p. 55). In a parallel vein, Slavin (1984b) warned that "meta-analysis can pull a veil of numbers over the critical information" (p. 26).

Clearly, there is always a risk in quantitative research that numbers will be treated as if they are the reality, and that reviewers and readers will forget to inquire about the basis for the numbers and their meaning. For that reason, a quote from William Thompson in the front pages of a recent book on meta-analysis (Mullen & Rosenthal, 1985) was disquieting, if not perturbing:

When you can measure what you are speaking about, and express it in numbers, you know something about it; but when you cannot measure it, when you cannot express it in numbers, your knowledge is of a meager and unsatisfactory kind: it may be the beginning of knowledge, but you have scarcely, in your thoughts, advanced to the stage of science. (p. xi)

The fallaciousness of such an extreme conception of the role of numbers does not, of course, mean that all use of numbers should be rejected. As Pillemer (1984) suggested, "the complaint that meta-analysis can be misused should be a plea for careful application rather than a rejection of the approach" (p. 32). Hedges (1986, p. 393) (who has as strong an inferential statistics orientation as any other current writer on meta-analysis) has urged the recognition that quantitative analysis alone will not suffice. There are some issues that cannot be settled by quantitative methods; moreover, the fruitful use of those methods depends on qualitative conceptualization to set context, guide the review, and aid in interpretation.

CONCLUSION

One purpose for this chapter has been to indicate the intellectual origins and potential contributions of quantitative review methodology, as well as to give a sense of the burgeoning

methodological literature. The dominant intent, however, has been to indicate the nature of the issues to be faced in using that methodology, emphasizing that quandaries of subjectivity, bias, and interpretation do not vanish with the benefits that come from more systematic, quantitative reviews.

If proper attention is paid to those issues—such as how to address the diversity in outcomes from a set of studies—the result may be more substantial findings to guide practice in social studies education. However, what is revealed may instead be further verification of the inadequate quality of the primary research (Fraenkel & Wallen, 1988) as a basis for decisions about social studies education. Another possibility is the clearer revelation of the complexity of the phenomenon of social studies education (Shaver, 1986), which may make the formulation of scientific-type knowledge unlikely, perhaps even impossible. As Light and Smith (1971) observed "genuinely contradictory results" may be "a valid description of reality" (p. 438). Along similar lines, Glass (1979) concluded that it is not now possible to "explain any appreciable proportion of the variance in success of different methods of schooling implemented in different places." Perhaps, he ruminated, we should give up the hunt for "the elusive consistencies and patterns to which we seem no nearer now than 20 years ago," recognizing that education deals with phenomena that are "unlawful, unpredictable, and unknowable *in the traditional scientific sense*" (p. 14, italics added). His call is similar to my own musing (Shaver et al., 1987, pp. 295–298) that conflicting research findings in education may reflect a reality that is indeed chaotic (Crutchfield, Farmer, Doyne, Packard, & Shaw, 1986)—lawful, with many regularities, but with such reactivity to minor perturbances that specific behavior is largely unpredictable.

These critical appraisals of the potential of education research and of reviews of that research should be taken not as discouragement but as indicators of the need to reformulate our goals and thus redirect our efforts in social studies research. Light (1979) and his colleagues (Light & Pillemer, 1984; Light & Smith, 1971) have argued that analyzing contradictory research results can yield valuable insights into teaching and learning. That argument is especially compelling if our purpose as researchers is consciously taken to be to inform and sensitize those who make decisions about social studies education, rather than the unrealistic goal of building nomothetic scientific theory (Shaver, 1982). The improvement of the quality of primary research and the appropriate, productive use of review methodologies is no less a challenge from that perspective.

References

Abrami, P. C., Cohen, P. A., & d'Apollonia, S. (1988). Implementation problems in meta-analysis. *Review of Education Research, 58,* 151–179.

Bangert-Drowns, R. L. (1986). Review of developments in meta-analytic methods. *Psychological Bulletin, 99,* 388–399.

Becker, B. J., & Hedges, L. V. (1984). Meta-analysis of cognitive gender differences: A comment on an analysis of Rosenthal and Rubin. *Journal of Education Psychology, 76*(4), 583–587.

Beem, A. L., & Brugman, D. (1986). The effects of values development

lessons on pupils' well-being, pleasure in school, mutual relationships, and on pupils' valuational behavior during classroom dialogues. *Theory and Research in Social Education, 14,* 97–112.

Biddle, B. J., & Anderson, D. S. (1986). Theory, methods, knowledge, and research on teaching. In M. C. Wittrock (Ed.), *Handbook of research on teaching* (3rd ed., pp. 230–252). New York: Macmillan.

Borg, W. R., & Gall, M. D. (1989). *Educational research: An introduction* (5th ed.) New York: Longman.

Bracey, G. W. (1985). Breakdown. *Phi Delta Kappan, 66,* 518.

Bracey, G. W. (1986). Tips for readers of research. *Phi Delta Kappan, 67,* 395–396.

Bryant, F. B., & Wortman, P. M. (1985). Methodological issues in the meta-analysis of quasi-experiments. *Evaluation Studies Review Annual, 10,* 629–648.

Bullock, R. J., & Svyantek, D. J. (1985). Analyzing meta-analysis: Potential problems, an unsuccessful replication, and evaluation criteria. *Journal of Applied Psychology, 70*(1), 108–115.

Carlberg, C. G., Johnson, D. W., Johnson, R., Maruyama, G., Kavale, K., Kulik, C. C., Kulik, J. A., Lysakowski, R. S., Pflaum, S. W., & Walberg, H. J. (1984). Meta-analysis in education: A reply to Slavin. *Educational Researcher, 13*(8), 16–27.

Carlberg, C. G., & Miller, T. L. (1984). Introduction. *The Journal of Special Education, 18,* 9–10.

Carlberg, C. G., & Walberg, H. J. (1984). Techniques of research synthesis. *The Journal of Special Education, 18,* 12–49.

Carver, R. P. (1978). The case against statistical significance testing. *Harvard Education Review, 48,* 378–399.

Center, B. A., Skiba, R. J., & Casey, A. (1985–1986). A methodology for the quantitative synthesis of intra-subject design research. *The Journal of Special Eduacation, 19,* 388–400.

Chipman, S. F. (1988). Far too sexy a topic [Review of *The psychology of gender: Advances through meta-analysis*]. *Educational Researcher, 17*(3), 46–49.

Chow, S. L. (1988). Significance test or effect size? *Psychological Bulletin, 103,* 105–110.

Cohen, J. (1988). *Statistical power analysis for the behavioral sciences* (2nd ed.). Hillsdale, NJ: Lawrence Erlbaum.

Cohen, S. A., & Hyman, J. S. (1979). How come so many hypotheses in educational research are supported? (A modest proposal). *Educational Researcher, 8*(11), 12–16.

Cohen, S. A., & Hyman, J. S. (1981, April). *Testing research hypotheses with critical ES instead of statistical significance in educational research.* Paper presented at the Annual Conference of the American Educational Research Association, Los Angeles.

Cook, T. D. (1987). Postpositivist critical multiplism. In W. R. Shadish, Jr., & C. S. Reichardt (Eds.), *Evaluation Studies Review Annual* (Vol. 12, pp. 458–499). Newbury Park, CA: Sage.

Cook, T. D., & Leviton, L. C. (1980). Reviewing the literature: A comparison of traditional methods with meta-analysis. *Journal of Personality, 48,* 449–472.

Cooper, H. M. (1981). On the significance of effects and the effects of significance. *Journal of Personality and Social Psychology, 41,* 1013–1018.

Cooper, H. M. (1982). Scientific guidelines for conducting integrative research reviews. *Review of Educational Research, 52,* 291–302.

Cooper, H. M. (1989). *Integrating research: A guide for literature reviews* (2nd ed.) Newbury Park, CA: Sage.

Cornbleth, C. (1985). Critical thinking and cognitive processes. In W. B. Stanley (Ed.), *Review of research in social studies education: 1976–1983* (pp. 11–63). Washington, DC: National Council for the Social Studies.

Crutchfield, J. P., Farmer, J. D., Doyne, J., Packard, N. H., & Shaw, R. S. (1986). Chaos. *Scientific American, 255*(6), 46–57.

Curtis, C. K., & Shaver, J. P. (1987). Modifying attitudes toward persons with disabilities: A review of reviews. *International Journal of Special Education, 2*(2), 103–129.

Davis, P. J., & Hersh, R. (1987). Rhetoric and mathematics. In J. S. Nelson, A. Megill, & D. N. McCloskey (Eds.), *The rhetoric of the human sciences* (pp.53–68). Madison, WI: The University of Wisconsin Press.

Eagly, A. H., & Carli, L. L. (1981). Sex of researchers and sex-typed communications as determinants of sex differences in influenceability: A meta-analysis of social influence studies. *Psychological Bulletin, 90,* 1–20.

Eysenck, H. J. (1978). An exercise in mega-silliness [Letter to the editor]. *American Psychologist, 33,* 517.

Eysenck, H. J. (1984). Meta-analysis: An abuse of research integration. *The Journal of Special Education, 18,* 41–59.

Feldman, K. A. (1971). Using the work of others: Some observations on reviewing and integrating. *Sociology of Education, 44,* 86–102.

Ferguson, G. A., & Takane, Y. (1989). *Statistical analysis in psychology and education* (6th ed.). New York: McGraw-Hill.

Fiske, D. W. (1983). The meta-analytic revolution in outcome research. *Journal of Consulting and Clinical Psychology, 51,* 65–70.

Fraenkel, J. R., & Wallen, N. E. (1988). *Toward improving research in social studies education.* Boulder, CO: Social Science Education Consortium.

Friedman, S. J. (1985). *Testing language, language dominance and math scores of bilingual Hispanic students.* Unpublished doctoral dissertation, Utah State University, Logan.

Gallo, P. S., Jr. (1978). Meta-analysis—A mixed meta-phor? [Letter to the editor]. *American Psychologist, 33,* 515–517.

Gilmore, A. C., & McKinney, C. W. (1986). The effects of student questions and teacher questions on concept acquisition. *Theory and Research in Social Education, 14,* 225–244.

Glass, G. V. (1976). Primary, secondary, and meta-analysis of research. *Educational Researcher, 5*(10), 3–8.

Glass, G. V. (1977). Integrating findings: The meta-analysis of research. *Review of Research in Education, 5,* 351–379.

Glass, G. V. (1979). Policy for the unpredictable (uncertainty research and policy). *Educational Researcher, 8*(9), 12–14.

Glass, G. V, & Hopkins, K. D. (1984). *Statistical methods in education and psychology* (2nd ed.). Englewood Cliffs, NJ: Prentice-Hall.

Glass, G. V, McGaw, B., & Smith, M. L. (1981). *Meta-analysis in social research.* Beverly Hills, CA: Sage.

Green, B. F., & Hall, J. A. (1984). Quantitative methods for literature reviews. *Annual Review of Psychology, 35,* 37–53.

Guskin, S. L. (1984). Problems and promises of meta-analysis in special education. *The Journal of Special Education, 18,* 73–80.

Haase, R. F., Waechter, D. M., & Solomon, G. S. (1982). How significant is a significant difference? Average effect size of research in counseling psychology. *Journal of Counseling Psychology, 29,* 58–65.

Hedges, L. V. (1986). Issues in meta-analysis. *Review of Research in Education, 13,* 353–398.

Hedges, L. V., & Olkin, I. (1982). Analyses, reanalyses, and meta-analysis [Review of *Meta-analysis in social research*]. *Contemporary Education Review, 1,* 157–165.

Hedges, L. V., & Olkin, I. (1985). *Statistical methods for meta-analysis.* New York: Academic Press.

Hedges, L. V., & Olkin, I. (1986). Meta analysis: A review and a new view. *Educational Researcher, 15*(8), 14–21.

Holmes, C. T. (1984). Effect size estimation in meta-analysis. *Journal of Experimental Education, 52,* 106–109.

Hunter, J. E., & Schmidt, F. L. (1990). *Methods of meta-analysis: Correcting error and bias in research findings.* Newbury Park, CA: Sage.

Hunter, J. E., Schmidt, F. L., & Jackson, G. B. (1982). *Meta-analysis: Cumulating research findings across studies.* Beverly Hills, CA: Sage.

Jackson, G. B. (1978). *Methods for reviewing and integrating research in the social sciences.* Final Technical Report to National Science Foundation for Grant #DIS 76-20398. Washington, DC: George Washington University, Social Research Group.

Jackson, G. B. (1980). Methods for integrative reviews. *Review of Educational Research, 50,* 438–460.

Kraemer, H. C., & Andrews, G. (1982). A nonparametric technique for meta-analysis effect size calculation. *Psychological Bulletin, 91*(2), 404–412.

Kulik, J. A., & Kulik, C. L. C. (1989). Meta-analysis in education. *International Journal of Education Research, 13*(3), 220–340.

Kupfersmid, J. (1988). Improving what is published: A model in search of an editor. *American Psychologist, 43,* 635–642.

Ladas, H. (1980). Summarizing research: A case study. *Review of Educational Research, 50,* 597–624.

Leming, J. S. (1981). Curricular effectiveness in moral/values education: A review of research. *Journal of Moral Education, 10,* 147–164.

Light, R. J. (1979). Capitalizing on variation: How conflicting research findings can be helpful for policy. *Educational Researcher, 8*(9), 7–11.

Light, R. J., & Pillemer, D. B. (1982). Numbers and narrative: Combining their strengths in research reviews. *Harvard Educational Review, 52,* 1–26.

Light, R. J., & Pillemer, D. B. (1984). *Summing up: The science of reviewing research.* Cambridge, MA; Harvard University Press.

Light, R. J., & Smith, P. V. (1971). Accumulating evidence: Procedures for resolving contradictions among different research studies. *Harvard Educational Review, 41,* 429–471.

Mansfield, R. S., & Busse, T. V. (1977). Meta-analysis of research: A rejoinder to Glass [Letter to the editor]. *Educational Researcher, 6*(9), 3.

McDaniel, M. A. (1986). Computer programs for calculating meta-analysis statistics. *Educational and Psychological Measurement, 46,* 175–177.

McGaw, B. (1988). Meta-analysis. In J. P. Keeves (Ed.), *Educational research, methodology, and measurement: An international handbook* (pp. 678–685). New York: Pergamon Press.

McGaw, B., & Glass, G. V. (1980). Choice of the metric for effect size in meta-analysis. *American Educational Research Journal, 17*(3), 325–337.

Messick, S. (1989). Meaning and values in test validation: The science and ethics of assessment. *Educational Researcher, 18*(2), 5–11.

Morrison, D. E., & Henkel, R. E. (1970a). *The significance test controversy—A reader.* Chicago: Aldine.

Morrison, D. E., & Henkel, R. E. (1970b). Significance tests in behavioral research: Skeptical conclusions and beyond. In D. E. Morrison & R. E. Henkel (Eds.), *The significance test controversy—A reader* (pp. 305–311). Chicago: Aldine.

Mullen, B., & Rosenthal, R. (1985). *Basic meta-analysis: Procedures and programs.* Hillsdale, NJ: Lawrence Erlbaum.

Murray, L. W., & Dosser, D. A., Jr. (1987). How significant is a significant difference? Problems with the measurement of magnitude of effect. *Journal of Counseling Psychology, 34,* 68–72.

Noblit, G. W., & Hare, R. D. (1988). *Meta-ethnography: Synthesizing qualitative studies.* Beverly Hills, CA: Sage.

O'Grady, K. E. (1982). Measures of explained variance: Cautions and limitations. *Psychological Bulletin, 92,* 766–777.

Oliver, L. W., & Spokane, A. R. (1983). Research integration: Approaches, problems, and recommendations for research reporting. *Journal of Counseling Psychology, 30*(2), 252–257.

Orwin, R. G., & Cordray, D. S. (1985). Effects of deficient reporting on meta-analysis: A conceptual framework and reanalysis. *Psychological Bulletin, 97,* 134–147.

Pillemer, D. B. (1984). Conceptual issues in research synthesis. *The Journal of Special Education, 18,* 27–40.

Preece, P. F. W. (1983). A measure of experimental effect size based on success rates. *Educational and Psychological Measurement, 43,* 763–766.

Presby, S. (1978). Overly broad categories obscure important differences between therapies [Letter to the editor]. *American Psychologist, 33,* 514–515.

Raudenbush, S. W., Becker, B. J., & Kalaian, H. (1988). Modeling multivariate effect sizes. *Psychological Bulletin, 103,* 111–120.

Rosenthal, R. (1976). *Experimenter effects in behavioral research.* New York: Irvington.

Rosenthal, R. (1978). Combining results of independent studies. *Psychological Bulletin, 85,* 185–193.

Rosenthal, R. (1979). The "file drawer problem" and tolerance for null results. *Psychological Bulletin, 86,* 638–641.

Rosenthal, R. (Ed.). (1980). *New directions for methodology of social and behavioral science: Quantitative assessment of research domains* (No. 5). San Francisco: Jossey-Bass.

Rosenthal, R. (1984). *Meta-analytic procedures for social research.* Beverly Hills, CA: Sage.

Rosenthal, R., & Rubin, D. B. (1982). A simple, general purpose display of magnitude of experimental effect. *Journal of Educational Psychology, 74,* 166–169.

Rosnow, R. L., & Rosenthal, R. (1989). Statistical procedures and the justification of knowledge in psychological sciences. *American Psychologist, 44,* 1276–1284.

Royall, R. M. (1986). The effect of sample size on the meaning of significance tests. *American Statistician, 40,* 313–315.

Salzberg, C. L., Strain, P. S., & Baer, D. M. (1987). Meta-analysis for single-subject research: When does it clarify, when does it obscure? *Remedial and Special Education, 8,* 43–48.

Sampson, G. E., Strykowski, B., Weinstein, T., & Walberg, H. J. (1987). The effects of teacher questioning levels on student achievement: A quantitative synthesis. *The Journal of Educational Research, 80,* 290–295.

Schlaefli, A., Rest, J. R., & Thoma, S. J. (1985). Does moral education improve judgement? A meta-analysis of intervention studies using the Defining Issues Test. *Review of Educational Research, 55,* 319–352.

Scruggs, T. E., Mastropieri, M. A., & Casto, G. (1987). The quantitative synthesis of single-subject research: Methodology and validation. *Remedial and Special Education, 8,* 24–33.

Scruggs, T. E., White, K. R., & Bennion, K. (1986). Teaching test-taking skills to elementary grade students: A meta-analysis. *The Elementary School Journal, 87,* 69–82.

Shapiro, D. A., & Shapiro, D. (1982). Meta-analysis of comparative therapy outcome studies: A replication and refinement. *Psychological Bulletin, 92,* 581–604.

Shapiro, D. A., & Shapiro, D. (1983). Comparative therapy outcome research: Methodological implications of meta-analysis. *Journal of Consulting and Clinical Psychology, 51*(1), 42–53.

Shavelson, R. J., Webb, N. M., & Burstein, L. (1986). Measurement of teaching. In M. C. Wittrock (Ed.), *Handbook of research on teaching* (3rd ed., pp. 50–91). New York: Macmillan.

Shaver, J. P. (1979a). The productivity of educational research and the applied-basic research distinction. *Educational Researcher, 8*(1), 3–9.

Shaver, J. P. (1979b). The usefulness of educational research in curricular/instructional decision-making in social studies. *Theory and Research in Social Education, 7*(3), 21–46.

Shaver, J. P. (1982). Reappraising the theoretical goals of research in social education. *Theory and Research in Social Education, 6*(1), 31–43.

Shaver, J. P. (1983). The verification of independent variables in teaching methods research. *Educational Researcher, 12*(8), 2–9.

Shaver, J. P. (1985a). Chance and nonsense: A conversation about interpreting tests of statistical significance, Part 1. *Phi Delta Kappan, 67,* 57–60.

Shaver, J. P. (1985b). Chance and nonsense: A conversation about interpreting tests of statistical significance, Part 2. *Phi Delta Kappan, 67,* 138–141. Erratum, 1986, *67,* 624.

Shaver, J. P. (1986). *Scholarship in social education: Issues from an empirical, meta-analysis research perspective.* Paper presented at the annual meeting of the National Council for the Social Studies, New York. (ERI Document Reproduction Service No. ED 278 594).

Shaver, J. P., Curtis, C. K., Jesunathadas, J., & Strong, C. J. (1987). *The modification of attitudes toward persons with handicaps: A comprehensive integrative review of research.* Final Report to the U.S. Department of Education, Office of Special Education and Rehabilitative Services. Logan, UT: Utah State University, Bureau of Research Services. (ERIC Document Reproduction Service No. ED 285 345).

Shaver, J. P., Curtis, C. K., Jesunathadas, J., & Strong, C. J. (1989). The modification of attitudes toward persons with disabilities: Is there a best way? *International Journal of Special Education, 49*(1), 33–57.

Slack, J. P., & Larkins, A. G. (1982). The effect of two instructional treatments on college students' map skills achievement. *Journal of Social Studies Research, 6*(1), 13–16.

Slavin, R. E. (1984a). Meta-analysis in education: How has it been used? *Educational Researcher, 13*(8), 6–15.

Slavin, R. E. (1984b). A rejoinder to Carlberg et al. *Educational Researcher, 13*(8), 24–27.

Slavin, R. E. (1986). Best-evidence synthesis: An alternative to meta-analytic and traditional reviews. *Educational Researcher, 15*(9), 5–11.

Slavin, R. E. (1987). Best-evidence synthesis: Why less is more. *Educational Researcher, 16*(4), 15–16.

Smith, M. L., & Glass, G. V. (1977). Meta-analysis of psychotherapy outcome studies. *American Psychologist, 32,* 752–760.

Stanley, J. C. (1987). Note about possible bias resulting when understatisticized studies are excluded from meta-analysis. *Journal of Educational Measurement, 24*(1), 72–76.

Sternberg, L., & Taylor, R. L. (1982). The insignificance of psycholinguistic training: A reply to Kavale. *Exceptional Children, 49,* 254–256.

Stock, W. A., Okun, M. A., Haring, M. J., Miller, W., Kinney, C., & Ceurvorst, R. W. (1982). Rigor in data synthesis: A case study of reliability in meta-analysis. *Educational Researcher, 11*(6), 10–14, 20.

Strong, C. J. (1989). *Stability of oral cohesion skills of language-impaired and normally developing school-aged children.* Unpublished doctoral dissertation, Utah State University, Logan.

Strube, M. J. (1988). Some comments on the use of magnitude-of-effect estimates. *Journal of Counseling Psychology, 35,* 342–345.

Strube, M. J., Gardner, W., & Hartmann, D. P. (1985). Limitations, liabilities, and obstacles in reviews of the literature: The current status of meta-analysis. *Clinical Psychology Review, 5,* 63–78.

Strube, M. J., & Hartmann, D. P. (1983). Meta-analysis: Techniques, applications, and functions. *Journal of Consulting and Clinical Psychology, 51,* 14–27.

Taylor, M. J., & White, K. R. (1990, April). *An evaluation of alternative methods for computing standardized mean difference effect sizes.* Paper presented at the annual meeting of the American Educational Research Association, Boston.

VanSickle, R. L. (1986). A quantitative review on instructional simulation gaming: A twenty-year perspective. *Theory and Research in Social Education, 14,* 245–264.

Wachter, K. W. (1988). Disturbed by meta-analysis? *Science, 241,* 1407–1408.

Wade, S. E. (1983). A synthesis of the research for improving reading in the social studies. *Review of Educational Research, 53,* 561–497.

Waxman, H. C., & Walberg, H. J. (1982). The relation of teaching and learning: A review of reviews of process-product research. *Contemporary Education Review, 1*(2), 103–120.

White, K. R. (1982). An integrative review of the relationship between socioeconomic status and academic achievement using meta-analysis techniques. *Psychological Bulletin, 91,* 461–481.

White, K. R. (1985–1986). Efficacy of early intervention. *The Journal of Special Education, 19,* 401–416.

White, K. R., Bush, D. W., & Casto, G. C. (1985–1986). Learning from reviews of early intervention. *The Journal of Special Education, 19,* 417–428.

White, K. R., & Greenspan, S. I. (1987). An overview of the effectiveness of preventive early intervention programs. In I. F. Berlin and J. Nashpitz (Eds.), *Basic handbook of child psychiatry* (pp. 541–553). New York: Basic Books.

White, O. R. (1987). Some comments concerning "The quantitative synthesis of single-subject research". *Remedial and Special Education, 8,* 34–39.

Wilson, G. T., & Rachman, S. J. (1983). Meta-analysis and the evaluation of psychotherapy outcome: Limitations and liabilities. *Journal of Consulting and Clinical Psychology, 51*(1), 54–64.

Winer, B. J. (1971). *Statistical principles in experimental design* (2nd ed.). New York: McGraw-Hill.

Wolf, F. M. (1986). *Meta-analysis: Quantitative methods for research synthesis.* Beverly Hills, CA: Sage.

·8·

LAYERED UNDERSTANDINGS OF ORIENTATIONS
IN SOCIAL STUDIES PROGRAM EVALUATION

Ted T. Aoki

UNIVERSITY OF ALBERTA (EMERITUS)

Since the mid-1960s, about the time of the publication of Scriven's *Perspectives of Curriculum Evaluation* (1976), the field of evaluation in education has begun to come into its own. In program evaluation in particular, significant advances have been made, led by scholars such as Eisner (1979); Stake (Stake & Easley, 1978); MacDonald and Walker (1974); House (1973); Apple (1974); Hamilton (Hamilton, Jenkins, King, MacDonald, & Parlett, 1977); and Patton (1975). Within this growing field, it has become increasingly challenging for curriculum evaluators not only to become acquainted with the burgeoning literature, but also to be insightful in trying to understand the world views from which approaches to evaluation have been propounded. Social studies evaluators have an added challenge for they find themselves in the midst of multiplicities: multiple understandings of evaluation approaches and multiple interpretations of social studies. The intent in this chapter is not to provide a compendium of evaluation models or of social studies evaluation reports, or a history of evaluation approaches in social studies education, but to begin to address the social studies evaluators' challenge by attempting to disclose orientations towards evaluation.

More than a decade ago in a probing article, "Research on Teaching Social Studies", Shaver and Larkins (1973), concerned with the confining nature of traditional approaches to research in social studies including evaluation research, called for an opening up of the basic research frame. In the field of evaluation practice in social studies, in spite of the numerous evaluation activities in social studies at the local, state/provincial, and national levels, the call of Shaver and Larkins seems to have gone largely unheeded. It is only within the last decade that those in the field of social studies curriculum evaluation have begun to put to serious questioning the notion of "evaluation" itself.

Social studies evaluators, like other researchers, have been prone to approach their evaluation tasks with their favorite evaluation models, approaches, and techniques. In education, the prevailing research ethos is technological. Evaluation is a part of this ethos, and evaluators have approached their tasks from that perspective. In fact, the prominent use of "assessment" in its strict instrumental sense within the language of evaluation speaks of the epistemological tradition to which many evaluators hold allegiance.

In itself there is little reason to be concerned about the dominance of any single mode of evaluation. What is of concern is that the dominance may lead evaluators to forget that the form of evaluation should be appropriate to the phenomenon to be evaluated and that the evaluation approach should be responsive to the interests to be served by the evaluation. In accord with what Kaplan (1964) has termed "the law of the instrument" (p. 28), in educational research the availability of a research tool often determines the nature of the research done and how research is understood; so, too, in evaluation, the evaluation methods and instruments available may determine the nature of the evaluation done and how evaluation is understood. We need to be alert to the law of the instrument in social studies evaluation.

In recent years, some have questioned the tendency of educators to reduce educational evaluation to the paradigm of scientific research. Much of this questioning has come from Continental European scholars who did not succumb, as did many North American scholars, to the persuasions of logical positivism expounded by members of the Vienna Circle. Among these

Reviewers were J. Nicholls Eastmond, Jr., Utah State University; Michael Hartoonian, Wisconsin State Department of Education; Daniel Stufflebeam, Western Michigan University.

is Jurgen Habermas (1972), a German scholar affiliated with the Frankfurt School. He, together with others such as Horkheimer and Adorno (1972) and Marcuse (1968), decried what they saw as a serious crisis in Western intellectualism because of the domination of instrumental reasoning based on scientism and technology. Habermas apppealed to philosophical anthropology, a cultural study of philosophic orientations, to reveal knowledge-constitutive human interests embedded in basically different orientations. His threefold orientations (the empirical-analytic, the critical-reflective, and the situational-interpretive) have inspired many human scientists in their endeavors to reexamine not only the issue of research frameworks noted by Shaver and Larkins (1973), but also the issue of evaluation frameworks.

In this chapter, which leans heavily on Habermas, the empirical-analytic orientation has been recast as an *ends-means* model, the critical-reflective orientation has been retained under the name of *praxis,* and the situational-interpretive orientation has been unfolded into *emic* and *critical-hermeneutic* evaluation orientations. Moreover, rather than merely suggest a plurality of alternative orientations, the orientations have been gathered, admittedly loosely, into layers that suggest some distinction between the world of concretely lived experiences and the formulations of evaluation that are abstractions of and somewhat distant from the lived experiences.

As might be expected, the world of lived experiences is considered as the ground for the four evaluation orientations, layered as follows:

1. Ends-means evaluation orientation.
2. Praxical evaluation orientation.
3. Emic evaluation orientation.
4. Critical-hermeneutic evaluation orientation.

Each of these evaluation orientations is discussed briefly. To provide some contact with the practical world of evaluation, illustrations are provided from the province-wide British Columbia Social Studies Assessment of which the author was team director (Aoki, Langford, Williams, & Wilson, 1977a, 1977b).

Our experiences in evaluating British Columbia social studies, guided by Habermas's interpretation of multiple interests, provide an exemplar of how evaluation can be viewed from multiple perspectives. From the outset as we ventured into various centers of British Columbia seeking out and trying to make sense of social studies interests expressed by teachers, students, parents, school trustees, administrators, and professors of social studies education, we seriously asked ourselves: "What evaluation frameworks and approaches should we employ in evaluating the phenomenon called *social studies* in British Columbia?"

We took a cue from what Beittel (1973, p. 6) called appropriately the "Rashomon effect," a notion from an acclaimed film by Kurosawa in which he disclosed the same event from several perspectives. Simultaneously, we were mindful of the possibility of inadvertently reducing our evaluation to the dominant ends-means orientation. As early as in the mid-1970s, Patton (1975) had pointed out this concern in the following way:

The very dominance of the scientific method in evaluation research

appears to have cut off the great majority of practitioners from serious consideration of any alternative research paradigm. The label "research" has come to mean the equivalent of employing the Scientific Method—of working within the dominant paradigm. (p. 6)

In the following sections, the four evaluation orientations, which are summarized in Table 8–1, are illuminated.

ENDS-MEANS EVALUATION ORIENTATION

The interests of evaluators acting within the ends-means orientation are reflected in the evaluation questions they entertain. The following questions illustrate these interests:

1. How effective and efficient are the means used in achieving the curricular goals and objectives?
2. What is the degree of congruency between and among intended outcomes, the content of the instructional materials, and the teaching approaches specified?
3. How good is Curriculum A compared with Curriculum B in achieving given ends?
4. Of given curricula, which one is the most cost effective and time efficient?
5. What valid generalizations can be made for all schools in a district?

These ends-means interests reflect an orientation to evaluation that can be characterized as technical or instrumental. As such, they reflect the dominant evaluation approach in use, going hand in hand with the technically oriented mainstream curriculum development/evaluation rationale, known popularly as the Tyler Rationale. We know it by Tyler's (1949) sequentially arranged four-step formulation. The steps are as follows:

1. What educational purposes should the school seek to attain?
2. How can learning experiences be selected which are likely to be useful in attaining these objectives?
3. How can learning experiences be organized for effective instruction?
4. How can the effectiveness of learning experiences be *evaluated?*

The ends-means evaluation orientation has for the pragmatically oriented a commonsensical ring that carries with it the validity of popular support. Further, its congruency with the mainstream social theory idioms of basically instrumental reason, such as behaviorism, systems analysis, and structural functionalism—from which educators have borrowed heavily—lends ends-means evaluation a credibility that assumes the status of consensual validity. Such legitimated authenticity has led many evaluators to regard this evaluation orientation reductively as *the* orientation.

But what does this orientation imply in terms of interests and assumptions usually held tacitly? Underneath the avowed interest in efficiency, effectiveness, predictability, and certainty, as reflected in the above list of interests, is a more deeply rooted interest—that of *control.* The orientation is immersed in a manipulative ethos that leads evaluators of this orientation

TABLE 8–1. A Summary of Layered Understandings of Evaluation Orientations

Evaluation Orientation	Evaluation Interests	World of Knowing	Mode of Evaluation
Ends-means	Control as reflected in values of efficiency, effectiveness, certainty, and predictability. Fidelity between ends and means.	Finite world of facts, information, concepts, generalizations, laws, and theories. Objectives are often stated in terms of knowledge, skills, and attitude. Possibility of progress is key belief.	Measurement of discrepancy between ends and means. Goal-based, criterion-referenced, cost-benefit assessment of achievement.
Praxical	Emancipatory action that improves human condition. Quality of reflection and action.	Critical knowing in the sense of understanding hidden assumptions, perspectives, motives, rationalizations, and ideologies. Critical knowing coupled with action.	Uncovering of ideology underlying knowledge and action.
Emic	Quality of everyday cultural life. Tacit rules people live by in daily life.	Thick, descriptive knowledge of lived cultural layer. Social life understood as socially constructed rules of everyday living.	Ethnographic case studies approach. Ethnomethodological approach.
Critical-hermeneutic	Disclosure of existential meanings in lived experience. Quality of human beingness.	A world of insights (rather than generalizations) into unique human situations. Concretely lived world as earth dwellers. Infinite world of being.	Phenomenological-hermeneutic approach. Critical quest for what it means to be human.

to value such evaluation questions as, "How well have the ends been achieved?" "Which is a better program, Curriculum A or Curriculum B?"

Within this framework, the form of knowledge that is prized is empirical data; the harder and the more objective the data, the better. Data are seen as brute facts. In scientific terms, the form of knowledge confers nomological status, with empirical validation demanded and levels of generalizability sought. Knowledge is assumed to be objective, carrying with it the dignity of value-free neutrality.

Evaluators who subscribe to the ends-means view are technologically oriented, primarily interested in seeing how well the system is able to control its own components in struggling to achieve system goals. These evaluators seek efficient tools and instruments such as tests and questionnaires, and seek rigor by bringing to bear the expertise of psychometricians and statisticians. They tend to resort to measurable quantitative data subjected to sophisticated statistical analyses.

In our British Columbia Social Studies Assessment, we administered achievement tests to randomly selected classes in Grades 4, 8, and 12 throughout the province and we sent questionnaires to randomly selected teachers in order to seek the teachers' assessment of instructional resources. In our evaluation project, the largest portion of the evaluation grant budget was allocated to this phase, indicating how we, ourselves, were held in the sway of this orientation.

In summary, the ends-means evaluation mode is framed within the framework of the following interests, world of knowing, and mode of evaluation:

Interests in: The ethos of control as reflected in the values of efficiency, effectiveness, certainty, and predictability. Fidelity to given ends is a major concern.

World of Knowing: Assumed is a finite world of nomological knowing. Understanding is in terms of facts, generalizations, concepts, laws, and theories. Objectives are often given in terms of knowledge, skills, and attitudes.

Mode of Evaluation: Ends-means evaluation that is achievement-oriented, goal-based, criterion-referenced, and cost-benefit-oriented.

PRAXICAL EVALUATION ORIENTATION

Evaluators thinking and acting within the praxical mode express their interests by committing themselves to a set of evaluation concerns that differ markedly from those of technically oriented evaluators. The following questions illustrate the concerns of praxical evaluators:

1. What is the orientation underlying Curriculum X in terms of root interests, root assumptions, root approaches?
2. What is the implicit view of the student or the teacher held by the curriculum planner?
3. At the most basic level, whose interests does Curriculum X serve?
4. What are the fundamental metaphors that guide the curriculum developer, curriculum implementer, or curriculum evaluator?
5. What is the basic bias of the publisher, author, or developer of prescribed or recommended resource materials?
6. What is the world view underlying the curriculum?

These evaluation interests reflect an orientation to evaluation that is rooted in neo-Marxian critical social theory. In this approach to evaluation, the evaluator attempts to bring into fuller view the underlying elements of programs that are typically taken for granted and, therefore, hidden from view. Implied within any curriculum or evaluation orientation are root metaphors, deep-seated human interests, assumptions about humans, world views, and knowledge, as well as stances that people take in approaching self or world. Praxical evaluators are interested in making these visible. But they do not stop there.

In ends-means evaluation the task is seen within the framework of instrumental or technical action; in praxical evaluation, it is seen within the dialectical framework of practical action and critical reflection, what Paulo Freire (1968) referred to as *praxis*. In critical reflection, the actor through the reflective process discovers and makes explicit tacit and hidden assumptions and intentions. Such reflective activity is guided by an interest in revealing the ideological condition that makes knowing possible, or in revealing the underlying human and social conditions that distort human existence, distortions that tend to produce alienation. Thus, praxical evaluators attempt to determine the regularities of human and social action that express ideologically frozen relations of dependence that can be transformed. Schaull (1968) captured aptly this praxical orientation in the following way:

There is no such thing as a *neutral* educational process. Education either functions as an instrument which is used to facilitate the integration of the younger generation into the logic of the present system and bring about conformity to it, *or* it becomes "the practice of freedom," the means by which men and women deal critically and creatively with reality and discover how to participate in the transformation of their world. (p.15)

Thus, a praxically oriented evaluator's self may become a part of the object of the evaluation research. The evaluator, in becoming involved with his or her subjects, enters into their world and attempts to engage them mutually in reflective activity. The evaluator questions the subjects and self, and encourages subjects to question him or her and themselves. Reflection by self and the participants allows new questions to emerge from the situation that, in turn, lead to further reflective activity. Reflection, however, is oriented not only toward making conscious the unconscious by discovering underlying interests, assumptions, and intentions, but also toward action guided by the newly gained conscious and critical knowledge. Hence, in the ongoing dialectical and transformative process, both evaluator and subjects become participants in an open dialogue.

Reflection in the foregoing sense is not the kind of activity in which school people typically engage in their ongoing daily lives. For, in their everyday existence people deal with their concerns in routine ways guided by the commonplace recipes that sustain them. What is missing is a conscious effort to examine critically the assumptions and intentions underlying their practical thoughts and acts. Evaluators may be reflective but not necessarily critically reflective. Critical reflection leads to an understanding of what is beyond the actor's ordinary view by making the familiar unfamiliar, by making the invisible visible. Such reflective activity allows liberation from the unconsciously held assumptions and intentions that lie buried and hidden. For example, at the personal level the content of reflection may be the rationalization an actor uses to hide underlying motives for his actions. At the societal level, the content reflected on may be the ideology used to support social practices and policies that render obscure society's manipulative ethos and the underlying interests.

But more than that, such critical reflection in intended to bring about the reorientation, through transformative action, of the assumptions and intentions upon which reflection and action rest. The praxical orientation to evaluation, then, with its guiding interest of liberating people from hidden interests and approaches, promotes a theory of individuals and society that is grounded in the moral attitude of emancipation.

Within the British Columbia Social Studies Assessment, praxical evaluation was included under the innocuous title "An Interpretation of Intents of the Elementary and Secondary Curriculum Guides." In that part of the project we examined the official text of the social studies curriculum-as-plan. The concluding statement of the praxical analysis gives a sense of the flavor of this evaluation:

The British Columbia Social Studies program approaches the study of man-in-his-world from three different perspectives: scientific, situational and critically reflective knowing. Through each of these, students are exposed to various interpretations of how the social world has been constructed. The program, however, does not provide a balance between these perspectives: rather, it emphasizes scientific knowledge. Through such an emphasis teachers and students are made dependent on one particular way of viewing the social world. Such dependence limits the possibilities which the participants have available for exploring their social environment. The extent to which the perspectives influence classroom presentations (passive vs. active, non-committal vs. committal) stresses the importance of providing a balance of knowledge perspectives in the program. (Aoki & Harrison, 1977, p. 62)

We tried to bring the official B. C. Social Studies Program into fuller view by revealing the tacitly held assumptions and intentions. Following the above comment, we added as a recommendation to the Ministry of Education the following:

To aid teachers in moving towards consideration of perspectives, it is recommended that a full description of the perspectives incorporated into the British Columbia Social Studies program be carefully described in the Curriculum Guides. Students and teachers are entitled to a full explanation of the curriculum developers' knowing stance. The curriculum developers' perspective toward the social world should not, in other words, be hidden from users of the curriculum. (Aoki & Harrison, 1977, p. 62)

The praxical evaluation orientation can be summarized as follows:

Interests in: Emancipation from hidden assumptions of underlying human conditions that distort human life. Quality of reflection/action.

World of Knowing: Critical knowing in the sense of understanding hidden assumptions, perspectives, motives, rationalizations, and ideologies. To explain within critical knowing is to trace down and bring into fuller view the underlying ideology. As praxis, this critical knowing is coupled with action.

Mode of Evaluation: Praxical evaluation involves (a) discovering through critical reflection the underlying human conditions, assumptions, and intentions and (b) acting upon self and world to improve the human condition or to transform the underlying assumptions and intentions.

EMIC EVALUATION ORIENTATION

In contrast to the technical interests of evaluators in the ends-means approach to evaluations and the emancipatory interests of those in the praxical approach, the central interest of emic evaluators is in seeking understanding of the situated cultural activities, values, and beliefs of participants in social studies. (*Emic* is an anthropological term referring to the insiders' subjective understanding.) Hence, these evaluators are guided by interests embedded in such questions as the following:

1. How can we understand the quality of this social studies class as a microculture of the classroom?
2. How do various groups such as teachers, students, parents, and administrators view Curriculum X? How worthy are these views?
3. In what ways do various groups approve or disapprove the school's social studies program?
4. How do the various groups view Curriculum X in terms of relevance? How worthy are these views?
5. How do the various groups understand the strengths and weaknesses of the social studies program?
6. What are the group-constructed rules for the social studies activities in this class?

The interests expressed in these questions reflect an approach to evaluation in which evaluators show interest in the ethnocultural patterns of life in the social studies situation. Hence, many of these evaluators have a kinship with cultural anthropologists or sociologists whose interest is in the social construction of reality. Characteristically, rather than be strictly objective observers, these evaluators attempt to place themselves in situ in order to be near the culture or society they wish to understand, while at the same time attempting to maintain a distance that will enable them to observe the construct of interest. Case studies are frequent within this orientation.

Related to the work of ethnographers is the work of ethnomethodologists who attempt to understand group life as a game consisting of tacitly acknowledged socially constructed rules. They also place themselves in situ. Tactically, they often introduce a break in the pattern of living and observe how members of a group respond to the break, attending to the way they reconstitute their way of life. In this reconstitution, the ethnomethodolgically oriented evaluator seeks out the socially constructed rules of the game that is life.

In the British Columbia Social Studies Assessment, we attempted to be sensitive to the etic/emic (outsider/insider) perspectives distinguished by cultural anthropologists. (The etic/emic perspective in this study was a contribution of Donald C. Wilson who, in his doctoral study (1976), explored epistemological issues underlying etic and emic approaches to research and evaluation.) In our emic effort, we strove to capture aspects of the subjective world of teachers, students, parents, and administrators as they lived in their social studies situations in school. In rendering emic views of their lives, we came to recognize a way of knowing that countered the standardized way in which people recognize correctness and incorrectness based on the strict outsiders' objective format that dominates the view of knowing stressed in ends-means evaluation.

A flavor of our effort in emic evaluation is offered in the following excerpt from a summary of the "Interpretive Studies of Selected School Situations" subreport of the B. C. Social Studies Assessment (Aoki et al., 1977b). It is

an account of five in-depth studies in school situations.... Each study is based on a series of school visits and interviews with educators and students. This personal contact provides evaluative information consisting of the thoughts and experiences individuals have of learning and teaching Social Studies in particular situations. Information concerned with the everyday activities of students and teachers enriches and therefore complements the generalizations arising from information obtained from the paper-and-pencil instruments. Hence, each study outlines the setting of the situation and describes the nature of the Social Studies programs, and interprets the meaning or significance which educators and students ascribe to them. Conclusions are made in terms of the schools visited in each particular situation and not with reference to all schools in British Columbia....

In most cases, paper/pencil instruments collect data according to certain reporting categories identified as important prior to collection procedures. Understanding, therefore, becomes expressed in terms of relational knowledge that can become generalizable to other situations.... Based on the premise that educators and students interpret social studies according to their experiences within their social context, the [interpretive] studies not only describe particular situations according to what was observed by evaluators and stated by teachers and students, but also interpret those descriptions with reference to frameworks that acknowledge the process of instruction and the "insider's" perspective. (p. 26)

A framework "used to interpret how teachers view a program" is described below:

1. *Intents:* These are expressions of desired goals or possibilities for a program. They may be manifestations of written instructional objectives or implicit desires of individuals.
2. *Resources:* These are resource materials that display a particular means with which students and teachers interact in an instructional setting. A resource might be a picture, a page in a textbook, a map, or a film that displays some object of the environment.
3. *Activities:* This component of a program refers to student and teacher activities defined in the context of intents and resources. Class activities may either be predefined by teachers or result from interactions of students and teachers. Activities that are often a part of a social studies program as lectures, class discussions, field studies, or simulations.

These components of a program do not exist in isolation but are closely interrelated. For example, the intent a teacher has for teaching social studies will also be manifested in his or her view of resources and desired class activities. Again, the concern for certain kinds of resources and class activities will reflect certain interests one has for teaching social studies. It is this "total picture" of how teachers interpret a program in a particular context that becomes the focus of the interpretation (Aoki et al., 1977b, p. 27).

In approaching emic evaluation with a preset framework, we were mindful of the risk of imposition of external categories and attempted to be open to the insiders' interpretations of our categories and sensitive as well to their own categories.

The emic evaluation orientation can be summarized as follows:

Interest in: The quality of everyday cultural and social life or of the tacit rules people live by in their daily lives.
World of Knowing: Thick descriptive knowledge of a cultural layer; understanding of socially constructed rules governing everyday living.
Mode of Evaluation: In situ evaluation that embodies ethnographic and/or ethnomethodological approaches.

CRITICAL-HERMENEUTIC EVALUATION ORIENTATION

Within the critical-hermeneutic orientation, the evaluators' interest is directed not so much to the level of attainment of knowledge, skills, or attitudes; nor to the merit of ideological interests, assumptions, and approaches; nor to in situ portrayals that constitute the cultural lives of people. Rather, the interest is in seeking out the quality of ontological meanings in the lived experiences of students, teachers, administrators, and parents.

The interests in the nature and quality of the beingness of human beings are reflected in questions such as the following:

1. What is it like being a teacher or student of social studies in this school?
2. What is it like to experience social studies classes in this school?
3. What is the quality of the lived experiences of teachers and students in social studies?
4. What *is* social studies? (Not, *what* is social studies?)
5. In what ways do teachers and taught belong together pedagogically?

Within this orientation social studies is understood not so much in terms of studies *about,* cast within the realm of positivistic objectivity, somewhat distanced from the lives of teachers and students, but in terms of life as humanly lived in social studies classes. Labels such as *social living* or *social education* that have appeared in the social studies lexicon in the past can be seen as early efforts to break out of the reductive objectivity from which social studies is understood as studies *about.* Hence, evaluators within this orientation try to transcend evaluation modes that are oriented to objectivity.

Since the guiding interests of critical-hermeneutic evaluation are insights into human experiences as humanly lived, the evaluators direct their efforts toward clarifying, authenticating, and bringing into human awareness the meaning structures of lived experiences of people in the situation. Thus, the form of knowledge sought by the evaluator within this orientation is not nomological statements, but rather the structures of existential meaning as people meaningfully experience and appropriate the natural and social world. Hence, a critical-hermeneutic evaluator comes to "know" the evaluated reality in a different form and in a different way than the knowledge gained by, for instance, an ends-means evaluator.

In seeking out understandings that are not accessible from an ends-means evaluation orientation, those in the critical-hermeneutic orientation attempt to provide explanations of a different kind. Whereas *explaining* within the ends-means orientation means giving causal, functional, or hypothetico-deductive statements, within the critical-hermeneutic orientation *explaining* requires the striking of resonance among people in dialogue situations by clarifying motives, authentic experiences, and common meanings. The evaluator, hence, cannot stand aloof as an observer, as is done in the ends-means evaluation and the in situ participation of emic evaluation, but must enter deeply into intersubjective conversation with the people in the evaluation situation.

Conversation that is hermeneutic moves beyond the chit-chat that so often remains at the informational level as simply exchanges of messages, not requiring true human presence. Exchanges of computerized messages based on bits and bytes characterize our Age of Technology and the Age of Information. Acknowledgement of the informational structure of our age and attempts to humanize the age can be seen in the efforts towards "user friendly" techniques. Hermeneutic conversation is a dialectic of questions and answers which in their interpretive turnings are attempts to move to deeper ontological realms of meanings. Successful hermeneutic conversations lead conversationalists, human beings that they are, toward questions concerning who they are. In such conversations existential themes often emerge, and the questionings and the answerings are guided by these emerging themes. Critical hermeneutics is an activity that deepens existential themes, as the source of our human beingness is sought in the realms of the finite and infinite.

The enterprise for critical hermeneutic evaluators is often linguistic. That is, for them language is not merely a tool of communication in which thoughts are put into words, nor is it merely a bearer of representational knowledge, but language is a way that humans live humanly in this world. We are reminded of Heidegger (1971) who called language a House of Being. The challenge to evaluators of this persuasion is to disclose life as lived in and through language, thereby disclosing in some way what it means to be human. These evaluators, therefore, are called upon to work beyond the prosaic language of representation and to dwell in a language world of metaphors. Hence, they entertain questions such as, "What is it *like to be* a teacher or student in social studies classes?"

Within the British Columbia Social Studies Assessment, a modest attempt was made to embody the critical-hermeneutic evaluation orientation. We were guided by an understanding of existential realms of being as follows:

Passive Realm of Being: From this stance a person does not view self as the one who lives out the expectancies of others. Values and meanings are perceived as given in the situations in which one exists.

Immediate Realm of Being: Within this attunement to the world, a person tends to be concerned only about pleasurable experiences to fight off boredom. It is the present that is of paramount importance, and little responsibility is taken for choices made.

Responsible Realm of Being: Here, decisiveness and self-determination are key qualities. Such a person makes choices and assumes full responsibility for them in terms of other people's welfare. Such a person knows that others are affected by his or her decisions.

Immanent Realm of Being: Living in this realm, a person experiences the self truly. Experiences in life are vivid. Choices are increasingly based on trusting personal understandings and on a sense of the spiritual dimensions of living. Authentic being with others is the person's prime concern. (Adapted from Aoki et al. (1977b, pp. 27–28). This segment of the report was contributed by Peter Rothe (1979), who made existential phenomenology the core of his doctoral study. An evaluation study incorporating critical hermeneutics was reported by Stephen W. Y. Bath (1988). He was concerned with the immanence of ethical being-with-others in evaluation situations.)

The following brief extract from the B. C. Social Studies Assessment Report (Aoki et al., 1977a) provides a flavor of what we meant by realms of being:

An interpretation of grade 4 responses indicates a wide range of meanings Social Studies has for pupils. Their varied responses suggest a "shift" in meanings when discussing Social Studies subject matter ... and classroom activities, indicating differing concerns about different aspects of a social studies class, usually pre-supposed or overlooked by educators. For example, when pupils were asked questions concerning what social studies topics they would like to spend more time studying, their answers suggested an immediate area of being. Their replies focus on momentary enjoyment, personal and appealing aesthetics....

Uncommitted reasons of ephemeral interest and boredom indicating classroom meanings within the Immediate area were also evident when pupils responded to the questions: "Of all the topics you have studied, what topics would you *not* like to spend more time studying?" "Why did you select this topic?"...

Reasons constituting meanings within the Responsible rather than Immediate area of being were prevalent when the grade 4 pupils interviewed were asked what classroom activities they prefer to participate in when doing Social Studies. Their responses indicate committed and responsible efforts to acquire maximum learning. It seems that the grade 4 pupils interviewed gave responsible meanings to circumstances involving relevant areas of ... classroom activities but uncommitted ephemeral responses indicating immediate meanings when answering ... questions pertaining to curricular subject matter. (pp. 76–78)

Even the brief extract given above suggests that pupils interpret social studies according to their experiences within their social contexts. Individuals give meanings to social studies based on their daily life situations, comprised of activities with people, learnings, social tasks, physical objects, and circumstances. For evaluators interested in the quality of life lived in social studies, inclusion of the critical-hermeneutic mode is a desirable possibility.

The critical hermeneutic evaluation framework can be summarized in terms of its interests, world of knowing, and mode of evaluation as follows:

Interest in: Disclosure of existential meanings in lived experiences.

World of Knowing: A world of insights (rather than generalizations) in each unique, personal situation as it is lived concretely. It is an open world, infinite in its layers of beingness.

Mode of Evaluation: A critical quest for what it means to be human. Often called existential inquiry or phenomenological hermeneutics.

A CONCLUDING NOTE

A modest attempt has been made in this chapter to trace out four evaluation orientations, reflecting the polysemic nature of both social studies and evaluation. The discussion of the orientations is not meant to exhaust all possibilities. What it does point to is the possibility of openness of discourses in social studies program evaluation.

At the outset, the contribution of Continental European scholarship in the human sciences, notably that of Jürgen Habermas, was acknowledged. Social studies educators and evaluators should open themselves to discussions in the human sciences that have provided us with disciplines such as critical social theory, phenomenology, sociology of knowledge, and hermeneutics. More recently, led by scholars such as Foucault (1972), Derrida (1978), Lyotard (1984), and Deleuze and Guttari (1987), there have been new stirrings with scholarship in post-modernism, post-structuralism, and deconstructionism that challenges the centrality of the metaphysical grounds of western tradition. We live in a turbulent and exciting time. Implications for social studies and evaluation abound.

It has been said that educators' understanding of their task as educators is most clearly demonstrated by their favored mode of evaluation. Conversely, evaluators' understanding of what evaluation is discloses their understanding of what it means to be an educator and what it means to be educated. At stake is what our children and adolescents experience in the name of social studies education. Hence, there is, at this time, a deep challenge confronting social studies evaluators.

At the end point of the British Columbia Social Studies Assessment, we asked ourselves this question: "Has the job of evaluation been done?" In response, we made the following admission which is a fitting conclusion to this chapter:

Whenever we see a picture of ourselves taken by someone else, we are anxious that justice be done to the "real me." If there is disappointment, it is because we know that there is so much more to the "real me" than has been momentarily captured by the photographer's click. So too with this assessment: there are deeper and wider dimensions to the total subject than can be justly dealt with from such a hasty glance. Any ensuing dissatisfaction should not be simply taken as a measure of the assessment's failing but as testimony to that crucial vitality of the subject that eludes captivity on paper. We know that the true magic of the educating act is so much more than a simple, albeit justifiable, concern for improved resources, more sensitively stated objectives, better pre-service and in-service training for teachers, or improved bureaucratic efficiency. Rather, it has to do with the whole meaning of a society's search for true maturity and responsible freedom through its young people. (Aoki et al., 1977b, p. 49)

References

Aoki, T. T., & Harrison, E. (1977). The intents of the B. C. Social Studies Curriculum Guides: An interpretation. In T. T. Aoki, C. Langford, D. M. Williams, & D. C. Wilson (Eds.), *The British Columbia social studies assessment summary report: A report to the Ministry of Education* (pp. 55–63). Victoria, B. C.: Ministry of Education.

Aoki, T. T., Langford, D., Williams, D. M., & Wilson, D. C. (Eds.). (1977a). *The British Columbia social studies assessment: A report to the Ministry of Education* (Vol. 1). Victoria, B. C.: Ministry of Education.

Aoki, T. T., Langford, D., Williams, D. M., & Wilson, D. C. (Eds.). (1977b). *The British Columbia social studies assessment summary report: A report to the Ministry of Education*. Victoria, B. C.: Ministry of Education.

Apple, M. W. (1974). The process and ideology of valuing in educational settings. In M. W. Apple, M. J. Subkoviak, & H. S. Lufler, Jr. (Eds.) *Educational evaluation: Analysis and responsibility* (pp. 3–34). Berkeley, CA: McCutchan.

Bath, S. W. Y. (1988). *Justice in evaluation: Participatory case study evaluation*. Unpublished doctoral dissertation, University of Alberta, Edmonton.

Beittel, K. R. (1973). *Alternatives for art education research*. Dubuque, IA: Wm. C. Brown.

Deleuze, G., & Guttari, F. (1987). *A thousand plateaus: Capitalism and schizophrenia*. Minneapolis: University of Minnesota Press.

Derrida, J. (1978). *Writing and difference*. Chicago: University of Chicago Press.

Eisner, E. W. (1979). *The educational imagination: On the design and evaluation of school programs*. New York: Macmillan.

Foucault, M. (1972). *The archaeology of knowledge*. London: Tavistock.

Freire, P. (1968). *Pedogogy of the oppressed*. New York: Herder and Herder.

Habermas, J. (1972). *Knowledge and human interest*. Boston: Beacon.

Hamilton, D., Jenkins, D., King, C., MacDonald, B., & Parlett, M. (Eds.). (1977). *Beyond the numbers game: A reader in educational evaluation*. Berkeley, CA: McCutchan.

Heidegger, M. (1971). *On the way to language*. San Francisco: Harper and Row.

Horkheimer, M., & Adorno, T. (1972). *Dialectic of enlightenment*. New York: Continuum.

House, E. R. (Ed.). (1973). *School evaluation: The politics and process*. Berkeley, CA: McCutchan.

Kaplan, A. (1964). *The conduct of inquiry*. San Francisco: Chandler.

Lyotard, J. F. (1984). *The postmodern condition: A report of knowledge*. Minneapolis, University of Minnesota Press.

MacDonald, B., & Walker, R. (Eds.). (1974). *SAFARI papers one: Innovation, evaluation, research and the problem of control*. Norwich, Eng.: University of East Anglia (CARE).

Marcuse, H. (1968). *Essays in critical theory*. Boston: Beacon.

Patton, M. Q. (1975). *Alternative evaluation research paradigm*. (Monograph of the North Dakota Study Group on Evaluation). Grand Forks: University of North Dakota Press.

Rothe, P. (1979). *An exploration of existential phenomenology as an approach to curriculum evaluation*. Unpublished doctoral dissertation. University of British Columbia, Vancouver.

Schaull, R. (1968). Foreword. In Paulo Freire, *Pedagogy of the oppressed* (pp. 9–15). New York: Herder and Herder.

Scriven, M. (1967). *Perspectives of curriculum evaluation*. Chicago: Rand McNally.

Shaver, J. P., & Larkins, A. G. (1973). Research on teaching social studies. In R. M. W. Travers (Ed.), *Second handbook of research on teaching* (pp. 1243–1262). Chicago: Rand McNally.

Stake, R., & Easley, J. (1978). *Case studies in science education: Vol. 2. Design, overview, and general findings*. Urbana-Champaign: University of Illinois, Center for Instructional Research and Curriculum Evaluation.

Tyler, R. W. (1949). *Basic principles of curriculum and instruction*. Chicago: University of Chicago Press.

Wilson, D. C. (1976). *Emic evaluation inquiry: An approach for evaluating school programs*. Unpublished doctoral dissertation, University of Alberta, Edmonton.

Section

·II·

THE STUDENT IN SOCIAL STUDIES EDUCATION

·9·

COGNITIVE, EMOTIONAL, AND SOCIAL DEVELOPMENT: EARLY CHILDHOOD SOCIAL STUDIES

Nancy B. Wyner
UNIVERSITY OF LOWELL

Elizabeth Farquhar
U.S. DEPARTMENT OF EDUCATION

Awareness of recent research on children's cognitive, affective, and social development is crucial for researchers and teachers working toward the improvement of teaching and learning in early childhood social studies. Early childhood education, as described in the position statement of the National Association for the Education of Young Children (Bredekamp, 1987), includes programs serving children from birth through age 8. This chapter is focused on research pertinent to children from 4 through 8 years of age, a period characterized in formal schooling as preschool through second grade.

In this review, we discuss developmental theory from which change in the individual is viewed as the result of multiple influences (Spodek, 1988), including family life, socioeconomic conditions, health, and schooling. Research is described that supports a view of the young child as an active learner, seeking regularities, underlying concepts, and similarities; engaged in building and interpreting self and social understandings. Attention is focused on studies of thought and affect related to the emergence of self-knowledge and emotion; social cognition in relation to prosocial behavior, perspective taking, friendships, and peer relations; and development of economic, political, and moral understandings. We also discuss needed research and issues concerned with methodology in the study of the young child's thought, affect, and social cognition.

The dominant purposes of early childhood education (Weber, 1984) have been to foster in children a sense of themselves as autonomous learners, questioners, problem solvers; to provide children with the knowledge and self-esteem essential for later learning; to encourage the child's sense of the teacher as a guide, helper, and source of useful information rather than an authoritarian judge of behavior; and to nurture the child's "sense of the school as a democratic social system in which exchange with peers is as highly valued as any other endeavor" (Biber, 1984, p. 286). In that context, social studies educators should consider the importance of broadly based early education, appropriately suited to children's developmental capabilities, as important to the realization of the purposes of social education.

Today, developmentally appropriate practice in early childhood programs is threatened by the belief that more academic learning should be accomplished earlier. Pressure to learn occurs at a formative time as preoperational children are pushed prematurely to perform concrete mental operations. However, high-quality, developmentally appropriate teaching and curricu-

Reviewer was Dorothy J. Skeel, George Peabody College for Teachers, Vanderbilt University.

Work on this chapter was undertaken by Dr. Farquhar in her private capacity. No official support or endorsement by the U.S. Department of Education is intended or should be inferred.

lar practices will be based on consideration of the developmental needs of young children (for expressions of concern, see Biber, 1984; Damon, 1989; Elkind, 1986; Katz, 1988; Shaver, 1979).

The developmental concept in early education has two dimensions: *age* appropriateness, referring to universal, predictable sequences of growth and change during the early years, and *individual* appropriateness, related to growth patterns and personalities unique to each child (Bredekamp, 1987, p. 4). Knowledge of child development "can help educators understand what young children are capable of knowing, how children come to know what they know, and how they validate their knowledge" (Spodek, 1988, p. 207). Child development researchers argue that effective practice will be realized only when the environment, materials, and teaching practices employed in teaching young children are appropriate to their levels of understanding and to their unique modes of learning (Elkind, 1989). Although many factors influence the quality of teaching and learning in developmentally appropriate early childhood programs, knowledge of child development is considered a crucial component in teacher training, curriculum planning and instruction, and assessment and documentation of learning (Elkind, 1989; Biber, 1984).

Researchers and educators agree that an enhanced understanding of cognitive development, more than any other area of social science research, can help in the clarification of early education (Kuhn, 1989). Furth (1979) argued that we can do no greater service to children and to the well-being of our society than to give children the repeated and continuing experience of being thinkers, to expose children to the whole gamut of life areas to which they can apply their thinking. Curriculum developers and teachers with knowledge of cognitive development can design appropriate social learning experiences to enable young children to begin to think about and conceptualize their life experiences.

COGNITIVE DEVELOPMENT

During the last two decades, significant changes in thinking about early development have evolved. Piaget's theories (1963) focused attention on how children learn as they interact with their social and physical environment, and how children develop cognitive structures to mediate between them and their experiences. In his research, Piaget described a general progression of cognitive growth from early sensorimotor and concrete organization of experience to abstract modes of thought. Influenced by Piaget's pioneering studies, other researchers made progress in studying cognition from a developmental viewpoint. Although Piaget is largely known for his emphasis on logical-deductive thought, he did acknowledge the essential role of social interaction and affect in cognitive development.

Some post-Piagetian researchers have sought to counter perceived shortcomings in Piaget's work, notably a stress on cognitive over affective development, the failure to address individual variability and creativity, and an exclusive emphasis on the Western scientific and philosophical perspective (Chazan, Laing & Harper, 1987; Gardner, 1983; Richards & Light, 1986; Zigler, Lamb & Child, 1982). New research on cognitive development is characterized by comprehensive descriptions of the young child's active construction of knowledge through interactions with the environment and a focus on the influence of cultural variations as children cope with and adapt to their environment (LeVine, 1980).

Researchers have reviewed Piaget's recognition of the social foundation and affective features of knowledge to account for processes in cognition, affect, and social development. The work of these researchers reflects an increased recognition of the child as an active learner constructing knowledge in the sociocultural environment of home, school, and community (Bearison & Zimiles, 1986; Biber, 1984; Comer, 1989; Damon 1989; Eisenberg, 1982; Miller-Jones, 1988; Slaughter & Dombrowski, 1989; Spencer, 1988).

THOUGHT AND AFFECT

Piaget rejected the separation of emotion and cognition as artificial, a theorist's ploy. He saw emotions as the energy source for intellectual functioning (Izard, 1986; Piaget, 1963). When thought and emotion are viewed as interactive and inseparable, the investigator cannot study intellectual development without considering affect, nor can emotional development be studied apart from cognition (Bearison & Zimiles, 1986; Zimiles, 1981). Sigel (1986) referred to the relationship of thought and emotions as a "fundamental psychological riddle" and argued that the cognition-affect dichotomy is an artifact of conceptualization, disputing Izard (1977), Zajonc (1980), and Lazarus (1982). He suggested that the problem now is how to conceptualize and study the interaction of thought and affect.

In recent years, studies of emotions in young children have documented the cultural universality of several basic emotions from early infancy, including anger, sadness, fear, joy, and love or attachment (Fischer, Shaver, & Carnochan, 1989). Harris (1989) found that 6-year-olds have an understanding of emotion that is far from egocentric, in contrast with research on Piagetian tasks that indicated that children prior to the concrete operations stage (age 7 or 8) lacked the ability to take another's perspective. Lee (1989) argued that evidence for the Piagetian theory of egocentricity was an artifact of testing.

Children's understanding of emotion is one part of a much more general understanding of other people's psychological states according to Harris (1989). He proposed that to anticipate what emotion someone else will feel, children apply the key concepts of desire and belief. Harris concluded that play helps children understand that whether someone feels sad or happy must be explained in terms of the relationship between states such as belief and desire. He suggested that young children are able to report their beliefs and desires, and that they base their psychological understandings on their own experience rather than on deduction from a set of theoretical postulates. Children's understanding of people's psychological states is an intriguing area for further study.

Self-Understanding and Self-Concept

Self-understanding and self-concept, recognized as crucial components of a person's understanding of his or her social world, are aspects of cognitive-affective interaction. Data regarding the nature of the self and ideas about the self are amassed by the growing child. Growth of self-concept calls upon the child's integrative skills (Zimiles, 1981).

Self-understanding provides the growing child with a basis for differentiating himself or herself from others in society. Concepts of self shift from the child's concrete, externalized definitions, based on observable characteristics and behaviors, to later descriptions, in middle adolescence, of self in terms of internal dispositions and beliefs.

Nucci (1989) pointed to a dilemma inherent in self-definition. He observed that we can speak meaningfully of the self in the singular as a way of referring to individual actions. Yet the multidimensionality of the self is evident in the school-aged child as a physical, social, and academic being. Although the child does not comprehend this multidimensionality as theories of what constitutes "me," studies demonstrate that children construct both a general sense of self-worth and domain-specific evaluations of their own competence, as well as differentiated notions of themselves as actors within different social contexts (p. 124).

There is evidence that children's academic self-concept may differ according to the area of the activity in which the child is involved, for example, math or social studies. Activities important to the child's self-image also may be a function of gender or race (Harter, 1983; Marsh & Smith, 1985). Harter (1983) provided a comprehensive picture of children's ability at age four, to make reliable differentiated judgments about their self-worth in terms of gender competence and social acceptance with age-mates. Zimiles (1981) proposed that "the more [positive] information about the self communicated to the child, the more references to the self are made during interactions with the child, the greater will be the clarity and sharpening of self-knowledge" (p. 56). In sum, principal features of the self-system—the solidity of the self, the sense of self-worth, and its accessibility to the individual—call for a focus of thought on feelings and ideas, which lie at the core of an individual's affective system.

Classroom observations can help the teacher to recognize children's specific evaluations of their own competence—for example, who is willing to take a leadership role and which students are confident in group discussions. The educational challenges then, are to help all children expand their own feelings of self-worth and competence among peers, and to encourage children to recognize strengths and competencies in themselves and each other. Uncertainties in the child's perceptions of his or her own self-worth and general competence may not be simply the consequence of preoperational thought, but may be related to the nature of "personhood" and the likelihood that "personness" is not firmly established in young children (Harter, 1983). Yonemura (1986) reported that in her work she has seen that children learn best when they are viewed as people, rather than locked into pupil roles, and are thus free to bring themselves and their views into the classroom world.

Self-Concept: Race, Racism, and Ethnicity

Culture has greater influence than many child development researchers anticipated, resulting in significant changes in the

view of the role of cultural diversity in self-concept development. LeVine (1989) observed that as research findings accumulate and the analytic sophistication of researchers deepens, we are learning more than ever about the impacts of the cultural, social, and psychological conditions in which children are raised. For example, researchers have documented the negative impacts of racism, gender discrimination, and developmentally inappropriate teaching methods on racially different children (Comer, 1989; Grant, 1984; Spencer 1985, 1988; Stangor & Ruble, 1987; Sue, Sue & Sue, 1983; Williams, 1989).

While early reseachers viewed self-esteem as the important dimension in self-concept, today self-esteem is regarded as only one element in self-concept. Rosenberg (1985) suggested that race is one of a large number of self-concept components such as social status, that mold the child's feelings of self-worth. Most of the early researchers on the effects of racism on African-American children concluded that it resulted in damaged self-esteem.

Studies of race as a category used by children indicate that children are inconsistent in their conception and application of race distinctions. Alejandro-Wright (1985) argued that we cannot gain an adequate understanding of racial self-concepts without understanding the child's perspective. Her research demonstrated that children's racial awareness is chiefly a response to skin color, not to the concept of race as defined by adults. In exploratory studies, Alejandro-Wright found substantial support for the hypothesis there is an age-related developmental progression to children's conceptions of racial categories. The child's concept of race was found to be qualitatively different from that of an adult. The child had his or her own unique way of thinking about racial and color categories. Her findings indicate that the developmental process of racial classification is more complex and gradual than previously proposed. These studies emphasized the importance of examining the child's spontaneous response patterns, knowledge of racial subclasses, and understanding of the properties by which racial categories are identified.

Much of the research on African-American children's development since the late 1960s has been oriented toward poverty and social problems (McLoyd & Randolph, 1985; Miller-Jones, 1988). Poverty is only one theme, yet it dominates other realities that challenge the myths and stereotypes of African-American children and other minority children—children who cope, students who tenaciously pursue academic excellence, parents and children who demonstrate resilience in their lives. The deficit views of minority children continue to influence interpretations and expectations of behavior and development. While poverty and social inequities will continue to be a priority concern in the future, researchers committed to the well-being of minority children can study, portray, and confirm the strong values that can be exhibited in school to foster achievement, self-improvement, and prosocial behavior. Findings from recent studies compel rethinking of earlier developmental paradigms in which deficits, deviance, and pathology in African-American communities were highlighted (McAdoo, 1985; Slaughter, 1988; Spencer, 1988). Slaughter (1988) reported that from a developmental perspective, research on poverty in African-American communities did not automatically connote weakness, pathological problems, deficit, or deviance.

Until the decade of the 1970s, the consistent finding of Euro-centric racial attitudes among young African-American children was interpreted as suggesting general psychopathology or self-rejection. However, Spencer (1988) reviewed research on African-American children's self-esteem that consistently demonstrated the independence of personal identity (i.e., self-esteem, self-concept, and reference group identification) from race awareness, race identification, and racial attitudes.

Spencer (1988) argued that teachers who lack specific knowledge about the development of minority children cannot be expected to be successful in teaching minority children. In fact, she suggested that teachers' understandings of minority students are often inhibited by a focus on deviance.

Given the importance of the young learner's real life experiences, early childhood teachers need to build their curriculum on the rich gifts of social knowledge and experience that minority children bring into the classroom. Williams (1989) suggested that teachers overlook opportunities for the expansion of repertoires that come from the social and cultural contexts within which children are raised. Rather than relying on worksheets and direct instruction, teachers can optimize growth of the child's self-knowledge and social skills with instruction that emphasizes thinking about positive role models, cultural histories and traditions, and daily life. For example, group discussions can be facilitated to generate cooperative efforts to "think about" and resolve problems that are real to minority children (Damon, 1977; Katz, 1988).

Gender Roles and Gender Stereotypes

Some researchers have found converging evidence from accuracy and memory measures to support the hypothesis that children's understanding of gender roles and gender stereotypes increases with age. There is substantial indication that children become insistent on the appropriateness of gender-stereotyped behavior as they attain consistency in their gender roles. Also, children's insistence on gender constancy associated with gender-stereotyped behaviors has been found (Stangor & Ruble, 1987). In the decade of the 1980s, studies demonstrated that the children had knowledge about normative gender stereotypes and gender roles, and that these perspectives do not seem to be changing (Liben & Bigler, 1987).

Race-Gender Status

The effects of race-gender status on classroom experiences has had limited attention from early-childhood researchers. Although race and gender are closely interrelated in their effects, the research has developed along separate paths of inquiry. But one ethnographic study conducted by Grant (1984) is a counter-example. Grant studied race and gender in six desegregated first-grade classrooms. She focused on the socialization of one race-gender group, African-American females, and their "place" in desegregated classrooms. Despite the rhetoric of equal opportunity, Grant concluded that public schools function as critical agencies in the intergenerational transmission of status arrangements, so that children of each race-gender group learn the intellectual and social skills for the roles played by adults in their own status relationships. The study concluded that African-American girls' everyday schooling experiences "seem more likely to nudge them toward stereotypical roles of black women than toward alternatives. These include serving others and maintaining peaceable ties among diverse persons rather than developing one's own skills" (p. 109).

Recent studies of prejudice in children have demonstrated that children are aware of differences among people and that at a young age, children learn the prevailing social attitudes toward these differences (Byrnes, 1988; Katz, 1983). A growing body of research literature (Pate, 1987) suggests that children may become less prejudiced if they are helped to identify over-generalizations and stereotypes and focus on positive social behaviors. Byrnes (1988) referred to this approach as development of children's awareness of inappropriate prejudgments. Instruction that interrupts stereotypic thinking and generalizations can help children to reflect on their viewpoints through discussion with peers, while providing the opportunity to present accurate information about social groups and social behaviors.

SOCIAL COGNITION—A "NEW" LOOK

In search of a response to a growing theoretical gap between reflective social cognition and experience, Bearison (1986) described theoretical models that represent the transactional features of social cognition. He argued that social cognition involves both the process of social development and the acquisition of social knowledge, referring to two distinct but complementary theories of cognitive development, those of Vygotsky (1962), who stressed the function of language as a symbolic dialogical social system that structures thinking, and of Piaget. Vygotsky and others (e.g., Light, 1986; Tizard & Hughes, 1984; Wells, 1981) have argued that language and social interactions organize the mental processes. Some theorists emphasize that the level of development varies across different domains of thought (Damon, 1977; Gardner, 1983; Turiel, 1983). Vygotsky suggested that "cognitive development 'first appears between people as an interpsychological category and then within the child as an intrapsychological category.' In other words, 'what the child can do in cooperation today, he can do alone tomorrow' " (Vygotsky, 1962, cited in Bearison, 1986, p. 130).

Prosocial Behavior

Increasingly, researchers have used the term *prosocial behavior* to designate helping, sharing, and other seemingly intentional and voluntary positive social behaviors. When and how these behaviors are acquired has become a growing focus of investigation with younger children (Denham, 1986). There is general consensus that maturing capacities, societal values and norms, and socialization experiences influence prosocial behavior (Radke-Yarrow, Zahn-Waxler, & Chapman, 1983).

Developmental theorists define prosocial behavior in terms of action intended to aid or benefit another person or groups of people without the actor's anticipation of external rewards (Mussen & Eisenberg-Berg, 1977). They distinguish prosocial behavior from altruistic behavior, which, according to Staub (1978), is action intended to benefit others generally, not specific persons. Dispositions to prosocial behavior emanate from parent-child relationships, with sufficient evidence to conclude that modeling and identification are powerful antecedents (Mussen & Eisenberg-Berg, 1977).

Research is limited concerning affective motives, including the interaction of affective and cognitive motivation as guides to perception, thought, and action (Eisenberg, 1982). Some young children typically respond to others' distress in a nonemotional, cognitive manner, and others respond emotionally (Radke-Yarrow et al., 1983). It is assumed that children who can imaginatively take the perspective of another, and thus have some understanding of the other's affective state and cognitive processing, are more likely to comprehend and respond to another's needs.

Cultural variations have been studied as a force shaping the child's disposition toward competition, cooperation, and prosocial behavior. In many cultures, prosocial behavior is predominant, whereas in others, egoistic and selfish qualities are the norm (Eisenberg & Mussen, 1989, p. 4). These researchers synthesized data pooled from many cultures and drew tentative conclusions about the features of cultures that seem to affect prosocial development. Some of the findings indicated that children apparently develop high levels of prosocial behavior if they are raised in cultures characterized by (a) parental and peer stress on consideration for others, sharing, and orientation toward the group; (b) a simple social organization and/or a traditional, rural setting; (c) assignment to women of important economic functions; (d) living in an extended family; and (e) early assignment of tasks and responsibility to children (p. 53).

Karniol (1982) suggested that prosocial behavior is the outcome of information-processing activities initiated by the stimulus situation (p. 273). She proposed that children acquire information concerning others' internal states by an inferential process in which they use stored knowledge. Karniol encouraged researchers to examine the informational sources, both stored and situational, that are available to the child for making inferences about the possible need for help. Although no reported study has directly examined the types of information "scripts" children actually have, evidence supporting their existence comes from studies that have examined children's friendship formation or their perceptions of people they like. Damon (1977) found, for example, that children ages 6 to 12 stated that they only share or help people they know and like (cited in Karniol, 1982, p. 272). Karniol proposed that children's offers to help may be limited to situations in which either of these variables are present, concluding that unless the child wants the other person to like him or her, expects future interaction with the other person, or expects the other person will give him or her something in return, he or she will be unlikely to help.

Schools provide unique settings for promoting the ability to perform high-quality prosocial behaviors. In everyday school life, teachers and administrators devote their energies to children's social development as well as academic learning. Although there is growing documentation of the importance of interpersonal interactions as predictors of social development and academic performance, few standards for assessing the characteristics of these predictors have been established.

Peer Interaction

Peers are both reinforcing models and agents in the process of social cognition and development. Children learn the concept of reciprocity through daily encounters and observations of their own interactions and the interactions of others. These social exchanges have been the focus of study over the years. Hartup and Moore (1990) discussed the developmental course of early peer relations. According to these researchers, family relations and peer socialization combine in a synergistic relationship to determine the child's adaptation. Their review of research confirms that children with good family relations in infancy and early childhood often are more popular in nursery school, tend to engage more frequently in social contact, and are more effective in offering guidance and suggestions to others than children with insecure relationships (p. 8).

Conversely, poor family relationships are accompanied by dependence on the teacher and poor impulse control (Sroufe & Fleeson, 1986, p. 10, cited in Hartup & Moore, 1990). Disruptive, disagreeable, and impulsive children create negative impressions that lead to rejection and negative peer expectations. Gradually, their opportunities to engage in constructive interactions with other children disappear. "Progressively, the companions available to the aggressive/rejected child include a disproportionate number of unskilled, unpopular children. That is, children select associates who provide rough matches for their own social skills" (Hartup & Moore, 1990, p. 11).

Patterson and Bank (1989) referred to "shopping for social opportunities" as the process in which children associate with others who are similar to themselves. Over time this process results in the emergence of relatively homogeneous peer groups in terms of values, interests, and activities. They indicated that multivariate studies are leading to verification of a conjunctive model of social development. (p. 11) As children act and interact with others, they become aware of their self and social self within their world. As social thinkers, they build on real relationships within their social world.

Research is needed on children's thinking about the nature of group life in the context of the classroom, particularly as related to peers, friendship, authority, and group membership. Knowledge and understanding of the social world of the classroom is needed for teachers to help children understand how social relationships are formed by caring, interest, trust; regulated through rules, agreements and governance; transacted by sharing, helping, negotiating; and ended by conflict, abuse of power, growth of independence, and loss (Wyner, 1978). In particular, too few careful studies have been done of peer influences on socialization among African-American children and children from other ethnic groups. Are different social processes used by minority children within different minority groups (Spencer, Brookins, & Allen, 1985)?

Friendships

The study of friendships in early childhood did not become a focus of interest until the late 1970s (Hartup, 1979). Empirical research and theoretical analysis applied to the study of friendships are considered to be important sources for increased understanding of the contributions of peer relationships to children's development. Current knowledge indicates a range of issues pertinent to research on friendships in childhood and the child's conceptions of friendships (Berndt, 1989; Hartup, 1983; Selman & Selman, 1979).

Berndt (1989) identified the place of friendships in the child's social world as "basic elements in the elaborate social structure that constitute the social world of peers" (p. 333). Studies have revealed that children think about friendships as sets of relationships among small groups of children. They also have substantial knowledge about friendships, for example, differences in the degrees of friendship among close friends (Berndt, 1982). The social influence of particular friends on children's attitudes and behaviors is another important theme in the study of children's friendships. Berndt (1989) suggested that friends' influence may lead to socially desirable as well as to socially undesirable behavior. He suggested the influence of friends and ways in which friends influence each other deserve more systematic research. One hypothesis is that developmental changes in friends' influence are partly determined by developmental changes in the nature of friendships themselves. The nature of these changes during childhood is proposed as a significant matter for future research.

From a Piagetian perspective, theorists and researchers have argued that equality is a guiding principle for friendships in childhood and adolescents (Berndt, 1982, 1989; Youniss, 1980). However, interactions among friends are often inconsistent with the concept of equality. Children compete with their friends and complain about how they boss them around, suggesting violations of equality. Faced with these incompatibilities, Berndt proposed a more plausible position, that the quest for status or rivalry is common in all human groups. Closer study of the peer social world and the attitudes, social perceptions, and social self-concepts of children could provide a fuller picture of the functions of peers and social structure in early childhood education (Berndt, 1989).

Play and Learning

Increased attention to theories of play has developed during the past 25 years. Vandenberg (1986) attributed Sutton-Smith's (1966) theoretical focus on play and his published correspondence with Piaget as factors underlying contemporary perspectives of play. According to Vandenberg, Sutton-Smith disagreed with Piaget's assimilation model of play. He argued that a more divergent view of cognitive functioning would place play in a central role in development. His work resulted in research on the contributions of play to divergent thinking. In his analysis of sex differences in children's play, Sutton-Smith argued that children's play reflects changes in the values and lifestyles of the culture.

Play is the young child's response to basic impulses to experiment and to explore the imagined and the real world, and to rehearse and to master what is perceived to be important to the child. For example, Biber (1984) stated,

In playing, it is possible to think through, to assimilate experience in piecemeal fashion, stripped of the contextual complexity of experience-in-the-real. The thinking, judging, problem-solving is child generated; situations are created that lead to new questions and new problems to be solved. (p. 237)

Biber theorized that as play progresses and the symbolization process develops, developmental cognitive changes occur in the interpersonal relationships and adaptive thinking of young children as they explore cooperative planning and helping roles. Seefeldt (1977) noted the importance of play in helping children form concepts, a central goal of social studies.

Researchers continue to study the important role of play in early cognitive growth and social understanding. Advocates for developmentally appropriate early childhood schooling argue that part of the curriculum should be play in which problem solving, cooperation, self-awareness, and school achievement are significant components (Yawkey & Pellegrini, 1984). Play, particularly in primary programs, continues to be a leisure time activity after schoolwork is done. This dichotomy between work and play diminishes important, natural inclinations or dispositions for student learning. Katz (1985) reported data on children's learning that suggested young children require learning environments that encourage spontaneous play and intellectually oriented experiences to strengthen their dispositions to observe, experiment, inquire, and interact.

In reframing the role of play in learning, Harris (1989) argued that children understand other people's mental states by relying on a distinctive type of imaginative understanding. Harris proposed that the capacity for imagination and make-believe allows the child:

to escape from his or her current reality but . . . such an escape is functional. It allows the child to entertain possible realities and, what is especially important, to entertain the possible realities other people entertain. It is a key that unlocks the minds of other people and allows the child temporarily to enter into their plans, hopes and fears. (p. 52)

The significance of pretend play, in which objects and actions are used to symbolize imaginary persons and situations, might be more evident if we understood the function of pretend play among low-income and minority children. McLoyd (1985) reported that the assumption that low-income children engage in less frequent, lower-quality pretend play, or play that is characteristically unimaginative, is widely accepted in the literature. Descriptions of play or games and the social, psychological, or environmental contexts in which play occurs are needed to understand the lasting importance and universality of play in the lives of low-income children. Research on the play of low-income and nonwhite minority children that was relatively free of adult constraints and interventions could provide valuable information on the relationships between children's play and valued social and cognitive outcomes. Research on how children's play reflects the unique aspects of African-American, Hispanic, or Southeast Asian cultures, for example, might provide opportunities for improving early childhood education for minority children, as well as knowledge by which to promote the racial and ethnic cultural awareness of White children.

In current play-theorizing, researchers express the need to study the importance of play in problem solving, cooperation, and self-awareness (Yawkey & Pellegrini, 1984). From this perspective, play is important because it enhances other aspects of development. Vandenberg (1986) argued that an alternative perspective would be to see humans as fundamentally myth-making creatures and reality as a set of trusted myths shared by other members of the culture. Vandenberg argued that "to be human, and to live in a meaningful way in a culture requires that we live in and through a very sophisticated, abstract, and symbolic system that is largely imaginary" (p. 25). From this alternative perspective, play and imagination are central features of what it means to be human. This view offers another possible direction for the future of play theory.

Understanding Societal Institutions and Moral Principles

Having explored how children develop understandings about themselves and others, we now move to the child's emerging understandings of societal institutions and moral principles. The roots of children's knowledge about society are in social experiences with important individuals in their family, with caregivers and family friends, peers, professionals such as doctors and teachers, people in stores and other public places, and fantasy or entertainment figures from books, stories, and television. These people comprise the child's interactive world (Borman, 1982).

Children first experience societal institutions at home as they learn family norms and values through personal interactions, observation, exploration, trial and error, and, generally, as they work to make sense out of their experiences. Dunn (1985) found that toddlers are aware of family rules and the consequences of breaking them. They even joke about rules, knowing this will arouse interest among family members.

Through symbolic play, young children augment their direct experiences, mixing fantasy and reality. In addition, they learn the meaning of authority both through unilateral power relationships with adults and older children and through reciprocal relationships with peers. Concepts of justice emerge from their childhood encounters with issues of fairness, sharing, and kindness (Damon, 1977).

Researchers such as Piaget (1963) have determined that children's social cognition develops in predictable, sequential fashion. At the same time, because young children lack the ability to generalize (Smetana, 1981) and have limited and uneven contacts with the social world, their social knowledge is fragmented. Mastery of diverse social concepts proceeds at dissimilar rates (Damon, 1977; Furth, 1980; Gardner, 1983; Schug & Birkey, 1983; Turiel, 1978).

Furth (1980) noted that 5- to 6-year-olds are in a period of prelogical, personalized thinking. They lack the ability to separate personal and societal roles and are unable to imagine that personal and societal needs might conflict. In Furth's interviews with English children, those in the youngest group projected a harmonious world in which personal needs and outside events were never in conflict.

The unreflective nature of young children's economic reasoning was described by Furth (1980) and by Schug and Birkey (1983). The latter noted that, when presented with hypothetical problems involving economics, preschool and kindergarten children generally failed to give reasons to support their answers. They responded in terms of their own immediate needs or with respect to the physical property of an object, or they employed tautological reasoning. Paramount in the responses were references to parental authority, indicating that children's reasoning reflects their own experiences.

Other evidence from Furth's (1980) study verifies the role of experience. The children's thinking was assessed relative to seven economic concepts. The results showed that children's understanding of aspects of exchange and television advertising developed more quickly than other basic but more remote concepts such as choice, monetary value, and opportunity cost. The majority of even the youngest children had some ideas about why shoppers give money at a store, and one third of preschool and kindergarten children showed some awareness of the purposes of advertising.

At about age 7 children enter a new stage, one that Furth (1980) called "playful images" (p. 78) and Schug and Birkey (1983), "emerging reasoning" (p. 3). They begin to speculate about occurrences, often using play to explore what they have not directly experienced. By age 8 or 9, children begin to search for logical and factual explanations and start to develop systemic understandings of societal institutions. Their notions of economics, for example, become more realistic.

Researchers who have examined the political socialization of young children include Connell (1971), Furth (1980), and Berti (1988), who have documented the knowledge of young children about political institutions and authority figures. For example, Berti (1988) interviewed 80 Italian children aged 6 to 15 to probe their ideas about political organization and conflict. She found a developmental progression in children's thinking, with the youngest children showing no understanding of conflict or the need for government or laws. Policemen were the only public authorities mentioned by this group. At the next level, 8- and 9-year-olds showed recognition of the likelihood of conflicts and, with prompting, the concept of rulers. The findings lend further support to a developmental approach to social learning and are consonant with Furth's (1980) description of the way in which young children envision the adult world.

Moral Development

Moral development is one of the most heavily researched areas in the social development of young children. Definitions of the domain vary, with researchers focusing on such concepts as rules, authority, punishment, social conventions, prosocial behavior, and justice. As with the other areas explored earlier in this chapter, a variety of explanations of the development of morality and moral reasoning has emerged. Freud (1921, 1923) described the conflict between the unsocialized child and the social system. In a theory that emphasized the irrational aspects of development, Freud declared that the Oedipal conflict and a subsequent rechanneling of aggression toward the same-sex parent into guilt led to creation of the superego.

From a diametrically opposed position, Skinner (1974) explained morality in terms of conditioned responses. Bandura (1979) and other social learning theorists (e.g., Aronfreed, 1968; Bandura & Walters, 1963; Mischel & Mischel, 1976) expanded behavioristic explanations. These researchers speculated that children learn by observing and imitating others, deciding whom to imitate based on the salience of the model and the consequences of both the model's action and children's own imitative behavior. In recent years, Bandura (1986) has revised social learning theory, emphasizing internal cognitive factors more strongly than in earlier versions. According to Bandura's most recent work, intentions and self-evaluation processes act as cognitive regulators and play important roles in the self-regulation of behavior. Eisenberg and Mussen (1989) concluded that "reinforcement, punishment, observational learning, cognitive representations, and self-regulation are all important concepts in current social cognitive theory." They also noted that self-satisfaction in this framework is contingent on living up to internal cognitive standards. Children acquire internal standards and rules by imitating models and by understanding socializers' explanations of moral behavior (p. 28).

In their efforts to explain how children come to internalize normative values, Aronfreed (1968), Hoffman (1970, 1977), and Hoffman and Saltzstein (1967) examined the socialization practices of parents. Hoffman's research demonstrated that neither punishment nor the withdrawal of love was successful in promoting morality. Far more effective were parents' explanations of why they behaved as they did, expressions of warmth, and attempts to encourage their children to empathize with victims. These researchers, then, have pointed to the contributions of cognition and emotion in social learning.

Developmentalists such as Kohlberg (1976) and Zigler et al. (1982) have criticized social learning theorists for underestimating the importance of internal cognitive processes in moral development and for failing to consider developmental issues. Piaget (1932), Kohlberg (1976), Damon (1977), and Turiel (1983) have described levels of moral and social-conventional reasoning, using structured interviews and observations. The morality of children between the ages of three and eight, according to Piaget, is based on the desire to please adults. Children's dependence on adults, Piaget argued, creates a respect for adult authority that underlies children's compliance. Children's morality becomes more sophisticated as they interact in reciprocal relationships with their peers; mutuality develops and, with it, concepts of justice. Gradually children move from morality based on seeking approval or avoiding punishment to an understanding of the function of rules in maintaining a smooth social order.

Kohlberg (1976) also organized morality around concepts of justice and the development of rational thinking. In his theory, the very young child displays an obedience and punishment orientation; at the next level (about age seven), children begin to make judgments to satisfy their own personal needs and, occasionally, those of others. Thus, children move from egoistic to conventional understanding.

In his developmental theory, Turiel (1975) described seven levels in the development of concepts about authority. Interviews with 109 subjects (aged 6 to 25) to probe the ways in which they reasoned indicated at the first level an awareness and acceptance of social uniformities. Children at Level 1, ages 6 to 7, lacked systematic ideas of social organization, but showed an awareness of differences in power and status. They accepted the right of those in positions of authority to set policy for others to obey. Children at ages 8 to 9 (Level 2) displayed more differentiated notions. They began to see that compliance with rules maintains uniformity but that rules are not always obeyed, calling into question the validity of individual power as a basis for authoritative rule (Glick & Clark-Stewart, 1978).

Damon (1977) assessed multiple areas of children's moral and social development—authority, friendship, justice, and social regulation—using children's everyday experiences to structure assessment tasks. Although he found general consistency in developmental progression, reasoning about one concept only roughly predicted development of reasoning about a second, and hypothetical reasoning about justice was not consistently associated with performance on real-life tasks in a controlled environment. The types of assessment measures used and the influence of different situational contexts may explain the inconsistencies.

Damon (1977) extended Turiel's (1975) research with 6-year-olds down to 4-year-olds, categorizing their reasoning about authority and rules. Like Turiel, he found a close relationship between age and reasoning. Damon questioned 56 girls and boys between the ages of 4 and 9 about sex role conventions, table manners, and stealing. The 4- to 5-year-olds he categorized as libertarians. They confused customs with rules, conventions, and also with personal desire. They lacked the capacity to see patterns and did not understand that personal desire may conflict with societal rules. At ages 5 to 6, although children could occasionally provide rationales for rules, they obeyed them to meet the expectations of authority figures, avoid punishment, and conform. They were aware of the potential conflict between self and social regulation. At the next level, according to Damon, children (ages 6 to 9) differentiated between some moral and conventional rules, having learned that the former were often more consistently followed and more strongly upheld.

Damon (1977) found a developmental progression in children's moral judgment: 37% of 4- to 5-year-olds, 60% of 6-year-olds, and 84% of 7- to 9-year-olds evaluated stealing as worse than poor table manners. Also, although half of children in the sample gave empathetic reasons for not stealing, the youngest children did not conclude that, therefore, rules against stealing were very important. Damon emphasized that everyday experiences with issues such as fairness and sharing were as important as adult constraint and example in shaping the moral development of children.

In recent years, much of the discussion of moral development has focused on Turiel's (1983) argument that even children as young as 6 make distinctions between the moral and conventional domains and appear to recognize the overriding importance of moral rules when asked about concrete situations relevant to their personal experiences. This proposition represents a departure from Piaget (1932) and Kohlberg (1976, 1984), who found that young children did not understand any type of rules and that not until they were much older did they feel an affinity for principles of justice. It should be pointed out, however, that methodology is likely to have influenced these results. Kohlberg, for example, employed problems centered around the adult world that were unlikely to have meaning for young children.

The research of Turiel (1975) and others reveals a strong tendency for even very young children to distinguish in interviews among moral principles, social conventions, and personal rules. For example, Smetana (1981) found that 3 and 4-year-olds judged moral transgressions as more serious and more deserving of punishment than conventional misbehavior, whether or not a rule existed concerning the moral act. Nucci and Turiel (1978) similarly demonstrated that preschool children responded differently to moral and conventional transgressions, paying far more attention to moral violations than to problems involving social norms.

Weston and Turiel (1980) asked children, ages 5 to 11, whether it was right or wrong for a school to have rules such as allowing children to (a) hit each other or (b) undress on the playground. Eighty-eight percent of children of all ages labeled the first rule wrong and harmful; 68% of them accepted the right of authorities to set the second policy, even though many objected to it.

Dodsworth-Rugani (1982) examined 88 children, ages 6 to 18, on family rules, game rules, and moral rules. A statistically significant percentage of all children said that moral rules (e.g., against stealing) could not be changed but that game and home rules (e.g., for using the telephone) could be altered.

The results of these studies suggest that as they think about their social world, children of all ages make distinctions, pay attention to context, and view moral functions as different from social organizational ones. "Qualitatively distinct types of social interactions with different classes of events or actions lead to the construction of different types of social knowledge" (Smetana, 1983, p. 134).

Turiel's (1975) analysis of moral development has been criticized by those engaged in cross-cultural research. Kagan and Lamb (1987), Schweder, Mahapatra, and Miller (1987), Edwards (1987), and Nisan (1988) have questioned the universality of moral principles and argued for the important influence of culture. Schweder et al. (1987) noted that while some moral principles appear to be universal, what is a social convention in one culture may be a moral principle in another. They also suggested that Turiel's theory of separate domains ignores the relationships that exist between social customs and morality. Further, they argued that although there may be cross-cultural agreement on principles such as justice, reciprocity, and keeping promises, their application in real life is situationally and culturally dependent.

A key and unresolved question from the literature on moral and social development is how children come to make distinctions between moral concepts such as justice, authority, and obedience, and social conventions such as manners and dress.

Does the evidence represent an innate predisposition toward morality over convention, as some attribute to Turiel (and he denies) (Edwards, 1987; Nisan, 1988; Turiel, Nucci & Smetana, 1988), an interactive cognitive process, culturally-transmitted learning, or some combination of these and other factors?

According to Turiel and his associates, "children generate understandings of the social world by forming intuitive theories regarding experienced social events" (Turiel, Killen, & Helwig, 1987, p. 170). What remains to be determined is the extent to which other persons, cultural events, emotion, and cognition help shape children's experiences and the relationships between young children's rudimentary knowledge and their later moral development.

METHODOLOGY

Recognition that cognitive processes are intertwined with emotional and social development points to methodological issues in the study of child development. The research reported in this chapter reflects growing emphasis on the complex interactions of affect and social cognition in the child's development. Until recently, researchers have demonstrated a preference for the experimental method. Zimiles (1981) described a "paradoxical methodological dilemma that tends to undermine efforts to study complexity." Fashioned by a tradition concerned with generating lean, simplified, quantifiable data, the experimental method is largely concerned with manipulable variables. Since the emotional state of an individual cannot be assessed quantitatively, it is much less studied. The net effect is "to stultify the study of complexity." (p. 60–61)

There is growing recognition of the importance of studying context through natural observations, narratives, and open-ended questioning, of documenting the child's thoughts and complex social relationships, and of providing more adequate accounts of developmentally and culturally diverse children. For example, McLoyd and Randolph (1985) summarized research on African-American children from 1936 to 1980. They reported an increase from 13% to 44% in the use of naturalistic, multivariate methods since the late 1970s.

Qualitative strategies enable the researcher to better capture the dynamic and complex nature of children's learning and interactions. The effective use of qualitative, interactional research tehcniques could expand the range of questions and new conceptions of development and learning that can be addressed. In this context, social studies researchers are encouraged to study children as group members or as individuals interacting with friends, peers, and adults in the schooling environment.

Descriptive developmental research opens the way for increased understanding of the emergence of prosocial behavior, the formation of friendships and peer relationships, and the connections children make in their conceptualizations of social events. One example of such research is a study by Selman and Selman (1979) of children's ideas about friendship. Open-ended, semi-structured interviews were part of the methodological design of the study. Children aged 3 to 15 were presented with a dilemma in an open-ended story. They were encouraged to share their thoughts and not just tell what they thought the researchers wanted to hear. Data were transcribed from 93 interviews to be analyzed for regular patterns of thought about the nature of friendships. The researchers found that stage-related responses in children's thinking were more evident in the justifications, the arguments, and the explanations for choices that followed probes of the "why" of the children's answers, than in the children's initial responses to the dilemma. They also noted a wealth of information when children's understanding of friendship, their reasoning, conceptions, and their theories about what friendship is and how it works were explored in the calm of interviews. While open-ended, semi-structured interviews are commonly used, this study engaged the children as coinvestigators, drawing on their unique knowledge and experiences in thinking and learning about friendships.

Collaborative interdisciplinary research between cognitive psychologists and social studies researchers is needed to mobilize expertise, broaden perspectives, and accelerate the transfer of theories into practice. Collaborative research offers the option of participating in theory building and educational practice. For example, few studies of kindergarten classrooms currently include classroom organization as a variable. Nor have researchers focused on the attitudes and social behaviors of young children (Fromberg, 1989), factors that are significantly related to concerns in social education. Collaborative research teams could bring the strength of multiple perspectives and diverse knowledge to the study of these complexities.

References

Alejandro-Wright, M. N. (1985). The child's conception of racial classification: A socio-cognitive developmental model. In M. B. Spencer, G. K. Brookins, W. R. Allen (Eds.), *Beginnings: The social and affective development of Black children* (pp. 185–200). Hillsdale, NJ: Erlbaum.

Aronfreed, J. (1968). *Conduct and conscience: The socialization of internalized control over behavior.* New York: Academic Press.

Bandura, A. (1979). *Social learning theory.* Englewood Cliffs, NJ: Prentice Hall.

Bandura, A. (1986) *The social foundation of thought and action: A social cognitive theory.* Englewood Cliffs, NJ: Prentice-Hall.

Bandura, A., & Walters, R. (1963). *Social learning and personality development.* New York: Holt, Rinehart & Winston.

Bearison, D. J. (1986). Transitional cognition in context: New models of social understanding. In D. J. Bearison and H. Zimiles (Eds.), *Thought and emotion: Developmental perspectives* (pp. 129–146). Hillsdale, NJ: Erlbaum.

Bearison, D. J., & Zimiles, H. (1986). Developmental perspectives on thought and emotion: An introduction. In D. J. Bearison and H. Zimiles (Eds.), *Thought and emotion: Developmental perspectives* (pp. 1–11). Hillsdale, NJ: Erlbaum.

Berndt, T. J. (1982). Fairness and friendship. In K. H. Rubin & H. S. Ross (Eds.), *Peer relationships and social skills in childhood* (pp. 253–278). New York: Springer Verlag.

Berndt, T. J. (1989). Friendships in childhood and adolescence. In W. A. Damon (Ed.), *Child development today and tomorrow* (pp. 332–348). San Francisco: Jossey-Bass.

Berti, A. E. (1988). The development of political understanding in children between 6–15 years old. *Human Relations, 41*(6), 437–446.

Biber, B. (1984). *Early education and psychological development.* New Haven, CT: Yale University Press.

Borman, K. M. (Ed.) (1982). *The social life of children in a changing society.* Hillsdale, NJ: Erlbaum.

Bredekamp, S. (Ed.). (1987). *Developmentally appropriate practices in early childhood programs serving children from birth through age 9* (expanded edition). Washington, DC: National Association for the Education of Young Children.

Byrnes, D. A. (1988). Children and prejudice. *Social Education, 52,* 267–271.

Chazan, M., Laing, A., & Harper, G. (1987). *Teaching five to eight year olds.* London: Basil Blackwell.

Comer, J. P. (1989). Racism and the education of young children. *Teachers College Record, 90,* 352–361.

Connell, R. (1971). *The child's construction of politics.* Carlton, Australia: Melbourne University Press.

Corsaro, W. A. (1985). *Friendship and peer culture in the early years.* Norwood, NJ: Ablex.

Damon, W. A. (1977). *The social world of the child.* San Francisco: Jossey-Bass.

Damon, W. A. (Ed.) (1989). *Child development today and tomorrow.* San Francisco: Jossey-Bass.

Denham, S. A. (1986). Social cognition, prosocial behavior, and emotion in preschoolers: Contextual validation. *Child Development, 57,* 157–201.

Dodsworth-Rugani, K. J. (1982). The development of concepts of social structure and their relationship to school rules and authority. Unpublished doctoral dissertation, University of California, Berkeley.

Dunn, J. (1985). Growing up in a family world: Issues in the study of social development in young children. In M. Richards & P. Light (Eds.), *Children of social worlds: Development in a social context* (pp. 98–115). Cambridge, MA: Harvard University Press.

Edwards, C. P. (1987). Culture and the construction of moral values: A comparative ethnography of moral encounters in two cultural settings. In J. Kagan & S. Lamb (Eds.), *The emergence of morality in young children* (pp. 123–150). Chicago: University of Chicago Press.

Eisenberg, N. (Ed.) (1982). *The development of prosocial behavior.* New York: Academic Press.

Eisenberg, N., & Mussen, P. H. (1989). *The roots of prosocial behavior in children.* New York: Cambridge University Press.

Elkind, D. (1986). Formal education and early childhood education: An essential difference. *Phi Delta Kappan, 67,* 631–636.

Elkind, D. (1989). Developmentally appropriate practice: Philosophical and practical implications. *Phi Delta Kappan, 70,* 113–117.

Fischer, K. W., Shaver, P. R., & Carnochan, P. (1989). A skill approach to emotional development: From basic to subordinate-category emotions. In W. A. Damon (Ed.), *Child development today and tomorrow* (pp. 107–132). San Francisco: Jossey-Bass.

Freud, S. (1921). *Group psychology and the analysis of the ego.* New York: Liveright, 1951.

Freud, S. (1923). *The ego and the id.* New York: Norton, 1960.

Fromberg, D. P. (1989). Kindergarten: Current circumstances affecting curriculum. In F. O'Connell, F. Rust, & L. Williams (Eds.), *The care and education of young children* (pp. 56–67). New York: Teachers College Press.

Furth, H. G. (1979). How the child understands social institutions. In

F. B. Murray (Ed.), *The impact of Piagetian theory* (pp. 135–137). Baltimore: University Park Press.

Furth, H. G. (1980). *The world of grown-ups: Children's conceptions of society.* New York: Elsevier.

Gardner, H. (1983). *Frames of mind: The theory of multiple intelligences.* New York: Basic Books.

Glick, J., & Clarke-Stewart, A. (Eds.) (1978). *The development of social understanding.* New York: Gardner Press.

Grant, L. (1984). Black females' "place" in desegregated classrooms. *Sociology of Education, 57,* 98–111.

Harris, P. L. (1989). *Emotions in children.* New York: Basil Blackwell.

Harter, S. (1983). Developmental perspectives on the self-system. In P. H. Mussen (Ed.), *Handbook of childhood psychology: Vol. IV. Socialization, personality and social development* (pp. 275–285). New York: John Wiley & Sons.

Hartup, W. W. (1979). The social worlds of childhood. *American Psychologist, 34,* 944–950.

Hartup, W. W. (1983). Peer relations. In E. M. Hetherington (Ed.), *Handbook of child psychology: Vol. IV. Socialization, personality, and social development* (pp. 469–545). New York: John Wiley & Sons.

Hartup, W. W., & S. G. Moore (1990). Early peer relations: Developmental significance and prognostic implications. *Early Childhood Research Quarterly, 5(1),* 1–17.

Hoffman, M. L. (1970). Moral development. In P. H. Mussen (Ed.), *Carmichael's manual of child psychology, 2* (pp. 261–359). New York: John Wiley & Sons.

Hoffman, M. L. (1977). Moral internalization. In L. Berkowitz (Ed.), *Advances in experimental social psychology (Vol. 10,* pp. 85–133). New York: Academic Press.

Hoffman, M. L., & Saltzstein, H. D. (1967). Parent discipline and the child's moral development. *Journal of Personality and Social Psychology, 5,* 45–47.

Izard, C. E. (1977). *Human emotions.* New York: Plenum.

Izard, C. E. (1986). Approaches to developmental research on emotion-cognition relationships. In D. J. Bearison & H. Zimiles (Eds.), *Thought and emotion* (pp. 21–29). Hillsdale, NJ: Erlbaum.

Kagan, J., & Lamb, S. (Eds.). (1987). *The emergence of morality in young children.* Chicago: University of Chicago Press.

Karniol, R. (1982). Settings, scripts and self-schemata: A cognitive analysis of the development of prosocial behavior. In N. Eisenberg (Ed.), *The development of prosocial behavior* (pp. 251–274). New York: Academic Press.

Katz, L. G. (1985). Dispositions in early childhood. *ERIC/EECE Bulletin, 18(2).*

Katz, L. G. (1988). Engaging children's minds: The applications of research for early childhood education. In C. Warger (Ed.), *Resource guide to public school early childhood programs* (pp. 32–52). Washington, DC: Association for Supervision and Curriculum Development.

Katz, P. A. (1983). Developmental foundations of gender and racial attitudes. In R. I. Leahy (Ed.), *The child's construction of social inequality* (pp. 41–78). New York: Academic Press.

Kohlberg, L. (1976). Moral stages and moralization: The cognitive-developmental approach. In T. Lickona (Ed.), *Moral development and behavior: Theory, research and social issues* (pp. 31–53). New York: Holt, Rinehart & Winston.

Kohlberg, L. (1984). *Essays on moral development: Vol. 2. The psychology of moral development.* New York: Harper & Row.

Kuhn, D. (1989). Making cognitive developmental research relevant to education. In W. Damon (Ed.), *Child development today and tomorrow* (pp. 261–287). San Francisco: Jossey-Bass.

Lazarus, R. (1982). Thoughts on the relations between emotion and cognition. *American Psychologist, 37,* 1019–1024.

Lee, P. (1989). Is the child egocentric or sociocentric? *Teachers College Record, 90(3),* 375–391.

LeVine, R. A. (1980). Studies in anthropology and child development. In C. M. Super and S. Harkness (Eds.), *Anthropological perspectives on child development* (pp. 71–86). New Directions in Child Development, No. 8. San Francisco: Jossey-Bass.

LeVine, R. A. (1989). Cultural environments in child development. In W. A. Damon (Ed.), *Child development for today and tomorrow* (pp. 52–68). San Francisco: Jossey-Bass.

Liben, L., & Bigler, R. S. (1987). Reformulating children's gender schemata. In L. Liben, & M. L. Signorella (Eds.), *Children's gender schemata* (pp. 117–123). New Directions in Child Development. San Francisco: Jossey-Bass.

Light, P. (1986). Context, conservation and conversation. In M. Richards & P. Light (Eds.), *Children of social worlds: Development in a social context* (pp. 170–190). Cambridge, MA: Harvard University Press.

Marsh, H. W., & Smith, C. (1985). Moral reasoning and moral conduct: An investigation prompted by Kohlberg's theory. *Journal of Personality and Social Psychology, 49,* 1016–1021.

McAdoo, H. P. (1985) Racial attitude and self-concept of young black children over time. In H. P. McAdoo & J. L. McAdoo (Eds.), *Black Children's Social, Educational and Parental Environments* (pp. 213–242). Beverly Hills, CA: Sage.

McLoyd, V. C. (1985). Are toys (just) toys? Exploring their effects on pretend play of low income preschoolers. In M. B. Spencer, G. R. Brookins, & W. R. Allen (Eds.), *Beginnings: The social and effective development of black children* (pp. 81–100). Hillsdale, NJ: Erlbaum.

McLoyd, V. C., & Randolph, S. M. (1985). Secular trends in the study of Afro-American children: A review of child development, 1936–1980. *Monographs of the Society for Research in Child Development, 50(4–5),* 78–92.

Miller-Jones, D. (1988). The study of African-American children's development: Contributions to reformulating developmental paradigms. In D. T. Slaughter (Ed.), *Black children and poverty: A developmental perspective* (pp. 75–93). New Directions in Child Development, No. 42. San Francisco: Jossey-Bass.

Mischel, W., & Mischel, H. (1976). A cognitive social learning approach to morality and self-regulation. In T. Lickona (Ed.), *Moral development and behavior* (pp. 84–107). New York: Holt, Rinehart & Winston.

Mussen, P., & Eisenberg-Berg (1977). *Roots of caring, sharing and helping: The development of prosocial behavior.* San Francisco: W. H. Freeman.

Nisan, M. (1988). A story of a pot, or a cross-cultural comparison of basic moral evaluations: A response to the critique by Turiel, Nucci, and Smetana. *Developmental Psychology, 24(1),* 144–146.

Nucci, L. P. (1989). Knowledge of the learner: The development of children's concepts of self, morality, and societal convention. In M. C. Reynolds (Ed.), *Knowledge base for the beginning teacher* (pp. 117–127). Washington, DC: American Association of Colleges for Teacher Education.

Nucci, L. P., & Turiel, E. (1978). Social interactions and the development of social concepts in preschool children. *Child Development, 49,* 400–407.

Pate, G. (1987). *What does research tell us about the reduction of prejudice?* Paper presented at the 1987 AntiDefamation League Conference on American Citizenship in the Twenty-First Century: Education for a Pluralistic, Democratic America. Cited in D. Byrnes, Children and prejudice. *Social Education,* 1988, *52,* 269.

Patterson, G., & Bank, L. (1989). Some amplifier and dampening mechanisms for pathologic processes in families. In M. Gunnar & E. Thelen (Eds.), *Minnesota Symposia on Child Psychology. Vol. 22* (pp. 169–209). Hillsdale, NJ: Erlbaum.

Piaget, J. (1932). *The moral judgment of the child.* Glencoe, IL: Free Press, 1948.

Piaget, J. (1963). *The child's conceptions of the world.* Paterson, NJ: Littlefield Adams.

Radke-Yarrow, M., Zahn-Waxler, C., & Chapman, M. (1983). Children's prosocial dispositions and behavior. In P. Mussen (Ed.), *Handbook of child psychology Vol. IV: Socialization, personality, and social development* (pp. 469–545). New York: John Wiley & Sons.

Richards, M., & Light, P. (Eds.) (1986). *Children of social worlds: Development in a social context.* Cambridge, MA: Harvard University Press.

Rosenberg, M. (1985). Summary. In M. B. Spencer, G. K. Brookins, and W. R. Allen, (Eds.) *Beginnings: The social and affective development of black children* (pp. 231–234). Hillsdale, NJ: Erlbaum.

Schug, M. C., & Birkey, C. J. (1983). *The development of children's economic reasoning.* Paper presented at the College and University Faculty Association of the National Council for the Social Studies. San Francisco. (ERIC Document Reproduction Service No. ED 236 099).

Schweder, R. A., Mahapatra, M., & Miller, J. G. (1987). Culture and moral development. In J. Kagan & S. Lamb (Eds.), *The emergence of morality in young children* (pp. 1–82). Chicago: University of Chicago Press.

Seefeldt, C. (1977). *Social studies for the preprimary child.* Columbus, OH: Merrill.

Selman, R., & Selman, A. (1979). Children's ideas about friendships. *Psychology Today, 9,* 71–80.

Shaver, J. P. (1979). The usefulness of educational research in curricular/instructional decision-making in social studies. *Theory and Research in Social Education, 7*(3), 21–46.

Sigel, I. E. (1986). Cognition-affect: A psychological riddle. In D. J. Bearison and H. Zimiles, *Thought and emotion: Developmental perspectives* (pp. 211–229). Hillsdale, NJ: Erlbaum.

Skinner, B. F. (1974). *About behaviorism.* New York: Appleton-Century-Crofts.

Slaughter, D. T. (Ed.). (1988). *Black children and poverty: A developmental perspective.* New Directions in Child Development. San Francisco: Jossey-Bass.

Slaughter, D. T., & Dombrowski, J. (1989). Cultural continuities and discontinuities: Impact on social and pretend play (pp. 30–46). In M. N. Block & A. Pellegrini (Eds.), *The ecological context of children's play.* Norwood, NJ: Ablex.

Smetana, J. G. (1981). Preschool children's conceptions of moral and social rules. *Child Development, 52,* 1333–1336.

Smetana, J. G. (1983). Social-cognitive development: Domain distinctions and coordinations. *Developmental Review, 3,* 131–147.

Spencer, M. B. (1985). Cultural cognition and social cognition as identity correlates of black children's personal-social development. In M. B. Spencer, G. Brookins, & R. Allen (Eds.), *Beginnings: Social and affective development of Black children* (pp. 215–230). Hillsdale, NJ: Erlbaum.

Spencer, M. B. (1988). Self-concept development. In D. T. Slaughter (Ed.), *Black children and poverty: A developmental perspective* (pp. 59–72). New Directions in Child Development, no. 42. San Francisco: Jossey-Bass.

Spencer, M. B., Brookins, G. K., & Allen, R. A. (1985). Synthesis: Black children keep growing. In M. B. Spencer, G. K. Brookings, & W. R. Allen (Eds.), *Beginnings: The social and affective development of black children* (pp. 301–314). Hillsdale, NJ: Erlbaum.

Spodek, B. (1988). Conceptualizing today's kindergarten. *The Elementary School Journal, 89*(2), 203–211.

Sroufe, L. A., & Fleeson, J. (1986). Attachment and the construction of relationships. In W. W. Hartup & Z. Rubin (Eds.), *Relationships and development* (pp. 51–71). Hillsdale, NJ: Erlbaum.

Stangor, C., & Ruble, D. N. (1987). Development of gender role knowledge and gender constancy. In L. S. Liben and M. L. Signorella (Eds.), *Children's gender schemata* (pp. 15–31). New Directions in Child Development. San Francisco: Jossey-Bass.

Staub, E. (1978). *Positive social behavior and morality: Social and personal influences (Vol. 1).* New York: Academic Press

Sue, D., Sue, D. W., & Sue, D. M. (1983). Psychological development of Chinese-American children. In G. J. Powell (Ed.), *The psychosocial development of minority group children* (pp. 159–166). New York: Brunner/Mazel.

Sutton-Smith, B. (1966). Piaget on play: A critique. *Psychological Review, 73,* 104–110.

Tizard, B., & Hughes, M. (1984). *Young children learning.* Cambridge, MA: Harvard University Press.

Turiel, E. (1975). The development of social concepts: Mores, customs and conventions. In D. J. DePalma & J. M. Foley (Eds.), *Moral development: Current theory and research* (pp. 7–38). Hillsdale, NJ: Erlbaum.

Turiel, E. (1978). The development of concepts of social structure: Social convention. In J. Glick & A. Clarke-Stewart (Eds.), *The development of social understanding* (pp. 25–107). New York: Gardner Press.

Turiel, E. (1983). *The development of social knowledge: Morality and convention.* Cambridge: Cambridge University Press.

Turiel, E., Killen, M., & Helweg, C. (1987). Morality: Its structure, function, and vagaries. In J. Kagan & S. Lamb (Eds.), *The emergence of morality in young children* (pp. 155–243). Chicago: University of Chicago Press.

Turiel, E., Nucci, L. P., & Smetana, J. G. (1988). A cross-cultural comparison about what? A critique of Nisan's (1987) study of morality and convention. *Developmental Psychology, 24,* 140–143.

Vandenberg, B. (1986). Play theory. In G. Fein & M. Rivkin (Eds.), *The Young Child at Play* (pp. 17–27). Washington, DC: National Associates for the Education of Young Children.

Vygotsky, L. (1962). *Thought and language.* Cambridge, MA: MIT Press.

Weber, E. (1984). *Ideas influencing early childhood education.* New York: Teachers College Press.

Wells, G. (1981). *Learning through interaction.* Cambridge: England: Cambridge University Press.

Weston, D., & Turiel, E. (1980). Act-rule relations: Children's concepts of social rules. *Developmental Psychology 236,* 417–424.

Williams, L. (1989). Diverse gifts: Multicultural education in the kindergarten. *Childhood Education, 66*(1), 2–3.

Wyner, N. B. (1978). Children becoming citizens. In A. L. Pagano (Ed.), *Social studies in early childhood: An interactionist point of view* (pp. 40–54). Washington, DC: National Council for the Social Studies.

Yawkey, T., & Pellegrini, A. (1984). *Child's play: Developmental and applied.* Hillsdale, NJ: Erlbaum.

Yonemura, M. V. (1986). *A teacher at work.* New York: Teachers College Press.

Youniss, J. (1980). *Parents and peers in social development.* Chicago: University of Chicago Press.

Zajonc, R. B. (1980). Feeling and thinking: Preferences need no inferences. *American Psychologist, 35,* 151–175.

Zigler, E. F., Lamb, M. E., & Child, I. L. (1982). *Socialization and personality development.* New York: Oxford University Press.

Zimiles, H. (1981). Cognitive-affective interaction—a concept that exceeds the researcher's grasp. In E. K. Shapiro and E. Weber (Eds.) *Cognitive and affective growth* (pp. 47–63). Hillsdale, NJ: Erlbaum

·10·

THE COGNITIVE, SOCIAL-EMOTIONAL, AND MORAL DEVELOPMENT CHARACTERISTICS OF STUDENTS: BASIS FOR ELEMENTARY AND MIDDLE SCHOOL SOCIAL STUDIES

Janet Elaine Alleman and Cheryl L. Rosaen
MICHIGAN STATE UNIVERSITY

WHAT IS CITIZEN EDUCATION?

Research on children's cognitive, social-emotional, and moral development has implications for what is possible in meaningful citizen education, a primary goal of the social studies. The discussion in this chapter of children's developmental characteristics in the elementary and middle school years is aimed toward developing the kind of citizen described by Brophy (1988):

one who is an *informed* person *skilled* in the processes of a free society, who is committed to *democratic values* and who not only is able to but *feels obligated to participate* in social, political, and economic processes [Parker & Jarolimek, 1984]. Parker and Kaltsounis (1986) add that the thinking and actions of such a citizen would be characterized by the following three perspectives: (a) *global* (commitment to liberty and justice for all extends to people everywhere); (b) *pluralistic* (cultural diversity and differences of opinion are seen as acceptable or even desirable); and (c) *constructive or critical* (democracy is seen as unfinished business; the nation is seen as in need of maintenance and improvement) (p. 3; italics in original).

A citizen is a whole person, not just a cognitive, social-emotional, or moral entity. Accordingly, the education of a citizen who is vested with the rights, privileges, and duties associated with a democratic government must be understood in terms of how cognitive, social-emotional, and moral characteristics interact as young people develop. In addition, the word "development" connotes growth, so that children must be understood as emerging citizens, not deficient or incomplete citizens, and their development must be understood in relation to ways in which their experiences influence their further development.

The research to be reviewed supports the need to examine development from three viewpoints: (a) the cognitive, social-emotional, and moral characteristics that individuals bring to elementary and middle school classrooms, (b) the interactions among the three domains, and (c) the interactions between individuals' characteristics and their experiences in and out of school. Those three viewpoints, represented by the three overlapping circles in Figure 10–1, provide a perspective on the competencies that young citizens bring to the classroom as an alternative to the more common focus on what children cannot do or are not capable of learning. Within each domain, more specific aspects of development interact to influence ongoing development (represented by the smallest overlapping circles in Figure 10–1). Additionally, children's developmental characteristics interact across the three domains (represented in Figure 10–1 by the three larger overlapping circles) and are shaped by the children's experiences and environments (represented by the largest circle that encompasses all three do-

Reviewers were Marlowe Berg, San Diego State University; Jere Brophy, Michigan State University; Theodore Kaltsounis, University of Washington. Shawn Silver contributed to the preparation of the manuscript.

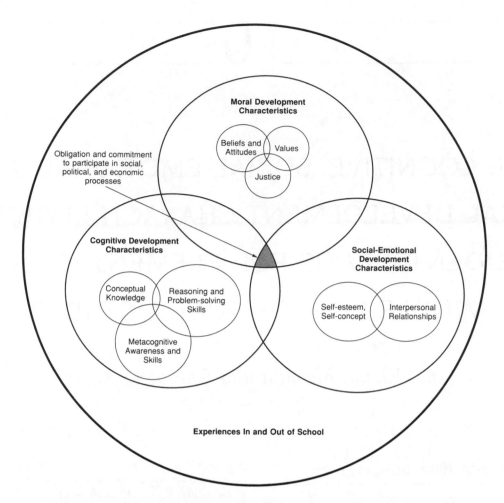

FIGURE 10–1. Interaction Within, Between, and Among Three Domains of Developmental Characteristics in Elementary and Middle School Children

mains). Figure 10–1, then, presents graphically the structure of this chapter, in which we review recent research and construct hypotheses regarding what elementary and middle school students, as emergent citizens, are capable of learning and doing in social studies.

A NONDEFICIENCY VIEW OF DEVELOPMENT

Research on language acquisition (Teale & Sulzby, 1986; Wells, 1986), concept development (Rogoff, Malkin, & Gilbride, 1984; Saxe, Gearhart, & Guberman, 1984), and socialization patterns (Corsaro, 1988) in early childhood is informative for conceptualizing the potential of elementary and middle school children for school learning. In particular, it is now understood that, as they interact with their caregivers at home, preschool children display increasingly complex competencies (e.g., communicative intent in interactions; maintaining a problem-solving focus on a task; use of facial expression and hand gestures to communicate) that are foundational for later school learning

(e.g., number concepts, letter recognition, sound-symbol correspondence, effective social interaction and communication). Moreover, instead of viewing the understandings that children bring to school as deficient, it is more accurate to see their expertise as developing, or as "emergent" (Teale & Sulzby, 1986).

In addition, adults can facilitate young learners' development of competencies in the home by acknowledging and interactively supporting them (Rogoff & Wertsch, 1984; Wells, 1986). Educators can learn from the early childhood research (reviewed in another handbook chapter) about ways to design curriculum and instruction for elementary and middle school social studies that build on the characteristics that learners bring to classrooms (Florio-Ruane, 1988). Many common curriculum and instructional practices "disenfranchise" children of their competencies when they come to school (Searcy, 1988), instead of supporting their ongoing development. Thus, children who enter school believing that they can communicate, read, count, or participate in group activities may come to believe—through discontinuities in the interactions through which they learn at home and at school—that they cannot (Michaels, 1986; Wells, 1986).

Similarly, there are discontinuities between the activities of daily life and the activities required of school children. Resnick (1987) identified four: (a) school tasks are individual, whereas outside tasks are shared; (b) school tasks require "pure mentation," and outside tasks encourage and often require tool manipulation; (c) school tasks typically require symbol manipulation, and daily-life tasks are connected with objects and events; and (d) in-school competencies are taught as generalized learning, while out-of-school tasks require situation-specific competencies. Thus, knowledge and skill development and their use are often decontextualized in schools and are learned in the absence of a "shared intellectual functioning such as we see in our best work environments" (Resnick, 1987, p. 19). Resnick suggested that educators make in-school learning more continuous with the shared thinking and problem solving seen in other contexts. This implies the need for realistic citizen education activities, not just practice using knowledge and skills in isolation.

COGNITIVE DEVELOPMENT CHARACTERISTICS: A BASIS FOR BECOMING AN INFORMED PERSON

Elementary- and middle-school-aged children come to school with three types of emerging cognitive characteristics that provide a basis for becoming informed citizens: conceptual knowledge, reasoning and problem-solving skills, and metacognitive awareness and skills. Much of the social studies literature has focused on what children *cannot* learn according to their presumed developmental level (Cornbleth, 1985). Many, especially those who support the "expanding horizons" approach embedded in many elementary social studies textbook series, argue that elementary-aged children are not ready to learn abstract and complex concepts related to history, geography, or economics. For instance, there is a question as to whether children have an adequate conception of time and, therefore, whether they should be taught history at younger ages (Zaccaria, 1978).

More recent research, however, supports a different way of thinking about readiness for conceptual learning. In *constructivist* theory, learners at any age are considered to be active constructors of meaning. When learners confront new information, they relate it to existing knowledge that they have already organized in a particular way, giving the new information organization and meaning (Bruner, 1982; Vygotsky, 1962, 1978). When the existing knowledge that learners bring to classrooms is more complex (organized around principles and abstractions, and incorporating more interconnections among ideas), they interpret new knowledge differently than learners with less complex knowledge structures or "schemata" (Chi, Glaser, & Rees, 1982; Glaser, 1984). For example, children who bring well-developed schemata to learning situations are able to examine simultaneously both abstract ideas (organizing principles related to a domain) and concrete referents of these ideas (Jantz & Klawitter, 1985). Moreover, learning is a socially mediated process whereby the meaning that is constructed is influ-

enced by the social context in which it takes place (e.g., interactions with others, social norms governing the patterns of interaction) (Vygotsky, 1962; Mehan, 1980; Erickson, 1982). This cognitive mediational view of the learning process (Anderson, 1989; Winne & Marx, 1982) focuses attention on understanding what elementary and middle school students learn as they make sense of their experiences and individually construct meanings during social interaction in the classroom.

Conceptual Knowledge Development

Concepts are abstractions that enable learners to organize knowledge and thus make meaning of their experiences. A cognitive-mediational perspective on learning implies that concepts evolve in learners over time and therefore will be more or less complete at a given age rather than being either present or absent.

Understanding the knowledge structures that children bring to learning situations is important for making decisions about what they are ready or able to learn. Instead of thinking of knowledge change as development occurring on a general structural level (according to fixed stages as in Piagetian theory), it is more helpful to think of domain-specific changes in knowledge structures that take place in response to interrelated factors that include the child's maturation, out-of-school experiences, and instructional experiences (Anderson, 1989).

Research on social studies knowledge development has focused more on children's understanding of particular concepts than on their knowledge structures or schemata (hierarchical networks of concepts). However, most reviewers (e.g., Cornbleth, 1985; Jantz & Klawitter, 1985; Downey & Levstik, 1988; Evans, 1987; NCSS Task Force, 1989) have concluded that children are capable of learning concepts and thinking at higher levels at earlier ages than was previously indicated by stage theory, and that social studies instruction should focus on particular concepts as they relate to children's developing schemata. Examples follow.

Time. Time has been investigated mostly in relation to whether young children are capable of learning history, but the time concept also enters into understanding of geography, anthropology, sociology, economics, and political science. It is generally agreed that elementary-aged children have difficulty understanding temporal concepts, although the aspect of time being referred to varies a great deal. For example, Poster (1973) discussed several "times" that can be associated with a particular cultural context: social, literary, personal, physical (clock), and historical. Similarly, Patriarca and Alleman (1987) pointed out other characteristics of time that enter into elementary-aged children's evolving conceptions: time is unobservable and untouchable (abstract); time is elusive because personal and conventional time may vary; time has a variety of units of measurement (e.g., milliseconds and millenia) and is measured in a variety of ways.

Thus, it is difficult to identify just which conception(s) of time enter into students' potential for learning particular subject matter. Moreover, some have argued that acquiring physical time concepts may not be important for developing historical or geographical understanding (Kennedy, 1983; NCSS Task Force, 1989; Thornton & Vukelich, 1988). Others (e.g., Poster, 1973) have posited that children's development of conceptions of historical time may be limited by societal norms that place little value on such time. Even so, there is evidence that elementary-aged children understand different aspects of historical time. For example, they can see patterns and sequences in real events, and gradually refine their understandings of broad categories into understandings of specific historical eras (Levstik & Pappas, 1987).

Spatial and Temporal Relationships. Research on children's sensitivity to and use of conceptual organizations that emphasize spatial and temporal relationships provides support for the argument that even elementary-aged children can understand different types of causal relationships (Downey & Levstik, 1988). Moreover, the use of narrative has been suggested by educational theorists (e.g., Bruner, 1986; Egan, 1982) as an effective means of helping children develop time and causation concepts. For example, temporally connected events in narrative imply causality, and causality can be explored by examining a series of temporally related historical events. In addition, elementary-age children's understandings of concepts such as "before" and "after" are starting points for deepening their understanding of historical time. Levstik (1989a) reported a year-long case study of a fifth-grade child's developing historical understanding, in which she showed how historical narrative helped the child to impose order on events and assign causation.

Spatial understanding, used in map and globe skills, is fundamental to the learning of geography. Jantz and Klawitter (1985) questioned the long-held claim that elementary-aged children may lack the cognitive structures needed to learn to read, analyze, and infer information from maps, citing studies that pointed toward the presence of such capabilities in certain situations. They concluded that beginning instruction should be focused on the concrete, moving progressively to the abstract at appropriate ages. Moreover, other researchers such as Crabtree (1976) and Rice and Cobb (1978) have reported on how children can profit from geographic studies, particularly when instruction is highly structured, sequential, and designed to get the students actively involved (NCSS Task Force, 1989). Elementary school children's emerging conceptual knowledge can be further developed by experiences that build appropriately on the characteristics that the youngsters bring to learning situations.

Political Socialization. Political socialization has been defined to include all political learnings such as: knowledge and understanding of political, social, and economic systems; attitudes toward government; and ways in which civic culture is presented to and interpreted by children (Palonsky, 1987). Children's developing political lives are constructed out of personal and school experiences, as well as out of learnings from school subjects.

There is a long history of research on construction of political knowledge in elementary- and middle-school-aged children, but the results are mixed as to which factors are most influential (Easton & Dennis, 1969; Ehman, 1980; Hess & Torney, 1967; Hyman, 1959; Metzger & Barr, 1978). Elementary children come to school with basic trust in the benevolence of the political system. This is tested against experiences, including those encountered in school, as children become older (Crabtree, 1983; Metzger & Barr, 1978). Thus, whether through direct instructional experiences or through the "hidden curriculum" of social norms and patterns of interaction favored in schools (Apple, 1986; Giroux, 1983), children do construct understandings of political, economic, and social systems as well as basic orientations towards, and attitudes and beliefs about, political participation.

Economic Concepts. Research on children's understanding of economic concepts has generated three major findings relevant to this discussion: children develop economic values at an early age; their economic reasoning follows a developmental pattern that evolves from the concrete to the abstract; and they are likely to have misconceptions about particular economic concepts. Concepts such as scarcity, money, exchange, and profit play an important role in children's developing understanding of and attitudes toward the economic system (Walstead, 1987). Moreover, research on children's reasoning about these concepts shows that it follows a developmental pattern, although this may vary by concept and differ to some extent according to the child's experience (Crabtree, 1983; Kourilsky, 1987; Schug, 1987).

Kourilsky (1987) interpreted examples of children's understanding of economic concepts using a developmental continuum that took their emerging competencies into account. For instance, although younger children (aged 2 through 7) may be able to interpret a concept such as demand from its symbolic representation in a demand curve, they may not be able to manipulate information on the curve into other forms such as a graph. As logical thought develops across the ages 7 through 11, children are still tied to the need for concrete materials. By middle school, however, many children develop the ability to reason logically and abstractly, such as by differentiating scarcity and economic shortage. Thus, instruction about economic concepts must take into consideration selection of appropriate concepts, appropriate sequencing and clustering, and provision of appropriate developmental support (Crabtree, 1983; Kourilsky, 1987; Schug, 1987).

Finally, since children come to school with prior knowledge of and experience with economics, they have misconceptions (Eaton, Anderson & Smith, 1984) or "learning hurdles" (Kourilsky, 1987) to be confronted. For example, students typically have difficulty with the concepts of scarcity, opportunity cost, the circular flow of income, and price (Kourilsky, 1987; Schug, 1987). As educators plan curricula and carry out instruction, they must pay attention to the understandings children bring so that they can help children change their thinking to develop an accurate conception (Anderson & Roth, in press; Eaton et al., 1984). This may require spending more time on fewer concepts to teach them well.

Developing a Global Perspective. Crabtree (1983) and Parker and Kaltsounis (1986) have argued for a global perspective in teaching about political, social and economic systems. This includes helping children to view the world as a planet-wide society and to understand the interdependence of human beings (Evans, 1987). Children are capable of understanding political, social, and economic systems from this perspective in the elementary years, and in fact, this is an optimal time for such learning (Evans, 1987; NCSS Task Force, 1989). For example, children under 10 are more receptive than older children to learning about other people, and more likely to develop a more positive outlook toward people from other countries and their homelands.

Development of Reasoning and Problem-Solving Skills

The informed person must be able to think and to critically appraise new knowledge for use in making decisions, solving problems, and participating in society (Brophy, 1988; Parker & Jarolimek, 1984). It has been argued that children of elementary age are not yet able to learn such school subjects as history, geography, government, or economics because they lack sufficient reasoning capacity and thinking skills. Recent research on the relationship between general cognitive skills and domain expertise offers an alternative viewpoint. Perkins and Solomon (1989) pointed out that, "There *are* general cognitive skills; but they always function in contextualized ways" (p. 19, italics in original). These authors went on to say, "general cognitive skills can be thought of as general gripping devices for retrieving and wielding domain-specific knowledge" (p. 23). The relationship between domain and strategic knowledge in academic performance was described by Alexander and Judy (1988) as follows:

As learners acquire more knowledge, they also seem to acquire the ability to abstract or mentally represent a given problem. Furthermore, more knowledgeable individuals categorize or classify problems on the basis of their underlying structures. (p. 394)

There is, then, a relationship between the two areas of cognitive development (conceptual knowledge and reasoning and problem solving skills) which must be attended to. Knowledge levels and organization affect the use of thinking skills, and thinking skills affect the way individuals perceive and organize new knowledge. Chi (1985) and Carey (1985) have described how children in early elementary years, not just older learners, develop domain-specific expertise. However, Carey (1985) argued that "by far the most important source of variance [in thinking] is in domain-specific knowledge. Children know less than adults. Children are novices in almost every domain in which adults are experts" (p. 514).

Recent research, particularly in science education, has pointed out the need to replace Piaget's notion of global restructuring (i.e., developmental changes take place in stages) with the notion of "domain-specific restructuring" (Vosniadou & Brewer, 1987)—that is, that children restructure their theory-like conceptual structures into new theories. Restructuring may take two forms: weak restructuring involves enrichment of existing structures; radical restructuring requires creation of new structures. However, Vosniadou and Brewer pointed out that these changes in the products—knowledge structures—of the learning process do not account for how the changes come about. Piaget attributed changes in knowledge structures to children's capacity for representational thought at particular ages. The research reviews discussed here point toward close interaction between general cognitive capacities and domain knowledge even at the elementary and middle school ages. This view implies a need for helping children begin to develop a knowledge base at younger ages, because without an adequate knowledge base, more complex knowledge structures cannot be formed, and categorization of particular kinds of problems (and accompanying problem-solving strategies) cannot take place.

Developing Metacognitive Awareness and Skills

As well as needing an adequate knowledge base and ability to think critically, make decisions, and solve problems, the citizen should be able to take responsibility for learning independently and to continue learning across the lifespan. Wang and Palincsar (1989) defined *metacognition* as domain-general knowledge that comprises a "broad spectrum of information that is related to efficiently "learning how to learn" (p. 73). They further described domain-general knowledge as including knowledge of strategies or rules for successful problem solving and completion of new tasks, and an understanding of how one's own learning characteristics interact with the learning environment. Planning and monitoring abilities are essential characteristics of successful learners, and helping learners develop purposeful awareness of these abilities can help them improve their capacity to learn from school tasks. When students take responsibility for and reflect on their strategic efforts, and when they are helped to have a series of successes on which to reflect, sustained use of effective cognitive strategies can be encouraged. Thus, effective learners take an active role in initiating and managing their learning.

Wang and Palincsar (1989) also pointed out that students who come to a learning task with more applicable knowledge are more likely to be successful. This point is related to Alexander and Judy's (1988) hypothesis that more capable learners perceive the "relatedness" among seemingly diverse tasks or domains and use that "relatedness" to guide their performance. This again underscores the importance of the relationship between knowledge structures and generalized strategies for successful learning (also see Prawat, 1988).

Finally, learning how to learn is a process that evolves over time, following a developmental progression (Anderson, 1989). Children of middle school age control their own learning more successfully than elementary-aged children; but teachers can help elementary-grade students develop the necessary knowledge and skills for learning how to learn by modeling and explaining thinking strategies, coaching students in their use, providing appropriate practice and gradually withdrawing support (Anderson, 1989; Collins, Brown, & Newman, in press). This kind of learning must take place within a problem-solving context that gives students the opportunity to practice exercising control over the learning process and helps them become aware of their developing expertise. (See Anderson, 1989, p.

92, for a list of instructional programs that foster self-regulation; also see Hunkins, 1985, for examples of how students can be helped to ask their own questions in social studies.)

Summary

Concepts are abstractions that enable learners to organize knowledge and make meaning of their experiences. The research reviewed supports the following hypotheses which could guide future research: (a) It is possible (as well as desirable) to begin teaching children to become informed citizens in the elementary years. (b) Although children's knowledge structures are less complex than adults' knowledge structures and their developing concepts may be incomplete, they nevertheless construct meaning from their experiences. (c) Learning school subjects such as history, geography, government, or economics can help children to organize their experiences and deepen their understandings of the social, political, and economic systems in which they will participate as adults. (d) There is a close interaction between general cognitive capabilities and domain knowledge; development of these characteristics goes hand in hand rather than one preceding the other. (e) There is a close interaction between domain knowledge and generalized strategies that leads to successful and continued learning, and citizens cannot stay informed without a sustained pattern of self-directed learning throughout their lives.

In the next two sections, we discuss ways in which characteristics in the domain of cognitive development interact with characteristics in the domains of social-emotional and moral development.

SOCIAL-EMOTIONAL CHARACTERISTICS: SELF-CONCEPT AND SELF-ESTEEM

In this section, the social-emotional domain is dealt with in terms of the elementary and middle school child's self-concept and self-esteem. Three aspects are considered: (a) the meanings of self-concept and self-esteem; (b) how each develops; and (c) how they relate to each other and are both determinants and consequences of social interaction. In addition, four influences on self-concept and self-esteem, as related to the child's capacity to become an involved citizen, are considered: cognitive development, ethnicity, gender, and opportunities for participation.

Definitions

Self-concept or identity is the awareness of understanding of self. It includes "all these aspects of the perceptual field to which we refer to as 'I or me'. It is the organization of perception about self which seems to the individual to be who he is" (Combs, Avila, & Purkey, 1971, p.39). Damon (1980) referred to self-concept as everything a child knows about his or her experience, position, and status in the social order, personal characteristics, and identity.

Self-esteem is the value people place on themselves and their behavior (McCandless & Evans, 1973), usually assessed in terms of positive or negative value. While the self-concept focuses on the understanding of "I or me," esteem draws its meaning from "I or me" in relation to others.

Development of Self-Concept and Self-Esteem

As children move through the elementary and middle school years, they have to respond to new situations, frequently perceived as sources of conflict and often labeled crises. How they react depends on and affects their self-concept and self-esteem. Erikson's (1968) stage theory provides a fruitful basis for research on major sources of conflict for children. He identified eight stages in the life cycle, with elementary and middle schoolers generally moving through two stages. Each stage involves a central developmental crisis, and Erikson posited that the child's success in coping with that crisis affects his or her more general development during and after that stage.

Elementary children are generally in Stage IV, the crisis of *industry versus inferiority*. During this stage, the major focus changes from self and home to concern with the neighborhood, peer group, and the school. These changes present new opportunities and expectations that children are usually motivated to fulfill. They learn to cooperate and get along with others. In the classroom, if they are successful, Stage IV youngsters learn to master school tasks, generally learn the role of being a student, and begin to develop a sense of efficacy through work accomplishments. They turn more outward; clubs, television, social and video games become important, and they immerse themselves in school work and play. They continually grow more independent of parents and adults. Their sense of success and recognition of progress, both in and out of school, greatly influence their emotional and social development. Gradual letting go by adults will permit the child to experience the pleasures of self-accomplishment and industry and avoid the feelings of inferiority that impede later development.

As children move through the transitional or middle school years between childhood and adolescence (ages 11–13), the need to discover "who they are" takes on crisis proportions. They enter Stage V, referred to by Erikson (1968) as the crisis of *identify versus identity confusion*. Activities begin to shift from large groups to smaller groups; friendships become more intimate, especially among girls, and individuals in this stage try to achieve mutually satisfying outcomes. Thornburg (1982) found that during these transitional years, relationships shift from same-gender to both-gender to opposite-gender. At school, there is a shift from a strong identification with teacher to identification with peers. During this transitional period, many students actually resent the teacher and the accompanying designated authority. How they resolve their identity crisis in terms of their self-concept and self-esteem has serious consequences for later school success and for adult citizenship participation.

Self-Concept, Self-Esteem, and Social Interaction

The value that elementary and middle school children place on themselves as individuals—their feelings of industry or inferiority, and of identity or identity confusion—is both a determinant and consequence of interaction (Lewis, 1979). Constant fluctuations in children's social lives (Erikson, 1968; Furth & Pickert, 1980) have effects on their understanding of themselves.

The child comes to school with a sense of self influenced and developed largely in response to social expectations, including reinforcement or modeling by significant others, especially his or her parents. Despite tendencies toward family resemblances in everything from food preferences (Rozin, Fallon, & Mandell, 1984) to political philosophies (Boshier & Thom, 1973), most personal and social traits develop in response to environmental rather than genetic influences (Ahern, Johnson, Wilson, McClearn, & Vandenberg, 1982). Parents are obviously a significant part of the child's environment, and the effects of parents' behavior on their children's development have been investigated by numerous researchers, including Baumrind (1971), Brophy (1977), Henderson (1981), and Maccoby and Martin (1983). Among the parental attributes that seem consistently and continuously vital in fostering optimal development as children move through the elementary and middle school years are basic acceptance of the child as an individual, warm and affectionate interactions, an approach to socialization that includes both instruction and discipline, expectations that communicate respect for the individual, and the practice, as well as advocacy of an articulated value system (Good & Brophy, 1990).

Interactions in school are vital, too. Combs, Avila, and Purkey (1971) found that self-concept and esteem are influenced by teachers. In addition, children learn much about who they are through their day-to-day contacts with peer groups (Coppersmith, 1967; Rogers, Smith, & Coleman, 1978).

Purkey (1970) has proposed ways for teachers to use the classroom setting to enhance students' self-concept and achievement. The opportunities of teachers to enhance elementary students' personal development is illustrated by the work of Schempp, Cheffers, and Zaichkowsky (1983). They found that children who were encouraged to share in classroom decision making felt more positive about themselves than those in classrooms where decisions were made exclusively by the teacher. The use of informal instructional opportunities has also been found to be influential in the development of children's abilities to relate to others successfully. Included is helping children to accept their gender or physical attributes, to develop empathy for others, to acquire social awareness, and to develop role-taking skills (Eisenberg, Lennon, & Roth, 1983; Rushton & Sorrentino, 1981; Smith, 1982).

Other Influences on Self-Concept and Self-Esteem

Among the factors that influence children's self-concept and esteem and affect their overall development of self-concept and self-esteem are cognitive capacity, ethnicity, gender, and opportunities to participate. These influences and the interactions that exist among them are discussed next.

Self-Concept and Cognitive Capacities. Purkey (1970) found that the affective value children place on themselves is related to their sense of accomplishment or academic achievement and that changes in one effect changes in the other. Shavelson and Bolus (1982) and Marsh, Parker and Smith (1983) also found correlations between regard for self and achievement. Stevens and Pihl (1982) found that the most academically able students (grade 6) have better auditory comprehension, spoken language, knowledge of time and space, and verbal and nonverbal competence than less academically able students. Each of these cognitive characteristics contributes to the child's social-emotional development. Stevens and Pihl also found statistically significant correlations ($r = .21$ to $.35$) between final grades and scores on a measure of self-concept. Yeger and Miezitis (1980) found that children with low self-concepts had more academic problems and were more socially withdrawn than were children with high self-concepts. In a study of the self-concepts and higher-level thought processes of minority children, Campbell (1981) found a positive relationship between self-concept and reading achievement, between self-concept and listening comprehension achievement, between self-concept and higher-level thinking, and between self-concept and social studies achievement. These findings reinforce the belief that cognitive abilities and self-concept are related, although causal relationships have not been proven.

Ethnicity, Self-Concept, and Self-Esteem. The attitudes of others toward ethnic groups and of ethnic minority children toward themselves affect self-concept and self-esteem. Comparisons between the work of Clark and Clark (1947) and Farrell and Olson (1983) suggest that the gaps between African-American children's ethnic identification and skin color preference are decreasing, with important positive implications for their self-concepts. In terms of the development of attitudes toward others, Katz (1976), identified eight overlapping stages of racial attitudes in children. The stages occurred over a period of approximately 10 years, with some crystallization of racial attitudes occurring at about the conclusion of the elementary grades. Although the stages were somewhat age-related, the child's acquisition of more complex racial concepts was an important variable. Environment is important, too. Children in ethnically heterogeneous classrooms tend to develop more accepting attitudes about ethnicity (Asher & Singleton, 1978; Friedman, 1980; Goldstein, Koopman, & Goldstein, 1978) and cooperative class groupings have been found to contribute to positive relations between ethnic groups (Johnson & Johnson, 1982).

Gender, Self-Concept, and Self-Esteem. Gender is another influence on the elementary and middle schooler's development of self-concept and self-esteem. Gender differences are observable from birth and at a very early age, children begin to define themselves and their peers in terms of these differences. Most children are strongly motivated to learn about their own gender and the role expectations that apply (Bradbard & Endsley, 1983; Masters, Ford, Arend, Grotevan, & Clark, 1979). While the preoccupation with gender identification declines in elementary schools, relations among peers at play as well as in the classroom tend to be primarily sex segregated (Eder & Halliman, 1978; Gilligan, 1982; Lever, 1976; Waldrop & Halverson, 1975).

In fact, there is some evidence that elementary and middle school children have negative attitudes about interacting in mixed sex groups (Lockheed, 1985).

Although the role of genetics in producing gender-related differences in social behavior, self-concept and self-esteem, and cognitive functions has been debated, Brooks-Gunn and Matthews (1979), Wittig and Petersen (1979), and Maccoby and Jacklin (1974) concluded that such differences are heavily affected by socialization. The differences can be influenced by changes in the environment in and out of school.

Gender is particularly relevant in terms of the nature of class participation and the potential effects on self-concept and self-esteem. Girls are more likely to be criticized for poor academic performance and praised for nonacademic qualities such as appearance, neatness, and politeness (Dweck, 1975). Boys, on the other hand, are more likely to be reprimanded for misbehavior and praised for good academic performance. They receive many more prohibitory control messages from teachers than girls do, and when teachers criticize boys, they are more likely to use harsh or angry tones (Meyer & Thompson, 1963). Scott (1985) proposed that teachers could facilitate equal-status interaction and cooperation between boys and girls by increasing cross-sex interaction in the classroom, by increasing students' understanding of the effects of gender on human interaction, and by expanding the students' competence in social skills.

Social Participation, Self-Concept, and Self-Esteem. Concern has been expressed about the lack of opportunities for participation in elementary and middle school classrooms that would lead to a sense of personal power, favorable feelings about self, and successful academic achievement (e.g., Pratte, 1988; Strike, 1988). Shermis and Barth (1982), for example, argued that when participation occurs it is only passive.

The research addressing participatory classroom climate as a significant variable in developing citizenship is, however, limited with most studies focused on adolescents (Conrad & Hedin, 1981, 1982, Corbett, 1977; Jones, 1974, 1975; Newmann, 1979; Reck, 1978). It should be noted, however, that elementary and middle school children are at the stage of acquiring new roles in their peer groups and that they have the capacity to cooperate, share, and generally get along with others. The effects of active participation during those school years merit greater research effort. In particular, cooperative learning, in which equal status interaction and cooperation are facilitated, seems to have the potential for offsetting some of the influences of cognitive capacity, ethnicity, and gender on self-concept and self-esteem (Johnson & Johnson, 1982). That is a potentially fruitful area of research.

Summary

Social-emotional development has been discussed in terms of self-concept and self-esteem within the context of interpersonal relationships. The research review supports the hypotheses that (a) elementary and middle school is an important period for social and emotional development, and (b) self-concept and self-esteem are related to each other and to such variables as cognitive capacity, ethnicity, gender, and opportunities to participate.

MORAL DEVELOPMENT: A BASIS FOR COMMITMENT TO DEMOCRATIC VALUES

Social studies goals include fostering behavior, thinking, and action consistent with such democratic values as justice, equity, freedom, and dignity. The school environment can influence children's learning of these values (Banks & Clegg, 1985; Parker & Jarolimek, 1984). The literature on the moral development of elementary and middle schoolers provides a basis for understanding the capacity of children to formulate and clarify their values and make choices about actions. There appear to be sequential stages, with intellectual development a necessary precursor to moral stage development. Stage developments may be enhanced by the appropriate interaction between the individual's cognitive structure and his or her environment. In this section we: (a) discuss the development of moral reasoning and (b) consider three influences on moral development—gender, cognitive capacity, and social participation.

Development of Moral Reasoning

The leading contemporary advocate for the position that moral judgment develops through changes in reasoning structures was Lawrence Kohlberg. Much of his work was an outgrowth of Piaget's stage theory. Piaget (1932) studied the changes in moral reasoning that accompany changes in cognitive development. He found that as children moved out of the egocentric stage (early elementary age) and acquired the cognitive abilities needed to assume the view of another individual, they began to understand such moral concepts as fairness and reciprocity.

Kohlberg (1969, 1984) elaborated on Piaget's ideas in his stage theory of the development of moral judgment. His theory includes three general levels of moral thinking with two stages at each level, described in detail elsewhere (e.g., Kohlberg, 1969). Briefly, the orientations of persons at various stages are: Stage 1—avoidance of punishment; Stage 2—reciprocity to obtain rewards; Stage 3—avoidance of disapproval; Stage 4—maintenance of social order; Stage 5—adherence to social contractual values; and Stage 6—accordance with universal principles of justice. However, Kohlberg's conception of Stage 6 has been heavily criticized (see Shaver & Strong, 1982, p. 150) for a too-narrow emphasis on justice (Peters, 1975) and for an overconcern with individual rights at the expense of other possible universal values (Hall & Davis, 1975). Also, Kohlberg's theory is limited to the cognitive or logical aspects of moral thinking; the emotional and social aspects are not addressed (Hoffman, 1983).

Although Piaget was able to link age and stage of cognitive development, the age-stage relationship in moral reasoning is less evident. However, Likona (1977) noted, "In general ..., Stages 1 and 2 dominate in the primary school years and persist in some individuals beyond that. Stage 3 gains ground during the upper elementary grades and often remains the general orientation through the end of high school" (p. 39). Changes in reasoning ability occur gradually, and age suggests a capacity to develop rather than being a determinant of development. Most elementary and middle schoolers are capable of using logical thought on specific problems that involve concrete examples. Many become capable of abstract, formal reasoning. That is the basis for Stage 3 "good boy–good girl" moral reasoning. In this stage, children become more cooperative and more willing and able to communicate with peers and adults. They begin to elicit validation for their ideas and decisions. As Stage 3 children become more socially oriented, they begin to realize that others may come to different conclusions in making decisions, and, as a result, they begin to see a need for rules as guides to behavior (Wadsworth, 1971). Classrooms, places where these youngsters spend a large portion of their time, have the potential for becoming social laboratories—safe environments for learning how to build consensus (Harshman & Gray, 1983) and places for open discourse regarding moral issues.

Kohlberg's theories have been used in designing educational programs to increase moral judgment levels (Damon & Killen, 1982). Typically, these programs have involved the use of moral dilemmas similar to those that Kohlberg asked children to cope with in his efforts to assess moral reasoning. These programs have been found to raise the children's levels of judgment, especially when the discussions are accompanied by empathy training, peer counseling, and a role playing (Lockwood, 1978). After examining several studies, Lockwood concluded, however, that the changes in stage development were small, were not consistent for all children, and tended to occur only in Stages 2 and 3 (Shaver & Strong, 1982, p. 151).

There is conflicting evidence about how teachers should challenge students in order to promote moral development. Mosher (1980) and Walker (1983) are among the researchers who have found it to be effective for teachers to confront the student's moral reasoning one level above his or her present stage. The rationale is that with "plus-one" challenges, cognitive conflict is introduced, inducing learners to be dissatisfied with their reasoning and leading to expanded reasoning ability. As Shaver and Strong (1982, p. 152) have noted, however, this approach continues to be questioned due to (a) the difficulties teachers have in assessing students' levels of reasoning, (b) the difficulties teachers experience in reacting to students' statements appropriately on an impromptu basis, and (c) the likely confusion—if the theory is correct that higher than plus-one arguments are not understood—when a class includes students at several moral stages (see, e.g., Rest, 1974). The evidence is clear, however, that concern for moral development must be integrated throughout the curriculum (Hersh, Paolitto, & Reimer, 1979; Shaver & Strong, 1982) rather than treated as a separate unit (Nucci, 1987), and that such a curriculum should be structured to promote debate among peers about moral issues (Nucci, 1987).

Other Influences on Moral Development

The adequate consideration of moral development must include not only the child's age and stage and the effects of classroom discussion, but the possible effects of gender, cognitive development, and social participation.

Gender and Moral Development. Kohlberg's theory has often been criticized on the grounds that only males' responses to moral dilemmas were used to develop the theory, and thus the scoring scheme was biased against females (Gilligan, 1982; Pratt, Golding, & Hunter, 1984). Research by Walker, DeVries, and Trevethan (1987) indicated, however, that gender is not associated with differences in the moral judgment of elementary and middle school students, as measured by Kohlberg's methods. Along a somewhat different line, Colangelo and Dettmann (1985) analyzed moral problems written by elementary and middle schoolers and found that gender and age were related to the way the students thought about moral problems and solutions. Boys tended to write about boys, and girls tended to write about girls, although girls used both sexes in stories more often then boys. These findings do not reflect gender differences in levels of reasoning, but suggest that boys and girls are interested in different types of moral issues.

Cognitive Capacities and Moral Development. As noted above, the major cognitive developmental considerations are that the concrete operational period is a prerequisite to Stage 2 moral reasoning, and the formal operational period must be reached before the child can move into Stage 3 moral reasoning (Hersh et al., 1979). Most elementary school children have the capacity to reason at Stage 2, and by the time they reach middle school most are able to reason at Stage 3.

Social Participation and Moral Development. The research indicates that moral reasoning and moral behavior are not highly related. In fact, early studies suggested almost no correlation, but more recent studies have revealed a moderate relationship. For example, students who score particularly low on moral judgments are more likely to be disruptive in school (Bear & Richards, 1981) and delinquent outside of school (Fleetwood & Parish, 1976). An emphasis on prosocial behavior—encouraging actions intended to aid or benefit another person or group without the anticipation of external rewards (Mussen & Eisenberg-Berg, 1977)—and the provision of opportunities to practice positive behavior seem to enhance the correlation between judgment and action (Eisenberg, 1982; Honig, 1982; Leming, 1981; Radke-Yarrow, Zahn-Waxler, & Chapman, 1983).

Teachers can promote moral development and behavior by modeling such thoughtfulness, by explaining the need for responsible behavior, by encouraging participation in dialogue about moral issues among peers, and by rewarding responsible behavior (Gibbs & Schnell, 1985). This view was operationalized at a school in Pittsburgh in 1977. Kubelick's research (1977) indicated that children ranging from ages 8 to 10 who took part in a curriculum that included role-taking opportunities, conflict situations that stimulated moral discussions, problem-solving opportunities, dialogue among peers in small groups, exposure to higher-reasoning stages, and a management structure perceived as fair and just made statistically significant stage changes and increased their reasoning abilities.

Summary

Research on moral development supports the hypotheses that (a) elementary and middle schoolers have the capacity to develop morally, with age an indicator of potential rather than a guarantee of development; and (b) development is influenced by variables such as gender, cognitive capacity, and social participation, as well as cognitive development.

RECOMMENDATIONS FOR FURTHER RESEARCH

The studies cited in this chapter were typically conducted from an unidimensional research model. That is, the researcher investigated cognitive development as related to age or development stage, or self-concept as related to ethnicity or gender, with no consideration of the ways in which cognitive, social-emotional, and moral development might interact, or of ways in which development within domains might be influenced by the environment. A more complex, interactive approach to research on children's development is needed (e.g., Cornbleth, 1985; Downey & Levstik, 1988; Palonsky, 1987).

Interpretive research methodology (Erickson, 1986a) that has grown out of ethnographic, anthropological, and sociolinguistic traditions shows promise for describing children's developmental characteristics and accounting for influences on further growth (also see the chapters by Cherryholmes and by Goetz & LeCompte in this volume). Interpretive researchers use a narrative approach to the documentation and analysis of development within its natural context. They use a limited sample (often developing case studies of individual learners' development in classrooms) to study in depth the interactions of multiple variables that may account for changes within or among domains of development across time. Erickson (1982) referred to this research approach as ethnographic inquiry with teaching and learning in its natural context as the primary focus.

The model used in Rosaen's study (1987), adapted from Erickson's work (1982), is one example of how research initiatives could be focused on describing the interaction among multiple aspects of children's development in the context of the social studies classroom environment. Rosaen documented the evolution of teaching and learning during seven weeks of an American history unit in an elementary classroom. Analyzing field notes, interviews, videotapes, audiotapes, and student work as primary data sources, Rosaen studied changes in event structure, subject-matter content, social interaction, teacher plans, and student work as they were negotiated and transformed across the unit. Use of this research model enabled Rosaen to describe ways in which changes in students' cognitive development (the nature and content of what they learned about history) were linked to changes in the learning environment (the social participation structure).

A second example of recent research drawing on Erickson's (1982) suggestions is Levstik's (1989a) year-long case study of the impact of the use of historical fiction on one fifth-grade student's understanding of history. Levstik outlined several ways in which narrative, as used in the classroom, influenced the way the child responded to and made sense of history. Levstik's approach allowed her to focus on the cognitive developmental characteristics that the student brought to the learning situation, and to account for ways in which the fifth-grader developed knowledge, skills, and understanding over time.

Rosaen (1987) and Levstik (1989a) uncovered some interconnections among aspects of the cognitive development domain and the environment by taking a narrative approach to understanding development within its natural context and by focusing on discourse as a centerpiece of instruction (Cazden, 1986). (For additional examples of this methodology, see Levstik, 1989b; Rowland, 1986; and Thornton & Wenger, 1989). What is relatively new in these research projects is the potential for understanding how the cognitive, social-emotional, and moral domains interconnect within the classroom context (Erickson, 1989b; Rowland, 1986). What must be of concern is the generalizability of conclusions from limited samples of classrooms, students, and observers. Nevertheless, interpretive approaches to investigating how children's developmental characteristics influence and are influenced by classroom life show promise for research that will stimulate thinking about how to improve social studies curriculum and instruction in order to develop a more intelligent and successful citizenry.

References

Ahern, L., Johnson, R., Wilson, J., McClearn, G., and Vandenberg, S. (1982). Family resemblance in personality. *Behavior genetics, 12,* 261–280.

Alexander, P. A., & Judy, J. E. (1988). The interaction of domain-specific and strategic knowledge in academic performance. *Review of Educational Research, 58*(4), 375–404.

Anderson, L. M. (1989). Learners and learning. In M. C. Reynolds (Ed.), *Knowledge base for the beginning teacher* (pp. 85–99). New York: Pergamon Press.

Anderson, C., & Roth, K. (in press). Teaching for meaningful and self-regulated learning of science. In J. Brophy (Ed.), *Advances in research on teaching, Vol. I: Teaching for meaningful understanding and self-regulated learning.* Greenwich, CT: JAI.

Apple, M. W. (1986). *Teachers and texts: A political economy of class and gender relation in education.* New York: Routledge & Kegan Paul.

Asher, S. R., & Singleton, L. C. (1978). Cross-race acceptance in integrated schools. *Integrated Education, 16,* 17–20.

Banks, J., with Clegg, A. (1985). *Teaching strategies for the social studies: Inquiry, valuing, and decision making* (3rd ed.). New York: Longman.

Baumrind, D. (1971). Current patterns of parental authority. *Developmental Psychology Monograph, 4*(1, Pt. 2).

Bear, G., & Richards, H. (1981). Moral reasoning and conduct problems in the classroom. *Journal of Educational Psychology, 73,* 644–670.

Boshier, R., & Thom, E. (1973). Do conservative parents nurture conservative children? *Social behavior and personality, 1,* 108–110.

Bradbard, M., & Endsley, R. (1983). The effects of sex-typed labeling on preschool children's information-seeking and retention. *Sex Roles: A Journal of Research, 9,* 247–260.

Brooks-Gunn, J., & Matthew, W. (1979). *He and she: How children develop their sex role identity.* Englewood Cliffs, NJ: Prentice Hall.

Brophy, J. (1977). *Child development and socialization.* Chicago: Science Research Associates.

Brophy, J. (1988). *Higher order thinking problem solving in social studies.* (Elementary Subjects Center Series No. 3). East Lansing: Michigan State University, The Center for the Learning and Teaching of Elementary Subjects, Institute for Research on Teaching.

Bruner, J. S. (1982). *The process of education.* Cambridge, MA: Harvard University Press. (original work published 1960)

Bruner, J. S. (1986). *Actual minds, possible worlds.* Cambridge, MA: Harvard University Press.

Campbell, R. L. (1981). Intellectual development, achievement, and self concept of elementary minority school children. *Social Science and Mathematics, 81,* 200–204.

Carey, S. (1985). Are children fundamentally different kinds of thinkers and learners than adults? In S. F. Chipman, J. W. Segal, & R. Glaser (Eds.), *Thinking and learning skills* (Vol. 2, pp. 485–517). Hillsdale, NJ: Erlbaum.

Cazden, C. (1986). Classroom discourse. In M. Wittrock (Ed.), *Handbook of research on teaching* (3rd ed., pp. 432–463). New York: Macmillan.

Chi, M. T. H. (1985). Interactive roles of knowledge and strategies in the development of organized sorting and recall. In S. F. Chipman, J. W. Segal, & R. Glaser (Eds.), *Thinking and learning skills* (Vol. 2, pp. 57–484). Hillsdale, NJ: Erlbaum.

Chi, M., Glaser, R., & Rees, E. (1982). Expertise in problem solving. In R. Sternberg (Ed.), *Advances in the psychology of human intelligence, 1* (pp. 7–75). Hillsdale, NJ: Erlbaum.

Clark, K. B., & Clark, M. P. (1947). Racial identification and preference in negro children. In E. E. Maccohy, T. M. Newcomb, & E. L. Hartley (Eds.), *Readings in social psychology* (pp. 159–169). New York: Holt, Rinehart & Winston.

Colangelo, N., & Dettmann, D. (1985). Characteristics of moral problems and solutions formed by students in grades 3–8. *Elementary School Guidance and Counseling, 19(4),* 261–271.

Collins, A., Brown, J. S., & Newman, S. E. (in press). Cognitive apprenticeship: Teaching the craft of reading, writing, and mathematics. In L. B. Resnick (Ed.), *Cognition and instruction: Issues and agendas.* Hillsdale, NJ: Erlbaum.

Combs, A., Avila, D., & Purkey, W. (1971). *Helping relationships: Basic concepts for the helping professions.* Boston: Allyn and Bacon.

Conrad, D., & Hedin, D. (1981). *Executive summary of the final report of the experiential education project.* St. Paul: University of Minnesota, Center for Youth Development and Research.

Conrad, D., & Hedin, D. (1982). The impact of experiential education on adolescent development. *Child and Youth Services 4,* 57–76.

Coppersmith, S. (1967). *The antecedents of self esteem.* San Francisco: Freeman.

Corbett, F. (1977). *The community involvement program: Social service as a factor in adolescent moral and psychosocial development.* Unpublished doctoral dissertation, University of Toronto.

Cornbleth, C. (1985). Critical thinking and cognitive processes. In W. Stanley (Ed.), *Review of research in social studies education: 1976–1983* (pp. 11–63). Washington, DC: National Council for the Social Studies.

Corsaro, W. A. (1988). Peer culture in the preschool. *Theory Into Practice, 27(1),* 19–24.

Crabtree, C. (1976). Sequence and transfer in children's learning of the analytic process of geographic inquiry. *Journal of Experimental Education, 45,* 19–30.

Crabtree, C. (1983). A common curriculum in the social studies. In G. Fenstermacher & J. Goodlad (Eds.), *Individual differences and the common curriculum; Eighty-second yearbook of the National Society for the Study of Education, Part I* (pp. 248–281). Chicago: University of Chicago Press.

Damon, W. (1980). Patterns of change in children's social reasoning: A two-year longitudinal study. *Child Development, 46,* 301–312.

Damon, W., & Killen, M. (1982). Peer interaction and the process of change in children's moral reasoning. *Merrill-Palmer Quarterly, 28,* 347–367.

Downey, M. T., & Levstik, L. S. (1988). Teaching and learning history: The research base. *Social Education, 52,* 336–342.

Dweck, C. A. (1975). *Sex differences in the meaning of negative evaluation situations: Determinants and consequences.* Paper presented at the Annual Meeting of the Society for Research on Child Development, Denver.

Easton, D., & Dennis, J. (1969). *Children in the political system: Origins of political legitimacy.* New York: McGraw-Hill.

Eaton, J. F., Anderson, C. W., & Smith, E. L. (1984). Students' misconceptions interfere with science learning: Case studies of fifth grade students. *The Elementary School Journal, 84(4),* 365–379.

Eder, O., & Halliman, M. T. (1978). Sex differences in children's friendships. *American Sociological Review, 43(2),* 237–250.

Egan, K. (1982). Teaching history to young children. *Phi Delta Kappan, 63,* 439–441.

Ehman, L. H. (1980). The American school in the political socialization process. *Review of Educational Research, 50,* 99–119.

Eisenberg, N. (1982). The development of reasoning regarding prosocial behavior. In N. Eisenberg, (Ed.), *The development of prosocial behavior* (pp. 219–246). New York: Academic Press.

Eisenberg, N., Lennon, R., & Roth, K. (1983). Prosocial development: A longitudinal study. *Developmental Psychology, 19,* 846–855.

Erickson, F. (1982). Taught cognitive learning in its immediate environments: A neglected topic in anthropology of education. *Anthropology and Education Quarterly, 13(2),* 149–180).

Erickson, F. (1986a). Qualitative methods in research in teaching. In M. Wittrock (Ed.), *Handbook of research on teaching* (pp. 119–161). New York: Macmillan.

Erickson, F. (1986b). Tasks in times: Objects of study in a natural history of teaching. In K. Zumwalt, (Ed.), *1986 yearbook of the Association for Supervision and Curriculum Development* (pp. 131–147). Washington, DC: ASCD.

Erikson, E. (1968). *Identity, youth, and crisis.* New York: Norton.

Evans, C. S. (1987). Teaching a global perspective in elementary classrooms. *Elementary School Journal, 87 (5),* 545–555.

Farrell, W. C., Jr., & Olson, J. L. (1983). Kenneth and Mamie Clark revisited: Racial identification and racial preference in dark skinned and light skinned black children. *Urban Education, 18,* 284–297.

Fleetwood, R., & Parish, T. (1976). Relationship between moral development test scores of juvenile delinquents and their inclusion in a moral dilemma discussion group. *Psychological Reports, 39,* 1075–1080.

Florio-Ruane, S. (1988). How ethnographers of communication study writing in school. In J. Reodence, R. Baldwins, J. Konopak, & P. O'Keefe (Eds.), *Dialogues in literacy research,* 37th Yearbook of the National Reading Conference (pp. 269–283). Chicago: National Reading Conference.

Friedman, P. (1980). Racial preferences and identifications of white elementary school children. *Contemporary Educational Psychology, 5,* 256–265.

Furth, H. G., & Pickert, S. M. (1980). How children maintain a conversation with adults. *Human Development, 23(3),* 162–176.

Gibbs, J. C., & Schnell, S. V. (1985). Moral development "versus" socialization. *American Psychologist, 40(10),* 1071–1080.

Gilligan, C. (1982). *In a different voice: Psychological theory and women's development.* Cambridge, MA: Harvard University Press.

Giroux, H. A. (1983). *Theory and resistance in education: A pedagogy for the opposition.* South Hadley, MA: Bergin & Garvey.

Glaser, R. (1984). Education and thinking: The role of knowledge. *American Psychologist, 39,* 93–104.

Goldstein, C. G., Koopman, E., & Goldstein H. (1979). Racial attitudes in young children as a function of interracial contact in the public schools. *American Journal of Orthopsychiatry, 48,* 89–99.

Good, T., & Brophy, J. (1990). *Educational psychology: A realistic approach* (4th ed.). New York: Longman.

Hall, R. T., & Davis, J. U. (1975). *Moral education in theory and practice.* Buffalo, NY: Prometheus Books.

Harshman, R. E., & Gray, C. (1983). A rationale for value education. *Theory and Research in Social Studies, 11*(3), 45–66.

Henderson, R. (Ed.). (1981). *Parent-child interaction: Theory, research, and prospects.* New York: Academic Press.

Hersh, R. H., Paolitto, D. P., & Reimer, J. (1979). *Promoting moral growth: From Piaget to Kohlberg.* New York: Longman.

Hess, R. D., & Torney, J. V. (1967). *The development of political attitudes in children.* Chicago: Aldine.

Hoffman, M. (1983). Affective and cognitive processes in moral internalization. In E. Higgins, D. Ruble, & W. Hertup (Eds.), *Social cognition and social development: A sociocultural perspective* (pp. 236–274). Cambridge: Cambridge University Press.

Honig, A. S. (1982). Research in review: Prosocial development in children. *Young Children, 37,* 51–62.

Hunkins, F. P. (1985). Helping students ask their own questions. *Social Education, 49,* 293–296.

Hyman, H. H. (1959). *Political socialization: A study in the psychology of political behavior.* Glencoe, IL: Free Press.

Jantz, R. K., & Klawitter, K. (1985). Early childhood/elementary social studies: A review of recent research. In W. Stanley (Ed.), *Review of research in social studies education: 1976–1983* (pp. 65–121). Washington, DC: National Council for the Social Studies.

Johnson, D. W., & Johnson, R. J. (1982). Effects of cooperative, competitive, and individualistic learning experiences on cross-ethnic interaction and friendships. *Journal of Social Psychology, 118,* 47–58.

Jones, S. (1974). Changing student attitudes: The impact of community participation. *Social Science Quarterly, 55,* 439–450.

Jones, S. (1975). Evaluating student involvement as a technique for improving citizenship education. *Theory and Research in Social Education, 3*(1), 73–78.

Katz, P. A. (1976). The acquisition of racial attitudes in children. In P. A. Katz (Ed.), *Towards the Elimination of Racism* (pp. 125–154). New York: Pergamon Press.

Kennedy, K. J. (1983). Assessing the relationship between information processing capacity and historical understanding. *Theory and Research in Social Education, 11*(2), 5–16.

Kohlberg, L. (1969). Stage and sequence: The cognitive-developmental approach to socialization. In D. Goslin (Ed.), *Handbook of socialization theory and research* (pp. 347–480). Chicago: Rand McNally.

Kohlberg, L. (1984). *Essays on moral development. Vol. 2. The psychology of moral development: The nature and validity of moral stages.* San Francisco: Harper & Row.

Kourilsky, M. L. (1987). Children's learning of economics: The imperative and the hurdles. *Theory Into Practice, 26*(3), 198–205.

Kubelick, C. (1977). *A study of the effects of a social skills intervention in the cognitive moral development of 8, 9, and 10 year olds.* Unpublished doctoral dissertation. University of Pittsburgh.

Leming, J. (1981). On the limits of rational moral education. *Theory and Research in Social Education, 9*(1), 7–34.

Lever, J. (1976). Sex differences in the games children play. *Social Problems, 23,* 478–487.

Levstik, L. S. (1989a). Historical narrative and the young reader. *Theory Into Practice, 23*(2), 114–119.

Levstik, L. S. (1989b, March). *Subverting reform in the social studies: A fourth grade case study.* Paper presented at the annual meeting of the American Educational Research Association, San Francisco.

Levstik, L. S., & Pappas, C. C. (1987). Exploring the development of historical understanding. *Journal of Research and Development in Education, 21,* 1–15.

Lewis, M. (1979). The self as a developmental concept. *Human Development, 22,* 416–419.

Lickona, T. (1977). How to encourage moral development. *Learning, 5,* 37–43.

Lockheed, M. (1985). Sex and social influence: A meta-analysis guided by theory. In J. Berger and M. Zelditch (Eds.), *Status attributions and rewards* (pp. 406–429). San Francisco: Jossey-Bass.

Lockwood, A. (1978). The effects of values clarification and moral development curricula on school-age subjects: A critical review of recent research. *Review of Educational Research, 48,* 325–364.

Maccoby, E., & Jacklin, C. (1974). *The psychology of sex differences.* Stanford: Stanford University Press.

Maccoby, E., & Martin, J. (1983). Socialization in the context of the family: Parent-child interaction. In P. Mussen (Ed.), *Handbook of child psychology* (4th ed.) (*Vol. 4,* pp. 1–101). New York: Wiley.

Marsh, H. W., Parker, J. W., & Smith, I. D. (1983). Pre-adolescent self-concept: Its relation to self-concept as inferred by teachers and to academic ability. *British Journal of Educational Psychology, 53,* 60–78.

Masters, J., Ford, M., Arend, R., Grotevan, H., & Clark, L. (1979). Modeling and labeling as integrated determinants of children's sex-typed imitative behavior. *Child Development, 50,* 364–371.

McCandless, B., & Evans, E. (1973). *Children and youth: Psychosocial development.* Hinsdale, IL: Dryden.

Mehan, H. (1980). The competent student. *Anthropology and Education Quarterly, 11*(3), 131–152.

Metzger, D. J., & Barr, R. D. (1978). The impact of school political systems on student political attitudes. *Theory and Research in Social Education, 6*(2), 48–79.

Meyer, W., & Thompson, G. (1963). Teacher interactions with boys, as contrasted with girls. In R. Kuhlens & G. Thompson (Eds.), *Psychological studies of human development* (pp. 510–518). New York: Appleton-Century-Crofts.

Michaels, S. (1986). Narrative presentations: An oral preparation for literacy with first graders. In J. Cook-Gumperz (Ed.), *The social construction of literacy* (pp. 94–116). New York: Cambridge University Press.

Mosher, R. (Ed.). (1980). *Moral education: A first generation of research and development.* New York: Preager.

Mussen, P., & Eisenberg-Berg, N. (1977). *Roots of caring, sharing, and helping: The development of prosocial behavior in children.* San Francisco: W. H. Freeman.

National Council for the Social Studies Task Force on Early Childhood/Elementary Social Studies (1989). Social studies for early childhood and elementary school children preparing for the 21st century: Task Force Report. *Social Education, 53,* 14–23.

Newmann, F. M. (1979). *Evaluation of the community studies program, 1978–1979, Memorial High School, Madison, Wisconsin.* Madison WI: University of Wisconsin.

Nucci, L. (1987). Synthesis of research on moral development. *Educational Leadership, 44*(5), 86–92.

Palonsky, S. B. (1987). Political socialization in elementary schools. *The Elementary School Journal, 87*(5), 493–505.

Parker, W. C., & Jarolimek, J. (1984). *Citizenship and the critical role of the social studies,* (NCSS Bulletin 72). Washington, D.C.: National Council for the Social Studies.

Parker, W. C., & Kaltsounis, T. (1986). Citizenship and law-related education. In V. Atwood (Ed.), *Elementary school social studies: Research as guide to practice* (NCSS Bulletin No. 79, pp. 14–33). Washington, DC: National Council for the Social Studies.

Patriarca, L. A., & Alleman, J. (1987). Studying time: A cognitive approach. *Social Education, 51,* 273–277.

Perkins, D. N., & Salomon, G. (1989). Are cognitive skills context-bound? *Educational Researcher, 18*(1), 16–25.

Peters, R. S. (1975). A reply to Kohlberg: Why doesn't Lawrence Kohlberg do his homework? *Phi Delta Kappan, 56,* 678.

Piaget, J. (1932). *The moral judgement of the child.* (M. Worden, Trans.). New York: Harcourt, Brace, and World.

Poster, J. B. (1973). The birth of the past: Children's perception of historical time. *The History Teacher, 6,* 87–98.

Pratt, M., Golding, G., & Hunter, W. (1984). Does morality have a gender? Sex, sex role, and moral judgement relationships across the adult lifespan. *Merrill-Palmer Quarterly, 30,* 321–340.

Pratte, R. (1988). Civic education in a democracy. *Theory Into Practice, 27*(4), 303–308.

Prawat, R. (1988). *Access: A framework for thinking about student empowerment.* (Elementary Subject Series No. 1). East Lansing, MI: Michigan State University, Institute for Research on Teaching.

Purkey, W. (1970). *Self–concept and school achievement.* Englewood Cliffs, NJ: Prentice Hall.

Radke-Yarrow, M., Zahn-Waxler, C., & Chapman, M. (1983). Children's prosocial dispositions and behavior. In P. Mussen (Ed.), *Handbook of child psychology: Vol. IV. Socialization, personality, and social development* (pp. 469–545). New York: John Wiley.

Reck, C. J. (1978). *A study of the relationship between participation in school service programs and moral development.* Unpublished doctoral dissertation, St. Louis University.

Resnick, L. B. (1987). Learning in school and out. *Educational Researcher, 16*(9), 13–20.

Rest, J. (1974). Developmental psychology as a guide to value education: A review of Kohlbergian programs. *Review of Educational Research, 44,* 241–259.

Rice, M. J., & Cobb, R. L. (1978). *What can children learn in geography? A review of the research.* Boulder, CO: ERIC/CHESS and Social Science Educational Consortium.

Rogers, C., Smith, M., & Coleman, J. (1978). Social comparison in the classroom: The relationship between academic achievement and self concept. *Journal of Educational Psychology, 70,* 50–57.

Rogoff, B., Malkin, C., & Gilbride, K. (1984). Interaction with babies as guidance in development. In B. Rogoff & J. V. Wertsch (Eds.), *Children's learning in the "zone of proximal development"* (pp. 31–44). San Francisco: Jossey-Bass.

Rogoff, B., & Wertsch, J. V. (Eds.). (1984). *Children's learning in the "zone of proximal development".* San Francisco: Jossey-Bass.

Rosaen, C. (1987). *Children as researchers: A descriptive study of intentions, interpretations, and social interaction in an elementary classroom.* Unpublished doctoral dissertation, Michigan State University, East Lansing.

Rowland, S. (1986). *The enquiring classroom: An introduction to children's learning.* New York: The Falmer Press.

Rozin, P., Fallon, A., & Mandell, R. (1984). Family resemblance in attitudes to foods. *Developmental Psychology, 20,* 309–314.

Rushton, J., & Sorrentino, R. (Eds.). (1981). *Altruism and helping behavior: Social, personality, and developmental perspectives.* Hillsdale, NJ: Erlbaum.

Saxe, G. B., Gearhart, M., & Guberman, S. R. (1984). The social organization of early number development. In B. Rogoff & J. V. Wertsch, (Eds.), *Children's learning in the "zone of proximal development"* (pp. 19–30). San Francisco: Jossey-Bass.

Schempp, P. G., Cheffers, J., & Zaichkowsky, L. (1983). Influence of decision-making on attitudes, creativity, motor skills and self concept in elementary children. *Research Quarterly for Exercise and Sport, 54,* 183–189.

Schug, M. C. (1987). Children's understanding of economics. *The Elementary School Journal, 87*(5), 507–518.

Scott, K. (1985). Social interaction skills: Perspectives on teaching cross-sex communication. *Social Education, 49,* 610–615.

Searcy, B. (1988). Getting children into the literacy club—And keeping them there. *Childhood Education, 65*(2), 74–77.

Shavelson, R. J., & Bolus, R. (1982). Self-concept: The interplay of theory and methods. *Journal of Educational Psychology, 74,* 3–17.

Shaver, J. P., & Strong, W. (1982). *Facing value decisions: Rationale-building for teachers* (2nd ed.). New York: Teachers College Press.

Shermis, S. S., & Barth, J. L. (1982). Teaching for passive citizenship: A critique of philosophical assumptions. *Theory and Research in Social Education, 10*(4), 17–37.

Smith, C. (1982). *Promoting the social development of young children: Strategies and activities.* Palo Alto, CA: Mayfield.

Stevens, R., & Pihl, R. O. (1982). The identification of the student at-risk for failure. *Journal of Clinical Psychology, 38,* 540–545.

Strike, K. A. (1988). Democracy, civic education, and the problem of neutrality. *Theory Into Practice, 27*(4), 256–261.

Teale, W., & Sulzby, E. (1986). *Emergent literacy: Writing and reading.* Norwood, NJ: Ablex.

Thornburg, H. (1982). *Development in adolescence* (2nd ed.). Monterey, CA: Brooks/Cole.

Thornton, S. J., & Vukelich, R. (1988). Effects of children's understanding of time concepts on historical understanding. *Theory and Research in Social Education, 16*(1), 69–82.

Thornton, S. J., & Wenger, R. N. (1989, March). *Geography in elementary social studies.* Paper presented at the annual meeting of the American Education Research Association, San Francisco.

Vosniadou, S., & Brewer, W. F. (1987). Theories of knowledge restructuring in development. *Review of Educational Research, 57*(1), 51–67.

Vygotsky, L. C. (1962). *Thought and language.* Cambridge, MA: MIT Press.

Vygotsky, L. C. (1978). *Mind in society: The development of higher psychological processes.* Cambridge, MA: Harvard University Press.

Wadsworth, B. J. (1971). *Piaget's theory of cognitive development: An introduction for students of psychology and education.* New York: David McKay.

Waldrop, M. I., & Halverson, C. F. (1975). Intensive and extensive peer behavior: Longitudinal and cross sectional analysis. *Child Development, 46,* 19–26.

Walker, L. (1983). Sources of cognitive conflict for stage transition in moral development. *Developmental Psychology, 19,* 103–110.

Walker, L., Devries, B., & Trevethan, S. (1987). Moral stages and moral orientations in real life and hypothetical dilemmas. *Child Development, 58,* 842–858.

Walstead, W. B. (1987). Attitudes, opinions, and economic understanding. *Theory Into Practice, 26*(3), 223–230.

Wang, M. C., & Palincsar, A. S. (1989). Teaching students to assume an active role in their learning. In M. C. Reynolds (Ed.), *Knowledge base for the beginning teacher* (pp. 71–84). New York: Pergamon Press.

Wells, G. (1986). The language experience of five-year-old children at home and at school. In J. Cook-Gumperz (Ed.), *The social construction of literacy* (pp. 69–93). New York: Cambridge University Press.

Winne, P. H., & Marx, R. W. (1982). Students' and teachers' views of thinking processes for classroom learning. *Elementary School Journal, 82,* 493–518.

Wittig, M., & Petersen, A. (Eds.). (1979). *Sex-related differences in cognitive functioning: Developmental issues.* New York: Academic Press.

Yeger, T., & Miezitis, S. (1980). Self concept and classroom behavior of preadolescent pupils. *Journal of Classroom Interaction, 15,* 31–37.

Zaccaria, M. A. (1978). The development of historical thinking: Implications for the teaching of history. *The History Teacher, 11,* 323–340.

ADOLESCENTS' SOCIAL, COGNITIVE, AND MORAL DEVELOPMENT AND SECONDARY SCHOOL SOCIAL STUDIES

James A. Mackey

UNIVERSITY OF MINNESOTA

Psychological theories outline the period between the ages of about 12 and 21 as a separate stage of personal and social development in our society. This concept of adolescence as a distinct period is bolstered by social and economic forces, including businesses dependent upon an acquisitive youth culture and schools dependent upon age-segregated social grouping. In short, the definition of adolescence, although psychological in form, is largely the result of modern social forces.

Adolescence is the period of development between puberty and maturity. It is the time when young people acquire their adult identities, define sexual roles, and begin to think and behave as adults. In Western culture, this period of psychological, social, and economic dependence has been growing in length. On the younger end, adolescence begins with sexual maturation, which has been occurring at earlier ages. On the older end, young adults live at home longer and remain economically dependent upon their parents at later ages. This expanded period of adolescence has increased the economic and psychological dependence of people at the very time they claim greater emotional maturity.

In this chapter, the research on the American adolescents' behavior and thinking is reviewed. Portrayed are the belief systems and thinking capacities that adolescents bring to social studies in the secondary school. First, a social portrait of adolescent life is sketched, then how adolescents learn in social studies is discussed. The emphasis is on the types of social thinking that typify adolescence. The chapter concludes with a brief discussion of adolescents' changing conceptions of morality and social conventions.

THE CREATION OF THE IDEA OF ADOLESCENCE

Although a separate period between childhood and maturity has been recognized since ancient times, scholars did not give special attention to this period until the 20th century. G. Stanley Hall of Clark University popularized the term *adolescence* in 1904 with the first edition of *Adolescence: Its Physiology and Its Relations to Psychology, Anthropology, Sociology, Sex, Crime, Religion, and Education.* (Hall's typesize in his title gave special emphasis to the words *psychology* and *education*.) Hall defined adolescence as "a time of storm and stress characterized by an inherent instability, emotional turmoil and psychic disturbance" (quoted in Rutter, 1980, p. 1). For Hall, adolescence was very different from the stages of personal development that precede and follow it.

Hall's philosophy was a study in contrasts, possessing equal parts of evolutionary biology and American puritanism. To Hall, each stage of early human development—infancy, childhood, and adolescence—repeated a stage in the evolution of humanity. Coincidentally, Hall argued that adolescence offered the greatest opportunity for efforts to reform the human race. Adolescence was so rich in the possibility for improvement, he argued, that it ought to be a time of reflection and delayed gratification. Adolescents, he asserted, needed to aspire to a rigid chastity of "fancy, heart, and body" (quoted in Kaplan, 1984, p. 78). This process could be accomplished most conveniently if adolescents were isolated from the corruption of society even if only for part of a day. Hall advocated the creation of separate

Reviewers were Patricia Avery, University of Minnesota; Janet Eyler, Peabody College.

social institutions, like junior high schools and scouting groups, to temper adolescent intensity. While in isolation, Hall contended, adolescents could be infused with intellectual, religious, and ethical values, and their intense sexual drives could be curtailed.

Like most social labels, the term *adolescence* served a function; it reflected the contemporary fear of young people who were becoming a distinguishable group in the newly created public secondary schools. The discussion of those youth, past puberty and not yet adults, centered mostly on adolescent street gangs and other delinquents from the "dangerous classes." Although Hall's ideas have been endlessly examined, debated, and mostly discredited, he laid the groundwork for the study of adolescents for nearly three fourths of a century.

Hall's work had clear limitations. He distorted the influence of biological forces, especially in his "recapitulation theory" that a child's life goes through stages reflecting those in the history of humanity. But he called attention to the turbulence of adolescence and provided "a view of human life that had not existed before his description" (Keniston, 1970, p. 632).

His work contained race, sex, and class biases. Hall and his successors typically studied white, upper-class, male adolescents. Much of the subsequent misunderstanding of adolescence grows out of this bias. He dismissed female adolescence with a call for male role models. In describing girls' needs, Hall (1904) asserted:

In most groups in this series of ideal departments there should be at least one healthful, wise, large-souled, honorable, married and attractive man. His very presence in an institution for young women give poise, polarizes the soul, and gives wholesome but long-circuited tension at root no doubt sexual, but unconsciously so. This mentor should not be more father than brother. (vol. 2, p. 645).

Hall said he shared the "growing fear that modern woman is in danger of declining from her orbit; that she is coming to lack just confidence and pride in her sex as such, and is just now in danger of lapsing into mannish ways, methods, and ideals until her original divinity becomes obscured" (vol. 2, p. 646). The study of adolescence, especially early adolescence, continues to suffer from gender bias and to lack a viable conceptual framework.

Social studies researchers need to be aware that some contemporary research continues to contain serious gender biases. Gilligan (1982), for example, has argued that Lawrence Kohlberg's stage theory is biased because he used only males in his foundational research.

A SOCIAL PORTRAIT OF ADOLESCENTS

Although there is not a great deal of systematic research on adolescents, some hypotheses can be drawn about adolescence as a period of personal development. In this section, a social picture of adolescents is sketched, organized around a series of hypotheses and generalizations drawn from a review of existing research.

Adolescents Do Not Fit Stereotypes

Much of what Americans believe about teenagers comes from speculation, preachment, and popular images. Even academic sources of information have focused on delinquent rather than normal teens, resulting in a literature on the pathology of deviance. Far more is known, for example, about teenage car thieves than about merit scholars. These imbalanced inquiries reinforce the idea of a separate "youth culture," and promote adult misunderstanding, fear, and envy of adolescents.

To correct the imbalance, a University of Chicago research team conducted a major study of adolescent behavior. Seventy-five 13 to 18 year-old subjects, randomly selected from a 4,000-student Chicago high school, were asked to carry beepers similar to those worn by doctors. When researchers beeped one of the subjects at randomly selected times during a week, the teenager was to stop and describe in writing his or her activities at the time. The subjects responded while eating breakfast, sitting in class, playing basketball, using drugs, and even having sex. Research participants filled out a form in a data book containing such questions as: "What are you doing?" "How much choice did you have in selecting this activity?" "How well are you concentrating?" "What are you thinking about? Are you in control of your actions?" "Is there anything at stake for you in this activity?" The research team also asked the participants to describe their mood at the time: from alert to drowsy, from sociable to lonely, from excited to bored.

Csikszentmihaly and Larsen (1984) described the research in *Being Adolescent: Conflict and Growth in the Teenage Years*. They reported the following conclusions. First, drastic swings in mood seemed to be a normal feature of life for the adolescents in the study. These mood swings were not necessarily evidence of psychological problems, but confirmed what Erik Erikson (1964) called the "normal identity crisis" of adolescence. In fact, Csikszentmihaly and Larsen (1984) claimed, "Adolescents whose moods changed most reported being as happy and as much in control as their peers, and appeared to be as well adjusted in other areas of their lives" (p. 123). Adolescent mood swings appeared to be short-lived, like a flash of emotion. Of teenagers' mood swings, Csikszentmihaly said: "If anything, it's the lack of both higher euphoria and low despair that might be an indication of potential pathology. Many of teenagers' moods have a half-life of fifteen minutes. This means that a high positive mood, or a low negative mood is back to the midpoint in fifteen minutes" (quoted in Collins, 1984, p. 4).

Second, school took up to one fourth of the adolescents' waking hours. This portion of their time represented 38 hours a week spent either in classes or studying. Interestingly, the authors claimed that of the 20 or so hours a week their adolescent subjects were in class, only 4 hours were spent listening to teachers.

Teenagers spent much more time outside of school. They devoted 42 hours per week to leisure activities such as socializing, watching television, non-school reading, and listening to music. Conversing with other teenagers—the single most prevalent activity in their lives—took up one third of the adolescents' waking hours. Time spent with parents consumed only 4.8% of the adolescents' waking hours.

Third, solitude was an important part of the adolescent subjects' lives; the teenagers in the study reported that they spent an average of 25.6% of their time alone. Although the subjects experienced some of their lowest moods while alone, they claimed that they were better able to focus on hobbies and homework in private. Solitude, they claimed, "heightened their subsequent enjoyment of friends, family and activities" (Csikszentmihaly & Larsen, 1984, p. 123).

In an interview, one of the researchers, Larsen, claimed that a major solitary activity of teenagers, was grooming and looking in the mirror. Adolescents, Larsen contended, need the time alone to experience themselves in ways that they cannot with other people and "to really be free from their constant social lives" (quoted by Merrow, 1977, p. 14).

Fourth, the boys in the sample preferred being with friends and tended to be uncomfortable with their parents, while the girls did not mind spending time with their parents. When boys were with parents, they reported themselves as "being less alert, less friendly, and less sociable" (quoted by Merrow, 1977, p. 3). While boys wanted to shut out the family, the girls in the study said they would share "everything with their families". The boys claimed that they did not tell their families anything if they could avoid it.

How to incorporate aspects of teenagers' social life into the social studies curriculum is a major challenge. Closer connections between the curriculum and that life could be not only a vehicle for classroom discussions that could enliven the social studies curriculum, but also a means of making the *social* part of social studies more meaningful.

Adolescents Are Not Economically Useful

Today's adolescents are rarely needed economically. Even in rural areas, machines have become so large and so expensive that young people often are not allowed to operate them. Some laws and insurance regulations even prevent young people from running the machinery.

Adolescents are typically no longer needed to care for younger children, because the modern family has fewer children and most of them are close in age. All children are sent to a school where school district personnel monitor their lives and activities. A host of custodial institutions have been created to care for and regulate adolescents.

A recent attempt to improve the adolescents' adjustment has been employment programs that encourage young people to take retail jobs. But these minimum-wage jobs have little relevance to later careers and take an unexpectedly high toll in the lives of adolescents. In their study of teenage employment, Greenberger and Steinberg (1986) found that the costs of such programs were hardly worth the benefits. "Experience in the adolescent workplace," they concluded,

often breeds contempt for the idea that work can be enjoyable and satisfying. Extensive involvement in a job takes a toll on young people's education, and lower educational attainment has implications for young people's long-run occupational success and life satisfaction. Intensive work leads to increased use of alcohol and marijuana, especially when jobs are stressful. And because the paychecks that reward long hours at

work are unencumbered by adult responsibilities, youngsters experience premature affluence: they engage in a level of consumption that is inconsistent with the obligations that many of them will face in the ensuing years. Finally, long hours spent in the workplace curtail opportunities for other, developmentally productive activities. (p. 237)

Working in fast-food restaurants and other menial jobs, Greenberger and Steinberg's young subjects often found themselves in jobs that adults refused to take. As a result, the authors found, the "youthwork" system increased rather than decreased *age* segregation.

Does work influence the social conceptions of adolescents? Does work make teenagers more tolerant toward and accepting of others? Does laboring in the workplace give adolescents a more accurate knowledge of the economic system? These are questions that merit attention by social studies researchers.

Adolescents Live in an Age-Segregated Society

Until the end of the Middle Ages, children were, from the time they were weaned, regarded as small adults who "mingled, competed, worked, and played with mature adults" (Aries, 1962, p. 411). Gradually, as an entrepreneurial class developed in European society, parents unconsciously began to encourage the separation of adults and children and to develop a new family attitude.

Centuries later, age segregation proceeded slowly in the United States as the agricultural society became industrialized. Children had been regarded as an economic asset until a new American conventional wisdom emerged that children were not ready for adult life. To equip adolescents for adult life, a series of social institutions evolved around new organizations. Intellectual support for the changes came from a new body of literature on child rearing. This literature argued for compulsory education, child-labor laws, and a special juvenile justice system to protect adolescents (Bakan, 1972). Although each of the changes carried social benefits, each also increased social segregation by age. Combined with the theoretical work of Hall and his successors, these social movements served to establish clearly the idea of adolescence and the acceptance of separation of activities by age.

As a result of this separation, young people often find their identities in negative rather than positive ways; that is, adolescents know more about who they are *not* than about who they are. Desperate for an identity, those individuals treated as delinquents tend, as Erikson (1964) has written, to over-identify with cliques, often "to the point of complete loss of individual identity." This lack of positive identify or self-image stimulates a search for identity or wholeness outside of oneself. Ideology can become a source of refuge, as Erikson (1964) wrote:

Where the human being despairs of an essential wholeness of experience, he restructures himself and the world by taking refuge in a totalistic world view. Thus there appears both in individuals and in groups a periodic need for a totality without further choice or alternative, even if it implies the abandonment of a much-needed wholeness. This can consist of a lone-wolf negativism; of a delinquent group's seeming nihilism; or in the case of national or racial groups, in a defiant glorification of one's own caricature. (p. 223)

Group identity and ideology, Erikson argued, are parts of the same process. Both provide for the maturation of individuals while allowing for identity through group membership. In their search for identity and personal meaning, adolescents can become compulsively ideological, moral, conservative, or radical. Left to their own devices at this crucial stage of their lives, some adolescents develop negative goals and engage in dysfunctional behavior. This isolation could be broken down in numerous ways. Perhaps the simplest way would be to create circumstances in which adolescents come together with other age groups for community activities and shared responsibilities.

Social studies educators, both teachers and researchers, need to recognize that the alienation adolescents feel is a natural consequence of serious reflection on the complexities of life. Adolescents need to know that they are not alone in their alienation. At the same time, young people and educators need to be able to discriminate between normal feelings of estrangement and pathological ones.

Adolescence Starts Earlier and Lasts Longer

Adolescence in America has stretched; it begins earlier and often lasts beyond the teenage years. While the sequence of adolescent biological events has remained the same, the events begin at an earlier age than ever before. Earlier biological maturation has been attributed to a variety of causes; better diet, the lessening of disease, warmer planetary climatic conditions, and greater psychosexual stimulation. The diet hypothesis involves the consumption of more protein and carbohydrates in early infancy.

Although physical maturation happens sooner, two major biological facts remain unchanged. On the average, girls develop two years earlier than boys, and some boys only *begin* their physical maturation while others of the same age are *finishing* theirs. Puberty appears to begin later and extend over a slightly longer time period for boys than it does for girls (Tanner, 1972).

The differences in maturation rates among children have life-long implications for some of them. Early maturing adolescents, especially boys, have a decided advantage over their peers. Rutter (1980) studies the difference in maturation rates among adolescents and surveyed the same group of people at 30 years of age. He found that early developers were likely to be more stable, more sociable, less neurotic, and more successful as adults. The advantaged group retained its advantages at age 30. Some early maturing boys had advantages over the girls.

Physical prowess and athletic success often accompanied early maturation. With such prowess comes respect from one's peers. This respect, in turn, gives the early maturing adolescent boy a head start in the development of leadership skills (Rutter, 1980). Adolescents' physical appearance also affects how people treat them. Most adults react more favorably to mature-looking adolescents than to their childish-looking companions.

Earlier puberty and maturation is associated with sexuality. Sexually mature boys and girls are more likely to associate with members of the other sex. This behavior affords them earlier opportunities to model adult behavior. Earlier sexual maturity has some negative side effects, of course, such as emotional immaturity, self-consciousness, a longer period of sexual frustration, and alienation from one's same-sex peers (Rutter, 1980). Actress Cheryl Ladd, for example, whose physical attractiveness has contributed to her success, claims that she spent much of her time in junior high school concealing breasts that had developed prematurely (Elkind, 1984).

Adolescence not only begins earlier, it also lasts longer. Young people spend more time in school than they did a century ago; average students spend six more years in school than they did at the turn of the century. More than 70% of young Americans complete high school, compared with 6.4% in 1900. About 9 million young Americans attended college each year in the 1980s, compared with about 230,000 in 1900 (Snyder, 1988). For many young people, this extended period of education means an increased length of time during which they are dependent upon family for economic, physical, and psychological support. The extended period of adolescence has implications for social studies that have not yet been adequately addressed by researchers or educators.

Adolescents' Psychological Needs Are Increasing

Until recently, adolescence was viewed by nearly everyone as a safe haven in which teenagers were able to devote their energies to the tasks of personal, social, and occupational growth without pressure from the "real world." In other words, they were given a special time in which to forge a strong personal identity. Nowadays most adults no longer consider adolescents to be a privileged group requiring special nurturing, and most adults are themselves confused about their roles. So teenagers are denied this freedom from social and economic pressure (Elkind, 1984). Adolescents thus become more vulnerable and less able to handle stress at the very time when the sources of stress are multiplying.

The stress on adolescents comes from three distinct sources: loss, failure, and freedom (Elkind, 1986). A sense of loss comes from a realistic adolescent fear that they face a world of shrinking resources in which they will not do as well as their parents did. The feelings of loss are reinforced by the large number of children who have experienced the pain of their parent's divorces and the permanent absence of one parent. Failure and the fear of failure result from intense competition and unrealistic expectations imposed upon adolescents in modern life. The freedom is illustrated by the early choice that adolescents face regarding drugs, alcohol, and sexual activity. This new freedom is enhanced by the amount of money adolescents have to spend. Adolescents have the largest disposable income of any age group. The stress that results from the freedom is aggravated by ambivalent messages from role models, peer groups, and the mass media.

Historically, the family, in close concert with the school, helped teenagers come of age. As the number of families in which both parents work at demanding jobs increases, the school is often expected to provide the needed personal guidance. Overburdened school personnel are frequently not able to respond in the precise fashion that the parents expect, and some of the parents—filled with their own sense of importance—are quick to protest.

What typical adults do not recognize is that the adolescent experience today is profoundly different from their own adolescence in several distinct ways. Adolescence has become tremendously competitive. Children know from an early age that they had better start running fast because, although the number of their peers has doubled in the past years, the number of opportunities has not kept pace. In order to succeed, the teenager knows he or she has to be nearly perfect. The number of young people who become discouraged by their prospects at an early age is growing at an alarming rate (Breskin, 1984).

Alert to these social changes, many high-achieving teenagers realize that their relationship with their parents is akin to a marketplace governed by a simple equation: good grades, athletic awards, and other tangible achievements become the currency with which to trade for parental approval and permissiveness (Breskin, 1984). In turn, many parents are driven by guilt, a desire to befriend their children, and uncertainty about the changing rules governing parental behavior. The spin-off to the social studies curriculum, largely ignored by researchers, is a fertile area for investigations.

THE DEVELOPMENT OF SOCIAL THINKING IN ADOLESCENTS

Children view their social world through a narrow, highly individualistic lens. Just before puberty, this narrow view widens dramatically as children begin thinking about their social world in new ways. This startling, profound change affects the way early adolescents learn from history, civics, geography, economics, and other forms of social studies. The dramatic shift in outlook involves "a fairly complete reorganization of how social issues are perceived and interpreted" (Adelson, 1982: p. 10). The essence of the change is a shift from a concrete to an abstract mode of thinking.

The change in mode of thinking is of special importance to social studies educators. Following is an extensive examination of adolescents' knowledge of government and politics, a research area that is well developed. The next section is on economic thinking, where research has been less extensive.

Adolescent Political Thinking

Political scientists and political educators have studied children's political socialization actively since Herbert Hyman (1959) gave the term prominence. In the early 1970s, however, the research activity slowed almost to a stop. An early researcher in political socialization saw a renewal of interest in the topic in the late 1980s (Torney-Purta, 1988).

Political socialization researchers study what children of a given age know about politics. The researchers also study the development of myths about the political system, the transmission of the myths across generations, and the mechanisms by which society passes on its political values and culture. Although a considerable amount of research has accumulated, to

this point, the goals pursued have been rather narrow. Berti and Bombi (1988, p. 114), for example, claim that most political socialization research has been undertaken by political scientists interested in examining the childhood antecedents of adult political choices or in outlining from whom and in what circumstances children obtain political information.

Although narrow in approach, the research has yielded some important findings. Political development apparently begins long before the student is exposed to formal civics. Preadolescent children tend to be favorably disposed toward the political objects they know about. Some cynicism and distrust sets in as children reach the end of junior high school, but adolescents continue to take pride generally in their country and its government (Torney-Purta, 1988). Students from higher socioeconomic backgrounds are less cynical than their parents, and they receive a more participant-oriented political education than their working-class peers (Coles, 1986).

American teenagers have a considerable reservoir of relative pride in American institutions, but they are sometimes ashamed (Sigel & Hoskin, 1981). This collective sense of guilt reflects general feelings about such events as the Vietnam war and Watergate, even though the adolescents may not have any specific, factual knowledge about those events. Their feelings seem to be unaffected by the addition of factual information.

Although a popular myth holds that adolescence is a time of idealism, investigations have shown that adolescent idealism has been overstated. Political psychologist Joseph Adelson (1972) found few signs of political idealism in his studies of adolescents. Instead, he found a prevalence of anti-utopian views growing out of the adolescent's striving toward realism. Adelson said anti-utopianism is an essential stage of adolescent intellectual development. Adolescents believe they are relinquishing childish naivete and straining toward maturity by adopting "adult" attitudes of coolness, prudence, and sober judgment.

Few of the adolescents in Adelson's studies (1972) had given much thought to radical visions of society. He found little critical thinking until late adolescence when the capacity for political reasoning is established. Even then, Adelson claimed, the adolescents' attitudes spanned a narrow range, extending "from fatuous complacency to sharp and succinct wishes for change, the latter very much within the system" (p. 130).

Studies by cognitive scientists make important contributions to our understanding of the adolescent's orientation to politics. Although most political socialization research concerns the content of children's political beliefs, cognitive psychologists seek to determine the structure, form, and level of rationality of adolescent political thinking. In essence, cognitive researchers attend to "how adolescents use their cognitive abilities to construct an integrated vision of political life" (Berti & Bomb, 1988, p. 114).

Much cognitive science originates from the theoretical framework erected by Jean Piaget (1965). Between 11 and 14 years of age, Piaget asserted, adolescents develop, elaborate, and integrate thinking abilities that existed previously only in an embryonic state (Sprinthall & Collins, 1988). Adolescence represents a period of potential for the development, enhancement, and integration of adult thinking skills. If the potential for thinking is not developed in adolescence, it likely will never occur, Piaget asserted.

Adolescent constructions of politics have been examined in great depth from two cognitive science perspectives. The first of these bodies of research was developed by Adelson (1982) and his students who investigated the way adolescents develop the idea of political community. The second examination is contained in Connell's (1971) evocative account of his research on how Australian children and adolescents perceive political symbols and objects.

Adelson (1982) proceeded in two steps. In the first, a cross-national inquiry, he compared youngsters in England, Germany, and the United States. For the second study, he analyzed data from urban, blue-collar children and adolescents in the United States. The subjects in each of the two studies—ranging in age from 10 to 18—were asked questions using an open-ended interview schedule that began with the following hypothetical situation: A thousand people leave their country and move to a Pacific island to start a new society.

Based on this hypothetical situation, the subjects were presented with political, social, and moral issues. They were asked, among other things, to comment on the range of political authority, the obligations of an individual to the community, the nature of crime and justice, and the prospects for utopia.

After summarizing his cross-sectional research, Adelson (1972) stated the essential change in political thinking during adolescence:

During adolescence the youngster gropes, stumbles, and leaps toward political understanding. Prior to these years the child's sense of the political order is erratic and incomplete—a curious array of sentiments and dogmas, personalized ideas, randomly remembered names and party labels, half-understood platitudes. By the time adolescence has come to an end, the child's mind much of the time moves easily within and among categories of political discourse. (p. 110)

Connell (1971) moved a step beyond most of the political socialization inquiries in his studies of 119 Australian children aged 6 to 16 years. He began his Piagetian protocol by posing a hypothetical situation, following with a series of questions on the social issues suggested by the situation. The interviewer's task was to tease out with probing questions the subject's thinking on a variety of issues. The success of the interview depended upon the interviewer's ability to probe. Connell's study and the interview schedule were less structured than Adelson's use of the hypothetical Pacific island prompt.

Connell (1971) sought to determine children's and adolescents' sources of political news, their perceptions of the most important political figures in their communities, and their beliefs about elections and political parties. Throughout the study, Connell concentrated on how children learn and structure politics, rather than on their knowledge of specific political facts. Connell said he was searching for a collective portrait of a group of children and the political development to be seen among them. From his findings, Connell concluded that preadult political thinking grows through four stages: intuition, primitive realism, construction of a political order, and ideology.

Connell found that the age of 11 marked a great leap forward for many of the children in his sample because, at that age, they acquired the intellectual capacity to construct a political order. For example, they could construct hierarchical organizations. Connell's adolescent subjects understood that a queen, for example, commands the prime minister, and that a mayor could become the prime minister. Conceiving of hierarchies gives adolescents a more accurate notion of power and leads them into abstract and deductive thinking. Abstract thinking and expanding political knowledge permits adolescents "to conceive of conflicts of opinions and interests, and to express their own opinions about the conduct of political leaders" (Berti & Bombi, 1988, p. 116). Even in middle adolescence, however, only a very few individuals possess the capacity for ideological thinking. Those few, Connell claimed, come from highly politicized homes.

Two central points can be drawn from Connell's work. First, children and adolescents do not receive politics passively, as much of the political socialization literature implies. Instead, they develop political understanding as far as their individual environment and intellectual capabilities allow. Second, the acquisition of the concept of hierarchy is the crucial step in the adolescents' movement toward adult political thinking. This concept of hierarchy permits adolescents to begin to see politics in terms of underlying wholes, with hierarchies of judgments, generalizations, and underlying themes. With these concepts, adolescents can perform classification and serialization tasks.

A contemporary example illustrates Connell's findings about classification and serialization skills. My son, Martin, when he was 14, studied Nicaragua and acquired a great deal of factual information about the country. Previously, Martin was content to keep the jumble of facts in his mind without concern about historical, political, or social structural patterns. Suddenly, in the middle of his 14th year, Martin became interested in finding patterns and tracing relationships between the facts he possessed. He made comments such as "I want to get this straight: Did Somoza come before Sandino?" Although Martin was hesitant in his thinking about relationships, he acquired classification and serialization capacities. He became eager to use facts to explain a large-scale social situation—Central American turmoil—he had encountered. Martin also became extremely concerned about the morality of American involvement in Nicaragua. The boy's concern reflected the Australian teenagers' development as discovered by Connell. Classification and serialization skills give adolescents a tool with which they eagerly examine their social concerns.

Although adolescents are not likely to be ideological thinkers, their thinking acquires a decidedly social cast (Connell, 1971). In adolescence, young people begin to understand their obligations and rights, to see conflicts over issues, and to perceive politics as the struggle for the control of public policy.

Social studies researchers should continue to pursue the kinds of inquiries begun by Adelson and Connell, to further portray the differences between children's and adolescents' thinking and to provide evidence as to the structure and form of adolescent thinking. These findings could provide a firmer foundation for social studies curriculum decisions.

Adolescent Economic Thinking

Most discussions of adolescents' economic knowledge have been focused on teenagers' deficiencies. Few scholars have published studies examining the development, structure, or form of teenagers' economic understanding. Typical of the genre is a recent study which was reviewed in the *New York Times* as indicating that the "level of economic knowledge among high school students is shocking. Our schools are producing a nation of economic illiterates" (Carmody, 1988, p. 1).

The investigators administered a multiple-choice test of 46 questions to 8,000 high school students (Walstad & Soper, 1988). Analyses of the data revealed serious gaps in the adolescents' knowledge of economics, including tariffs and trade, supply and demand, and the federal deficit. The authors argued that the adolescents' lack of economic knowledge makes it difficult for them to understand the American economic system. The report is but the latest in a series of such reports and essays in which American students are labeled as deficient in economic knowledge.

Despite the consensus on how little adolescents know, little is known about how they acquire economic knowledge. More research, for example, has been devoted to the study of adolescents as consumers than to the processes through which adolescents develop ideas and attitudes about economic questions.

Recently, the dearth of research has been remedied somewhat by the translation into English of the work on children and adolescents' economic understanding by Berti and Bombi (1988). Their book includes a summary of research on adolescents' economic thinking as well as the results of a study, based on a Piagetian framework, of 916 Italian children between the ages 3 and 14. Among the areas investigated were understandings of the relationship between work and remuneration, the concept of "the boss," banks and interest, differences between rich and poor, and the production and distribution of goods.

In his review of Bombi and Berti's book, Furth (1988, p. 420) commented on the "childish" quality of adolescents' economic thinking. He claimed that it takes years for adolescents to accept the impersonal qualities of monetary exchange because they do not "want to give up their childish, playful conceptions of human society where personal desire determines an action and fulfillment of desire is unproblematic" (p. 450).

Although adolescents' economic thinking retains a childish quality, their thinking also begins to assume distinct adult characteristics after the age of 11. The changes in adolescents' economic understanding that Bombi and Berti noted are strikingly similar to the structural changes that Connell (1971) and Adelson (1972) found in adolescents' understanding of political concepts. Berti and Bombi (1988), for example, claimed that children's reasons and justifications for the difference between the rich and the poor were concrete and personalized. In a related study, the young people in Leahy's (1983) sample said: "the rich are rich because they have money, to become rich you have to ask rich people to give you money. To solve the problem of poverty all you have to do with the poor is send them away" (p. 121, quoted in Berti & Bombi 1988, p. 13). Unlike children, adolescents can consider the perspectives of others when they make economic decisions, that is, they have developed role-taking abilities that children do not possess. When adolescents defined poverty, for example, they considered the factors that regulated the economic systems, as well as the elements making up the system (Berti & Bombi, 1988).

Berti and Bombi found that adolescents could coordinate the various economic roles into a single system. Their adolescents understood, for instance, that a factory owner pays his workers with money received from the sale of goods from his factory. And their adolescents understood that the price of goods is a function of the owner's profit margin and the costs of materials and labor.

Adolescents also developed a vision of other economic exchanges. The idea of a single system permits adolescents to use information obtained through a variety of experiences. Adolescents can construct broader connections about economic processes:

The boss sells the products and pays the workers. A bank is somewhere to put money and somewhere to get loans from. Comic books cost 500 lire because the publisher checks how much he's paid for the paper, the ink, and the people who work there (Berti & Bombi, 1988, p. 185).

Adolescents' economic thinking expands in other ways. They can perform intellectual operations such as classification, serialization, and correspondence. This permits them to organize different economic factors into a single system. Adolescents can then see what contributes to the formation of prices and see the correspondence between loans and repayments, deposits and withdrawals.

In short, early adolescent economic thinking, although still in an embryonic state, resembles adult economic thinking while childish views fade.

Social studies researchers need to examine the relation between the economics curriculum in school and the structure of adolescent economic thinking. An accurate match between the two could make the curriculum more effective. The adolescents' ability to perceive economic issues ought to be the foundation of the curriculum.

MORALITY AND SOCIAL CONVENTIONS

Moral Thought

Adolescents think differently about moral issues than other groups in American society. Lawrence Kohlberg (1979) created the conceptual scheme most commonly used to explain adolescent moral development. He stepped onto ground prepared by Piaget (1965), who did the first major research on childhood morality. Piaget's critics claimed that in his questions to children about rules, he failed to make distinctions between different kinds of rules (Sprinthall & Collins (1988). As a result, Kohlberg and other critics said Piaget's conclusions lacked sublety and contained an insufficient number of moral categories. On the other hand, Kohlberg, who posed moral dilemmas for his subjects, forced choices containing implicit adult assumptions and ignored the possibility that children might make choices in their own words on their own terms (Cook, 1984).

Rather than a series of fixed either/or traits or beliefs, morality became thought of as a series of identifiable stages or developmental sequences. Kohlberg said each stage of moral development grew out of a previous, more simplistic one. The child must pass through each stage before reaching a higher, more complex one. At the more complex, higher stages, a person can do a better job of reasoning (Rest, 1975). In Kohlberg's model, a person's moral reasoning changes as the individual encounters situations for which he or she has no moral schema. Because the new moral outlook is more complex, the individual steps up a rung on the ladder of moral development. All moral reasoning, Kohlberg maintained, takes place within six distinct stages. Since this model is well known to social studies educators it is not explicated here.

Most teenagers score at Stage 3 on Kohlberg's scale. Kohlberg found 13-year-olds, however, evenly split between Stage 2 and Stage 3. Stage 3 thinking involves responses to moral issues in terms of what others think. In one longitudinal study (Kohlberg, 1979), 42% of the students were at Stage 3 and 45% remained at Stage 2. By the time the adolescents reached the 16- to 18-years-of-age group, the proportions had changed. A solid majority (60%) scored at Stage 3, and only 20% remained at Stage 2. Less than 15% of these older adolescents scored at Stage 4 (Kohlberg, 1979). Most teenagers, then, view moral questions in terms of what they can gain for themselves or of what others will think of them. The other-directed orientation ascends as they grow through their teenage years (Sprinthall & Collins, 1988).

The most dramatic change in adolescence is not a large rush up the ladder of moral reasoning—a considerable number of elementary school students have reached Stage 3—but it is an alteration in the reference point of approval. During childhood, students commonly seek approval from parents and teachers. As adolescents, their focus changes to the peer group. Even though the teenagers' moral reasoning has advanced, the majority are still not able to process "judgment according to rational and stable self-directed and democratic values. . . . Teenagers [can] be directed by a variety of others: parents, peers, or perhaps some cult leaders" (Sprinthall & Collins, 1988, p. 194). They remain vulnerable, susceptible to fads, and captive to the peer group. The simplistic thinking inherent in this stage relates not only "to the superficial aspects of life at this age, such as looks, hairstyle and clothing, but also to much more significant value questions, such as racism and other forms of ethnocentrism" (Sprinthall & Collins, 1988, p. 194).

Stage 3 reasoning has several positive aspects. A dominant one is the development of role taking and empathy which cause the adolescent to move away from the narrow self-interest of Stage 2 thinking. Most issues, however, are still resolved by the values of the leading adolescent crowd, the trendsetters.

For social studies educators, the most important aspect of adolescence is the movement toward Stage 4. Young people at this stage can understand a broad set of rules and see the world in terms of society's needs. Although only a small group reaches this stage by the age of 18, the majority seems to be moving in this direction.

Kohlberg's model has elicited some criticism, especially for his seeming neglect of gender differences. Kohlberg's original sample was all male, and his colleague, Carol Gilligan (1982), charged that his theory was sex-biased. She argued that his higher stages of reasoning, with their narrowly rational orientation, ignored human compassion and caring.

Gilligan's criticism stimulated a series of investigations of the alleged sex-bias in Kohlberg's research. For example, Rest (1979), the developer of an objective test to measure stages of moral development, undertook a review of the research. He concluded that the research did not support Gilligan's charge of sex-bias. Instead of scoring low on Kohlberg's scale, females actually scored as high or higher than males. Two other researchers, Braebeck (1982) and Walker (1984) also found no gender difference in their reviews of research based on Kohlberg's theories. After Gilligan published her criticism, Kohlberg, with whom Gilligan coauthored several articles, revised his scoring manual to discourage classifying "caring" as a lower-stage response.

Sprinthall and Collins (1988) found another potential bias, pointing out that the content of the moral dilemmas influenced adolescents' score on the moral reasoning assessment. Students scored lower on Kohlberg's scale when dilemmas involved personal issues, such as sexual experimentation, than when they involved more distant social issues. In their review, Sprinthall and Collins concluded that adolescents' discomfort with some personal issues influenced their responses to questions about moral dilemmas. Their contention has serious implications for a social studies curriculum built around the "closed areas," such as sex and morality.

THINKING ABOUT SOCIAL CONVENTIONS

Another of Kohlberg's former colleagues, Elliot Turiel (1983), offered a subtle disagreement, identifying more categories of social knowledge than Kohlberg. Turiel called his own set of principles *social conventions* Social conventions are predictable patterns of behavior and shared rules, such as styles of dress and forms of greeting, that underlie social interactions. Adolescents' knowledge of social conventions—for example, the way they address their elders or wear their hair—reflects their understanding of social organization.

Children, Turiel (1983) argued, can make clear distinctions between morality (what is right and wrong) and social convention (what is acceptable). Two of his points are central to the consideration of adolescent thinking: First, children are "intuitive moralists," and, second, not all young people see all rules in the same way. Children structure their social world in three general domains:

(1) concepts of persons or psychological systems (the psychological domain), (2) concepts of systems of social relations and organizations (the societal domain)—of which convention is but one component, and (3) prescriptive judgments of justice, rights, and welfare (the moral domain). (p. 4)

Attitudes toward social conventions change as the children and adolescents grow. Through both cross-sectional (1978) and longitudinal (1983) studies, Turiel identified seven levels of development involving the relationships among rules, social conventions, and the social system. Young children (at about the ages of 6 and 7) begin to develop attitudes about social convention by observing other people behaving in uniform ways. (For example, children will not call teachers by their first names unless other children do.) At about ages 8 or 9, children begin to question conventional behavior. The uniform behavior of others is no longer sufficient to maintain social conventions. By the time they are 10 or 11, children are more likely to adhere to rules than to conventions, which are seen as arbitrary and changeable. (You cannot call teachers by their first names because the principal and teacher have a rule against it.) Between the ages of 12 and 16, adolescents accept conventions based on general knowledge and shared norms as necessary to facilitate social interactions. (It would not be wrong to call teachers by their first names. But it could be inconvenient if students began to regard themselves as just as authoritative as the teacher.)

Turiel (1983) said that most adolescents (Levels 3 to 5) move through affirmation of social conventions, negation, and a second affirmation. On the threshold of adolescence (Level 3), children believe social relations are governed by authority figures, such as principals and teachers. The reason to adhere to the convention is the authority figure and the rules. As the child matures, his or her thinking moves into Level 4 in which the adolescent begins to think it is silly to follow rules just because someone says so. As they grow out of Level 4, adolescents see the system as more complex. They begin to follow the adage, "To go along you have to get along" with people and vice versa. At this level, the adolescents see that going along is necessary for the maintenance of the general social order.

Level 4 thinkers fail to see any need for many conventions and rules; they become critical of authority. This thinking causes many adolescents to see conventions as arbitrary expectations. When asked about teachers' last names a 12-year-old said "a name is just like a symbol or something and it doesn't really matter what (teachers) are called" (Turiel, 1983, p. 109). It is no coincidence that disruptive behavior in classrooms peaks in junior high school when most adolescents are immersed in this stage of thinking (Geiger & Turiel, 1983).

Most adolescents begin to construct systematic concepts of a social system when they reach Level 5 at about age 14. These teenagers no longer perceive authority as uncoordinated, but they see "social interactions as forming an organization, in which the individual is considered part of a general collective and cultural system" (Turiel, 1983, p. 110). At this level, individuals believe that adhering to conventions is a necessary accommodation to the groups in which they participate. When a Level 5 adolescent was queried on the teacher-name issue, he said, "I think he was wrong [the boy who called the teacher by his first name], because you have to realize that you should have respect for your elders and that respect is shown by addressing them by their last names" (Turiel, 1983, p. 110). Interestingly, as students reach Level 5, their disruptive behavior in the classroom declines (Geiger & Turiel, 1983).

Turiel and his associates have published more than 30 research articles reporting how children differentiate between morality and social convention (e.g., Turiel, 1983; Turiel, Killen, & Helwig, 1987; Nucci, 1989). In these studies, the researchers found that children and adolescents respond to moral issues on the basis of features intrinsic to the acts, such as physical harm and injustice. They responded to conventions on the basis of the social order (e.g. rules, regulations, normative expectations). The subjects viewed moral transgressions as more serious than violations of conventions and as deserving of more serious punishment (Nucci, 1989).

The findings of research on social conventions bears striking similarities to the previously reviewed research on adolescents' political, economic, and moral thinking. In essence, soon after the onset of adolescence, at about age 14, there is a dramatic change in the capacity of teenagers to think about social phenomena. At this time, many adolescents begin to think abstractly and are able to engage in thought processes that characterize adult thinking.

CONCLUSIONS AND NEEDED RESEARCH

In this chapter, adolescence in contemporary America has been explored, some generalizations about adolescents have been examined, and a portrait of adolescent thinking has been drawn. Four general conclusions emerge.

First, adolescence is no longer as safe as it once was. Increasingly, social problems have invaded the previously protected province of adolescence. Contemporary adolescents are frequently hurried into adulthood and denied the opportunity to test tentative social theories and ways of behaving.

Research examining how the changing social environment of adolescence influences adolescent social thinking is needed. After researchers locate the adolescents' social thinking, curriculum materials based on the adolescent conceptions should be developed for social studies and the effects of the more socially oriented curriculum subjected to research.

Second, American adults are increasingly afraid of adolescents. Adult prejudice has resulted in the creation of situations that isolate adolescents from the larger society. The effect of this fear and isolation on adolescent development has not been healthy. Because many teenagers feel isolated and alone and are often estranged from adults, they are coming of age without useful role models. Social studies researchers need to examine adolescent alienation and estrangement. How prevalent, for example, is adolescent alienation? Are some teenagers more vulnerable than others? What social and intellectual characteristics do alienated adolescents possess? Does work outside school or do certain kinds of social activities inside school affect adolescent alienation? Are some school structures useful in reducing disaffection? Is community involvement important during adolescence? Does it reduce estrangement from society?

Third, social studies research will be enhanced if more cognitive science theories and methods are used. Cognitive science models should be used to examine a wide variety of research questions. How do adolescents process textual materials? how do they relate new social information to prior knowledge? And what kinds of misconceptions do adolescents bring to the study of social issues? The most important contribution that cognitive science can make to social studies research is, however, to focus attention on how adolescents perceive the social world and make choices in their own words on their own terms.

A fourth conclusion is the shocking lack of empirical knowledge about adolescence and adolescent life. The study of adolescence remains primitive, despite the subject's importance and the pervasiveness of adolescent problems. Most writing is theoretical without empirical foundation—essentially lectures to young people and their parents. Or if empirical, it is based on collections of isolated data unconnected by theory. The shadow of G. Stanley Hall still looms over the field of research on adolescence. The influence of Hall's primitive beliefs seriously inhibits inquiry into adolescence and its problems. The most dramatic instance of this inhibition is the lack of attention to the problems of young women. Research on adolescence must be conducted from a more balanced perspective if a viable conceptual framework is to be developed that can have a significant influence on social studies education.

References

Adelson, J. (1972). The political imagination of the young adolescent. In J. Kagan and R. Coles (Eds.), *Twelve to sixteen: Early adolescence* (pp. 106–144). New York: Norton.

Adelson, J. (1982, Summer). Rites of passage. *American Education, 62,* 6–13.

Aries, P. (1962). *Centuries of childhood.* (1962). New York: Knopf.

Bakan, D. (1972). Adolescence in America, From idea to social fact. In J. Kagan and R. Coles (Eds.), *Twelve to sixteen: Early adolescence* (pp. 73–89). New York: Norton

Berti, A. E., & Bombi, A. S. (1988). *The child's construction of economics.* Cambridge: Cambridge University Press.

Braebeck, M. (1982). Moral judgement: Theory and research on differences between males and females. *Developmental Review, 3,* 274–291.

Breskin, D. (1984, November 8). Teen suicide. *Rolling Stone,* pp. 26–37.

Carmody, D. (1988, December 29). Many students fail quiz on basic economics. *New York Times,* pp. 1, 8.

Coles, R. (1986). *The political life of children.* Boston: Houghton Mifflin

Collins, G. (1984, July 15). Beeper study finds solitude, mood swings normal for teenagers. *Minneapolis Star-Tribune,* 1F, 4F.

Connell, R. (1971). *The child's construction of politics.* Carleton, Australia: Melbourne University Press.

Cook, T. E. (1984). Review of the development of social knowledge. *American Political Science Review, 78,* 1202–1203.

Csikszentmihalyi, M., & Larson, R. (1984). *Being adolescent: Conflict and growth in the teenage years.* New York: Basic Books.

Elkind, D. (1984). *All grown up and no place to go: Teenagers in crisis.* New York: Addison-Wesley.

Elkind, D. (1986, May 22) *Stresses on adolescents.* A presentation at the School of Public Health, University of Minnesota.

Erikson, E. H. (1964). A memorandum on Negro identity and Negro youth. *Journal of Social Issues, 20,* 617–624.

Furth, H. (1988). Playful conceptions. *Science, 242,* 450.

Geiger, K. M., & Turiel, E. (1983). Disruptive school behavior and concepts of social convention in early adolescence. *Journal of Educational Psychology, 75,* 677–685.

Gilligan, C. (1982). *In a different voice.* Cambridge, MA: Harvard University Press.

Greenberger, E., & Steinberg, L. (1986). *When teenagers work: The psychological and social costs of adolescent employment.* New York: Basic Books.

Hall, G. S. (1904). *Adolescence: Its physiology and its relations to psychology, anthropology, sociology, sex, crime, religion and education.* New York: D. Appleton.

Hyman, H. H. (1959). *Political Socialization.* New York: Free Press.

Kaplan, L. J. (1984). *Adolescence: The farewell to childhood.* New York: Simon and Schuster.

Keniston, K. (1970). Youth: A "new" state of life. *American Scholar, 39,* 631–641.

Kohlberg, L. (1979). *Measuring moral judgment.* Worcester, MA: Clark University Press.

Leahy, R. L. (1983). Development of the conception of economic equality: Explanations, justifications and concepts of social mobility and change. *Developmental Psychology, 19,* 111–125

Merrow, J. (October, 1977). "Portrait of American Adolescence." A four part series on National Public Radio.

Nucci, L. (1989). Knowledge of the learner: The development of children's concepts of self, morality and societal convention. In M. Reynolds (Ed.), *Knowledge base for beginning teachers* (pp. 117–127). New York: Pergamon Press.

Piaget, J. (1965) *The moral judgement of the child.* New York: Free Press. (originally published 1932)

Rest, J. (1975). Developmental psychology as guide to curriculum development. *MCSS Journal, 13,* 2–7.

Rest, J. (1979). *Development in judging moral issues.* Minneapolis: University of Minnesota Press.

Rutter, M. (1980). *Changing youth in a changing society. Patterns of adolescent development and disorder.* Cambridge, MA: Harvard University Press.

Sigel, R., & Hoskin, M. (1981). *The political involvement of adolescents.* New Brunswick, NJ: Rutgers University Press.

Snyder, T. D. (1988). *Digest of education statistics.* Washington, DC: National Center For Education Statistics.

Sprinthall, N. A., & Collins, W. A. (1988). *Adolescent psychology: A developmental view.* New York: Random House.

Tanner, J. M. (1972). Sequence, tempo, and individual variation in growth and development of boys and girls aged twelve to sixteen. In J. Kagan and R. Coles (Eds.), *Twelve to sixteen: Early adolescence* (pp. 1–25). New York: Norton.

Torney-Purta, J. (1988). *Political socialization.* Paper presented at Citizenship for 21st Century: A National Conference on the Future of Civic Education, Washington, DC.

Turiel, E. (1978). The development of concepts of social structure: Social convention. In J. Glick and A. Clark-Stewart (Eds.), *The development of social understanding* (pp. 25–107). New York: Gardner Press.

Turiel, E. (1983). *The development of social knowledge.* Cambridge: Cambridge University Press.

Turiel, E., Killen, M., & Helwig, C. H. (1987). Morality: Its structure, functions and vagaries. In J. Kagan and S. Lamb (Eds.), *The emergence of morality in young children* (pp. 155–243). Chicago: Univeristy of Chicago Press.

Walker, L. K. (1984). Sex differences in the development of moral reasoning: A critical review. *Child Development, 55,* 677–691.

Walstad, W. B., & Soper, J. (1988). *A report card on the economic literacy of U.S. high school students.* New York: Joint Council of Economic Education.

·12·

CULTURALLY DIVERSE STUDENTS AND SOCIAL STUDIES

Geneva Gay

Little recently reported research has been focused directly on the effects of various curricular content and instructional strategies on the social studies achievement of culturally different students (Armento, 1986). The exception is studies on political socialization in the late 1960s and early 1970s. This void is somewhat paradoxical because advocates of cultural diversity have argued persistently that social studies is a natural medium for teaching cross-cultural understanding and making education more meaningful for students from different ethnic, social, and cultural backgrounds.

Some of the research on political socialization has been helpful in explaining how gender, socioeconomic status, ethnicity, and academic ability are related to the performance of students on differnt measures of political efficacy (Abramson, 1977; Armento, 1986; Ehman, 1970). Most frequently, the research did not explain why the relationships óccurred. The investigations conducted by Button (1974), Garcia (1973), and Hirsch (1971) were exceptions to this general trend. They included additional explanatory variables in their analyses, such as the interest appeal of instructional materials, levels of acculturation among ethnic minorities, and the political role models available to students. Unfortunately, this promising line of inquiry for teaching social studies content and skills to culturally different students has not been continued. Nor have its precedents been extended to other curricular components and instructional methodologies.

However, research studies on the interaction between cultural diversity and learning in general are producing some findings that are instructive for social studies education. Studies that describe the information processing systems, communication patterns, and interactional styles of students from different economic, social, ethnic, cultural, and racial backgrounds are especially pertinent. In this chapter, the attempt is made to make the linkage with social studies more explicit. The chapter is organized into three parts. In the first section, the general attributes of cultural discontinuities in learning are discussed. Research on specific cultural characteristics of different groups that may lead to discontinuities in teaching and learning is summarized in the second part. Suggestions for research on cultural diversity and social studies education are discussed in the final section. Research on teaching content about cultural pluralism is excluded because it is discussed elsewhere in this volume.

ATTRIBUTES OF DISCONTINUITIES IN LEARNING

Research on cultural diversity has revealed several common attributes of cultural-classroom discontinuities. One of these is the negative effect that mismatches in the structural and procedural elements of teaching and learning can have on the academic achievement of culturally different students. Alexander, Entwisle, and Thompson (1987) found evidence of this in the socioeconomic status differences of students and teachers. They monitored the achievement of first graders in 20 elementary schools. The results showed that high-SES teachers had difficulty forming a bond of common identity with and establishing positive performance expectations for low-SES students.

Some of the incompatibilities that exist between the learning styles of many culturally different students and those expected in many classrooms occur without deliberate or conscious intent. They happen when people from different cultural back-

Reviewers were Christine Bennett, Indiana University; Carlos E. Cortés, University of California, Riverside; Josiah Tlou, University of Botswana.

grounds simply act naturally, inasmuch as many social and interpersonal interactions are culturally patterned at a level below conscious awareness and control (Au, 1980b; McDermott, 1987; Spindler, 1987).

Cultural discontinuities are not restricted to any selected areas of human behavior. They can appear across the full range of teaching-learning interactions. Of particular significance for teaching culturally different students are discontinuities in patterns of interpersonal relations, communications, problem solving, time usage, performance styles, and cognitive processing (Boggs, Watson-Gegeo, McMillen, 1985; Jordan & Tharp, 1979).

In addition to occurring without conscious thought and being pervasive, the causes of cultural discontinuity do not necessarily diminish over time. Keefe and Padilla (1987) confirmed the power of cultural socialization in their study of acculturation among Mexican-Americans. They concluded that "some ethnic traits ... are sustained and surprisingly even strengthened from generation to generation" (p. 189).

Some of the most serious discontinuities between classroom styles and the behavioral patterns of culturally different students are structural or procedural. Florio and Shultz (1979) argued that the creative challenge imposed upon culturally different students to function well in both their school and nonschool lives involved more structural and procedural adaptations than academic ability. McDermott (1987) added that sometimes the ways of knowing and behaving in home and school are mutually exclusive. His observation was substantiated by Holliday's (1985) study of 9- and 10-year-old African-Americans in desegregated schools. These students routinely changed their behavioral styles between home and the school. At home and in the neighborhood they demonstrated high competence in problem-solving skills; in school their greatest competence was in the area of interpersonal and social skills.

Discontinuities between culturally different students and classroom teachers are particularly evident in verbal interactions. Greenbaum (1985), Philips (1985), and Zeuli and Floden (1987) located these more specifically in differences in attention giving, questioning, turn taking, length of utterances, and response timing. Students and teachers from different cultural backgrounds may not share common vocabulary meanings, language experiences, or referent points. Consequently, when they attempt to communicate, they often miss each other with their intended meanings. These bypasses happen in verbal exchanges as well as perceptions, nonverbal behaviors, and symbolic language (Blubaugh & Pennington, 1976).

The research on the general attributes of cultural discontinuity between home and school suggests, therefore, that African-American, Hispanic, American Indian, Asian-American, and poor students may have to develop both social and academic competence to succeed in school. Social competence involves using adaptive abilities and coping skills to adjust indigenous performance styles to the learning procedures used in the classroom. Academic competence deals with intellectual abilities, knowledge acquisition, and task mastery in the subject matter and skills being taught. Most often the social competence must precede the academic competence (Holliday, 1985). For researchers to design investigations to examine the expressions and effects of cul-

tural discontinuities in social studies education, as well as to create appropriate remediation strategies, it is helpful to know some of the specific causes of these disjunctures.

CULTURAL CHARACTERISTICS THAT CAUSE DISCONTINUITIES

Discontinuities between the normal structures and procedures of classroom teaching and those used by culturally different students in learning can be attributed to several categories of cultural characteristics. The ones discussed here are participation structures, learning modalities, and intragroup variabilities. The categories descriptive characteristics were derived from empirical investigations and ethnographic observations that have been conducted primarily with racial minorities, in urban areas, and with subjects from low-SES backgrounds.

Participation Structures

Participation structures involve the rights and obligations of teachers and students with respect to who can say what, when, and to whom (Cazden, 1986). As a result of their study of the communication behaviors of teachers and Odawa Indians in Canada, Mohatt and Erickson (1981) identified several common features of participation structures used in conventional classrooms. They are the overall tempo, pace, and directiveness of teaching; techniques for calling attention to students' behavior; how student attention is elicited, managed, and reinforced; amount of time allowed for compliance to directives; and the strategies used to stimulate speaking and participation in classroom interactions. In an extensive review of research on classroom discourse, Cazden (1986) emphasized the impact of social contexts and cultural experiences on communication and the important role speech protocols play in determining the learning opportunities of students in the classroom.

The participation structure commonly used by teachers presents the classroom as a highly structured and ordered system with clear distinctions between the roles of teacher and student. The teacher talks, controls, and directs while the student listens, obeys, and follows. The teacher determines the sociospatial arrangements of interactions, the amount of movement allowed, and who will talk, when, and under what conditions (Cazden, 1986; LeCompte, 1981). Students are taught to value rational thought, control implusive behavior, compress physical movement, and depend primarily upon visual perceptual cues and performance styles. Learning is perceived as a work task that is best executed by competitive individual efforts in an environment of persistent and prolonged perseverance (Boykin, 1986; Goodlad, 1984; Keating & Oakes, 1988; White, 1985).

Philips (1985) called this protocol for classroom interactions a "switchboard participation structure." She attributed this character to it for two reasons. The first was the dominate role played by the teacher in the operations of the system. Students almost never give directions to teachers, they rarely ask questions except for procedures and permissions, and all of their verbal behaviors are expected to conform to the conditions established by teachers (Cazden, 1986). The second switchboard feature of classroom communication is the serialized style of presentation. Usually only one student talks to the teacher at a time, and the teacher controls how this talk occurs through the use of questions, cues, feedback, and response wait-time.

Research on the participation structures of culturally different students reveal differences among ethnic, SES, gender, and ability groups on the kinds of questions asked, role relationships between speakers and listeners, turn-taking patterns, length of response time, and the preferred social context of learning (Cazden, 1986). Greenbaum (1985) provided more specific characteristics of the communication styles of American Indians from his study of Choctaw children in elementary school. He used Philips' (1985) conception of switchboard participation structures to analyze the nonverbal speech behaviors of 78 fifth- and sixth-grade students and four teachers in four different classrooms. Two of the classrooms were located in a school on the Mississippi Choctaw Indian Reservation, and two were in a predominately middle-class Anglo school in Lawrence, Kansas. Eleven class sessions were videotaped to collect data on such sociolinguistic features as length of utterances, listening-gaze behaviors, turn-taking patterns, and chorus versus individual speaking. The results indicated that the Choctaw students spoke individually less often, interrupted the teacher more, used shorter utterances, responded more frequently in chorus, and spent more time gazing at peers when the teacher was talking than did the Anglo students. The differences between the two groups were statistically significant ($p < .05$); mean differences ranged from a low of .18 on turn-switching pause duration to a high of 29.3 on percentage of choral speaking.

Teachers at the two school sites communicated differently, too. Those in the reservation schools used longer turn-switching pauses and shorter utterances. They also asked more questions of the group but fewer of individual students than did their counterparts in the public schools. Their behavioral patterns seemed to be adaptive responses to the participation styles of the Choctaw students.

Whereas Greenbaum used quantitative data, Durmont (1985), Mohatt and Erickson (1981), and Philips (1985) applied ethnographic techniques to describe the sociolinguistic characteristics of the communication styles of Indian groups. They found patterns similar to the Choctaw among the Sioux, Cherokee, Odawa, and Warm Springs Reservation Indians. Common behaviors observed included students being reluctant to participate when teachers expected them to speak out individually or compete with each other; rarely volunteering to respond to teacher-initiated requests; not waiting to be recognized by teachers before speaking; and talking more to each other than to the teacher, even as the teacher talked. In self-controlled, small groups, the students talked more and spent more time on task, their attention spans increased, and the duration and quality of academic efforts improved. Participation styles almost identical to these have been observed among Hispanics (Grossman, 1984; Justin, 1975; Ramírez & Castañda, 1974), African-Americans (Akbar, 1978; Boykin, 1978, 1983; Hale, 1982; Kochman, 1981; Shade, 1982, 1984a, 1986; Smitherman, 1977), and

native Hawaiians (Au, 1980a, 1980b; Boggs et al., 1985; Jordan, Au, & Joestring, 1981).

The differences Kochman (1981) observed in the communication patterns of Anglos and African-American college students led him to describe the Anglo participation style as one that favored rational and objective modes of expression, with turn taking regulated by clearly defined rules that were closely controlled by the teachers. The African-Americans tended to use a more personal and passionate communication style, with more loosely structured turn-taking rules that were regulated by the assertiveness of individual speakers. Whereas the Anglos in the study thought emotionalism interfered with rational thinking, the African-Americans used emotions to heighten reasoning abilities. Such differences can become major barriers to effective performance in social studies learning experiences dealing with critical thinking, problem solving, intergroup relations, civil rights, and moral-dilemma discussions. While the content used to develop these skills is often affective and emotional, the skills themselves are considered by curriculum developers and teachers to be highly rational.

Heath (1982) provided other evidence of Anglo and African-American communication styles. Although her study was conducted with much younger subjects and her results were somewhat different from Kochman's they are related. Her findings revealed that white children tended to be more topic-focused in the stories they told, while the African-American children used a topic-chaining style of presentation. Their accounts were largely about personal relations, compared to the Anglos' stories about possessions.

Michaels and Cazden (1986) asked Anglo and African-American teachers to comment on the quality of these two types of stories. The Anglo teachers found topic-chaining stories harder to follow and they described the narrators as low-achieving students. The African-American teachers evaluated both the topic-centered and topic-chaining stories and their narrators more positively.

These findings suggest that the problems inherent in discontinuities between home and school participation structures are not limited to ineffective communication between teachers and culturally different students. They may also cause these students' academic abilities to be assessed negatively.

Classroom Compatibility. Not all ethnic minority groups' participation structures are incompatible with those of the classroom. The emphasis accorded to self-discipline, control, and conformity to rather formal rules of interpersonal relations in traditional Japanese, Chinese, and Indochinese cultures (Kitano & Daniels, 1988; Montero, 1980; Thu, 1983) may explain why students from these backgrounds adjust rather well to the normal participation structure of the classroom.

Tong (1978) explained these connections further in his description of traditional Chinese culture. According to him, the Chinese orientation to learning was analogous to the training of traditional warriors. It stressed obedience, form, rhythm, precision, and total control of one's actions. The training was perfected through a process of observation, imitation, memorization, and repetition. It produced in individuals a tendency to be cautious, deliberate, and methodical about their decisions and actions. Consequently, some Chinese-American students may have a more reflective and slower, yet more meticulous response style than other ethnically different students (Pickcunas, 1986). They may require more wait-time to respond to questions asked by teachers and find it difficult to adjust to instructional techniques that emphasize learning by doing, discovering, critical thinking, and values analysis. But, they may adjust readily to those aspects of typical classroom participation structures that stress student passivity, repetition, and rote memory in learning. Some Japanese-American and Indochinese students have similar learning orientations (Chan, 1981; Thu, 1983).

Effects on Social Studies. The participation structures of many culturally different students raise interesting questions about how they may affect students' response patterns to some of the instructional techniques frequently used in social studies education. It might be hypothesized that because of their cultural socialization and preferred participation structures, (a) most Asian-American students will be reluctant to participate in open-ended discussions, values analysis, and inquiry teaching; (b) informal social contexts in social studies classrooms will improve the participation and performance of Hispanics, African-Americans, and American Indians; (c) as teachers use more cooperative learning strategies the involvement, time on task, and academic achievement of African-American, Hispanic, and Indian students will increase; and (d) divergent questioning and indirect teaching strategies are more suited to the participation structures of some culturally different students than others.

Another possible effect of culturally determined participation structures is that students from some cultural groups may respond differently to various phases of a given social studies instructional strategy. For example, within the critical thinking, decision-making, and problem-solving models of teaching, Asian-Americans may be less involved when speculating about the causes, consequences, and potential solutions to targeted problems, but more involved during the data-gathering phase. The reverse may be true for African-Americans and Hispanics. They may be more adept at speculating, hypothesizing, and brainstorming than collecting information and systematically testing hypotheses against facts. All of these hypotheses need to be empirically tested.

The investigation that Knight, Waxman, and Padron (1987) conducted on the cognitive strategies Hispanic students use to solve social studies problems supported the need for this kind of research. The elementary students who participated in the study reported regularly using only 3 of the 12 cognitive strategies identified as effective elements of high-level critical thinking. These were writing down important information, brainstorming, and imaging. They rarely organized information in lists or charts, looked for patterns, categorized information, worked backwards from end-goals to find solutions, made guesses when unable to solve problems, or related the problems studied to familiar events in their personal lives.

Modality and Climate Preferences in Learning

The perceptual sensations students use most persistently in learning and the kinds of environments in which they prefer to learn are influenced as much by cultural conditioning, and are as much a potential source of discontinuity in learning, as are participation structures (Shade, 1984a). Perceptual modalities are the sensory channels through which information is received, processed, and retained. They are either visual, verbal, auditory, tactile, or kinetic (Barbe & Swassing, 1979; Shade, 1982). Learning climates are the social contexts that surround task effort and performance. They may be formal or informal, individual or communal, competitive or cooperative, autocratic or democratic.

Visual and auditory modalities are used most often in classroom teaching. In his comprehensive *Study of Schooling*, Goodlad (1984) documented the extent to which these modalities dominate teaching. The investigation involved detailed observations of over 1,000 classrooms in 38 elementary and secondary schools nationwide. His data supported the popular image of teachers "standing or sitting in front of a class imparting knowledge to a group of students, explaining and lecturing ... [or] observing students at work or monitoring their seatwork" (p. 105). The incidence of active modes of learning were shockingly low.

Compared to this rather passive, verbal, and individualistic approach to learning, some culturally different students prefer more kinetic and tactile stimulation, active involvement, and cooperative social environments. American Indians have been described as preferring to learn through collaborative efforts with peers and the indirect participation of teachers (Cazden & John, 1971; Greenbaum 1985; Lockart, 1978; Mohatt & Erickson, 1981; Philips, 1985). These characteristics suggest a learning-style inclination toward field dependency. This hypothesis was investigated by Dinges and Hollenbeck (1978). Contrary to expectation, the 9-year-old Navajos who participated in their study were more field independent than their Anglo counterparts. The males were even more so than the females, as indicated by their higher scores on the Children's Embedded Figures Test. The investigators attributed these results to cultural and linguistic factors within Navajo life that simultaneously cultivate self-reliance and autonomous action, and group alliance and conformity. For example, the form-dominated linguistic structure of the Navajo language emphasizes matching objects by form and material instead of size and color.

The research studies conducted on the Kamehameha Early Education Program (KEEP) revealed that native Hawaiian children encountered difficulties in school partially because they used learning modalities that are not favored in the classroom. These children valued establishing a social context prior to task performance, the mutual participation of peers, conarration in verbal interactions, and physical movement in learning (Au, 1980a, 1980b; Au & Jordan, 1981; Boggs et al., 1985; Jordan et al., 1981). Conarration is a style of verbal performance in which several individuals work together to deliver a single speech event. It resembles the active-participatory and call-response interaction patterns between speakers and listeners that have been observed among African-Americans (Boykin, 1983, 1986; Kochman, 1981; Smitherman, 1977). When used in the classroom, conarration presumes the existence of a friendly and informal relationship between students and teachers. Boggs (1985) found that when this was indeed the case, native Hawaiian children were verbally active and more attentive to learning tasks. In the absence of a positive social relationship with teachers and the presence of the peer group, the same verbally astute children became virtually mute.

Many of the same perceptual modalities and environmental preferences attributed to American Indians and native Hawaiians have been observed among Hispanics and African-Americans, too. Research summarized by Ramírez and Castañeda (1974), as well as their own investigations, indicated that Mexican-American children had different incentive, motivational, relational, perceptual, and cognitive processing styles than Anglos. These differences gave priority to cooperative efforts, achievement for family benefit over self, reliance upon the social group for assistance in task performance, human and social content, and activities that required physical movement, tactical manipulation, and free association.

Grossman (1984) validated Ramírez and Castañeda's findings. His investigation was undertaken to determine the extent to which cultural traits and learning-style preferences usually attributed to Mexican-Americans existed across the larger Hispanic cultural community, including Puerto Ricans, Cubans, and individuals from various South American origins. Grossman used a 400-item questionnaire to collect data. It was administered to 469 individuals in 19 states, the District of Columbia, Puerto Rico, and Ecuador. The participants included mostly professional Hispanic and Anglo educators (85%) and a few parents and students. Sixty-five percent of the Anglo participants (who were 37% of the sample) considered themselves to have either good or excellent knowledge of Hispanic culture as a basis for responding to the questionnaire. Based on the results he obtained, Grossman concluded that Hispanics shared a culturally determined preference for learning by doing, global perspectives in task performance, poetic expressions and analogies in speaking, and working at a relaxed, leisurely pace. Similar findings came from Justin's (1975) examination of cultural conflict and Mexican-American achievement.

The perceptual modalities and preferred social learning environments of African-Americans tend to be as different from the classroom norms as those of American Indians and Hispanics. Many African-American students use predominately verbal, tactile, and kinetic learning modes, rather than the visual and auditory ones that dominate in the classroom. They have a facility for perceiving minute body movements and engaging in elaborate, spontaneous motoric responses, as well as preferring affective instructional materials and socially interactive learning environments. African-American students also tend to use relational, holistic, and functional criteria for sorting information, whereas middle-class Anglocentric teachers encourage analytical, detail-specific, taxonomic, and descriptive strategies in learning (Shade, 1982, 1984a; 1984b). Boykin (1978, 1986) and Gay and Baber (1987) provided additional confirmation of these cultural attributes. They described the African-American cultural values (from which learning modalities derive) of affective expression, energetic and dynamic self-presentation, communal efforts, kinetic movement, verbal dexterity, and creating social settings before engaging in task performance.

The learning modalities of African-American students were established from investigations of several different variables and experimental conditions. Damico (1985) investigated the hypothesis that African-American students are more people-oriented and Anglos more object-oriented. The students were asked to take photographs of things that best described their school. The photographs taken by the African-Americans were almost exclusively of people, and they included both males and females in the compositions. The Anglo students took more photographs of objects, same-sex groups, and the physical facilities of their school. Both groups took pictures primarily of same-race individuals. Damico interpreted these results as substantiation of the value some African-Americans place on people and social relations, compared to the priority given to material possessions by many Anglos. This study demonstrated the value of using photography as a research tool.

[A] variety of reliable evidence can be read directly from photographs of social and ceremonial activity, for in them is reflected complex dimensions of social structure, cultural identity, interpersonal relations, and psychological expression. (Collier & Collier, 1986, p. 77)

A second variable frequently used to determine the perceptual modalities of African-Americans is affectivity. Researchers (Gitter, Black, & Mostofsy, 1972; Hirschberg, Jones, & Haggerty, 1978; Orasanu, Lee, & Scribner, 1979; Shade, 1986; Shade & Edwards, 1987) who have investigated this variable have reported similar findings. Compared to Anglos, African-Americans generally were better at discerning emotions from expressions, paid more attention to social reactions and interpersonal nuances, were more social and kinetic, and engaged in pretend and creative play more frequently.

African-American preferences for kinetic and affective learning modes are demonstrated consistently on tests of intellectual abilities, cognitive styles, and creativity. Shade (1984b, 1986) found that African-American youths scored higher on perceptual speed and accuracy, social observation, and verbal skills than visual-spatial and analytical tasks on the Group Embedded Figures Test, the Clayton-Jackson Object Sorting Task, and the Myers-Briggs Type Indicator. Richmond (1971) used Level 4 of the Lorge-Thorndike Tests and the Torrence Tests of Creative Thinking, Verbal and Figural, Form B, to assess the cognitive and creative abilities of eighth-grade African-American and white students. The findings supported differences in favor of the Anglos on all measures (verbal and figural fluency, flexibility, and originality) except figural elaboration where African-Americans performed better.

In addition to studies of preference for social environments and the affective, African-Americans learning modalities have been determined by examining the effects of stimulus variation and physical movement on task performance. Boykin (1979, 1982) reported that African-American students performed better when problem-solving tasks were presented in different styles than when the same format was used. Guttentag (1972) unobtrusively observed African-American and Anglo preschool children with and without toys, with and without music, and alone and with another child to determine differences in kinetic styles. The Anglo children used less of the total play space and engaged in low intensity activities such as lying down, sitting, and squatting. The African-American children engaged in more high-energy activities like walking, running, jumping, and dancing. In a related study, Guttentag and Ross (1972) examined the effectiveness of using movement to teach simple verbal concepts to lower-class preschool African-American children. The results were positive, and indicated that kinetics facilitated the achievement of the African-American students.

The findings of research on the perceptual modalities, social environments, and participation structures of many culturally different students have revealed attributes that are consistent with the portrayals of object-centeredness and person-centeredness developed by Cutrona and Feshbach (1979). They described object-centered individuals as more adept at differentiating concepts, and at organizing and analyzing physical materials, abstractions, and inanimate materials. Person-oriented individuals are good at interpersonal relationships, empathizing with others, and learning content about social issues. Many poor and ethnic minority students fall into the latter category.

The learning modalities and preferences of culturally different students have implications for two essential components of social studies: what is taught and how it is taught. Research into the compatibility between these components of social studies education and the learning modalities of culturally different students should lead to improved academic achievement. This hypothesis should be a major part of future research on social studies and cultural diversity.

Variability Within Cultural Patterns

Since no ethnic, cultural, or social group is a monolith, intragroup variability within participation structures and learning modalities is a necessary complement to intergroup differences. The research to date on intragroup differences in cultural discontinuity and learning is not extensive. The little that does exist has focused on referent group orientation, generational identity, and gender (Keefe & Padilla, 1987; Ramírez & Castañeda, 1974; Thu, 1983).

Level of Acculturation. Typical measures of referent group orientation are levels of acculturation, and ethnic identification and affiliation. Level of acculturation is the extent to which culturally different individuals ascribe to the values and norms of the mainstream culture. Chow (1981), Kitano and Daniels (1988), and Montero (1980) studied this phenomenon among Asian-Americans. They found that as the level of acculturation increased, compliance to indigenous cultural values declined, as did the amount of functional discontinuity individuals experienced in mainstream institutions. The rate of acculturation was affected by generational identity, gender, proximity to cultural community, and the prejudice against the cultural or social group (Keefe & Padilla, 1987).

Chow (1981) added personality type to his analysis of acculturation among Asian-American females. He argued that how Asian-American females engaged in social interactions was influenced by one of four personality types. *Traditionalists* tended to be subservient to traditional social codes and expectations. *Assimilationists* had strong affiliations with mainstream values, rejected ethnic identity, and sometimes experienced intense feelings of guilt, self-denial, and self-hate. *Pluralists* were bicultural in that they integrated Asian and American cultural heritages into their values and behaviors. Their self-worth was defined by both ethnic pride and affiliation with and participation in mainstream culture. *Ambivalents* rejected both their indigenous and American cultures, were culturally and socially alienated, and often had high levels of anomie.

Presumably, those personality types that most closely resemble the values and participation structures of the classroom, experience fewer discontinuities in learning. Prior research findings suggest that the values and relational styles of some Asian-American cultures are compatible with common classroom routines and modes of teaching. If these are valid and generalizable, the traditionalists, assilimationists, and pluralists in Chow's typology should do equally well in academic achievement. This hypothesis needs to be tested with empirical data.

Levels of acculturation may also be influenced by generational identity. Kitano and Daniels (1988) and Montero (1980) found this to be true among the Japanese-Americans they studied, as did Palleja (1987) with Puerto Ricans. Second-generation immigrants tended to be more acculturated than first-generation immigrants and were able to function better in mainstream culture. Keefe and Padilla (1985) disagreed that generational identity was the best predictor of acculturation. The more reliable predictors that emerged from their three-year study of Hispanics in California were the extent of perceived discrimination, strength of community kinship, and intergroup contact. Exactly how these affect the academic achievement of culturally different students is uncertain.

Ethnic Identity. Self-ethnic identification is another variable that can cause variations in the amount of cultural discontinuity in learning that individuals within the same cultural group experience. Whereas, in research on acculturation, acceptance of mainstream norms is used as the unit of analysis, researchers of ethnic identification exmine how individuals relate to their own ethnicity. Conceptual models of this process have been developed by Banks (1979), Cross (1971; 1978), Gay (1982, 1987), and Thomas (1971). They have been empirically tested by Bennett (1982), Cross (1976), and Williams (1975). The findings from investigations with college-age students and adults have validated the conceptual features. The most significant ones for social studies teaching and research are that as individuals develop psychologically from negative to positive perceptions of their ethnicity they become more self-assured, less intransigent in attitudes and values, more empathetic and receptive toward other ethnic groups, more willing to engage in interethnic group relations, and more committed to social activism and social justice.

The effects of stages of ethnic identity on the academic performance and interpersonal relations of K–12 students are yet to be established. However, the idea offers some promising directions for social studies research. There may be a relationship between stages of ethnic identity and how different students respond to prominent social studies curricular goals and content, such as intergroup relations, self-concept development, equality and justice, and interdependence. Stages of ethnic identification may also affect how students respond to instructional strategies like moral-dilemma discussions, cooperative learning, perspective taking, and problem solving. These possibilities should be essential components of future research on teaching social studies to culturally different students.

Gender. Along with levels of acculturation and ethnic identification, gender can have a significant impact upon intragroup variability in cultural discontinuities. For example, Dyk and Witkin (1965) and Witkin (1967) reported that how males and females were socialized in the middle-class mainstream culture produced differences in cognitive styles. Males were taught sex-role attributes that resembled field independent learning traits, including competition, individual assertiveness, exploration of novel and challenging situations, and task orientation. Female socialization emphasized such field dependent traits as social convention, protectiveness, interpersonal relations, and affective expression. When the socialization was transmitted through communication behaviors, different gender patterns of aggressiveness and submissiveness emerged. Males talked, interrupted, and engaged in overlapping speech more frequently than females. The females were more cautious talkers, but they were more attentive to details, asked more questions, used more delayed responses, and were silent for longer periods of time (Eakins & Eakins, 1978).

There appears to be an interaction between gender and ethnicity in preferred participation structures and learning modalities. Perney (1976) found this effect among the sixth graders she studied. The African-American students took more time than Whites to complete the Embedded Figures Test, and girls in each of the ethnic groups required more time than the boys. The African-American females accounted for most of the performance differences between the races. They took almost twice as much time as the other three groups to find the embedded figures. Perney thought that these differences could not be attributed to gender alone, since the African-American and White females did not perform similarly. Nor could they be considered true racial differences because the performance of the African-American males differed from the African-American females. Therefore, she concluded that their cultural socialization probably fostered field dependence in African-American females. The extent to which Perney's interpretations are correct, whether intragroup differences in gender socialization are transferred to classroom participation and academic performance, and whether any differences are generalizable across cultural groups are yet to be determined. The existing findings are too preliminary to be conclusive, but they do offer some important possibilities for future research.

The findings derived from research on the specific cultural characteristics of different ethnic, cultural, and social groups substantiate the existence of serious discontinuities between their natal cultures and the school. These discontinuities are particularly prominent among African-Americans, Puerto Ricans, Mexican-Americans, American Indians, and low-SES groups. The causes stem from both intergroup and intragroup differences, and may be located in participation structures, learning modalities, referent group orientations, generational identity, age, and gender. The effects of these discontinuities are numerous, too. They are evident in academic achievement, social adjustment to school, interracial relations, and individual self-concepts.

Social Studies Implications. Almost all of the results on the effects of cultural diversity on learning were obtained from investigations that did not directly involve social studies education. Yet, they have clear implications for social studies research and practice with culturally different students. White (1985) described the general character of these implications, based upon reviews of ethnographic research studies and analyses of their potential contributions to social studies education. She concluded that these studies indicated that neither the type of authority structure alone nor the instructional strategy or the type of academic knowledge generated determines what works in culturally pluralistic classrooms. Rather, it is the existence of a core of shared values and social relationships which are accepted by both students and teachers as being in their best interests. In the absence of these, the classroom can become a battleground with constant skirmishes over self-worth, status, and power, with the time and energy of both students and teachers being distracted from academic tasks and educational processes.

IMPLICATIONS FOR RESEARCH

Two levels of implications for social studies research can be derived from prior studies on cultural diversity and learning. On the first level are some general conceptual guidelines for minimizing discontinuities in learning for culturally different students and designing related research. The second level includes more specific questions, hypotheses, and variables to be empirically tested.

General Conceptual Guidelines

Four different conceptual models have been proposed for improving the academic success of culturally different students by increasing compatibility between their home and school experiences. These are sociolinguistic facilitation, shared cognitive frameworks, modified activity structures, and cooperative task structures.

Sociolinguistic Facilitation. The use of participation structures and communication interactions that are similar to the ones students use in their homes and communities is one suggested strategy. It may require modifications in turn-taking rules, duration of utterances, turn-switching pauses, wait-time for responses, questioning strategies, and the distribution of opportunities for individuals and groups to participate in verbal interactions with teachers (Au, 1980b; Greenbaum, 1985; Mohatt & Erickson, 1981). The major hypotheses embedded in this strategy are that conflicts in teaching and learning styles will be minimized, and that culturally different students can spend more of their energy, attention, and efforts on academic tasks. Thus, the students will no longer need to develop social competence *before* they can attend to academic competence (Holliday, 1985).

The intervention strategies used in the Kamehameha Early Education Program (KEEP) to teach reading and language arts skills to native Hawaiian students exemplified sociolinguistic facilitation. By using some of the learning-style characteristics of the children, KEEP succeeded in raising reading scores from the 13th to the 67th percentile in four years. The program represented "a cultural synthesis of familiar and novel routines and participation structures which enable Hawaiian children to use their sociolinguistic skills in learning to read' (Boggs et al., 1985, p. 140).

Additional evidence on the effects of sociolinguistic facilitation in teaching culturally different students came from research on American Indians. Mohatt and Erickson (1981) observed that teachers who increased the verbal classroom participation of Odawa students paid close attention to the rhythm of the students' activities and used that rhythm as a basis for determining their own rates of beginning, pacing, and finishing tasks in formal instruction. When teachers adjusted their communication styles to accommodate the cultural patterns of Choctaw Indians, the children's verbal participation and time on task increased. Their adaptative accommodations included using longer turn-switching pauses, providing more wait-time for responses to questions, and asking shorter questions (Greenbaum, 1985). Durmont (1985) found similar positive effects of sociolinguistic facilitation with Sioux children.

Piestrup (1973) and Foster (1987) examined another form of sociolinguistic facilitation with African-American students. They investigated the effects of teachers incorporating features of African-American communication style into their own instructional language behaviors. Piestrup (1973) reported that first graders in predominately African-American classrooms who were taught with this African-American artful teaching style achieved higher scores on standardized reading tests than those taught with a more traditional style. Foster's (1987) ethnographic analysis of an African-American teacher's verbal interactions with African-American students in a community college class indicated positive results, too. When the teacher used participation structures and language behaviors familiar to the students, the quantity, intensity, and quality of their involvement was much better than when the more traditional, professorial instructional style was used. The students were able to recall information with a greater degree of accuracy, were more attentive and enthusiastic about learning, and grasped concepts much quicker. Piestrup and Foster described an African-American artful teaching style as the inclusion of African-American rhythmic language, intonation patterns, gesticulations, metaphoric imagery, pace and rhythm of speaking, repetition, and creative verbal play into the teacher's verbal and nonverbal behaviors.

Both forms of sociolinguistic facilitation and their effects suggest variables and experimental treatments that should be tested in social studies research. Particularly appropriate would be the examination of the effects of changing questioning strategies, using more informal interactional styles, and including more group activities on the performance of students from different ethnic, social, and cultural backgrounds.

Shared Cognitive Frameworks. Another strategy proposed for improving the education of culturally different students is to establish closer linkages between cognitive frameworks present in the home and school cultures. The emphasis is on common patterns of thought, frames of reference, and styles of information processing that people use to interpret their worlds, resolve conflicts, and solve problems (Wilson, 1979). Several benefits of this technique have been documented. In a review of the research on the reading comprehension of linguistically different students, Pandolfo (1985) discovered that "the closer the match between the content schema used by the author in writing the text and the schema chosen by the reader to interpret the text, the better the level of comprehension" (p. 5). Smith and Lewis (1985) reported similar results in their analyses of the effects of self-schema on the information recall of African-American 6- and 7-year olds. They recalled more details of stories about African-American characters than white characters. However, the females had less clearly defined racially determined self-schemata than did the males. Their self-schemata seemed to be affected by their gender as well. The bidialectic students who participated in the investigations of Hall, Reder, and Cole (1979) recalled more information when they were tested in their cultural dialects than in standard English.

Shared cognitive frameworks have implications for the selection of social studies content, instructional strategies, and performance evaluation techniques to be used with culturally different students. Culturally pluralistic content and more kinetic and auditory instructional and evaluation strategies should improve the academic achievement of some African-American, Hispanic, Indian, and lower-SES students.

Modifying the Structure of Learning Activities. Changing the structure of learning activities may positively affect the academic achievement of some culturally different students, too. This intervention strategy has been empirically tested by examining the hypothesis that African-American students perform better in learning activities that involve kinetic movement, multiple sensory stimulation, and frequently varied structural formats. Boykin (1979, 1982) examined the effects of task-format variability on the problem-solving abilities of third- and fourth-grade African-American and Anglo students. The tasks were presented in unvaried and varied formats. In the unvaried format all tasks of the same kind were presented to the students before tasks of a different kind were introduced. In the varied format all of the experimental tasks were randomly ordered, with no more than two of the same kind presented sequentially. The African-American students did better on tasks presented in the varied format, but the Anglo students did as well in either the varied or unvaried format.

Two other results of Boykin's study have implications for other studies of the effects of modified activity structures on student performance. First, the preference of African-American students for the varied formats was not related to ability. Both high- and low-achieving students preferred the varied approach. Second, the adaptive responses of African-American and Anglo students toward their least-preferred learning formats were qualitatively different. The Anglo students tried to make the task more interesting and to keep their efforts focused on it. The African-American students engaged in non-task-specific behaviors and avoided continuing with the task. These different reactions suggest why unvaried styles of instruction do not interfere as much with Anglo students' academic concentration as with African-Americans: the latter have a lower tolerance for monotony and repetition in teaching than Anglos (Boykin, 1979).

A study of performance on a color discrimination task among kindergarten children extended Boykin's findings about the effect of format variability to low-SES groups. Marshall (1969) measured the impact of novelty and stimulus changes on the quality of tasks performed by lower-class and middle-class children. When the lower-class children were given a high-interest task, they performed as well and as quickly as the middle-class students. The middle-class students performed better on low-interest than high-interest tasks. While the game-like character of the high-interest tasks distracted the middle-class students from the learning task, it facilitated task mastery for the lower-class children by maintaining their attention and involvement.

Research conducted by Guttentag and Ross (1972) on the impact of physical movement on learning revealed positive results among African-American preschoolers. The use of spontaneous and directed gross- and fine-motor responses associated with such concepts as big-small, loud-soft, and high-low enhanced the recall and use of the concepts for all the students, but even more so for the African-American children.

These findings pose the question of whether other cultural groups will respond similarly to modified activity structures, and if the same reactions will occur in social studies. If so, then a wide variety of instructional strategies and learning arrangements that include multiple-sensory stimuli, physical movement, and varied formats should be employed. Learning centers, individualized programs, and small group activities may be especially effective. The differential effects of these on the academic achievement of various culturally different students need to be carefully documented.

Cooperative Task Structures. Research on the participation structures and learning modalities of ethnic minority students indicate that many of them prefer to learn within the context of group settings and communal efforts. This inclination led to the recommendation that cooperative task structures be used to facilitate cultural continuity in learning. Task structures refer to the many ways in which teachers arrange activities designed to result in student learning (Slavin, 1983). The conarration of stories by native Hawaiian children (Au, 1980a; Boggs et al., 1985), the choral response patterns of American Indian students (Greenbaum, 1985; Philips, 1985), the tendency of some Hispanics to rely upon group assistance in task performance (Grossman, 1984; Ramírez & Castañeda, 1974), and the call-response communication style observed among African-Americans (Kochman, 1981; Smitherman, 1977) are examples of how cooperative task structures may be activated in learning by culturally different students.

Although most of the reported research on cooperative learning was not cast in the conceptual framework of cultural discontinuity and did not involve social studies education, the strategy and its results have strong inferential linkages to both. By 1987, more than 70 high-quality studies had been conducted to evaluate various cooperative learning strategies. They showed that cooperative learning was of equal benefit to all types of students, irrespective of gender, ability level, ethnicity, or the achievement measure used. The positive effects included improved academic achievement, better intergroup race relations, more cross-ethnic-group friendships, improved self-esteem, the development of peer norms in favor of doing well academically, and greater feelings of control over their own fate in school among students (Slavin, 1983, 1987).

Despite these positive effects, Webb (1982) suggested that more research attention be given to the interactions within small groups in order to capitalize on the maximum potential of this instructional strategy. Two variables emerged from her studies which are pertinent to research on social studies and cultural diversity. These are the ability and the racial composition of the groups. The evidence indicated that a mixture of ability among group members affected the interaction and performance of the group, but the directions of these effects were inconsistent. The data on the racial composition of groups were more conclusive. Studies of interactions within multiracial groups showed that white students tended to be more active and influential, whereas minority students were less assertive, less talkative, more anxious, and gave less information or fewer suggestions toward task completion. This pattern is not immutable. It can be altered by manipulating expectations for competent perfomance of group members and by skill-training interventions.

Further studies of the interactions within small multiracial, culturally diverse, and varied ability groups, and their effects on performance achievement are strongly warranted in social studies research on cultural diversity. Cooperative learning is a teaching technique that is highly congruent with how some culturally different students prefer to learn, and it is frequently employed in social studies instruction. Furthermore, some of the results of cooperative learning parallel desired outcomes of the social studies. These include improved self-concepts, positive intergroup relations, personal empowerment, and negotiated decision-making.

Cooperative task structures, sociolinguistic facilitation, shared cognitive frameworks, and modified activity structures provide some useful general guidelines for conceptualizing research on social studies and cultural diversity. From these general suggestions, more specific questions, variables, and experimental treatments related to curriculum content, instructional strategies, classroom climates, and evaluation techniques can be derived.

Specific Research Possibilities

The various attributes of the learning styles of some culturally different students suggest that they may find social studies more meaningful, and therefore their achievement will be better than for some other subjects. This hypothesis should be examined empirically by investigating such questions as: How does the achievement of culturally different students in social studies compare with their performance in other subjects? What cultural characteristics correlate more highly with social studies achievement? What social studies content, skills, instructional strategies, and learning environments are most effective with which culturally different students?

Previous research has suggested that the academic performance of culturally different students may be affected by generational identity, levels of acculturation and ethnic identification, perceptual modalities, and participation structures, as well as by ethnic group membership, age, gender, SES, and ability. Additional research should be conducted to determine how these different variables influence social studies achievement, what kinds of interaction effects exist among these variables, and whether patterns of influence are generalizable across school levels, classroom environments, instructional strategies, and curriculum content.

To answer these questions, social studies researchers need to depart from some of the established precedents in studying cultural diversity. Frequently, investigations have concentrated on urban classrooms, treated the groups studied as monoliths, compared lower-class minorities with middle-class Anglos, and used output data in the form of standardized achievement test scores as the primary dependent measures. More input variables and interaction effects should be examined to complement the output variables; the populations sampled and the research sites should be more widely diversified; and more attention should be given to within-group variability. The interaction effect might include participation structures, task structures, perceptual and stimulus response patterns, referent group orientations, and styles of cognitive processing. Performance measures of achievement in nonacademic areas, and with different instructional strategies, need to be investigated. The subjects selected for study should be chosen from an array of low- and high-achieving students, socioeconomic backgrounds, ethnic groups, urban, rural, and suburban settings, and different geographic locations. Social studies researchers should make greater use of ethnographic techniques to collect data on these relationships and effects. The findings from these more comprehensive studies will be more generalizable, and will improve the criteria used to diagnose students' needs, evaluate performance, identify obstacles to learning, and modify curriculum content and instructional strategies to better serve culturally different students.

Verbal communication behaviors are fundamental elements of classroom participation structures in general (Au, 1980a; Cazden, 1986; Greenbaum, 1985; Mohatt & Erickson, 1981; Philips, 1985) and social studies education in particular. They are major determinants of the kinds of learning opportunities that different students receive. This reliance on verbal communication makes research on the participation structures of culturally different students especially pertinent to social studies. Specific investigations might examine how students from various ethnic groups who are reluctant to engage in public self-disclosure respond to moral-dilemma discussions and value-clarification techniques. Other related questions worthy of research are: How do groups such as African-Americans, Hispanics, and American Indians who value group effort perform in cooperative learning strategies, as compared to others, like middle-class Anglos, who are more individualistic and competitive? How does gender affect student performance on various social studies instructional strategies and curriculum content? How do other instructional strategies, such as inquiry teaching, questioning strategies, and concept mastery, affect the classroom participation and academic achievement of students from different ethnic and cultural groups, in rural and urban settings, and from lower- and middle-class backgrounds?

Another potentially fruitful area for research is the study of the effects of multicultural social studies curricula on student attitudes, social skill development, and academic achievement. Some previous investigations (Hall et al., 1979; Pandolfo, 1985; Smith & Lewis, 1985) indicated that shared cognitive frameworks improved academic achievement for culturally different students. Button (1974) demonstrated the differential effects on the attitudes and achievement of Anglos, Hispanics, and African-Americans of using ethnic content to teach political efficacy. More social studies research of this kind is needed to determine the differential effects for students from various cultural groups of teaching knowledge about other cultures on prejudices, intergroup relations and self-esteem, and the mastery of other social studies concepts, topics, and skills. The findings will contribute significantly to deciding where to incorporate content about cultural pluralism into social studies curriculum and instruction.

Previous research suggested that the sucessful academic performance of some culturally different students is contingent upon the existence of an appropriate social and interpersonal context for learning (Boggs et al., 1985; Grossman, 1984; Holliday, 1985). The existence of such environments apparently minimizes psychological distractors to learning and maximizes the academic-attending behaviors of students. Further investigations are needed to determine if compatibility in the structures and procedures of social studies teaching with how culturally different students learn will decrease feelings of alienation, increase feelings of personal empowerment, and improve time on task. Also bearing investigation is how the creation of a social context for learning affects the achievement of such social studies goals and skills as consensus building, social activism, problem solving, collaborative efforts, and participatory democracy. A third needed approach to studying the effects of social contexts on learning is to determine how the self-initiated grouping patterns and social interactions among culturally different students are affected by task assignment, teacher expectations for performance, and the ethnic, racial, and economic mix of the classroom.

Finally, in other studies on cultural diversity some measurement instruments and treatments have been used that can be applied in social studies research. Among these are sociolinguistic features of participation structures, the Torrence Test of Creative Thinking, the Group Embedded Figures Test for diagnosing learning styles, indicators of learning modalities, stages of ethnic identification, photographic inventories, and cooperative learning strategies. These techniques have the potential for helping social studies educators better understand *how* culturally different students engage in learning and *why* their learning processes may conflict with the routines of teaching that are regularly used in the classroom.

CONCLUSION

The primary message from previous research on cultural diversity and learning for social studies research is that cultural socialization affects how students learn. The ease or difficulty with which students learn may be influenced as much by congruency in the processes of teaching and learning as by intellectual ability. Therefore, a major focus of social studies research should be the effects various teaching styles and learning arrangements have on the academic achievement of low-SES, African-American, Hispanic, Indian, Asian-American, and male and female students.

The research summarized in this chapter suggested some potential linkages between general studies of cultural diversity and the specific concerns of social studies educators. Hopefully, researchers will use some of the major conceptual frameworks, variables, methodologies, treatments, and hypotheses offered to guide their investigations of teaching social studies to culturally different students. The essence of these can be summarized as follows:

- Cultural discontinuities exist between the routine procedures of classroom teaching and how some culturally different students learn.
- Cultural discontinuities in approaches to learning can jeopardize academic achievement.
- Variables contributing to cultural discontinuities in learning exceed the traditional demographics of age, gender, education, SES, ethnicity, and ability. Other significant variables are referent group orientation, levels of ethnic identification and disaffiliation, participation structures, learning modalities, and task structures.
- Continuity in learning for culturally different students may be achieved through sociolinguistic facilitation, shared cognitive frameworks, culturally adaptive task structures, and cooperative learning structures.
- Congruency in the procedural structures of teaching and learning has a positive effect on academic performance.

The results generated from empirical investigations of these hypotheses can make quality social studies education and greater academic success more accessible to a greater number of culturally different students.

References

Abramson, P. R. (1977). *The political socialization of Black America: A critical evaluation of research of efficacy and trust.* New York: Free Press.

Akbar, N. (1978). *Cultural expressions of the African American child.* (ERIC Document Reproduction Service No. ED 179 633).

Alexander, K. L., Entwisle, D. R., & Thompson, M. S. (1987). School performance, status relations, and the structure of sentiment: Bringing the teacher back in. *American Sociological Review, 52,* 665–682.

Armento, B. J. (1986). Research on teaching social studies. In M. C. Wittrock (Ed.), *Handbook of research on teaching.* (3rd ed., pp. 942–951). New York: Macmillan.

Au, K. H. P. (1980a). Participation structures in a reading lesson with Hawaiian children: Analysis of a culturally appropriate instructional event. *Anthropology and Education Quarterly, 11,* 91–115.

Au, K. H. P. (1980b). *Theory and method in establishing the cultural congruence of classroom speech events.* (ERIC Document Reproduction Service No. ED 204 465)

Au, K. H. P., & Jordan, C. (1981). Teaching reading to Hawaiian children: Finding a culturally appropriate solution. In H. T. Trueba, G. P. Guthrie, & K. H. P. Au (Eds.). *Culture and the bilingual classroom: Studies in classroom ethnography* (pp. 139–152). Rowley, MA: Newbury House.

Banks, J. A. (1979). *Teaching strategies for ethnic studies.* Boston: Allyn & Bacon.

Barbe, W. B., & Swassing, R. H. (1979). *Teaching through modality strengths: Concepts and practice.* Columbus, OH: Zaner-Bloser.

Bennett, C. (1982, March). *Factors related to the retention of minority and non-minority students in a White predominated university: Part one—stage of ethnicity.* Paper presented at the annual meeting of the American Educational Research Association, New York.

Blubaugh, J. A., & Pennington, D. L. (1976). *Crossing differences . . . Interracial communication.* Columbus, OH: Merrill.

Boggs, S. T. (1985). The meaning of questions and narratives to Hawaiian children. In C. B. Cazden, V. P. John, & D. Hymes (Eds.), *Functions of language in the classroom* (pp. 299–327). Prospect Heights, IL: Waveland Press.

Boggs, S. T., Watson-Gegeo, K., & McMillen, G. (1985). *Speaking, relating, and learning: A study of Hawaiian children at home and at school.* Norwood, NJ: Ablex.

Boykin, A. W. (1978). Psychological/behavioral verve in academic task performance: Pretheoretical considerations. *Journal of Negro Education, 47,* 343–354.

Boykin, A. W. (1979). Psychological/behavioral verve: Some theoretical explorations and empirical manifestations. In A. W. Boykin, A. J. Franklin, & J. F. Yates (Eds.), *Research directions of Black psychologists* (pp. 351–367). New York: Russell Sage Foundation.

Boykin, A. W. (1982). Task variability and the performance of black and white schoolchildren: Vervistic explorations. *Journal of Black Studies, 12,* 469–485.

Boykin, A. W. (1983). The academic performance of Afro-American children. In J. T. Spencer (Ed.), *Achievement and achievement motives: Psychological and sociological approaches* (pp. 321–371). San Francisco: W. H. Freeman.

Boykin, A. W. (1986). The triple quandary and the schooling of Afro-American children. In E. Neisser (Ed.), *The school achievement of minority children: New perspectives* (pp. 57–92). Hillsdale, NJ: Lawrence Erlbaum.

Button, C. B. (1974). Political education for minority groups. In R. G. Niemi (Ed.), *The politics of future citizens* (pp. 167–198). San Francisco: Jossey-Bass.

Cazden, C. (1986). Classroom discourse. In M. C. Wittrock (Ed.), *Handbook of research on teaching* (3rd ed., pp. 432–463). New York: Macmillan.

Cazden, C. B., & John, V. P. (1971). Learning in American Indian children.

In M. L. Wax, S. Diamond, & F. O. Gearing (Eds.), *Anthropological perspectives on education* (pp. 252–272). New York: Basic Books.

Chan, K. N. (1981). Education for Chinese and Indochinese. *Theory Into Practice, 20,* 35–44.

Chow, E. N. L. (1981). *Acculturation and self concept of the Asian American woman.* (ERIC Document Reproduction Service No. ED 224 848)

Collier, J., & Collier, M. (1986). *Visual anthropology: Photography as a research method.* Albuquerque: University of New Mexico Press.

Cross, W. E., Jr. (1971). Discovering the Black referent: The psychology of black liberation. In V. J. Dixon & B. G. Foster (Eds.), *Beyond Black and White: An alternate America* (pp. 95–110). Boston: Little, Brown.

Cross, W. E., Jr. (1976). *Stereotypic and non-stereotypic images associated with the Negro to Black conversion experiences: An empirical analysis.* Unpublished doctoral dissertation, Princeton University.

Cross, W. E., Jr. (1978). The Thomas and Cross models of psychological nigrescence: A review. *The Journal of Black Psychology, 5,* 13–31.

Cutrona, C. E., & Feshbach, S. (1979). Cognitive and behavioral correlates of children's differential use of social information. *Educational Psychologist, 50,* 1036–1042.

Damico, S. B. (1985). The two worlds of school differences in the photographs of Black and White adolescents. *The Urban Review, 17,* 210–222.

Dinges, N. C., & Hollenbeck, A. R. (1978). Field-dependence-field-independence in Navajo children. *International Journal of Psychology, 13,* 215–220.

Durmont, R. V., Jr. (1985). Learning English and how to be silent: Studies in Sioux and Cherokee classrooms. In C. B. Cazden, V. P. John, & D. Hymes (Eds.). *Functions of language in the classroom* (pp. 344–369). Prospect Heights, IL: Waveland Press.

Dyk, R. B., & Witkin, H. A. (1965). Family experiences related to the development of differentiation in children. *Child Development, 36,* 21–55.

Eakins, B. W., & Eakins, R. G. (1978). *Sex differences in human communication.* Boston: Houghton Mifflin.

Ehman, L. H. (1970). Normative discourse and attitude change in the social studies classroom. *The High School Journal, 54,* 76–83.

Florio, S., & Shultz, J. (1979). Social competence at home and at school. *Theory Into Practice, 18,* 234–243.

Foster, M. (1987). *It's cookin' now: A performance analysis of the speech events of a Black teacher in an urban community college.* Paper presented at the Symposium on Afro-American Perspectives on Issues of Learning, Ethnicity and Identity at the American Anthropological Association, Chicago.

Garcia, F. C. (1973). *Political socialization of Chicano children: A comparative study with Anglos in California schools.* New York: Praeger.

Gay, G. (1982). Developmental perspectives for multicultural education in the social studies. In L. W. Rosenzweig (Ed.), *Developmental perspectives on the social studies* (pp. 67–81). Washington, DC: National Council for the Social Studies.

Gay, G. (1987). Ethnic identity development and Black expressiveness. In G. Gay & W. L. Baber (Eds.), *Expressively Black: The cultural basis of ethnic identity* (pp. 35–74). New York: Praeger.

Gay, G., & Baber, W. L. (Eds.). (1987). *Expressively Black: The cultural basis of ethnic identity.* New York: Praeger.

Gitter, A. G., Black, H., & Mostofsy, D. (1972). Race and sex in the perception of emotion. *Journal of Social Issues, 28,* 63–78.

Goodlad, J. I. (1984). *A place called school: Prospects for the future.* New York: McGraw-Hill Book Company.

Greenbaum, P. E. (1985). Nonverbal differences in communication style between American Indian and Anglo elementary classrooms. *American Educational Research Journal, 22,* 101–115.

Grossman, H. (1984). *Educating Hispanic students: Cultural implications for instruction, classroom management, counseling and assessment.* Springfield, IL: Charles C. Thomas.

Guttentag, M. (1972). Negro-White differences in children's movement. *Perceptual and Motor Skills, 35,* 435–436.

Guttentag, M. & Ross, S. (1972). Movement responses in simple concept learning. *American Journal of Orthopsychiatry, 42,* 657–665.

Hale, J. (1982). *Black children: Their roots, culture and learning style.* Provo, UT: Brigham Young University Press.

Hall, W. S., Reder, S., & Cole, M. (1979). Story recall in young Black and White children: Effects of racial group membership, race of experimenter, and dialect. In A. W. Boykin, A. J. Franklin, & J. F. Yates (Eds.), *Research directions of Black psychologists* (pp. 253–265). New York: Russell Sage Foundation.

Heath, S. B. (1982). Questioning strategies at home and at school: A comparative study. In G. Spindler (Ed.), *Doing the ethnography of schooling: Educational anthropology in action* (pp. 102–131). New York: Holt, Rinehart & Winston.

Hirsch, H. (1971). *Poverty and politicization: Political socialization in an American sub-culture.* New York: Free Press.

Hirschberg, N., Jones, L., & Haggerty, E. (1978). What's in a face: Individual difference in face perceptions. *Journal of Research in Personality, 12,* 488–499.

Holliday, B. G. (1985). Towards a model of teacher-child transactional processes affecting Black children's academic achievement. In M. B. Spencer, G. K. Brookins, & W. R. Allen (Eds.), *Beginnings: The social and affective development of Black children* (pp. 117–130). Hillsdale, NJ: Lawrence Erlbaum.

Jordan, C., Au, K. H. P., & Joestring, A. K. (1981). *Patterns of classroom interaction with Pacific Islands children: The implication of cultural differences.* (ERIC Document Reproduction Service No. ED 221 632)

Jordan, C. & Tharp, R. G. (1979). Culture and education. In A. J. Marsella, R. G. Tharp, & I. J. Ciborowski (Eds.), *Perspectives in cross-cultural psychology* (pp. 265–285). New York: Academic Press.

Justin, N. (1975). Culture conflict and Mexican-American achievement. In E. J. Ogletree & D. Garcia (Eds.). *Education of the Spanish-speaking urban child: A book of readings* (pp. 269–274). Springfield, IL: Charles C. Thomas.

Keating, P., & Oakes, J. (1988). *Access to knowledge: Breaking down school barriers to learning.* Denver: The Education Commission of the States.

Keefe, S. E., & Padilla, A. M. (1987). *Chicano ethnicity.* Albuquerque: University of New Mexico Press.

Kitano, H. H. L., & Daniels, R. (1988). *Asian Americans: Emerging minorities.* Englewood Cliffs, NJ: Prentice-Hall.

Knight, S. L., Waxman, H. C., & Padron, Y. N. (1987). Investigating Hispanic students' cognitive strategies in social studies. *Journal of Social Studies Research, 11,* 15–19.

Kochman, T. (1981). *Black and White styles in conflict.* Chicago: University of Chicago Press.

LeCompte, M. D. (1981). The Procrustean bed: Public schools, management systems, and minority students. In H. T. Trueba, G. P. Guthrie, & K. H. P. Au (Eds.), *Culture and the bilingual classroom: Studies in classroom ethnography* (pp. 178–195). Rowley, MA: Newbury House Publishers.

Lockart, B. L. (1978). *Cultural conflict: The Indian child in the non-Indian classroom.* (ERIC Document Reproduction Service No. ED 195 379)

Marshall, H. H. (1969). Learning as a function of task interest, reinforcement, and social class variables. *Journal of Educational Psychology, 60,* 133–137.

McDermott, R. (1987). Achieving school failure: An anthropological approach to illiteracy and social stratification. In G. D. Spindler (Ed.), *Education and cultural process: Anthropological approaches.* (2d ed., pp. 173–209). Prospect Heights, IL: Waveland Press.

Michaels, S., & Cazden, C. B. (1986). Teacher/child collaboration as oral preparation for literacy. In B. B. Schieffelin & P. Gilmore (Eds.), *The acquisition of literacy: Ethnographic perspectives* (pp. 132–154). Norwood, NJ: Ablex.

Mohatt, G., & Erickson, F. (1981). Cultural differences in teaching styles in an Odawa school: A sociolinguistic approach. In H. T. Trueba, G. P. Guthrie, & K. H. P. Au (Eds.), *Culture and the bilingual classroom* (pp. 105–119). Rowley, MA: Newbury House.

Montero, D. (1980). *Japanese Americans: Changing patterns of ethnic affiliation over three generations*. Boulder, CO: Westview Press.

Orasanu, J., Lee, C., & Scribner, S. (1979). Free recall: Ethnic and economic gap comparisons. *Child Development, 50,* 1100–1109.

Palleja, J. (1987). The impact of cultural identification on the behavior of second generation Puerto Rican adolescents. *Dissertation Abstracts International, 48,* 1541A. (University Microfilm No. 871543)

Pandolfo, J. M. (1985). Prior knowledge and the reading comprehension of linguistically/culturally diverse students. (ERIC Document Reproduction Service No. ED 255 863)

Perney, V. H. (1976). Effects of race and sex on field dependence-independence in children. *Perceptual and Motor Skills, 42,* 975–980.

Philips, S. U. (1985). Participant structures and communicative competence: Warm Springs children in community and classroom. In C. B. Cazden, V. P. John, & D. Hymes (Eds.). *Functions of language in the classroom* (pp. 370–394). Prospect Heights, IL: Waveland Press.

Pickcunas, D. D. (1986). *Analysis of Asian American early childhood practices and their implications for early childhood education.* (ERIC Document Reproduction Service No. ED 274 422)

Piestrup, A. M. (1973). *Black dialect interference and accommodation of reading instruction in first grade.* Monograph of the Language Behavior Research Laboratory. Berkeley: University of California.

Ramírez, M. III, & Castañeda, A. (1974). *Cultural democracy, bicognitive development and education.* New York: Academic Press.

Richmond, B. O. (1971). Creative and cognitive abilities of white and Negro children. *Journal of Negro Education, 40,* 111–116.

Shade, B. J. (1982). Afro-American cognitive style: A variable in school success? *Review of Educational Research, 52,* 219–244.

Shade, B. J. (1984a). *Afro-American patterns of cognition: A review of research.* (ERIC Document Reproduction Service No. ED 244 025)

Shade, B. J. (1985b). *The perceptual process in teaching and learning: Cross-ethnic comparisons.* (ERIC Document Reproduction Service No. ED 252 634)

Shade, B. J, (1986). Is there an Afro-American cognitive style? An exploratory study. *The Journal of Black Psychology, 13,* 13–16.

Shade, B. J., & Edwards, P. A. (1987). Ecological correlates of the educative style of Afro-American children. *Journal of Negro Education, 56,* 88–99.

Slavin, R. E. (1983). *Cooperative learning.* New York: Longman.

Slavin, R. E. (1987). *Cooperative learning: Student teams.* (2d ed.). Washington, DC: National Education Association.

Smith, R. R., & Lewis, R. (1985). Race as a self-schema affecting recall in black children. *The Journal of Black Psychology, 12,* 15–29.

Smitherman, G. (1977). *Talkin' and testifyin': The language of black America.* Boston: Houghton Mifflin Company.

Spindler, G. D. (1987). Why have minority groups in North America been disadvantaged by their schools? In G. D. Spindler (Ed.), *Education and cultural process: Anthropological approaches.* (2d ed., pp. 160–172). Prospect Heights, IL: Waveland Press.

Thomas, C. W. (1971). *Boys no more: A black psychologist view of community.* Beverly Hills, CA: Glencoe Press.

Thu, H. B. (1983). Meeting the needs of Indochinese students. *Momentum, 14,* 20–22.

Tong, B. R. (1978). Warriors and victims: Chinese American sensibility and learning styles. In L. Morris, G. Sather, & S. Scull (Eds.), *Extracting learning styles from social/cultural diversity: A study of five American minorities* (pp. 70–93). Normal, OK: Southwest Teacher Corps Network.

Webb, N. M. (1982). Student interaction and learning in small groups. *Review of Educational Research, 52,* 421–445.

White, J. J. (1985). What works for teachers: A review of ethnographic research studies as they inform issues of social studies curriculum and instruction. In W. B. Stanley (Ed.), *Review of research in social studies education, 1976–1983* (pp. 215–307).

Williams, I. J. (1975). *An investigation of the developmental stages of black consciousness.* Unpublished doctoral dissertation, University of Cincinnati.

Wilson, S. H. (1979). *Analysis of the concept of shared cognitive frameworks as a key to promoting school improvement.* (ERI Document Reproduction Service No. ED 229 474)

Witkin, H. A. (1967). A cognitive style approach to cross-cultural research. *International Journal of Psychology, 2,* 233–250.

Zeuli, J. S., & Floden, R. (1987). *Cultural incongruities and inequities of schooling: Implications for practice from ethnographic research.* (ERIC Document Reproduction Service No. ED 285 963)

13

SOCIAL STUDIES FOR STUDENTS AT-RISK AND WITH DISABILITIES

Charles K. Curtis

THE UNIVERSITY OF BRITISH COLUMBIA

Special educators are in general agreement with their social studies colleagues that preparation for citizenship is a primary function of social studies instruction (Curtis, 1978). Arguments for including citizenship in social studies for special education students are based on the concept of participatory democracy: All citizens in a democratic society are expected to share in the decision-making process. That is, they can vote in elections, join political parties and advocacy groups, run for public office, and take part in legitimate political activities. Failure to provide a particular group with instruction in the means of participation violates a basic tenet of our society by serving to exclude individuals from the democratic process. In this chapter, the research on social studies for disabled and at-risk students is examined, with particular focus on citizenship.

DEFINITIONS OF TERMS

A variety of terms has been used to identify the students with whom this chapter is concerned. Some terms used in the studies reviewed, such as *visual* or *hearing impairment, learning disabilities,* and *emotional disturbance,* are similar to the descriptors in The Education of All Handicapped Children Act of 1975 (PL 94-142). Subjects identified as EMR (educationally mentally retarded) students in studies conducted prior to 1975 would, under that legislation, have been identified as mildly mentally retarded. Several of the earlier studies were conducted with subjects referred to as *slow learners, low achievers, low ability students,* or *educationally disadvantaged students.* Throughout this chapter, these students will be referred to as

at-risk, a contemporary term that has been loosely defined (see, e.g., Slavin & Madden, 1987) to include students previously referred to by these and similar designations.

LITERATURE SEARCH PROCEDURES

The primary studies reviewed here were located by computer searches of *ERIC, Dissertation Abstracts, CEC Abstracts,* and *Psychological Abstracts,* using a number of descriptors of broad subject categories (e.g., handicapped children, slow learner, educable mentally retarded), programs (e.g., social studies, history, geography) and instructional methods (e.g., cooperative education, peer-tutoring). Additionally, a manual search was conducted. Included were the bibliographies and reference lists in over 200 articles, 59 *ERIC* reports, 15 dissertations, 14 National Council for the Social Studies and National Education Association publications, and 276 college-level textbooks for social studies or special education methods courses. This search yielded 39 primary studies of treatments to increase the knowledge, improve the skills, or modify the attitudes of disabled or at-risk students. Several studies were also located in which social studies curricula for special programs were analyzed, teaching practices in integrated and nonintegrated settings were examined, or student characteristics were investigated. The literature search failed to reveal any prior reviews in this area, although references to research conducted with disabled or at-risk students were found in several general reviews of social studies research (Armento, 1986; Crabtree, 1983; Shaver, 1987).

Reviewers were: John G. Herlihy, State University of New York at Geneseo; Julie Landeen, Cache County School District, Logan, Utah.

REVIEWS OF CURRICULA AND PROGRAMS FOR SPECIAL STUDENTS

Public Law 94-142 mandated in 1975 that disabled students are to be educated in the least restrictive environment with their nonhandicapped peers to the extent possible. Prior to PL 94-142, many students currently categorized as mildly mentally retarded or at-risk were educated in either separate schools or special classes. Examination of social studies curricula developed during the period between 1950 and 1975 for special education programs in a number of cities, states, and provinces in the United States and Canada (Curtis, 1978) indicated that although in the majority of the curricula citizenship was acknowledged as an instructional objective, for the most part, the curricula were simplifications of traditional history and civics courses. They were often designed to inculcate a sense of duty toward the maintenance of one's self, family, and home; to provide information about making and keeping friends; and to encourage the acceptance of community responsibilities. Other reviews of social studies curricula for special students prior to 1975 produced similar results (e.g., Bailey, 1968; Gozali & Gonwa, 1973; Stevens, 1958; Stroud, 1976; Uphoff, 1967): low expectations and an emphasis on law-abiding behavior and social living.

Several recent reports of investigations of social studies programs in both separate and mainstreamed settings were located. Sunal, Paul, and DeMary (1981) examined social studies curricula in elementary and secondary programs for students with hearing impairment and concluded that "curricula in a majority of programs provide minimal social studies education" (p. 71). Where social studies goals were listed, they tended to be focused on the learning of facts, rather than on process skills, and there were few suggestions to modify instructional approaches to accommodate hearing impaired students.

Patton, Polloway, and Cronin (1987) surveyed special education teachers in seven states to investigate the present state of social studies instruction for handicapped students. The majority (89%) of the 284 respondents were teaching mildly handicapped or learning-disabled students. Large percentages of special education teachers in resource-room programs (70%) and half-day instructional programs (61%) reported that their students received no social studies instruction. Furthermore, almost one quarter of the elementary teachers and one half of the secondary teachers of full-day, self-contained classes reported that they did not include instruction in social studies in their programs, and 20% of the teachers who taught social studies in their programs did so because they chose to, not because it was mandated.

Teaching practices in elementary mainstreamed social studies classes in Maryland were investigated in a survey conducted by Moore (1980). On the basis of 125 completed questionnaires (84% response rate), she concluded that most teachers presented information to integrated students in small amounts, divided assignments into short distinct parts, allowed the students more time to complete assignments, and asked questions that required less abstract thinking. Along similar lines, Romanoff (1987) observed teacher behavior in 18 mainstreamed and 18 self-contained special-education history classes in nine randomly selected high schools in New York City. He found that social studies teachers in mainstreamed classes had clearer objectives, were better organized, used a wider variety of methods and materials, used more reviews, and demonstrated a greater knowledge of their subject than did special-education teachers in self-contained settings.

STUDENT CHARACTERISTICS

Two studies were located (Curtis, 1978, 1981; Rosenberg, 1968) that pertained to the attributes of at-risk students. In one (Curtis, 1978, 1981), the attitudes toward fundamental freedoms of at-risk students were compared with those of other high school students in vocational and academic programs using the The Freedoms Scale (Curtis & Shaver, 1983). The at-risk students were less committed to democratic freedoms than were the other students.

At-risk learners are frequently characterized as possessing low self-esteem (Curtis, 1978). Self-esteem is particularly relevant for social studies as citizenship education. Rosenberg (1968) found that for a sample of over 1,000 high school students, political apathy was directly related to low self-esteem: Students with low self-esteem were less likely to engage in political discussions, demonstrated less interest in and knowledge of public affairs, were less able to identify political figures, and tended not to follow reports of significant events in the media.

STUDIES CONDUCTED WITH AT-RISK AND DISABLED STUDENTS

The 39 studies reviewed here were reported in journals ($n = 22$), doctoral dissertations ($n = 12$), unpublished reports ($n = 4$), and in a book chapter.

Theory as a Basis for Research

The theoretical bases for treatments were stated in 14 of the 39 reports. Of these, 6 also cited prior research to support experimental hypotheses. For 11 studies, treatments were based on prior research findings, but with no reference to theoretical underpinnings. The treatments for the remaining 14 studies appeared to be based on neither theory nor research.

Internal Validity

The 39 studies were coded for threats to internal validity (Campbell & Stanley, 1963). Experimental mortality was a threat in over one third ($n = 15$) of the students. In several studies that were conducted with intact classes, the number of subjects lost was large enough to seriously bias the results. Selection was a threat in 11 studies in which subjects were not randomly assigned. (As a matter of external validity, subjects were randomly selected from a population in only 2 studies.) Students from intact classes were randomly assigned to treatment and control groups in 16 studies. In 3 studies, intact classes were randomly assigned as treatment and control classes. In an additional 3 studies, school districts or schools were selected at random and then intact classes that met criteria for the study were either randomly assigned as treatment and control classes or used with the single-group, pretest-posttest design. It was not possible to discern the selection process in 5 studies.

History was of particular concern in 9 studies, where either no comparison group was used or the treatment was a curriculum project conducted over a long period of time. In at least 8 studies, pretest-posttest differences might have resulted from maturation.

Testing was a possible threat in 15 studies in which the dependent measures were judged to be highly reactive. Instrumentation posed a threat to internal validity in 9 studies; in several, instruments were modified between pretest and posttest administrations and even during the posttest administration.

Treatment validity was a possible threat in most of the studies: In only 9 studies did researchers attempt to verify that the treatment was implemented as designed.

Instrumentation

Researcher or teacher-made tests comprised the assessment instruments in half ($n = 20$) of the studies. Standardized tests were used in 5 studies, while assessment programs in 9 studies were composed of both researcher-made and standardized instruments. The source of the test for 1 study could not be determined. Reliability and/or validity data were reported in only 17 studies. Four researchers reported both reliability and validity data for scores on their dependent measures. Another 11 reported only reliability data, and 2 reported only validity information.

THE RESEARCH FINDINGS

Instructional Approaches

Among the instructional approaches investigated, two—inquiry and contemporary problems—are commonly described in the social studies literature. In a study by Miller and Weston (1947), pupils in a 10th-grade, "low-IQ geography class" were to examine the problem of diminishing water resources. A primary objective of the study was the development of critical-thinking skills through inquiry activities. No reference to sample selection was found in either the authors' article or the report of the Detroit Citizenship Education Study (Dimond, 1953), of which the study was a part. The mean posttest scores of the experimental students on the Wrightstone Test of Critical Thinking exceeded those of a control group on only one of the three aspects of critical thinking assessed by this instrument— "the ability to draw conclusions." When reports contained adequate information (means and standard deviations), standardized mean differences (*SMDs*) were computed as indicators of the magnitude of results. Where that information was missing but tests of statistical significance were reported (e.g., a *t*-ratio), SMDs were estimated (see, e.g., Glass, McGaw, & Smith, 1981).

However, for this study, neither the mean scores of the groups, the statistical tests, nor statistical significance were reported.

In another study (Curtis, 1978; Curtis & Shaver, 1980), 225 subjects were enrolled in special programs for at-risk high school students in six communities in British Columbia. During the 5-month period of the project, students used an inquiry approach to investigate the lack of adequate low-income housing in their community. Sources for the study included newspapers, magazine articles, government publications, and brochures from private interest groups. In critical-thinking lessons, students analyzed taped radio interviews and the publications of advocacy groups. They also undertook extensive field studies in their communities.

School districts were randomly selected for the study. In school districts where two comparable classes existed, the classes were randomly assigned to treatment or control groups. A single-group, pretest-posttest design was used where only one class was available. Based on theory and prior research, gains were predicted in interest in contemporary problems, open-mindedness, critical thinking, self-esteem, reading comprehension, and attitudes toward democratic freedoms. The assessment program included both published and researcher-developed instruments. Statistically significant differences in favor of the experimental group were found for all dependent variables except attitudes toward democratic freedoms. Similarly, the posttest scores of the classes in the single-group design were statistically significantly greater than their pretest scores on all measures. Attitude toward democratic freedoms was assessed only as a posttest and so no comparison could be made with the single-group design. As shown in Table 13–1, standardized mean differences (*SMDs*) from both designs for all variables except attitudes toward democratic freedoms ranged from just below medium (.44) for reading comprehension to very large (1.39) for interest in contemporary problems. Parents' responses (42% response rate) to a mailed questionnaire indicated that they supported the study of contemporary issues.

Inquiry was also the approach employed in the *Living in an Urban World* series, which was developed for at-risk high school students. Two dissertations (Sauers, 1974; Schubert, 1973) described the development and field testing of two series units. For each unit, students were to examine the historical and contemporary problems of a particular city. Materials produced and used in each study were a student textbook, a teacher's manual, and audiovisual aids. Historical and sociological concepts were taught to the students to be used to define problems, formulate and test hypotheses, and arrive at conclusions. Tests to assess knowledge, critical thinking, and inquiry skills, as well as attitudes towards learning, were developed for the studies. Both Sauers and Schubert concluded that pretest-posttest gains on these instruments indicated substantial gains in the areas assessed. However, the data were not analyzed statistically. Mean test scores were simply listed in tables and discussed. Since both of these were field studies, no attempt was made to control for extraneous variables, and no comparison groups were used.

Contemporary Problems. The Humanities Curriculum Project (Hamingson, 1973), which was conducted in a large number of

TABLE 13–1. Studies of Instructional Approaches

Author(s) Date	Randomly Selected	Randomly Assigned	Subjects	Grade(s)	N	Treatment	Treatment Length	Dependent Variable(s)	SMD[a]	p
Curtis (1978) Curtis & Shaver (1980)	By school district	By class	Slow learners Nonacademic	Special classes 9,10,11	E = 147 C = 78	Contemporary problems, inquiry	5–6 mos.	Interest in contemporary problems	1.39	.01
								Closed-mindedness	−.64	.01
								Critical thinking	.54	.01
								Self-esteem	.60	.05
								Reading	.44	.05
								Attitude toward democratic freedoms	−.14	ns
Fleming (1980)	By school		Learning disabled	4	6	Reinforcement for recall and explanation of teacher directions	25 periods	Social studies assignments	1.67	.00
Hamingson (1973)			Early school leavers of average to below-average ability	8,9	E = 228 C = 145	Controversial issues	3–5 years	Reading comprehension		.05
								Vocabulary		.05
								Hostility reduction		.05
								Self-esteem		.05
								Personality		
								Awareness of social problems		.05
Miller & Weston (1947)			Slow learners	10	E = 1 class C = 1 class	Contemporary problems, inquiry	1 semester	Critical thinking		
Rackman (1974)	By school	By individual	EMR students	Special classes high school	E = 19 P = 19 C = 19	Moral-judgment training	7 weeks	Stages of moral development		
								Posttest		
								E vs. P	.99	.05
								E vs. C	.45	.05
								Follow-up		
								E vs. P	.11	ns
								E vs. C	.12	ns
Sauers (1974)			Slow learners	10,11	17	Historical and contemporary problems, inquiry, concept development, values clarification and analysis	1 term	Attitude toward learning		
								Study skills		
								Inquiry skills		
								Knowledge of content		
Schubert (1973)			Slow learners, low achievers	10	21	Historical and contemporary problems, inquiry, concept development, values clarification and analysis	2 mos.	Lower-level thinking		
								Higher-level thinking		
								Self-concept		
								Attitude toward learning		
								Knowledge of content		

[a]Standardized mean differences (SMDs) were computed as effect sizes in 3 studies. Criteria for small (.20), medium or moderate (.50), and large (.80) SMDs were those suggested by Cohen (1977).

British secondary schools during the period 1968 to 1972, was a major study involving at-risk students in investigations of contemporary problems. The purpose of this study was to examine a strategy for teaching about controversial problems in areas such as poverty, employment, and family responsibilities with 16-year old, average to below-average students during their final school year. Discussions in project classrooms were to be based on materials prepared for the project. These discussions were chaired by teachers who were to refrain from expressing opinions and who were responsible for keeping students' comments focused on the topic.

Based on classroom observations and interviews with teachers and students, Hamingson concluded that treatment differences existed not only between but also within project schools and that support for the project varied among teachers and administrators. Consequently, Hamilton recommended that the findings of the study be considered with caution.

Student outcomes were assessed by a battery of 21 instruments, either modified from existing tests or developed by project staff. Reliability and validity information were not reported, nor were the statistical tests used to analyze the data. It appears likely that only within-group pretest-posttest means were compared, rather than the mean gain scores of the project students and control students selected from nonproject schools. Tests were administered at several times and to different groups of project and control students throughout the four-year period. For a sample of 226 16-year old students leaving school at the end of the ninth grade who had been in the project for one year, pretest to posttest mean gains were statistically significant for measures of reading and self-concept. Mean gains for vocabulary, abstract thinking, emotional stability, and self-sufficiency were not statistically significant. Based on the data for all project students, Hamingson concluded that the "most stable effects of the project . . . are increased reading levels, vocabulary levels, and self-esteem" (p. 453).

Moral Education. One study (Rackman, 1974) was located in which a strategy for modifying stages of moral development was the treatment. In this study, Kohlberg's cognitive-developmental model of moral reasoning provided the theoretical basis for the intervention for raising moral-reasoning levels in EMR students. Fifty-seven EMR students were randomly assigned to experimental, placebo, and control groups. Students in the treatment group were presented with moral dilemmas. As they considered each dilemma, the teacher conducted the discussion on a moral level one stage higher than the average for the class. The placebo students played mathematics and word games and discussed current events. Activities in the experimental and placebo classrooms continued over a 7-week period with three 45-minute sessions each week. Pretreatment stages of moral development were assessed by an individually administered test that had each student respond to questions about moral dilemmas. The posttest and a follow-up test three months later were administered in a similar manner. Stages of moral development were recorded in a contingency table with two levels (preconventional and conventional) and analyzed with the chi-square test of independence.

A χ^2 of 2.37 for pretest stages was not statistically significant

($p > .05$). A χ^2 of 6.76 ($p < .05$) indicated a statistically significant difference among the three groups on the posttest, attributed to a greater proportion of the experimental students who achieved higher moral stage scores. An *SMD* of .92 was estimated for the experimental and placebo group comparison and .45 for the experimental and control group comparison. No statistically significant differences were reported for the moral stages of the three groups on the follow-up test. Comparisons of the stages of the experimental students with stages of students in the placebo and control groups on the follow-up test yielded estimated *SMD*s of .11 and .12, respectively. Rackman suggested that pretest sensitization serving as an advanced organizer might have been a factor in the pretest-posttest increase of the experimental students. He proposed that moral dilemmas that are more relevant and personal to EMR students might increase the duration of the effects.

Reinforcement. In a study by Fleming (1980), reinforcement theory underlay a treatment to reduce the degree to which six learning-disabled students in two mainstreamed fourth-grade social studies classes relied on their tutor for assistance and to increase their ability to work independently, to follow written and oral directions, and to complete in-class assignments. Daily lessons consisted of directions by the teacher at the beginning of the period followed by questions from either the textbook or a work sheet to be completed during the remainder of the period. The treatment consisted of the tutor awarding each child points for being able to identify the page of the textbook or worksheet that was assigned and stating which items were to be completed and how this was to be done. Points awarded at the end of each period could be used to purchase, among other rewards, pencils, felt markers, and lunch with the tutor.

The mean z-scores for the learning disabled students' daily assignments increased from a baseline of -1.19 to .49 during treatment, indicating, on the average, improvement in the position of their achievement scores in the distributions of scores for the total classes. Fleming concluded that reinforcement techniques that strengthen attention to teacher directions can result in increases in achievement.

Teaching Strategies

Strategies for teaching about democratic rights, increasing thinking skills, helping students identity problems in value dilemmas and social situations, and assisting students to learn textbook content were examined in 13 of the 39 studies.

Teaching About Democratic Rights. Jones (1964) examined the efficacy of the case method for teaching the Bill of Rights. At-risk students ($n = 123$) enrolled in 4 of the 14 eighth-grade American history classes included in the study comprised 23% of the sample. Sixty-eight percent of these students scored below 90 on the Henman-Nelson Test of Mental Ability. Students in classes selected from among those volunteered by their teachers read sections of the textbook which described the history of the Bill of Rights, viewed and discussed a film, and then examined five case studies. Assignments consisted of complet-

TABLE 13-2. Studies of Teaching Strategies

Author(s) Date	Subjects	Randomly Selected	Randomly Assigned	Grade(s)	N	Treatment	Treatment Length	Dependent Variable(s)	SMD[a]	p
Teaching About Democratic Rights										
Jones (1964)	Low-ability students			8	103	Case studies of the Bill of Rights	2 weeks	Knowledge of and acceptance of democratic principles		
Thibeault (1971)	Low-IQ students		By class	12	One-sided = 4, Two-sided = 9, C = 11	One-sided and two-sided arguments	22–25 min.	Acceptance of democratic rights		.01
Teaching Higher-Level Thinking Skills										
Holdt (1976)	Hearing-impaired students		By class	2nd-grade reading ability	76; A = 7 classes, B = 7 classes	A = 70% knowledge and 30% higher-level questions; B = 30% knowledge and 70% higher-level questions	8 weeks	Higher-level thinking skills	−1.12	.01
Teaching Problem Recognition										
VanSickle (1978)	Slow learners from 3 high schools	By individual		9,10	$E_1 = 12$, $E_2 = 12$, $E_3 = 12$, $E_4 = 12$, $E_5 = 12$	Variations in concreteness (utilizing pictures and audio tapes)	5–10 min.	Identification of dilemma		ns
								Courses of action to resolve dilemma		ns
Woolard (1974)	Slow learners	By individual		9–12	E = 22, C = 21	Perceptual readiness through simulation	?	Problem recognition		ns
Teaching Textbook Content										
Baines (1967–1968)	Slow learners		By class	10	E = 2 classes, C = 2 classes	Modified textbook and audio and visual materials	1 year	Knowledge of content		.01
Bean & Pardi (1979)	Corrective readers			7	$E_1 = 18$, $C_1 = 21$, $E_2 = 19$, $C_2 = 17$	Guided reading strategy	?	Knowledge of content — Posttest	1.13	.01
								Follow-up	.71	ns
								Posttest	.79	.05
								Follow-up	1.04	.00
Darch & Carnine (1986)	Learning disabled	By individual		4,5,6	E = 12, C = 12	Visual spatial displays and group learning	9 periods	Knowledge of content	1.59	.01
								Transfer	.70	ns
LeSourd (1985)	Poor readers	By individual			E = 30, C = 30	Textual structuring for concept attainment	1 period	Concept attainment	.44	ns
Mosby (1979)	Learning disabled			junior high school	50	Regular social studies program supplemented by audio materials	1 year	SAT Social Studies	.54	.05
								Social Studies grades	.10	ns
Tyo (1980)	Poor readers			junior high school	104; E = ?, C = ?	Audio tapes of selections from textbook	1 semester	Knowledge of content	.68	.01
Wilson (1967)	Slow learners			11	167	Modified textbook	1 year	MAT Reading	.35	.01
								MAT SS Skills	.16	.05
								MAT SS Vocabulary	.21	.05
								MAT SS Information	.17	ns
								Knowledge of content	.66	.01
Wong et al. (1986)	Learning disabled			7, 8	5, 3	Summarization strategy	2–3 mos	Summarization skills	Data indicated improvement	

aStandardized mean differences (SMDs) were computed as effect sizes in 7 studies. Criteria for small (.20), medium or moderate (.50), and large (.80). SMDs were those suggested by Cohen (1977).

ing worksheets, taking part in debates, reading newspapers, interviewing guest speakers, and, finally, writing their own cases.

Mean pretest and posttest scores on a researcher-developed test to measure attitudes toward and knowledge of the Bill of Rights were placed on graphs and described, without the use of statistical tests. The mean gain scores of the at-risk students for both attitude and knowledge were modest. An instrument to assess ability to discern whether rights in a case study had been violated was revised during the posttest administration when it was found that students had difficulty recording subjective responses. According to Jones, data collected with this instrument revealed that students in low-ability classes could identify rights in a case study but had difficulty determining whether they had been violated.

Thibeault (1971) compared a single-argument approach with a balanced or two-argument approach for increasing acceptance of basic rights with students ($N = 742$) in Grade-12 civics classes. Intact classes were randomly assigned either to one of two treatment groups or to a control group. Treatment A, the propaganda approach, consisted of a 22-minute slide-tape presentation that contained strong arguments in favor of the principles in the Bill of Rights. Treatment B, the augmented approach, consisted of the same slides but the 25-minute audio tape presented "emotional and conflicting points of view" concerning civil rights. The treatments were administered in the school auditorium. Students in the control class continued on with their regular work.

The assessment program consisted of the pre-posttest administration of a researcher-developed test purported to measure attitudes toward the rights and legal procedures in the Bill of Rights. Thibeault interpreted the statistically significant difference among treatment means as indicating that the mean scores of the treatment groups were significantly greater than the mean score of the control group, although group means were not paired and compared.

The data were also grouped according to four levels of IQ scores and analyzed. The interaction of treatment and IQ was statistically significant, but means and standard deviations for IQ levels were not reported. Correlation coefficients (Pearson product-moment r) for the relationship between IQ and treatment in each group (A = $-.40$; B = $.38$; Control = $.04$) were interpreted by Thibeault to indicate that at-risk students are more likely to accept civil rights when presented with a one-sided argument than with a balanced approach. The loss of 123 subjects (17%) creates difficulty in interpreting the results. Threats to internal validity and incomplete data analysis characterized both this study and the preceding study by Jones (1964).

Teaching Higher-Level Thinking Skills.

Higher-level cognitive skills constituted the dependent variable in a study conducted with students enrolled in residential facilities and regional day programs for hearing-impaired children (Holdt, 1976). Knowledge and higher-level questions based on Bloom's taxonomy were developed for teaching the concepts *rules* and *location*. Students grouped according to communication system were randomly assigned to either Treatment A, which consisted of 70% knowledge-level questions and 30% higher-level questions, or Treatment B, the reverse. Within each treatment, two

communications systems were compared. Students in classes in which a total communication system was utilized used signed English to complement speech, speechreading, and the amplification of residual hearing. Students in the partial communication classes did not use signed English.

The posttest mean score of the students in Treatment B on a researcher-developed instrument designed to measure understanding of the concepts and the ability to use high-level cognitive skills was significantly greater ($p < .01$) than the mean for students in Treatment A. The *SMD* for this difference was large (1.12). This finding was consistent with the findings from earlier studies (e.g., Ryan, 1973) conducted with normal-functioning students. A second important finding was that regardless of the treatment, the mean scores of students in the partial communications classes were statistically significantly higher than the mean scores of the students in the total communications classes (*SMD* = 1.08).

Teaching Problem Recognition.

Value dilemmas frequently involve events or conditions that are foreign to students' experiences. VanSickle (1978) investigated the use of audio and visual materials for making such value dilemmas comprehensible to at-risk students. Students in 9th and 10th-grade slow-learner classes in two junior high schools were randomly assigned to one of five treatment groups. Treatment conditions lasted from 5 to 10 minutes and varied in degree of "experimental concreteness." Treatments were: (a) an audio tape of the teacher describing an international crisis faced by the president of the United States; (b) the teacher describing the president's crisis; (c) an audio tape of the teacher's description accompanied by eight pictures related to the audio description; (d) an audio tape of the teacher role-playing the president describing his crisis; and (e) the same audio tape as used in (d) but accompanied by the pictures in (c).

On the posttest the students were asked to describe the dilemma, identify possible courses of action, and suggest the possible consequences of each. No statistically significant differences were found among the mean scores of the five groups. However, mean z-scores for students in Treatment C were almost half a standard deviation greater than the mean z-scores for students in Treatments A, B, and D for description of the dilemma, and for students in Treatments B, D, and E for prediction of consequences. Nevertheless, VanSickle concluded that the findings failed to support the supposition that "concrete, experiential presentations will enable naive learners to learn a body of information more easily" (p. 66).

The first step in the inquiry model is the recognition of a problem or incongruity. Whether at-risk learners can recognize problems or incongruities in social situations was the question investigated by Woolard (1974). At-risk students enrolled in 9th through 12th-grade social studies classes were randomly assigned to treatment or control groups. The treatment, based on Bruner's (1975) model of problem perception, consisted of having students view cartoons of social situations that contained incongruities (e.g., a meeting of the Ku Klux Klan at which the members are told by the Grand Dragon to recruit Blacks). As they considered the situation in each cartoon, they responded to questions that caused them to focus on their own expectations. If students failed to perceive incongruities, they were given a series of questions intended to make them reexamine their perceptions of the events portrayed in the cartoons.

A posttest designed to assess problem recognition consisted of six cartoons, four with incongruities and two without. Absenteeism was high (35%) during the posttest administration. Nonparametric tests used to treat nominal and ordinal posttest data yielded statistically nonsignificant results.

Teaching Textbook Content. Mildly retarded, learning-disabled, and hearing-impaired students are likely to experience serious reading difficulties in integrated classrooms (Gearheart & Weishahn, 1980). This is a particular problem in social studies, where many textbooks have readability levels well beyond grade level (Bradley, Ames, & Mitchell, 1980).

Two studies were located in which strategies for helping at-risk and disabled students read and understand textbook material were investigated. Bean and Pardi (1979) employed a guided reading strategy to increase the reading comprehension of 7th-grade geography students indentified as corrective readers. Comparable students in a second geography class comprised the control group. Students in the experimental group read chapters in the textbook concentrating on titles, subtitles, vocabulary lists, graphs, charts, maps, and chapter questions. When each chapter was completed, the teacher asked what the students could remember about the content and recorded their answers on the board. Missing information was searched out and added to the information on the board, which was organized into a topical outline.

Short-term comprehension was assessed by a teacher-made, 10-item true-false test. The difference between the posttest means of the experimental students and the control students, who had simply read the textbook without guidance from the teacher, was statistically significant and yielded an estimated *SMD* of 1.13. A follow-up test administered one week later to assess long-term comprehension yielded an estimated *SMD* of .71. The study was replicated with the two groups exchanging positions. Differences between the means of the experimental and control groups were statistically significant in favor of the experimental students for both immediate (estimated *SMD* = .79) and delayed tests (estimated *SMD* = 1.21).

Five seventh- and three eighth-grade students categorized as underachievers and learning disabled were the subjects in a study by Wong, Wong, Perry, and Sawatsky (1986). During a baseline period, students summarized and then attempted to recall the information in an expository passage. Treatment consisted of teaching students how to identify the main sentence in a paragraph and how to summarize paragraphs. Worksheets for recording main-idea sentences and important details were provided to assist them. For a 3-month period, students met individually with researchers for three 30-minute (seventh-graders) or 50-minute (eighth-graders) sessions a week, during which time they summarized selections from their social studies textbooks. This was followed by the maintenance phase of the study, as students continued to summarize and recall information from paragraphs.

On transfer and follow-up tests, the students were asked to summarize selections from textbooks not used previously. On the basis of individual test scores that varied from 50% to 90%, the authors concluded that summarization skills had been learned successfully. They noted, however, that the length of time required for the process was almost 5 1/2 months and that some teachers might object to treatments of this length, regardless of their effectiveness. Moreover, they reported motivational problems with several of the students. For reasons not explained in their report, they did not assess social studies achievement.

Mosby (1979) and Tyo (1980) sought to bypass the effects of deficit reading skills by providing students with recorded selections from the textbook. Neither researcher attempted to increase reading skills. Mosby's sample of junior high school students with learning disabilities attended regular social studies classes but listened to required readings on audio tapes. Their pretest-posttest mean gain on the Stanford Achievement Test (SAT), Social Studies Subtest, was statistically significant and yielded a medium estimated *SMD* (.54). No improvement was found for teacher-assigned grades (estimated *SMD* = −.10).

Tyo (1980) also selected his sample from junior high school students, in this case, from among "poor readers." Students in the experimental group listened to audio tapes of the selections as they read from the social studies textbook. Comparable students in the control group read the same selections but were not provided with taped versions. Classes for both groups met one period daily for a semester. A medium *SMD* (.68) estimated for a test to assess comprehension of social studies content indicated a higher mean for the students who used audio tapes.

Darch and Carnine (1986) attempted to bypass reading deficits by employing visual spatial displays. Elementary learning-disabled students were randomly assigned to either a visual display group or a text group. Treatment in the visual display group consisted of the teacher showing and discussing a picture that illustrated the interrelationships among several concepts (e.g., flora, fauna, and industry in a mountainous region). Students were given an outline of the picture and asked to fill in the blank areas. Then, divided into small groups, they played games that required them to identify specific detail (e.g., changes in vegetation that occur with increased elevation). Students in the text group read passages aloud that covered the same content. Then, organized into small study groups, they practiced an outlining procedure that had them identify headings and subheadings, develop questions related to the passage, and identify important details.

A 9-item multiple choice test to measure recall of information was administered as a posttest. A transfer test was also administered to assess students' ability to apply a visual display after reading a passage unrelated to the topic studied. An *SMD* of 1.67 for the information test was due to a higher mean for the visual group. Similarly, the mean score of the visual group exceeded that of the text group on the transfer test (*SMD* = .70). The authors concluded that visual spatial displays combined with a group task structure comprised an effective strategy for increasing comprehension.

LeSourd (1985) hypothesized that students using a passage of text organized according to a concept presentation model would score significantly higher on a concept attainment test than control students who read expository material. Both groups, consisting of students reading three years below grade level, read passages describing political interest groups; however, the passage prepared for the experimental group included a clear specification of the concept name, a formally stated concept definition, a list of necessary attributes, an explanation of irrelevant attributes, and the extensive description of two concept examples and one nonexample. A comparison of the means of the two groups on the posttest yielded a median *SMD* (.44), with the higher mean that of the students taught with the concept attainment model.

Whether social studies texts prepared specifically for at-risk students enhance learning was the question investigated by Baines (1967–1968) and Wilson (1967). Two textbooks by Abramowitz, *American History Study Lessons* and *Basic Learning Program in World History* were examined. Both textbooks were prepared for high school slow-learner classes, with reading levels that varied from the sixth to ninth-grade. Vocabulary development was emphasized, and chapters were introduced with outlines and significant questions. Documents, pictures, maps, charts, and graphs were included in each chapter.

The subjects in Baines' (1967–1968) study were enrolled in Grade-10 world history classes. Four intact classes were randomly assigned as experimental or control groups. Students in the experimental classes were taught from the Abramowitz textbook, whereas students in the control group used the regular textbook. Lessons in the experimental classes were supplemented by additional texts and audiovisual materials not available to the control classes. The addition of these materials confounded the treatment, and the finding that the posttest mean score on the Cooperative Social Studies Test and teacher-assigned grades were statistically significantly higher for the treatment group must be viewed in that light. Absenteeism declined in the experimental classes, and teachers noted increased interest, motivation, a more relaxed attitude, and a greater willingness to participate on the part of their students. Nevertheless, teachers of the experimental classes concluded that world history was too "sophisticated" for a slow-learning students.

Wilson's (1967) report described a pilot study designed to examine procedures for setting up a program for at-risk learners. The use of the Abramowitz text with at-risk students (*N* = 167) enrolled in a grade-11 American history course was evaluated. A battery of standardized tests were administered to assess social studies achievement and reading. Students' scores were described as percentile rankings. Standardized mean differences calculated from these data varied from very small (.16) to medium (.66) for social studies achievement, with an average *SMD* of .30. A small *SMD* (.35) was determined for reading achievement. Contrary to the findings of the preceding study, behavioral problems did not decrease as this study progressed.

Procedures for Organization Instruction

Fifteen of the 39 studies examined procedures for organizing instruction in segregated or mainstreamed social studies classes. In the majority of these studies, the cooperative learning approach was compared with competitive and/or individualistic approaches. Other studies investigated the effects of peer-tutoring and individualized instruction on social studies achievement.

Cooperative Learning. Most of the studies conducted by David and Roger Johnson and their associates were characterized by the following: (a) students in several intact mainstreamed classes in a "midwestern metropolitan area school" were randomly assigned to treatment and control classes; (b) initial differences between classes were neither assessed nor considered in the analysis of the posttests; (c) handicapped children, usually with learning disabilities or behavioral problems, were equally represented in all learning groups; (d) treatment verification consisted of classroom observations by project staff; and (e) assessment programs included researcher-developed instruments for recording sociometric choices and for observing student interactions.

Johnson and Johnson (1981, 1984) and Smith, Johnson, and Johnson (1982) compared cooperative learning with individualistic instruction in elementary classes in which learning disabled and emotionally disturbed children were integrated. Approximately one quarter of the students in two studies (Johnson & Johnson, 1981; 1984) were handicapped learners. In the remaining study (Smith et al., 1982), 7 of the 55 students fit this category. Social studies topics included lifestyles of the Ojibwe and Dakota Indians (Johnson & Johnson, 1981) and a recreation area in Minnesota (Johnson & Johnson, 1984; Smith et al., 1982). Students in the cooperative conditions were organized into groups of four members each and assigned tasks to be completed as a group. Teachers praised and rewarded the group as a whole. Students in the individualistic conditions worked on their own on the same tasks, avoiding interactions with other students. In this setting, individual achievement was praised and rewarded.

Assessment programs consisted of measures of interaction and attitude between handicapped and nonhandicapped students. Mean scores were reported in tables by group but analyzed by treatment condition. The authors concluded (based on levels of statistical significance that varied from .01 to .15) that in each study, interpersonal attraction between handicapped and nonhandicapped students in the cooperative condition exceeded that for the individualistic condition. In the two studies (Johnson & Johnson, 1984; Smith et al., 1982) in which social studies achievement was also assessed, the mean scores for the handicapped students in the cooperative conditions on teacher-made tests were higher than the mean scores for comparable students in the individualistic groups. In the Smith et al. study, the mean score of the handicapped students in the cooperative condition on a measure of self-esteem also exceeded the mean score for comparable students in the individualistic group. In the one instance (Johnson & Johnson, 1981) where handicapped students were compared on participation, a moderate to large *SMD* (.77) was estimated (in favor of the students in the cooperative group).

In another study, Johnson and Johnson (1982) compared the effects of cooperative and competitive learning on interpersonal attraction between handicapped and nonhandicapped students. Ten of the 51 fourth-grade students were either learning disabled or behaviorally disturbed. Coal as an energy

TABLE 13-3. Studies of Procedures for Organizing Instruction

Author(s) Date	Subjects	Randomly Selected Assigned	Grade(s)	N	Treatment	Treatment Length	Dependent Variable(s)	SMD[a]	p
					Cooperative Learning				
Allen & VanSickle (1984)	Low achievers	By class	9	E = 23 C = 28	Student teams-achievement divisions (STAD)	6 weeks	Knowledge of content Self-concept	.94 .22	.05 ns
Cooper, Johnson, et al. (1980)	Nonhandicapped, learning-disabled, & emotionally disturbed students	By individual	7	60 (H = 12)	Cooperative vs. competitive vs. individual learning	15 periods	Helping H students to learn (coop. vs. comp. & indiv.) Making friends with H (coop. vs. comp. & indiv.)	.96 .62	.01 ns
Farran (1969)	Underachievers	By individual	8	123	Group competition vs. individual competition	16 hours	Knowledge of content Attitude toward learning	−.47 −.47	.01 .01
Johnson & Johnson (1981)	Nonhandicapped, learning-disabled, & behaviorally disturbed students	By individual	4	51 (H = 12)	Cooperative vs. individual learning	16 periods	Intergroup interaction H participation	.46–2.89 .77	.01–.15 ns
Johnson & Johnson (1982)	Nonhandicapped, learning-disabled, & behaviorally disturbed students	By individual	4	51 (H = 10)	Cooperative vs. competitive learning	15 periods	Intergroup interaction Cross-handicap helping		.01–.05 .01
Johnson & Johnson (1983)	Nonhandicapped, learning-disabled, & behaviorally disturbed students	By individual	4	59 (H = 12)	Cooperative vs. competitive vs. individual learning	15 periods	Intergroup interaction (coop. vs. comp. & indiv.) Self-esteem (coop. vs. comp. & indiv.)	−.95–3.30	.01 .01–.10
Johnson & Johnson (1984)	Nonhandicapped, learning-disabled, & emotionally disturbed students	By individual	4	48 (H = 12)	Cooperative vs. individual learning	15 periods	H knowledge of content Cross-handicap attraction	1.12 .47–2.45	.05 .01–.05
Johnson & Johnson (1985)	Nonhandicapped, learning-disabled, & behaviorally disturbed students	By individual	6	72 (H = 27)	Cooperative controversy vs. cooperative debate vs. individual learning	11 periods	Interpersonal attraction (highest X for coop. controversy) Cross-handicap interaction		.00–.10

Study	Subjects	Assignment	N	Grade	Treatment	Duration	Dependent variable	Effect size[a]
Slavin (1977)	Special-needs students	By individual	39 E = 21 C = 18	8,9	Teams-games-tournament (TGT)	12 weeks	(highest X for coop. controversy) Attitude toward learning (greatest no. of frequencies for coop. controversy) On-task and peer-task behavior Follow-up test of the above	.00–.05 .00–.10 .05 .00
Smith et al. (1982)	Nonhandicapped (regular & gifted), & academically handicapped students	By individual	55 (H = 7)	6	Cooperative vs. individual learning	5 65-min. periods	Mutual attraction, helpfulness, and interaction on task Knowledge of content Retention (same as above) Liking for peers Self-esteem as a student	.10 .01 .01 .01 .05
Yager et al. (1985)	High-, medium-, & low-ability students	By individual	84 (low ability = 28)	3	Cooperative with group processing vs. cooperative and individual learning	25 periods	Knowledge of content Retention (same as above)	.00 .00
Individualized Instruction								
Kourilsky, Ballard-Campbell (1984)	Low-ability (X̄ IQ = 82)	From IQ strata	60	3–6	Minisociety instructional system	?	Economic decision-making Attitude toward school Attitude toward learning	1.35 .61 .98
Peer-Tutoring								
Maheady, Harper, & Sacca (1988)	Learning-disabled, behaviorally disordered, & EMR students		20	9, 10-12	Classwide peer-tutoring system (CWPT)	1 semester	Knowledge of content	Data indicated improvement
Maheady, Sacca, & Harper (1988)	Nonhandicapped & mildly handicapped students		50 (H = 14)	10	Classwide peer-tutoring system (CWPT)	1 semester	Knowledge of content	Data indicated improvement

[a]Standardized mean differences (SMDs) were computed as effect sizes in 7 studies. Criteria for small (.20), medium or moderate (.50), and large (.80) SMDs were those suggested by Cohen (1977).

source and the wolf as an endangered species were the topics studied. Students in the cooperative condition worked in groups as in the preceding studies. Students in the competitive condition worked individually as in the individualistic condition, but, in addition, they were instructed to work better than their peers. Assignments were collected and graded daily. The five highest-ranking students in the competitive condition received praise from the teacher. The mean scores on several measures purported to assess interpersonal attraction between handicapped and nonhandicapped students were reported and analyzed by condition but not by student group. Based on levels of statistical significance that varied from .01 to .10, the authors concluded that the cooperative group exceeded the competitive group on both number of handicapped-nonhandicapped free-time interactions and instances of cross-handicapped helping.

Cooperative learning was compared with competitive and with individualistic learning by Johnson and Johnson (1983) and Cooper, Johnson, Johnson, and Wilderson (1980). In the former study, fourth-grade students studied the units developed for the Johnson and Johnson (1982) study described above. In the Cooper et al. study, seventh-grade students studied map reading in geography. In both groups, 12 students were described as being learning disabled or behaviorally disturbed. Data in both studies were reported and analyzed only by treatment condition. Levels of statistical significance varied from .01 to .10, with the findings similar to the findings in the preceding studies. Interpersonal relationships between handicapped and nonhandicapped students were greater, and more nonhandicapped students choose handicapped peers as friends in the cooperative groups (estimated *SMD*s varied from .62 to .96). In the Johnson and Johnson study, estimated *SMD*s for the three measures of self-esteem varied from $-.95$ to 2.45 for the cooperative versus competitive and individual comparisons.

Several variations of the preceding studies were also located. Johnson and Johnson (1985) compared the effects of cooperative controversy, cooperative debate, and individualistic learning on cross-handicap interaction, peer support, and self-esteem. Twenty-seven of the 72 sixth-grade students in the study had severe learning or behavioral problems. The treatment in the cooperative controversy condition consisted of presenting one pair of students in each four-member group with arguments for protecting and conserving wolves and the second pair with arguments for hunting and killing wolves. Members of each group assumed roles within their position (e.g., hunter, conservationist) and presented their opinions to the other members. Each group prepared a report in which a consensus opinion was argued. Students in the cooperative debate condition were organized in a similar manner, but each group member competed with the other members to see who could present the best argument for his or her position. In the individualistic condition, students were asked to examine the materials and to learn as much as they could about the two positions.

The analysis of data revealed more interactions ($p < .001$ to .10) between handicapped and nonhandicapped students in the two cooperative conditions than in the individualistic condition. Additionally, the nonhandicapped students in the cooperative controversy groups were more concerned ($p < .001$) than similar students in the cooperative debate groups that handicapped members learn the materials. Mean self-esteem (success as a student) scores were highest for the handicapped students in the cooperative groups.

Another variation (Yager, Johnson, Johnson, & Snider, 1985) included group processing in one of the two cooperative conditions. Third-grade students ($N = 84$) were stratified according to ability levels and randomly assigned to one of three treatments. In the cooperative condition with group processing, students discussed how well their group was functioning and what could be done to make it more effective. The second cooperative condition and the individualistic condition were similar to those in other studies. Students in all conditions studied a unit on transportation. The dependent variable was achievement, as assessed by teacher-made tests to measure factual recall. Ability groups were not compared; however, the overall mean of the cooperative condition with group processing was greater ($p < .001$) than the overall means for the two other conditions. A similar pattern occurred for the overall mean scores of the groups on a retention test administered three weeks after the completion of the unit.

In his report of a cooperative learning study, Slavin (1977) described the teams-games-tournament (TGT) approach. This study was conducted in two social studies classes in a middle school for students of normal intelligence who have been identified as having "difficulties with academic tasks, human relationships, and/or self-organization" (p. 79). The 39 students were randomly assigned to experimental and control groups. The treatment period covered 12 weeks, during which time students studied American history. In the experimental class, students as members of teams prepared for tournaments by attempting to answer history questions from cards developed for the study. Students representing their respective teams played in tournaments once a week. Students in the control class worked occasionally with friends on assignments, but for the most part they worked individually.

The dependent variables were time on task and selection of class friends. The analysis of frequency data collected during classroom observations revealed that the TGT students were on task significantly more often than the control students (84.6% vs. 81.1%; $p = < .01$). A number of statistically significant differences on items in the sociometric measure of class friends indicated to Slavin that a higher level of mutual peer attraction existed in the TGT class than in the control class. Follow-up observations five months after the conclusion of the study and with the students now in different classes revealed that the students who had been in the TGT program still interacted more with their peers than did the students who had been in the control class (8.6% vs. 1.5%; $p = < .001$). A statistically significant ($p < .05$) portion of this time, however, consisted of inappropriate behavior.

Other researchers have also examined the effects of team learning with at-risk learners. Farran (1969) hypothesized that games played in a group competitive situation would result in greater learning and more positive attitudes than would games in which competitors played individually. Underachievers enrolled in a summer session at a residential school were randomly assigned to eight house groups. Students in four houses played the Consumer Game and the Life Career Game in a group competitive manner. Student scores were totaled by house and compared. In the remaining four houses, individual winners were named and total game scores for houses were not compared. Mean posttest scores on researcher-made tests to assess game knowledge and its applicability to real life were statistically significantly higher (estimated SMD = .47) for the individual competition group. The pretest-posttest mean increase in scores on a standardized measure of attitude toward learning was greater (p < .01) for the individual group (estimated SMD = .47). Farran rejected his initial hypotheses.

In Allen and VanSickle's (1984) study, students in a ninth-grade class for low achievers were organized into teams during a six-week study on sub-Saharan Africa. Similar students in a second ninth-grade class were the comparison group. The independent variable was team learning. Working in teacher-assigned teams, the experimental students read selections from the text, discussed films, did map assignments, and completed worksheets. Points were earned for scores on quizzes. The difference between the posttest means of the groups on a test of knowledge of sub-Saharan Africa was statistically significant, in favor of the experimental group (SMD = .94). However, the difference between the posttest means of the two groups on a measure of self-esteem was not statistically significant and the SMD was small (.22).

Peer-Tutoring. Maheady, Sacca, and Harper (1988) examined the effects of a peer-tutoring program on achievement with 14 mildly handicapped students in three mainstreamed 10th-grade history classes. Following the collection of baseline scores on weekly teacher-made tests, the students (both handicapped and nonhandicapped) were randomly placed into two teams and then randomly paired within teams in tutoring dyads. During each 30-minute tutoring session, the tutor in each dyad asked the other student questions from a worksheet. When all of the questions had been answered correctly, students reversed roles. Points were awarded for correct responses and for "good tutoring behaviors" (e.g., the use of praise and support). The scores of each team were posted and the results were printed in the school's weekly bulletin.

The dependent variable was the percentage of correct responses on weekly tests. During baseline, approximately 13% of the students received "A" grades, while 33% received "E" grades. During intervention, the percentage of students receiving "A's" for weekly tests averaged 58%, with 90% receiving "A" grades on 5 of the 13 weekly tests. During intervention, no handicapped student received a weekly grade below "C". The mean gain on weekly tests for the total student group during the 18-week period of the study was 21.66%. A mean gain of 23.15% for the handicapped students resulted in the authors concluding that the "intervention proved to be . . . academically beneficial" for the handicapped students (Maheady, Sacca, & Harper, 1988, p. 59). However, they did not report the extent to which the peer-tutoring procedures had been followed, and they were unable to identify critical aspects of the program that contributed to its success.

A second study by the same researchers (Maheady , Harper, & Sacca, 1988) was conducted in a resource room with 9th- and 10th-grade handicapped students who received instruction in several subjects, including social studies. The peer-tutoring program described for the preceding study was the independent variable. During intervention, scores on weekly quizzes increased by 20% for the 9th-grade students and by 17% for the 10th-grade students. Students' responses to a teacher-made test to assess attitudes toward peer-tutoring were interpreted as indicating acceptance of the process.

Individualizing Instruction. Kourilsky and Ballard-Campbell (1984) examined a minisociety experience as a means for individualizing instruction in mainstreamed classrooms. Elementary students were randomly selected from ability strata and assigned to classes so that each class had similar proportions of high-, medium-, and low-ability students. Intelligence scores for students in the low-ability group varied from borderline to mildly mentally retarded Each class was organized as a small society in which students set up businesses, conducted trade, and established a monetary system, as they investigated ways for dealing with scarcity. SMDs for pretest-posttest gains of the low-ability group on researcher-made tests ranged from medium (.61) for attitude toward school to large for attitude toward learning (.98) and economic decision making (1.35). Although the methods of individualizing instruction were not clearly described in their report, the authors suggested that the minisociety experience permits low-ability students to achieve success without having to rely entirely on verbal skills. It is not possible, however, to separate the effects of the individualization processes from the knowledge component of the minisociety experience.

Social Studies Curriculum Projects

Several curriculum projects conducted with at-risk students were examined. The Milwaukee Studies Program for educationally disadvantaged students (*Seventh Grade Social Studies,* 1967) involved 41 junior high school classes. This program was designed to strengthen study and cognitive skills, and to increase knowledge of social studies content. Moreover, it was anticipated that students' attitudes toward their role in society would improve with increased knowledge of their culture. In addition to an in-depth consideration of citizenship participation, the treatment consisted of a brief survey of Western civilization and the evolvement of social institutions, and of the application of a modified anthropological approach to study ways for meeting basic needs. The assessment program included the SAT Study Skills Subtest, a researcher-made test to measure cognitive skills, and a scale to assess attitudes toward citizenship. The pretest-posttest mean gains for four randomly selected classes were statistically significant on all dependent variables. SMDs varied from medium for attitude (.48) to large for study skills (.79) and knowledge of content (1.77).

Sutton, Barnhart, and Palter (1968) and Tobias (1982) described curriculum projects that involved at-risk students in a number of subject areas including social studies. In both projects, teacher-assigned grades for social studies improved; however, in comprehensive curriculum projects such as these, it is difficult to identify the specific factors that affected the results in a particular subject area.

Special Class vs Mainstreaming

Two studies designed to identify the most effective setting for teaching social studies to at-risk and mildly mentally retarded students were located. In a study by Stoakes (1964), 48

TABLE 13-4. Curriculum Projects and Special Class vs. Mainstreaming Studies.

Author(s) Date	Subjects	Grade(s)	N	Treatment	Treatment Length	Dependent Variable(s)	SMD[a]	p
				Social Studies Curriculum Projects				
Seventh Grade Social Studies (1966–1967)	Educationally disadvantaged	7	594 41 classes n's of subjects sampled = 66–299	Modified anthropological study of historical and contemporary institutions	2 semesters	Knowledge of content SAT Social Studies Attitude toward citizenship	1.77 .76 .48	.01 .01 .01
Sutton et al. (1968)	Low-achieving students	10–12	73	A: student seminars, group guidance, team teaching, audiovisual materials, field trips B: same as A, but without seminars C: regular program	3 years	Knowledge of content (end of 12th grade) A vs. B A/B vs. C		ns .01
Tobias (1982)	Hispanic EMR & learning-disabled students	elem.–sec.	132 (classes = 11)	Individualized instruction, resource assistance, staff development, parental training and involvement, Hispanic studies (included all academic subjects)	1 year	Knowledge of content (86% of students scored 70% or better on social studies test)		
				Special Class vs. Mainstreaming				
Stoakes (1964)	Slow learners	7–8	48	Homogeneous grouping vs. heterogeneous grouping	2 years	Knowledge of content SAT Social Studies CTP Personal Section CTP Social Section	−.83 −.88 .12 −.43	ns ns .05 ns
Stroud (1976)	EMR students	1–12	550	Self-contained (SC) vs. Selected Academic Placement (SAP) vs. Learning Center Model (LC) vs. Mainstreaming (MS)		Basic practical knowledge SC vs SAP SC vs LC SC vs MS	−.33 −.05 −.07	ns ns ns

[a]Standardized mean differences (SMDs) were computed as effect sizes in 3 studies. Criteria for small (.20), medium or moderate (.50), and large (.80) SMDs were those suggested by Cohen (1977).

at-risk junior high school students selected from three junior high schools were assigned to either homogeneous or heterogeneous classes. Teacher-made tests and the SAT Social Studies Subtest were used to assess social studies achievement during the two-year period of the study. The California Test of Personality (CTP) was administered to assess personality change. Posttest mean differences for achievement yielded large *SMDs* (.88 for teacher-made tests; .88 for the SAT Social Studies Subtest), with higher means for the heterogeneous classes. Data collected using the CTP were less consistent. An *SMD* of .12 for the Personal Section reflected a higher mean for students in the homogeneous group, while an *SMD* of .43 for the Social Section was due to a higher mean for the students in the heterogeneous group. Whether grouping was the sole treatment variable in this study is questionable; for example, the teachers of the homogeneous classes received in-service training and used more enrichment materials in their courses.

Stroud's (1976) study involved comparing the achievement of EMR students in primary, intermediate, junior, and senior high school classes in four settings: self-contained classes, selected academic placement (part integration) classes, classes with learning center support, and mainstreamed classes with occasional support from an EMR teacher. Students in the self-contained program were to be taught the Persisting Life Problems (PLP) curriculum, a grade 1 through 12 program that consisted of basic, practical knowledge (e.g., earning a living, homemaking) required to function as an independent adult. Students in the other settings were taught the regular social studies curricula, primarily history and geography.

Whether the basic objectives of the PLP program were achieved in these classes was the question examined in this study. The loss of 200 subjects (from a sample of 550 at pretest) makes interpretation of the results difficult. Furthermore, it was not known whether the PLP curriculum was taught in all of the self-contained classes because it was not prescribed by the school district. Additionally, the number of EMR students in the academic placement classes actually taking social studies in regular classes was not determined.

An instrument developed to measure the objectives of the PLP was administered at the beginning and end of the school year to 10 randomly selected students from each class. Differences among the mean scores for the four alternative settings across grade levels were not statistically significant. Comparison of the several settings with the self-contained classes yielded very small *SMDs*, with higher means for the alternative arrangements (see Table 13–4). The author concluded that the three alternative settings were as effective for achieving PLP objectives as was the program in the self-contained classes.

DISCUSSION

Reviews of social studies curricula and programs for at-risk and handicapped students reveal a general pattern of simplified courses that are of questionable validity as citizenship education, particularly if a primary purpose of social studies instruction is the development of informed citizens who are open-minded, committed to the resolution of societal problems and inequities, and who participate effectively in the democratic process (Curtis, 1978). In fact, the findings of these reviews imply that the preparation of special-needs students for active citizenship roles has not been a fundamental objective of social studies instruction, especially in self-contained classes.

What are the inferences for classroom practice, and in particular for citizenship education, to be drawn from the findings of the studies reviewed in this chapter? One must proceed cautiously with this question, since problems with study quality, the number of studies without comparison groups, the over-reliance on researcher and teacher-made tests without reliability and validity data, and the small number of studies in any area make it difficult to construct reliable generalizations. Nevertheless, several patterns emerge with implications for teaching at-risk and handicapped students.

The study of contemporary problems, considered by some educators to be an integral part of citizenship preparation, has been investigated with at-risk students with encouraging results. In several studies, contemporary problems provided the context for teaching critical-thinking skills and for increasing awareness of community issues, in addition to developing self-esteem and reading comprehension. Furthermore, these studies utilized a wide variety of resources available in the community, rather than modified materials specifically prepared for poor readers.

Contemporary problems involve the examination of controversial and diverse opinions. Less-able students in mainstreamed classes may be reluctant to engage in controversy or to express their opinions in the presence of their nonhandicapped peers. The finding that controversy can be dealt with in cooperative groups without the loss of self-esteem on the part of these students suggests an approach for dealing with controversy in integrated settings.

In the largest single group of studies reviewed, the effects of cooperative learning were assessed, in particular for the models described by Johnson and Johnson. Although the point is not argued in these studies, cooperative learning may be conceived of as citizenship training by providing a model for developing the skills necessary for functioning effectively in democratic groups.

The specific effects on handicapped students in several of the cooperative learning studies are difficult to discern inasmuch as learning conditions, rather than student groups within learning conditions, were compared. As might well be anticipated, the findings of these studies suggest that cooperative learning tends to promote interactions between handicapped and nonhandicapped children. Furthermore, it appears from several of the studies that these interactions are likely to be positive, consisting for the most part of nonhandicapped students helping handicapped students to learn, and to promote friendships outside the classroom—at least for the duration of the study. It is possible that cooperative learning leads to increased self-esteem in handicapped children, but this is difficult to discern in the studies reviewed here. Whether cooperative learning is an effective approach for teaching social studies content is not clear from these studies, because achievement was a variable in too few studies.

Whether organizing students into cooperative groups to play games results in positive interactions between handicapped and nonhandicapped or at-risk students in social studies classes cannot be inferred from the two studies reviewed here, because both studies were conducted in segregated classes. In Slavin's (1977) study, mutual peer attraction and on-task behavior were greater in the class where students worked cooperatively. Farran's (1969) finding that students playing games individually scored higher on tests assessing knowledge of content than did students playing in groups was not tested in Slavin's study.

Other ways to organize instruction include peer-tutoring and individualized learning. Both techniques have yielded increases in social studies achievement. However, the treatment in the single study in which an individualized approach was used was complex and involved a number of factors, and the effects of individualization alone were difficult to ascertain.

The question of how best to help poor readers learn content in social studies textbooks has been examined in a number of studies which, for the most part, have yielded promising results. Simplifying language in textbooks, recording textbooks on audio tapes, and supplementing textbooks with visual materials have all resulted in increased knowledge, as has teaching students to use summarization strategies.

Whether handicapped students are best taught in segregated or integrated settings has been the subject of some research. Carlberg and Kavale's (1980) meta-analysis of studies comparing self-contained and mainstreamed classes revealed small but positive effect sizes for achievement and social/personality factors, with higher means for mainstreamed classes. Some support for these findings is provided in two of the studies reviewed here. The achievement gains for mainstreamed classes were higher in both studies; however, standardized mean differences were large in one study and small to negligible in the other study. In the single study where personality changes were assessed, the results were conflicting.

SUGGESTIONS FOR FUTURE RESEARCH

A number of questions raised by this review suggest topics for future research. For example, how to develop commitment to basic democratic values and principles in a manner that permits informed choice and rational discussion is an important question that bears consideration. Treatments in several studies included strategies for teaching democratic values, but the findings of these studies were inconclusive. This is perplexing, because the strategies were grounded in theory and developed from suggestions commonly found in the literature. Similarly, a treatment based on Kohlberg's moral-development theory resulted in only temporary gains in moral stage reasoning that were not maintained on a follow-up assessment. The finding in one study that at-risk students' acceptance of democratic principles is more likely to occur with a propaganda approach than with the examination of diversity of opinion is disturbing, particularly because commitment to rational thought and informed choice is a basic tenet in democratic societies.

A number of important questions are suggested by the cooperative learning studies. How to use this strategy with at-risk and disabled students to develop skills such as problem solving and decision making—which are so much a part of citizenship education—is a question that has yet to be examined, as is the frequency with which cooperative learning can be used effectively in mainstreamed social studies classes. Furthermore, the specific roles that at-risk and disabled children assume in cooperative groups, whether the effects of cooperative learning correlate with specific disabling conditions, and whether cooperative learning results in long-term acceptance of individual differences are also questions for future researchers.

Peer-tutoring and individualization are appropriate topics for research, since few studies have been conducted with special-needs students in social studies classes. How to help students read information in the form in which it occurs in real life is a major question. In particular, researchers might examine strategies such as guided reading and summarization, or ways to augment and clarify reading passages through the use of audiovisual materials.

Most of the studies reviewed were conducted with at-risk, mildly mentally retarded, learning-disabled, or behaviorally disturbed children. Studies in which subjects had other disabling conditions are missing from the literature. How do conditions such as quadriplegia, cerebral palsy, spina bifida, and severe hearing loss, for example, impact learning in social studies? How to reduce the degree to which disabling conditions inhibit participation in activities such as discussions, debates, and field studies is also an important question.

Certainly, how to convince curriculum developers to include citizenship preparation in their social studies curricula for special-needs students is a compelling question that needs to be addressed.

References

Allen, W., & VanSickle, R. (1984). Learning teams and low achievers. *Social Education, 48,* 60–64.

Armento, B. J. (1986). Research on teaching social studies. In M. Wittrock (Ed.), *Handbook of Research on Teaching* (3rd ed., pp. 942–951). New York: Macmillan.

Bailey, J. D. (1968). *A study and analysis of the content of selected social studies curricula for secondary educable mentally retarded students.* Unpublished master's thesis, University of Kansas.

Baines, T. (1967–1968). *The use of selected materials, based on reading level, to improve achievement of slow learners in a world history course.* Newport News, VA: Newport News Public Schools.

Bean, W., & Pardi, R. (1979). A field test of a guided reading strategy. *Journal of Reading, 23,* 144–147.

Bradley, J., Ames, W., & Mitchell, J. (1980). Intrabook reliability: Variations within history textbooks. *Social Education, 44,* 524–528.

Bruner, J. (1975). On perceptual readiness. *Psychological Review, 64,* 123–141.

Campbell, D. T., & Stanley, J. C. (1963). *Experimental and quasi-experimental designs for research.* Chicago: Rand McNally.

Carlberg, C., & Kavale, K. (1980). The efficacy of special versus regular class placement for exceptional children: A meta-analysis. *Journal of Special Education, 14,* 295–309.

Cooper, L., Johnson, D. W., Johnson, R. T, & Wilderson, F. (1980). The effects of cooperative, competitive, and individualistic experiences on inter-personal attraction among heterogeneous peers. *The Journal of Social Psychology, 111,* 243–252.

Crabtree, C. (1983). A common curriculum in the social studies. In G. Fenstermacher & J. Goodlad (Eds.), *Individual Differences and the Common Curriculum* (pp. 248–281). Chicago: University of Chicago Press.

Curtis, C. K. (1978). *Contemporary community problems in citizenship education for slow-learning secondary students.* Unpublished Doctoral dissertation, Utah State University.

Curtis, C. K. (1981). Slow learners' attitudes toward fundamental freedoms. *Journal of Social Studies Research, 5,* 35–39.

Curtis, C. K., & Shaver, J. P. (1980). Slow learners and the study of contemporary problems. *Social Education, 44,* 302–309.

Curtis, C. K., & Shaver, J. P. (1983, March). *A measure of attitudes toward civil liberties.* Vancouver: Faculty of Education, University of British Columbia. (ERIC Document Reproduction Service No. ED 231 677)

Darch, C., & Carnine, D. (1986). Teaching content area material to learning disabled students. *Exceptional Children, 55,* 240–246.

Dimond, S. E. (1953). *Schools and the development of good citizens.* Detroit: Wayne University Press.

Farran, D. (1969). Competition and learning for underachievers. In S. Boocock & E. Schid (Eds.), *Simulation games in learning.* Beverly Hills, CA: Sage.

Fleming, J. (1980). *An investigation of the effects of reinforcement for recall and explanation of teacher directions on social studies performance.* Unpublished doctoral dissertation, University of Washington,

Gearheart, W. R., & Weishahn, M. W. (1980). *The handicapped student in the regular classroom.* St. Louis: C. V. Mosby.

Glass, G. V., McGaw, B., & Smith, M. L. (1981). *Meta-analysis in social research.* Beverly Hills, CA: Sage.

Gozali, J. & Gonwa, J. (1973). Citizenship training for the EMR: A case of educational neglect. *Mental Retardation, 11* (1), 49–50.

Hamingson, D. (Ed.). (1973). *Towards judgement.* East Anglia, Eng.: University of East Anglia, Centre for Applied Research in Education.

Holdt, B. (1976). *The relationship of levels of classroom questions and social studies achievement of second-grade achieving hearing impaired children.* Unpublished doctoral dissertation, Utah State University.

Johnson, D. W., & Johnson, R. T. (1981). The integration of the handicapped into the regular classroom: Effects of cooperative and individualistic instruction. *Contemporary Educational Psychology, 6,* 344–353.

Johnson, D. W., & Johnson, R. T. (1984). Building acceptance of differences between handicapped and nonhandicapped students: The effects of cooperative and individualistic instruction. *The Journal of Social Psychology, 122,* 257–267.

Johnson, D. W., & Johnson, R. T. (1985). Classroom conflict: Controversy versus debate in learning groups. *American Educational Research Journal, 22,* 237–256.

Johnson, R. T., & Johnson, D. W. (1982). Effects of cooperative and competitive learning experiences on interpersonal attraction between handicapped and nonhandicapped students. *The Journal of Social Psychology, 116,* 211–219.

Johnson, R. T., & Johnson, D. W. (1983). Effects of cooperative, competitive, and individualistic learning experiences on social development. *Exceptional Children, 49,* 323–328.

Jones, W. E. (1964). *An investigation of the case method of instruction in selected eighth grade civics classes.* Unpublished doctoral dissertation, University of California, Berkeley.

Kourilsky, M., & Ballard-Campbell, M. (1984). Mini-society: An individualized social studies program for children of low, middle, and high ability. *The Social Studies, 78,* 224–228.

LeSourd, S. (1985). Using text structure to improve social science concept attainment. *Journal of Social Studies Research, 9*(2), 1–14.

Maheady, L., Harper, G., & Sacca, K. (1988). A classwide peer-tutoring system in a secondary resource room program for the mildly handicapped. *Journal of Research and Development in Education, 2*(3), 76–83.

Maheady, L., Sacca, K., & Harper, G. (1988). Classwide peer-tutoring with mildly handicapped high school students. *Exceptional Children, 55,* 52–59.

Miller, J., & Weston, G. (1947). Slow learners improve in critical thinking. *Social Education, 13,* 315–318.

Moore, B. A. (1980). *Classroom teachers' use and modification of instructional materials for mainstreamed, handicapped students and perceived need for assistance and training.* Unpublished doctoral dissertation, The American University.

Mosby, R. (1979). A bypass program of supported instruction for secondary students with learning disabilities. *Journal of Learning Disabilities, 12*(3), 187–190.

Patton, J., Polloway, E., & Cronin, M. (1987). Social studies instruction for handicapped students: A review of current practices, *The Social Studies, 78,* 131–135.

Rackman, B. M. (1974). *Improving moral judgments made by educable mentally retarded adolescents.* Unpublished doctoral dissertation, Columbia University,

Romanoff, A. M. (1987). *An observational study of high school history instruction in self-contained and mainstreamed classes on four dimensions of teacher behavior pertinent to the instruction of learning disabled adolescents.* Unpublished doctoral dissertation, Columbia University.

Rosenberg, M. (1968). *Society and the adolescent self-image.* Princeton, NJ: Princeton University Press.

Ryan, F. (1973). Differentiated effects of levels of questioning on student achievement. *The Journal of Experimental Education, 41,* 63–67.

Sauers, B. J. (1974). *Living in an urban world—Mexico City: A history unit for tenth-grade slow learners.* Unpublished doctoral dissertation, Carnegie-Mellon University.

Schubert, J. G. (1973). *Living in an urban world—Ibadan: A history unit for tenth-grade slow learners.* Unpublished doctoral dissertation, Carnegie-Mellon University.

Seventh Grade Social Studies Program Evaluation. (1967). Milwaukee, WI: Milwaukee Public Schools. (ERIC Document Reproduction Service No. ED 019 334)

Shaver, J. P. (1987). Implications from research: What should be taught in social studies? In V. Richard-Kohler (Ed.), *Educator's handbook: A research perspective* (pp. 112–138). New York, NY: Longman.

Slavin, R. E. (1977). A student team approach to teaching adolescents with special emotional and behavioral needs. *Psychology in the Schools, 14*(1), 77–84.

Slavin, R. E., & Madden, N. A. (1987). *Effective classroom programs for students at risk.* Baltimore: Johns Hopkins University, Center for Research on Elementary and Middle Schools. (ERIC Document Reproduction Service No. ED 288 922)

Smith, K., Johnson, D. W., & Johnson, R. T. (1982). Effects of cooperative and individualistic instruction on the achievement of handicapped, regular, and gifted students. *The Journal of Social Psychology, 116,* 277–283.

Stevens, G. D. (1958). An analysis of objectives for the education of children with retarded mental development. *American Journal of Mental Deficiency, 63,* 225–235.

Stoakes, D. W. (1964). *An educational experiment with the homogeneous grouping of mentally advanced and slow learning students in the junior high school.* Unpublished doctoral dissertation, University of Colorado.

Stroud, M. B. (1976). *The achievement of social studies objectives of a persisting life problems curriculum by educable mentally retarded pupils in four alternative mainstreaming settings in Ohio.* Unpublished doctoral dissertation, Kent State University.

Sunal, C., Paul, M., & DeMary, J. (1981). Social studies for the hearing impaired: The state of the art. *Theory and Research in Social Education, 9*(3), 61–72.

Sutton, J., Barnhart, B., & Palter, G. (1968). *A Program to increase the motivation of low achieving students*. Syosset, NY: Central School District Number Two. (ERIC Document Reproduction Service No. ED 036 954)

Thibeault, D. (1971). *The effects of "single" versus "augmented" treatment in changing the views of high school youth concerning the principles of freedom embodied in the Bill of Rights*. Unpublished doctoral dissertation, University of California, Los Angeles.

Tobias, R. (1982). *Bronx Multidiscipline Special Education Bilingual Program. ESEA Title VII Annual evaluation report, 1981–82*. Brooklyn: New York City Board of Education. (ERIC Document Reproduction Service No. ED 230 634)

Tyo, J. (1980). An alternative for poor readers in social science. *Social Education, 44*, 309–310.

Uphoff, J. K. (1967). *Senior high school social studies programs for low achievers*. Unpublished doctoral dissertation, University of Nebraska.

VanSickle, R. (1978). Experiential concreteness and the presentation of value dilemmas to slow learning students. *Social Education, 42*, 64–66.

Wilson, J. B. (1967). *A pilot study using selected published materials in American History for slow learners*. Unpublished doctoral dissertation, Baylor University.

Wong, B., Wong, R., Perry, N., & Sawatsky, D. (1986). The efficacy of a self-questioning summarization strategy for use by underachievers and learning disabled adolescents in social studies. *Learning Disabilities Focus, 2*(2), 20–35.

Woolard, S. H. (1974). *A Simulation of a model of perception to shape problem recognition behavior of slow learners in social studies*. Unpublished doctoral dissertation, Florida State University.

Yager, S., Johnson, R. T., Johnson, D. W., & Snider, B. (1985). The impact of group processing on achievement in cooperative learning groups. *The Journal of Social Psychology, 126*, 389–397.

14

GIFTED STUDENTS AND SOCIAL STUDIES

James R. Delisle
KENT STATE UNIVERSITY

Gifted education: It is controversial and commonplace, new-fangled and old fashioned, a legitimate educational endeavor and "a frill" to be cut when a school district faces budget problems. John Gowan, past president of the National Association for Gifted Children, in responding to society's love–hate relationship with gifted children and gifted programs, wrote that "gifted education is a passionless issue in a society geared to emergencies" (1972; p. 8).

To understand fully the reasons behind our nation's on again–off again interest in gifted education programs, one needs a perspective on two concepts: the definition of giftedness and the concept of differential education for gifted children.

THE CONCEPT OF GIFTEDNESS IN A HISTORICAL CONTEXT

Interest in gifted children and their education has been noted in virtually every society since ancient times. Plato suggested that evidently gifted children be segregated from others at an early age, and he argued that "a better social order could be achieved if those who governed were selected from among the most intellectually able" (cited in Kitano & Kirby, 1986, p. 10). Around A.D. 800, Emperor Charlemagne urged that promising children found among the common people be educated at state expense (cited in Whitmore, 1980). And in China from the Dark Ages to the Renaissance, child prodigies were identified and nurtured (Tsuin-chen, 1961). In fact, Confucius established a private school around 2,000 years ago and advocated teaching students in accordance with their aptitude (Li & Delisle, in press).

This early, worldwide interest in gifted persons continued through the Renaissance and into modern times. In various eras, giftedness, or *genius* as it came to be called, was linked with national prosperity (Tsuin-chen, 1961), insanity (Lombroso, 1891), and an abnormally developed nervous system (Ellis, 1904).

The researcher generally attributed to be the first person to study giftedness in children over a sustained period of time was Lewis M. Terman. In his now-classic six-volume series, *Genetic Studies of Genius,* published between 1924 and 1969 by the Stanford University Press, Terman provided evidence to refute the claims that gifted children were biological anomalies, genetically inferior, or subject to mental illness. Using a Stanford Binet IQ score above 135 as the determining factor for qualifying an individual as gifted, Terman studied 1,528 children, starting in 1921. Both these persons and their descendants continue to be studied today (more than 75% of the original Terman subjects are still alive). A comprehensive review of his results is available (Goleman, 1980), but the Terman legacy is this: Gifted individuals begin with and maintain "superiority to nongifted peers in physical and emotional health as well as in intellectual capacities" (Kitano & Kirby, 1986, p. 57). Or, as stated directly by Terman, "no one as yet has developed post-adolescent stupidity" (1954, p. 229).

More recently, educators and scientists have expanded their conceptions of giftedness beyond exceptional performance on an IQ test. Witty (1940) described gifted children as those "whose performance is consistently remarkable in any potentially valuable area" (p. 516), and the Education Consolidation and Improvement Act, passed by the U.S. Congress in 1981, includes within its definition of giftedness high performance capability in intellectual, creative, artistic, and leadership capacities. Given the differences in conceptions of giftedness throughout the centuries, it is expected that society's interpretation of giftedness will continue to expand and evolve.

THE CONCEPT OF DIFFERENTIAL EDUCATION FOR THE GIFTED

Even though the definition of giftedness continues to be debated, few would argue against the fact that people do differ in

Reviewers were Jerry Flack, University of Colorado; Jay A. Monson, Utah State University.

intellectual potential. In this regard, authors have recognized the need to provide highly able students with educational experiences commensurate with their talents (e.g., McClelland, Baldwin, Bronfenbrenner, & Strodtbeck, 1958):

Talent potential may be fairly widespread, a characteristic which can be transformed into actually talented performance of various sorts by the right kinds of education. If so, the emphasis should shift from identifying talent potential to studying the process by which talent becomes actual, by which it develops. Such a focus requires above all a knowledge of theory—an understanding of what we are measuring, how it develops under different circumstances, and how it is related to the ultimate criteria of talented performance which we want to predict.(p. 25)

There is no lack of suggestions for methods of educating gifted students; there is also no consensus on what works best, or why. Some authors (Newland, 1976; Ward, 1980) contend that this lack of agreement on effective practices is the result of our society's limited acceptance of the needs for special educational provisions for students who already succeed academically. As stated by Newland;

Especially in the late '50's and during the '60's, educational changes intended to be in the interests of the gifted were effected more under pressure than as a result of a deep and abiding philosophical comprehension of the potential contributive value of such provisions. (p. 119)

Research evidence on the effectiveness of various programs and classroom structures for gifted students is generally positive, as Kulik and Kulik (1984) found in their meta-analysis of 126 school projects reported between 1920–1984. The Kuliks examined the effectiveness of three major approaches to educating gifted students: grouping, acceleration, and enrichment. Using the meta-analytic approach suggested by Glass (1976), Kulik and Kulik analyzed data from 81 separate studies of interclass grouping, 26 programs of acceleration, and 19 studies of heterogeneous classroom enrichment.

Because the 126 separate studies were so diverse regarding duration of treatment, subject assignment to groups, grade levels of subjects, and other factors, Kulik and Kulik calculated only one effect size (ES) for each outcome of each study. When comparisons differed in methodological adequacy, the ES was calculated "from what would ordinarily be considered the most methodologically sound comparison" (Kulik & Kulik, 1984, p. 12). Thus, when a particular study presented the results of both an experimental and a quasi-experimental comparison, only results of the true experiment were coded; similarly, when results from both long- and short-term program implementation were reported, results from the longer implementation were used.

The results of this meta-analysis were both vast and varied, prohibiting full discussion here. However, some overall findings are worth review.

1. In studies designed to detect differences in student achievement using heterogeneous and homogeneous class groupings as the independent measure, the achievement of gifted students in homogeneously grouped classes was great enough to be statistically significant. The average ES in these studies, 0.33, "means that teaching talented students in homogenous classes raises their scores on achievement tests by 0.33 standard deviation" (p. 21).

2. In studies of acceleration (when younger gifted students attended classes with older pupils), the results were unequivocal: Acceleration settings contributed to gifted student's achievement. The mean ES in the studies examined was 0.88, the ES standard deviation was .66, and the standard error was .19. Because approximately 81% of the area of the standard normal curve falls below a z-score of 0.88, Kulik and Kulik concluded that 81% of accelerated-class students outperformed the typical student in the control class.

3. A mean ES of 0.62 for studies of intraclass enrichment programs for gifted students indicated greater impact on student achievement than for classes in which gifted students were not grouped for enrichment options with intellectual peers, for which the mean ES was 0.17.

Kulik and Kulik summarized their meta-analysis by stating that "talented students in these programs almost invariably gain academically from them" (p. 43), as well as sometimes developing positive attitudes toward both their schools and academic subjects.

The Kulik and Kulik study provided research evidence of the effectiveness of grouping and acceleration options for gifted students. It did not, however, provide guidance for practitioners who want to structure lessons within these particular groupings. Other authors (Clark, 1988; Gallagher, 1985) have done so, and have suggested that the educative experiences for gifted students should:

1. involve the use of higher levels of thinking such as synthesis, analysis, and evaluation;
2. imbue in students the ability to learn independently, free from teacher direction;
3. stress broad-based inquiry, rather than the study of discrete facts and ideas;
4. be paced according to the child's developmental need, rather than to a prescribed grade-level sequence.

SOCIAL STUDIES INSTRUCTION FOR GIFTED STUDENTS

Several questions can be raised about the role of the social studies educator with gifted students. The first question, more easily asked than answered, is this: "Why is social studies an especially appropriate content focus for gifted students?"

The answers to this question vary, but most responses are based on the natural link that exists between the goals of gifted education and social studies education. As highlighted by Stewart (1985), "The objectives of both fields frequently overlap—encouraging inquiry, critical thinking skills, creative thinking skills, decision-making skills, investigation of real problems, and leadership skills" (p. 238). Breiter (1987) concurred. She wrote that "since social studies is an area of the curriculum which allows for almost unlimited diversity, it is an excellent vehicle for gifted education" (p. 43).

An additional and related rationale for the instruction of gifted students in the social studies relates to the highly able student's role as a future leader in our global society. Frequently, gifted programs are begun in school districts under the premise that to-day's most intellectually capable students will become tomor-row's leaders in business, politics, and other professions. Thus, in this utilitarian view, the education of gifted students becomes an investment in the future; to ignore our "moral mandate" to ed-ucate gifted students is to risk the very future of our society. As stated by Whitmore (1980), "If Americans are serious about want-ing to conserve and develop our most talented human resources . . . they must become genuinely committed to better meeting the needs of gifted students" (p. 410).

Others believe that the role of the gifted child in the future is a concern secondary in importance to the full personal devel-opment of the student. From this vantage, gifted education ser-vices are required so that highly able children can learn to un-derstand and accept their strengths; if society benefits from a gifted child's talents, that is an added bonus.

This ambivalence toward the primary rationale for educating gifted students has been expressed by gifted students them-selves. For example, Delisle (1984) surveyed over 4,000 gifted students to determine their own impressions of giftedness and received such conflicting responses as "I think being gifted means having a special gift from God. I feel that if you are gifted you are on Earth to fulfill a need that maybe other people can't fulfill" (girl, 12, Arkansas, p. 5), and "I don't want to be noticed as being smart. I just want to be a regular housewife because I don't think it's fair that just because I'm smart I have to be a scientist or something" (girl, 10, New York, p. 105).

This controversy over the most vital reason for providing gifted education services has been addressed by Gallagher (1985), who stressed that the emphasis on social studies instruc-tion should be on developing student understanding of self *and* society. In this view, both the personal and societal benefits of gifted education were considered equally important, and the types of instruction provided to gifted students, if constructed carefully, would address these two important needs.

Another rationale for providing social studies instruction specifically to gifted students concerns two related factors: the current inadequacy of social studies texts for gifted students, and research concerning gifted students' preferred learning styles. In a study of student knowledge of textbook content (Ed-ucation Products Information Exchange, 1979), it was found that a majority of students had mastered 80 percent of the material in some of their subject-matter texts (including social studies) before they had even opened their books. Further, the National Commission on Excellence in Education (1983) reported that "during the past decade or so a large number of texts have been 'written down' by their publishers to ever-lower reading levels" (p. 21).

The issue of gifted students' preferred modes of learning has also been addressed in the research. Bireley and Hoehn (1987) reported that the learning-style preferences of average, learning disabled (LD), and gifted children differed greatly. Both average and LD children preferred to learn in a step-by-step approach, but gifted students preferred intuitive learning experiences that stressed a holistic approach to instruction. Us-ing the *Learning Preference Inventory* (Hanson & Silver, 1978), a group-administered instrument to assess student preference on the factor of introversion–extroversion and four "routes" for

learning (sensing, intuition, thinking, and feeling), Bireley and Hoehn found that 60% of average and LD children preferred sensing as a way of learning. Sixty-two percent of gifted students chose intuition as their preferred mode of learning. According to the authors, these findings have implications for educators, in terms of both methods and materials used for instruction.

Likewise, in a comprehensive review of research related to the interaction of aptitude and instructional style, Howley, How-ley, and Pendarvis (1986) concluded that

1. Gifted students appear to be the only ones capable of gaining more from inductive teaching than from didactic teaching.
2. Gifted students learn more in an environment in which they can give opinions and ask questions.
3. Independent study is an effective means of learning for gifted students (p. 77).

The research on learning styles and preferences, the appropri-ateness of textbook content, and the meta-analysis of findings related to the advantages of grouping gifted students have served as the bases upon which other researchers have de-signed specific instructional models appropriate for gifted stu-dents, several of which are described in the following section.

INSTRUCTIONAL MODELS IN THE SOCIAL STUDIES FOR GIFTED STUDENTS

Although several organizational models for teaching social studies to gifted students have emerged since the 1970s (Betts, 1985; Renzulli, 1977), the instructional designs used within these models come from the general education field. Thus, as one reads the literature on gifted education and social studies, some familiar names emerge; the contributions of Hilda Taba, Benjamin Bloom, Jerome Bruner, and Lawrence Kohlberg are the mainstays of social studies instruction for highly able stu-dents.

In her review of issue-based curriculum for gifted students, Tomlinson (1987) emphasized that "processes for a social stud-ies class for gifted students should differ from those of a regular classroom . . . focus[ing] on processes such as hypothesizing, creating, predicting, judging, experimenting, debating, critiqu-ing and investigating" (pp. 149–150). Each of those processes fits well with the theories of Taba (Taba, Durkin, Fraenkel, & McNaughton, 1971), Bloom (1956), and Kohlberg (1978), who believed that an inquiry approach to teaching could be achieved through sophisticated classroom questioning. They are consistent, too, with Bruner's (1966) discovery approach to social studies content, which incorporated the intuitive learning strategies found effective with gifted students (Maker, 1982).

Although it is beyond the scope of this chapter to review all the contributions of these researchers to social studies and gifted education, Table 14–1 presents an overview of each au-thor's work as it relates to the education of gifted students.

Two authors (Betts, 1985; Renzulli, 1977) have proposed or-ganizational models for gifted programs that incorporate the suggestions of Bloom, Bruner, and others. Adaptable for use with both elementary and secondary students, *The Enrichment*

TABLE 14–1. General Curriculum Theorists and Their Impact on Gifted Education

Researcher	Major Contribution	Usefulness in Gifted Education	Research Effectiveness with Gifted Students
Benjamin Bloom (1956)	Established a taxonomy of higher level thinking skills designed to classify educational objectives according to the level of complexity of thinking required.	Assists teachers in developing lessons, learning centers, and independent study projects that help students generate new knowledge instead of merely rephrasing existing knowledge.	Although Bloom's *Taxonomy* is often used in gifted programs, no comparative studies using this method of instruction have been conducted. However, development of *The Ross Test of Cognitve Processes* (Ross & Ross, 1976) was based on the *Taxonomy* and may yet foster research effectiveness studies.
Jerome Bruner (1966)	Designed curricular content and processes that teach children about the structure of a particular discipline (e.g., the concept of revolution, the theory of supply and demand). When concepts are understood and interrelated, the various disciplines are more thoroughly comprehended.	Many concepts espoused by Bruner require abstract and complex thinking, which may not be suitable for all students. Although inquiry teaching can be appreciated to some degree by all students, the process seems especially suitable for able children.	Most studies of the effectiveness of inquiry approaches with gifted students have focused on mathematics instruction (Lowman, 1961) and science instruction (Wallace, 1962), although an evaluation of *Man: A Course of Study* (Hanley, Whitla, Moo, & Walter, 1970) showed high IQ to be a factor in student success in some MACOS units.
Lawrence Kohlberg (1978)	Postulated that moral reasoning is sequential and developmental and that children can develop higher levels of moral reasoning by discussion of "classroom dilemmas."	Because gifted individuals are theorized to have greater capacity than others to transfer moral reasoning into moral behavior (Ward, 1980), this system allows for practice of and exposure to common dilemmas.	A study by Karnes and Brown (1981) found significant correlations between IQ and the presence of moral reasoning in children aged 9–15 years. Research by Selman (1971) indicated that gifted students progress more rapidly than others through Kohlberg's stages.
Hilda Taba (1971)	Developed a series of structured, sequential questioning techniques to lead children to develop higher levels of cognitive thinking. Taba's theory assumes that "knowledge precedes thinking," and, therefore, her strategies build upon students' factual knowledge.	Assumed that high levels of abstract thinking can only be developed in bright or creative children. Although Taba's strategies can be used with all students, pacing rates differ, making grouping by ability the most economical use of both teachers' and students' time.	Research with Taba's techniques has focused on heterogeneous classes of children, so effectiveness with gifted students exclusively is not known.

Triad Model (Renzulli, 1977) and *The Autonomous Learner Model* (Betts, 1985) have gained widespread acceptance and use by educators responsible for directing gifted programs.

In the Enrichment Triad Model, Renzulli proposes that gifted program instruction be centered around three types of experiences. Type I enrichment consists of general exploratory activities such as field trips, films, and guest speakers that expose students to new areas of the curriculum or their world. Type II enrichment involves training activities that give students the tools to pursue further learning. Library research skills, Kohlbergian discussions, and creative-thinking activities are examples of Type II enrichment. Type III enrichment is the independent investigation of a problem of interest to the student. What differentiates Type III enrichment from more typical independent study projects are the focus on firsthand inquiry and the sharing of results with an audience other than the teacher. As explained by Renzulli, "a group of youngsters who have become involved in public opinion polling . . . have transcended the role of merely being students acting like researchers . . . to *become* social scientists' (p. 32). The Enrichment Triad Model is widely used, especially in gifted programs at the elementary level. Several descriptions of sample social studies units for gifted students using the Triad Model are available (Cellerino & Story, 1986; Reis & Hebert, 1985).

Betts's Autonomous Learner Model "was developed to meet the diversified cognitive, emotional and social needs of gifted and talented students" (1985, p. 1). It involves a 5-dimensional series of activities that mesh well with social studies instruction. Figure 14–1 shows the various dimensions of the model. As can be noted, the suggested activities require both in-school and out-of-school involvement. Intended to be used over a 3-year span during middle school or high school, the model is fre-

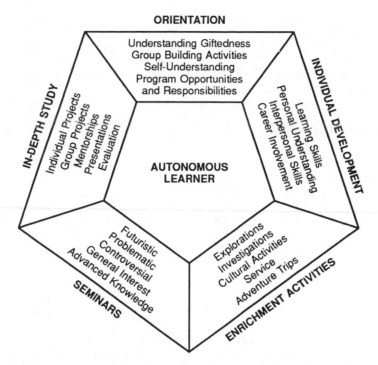

FIGURE 14–1. Note: From *The Autonomous Learner Model for the Gifted and Talented* (p. 2) by G. T. Betts. 1985. Greeley, CO: Autonomous Learning Publications and Specialists. Copyright by Autonomous Learning Publications and Specialists. Reprinted by permission.

quently offered to students in the form of an elective class to be taken within the structure of the school day. Thus, students are not pulled out of one class to participate in Autonomous Learner activities; rather they attend the regularly scheduled Autonomous Learner class, during which time they participate in one or more of the options presented in Figure 14–1. Although Betts does suggest a time line for implementing the various dimensions of the model, the Autonomous Learner is not considered by him to be hierarchical. Thus, seminars, orientation, and in-depth study take place each year of the 3-year duration of the model.

Neither The Enrichment Triad Model nor The Autonomous Learner Model has been studied for its effectiveness in relation to other program options available to gifted students. Maker (1982) criticized the lack of research on the Enrichment Triad Model. Still, no controlled studies have emerged. Instead, both Renzulli and Betts, in their respective work, challenged educators to evaluate the effectiveness of the models by using data derived from student, teacher, and parent reactions to specific program features.

WHAT WORKS: RESEARCH EVIDENCE SUPPORTING SOCIAL STUDIES INSTRUCTION FOR GIFTED STUDENTS

Empirical evidence of the effectiveness of specific social studies programs for gifted students is limited, but what data do

exist are encouraging. The relative paucity of "hard evidence" is true of the entire field of gifted education, not only social studies instruction for gifted students, as explained by Coleman (1985).

> Criticism leveled at gifted education comes from the field's inability to provide non-contradictory evidence on the efficacy of program practices, and the field's difficulty maintaining that serious and meaningful study, rather than fun and games, is occurring in programs. (p. 290)

Nonetheless, some researchers have conducted studies showing both academic and nonintellective benefits of various social studies programs for gifted students.

Many of these studies have concentrated on short-term gains in student achievement or attitude resulting from participation in a specific program option. Thompson (1986) investigated the instructional styles of teachers in charge of Advanced Placement (AP) American history classes in an effort to determine whether an expository/lecture style of teaching or an inquiry learning approach was used more often. Thompson sent questionnaires to teachers in 76 public school districts in California, seeking information on the districts' gifted program and on AP options. Then, the researcher visited all available AP American history classes in these districts, recording and analyzing instructional techniques used by the teachers. He found that AP classes, though the most common method of providing differentiated instruction for gifted high school students, were taught in a typical lecture format. Commenting that this method of instruction was inconsistent with research on the most effective techniques for teaching gifted students, Thompson advocated that AP classes be taught using processes as differentiated as the content of the lessons.

Pollins (1985) investigated whether school districts were more likely to provide enrichment and acceleration options to junior high students eligible to participate in social studies and other courses at Duke University. Five hundred and twenty-nine students eligible for summer enrollment at Duke were sent questionnaires on which they were to list any special academic options open to them as gifted students. Of this number, 151 eventually attended the Duke Talent Identification Program (TIP): These students were sent a follow-up questionnaire 3 months after their return from TIP, to determine whether additional program services for the gifted had been made available to them. In effect, Pollins wished to determine "the quality of the interface between the university program and the schools of the students served by the program" (p. 103).

The results of the study were that 76% of the summer program students had at least one type of special arrangement made for them as a direct result of their participation in TIP. Subject acceleration was the most common provision (66% of the students), with placement in gifted programs (27%) and independent study options (22%) also provided. A Fisher's exact test was performed to analyze the relationship of gender to the availability of special provisions; special arrangements were more likely to be made for males (82%) than for females (63%) ($p < .05$). According to the author, "the results of this study indicated clearly that schools and university-based programs can work together rather well to best serve the extremely gifted student" (p. 110).

Individual school districts have investigated the impact of social studies instruction on gifted students, but these investigations have generally been in-house evaluations, rather than controlled studies (Juntune, 1986). This situation is frustrating for the researcher, as more theories concerning what works best with gifted students are available than are actual data to provide substantiating evidence for these theories. One of the main stumbling blocks to overcome is the nature of assessment for gifted students. As stated by Sosniak (1987):

When a school system uses students' high scores on a standardized, norm-referenced test to define them as gifted and talented, the last thing these youngsters need is a special program to help them attain high scores on yet another standardized, norm-referenced test. (p. 536)

The use of an inappropriate dependent measure (i.e., standardized test scores), coupled with the lack of suitable alternative measures, is a continuing problem for researchers interested in gifted children and their education.

Another dilemma involves the use of gain scores. Although pretest-postest gains are often used as indicators of treatment effect, they are often inappropriate for use with gifted students because of such students' initially high pretreatment scores. As a consequence, program personnel frequently rely on informal data sources as measures of outcomes—for example, questionnaires sent to teachers and parents involved in gifted programs.

The problem is exacerbated by the lack of valid and reliable instruments for measuring higher cognitive processes, especially of young children; even researchers who wish to conduct empirical studies on the effects of various gifted programs find themselves limited by the lack of suitable measurement instruments (Hoge, 1988; Tannenbaum, 1983).

In the late 1980s there was controversy over which was more vital in evaluating gifted programs, empirical precision or practical relevance? Rarely has the assessment of outcomes in a single study satisfied both practitioners and researchers in the field of gifted education.

FUTURE DIRECTIONS FOR GIFTED STUDENTS AND SOCIAL STUDIES

Many areas within gifted education could be refined. The definition of giftedness, the identification of gifted students, and appropriate student placement programs for the gifted all need continued study, as does curriculum design. Two particular areas of concern raised by educators and researchers in gifted education are (a) the content of social studies instruction and the instructional processes used to teach this content and (b) the assessment and evaluation of student performance.

Improving Social Studies Instruction for Gifted Students

Maker (1986) contended that "educators of the gifted have often placed so much emphasis on process that they have neglected the development of ideas/conclusions in the academic disciplines and the teaching of important concepts necessary as a foundation for further learning and creativity' (p. 152). To address this criticism, various authors have presented schemes for introducing gifted students to important concepts and issues in social studies. For example, Kitano and Kirby (1986) proposed a general plan for curriculum development applicable to gifted students, Grades 4–6. This model, presented in Figure 14–2, includes the interrelatedness of key social studies concepts from the disciplines of sociology, anthropology, ecology, history, and other areas of study. The authors elaborated on this plan by suggesting methods of incorporating various disciplines into the study of resources. For example, an economist would explore the theme of resources through investigating scarcity, consumption, and division of labor, whereas a geographer would view the same concept from the vantages of climate, human–land relationships, and land forms. Beyond the social sciences, other content areas might be studied; chemistry, ethics, and literature have been suggested as options. The goal in the study of resources by gifted students was summed up by Kitano and Kirby (1986):

Gifted youngsters will group and extend disciplinary applications to real environmental problems and their solutions ... As they acquire new insights from the concepts and content of the social sciences and

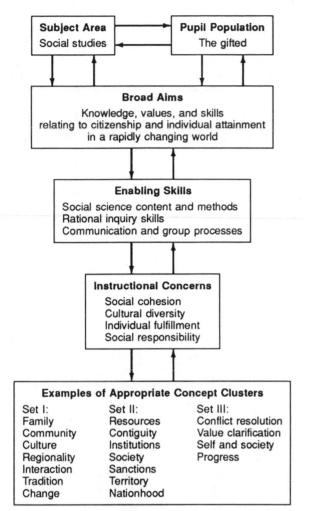

Subject Area	Pupil Population
Social studies	The gifted

Broad Aims

Knowledge, values, and skills
relating to citizenship and individual attainment
in a rapidly changing world

Enabling Skills

Social science content and methods
Rational inquiry skills
Communication and group processes

Instructional Concerns

Social cohesion
Cultural diversity
Individual fulfillment
Social responsibility

Examples of Appropriate Concept Clusters

Set I:	Set II:	Set III:
Family	Resources	Conflict resolution
Community	Contiguity	Value clarification
Culture	Institutions	Self and society
Regionality	Society	Progress
Interaction	Sanctions	
Tradition	Territory	
Change	Nationhood	

FIGURE 14–2. *Note.* From *Gifted Education: A Comprehensive View* (p. 138) by M. K. Kitano and D. F. Kirby, 1986, copyright 1986 by Margie K. Kitano and Darrell I. Kirby. Reprinted by permission of Harper Collins, Publishers.

other disciplines, gifted youngsters will be able to discover, develop, and apply the methods of investigation of disciplinary inquiry. (p. 145)

In addition to presenting gifted students with social studies instruction that integrates several disciplines, it is also recommended that a variety of teaching approaches be used. The specific suggestions cited earlier in the work of Taba, Bloom, Bruner, and Kohlberg are often found in texts and curricular materials designed for use by educators of gifted students. To date, no research comparing different instructional paradigms for the gifted in social studies has been reported. However, Horowitz and O'Brien (1986) presented a reality with which it is hard to disagree: "We cannot wait until we know all we need to know to provide challenging educational environments for [gifted] children" (p. 1151).

To help educators plan appropriate instruction for gifted students, Kaplan (1986) presented the following suggestions, which, though general in nature, relate well to social studies:

1. Curricula should be designed to meet the individual needs of students and not be generalized sets of goals deemed appropriate for all gifted students.
2. Curriculum content must not be purposeless or disjointed. For example, to merely teach gifted students from chapters in a textbook that are not covered in the regular curriculum is to disregard these students' individual needs and interests.
3. Curriculum content and processes in the social studies should have some connection with the world outside of the classroom, so that their applications to real problems are reinforced.

Passow (1987) agreed with these propositions and added one more note that is especially appropriate for social studies educators:

If the gifted are to be our "leaders of tomorrow", for what kinds of leadership should we be educating them? Is it sufficient for them to be creative, productive scientists, or should we be concerned with their morality, their ethics, and their social responsibility as well? . . . If we indeed are "one planet, one family", what kind of curricular experiences will contribute to bringing that notion to a reality instead of a pious phrase? (pp. 7, 10)

The last question, the most important and fundamental one raised in this chapter, may not be answered solely by pretest-posttest results or empirical research. The true answer will emerge only later, in the next generation, when today's children must decide the future course of our world. Our charge, then, as educators is to provide curriculum and instruction that are focused on attitudes and values, as well as on the acquisition of facts.

SUMMARY

The field of education for the gifted is filled with challenges, for both the students involved in the programs and the educators involved in the program operations. If we were to listen to the critics, we would hear that education for the gifted is a vast wasteland, a subsection of education so amorphous that those in it cannot even agree on a definition of the population they are trying to serve. If we were to listen to the proponents, we would hear about the varied nature of the gifted population and that the range of services provided them is the field's greatest strength. In effect, the proponents argue, educators should not be criticized for offering program models and services that are so visionary they do not fit discretely into typical patterns of curricular design or research.

The reality, of course, is that neither extreme is completely legitimate. As the field of education for the gifted heads toward the next century, its practitioners should be more conscious of the need to articulate better how their programs have improved the education of gifted students, in social studies and in other fields. Much research-based knowledge must be added to what little has been learned to date about effective programs for gifted students.

References

Betts, G. T. (1985). *The autonomous learner model for the gifted and talented.* Greeley, CO: Autonomous Learning Publications and Specialists.

Bireley, M., & Hoehn, L. (1987). Teaching implications of learning styles. *Academic Therapy, 22*(4), 437–441.

Bloom, B. S. (1956). *Taxonomy of educational objectives: Cognitive domain.* New York: David McKay.

Breiter, J. (1987). What's happening for gifted children in the social studies? *Southern Social Studies Quarterly, 13*(1), 43–54.

Bruner, J. (1966). *Toward a theory of instruction.* Cambridge, MA: Harvard University Press.

Cellerino, M. B., & Story, C. M. (1986). An energetic evolution: Meeting the needs of the gifted in the regular classroom. *Roeper Review, 8*(2), 104–107.

Clark, B. (1988). *Growing up gifted* (3rd ed.). Columbus, OH: Merrill.

Coleman, L. C. (1985). *Schooling the gifted.* Reading, MA: Addison-Wesley.

Delisle, J. R. (1984). *Gifted children speak out.* New York: Walker.

Education Products Information Exchange. (1979). Grant Progress Report NEI-G-790083 (Mimeograph). Stony Brook, NY: Author.

Ellis, H. (1904). *A study of British genius.* London: Hurst and Blackett.

Gallagher, J. J. (1985). *Teaching the gifted child* (3rd ed.). Boston: Allyn & Bacon.

Glass, G. V. (1976). Primary, secondary and meta-analysis of research. *Educational Researcher, 5,* 3–8.

Goleman, D. (1980, February). 1,528 little geniuses and how they grew. *Psychology Today,* pp. 28–43.

Gowan, J. C. (1972). Improving the mental health and performance of children. In *Emotional disturbance and the gifted child: Implications for school people* (pp. 8–12). Westmoreland, PA: Pennsylvania Department of Education.

Hanley, J. P., Whitla, D. K., Moo, E. W., & Walter, A. S. (1970). *Man: A course of study: An evaluation.* Cambridge, MA: Education Development Center.

Hanson, J. R., & Silver, H. F. (1978). *The learning preference inventory.* Moorestown, NJ: Hanson, Silver.

Hoge, R. D. (1988). Issues in the definition and measurement of the giftedness construct. *Educational Researcher, 17*(7), 12–22.

Horowitz, F. D., & O'Brien, M. (1986). Gifted and talented children: State of knowledge and directions for research. *American Psychologist, 41*(10), 1147–1152.

Howley, A., Howley, C. B., & Pendarvis, E. D. (1986). *Teaching gifted children: Principles and strategies.* Boston: Little, Brown.

Juntune, J. (1986). *Successful programs for the gifted and talented* (2nd ed.). Circle Pines, MN: National Association for Gifted Children.

Kaplan, S. N. (1986). Qualitatively differentiated curricula. In C. J. Maker (Ed.), *Critical issues in gifted education* (pp. 121–134). Rockville, MD: Aspen Systems.

Karnes, F. A., & Brown, K. E. (1981). Moral development and the gifted: An initial investigation. *Roeper Review, 3,* 8–10.

Kitano, M. J., & Kirby, D. F. (1986). *Gifted education: A comprehensive view.* Boston: Little, Brown.

Kohlberg, L. (1978). The cognitive-developmental approach to moral education. In P. Scharf (Ed.), *Readings in moral education* (pp. 136–51). Minneapolis: Winston Press.

Kulik, J. A., & Kulik, C. C. (1984). *Meta-analysis of evaluation findings on education of gifted and talented students,* (Final Report, Grant No. NIE-G-83-0053). Ann Arbor, MI: Center for Research on Learning and Teaching.

Li, L., & Delisle, J. R. (in press). Gifted education in China. *Gifted Education International.*

Lombroso, C. (1891). *The men of genius.* London: Robert Scott.

Lowman, L. M. (1961). An experimental evaluation of two curriculum digests for teaching first year algebra in a ninth grade class. (Doctoral Dissertation, University of Oklahoma). *Dissertation Abstracts, 22,* 502. (University Microfilms No. 61-2864).

Maker, C. J. (1982). *Teaching models in education of the gifted.* Rockville, MD: Aspen Systems.

Maker, C. J. (1986). Integrating content and process in the teaching of gifted students. In C. J. Maker (Ed.), *Critical issues in gifted education* (pp. 152–155). Rockville, MD: Aspen Systems.

McClelland, D. C., Baldwin, A. L., Bronfenbrenner, V., & Strodtbeck. F. L. (1958). *Talent and society.* Princeton: D. Van Nostrand.

National Commission on Excellence in Education. (1983). *A nation at risk.* Washington, DC: U.S. Department of Education.

Newland, T. E. (1976). *The gifted in socio-educational perspective.* Englewood Cliffs, NJ: Prentice-Hall.

Passow, A. H. (1987, January–February). Issues and trends in curriculum for gifted. *Michigan Council for the Gifted and Talented News* (pp. 6–10). East Lansing, MI: Michigan Council for the Gifted and Talented.

Pollins, L. D. (1985). Quality of in-school special services and the school/university program relationship for extremely gifted students. *Journal of Special Education, 19*(1), 103–110.

Reis, S. M., & Hebert, T. (1985). Creating practicing professionals in gifted programs: Encouraging students to become young professionals. *Roeper Review, 8*(2), 101–104.

Renzulli, J. S. (1977). *The enrichment triad model.* Mansfield Center, CT: Creative Learning Press.

Ross, J. D. & Ross, C. M. (1976). *The Ross Test of Higher Cognitive Processes.* Novato, CA: Academic Therapy Publications.

Selman, R. (1971). The relation of role-taking to the development of moral judgment in children. *Child Development, 42,* 79–91.

Sosniak, L. A. (1987). Gifted education and boondoggles: A few bad apples or a rotten bushel? *Phi Delta Kappan, 68*(7), 535–538.

Stewart, E. D. (1985). Social studies. In R. H. Swassing (Ed.), *Teaching gifted children and adolescents* (pp. 232–275). Columbus, OH: Charles E. Merrill.

Taba, H., Durkin, M. C., Fraenkel, J. R., & McNaughton, A. H. (1971). *A teacher's handbook to elementary social studies: An inductive approach.* Reading, MA: Addison-Wesley.

Tannenbaum, A. J. (1983). *Gifted children: Psychological and educational perspectives.* New York: Macmillan.

Terman, L. M. (1954). The discovery and encouragement of exceptional talent. *American Psychologist, 9,* 221–230.

Thompson, R. R. (1986). Giftedness and Advanced Placement American history: An investigation into the use of inquiry, conceptual and direct instructional techniques (Doctoral dissertation, Stanford University). *Dissertation Abstracts International, 47*(6), 2011A–2012A. (University Microfilms No. DA8619837)

Tomlinson, S. (1987). Issue based curriculum in the social studies for the gifted and talented. *The Social Studies, 78*(4), 148–154.

Tsuin-chen, O. (1961). Some facts and ideas about talent and genius in Chinese history. In G. Z. F. Bereday & J. A. Lauwerys (Eds.), *Concepts of excellence in education: The yearbook of education* (pp. 54–58). New York: Harcourt, Brace and World.

Wallace, W. L. (1962). The BSCS 1961–62 evaluation program: A statistical report. *Biological Sciences Curriculum Study Newsletter, 19,* 22–24.

Ward, V. S. (1980). *Differential education for the gifted.* Ventura, CA: Ventura County Superintendent of Schools.

Whitmore, J. R. (1980). *Giftedness, conflict and underachievement.* Boston: Allyn & Bacon.

Witty, P. A. (1940). Some considerations in the education of gifted children. *Educational Administration and Supervision, 26,* 512–521.

Section

·III·

TEACHERS IN SOCIAL STUDIES EDUCATION

·15·

CHANGING CONCEPTIONS OF RESEARCH ON THE TEACHING OF SOCIAL STUDIES

Beverly J. Armento

GEORGIA STATE UNIVERSITY

This chapter has been written with a sense of optimism. Recent reviews of research on teaching social studies (Armento, 1986; Fraenkel, 1987; Shaver, 1982; Stanley, 1985) have documented the serious problems that characterize the field: too few studies, with too few of those being methodologically sound and theoretically grounded. And most critics have argued that social studies researchers have not addressed the major issues in the field. In addition, the empirical research in social studies has been characterized by Fraenkel (1987) and others (e.g., Armento, 1986) as fragmented and noncumulative.

In spite of these criticisms, there are several countervailing forces that are prompting a quiet revolution in the research on teaching social studies. These forces will continue to influence the field well into the 1990s. First of all, there has been a considerable amount of public and professional dialogue on the state of education in general, and on the nature, goals, and content of the social studies curriculum in particular. Notable among the reports calling for reform in social studies are those by the Bradley Commission on History in Schools (1989; see also Gagnon, 1987, 1988) and by the National Commission on Social Studies in Schools and the National Social Science Disciplinary Associations (1989). In addition, numerous books and articles, representing a range of perspectives and voices, that have appeared recently provide new dimensions to the issues (e.g., Aronowitz & Giroux, 1985; Butts, 1988; Engle & Ochoa, 1988; Giroux, 1983a, 1983b; Goodlad, 1984; Greene, 1988; Purpel, 1989; Wexler, 1987).

Second, senior researchers associated with large funded projects or with research and development centers are now conducting research on the teaching of social studies. Included here are such researchers as: (a) Fred Newmann at the National

Center on Effective Secondary Schools at the University of Wisconsin-Madison; (b) Jere Brophy at the Institute for Research on Teaching at Michigan State University (see Porter & Brophy, 1987); (c) Lee Shulman with both the Teacher Assessment Project and the Knowledge Growth in a Profession Project at Stanford University; and (d) James Voss at the Learning Research and Development Center at the University of Pittsburgh.

These researchers and their colleagues are engaged in large-scale and multifaceted programs of social studies inquiry. Unlike doctoral students and independent faculty researchers, those who direct these (and other) funded projects have the resources to conduct the more complex, long-term, and cumulative investigations that are needed in research on teaching social studies.

Research on teaching social studies has also been influenced by the cognitive psychology movement which prompted changes in the research on teaching reading, mathematics, and science beginning some 10 years ago. Social studies researchers are asking new questions suggested by the field of cognitive psychology. In particular, the renewed emphasis on conceptualizing teaching and learning as integrated, interdependent processes has changed the character of empirical analytic research on teaching. Research on teaching social studies has also benefited from the spin-off effects of the cognitive research on teaching reading within the social studies content areas.

Recurring philosophic controversies regarding the nature of social knowledge and of inquiry have also affected (and will continue to affect) not only the research on teaching social studies but also the content and form of the social studies curriculum itself. As a result of this ferment, scholars are exploring alternative orientations toward science (Gergen, 1982). Many of

Reviewers were Jere E. Brophy, Michigan State University; Alan R. Tom, Washington University; Merlin C. Wittrock, University of California, Los Angeles.

these alternative paradigms are evident in the current research on teaching social studies.

These four societal forces—public debate, funded projects, the cognitive psychology movement, and fervor in the social sciences—have influenced social studies researchers to think and behave differently over the last several years. As a result, a quiet revolution has occurred in the research on teaching social studies. Today there are new faces, new issues, and new research paradigms. At least five fundamental shifts in the research on teaching social studies can be identified:

1. New epistemological traditions are being employed to study the teaching of social studies. Interpretive and critical analysis, as well as positivistic research paradigms, are now actively used. With these traditions, a more inclusive range of perspectives has become evident, including cognitive psychology, literary criticism, ethnography, sociolinguistics, humanism, and feminism.
2. The conceptualization of the roles of teachers has changed from unidimensional and simple toward more multidimensional and complex.
3. The units of analysis are no longer only observable teaching acts, but more holistic structures and internal belief and knowledge schemata.
4. The instructional focus has shifted from an emphasis on isolated elements in classroom life toward more integrative analyses that take into account student learning as well as various contextual elements.
5. Changes have occurred in the ways the domain of social studies itself is conceptualized, defined, and analyzed.

The quiet revolution has, however, yet to capture the imagination of most social studies researchers and educators or to have an impact on most social studies teacher preparation institutions and elementary and secondary school studies classrooms. The purpose of this chapter is to describe and document the emerging quiet revolution in the research on teaching social studies and to propose ways to extend and enrich this work. The five characteristics that mark the recent changes in the field form the outline of this chapter: changes in paradigms, in views of teachers, in the units of analysis, in instructional foci, and in the definition of the field. Specific works are cited to illustrate the trends; an exhaustive survey is not intended.

CHANGING RESEARCH PARADIGMS: FROM POSITIVISM TO POSTPOSITIVISM

The major function of science, from a positivistic perspective, is to discover lawlike principles that describe relationships among sets of observable phenomena. These laws are constructed from empirical observations and are assumed to form a cumulative body of knowledge. The positivistic paradigm has been highly successful for studying phenomena of the natural world. For the study of humans and of social phenomena, this model of inquiry has serious limitations. Those limitations and the search for more viable models of inquiry have been topics

of debate among philosophers and social scientists for many years (Gergen, 1982, pp. 7–8).

One of the central issues has to do with the stability of the phenomena under investigation. Although many behavioral scientists continue to believe in the underlying stability of human behavior, others recognize the extent and nature of change in the social world and the wide range of variation in human behavior and interaction. Many social scientists question also the capacity of humans to stand outside of their culture and their time in history to be fully conscious and objective in their observations of human behavior (Gergen, 1982). Given the realities of change and variation in social life, in human behavior, and in educational settings, many social scientists are no longer optimistic that their inquiry will lead to the discovery of "objective and enduring truth" (Gergen, 1982, p. 1). Realizing the inadequacies of traditional inquiry, social scientists have sought alternative orientations as well as a broader definition of positivism to reorient empirical investigations and bring inquiry more in line with their new assumptions about human and social behavior.

The Interpretive Perspective

Many researchers have come to view the social sciences primarily as interpretive disciplines (Gergen, 1982, p. 90), concerned with the processes humans use to construct reality. In order to fully understand the meaning of human actions, one must examine the cultural and historical milieu or the context within which those actions occur. In addition, human action is couched in intention and prompted by one's beliefs, values, motivations, and cognitions of the world; one's language as well as one's overt behavior are used to express the underlying meaning of human actions. Thus, human action must be examined in its full context if it is to be understood.

Consistent with these ideas is the notion that human behavior is subject to multiple interpretations (Gergen, 1982; Mannheim, 1952). Actions or events occur not in isolation, but rather in networks of interdependent beliefs and actions. Actions occurring before and after the event in question are pertinent if one is to attach meaning and significance to the happening. And, because each of these "pieces of the puzzle" of social interaction is open to interpretation, so is the "final interpretation" open to multiple interpretations (Gergen, 1982).

A number of new perspectives on the nature of social knowledge have emerged from this dialogue within the social sciences. Many of these ways of knowing have been applied to the study of teaching and to the study of the teaching of social studies. Included in the interpretive paradigm is ethnographic research (see Erickson, 1986; Fenstermacher, 1986; Goetz & LeCompte, 1984; Palonsky, 1987; White, 1985); the study of ordinary language or the linguistic perspective (see Green, 1983; Green & Smith, 1983; Green & Weade, 1988); the study of social knowledge from the perspective of women, or feminism (see Blair, 1985; Boydston, 1975; Dietz, 1987; Maher, 1987; Maher & Tetreault, 1987; Martin, 1982; Sherman, 1984; Westkott, 1979); the study of social behavior from a range of humanistic disciplines including art, theatre, music, architecture, and journalism (see Barone, 1983; Eisner, 1979; Elbaz & Elbaz, 1981; Milburn, 1985); and the study of social behavior from a cognitive perspective that focuses on such internal processes as attention, motivation, memory and knowledge schemata (e.g., see Magoon, 1977; Pressley & Levin, 1983; Winne & Marx, 1982; Wittrock, 1974, 1977, 1978, 1986).

Critical Theory

The third research tradition, in addition to the positivist and interpretive orientations, is that of critical theory. Proposing an alternative and more egalitarian social order based on justice and equality, the critical theorist begins research from a normative perspective and aims to illuminate the hidden political, economic, and social arrangements which lead to injustice and maldistribution of wealth and power. The intent of the critical theorist is openly emancipatory: the goals are enlightenment and empowerment and transformation of society (see Arendt, 1954; Bourdieu & Posseron, 1977; Cherryholmes, 1982; Clements, 1981; Giroux, 1983b; Livingstone, 1987; Popkewitz, 1981, Shor, 1986).

The critical theorist not only rejects the assumptions of the positivist that research can be value-free, but argues that positivistic methodologies are obsolete and that new conceptions for generating knowledge are needed (Lather, 1986, p. 260). Whereas the positivist tends to study elements of social behavior as independent units and the interpretive researcher examines behavior within its immediate contexts, the critical theorist assumes that particular social situations "form a dynamic relationship to the whole of social existence." That is, the "past, the present, and the possible future of the situation including its relationships to the large social context" (Shannon, 1989, p. xx) must be considered.

Much ferment has been stimulated within the social sciences by critical discourse about the nature of knowing and of knowledge in history, philosophy, and the social sciences.

The past decade has witnessed a virtual explosion of American interest in social theory. A panoply of Marxism, neo-Weberianism, poststructuralism and several others have been taken up by intellectuals as means to critique the dominant pluralist traditions of American social science, humanistic studies, and philosophy. (Giroux, 1983b, p. xi)

Feminist, liberal, and Freirian calls for emancipatory goals are also influences in the current literature addressed to educational issues (Aronowitz & Giroux, 1985; Freire & Macedo, 1987; Giroux, 1983b, 1984, 1988; Greene, 1986, 1988; Kickbusch, 1985; Livingstone, 1987; Shor & Freire, 1987).

A range of ideological perspectives is evident within the critical theorists, with conceptual debates over educational definitions and issues. For example, Giroux (1988) and Giroux and McLaren (1986) have proposed the concept of the teacher as an intellectual transformer:

A transformative intellectual [is one] who exercises forms of intellectual and pedagogical practice which attempt to insert teaching and learning directly into the political sphere by arguing that schooling represents both a struggle for meaning and a struggle over power relations. (p. 215)

This teacher is one who would "treat students as critical agents, question how knowledge is produced and distributed, utilize dialogue, and make knowledge meaningful, critical, and ultimately emancipatory" (Giroux & McLaren, 1986, p. 215).

But just how emancipatory, critical, and transformative should teachers be? Liston and Zeichner (1987) disagreed with Giroux and McLaren's concept of the intellectual transformer, suggesting that this concept "blurs an essential distinction between the teacher as educator and the teacher as political activist" (p. 122). "Teachers, as educators," argued Liston and Zeichner, "should be more concerned with enabling students to acquire and critically examine moral beliefs". This entails a careful and impartial consideration of the *plurality* of moral issues (p. 122). The concept of intellectual transformer, they argued, discourages a range of thought by proposing only one ideological perspective for the teacher to embrace, thus denying the opportunity to hold alternative positions.

On another matter, Newmann (1985) challenged critical theorists to be more specific in their answers to educational issues. "Specific social visions consistent with the value of emancipation" should be developed "to determine what organizational changes need to be made in schools, and to identify specific teaching practices that maximize the intellectual accomplishment and emotional rewards of critical inquiry" (p. 1). In other words what would a more just world look like? Would the model be a socialistic democracy? If so, how would society and schools be organized and what are the implications for social studies teachers and curriculum? These questions are yet to be addressed adequately by critical theorists.

Although there has been some critically grounded empirical work in social studies (see especially Anyon, 1978, 1979, 1980; Kickbusch, 1981; McNeil, 1986) and in education in general (McLaren, 1986), there has not been a considerable amount of such work. And, some of these researchers have been criticized for forcing the data to match the theory (Lather, 1986). What does empirical rigor mean from a critical perspective?

Methodological concerns are part of the current dialogue among critical theorists. There are few clear and commonly agreed upon strategies for linking the voluminous amount of critical theory writing with empirical research on teaching social studies. Lather (1986) has suggested that critical theory implies new methodologies to serve both the purposes of emancipatory knowledge and the empowerment of the researched, including teachers (p. 261). She took the constructs of triangulation, reflexivity, and research subject checks and reconceptualized them in a new context of "research as praxis." Research as praxis means to "involve the researched in a democratized process of inquiry characterized by negotiation, reciprocity, and empowerment" (Lather, 1986, p. 25).

That is, the subjects of an investigation should have opportunities to participate, to collaborate with the researcher and to engage in interpretation of the data. Thus, research subjects would engage in open-ended dialectical theory building. These open and collaborative activities should minimize the problems of theoretical imposition on the data, should maximize the participants' opportunities for awareness building and empowerment, and should establish greater credibility for the data (Lather, 1986, p. 272).

Although a critical theorist investigating the teaching of social studies might employ much of the same ethnographic methodology as a researcher operating out of an interpretive paradigm—case studies, interviews, observations—there are differences between interpretive and critical investigators. The critical theorist's a priori value assumptions guide data selection and interpretation, whereas the more traditional use of ethnographic inquiry is inductive. That is, the ethnographer tries to suspend preconceived ideas or categorization systems to allow the interpretive constructs to evolve from the data. Because interpretive researchers believe that situations are unique, their reports are written as descriptions (rather than as critiques and uncoverings as in critical theory research or as generalizations as in positivistic research). The aim for the critical theorist is to have the descriptions illuminate the reality of others in similar situations—in this case, other social studies teachers.

Continuing Positivistic Research

While the philosophic debates within the social sciences have encouraged work from interpretive and critical perspectives, positivistic research on teaching social studies continues as well. Some researchers have attempted to uncover the presage-process-product patterns in the teaching-learning process (Dunkin & Biddle, 1974). The process-product research paradigm, at its peak of popularity in the mid-to-late 1970s, has had a fundamental effect on educational policy and practice in the United States. Teacher variables such as enthusiasm, clarity, organization, use of advance organizers, and time on task were found to relate to student achievement outcomes (Brophy & Good, 1986; Fenstermacher, 1978; Gage, 1972; Medley, 1979; Mitzel, 1960; Rosenshine & Stevens, 1986). Today, these constructs are part of many teacher preparation and evaluation systems.

Current examples of empirical-analytic research on teaching social studies from a process-product perspective include studies of the use of behavioral objectives by the teacher (Ahlawat, Saadeh, Bader, & Khalifeh, 1988; O'Brien, Meszaros, & Pulliam, 1985) and of teacher enthusiasm (Burts, McKinney & Burts, 1985; McKinney, Larkins, & Burts, 1984). Other researchers have attempted to discover principles for teaching to achieve such social studies outcomes as fact or conceptual learning or critical thinking. Examples here include McKenzie and Sawyer's (1986) work on teachers' use of mnemonic devices and practice with fifth graders learning geographic locations, Gilmore and McKinney's (1986) work on teachers' use of questions with fifth and sixth graders during concept instruction, and Yoho's (1986) study of teachers' use of structured lessons during ninth-grade world history concept lessons.

As researchers have been influenced by the philosophic debates ongoing within the social sciences, the theoretical and empirical work on the teaching of social studies has gained in richness and diversity. Further evidence of this can be seen in the range of ways the roles of the social studies teacher have been conceptualized by researchers over the last several years.

CHANGING VIEWS ABOUT TEACHERS: FROM PRESENTER TO DECISION MAKER TO TRANSFORMER

Social studies teachers have been conceptualized variously as transmitters of culture (Barr, Barth, & Shermis, 1977) decision makers (Barr et al., 1977; Engle & Ochoa, 1988), moral craftspersons (Tom, 1980, 1984; Van Manen, 1977), brokers of scholarly knowledge (White, 1987), reflective thinkers (Schon, 1983, 1987; VanSickle, 1985; Zeichner, 1983; Zeichner & Liston, 1987), and as transformative intellectuals (Giroux, 1988; Giroux & McLaren, 1986). These conceptions of teachers' roles range from the simple to the complex, from the apolitical to the political. In most cases, the work on these views of teachers has been theoretical rather than empirical. That conceptual work is highlighted in this section.

Presenter of Knowledge

The current view of the teacher as a presenter of knowledge emerged from the process-product literature in Rosenshine's conception of direct instruction (Brophy & Good, 1986; Rosenshine, 1976; Rosenshine & Furst, 1973; Rosenshine & Stevens, 1986). The direct instruction assumption is

that students learn more efficiently when their teachers first structure new information for them and help them relate it to what they already know, and then monitor their performance and provide corrective feedback during recitation, drill, practice, or application activities. (Brophy & Good, 1986, p. 366)

This view of the teacher as a presenter of knowledge and skills was derived from positivistic research programs designed to identify the generic forms of teaching behavior that consistently relate with student cognitive achievement. However, in this process-product research,

critical features of teaching, such as the subject matter being taught, the classroom context, the physical and psychological characteristics of the students, or the accomplishment of purposes not readily assessed on standardized tests, [were] typically ignored in the quest for general principles of effective teaching. (Shulman, 1987, p. 6)

Shulman (1987) proposed that a more comprehensive view of the roles of teachers and of teaching should guide inquiry. In the model he proposed, teaching begins with a

teacher's understanding of what is to be learned and how it is to be taught. It proceeds through a series of activities during which the students are provided specific instruction and opportunities for learning. Teaching ends with new comprehension by both the teacher and the student. (Shulman, 1987, p. 7)

A teacher's *pedagogical content knowledge* and *pedagogical reasoning* are major elements in any teacher's role, proposed Shulman (1987). The key, he argued,

lies at the intersection of content and pedagogy, in the capacity of the teacher to transform the content knowledge [possessed] into forms that are pedagogically powerful and yet adaptive to the variations in ability and background presented by the students. (p. 15)

Exploring the social studies content-knowledge that teachers employ is the focus of a research program at Stanford (Gudmundsdottir, 1987). Although the teacher's role is basically still defined as a presenter of knowledge, ethnographic techniques are being employed to examine the nature and structure of teachers' content knowledge and the ways teachers structure and use knowledge during instruction. Research such as this can provide rich information not only about the procedural actions of teachers as they present social studies instruction, but also data about the accuracy, misconceptions, completeness, and degree of interpretation that teachers employ in their presentation of social studies knowledge.

Presenter of Knowledge

This is probably the most dominant role that most social studies educators play. Nevertheless, little is known currently about teachers' beliefs regarding the nature of social knowledge or about the nature of their content knowledge. In addition, researchers should ask: How do social studies teachers *present* knowledge to students of various ages? How do teachers present alternative interpretations of social knowledge? What are the relationships between the ways teachers interpret critical social studies topics and issues and the ways students understand these topics?

Decision Maker

Some have argued that the heart of the social studies teacher's role is decision making (Engle & Ochoa, 1988; Shavelson, 1973). This is especially so for the social studies teacher who intends to foster in students an attitude of reflective decision making:

In a reflective classroom, the teacher's role is to stimulate thinking, encourage dialogue, and guide students in evaluating the worth of ideas. The role of teachers becomes a facilitative one where teachers raise questions, foster doubt, present competing views, challenge the ideas of students, and promote rigorous and democratic dialogue. At the same time, the teacher must be informed with respect to the issues under discussion. (Engle & Ochoa, 1988, p. 162)

The idea of the teacher as a reflective decision maker has gained popularity in the educational literature during the last several years. However, the careful reader of the literature will find a range of views on and definitions of the *reflective teacher*. For example, when Shulman (1987) uses the term *reflection,* he means:

This is what a teacher does when he or she looks back at the teaching and learning that has occurred, and reconstructs, reenacts, and/or recaptures the events, the emotions, and the accomplishments. It is that set of processes through which a professional learns from experience . . . not merely a disposition . . . nor a set of strategies . . . but also the use of particular kinds of analytic knowledge. (p. 327)

The critical theorist's conception of a reflective teacher goes beyond Shulman's by proposing that such teachers

treat others responsibly and justly and link knowledge to the biography and personal meanings of students, raise questions about the epistemological, political, and economic uses of knowledge, and situate all of the above within an historical analysis of education. (Landon & Apple, 1988, p. 5; see also Noffke & Brennan, 1988; Zeichner & Liston, 1987)

How do social studies teachers make decisions? What decisions do they make? How do social studies teachers model decision-making processes for students? How, indeed, is social decision making made a part of students' lives by teachers? These are only a few of the many questions awaiting social studies researchers who seek to better understand the role of the teacher as decision maker.

The Caring Role

Most social studies teachers daily play a range of roles in their complex relationships with students: presenter of knowledge and ideas, inquirer, prober, decision maker, and reflector. But a social studies teacher should be much more according to Bryk (1988), Greene (1988), and Noddings (1988), who have pointed out that there is a personal and a caring side to teaching. Classrooms and schools are places where people have many meaningful relationships—where people care about one another—and where that caring (or lack of it) influences the beliefs, attitudes, knowledge, actions, and aspirations of students as well as teachers.

While no one theory of the ethic of caring exists, there are ingredients for theories and models of caring which have particular relevance to research on teaching social studies. For example, Noddings's (1988) concept of caring relates to "connected teaching" or the ability to look into the eyes of students, to inspire them to not only comprehend social issues but to relate to the issues and to understand them from a range of perspectives. Caring has to do with wanting to grapple with serious issues and with feeling a commitment to take social action.

Empathy, civic responsibility, and perspective taking have long histories as stated goals for social studies programs in a democratic society. Yet, our understanding of these goals and the instructional means to achieve them is minimal. A purely cognitive analysis has proven insufficient for understanding the complex nature of teaching for these goals. Social studies researchers must go beyond narrow academic orientations to find new ways to study the role of such constructs as teacher caring, imagination, identification, and role taking in social studies teaching. Questions include: How do social studies teachers demonstrate human caring, and how do they encourage students to "connect" with social studies content and with important social issues? How do teachers influence students to want to participate in sociopolitical activities and to care to learn more about and to address civic concerns? How do teachers learn to care about civic issues themselves? What role does teacher preparation play in nurturing caring attributes?

As researchers have explored a broader range of roles of the social studies teacher over the last several years, the ways in which they have defined the units of analyses have also changed.

CHANGING VIEWS ABOUT UNITS OF ANALYSIS: FROM MICRO TO MACRO

Researchers operating from a positivistic orientation tend to focus on overt, quantifiable elements of teacher behavior in a search for patterns of effective teaching-learning relationships. The research focus has traditionally been on such variables as the number and type of questions asked; directions, praise, or feedback given; or the nature, quantity, and timing of practice and review.

Two distinct shifts away from this observable bits-of-behavior approach to research on teaching social studies can be seen in the more recent research: (a) defining the unit of analysis as internal teacher processes—goals, plans, judgments, knowledge, decisions, and beliefs; and (b) defining teaching as a social event and thus conceptualizing the unit of analysis as a social structure, such as an activity, a lesson, an entire classroom, or a school.

Since there are other chapters in this handbook addressing the research on teachers' internal beliefs, plans, and knowledge, this aspect of the shift in the research focus will not be discussed here (see, however, Calderhead, 1987; McNair, 1979; Shavelson, 1983; Shavelson & Stern, 1981). Rather, examples will be given of social studies research in which the unit of analysis is a type of social structure. The units of analysis featured in these studies are the activity event, the classroom, or the school.

Stodolsky (1988) observed 39 fifth-grade mathematics and social studies classes taught by 21 teachers in more than a dozen schools. In this extensive study of a range of instructional factors (content of lessons, forms of instruction, goals, student attitudes, and the roles of teachers), Stodolsky used the *activity structure* as the unit of analysis. An activity structure is a broader conception of classroom activity than the notion of single teacher-student interactions; the activity structure represents the sum of the instructional arrangements employed for teaching different content areas.

Using the activity structure construct, Stodolsky found a great range of instructional diversity in social studies classes. Activities included the typical textbook reading and recitation; however, there were also peer work groups, simulation activities, and projects. High-level thinking skills and problem solving as well as affective and social skills were emphasized; in addition, research skills as well as factual knowledge were stressed. Students worked with one another, with the teacher, and with a range of materials and a range of topics (Stodolsky, 1988).

These rich observations of elementary social studies activity structures provide a contrast to the typical descriptions in which elementary social studies classrooms are portrayed as boring, teacher-dominated, textbook-driven places. The use of the activity structure as the unit of analysis provided a way to capture previously unnoticed elements of social studies classrooms.

The classroom itself was the unit of analysis for Newmann's (1988) study of higher level thinking and thoughtfulness in social studies classes in five high schools. After developing a rationale for the importance of higher level thinking and a broad conception of thinking, Newmann developed instruments to guide the classroom observational process. Characteristics of the lesson, of teacher behavior, and of student behavior were identified. Total class periods were rated, for example, on such teacher behaviors as: the thoughtful teacher must ask challenging questions, carefully consider student explanations and reasons for conclusions, and press individual students to justify or clarify their assertions (Newmann, 1988, p. 5).

Newmann's research is clearly empirical-analytic work with positivistic assumptions; however, unlike some earlier work, it is well grounded in theory, methodologically sound, and focused on an important social studies issue, teaching for higher level thinking. Newmann (1988) asserted:

One way to learn to promote higher order thinking is to find teachers who do it rather consistently and to look for the ways in which they differ from those who demonstrate less success. If we can distinguish between more and less thoughtful classrooms, we can then inquire more systematically about the possible factors that influence the promotion of higher order thinking in classrooms. (p. 2)

Indeed, there were differences among classes. Some were rated more thoughtful by Newmann's definition: that is, the teachers were judged to demonstrate more careful consideration of students' reasons and explanations and to use more socratic questioning; students were rated as more engaged during the observation period, and they generated more original ideas and were rated to be more articulate in expressing their ideas. Lecture and recitation characterized the classes rated as least thoughtful, and teacher-led discussion characterized those rated as most thoughtful. There was also more use of primary sources and less reliance upon textbooks in the classes rated as more thoughtful (Newmann, 1988, p. 21).

In a very different focus on the classroom as the unit of analysis, Milburn (1985) applied a humanistic metaphor (Beckerman's, 1970, concept of drama) in his interpretive study of a high school economics class. He noted that "such a perspective focusses attention on teaching, not as a series of categorical behaviors, not as a script, not as a series of intended learning outcomes, but as a humanistic undertaking" (p. 23). The aim of the case study was an "illumination of human performances in the social studies classroom, with both teachers and students engaged in educational acts over a particular time and in a particular space" (p. 23).

Using the school as the unit of analysis, McNeil (1986) examined how social studies knowledge in four high schools was shaped and controlled by the organizational context of the school itself. Grounding the study in a critical perspective, McNeil documented the ways in which social studies teachers fragment, simplify, and mystify social studies knowledge in their efforts to control students. This "defensive teaching," contributes to the de-skilling of teachers as well as robbing students of meaningful learning. Defensive teaching was seen by McNeil as an accommodation by teachers "to a complex organization which embodied conflicting goals (student control and learning) and gave powerless teachers the responsibility of resolving the conflicts" (p. 211).

Each of the four studies on the teaching of social studies cited above illustrates an important characteristic of the new wave of research: that is, the search for deeper meaning through the ways in which the complex phenomena of social studies teaching and learning are described and illuminated. These studies, representing different research traditions (Stodolsky and Newmann, empirical-analytic; Milburn, interpretive; and McNeil, critical) provoke new insights, images, and questions for social studies teachers, teacher educators, and researchers alike.

CHANGING VIEWS OF THE INSTRUCTIONAL FOCI: FROM ISOLATED TO INTEGRATED

Behavioral psychological principles have long dominated educational psychology and the research on teaching. Associationist views led educators and researchers to think that knowledge and skills could be analyzed into "hundreds of components to be placed in learners' heads through practice and appropriate rewards" (Resnick & Klopfer, 1989, p. 2). From that orientation came the idea that knowledge, skills, and various instructional components could be conceptualized in a linear fashion, from simple to difficult; thus, the hierarchies of types of knowledge (Gagne, 1974) and questions (Bloom, 1954) that have influenced curriculum development, teacher education, and research on teaching social studies in profound ways. For example, researchers have often examined the number and types of questions teachers asked but seldom inquired into the accuracy, completeness, and relevance of the content of those questions. Or, researchers have counted the frequency of praise or quantified evidence of teacher enthusiasm but neglected to take into account relevant classroom contextual factors that might illuminate and explain such teacher behavior and its effects.

However, today researchers are being influenced primarily by advances in cognitive psychology and in cultural anthropology to view teaching-learning settings in more holistic, integrated, and interactive ways. For example, the cognitive movement in psychology has led to new conceptualizations of human learning. From these understandings, an educational researcher can develop theoretically grounded hypotheses about teaching, which can be then be explored in naturalistic or laboratory settings. Cognitive psychologists, for example, believe that learning occurs through active construction of new knowledge or reorganization of prior knowledge. Meaningful learning implies active processes of motivation, attention, memory, and visualization as well as thinking and problem solving (Glaser, 1988; Wittrock, 1974, 1977, 1978, 1986). Further, it is thought that knowledge of the social world is organized and held in memory in schemata, or conceptual structures, that represent the relationships the learner has built among a category of events, objects, and ideas.

From these and other basic principles of learning, some cognitive psychologists have derived and tested propositions for teaching. Wittrock's (1978) generative approach to teaching, for instance, suggests many ways teachers can facilitate students' active reorganization and coding of new ideas. While there has been considerable testing of Wittrock's generative approach to teaching in mathematics and reading, few studies can be found using social studies content. For social studies researchers who seek to ground their hypotheses about teaching in cognitive psychology, the generative theory of teaching holds considerable promise.

Vosniadou and Brewer (1987) have also proposed instructional hypotheses based on cognitive psychology principles of human learning. The research on cognitive schemata and radical knowledge restructuring suggests that learners who hold serious misconceptions about a topic must develop completely new schemata for that topic; they cannot simply reorganize their previously held ideas. Vosniadou and Brewer have hypothesized two instructional teaching strategies for use in such cases: (a) Socratic dialogues and (b) analogies, metaphors, and visual representations of the new ideas (p. 61).

It is often the case in social studies that students hold serious misconceptions about other people, places, and ideologies. The role of the social studies teacher in such cases, according to Vosniadou and Brewer, is to diagnose student misconceptions, understand the student's point of view, propose new frameworks, raise questions to illuminate inconsistencies and errors, and guide the learner to the construction of more meaningful schemata (p. 61). In addition to such Socratic methods, teachers can use visual representations of the topic to aid the student in the development of a new conceptualization.

Currently, such theoretically grounded hypotheses on social studies teaching are untested. And, the contributions of cognitive psychology for research on social studies teaching go far beyond the few examples cited above. In this chapter, only surface attention could be given to the extensive theoretical and empirical work in cognitive psychology and to the possible applications to social studies research. In-depth readings are available, such as: Bransford, Sherwood, Vye, and Rieser (1986), Carey (1986), Glaser (1984, 1988), Lepper and Greene (1978), Resnick and Klopfer (1989), Vosniadou and Brewer (1987), Voss (1986), Voss, Greene, Post, and Penner (1983), and Voss, Tyler, and Yengo (1983).

CHANGING VIEWS OF SOCIAL STUDIES: WHOSE INTERPRETATION IS "RIGHT"?

History and social studies education have been charged frequently with being ethnocentric, Eurocentric, and lacking in objectivity and in multiple perspectives. These criticisms have been applied not only to the content of textbooks but also to the language of teachers and to the omissions and commissions of classroom dialogue (e.g., Berman, 1988; Kickbusch, 1987; Nash, 1974; White, 1988).

Descriptions of historical events are often presented as fact, seen from one point of view, rather than as one of many interpretations. History is seldom presented through the voices of its many participants, and the sensitive issues of the past and present are often hidden from students' view. These criticisms of social studies education continue to confront the field. Juxtaposed against these criticisms are the ferment and excitement within the fields of history and the social sciences as revisionist scholars look with new eyes and new data at their fields. For example, historian Gary Nash's *Red, White, and Black* (1974) is written:

from the belief that to cure the historical amnesia that has blotted out so much of our past we must look at American history as the interaction of many people from a wide range of cultural backgrounds over a period of many centuries. (p. 3)

Assessments of currently used social studies textbooks, however, continue to present a picture not of revisionist views of history and social studies, but rather of one-sided, simplistic descriptions of events (e.g., Berman (1988); White, 1988).

How do social studies teachers use such textbooks? How do social studies teachers present social knowledge? Are multiple perspectives and interpretations encouraged and presented? Are multiple interpretations compared, analyzed? What role does the teacher-preparation program play in the development of teachers' knowledge of the nature of social knowledge? Do teachers themselves question social knowledge and do teachers encourage students to question the sources and accuracy of data?

Researchers are beginning to ask such important questions. For example, using ethonographic techniques, Wilson and Wineburg (1988) explored in depth the historical and social science knowledge possessed by four high school social studies teachers. The researchers also examined how the teachers used their knowledge in classroom interaction.

Examination of the domain-specific knowledge of teachers and of students has provided new insights into what happens in social studies classes. Much of what happens depends on what is in the minds of teachers and learners who participate daily in social studies classes. Most of the current research along these lines has been influenced by the cognitive psychology movement (Alexander, Judy, & Kim, 1988; Carlsen & Wilson, 1988; Evans, 1988; Gudmunsdottir, 1987; Leinhardt, 1983; Voss, Greene, Post & Penner, 1983; Voss, Tyler, & Yengo, 1983; Wilson, Shulman, & Richert, 1987; Wilson & Wineburg, 1988; Wineburg & Wilson, in press). A range of methodological tools have been employed in these studies, including such techniques as interview, instructional protocol analysis, and postlesson interpretation by the teacher.

Describing teachers' and students' schemata for topics and ideas in the social sciences and history and in social studies classes is an important research emphasis. However, this knowledge is not a substitute for the adequate conceptualization of the characteristics of social knowledge and of the knowledge and skills needed for citizenship. Without a clear image of the goals of the field, there will be no standard against which to compare any person's view of history. Just what is wrong with the thinking of a teacher such as Fred, discussed by Wilson and Wineburg (1988), who thinks history is just "knowing the facts" (p. 529)?

What is problematic or useful and powerful about a Fred's preparation to become a social studies teacher? And what interventions might influence a Fred to think, believe, and act in more empowered ways in his role as a social studies teacher? How do school organization and climate facilitate or inhibit a Fred's intellectual and professional growth as a social studies educator? And in what ways do a Fred's ideas and knowledge influence the ideas and knowledge of his students? These are important research questions for social studies education.

CHANGING CONCEPTIONS OF RESEARCH ON TEACHING SOCIAL STUDIES

The quiet revolution in the research on teaching social studies means that today there are new theoretical constructs, new research paradigms, new methodological tools. And social studies researchers and educators will have to draw from among the best of these ideas if we are to address the serious problems currently facing the teaching of social studies.

The National Council for the Social Studies Curriculum Guidelines propose that: "The basic goal of social studies education is to prepare young people to be humane, rational, participating citizens in a world that is becoming increasingly interdependent" (Osborn, 1979, p. 262). Such a citizen should hold attitudes of and a commitment to human dignity, possess usable and meaningful knowledge, and be able and willing to critically assess and help resolve the important issues facing society (Osborn, 1979). Researchers interested in the teaching of social studies should be in the service of these goals: How, organizationally and pedagogically, can schools and teachers better achieve the goals of social studies for all students?

A Research Agenda

The quiet revolution described in this chapter has yet to influence the bulk of the research on teaching social studies. Researchers who hold positivistic, interpretive, or critical perspectives must raise new questions and offer new ways of illuminating old problems. Potentially fruitful areas of the research on teaching social studies include the development and testing of curriculum alternatives, the teaching and preparation of social studies teachers, pedagogical effectiveness, and organizational effect. In addition, research on research is needed. What are some of the questions awaiting new approaches?

Research and Development of Curriculum Alternatives. Research on teaching social studies should begin with questions concerning goals and curricular alternatives. What should be taught? In what form? To whom? Changes in society should prompt social studies educators to address curricular issues, and so should changes within the fields of history and the social sciences. How should revisionist historical perspectives, for example, be translated into social studies instruction? What alternative forms might curriculum and instruction take, based on what is known about human motivation and learning? What do teachers need to know and be able to do to effectively use alternative social studies curriculum materials?

Research on the Education of Social Studies Teachers. What knowledge, skills, and attitudes do social studies teachers need in order to effectively address social studies goals? How can social studies teachers interact with students to achieve important goals? Ethnographic studies of social studies classrooms have provided rich but incomplete data on these questions. Studies of teachers' pedagogical content knowledge have opened new lines of inquiry. Yet, we know very little about the most effective ways of empowering social studies teachers with the knowledge, critical thinking skills, and attitudes they need in order to facilitate these attributes in students.

Research on Pedagogical Effectiveness. The extensive work in cognitive psychology should provide a theoretical base for social studies researchers to develop hypotheses about more effective ways of teaching for goals of thinking, knowing, and doing. More is known now than ever before about such constructs as motivation, memory, cognition, critical thinking, and role taking. Descriptive looks at classrooms to see what is happening are useful. However, social studies researchers must also test viable instructional alternatives that will enable teachers to better address some of the more difficult goal areas, such as the critical assessment of social issues.

New theoretical constructs, such as the ethic of caring, should be carefully considered for their relevance to research on teaching social studies. Social studies goals cut across the traditional boundaries of knowledge, values, and skills; the approaches researchers take to explore pedagogical effectiveness must address the multidimensionality of teaching for such goals.

Research on Organizational Effects. What school and classroom social structures maximize social studies instruction? What contextual factors inhibit teachers and students from achieving social studies goals? What influences do political-legal factors have on social studies teachers and on what they choose to emphasize or omit?

Research on Research. How might those who do research on teaching social studies relate with teachers of social studies? Should the researcher and the teacher be collaborators, as Lather (1986) suggested in her concept of research as praxis? How might such collaboration change researchers? Teachers? Research results? The use of research findings? These are especially important questions if researchers hope that their research on teaching social studies will be intimately related with teaching social studies.

Social studies researchers have a unique opportunity today to become part of the quiet revolution. The challenges to the field are many; it will take the best minds and the best of the new ideas to address the problems facing social studies education. And although research alone will not solve the issues, perhaps research can enable those in the field to narrow the gap between our stated goals and the current reality of life in social studies classrooms.

References

Ahlawat, K. S., Saadeh, J. A, Bader, Q. H., & Khalifeh, G. (1988). An investigation of the use of behavioral objectives in Jordanian social studies classrooms. *Theory and Research in Social Education, 16*(3), 227–243.

Alexander, P. A., Judy, J. E., & Kim, Y. H. (1988, April). *Domain-specific and strategic knowledge: A review of the literature.* Paper presented at the annual meeting of the American Educational Research Association, New Orleans.

Anyon, J. (1978). Elementary social studies textbooks and legitimating knowledge. *Theory and Research in Social Education, 6,* 40–55.

Anyon, J. (1979). Ideology and United States history textbooks. *Harvard Educational Review, 49,* 361–386.

Anyon, J. (1980). Social class and the hidden curriculum of work. *Journal of Education, 162,* 69–92.

Arendt, H. (1954). *Between past and future: Eight exercises in political thought.* New York: Viking.

Armento, B. J. (1986). Research on teaching social studies. In M. C. Wittrock (Ed.), *Handbook of research on Teaching* (3rd ed., pp. 942–951). New York: Macmillan.

Aronowitz, S., & Giroux, H. A. (1985). *Education under siege: The conservative, liberal, and radical debate over schooling.* Westport, CT: Bergin & Garvey.

Barone, T. (1983). Education as aesthetic experience: "Art is germ." *Educational Leadership, 40*(4), 21–26.

Barr, R. D., Barth, J. L., & Shermis, S. S. (1977). *Defining the social studies.* Washington, DC: National Council for the Social Studies.

Beckerman, B. (1970). *Dynamics of drama: Theory and method of analysis.* New York: Knopf.

Berman, D. M. (1988). "Every Vietnamese Was a Gook" My Lai, Vietnam, and American Education. *Theory and Research in Social Education, 16*(2), 141–159.

Blair, J. (1985). Women's self concept and belief: A feminist approach to empowerment symbolism. *Women's Studies International Forum, 8*(4), 323–334.

Bloom, B. S. (1954). *Taxonomy of educational objectives. Handbook I: Cognitive domain.* New York: Longmans, Green & Co.

Bourdieu, P., & Posseron, J. (1977). *Reproduction in education, society, and culture.* Beverly Hills, CA: Sage.

Boydston, J. A. (1975). John Dewey and the new feminism. *Teachers College Record 76*(3), 443–446.

Bradley Commission on History in Schools. (1989). Building a history curriculum: Guidelines for teaching history in schools. In P. Gagnon & the Bradley Commission (Eds.), *Historical literacy: the case for history in American education* (pp. 16–47). New York: Macmillan.

Bransford, J., Sherwood, R., Vye, N., & Rieser, J. (1986). Teaching thinking and problem solving. *American Psychologist, 41*(10), 1078–1089.

Brophy, J., & Good, T. L. (1986). Teacher behavior and student achievement. In M. C. Wittrock (Ed.), *Handbook of research on teaching* (3rd ed., pp. 328–375). New York: Macmillan.

Bryk, A. S. (1988). Musings on the moral life of schools. *American Journal of Education, 96,* 256–290.

Burts, D. C., & C. W. McKinney, & B. L. Burts. (1985). Effects of teacher enthusiasm on three and four year old children's acquisitions of four concepts. *Theory and Research in Social Education. 13*(1), 19–29.

Butts, R. F. (1988). *The morality of democratic citizenship: Goals for civic education in the republic's third century.* Calabasas, CA: Center for Civic Education.

Calderhead, J. (Ed.). (1987). *Exploring teachers' thinking.* London: Cassell.

Carey, S. (1986). Cognitive science and science education. *American Psychologist, 41*(10), 1123–1130.

Carlsen, W. S., & Wilson, S. M. (1988, April). *Responding to student questions: The effects of teacher subject-matter knowledge and experience on teacher discourse strategies.* Paper presented at the annual meeting of the American Educational Research Association, New Orleans.

Cherryholmes, C. H. (1982). Discourse and criticism in the social studies classroom. *Theory and Research in Social Education, 9*(4), 57–73.

Clements, M. (1981). A social paradigm: An ethical perspective. *Theory and Research in Social Education, 9*(3), 1–23.

Dietz, M. G. (1987). Context is all: Feminism and theories of citizenship. *Daedalus, 116*(4), 1–24.

Dunkin, M. J., & Biddle, B. J. (1974). *The study of teaching.* New York: Holt, Rinehart & Winston.

Eisner, E. W. (1979). *The educational imagination: On the design and evaluation of school programs.* New York: Macmillan.

Elbaz, F., & Elbaz, R. (1981). Literature and curriculum: Toward a view of curriculum as discursive practice. *Curriculum Inquiry, 11,* 105–122.

Engle, S. H., & Ochoa, A. S. (1988). *Education for democratic citizenship: Decision-making in the social studies.* New York: Teachers College Press.

Erickson, F. (1986). Qualitative methods in research on teaching. In M. C. Wittrock (Ed.), *Handbook of research on teaching* (3rd ed., pp. 119–161). New York: Macmillan.

Evans, R. W. (1988). Lessons from history: Teacher and student conceptions of the meaning of history. *Theory and Research in Social Education, 16*(3), 203–225.

Fenstermacher, G. D. (1978). A philosophical consideration of recent research on teacher effectiveness. In L. S. Shulman (Ed.), *Review of research in Education* (Vol. 6, pp. 157–185). Itasca, IL: Peacock.

Fenstermacher, G. D. (1986). Philosophy of research on teaching: Three aspects. In M. C. Wittrock (Ed.), *Handbook of research on teaching,* (3rd ed., pp. 37–49). New York: Macmillan.

Fraenkel, J. R. (1987). Toward improving research in social studies education. *Theory and Research in Social Education, 15*(3), 203–222.

Friere, P., & Macedo, D. (1987). *Literacy: Reading the word and the world.* Westport, CT: Bergin & Garvey.

Gage, N. L. (1972). *Teacher effectiveness and teacher education: The search for a scientific basis.* Palo Alto, CA: Pacific Books.

Gagne, R. M. (1974). *The conditions of learning.* (2nd ed.). New York: Holt, Rinehart & Winston.

Gagnon, P. A. (1987). *Democracy's untold story: What world history textbooks neglect.* Washington, DC: American Federation of Teachers.

Gagnon, P. A. (1988). Why study history? *Atlantic Monthly, 262*(5), 43–66.

Gergen, K. J. (1982). *Toward transformation in social knowledge.* New York: Springer-Verlag.

Gilmore, A. C., & McKinney, C. W. (1986). The effects of student questions and teacher questions on concept acquisition. *Theory and Research in Social Education, 14*(3), 225–244.

Giroux, H. A. (1983a). Theories of reproduction and resistance in the new sociology of education: A critical analysis. *Harvard Educational Review, 53*(3), 257–293.

Giroux, H. A. (1983b). *Theory and resistance in education.* MA.: Bergin & Garvey.

Giroux, H. A. (1984). Public philosophy and the crisis in education. *Harvard Educational Review, 54*(2), 186–194.

Giroux, H. A. (1988). *Teachers as intellectuals: Toward a critical pedagogy of learning.* Westport, CT: Bergin & Garvey.

Giroux, H. A., & P. McLaren. (1986). Teacher education and the politics of engagement: The case for democratic schooling. *Harvard Educational Review, 56*(3), 213–238.

Glaser, R. (1984). The role of knowledge. *American Psychologist, 39*(2), 93–104.

Glaser, R. (1988). Cognitive science and education. *International Social Science Journal, 40,* 21–44.

Goetz, J. P., & LeCompte, M. D. (1984). *Ethnography and qualitative design in educational research.* Orlando, FL: Academic Press.

Goodlad, John, I. (1984). *A place called school: Prospects for the future.* New York: McGraw-Hill.

Green, J. L. (1983). Research on teaching as a linguistic process: A state of the art. In E. W. Gordon (Ed.), *Review of research in education* (Vol. 10, pp. 151–252). Washington, D. C.: American Educational Research Association.

Green, J. L., & Smith, D. (March, 1983). Teaching and learning: A linguistic perspective. *The Elementary School Journal, 83*(4), 353–391.

Green, J. L., & Weade, R. (1988, April). *Teaching as conversation and the construction of meaning in the classroom.* Paper presented at the 1988 annual meeting of the American Educational Research Association, New Orleans.

Greene, M. (1986). In search of a critical pedagogy. *Harvard Educational Review, 56*(4), 427–441.

Greene, M. (1988). *The dialectic of freedom.* New York: Teachers College Press.

Gudmundsdottir, S. (1987, April). *Pedagogical content knowledge: Teachers' ways of knowing.* Paper presented at the annual meeting of the American Educational Research Association, Washington, DC.

Kickbusch, K. W. (1981). *An investigation of relationships between epistemological systems in social studies classrooms and the effects of the hidden curriculum on knowledge reproduction.* Unpublished doctoral dissertation, University of California, Santa Barbara.

Kickbusch, K. W. (1985). Ideological innocence and dialogue: A critical perspective on discourse in the social studies. *Theory and Research in Social Education, 13*(3), 45–56.

Kickbusch, K. W. (1987). Civic education and preservice educators: Extending the boundaries of discourse. *Theory and Research in Social Education, 15* (3), 173–188.

Landon, B., & Apple, M. (Eds.) (1988). *The curriculum: Problems, politics and possibilities.* Buffalo: State University of New York Press.

Lather, P. (1986). Research as praxis. *Harvard Educational Review, 56*(3), 257–272.

Leinhardt, G. (1983). Novice and expert knowlege in individual student's achievement. *Educational Psychologist, 18*(3), 165–179.

Lepper, M. R., & Greene, D. (1978). *The hidden costs of reward: New perspectives on the psychology of human motivation.* Hillsdale, NJ: Lawrence Erlbaum.

Liston, D. P., & Zeichner, K. M. (1987). Critical pedagogy and teacher education. *Journal of Education, 169*(3), 119–137.

Livingstone, D. W. (Ed.) (1987). *Critical pedagogy and cultural power.* Westport, CT: Bergin & Garvey.

Magoon, J. (1977). Constructivist approaches in educational research. *Review of Educational Research, 47,* 651–693.

Maher, F. A. (1987). Toward a richer theory of feminist pedagogy: A comparison of "liberation" and "gender" models for teaching and learning. *Journal of Education 169*(3), 91–100.

Maher, F. A., & Tetreault, M. K. (1987, April). *Breaking through illusion I.* Paper presented at the American Educational Research Association meeting, Washington, DC.

Mannheim, K. (1952). *Essays on the sociology of knowledge.* London: Routledge & Kegan Paul.

Martin, J. R. (1982). Excluding women from the educational realm. *Harvard Educational Review,* 52(2), 133–148.

McKenzie, G. R., & Sawyer, J. (1986). Effects of test-like practice and mnemonics on learning geographic facts. *Theory and Research in Social Education, 14*(3), 201–209.

McKinney, C. W., Larkins, A. G., & Burts, D. C. (1984). Effect of overt teacher enthusiasm on first grade students' acquisition of three concepts. *Theory and Research in Social Education, 11*(4), 15–24.

McLaren, P. (1986). *Schooling as a ritual performance: Towards a political economy of educational symbols and gestures.* London: Routledge and Kegan Paul.

McNair, K. (1978–1979). Capturing inflight decisions: Thoughts while teaching. *Educational Research Quarterly, 3*(4), 26–42.

McNeil, L. M. (1986). *Contradictions of Control: School structure and school knowledge.* New York: Routledge.

Medley, D. M. (1979). The effectiveness of teachers. In P. L. Peterson and H. J. Walberg, (Eds.), *Research on teaching: Concepts, findings, and implications.* (pp. 11–27) Berkeley, CA: McCutchan.

Milburn, G. (1985). Deciphering a code or unraveling a riddle: A case study in the application of a humanistic metaphor to the reporting of social studies teaching. *Theory and Research in Social Education, 13*(3), 21–44.

Mitzel, H. E. (1960). Teacher effectiveness. In C. E. Harris (Ed.). *Encyclopedia of Educational Research* (3rd ed., pp. 1481–1486). New York: Macmillan.

Nash, G. B. (1974). *Red, white, and black: The peoples of early America.* Englewood Cliffs, NJ: Prentice-Hall.

National Commission on Social Studies in Schools. (1989). *Charting a course: Social studies curriculum for the 21st century. A report of the Curriculum Task Force.* Washington, DC: Author.

Newmann, F. M. (1985). The radical perspective on social studies: A synthesis and critique. *Theory and Research in Social Education, 13*(1), 1–18.

Newmann, F. M. (1988). *Higher order thinking in high school social studies: Analysis of classrooms, teachers, students and leadership.* National Center on Effective Secondary Schools, University of Wisconsin-Madison.

Noddings, N. (1988). An ethic of caring. *American Journal of Education, 96,* 256–290.

Noffke, S. E., & Brennan, M. (1988, April). *The dimensions of reflection: A conceptual and contextual analysis.* Paper presented at the annual meeting of the American Educational Research Association, New Orleans.

O'Brien, L. M., Meszaros, B., & Pulliam, W. E. (1985). Effects of teachers' use of objectives on student achievement in social studies. *Theory and Research in Social Education, 13*(3), 57–65.

Osborn, R. (Ed.). (1979). Revision of the NCSS social studies curriculum guidelines. *Social Education, 43*(4), 261–273.

Palonsky, S. B. (1987). Ethnographic scholarship and social education. *Theory and Research in Social Education, 15*(2), 77–87.

Popkewitz, T. S. (1981). The social contexts of schooling, change, and educational research. *Journal of Curriculum Studies, 13,* 189–206.

Porter, A. C. & Brophy, J. E. (1987). *Good teaching: Insights from the work of the Institute for Research on Teaching.* East Lansing, MI: The Institute for Research on Teaching.

Pressley, M., & Levin, J. (Eds.). (1983). *Cognitive strategy research: Educational applications.* New York: Springer Verlag.

Purpel, D. E. (1989). *The moral and spiritual crisis in education: A curriculum for justice and compassion in education.* Westport, CT: Bergin & Garvey.

Resnick, L. B., & Klopfer, L. E. (Eds.) (1989). *Toward the thinking curriculum: Current cognitive research,* Washington, DC: Association for Supervision and Curriculum Development.

Rosenshine, B. (1976). Classroom Instruction. In 75th Yearbook, National Society for the Study of Education, *The psychology of teaching methods.* Chicago: University of Chicago Press.

Rosenshine, B., & Furst, N. (1973). The use of direct observation to study teaching. In R. M. W. Travers (Ed.), *Second handbook of research on teaching* (pp. 122–183). Chicago: Rand McNally.

Rosenshine, B., & Stevens, R. (1986). Teaching functions. In M. C. Wittrock (Ed.), *Handbook of research on teaching* (3rd ed., pp. 376–391). New York: Macmillan.

Schon, D. A. (1983). *The reflective practitioner: How professionals think in action.* New York: Basic Books.

Schon, D. A. (1987). *Educating the reflective practitioner.* London: Jossey-Bass Limited.

Shannon, P. (1989). *Broken promises: Reading instruction in twentieth-century America.* Westport, CT: Bergin and Garvey.

Shavelson, R. J. (1973). What is the basic teaching skill? *The Journal of Teacher Education, 24*(2), 144–151.

Shavelson, R. J. (1983). Review of research on teachers' pedagogical judgments, plans, and decisions. *The Elementary School Journal, 83*(4), 392–411.

Shavelson, R. J., & Stern, P. (1981). Research on teachers' pedagogical thoughts, judgments, decisions, and behavior. *Review of Educational Research, 51*(4), 455–498.

Shaver, J. P. (1982). Reappraising the theoretical goals of research in social education. *Theory and Research in Social Education, 9*(4), 1–16.

Sherman, A. L. (1984). Genderism and the reconstitution of philosophy of educaton. *Educational Theory, 34*(4), 341–353.

Shor, I. (1986). Equality is excellence: Transforming teachers education and the learning process. *Harvard Educational Review, 56*(4), 406–426.

Shor, I., & Freire, P. (1987). *A pedagogy for liberation: Dialogues on transforming education.* Westport, CT: Bergin and Garvey.

Shulman, L. S. (1986). Paradigms and research programs in the study of teaching: A contemporary perspective. In M. C. Wittrock (Ed.), *Handbook of research on teaching* (3rd ed., pp. 3–36). New York: Macmillan.

Shulman, L. S. (1987). Knowledge and teaching: Foundations of the new reform. *Harvard Educational Review, 57*(1), 1–22.

Stanley, W. B. (Ed.). (1985). *Review of research in social studies education: 1976–1983.* Washington, DC: National Council for the Social Studies.

Stodolsky, S. (1988). *The subject matters: Classroom activity in math and social studies.* Chicago: University of Chicago Press.

Tom, A. R. (1980). Teaching as a moral craft: A metaphor for teaching and teacher education. *Curriculum Inquiry, 10*(3), 317–322.

Tom, A. R. (1984). *Teaching as a moral craft.* New York: Longman

VanManen, M. (1977). Linking ways of knowing with ways of being practical. *Curriculum Inquiry, 6,* 205–228.

VanSickle, R. L. (1985). Research implications of a theoretical analysis of John Dewey's *How we think. Theory and Research in Social Education, 13*(3), 1–20.

Vosniadou, S., & Brewer, W. F. (1987). Theories of knowledge restructuring in development. *Review of Educational Research, 57*(1), 51–67.

Voss, J. F. (1986). Social Studies. In R. F. Dillon & R. J. Sternberg (Eds.), *Cognition and instruction.* New York: Academic Press.

Voss, J. F., Greene, T. R., Post, T. A., & Penner, B. C. (1983). Problem solving skill in the social sciences. In G. Bower (Ed.), *The psychology of learning and motivation: Advances in research theory* (Vol. 17, pp. 165–213). New York: Academic Press.

Voss, J. F., Tyler, S. W., & Yengo, L. A. (1983). Individual differences in the solving of social science problems. In R. F. Dillon & R. R. Schnech (Eds.), *Individual differences in cognition* (pp. 205–232). New York: Academic Press.

Westkott, M. (1979). Feminist criticism of the social sciences. *Harvard Educational Review, 49*(4), 422–430.

Wexler, P. (1987). *Social analysis of education: After the new sociology.* London: Routledge & Kegan Paul.

White, J. J. (1985). What works for teachers: A review of ethnographic research studies as they inform issues of social studies curriculum and instruction. In W. B. Stanley (Ed.), *Review of research in social studies education, 1976–1983* (pp. 215–307). Washington, DC: National Council for the Social Studies.

White, J. J. (1987). The teacher as broker of scholarly knowledge. *Journal of Teacher Education,* 19–24.

White, J. J. (1988). Searching for substantial knowledge in social studies texts. *Theory and Research in Social Education, 16* (2), 115–140.

Wilson, S. M., Shulman, L. S., & Richert, A. E. (1987). 150 different ways of knowing: Representations of knowledge in teaching. In J. Caldershead (Ed.), *Exploring Teachers' Thinking* (pp. 104–124). London: Cassell.

Wilson, S. M., & Wineburg, S. S. (1988). Peering at history through different lenses: The role of disciplinary perspectives in teaching history. *Teachers College Record, 89*(4), 525–539.

Wineburg, S. S., & Wilson, S. M. (In press). Subject matter knowledge in the teaching of history. In J. E. Brophy (Ed.), *Advances in research on teaching.* Greenwich, CT: JAI.

Winne, P. H., & Marx, R. W. (1982). Students' and teachers' views of thinking processes for classroom learning. *The Elementary School Journal, 82*(5), 493–518.

Wittrock, M. C. (1974). Learning as a generative process. *Educational Psychologist, 11,* 87–95.

Wittrock, M. C. (Ed.). (1977). *The human brain.* Englewood Cliffs, NJ: Prentice Hall.

Wittrock, M. C. (1978). The cognitive movement in instruction. *Educational Psychologist, 13,* 15–29.

Wittrock, M. C. (1986). Students' thought processes. In M. C. Wittrock (Ed.), *Handbook of research on teaching* (3rd ed., pp. 297–314). New York: Macmillan.

Yoho, R. F. (1986). Effectiveness of four concept teaching strategies on social studies concept acquisition and retention. *Theory and Research in Social Education. 14*(3), 211–223.

Zeichner, K. M. (1983). Alternative paradigms of teacher education. *Journal of Teacher Education, 34*(3), 3–9.

Zeichner, K. M., & Liston, D. P. (1987). Teaching student teachers to reflect. *Harvard Educational Review, 51*(1), 23–48.

HISTORY OF TEACHING IN SOCIAL STUDIES

Larry Cuban
STANFORD UNIVERSITY

History is the study of both stability and change. The familiar view is that change is divorced from stability; it is either one or the other. Yet change and stability coexist in the same person, group, organization, and culture. Psychologists often point to the durability of personality traits over time, even as an individual changes from infancy to adulthood. Sociologists stress the persistent features that mark organizations as they evolve from their origins to maturity. Anthropologists record how both exotic and familiar cultures adapt, that is, change traditions. Political scientists underscore the continuity of national impulses through centuries amid radical political changes. So, too, for the history of public schooling.

Established as a social instrument to maintain what the community felt had to be passed on to the next generation, schools were also expected to provide opportunities for social mobility while getting the young ready to remedy economic and social ills harming the community. Constancy and change, then, have been tangled together since the very development of public schooling in America; it is not oxymoronic to speak of stable forms of change, continuity amidst change, or even persistence of reform (Cremin, 1988; Kaestle, 1983; Tyack, 1974).

The concept of change, however, is both complex and subtle (Nisbet, 1969). To better understand how teachers taught social studies in settings in which both stability and change were prized, at least one distinction needs to be made between types of planned change, that is, between first- and second-order changes.

Planned Changes

Planned changes are the designs and blueprints that policymakers initiate, adopt, and direct subordinates to implement. Many of the innovations described in journals and books—berated or blessed—are planned changes.

Designers of planned changes can be national officials (Congress authorizing Title I of the Elementary and Secondary Education Act in 1965); state policymakers (governors initiating reform bills); district school boards mandating specific curricula to be taught in their communities; a principal producing a new reading program to raise test scores in the school; or history teachers deciding to use computers in their classes to teach students different forms of thinking. But there are different types of planned changes: those that aim at improving the organization and those that aim at fundamentally altering what routinely occurs.

First- and Second-Order Changes. First-order, or incremental, changes are intentional efforts to enhance existing arrangements while correcting deficiencies in policies and practices. Such planned changes are efforts to make what exists more efficient and effective without disrupting the basic organizational features of the classroom, school, or district. Those who propose incremental changes, then, assume that the current goals and structures of schooling are both adequate and desirable.

Examples of first-order changes in classrooms would be procuring better textbooks, introducing a new technique to maintain order, and trying out lessons different from those of the previous year. For the school, incremental changes might be adding or deleting a course, introducing a set of rules for schoolwide student behavior, or starting a staff-development program for all teachers that is concentrated on improving the school climate. At the district level, first-order changes might include changes in evaluation procedures, introduction of new district attendance rules, realignment of district boundaries to accommodate shifts in enrollment, and raising of salaries.

The school effectiveness movement that spread among states and districts beginning in the early 1980s is one instance of incremental changes that penetrated all levels of schooling. Within the movement, there was stress on higher expectations

Reviewers were Richard S. Knight, Utah State University; Gary McKenzie, University of Texas, Austin.

for students, more student time spent on academic tasks, strong instructional leadership at the school site, and tighter district alignment of goals with curriculum, texts, and tests. The movement was anchored in the belief that the existing system of schooling could be improved.

Second-order, or fundamental, changes are efforts to alter the ways that organizations are put together because of major dissatisfaction with the present arrangements. Second-order changes introduce new goals, structures, and roles that transform familiar ways of performing duties into novel solutions to persistent issues.

The clearest instance of fundamental change occurred in the middle of the nineteenth century and transformed both the structures and practices of schooling by the end of that century. With the introduction of the graded school in the 1840s, reformers sought to restructure one-room schools (the then dominant form of providing public education) and the role of the teacher to fit the reformers' vision of social order, efficiency, and democracy (Kaestle, 1973; Katz, 1968).

The one-room schoolhouse of the 1840s usually had an untrained, unsupervised teacher responsible for children ranging in age from 4 through 18 who could give each child a few minutes of her attention. Moving from that to a graded elementary school—a school bringing together hundreds of children separated by age into six or more grades with a curriculum divided into grade-level segments, a separate classroom for each teacher, an annual promotion, and a principal—is a vivid instance of a basic change.

Other, more recent, second-order changes that penetrate both the school and classroom are open-space buildings and open classrooms. In these settings, teachers and principals view children as individuals who need to make their own decisions, to work together, and to connect knowledge learned in school with what occurs outside the walls of the school. These educators have relationships quite unlike colleagues who view children as students who have to be filled with correct knowledge and trained to be adults (Barth, 1972; Silberman, 1971; Sizer, 1985; Wigginton, 1985).

Presently, there are some reform proposals that are intended to make fundamental changes. Frequently they are aimed at a particular structure rather than at the entire system. For example, vouchers would give parents a choice of places to send their children to school. A variation on expanding parental choice is the elimination of all attendance boundaries within a district, parents choosing to send their sons and daughters to any school they wished (thus introducing marketplace competition into what was once a monopoly). Another example is the proposal that school staffs be allowed to make budgetary, personnel, and curricular decisions now made in the district office. In each case, the intention is to alter a basic part of the fundamental design of schooling through enlarging parental choice and teacher autonomy or rearranging how schools are funded and operated.

Generally, since 1900, school reforms have been a series of first-order improvements to those graded schools and governance structures that were introduced over a century ago. Often the impetus for these planned changes came from outside the schools (e.g., progressive reforms at the turn of the 20th century that were aimed at improving life in the cities, the civil rights movement in the 1960s, governors and legislatures mandating changes in schools to keep their states economically competitive in the 1980s).

Occasionally, certain fundamental reforms such as student-centered instruction in elementary schools, ungraded schools, team teaching, open-space architecture, and flexible scheduling got launched in isolation. They were detached from other reforms, leaving, after the hoopla had evaporated, little more than a bare residue, acknowledged, perhaps, as a footnote in a history of reform.

Finally, there are two ways that second-order reforms get adapted by schools and districts. First, there are those fundamental changes that get packaged into special programs and placed on the periphery of the school system, that is, school and district programs that are restricted to students labeled "different", a minority in the school, while leaving the core program for most students untouched. Often, innovative programs for pregnant teenagers, potential dropouts, at-risk children, handicapped students, and others are fundamentally different in class size, student–teacher relationships, content organization and teaching, and students' activities. Thus, some second-order changes are encapsulated and placed on the periphery; yet they still exist within the system (Farrar, Powell, & Cohen, 1985).

Another way that schools and districts deal with fundamental reforms is to convert them into incremental ones. Recall the efforts to modify what teachers taught and students learned in the late 1950s and early 1960s in a star burst of curricular reforms such as the "new math" and "new physics." Within less than a decade, those federally funded renovations of existing curricula were converted into another set of textbooks used by teachers (Atkin & House, 1981).

Thus, to argue that public schooling is the same as it has always been is to miss an important point: Districts and schools have changed, mostly in incremental ways, since the introduction of the graded school in the mid-nineteenth century. District governance has changed from large, politically appointed school boards to smaller, elected boards; turn-of-the-century teachers and administrators who seldom needed anything beyond a grammar school or high school education have given way to heavily credentialed educators; new structures have been added to the graded school such as kindergarten and the junior high school; new curricula such as vocational education have become commonplace in high schools; new specialties have been established such as counselors, reading teachers, bilingual staff, and Chapter 1 teachers (Kirst & Meister, 1985; Orlosky & Smith, 1972; Tyack, Hansot, & Kirst, 1980). The point is clear: Districts and schools have, indeed, embraced numerous first-order changes. But has teaching changed?

CHANGE AND STABILITY IN TEACHING

The evidence is spotty. A few studies have seen efforts to reconstruct what has occurred in the nation's classrooms over the last century (Cuban, 1984; Finkelstein, 1970; Tyack, Lowe, & Hansot, 1984; Zilversmit, 1976). In recounting the findings of this limited body of research, I need to caution the reader that, in trying to recapture what has disappeared—i.e., teacher intentions and actions, student–teacher exchanges, classroom culture, what children learned,—historians and other researchers have access to few sources. Written and oral recollections, interviews, lesson plans, tests, textbooks, a description from an occasional visitor, and the like produce only a bare outline of what might have happened and nary a word about the tedium or exhilaration of a lesson, the flair or flop of a teaching style. Thus, in the report of the results of the few studies on how teachers taught, several things are absent: teaching styles, classroom climate, indices of effectiveness, whether reasoning flourished, and appreciation of ethnic differences. Important as these dimensions are to what occurs in classrooms, they are beyond the historian's reach so far. What is offered here is a skeletal behavioral description, much of it inferred from primary and secondary sources.

One study, for example, was concentrated upon what teachers did over the 20th century, before and after major reforms aimed at getting teachers to alter fundamentally the role they usually performed in classrooms, at how they made instructional and curricular decisions, and at the methods they used (Cuban, 1984). Including both elementary and secondary school teachers across the academic curriculum, I concluded the following:

Since 1900, most elementary and secondary school teachers used a repertoire dominated by techniques categorized as "teacher-centered instruction." This form of instruction was present in its purest form in high school and less so in the lower grades. Teachers relied heavily upon teacher talk (lecturing, explaining, questioning students to determine understanding), use of a textbook, seatwork, and review of assignments. This repertoire was executed by instructing the entire group at once except . . . in the lower grades where small group instruction in certain subjects and skills became common by the fourth decade of this century.

Even at the height of efforts to reform teacher-centered instruction (such as what child-centered progressives introduced in the 1920s and 1930s; what partisans of informal education in the late 1960s and early 1970s advocated insofar as individual and small group work, and instruction that encouraged student planning and decisionmaking) pedagogy remained largely teacher-centered in urban and rural, rich and poor, small and large school settings.

Changes in classrooms did occur more frequently in elementary than in secondary schools. Certain aspects of the second-order reforms were adapted into first-order improvements in classrooms where teachers created hybrids, mixes of teacher- and student-centered instruction. Over the last century, elementary classrooms featured increasingly movable furniture, varied materials, less formal relationships, more physical movement of students, and use of small groups. While some of these features did penetrate particular secondary school classrooms, most did not. Even with these noticeable differences between the two classroom levels, teacher-centered instruction still dominated elementary schools. (pp. 135–137, 237–239; see also Goodlad, 1984; Tyack, Lowe, Hansot, 1984)

The glimpses of classroom teaching in general that emerge from these scattered studies suggest that both constancy and change were entangled within the nation's classrooms over the last 100 years of public schooling. Moreover, the changes that

did occur were mostly incremental, even in those instances when the intentions were to revolutionize dominant patterns of pedagogy. In an examination of how teachers taught social studies, a similar tension between constancy and change becomes apparent.

HOW SOCIAL STUDIES TEACHERS TAUGHT

In trying to reconstruct what happened in classrooms, I need to stress two obvious features of the literature on the teaching of social studies: the scarcity of descriptions and analyses of social studies classrooms and the abundance of advice on how social studies teachers *should* teach. The tilt toward surveys; experimental, correlational studies; and advice is as evident here, as elsewhere in educational research, especially in doctoral dissertations (Connors, 1959; Massialas, 1963; McGill, 1949; Penix, 1964). Moreover, those comprehensive articles and studies written from a historical perspective that are summaries of research often argue a point of view or advocate a particular curricular or instructional approach (Brophy, 1988; Hertzberg, 1981).

The scarcity of accounts about what occurs in social studies classrooms is remarkable, given the advice amply supplied by researchers to both practitioners and policymakers. In the three editions of the *Handbook of Research on Teaching,* covering over 3 decades of research, for example, articles on the teaching of social studies appeared. In none of them were studies cited of teacher behavior in classrooms. In the 49 issues of *Theory and Research in Social Education* published since 1973 there were 221 articles excluding book reviews. Of that total, 3 articles described and analyzed teaching behaviors: two dealt with elementary teachers (one examined planning), and the other was an investigation of Australian high school teachers. Occasional ethnographies to investigate the topography of social studies classrooms have begun to appear, but they remain rare. Researchers concerned about both the quality and the gaps in the knowledge base for the social studies have commented, even railed, at this state of affairs for over a quarter of a century (Armento, 1987; Fraenkel, 1985; Metcalf, 1963; Palonsky, 1987; Shaver & Larkins, 1973; White, 1985).

What evidence there is, then, offers a partial, if fragmented, answer to the question; How did social studies teachers teach? Wherever possible, I cite studies that include direct observations of classrooms. In the absence of these studies, I use surveys, self-reports, and other sources where appropriate. Because social studies as an explicit curriculum spread in high schools after World War I (although its sources can be traced back to the closing decades of the 19th century), I begin with secondary school classrooms (Robinson, 1980; Singleton, 1980).

Teaching Social Studies in the Secondary School: 1900s to 1930s

The earliest classroom observation of social studies teachers that I could find was part of a larger study of how teachers

TABLE 16–1. Percentages of Time Devoted by Social Studies Teachers in Short- and Long-Period Classes

	Short	Long
Recitation	64.1	45.4
Assignment	17.8	9.4
Supervised study	8.2	21.1
Testing	4.5	4.7
Other	5.4	19.4

Note. From "A Comparison of Teaching Procedures in Short and Long Class Periods" by L. Koos and O. Troxel, 1927, School Review, 35, p. 345. Copyright 1927 by University of Chicago Press. Reprinted by permission.

question students (Stevens, 1912). Stevens visited an unspecified number of schools in and near New York City between 1907 and 1911 to study teacher questioning. Using a stopwatch and a stenographer, she observed 100 teachers whom principals had identified as superior. In addition to noting what both teachers and students did in each period, she recorded the number of questions asked by both. For 20 teachers of history, within a 45-minute period, the number of questions ranged from 47 to 142. The percentage of teacher talk in these history classes ranged from a low of 57% to a high of 80%; the average was 64% (p. 22).

The pattern of instruction was heavily tilted toward students' answering rapid-fire questions from a teacher on the content of a textbook chapter. Stevens found such teaching distasteful because it made teachers "drillmasters instead of educators" and left little chance for students to either express themselves or even think (pp. 23, 25).

Another study completed 2 decades later was conducted to determine if teachers in Minneapolis, Minnesota high schools taught differently in regular periods (45 minutes) and extended periods (55–60 minutes). University of Minnesota seniors and graduate students, most of whom "had had teaching or supervisory experience or both," observed four classes in a high school—two with short periods and two with long periods—and recorded the procedures that teachers used (Koos & Troxel, p. 341, 1927). The categories were teacher-led question-and-answer exchanges with students about content; making and explaining the assignment; supervised study, that is, students working at their desks on homework or tasks assigned by the teacher; testing and other, unspecified, activities (see Table 16–1). Of the 346 classes observed, 100 were social studies.

Another study, of 116 social studies teachers in 20 high schools, was completed in the Chicago area (Hughes & Melby, 1930). Unusual for the times, observers were trained to use an instrument that described exactly what activities teachers used every second of a class period. An observer documented one class period of each teacher. Issues of interrater reliability and validity were specifically dealt with in the study. The purpose of the study was to improve the supervision of teaching, but a picture of what happened in these classrooms also emerged.

The dominant practice used by the social studies teachers was questioning (82%); students asked questions 10% of the time. The next most frequent activity was "making informal comments" (74%); I translate that to mean teacher lecturing, explaining, and clarifying. Students made "informal comments" 8% of the time. The third most frequent teacher behavior was "answering questions" (54%); student talk was highest in this category (51%). The fourth most frequent behavior was "assignment activities" (45%); students did these tasks for 40% of their time.

For the dominant teaching practice of questioning, researchers found that the median number of questions asked was 44 during a class period, about one per minute. Almost one out of three teachers was observed to ask 70 or more questions during a period (Hughes & Melby, 1930, pp. 141–144). Students seldom voluntarily entered the exchanges in these classes. Ten percent of all students "raised queries during the recitations" and "only 8% made any form of informal comment" (p. 142).

A third study of social studies teachers was completed by a professor at Teachers College, Columbia University, who sent a "professionally trained graduate student" into 21 public high schools in the metropolitan New York City area to "observe the work of the best teachers of any subjects" (Briggs, 1935). The graduate student visited 104 classes of teachers identified by the principal as "best." Of those classes, 21 were social studies. According to Briggs, "four in every five were conventional teaching from the textbook" (p. 746). Of the 19 exceptions to conventional teaching (20%), Briggs identified only one in American history. Thus, 20 of the 21 social studies teachers "merely taught lessons as presented in the textbooks" (p. 747).

Of these four studies, only two (Hughes & Melby, 1930; Stevens, 1912) might pass muster by today's standards for conducting classroom research and producing descriptions of teacher and student behavior. The others contain substantial flaws in design, methods, and implementation. Nonetheless, taken together they have partial value in that a few individuals actually sat in classrooms and tried to capture systematically a small portion of what occurred there. These imperfect descriptions go beyond those familiar self-reports submitted by teachers or surveys of principals' opinions about what teachers do in their classes. Marred and blurred as these snapshots of social studies teachers are, they do offer a glimpse of teaching practices in the early decades of the 20th century to researchers interested in reconstructing how teachers taught. They offer little evidence of student-centered instruction, with its emphasis on group and independent work in class.

Of course, there are other sources that report what social studies teachers did in their classrooms. Commonly such reports, appearing in books, journals, magazines, and newspapers, advocated innovative practices that challenged what Briggs called in 1935 "conventional teaching." Such evidence frequently suggested that novel teaching methods aimed at increasing student-centered instruction and critical thought, goals of pedagogical progressives in the early decades of the twentieth century, were on the brink of becoming mainstream practice. Representative of these reports would be articles that appeared in such journals as The Clearing House ("A History Project in an Eighth Grade Social Studies Class" [Norman, 1934]) and High Points ("The Laboratory Plan in Community Civics" [Goldstein, 1926]).

Historians, however, must ask about the representativeness

of these sources. Are they typical of what mainstream teachers were doing? Are claims of widespread use of innovative approaches to social studies warranted? To test such claims, I reanalyzed data available from five high schools in Denver, Colorado, enrolled in the major curricular innovation undertaken in the 1930s, the Eight Year Study (*Thirty Schools Tell Their Story*, 1942). Examining the primary sources available for each of the high schools, I reconstructed a picture, albeit a fragmentary one, of what high school teachers did, especially social studies teachers, at the very height of the innovation in the schools (Cuban, 1984).

Beginning in 1933 with one class of 40 students in each of the five high schools, the principal chose two teachers, one in English and one in social studies, to work with the experimental group as both teachers and counselors for at least half of the school day. Each succeeding year another class was added during the life of the program; but at no time did any school have more than 30 percent of the student body enrolled in the "progressive" classes, as they were called. Today, such a program would be labeled a school-within-a-school (Cuban, 1984, pp. 75–78).

Teams of teachers taught "core subjects." They were expected to plan together the coursework, replace existing systems of grades and punishment with "new drives for learning," and, in choosing subject matter, pick content that "assists in the solving of problems and in the meeting of the needs of pupils" (p. 77). Time was set aside for students to explore their interests and to study and work in the community.

The number of teachers directly participating in the experiment remained a minority of each school's faculty. In 1939, for example, there were 12 out of 42 teachers (29%) at Manual Training High School in the program; at North High there were also 12 teachers, but this staff had 80 on its faculty (15%). For those social studies teachers who became directly involved, there is ample evidence of a broader repertoire of teaching approaches including greater student participation in planning lessons, speaking in class, leading discussions, and working independently. Such teachers, however, were outnumbered by the majority uninvolved with the project, who seemingly taught in the "conventional manner" (Cuban, 1984).

How Social Studies Teachers Taught: 1940s–1980s

How is the narrow glimpse just offered of secondary school teaching similar to and different from what has occurred since 1945? In turning to empirical research, the same barrenness in description and analysis of earlier decades is, again, apparent. One researcher who summarized what was available in 1975 minced few words in concluding, "It can be safely said that we know very little about what were the most commonly used classroom practices in social studies throughout the U.S. at any particular time during the last 20 years" (Wiley, 1977, p. 77).

Although there are more studies of social studies teaching available in these years, many lean heavily on self-reports of classroom practices. Inflated estimates, atypical samples, and other inherent flaws in the research surface repeatedly. Nonetheless, by examining these data and supplementing them with direct observation of classrooms, a recognizable snapshot emerges (see Table 16–2).

In one major study, undertaken in the 1970s and funded by the National Science Foundation (NSF), ethnographic methods were used at 11 sites, each of which included a high school and its feeder elementary schools. Trained observer-participants drawn from many disciplines entered rural and urban schools, of high and low socioeconomic status and in diverse parts of the nation, to produce an unusual descriptive and analytical study of academic subjects including social studies (Stake & Easley, 1978).

In reviewing this study and two companion efforts, three scholars in the social studies found that multiple studies, which included a review of the literature (Wiley, 1977) and a national survey (Weiss, 1978), corroborated one another. These researchers concluded that, even in the wake of the New Social Studies from the late 1960s and early 1970s, most students' "social studies classes will be strikingly similar to those that many of us experienced as youngsters: textbook assignments followed by recitation led by a teacher who, in his or her own way, likes students and tries to show concern for them—and avoids controversial issues, but tries to pitch the class at the students' level" (Shaver, Davis, & Helburn, 1980, p. 7). Although one historian questioned their interpretation (Herzberg, 1981), my reading of the cases supports the views expressed by Shaver and his colleagues. The three NSF-funded studies "indicated that there had been great stability in the social studies curriculum" (p. 17).

The NSF case studies brought researchers into social studies classrooms. Not many have followed. Faced with a lack of direct observation of teaching, researchers need to examine sources that offer clues to what occurred once the classroom door closed. For example, what students report about their teachers' methods is important indirect evidence. Recent data (Applebee, Langer, & Mullis, 1987) drawn from student reports of practices in U.S. history classrooms portray teacher-centered instruction. In 89% of these classrooms, textbooks were used weekly; 5% of the students reported using no text (p. 30). Eighty-three percent of the students reported that they memorized information for U.S. history at least sometimes, and 64% said they did so at least once a week (p. 30). As for writing, 68% of 11th graders reported that they never wrote long reports for their classes (p. 31). One-third of the students saw a film once a week; 93% reported that they never visited museums or exhibits (p. 32). The most frequently reported instructional practice used at least some of the time was whole-group lecturing (97%); 57% of the students reported participation in small group work at least some of the time. The authors concluded that the students' descriptions of their work in history "reflect a very traditional approach to instruction" (p. 34).

Another source of indirect evidence about instruction are teacher-made tests, because they dominate classroom assessment. Popenfus (1978) and Kurfman (1982), for example, concluded that teacher-made tests in social studies stress factual recall, with multiple-choice items used rather than essays. We can infer from these assessment tools that coverage of content is highly valued, and it is no great leap of faith to extend the inference to the conclusion that the textbook and teacher pre-

Table 16–2. Research on Social Studies Teaching in Secondary Schools, 1950s–1980s

Year of Data Collection	Author	Subject	Place	Instrument	Respondents	N =	Findings/Conclusions
1950	Gross (1951)	U.S. history	California	Survey (60% return of random sample)	Secondary school department chairs	100	"On the whole, United States history is presented in a traditional manner … probably more so than in the late 30s and early 40s. Although some of the newer techniques are used at times, traditional methods remain the most common approach. Also, some of these means employed in teaching are not of the type that will really help develop the important skills, attitudes, and behaviors stated in the teachers' lists of ojectives."
1959	Siemers (1960)	World history	California	Survey (non-random sample)	Teachers	100	○ 67% used lectures and class discussions as primary teaching devices ○ 80% used memorization of key dates weekly ○ 92% used a basic textbook
1964	Baxter, Ferrell, & Wiltz (1964)	U.S. history	Indiana	Survey (80% response of total U.S. history teachers)	Teachers	1084	○ 78% favored chronological approach, with 33% using it exclusively ○ 85% organized U.S. history chronologically and topically ○ 70% "give about equal emphasis to recitation and interpretation while remainder either do not specify what they do or stated that they emphasize recitation." ○ 66% "lecture to their classes on occasion but less than 40% of the time" ○ 70% "set aside a portion of the hour for supervised study, usually for reading the assignment in the text book …"
Late 1970s	Sirotnik (1981)	Social studies	Nation	Direct Classroom Observation (representative sample)	Teachers	53 (Jr. High)	○ "teachers 'out-talk' students by a ratio of three to one." ○ "the model classroom(s) … look like this: the teacher explaining/lecturing to the total class (or a single student), asking direct, factual-type questions or monitoring or observing students; the students 'listening' to the teacher or responding to teacher-initiated interaction."
1976–1977	Stake & Easley (1978)	Social sciences	Nation	Direct Classroom Observation & Interviews (case studies)	Teachers, students	11 (Elem. & Sec. schls.)	○ "student response to social studies was widely observed to be apathetic." ○ "we concluded that the social studies were capable of interesting the students more, but often failed to do so." ○ "we saw no evidence of contact with the High School Geography Project, Project Social Studies, the Anthropology Project … or other course content improvement projects."
1977	Weiss (1978)	Social sciences	Nation	Survey (76% return of random sample)	Teachers	943 (Jr. and Sr. High)	○ 94% of secondary teachers use lecture and discussion daily ○ 35% of junior high teachers use individual assignments daily ○ 18% of senior high teachers use individual assignments daily ○ 62% of junior high teachers give test or quiz once a week ○ 54% of senior high teachers give test or quiz once a week
1986	Applebee, Langer, & Mullis (1987)	U.S. history	Nation	Questionnaire Items	Students	8000	○ "The students' descriptions of their course in history reflect a very traditional approach to instruction."

sentation bear the burden of making that content available to students. If the inferences have merit, both would be related to teacher-centered instruction. Risky as inference atop inference is, in the absence of direct observation, such evidence provides mild corroboration for the results of other classroom studies.

A recent and different line of inquiry into how teachers teach (that includes high school social studies teachers) has been undertaken by Shulman (1987) and a cadre of researchers. Shulman has pursued the question, What do teachers have to know in order to teach? He argues that the teacher

must understand the structures of the subject matter, the principles of conceptual organization, and the principles of inquiry that help answer two kinds of questions in each field: What are the important ideas and skills in this domain? and How are new ideas added and deficient ones dropped by those who produce knowledge in this area? (p. 9)

Central to this line of investigation is the notion of pedagogical content knowledge, that is, what a teacher knows of key subject matter that can be transformed into specific curricular material and the ways a teacher uses metaphors, analysis, and demonstrations with a particular group of youngsters. A number of researchers have examined how novice and expert social studies teachers teach the same lessons, how teachers come to develop their perspectives on history, and what students know about history as they learn it (Wilson & Wineburg, 1988). These researchers have stressed the impact of a teacher's knowledge of social studies, especially the discipline in which the teacher was originally trained, upon the instructional choices she or he makes each day. Although these investigators have not directly challenged the durable descriptions of how social studies teachers have taught, in their richly textured accounts they have underscored the impact of beliefs and disciplinary perspective upon the lessons taught, indeed, upon the repertoires teachers used. In concentrating on the importance of pedagogical content knowledge, Wilson and Wineburg, as few other researchers have done, have pointed with crisp clarity to the importance of one contextual factor, subject-specific pedagogical knowledge, that shapes teaching practice.

From the studies done since 1945, a plausible inference to be drawn from the available evidence on the teaching practices of secondary school social studies teachers is that a few key patterns continued to dominate teaching in the closing decades of the 20th century as they did earlier in the century.

Teaching Social Studies in the Elementary School

Because the structures of secondary and elementary schools, the ages of students, and the expectations for teachers and students differ, one would expect teaching in each setting to differ. In the upper grades, teachers see 150 or more students for 50 minutes a day; in the lower grades, teachers may teach social studies for a lesser amount of time (Weiss, 1978) to 30 or so children, but the students stay with the same teacher for almost the entire day. If secondary school teachers see themselves as discipline-based specialists, elementary school teachers see themselves as generalists. Between kindergarten and the sixth grade, for example, most teachers are responsible for instruc-

tion in five to eight different subject and skill areas, depending on the school district. Language arts and mathematics absorb much of the mornings. Science, social studies, and other content areas frequently find their niche in the afternoons, times when the energies, much less the attention, of both teachers and students slip. Finally, external demands made by accreditation standards, the Carnegie unit, college entrance requirements, standardized achievement exams, and similar expectations shape the contours of social studies knowledge and skills presented in secondary school classrooms. Fewer of those external demands reach down into the primary and intermediate grades of elementary schools.

Amid these instructional differences, however, research done in elementary school social studies has been similar to that done in secondary schools, that is, there has been little that is descriptive and analytical about what occurs in classrooms. The limited research does reveal sparingly and in fragments that elementary teachers teach social studies both similarly to and differently from their colleagues in the upper grades. The similarities are in the dominant activities: homework assigned from a textbook, review of assignment in class, extensive teacher talk (lecturing, clarifying, explaining), recitation, and seatwork, interspersed with occasional use of audiovisual aids and field trips (Goodlad, 1984; Herman, 1977; Jackson, 1968; Sirotnik, 1981; Weiss, 1978).

Differences do emerge also. Elementary teachers use small groups and independent work more frequently than do secondary school teachers (Bliss, 1986; Sirotnik, 1981; Stodolsky, 1988). Their arsenal of techniques is slightly larger than that of their upper-grade peers, including the use of materials that can be manipulated, films, television, computers, and other forms of student involvement (Sirotnik, 1981; Weiss, 1978, Appendix B, 64–67). Also, elementary teachers integrate social studies into other daily activities, especially tasks linked to citizenship (Stodolsky, 1988; Wilkinson, 1964).

One researcher (Stodolsky, 1988) has gone further in concluding that elementary teachers vary their instruction depending upon the subject they are teaching. They use, for example, small groups working together in social studies far more than in the teaching of elementary mathematics, suggesting that there may be something in the subject matter itself or in the teachers' goals and beliefs that influence practice.

Stodolsky examined 39 fifth-grade classes (19 social studies and 20 mathematics) in 11 different Chicago area districts. The classes were drawn from districts with high, middle, and low socioeconomic status and different levels of per-pupil expenditure. The social studies data came from trained observers who spent 6,649 minutes in classrooms over 153 days. The average number of days of observation for social studies lessons was 8. Carefully designed and implemented, this study was concentrated upon student–teacher exchanges, teaching activities, and the organization of classroom tasks into lessons.

Stodolsky and her colleagues found that, even though an "extremely small number of instructional patterns were used", there was more variety in social studies lessons than in mathematics (p. 73). In mathematics, two patterns dominated: teacher-centered instruction (whole-class instruction with heavy use of textbook, seatwork, and recitation) and individualized instruction. In social studies lessons, Stodolsky found three patterns: teacher-centered activity (10 of 19 classes), group work (6 of the 19), and hybrids (3 of the 19 used mixes of the two and other instructional activities) (pp. 73–74).

Stodolsky's findings suggest that the subject matter that elementary teachers present shapes their instructional practices. In particular, small-group work in these fifth-grade social studies lessons may well be due to the nature of social studies and teachers' beliefs about the subject, a line of inquiry that would need further elaboration in the lower and upper grades. The work of Shulman, Wilson, and Wineburg in exploring the impact of subject-specific pedagogical knowledge among high school history teachers appears to be linked to Stodolsky's study. Clues from other studies in secondary schools suggest the possibility of instructional variation by content. Sirotnik's (1981) data on secondary school teachers arrayed by subject area (Tables 8 and 9, p. 16) and a year-long observational study in a midwestern high school (Anang & Lanier, 1982) provide additional hints about the importance of subject matter.

Summary

Acknowledging the flaws inherent in the limited evidence drawn from diverse lines of research over the last 6 decades, I offer these (numbered) statements:

1. *Instruction in the social studies has been (and is) marked more by stability than change.* At least two durable patterns of instructional activities and teacher behavior seem to have prevailed in elementary and secondary classrooms in the past and are present now.

The most common pattern, employed by the vast majority of social studies teachers, is that of teacher-centered instruction. This pattern includes activities using the textbook and teacher as sources of information for assignments, recitation (now commonly called *discussion*), tests, and individual seatwork. Talking by the teacher (presenting information, explaining, and clarifying) exceeds talking by students, whose responses are generally confined to answering the teacher's questions. Occasional use of films, videos, and other devices supplements these activities. This core pattern is most frequently enacted when the entire class is taught as a group. Infrequently at the high school level, but with slightly more frequency at the elementary level, small-group work is a vehicle for classroom activities.

A second pattern is evident among a small number of teachers who combine teacher-centered instructional activities with ones that incorporate greater levels of student involvement, such as discussion, role playing, debate, and choice of subjects to study. These hybrids include more small-group work and independent study than the dominant pattern. The hybrids appear more frequently in elementary than in secondary classrooms.

2. *Most changes that have been planned and introduced into social studies classrooms have been incremental; fundamental changes that have been tried have been adapted into incremental ones or have gradually disappeared.* Changes that have most frequently influenced social studies classes have been shifts in ability grouping, improvements in texts and tests, expanded range in instructional materials sensitive to ethnic diversity and gender, increased supplies, and the like. These are incremental changes aimed at improving how social studies teacher teach.

Occasional reforms intended to alter fundamentally what social studies teachers do (such as inquiry teaching, or instruction in reasoning and problem solving, or learning-how-to-learn skills) have, for the most part, been converted into first-order changes. For more than a half century, then, particular patterns of instruction have persisted; yet teachers have also demonstrated a capacity to make incremental changes in the delivery of that instruction.

These findings go beyond general statements, often unsupported, about teaching practices in social studies classrooms made by authors since 1960, such as the following:

> Although lecturing at the lower school level, as well as formalized recitation, has been long under attack, both techniques continue to be used to a considerable degree by many teachers. (Gross & Badger, 1960, p. 1306)

> In actual classroom practice, far too little innovation in instructional approach can be found, with the traditional teacher-led discussion based on textbook assignments being the dominant mode. (Skretting & Sundeen, 1969, p. 1235)

> Social studies classrooms of today are little different from those 20 years ago, despite the expenditure of millions of dollars and the involvement of many creative minds in the development of innovative curricular materials . . . Lecture and discussion are still the most frequently used strategies in social studies classrooms with teacher talk dominating; and the conventional textbook remains the primary instructional tool. (Armento, 1986, p. 944)

Except for Armento, who cited Stake and Easely (1978), none of these authors felt compelled to document their statements about dominant teaching patterns. The conventional wisdom of only one pattern of teaching apparently is fixed in the minds of prominent writers and seemingly goes unquestioned except for the occasional surprise or annoyance expressed by individual scholars who cannot understand the durability of a particular set of practices. What emerges out of this review of how social studies teachers have taught since the early 1900s is a similar but, of some importance, a more complex, if incomplete, series of snapshots that suggests both stability in at least two patterns of teaching and incremental changes in practice over time.

Meaning

Of what significance are these statements surrounded by qualifiers? In light of the earlier warning given to readers that what is recaptured in empirical studies of teaching, particularly historical ones, is merely a glimpse of what occurred in classrooms, the question of significance is deserved. After all, a glimpse through the rearview mirror of history cannot reconstruct the teaching styles, the classroom climates, the student learning, or a dozen other dimensions of teaching and learning that would fill out a livelier and fuller classroom portrait. Moreover, there are reservations about how much one can lean on the slender body of evidence reported here.

Yet, even with these substantial doubts, I do see significance in these findings, imperfect as they are. These findings raise puzzling questions that are important to practitioners (teachers and school administrators), researchers and policymakers. Why has the core pattern of teaching practice endured over most of the 20th century? Why did some teachers and not others adopt a hybrid pattern? Finally, what I believe is a central question raised by this review: In view of the changes that have occurred in the occupation of teaching since the early 1900s and the advice that researchers and policymakers have given to social studies teachers to improve practice, why have there been a pervasive constancy in teaching practices—what many have labeled a *limited repertoire*—and so little second-order change? This last question needs elaboration. Consider the changes that have occurred in the occupation of teaching in the 20th century.

Teachers Are Far More Educated Now Than in Earlier Decades. In the later nineteenth century, a high school degree and one or two years of normal school were considered more than sufficient to become licensed as a teacher (Tyack, 1974). In 1935, 10% of elementary, 56% of junior high, and 85% of senior high school teachers had bachelor's degrees. By 1981, about half of all teachers held master's degrees (Sedlak & Schlossman, 1986).

Classes Are Smaller Now. Actual class size has dropped from averages of 50 to 70 students in urban classrooms in the early decades of the 20th century to 30 or less in both elementary and secondary schools (Glass, Cohen, Smith & Filby, 1982; Tyack, 1974). Although 30 students are more than most teachers desire, the reduction is still substantial.

Teachers Have More Autonomy. Beginning in the 1920s and expanding since the 1960s, the notion that teachers should make curricular and instructional decisions for their classes has become broadly accepted, although exceptions still occur. Teachers largely determine which materials and methods they will use in their classes (Shaver et al., 1979).

More Materials Are Available. Although critics of social studies textbooks persist (e.g., Fitzgerald, 1979), the information presented and the concerns for ethnic and gender issues have clearly broadened what was previously available. Moreover, the range of materials, both print and nonprint, vastly exceeds what was available to teachers a generation, much less a half-century, ago.

Teachers Receive more Protection of Their Academic Freedom Than Earlier. Historically, teachers have been vulnerable to external pressures to conform in their teaching of certain subjects. Since the 1950s, however, teacher rights to introduce topics that may be considered controversial in a community have been tested and expanded. Although precollegiate teachers still get challenged over what they teach (e.g., Man, a Course of Study, MACOS), collective bargaining contracts and district policies protect teachers' right to speak and choose content far more than in earlier decades. There are, for example, far fewer dismissals of teachers from their posts for what has been said in classrooms or for the materials used (Beale, 1941; Bridges, 1986; Waller, 1931).

Given these substantial changes, which many informed observers would call improvements in making teaching a profession, there still have been (and continue to be) durable patterns of practice, which others have called a limited range of techniques, in use. The question is, Why?

What makes the question even more puzzling is another enduring pattern in social studies classrooms apart from teaching practices. A consistent and familiar complaint, fully documented in the research literature, comes from students about the tedium, uselessness, and forgettability of social studies (Chase, 1949; Goodlad, 1984; Harper, 1937; Herman, 1977; Outland & Jones, 1940; Stake & Easley 1979). Here, then, is a paradox that emerges from the many studies I have examined: Remarkable improvements in the occupation of teaching are paralleled by constancy in a narrow band of teaching practices and students' complaints about that teaching. Why?

These questions are not only puzzling, but they also pose important policy issues for practitioners, researchers, and policymakers. It is to these issues, that I turn in the final section of this chapter. Here I elaborate on why these questions are important and then suggest what directions interested researchers might pursue in trying to answer them.

THE IMPORTANCE OF THE QUESTIONS

When researchers ask questions derived from investigating actual teaching practices over the last 50 years, they substitute one line of inquiry for another used by policymakers. This is important because of the linkages between research and policy formation. When state and local policymakers use research findings they often initiate innovations, justify policy directions already decided upon, or employ some combination of the two strategies. Because of the traffic between research and policy in education, policy agendas are partially influenced by the research questions that are asked.

The question implicit in many researchers' studies has been, How should teachers teach? Studies that show one approach superior to another in the classroom get converted into demonstration projects, districtwide programs, or elaborate staff-development efforts aimed at preparing teachers to use new materials and methods. By asking, How did teachers teach? the center of gravity shifts from "should" to description, and then to, Why? Rather than policymakers and researchers trying to figure out how a particular "should" can be implemented in classrooms, a different set of issues arise.

Asking prior, more fundamental, questions about why teachers teach the way they do and what changes they have embraced and rejected results in defining the problem differently. Why did certain patterns of teaching in the social studies persist over time? Why did some teachers alter what they did and others did not? Why have teaching repertoires been fairly limited even in the face of student boredom and substantial improvements in converting an occupation into a profession? These questions reframe a problem.

By defining the problem initially in terms of how to get social studies teachers to install a curricular or instructional inno-vation in their classrooms, researchers and policymakers slide easily into framing solutions in terms of getting teachers, indi-vidually or in groups, to alter routine behaviors. Such a familiar definition of the problem assumes that all that is necessary to get teachers to change is to convince them to do so. Teachers, then, are both the problem and the solution.

To ask different questions, however, for example, Why do teachers teach as they do? directs researchers and policymakers to investigate the many factors that shape teachers' behavior beyond their individual wills to make classroom changes. In the examination of other factors and conditions that shape the practice of teaching, very different approaches to getting teach-ers to alter their classroom instruction arise.

Finally, what makes reframing the problem and asking dif-ferent questions important is that policymakers at the district, state, and federal levels are responsible for setting new, or re-aligning old, goals; securing and allocating resources; and adopting policies that will achieve desirable ends. Policymak-ers, for example, want to influence teachers of social studies in what and how they teach. This becomes crucial in achieving such prized goals as improvement of students' problem-solving skills, critical reasoning, and flexibility in coping with novel sit-uations. Reforms in the last decade of the 20th century will be based on policymakers' aspiration that students who graduate from high school be able to perform complex cognitive skills. Reframed questions can better inform policymakers' intentions to pursue the improvement of reasoning and, at the same time, help classroom teachers reach the same goal.

EXPLORING ANSWERS TO THE QUESTIONS: SUGGESTIONS TO RESEARCHERS

What accounts for both stability and change in social studies teaching? Given the substantial move toward professionaliza-tion, why have social studies teachers displayed a fairly limited range of teaching practices in the classroom, and why have stu-dents persistently complained about the tedium of the subjects?

Basically, there are four lines of potential explanation that researchers might pursue in trying to answer these queries: the individual, the setting, the environment external to the setting, and combinations of these. By the "individual", I mean seeking answers in how teachers think and behave, but with an empha-sis on the will of teachers to make choices and bend situations to meet their goals. By "setting", I mean the immediate context of the work that teachers do, that is, the classroom and school. By "environment", I mean the district, the community, the state, and the federal structures that influence the school, and the larger culture with its values that inevitably penetrate the class-room. To differing degrees, researchers seeking answers to why teachers practice as they do have explored one or more of these lines of inquiry.

Some researchers and policymakers, however, have used two extreme explanations in seeking answers to these ques-tions. Some have concentrated excessively on the individual teacher as being the person who solely makes decisions about pedagogy, and they end up citing teacher willfulness as the an-swer to the questions just posed. It is as if most teachers inde-pendently reached the same conclusion about practicing the dominant pattern described earlier. Implicit in this viewpoint is the belief that teachers could alter what they do tomorrow if they only chose to do so This explanation, focused on individ-ual teachers, is understandable from a policy perspective, that is, school and classroom improvement is far more possible if one believes the solution lies in changing an individual's behav-ior, but still it omits so many other factors as to be almost a caricature of a reasonable explanation (National Commission on Excellence in Education, 1983).

Similarly, there are some researchers who pursue an ex-treme variation of the environmental explanation. Teachers, they argue, are mere agents of a larger social system that is driven by socioeconomic imperatives to sort out those students who will be workers from those who will be managers and professionals (e.g., Bowles & Gintis, 1976). More complex and less deterministic versions of this view argue that the schools recreate the conditions that sustain social norms and values in everyday classroom activities, thereby maintaining the eco-nomic and cultural inequalities that exist in the larger society (Apple, 1982; Giroux, 1981).

I have excluded both extreme versions of these two explana-tions, because my understanding of the research on the nature of teaching in general and social studies in particular, harnessed to my experiences as a practitioner, convinces me that far more sophisticated answers are necessary for the questions raised. Simple-factor answers to complex questions about teacher be-haviors challenge both experience-based and research-based knowledge about teaching. Adequate answers, I believe, must include concrete linkages between abstract concepts (e.g., set-ting and environment) and actual classroom practices.

These questions about social studies teachers are very simi-lar to the ones asked in a previous study about all academic teachers (Cuban, 1984). The tentative answer given then as a way of expanding the limited inquiry into why teachers teach as they do is relevant here. In that study, I offered an answer "midway between speculation and conclusion." More informed than a guess, it still fell short of being a confident assertion (p. 249).

In combining the explanations mentioned earlier, I called the quasi-speculative answer "situationally-constrained choice." I labeled the teaching practices that appeared constant over the last 100 years (1890s–1980s) "practical pedagogy" (similar to what has been identified earlier in this chapter as the core pat-tern of teaching dominant in social studies classrooms). This practical pedagogy was tailored to classrooms and designed to meet the demands arising from conflicting values that teachers had to satisfy in order to survive in the job. In short, the class-room setting and the culture that teachers found themselves in, that is, the graded school and multiple expectations, required them to develop practices to cope with the complexity of the workplace in which they found themselves. After all, to ask teachers already trying to cope with too many students and diffi-cult conditions to transform their classrooms into student-cen-tered ones would demand major expenditures of their time and energy, with few incentives offered by their organizations to do so.

To put it another way, I offered an umbrella explanation, crudely stated and undefined, of the organizational setting as one of two driving forces shaping the conditions within which teachers acted. The other driving force was the occupational culture of hierarchically organized schools. Within public schools, teachers implicitly embraced norms, beliefs, attitudes, and rituals that reached back many decades in their own lives, first as students, then as novices in classrooms, and eventually as licensed teachers. Both of these forces, deriving from the nature of the organization and the culture of teaching, shaped how teachers taught.

To moderate the deterministic thrust of the argument, to explain how some teachers did change by creating hybrids which were clear departures from dominant practices, I introduced the notion of individual choice. Teachers had a sufficient margin of autonomy once they closed their doors to pursue prized beliefs and norms that differed from those embedded in the practical pedagogy. Some teachers experimented with different techniques, materials, and styles of teaching and, over time, created hybrid patterns of instruction. Thus, the preliminary explanation offered in the earlier study was called "situationally-constrained choice."

In the years since that study, I have had the benefit of criticisms of this argument, read many studies of teaching that have been published, taught a high school U.S. history class for a semester, and completed this review of the slim body of literature on how social studies teachers have taught. Nothing that I have read, thought about, or experienced has convinced me to reject the earlier explanation. There is, however, a clear need to refurbish it for application to social studies instruction.

What is missing from the earlier argument is an elaboration of what is meant by *setting* and *context*. I omitted a number of factors that may have substantial influence upon how teachers teach, such as the socioeconomic status (SES) of the children, the subject matter taught by the teacher, the school goals and policies, and how teachers themselves, members of and value bearers of the larger culture, extract meaning from these factors in choosing what and how to teach. Finally, the penetration of economic and political forces that shape the school as a setting was omitted.

The background of students and their perceived ability to achieve as influences on teaching practices have been explored at both the elementary and secondary school levels by researchers (Anyon, 1980; Goodlad, 1984; Metz, 1978; Oakes, 1987; Rist, 1970; Stodolsky, Ferguson, & Wimpelberg, 1981; Wilcox, 1982). The meaning of the students' SES is filtered by teachers' culturally shaped beliefs into their expectations of what students are capable of achieving and then converted into teacher actions. Helping to transform teacher beliefs into classroom decisions about content and method is the school's formal assignment of students to teachers.

Since World War I, grouping by ability, as measured by the growing technology of paper-and-pencil tests, has reinforced socioeconomic differences among children. Classes in lower-ability groups in both elementary and secondary schools have larger than expected numbers of low SES students, usually drawn from immigrant and ethnic minorities. These grouping policies assign a label to individual children and then similarly labeled students are gathered into classes. Of concern here are those students given low-status labels, that is, low-ability, because of what such labels trigger in the minds of students and teachers as to what can and cannot be learned in class. Hence, the teacher's beliefs and school grouping policies intersect to create within the teacher's and the student's mind a set of expectations about what content the student can learn (Goodlad, 1984; Oakes, 1985; Rosenbaum, 1976).

Add to these contextual factors the recent research on subject-specific pedagogical knowledge (Shulman, 1987; Stodolsky, 1988; Wineburg & Wilson, in press), which suggests that teacher decision making is, in part, shaped by the teacher's disciplinary knowledge, awareness of curricular materials in the field, and range of skills linked to this knowledge. Putting the two factors of SES and pedagogical knowledge in a discipline together produces a growing body of research that points to the school's role in permitting students varied access to knowledge (Apple, 1982, 1986; Goodlad, 1984; Hanson, 1985; Oakes, 1985).

There are, of course, other contextual factors that may well influence content and practice. Some researchers have pointed to how districts, schools, and classrooms allocate resources and how those decisions affect the instructional choices that teachers make about within-class grouping and pacing in covering content (Barr & Dreeben, 1983). Consider, too, the role of departments in secondary schools. Bliss (1986) described how teachers in one social studies department of the four that she studied pursued small-group work as a consequence of departmental norms established over the years. Newmann (1988), who studied the presence of higher order thinking in social studies classrooms, found in five social studies departments the importance of departmental leadership and departmental norms supportive of teaching those skills. Moreover, he noted the principal's direction as a critical factor in sustaining instruction in those cognitive skills.

These studies are few. The point I stress is, not the lack of evidence for any particular explanation, but the need to establish with some degree of confidence what factors can be linked concretely to the daily practices of social studies teachers. Identifying, elaborating, and mapping these factors onto the school and classroom terrain offer some promise in improving what social studies teachers do, even if that terrain becomes far more complicated than what we now have. At the very least, the map will be more faithful and less likely to lead to fool's gold and disillusionment.

Thus far, my suggestions to researchers have been confined to unpacking the contextual elements encased in the concept of *setting*. By concentrating on the flaws of an earlier explanation that combined individual choice, the setting, and the environment, I have tried to demonstrate that much research remains to be done in this area. However, the focus on how one scholar tried to answer questions about stability and change in teaching risks ignoring other directions that could be taken in seeking answers to these questions.

Ethnographers from varied disciplines, for example, have investigated the effects of the larger culture on teachers' beliefs and the pedagogy they practice in their classrooms. The beliefs teachers bring into their classrooms about what knowledge is of most value, how teaching should occur, how learning occurs, and the role of the school get transformed into classroom practices in spite of state curricular and organizational mandates contrary to those beliefs (Popkewitz, Tabachnick, & Weklege, 1982; Spindler, 1982; Wolcott, 1977). Although a few scholars have studied the connective strands between folk beliefs in the culture about knowledge, learning, and teaching and what occurs in the classroom, the social studies has received little attention. Researchers in this line of inquiry examine the potent intersection between what individual social studies teachers believe about what they do and how those beliefs reinforce and challenge cultural beliefs that are embedded—hidden might be a more apt word—so deeply in their minds, the structures within which they work, and the tools they use (Cohen, 1988).

So, the available answers to the complex questions asked earlier leave much to be desired. They are suggestive and, at best, tentative. None is yet compelling. Cross-national studies of social studies to determine if the same patterns of stability and incremental change exist in other countries where the cultures are different from the United States might also shed further light on the questions and the answers. Also, cross-institutional studies of social science teaching in colleges and universities where the organizational structures are very different might bring more understanding to the puzzling patterns examined here.

In inquiring how social studies teachers taught in the 20th century, this chapter recovered a slim body of evidence that suggests, albeit incompletely, that both stability and change existed simultaneously in the classroom. Even in the midst of strenuous efforts to market reforms in curriculum, instruction, and classroom organization, social studies teachers blended continuity and change into their dominant ways of instruction. Few, if any, fundamental changes have penetrated these classrooms permanently, but many incremental ones have occurred with the eager help of teachers themselves. What explains these apparent patterns of classroom behavior? No firm answers are now available. Yet answers to these questions will provide surer, more certain, and more reliable guides to changes in practice than existing lines of investigation, because such research will be anchored in what teachers did rather than in what they ought to have done.

References

Anang, A., & Lanier, P. (1982). Where is the subject matter? How the social organization of the classroom affects teaching. East Lansing, MI: Michigan State University, Institute for Research on Teaching.

Anyon, J. (1980). Social class and the hidden curriculum of work. *Journal of Education, 162,* 67–91.

Apple, M. (1982). *Cultural and economic reproduction in education.* New York: Routledge and Kegan Paul.

Apple, M. (1986). *Teachers and texts.* New York: Routledge and Kegan Paul.

Applebee, A., Langer, J., & Mullis, I. (1987). *The nation's report card: Literature and U.S. history.* Princeton, NJ: Educational Testing Service.

Armento, B. (1986). Research on teaching social studies. In M. Wittrock (Ed.), *Handbook of research on teaching* (2nd ed., pp. 942–951). New York: Macmillan.

Atkin, M., & House, E. (1981). The federal role in curriculum development, 1950–1980. *Educational Evaluation and Policy Analysis 3,* 5–36.

Barr, R., & Dreeben, R. (1983). *How schools work.* Chicago: University of Chicago Press.

Barth, R. (1972). *Open education and the American school.* New York: Agathon.

Baxter, M., Ferrell, R., & Wiltz, J. (1964). *The teaching of American history in high schools.* Bloomington, IN: Indiana University Press.

Beale, H. K. (1941). *A history of freedom of teaching in American schools.* New York: Charles Scribners Sons.

Bliss, T. (1986). *Small group work in high school social studies.* Unpublished doctoral dissertation, Stanford University.

Bowles, S., & Gintis, H. (1976). *Schooling in capitalist America.* New York: Basic Books.

Bridges, E. (1986). *The incompetent teacher.* London: Falmer Press.

Briggs, T. (1935). The practices of best high school teachers. *School Review, 43,* 745–752.

Brophy, J. (1988). *Teaching for conceptual understanding and higher order applications of social studies content.* East Lansing, MI: Michigan State University, Institute for Research on Teaching.

Chase, W. L. (1949). Subject preferences of fifth grade children. *Elementary School Journal, 50,* 204–211.

Cohen, D. (1988). Teaching practice, Plus Que Ca change . . . In P. Jack-son (Ed.), *Contributing to educational change.* Berkeley, CA: McCutchan.

Conners, R. (1959). *Geographic problem solving behavior of eighth grade students in the Warren Beatty Junior High School.* Unpublished dissertation, Pennsylvania State University.

Cremin, L. (1988). *American education: The metropolitan experience, 1876–1980.* New York: Harper & Row.

Cuban, L. (1984). *How teachers taught: Constancy and change in American classrooms, 1890–1980.* New York: Longman.

Farrar, E., Powell, A., & Cohen D. (1985). *The shopping mall high school.* Boston: Houghton Mifflin.

Finkelstein, B. (1970). *Governing the young: Teacher behavior in American primary schools, 1820–1880.* Unpublished doctoral dissertation, Teachers College, Columbia University.

Fitzgerald, F. (1979). *America revised.* Boston: Little, Brown.

Fraenkel, J. (1987). Toward improving research in social studies education. *Theory and Research in Social Education, 15*(3), 77–87.

Giroux, H. (1981). *Ideology, culture, and the process of schooling.* Philadelphia: Temple University Press.

Goodlad, J. (1984). *A place called school.* New York: McGraw-Hill.

Gross, R. (1951). *Trends in the teaching of United States history in the senior high school of California.* Unpublished doctoral dissertation, Stanford University, Stanford, CA.

Gross, R., & Badger, W. (1960). Social studies. In C. Harris (Ed.), *Encyclopedia of educational research* (3rd ed., pp. 1296–1319). New York: Macmillan.

Hanson, S. (1985). *The college preparatory curriculum at two high schools in one school district.* Unpublished doctoral dissertation, Stanford University.

Harper, C. (1937). Why do children dislike history? *Social Education, 1,* 492–494.

Herman, W. L. (1977). Teacher behavior in the elementary school social studies. *Theory and Research in Social Education, 4*(3), 39–63.

Hertzberg, H. (1981). *Social studies reform, 1880–1900.* Boulder, CO: Social Science Education Consortium.

Hughes, J., & Melby, E. (1930). *Supervision of instruction in high schools.* Bloomington, IL: Public School Publishing.

Jackson, P. (1968). *Life in classrooms.* New York: Holt, Rinehart & Winston.

Kaestle, C. (1973). *The evolution of an urban school system.* Cambridge, MA: Harvard University Press.

Kaestle, C. (1983). *Pillars of the republic.* New York: Hill and Wang.

Katz, M. (1968). *The irony of early school reform.* Boston: Beacon Press.

Kirst, M., & Meister, G. (1985). Turbulence in American secondary schools: What reforms last? *Curriculum Inquiry, 15*(2), 169–186.

Kurfman, D. (1982). Evaluation in social studies. In Project Span Staff (Eds.), *Working papers from Project Span* (pp. 3–27). Boulder, CO: Social Science Education Consortium.

Massialias, B. (1963). Developing a method of inquiry in teaching world history. In B. Massialias (Ed.), *The Indiana experiments in inquiry: Social studies* (Bulletin of the School of Education, Indiana University, Vol. 39), (pp. 1–35).

McGill, J. (1949). *Comparative values of assigned homework and supervised study: An experimental study of the two methods of preparation as used by students of the social studies at the high school level.* Unpublished doctoral dissertation. New York University.

Metcalf, L. (1963). Research in teaching the social studies. In N. Gage (Ed.), *Handbook of research on teaching.* Chicago: Rand McNally, 929–965.

Metz, M. (1978). *Classroom and corridors.* Berkeley, CA: University of California Press.

National Commission on Excellence in Education. (1983). *A nation at risk.* Washington, DC: U.S. Government Printing Office.

Newmann, F. M. (988). *Higher order thinking in high school social studies: An analysis of classrooms, teachers, students, and leadership.* Madison, WI: University of Wisconsin, National Center on Effective Secondary Schools.

Nisbet, R. (1969). *Social change and history.* London: Oxford University Press.

Norman, R. H. (1934). A history project in an eighth grade social studies class. *The Clearing House, 13*(4), 274–275.

Oakes, J. (1985). *Keeping track: How schools structure inequality.* New Heaven, CT: Yale University Press.

Orlosky, D., & Smith, B. O. (1972). Educational change: Its origins and characteristics. *Phi Delta Kappan, 53,* 412–414.

Outland, G., & Jones, L. (1940). High school pupils evaluate the social studies program. *School Review, 48,* 592–599.

Palonsky, S. B. (1987). Political socialization in elementary schools. *Elementary School Journal, 87*(5), 493–505.

Penix, F. Teaching social studies in elementary schools: Experiments in method. In B. Massialias & F. Smith, *Current research in social studies* (Bulletin of the School of Education, Indiana University, Vol. 40), (pp. 31–42).

Popenfus, J. R. (1978). *Classroom applications of theory and practice in secondary school social studies.* Washington, DC: University Press of America.

Popkewitz, T., Tabachnick, B., & Weklege, G. (1982). *The myth of education reform.* Madison, WI: University of Wisconsin Press.

Rist, R. (1970) Student social class and teacher expectations: The self-fulfilling prophecy in ghetto education. *Harvard Educational Review, 40,* 411–451.

Robinson, P. (1980). The conventional histories of the social studies. *Theory and Research in Social Education, 8*(3), 65–87.

Sedlak, M., & Schlossman, S. (1986). *Who will teach?* Santa Monica, CA: Rand Corporation.

Shaver, J., & Larkins, G. (1973). Research on teaching social studies. In R. M. W. Travers (Ed)., *Second handbook on research on teaching* (pp. 1243–1262). Chicago: Rand McNally.

Shaver, J. P., Davis, O. L., & Helburn, S. W. (1980). An interpretive report on the status of precollege social studies education based on three NSF-funded studies. In *What are the needs in precollege science, mathematics, and social science education?* Washington, DC: National Science Foundation.

Shulman, L. (1987). Knowledge and teaching: Foundations of the new reform. *Harvard Educational Review, 57*(1), 1–22.

Siemers, A. (1960). World history: Practices and problems. *Social Education, 27*(4), 153–157.

Silberman, C. (1971). *Crisis in the classroom.* New York: Alfred A. Knopf.

Singleton, H. W. (1980). Problems of democracy: The revisionist plan for social studies education. *Theory and Research in Social Studies Education, 8,* 89–104.

Sirotnik, K. (1981). What you see is what you get: A summary of observations in over 1,000 elementary and secondary classrooms. In *A study of schooling.* Los Angeles: University of California, Graduate School of Education.

Sizer, T. (1984). *Horace's compromise.* Boston: Houghton Mifflin,

Skretting, J., & Sundeen, J. (1969). Social studies education. In R. Ebel (Ed.), *Encyclopedia of educational research* (4th ed., pp. 1231–1241). New York: Macmillan.

Spindler, G. (1982). General introduction. In G. Spindler (Ed.), *Doing the ethnography of schooling: Educational anthropology in action* (pp. 1–13). New York: Holt, Rinehart & Winston.

Stake, R. E. & Easley, J. A. (1978). *Case studies in science education. Vol. 2. Design, overview and general findings.* Urbana, IL: Center for Instructional Research and Curriculum Evaluation, University of Illinois.

Stevens, R. (1912). *The question as a measure of efficiency in instruction.* New York: Columbia University, Teachers College.

Stodolsky, S. (1988). *The subject matters.* Chicago: University of Chicago Press.

Stodolsky, S., Ferguson, T., & Wimpelberg, K. (1981). The recitation persists, but what does it look like? *Journal of Curriculum Studies, 13*(2), 121–130.

Thirty schools tell their story (Vol. 5). (1942). New York: Harpers and Brothers.

Tyack, D. (1974). *The One best system: A history of American urban education.* Cambridge, MA: Harvard University Press.

Tyack, D., Kirst, M., & Hansot, E. (1980). Educational reform: Retrospect and prospect. *Teachers College Record, 81,* 253–270.

Tyack, D., Lowe R., & Hansot, E. (1984). *Public schools in hard times.* Cambridge, MA: Harvard University Press.

Waller, W. (1965). *The sociology of teaching.* New York: John Wiley & Sons.

Weiss, I. (1978). *Report of the 1977 national survey of science, mathematics, and social studies education.* Research Triangle Park, NC: Research Triangle Institute.

White, J. J. (1985). What works for teachers: A review of ethnographic research studies as they inform issues in social studies curriculum and instruction. In W. B. Stanley (Ed.), *Review of Research in Social Studies Education, 1976–1983* (pp. 215–307). Washington, DC: National Council for the Social Studies.

Wigginton, E. (1985). *Sometimes a shining moment.* Garden City, NY: Doubleday, Anchor Press.

Wilcox, K. (1982). Differential socialization in the classroom: Implications for equal opportunity. In G. Spindler (Ed.), *Doing the ethnography of schooling.* New York: Holt, Rinehart & Winston.

Wiley, K. B. (1977). *The status of pre-college science, mathematics, and social studies education: 1955–1975; Vol. 3. Social science education.* Boulder, CO: Social Science Education Consortium.

Wilkinson, R. (1964). Social studies in the elementary schools. *Education, 34*(5), 280–285.

Wilson, S. M., & Wineburg, S. W. (1988). Peering at history through different lenses: The role of disciplinary perspectives in teaching history. *Teachers College Record, 89*(4), 525–539.

Wineburg, S., & Wilson, S. (in press) Subject matter knowledge in the teaching of history. In J. E. Brophy (Ed.), *Advances in Research on Teaching.* Greenwich, CT: JAI Press.

Wolcott, H. (1977). *Teachers versus technocrats.* Eugene, OR: University of Oregon, Center for Educational Policy & Management.

Zilversmit, A. (1976). The failure of progressive education, 1920–1940. In L. Stone (Ed.), *Schooling and society.* Baltimore: Johns Hopkins Press.

·17·

THE EDUCATION OF SOCIAL STUDIES TEACHERS

Susan A. Adler

UNIVERSITY OF MISSOURI, KANSAS CITY

In his landmark book, *A Place Called School* (1984), John Goodlad described the social studies as potentially engaging school subjects. After all, he wrote, the topics ought to be of great human interest. What he found, however, was that the social studies are often the least liked subjects in school: "Something strange seems to happen to them on the way to the classroom. The topics of study become removed from their intrinsically human character, reduced to the dates and places readers will recall memorizing for tests" (p. 212).

As Goodlad and others (see, e.g., Shaver, Davis, & Helburn, 1979) have documented, social studies in the schools is characterized by an emphasis on authority and memorization. Most of the activities learners engage in are passive: reading texts, listening quietly, completing work sheets, and taking quizzes and examinations. At the same time, the social studies literature is replete with such goals as reasoning and decision making, increasing learners' conceptual understanding, drawing conclusions from data, and developing skills for participatory citizenship.

There seems to be little doubt that there is a gap between theory, what social studies ought to be, and practice, what happens in many classrooms. What is far less certain is how to account for this gap and what, if anything, to do to narrow it. Certainly, there is no simple answer to this complex question, but understanding and improving the education of social studies teachers offers one direction. The classroom teacher is the mediator of the curriculum, the one who makes decisions that profoundly influence what is actually taught (Parker, 1987). How are teachers prepared for the work of teaching social studies? How does their ongoing education help them deal with issues and concerns related to achieving the goals of the field? What practices in the education of social studies teachers hold promise for improved teaching and learning in social studies classrooms?

A review of the literature on social studies teacher education over the decade 1978–1988 reveals no shortage of criticism, nor any shortage of ideas about what social studies teacher education *ought* to be and *ought* to accomplish. The concerns and the proposed solutions cover a myriad of interests. The failure of teacher-preparation programs to prepare teachers who can teach their students critical thinking skills is noted by several authors. Jantz, Weaver, Cirrincione, and Farrell (1985) argued that teacher-preparation programs failed to prepare preservice teachers to use inquiry techniques. Paul (1986) and Unks (1985) questioned how we could expect to find critical thinking skills being taught in schools when teachers themselves do not possess these skills.

A variety of other concerns are also cited in the literature. Beginning teachers don't have an adequate knowledge of social studies content or appropriate pedagogy, according to Berryman and Schneider's survey of social studies supervisors (1984). Teacher educators should place more emphasis on citizenship education (Butts, 1983) and try to learn how to create a classroom climate that is congruent with the content and processes of civic values (Torney-Purta, 1983). Teachers should have more course work in economics (Diem, 1981), and more should be done to help pre- and inservice teachers become computer literate (Martorella, 1984; Napier, 1983). Preservice teachers ought to be introduced to a global perspective (Gilliom & Harf, 1985).

Methods courses must help the preservice elementary teacher develop a definition of social studies, an understanding of its goals and objectives, a knowledge of major concepts and how they are to be sequenced, and appropriate methods of evaluation (Skeel, 1981). There is a need for social studies teacher educators to confront the disarray in the field with a unified voice and a national plan (Tucker & Joyce, 1979). In sum, it would seem that there is much that *ought* to be done. But teacher education must proceed with a knowledge of what *is* being done and to what effect.

Reviewers were Jesse Goodman, Indiana University; E. Wayne Ross, State University of New York at Albany.

In this chapter current research is examined on the education of both preservice and inservice social studies teachers, at both the elementary and the secondary levels. One major goal is to identify common and promising practices in the education of social studies teachers. A second important goal is to identify common and promising practices in the research about the education of social studies teachers. These are two separate, but related, goals. Research should enable us to improve practice, but, to do so, we must look both to the subjects of research and to the research processes themselves.

The first goal, then, is to synthesize what recent research says about social studies teacher education. One would hope that a review of research would provide generalizations about social studies teacher education, about long-term and short-term gains, and point toward theories that would guide those responsible for the education of social studies teachers.

This review also goes beyond synthesis in looking toward what needs to be known and suggesting how researchers might proceed. What questions have researchers not asked or only begun to ask? What new questions and approaches hold promise for extending our knowledge about social studies teacher education and improving our practices? How are we conducting research and how might we conduct research? This review aims to point in new directions, toward new questions and new methodologies, as well as to synthesize work already done.

Included in this review of research are descriptions of practice, as well as of experimental and field studies. Research here is taken broadly as purposeful, systematic inquiry that facilitates better knowing and understanding of social phenomena (Stanley, 1985, p. 3). It is argued that the practitioners of teacher education, those who work most directly and intensely with preservice education, can function as practitioner–researchers (Schön, 1983) when they engage in systematic, purposeful reflection on their own practices.

Research on social studies teacher education is an integral part of research on teacher education in general. To facilitate the development of a coherent body of work, it seems reasonable, then, to parallel the organization of this chapter with that of Lanier and Little's (1986) chapter, "Research on Teacher Education", in *Handbook of Research on Teaching*. Therefore, headings are organized around Schwab's (1978) commonplaces of teaching: the curriculum, the teacher, the students, and the context or milieu. Much of the research specifically directed at social studies teacher education has been done on the curriculum of teacher education; it is this work, then, that is discussed first and at greatest length.

THE CURRICULUM

The term *curriculum* here refers to the teaching and learning of pedagogy and of subject-matter content. Social studies teacher education is distinguished from teacher education in general by the social studies methods class and course work in history and the social sciences. It is no surprise, then, that research in the curriculum of social studies teacher education has been focused primarily on these two areas, with the strongest emphasis on the social studies methods class.

Social Studies Methods

Given the concern with the social studies methods course as a special feature of social studies teacher education, one might expect that here, at least, a synthesis of recent research would give some direction toward improved practice and the development of theory. This is not, however, the case. Research on the teaching of social studies methods has been, on the whole, particularistic and unsystematic. Robinson's (1982) assertion that there is little cumulative impact to this line of inquiry still holds; there is little building of one study upon another.

Articles and papers reviewed in this category include those focused on both overall course design and particular practices in the teaching of social studies methods. Studies that are primarily descriptions of practice or course design are included along with the more traditional experimental and survey approaches, because each has the potential to contribute to our knowledge about social studies methods classes and to improve practice. The work on overall course design is discussed first.

The research on methods course design and structure has covered a variety of possibilities. The greatest research emphasis has been given to field-based methods courses, but, despite a common topic, a synthesis of these studies did not produce any systematic data from which to draw conclusions. Dibella and Fitzgerald (1982) described the experience of integrating fieldwork into the methods class by assigning preservice teachers enrolled in social studies methods to teach a unit of study once a week over a period of 9 weeks. Student and faculty responses on a questionnaire indicated that the program had been successful.

Merwin and Templeton (1978) reported the findings of a study in which three groups of students enrolled in social studies methods classes at one institution were used to evaluate the efficacy of Self-Instructional Modules (SIMs) developed by the authors. Efficacy was measured by the authors' observations of the students' teaching in their field placements. Students who experienced the SIMs in conjunction with a field-based methods course were rated most highly; those who used the modules along with the conventional methods class were also rated highly; those who did not use the modules were rated last. No group experienced the field-based course without the use of SIMs.

Foster (1979), Phillips (1979), and Staton-Spicer, Colson, and Bassett (1979) described different perspectives on a collaborative program that emphasized fieldwork during methods courses in order to facilitate the application of theory to practice. Van Cleaf, Schroder, and Frataccia (1980) examined the effects of varying amounts of time allocated to experience with children on the participating preservice teachers' perceptions of the value of various components of their methods course. Interestingly, those who had spent the most time with children as part of their methods course (30% of the time) ranked that component of the course least important. Those who had spent less time (from 2.5 to 5% of their time) ranked that experience as most valuable. During student teaching, however, the group that had spent more of their time in the early field experience ranked that experience as more valued. The authors assumed that student perceptions, as measured by a survey instrument with Likert-scale items, are an important factor in determining whether the balance between course work and field experiences is appropriate.

Positive results are claimed in the reports of studies on field-based methods courses, but the data supporting these assertions are generally superficial, based on questionnaires and observers' impressions. Importantly, researchers have not investigated the effects of field experiences on preservice teachers' long-term development in teaching.

Articles that described overall course design, other than those studies that were focused on field-based programs, covered a variety of often unrelated ideas. Metzger (1985) presented a rationale for increasing the number of required hours for the social studies methods course, along with a description of expanded courses. However, he provided no empirical evidence that students actually gain from this expanded experience. Herman (1982) argued that methods courses can be improved through the development of closer relationships with schools. Data from schools describing what school people believe methods courses ought to include can be helpful to methods instructors, the author argued in identifying the competencies needed in the real world of classrooms. Hoffman (1979) presented a description of a social studies methods class designed to make the class more personal and allow for mutual sharing of ideas and interests.

For the most part, these authors described course structure and presented little systematic evidence to support their recommendations. Although some rationale was given for each idea, by and large there was little attention paid to any theoretical base. Hoffman (1979) made mention of developmental theory in arguing for the importance of modeling trust and rapport; nonetheless, he made no systematic effort to apply a particular theory to teaching the methods course.

A different approach to the discussion of overall course design is represented by the work of Goodman (1986), Adler and Goodman (1986), and Ross and Hannay (1986). These authors discussed attempts to base a methods course on theory and rationale by applying the work of critical theorists to the teaching of methods courses. The studies were primarily descriptive and did not include assessments of outcomes; there was no assessment of the ways in which students were actually changed by their participation in the course or whether those changes were reflected in their eventual classroom teaching. These studies were not empirical in nature, but they do represent a systematic approach to applying theory to practice and suggest a direction for future research.

The work just described was focused on methods classes in general; the more common approach was to examine particular assignments or elements of the methods course. Several authors have discussed ways in which they incorporated issues of ethnic and gender diversity into the methods class. Carlson (1986) discussed the use of videodiscs to increase preservice teachers' understanding of cultural diversity. A survey, "Understanding Cultural Diversity," and the author's observations were presented to support the technique discussed. Bennett (1979) described a variety of class activities in a secondary methods class, labeled the experimental group and designed to change preservice teachers' perceptions of racial and cultural groups. He contrasted this approach with what he described as the more traditional competency-based approach of another class, the control group. In this study, the author reported, responses to survey instruments did indicate some statistically significant positive changes in experimental groups' perceptions of ethnic groups.

Smith (1978) studied the effects of materials he developed to help elementary preservice teachers investigate their own attitudes toward gender and gender roles. Although there was no statistically significant difference between the non–randomly assigned experimental and control groups on the posttest attitude survey administered in this study, the author argued that the experimental group did show greater willingness to develop nonsexist lesson plans with regard to family roles and careers.

It is no surprise that the instructors of social studies methods classes should address issues of ethnic and gender diversity; these are topics that seem natural to social studies. What is surprising is what is not included in this research. Given the changing demographics of the school-age population, one would hope that research on social studies teacher education would in the future include reports on efforts to prepare white, middle-class teachers to teach social studies to students of diverse ethnic backgrounds and from poverty-level homes.

Other studies on strategies for teaching methods classes range over diverse approaches. The emphasis is on the description of practices, with some data presented to support the particular thesis. Weaver, Gardner, Williams, Cole, and Saracho (1984) and Kincheloe (1985) described ways of using community resources and getting preservice teachers involved in doing primary source research. In the Weaver et al. report, students enrolled in one methods class were used as an experimental group and those in another class were used as a control group. The description of the teaching strategy used was informative, but the measures used to compare the two groups were unclear. The Kincheloe report included a description of a student research project and a report on its observed success; the author did not make clear what evidence for success was used.

Marsh (1983) presented the results of a survey of Australian social studies methods professors in which 58% of the respondents indicated that teaching preservice students to develop criteria for the selection of curricular materials was very important. However, on the same survey, a majority of respondents reported using less than 20% of their course to involve students in such activities. The author concluded that this is insufficient time, and, despite its perceived importance, little emphasis is given by methods instructors to teaching students to develop criteria for selecting curricular materials.

Ellington (1985) described the practice of having preservice teachers interview practicing teachers and, thus, gain insight into teaching while learning an important skill. Student comments and course evaluations were presented to support the usefulness of the activity. Walton, Kutz, and Thompson (1986) discussed the use of Carl Sagan's book *Cosmos* during the methods class as a vehicle to demonstrate and promote integrated curricula for the schools. A questionnaire and observations of small-group discussions about the theory, applications, and benefits of an integrated curriculum were used to assess students' reactions, seen as positive, to the approach.

Freeland (1983) divided students enrolled in social studies

methods courses into an experimental group ($n = 45$), which used self-instructional modules to teach about the social sciences, and a control group ($n = 55$), which used a textbook to teach the same topic. Results of pre- and posttests, according to the author, indicated that those using the self-instructional modules learned more. Lee (1984) described a process used to help students learn power-sharing and decision-making skills and included a discussion of student reactions to the experiences.

Thus, research on social studies methods courses conducted in the period 1978–1988 ranged widely, but not deeply, over an array of topics. Some of these studies were simply descriptive pieces, detailing the implementation of particular practices or orientations (Foster , 1979; Herman, 1982; Hoffman, 1979; Metzger, 1985; Phillips, 1979; Staton-Spicer et al., 1979). Although not systematic in their discussion of outcomes or in the connections they made with one another, the reports can be useful in stimulating ideas for individual readers who, themselves, teach methods courses.

Other studies were more empirically grounded. Among these were studies in which data were gathered through questionnaires, surveys, or observations of the preservice students involved (Carlson, 1986; Dibella & Fitzgerald, 1982; Ellington, 1985; Kincheloe, 1985; Marsh, 1983; Walton, et al., 1986). In still other efforts, experimental research design was used in the natural settings of teacher education programs (Bennett, 1979; Freeland, 1983; Merwin & Templeton, 1978; Smith, 1978; Van Cleaf, et al., 1980; Weaver et al., 1984). However, claims to the validity of these studies were weak when measured against the standards for experimental research (Campbell & Stanley, 1963). Samples were randomly selected from too narrow a population or not randomly selected at all, jeopardizing the validity of generalizing to a wider population. The internal validity of these studies was not clear; changes documented may have resulted from any one of a number of factors. A change in attitude, as measured by a survey instrument administered by a methods class instructor, for example, may have been the result of knowing what the professor wanted. Further, the researchers did not build upon or make reference to related research; rather, they tended to be ahistorical in their approach.

No evidence was presented that findings translated into meaningful recommendations for practice. None of the studies discussed examined whether changes in attitudes and/or knowledge had an impact on the teaching practices developed by the preservice teachers under study. Did the strategies used in methods classes and described in these studies make any difference to the teaching of social studies?

Further, in the research on social studies methods classes, the relationship of the methods class to the broader education program of which it is a part was not examined. Decontextualization of the elements of teacher education under study is a common problem in research on teacher education generally (Zeichner, 1985). Does it matter, for example, whether students take the methods class at the graduate or undergraduate level? Are there any meaningful differences when the same strategies in a methods class are used in a small program or a large one, at a small college or a large university? How do the expectations from other courses, both implicit and explicit, influence what is learned in a methods class? Finally, little attention was paid

to how participants, including the researchers, structured the meaning of tasks or how the contexts of those tasks influenced those meanings and shaped intentions and practices.

The nature of the research discussed suggests that most researchers cited in this review were describing their own teaching experiences. Certainly, among those interested in methods courses are those who teach them, although these are often not the people involved in large-scale research. Teacher educators are practitioners, who, although often limited in time and resources, can reflect on their own practices and contribute to a body of literature that reflects "wisdom of practice." Rather than separate the knower and the known, researchers of teacher education can look to a knowledge base developed from practice "continually being created and interpreted, especially by practitioners" in their particular situations (Diez, 1987, p. 2). The work of practitioner researchers need not be aimed at building timeless generalizations; rather, such researchers can develop and utilize alternative approaches to research that might enable methods class practitioners to make informed choices about the nature and activities of their classes.

A stress on intrapersonal processes, introspection, and self-reports can serve as a valid component of a broader set of research practices (Allender, 1986). Reflection on one's own practice, done systematically and thoughtfully, can contribute to an accumulation of knowledge about the social studies methods class.

Some of the studies of methods classes described (Adler & Goodman, 1986; Goodman, 1986; Lee, 1984; Little, 1984) were more self-consciously reflective. These authors explicitly examined their own involvement as practitioners of teacher education. All included descriptions of the problems encountered as they sought to implement their particular ideas. Little's (1984) study was explicitly "dedicated to an introspective analysis" (p. 1) of his work to implement social studies methods courses within the particular demands of two thematically different teacher education programs at Michigan State University. In the other studies also, the authors attended to the ways in which the particulars of context and situation influenced the practice of methods courses.

Quantitative, experimental studies can contribute to our knowledge of methods classes when carefully designed and when placed in a context of related theory and research. But this is only one framework for study and, as such, is limiting (Cornbleth, 1986). Too often, the methods class practitioner has neither the time nor the resources to conduct well-designed experiments. But the practitioner–researcher can bring other perspectives to the field, particularly the thoughtful description of and reflection upon practice.

Methods Texts

Textbooks used in methods classes are often the primary source of information about social studies teaching for preservice teachers. Texts may define what content is covered in the methods course and the nature of that coverage. An examination of methods texts is, therefore, an important direction for research in social studies teacher education.

Cherryholmes (1982) examined the power relationships

embedded in what he termed the discursive practices found in three social studies methods texts, as well as in several other printed social studies documents. He found that concerns with teacher control of classroom instruction and explanations that reinforced the social status quo dominated the text of these documents. Cherryholmes argued that the language used in these texts served to reinforce preservice teachers' concerns with pupil control and maintenance of status quo, rather than encouraging them to raise questions and reflect on the nature of the social world.

Stanley (1983,1984) found that frequently used methods texts gave insufficient attention to the teaching of concepts and inadequate coverage to values education. Further, in the area of values education, almost all the texts failed to discuss criticisms of the prevailing approaches to values education.

No studies could be located that examined the actual use of textbooks in social studies methods classes or the meanings that preservice teachers actually take from the texts they use. The assumption that textbooks tell us something about the content of methods courses may be unwarranted. What is the role of the textbook in a methods class? To what extent are courses actually organized around text content? How are these texts supplemented by other readings and by class activities? What happens when methods instructors do not use any text?

Field Experiences

One of the common wisdoms of teacher preparation is that time in the public school classroom is the most important and meaningful aspect of teacher-preparation programs. Teacher educators and preservice teachers see field experiences as opportunities for prospective teachers to apply learned skills and gain real-world experience. But a substantial amount of research on field experiences calls into question the actual learning that takes place in the field. Early in the century, John Dewey (1904/1964) made a distinction between laboratory experiences and apprenticeships. In the latter, according to Dewey, students learn what works to make a class run smoothly; in the former, students are given the opportunity to reflect on classroom decisions and to consider the consequences of their acts in terms of what their students would actually learn and in terms of ethical and social principles. Research on field experiences since Dewey's time suggests that the apprenticeship model dominates. In the field, preservice teachers seem, by and large, to take on a managerial mentality, to use trial-and-error to determine what works and to define what works by what keeps the class running smoothly.

The distinction posed by Dewey is a significant one. Cox (1981) studied a student-teaching experience designed to promote reflectivity, to make the student-teaching experience less of an apprenticeship and more of a laboratory experience. Six student teachers were assigned to cooperating teachers in pairs, in order to promote collaborative interaction among peers. The pair-placed teachers did, on the average, use more teaching techniques per class and more diverse approaches to evaluation than did the four single-placed student teachers who served as the control group. Further, there were some indications that

the content of their discussions dealt, according to Cox, with more reflective concerns. Cox did not find that pairs moved more rapidly from concerns with self to concerns with others.

Although the Cox study was an attempt to describe an experience for student teachers that would promote reflection and would thereby be a laboratory experience in the Deweyean sense, the question of what the preservice teachers actually learned was not directly addressed. To what extent do field experiences, as they are generally practiced, contribute to social studies teaching as it ought to be? To what extent do preservice teachers learn, from these experiences, to fit into the status quo? What does the experience of work in classrooms mean to those learning to teach?

Several studies have undertaken to examine just these sorts of questions. The following studies are significant for their emphasis on the perceptions and perspectives of the student teacher. These researchers have sought to determine the meanings that social studies student teachers give to their experiences, the factors that influence those meanings, and the possible consequences of those experiences.

Nelson and Palonsky (1980) investigated the conceptions of social studies held by preservice teachers as they completed their student teaching. They got very mixed responses to questions of definition and purpose, perhaps reflecting, the authors suggested, the lack of consensus in the field. Palonsky and Nelson (1980) also used an interview technique to investigate student teachers' perceptions of political restraint, of power and control within the school setting, during student teaching. Most of these student teachers expressed an awareness of role conflict. They saw themselves as politically slightly to the left of their cooperating teachers and more to the left of the school administration; they believed they could not fully implement strategies and processes they thought to be appropriate. Thus, they perceived restraints on their teaching that were informal, rather than explicit. The student teachers sought to avoid conflict and to accommodate to the restraints. However, their accommodations were conscious decisions in particular contexts and not necessarily internalizations of more conservative beliefs.

Kickbusch's (1987) observations and interviews yielded similar findings. Student teachers in social studies classrooms exhibited a narrow range of pedagogical skills in support of narrow civic education goals. For two of the student teachers observed, this behavior was dissonant with their expressed personal beliefs, the result of their perceptions of the prevailing mechanisms of power and control at the school sites and their own perceived lack of power.

Ross (1988) examined the extent to which student teachers felt free to exercise independent judgment or felt pressured to conform to institutional constraints. His findings confirmed Lacy's (1977) that, not only did some students conform while others acted more independently, but also some students conformed only outwardly, seeming to comply while retaining their own differing viewpoints. The student teachers' past experiences and perceptions of the situation, as well as the evaluative power of the cooperating teacher and university supervisor, were important factors in shaping student teachers' responses to institutional demands.

In another study, which addressed student teacher perspectives, Adler (1984) examined the perspectives on social studies of four elementary school student teachers whose beliefs, as determined by a questionnaire and observations during their methods classes, seemed to reflect an understanding of social studies that was consistent with that expressed by many social studies educators. These student teachers wanted to implement a curriculum that would reflect a process, interdisciplinary orientation, and that would be personally meaningful to pupils. The perspectives on social studies that emerged during student teaching were, however, more diverse, reflecting meanings that emerged from the student teachers' experiences as they interpreted them. Once again, at least two of the four student teachers studied perceived restraints that prevented them from acting in ways they had thought would be appropriate. It is important to note that it was these students' interpretations of their teaching situation, not explicit rules or pressures, that shaped their teaching practices.

Goodman and Adler (1985) extended the Adler study, which had been focused on four preservice teachers, and described the perspectives on social studies of 16 elementary school student teachers. Again, the perspectives that emerged in practice did not necessarily correspond with these preservice teachers' orientation toward social studies as demonstrated by questionnaires and interviews prior to student teaching. However, the student-teaching experience alone did not create their perspectives or shape their teaching practices. What was learned during student teaching was shaped by these individuals' interpretations of the situation, and this, in turn was influenced as much by personal biography and beliefs as by the situation itself.

This same line of inquiry was followed by Ross (1987) in a study of the perspectives on social studies of 25 secondary social studies student teachers. Using a series of interviews with the informants, Ross concluded that individuals' perspectives were the product of a dialectical process involving the interaction of personal variables, such as past experiences, and structural variables, such as teacher education course work. Individual preservice teachers played an active role in mediating their experiences.

The studies just cited point to the complexity of the process of becoming a teacher. Just what preservice teachers learn from their field experiences depends a good deal on what they bring with them (Tabachnick & Zeichner, 1984). One promising direction in research on social studies teacher education is that of exploring further the factors that influence teachers' socialization and the ways to build upon personal past experiences to improve teaching practice.

The Teacher Education Program

Teacher educators throughout the 20th century have been concerned with determining an appropriate balance of general and professional education (Borrowman, 1956). Social studies teacher educators have shared that concern, with special attention paid to how much and what sort of social science education would be appropriate.

The results of Berryman and Schneider's (1984) survey of social studies supervisors suggested that, at least from the point of view of the supervisors surveyed, beginning teachers have an inadequate knowledge of social science content. These supervisors also indicated that beginning teachers have inadequate knowledge of teaching methods. One cannot use these data to argue, therefore, that professional course work is emphasized at the expense of subject matter.

The supervisors' concern about inadequate social science preparation, however, is echoed by other educators. Martin and Saif (1987) present the case for adding more political science, economics, and history courses to the required preparation of social studies teachers. Diem (1981) used the scores of Texas elementary and secondary social studies teachers on the nationally administered Test of Economic Literacy to argue that more academic course work in economics, as contrasted with inservice workshops, should be required of social studies teachers. Napier (1983) argued for greater emphasis on computer literacy in the preparation of social studies teachers. Each makes a case for greater preparation in some particular field, generally with little attention to broader program demands.

Another perspective was presented by Wendling, Merritt, Beal, Olstad, and Kaltsounis (1986), who questioned the common wisdom that social studies teachers are not equipped to handle the broad range of subjects demanded by their certification. They argued that some preservice teachers, at least, are adequately prepared in the social sciences, despite lack of indepth course work in all fields. Their sample consisted of the 16 student teachers enrolled in the University of Washington social studies teacher-preparation program, a program that, the authors noted, had rigorous admission standards. These preservice secondary social studies teachers achieved high scores on the National Teacher Examination social studies specialty area, despite the fact that most majored in narrowly defined traditional discipline.

Generally, arguments for more of one course or another are not well supported. Even when data, and not simply common-sense appeal, are presented, the link from more course work to improved classroom practice has not been made. These studies shed little light on the relationship of courses taken in history and the social sciences or related areas to excellence in social studies teaching. Certainly social studies teachers ought to be well grounded in history and the social sciences, but how much is enough to get started? To what extent is a teacher's social science education ongoing, rather than completed during the preservice?

The question of how much is enough may be the wrong question to ask about the social science/history education of a social studies teacher. The search for the most efficient input–output model has not yielded any insights. What do students learn from their social science courses and what influences that learning? Are students being socialized to a model of teaching that is inappropriate to the precollege level? Metzger (1985) argued that the preparation of social studies teachers has to undo what preservice teachers have learned about teaching and the nature of social studies from their undergraduate social science professors.

Lacy (1977) suggested that preservice teachers' subject-matter specialty is one of the factors that influence their socialization into teaching. A subject-matter specialty is one of the factors each teacher brings to the teaching experience that form the "filter" through which the teacher understands the classroom and the curriculum. In what ways does content-matter specialization come to bear on a teacher's classroom practice? How do teachers learn to translate what knowledge they do have into curriculum that is appropriate for their students?

Teacher Certification

The courses that students take to receive their initial certification and, in some states, continuing certification are influenced by state and National Council for Accreditation of Teacher Education (NCATE) requirements. These requirements are, in turn, influenced by the recommendations of a variety of organizations such as the American Association of Colleges for Teacher Education, the National Council for the Social Studies, and the National Association of State Directors of Teacher Education and Certification. Weible and Dumas (1986) investigated the certification requirements for elementary school teachers in all 50 states. They described the requirements in general and professional education, providing an overview of a framework within which teacher education programs must function. As Ochoa (1981) noted, such requirements tend to be based more on a commonsense appeal than on empirically grounded research. Furthermore, state and NCATE requirements affect the frameworks within which teacher education is structured, but knowing the framework tells us little, in fact, about what actually goes on in programs. Nor has there been research on the connections among certification criteria, what goes on in classrooms, and student learning.

Inservice Education

Inservice education is a given of most professions, including teaching. To be a teacher, in the best sense, is to continue to be a learner as well—a student of pedagogy, of youth, of one's content field. Some, like Shaver (1983), even suggest that we've put the cart before the horse, that the greater bulk of professional education ought to come in the form of inservice or graduate work rather than preservice education. Only after teachers have encountered the realities and perplexities of teaching, Shaver argued, can they be thoughtful about the study of teaching.

Research in the area of social studies inservice education, however, has been focused more upon particular outcomes of particular interventions than on whether teachers have become more reflective practitioners or, often, on whether they've become better teachers in any sense. Many of the studies on the inservice component of social studies teacher education to be discussed were concerned with whether teachers had developed particular attitudes or skills or acquired some new knowledge. As in the area of preservice education, many of the studies reviewed were descriptive, whereas others were based on a more experimental approach.

Inservice experience in the area of international education was an interest common to several researchers. Barnes and Curlette (1985) described a graduate course designed to increase

global-mindedness. They administered pre- and posttest measures to their experimental group (those enrolled in the course) and to a control group (those education students enrolled in other courses). The former became more "world-minded" than the control group while continuing to value their national identity.

Gilliom, Remy, and Wayach (1980), Brown (1984), Tucker (1982), and Lamy (1982) have described inservice programs and resources for international education. These articles contain useful information for those interested in inservice education that promotes an international dimension. The descriptive nature of these articles provided readers with information about programs, but no research was reported on the impacts of programs on the practices of classroom teachers.

No one topic, other than international education, has served as a major interest area for research on inservice education. As in the research on methods courses, this work tends to be particularistic, providing little more than a surface look at an array of ideas. Greenfield (1982) described the economics portion of an inservice program designed to improve the social science background of teachers. He ended his description with a call for the establishment of more linkages between economists and teachers. Schug (1983) presented a framework for developing a program to introduce teachers to community resources and institutions: Readers are told that the teachers involved in this program expressed new enthusiasm for their teaching. Diem (1980) described a program in which 9 middle and 12 high school social studies teachers were trained to teach functional reading skills along with social studies content. Student performance in reading increased somewhat. Von Eschenback and Noland (1982) provided a model for allowing social studies teachers to participate in selecting the form of inservice programs and follow-up evaluation of teachers. Interestingly, although they focused on teacher participation, they did not consider letting teachers choose the content of the program or even whether there would be a program.

Holden (1980) reported the evaluation of an inservice program designed to familiarize teachers with theories of moral and ethical development and to identify and use curricular materials in this area. Extensive description of the program, the materials used, and the results was provided. The 244 participating social studies, language arts, health and humanities teachers and their administrators became increasingly more favorable toward the program as determined through interviews, classroom observations, and videotapes of teaching sessions. There was some evidence, from pre- and posttests and classroom observation, that their students were moved to visible levels of concern. The thoroughness of this report provides an opportunity for others to adopt and adapt as they see fit.

Berg (1983) presented the argument that computer technology ought to be introduced into the classroom and that the concerns of teachers are one of the "resisting forces" to successful implementation of this new technology. Successful inservice, he argued, must address the concerns of teachers. Although Berg assumed a deficit model of teachers and left unquestioned the assumption that computer technology ought not be resisted, he did acknowledge the importance of teachers' conceptions and understandings in the implementation of new curriculum. McCutcheon (1981) argued that many factors affect teachers' planning: teachers' skills and knowledge; their perception of context, both formal and covert; and their attitudes and beliefs.

To understand how an inservice program or graduate course affects teaching practice, we must, once again, move beyond an input–output model. How does the teacher make sense of the inservice program and work to incorporate, or fail to incorporate, these new understandings into an established teaching repertoire in a particular context?

THE TEACHERS OF TEACHERS

Few researchers have shown any inclination to study social studies teacher educators. Cornbleth (1982) argued that an understanding of the internal processes of teacher education involves understanding the belief systems that underlie the practice of teaching educators. Research on the teachers of social studies teachers during the 1980s involved primarily data gathered from attitude surveys and questionnaires.

Teacher educators' responses to surveys can give a glimpse into the conceptions of social studies teacher educators; however, the researcher's intention has often been to gather information about the field rather than about the teacher educators themselves. An example of such a survey is that conducted by Joyce and Tucker (1980). A sample of 58 social studies teacher educators was surveyed about their views on current trends, needs, and practices in social studies teacher education at the end of the 1970s. Similarly, Gross (1984) conducted a national survey of social studies methods professors regarding current educational practices in their teaching. Along with demographic information, his survey sought information about course content, teaching strategies, materials of instruction, and instructors' perceptions of the methods course. Some insight into these teacher educators' assumptions and beliefs may be inferred from the report of these data; however, the focus is on instructors' descriptions of practices and not on the assumptions and beliefs that guide those practices.

A survey was administered by Katz and Rath (1982) to 88 teacher educators who regularly taught social studies methods classes in Illinois. The study was, however, focused more explicitly on preservice teacher educators' goals and on the teaching methods and attributes teacher educators believe essential for teaching success. Katz and Rath concluded that there was a lack of congruence between stated course goals and statements designating the attributes of the successful teacher. However, they did not explore the instructors' thinking in any depth beyond the survey responses. These instructors might be able to account for the incongruities in quite reasonable ways; it should not be assumed that they were necessarily acting in mindless ways.

Shermis and Washburn (1986) surveyed 25 social studies methods instructors in Indiana. The instrument was designed to gather data on the demographics, background experiences, values, and political views of the professors, along with their perceptions of curricular materials and of the goals of social studies. The investigators concluded from this sample that, as a group, social studies methods professors were liberal, humane, and egalitarian. They appeared to be committed to enhancing critical thought and to the responsibilities of democratic citizenship.

Their social science background was described as limited. And they were prone, concluded the authors, to accept the status quo.

These studies only begin to hint at the possibilities of research into the practices, assumptions, and beliefs of social studies teacher educators. Researchers have begun to look more purposefully at the mental lives of teachers, at their intentions and perceived restraints (Clark & Peterson, 1986; Peterson, 1988). Teacher educators are also teachers, practitioners guided by beliefs and understandings formed from past experience and influenced by current context. Surveys and questionnaires can provide an initial data base, but in-depth interviews and observations could provide a more detailed and refined picture (LeSourd, 1984).

THE STUDENTS

Despite the apparent importance of knowing about those who become social studies teachers, relatively little work has been done in this area. Lanier and Little (1986) reported that research on students of teaching tended to be "desultory in nature, poorly synthesized and weakly criticized (p. 535)." Research on students of social studies teaching adds little to the literature. Information as straightforward as academic background and test scores, social class, and career goals could shed light on this population. More important are questions of biography and the interplay of biography and the formal institutions of teacher education. In this area, the literature on prospective social studies teachers sheds some light.

Individuals do not come to the occupation of teaching tabula rasa; they bring with them their backgrounds, the experiences and the assumptions and beliefs that they have formed from those experiences. Those assumptions and beliefs are important factors in their development as teachers. As Lanier and Little (1986) noted, "The expectations, aspirations, academic abilities, and motivation for learning that prospective and practicing teachers bring to teacher education are as influential and important as those same learner qualities in all teaching situations" (p. 545).

Researchers interested in the development of social studies teacher perspectives (Alder, 1984; Goodman & Alder, 1985; Ross, 1987, 1988) have begun to examine the ways in which past experiences shape preservice teachers' intentions and practice. In contrast, the influence of the teacher education program seems minimal; these programs do not appear to produce deep changes in preservice teachers' belief systems. Similarly, the socialization process experienced in student teaching is not necessarily overbearing or direct. Student teachers actively mediate these experiences, responding to them and learning from them according to their individual belief structures.

THE MILIEU

Understanding the contexts of teacher education could contribute greatly to our understanding of the processes of teacher education. In what ways do the various communities responsible for the education of social studies teachers contribute to that education? In what ways do they support or fail to support the goals of social studies education? In what ways do they support or fail to support one another? What about the broader social contexts of dominant and nondominant ideologies?

Researchers in teacher education have begun to raise questions that address issues of context (Lanier & Little, 1986), but these questions have not been raised in research on social studies teacher education. Particularly striking is the absence of research on the professional socialization of social studies teachers. A number of studies have demonstrated that socialization into the school environment is a powerful learning experience (see, e.g., Lortie, 1975). McNeil 1986 described significant connections between the bureaucratic nature of schools and the content taught. Yet researchers generally have not addressed the issue of what teachers learn about social studies teaching as they become part of a school community. In what ways do both formal and informal induction processes educate new teachers? What, for example, do new teachers learn in those schools and districts that have formal mentoring programs and career ladders? What is learned informally from peers and students?

In addition, little research in teacher education has addressed the role of professional organizations in the ongoing education of teachers. Social studies educators would do well to ask about the role of such organizations as the National Council for the Social Studies and the Joint Council for Economic Education in teaching teachers. Do these organizations make a difference in what teachers learn as they develop in their teaching roles and, if so, what sorts of differences?

In what ways do these various contexts support and reinforce one another or provide conflicting messages about what is possible and what is desirable in social studies education. One taken-for-granted wisdom is that the liberalizing influences of the university context are canceled by the generally conservative contexts of schools. That assumption has been called into question (Zeichner & Tabachnick, 1981); students of social studies education may learn a conservative approach to teaching from their university experiences as much as from their past experiences and their socialization into the classroom.

In sum, the contexts of learning to teach social studies play a role in what teachers, both preservice and inservice, learn and do: reinforcing and/or changing preconceived notions of teaching and learning, developing and/or stifling teaching skills, encouraging or discouraging reflection and growth in the teachers of social studies. But we know little about that role and those processes.

CONCLUSIONS

As described in this chapter, most research in social studies teacher education has been conducted from a descriptive or quasi-experimental perspective, with the researcher generally focusing on one treatment or innovation and its effect on preservice or in-service teachers' skills. Thus, an array of unrelated or random aspects of social studies teacher education has been studied and described. These particularistic approaches can stimulate readers to try new ideas in their methods courses or in-service programs. Little attempt, however, has been made by researchers to build upon one another's work systematically in order to develop knowledge about the field.

At the beginning of this chapter, well-known criticisms of social studies teaching were cited as an impetus to improve research on social studies teacher education. Most of those critiques were directed at the lack of skills and knowledge of social studies teachers. Such critiques, implicitly at least, acknowledge the importance of the role of the classroom teacher. However, recommendations for the improvement of teachers' skills or remediation of teacher shortcomings ignore the structural problems of schooling that contribute to the perceived failure of social studies teaching. Both the contexts of schooling and teachers' perceptions of the contexts shape the course of classroom teaching. It is encouraging to note that researchers have begun to explore the interrelationships in social studies teacher education among teacher practice, the contexts in which practices are learned and developed, and teachers' mental lives.

The complexities of becoming a teacher—the multiple tasks, the diverse individuals involved as teachers and learners, the multiple contexts for learning and practice—demand that our study of the processes of learning to teach be approached from multiple perspectives. Studies of teacher development need to be made over time, ought to include the perspectives and understandings of the participants, and need to situate both behavior and intentionality in institutional and social contexts.

Few generalizations about effective practices in the education of social studies teachers can be made from the research conducted in the decade 1978–1988. Researchers on the education of social studies teachers are, however, beginning to build upon and extend research in teacher education more generally in areas such as teacher socialization and the development of teacher perspectives. In addition, teacher education researchers are beginning to examine the pedagogical and content knowledge of pre- and inservice teachers (Shulman, 1986). In this area as well, researchers interested in the education of social studies teachers can make a contribution.

Thus, there are indications that researchers are exploring new ways to understand the complex processes of teacher education. In keeping with the acceptance of multiple perspectives toward research on the education of social studies teachers is the argument that the perspectives of those who teach teachers would be a meaningful addition to the literature. Such a perspective would mean not merely the reporting of an innovation or fresh idea or shaping that report to fit a quasi-experimental framework. Rather, it would mean a reflection on practice in which innovations and ideas were situated within the framework of other research and within the teacher education's broader institutional and political contexts. It would mean maintaining a skeptical view toward accepted practices and points of view. It would mean understanding the tasks of teaching teachers as problematic. It would mean attempting to reconstruct experiences in ways that enable the researcher and the reader to arrive at greater understanding of those tasks and of the experiences of individuals involved in teacher education.

Research is an effort to develop an understanding of the factors that influence thought and behavior. In this sense, reflection on practice is one of several approaches to research and understanding. With the multiple vision gained from the new, along with the traditional, approaches to research, the possibilities for understanding and improving the education of social studies teachers seem greater.

References

Adler, S. (1984). A field study of selected student teacher perspectives toward social studies. *Theory and Research in Social Education, 12*(1), 13–30.

Adler, S., & Goodman J. (1986). Critical theory as a foundation for methods courses. *Journal of Teacher Education, 37*(4), 2–8.

Allender, J. S. (1986). Educational research: A personal and social process. *Review of Educational Research, 56*(2), 173–193.

Barnes, B., & Curlette, W. (1985). Effects of instruction on teachers' global mindedness and patriotism. *Theory and Research in Social Education, 13*(1), 43–49.

Bennett, C. (1979). The preparation of pre-service secondary social studies teachers in multiethnic education. *High School Journal, 62*(5), 232–237.

Berg, R. (1983). Resisting change: What the literature says about computers in the social studies classroom. *Social Education, 47*(5), 314–316.

Berryman, C., & Schneider, D. (1984). Social studies teacher education: More academic content and less teaching methodology? *Social Education, 48*(7), 507–509.

Borrowman, M. (1956). *The liberal and the technical in teacher education.* New York: Teachers College Press.

Brown, J. (1984). *Global learning teacher education manual: A model inservice or graduate course for elementary and secondary teachers.* Montclair, NJ: Global Learning. (ERIC Document Reproduction Service No. ED 286 770)

Butts, R. A. (1983). Teacher education and the revival of civic learning: A reprise of yesteryear's theme. *Journal of Teacher Education, 34*(6), 48–51.

Campbell, D., & Stanley, J. (1963). *Experimental and quasiexperimental designs for research.* Chicago: Rand McNally.

Carlson, H. L. (1986). *Social studies teacher education: The role of interactive videodisc in understanding cultural diversity.* Paper presented at the annual meeting of the National Council for the Social Studies, New York. (ERIC Document Reproduction Service No. ED 278 588)

Cherryholmes, C. (1982). *Knowledge and power in social studies education.* Paper presented at the annual meeting of the Social Science Education Consortium, East Lansing, MI. (ERIC Document Reproduction Service No. ED 218 177)

Clark, C. M., & Peterson, P. L. (1986). Teachers' thought processes. In M. Wittrock (Ed.), *Handbook of research on teaching* (3rd ed., pp. 255–296). New York: Macmillan.

Cornbleth, C. (1982). *Mirroring ourselves: Reflection on social studies teacher education.* Paper presented at the Mid-Atlantic Regional Conference for the Social Studies, New York. (ERIC Document Reproduction Service No. ED 214 814)

Cornbleth, C. (1986). The invitation. In C. Cornbleth (Ed.), *An invitation to research in social education* (pp. 1–9). Washington, DC: National Council for the Social Studies.

Cox, C. B. (1981). *A study of the effects of pairing social studies student teachers.* (ERIC Document Reproduction Service No. ED 222 429)

Dewey, J. (1964). The relation of theory to practice in education. In R. D. Archambault, *John Dewey on Education* (pp. 313–337). Chicago: University of Chicago Press. (Original work published 1964)

Dibella, M. F., & Fitzgerald, J. D. (1982). *A high intensity social studies program in a clinical setting for teacher education students.* Paper presented at the Annual meeting of the National Council for the Social Studies, Boston. (ERIC Document Reproduction Service No. ED 182 221)

Diem, R. (1980). *An analysis of a staff development training program in reading and social studies.* Paper presented at the annual meeting of the Southwest Educational Research Association, San Antonio. (ERIC Document Reproduction Service No. ED 182 221)

Diem, R. (1981). *Competency testing for teachers: A case study in economic education.* Paper presented at the annual meeting of the Southwest Education Research Association, Dallas. (ERIC Document Reproduction Service No. ED 198 050)

Diez, M. E. (1987). *The knowledge base: Issues for liberal arts colleges* (AILACTE Occasional Paper No. 7). Association of Independent Liberal Arts Colleges for Teacher Education.

Ellington, L. (1985). The dual benefits of the interview assignment in the social studies methods course. *Social Studies, 76*(3), 103–105.

Foster, C. D. (1979). Field oriented teacher education as a vehicle for the professional development of elementary social studies teachers. *Social Education, 43*(5), 374–377.

Freeland, K. (1983). A study of the effects of self-instructional modules on achievement in college social studies. *Social Studies Review, 22*(2), 61–65.

Gilliom, M. E., & Harf, J. (1985). Paper commissioned by the American Association of Colleges for Teacher Education on guidelines for International Teacher Education Project. (ERIC Document Reproduction Service No. ED 265 115)

Gilliom, M. E., Remy, R. C., & Wayach, R. (1980). Using the local community as a resource for global education. *Teaching Political Science, 7*(3), 251–264.

Goodlad, J. (1984). *A place called school.* McGraw Hill.

Goodman, J. (1986). Social studies curriculum design: A critical approach. *Curriculum Inquiry, 16*(2), 179–201.

Goodman, J., & Adler, S. (1985). Becoming an elementary social studies teacher: A study in perspectives. *Theory and Research in Social Education, 13*(2), 1–20.

Greenfield, H. (1982). Economics in secondary schools: Some problems of inservice teaching. *Social Studies, 73*(5), 217–219.

Gross, R. (1984). Is there a method to our madness or a madness to our methods? *Social Studies, 75*(4), 158–165.

Herman, W., Jr. (1982). A research proposal for social studies methods courses. *Social Studies, 73*(2), 68–73.

Hoffman, A. (1979). Try to make social studies methods personal. *Social Studies, 70*(3), 129–132.

Holden, L. (1980). *The ethical quest in a democratic society. A program in moral/ethical education* (1975–1980 Evaluation Report). Tacoma, WA: Tacoma Public Schools, Office of Research and Evaluation. (ERIC Document Reproduction Service No. ED 224 741)

Jantz, R., Weaver, V. P., Cirrincione, J. M., & Farrell, R. T. (1985). Inquiry and curriculum change: Perceptions of school and college/university faculty. *Theory and Research in Social Education, 13*(2), 61–72.

Joyce, W., & Tucker, J. (1980). Toward a constructive plan of action in elementary social studies teacher education. *Social Education, 44*(6), 508–512.

Katz, L., & Rath, J. (1982). The best of intentions for the education of teachers. *Action in Teacher Education, 4*(1), 8–16.

Kickbusch, K. W. (1987). Civic education and preservice education. *Theory and Research in Social Education, 15*(3), 173–188.

Kincheloe, J. (1985). Using primary research to teach elementary school social studies methods: Exploring Shreveport's water. *Social Studies, 76*(4), 180–183.

Lacey, C. (1977). *The socialization of teachers.* London: Metheun.

Lamy, S. (1982). Teacher training in global perspectives education: The center for teaching international relations. *Theory Into Practice, 21*(3), 206–211.

Lanier, J. E. & Little, J. W. (1986). Research on teacher education. In M. C. Wittrock (Ed.), *Handbook of Research on Teaching* (3rd ed., pp. 527–569). New York: Macmillan.

Lee, H. (1984). *Power sharing and the social studies.* (ERIC Document Reproduction Service No. ED 248 157)

LeSourd, S. J. (1984). An exploratory comparison of two methods of assessing teacher attitude toward instructional strategies. *Theory and Research in Social Education, 12*(1), 31–41.

Little, T. (1984). *Alternative programs in teacher education and social studies methods course design: A case study.* Paper presented at the annual meeting of the National Council for the Social Studies, Teacher Education Special Interest Group, Washington, DC. (ERIC Document Reproduction Service No. ED 265 095)

Lortie, D. C. (1975). *Schoolteacher: A sociological study.* Chicago: University of Chicago Press.

Marsh, C. (1983). Curriculum materials analysis in social studies methods classes. *Social Studies, 74*(3), 107–111.

Martin, D., & Saif, P. (1987). The social sciences in teacher preparation: A special place. *Social Education, 51*(5), 358–360.

Martorella, P. (1984). *Developing computer literate social studies teachers.* Paper presented at the annual meeting of the National Council for the Social Studies, Washington, DC. (ERIC Document Reproduction Service No. ED 254 434)

McCutcheon, G. (1981). Elementary social studies teachers' planning for social studies and other subjects. *Theory and Research in Social Education, 9*(1), 45–66.

McNeil, L. (1986). *Contradictions of control: School structure and school knowledge.* New York; Routledge and Kegan Paul.

Merwin, W., & Templeton, R. (1978). A study of a field-based special methods course. *High School Journal, 62*(1), 20–25.

Metzger, D. (1985). *Challenging the trend: Expanding the social studies education course.* (ERIC Document Reproduction Service No. ED 278 578)

Napier, J. (1983). *Computer literacy and social studies teacher education: Changes in form and content.* Paper presented at the meeting of the Social Science Education Consortium, Athens, GA. (ERIC Document Reproduction Service No. ED 231 740)

Nelson, J., & Palonsky, S. (1980). Preservice teachers' perceptions of social education. *Journal of Social Studies Research, 4*(1), 5–12.

Ochoa, A. S. (1981). The education of social studies teachers. In H. Mehlinger & O. L. Davis (Eds.), *The social studies. 80th Yearbook of the study of education* (Part II, pp. 151–169). Chicago: University of Chicago Press.

Palonsky, S., & Nelson, J. (1980). Political restraint in the socialization of student teachers. *Theory and Research in Social Education, 7*(4), 19–34.

Parker, W. (1987). Teachers' mediation in social studies. *Theory and Research in Social Education, 15*(1), 1–22.

Paul, R. (1986). *Critical thinking and the critical person.* (ERIC Document Reproduction Services No. ED 273 511)

Peterson, P. (1988). Teachers' and students' cognitional knowledge for classroom teaching and learning. *Educational Researchers, 17*(5), 5–14.

Phillips, L. (1979). Promoting and improving social studies instruction in schools through a field-oriented methods course. *Social Education, 43*(5), 381–384.

Robinson, P. (1982). *Patterns in social studies methods courses: A review of the literature.* Paper presented at the Annual meeting of the National Council for the Social Studies; Boston. (ERIC Document Reproduction Services No. ED 227 020)

Ross, E. W. (1987). Teacher perspective development: A study of preservice social studies teachers. *Theory and Research in Social Education, 15*(4), 225–244.

Ross, E. W. (1988). Preservice teachers' responses to institutional constraints: The active role of the individual in teacher socialization. *Educational Foundations, 2*(1), 77–92.

Ross, E. W., & Hannay, L. (1986). Towards a critical theory of reflective inquiry. *Journal of Teacher Education, 37*(4), 9–15.

Schön, D. A. (1983). *The reflective practitioner: How professionals think in action.* New York: Basic Books.

Schug, M. (1983). Community study for social studies teachers. *Social Studies, 74*(6), 237–241.

Schwab, J. J. (1978). *Science, curriculum and liberal education: Selected essays.* I. Westbury & N. J. Wilkof (Eds.), Chicago: University of Chicago Press.

Shaver, J. P. (1983). A call for the reexamination of teacher education in social studies. In C. Berryman & M. Rice (Eds.), *New directions in social science teacher education* (pp. 10–15). Athens, GA: University of Georgia.

Shaver, J. P., Davis, O. L., & Helburn, S. W. (1979). The status of social studies education: Impressions from three NSF studies. *Social Education, 43,* 150–153.

Shermis, S., & Washburn, P. (1986). Social studies educators and their beliefs: Preliminary data from Indiana Colleges and Universities. *Theory and Research in Social Education, 14*(2), 331–340.

Shulman, L. S. (1986). Those who understand: Knowledge growth in teaching. *Educational Researcher, 15*(4), 4–14.

Skeel, D. (1981). *What are the crucial elements of a social studies methods course?* Paper presented at the meeting of the National Council for the Social Studies, Detroit. (ERIC Document Reproduction Services No. ED 209 161)

Smith, W. (1978). Elimination of sex role stereotyping through elementary teacher education. *Teacher Educator, 14*(2) 21–27.

Stanley, W. B. (1983). Training teachers to deal with values education: A critical look at social studies methods texts. *Social Studies, 74*(6), 242–246.

Stanley, W. B. (1984). Approaches to teaching concepts and conceptualizing: An analysis of social studies methods textbooks. *Theory and Research in Social Education, 11*(4), 1–14.

Stanley, W. B. (1985). Research in social education: Issues and approaches. In W. B. Stanley (Ed.), *Review of research in social studies education: 1976–1983* (pp. 1–9). Washington, DC: National Council for the Social Studies.

Staton-Spicer, A. Q., Colson, E., & Bassett, R. (1979). A field oriented teacher education program: Forum for resolving communications concerns. *Social Education, 43*(5), 378–380.

Tabachnick, B. R., & Zeichner, K. M. (1984). The impact of the student teaching experience on the development of teacher perspectives. *Journal of Teacher Education, 35*(6), 28–36.

Torney-Purta, J. (1983). Pedagogical perspectives on enhancing civic education through the education of teachers. *Journal of Teacher Education, 34*(6), 30–34.

Tucker, J. L. (1982). Developing a global dimension in teacher education. *Theory Into Practice, 21*(3), 212–217.

Tucker, J., & Joyce, W. (1979). *Social studies teacher education: Practices, problems and recommendations.* Boulder, CO: Social Science Education Consortium. (SSEC Publication No. 237)

Unks, G. (1985). Critical thinking in the social studies classroom. Do we teach it? *Social Education, 49,*(3), 244–246.

Van Cleaf, D. W., Schroder, A. M., & Frataccia, E. V. (1980). *Differentiated needs of teacher trainees: Implications for social studies.* Paper presented at annual meeting of the National Council for the Social Studies, New Orleans. (ERIC Document Reproduction Services No. ED 196 754)

Von Eschenback, J., & Noland, R. (1982). In-service delivery system preferences among social studies teachers. *Social Studies, 73*(1), 16–20.

Walton, S., Kutz, R. E., & Thompson, L. (1986). The integrated day comes to college. *Social Studies, 77*(2), 83–87.

Weaver, V. P., Garner, R., Williams, D. L., Cole, M. B., & Saracho, O. N.

(1984). Teacher education on the mall. *Social Studies, 75*(3), 117–121.

Weible, T., & Dumas, W. (1986). Elementary teacher education and certification. In V. A. Atwood (Ed.), *Elementary school social studies: Research as a guide to practice* (pp. 137–145). Washington, DC: National Council for the Social Studies.

Wendling, L., Marrett, A. V., Beal, J. L., Olstad, R. G., & Kaltsounis, T. (1986). *The effectiveness of a narrow social science major in preparing students to teach in the broad field of social studies.* Paper presented at the annual meeting of the College and University Faculty Assembly of the National Council for the Social Studies, New York. (ERIC Document Reproduction Service No. ED 278 606)

Zeichner, K. M. (1985). *Content and contexts: Neglected elements in studies of student teaching as an occasion for learning to teach.* Paper presented at the meeting of the American Educational Research Association, Chicago.

Zeichner, K. M., & Tabachnick, B. R. (1981). Are the effects of university teacher education "washed out" by school experience? *Journal of Teacher Education, 32*(3), 7–11.

18

TEACHER CHARACTERISTICS AND SOCIAL STUDIES EDUCATION

James S. Leming

SOUTHERN ILLINOIS UNIVERSITY AT CARBONDALE

The appearance of the first *Handbook of Research on Teaching* marked a significant point in the study of teacher characteristics. Gage (1963), the editor of the volume, concluded that "these studies have yielded disappointing results: correlations that are nonsignificant, inconsistent from one study to the next, and usually lacking in psychological and educational meaning" (p. 118). Getzels and Jackson (1963), in the same volume, undertook what, to this date, remains the most comprehensive review of research on teacher characteristics. In their review they critically analyzed 800 studies completed between 1950 and 1963. Their conclusion echoed that of Gage: "Despite the critical importance of the problem and a half-century of prodigious research effort very little is known for certain about . . . the relation between teacher personality and teaching effectiveness" (p. 574). In a more recent review of the research on teacher characteristics, Lewis (1985) concluded that the research of the 1960s and 1970s on this topic did not provide evidence for a more optimistic view of the relationship between personality and teacher effectiveness.

Following the dismal assessment in the first *Handbook,* research on teacher characteristics ceased to be a major topic of interest among educational researchers. Neither the second (Travers, 1972) nor the third (Wittrock, 1985) edition contains a chapter on the topic. The subject index of neither volume contains a heading for teacher characteristics or for teacher personality. To a great extent research on teacher characteristics floundered on the shoals of nonsignificant findings; yet another reason for its demise was the appearance of a research program that promised better results. This program of research was directed to teacher and student behavior in classrooms. One example of this new line of research was that of Flanders (1960) and his interaction analysis, which focused on the patterns of verbal exchange in classrooms. This research thrust began in the 1950s, but it was the appearance in 1971 of Rosenshine and Furst's analysis of teacher behaviors associated with student achievement that completed the shift in focus of educational research from teacher characteristics to teacher behavior.

A BROADER FOCUS

Obviously, a chapter on teacher characteristics in a research handbook today, if it is not to be an anachronism, must contain a careful definition and justification of its approach to the topic. The standard dictionary definition of the word *characteristic* is a trait, quality, or property, or group of them, that distinguish an individual, group, or type. The research reviewed by Getzels and Jackson was focused only on one possible subset of teacher characteristics, the personality of teachers. That is, the concern was with the teacher as a psychological or unique whole and the dynamic organization of motives within that whole. This emphasis is evident from the organization of the Getzels and Jackson review, which included such areas as teachers' attitudes, values, interests, adjustment, needs, personality factors, and cognitive abilities. The assumption underlying the research that was reviewed was that these personal qualities would account for differential effectiveness among teachers. This perspective on teacher characteristics is a narrow one and one that has not proven useful in understanding teacher behavior in the classroom or its effects. For the purposes of this chapter, a broader conception of the topic of teacher characteristics is essential.

It should be noted at the outset that the literature review undertaken for this chapter revealed no new evidence linking

---

Reviewers were Linda Biemer, State University of New York at Binghamton; Anna Ochoa, Indiana University.

teacher characteristics, no matter how broadly defined, to learning outcomes of students. In the remainder of this chapter I do four things. *First,* I present a rationale for the study of characteristics of social studies teachers, given the results of 40 years of discouraging findings; *second,* I stipulate a framework for the analysis of research in this chapter; *third,* I review recent research within each of the components of the framework; and, *finally,* I provide an overall assessment of the state of research on this topic for social studies and suggest some avenues for future research.

Is the study of teacher characteristics a potentially fruitful topic for inquiry, or have the findings of past research sufficiently demonstrated that this research program is no longer viable and, therefore, should be abandoned? There can be little doubt that continuing to search for a relationship between teacher personality and student achievement is likely to be futile. The preponderance of the findings of previous research are consistent and overwhelming. Given the atheoretical nature of the research regarding how teacher personality and student achievement are linked, it is doubtful that any causal link can be established analytically, much less empirically. Clearly, the study of teachers' characteristics as defined in the prior literature is a dead horse and one that future researchers would be well advised not to saddle up.

A Viable Definition

There are, however, other possible interpretations of the topic of teacher characteristics that make its study a potentially valuable one. Before turning to the conception of teacher characteristics that will guide the remainder of this chapter, it is important to note the central problems associated with the prior research. First, the topic, teacher characteristics, has been defined too narrowly. Although the stress on teacher personality was an appropriate attempt to narrowly define the key variables, it has led to the neglect of many other facets of teaching personnel that may be potentially fruitful areas for inquiry. Likewise, the focus on student achievement has unnecessarily limited the research program.

. A variety of teacher characteristics, other than personality, have potential value for understanding the act of teaching and the influence of teachers. Such areas as teacher intelligence, enthusiasm, family background, experience, gender, political orientation, professional values, cognitive style, and moral reasoning, to name a few, are characteristics of teachers that have potential utility for the study of the teaching of social studies. Similarly, student outcomes other than academic achievement are of interest, particularly in a field like social studies education in which the commonly agreed-upon goal is citizenship. Attitudes, values, habits of mind, and citizenship behavior are accepted and valued outcomes of the social studies. Thus, both the predictor, or independent, variable and the dependent, or criterion, variable, depending on the research design, have been too narrowly defined in the previous research to rule out the possibility that teacher characteristics are an important area of study in social studies education. Freeing the topic of teacher characteristics from the definitional constraints of teacher per-

sonality and student academic achievement opens potentially fruitful avenues for future research.

Within the literature on teacher characteristics one finds the term used in four distinct senses. *First,* as discussed, *teacher characteristics* is interpreted as teacher personality. *Second,* it is defined as teacher instructional behavior. *Third,* the term is interpreted as referring to background demographics and opinions on professional and sociopolitical issues. *Finally, teacher characteristics* has recently been interpreted as beliefs about education and teaching, including conceptions of subject matter, that affect teacher judgments, decisions, and behavior.

One problem with personality as an adequate conception of teacher characteristics was the multiplicity of definitions of the word *personality;* Allport (1937) identified over 50 different meanings. Another problem was the lack of clear theoretical and empirical links between personality and student achievement. Defining social studies teacher characteristics as instructional behavior, as McMann and McMann (1984) suggested, is to make the study of teacher characteristics isomorphic with the teaching effectiveness literature. This literature has been reported extensively elsewhere (Berliner, 1987; Rosenshine, 1987). Demographic data on social studies teachers are culled from regional and national surveys, usually mailed to teachers. These data are highly variable from survey to survey and seldom contain any conceptual or theoretical link with teaching behavior or student outcomes. Beliefs about education and teaching are a relatively new area of research that has been recently reviewed by Shavelson and Stern (1981).

The interpretation of teacher characteristics that guides the review in this chapter is founded on a perspective on the preferable outcomes of social studies education. This chapter does not include a review of the literature on the knowledge outcomes of social studies; that topic is handled elsewhere in this handbook. Rather, in this chapter I am concerned with the reasoning, attitudes, and values of students. As a result, the teacher characteristics judged to be most relevant to this set of student outcomes are selected aspects of teacher demographics and teacher cognitive style and moral development. What are the potential connections between this interpretation of teacher characteristics and student outcomes?

Research Connections and Implications

In this section, arguments for the utility of the approach to the study of the research on teacher characteristics previously discussed are presented.

Demographic Data. Demographic data on the social studies profession has utility on two accounts. *First,* such knowledge provides a sense of identity by placing the profession in a contemporary and historical context. This helps those in the profession to know who they are and how they compare with other significant groups such as other subject-matter teachers and the general public. Such knowledge is potentially valuable in that it allows the tracking of shifts in the profession over time. One justification for such demographic research rests on the assumption that self-knowledge is intrinsically worthwhile. Beyond that, such knowledge may be of value to policymakers, teacher educators, and the general public whom the profession serves. Most doctors, even if one is in perfect health, recommend a regular electrocardiogram so that there will be a baseline against which to compare future readings. The analogy holds for the study of our profession. Are we getting older, more conservative, less academically able, more male dominated, more provincial, and the like? In addition, as potential links between teacher characteristics and professional performance are proposed, a data base of teacher characteristics for social studies teachers would be helpful in interpreting and responding to such claims.

Second, basic demographic information may have utility beyond the purposes just cited. The traditional idea that the character of the teacher is an important influence in shaping the values of children still holds considerable appeal among the educational community and the general public. This perspective is based on the observation that the teacher inevitably reveals to the student those values to which he or she attaches importance. Among the values likely to be revealed are honesty, diligence, considerateness, and political orientation. The results of the classic Hartshorne and May (1928) study indicated that the personal attributes of the teacher in the individual classroom had a significant and lasting impact on one form of moral behavior, deceit, whereas explicit curricular efforts to promote character were largely unsuccessful.

More recent research has not been focused on the influence of the teacher with regard to the development of attitudes or values; however, it is not uncommon to find significant differences between classrooms in studies that explore the influence of the various values-education approaches. A potentially fruitful approach to understanding the differential effect of teachers on student attitudes and values is through social learning theory (Bandura, 1977). In addition to the shaping of behavior through contingencies of reinforcement, social learning theory emphasizes the role of observation and imitation in the learning of social behavior and values. According to social learning theory, such factors as the extent to which the model is perceived as possessing a high degree of competence, status, and control over resources; the degree of prior nurturance; the degree to which the model's social background is similar to the child's; and the degree to which the observed behavior yields positive consequences for the model all increase the model's ability to induce the modeled behavior.

The implications of this perspective for the study of teacher characteristics are as follows. *First,* it is highly improbable that teachers can avoid revealing their character and values to students over the course of the school year. The components of the teacher's character, therefore, are important. In this analysis, the political orientations and behaviors of social studies teachers assume significance. *Second,* any characteristics that would affect the social studies teacher's salience in the eyes of students would also be relevant. Existing research suggests that teacher gender, age, and appearance may be important factors in student judgments of competence (e.g., Clayson & Maughan, 1986; Goebel & Cashen, 1978; Hunsberger & Cavanagh, 1988). In addition, the degree to which teachers are similar to socially familiar groups may also increase their effectiveness as models.

This chapter, therefore, although not focused on teacher personality or teacher instructional behavior, is based on the assumption that there is potential utility in the study of teacher characteristics from the perspective of the teacher's potential to influence student attitudes and values. The research on these characteristics is summarized in these three sections: demographics of the profession, professional characteristics, and the social studies teacher as citizen. It should be pointed out that studies in naturalistic settings concerned with teacher influence on student reasoning, attitudes, and values are few in number. This is a serious weakness in the field of the study of education and poses a major research agenda for the future.

Searching the research literature for positive effects of the social studies curriculum on students' political attitudes is a frustrating business. There are some encouraging findings, even though the effects are not dramatic. One such finding is a series of research studies and reviews of the literature in which researchers found that, when students have been exposed to classrooms where the open and free discussion of controversial issues was a part of the social studies experience, they tended to have more positive political system attitudes than students whose instruction followed more traditional patterns (Ehman, 1980a, 1980b). Another related area of research is that of democratic climates. The just-community approach to moral education (Power, 1988) is based on a democratic classroom and school environment. Evaluations of such programs have found that democratic environments are conducive to the development of sociomoral reasoning and action.

A New Perspective on Teacher Characteristics. One important question from the perspective of this chapter is, "Is there a set of teacher characteristics that differentiate traditional teachers from those who incorporate democratic climates and controversial issues into their classes?" As will be seen, little evidence exists on the question. However, certain characteristics such as tolerance for ambiguity, open-mindedness, intellectual flexibility, risk taking, and a provisional view of truth seem consistent with such a teaching style. On the other hand, a high need for order, dogmatism, intellectual rigidity, absolute notions regarding truth, and the like seem inconsistent with such a teaching style.

Two perspectives on the intellectual and social orientations required of teachers for such instruction are described next. Oliver and Shaver (1966/1974) discussed the characteristics of jurisprudential teachers in terms of intellectual orientations and attitudes toward students. With regard to orientation toward subject matter, the teacher must be

- open to the exploration of ideas;
- able to think in other than categorical terms;
- able to tolerate the conflict of ideas and ideals;
- able to recognize values embedded in controversies;
- have a tentative, probabilistic view of knowledge.

According to Oliver and Shaver, in terms of the attitudes toward students required by the jurisprudential approach, the teacher must

- perceive students as rational human beings with the right to be involved in decision making;
- value student opinions and problem-solving styles;
- be willing to interact freely with students in an exchange of ideas.

Newmann (in press) recently listed a number of dispositions that together constitute thoughtfulness:

- persistent desire to have claims be supported by reasons (and the reasons themselves be scrutinized);
- tendency to be reflective—to take time to think problems through for oneself, rather than to act impulsively or automatically accept the views of others;
- curiosity to explore new questions;
- flexibility to entertain alternative and original solutions to problems.

Presumedly, a teacher who serves as a model of thoughtfulness and who fosters thoughtfulness in the classroom possesses these dispositions.

The characteristics described are those deemed essential for the development of a classroom environment characterized by the open and free exchange of ideas and ideals. Such characteristics of teachers are thought to be essential if higher order thinking or the evaluation of social and public policy issues is to be promoted effectively.

Two further, and more speculative, perspectives have potential for the study of the relationship between teacher characteristics and student outcomes. To my knowledge there is no evidence to support either of these perspectives other than their strong appeal to common sense. First is the study of the characteristics of those teachers who, through strength of person, have had a significant impact on students' basic attitudes or values. Are there exemplary teachers who influence large numbers of students with respect to basic values of citizenship? If so, what are the characteristics of such teachers?

The second perspective is on the relationship between teachers' characteristics and their choice of teaching style. Some preservice teachers quickly and easily adopt teaching methods that require students to take active and questioning approaches to knowledge. Others appear to have an allergic reaction to such approaches. What characteristics differentiate between such teachers?

In the next section of this chapter, the available survey data on the demographic characteristics of social studies teachers are reviewed. This provides a snapshot of the profession and the data will be interpreted with a view to understanding the potential of teacher characteristics for the transmission of attitudes and values to students. In the following section, the research on teacher cognitive style and moral development is reviewed and analyzed. The data will be analyzed with a view toward understanding the extent to which teachers bring to the classroom the intellectual dispositions and the skills necessary for the creation of classroom environments that foster the development of reasoning, attitudes, and values in students. The

chapter concludes with a summary and recommendations for future research.

DEMOGRAPHICS OF THE PROFESSION

The purpose of this section is to review the available data on social studies educators as individuals, professionals, and citizens. The topics examined include gender mix, professional characteristics, political life, social life, and home background. The data reviewed for this section come from national surveys of social studies teachers and, as a point of comparison, surveys of the teaching profession as a whole. Twelve recent surveys, completed since 1977, were identified. It was decided that an in-depth look at data from that year on was preferable to a broader historical perspective.

Social Studies Surveys

Of the eight surveys of social studies teachers, five were national in scope, with sampling techniques intended to ensure results representative of the total population: the Agency for Instructional Television Survey (Fontana, 1980); the High School and Beyond Survey (Rutter, 1986); the National Science Foundation Survey (Weiss, 1978); the National Center for Education Information Survey, Social Studies Subset (Feistritzer, 1986); and the National Council for the Social Studies Survey (Educational Research Service, 1987).

The Agency for Instructional Television (AIT) Survey was based on a sample of 1,000 social studies teachers randomly selected from a population of 132,588 teachers on a list provided by Market Data Retrieval, Inc. Questionnaires were mailed to the 1,000 social studies teachers in January 1980. The response rate was 58.8% ($N = 588$).

The High School and Beyond (HSB) sample came from the 1984 Supplemental Teacher Survey collected by the Consortium for the Study of Effective Secondary Schools. The pool of eligible teachers was full-time social studies teachers. From 1–30 teachers in each of 537 schools were asked to fill out the questionnaire in the spring of 1984. Completed questionnaires were received from teachers in 482 of the schools. The actual response rate was not reported. In all, 10,370 teachers returned completed questionnaires, resulting in a national probability sample from a population of 574,212 teachers (493,794 in public schools).

In the National Science Foundation survey, a multistage, stratified cluster sampling design was used to insure that every superintendent, supervisor, principal, and teacher in the 50 states had an equal chance of being selected. A sample of approximately 400 public school districts was selected from 102 primary sampling units. In each district, one high school, one junior high school, two K–3 schools, and two 4–6 schools were selected. A list of teachers in each school was obtained from the principal, and teachers were randomly selected from this list. Questionnaires were sent out to 6,378 teachers in April 1977. Completed questionnaires were received from 4,829 teachers, for a response rate of 76%. The final sample contained

1,478 social studies teachers. The breakdown by grade level was K–3 (N = 254), 4–6 (N = 281), 7–9 (N = 453), 10–12 (N = 490).

The sample of the National Center for Education Information (NCEI) Survey, Social Studies (SS) Subset, consisted of the 280 social studies teachers contained within the full survey (N = 1,592). The sampling techniques and response rate are discussed later.

The National Council for the Social Studies Survey sample consisted of 1,298 NCSS members who responded to a mailed survey instrument. The response rate was 65%. A total of 407 nonmembers of NCSS responded. No response rate was provided for the nonmembers. In addition to schoolteachers, the NCSS sample included 105 supervisors and 414 college and university staff. The data reported in this chapter consist only of that from the 104 Grades K–6 teachers and the 530 grades 7–12 teachers, all of whom were members of NCSS. In cases in which data from supervisors and college faculty were lumped together with data from K–12 teachers, the results are not reported here.

Two surveys were of social studies teachers selected from states chosen to reflect geographical balance. The Indiana Survey (Ochoa, 1981) was mailed to 1,200 teachers selected randomly from professional mailing lists. Although the date of the mailing was not reported, it appeared to have been 1980 or early 1981. The six population states were Kansas, Mississippi, New Mexico, Washington, Wisconsin, and Vermont. The response rate was 33%, with a final sample size of 402. The Maine Survey (Farmer, 1984) was mailed during the 1982–1983 academic year to social studies teachers in Alabama, Arkansas, Delaware, Iowa, Maine, Montana, Oregon, and South Carolina. From lists of social studies teachers provided by state departments of education, between 100 to 200 teachers were randomly selected from each state, for a total of 1,150 potential respondents. Of the 1,150 instruments mailed out, 542 were returned, for a response rate of 47.1%. Because of the low response rates and the unrepresentative nature of the samples, the data from the Indiana and Maine surveys must be interpreted cautiously.

Finally, *Case Studies in Science Education* (Stake & Easley, 1978) contains reports of field observations of science, mathematics, and social studies teaching and learning collected during the 1976–1977 school year at high schools and feeder schools at 11 sites. The sites, selected to ensure a diverse but balanced view of American schools, were also selected to be accessible to the project researchers. The data-collection method was observation and data recording consistent with the current ethnographic paradigm in educational research.

General Surveys

As a basis for comparing social studies teachers with the remainder of the teaching profession, four national surveys of teachers were also reviewed: the Gallup Poll of Teacher Attitudes Toward the Public Schools (Gallup, 1984, 1985), the NCEI's *Profile of Teachers* (Feistritzer, 1986), the National Education Association's (NEA) *Status of the American Public School Teacher 1985–86* (NEA, 1987), and the *Metropolitan Life Survey of the American Teacher, 1988* (Harris & Associates, 1988).

The Gallup Poll findings come from questionnaires mailed to a representative sample of U.S. teachers. Questionnaires were mailed to 2,000 teachers selected to reflect the total national population. Forty-one percent returned the questionnaires. To insure that those not returning the questionnaires did not differ from those who returned them, follow-up telephone interviews were conducted with 100 nonrespondents. Their responses were similar to the mailed-in responses.

In the National Center for Education Information survey, a systematic random sampling procedure was used. The sample was randomly selected from a list of 1.4 million current public school teachers and 172,000 current private school teachers. A total of 2,621 questionnaires were mailed February 7, 1986. The final sample consisted of 1,592 completed questionnaires, for a response rate of 70%. The number of current public school teachers who completed the questionnaire was weighted to true proportion, by state, based on current population statistics.

For the NEA survey, a two-stage, stratified random sampling technique was used. First, a sample of public school systems was selected, based on enrollment data. A list of teachers was then obtained from each school district, and teachers were selected randomly from the list. The questionnaire was sent to 1,998 teachers; 1,505 questionnaires were returned, for a response rate of 72.4%.

The Metropolitan Life Survey sample was a random sample drawn from a nationwide list of 1.2 million teachers provided by Market Data Retrieval of Westport, Connecticut. Phone interviews were conducted with 1,208 teachers in April, May, and June of 1988.

Biographical Data

According to the national surveys reviewed, the teaching force in U.S. public schools consists of approximately 70% females and 30% males. As might be expected, the elementary-school picture is quite different from the high school one. At the elementary level, females outnumber males 3 to 1, whereas, at the secondary level, the split is 50 : 50. At the junior high/middle school level, the ratio is approximately 60 : 40 female to male.

Social studies teachers at the elementary level have the same male–female ratio as has the profession as a whole. However, at the secondary level, the ratio shifts dramatically. Instead of 50 : 50, the data from both the NSF and HSB surveys indicated that 75% of high school social studies teachers were male. In the remaining social studies surveys the percentage of males reported to be teaching in Grades 7–9 varied considerably: 55% (NCSS), 60% (NCEI-SS), 70% (Indiana), and 76% (Maine). It would appear, based on these surveys, that, at the secondary level, the social studies profession has a substantially higher percentage of male teachers than the profession as a whole.

The average age of the American teacher was found to be 42, according to the NEA and NCEI surveys. In 1966, 34% of teachers were under the age of 30 and almost 58% were under the age of 40 (NEA). In the 1986 NEA survey, only 11% of teacher were under the age of 30; 32% were under the age of 40. The profession is greying. Social studies teachers have approximately the same age demographics as the profession as a whole.

The teaching profession is overwhelmingly White and middle class. According to the results of the NCEI and NEA surveys, 90% of public school teachers are white. Since the mid-1970s, no significant shifts in this regard have been noted. The teaching profession is, however, only slightly more White than other professions that require a 4-year college degree. Eighty-seven percent of the members of those professions are White (NCEI). Public school males are 94% White, and public school females are 89% White. Social studies teachers also are overwhelmingly White. According to the NCSS, NCEI (SS), and HSB reports, 92% of social studies teachers are White. African-Americans are reported as 6% (HSB) and 2.5% (NCEI-SS) of the social studies teaching force. The NCSS survey found African-Americans to be 1.8% of Grades K–6 teachers and 1.2% of Grades 7–12 teachers. On the other hand, 27% of the public elementary and secondary school enrollment is from minority groups.

The families that teachers come from are largely middle class. Over 70% of teachers reported their father's occupation to be professional, managerial, or technical/skilled worker (NEA, NCEI). Seventeen percent of teachers reported that their father was a school administrator; 5% of fathers' and 11% of mothers' occupations were reported as teacher or professor (NCEI). One quarter of public school teachers' fathers and 16% of their mothers had completed 4 or more years of college, but two thirds of their fathers and mothers had a high school degree or less (NCEI). The only data with regard to the family background of social studies teachers come from the NCEI (SS) survey and are largely consistent with the data for all teachers reported earlier: The home background of social studies teachers is middle class.

Teachers are typically married. The NCEI and NEA surveys report that 75% of all teachers are married, compared with 60% of the adult working force. Eighty percent of male teachers are married, compared with 62% of female teachers. Approximately 10 percent of all teachers are divorced, widowed, or separated. The rate is 13% for females but only 2% for males. One in four married teachers has a teacher as a spouse (Feistritzer, 1986). Social studies teachers vary only slightly from the profession as a whole in these regards.

Most teachers who are married live in a two-income household. Seventy-eight percent of public school teachers have a spouse who works full time, according to the NCEI survey. Eleven percent have a spouse who works part time. These same figures hold for social studies teachers (NCEI-SS).

Teachers tend be a provincial lot. Two thirds of today's public school teachers received their college education within 150 miles of where they were born (NCEI). Nearly two thirds, 62%, are now teaching within 150 miles of their birthplace (NCEI). In the NEA survey, about one third of all teachers indicated that they were living in the community in which they had lived since childhood. Social studies teachers follow the same general pattern with respect to completion of degree and teaching within 150 miles of home. In addition to teaching fairly close to home, social studies teachers are not professionally mobile. One quar-

ter reported that they had taught only in one school; one quarter, only in two schools (NCEI-SS).

To sum up, social studies teachers appear little different from other teachers in the categories discussed. Social studies teachers are predominantly White, male (at the high school level), married, from middle-class backgrounds, work close to their family homes, and stable in terms of professional mobility. These characteristics suggest that social studies teachers are likely to embrace the social values of the local community and transmit those values through their teaching.

Professional Characteristics

In this section, the qualifications and experience of social studies teachers are examined, as well as their perceptions regarding issues facing the profession.

Academic Caliber and Preparation. No data on the academic caliber of social studies teachers were identified. There exists, however, a number of studies in which the Scholastic Aptitude Test (SAT) scores of education majors were examined and compared with those of other undergraduates. Two findings stand out. *First,* most teaching recruits are drawn from the bottom groups of SAT scores, *second,* there is a strong negative relationship between measured academic ability and retention in teaching (Darling-Hammond, 1984; Feistritzer, 1986; Vance & Schlechty, 1982). Schlechty and Vance (1981) found that, among a longitudinal sample of North Carolina teachers, 30% of those teacher education graduates who actually taught were drawn from the lowest quintile of SAT scorers. Only 10% of practicing teachers were drawn from the top quintile. The poorest teacher education students were the most likely to persist in teaching, with the academically better teachers more likely to move on to positions outside of education.

Years of Teaching Experience. Just as the profession is getting older, it is getting more experienced. In 1966, 30% of teachers had 10 or more years' experience in their current positions, according to the NEA. In 1986, that figure was 60%. Because the profession is aging, earlier figures, such as from the NSF survey in which the average years of experience were found to be 11.3, are now dated. In the NEA 1986 survey, it was found that the median years of experience was 15, with 25% of elementary teachers having 20 or more years of experience and 30% of secondary teachers with 20 or more years of experience.

Job Satisfaction. Overall, teachers are fairly satisfied with their choice of teaching as a profession. The NCEI survey results indicated that 34% were very satisfied and 52% somewhat satisfied. Only 16% reported that they were somewhat or very dissatisfied. In the NEA survey 49% of teachers reported they would probably or certainly choose teaching again as their profession. Twenty percent reported that they were ambivalent, and 31% reported that they probably or certainly would not choose to teach again. The NEA survey results indicated that, since the 1960s, dissatisfaction with the choice to teach has tripled (from 10% to 30%), and satisfaction with the choice has fallen by one third. The Metropolitan Life survey, on the other hand, contains data that indicate that teachers are generally satisfied with their teaching choice; 50% of teachers said they were very satisfied and 37% said they were somewhat satisfied with the choice of teaching as a career. Results from the Metropolitan Life survey, conducted annually since 1984, indicate a steady increase in teacher satisfaction, with a 10% increase in the very satisfied response category between 1987 and 1988. The aspect of teaching that teachers found most satisfying was relationships with other teachers, with 95% indicating that they are somewhat or very satisfied with this aspect of professional life (NCEI). Salary and status in the community are the areas with which teachers are most dissatisfied. Over 50% of the teachers indicated that they are somewhat or very dissatisfied with these aspects of their careers (NCEI).

Data from social studies teacher surveys indicated that social studies teachers' job-satisfaction levels were similar to those of the profession as a whole. Eighty-three percent indicated that they were very or somewhat contented as social studies teachers (NCEI-SS). Salaries and community status appeared to be the largest negative factors in social studies teachers' job satisfaction (NCEI-SS, Maine).

Professional Concerns, Opinions, and Perceptions. It is possible to compare the opinions of the general public, the teaching profession, and social studies teachers on two questions: "What are the major problems confronting education today?" and "What should the goals of education be?" According to the Gallup survey, teachers identified the following, in descending order of importance, as the major problems facing education today: parents' lack of interest and support, lack of proper financial support, pupils' lack of interest and their truancy, lack of discipline, and problems with administration. Parents, however, had a different set of concerns; for example, 31% of all teachers saw parent lack of interest as a problem, but only 1% of the general public listed this as a major problem (Gallup, 1988). Also, 10% of teachers listed problems with the administration as a concern, but only 1% of the general public shared this concern. The general public also had some concerns that were not widely shared by teachers. For example, 32% of the general public saw the rise of drug use as a major problem facing schools (Gallup, 1988), but only 14% of teachers saw drugs as a major problem at their schools, according to the Metropolitan Life survey.

Of all the surveys included in this study, only the NCSS survey included an attempt to elicit social studies teachers' opinions regarding the major issues facing the profession. The most important issues identified in the NCSS survey were "Impact of home life, after school work, peer culture, alcohol, drug use, etc. on students' performance, attitudes and behavior" (Educational Research Service, 1987, p. 8). Fifty-seven percent of elementary teachers and 67% of secondary teachers identified this as the major issue. Teaching for skill development was the second most cited issue facing the profession, with 45.7% of secondary and 50% of elementary school teachers citing the issue as a major problem. Student lack of interest in the curriculum was cited by 38% of secondary teachers and by 35% of elementary teachers. Other major areas of concern centered around

the low status of social studies and deficiencies in the curriculum. The NCSS survey did not include salary and financial support as possible responses.

Overall, a comparison of the three surveys (Gallup, Metropolitan Life, and NCSS) indicated that social studies teachers are almost twice as likely as other educators to report out-of-school influences as a major issue facing the profession. Social studies teachers also appeared much more concerned about their low status than did the profession as a whole. The effects of the students' home life, although a major concern with the profession and social studies teachers, did not concern the general public, only 1% of whom saw them as a major problem. The public's concern regarding drug use was also not shared by the profession; the general public was three times more likely than social studies teachers to see drugs as an important issue facing contemporary schools.

Views on the purposes of education provide another point of comparison. The NCEI survey presented teachers with six statements, and they were asked to check the two or three that they saw as most important. In the Gallup survey, the respondents were provided with 25 statements of goals and were asked to rate their importance on a scale of 1 to 10. In the NCEI survey, "to teach student reasoning and analytical skills" was the most highly rated goal, receiving an 85% response. Next in importance was "to help students develop sound character," cited by over 60% of the teachers. In the Gallup survey, 55% of the teachers gave the top rating to "to develop the ability to think—creatively, objectively, analytically." Only items that focused on work habits, written and oral expression, mathematical ability, and desire to continue lifelong learning received the highest rating from at least 50% of the teachers in the sample. In the Gallup poll, the goal, "development of character," was given the highest rating by only 33% of the teachers. About half of the NCEI survey respondents supported this goal. Obviously, the different ranges of possible responses and the different answer formats make comparisons between the two surveys speculative.

On the Gallup survey there was general consistency between the general public's ratings of goals and those of teachers. The major differences were with respect to vocations/jobs, desire to excel, standards of right and wrong, and adult responsibilities; the public felt more strongly that schools should be involved in these areas.

The only surveys in which social studies teachers' opinions were assessed regarding the general goals of education were the NCEI (SS) and HSB surveys. According to the NCEI (SS) survey report, social studies teachers rated educational goals in the same order as other teachers. That order, from high to low, was reasoning and analytical skills, social character, job skills, morals, and preparation for college. The top goal was rated twice as important as the bottom goal. In the HSB survey, social studies teachers ranked goals for education in the following order: basic literacy skills, good work habits and self-discipline, academic excellence, personal growth, citizenship, human relations, moral and religious values, occupational skills. The top goal received a mean rating of 2.4 on an 8-point scale; the bottom goal, a rating of 6.7. Although solid comparisons are difficult between the two lists, it is interesting to note that citizenship was given only a 4 rating on an 8-point scale in the HSB survey and that developing character and morals took a back seat to reasoning on the NCEI (SS) survey.

The most complete information regarding social studies teachers' views of the purpose of social studies comes from the AIT survey. When social studies teachers were asked about the purpose of social studies, 95.3% agreed that it was to teach students to think critically and constructively about society. Over 87% also agreed that teaching students to cope with issues in their own lives was an important purpose of social studies. To promote activity in social and political organizations and to teach knowledge of the past were supported as social studies goals by only 53% of teachers surveyed. When social studies teachers were asked to rank order attitudes (e.g., respect for others and patriotism), skills (e.g., map reading and library research), and knowledge (facts, names, dates), 51.8% ranked attitudes as most important, 29.6% ranked knowledge as most important, and 18.8% ranked skills as most important.

Overall, the information on the goals of education suggests that the areas of greatest agreement among the public, the profession, and social studies teachers are teaching students to think, express themselves, and develop work habits. The areas of greatest difference are with respect to teaching standards of right and wrong; the general public rates the goal as twice as important as the profession and social studies teachers. Promotion of understanding of and participation in the political process, a goal commonly accepted by many of the social studies intelligentsia, did not receive great support among teachers and the general public. In the Gallup survey that goal received the highest rating by only 31% and 33% of the teachers and general public, respectively. In the AIT survey that goal was ranked fourth among six possible goals by social studies teachers.

Other Studies. A widely discussed perspective on the purposes of social studies education can be found in the NCSS Bulletin, *Defining the Social Studies* (Barr, Barth, & Shermis, 1977). The authors argued that the social studies can be perceived in terms of three distinct historical traditions: social studies as citizenship transmission, as social science, and as reflective inquiry. The authors also reported empirical confirmation of the existence of these distinct orientations among social studies teachers. Subsequent studies by Andres (1981) and White (1982), using the same Social Studies Preference Scale (SSPS), have not supported Barr, et al.'s original analysis. The SSPS is a 45-item Likert response instrument with 15 items for each of the orientations.

The Andres study sample was selected using a stratified random design. The population was social studies teachers of Indiana, and the sample selected consisted of 193 secondary school teachers. White obtained a sample of convenience consisting of 190 secondary school social studies teachers in six Midwest and New England school districts. In both studies, factor analysis on the 45 SSPS items yielded similar results. Citizenship transmission emerged as the most distinct orientation. One additional factor emerged; it was neither social science nor reflective inquiry, but a mixture of the two.

In an ethnographic study of 16 elementary school teachers' perspectives toward social studies education, Goodman and

Adler (1985) found, not two or three orientations, but six. These were social studies as a nonsubject, as human relations, as citizenship indoctrination, as school knowledge, as the integrative core of the elementary curriculum, and as education for social action.

Citizenship appears to be the ideal that most social studies teachers acknowledge as an important goal; however, there are competing interpretations of the goal and enough disagreement to state safely that the profession is far from united under a single banner. Evidence for the two most prominent interpretations of citizenship comes from Andres' findings that 76% of social studies teachers in his sample possessed a strong commitment to teaching traditional American values and 98% favored the balanced and thoughtful discussion of controversial issues as a regular part of the social studies.

The Social Studies Teacher as Citizen

In an area of the school curriculum where the self-proclaimed responsibility is the education of youth for citizenship, the citizen characteristics of the teachers are of special interest. If all of teaching were nothing but drama, acting on a stage, then perhaps teachers' political beliefs and actions might be considered irrelevant. However, some of the teacher's politically relevant characteristics are likely revealed to students in the process of spending one hour per day for 9 months together in the same room. If the teacher is perceived as attractive and competent and reveals her or his political ideology, the opportunity for influence exists. For example, it is reported in the Metropolitan Life survey that 39% of high school students said that there were teachers whom they admired and would like to be like. Because of this potential and also because the citizenship qualities of the teachers who teach citizenship are an intrinsically interesting topic, teachers as citizens are considered next.

Political Ideology and Affiliation. In the NEA survey, teachers labeled themselves in the following manner: tend to be liberal (27.8%), liberal (11.7%), tend to be conservative (43.6%), and conservative (17%). Using a three-level classification in the NCEI survey, teachers labeled themselves as liberal (14%), moderate (56%), and conservative (30%). The only available data on social studies teachers come from the NCEI (SS) survey, in which the following pattern of ideological identification was found: liberal (15%), moderate (57%), and conservative (28%). It is apparent that social studies teachers are not different ideologically from other teachers.

How do the political orientations of teachers as a group compare with those of the general public? The varying numbers of response categories make such comparisons difficult, but the data from one recent summary (Robinson & Fleishman, 1988) permit some conclusions. Robinson and Fleishman noted that when a middle-of-the-road option was provided to the general public, 30% to 40% of the respondents chose it. The conservative to liberal ratio generally fluctuated between 1.5 and 2.0 to 1. This data set suggests that the conservative to liberal ratio for teachers and the general public is approximately the same. The difference is that the moderate, or middle-of-the-road, response is almost twice as large for teachers as for the general public.

Teachers tend to identify more with the Democratic party. When asked about party preference, about 41% of teachers reported that they were Democrats, 31% Republican, and 25% Independent (NEA, NCEI). Three percent indicated that they were not sure. Comparing the teacher profession to all college graduates within the 25–34 years age span, 47% of teachers said that they were Democratic, compared with 33% of all college graduates (NCEI).

Any differences with regard to party preference between social studies teachers and other teachers are minimal. Social studies teachers' party preferences, according to the NCEI (SS) survey are as follows: Democratic (40%), Republican (31%), and Independent (28%). According to the Indiana survey, 40% of social studies teachers indicated the Democratic party as the party of preference, but a lower percentage identified themselves as Republicans (22%) and a higher percentage (35%) identified themselves as Independent (Ganz, 1981).

Fifty-five percent of all teachers reported that they had voted for Reagan in the 1984 national election; 35% for Mondale (NCEI). Only 4% reported that they had not voted. Social studies teachers tended to vote slightly more for Reagan, with 60% voting for Reagan and 30% for Mondale (NCEI-SS). In the 1980 presidential election, according to social studies teachers' reports, they voted 46% for Carter, 38% for Reagan, and 13% for Anderson, compared with 42%, 50%, 6%, respectively, of the general public. Thus, between 1980 and 1984, Reagan gained 17 percentage points among social studies teachers. Even though only 28% to 30% of social studies teachers identified themselves as conservative and Republican, when in 1984 they had a liberal–conservative choice in the presidential election, 55% chose to vote for the conservative Republican candidate.

Participation in Community and Political Life. Social studies teachers appear to be much more actively involved in political affairs than the general public. According to the Indiana survey, which must be treated cautiously because of the low response rates, 98% of social studies teachers reported that they were registered to vote and they voted regularly. This is compared with 67% of the general public, who reported that they were registered to vote and voted regularly. Social studies teachers also reported that they were considerably more active (at a 5 : 1 ratio) than did the general public with regard to political contributions, writing letters to officials, displaying campaign paraphernalia, writing letters of opinion, attempting to get others to participate, and attending political meetings (Indiana). Unfortunately, the Indiana study report is the only one that contains information on political activity by social studies teachers. With one exception, no information was found on the level of political activity of teachers in general. According to the NEA survey, 13.8% of all teachers belonged to a political party organization.

Religion. Teachers tend to be more religious than the general public. In the NEA and NCEI surveys, almost 80% of teachers reported belonging to a church, compared with 71% of the general public (NCEI). Fifty percent of the general public considered themselves very or moderately religious (NCEI). Sixty-one percent of teachers reported that they had attended a church or synagogue in the previous 7 days compared with 42% of the general public (NCEI). Approximately 50% of all teachers said they believed that religion could answer all or most of today's problems, and 94% responded in the affirmative to the question "Do you ever pray to God?" (NCEI). Sixty percent of social studies teachers considered themselves very or moderately religious, and only 8.4% said they were not at all religious (Indiana).

Social studies teachers' religious beliefs and practices appear to be quite similar to those of the profession as a whole. Ninety-three percent of the profession reported that they sometimes prayed to God, 43% said that they believed religion could answer all or most of today's problems, 75% said they belonged to a church or synagogue, and 58% reported attending a religious service in the previous 7 days (NCEI-SS). According to the Indiana survey, 60% of social studies teachers reported they were Protestant, 21% Catholic, 1% Jewish, and 18% other or none.

Opinions on Major Social Issues. Abortion is one of the most divisive and emotional issues facing the United States today. In the NCEI survey 48% of public school teachers said they believed abortion should be legalized, 39% said it should be legal only to save a life, and 8% said it should not be legal under any circumstance. The general public was less likely to favor the legalization of abortion (38%) and more likely to support its legality only to save a life (45%) (NCEI). Social studies teachers tended to fall between the general public and teachers' positions: 41.5% of social studies teachers said they believed it should be legal, as it then was; 36% said it should be legal only to save a life (NCEI-SS); 12% reported believing that it should not be permitted at all; and 10% said they did not know. The Indiana survey found that two-thirds of social studies teachers approved of an anti-abortion constitutional amendment. This sentiment is similar to that of the general public.

Another issue that has aroused considerable debate in the United States is the place of religion in public schools. Among public school teachers, 47% reported believing that schools should be allowed to start each day with a prayer, 37% said they believed that religion did not belong in schools, and 16% were unsure on the question (NCEI). The general public feels more strongly that religious prayer in schools is appropriate, with 66% responding positively (NCEI, Gallup). Forty-two percent of social studies teachers favored starting the school day with a prayer, 44% said it did not belong in the school, and 14% were unsure (NCEI-SS). In the Indiana survey, only 25% of social studies teachers reported that they believed that religious practices were appropriate in schools (Soley, 1981).

Social studies teachers in the NCEI-SS sample were found to be more supportive of the death penalty than either public school teachers or the general public. Eighty-one percent of social studies teachers favored the death penalty for persons convicted of murder (NCEI-SS), and 70% of public school teachers and 75% of the general public shared this perspective (NCEI).

Data from the Indiana survey suggest that social studies

teachers in general supported the efforts during the 1970s and 1980s to extend civil rights to all members of our society. Eighty-eight percent said that the civil rights movement had been a positive influence, and 72% believed that discrimination was still a major problem. When, however, the issue of civil rights was tied to specific legislative action, the support weakened. For example, only 54% of social studies teachers supported the Equal Rights Amendment. Sixty-six percent of social studies teachers were opposed to busing to achieve racial integration, and over 50% said that busing had a negative effect on education. Fifty-five percent of social studies teachers have a negative view of affirmative action, believing it results in reverse discrimination.

Economic Opportunity. In 1984, the National Opinion Research Center conducted a General Social Survey that included five questions on the basic fairness of our economic system. Feistritzer (1986) used the same questions in the NCEI survey. Social studies teachers' responses to these questions were included in the NCEI (SS) survey data. Respondents answered the five statements on a 4-point Likert scale. The five statements were

America has an open society. What one achieves in life no longer depends on one's family background, but on the abilities one has and the education one acquires.

Everyone in this country has an opportunity to obtain an education corresponding to his or her abilities and talents.

In the United States there are still great differences between social levels, and what one can achieve in life depends mainly upon one's family background.

Only if differences in income and social standing are large enough is there an incentive for individual effort.

Differences in social standing between people are acceptable because they basically reflect what people are made out of. (p. 64)

The belief that America is an open society and that one's achievements are the result of one's efforts was positively endorsed by both teachers and the general public: 85% of the public and 72% of public school teachers responded affirmatively (strongly agree or somewhat agree). Seventy-one percent of the general public and 63% of teachers agreed that educational opportunity was a reality. Approximately 55% of the general public and teacher samples disagreed with the idea that current differences between social levels were primarily the result of family background; 45% agreed with the position.

The last two questions of the General Social Survey revealed major differences of opinion between teachers and the general public. The statement that incentive exists only if differences in income and social standing exist received much weaker support from teachers than from the general public. Fifty-nine percent of the general public agreed with the statement, 33% of social studies teachers agreed, and only 24% of public school teachers agreed. The most dramatic differences of opinion between teachers and the general public occurred with respect to whether differences in social standing are acceptable because they reflect differences in effort. Seventy-four percent of the general public found that position acceptable, but only 43% of teachers did. In general, the responses of social studies teachers mirrored those of all teachers (NCEI-SS).

Overall, it appears that the general public, more so than teachers, accepts the basic premises of our mixed-market, capitalistic society, namely, that we have an open society with true equality of opportunity and that one gets what one earns in life. Teachers are less likely to endorse this position, especially when it results in differences in social standing. Better than two-thirds of the teachers sampled accepted the open society ideal in general, but a majority rejected the idea that differences in social standing are an acceptable result of such a system. It is not clear from the survey data how teachers reconciled their belief in an open and free system with the belief that there should not be differences in social standing.

A pervasive characteristic of teachers' economic life is union membership. Eighty percent of public school teachers in the United States belong to a union, compared with only 20% of the adult workers in the United States. As might be expected, teachers have more favorable views toward unions than do the general public. For example, in the Gallup survey, 49% of teachers thought that unions had helped the quality of education in the United States. Only 18% of the general public shared this perception. Although teachers support unions, the NCEI survey found that the teaching profession was equally split on the question of whether unions stifle individual initiative. Teachers overwhelmingly agreed (85%) that unions improve salaries and that they are necessary to get fair treatment for employees (70%). No differences between social studies teachers and other teachers were reported with respect to opinions about unions.

It is apparent that, with regard to political ideology and opinions on a variety of social issues, social studies teachers are little different from their fellow professionals, and both are not greatly at variance with the general public. Teachers are less accepting of economic inequality as a necessary result of our economic system and less supportive of prayer in schools, but, on the whole, teachers' values and the values of the general public are similar. Thus, it is reasonable to expect that social studies teachers would have little difficulty supporting and transmitting community values to children. Findings from ethnographic studies suggest that, in fact, social studies teachers assume a role in schools as agents in the socialization of youth into community values (Lortie, 1975; McNeill, 1986; McPherson, 1972; Peshkin, 1978; Stake & Easley, 1978).

COGNITIVE STYLE AND MORAL DEVELOPMENT

The purpose for this section is to examine the evidence for relationships between teacher cognitive style and moral development and the creation of democratic classroom environments conducive to the examination of controversial issues as an ongoing part of social studies instruction. The reason for examining this set of variables is as follows. The classroom climate created by the teacher has been shown to be the strongest predictor of positive political attitudes and moral development among children (Leming, 1985). Teachers who create democratic climates and encourage student expression and consideration of diverse perspectives may be psychologically different from teachers who maintain rigid control of classroom processes and knowledge. The summaries by Newmann (1990) and Oliver and Shaver (1966/1974) of characteristics of teachers who hold to a more provisional view of knowledge and engage students in exploring issues and in higher order thinking were reported earlier. The research on the potential relationship between teacher characteristics and classroom environment may be organized around two sets of variables: cognitive style and moral development.

Cognitive Style

Cognitive styles are consistent individual patterns in organizing and processing information and experiences (Messick, 1984). Cognitive styles tend to be pervasive and to cut across cognitive, intellectual, personality, and interpersonal domains; they are intimately interwoven with affective, temperamental, and motivational structure as parts of the total personality. Promising links between stylistic aspects of cognitive functioning and personality or social functioning that have potential for the study of education have been reported in the literature (Kogan, 1971; Messick, 1984). Messick (1971) has identified nine separate cognitive styles that have been the object of systematic theoretical and empirical examination. Three of these styles of cognitive function are directly relevant to this chapter.

The first important style is field dependence as a characterization of the individual's perceptions, personality, intelligence, and social behavior (Witkin, Moore, Goodenough, & Cox, 1977). Field-dependent individuals, in comparison to field-independent persons, are more likely to exhibit reliance on the surrounding stimuli, rely on authority, and experience their environment in a relatively global fashion by conforming to the perceived context. With regard to social orientation, field-dependent persons are more likely to be attentive to and make use of prevailing social frames of reference; they are more attuned to the social aspects of situations. They are also more drawn to people in the sense of liking to be with them. This liking to be with people is reflected in field-dependent teachers' tendency to use discussion and discovery approaches that encourage interpersonal relations, whereas field-independent teachers tend to rely more on lecturing (Witkin et al., 1977).

With regard to cognitive outcomes, field-independent individuals may be more effective as teachers. Saracho and Dayton (1980) found, in a study of 36 elementary classrooms, that children with field-independent teachers showed greater cognitive gains than children with field-dependent teachers.

The second important cognitive style has to do with the dimension of abstractness–concreteness (Harvey, Hunt, & Schroder, 1961). Four distinct levels of abstractness–concreteness have been described, ranging from minimal differentiation at the concrete extreme to maximal differentiation and hierarchic integration at the abstract extreme.

Harvey, Prather, White, and Hoffmeister (1968) and Hunt (1976) have found relationships between levels of cognitive complexity and teacher behavior. Teachers who were assessed to be more toward the abstract end of the continuum tended to demonstrate greater warmth and sensitivity toward students, were less dogmatic and rule oriented with regard to discipline, manifested less need for structure, and were less punitive. Teachers with abstract belief systems were also more democratic and resourceful than teachers with concrete belief systems.

A third cognitive style that could have implications for social studies instruction is characterized by the extent to which the individual is tolerant of new and/or discrepant information. This style has been studied most often by using the Dogmatism Scale of Rokeach (1960). *Dogmatism* is used to refer to a closed system of beliefs that are highly resistant to change and not open to new information. Chalker (1972), using a sample of 178 secondary social studies teachers, compared the 10 teachers who scored highest on the Dogmatism Scale with the 10 teachers who scored lowest. Those teachers low in dogmatism encouraged greater classroom participation, had greater respect for students' opinions, and generally established a more intellectually open classroom.

Victor (1976), in a multidimensional study of the relationship between personality and teaching style with a sample of 163 special education teachers, found that dogmatism loaded consistently and strongly (+.70) on a teaching style identified as teacher centeredness—a system of beliefs emphasizing the value of subject matter and the maintenance of social distance between teacher and student.

As noted earlier in this chapter, in the 1960s the interests of researchers began to shift away from teacher characteristics. As a consequence, the research on the topic is now somewhat dated and limited. The little evidence available suggests that the relationship between cognitive style and teachers' approaches to instruction is an area in which further inquiry is warranted.

Moral Development

Teaching is a social enterprise. Morality, in its broadest terms, includes all interpersonal behavior that involves the rights, duties, and welfare of either party. Teaching, therefore, is a moral undertaking, both in its goal to enhance the well-being of others and through the necessary regulation of the social life of schools. It follows, therefore, that the teacher's conception of morality would influence his or her understanding of teaching and his or her behavior in the classroom. In addition, there are probably requisite levels of teacher moral development for particular forms of moral education to be effective. The research on these two questions is examined next.

Johnston and Lubomudrov (1987) examined the relationship between teachers' level of moral development and their understanding of rules and teacher–student roles in their classrooms. From a larger group of 27 teachers enrolled in a graduate program at the University of Utah, the four teachers who scored highest on the Defining Issues Test (Rest, 1979) and the four teachers who scored lowest were selected. The primary score from the Defining Issues Test is the P score, an index that reflects the percentage of the individuals reasoning at the principled level. The four high teachers had P scores above 33.

The four low teachers had P scores below 24. The eight teachers were then interviewed three times. The first interview dealt with a broad range of educational issues, the second interview was directed at issues related to the moral aspects of teaching, and the third interview was focused on an hour-long videotape of the teacher's classroom.

Johnston and Lubomudrov found that differences in the ways these teachers understood classroom rules and roles corresponded in a consistent way to their level of moral development. For teachers in the low-scoring group, rules served primarily to maintain a stable social order. They emanated from authorities and, once established, students were expected to comply with them. Teachers in the high group viewed rules as necessary to insure the rights of individual students as well as the rights of the group. Rules were perceived as less fixed, and the higher scoring teachers talked about balancing group and individual rights and the need to question and alter rules to meet changing situations. Higher scoring teachers also were concerned about students' understanding of the rules and tried to help them assume responsibility for the classroom climate.

With regard to teacher–student roles, marked differences were also apparent between high- and low-scoring teachers. Low-scoring teachers held to an autocratic role, with the teacher in total control and the student compliant and submissive. In contrast, high-scoring teachers thought that students should participate in establishing rules and share responsibility for upholding rules. High-scoring teachers valued democratic classroom interaction.

Bergem (1986) administered the Defining Issues Test to 83 student teachers at a midwestern university and then correlated their P scores with their cooperating teachers' ratings of student-teaching performance and scores on a measure of social sensitivity. Bergem found no statistically significant relationship between moral reasoning scores and ratings of teaching performance. A weak but statistically significant relationship ($r = .25$, $p < .05$) was found between social sensitivity scores and ratings of teaching performance. Although the rating of teaching performance consisted of evaluations in three general areas—instructional competencies, relationships, and professional attributes—Bergem analyzed the data using only the overall rating. It should be noted that Bergem did not analyze data by high–low teaching ratings or high–low moral scores.

Although there is little research on the relationship between teachers' moral reasoning and ratings of teacher performance in social studies education, evidence from the medical profession suggests that moral reasoning is an important factor in judgments of physician performance (Sheehan, Husted, Candee, Cook, & Bargen, 1980). In this study, physicians with higher moral reasoning scores were compared with physicians with lower moral reasoning scores. Both groups were rated by superiors on six criteria of performance: compassion, knowledge, dependability, critical attitude, teamwork, and efficiency. Although the context was different, these criteria are not that different from those frequently used to evaluate preservice and practicing teachers. There were clear differences in the performance ratings of the principled and pre-principled physicians. For the entire sample, the correlation between P score and performance rating was $r = .57$, $p < .001$. Whether social studies

teachers' sense of right and wrong, value priorities, and sense of responsibility to students and the institution are related to their teaching performance is a promising topic for further research.

The moral development of teachers is related in another way to teacher effectiveness. Recent reviews on the influence of the moral dilemma discussion approach of Kohlberg has demonstrated that, when teachers engage students in moral dialogue about the resolution of moral dilemmas and ensure that they are exposed to moderately higher reasoning, students will experience upward movement in moral development (Leming, 1985; Schlaefli, Rest, & Thoma, 1985).

The teacher characteristics required by the dilemma discussion approach are those that enable the creation of a climate that encourages open and free discussion and the orchestration of that dialogue in such a way that all students are exposed to a moderately higher level of moral reasoning. A teacher who is to be effective with the dilemma discussion approach must have attained a certain level of moral development. Rest, Turiel, and Kohlberg (1969) found that individuals have difficulty understanding moral reasoning above their own stage but have no such difficulty with lower stages. In addition, individuals tend to prefer the reasoning of the next higher stage and to reject reasoning that is below their own stage. It follows that, for a teacher to be effective at leading discussions focused on moral dilemmas, she or he would need to reason at a higher level than the students to understand their reasoning, but not reason at a level so much above that of the students as not to be understood. To assume this role requires not only that the teacher be able to understand a student's stage of moral reasoning, but also that the teacher have an awareness of her or his own moral reasoning and be able to "match" moral statements in a developmentally propitious manner.

Research on the levels of moral reasoning of teachers is sparse. The findings suggest that teachers are substantially lower in moral development than other college graduates, although sufficient in moral development to be able to lead moral discussions in the classroom. Rest (1976) reported that, among 2,479 college students, the mean P score was 42.3; among 183 graduate students, the mean was 53.3; and among a sample of 1,149 adults, it was 40.0 Bloom (1976) found that, among 82 education graduate students at William and Mary University, the mean P score was 29.8. This score is 23.5 points below the mean for graduate students reported by Rest. Griffore and Lewis (1978) reported the mean P score for 78 Michigan teachers taking graduate education courses to be 43.29.

If, as Johnston and Lubomudrov (1987) have suggested, low levels of moral development are related to more custodial and less democratic orientations to teaching, these data are not encouraging. On the other hand, the level of moral development among teachers, in general, is sufficiently advanced to allow most of them to be successful at leading moral discussions. Rest (1976) reported the mean P score for junior high school students in his sample to be 21.9 and for high school students to be 31.8. With the moral reasoning of high school students and teachers in one of the samples so similar, it might be difficult for the teachers to serve as an example of more advanced reasoning. Given the failure of the moral dilemma discussion approach to become a part of social studies practice (Colby, Kohlberg, Fenton, Speicher-Dubin, & Lieberman, 1977; Silver, 1982), such data may have only limited significance.

SUMMARY AND CONCLUSIONS

Since the 1960s the topic of teacher characteristics has not been of great professional interest to the educational research community. The literature reviewed in this chapter suggests that the study of teacher characteristics in social studies education is not moribund but, rather, incomplete and unexplored.

Two general perspectives on teacher characteristics were proposed that have potential for increasing the understanding of social studies education. The first general set of characteristics was labeled *demographic* and discussed with a view to understanding the frequently cited observation that social studies teachers in general see their role as transmitting existing civic and social values to students. Social studies teachers were found to vary little from other teachers and the general public in most demographic categories. Most social studies teachers come from middle-class backgrounds, live close to their family homes, and are stable and involved members of their community. To the extent that teachers are to reveal their values to students and, thereby, through their teaching reinforce dominant community values, the demographics suggest that social studies teachers are ideally suited for this activity. Based on the information identified in this chapter, it is unlikely that social studies teachers would be culturally trans-

formative (Giroux, 1985) in their roles as teachers of social studies.

The second major set of teacher characteristics considered in this chapter was cognitive style and moral development. The emphasis was on cognitive characteristics of teachers that might influence their approach to knowledge and classroom environment. Suggestive evidence was found that these variables may well be related to teachers' willingness to discuss issues openly with students and to create more democratic classrooms. Due to the recent general lack of interest among researchers regarding teacher characteristics, the number and variety of these studies were limited. This review suggests that the abandonment of teacher characteristics as a research topic was premature.

Teacher characteristics are a promising area for future research in social studies education. For the promise to be realized, however, two objectives must be met. *First,* a clearer understanding must be developed of the relationship between demographic factors and the roles teachers assume in schools. *Second,* clearer theoretical and empirical links must be established between teacher cognitive characteristics and teacher behavior with regard to content, methodology, and teacher–student relationships. In the first case, the study of teacher characteristics will illuminate the process of social studies education as a conservative and tradition-sustaining activity. In the second case, the study of teacher characteristics can illuminate the possibilities for social studies to achieve one of its most valued goals: active and critical citizenship. The study of the interaction between these two forces will provide deeper insight into the nature of the social studies education profession.

References

Allport, G. W. (1937). *Personality: A psychological interpretation.* New York: Henry Holt.

Andres, P. N. (1981). Social studies orientations and educational attitudes of secondary classroom teachers in the state of Indiana. *Dissertation Abstracts International, 42,* 5082A. (University Microfilms No. DA8209884)

Bandura, A. (1977). *Social learning theory.* Englewood Cliffs, NJ: Prentice-Hall.

Barr, R. D., Barth, J. L., & Shermis, S. S. (1977). *Defining the social studies* (Bulletin 51). Washington, DC: National Council for the Social Studies.

Bergem, T. (1986). Teachers' thinking and behavior: An empirical study of the role of social sensitivity and moral reasoning in the teaching performance of student teachers. *Scandinavian Journal of Educational Research, 30,* 193–203.

Berliner, D. (1987). Simple views of effective teaching and simple theories of classroom instruction. In D. Berliner & B. Rosenshine (Eds.), *Talks with teachers* (pp. 93–110). New York: Random House.

Bloom, R. B. (1976). Morally speaking, who are today's teachers? *Phi Delta Kappan, 59,* 624–625.

Chalker, J. W. (1972). A study using interaction analysis of the relationship between teacher dogmatism and the reflective method of teaching social studies. *Dissertation Abstracts International, 33,* 1073A. (University Microfilms No. 72-24, 175)

Clayson, D. E., & Maughan, M. R. C. (1986). Redheads and blondes: Stereotypic images. *Psychological Reports, 59,* 811–816.

Colby, A., Kohlberg, L., Fenton, E., Speicher-Dubin, & Lieberman, M. (1977). Secondary school moral discussion programs led by social studies teachers. *Journal of Moral Education, 6,* 90–111.

Darling-Hammond, L. (1984). *Beyond the commission reports: The coming crisis in education.* Santa Monica, CA: RAND Corporation.

Educational Research Service. (1987). *Survey of members and potential members of the National Council for the Social Studies.* Washington, DC: National Council for the Social Studies.

Ehman, L. H. (1980a). The American school in the political socialization process. *Review of Educational Research, 50,* 99–119.

Ehman, L. H. (1980b). Change in high school students' political attitudes as a function of social studies classroom climate. *American Educational Research Journal, 17,* 253–265.

Farmer, R. (1984). The social studies teacher in the '80s: Report from the national survey. *The Social Studies, 75,* 166–171.

Feistritzer, C. E. (1986). *Profile of teachers in the U.S.* Washington, DC: National Center for Education Information.

Flanders, N. A. (1960). *Teacher influence, pupil attitudes and achievement* (Final Report, Cooperative Research Program Project No. 397). Minneapolis: University of Minnesota.

Fontana, L. (1980). *Status of social studies teaching practices in secondary schools.* Bloomington, IN: Agency for Instructional Television.

Gage, N. L. (1963). Paradigms for research on teaching. In N. L. Gage (Ed.). *Handbook of research on teaching* (pp. 94–141). Chicago: Rand McNally.

Gallup, A. (1984). The Gallup poll of teachers' attitudes toward the public schools, Part I. *Phi Delta Kappan, 66,* 97–107.

Gallup, A. (1985). The Gallup poll of teachers' attitudes toward the public schools, Part 2. *Phi Delta Kappan, 66,* 323–329.

Gallup, A. (1988). The 20th annual Gallup poll of the public's attitudes toward the public schools. *Phi Delta Kappan, 20,* 33–46.

Ganz, R. (1981). Social studies teachers as political participants. *Social Education, 45,* 408–411.

Getzels, J. W., & Jackson, P. W. (1963). The teacher's personality and characteristics. In N. L. Gage (Ed.), *Handbook of research on teaching* (pp. 506–582). Chicago: Rand McNally.

Giroux, H. A. (1985). Teachers as transformative intellectuals. *Social Education, 49,* 376–379.

Goebel, B. L., & Cashen, V. M. (1978). Age, sex, and attractiveness as factors in student ratings of teachers: A developmental study. *Journal of Educational Psychology, 71,* 646–653.

Goodman, J., & Adler, S. (1985). Becoming an elementary social studies teacher: A study of perspectives. *Theory and Research in Social Education, 13*(2), 1–20.

Griffore, R. J., & Lewis, J. (1978). Characteristics of teacher's moral judgment. *Educational Research Quarterly, 3,* 20–30.

Harris, L., & Associates (1988). *The Metropolitan Life survey of the American teacher, 1988.* New York: Louis Harris and Associates.

Hartshorne, H., & May, M. (1928). *Studies in the nature of character: Vol. 1. Studies in deceit.* New York: Macmillan.

Harvey, O. J., Hunt, D. E., & Schroder, H. M. (1961). *Conceptual systems and personality organization.* New York: John Wiley & Sons.

Harvey, O. J., Prather, M., White, B. J., & Hoffmeister, J. K. (1968). Teachers' beliefs, classroom atmosphere and student behavior. *American Educational Research Journal, 5,* 151–166.

Hunsberger, B., & Cavanagh, B. (1988). Physical attractiveness and childrens' expectations of potential teachers. *Psychology in the Schools, 25,* 70–74.

Hunt, D. (1976). Teachers' adaptation: "Reading" and "flexing" to students. *Journal of Teacher Education, 27,* 268–275.

Johnston, M., & Lubomudrov, C. (1987). Teachers' level of moral reasoning and their understanding of classroom rules and roles. *Elementary School Journal, 88,* 65–77.

Kogan, N. (1971). Educational implications of cognitive styles. In G. S. Lesser (Ed.), *Psychology and educational practice* (pp. 242–292). Glenview, IL: Scott, Foresman.

Leming, J. S. (1985). Research on social studies curriculum and instruction: Interventions and outcomes in the socio-moral domain. In W. B. Stanley (Ed.), *Review of research in social studies education: 1976–1983* (pp. 123–213). Washington, DC: National Council for the Social Studies.

Lewis, D. S. (1975). Teacher personality and instruction. In T. Husen & T. N. Postlethwaite (Eds.), *The international encyclopedia of education* (Vol. 9, pp. 5016–5021). Elmsford, NY: Pergamon.

Lortie, D. C. (1975). *Schoolteacher: A sociological study.* Chicago: University of Chicago Press.

McMann, F. C., & McMann, C. J. (1984). Defining characteristics of social studies teachers: A response to Ochoa's challenge. *The Social Studies, 75,* 36–41.

McNeil, L. M. (1986). *Contradictions of control: School structure and school knowledge.* New York: Routledge and Kegan Paul.

McPherson, G. H. (1972). *Small town teacher.* Cambridge, MA: Harvard University Press.

Messick, S. (1971). The criterion problem in the evaluation of instruction: Assessing possible, not just intended outcomes. In M. C. Wittrock & D. E. Wiley (Eds.), *The evaluation of instruction: Issues and problems* (pp. 183–202). New York: Holt, Rinehart, & Winston.

Messick, S. (1984). The nature of cognitive styles: Problems and promise in educational practice. *Educational Psychologist, 19,* 59–74.

National Education Association. (1987). *Status of the American public school teacher 1985–86.* Washington, DC: Author.

Newmann, F. M. (1990). Higher order thinking in the teaching of social studies: A rationale for the assessment of classroom thoughtfulness. *Journal of Curriculum Studies, 22,* 41–56.

Ochoa, A. S. (Ed.). (1981). A profile of social studies teachers [Special section]. *Social Education, 45*(6), 401–421.

Oliver, D. W., & Shaver, J. P. (1974). *Teaching public issues in the high school.* Logan, UT: Utah State University Press. (Original work published 1966)

Peshkin, A. (1978). *Growing up American: Schooling and the survival of community.* Chicago: University of Chicago Press.

Power, C. (1988). The just community approach to moral education. *Journal of Moral Education, 17,* 195–208.

Rest, J. (1976). *Moral judgment related to sample characteristics: Final report* (Grant No. 8703-MH24988). Washington, DC: National Institute of Mental Health.

Rest, J. (1979). *Development in judging moral issues.* Minneapolis, N: University of Minnesota Press.

Rest, J., Turiel, E., & Kohlberg, L. (1969). Level of moral development as a determinant of preference and comprehension of moral judgments made by others. *Journal of Personality, 37,* 225–252.

Robinson, J. P., & Fleishman, J. A. (1988). Ideological identification: Trends and interpretations of the liberal–conservative balance. *Public Opinion Quarterly, 52,* 134–145.

Rokeach, M. (1960). *The open and closed mind.* New York: Basic Books.

Rosenshine, B. (1987). Explicit teaching. In D. C. Berliner & B. Rosenshine (Eds.), *Talks with teachers* (pp. 75–92). New York: Random House.

Rosenshine, B., & Furst, N. F. (1971). Research on teacher performance criteria. In B. O. Smith (Ed.), *Research in teacher education: A symposium* (pp. 37–72). Englewood Cliffs, NJ: Prentice-Hall.

Rutter, R. A. (1986). Profile of the profession. *Social Education, 50,* 252–255.

Saracho, O. N., & Dayton, C. M. (1980). Relationship of teachers' cognitive styles to pupils' academic achievement gains. *Journal of Educational Psychology, 72,* 544–549.

Schlechty, P. C., & Vance, U. S. (1981). Do academically able teachers leave education? The North Carolina case. *Phi Delta Kappan, 63,* 106–112.

Schlaefli, A., Rest, J. R., & Thoma, S. J. (1985). Does moral education improve moral judgment? A meta-analysis of intervention studies using the Defining Issues Test. *Review of Educational Research, 55,* 319–352.

Shavelson, R. J., & Stern, P. (1981). Research on teachers' pedagogical thoughts, judgments, decisions, and behavior. *Review of Educational Research, 51,* 455–498.

Sheehan, T. J., Husted, S. D. R., Candee, D., Cook, C., & Bargen, B. (1980). Moral judgment as a predictor of physician performance. *Evaluation and the Health Professions, 3,* 393–404.

Silver, M. (1982). Moral education and teaching. An interview study of teachers. *Dissertation Abstracts International, 43,* 3804A. (University Microfilms No. 8310943)

Soley, M. (1981). Controversial issues as viewed by social studies teachers. *Social Education, 45,* 412–417.

Stake, R. E., & Easley, J. A. (1978). *Case studies in science education: Vol. 2. Design, overview and general findings.* Urbana, IL: Center for Instructional Research and Curriculum Evaluation, University of Illinois.

Travers, R. M. W. (Ed.). (1972). *Second handbook of research on teaching.* Chicago: Rand McNally.

Vance, V. S., & Schlechty, P. C. (1982). The distribution of academic ability in the teaching force: Policy implications. *Phi Delta Kappan, 64,* 22–27.

Victor, J. B. (1976). Relation between teacher belief and teacher personality in four samples of teacher trainees. *Journal of Experimental Education, 45,* 4–9.

Weiss, I. R. (1978). *Report of the 1977 national survey of science, mathematics and social studies education* (Publication No. 038-000-00364-0). Washington, DC: Government Printing Office.

White, C. S. (1982). A validation study of the Barth-Shermis Social Studies Preference Scale. *Theory and Research in Social Education, 10*(2), 1–20.

Wittrock, M. C. (Ed.). (1985). *Handbook of research on teaching* (3rd ed.). New York: Macmillan.

Witkin, H. A., Moore, C. A., Goodenough, D. R., & Cox, P. W. (1977). Field-dependent and field-independent cognitive styles and their educational implications. *Review of Educational Research, 47,* 1–64.

19

TEACHER AS CURRICULAR-INSTRUCTIONAL GATEKEEPER IN SOCIAL STUDIES

Stephen J. Thornton
TEACHERS COLLEGE, COLUMBIA UNIVERSITY

In an overview of the comprehensive investigations of social studies education sponsored by the National Science Foundation in the 1970s, Shaver, Davis, and Helburn (1980) concluded that the teacher is the "key" to the curriculum experienced by students.

The teacher's beliefs about schooling, his or her knowledge of the subject area and of available materials and techniques, how he or she decides to put these together for the classroom—out of that process of reflection and personal inclination comes the day-by-day classroom experiences of students. This is not to say that social studies classes are not affected by factors such as the characteristics of the students enrolled, but only to emphasize that the teacher plays the primary structuring role. (p. 5)

TEACHER AS CURRICULAR–INSTRUCTIONAL GATEKEEPER

The key role of social studies teachers (hereafter, teachers) in day-to-day curriculum and instruction is the focus of this chapter. In particular, teachers will be characterized as curricular–instructional gatekeepers (hereafter, gatekeepers). As gatekeepers, teachers make the day-to-day decisions concerning both the subject matter and the experiences to which students have access and the nature of that subject matter and those experiences. As used in this chapter, *gatekeeping* encompasses the decisions teachers make about curriculum and instruction and the criteria they use to make those decisions. Curricular decisions are defined as decisions about appropriate teaching goals and the experiences to reach them. Instructional deci-

sions concern how to teach within some implicit or explicit curricular frame (Shaver, 1979, p. 21). As should become apparent, in practice curricular decisions and instructional decisions are interactive, rather than discrete entities.

Underlying how teachers tend the gate, whether consciously or not, are criteria drawn from what Beard (1934) called a "frame of reference":

Every human brought up in society inevitably has in mind a frame of social knowledge, ideas, and ideals—a more or less definite pattern of things deemed necessary, things deemed possible, and things deemed desirable; and to this frame or pattern, his thought and action will be more or less consciously referred. This frame may be large or small; it may embrace an immense store of knowledge or little knowledge; it may be well organized with respect to categories of social thought or confused and blurred in organization; and the ideal element in it may represent the highest or lowest aspirations of mankind. But frame there is in every human mind.... Since all things known cannot be placed before children in the school room, there must and will be, inevitably, a selection, and the selection will be made with reference to some frame of knowledge and values, more or less consciously established in the mind of the selector. (p. 182)

The term *frame of reference* is employed in this chapter; however, it should be noted that other researchers have employed terms that are similar in meaning, such as *personal perspective, personal theory, implicit theory,* and *personal knowledge* (see Clark & Yinger, 1979, pp. 251, 259; Connelly & Clandinin, 1988, p. 4; McCutcheon, 1981).

Three primary components of gatekeeping are considered in this chapter: (1) beliefs concerning the meaning of social studies, (2) decisions concerning planning, and (3) decisions

Reviewers were Edith Guyton, Georgia State University; William B. Stanley, University of Delaware; Suzanne M. Wilson, Michigan State University.

This chapter was written while the author was on the faculty of the University of Delaware, and he appreciates the support given him in the preparation of the manuscript.

concerning instructional strategy. Various other factors, sometimes ignored in discussions of curriculum and instruction, are also part of gatekeeping. For example, teachers make decisions about when to allow children to go out to recess, how to judge what students are learning, and how to accommodate to the culture of a particular school. Such decisions, as White (1985) has shown, influence curriculum and instruction, and they are considered in this chapter when relevant to the three primary components of gatekeeping just identified.

ORGANIZATION OF THIS CHAPTER

In this chapter, the aims are to (1) summarize the research literature relevant to gatekeeping, (2) identify themes in that literature, and (3) suggest directions for future research. The chapter is organized around the three primary components of gatekeeping. In practice, the three components are not discrete but interactive; however, they are treated separately in this chapter for purposes of discussion. The research studies reviewed were chosen on the basis of their relevance to gatekeeping. Although the term gatekeeping has seldom been used in the social studies literature, it provides an apt rubric for pulling together various studies on teachers' approaches to social studies curriculum and instruction.

Beyond what has been identified thus far, there are at least two other categories of research potentially relevant to gatekeeping. Clark and Peterson (1986), for instance, reviewed literature on teachers' "interactive thoughts and decisions," what teachers think and decide during instruction. In social studies, however, there are few studies of the thinking that teachers do during instruction. Therefore, interactive decision-making is included in a more general category, planning. Similarly, studies of curriculum implementation provide insights into how teachers make curricular–instructional decisions. The once-burgeoning interest in implementation of social studies curriculum (e.g., Hahn, 1977), however, has waned to such an extent that the editor of the last volume-length review of social studies research concluded that there were "not enough recent developments" to warrant separate consideration (Stanley, 1985b, p. 2). The few new implementation studies (e.g., Marsh, 1987) are cited herein where relevant.

Gatekeeping, of course, does not occur in a social vacuum. As several researchers have documented (e.g., Bruckerhoff, 1985; McNeil, 1986; White, 1985), the decisions that teachers make about curriculum and instruction in social studies are heavily influenced by contextual factors such as the school ethos. These factors have, however, generally been ignored in research on social studies teaching (Armento, 1986, p. 948). Because a basic assumption underlying this chapter is that knowledge is socially constructed—that is, dependent on and derived from social and historical contexts (Stanley, 1985b, p. 4)—every attempt is made to stress contextual influences on gatekeeping. At times, however, this is simply not possible, because such information was not provided in the reports. The reader is also referred to Section IV of this handbook on the "Contexts of Social Studies Education."

The research literature reviewed in this chapter comes from a variety of sources including published books and journal articles and less widely available conference papers. The major social studies research journal, *Theory and Research in Social Education,* was reviewed for the period since 1983, the termination point of the last volume-length review of research on social studies education (Stanley, 1985c). *Dissertation Abstracts International* was searched for the years 1973–1988.

TEACHER GATEKEEPING AND THE MEANING OF SOCIAL STUDIES

How teachers define social studies to a great extent determines what decisions they make about appropriate curriculum and instruction. The meaning of social studies, of course, is the object of continuing scholarly debate among researchers of social studies (Stanley, 1985a). They have paid much less attention, however, to teachers' beliefs about the meaning of social studies (Shaver, 1987, p. 114). Yet, as Shulman (1987) observed;

When we examine the quality of teaching, the idea of influencing the grounds or reasons for teachers' decisions places the emphasis precisely where it belongs: on the features of pedagogical reasoning that lead to or can be invoked to explain pedagogical actions. (p. 13)

How do teachers define social studies?

Two Large-Sample Studies

Case Studies in Science Education (CSSE) by Stake & Easley (1978) and *A Place Called School* by Goodlad (1984) are the two most comprehensive and nationally representative sources of empirical evidence on how teachers define social studies. (Readers are also referred to a useful summary of research on social studies curriculum and instruction edited by Morrissett, 1982). Summaries of the conclusions of those two studies relevant to this section are presented in turn.

Employing ethnographic methods, the *CSSE* researchers investigated 11 high schools and their feeder schools, ranging from urban to suburban to rural and located in diverse regions of the United States. Four findings from *CSSE* are especially relevant to how teachers define social studies. *First,* teachers usually equated the social studies curriculum with the content of the textbook. Moreover, they tended to treat the textbook as an authoritative source of knowledge. *Second,* teachers believed that factual information and basic reading and writing skills were the central knowledge goals for social studies. *Third,* teachers considered socialization to school, community, and national values more important goals than cognitive objectives. *Fourth,* teachers tended to conform to the norms of their communities and, reflecting those norms, did not appear concerned that they seldom dealt with controversial topics.

Goodlad (1984) reported the findings of a study of 38 schools, 1,350 teachers, and over 1,000 classrooms (pp. 18–21). Like those in *CSSE,* the schools selected were intended to represent urban, suburban, and rural settings in diverse regions of the United States. Many of the findings in the Goodlad report were not separated out by school subject. Nonetheless, some observations on social studies teaching and teachers were made.

Overall, Goodlad's findings supported the portrayal of gate-keeping in *CSSE*. *First,* teachers claimed that their goals for social studies included an array of complex thinking skills such as understanding relationships and drawing inferences and conclusions. The curricular priorities embodied in the tests teachers gave, however, revealed an emphasis on memorization of information (pp. 211–212). *Second,* teachers paid little attention to the role of the United States in an interdependent world. It seems, therefore, that social studies programs support an American-centered view of the world and concomitant values (pp. 212–213). *Third,* judging from the learning activities teachers employed, the abilities developed in social studies appear very similar to the listening, reading, and writing goals of language arts. In contrast, Goodlad reported a paucity of activities related to problem solving, achievement of group goals, and projects that one might expect in a social studies program (p. 213). *Fourth,* Goodlad reported that teachers and administrators seemed uncertain about the purposes of social studies programs: "There appears to be much less certainty [compared to English and mathematics] on the part of schools, particularly at the elementary level, about either the importance of the social studies subjects or what should be taught in them" (p. 210).

In sum, the characterization of social studies presented by Stake and Easley and by Goodlad suggests that the beliefs of teachers and administrators reflect uncertainty about appropriate social studies scope and sequence, as well as about the subject's status. Except for the transmission of mainstream, American values (see Barr, Barth, & Shermis, 1977), the views of the social studies curriculum propounded in the social studies literature do not seem much in evidence in the beliefs of teachers. Significantly, however, this characterization is mainly inferred from what curricular–instructional patterns reveal about what teachers apparently believe about social studies. In the remainder of this section of the chapter, discussion is centered on studies in which teachers' beliefs have been examined explicitly.

As Shaver and Berlak (1968) observed, beliefs are based on elements of teachers' frames of reference such as their conceptions of society, conceptions of the nature of subject matter, and conceptions of the nature of thinking (pp. 2–3). Two elements of teacher beliefs have been researched sufficiently to permit comment: teacher beliefs about subject matter and teacher beliefs about thinking. More is known about the former than the latter. Nevertheless, teacher beliefs in one area overlap with their beliefs in other areas. For example, the beliefs teachers hold about student thinking are related to their beliefs about socialization to school and societal norms. Consequently, although studies are classified under various headings in Tables 19–1—19–6, the classification scheme is inevitably somewhat arbitrary because many studies could be (and some are) included in more than one category.

Teacher Beliefs About Social Studies Subject Matter

At the elementary school level, the lack of consensus about social studies goals and status that Goodlad noted was supported by Goodman and Adler (1985). They reported that ele-mentary-level student teachers' beliefs about social studies curriculum were both idiosyncratic and largely unrelated to the expert views they had been exposed to in teacher education programs. As Goodman and Adler observed, given the uncertainty of many of the student teachers about the importance of social studies, their role as gatekeepers might lead to the lack of a substantive social studies program in the elementary school. For example, one student teacher summarized the experience of a number of others: "Well, in the afternoon, if we have some time to kill, we might show a filmstrip or movie on some social studies topic. We're supposed to teach it more often, but there are too many other things to do" (p. 7).

At the secondary level, social studies is a formal part of the course structure and not subject to exclusion on the basis of teachers' preferences. But even regularly scheduled courses are influenced by teachers' views of their purposes. Three studies of high school history teachers are illustrative. In one study (Thornton, 1985, 1988), three high school U.S. history teachers at the same school, using the same textbook, with comparable students had distinctly different views of the goals of teaching youngsters U.S. history. Evans (1988) also studied three high school U.S. history teachers. He found that the goals of each teacher were related to their life experiences, particularly their previous teachers and their home environments, resulting in different goals and pedagogy across teachers. Wilson and Wineburg (1988) observed that the four high school history teachers that they studied also had distinctly different views of appropriate subject-matter goals. The researchers attributed these different goals to the social studies subject (political science, anthropology, history, American studies) in which the teacher had majored. In all three studies, significantly for the purposes of this chapter, it was concluded that the teachers' beliefs about appropriate subject-matter largely shaped their curricular–instructional decision-making.

In sum, teachers' beliefs concerning social studies do influence what they plan to teach (the intended curriculum) and the curriculum that they actually provide in the classroom (the operational curriculum). It appears that most teachers have a great deal of freedom to define social studies as they see fit, although they might not exercise that freedom or even be aware of it.

Teacher Beliefs About Student Thinking in Social Studies

Most social studies teachers employ expository instruction frequently (Hertzberg, 1981, p. 168), which carries with it the implicit assumption that exposition makes contact with student thinking. In other words, teachers seem to assume that students learn mainly through teacher-led recitation and lecture. Although this assumed link between instruction and learning is a central feature of social studies instruction, few researchers have investigated tachers' beliefs about how students think.

McKee (1988) studied the responses of seven high school U.S. history teachers to the implementation of a critical-thinking skills program for which "critical thinking was defined as a dynamic process of questioning and reasoning, active inquiry as opposed to passive accumulation of knowledge" (p. 444). Al-

TABLE 19–1. Teacher Beliefs About Social Studies Subject Matter

Study	Methods	Selected Conclusions
Evans, 1988	Three high school (U.S. history) teachers. Interviews and observations.	1. Teachers hold very different conceptions of the meaning of history. 2. Teachers' conceptions influence content selection, emphasis, questions, and pedagogy.
Goodman & Adler, 1985	Sixteen elementary-level student teachers. Interviews and observations.	1. Official conceptions of social studies curriculum (as defined by scholars) have little to do with teachers' beliefs and actions in classroom. 2. Many factors contribute to teachers' conceptions, but it is unclear why some conceptions are more popular than others.
Thornton, 1985 (Summary of some major findings, Thornton, 1988)	Three 10th-grade social studies (U.S. history) teachers. Interviews and observations.	1. Teachers' conceptions of the purposes of U.S. history courses vary widely. 2. Teachers' conceptions are influenced by management considerations and contextual factors.
Wilson & Wineburg, 1988	Four beginning high school social studies (history) teachers. Interviews and observations.	1. Teachers' views of how to teach history changed as they gained experience in the classroom, but their conception of historical knowledge was much more resistant to change. 2. Teachers' conceptions of historical knowledge are heavily influenced by the social studies subject in which they were trained.

TABLE 19–2. Teacher Beliefs About Student Thinking in Social Studies

Study	Methods	Selected Conclusions
McKee, 1988	Seven 11th-grade social studies (U.S. history) teachers. Observations, interviews, documentation of meetings, analysis of materials.	1. Despite intentions of the developers of a new critical-thinking curriculum, teachers identified critical thinking as discrete skills. 2. Teachers presented consensus, "public" view of U.S. history, although "privately" they had a more skeptical view of knowledge. 3. Teachers believed that they were instructing for critical thinking. 4. Teachers modified the new curriculum to fit with existing classroom routines and student expectations.
Thornton & Wenger, 1989	Three 4th-grade teachers. Observations and interviews.	1. Teachers described ideal versions of how children learn geography, but this was usually distinct from their beliefs about what their students would actually learn. 2. Two of the teachers believed that the inculcation of facts and discrete skills provided a "framework" for higher-order thinking in later grades. 3. The remaining teacher believed that students learned best through activities of high cognitive complexity, but she usually emphasized students' learning of facts and discrete skills.

though privately the teachers believed that the study of U.S. history included raising questions and displaying skepticism, in the classroom their instruction remained dominated by the recall of facts. The teachers adapted the critical-thinking skills project to reduce ambiguity and risk and to conform to preexisting instructional arrangements and student beliefs about the kinds of thinking tasks normally encountered in social studies. The teachers insisted that critical thinking by the students first required the retention of information; little time was left for higher cognitive processes. Nonetheless, the teachers reported believing that they were teaching their students to think critically.

A contrast between what teachers privately believe about how students learn best and what can be accomplished in the daily grind of classrooms is also evident in another study (Thornton & Wenger, 1989). Three fourth-grade teachers described how students would ideally learn in social studies, particularly the kind of thinking tasks they would need to perform for their learning to be meaningful. For example, one teacher observed that students learned best when instruction was built around their interests. However, each of the teachers cited factors, such as shortage of instructional time and need to cover subject matter that students had to know for success in the next grade, as reasons why ideal learning strategies were not regularly employed. In contrast to their description of ideal learning environments, two of the teachers said that, in practice, their students learned to think effectively through the inculcation of facts and discrete skills. This subject matter provided, the teachers claimed, a "framework" or "foundation" for learning and, in the higher grades, the children would be ready for more cognitively complex learning activities.

The third teacher took a somewhat different view. She claimed that a facts-and-skills approach seldom resulted in engaging and meaningful learning. Although this teacher sometimes provided more cognitively complex learning activities for her students than did her two colleagues, she too, in practice, mostly did not adhere to her beliefs about meaningful learning. For example, she argued that there was insufficient instructional time available to emphasize more complex thinking tasks. Further, the evaluation procedures that she used frequently emphasized facts and discrete skills, rather than assessment of higher-order thinking.

Conclusions

The available research on teacher gatekeeping and the meaning of social studies obviously falls far short of being comprehensive. Nonetheless, the evidence leads consistently to the conclusion that social studies "experts" (social studies education professors, university-based subject-matter specialists, and curriculum developers) and teachers of social studies attribute quite different meanings to the subject. Although the curricular–instructional practices that teachers employ have been described in some depth, much less is known about their underlying beliefs about social studies. Because it appears beyond doubt that teachers' beliefs about the meaning of social studies strongly influence their curricular–instructional decision making, researchers should seek to explore fully how and why teachers come to define social studies as they do.

TEACHER GATEKEEPING AND THE PLANNING OF SOCIAL STUDIES

In the 1960s and early 1970s, curriculum reformers confidently proposed a New Social Studies. Subject-matter experts, educational psychologists, and social studies education specialists developed curriculum kits intended to promote inquiry or discovery teaching and learning. As several studies revealed (e.g., Gross, 1977; Shaver et al., 1980), however, most teachers did not use either the new materials or the innovative instructional strategies. The failure of the New Social Studies movement provided compelling evidence that the planning that makes a difference is not the materials and curriculum guides (official curriculum) developed by outside authorities but how teachers adapt those materials to their own purposes. As Ben-Peretz (1975) suggested, a curriculum is actually a series of "potentials" open to many possible interpretations and uses. The focus of this section of the chapter is on how teachers transform the official curriculum into the intended curriculum—what they plan to teach.

Teacher Conceptions of Planning Responsibilities

How teachers plan a social studies curriculum varies considerably from one teacher to the next (Peterson, Marx, & Clark, 1978; Smith, 1983). Nevertheless, it seems safe to conclude that all teachers have some image in mind of what they want to accomplish in the classroom, although this image may be altered during instruction.

Despite the central role of teachers in planning the intended curriculum, it appears that many teachers do not view themselves as key players in the determination of curriculum. Rather, they characterize their gatekeeping as pertaining to instruction. Curriculum decisions, many teachers believe, are made by outside authorities and school-district curriculum committees composed of teachers and supervisors. For example, White (1985) described a " 'can-do' mentality" among teachers, based on a 4-year ethnographic study of a White, working-class elementary school (White, 1980). The teachers believed that it was proper, appropriate, and even helpful for "experts" and administrative supervisors to redesign the curriculum about every 7 years to "help keep the teachers and this country up to date." Rather than having a personal investment in the designing of the new curriculum and in the specific academic content and substance of the units, the teachers' sense of worth was tied up in the notion that "the county can give me anything and I can teach it!" (p. 233).

Even when teachers are directly involved in curriculum planning, they may prefer not to be. One of the three high school teachers studied in an upper-middle-class community provides an example (Thornton, 1985). This veteran teacher said he enjoyed planning, but went on to note:

Well, actually it would be easier if someone handed me a curriculum and said here are the people the students have to know, here are the events and at the end said here are the values we would like you to push during the school year. That would be a lot easier, then all I would have to worry about is teaching. I've found it much easier to teach, than in deciding what to teach. That's the hard problem for me and you get very, very little, you don't get any guidance in this district, on that particular thing. There's no syllabus you have to follow. (p. 208).

Of the other two teachers, one used the official curriculum only insofar as it corresponded to his goals. He confidently planned his own curricular materials and instructional strategies. In contrast, the remaining teacher, new to the school, complained of the lack of guidance for curriculum decisions and closely adhered to the content of the textbook and to materials obtained from other teachers.

Cornett (1987), in an in-depth, naturalistic case study of one 12th-grade social studies teacher, found that the teacher believed that curriculum development "was a formal task imposed from the outside which was a distraction from the real task that should be attended to, teaching" (p. 222). The teacher contended "that she was expected to teach a particular content" although "she had the autonomy to decide how it should be presented and sequenced" (p. 223). Although she planned and implemented current events as a regularly scheduled activity in her classroom, the teacher did not consider this to be part of the curriculum.

TABLE 19–3. Teacher Conceptions of Planning Responsibilities

Study	Methods	Selected Conclusions
Brown, 1988	Twelve middle-school teachers (English, German, mathematics, science, social studies). Questionnaires, interviews, analysis of written plans, and think-aloud method.	1. Teachers operate as implementors and not curriculum planners. 2. Goals of planning varied according to the subject taught. For example, social studies teachers' planning was influenced by availability of audiovisual equipment.
Cornett, 1988	One 12th-grade social studies (problems of democracy) teacher. Interviews and observations.	1. Teacher believed she made decisions on instruction, rather than on curriculum. 2. Significant content beyond the textbook was designed by the teacher. 3. Parts of the curriculum (e.g., current events) teacher did not formally consider "curriculum."
Marsh, 1984	Twenty-two elementary-level teachers. Survey and interviews.	1. Most teachers were content to leave decisions on curricular materials to others, e.g., principals, librarians. 2. Teachers tended to rely on personal collections of curricular materials and standard items such as atlases and charts.
Thornton, 1985 (summary of some major findings, Thornton, 1988)	Three 10th grade social studies (U.S. history) teachers. Interviews and observations.	1. There was great variety across teachers regarding the extent to which they modified the official curriculum. 2. One teacher enjoyed the freedom of planning his own curriculum, whereas the other teachers wished for more guidance.
White, 1980 (summary of some major findings, White, 1985)	Twenty elementary-level teachers.[a] Ethnographic participant observation and interviews.	1. Teachers believed that outside experts designed the curriculum while they were concerned with instruction. 2. Teachers' sense of self-worth was connected to instructional, rather than to curricular expertise.

[a] J. J. White, personal communication, April 15, 1989.

Marsh (1984), employing case studies and questionnaires, investigated Australian public elementary school teachers' knowledge and use of social studies curricular materials. According to Marsh, few teachers were either knowledgeable about or much interested in the selection of new curricular materials. Rather, they were content to let others (such as principals and librarians) make those curriculum decisions for them.

Taken together, these four studies suggest that teachers distinguish between curriculum and instruction, and that they identify themselves with the latter and outside authorities with the former. Some researchers (e.g., Brown, 1988, p. 79) have argued that this distinction between curriculum and instruction means that teachers are "implementors" rather than "curriculum planners." This should not obscure, however, the fact that implementation is still an act of selection from some curriculum universe. Although teachers may claim as their own decisions about sequencing and learning activities, and not recognize these decisions as "curricular" it remains true that they are planning an intended curriculum.

Practicality and Socialization as Goals of Teacher Planning

Teachers' planning incorporates more than just subject matter (Shaver et al., 1980). Teachers plan with multiple, sometimes competing, goals in mind. Beyond subject matter, teach-

ers are greatly concerned with management and socialization (Cornbleth, Korth, & Dorow, 1983). Indeed, management and socialization may be *more* influential than subject matter: "The curriculum-in-use in each classroom appeared to be shaped less by courses of study than by institutionally sanctioned teacher beliefs and teacher–student interactions" (p. 20).

Convenience and adherence to established routines become part of the taken-for-granted culture of the school. In this scheme of things, teachers often identify the social studies curriculum as synonymous with the content of the textbook. Teachers view the routines as both practical and appropriate socialization for social studies instruction in higher grades. For example, Levstik (1989) reported the case of one fourth-grade teacher, new to the school, whose aspirations to reform the social studies curriculum met with stiff resistance from other teachers at the same grade level. These other teachers were set in their "text-and-workbook based" social studies program and saw no good reason to spend time and energy on a more process-oriented curriculum in an enrichment subject such as social studies. Through social ostracism and keeping back their students from components of the innovative program such as guest speakers, the other teachers coerced their new colleague into abandoning most of her innovations. Significantly, the students found the new program engaging, but, because it was not based on familiar "text-and-workbook" sources, they did not consider it to be social studies.

Levstik's account of subverting social studies reform appears to be an extreme case of gatekeeping. Many less extreme cases,

TABLE 19–4. Practicality and Socialization as Goals of Teacher Planning

Study	Methods	Selected Conclusions
Cornbleth, Korth, & Dorow, 1983	Nine middle-school teachers (English, science, social studies). Observations, log monitoring school office, informal interviews.	1. Operational curriculum was shaped more by institutionally sanctioned teacher beliefs and teacher–student interactions than by courses of study. 2. Classroom organizational rules were more explicit than substantive academic expectations.
Hyland, 1985	Four 8th-grade social studies teachers. Questionnaire, interviews, and observations.	1. Planning was heavily influenced by management considerations. 2. Teachers' beliefs about effective learning activities were not evident in their planning and teaching.
Levstik, 1989	One new 4th-grade teacher. Ethnographic participant observation and formal and informal interviews.	1. Other teachers resisted the new teacher's attempt to reform the curriculum. 2. Students also regarded the new curriculum as illegitimate but enjoyable.
McCutcheon, 1981	Twelve 1st- to 6th-grade teachers. Interviews, observations, and teacher collaboration.	1. Lessons were derived largely from textbooks. 2. Both formal (e.g., scheduling) and informal (e.g., interruptions) policies influenced planning. 3. Teachers seldom considered continuity of subject matter in planning.
Parker & Gehrke, 1986	Twelve elementary-level teachers (teaching social studies).[a] Stimulated-recall interviews about a social studies lesson.	1. Teachers' interactive decision-making is embedded in classroom activities that simultaneously concern subject matter and management. 2. Teachers are reluctant to abandon their original plans for a lesson during instruction.

[a]W. C. Parker, personal communication, September 27, 1988.

however, have also been reported. McCutcheon (1981), for instance, noted the strong influence of practicality and socialization on the planning of 12 elementary-level teachers. For example, the teachers planned for the likelihood that social studies would be interrupted periodically. The textbook, in whose authority the teachers trusted, provided the content for most of their lessons. The selection of content from the textbook, however, was guided by criteria such as the content's fit with available instructional time and its potential for being easily controlled by the teacher (p. 50). Central concerns for effective learning such as continuity of subject matter were not considered by 10 of the 12 teachers during their planning (p. 54). Similar planning priorities were described by Hyland (1985) in his study of four eighth-grade social studies teachers. Hyland concluded that classroom control and adherence to the textbook-as-authority were central concerns in the teachers' planning.

In addition to planning prior to instruction (preactive planning), teachers also modify old plans and conceive new ones during instruction (interactive planning). In a study of 12 elementary-level teachers, Parker and Gehrke (1986) concluded that the teachers' interactive decision making simultaneously concerned subject matter and management. Their preactive planning attempted to fit lessons into established classroom routines. During instruction, the teachers tried to adhere to their preactive plans unless they perceived that the lesson was going poorly. Changing preactive plans entailed risks such as time and content loss and student misbehavior that the teachers preferred to avoid.

Practicality and socialization appear to be central aims of the planning in which most teachers engage. This has major ramifications for curriculum-change proposals when one considers the emphasis that most reformers place on subject-matter objectives. Enmeshed in the daily grind of classrooms, teachers plan curricula that often owe as much to what they perceive as the realities of classrooms as to what subject-matter experts and social studies professors have identified as essential social studies content.

Teacher Planning and the Textbook

Few issues have created as much controversy among social studies educators as the content of textbooks (White, 1988). This interest is partly understandable, given the oft-reported dominance of textbooks in social studies instruction. Although it appears from some reports (e.g., Downey & Levstik, 1988; Stodolsky, 1988) that not *all* textbook-dominated curricula are the same and that not *all* social studies curricula are textbook-dominated—for example, curriculum kits, films, and small-group work are also used regularly in some classrooms—there are relatively few studies in which researchers have examined *how* and *why* teachers use textbooks to plan.

In the social studies literature, beyond practicality and socialization, two major explanations of how and why most teachers select content from textbooks (rather than some other source) have been advanced. First, although teachers often do not place much faith in social studies professors for guidance in curriculum and instruction (Shaver, et al., 1980), they do believe in the authority of the textbook. As McCutcheon (1981)

TABLE 19–5. Teacher Planning and the Textbook

Study	Methods	Selected Conclusions
Cornett, 1987	One 12th-grade social studies (problems of democracy) teacher. Interviews and observations.	1. Teachers' beliefs about appropriate goals guided planning. In practice, some goals were mutually contradictory. 2. Textbook units defined most curricular content.
Hyland, 1985	Four 8th-grade social studies teachers. Questionnaire, interviews and observations.	1. Teachers lacked substantive knowledge of content and looked to the textbook as the authority. 2. Poor knowledge of subject matter restricted content to the textbook, but this was not perceived by the teachers as a problem.
Lydecker, 1982	Twenty-one preservice and inservice teachers of grades 4,5,6. Survey and think-aloud during planning.	1. Teachers claimed values and processes as important goals, but these were not reflected in plans. 2. Teachers tended to rely on the textbook, even when planning units that did not require or directly relate to it.
Wilson & Wineburg, 1988	Four beginning high school social studies (history) teachers. Interviews and observations.	1. Teachers used textbook content in planning history lessons but modified the content according to their college majors (e.g., anthropology, political science, history). 2. Teachers who had not majored in history relied more on the textbook during planning.

noted, the teachers she studied uncritically accepted that textbooks would provide for continuity of subject matter. Cornett (1987) concluded that the teacher he studied seemed to regard coverage of the content of the textbook as a primary obligation. Although this teacher also regularly taught other content such as current events, she distinguished current events from the "curriculum," the content of the textbook. Similarly, Lydecker (1982) noted that the textbook had legitimacy in the eyes of teachers even when its content was largely irrelevant to their goals for a particular unit. Lydecker concluded that many teachers looked more to the textbook than to their personal goals. And, according to Marsh (1984), elementary-level teachers tend to rely on personal collections of readily available, standard materials such as atlases, rather than on resources that might have more potential for meeting goals such as inquiry (p. 240).

A second explanation for teacher reliance on textbooks seems, in recent years, to demand notice, given the growing attention to testing of teacher subject-matter knowledge: Teachers rely on the textbook because their subject-matter knowledge is inadequate. Although there is no consensus on what adequate teacher subject-matter knowledge is (Stanley, this volume), recent popular commentators such as E. D. Hirsch, Jr., in his *Cultural Literacy* (1987), have lambasted schools and, by implication, teachers for not including enough content, particularly factual content, in school programs. Nonetheless, there is very little persuasive evidence concerning what teachers know about social studies subject matter and how this knowledge influences their planning.

Hyland (1985), in his study of four eighth-grade teachers' planning and teaching of lessons about the Constitution, reported that they relied on the content of the textbook as their primary source of subject-matter understanding. According to Hyland, the teachers knew little about the historical events of the Constitutional period or about conflicting historical interpretations of those events. Unsurprisingly, their planning was highly derivative of the content of the textbook.

Wilson and Wineburg (1988) studied four novice teachers who had an undergraduate major in a social science, history, or a related field (political science, anthropology, American studies). However, each teacher had been assigned to teach history. Each teacher used a textbook that he or she interpreted according to criteria learned in the undergraduate major. The teacher trained in anthropology taught history with a strong anthropological slant, whereas the teacher trained in political science regarded history as facts about the past and had little appreciation of the role of interpretation in historical explanation. Both of these teachers placed little emphasis on central components of historical understanding such as causation. In contrast, the two teachers trained in the methods of history were better able to approach unfamiliar historical topics and plan appropriate lessons that included, for example, evaluation of conflicting interpretations of historical events (p. 535). Moreover, what Wilson and Wineburg referred to as the "disciplinary perspectives" that the teachers brought to history curriculum, particularly the ignorance of history of the two students who had majored in anthropology and political science, in large measure determined how much they relied on the textbook and what parts of the textbook they used (pp. 535–536).

In sum, there is ample evidence that teacher planning is often based on textbooks. As Marsh (1984) suggested concerning teachers' lack of interest in the selection of curricular materials, it may be that teachers do not question how or why they rely on textbooks. Nonetheless, there is surprisingly little direct evidence of how and why they decide to rely on textbooks and why they emphasize some parts of textbooks and not others. These questions, given the central role of textbooks in most social studies instruction, warrant more attention from researchers than they have received to date.

Conclusions

When teachers act as gatekeepers in the planning process, they transform some identified body of knowledge into curricu-

TABLE 19–6. Teachers' Choices of Instructional Strategies

Study	Methods	Selected Conclusions
McNeil, 1986	Thirteen (approximation) social studies teachers in 4 "typical American high schools." Ethnographic case studies.	1. Teachers exhibited a wide range of beliefs about appropriate curriculum and instruction. 2. Teaching was "defensive"; teachers' beliefs about appropriate instructional strategies and academic expectations of students were traded for student compliance with classroom rules. 3. Goals of teaching were contradicted by teaching styles.
Stodolsky, 1988	Fifth-grade classrooms, 19 social studies and 20 mathematics. Observations and data coding and analysis.	1. The ill-defined nature of social studies influenced teachers' decision making about it. 2. The same teachers arranged curricula and taught differently in social studies and mathematics. 3. How teachers used textbooks and the extent to which they used other materials varied within social studies. 4. Different kinds of instructional strategies elicited qualitatively different kinds of thinking from students.
Thornton, 1985 (Summary of some major findings, Thornton, 1988)	Three 10th-grade social studies (U.S. history) teachers. Interviews and observations.	1. How instruction was arranged varied greatly across teachers. 2. Textbook-based recitation in two classrooms differed in instructional effectiveness.
Wineburg & Wilson, in press	Two high school social studies (U.S. history) teachers. Interviews and observations.	1. Outstanding teaching may involve very different instructional arrangements from one teacher to another. 2. Seemingly traditional expository instruction can elicit high levels of student engagement.

lum and instructional strategies for some identified group of students. During this process, teachers may disregard beliefs about what social studies ideally should be in favor of what they believe can be accomplished with a particular group of students. Nevertheless, teachers tend to characterize their planning as concerning instruction, not curriculum. To many teachers, "curriculum" appears to be synonymous with a body of knowledge identified by "experts" and encapsulated in a textbook. In other words, many do not appear to be aware of, and may not be particularly interested in, the degree of control that their gatekeeping exercises over the curriculum they plan for their students. Rather, practicality and socialization to prevailing school norms are central features of what teachers consider when they plan. Although the guiding role of textbook content in instruction is well supported in many studies, it is less clear how and why teachers plan by the book.

TEACHER GATEKEEPING AND INSTRUCTIONAL STRATEGY

As has been discussed, social studies instruction traditionally has been dominated by textbook-based, large-group, teacher-controlled recitation and lecture (Goodlad, 1984; Hertzberg, 1981; Stake & Easley, 1978). McNeil (1986) argued that, rather than aberrations, practices such as the persistence of recitation and reliance on textbook-based knowledge are the logical outcomes of the organization of schools.

Based on ethnographies of social studies instruction in four "typical" (p. 19) American high schools, McNeil identified a wide range of curricular–instructional goals held by the various teachers. However, she found little variation in how they taught. McNeil characterized most of the teaching that she witnessed

as "defensive." Rather than actively engaging students in the meaning and significance of the subject matter, the teachers chose "to simplify content and reduce demands on students in return for classroom order and minimal student compliance on assignments" (p. 158). McNeil identified a number of techniques these teachers used to "control" knowledge in order to "control" students. For example, they fragmented information so that it was so disjointed as to be meaningless (p. 167). Further, the teachers assured student compliance during a lesson by promising that it would not be difficult and then presented the subject matter with the implicit expectation that students would not think deeply about it (pp. 174–175). Defensive teaching assured that subject matter was covered, but students seldom had the opportunity to think critically about knowledge. In effect, McNeil concluded, most teachers abandoned their often idealistic goals for instruction and adopted a contradictory instructional style that emphasized recitation of low-level knowledge (p. 157).

It should be apparent that McNeil's conclusions about the stifling effects of the culture of the school on creative and non–traditional teaching are more pointed than, but not inconsistent with, the findings of other studies already discussed (e.g., Levstik, 1989; Stake & Easley, 1978). Nonetheless, several recent studies have documented the existence of greater instructional variety than has been widely reported.

In a study of instruction in mathematics (20 teachers) and social studies (19 teachers) in fifth-grade classrooms in a variety of socioeconomic settings, Stodolsky (1988) found that the teachers played a larger gatekeeping role in an "enrichment," ill-defined subject like social studies than in a core subject like mathematics. This enhanced gatekeeping role in social studies frequently resulted in the same teachers employing markedly different instructional strategies in social studies and mathematics (p. 116). More important, however, Stodolsky noted that a great deal of social studies instruction diverged from the stereotypical textbook-based recitation and lecture: "Seatwork and recitation ... occurred in social studies, but group work, films and students reports were dominant formats in some classes" (p. 44). Moreover, in classes where instructional arrangements were less traditional, more complex intellectual goals such as higher mental processes and application were more common (p. 115). Stodolsky also observed that subject matter drawn from social sciences like anthropology and psychology tended to involve less teacher-dominated instruction than subject matter from "sequential subjects" such as history and geography (pp. 115–117).

Two case studies of high school U.S. history teachers also suggest that instruction may not be as uniform as has often been contended. In a study of three teachers in an upper-middle-class high school (Thornton, 1985, 1988), it was found that each had a distinctive view of the purposes of teaching adolescents U.S. history and that the resultant instructional arrangements also varied. Whereas one teacher seldom employed traditional expository teaching, it was also notable that the other more traditional teachers also varied in the degree of engagement their instruction elicited from their students.

The two teachers who employed more textbook-based, expository instructional strategies were more different than similar in instructional effectiveness. One teacher's instruction was frequently engaging: He related colorful historical anecdotes, used humor deftly, and supplemented classroom work with reading and writing assignments on topics such as the Black Sox scandal and Will Rogers that were intended to give students a feeling for life in the times being studied. Although this teacher did most of the intellectual processing of the subject matter for his students, his instruction was intellectually substantive and appealing to most of them. The other teacher also relied on recitation but was seldom able to elicit more than perfunctory participation from his students. Beyond student concern with what would be on the test, instruction in this class was generally repetitious and dull.

Research by Wineburg and Wilson (in press) also lends weight to the notion that frequent use of expository instructional strategies, often condemned in the social studies literature, may not necessarily be as dull and undemanding for students as has traditionally been assumed. The researchers studied two secondary-level teachers who shared a reputation in their districts for being excellent instructors. Both teachers, Wineburg and Wilson found, were indeed excellent instructors, much appreciated by their students. The researchers also found, however, that the two teachers were a study in contrasts: One hardly "taught" at all in the usual understanding of the term, preferring student-centered learning. The other, employing seemingly traditional teacher-centered techniques such as question-and-answer, was nonetheless very successful in engaging students. Upon analysis, however, this teacher was less traditional than a superficial view of his methods might suggest. His instruction was based on a wide variety of carefully organized learning activities, and, although he occupied center stage during discussion, his students were actively involved and challenged during lessons.

Conclusions

There seems to be little reason to doubt that teacher gatekeeping usually results in instruction that is textbook-based, teacher-dominated recitation and lecture. This type of instruction fits comfortably with the culture of most schools. Nevertheless, the traditional view of monolithic uniformity in social studies instruction is open to question in at least two ways. *First,* there seems to be at least the possibility that more variety exists in instructional strategies than has previously been reported. *Second,* and more important, it appears that recitation and lecture vary considerably in their educational effectiveness from one teacher to the next, and, therefore, it cannot be assumed that recitation and lecture, even when used regularly, necessarily result in student disengagement.

CONCLUSIONS

Gatekeeping is based on the idea of teacher agency. As researchers have increasingly found (e.g., Marsh, 1987), even careful implementation efforts do not circumvent gatekeeping. Parker (1987) noted in a recent review:

The claim that "teachers make a difference" does [not] mean that teachers make or break a development/implementation process and, consequently, must receive proper inservice training so that they make it rather than break it. This is the discourse of the teacher-as-curriculum conduit. Rather, the same claim, "teachers make a difference," is resituated in a prior question that regards teachers as curriculum agents, or inquirers-in-practice, whose practice, far from conduction, is intellectual, moral, and inventive. (p. 7)

The centrality of gatekeeping in social studies curriculum and instruction raises three issues for researchers and leaders in the field. *First,* although caution should be exercised so as not to overgeneralize from small samples, case study research appears to be a particularly rich source for understanding gatekeeping. Shaver et al. (1980) also noted that case studies provided "a strong[er] feeling of reality" than surveys and observational instruments (p. 14). As researchers such as Wineburg and Wilson (in press) have shown, merely knowing that instruction is teacher dominated provides an insufficient basis for concluding that instruction is not educationally propitious in a particular setting. Moreover, case studies are often revealing of the ecological character of gatekeeping. As Hertzberg (1981) noted, because social studies reformers have so often ignored school and classroom realities—the ecological system within which gatekeeping occurs—reforms have seldom penetrated to the classroom level.

Second, the education of teachers as gatekeepers should be considered a primary mission of teacher education. As has been discussed, gatekeeping decisions are frequently made by teachers on the basis of convention or even unconsciously. Teachers need to be made aware of both the inevitability and the importance of their gatekeeping. As early as the late 1960s Shaver and Berlak (1968) spoke to this issue when they discussed the importance of rationale building: To the extent that teachers move from nonspecified, nonexplicated frames of reference to the careful consideration of their beliefs and the implications for curriculum and instruction, they are developing rationales for what they do. Rationale building, it would appear, is not a nice extra but a fundamental condition for curricular–instructional improvement in social studies.

Third, it may be useful to identify outstanding cases of gatekeeping that could serve as images of the possible. Shulman (1983) has pointed out the advantages of studying images of the possible:

The well-crafted case instantiates the possible, not only documenting that it can be done but also laying out at least one detailed example of how it was organized, developed, and pursued. For the practitioner concerned with process, the operational detail of case studies can be more helpful than the more confidently generalizable virtue of quantitative analysis in many cases. (p. 495)

Although there is a great deal of scholarly debate about what social studies curriculum and instruction should be, there exist few well-crafted case studies of exemplary practices. This is not to say that theorists and researchers should be merely content with the status quo. Clearly, concerns raised by feminist theorists (e.g., Noddings, 1988) and critical theorists (e.g., Kickbusch, 1985), for example, have underscored areas often neglected in the social studies literature. However, it does appear that, in many instances, the problems of gatekeeping are well known, and it would be more informative to understand under what conditions and in what ways exemplary social studies curriculum and instruction thrive. Newmann's (1990) research on the conditions for the teaching of thinking is instructive in that regard.

Finally, this chapter is not intended as a further condemnation of teachers' gatekeeping. Although it must be recognized that much about teachers' gatekeeping surely contributes little to social studies goals, generations of criticism have done little to effect change. Rather, in this chapter, an underlying aim has been to suggest that most conceptualizations of implementation of social studies curricula have been insufficiently broad. Until social studies researchers account for teachers' gatekeeping, as well as experts' views, and how those two perspectives interact and to what educational effects, the lofty purposes propounded in social studies curricular guides will likely remain aspiration, rather than practice.

References

Armento, B. J. (1986). Research on teaching social studies. In M. C. Wittrock (Ed.), *Handbook of research on teaching* (3rd ed., pp. 942–951). New York: Macmillan.

Barr, R. D., Barth, J. L., & Shermis, S. S. (1977). *Defining the social studies.* Arlington, VA: National Council for the Social Studies.

Beard, C. A. (1934). *The nature of the social sciences in relation to objectives of instruction.* New York: Charles Scribner's Sons.

Ben-Peretz, M. (1975). *The concept of curriculum potential. Curriculum Theory Network, 5,* 151–159.

Brown, D. S. (1988). Twelve middle-school teachers' planning. *Elementary School Journal, 89,* 69–87.

Bruckerhoff, C. (1985). *Teachers at work: A case study of collegial behavior in a high school.* Paper presented at the meeting of the American Educational Research, Chicago. (Eric Document Reproduction Service No. ED 263 043)

Clark, C. M., & Peterson, P. L. (1986). Teachers' thought processes. In M. C. Wittrock (Ed.), *Handbook of research on teaching* (3rd ed., pp. 255–296). New York: Macmillan.

Clark, C. M., & Yinger, R. J. (1979). Teachers' thinking. In P. L. Peterson & H. J. Walberg (Eds.), *Research on teaching* (pp. 231–263). Berkeley, CA: McCutchan.

Connelly, F. M., & Clandinin, D. J. (1988). *Teachers as curriculum planners: Narratives of experience.* New York: Teachers College Press, and Toronto: OISE Press/The Ontario Institute for Studies in Education.

Cornbleth, C., Korth, W., & Dorow, E. B. (1983). *Creating the curriculum: Beginning the year in a middle school.* Paper presented at the annual meeting of the American Educational Research Association, Montreal. (ERIC Document Reproduction Service No. ED 232 948)

Cornett, J. W. (1987). *Teacher personal practical theories and their influence upon teacher curricular and instructional actions: A case study of a secondary social studies teacher.* Unpublished doctoral dissertation, Ohio State University.

Downey, M. T., & Levstik, L. S. (1988). Teaching and learning history: The research base. *Social Education, 52,* 336–342.

Evans, R. W. (1988). Lessons from history: Teacher and student conceptions of the meaning of history. *Theory and Research in Social Education, 16,* 203–225.

Goodlad, J. (1984). *A place called school.* New York: McGraw-Hill.

Goodman, J., & Adler, S. (1985). Becoming an elementary social studies teacher: A study of perspectives. *Theory and Research in Social Education, 13*(2), 1–20.

Gross, R. E. (1977). The status of the social studies in the public schools of the United States: Facts and impressions of a national survey. *Social Education, 41,* 194–200, 205.

Hahn, C. L. (1977). Research on the diffusion of social studies innovations. In F. P. Hunkins (Ed.), *Review of research in social studies education: 1970–1975* (pp. 137–177). Washington, DC: National Council for the Social Studies, and Boulder, CO: ERIC Clearinghouse for Social Studies/Social Science Education and Social Science Education Consortium.

Hertzberg, H. W. (1981). *Social studies reform: 1880–1980.* Boulder, CO: Social Science Education Consortium.

Hirsch, E. D., Jr. (1987). *Cultural literacy: What every American needs to know.* Boston: Houghton Mifflin.

Hyland, J. T. (1985). *Teaching about the constitution: Relationships between teachers' subject matter knowledge, pedagogic beliefs, and instructional decision making regarding selection of content, materials and activities.* Unpublished doctoral dissertation, University of California, Los Angeles.

Kickbusch, K. W. (1985). Ideological innocence and dialogue: A critical perspective on discourse in the social studies. *Theory and Research in Social Education, 13*(3), 45–56.

Levstik, L. S. (1989). *Subverting reform in the social studies: A fourth grade case study.* Paper presented at the annual meeting of the American Educational Research Association, San Francisco.

Lydecker, A. M. R. (1982). *Teacher planning of social studies instructional units: Relationships with selected variables.* Unpublished doctoral dissertation, University of Michigan.

Marsh, C. J. (1984). Teachers' knowledge of and use of social studies curriculum materials in public elementary schools. *Journal of Educational Research, 77,* 237–243.

Marsh, C. J. (1987). Implementation of a social studies curriculum in an Australian elementary school. *Elementary School Journal, 87,* 475–486.

McCutcheon, G. (1981). Elementary school teachers' planning for social studies and other subjects. *Theory and Research in Social Education, 9*(1), 45–66.

McKee, S. J. (1988). Impediments to implementing critical thinking. *Social Education, 52,* 444–446.

McNeil, L. M. (1986). *Contradictions of control: School structure and school knowledge.* New York: Routledge and Kegan Paul.

Morrissett, I. (Ed.) (1982). *Social studies in the 1980s: A report of Project SPAN.* Alexandria, VA: Association for Supervision and Curriculum Development.

Newmann, F. M. (1990). Higher order thinking in teaching social studies: A rationale for the assessment of classroom thoughtfulness. *Journal of Curriculum Studies, 22,* 41–56.

Noddings, N. (1988). An ethic of caring and its implications for instructional arrangements. *American Journal of Education, 96,* 215–230.

Parker, W. C. (1987). Teachers' mediation in social studies. *Theory and Research in Social Education, 15,* 1–22.

Parker, W. C., & Gehrke, N. J. (1986). Learning activities and teachers' decision making: Some grounded hypotheses. *American Educational Research Journal, 23,* 227–242.

Peterson, P. L., Marx, R. W., & Clark, C. M. (1978). Teacher planning, teacher behavior, and student achievement. *American Educational Research Journal, 15,* 417–432.

Shaver, J. P. (1979). The usefulness of educational research in curricular/instructional decision-making in social studies. *Theory and Research in Social Education, 7*(3), 21–46.

Shaver, J. P. (1987). Implications from research: What should be taught in social studies? In V. Richardson-Koehler (Ed.), *Educators' handbook: A research perspective* (pp. 112–138). New York: Longman.

Shaver, J. P., & Berlak, H. (1968). Curriculum decisions in the social studies. In J. P. Shaver & H. Berlak (Eds.), *Democracy, pluralism, and the social studies* (pp. 1–10). Boston: Houghton Mifflin.

Shaver, J. P., Davis, O. L., Jr., & Helburn, S. W. (1980). An interpretive report on the status of precollege social studies education based on three NSF-funded studies. In *What are the needs in precollege science, mathematics, and social science education? Views from the field.* Washington, DC: National Science Foundation.

Shulman, L. S. (1983). Autonomy and obligation: The remote control of teaching. In L. S. Shulman & G. Sykes (Eds.), *Handbook of teaching and policy* (pp. 484–504). New York: Longman.

Shulman, L. S. (1987). Knowledge and teaching: Foundation of the new reform. *Harvard Educational Review, 57,* 1–22.

Smith, B. D. (1983). Instructional planning: Attitudes, decisions, and preparation time among secondary social studies teachers. *Journal of Social Studies Research, 7*(1), 1–22.

Stake, R. E., & Easley, J. A., Jr. (1978). *Case studies in science education: Vol. II. Design, overview, and findings.* Urbana, IL: University of Illinois, Center for Instructional Research and Curriculum Evaluation.

Stanley, W. B. (1985a). Recent research in the foundations of social education: 1976–1983. In W. B. Stanley (Ed.), *Review of research in social studies education: 1976–1983* (pp. 309–399). Washington, DC: National Council for the Social Studies.

Stanley, W. B. (1985b). Research in social education: Issues and approaches. In W. B. Stanley (Ed.), *Review of research in social studies education: 1976–1983* (pp. 1–9). Washington, DC: National Council for the Social Studies.

Stanley, W. B. (Ed.). (1985c). *Review of research in social studies education: 1976–1983.* Washington, DC: National Council for the Social Studies.

Stodolsky, S. S. (1988). *The subject matters: Classroom activity in math and social studies.* Chicago: University of Chicago Press.

Thornton, S. J. (1985). *Curriculum consonance in United States history classrooms.* Unpublished doctoral dissertation, Stanford University.

Thornton, S. J. (1988). Curriculum consonance in United States history classrooms. *Journal of Curriculum and Supervision, 3,* 308–320.

Thornton, S. J, & Wenger, R. N. (1989). *Geography in elementary social studies classrooms.* Paper presented at the meeting of the American Educational Research Association, San Francisco.

White, J. J. (1980). *An ethnographic study of the construction of knowledge about different cultures in an elementary school.* Unpublished doctoral dissertation, University of Pennsylvania.

White J. J. (1985). What works for teachers: A review of ethnographic research studies as they inform issues of social studies curriculum and instruction. In W. B. Stanley (Ed.), *Review of research in social studies education, 1976–1983* (pp. 215–307). Washington, DC: National Council for the Social Studies, and Boulder CO: ERIC Clearinghouse for Social Studies/Social Science Education and Social Science Education Consortium.

White, J. J. (1988). Searching for substantial knowledge in social studies texts. *Theory and Research in Social Education, 16,* 115–140.

Wilson, S. M., & Wineburg, S. S. (1988). Peering at history from different lenses: The role of disciplinary perspectives in the teaching of American history. *Teachers College Record, 89,* 525–539.

Wineburg, S. S., & Wilson, S. M. (in press). Subject matter knowledge in the teaching of history. In. J. E. Brophy (Ed.), *Advances in research on teaching.* Greenwich, CT: JAI Press.

·20·

TEACHER COMPETENCE FOR SOCIAL STUDIES

William B. Stanley

UNIVERSITY OF DELAWARE

In this chapter, the major conceptions of competence that have oriented educational research or research on teaching over the past two decades are explored to assess their strengths, weaknesses, and relevance to social studies education. Three major approaches to this research have evolved. The first approach has been derived from the teacher effectiveness or process-product research which has dominated education for almost 20 years. A second approach is a reaction against the process-product approach in which the teacher's knowledge of content and context is emphasized. Finally, there is a critical approach to teacher competence which is a rejection of many of the assumptions and guidelines prescribed by the other two mainstream approaches. The critical approach is the most difficult to describe because it is composed of various positions that are not well integrated and even conflict on some points.

The reader should bear in mind that these approaches are used as heuristics for the purpose of analysis and discussion. They are not proposed as definitive or discrete categories. Nevertheless, they do refer to important tendencies regarding the ways in which teacher competence is defined. The position taken here is that in the move from the teacher effectiveness approach to the teacher content-knowledge approach and, finally, to the critical approach to competence, social studies is successively taken more seriously as an area of curriculum with unique attributes and goals. After an examination of each approach, the general implications for social educators are indicated along with areas where further research is needed.

COMPETENCE BASED ON TEACHER EFFECTIVENESS RESEARCH

The process-product or teacher effectiveness approach to research on teaching gradually became dominant during the 1970s. There are numerous reviews of earlier approaches based on teacher characteristics, psychological theories, or models of instruction not discussed in this chapter (e.g., Doyle, 1979, 1984, 1985; Dunkin & Biddle, 1974; Hunkins, 1977). Very little of the teacher effectiveness research has involved the social studies, but in this chapter an attempt is made to indicate how it has been applied by some social studies educators.

The goal of the teacher effectiveness researchers is to assess the impact of various kinds of teacher behavior (processes) on specific outcomes (products) that can be measured objectively, usually by achievement tests in reading or math. The characteristic behaviors of those teachers whose classes' mean scores are significantly higher (statistically) are used as the model for teacher competence. This is based on the assumption that these teacher behaviors are reliably correlated with higher student achievement. The reader can consult several excellent reviews of this teacher effectiveness research (see Brophy, 1973; Brophy & Good, 1986; Good, 1983; Rosenshine, 1983) for more detailed analyses of the research methodology.

A generic notion of the effective teacher has emerged from the teacher effectiveness research base (Brophy, 1987). Effective teachers tend to be goal directed and have a "businesslike and task-oriented" personality. They expect their students to master the specific instructional objectives prescribed by the curriculum and spend most classroom time on academic activities. Classroom management is carefully planned, and basic rules and expectations are made clear to students. Student behavior is continually observed and misbehavior corrected before it becomes a serious problem. Student learning is briskly paced with smooth transitions from one topic or activity to another. Effective teachers continuously monitor student progress and give students adequate, timely feedback regarding their performance. Instruction is broken into small steps that students can master with a high rate of success. Given the empha-

Reviewers were Wilma Longstreet, University of New Orleans; Stephen J. Thornton, University of Delaware; James A. (Tony) Whitson, Louisiana State University.

sis on direct instruction, relatively little time is spent on unsupervised small-group instruction or seatwork.

Effective teachers are enthusiastic. They also structure content to enable students to understand it as an "integrated whole." This includes the use of "advance organizers, outlining, signaling of transitions, calling attention to main ideas, and summarizing" (Brophy 1987, p. 3). Effective teachers state questions clearly and frame them at appropriate levels to facilitate student success. Adequate wait time and clear, relevant feedback to student responses are essential. Effective teachers also prompt more and better responses and incorporate student responses into the lesson. Their assignments involve experiences that are challenging and meaningful but easy enough to ensure a high rate of success. Effective teachers prepare students for homework or follow-up assignments by reviewing necessary material and providing adequate time for practice.

A recent review by McKenzie (1986) provides an example of how teacher effectiveness research has been interpreted by some social studies educators. McKenzie accepted the importance of dealing with complex problems in the social studies but argued that teachers must first "identify and teach the information the children need as background evidence, models, or premises" (p. 122). He recommended the use of clear goals, telling students the lesson objectives, providing assignments that ensure a high level of student success, trying to relate lessons to prior student knowledge, and focusing student attention by the use of questions and/or quizes (p. 124). He did acknowledge that the results of teacher effectiveness research findings must be qualified in application to social studies. For example, the guidelines seem most appropriate for teaching basic skills and knowledge to students from lower socioeconomic backgrounds and less so for teaching more complex knowledge to middle-class students. But even for complex knowledge, McKenzie advised a step-by-step approach to instruction guided by specific objectives. As a case in point, he recommended using the concept-teaching strategies proposed by Markle (1975) and Tennyson and Park (1980).

According to McKenzie (1986), because learning often moves from the acquisition of prerequisite bits of low-level information to more complex learning, the social studies teacher can take complex knowledge and break it into smaller bits of basic knowledge to teach. Once acquired, these bits can serve as the basis for learning more complex knowledge. In this sense, argued McKenzie, social studies is a fundamental source of "basic" knowledge in the curriculum, because it can provide the information that is required for making sense of complex life experiences or problems. Indeed, such knowledge is even a basic prerequisite to the acquisition of so-called "basic skills" (pp. 120–122).

McKenzie (1986) noted how the oral questioning of individual students might increase off-task behavior, but the use of "test-like events" where *all* students must answer without consulting sources, can help maintain attention (p. 129). He also suggested that the effectiveness of higher-level questions is not well supported by teacher effectiveness studies, probably because students need sufficient prior knowledge before they can give adequate responses to higher-level questions. Thus lower-

level questions might be as effective or better than higher-level questions (p. 130). McKenzie suggested that a basic, systematic approach to social studies teaching might be a more effective way to develop student problem-solving skills than a direct focus on problem solving, although he acknowledged that more research is required to determine if this hypothesis is warranted (p. 130). Much of the same generic teacher effectiveness research is also favorably cited in research reviews by Armento and Flores (1986) and Jantz and Klawitter (1986).

The area of concept instruction has also generated a great deal of research (e.g., Merrill & Tennyson, 1977; Park, 1984; Tennyson, Chao, & Younger, 1981; Tennyson & Park, 1980) that has had a significant influence on social studies education research and the strategies proposed in methods textbooks (Ford & McKinney, 1986; Gilmore & McKinney, 1986; McKinney, Larkins, Burts, & Davis, 1982; McKinney, Larkins, Ford, & Davis, 1983; Stanley, 1984; Yoho, 1986). Although this research is not usually mentioned in the surveys of teacher effectiveness research reviewed for this chapter, it has many similarities—for example, breaking learning down into specific bits, the use of specific instructional objectives, step-by-step lesson procedures, teacher-directed or active instruction, careful monitoring of student progress, and adequate time for guided practice.

Critical Reaction to the Teacher Effectiveness Approach

Teacher effectiveness research has had a strong influence on the back-to-basics movement as well as on various teacher accountability and competency-based teacher education programs, but it has also received a wide range of criticism. Teacher effectiveness research is rooted in a psychological tradition based on the assumption that complex human behavior in specific situations can be understood in terms of certain generic processes. Consequently, the aim of this research is to identify general teacher behaviors correlated with student achievement as measured by standardized tests (Shulman 1987a, p. 6). However, many important aspects of teaching, including subject matter knowledge, classroom context, student physical and psychological characteristics, or other things not easily measured by standardized tests, are generally ignored (p. 6). In many instances, the differences in teacher effectiveness would be better described as "tendencies or trends rather than sharp dichotomies" (Doyle, 1985, p. 31). Furthermore, it is often the case that teachers who use methods quite different from the teacher effectiveness model have high student achievement (Good, 1983, pp. 137–138; White, 1985, pp. 284–285). In other words, teachers can be very effective (in terms of the effectiveness definition of *effectiveness*) in a wide variety of ways.

In the main, teacher effectiveness research has been conducted with disadvantaged elementary students learning basic language or mathematical knowledge and skills (Doyle, 1985, p. 31). Furthermore, the bulk of the teacher effectiveness studies were not designed to address teacher evaluation or the process of teacher selection. The main concern was to provide a body of knowledge to better inform the process of teacher education. Such important limitations are usually ignored in the rush to apply recent research results (Darling-Hammond, Wise, & Pease, 1983).

Given these qualified results, it is quite likely that using teacher effectiveness findings to guide teacher selection will result in both the exclusion of some excellent teachers and the hiring of some false-positives, who fit the profile but are not effective in practice (Doyle, 1985, p. 31). Another critical point is that relatively small variations in the classroom performance of students cannot be explained solely by variations in teacher competence (p. 32). While teachers can make a difference in student learning, many other factors play a role. Thus, the results of effectiveness studies should be used to help guide and inform practice but not to prescribe a model appropriate to all, or even most, situations. For Doyle, effective teaching involves more than modeling a master teacher profile. It should be conceived instead as "the constructive adaptation of social and curriculum structures to specific contexts" (p. 32). At present, therefore, competence cannot and should not be reduced to a set of specific behavior indicators.

Ornstein (1985) has expanded on the concerns raised by Doyle. Noting the general failure to agree on what the measures of teaching outcomes should be, he argued that until this dispute is resolved there can be no adequate definition of teacher effectiveness (p. 399). In terms of methodology, in almost all of the teacher effectiveness studies, students' mean gains or mean residual gains were used as the dependent variable. Since individual scores are generally ignored, the relation of teacher effectiveness to student variation remains open. Also, most of this research has been focused solely on the teacher; student differences as an independent variable influencing teacher behavior have been ignored. There is, in addition, considerable confusion regarding the meaning of the variables used to define and assess teacher effectiveness, and some variables—such as democratic personalities, attitudes, or behaviors—are constructs that cannot be defined in a precise, operational way. However, should researchers or educators insist on reducing such "terms to precise, agreed upon, quantifiable constructs, the number of terms would increase to the point of trivia and the importance of each would be reduced to the specific study" (p. 400).

Ornstein (1985) also argued that teacher effects are often nearly indistinguishable from those of parents, peers, and others. Given these other influences, not only is it difficult to explain short-term effects, it is virtually impossible to control or explain long-term teacher effects on students. This process is further complicated because learning tends to come in irregular increments that vary according to "season, age, grade level, and subject" (p. 400). These factors might often be more important than teacher effectiveness in a given situation. In other words, some teachers might be penalized because their students' intellectual abilities are developing more slowly, whereas other teachers might be advantaged by reverse circumstances. Furthermore, we need to recall that a student's previous learning accounts for 60 to 80% of learning variation during a given school year. In short, the relevance of this research program is more limited than the effectiveness rhetoric seems to suggest.

Finally, the teacher effectiveness studies are prone to all of the limitations inherent in the human sciences. The complexity and interactive nature of human behavior and its causes make its study extremely difficult because the behaviors and outcomes studied cannot be defined or isolated as stable constructs without some distortion (Ornstein 1985, p. 400). It is always possible that the reductive behavior identified in a study does not really represent causal behavior. For instance, some studies, such as those conducted by Flanders, have indicated that indirect instruction has a significant positive impact on student's behavior and performance. But, it remains unclear in which direction causality runs. Is it really that teachers adapt to the behavior of students, causing them to teach in more or less directive ways (p. 401)? Detailed ethnographic studies may be required to determine what is really happening in direct and indirect instruction. But the results of such research would represent a different knowledge claim, one not congruent with the generalizability claims of teacher effectiveness studies.

Armento (1986), in a recent review of social studies research, also raised questions about the teacher effectiveness studies and their application to social education. Given the controversy over competing approaches or rationales for social studies education, Armento found it surprising that so little research has been conducted to assess the effectiveness of programs or teaching grounded in these different orientations. Furthermore, given the tendency to reduce teacher behavior and student performance in such studies to isolated, specific behaviors, little is actually known about how various individual instructional techniques relate to more comprehensive approaches to instruction. For example, studies of how teachers use questions are typically conducted apart from more general strategies for discussion or inquiry. In the case of student performance, the focus is normally on acquisition of either facts and concepts or specific thinking skills. This focus on isolated teacher and student behaviors promotes a narrow view of instruction, knowledge, and understanding that ignores the interrelationships among forms of knowledge and the social and affective dimensions of teaching (p. 944).

According to Armento (1986), students simply do not seem to respond in any uniform way to the techniques derived from teacher effectiveness studies. The kinds of teacher questions used, for instance, vary in effectiveness depending on the subject, the type of student, and prior student knowledge. It might be that the type of question used is only effective if it prompts the learner to think about ideas in ways he or she might not have done otherwise (p. 945). Following this line of thought, competent teachers would shift from an exclusive focus on generic techniques to an attempt to find better ways to help students to construct social meaning (p. 946). Such an attempt might include identifying how the ability to reorganize and reconstruct prior knowledge affects students' learning of new knowledge, their capacity to construct knowledge hierarchies and relationships, and their acquisition of skills required to analyze social issues.

Teacher effectiveness researchers have been sensitive to (and often anticipated) the charges of their critics. As Porter and Brophy (1988) argued, there has been a shift away from prescriptions of behavior to a search for principles to help develop teacher effectiveness. From this view, teachers are seen as "semi-autonomous professionals who negotiate and mediate among complex and sometimes contradictory task demands as they pursue goals of excellence and equity" (p. 74).

As Good (1983) has argued, the results of the empirical research do not yield rules for producing student achievement, because the requirements can vary from classroom to classroom. Indeed, following simple rules might do more harm than good. In other words, we should *not* attempt to give teachers a prescribed list of behaviors to perform routinely (p. 136). Although Good believes that there is considerable evidence to support the effectiveness of what he called "active teaching," this should be understood as a way of thinking about teaching rather than as a set of behavioral guidelines (p. 138). In teacher education, the findings of effectiveness research should be disseminated, but with careful qualification. Teachers must come to see that learning is problematic because of the variability among classroom contexts and different students (p. 142).

Along the same lines, Rosenshine (1986), making a point relevant to social studies educators, acknowledged that teacher effectiveness research has relatively little to say regarding how to teach students to understand complex textual knowledge, such as the critical interpretations presented in a lesson on the *Federalist Papers*. Thus, while effectiveness research can and should inform practice, it does not hold the solution to most educational problems (p. 142). Similar points have been made by Coker, Medley, and Soar (1980), Brophy and Good (1986), and Rosenshine and Stevens (1986). Undoubtedly, many of the teacher effectiveness researchers themselves would have been appalled by the simplistic application of their findings to teacher education programs, teachers evaluation, and the selection of new teachers. Unfortunately, such simplistic application is often the approach taken in state and local programs.

COMPETENCE RELATED TO TEACHER KNOWLEDGE OF SUBJECT MATTER

A rather different conception of teacher competence is proposed by those who focus on the specific subject-matter knowledge an expert teacher should possess. Proponents of the knowledge-of-subject-matter approach to competence do not deny the importance of teacher effectiveness research but argue that it is too limited to provide an adequate basis for defining teacher competence (e.g., Amarel & Chittenden, 1982; Clandinin, 1985; Leinhardt & Smith, 1985; Shulman, 1987a, 1987b; Wilson, Shulman, & Richert, 1987; Wilson & Wineburg, 1988; Wineburg & Wilson, in press). A more adequate conception of competence must include knowledge of how different content and classroom contexts influence effective teaching. In practice, different content areas can require different approaches to instruction. Content differences refer to those among disciplines (e.g., English, history, math, science) and those within disciplines (e.g., subtopics like grammar or literature as well as different schools of thought or approaches to research). Put another way, an individual teacher is not trying to teach

generically but toward some specific outcome, such as a student's understanding of the causes and effects of the Battle of Lexington and how this knowledge might relate to some present-day situation (Wilson et al., 1987).

The emerging research base used to support the view of competence based on a teacher's knowledge of subject matter is in general different from the more "objective" classroom studies and quasi-experimental methodologies employed by teacher effectiveness researchers. For the most part, those investigating how a teacher's content knowledge affects his or her performance employ ethnographic methodologies. These include long-term classroom observations during which the researchers take detailed field notes (and often video tapes) of the teacher and student behavior. In addition, teachers are interviewed to determine their background knowledge, how they view their disciplines, and how they approach instruction. Such methods lead to rich, thick descriptions of instruction that yield insights into how subject matter knowledge relates to teacher competence in various classroom contexts.

The results of research regarding how school subjects in general (and social studies in particular) have been taught have been remarkably stable for the past 25 years and, in many respects, throughout this century (e.g., Baxter, Ferrell, & Wiltz, 1964; Cuban, 1984; Goodlad, 1984; Shaver, Davis, & Helburn, 1979; Thornton, 1988; Wiley & Race, 1977). For this reason, some researchers interested in the relation of teacher content knowledge to competence have questioned what remains to be gained by studying representative or typical classrooms and have shifted their research focus to extraordinary or expert social studies teachers in an attempt to describe what levels of teacher competence are possible and how these are achieved (e.g., Shulman, 1987a; Wineburg & Wilson, in press). The teaching profession is unique in that most of the record of excellent practice is lost to others because most instruction takes place without peer observation. What is worse, expert teachers appear to have a knowledge base they are largely unable to articulate. In short, the teaching field lacks a comprehensive history of practice. Identification of the wisdom of practice revealed in the behavior of expert teachers is a central goal of the researchers studying teachers' subject-matter knowledge and how it relates to competence.

A better sense of the complexities of teaching is provided by the categories of teacher knowledge relevant to competence. Shulman (1987a, p. 8) identified seven types of knowledge: (a) *content knowledge;* (b) *general pedagogical knowledge*—a generic set of principles and strategies for organizing and managing classrooms; (c) *curriculum knowledge,* including the various programs and materials relevant to one's area; (d) *pedagogical content knowledge*—"a special mix of content and pedagogy unique to teaching, that is, teachers' special form of professional understanding"; (e) *knowledge of learners and their characteristics;* (f) *knowledge of educational contexts,* including group and classroom behavior, school culture and organization, and community and national cultural patterns; and (g) *knowledge of educational ends,* including educational values and the historical and philosophical grounds for their development.

Shulman argues that only pedagogical content knowledge is a distinctive knowledge base for teaching. Pedagogical content knowledge refers to how teachers blend content and pedagogy to determine the most effective means to teach particular topics or problems consistent with students' interests and abilities (p. 8).

In terms of content knowledge, teachers need to know the most recent knowledge in their discipline as well as the history and philosophy of that discipline, including schools of thought and how the knowledge base of a discipline informs or is informed by other disciplines and fields. All these kinds of content knowledge are important to teacher competence. Without them, teachers have no effective way to determine what subject matter is essential as opposed to peripheral. Knowledge of what is essential is critical because teachers are often a student's primary source for understanding a subject (Shulman, 1987a, p. 9). Teachers also influence how students come to understand the nature and sources of knowledge, what counts as valid knowledge and what does not.

Implicit (and often explicit) in this approach to competence is a world view or value system related to the purpose of knowledge, a conception of a preferred social order, and a view of the good person. This point indicates the importance of linking content knowledge to an understanding of the theoretical and normative scholarship on education. Similar observations were made by Beard (1934, pp. 181–182) and the social reconstructionists over 50 years ago (Stanley, 1981). Thus, this dimension of teacher competence has been a concern of some social educators for most of this century.

Specifically, a teacher's knowledge of subject matter influences how he or she modifies the materials used and the particular representations employed (e. g., metaphors, analogies, best examples) to teach concepts and other forms of knowledge (Wilson et al., 1987). Of the teachers observed by Wilson et al., those who had a high level of subject-matter knowledge were more likely to challenge textbook presentations of knowledge, detect student misconceptions, seize opportunities to relate subject content to other relevant areas, manage class activities effectively, and interpret student comments. Furthermore, the representations of content knowledge generated by less knowledgeable teachers tended to be more superficial and frequently inappropriate or inaccurate.

In sum, the more knowledgeable teachers not only knew more subject matter, but also knew more about the relationship among the parts of this knowledge; how this discipline or field related to other areas of knowledge; and, equally important, how best to represent this knowledge so students would come to understand it. Wilson, Shulman, and Richert (1987) also found, contrary to the results from Fuller and Brown's (1975) earlier research, that even novice teachers paid a great deal of attention to subject content as an important aspect of effective instruction.

In one of the recent "wisdom of practice" studies, the work of 11 experienced (as opposed to novice) teachers of high school history was examined (Wineburg & Wilson, in press). Each of the 11 teachers was nominated as an "expert" by other teachers, school administrators, and university professors. Each

teacher in the study was given a series of five detailed interviews, and the classes of each were observed at least six times. The data collection was limited to that part of a U.S. history course dealing with the American Revolution and the early formation of the United States government. The main reason for selecting this topic was the high probability it is included in American history courses throughout the nation.

The range of behaviors among the effective teachers studied was dramatic. Wineburg and Wilson (in press) described two of these teachers in great detail. One was an almost invisible debate facilitator who did little in class that resembled traditional teaching. Her teaching competence was reflected in the skills and knowledge of her students during a debate on the causes of the American Revolution. The teacher's low teaching profile was possible because of her in-depth historical knowledge and extraordinary abilities in planning the class. In particular, this teacher's lack of direct intervention during class was an intentional strategy to create opportunities for the students to learn to do things they would not likely learn to do via direct instruction. It was also clear that this teacher's approach to instruction was strongly influenced by her understanding of history as being held together by several key ideas. Consequently, she started the year with a unit on the ideas of great thinkers of world history as well as our nation's distant past. An overarching goal was to have students grasp the dynamic process of history as the result of human activity.

In this competent teacher's classroom a textbook did not drive instruction; teacher talk was minimal, and there were no student worksheets. Instead, students were involved in serious dialogue during which they came to understand new ideas which they analyzed in depth. In a sense, the students learned history by recreating it instead of just reading it.

A second competent teacher described by Wineburg and Wilson (in press) taught in a very different way. This teacher was highly visible and at the center of classroom activities. His teaching techniques were similar to well-developed acting skills. In addition, he was keenly sensitive to individual student needs and interests. Many low-level questions were asked to involve students, and the teacher expected the students to know the answers. He also urged them to seek additional evidence from many sources, including class notes, to document their views. All this was accomplished without a detailed lesson plan or use of a particular text. Instead, this teacher relied on a detailed notebook of relevant information and ideas gathered during 17 years of experience.

Again, practice was influenced by the teacher's understanding of content. He viewed history as the product of interpretations, shaped by the values one holds. While a certain amount of content was deemed essential, the more important goal was to have students become excited about history and to appreciate how historical knowledge is developed. This teacher emphasized the textbook as only *one* view of the past by referring to it as the author's view. He also personalized the lives of various historical figures, giving attention to motives for their behavior, to stimulate student interest. The stories of history were left open and unresolved, indicating that a new interpretation of events is always possible. Indeed, conflicting interpretations were presented as the norm for most historical stories. So while the class was taught in a rather traditional way, (e.g., teacher-centered, whole-group, lecture-recitation instruction), it appeared to be as exciting and enriching as the very different, indirectly taught class described earlier.

Although the teaching styles and behaviors of the two teachers described in detail by Wineburg and Wilson (in press) were quite distinct, their effects on students seemed to be more similar than different. Students of both teachers were highly stimulated and interested in history outside the bounds of the classroom. In each class they were actively involved in high-level, complex discussions and analyses of history. Both teachers planned carefully and developed strategies to stimulate student discussion. Each communicated clear goals for their lessons. And, significantly, both were masters of their subject matter, not only the specific historic content but a more general knowledge base that enabled them to relate and give structure to detailed information. Their knowledge included the ability to draw analogies to relevant contemporary situations. In both classes, the textbook was regarded as only one of several competing interpretations of events. For students in both classes, a critical, inquiring disposition and the requisite skills were primary goals.

Wilson and Wineburg (1988) observed four novice, secondary-school history teachers, each of whom has a different disciplinary training—American history, American studies, anthropology, political science. Each novice teacher was given a series of structured interviews to gain an understanding of the subject's own intellectual history, conceptions and knowledge of subject matter, and pedagogy. A particular focus was the teachers' understanding of the substantive and syntactic structures (Schwab, 1964) of their respective disciplines. The researchers were interested in both the subject's current level of knowledge as well as how that knowledge base had developed throughout their college education. In addition to the interviews, a series of "planning observation-reflection" cycles were conducted with each novice teacher. The teachers were asked to explain the purpose of specific lessons they were planning and their knowledge of the lesson content. Each lesson was observed, most were videotaped, and, in addition, field notes were taken. Finally, the researchers interviewed the teachers after each lesson to try to determine if any changes in teacher subject-matter knowledge had occurred and what the teachers perceived as the cause of any change.

Even though each novice teacher taught the same secondary-school subject (American history), they interpreted and taught it in very different ways. Specifically, each teacher constructed different ways of representing the subject matter to students—the kinds of analogies, examples, illustrations, and metaphors used—during teaching and for home assignments. For example, Fred, the novice teacher trained as a political scientist, viewed history as particularistic and fact-oriented and had no grasp of historiography or the structure of history. Consequently, he organized his U.S. history course around political science with a particular emphasis on political and economic themes. Fred believed knowledge of historical facts to be of little practical value, and he avoided them in class. Because he did not understand that history involves interpretation as well as fact, Fred did not seek or urge his students to seek alternative interpretations of historical topics. He also tended to overgeneralize, as when he taught that all revolutions were essentially the same.

In contrast, Jane, a novice teacher trained in history, possessed a complex historical framework for analyzing new knowledge. Jane viewed history as more than a collection of particular facts. History involves interpretation, and she presented historical topics as a series of complex events with multiple causes. Jane believed that historical knowledge was important to help students better understand the present, but she also wanted students to appreciate history for its own sake. Given her better understanding of history, Jane was more competent than Fred in presenting a sense of historical knowledge and how it relates to students' lives in contemporary society. The other teachers in the study also presented very different ways of teaching history to their students.

Wilson and Wineburg (1988) concluded that, generally, social studies teachers would be more competent to the extent that they understood the structure (in Schwab's sense) of the discipline(s) they taught. This involves far more than the accumulation of facts, concepts, and interpretations. Teachers' knowledge of a discipline is influenced as much by their beliefs as by the acquisition of new information. For example, Fred learned a great deal of new historical knowledge during his novice year as a teacher and scored high on the National Teachers Examination test of subject knowledge. But this knowledge had little effect on his understanding of history as a discipline. Indeed, his beliefs regarding history as facts remained so strong that when presented with new interpretations of historical figures, he persisted in assuming they must have come from some political scientist and been incorporated into a history text.

In any case, a competent social studies teacher should have a sense of the disciplines they will teach and the "ways of knowing" each employs. Although it might be unreasonable to expect social studies teachers to have an in-depth understanding of several disciplines, they will be less competent to the extent they are unaware that there are different ways of knowing and lack a sense of how these different forms of knowledge can be applied to disciplines other than the one is which they received their main training. Although the development of a research base for the knowledge-of-subject-matter approach to teacher competence is still in its early stages, there are sufficient data available to indicate that teacher knowledge of subject matter as applied to different classroom contexts is an important component of competence and a necessary addition to the rather narrow conception of competence presented in the previous section.

COMPETENCE BASED ON CRITICAL THINKING AND CRITICAL PEDAGOGY

Other views of competence represent alternatives to the teacher effectiveness and teacher knowledge-of-content approaches discussed in the previous two sections. Aspects of these approaches have been suggested by the work of Short (1984), Fenstermacher (1987a, 1987b), Sockett (1987), and Shulman (1987a, 1987b). Three other approaches are presented in this section: teacher competence as (a) critical thinking, (b) critical pedagogy, and (c) practical judgment. There is some overlap with the previous section (e.g., Shulman discusses critical thinking and practical competence). However, the focus here is more specifically on each of these particular approaches to competence.

Critical Thinking

Critical thinking has been a central rhetorical focus of social studies educators and curriculum theorists throughout most of this century. In practice, however, very little teaching for critical thought has been observed by researchers (e.g., Baxter, Ferrell, & Wiltz, 1964; Boyer, 1983; Christopoulos, Rohwer, & Thomas, 1987; Goodlad, 1984; Howard & Mendenhall, 1982; National Commission, 1983; Ravitch & Finn, 1987; Shaver et al., 1979; Sizer, 1984; Stake & Easley, 1978; Wiley and Race, 1977). Nonetheless, efforts continue to promote critical thinking as essential to citizenship in a democratic society where citizens are confronted by persistent and complex social problems (Nickerson, 1987; Stanley, 1985). From this perspective, a competent social studies teacher should demonstrate the capacity to think critically and have the ability to help students to acquire this competence.

Perkins (1987a, 1987b) argued that students' critical thinking develops very slowly and cited numerous studies to support the view that tactics for critical thinking must be taught directly (e.g., Ericsson & Simon, 1984; Palinscar & Brown, 1984; Schoenfield, 1979). This is consistent with the position taken by Shaver (1962) over 20 years earlier. Teachers also need to work to make student critical thinking tactics more automatic by giving students reinforcement and frequent opportunities for practice. And students need direct help to be able to transfer critical thinking tactics from one context to another (Perkins, 1987b, p. 51).

Knowledge of content is essential to developing a student's critical thinking abilities. Indeed, attempts to teach generic thinking skills or models without adequate attention to content are unlikely to have any impact on student performance in subject areas (Perkins, 1986, 1987a, 1987b). This point was reinforced by Cornbleth (1985) in a review of research on critical thinking as applied to teaching social studies. In several studies on problem solving (e.g., Voss, Greene, Post, & Penner, 1984; Voss, Tyler, & Yengo, 1983), the major finding was that those most skilled in using critical thinking to solve problems had both a detailed knowledge of the relevant subject matter and a good understanding of problem-solving strategies (Cornbleth, 1985, p. 36). These studies suggest that teachers should try to combine subject matter, skills, and thinking strategies in lessons to develop students' critical thought (Cornbleth, p. 37). Thus, competent social studies teachers will not be satisfied if students only learn content. They will include student practice with identifying and solving problems.

Problem analysis should be stimulated by presenting problematic situations that arouse student curiosity. Students should also be presented with opportunities to make connections between prior knowledge and various elements of new knowledge. The goal is to have control of thinking move from the teacher to the student. A student's attitude is important since successful student problem-solving strategies should include questioning the ideas they encounter as well as self-questioning (Cornbleth, pp. 44–49).

The opportunity for students to learn to think critically should also include the analysis of open-ended social problems that do not have a clear indication of origins, causes, or criteria for a solution. And since competent problem solvers might disagree on the best solution, the major test of a student's ability is how well the student analyzes the problem and argues to support the proposed solution (Cornbleth, 1985; Paul, 1987). Thus, recent research on critical thinking is consistent with frequent recommendations for teaching social studies and problem solving over the past several decades (e.g., Dewey, 1933; Engle, 1960; Hunt & Metcalf, 1968; Oliver & Shaver, 1966/1974; Shaver & Strong, 1982; Stanley, 1985).

The recent research by Newmann and his colleagues at the National Center on Effective Secondary schools is focused on thoughtfulness to help promote higher-order thinking (Newmann, 1988a, 1988b, in press). Newmann (1988c) has chosen not to emphasize specific conceptions like critical thinking but to utilize a broader view of higher-order thought in social education. Higher-order thinking involves the interpretation, analysis, and application of knowledge in a situation wherein one is confronted with a problem or problems that cannot be solved by the algorithmic application of prior knowledge. It also requires students to have detailed content knowledge, information processing skills, and certain attitudes regarding the value of reflective thought in order to deal with such open-ended problems.

By implication, the competent social studies teacher would teach fewer topics in more depth and try to show how these are related. Newmann also recommended placing students in genuine problematic situations in which they can have the opportunity to struggle toward problem resolution. Classroom problem-solving activities should be conducted within the framework of thoughtfulness, that is, a student's attitude and behavior should become consistent with the reflective inquiry process as a mode of social judgment. This approach to higher-order thought includes a willingness to reexamine one's assumptions, to analyze problems from alternative vantage points, to insist on reasons supported by evidence, and to constantly scrutinize the value of the evidence used.

Newmann (1988b) has developed several high-inference rating scales to help identify teachers who are competent in developing thoughtful social studies classrooms. These indicators include: in-depth coverage of content, instructional coherence and continuity, sufficient time to think and respond, encouraging students to explain and justify positions, modeling of thoughtfulness in problem solving, and the acceptance and frequent elicitation of original and unconventional student views.

Based on Newmann's (1988b) research, two teacher behaviors appear to be especially related to developing thoughtful social studies classrooms: a teacher's careful consideration of the quality of student reasons and Socratic questioning (p. 16). Other teacher behaviors noted above are theoretically related to thoughtful social studies classrooms but, to date, Newmann has not found supporting evidence. The research conducted by Newmann and his colleagues has all been in secondary schools. Nevertheless, the results seem to hold promise for elementary social studies instruction. Replication studies at the elementary level will be required to document this hypothesis.

Competence as Critical Pedagogy

A related but somewhat different approach to teacher competence is found in the literature on critical pedagogy. Apple (1983), for example, points out the way the curriculum is formed and organized to de-skill teachers. In his estimation, schools have come more and more to approximate the organization and form of industry. This has a tendency to make power over teachers less visible, because it is incorporated into the very structure of the work itself (p. 147). If the structure of teachers' work appears legitimate, the control over their practice is not seen as external or coercive. But, in fact, this sort of technical control places the majority of important decisions regarding teachers' work in the hands of external managers, curriculum developers, and other evaluators.

This technical approach to organizing teacher's work was strongly influenced by the industrial management practices associated with Frederick Taylor (1911) in the early part of this century. Scientific management usually involved breaking down relatively complex jobs into specified behaviors with specified outcomes. A technical rationality is reflected in the Competency Based Teacher Education (CBTE) programs as well as other teacher effectiveness guidelines noted in the earlier part of this chapter. This approach leads to the "separation of conception from execution", that is, practice is largely reduced to a set of discrete moves requiring relatively little intellectual ability. As less artistry and craft are required in practice, training and hiring are focused on narrow technical skills and abilities. Consequently, skills normally associated with teacher competence, like curriculum planning and designing teaching and curriculum strategies for different groups and individuals, are either eliminated or drastically reduced.

This technical approach to competence is not limited to the production of curriculum materials. As the reaction to the teacher effectiveness research presented earlier illustrates, it is solidly incorporated into teacher education programs, inservice programs, and systems to evaluate teachers. The effects of this influence are exacerbated by the increased inclusion of behavior-modification classroom-management techniques as part of the instructional repertoire (Apple, 1983, p. 151). Thus, the shift is also from a loss of teaching skills to an increase in management skills to control students.

The introduction of programmed teaching material goes back at least to the creation of so-called teacher-proof materials in the 1950s and 1960s. This approach has gained continued momentum in part because it meets a variety of needs, such as the desire of state or local governments to control the assessment of teacher accountability, the teacher's needs for practical materials, and the potential cost savings involved (Apple, 1983, p. 155).

A case could be made that Apple's fears are not warranted, because many—if not most—social studies teachers have not used curriculum guides and materials, at least not in the ways those who wrote these curriculum materials (e.g., "New Social Studies" materials) intended (e.g., Project SPAN Staff and Consultants, 1982; Shaver et al., 1979). But while the various New Social Studies materials were often prescriptive regarding competent teacher behaviors, most allowed for, indeed required, far more teacher input and judgment than the narrow technical approach described by Apple. Furthermore, Apple's (1983) argument does not depend on most teachers actually using technical curriculum materials in the prescribed manner. He has sensed a more sinister dimension to this new view of competence. It legitimates and helps reproduce a type of individual (and conception of individualism) who is almost entirely dependent on technical skills. To the extent that a teacher's sense of self and others is based on technical expertise, it is likely that such a teacher will give relatively little attention to moral and community values, an important component of social studies education (p. 157).

What is critical from a social studies perspective is that this new conception of individualism tends to displace an older conception that assumed individual autonomy and decision making to help control one's destiny (Lasch, 1984). Apple (1983) has argued that we need to resist these trends. Such resistance implies a very different conception of teacher competence, one in which teachers find ways to challenge a trend that appears to be eroding the individual autonomy of teachers and their students (pp. 159–162).

Paulo Freire (1970a, 1970b, 1970c, 1973, 1985; Freire & Macedo, 1987) is one educator who has provided guidelines for resistance to dominant forms of education that limit the conceptions of teacher's competence. Freire referred to traditional approaches to teaching as "banking education," that is, a process whereby teachers deposit a dominant and official form of knowledge in the minds of passive students. In this approach to instruction, teachers function primarily to transmit and legitimate the status quo. Within the framework of critical pedagogy, the competent teacher would challenge the banking education process by helping students understand those influences that shape official knowledge and prevent them from having an accurate conception of reality (e.g., racism, sexism, and distortion or suppression historical knowledge).

Freire's general goal is to help students acquire the competence to disrupt the attempts to accomodate them to the dominant culture and to enable them to eventually transform reality in ways more consistent with their interests (Freire, 1970b, pp. 452–477; 1970c, pp. 205–225). A basic assumption underlying his approach is that the kind of literacy that empowers students consists of more than functional or basic reading skills; literacy must enable students to become critical questioners of social reality. Freire and Macedo (1987) claim that mainstream conceptions of literacy (i.e., functional and cultural) in our society actually function to keep students from developing the competence to grasp the social construction of reality and challenge the dominant social order. Consequently, these mainstream views of literacy actually contribute to a growing political illiteracy and pose a threat to our democratic culture.

Shor (1986) has been strongly influenced by Freire's views

and has tried to develop an approach to teaching critical literacy. He has pointed to the need to develop a pedagogy of desocialization to counteract the dominant form of banking education. Desocialization would involve the gradual deconstruction of much of the student's original socialization. Unless this is accomplished, students will have great difficulty getting beyond the conceptual constraints imposed on them during early childhood. The concerns raised by Freire and Shor are similar to the earlier views expressed by Schwab (1964) in reference to helping students grasp how conceptual frameworks are socially constructed, and how they both facilitate and limit our understanding of social reality. The static and passive models of instruction documented by numerous researchers (e.g., Cuban, 1984; Goodlad, 1984; Sizer, 1984) illustrate that many of the concerns raised by advocates of critical pedagogy are well founded.

Shor (1986) has argued that competent teachers are those able to initiate desocialization because students, despite their alienation, cannot do it on their own. Desocialization will be extremely difficult to accomplish given the powerful influence of dominant approaches to education and the general level of student resistance to education that these practices have engendered. In fact, a teacher who wants to help empower students might be forced back into traditional roles by student resistance (p. 186). Irronically, in such a case student resistance itself might actually function to limit the student's ability to challenge the dominant social order (Giroux, 1983a, 1983b; McRobbie, 1978; Willis, 1977). For example, Willis (1977) described a situation where working class students consciously resisted the school's middle class ideology, in which intellectual labor was considered superior to manual labor. However, by rejecting intellectual labor, these students were unable to utilize the great potential of reflective inquiry to empower them as competent citizens capable of challenging the dominant order.

Furthermore, social studies teachers who work to promote a Freirean form of critical literacy by empowering students to challenge the dominant social order may risk sacrificing their careers (Shor, 1986, p. 186). Such an approach to teaching poses a curious situation in which a social studies teacher's competence might provoke a community reaction leading to dismissal. This paradoxical dilemma has been a concern of both mainstream and critical social educators (e.g., Giroux, 1983a; Shaver & Strong, 1982; Shor, 1986).

Giroux (1983a), understanding the risks facing critical social educators, has provided another explanation of how a critical pedagogy might be applied to citizenship education, a core goal of the social studies. Students, and by implication competent teachers, must learn "to display civic courage, i.e., the willingness to act *as if* they were living in a democratic society" (p. 201). To accomplish this purpose, teachers must become aware of the political nature of education and use it to help create a genuine democratic society by enabling students to evaluate society "against *its* own claims" and to "think and act in ways that speak to different societal possibilities and ways of living" (p. 202).

Toward this end, a competent teacher would stress active student participation in the learning process and reject most transmission models of instruction, including much of the teacher effectiveness model. Teachers can help develop student's citizenship competence by rendering knowledge problematic, focusing on its historical origins, and eliminating "its objective pretensions." In this way, students might come to understand their present world view and how they came to this stance. Students should also learn about the origins of other world views and how they contrast with their own (Giroux, 1983a, p. 202). This involves more than merely exposing students to different views and letting them select those that suit their own experiences. As Giroux (1988) explained, while "a teacher cannot demand a student not be a racist, he/she can certainly subject such a person to a critique that reveals it as an act of political and moral irresponsibility related to wider social and historical practices" (p. 67).

Competent teachers should also help students use their critical skills to construct their own biographies. Such teaching could help provide a necessary knowledge base for critically evaluating the truth of competing systems of meaning. Students need to clarify their values and understand the importance of certain democratic values to the reproduction of human life. Finally, students need to develop the knowledge and skills to act collectively to transform the social order and the "passion and optimism that speak to possibilities" for human betterment (Giroux, 1988, p. 203).

The power of the critical pedagogy approach to teacher competence lies in its demonstration of and insistence on the moral-political nature of teaching and the need to radicalize the process of critical thought to inform social action. But it is not just a case of adding a moral-political dimension to schooling. As Lasch (1979, 1984) has argued, values are not to be grafted on to education or other professions to make up for some perceived lack. Instead, we need to conceive of teaching as an essentially moral enterprise that operates within the social fabric. Educators should not seek to add a moral dimension to teaching; rather, they should recognize that teaching is an intrinsically moral enterprise. Consequently, the competent social studies teacher would not conceive of values education as a separate component of instruction, something he or she did at certain times and in certain contexts. Instead, social studies education would be planned and conducted in accordance with a moral-political framework, as posed by critical educators like Apple, Freire, Shor, and Giroux.

Teacher Competence and Practical Judgment

Practical judgment is a term that has been interpreted in various ways. Fenstermacher (1978, 1987a), influenced by the work of Green (1976), described practical judgment as "a reasonably coherent chain of reasoning leading from an expression of a desired end state, through various types of promises— some empirical, others situational—to an intention to act in a particular way" (Fenstermacher, 1987a, p. 359).

Another explanation of practical judgment has been provided by Schon (1983, 1987). Schon was critical of what he saw as a dominant technical rationality that seems to orient most research and practice in education. He did not reject the utility of technical knowledge (e.g., much of the knowledge derived from teacher effectiveness studies) but argued that more emphasis should be placed on various forms of knowledge in practice. Included would be tacit knowledge as posited by Polanyi (1964) and what Schon (1983) called reflection in action. To a large extent, the view of practical intelligence presented by Schon was derived from philosophical discourse, but an emerging research base also provided somewhat more empirical grounds (e.g., Schon, 1983; Shulman, 1987a; Sternberg & Wagner, 1986).

Arguments for the importance of practical judgment or knowledge for curriculum (and by implication teacher competence) are certainly not new. Schwab (1964) called our attention to this issue almost 30 years ago. He argued that all of the things schools should do, practical knowledge is given the least attention. Schwab described practical knowledge as essentially what teachers do when they act *deliberately,* as opposed to functioning as automatons (pp. 16–17).

Practical judgment is to some writers, then, an important criterion of teacher competence. That the development of students' practical competence should be *the* central purpose of social education is a claim that should not be ignored (Whitson & Stanley, 1988). A social studies teacher's level of competence is directly linked to his or her ability to promote students' practical judgment. Consequently, competent social studies teachers must understand and possess an adequate level of practical competence.

Social studies education, by definition, is concerned with social life, which consists of processes in which individual and social identities are formed and transformed. Social studies *is* about "the study of human action in the social world, and the activity of learning itself takes place within such social action" (Whitson & Stanley, 1988, p. 3). As such, a competence is entailed that goes beyond the skills to perform tasks with prespecified outcomes as envisioned in teacher effectiveness or other instrumentally oriented models of competence. Unfortunately, even some of the more sophisticated approaches to the teaching of critical thinking and the complex analysis of pedagogical content-knowledge proposed by Shulman suffer from a predominately technical orientation. These orientations seem to be driven by a functionalist view that students need to be educated so that they can survive successfully in the "real" world. Survival is an important consideration, but human action also requires a *practical* competence beyond functional skill (Beyer, Feinberg, Pagano, & Whitson, 1990; Whitson & Stanley, 1988).

Merton (1967), a leading functionalist, was critical of functionalists who overemphasized the value of existing social institutions, thereby taking an essentially conservative position. Merton cautioned that our institutions can have disintegrative as well as integrative consequences (p. 29). Consequently, competent social studies teachers must enable students to examine critically the function of extant institutions and not limit instruction to the development of the skills necessary to function within the present institutional structure. But competent social studies instruction must not be reduced to the purpose of "restoring a balance between the practical and the instrumental or technical; it must . . . [be based on] the realization that a purely instrumental or technical competence is not possible" (Whitson & Stanley, p. 3). Indeed, scientific knowledge itself is derived from practical judgment.

The practical tradition has all but disappeared in modern society and culture (Bernstein, 1983; Whitson & Stanley, 1988). It is a very old tradition rooted in Aristotle's conception of practical competence *(phronesis)* as different from technical or instrumental competence *(techne). Phronesis* is defined in *The Random House Dictionary* (2nd edition, unabridged, 1987) as "wisdom in determining ends and the means of attaining them." A major purpose of critical theory has been to reclaim the practical tradition in modern society (Bernstein, 1983; Beyer et al., 1990). Human social action or *praxis* involves the *enactment* or realization of more particular acts from among the virtually infinite possible alternative actions that humans might exercise in particular situations. The most applicable definition of *praxis* is "1. practice, as distinguished from theory; application or use, as of knowledge or skills" (Random House, 1987). In this chapter, *praxis* is used in Aristotle's sense as intelligible action directed toward human betterment in a communal setting (Bernstein, 1983). This is consistent with the pragmatic philosophy of Peirce and, to a somewhat lesser extent, Dewey. The process of exercising practical competence leads to the recognition of more diverging options or interpretations as one proceeds toward a social decision, and neither knowledge of social structures nor any level of technical competence is adequate to determine which of the possible social actions should be followed. Indeed, no technical process can be conceived unless "the underlying practical competence can be taken for granted. Without pragmatic definition of the task to be completed, there is no skillful performance possible" (Whitson & Stanley, 1988, p. 13).

The sort of practical competence central to both teacher and student action is closely linked to linguistic pragmatics and is the antithesis of literal reading or the cultural literacy espoused by E. D. Hirsch (1987) and others. Practical judgment is also opposed to the cult of the expert which pervades modern mass culture (Lasch, 1979, 1984). It is not that experts do not have important knowledge, but this is not sufficient for the citizen or client to take action (Bellah, Madsen, Sullivan, Swidler, & Tipton, 1985; Lasch, 1984; Shaver, 1980).

Practical judgment, or phronesis, as Bernstein (1983) explained, is used when a person is confronted with variable situations about which there can be different opinions. General principles are available, but no technical rules exist to determine the universal principles and the acts that would be relevant and appropriate in any particular situation (p. 54). This form of judgment should not be confused with forms of relativism that admit only to personal preference when making individual decisions or resolving public issues.

Practical judgment is also qualitatively different from neo-Kantian approaches to social studies education that posit a set of a priori core democratic values or an "American Creed" to be used to determine the appropriateness of social policy recommendations or decisions (e.g., Kohlberg, 1973; Oliver & Shaver, 1966/1974; Shaver & Strong, 1982). In the case of practical judgment, wisdom must be used to determine which ends are appropriate as well as the best means of attaining them.

Furthermore, following the Kantian tradition, social educators have tended to separate the analysis of aesthetic from ethical issues and argue that while aesthetic values are ultimately a matter of personal taste, moral or ethical values "are never merely matters of personal taste" (e.g., Shaver & Strong, 1982, pp. 31–32, chap. 5, 6). In contrast, practical judgment involves the sort of reasoning one uses when making an aesthetic judgment (Bernstein, 1983). Although the application of aesthetic reasoning to social issues might seem counterintuitive, a considerable body of literature has emerged that explains the relevance of this kind of judgment to deciding how to act in social (including moral) situations (Beiner, 1983; Bernstein, 1983; Gadamer, 1975). The scope of this chapter does not permit an adequate examination of this issue, but it is an important one that should be a focus of future research on social studies teacher competence.

CONCLUSION

In this chapter, three different conceptions of teacher competence were examined along with some discussion of the research relevant to each. The teacher effectiveness approach to teacher competence is supported by the most extensive research base. However, this approach implies a very narrow and technical conception of social studies education that is difficult to apply to the teaching for more complex goals such as the reflective examination of social issues. In addition, there are serious problems with the research methods used in teacher effectiveness studies (e.g., Coker, et al., 1980). Nevertheless, there do seem to be certain generic teacher behaviors that promote competence across a wide variety of contexts (e.g., Berliner, 1986; Fenstermacher, 1987a & 1987b).

Research based on other approaches has clearly demonstrated that teacher competence in social studies requires more than generic skills. A teacher's knowledge of subject matter and how to best teach this knowledge in widely different classroom contexts is a critical feature of teacher competence (Shulman, 1987a). This research has reinforced the view that context is a critical variable and that component teachers can be effective using dramatically different approaches to teaching the same subject matter. However, the research on how teacher knowledge of subject matter relates to effective instruction is still very limited. Although the research to date has given a clearer picture of the role of teacher knowledge of subject matter, it is still difficult to either generalize or point to many specific recommendations for teacher behavior. As Shulman rightly pointed out during his 1987 NCSS address in Dallas, social studies education lags behind the other major subject areas in research related to how teacher subject-matter knowledge relates to effective instruction. Obviously, much work needs to be done in this area.

Finally, approaches to teacher competence based on critical thinking, critical pedagogy, and practical judgment were examined. The case for critical approaches to reasoning as a central concern of social studies education rest, in the main, on philosophical and social theory. In addition, there is an emerging body of empirical research that gives some support to these philosophical and social theories (Cornbleth, 1985; Baron & Sternberg, 1987). However, what empirical research does exist is often inconclusive or contradictory. The limited research studies and results are not unexpected, given the great difficulty involved in conducting the kind of studies that would document this form of teacher competence. One major difficulty is that, while certain aspects of critical thinking might be taught directly, it also seems clear that students must be given the opportunity to develop this competence in practical situations. It is still far from clear how a competent teacher would best construct such learning situations and which kinds of situations are most effective. Obviously, there is a strong need to pursue this line of inquiry.

What can be determined is that there is a danger that teacher competence for social studies will be defined too narrowly. The pressure for a quick fix is great, and teachers and the public are understandably desperate for something that works. Such pressure needs to be resisted. Even though adequate information is still lacking, each of the approaches to competence discussed in this chapter offers suggestions for developing teacher competence. What a social studies teacher decides to take from each of these approaches to competence is a matter of practical judgment (consistent with the type of competence discussed in the last section of the chapter). Consequently, teacher competence for social studies is not merely a matter of eclecticism. Instead, practical judgment must be used to determine the ends of social studies as a field of study and then to select the best means to achieve these ends in particular classroom situations. This decision-making process is confused by the persistent failure to reach consensus on the purpose of social studies education (Stanley, 1985). It is also made problematic by the structures of schooling and teachers' work that function to block reflective and critical approaches to instruction (Apple, 1983; Cuban, 1984; Goodlad, 1984; McNeil, 1986).

Too often, proponents of teacher effectiveness have reduced competence to technical expertise (Short, 1984; Whitson & Stanley, 1988), but technical skill without the prior application of practical judgment is blind. It is also the case that practical competence without technical skill is empty (Bernstein, 1983, p. 161). So, teacher competence for social studies education will require technical, practical, and critical expertise. That is much to ask of teachers, but to ask less is to limit unduly their competence.

References

Amarel, M., & Chittenden, D. A. (1982). *A conceptual study of knowledge use in schools.* Princeton: Educational Testing Service.

Apple, M. W. (1983). Curricular form and the logic of technical control. In M. W. Apple & L. Weis (Eds.), *Ideology and practice in schooling* (pp. 143–165). New York: Cambridge University Press.

Armento, B. J. (1986). Research on teaching social studies. In M. C. Wittrock (Ed.), *Handbook of research on teaching* (3rd ed., pp. 942–951). New York: Macmillan.

Armento, B. J., & Flores, S. (1986). Learning about the economic world. In V. A. Atwood (Ed.), *Elementary school social studies: Research as a guide to practice* (Bulletin No. 79, pp. 85–101). Washington, DC: National Council for the Social Studies.

Baron, J. Steinberg, R. J. (Eds.). (1987). *Teaching thinking skills: Theory and practice.* New York: W. H. Freeman.

Baxter, M. G., Ferrell, R. H., & Wiltz, J. E. (1964). *The teaching of American history in high schools.* Bloomington: Indiana University Press.

Beard, C. A. (1934). *The nature of the social sciences in relation to objectives of instruction* (Report of the Commission on the Social Studies, part 7). New York: Charles Scribner's Sons.

Beiner, R. (1983). *Political judgment.* Chicago: University of Chicago Press.

Bellah, R. N., Madsen, R., Sullivan, W. M., Swidler, A., & Tipton, S. M. (1985). *Habits of the heart: Individualism and commitment in American life.* Berkeley: University of California Press.

Berliner, D. C. (1986). In pursuit of the expert pedagogue. *Educational Researcher, 15*(7), 5–13.

Bernstein, R. (1983). *Beyond objectivism and relativism: Science, hermeneutics, and praxis.* Philadelphia: University of Pennsylvania Press.

Beyer, L. E., Feinberg, W., Pagano, J. A., & Whitson, J. A. (1990). *The liberal arts, educational studies, and professionalism.* New York: Teachers College Press.

Boyer, E. (1983). *High school: A report on secondary education in America.* New York: Harper & Row.

Brophy, J. E. (1973). Stability in teacher effectiveness. *American Educational Research Journal, 10*, 245–252.

Brophy, J. E. (1987). *Research on teacher effects: Uses and abuses* (Occasional Paper No. 116). Lansing: Michigan State University, Institute for Research on Teaching.

Brophy, J. E., & Good, T. (1986). Teacher behavior and student achievement. In M. C. Wittrock (Ed.), *Handbook of research on teaching* (3rd ed., pp. 328–375). New York: Macmillan.

Christopolous, J. P., Rohwer, W. D., & Thomas, J. W. (1987). Grade level differences in students' study activities as a function of course characteristics. *Contemporary Educational Psychology, 12*, 303–323.

Clandinin, D. J. (1985). Personal practical knowledge: A study of teachers' classroom images. *Curriculum Inquiry, 15*, 361–385.

Coker, H., Medley, D. M., & Soar, R. S. (1980). How valid are expert opinions about effective teaching? *Phi Delta Kappan, 62*, 131–134.

Cornbleth, C. (1985). Critical thinking and cognitive processes. In W. B. Stanley (Ed.), *Review of research in social studies education: 1976–1983* (pp. 11–63). Washington, DC: National Council for the Social Studies.

Cuban, L. (1984). *How teachers taught: Constancy and change in American classrooms, 1890–1980.* New York: Longman.

Darling-Hammond, L., Wise, A. E., & Pease, S. R. (1983). Teacher evaluation in the organizational context: A review of the literature. *Review of Educational Research, 53*, 255–328.

Dewey, J. (1933). *How we think.* Boston: Heath.

Doyle, W. (1979). Making managerial decisions in classrooms. In D. L. Duke (Ed.), *Classroom management: Seventy-eighth yearbook of the National Society for the Study of Education (Part 2,* pp. 42–74). Chicago: University of Chicago Press.

Doyle, W. (1984). How is order achieved in classrooms: An interim report. *Journal of Curriculum Studies, 16*, 259–277.

Doyle, W. (1985). Effective teaching and the concept of master teacher. *The Elementary School Journal, 86*, 27–33.

Dunkin, M. J., & Biddle, B. J. (1974). *The study of teaching.* New York: Holt.

Engle, S. H. (1960). Decision making: The heart of social studies instruction. *Social Education, 24*, 301–304.

Ericsson, K. A., & Simon, H. A. (1984). *Protocol analysis.* Cambridge, MA: MIT Press.

Fenstermacher, G. (1987a). Prologue to my critics. *Educational Theory, 37*, 357–360.

Fenstermacher, G. (1987b). A reply to my critics. *Educational Theory, 37*, 413–422.

Ford, M. J., & McKinney, C. W. (1986). The effects of recycling and response sensitivity on the acquisition of social studies concepts. *Theory and Research in Social Education, 14*, 21–33.

Freire, P. (1970a). The adult literacy process in cultural action for freedom. *Harvard Educational Review, 40*, 205–225.

Freire, P. (1970b). *Cultural action for freedom* (Monograph Series No. 1). Cambridge, MA: Harvard Educational Review.

Freire, P. (1970c). *Pedagogy of the oppressed* (M. B. Ramos, Trans.). New York: Seabury Press.

Freire, P. (1973). *Education for critical consciousness.* New York: Seabury Press.

Freire, P. (1985). The politics of education: Culture, power, and liberation (D. Macedo, Trans.). South Hadley, MA: Bergin & Garvey.

Freire, P., & Macedo, D. (1987). *Literacy: Reading the word and the world.* South Hadley, MA: Bergin & Garvey.

Fuller, F. F., & Brown, O. (1975). Becoming a teacher. In K. Ryan (Ed.), *Teacher education: Seventy-fourth yearbook of the National Society for the Study of Education, Part 2* (pp. 25–52). Chicago: University of Chicago Press.

Gadamer, H. (1975). *Truth and method.* London: Sheed and Ward.

Gilmore, A. G., & McKinney, C. W. (1986). The effects of student questions and teacher questions on concept acquisition. *Theory and Research in Social Education, 14*, 225–244.

Giroux, H. A. (1983a). *Theories and resistance in education.* South Hadley, MA: Bergin & Garvey.

Giroux, H. A. (1983b). Theories of reproduction and resistance in the new sociology of education. *Harvard Educational Review, 53*, 257–293.

Giroux, H. A. (1988). *Schooling and the struggle for public life: Critical pedagogy in the modern age.* Minneapolis: University of Minnesota Press.

Good, T. L. (1983). Classroom research: A decade of progress. *Educational Psychologist, 18*, 127–144.

Goodlad, J. I. (1984). *A place called school: Prospects for the future.* New York: McGraw-Hill.

Green, T. F. (1976). Teacher competence as practical rationality. *Educational Theory, 26*, 249–258.

Hirsch, E. D., Jr. (1987). *Cultural literacy: What every American needs to know.* Boston: Houghton Mifflin.

Howard, J., & Mendenhall, T. (1982). *Making history come alive.* Washington, DC: Council for Basic Education.

Hunkins, F. P. (Ed.). (1977) *Review of research in social studies education: 1970–1975.* Washington, DC: National Council for the Social Studies.

Hunt, M. P., & Metcalf, L. E. (1968). *Teaching high school social studies* (2nd ed.). New York: Harper & Row.

Jantz, R. K., & Klawitter, K. (1986). Anthropology and sociology. In V. A. Atwood (Ed.), *Elementary school social studies: Research as a guide to practice* (Bulletin No. 79, pp. 102–118). Washington, DC: National Council for the Social Studies.

Kohlberg, L. (1973). Continuities in childhood and adult moral development revisited. In P. B. Baltes & L. R. Goulet (Eds.), *Lifespan developmental psychology* (2nd ed.). New York: Academic Press.

Lasch, C. (1979). *The culture of narcissism: American life in an age of diminishing expectations.* New York: Warner Books.

Lasch, C. (1984). *The minimal self: Psychic survival in troubled times.* New York: Norton.

Leinhardt, G., & Smith, D. A. (1985). Expertise in mathematics instruction: Subject matter knowledge. *Journal of Educational Psychology, 77*, 247–271.

Markle, S. M. (1975). They teach concepts, don't they? *Educational Researcher, 4*(6), 3–9.

McKenzie, G. R. (1986). Learning and instruction. In V. A. Atwood (Ed.), *Elementary school social studies: Research as a guide to practice*

(Bulletin No. 79, pp. 119–136). Washington, DC: National Council for the Social Studies.

McKinney, C. W., Larkins, A. G., Burts, D. C., & Davis, J. C. (1982). Teach social studies concepts to first grade students? Research on the Merrill and Tennyson model. *The Social Studies, 72,* 235–238.

McKinney, C. W., Larkins, A. G., Ford, M. J., & Davis, J. C. (1983). The effectiveness of three methods of teaching social studies concepts to fourth-grade students: An aptitude-treatment interaction study. *American Educational Research Journal, 20,* 663–670.

McNeil, L. M. (1986). *Contradictions of control.* London: Routledge & Kegan Paul.

McRobbie, A. (1978). Working class girls and the culture of femininity. In Women's Studies Group, Center for Contemporary Cultural Studies (Ed.), *Women take issue: Aspects of women's subordination* (pp. 96–108). London: Hutchinson.

Merrill, M. D., & Tennyson, R. D. (1977). *Teaching concepts: An instructional design guide.* Englewood Cliffs, NJ: Educational Technology Publication.

Merton, R. K. (1967). *Social theory and social structure.* New York: Free Press.

National Commission on Excellence in Education. (1983). *A nation at risk: The imperative for educational reform.* Washington, DC: U.S. Department of Education. (ERIC Document Reproduction Service No. ED 226 066)

Newmann, F. M. (1988a). *The assessment of discourse in social studies.* Madison: University of Wisconsin, National Center on Effective Secondary Schools.

Newmann, F. M. (1988b). The curriculum of thoughtful classes. In F. M. Newmann (Ed.), *Higher order thinking in high school social studies: An analysis of classrooms, teachers, students, and leadership* (Part 2, pp. 1–35). Madison: University of Wisconsin, National Center on Effective Secondary Schools.

Newmann, F. M. (in press). Higher order thinking in the teaching of social studies: Connection between theory and practice. In D. Perkins, J. Segal, & J. Voss (Eds.), *Informal reasoning and education.* Hillsdale, NJ: Erlbaum.

Nickerson, R. S. (1987). Why teach thinking? In J. B. Baron & R. J. Sternberg (Eds.), *Teaching thinking skills: Theory and practice* (pp. 27–38). New York: Freeman.

Oliver, D. W., & Shaver, J. P. (1974). *Teaching public issues in the high school.* Logan, UT: Utah State University Press. (Original work published 1966)

Ornstein, A. (1985). Considering teacher effectiveness. *The Clearing House, 58,* 399–402.

Palincsar, A., & Brown, A. L. (1984). Reciprocal teaching of comprehension fostering and comprehension-monitoring activities. *Cognition and Instruction, 1,* 117–175.

Park, O. (1984). Example comparison strategy versus attribute identification strategy in concept learning. *American Educational Research Journal, 21,* 145–162.

Paul, R. W. (1987). Dialogical thinking: Critical thought essential to the acquisition of rational knowledge and passions. In J. B. Baron & R. J. Sternberg (Eds.), *Teaching thinking skills: Theory and practice* (pp. 127–148). New York: Freeman.

Perkins, D. N. (1986). *Knowledge as design.* Hillsdale, NJ: Erlbaum.

Perkins, D. N. (1987a). Knowledge as design: Teaching thinking through content. In J. B. Baron & R. J. Sternberg (Eds.), *Teaching thinking skills: Theory and practice* (pp. 62–85). New York: Freeman.

Perkins, D. N. (1987b). Thinking frames: An intergrative perspective on teaching cognitive skills. In J. B. Baron & R. J. Sternberg (Eds.), *Teaching thinking skills: Theory and practice* (pp. 41–61). New York: Freeman.

Polanyi, M. (1964). *Personal knowledge.* New York: Harper & Row.

Porter, A. C., & Brophy, J. (1988). Synthesis of research on good teaching: Insights from the work of the Institute for Research on Teaching. *Educational Leadership, 45*(8), 74–85.

Project SPAN Staff and Consultants. (1982). The current state of the social studies: A report of Project SPAN. Boulder, CO: Social Science Education Consortium. (ERIC Document Reproduction Service No. ED 218 199)

Ravitch, D., & Finn, C. (1987). *What do our 17-year-olds know?* New York: Harper & Row.

Rosenshine, B. (1983) Teaching functions in instructional programs. *The Elementary School Journal, 83,* 335–351.

Rosenshine, B. (1986). Unsolved issues in teaching content: A critique of a lesson on Federalist Papers No. 10. *Teaching and Teacher Education, 2,* 301–308

Rosenshine, B., & Stevens, R. (1986). Teaching functions. In M. C. Wittrock (Ed.), *Handbook of research on teaching.* (3rd ed., pp. 376–391). New York: Macmillan.

Schoenfeld, A. H. (1979). Explicit heuristic training as a variable in problem solving performance. *Journal for Research in Mathematics Education, 10,* 173–187.

Schon, D. A. (1983). *The reflective practitioner: How professionals think in action.* New York: Basic Books.

Schon, D. A. (1987). *Educating the reflective practitioner.* San Francisco: Jossey-Bass.

Schwab, J. J. (1964). The structures of the disciplines: Meanings and significances. In G. W. Ford & L. Pugno (Eds.), *The structure of knowledge and the curriculum* (pp. 6–30). Chicago: Rand McNally.

Shaver, J. P. (1962). Educational research and instruction for critical thinking. *Social Education, 26,* 13–18.

Shaver, J. P. (1980). Toward the twenty-first century: Social studies goals for decision-making and research skills. *Journal of Research and Development in Education, 13*(2), 36–46.

Shaver, J. P., Davis, O. L., & Helburn, S. W. (1979). The status of social studies education: Impressions from three NSF studies. *Social Education, 43,* 150–153.

Shaver, J. P., & Strong, W. (1982). *Facing value decisions: Rationale-building for teachers* (2nd ed.). New York: Teachers College Press.

Shor, I. (1986). *Culture wars: School and society in the conservative restoration, 1969–1984.* Boston: Routledge & Kegan Paul.

Short, E. C. (1984). Competence reëxamined. *Educational Theory, 34,* 201–208.

Shulman, L. S. (1987a). Knowledge and teaching: Foundations of the new reform. *Harvard Educational Review, 57,* 1–22.

Shulman, L. S. (1987b). Sounding the alarm: A reply to Sockett. *Harvard Educational Review, 57,* 473–482.

Sizer, T. (1984). *Horace's compromise: The dilemma of the American high school.* Boston: Houghton Mifflin.

Sockett, H. T. (1987). Has Shulman got the strategy right?. *Harvard Educational Review, 57,* 208–219.

Stake, R. E., & Easley, J. A. (1978). *Case studies in science education.* Washington, DC: National Science Foundation.

Stanley, W. B. (1981). The radical reconstructionist rationale for social education. *Theory and Research in Social Education, 8,* 55–79.

Stanley, W. B. (1984). Approaches to teaching concepts and conceptualizing: An analysis of social studies textbooks. *Theory and Research in Social Education, 11,* 1–14.

Stanley, W. B. (1985). Recent research in the foundations of social education: 1976–1983. In W. B. Stanley (Ed.), *Review of research in social studies education: 1976–1983* (pp. 309–399). Washington, DC: National Council for the Social Studies.

Sternberg, R. J., & Wagner, R. K. (1986). *Practical intelligence: Nature and origins of competence in the everyday world.* London: Cambridge University Press.

Taylor, F. W. (1911). *The principles of scientific management.* New York: Harper.

Tennyson, R. D., Chao, J. N., & Younger, J. (1981). Concept learning effectiveness using prototype and skill development presentations. *Journal of Educational Psychology, 73,* 326–334.

Tennyson, R. D., & Park, D. C. (1980). The teaching of concepts: A review of instructional design research literature. *Journal of Educational Psychology, 50,* 55–70.

Thornton, S. J. (1988). Curriculum consonance in United States history classrooms. *Journal of Curriculum and Supervision, 3,* 308–320.

Voss, J. F., Greene, T. R., Post, T. A., & Penner, B. C. (1984). Problem solving skill in the social sciences. In G. Bower (Ed.), *The psychology of learning and motivation: Advances in research theory* (pp. 165–213). New York: Academic Press.

Voss, J. F., Tyler, S. W., & Yengo, L. A. (1983). Individual differences in the solving of social science problems. In R. F. Dillon and R. R. Schmeck (Eds.), *Individual differences in cognition* (pp. 205–232). New York: Academic Press.

White, J. J. (1985). What works for teachers: A review of ethnographic research studies as they inform issues on social studies curriculum and instruction. In W. B. Stanley (Ed.), *Review of Research in Social Studies Education: 1976–1983* (pp. 215–307). Washington, DC: National Clearinghouse for the Social Studies.

Whitson, J. A., & Stanley, W. B. (1988, November). *Practical competence: A rationale for social education.* Paper presented at the meeting of the National Council for Social Studies, Orlando, FL.

Wiley, K. B. (1977). *The status of pre-college science, mathematics, and social science education: 1955–1975: Vol. 3. Social science education.* Boulder, CO: Social Science Education Consortium.

Willis, P. (1977). *Learning to labour.* Lexington, MA: Heath.

Wilson, S. M., Shulman, L. S., & Richert, A. E. (1987). '150 different ways' of knowing: representations of knowledge in teaching. In J. Calderhead (Ed.), *Exploring teachers' thinking,* (pp. 104–124). London: Cassell Education.

Wilson, S. M., & Wineburg, S. S. (1988). Peering at history from different lenses: The role of disciplinary perspectives in the teaching of American history: *Teachers College Record, 89,* 525–539.

Wineburg, S. S., & Wilson, S. M. (in press). Subject matter knowledge in the teaching of history. In J. E. Brophy (Ed.), *Advances in research on teaching.* Greenwich, CT: JAI.

Yoho, R. F. (1986). Effectiveness of four concept teaching strategies on social studies concept acquisition and retention. *Theory and Research in Social Education, 14,* 225–244.

Section

·IV·

CONTEXTS OF SOCIAL STUDIES EDUCATION

·21·

RESEARCH ON CONTEXT, RESEARCH IN CONTEXT

Catherine Cornbleth

STATE UNIVERSITY OF NEW YORK AT BUFFALO

In a recent analysis of the contexts of policy change, Cornbleth and Adams (1987) qualified their interpretation as follows:

Recognizing that context is widely acknowledged but largely uncharted territory—not unlike the "new world" of 15th century European maps and perhaps for good reason—we proceed with caution and tentativeness. The complexity and elusiveness of . . . [educational] context, at least in the case of the U.S. educational system, makes it difficult to "pin down" and link empirically to particular policies. The resulting tendency to decontextualize . . . educational policy, however, limits our analysis and understanding of both policy and policymaking. (p. 331)

The risks, both of pursuing context and of decontextualization, are considerable whether one's focus is educational policy and policymaking or educational research and practice.

Until recently, decontextualization has been the norm in social studies education research and educational research more generally. There are now growing and compelling arguments and evidence for the contextualization of educational research. Efforts to contextualize research have been spurred both by disappointment with the yield and utility of conventional, decontextualized research and by alternative paradigms, or worldviews, in which context plays a major role in understanding and explanation. In this chapter, I explore the meanings of context associated with different paradigms and then examine different ways of addressing context in social studies and related research with examples from recent studies. Finally, based on this review and analysis, I offer suggestions for future social studies research.

MEANINGS OF CONTEXT

Different ways of conceptualizing and dealing with context are associated with different paradigms, or orientations toward the world. By paradigm, or worldview, I mean a framework of knowledge and belief through which one "sees" and investigates the world or some part of it such as social studies education; a paradigm consists of one's working assumptions about the world and how it is to be perceived, studied, understood, and acted upon. This framework of knowledge and belief includes interrelated concepts and values, questions, procedures, and actions. A paradigm is, in a sense, a window to the world. It enables us to see what is "out there." But, just as windows have frames that limit one's view, so do paradigms. Their conceptual, normative, and procedural frames limit what can be seen and how it is to be interrogated and interpreted.

Paradigms are not givens, although they are often taken for granted. Because they are omnipresent, people often do not recognize their own paradigms, or worldviews, as such, instead presuming that "that's the way things are." Paradigms, like theory and knowledge in general, are socially constructed, that is, created by human beings in a particular time, place, and social location. Commitment to one or another paradigm, whether or not recognized as such, involves affiliation with a community whose members share, sustain, and shape that paradigm through their language and research activity.

Three research paradigms and their associated conceptualizations and treatment of context are examined here. Based on Habermas's (1972) distinctions among forms of science and cognitive interests as elaborated with respect to social studies education research by Popkewitz (1986), the paradigms are empirical-analytic; symbolic, or interpretive; and critical (cf. Bredo & Feinberg, 1982). These three research paradigms are more appropriately viewed as occasionally overlapping segments of a continuum than as discrete or mutually exclusive categories. Research from an empirical-analytic paradigm usually is clearly distinguishable. At times, it may be more difficult to distinguish research studies from the interpretive and critical paradigms

---

Reviewers were Kathryn Borman, University of Cincinnati, Robert Stevenson, State University of New York at Buffalo.

The author appreciated the assistance of Machiko Matsui in the unpublished review, mentioned in this chapter, of the empirical studies reported in *Theory and Research in Social Education*, 1986–1988.

because of their several commonalities. It could be argued that critical research is an extension of some versions of interpretive research. A further qualification is that there are variations in the research associated with each paradigm that are not detailed in the following brief characterizations.

The Empirical-Analytic Paradigm

Empirical-analytic researchers are present- and future-oriented. Their focus is on what is or can be made observable (empirical), usually in the form of constituent elements or, presumably, discrete variables (analytic). Effective teaching, for example, is viewed in terms of observable teacher behaviors related to measurable student outcomes. The overriding interest of empirical-analytic researchers is technical; their purpose is to determine the effectiveness of means to predetermined ends, in order to foster efficiency and control. Effective strategies of classroom management or concept development, for example, are sought in order to efficiently control future student behavior and concept learning.

Among the assumptions underlying empirical-analytic research, two are particularly relevant to the present concern with context. One is the assumption that educational research can and should generate generalizations that, if not universal, are widely applicable across classroom and school situations. Statistical analyses "are used to decontextualize knowledge so that findings seem to have cross-situational and historical validity" (Popkewitz, 1986, p. 15). Theory consists of statements of lawlike regularities of social behavior. Although prominent educational researchers in the empirical-analytic tradition have questioned the possibility of universal rules, or laws, of human behavior (e.g., Shaver, 1982), the quest for law like regularities continues.

The second assumption is that the world, or some part of it such as a social studies lesson, is composed of distinct and distinguishable elements, or variables. Such variables can be measured and treated statistically to identify probabilistic relationships such as correlation and cause–effect. It follows that causation is usually viewed as linear and directional. For example, if the teacher follows strategy X, the result will be student behavior Y (within previously established limits of probability). However, if the evidence indicates that there are interactions between teaching strategies and student characteristics—for example, strategy X is effective with good readers but not with poor readers—then teachers are advised to differentiate their teaching by employing strategy X with good readers but not with poor ones.

At least two implications for conceptualizing and dealing with context follow from the empirical-analytical paradigm and the resultant research. One is that, where possible, context is to be ignored, avoided, or overcome. Because a major goal is to identify universal generalizations, empirical-analytic researchers are likely to (a) ignore context as irrelevant to their concerns; (b) attempt to control for, and thereby rule out, the possible influence of context factors; or (c) seek powerful treatments that are effective across contexts. The effort to control context factors is characterized by empirical-analytic research-

ers as minimizing threats to internal and external validity. It is often pursued statistically. For example, students' prior knowledge in a concept-teaching experiment is controlled by use of analysis of covariance techniques, in order to minimize a possible selection threat to internal validity and, perhaps inappropriately, to extend external validity or generalizability.

A second implication concerns the treatment of context when it cannot be ignored, avoided, or overcome, for example, when the results of concept-teaching experiments are found to vary systematically with the students, teachers, or schools involved in the studies. Then, context is likely to be acknowledged and treated as one or more variables such as subject area, grade level, community SES, or student racial-ethnic background. These so-called mediating, or intervening, variables are measured and treated quantitatively, along with other independent variables of interest in the study. The resulting generalizations are necessarily qualified according to the statistically identified relationships among context and other variables.

The Interpretive Paradigm

Although symbolic or interpretive researchers may examine the past and look to the future, they tend to be present-oriented as they examine what is happening in a given setting. Their focus extends beyond the observable to the meanings that participants give to their communication and interaction and to the context or "situation" in which the interaction occurs. Social interaction is seen as creating and maintaining social roles and rules; the latter are not viewed as lawlike social regularities awaiting discovery. Rather than presuming discrete variables or behaviors, attention is directed to patterns of interaction and their meanings to participants. Situated and situational understanding is sought, rather than cross-site generalizability. Teaching, for example, is viewed in terms of the interaction of a specific teacher and group of students in a specific classroom, time, and place, not in terms of generic teacher behaviors.

The overriding interest of interpretive researchers is practical; their purpose is to understand "what's happening," especially the operative social rules and meanings in the situation under study. Teacher and student norms and the "negotiated order" of the classroom, for example, are sought out in order to understand what students are or are not learning and why (e.g., traditional gender roles, how to think critically about social issues). Interpretive researchers seek to understand the particular setting being studied and to inform understanding of other, similar settings but not to formulate lawlike generalizations that might enable prediction and control.

Among the assumptions underlying interpretive research, two are especially relevant here. One is the assumption that the conceptions and interpretations of participants in a situation take precedence over those of outside observers. Consequently, imposition of predefined categories such as teacher praise or warmth are eschewed in favor of emergent categories based on the researchers' interpretations of the meanings given to events by their participants. There is a blending of the researchers' theoretical or other frame of reference with that of the participants.

The importance of incorporating participant conceptions

into educational research arises from the presumption that behavior is purposeful and that outsiders cannot adequately interpret the actions of insiders without access and attention to their meanings and purposes, as well as to the contexts and interactive course of observed behavior. Teachers and students do what they do because their actions serve desired ends. Their activity might seem absurd or worse to the observer unacquainted with their conceptions of the situation in question. What might count as teacher praise, reward, or reinforcement to the researcher (e.g., smiling, patting a student on the shoulder, saying "good work, I'm proud of you"), for example, might not be so perceived and acted upon by the student(s). Employment of only the researcher's definitions could result in misunderstanding of the situation by the researcher and invalid conclusions.

The second assumption is succinctly expressed by the title of Mishler's (1979) article, "Meaning in Context: Is There Any Other Kind?" Mishler argued that what is happening in a situation cannot be adequately understood apart from or outside of the situation. And, because situations differ in ways that may be important to understanding them, a priori generalization is undesirable. Contextualized understanding, however, does not preclude generalization by readers of an interpretive study to other situations that they see as similar. Here, generalization from one situation to others is the responsibility of the reader, rather than of the researcher.

Wineburg and Wilson's (1988) account of an exemplary teacher's U.S. history class provides a dramatic illustration of the importance of contextualized interpretation. Their commentary on this case of "wisdom of practice" is worth quoting at length.

The exchange between Price and his students takes less than five minutes. He dominates the conversation, uttering more than 750 words, compared to the 26 words that a subset of his students contribute.... A casual observer peering into Price's classroom door might claim to have seen what other researchers have observed—teacher-dominated, whole-group instruction, with activities centered on the teacher's questions and explanations.

But there is something that makes this class different from those described by the researchers. There is electricity in the air. Students lean forward in their seats, ask thoughtful and stimulating questions, and stay in the room to continue discussions after the bell has rung.... No ordinary teacher, John Price is a master performer who has seized the collective imagination of 35 adolescents and has led them on an expedition into the past. (pp. 54–55)

Interpretive theory is directed to the process and conditions of classroom interaction (i.e., the creation of social rules governing action) more than to its substance or products. Two types of causality are recognized as legitimate by interpretive researchers. One is "because of," when the cause or causes of an event are taken to be a previous event or events, as in empirical-analytic research. The second is "in order to," when the "individual intentionally does a particular act in order to bring about something in the future" (Popkewitz, 1986, p. 17) such as a student studying in order to score well on a test or participating in class in order to please the teacher and thereby "earn" a good grade.

The assumptions of interpretive research are in direct opposition to the empirical-analytic paradigm's assumptions of generalizable laws, or rules, and discrete variables. Implications for conceptualizing and dealing with context also are quite different. Here, context is an integral part of what is to be studied in order to understand what is happening, not something to be ignored, avoided, overcome, or separated into statistically manipulable variables. Context is studied descriptively by observation, interview, and documentation; it may be studied interpretively using categories derived inductively from the descriptive data. The context of interest to interpretive researchers usually is the immediate, or local, social context of interaction, that is, the reading group, the social studies classroom, or the curriculum study committee. The social context includes overlapping interpersonal, organizational, community, and societal layers. Examples include the dyad or group (interpersonal), the school, the school district, the state or provincial department of education and/or national educational system (organizational), the PTA or local chamber of commerce (community), and the national demographic trends or social movements (societal).

Interpersonal context, which is of particular interest to interpretive researchers, is the immediate setting shaping individual behavior. Behavior, even at the dyadic (e.g., teacher–student) level, is not simply a function of individual attributes such as age, gender, or race-ethnicity, but also of place and history. Goffman (1964), for example, detailed the "neglected situation," or interpersonal setting, demonstrating that interpersonal interactions such as those between a teacher and one or more students constitute social situations with distinguishing cultural characteristics and frameworks. They are not merely sequences of verbal and nonverbal behavior. "Cultural rules establish how individuals are to conduct themselves ... and these rules for comingling ... socially organize the behavior of those in the situation" (p. 135). Consider, for example, differences in "appropriate" teacher–student interaction in the classroom, the school corridor between classes, and a hardware store at the community shopping center.

Because interpersonal interactions are social contexts that shape the behavior of participants, understanding observed interpersonal behavior requires the identification of the operative cultural rules, rules generated in part by the participants. A common example is the social studies recitation consisting of teacher-question, student-response, teacher-reaction interactions, occasionally interspersed with teacher elaboration of important points and teacher reprimand of a student deemed inattentive or uncooperative. Typically, the recitation is mutually defined as one in which the teacher controls the interaction as director and judge while the students play the passive, dependent role of complying with teacher demands in order to obtain favorable evaluations. The differential status of teacher and students in these exchanges is evident in their respective rights and responsibilities. The teacher as questioner has the right to determine the topic and how it is to be pursued, to speak at any time, to select other participants, and to terminate their participation. The students have the obligation to respond when requested and to remain quietly cooperative and receptive at other times. If students resist or challenge the implicit or explicit rules, teachers tend to assert their authority or employ coercive power in an effort to regain control of the interaction.

Contrast the social situation of the recitation with that of the group discussion. Here the understood rights and responsibilities of teachers and students and their patterns of interaction are much different. The same behavior on the part of teacher or students, such as students asking questions of or responding directly to one another, has different meanings (and consequences) in the two contexts.

The Critical Paradigm

Critical researchers situate the present in historical and social context. The social context of concern here is not only the immediate situation of interest to interpretive researchers but also the larger organizational, or structural context that constitutes the educational system and the broader societal, or sociocultural, context that encompasses the educational system. (Structural and sociocultural contexts are elaborated and illustrated in later sections of this chapter and subsequent chapters of this volume.) The scope of critical research is wider and deeper than that of either empirical-analytic or interpretive research, extended beyond the observable to the larger, historically shaped structural and sociocultural contexts, as well as to participant meanings in the situation at hand. From a critical perspective, the patterns of social interaction that interpretive researchers view as creating and maintaining social roles and rules (and that empirical-analytic researchers see as instances of discoverable regularities of social life) cannot be understood adequately apart from history, biography, and social structure (Mills, 1959). Within this expanded conception of context, generalization is possible, although not a priority for most critical researchers.

The overriding interest of critical researchers is emancipation; their purpose is to "demystify the patterns of knowledge and social conditions that produce domination and restrict human possibilities" (Popkewitz, 1986, p. 19). Whereas Marxist variants of critical research stand "in opposition to the dominant culture, its values and institutions" and purport to "guide people in establishing new meanings, practices and relationships" (p. 19), researchers in the less deterministic sociology of knowledge variants of critical research are concerned with critiquing dominant cultural patterns and identifying alternatives.

Critical researchers are explicitly normative. For example, researchers from both critical traditions might examine the norms and values communicated through classroom interaction patterns and the ways in which these norms and values benefit some students (e.g., boys) but not others (e.g., girls). Their interpretations probably would differ, with neo-Marxists attributing more explanatory power to the national economic system, especially to the forms of production and the need to maintain societal structures.

The efforts of critical researchers to account for what is observed and to respond to the question of who benefits from classroom interaction patterns and the norms and values they communicate are not limited to the situation at hand. Rather, they attempt to relate the observed situation to the larger sociocultural and structural contexts that encompass and shape it.

From a critical perspective, differential teacher interaction with male and female students that fosters perpetuation of traditional gender roles, for example, is not simply a function of the classroom situation or of natural law. Rather, it is a socially and historically constructed practice that is amenable to reconstruction. The knowledge generated by critical research is intended to further educators' understanding of "the assumptions and implications of their practices, thus opening a search for alternatives providing greater social justice" (Popkewitz, 1986, p. 19). Emancipation is fostered by skepticism, questioning, and critique.

Two of the assumptions underlying critical research are especially relevant here. One is that society and its institutions, including schooling and social studies education, do not adequately embody democratic and humanitarian ideals. The corollary is that they can and should be moved toward such goals. The second, related, assumption is that schooling, like other social institutions, is a product of its social milieu and history. Given that social studies education is a function of its structural and sociocultural contexts over time, improving social studies education requires changing those contexts. Contextual change, in turn, requires understanding the nature of those contexts, their internal dymanics and interrelationships. Thus, context and contextual change become major foci of critical research. The point is not simply that one can deal with context from a critical perspective, but that context must be addressed.

Critical theory is directed to the substance, as well as the process and conditions, of schooling and classroom interaction. Beyond description and explanation, it is intended to critique and illuminate in ways that foster emancipatory action. The two types of causality recognized in interpretive research are also recognized here. However, "because of" causality tends to be more broadly construed to incorporate multiple historical and contemporary "causes," and "in order to" causality encompasses not only individual reasons or motives but also the social and historical experience that shaped them. Interpretive researchers could accommodate these broader conceptions of causality, but most tend not to do so. Importantly, causality and change are seen as involving contradictions and reciprocal transformations, rather than as linear or additive.

The implications for conceptualizing and dealing with context from a critical perspective can be seen as extensions of those stemming from an interpretive paradigm. Context is emphasized and extended in historical depth and social scope. The interactions of interest are those among groups and organizations, or institutions, as well as among individuals. Historical and contemporary context are examined and interrogated, quantitatively and qualitatively, through observation, interview, and documentary records. Expanding the definition of relevant context also renders causality and change more complex in theory and practice. In addition, critical research is explicitly normative and action-oriented. The knowledge it generates is for understanding that can empower practitioners, enabling them to improve practice consistent with values of human dignity and social justice.

WHICH CONTEXT?

One's implicit or explicit paradigmatic affiliation directs the conceptualization and treatment of context in social studies and other educational research and in the interpretation and evaluation of research. Beyond general conceptualization, however, the specific aspects of context that are selected for examination depend on what one is studying, that is, the context of what? In presenting the empirical-analytic, interpretive, and critical research approaches to context, I used teacher–student, or classroom, interaction as my common example. Other examples such as social studies teacher education, textbooks, and assessment of student learning would have directed attention to other context factors.

Making context manageable and meaningful requires distinguishing those aspects of the environment for which there is evidence or reason to expect influence on social studies education, or that part of it that is of interest in a particular study. For example, the activity of the religious right in U.S. society and politics influenced social studies curriculum and other aspects of education in the 1980s, but it seems not to have influenced social studies teacher education in substantial ways. However, social studies teacher education programs in colleges sponsored by fundamentalist religions or in heavily fundamentalist communities may well be shaped by their milieu; prospective teachers may learn about acceptable social studies topics and approaches from instructors who share or are influenced by community religious values.

The relevant context varies over time and with the local situation within the national milieu. Further variation is evident in the relative strength or intensity of particular context factors and how they interact with one another from case to case (e.g., are they complementary or do they conflict?). For example, the activities of groups such as the Eagle Forum, the Heritage Foundation, the American Civil Liberties Union (ACLU), and People for the American Way are part of the context of social studies curriculum; they may or may not be relevant in a particular case. Further, the activities of the Eagle Forum and People for the American Way probably would conflict and perhaps even cancel each other out, whereas the activities of the ACLU and People for the American Way probably would be complementary.

Aspects of context are more validly seen as overlapping and interacting clusters than as separate factors arranged in lists or nonoverlapping circles. Earlier, the organizational or structural context that constitutes the educational system was distinguished from the broader societal or sociocultural context that encompasses it. The structural (i.e., educational system) context of social studies education, nested within the sociocultural context, rarely has clear-cut or stable boundaries. Whatever the educational system boundaries, they are rarely impermeable. Nesting also occurs within structural and sociocultural contexts, for example, classrooms within departments within schools within school districts within states and communities within regions within the nation. Further, past events and experiences are potential context for subsequent ones.

Given its multifaceted, nested, and fluid nature, the relevant context cannot be predetermined. There is no generic context, no fixed set of parameters or invariant grid, that can be imposed. Instead, potentially relevant context factors can be identified, and their role in a particular case can be examined.

Prior research and conceptualization suggest several different contextual clusters or layers that are likely to be relevant to social studies education and different ways of partitioning them. However, there have been too few published works on context that go beyond listing potentially influential variables to offer an empirically grounded, integrated account of context relevant to educational research or school practice. Differences in the conceptualization of context can be linked to the author's paradigmatic affiliation and to the level of the phenomena of interest, from micro (classroom) to macro (national educational system). Illustrations reflecting interpretive and critical paradigms are drawn from the work of Warwick (1980), Popkewitz (1981), and Cornbleth (1988). Because of the nature of the empirical-analytic paradigm, there has been little work on or with context from that perspective.

National Context from an Interpretive Perspective

In his transactional model of national development planning and implementation, Warwick (1980) treated context at the macro level from a politically oriented, interpretive perspective. Warwick's framework of key context factors in national planning and program implementation also might be used to guide research aimed at understanding and accounting for national educational movements and change efforts.

Although noting that the salient environment or relevant context varies, depending on the area (e.g., social studies curriculum, teacher education) and kind of change (e.g., programmatic, accountability) in question, Warwick (1980) suggested that the following contextual factors be considered as potentially relevant. *Remote environment* refers to broader conditions whose influence is likely to be indirect or taken for granted and, therefore, ignored. *Proximate environment* refers to more immediate or contemporary conditions and actors whose influence is likely to be direct but not often taken into consideration in planning or research.

Remote Environment
    Social structure
    Culture
    Political institutions
    Formative historical experiences
Proximate Environment
    Power setting
        National authorities
        Bureaucratic rivals and allies
        Gatekeepers
        Interest groups
        International [external] donors
        Implementors
    Issue context
        Energizing issues
        Debilitating issues
Operating Environment
    Threat
    Uncertainty
    Complexity

Within Warwick's remote environment, *social structure* "refers to the patterns of interaction between or among individuals and groups in the society," whereas *culture* is defined as "the norms, values, beliefs, and symbols guiding the choices made by members of the society and shaping their interactions with each other" (p. 388). Within social studies education, cultural factors affected the fate of the Man: A Course of Study (MACOS) curriculum, and both cultural and social structural factors affected efforts to promote team teaching and cooperative learning. Political institutions and formative historical experiences, as well as culture, constrain efforts to establish a national social studies curriculum.

Within Warwick's proximate environment, influential actors (individuals, groups, organizations) constitute the power setting. They may have formal authority in the domain in question or informal influence. With respect to social studies curriculum, for example, assistant superintendents for instruction and social studies curriculum coordinators have formal authority, and textbooks publishers and their representatives and locally active interest groups can have considerable informal influence. External donors such as foundations or federal agencies can influence social studies curricula informally by offering funding for particular programs and formally through guidelines or regulations once funding is accepted by a school district. The implementors—the people who are to carry out the intended change, for example, social studies teachers—are too often overlooked despite their considerable influence on what does or does not occur.

Warwick (1980) defined the issue context of the proximate environment as "the points of discussion, debate, or controversy in the society" (p. 395). Whereas some issues are "energizing because they serve to arouse interest or mobilize support [for change]," others are "debilitating if they devitalize or contaminate the [change] policies with which they become associated" (pp. 395–396). For example, efforts to promote critical, or higher-order, thinking in social studies can be energized by association with issues of national economic competitiveness and debilitated by association with issues of erosion of traditional American values.

Conditions in the operating environment of a change effort that were identified by Warwick include threat or impending danger, uncertainty (i.e., political, economic, or social unpredictability), and complexity. All three are likely to discourage or impede change efforts. School personnel who see their positions as in danger of elimination because of political changes or possible budget cutbacks are unlikely to initiate curriculum-change projects. Complex curriculum-change efforts are less likely to be undertaken than simple ones, even if the former promise greater benefits.

Use of a multidimensional contextual framework such as that offered by Warwick could enhance studies of national movements and change efforts in social studies education in several ways. One is that the movement or change effort would be located in its broader historical, cultural, and sociopolitical context (Warwick's remote environment). When movements or change efforts such as the New Social Studies or attempts to establish a common, nationwide, social studies curriculum are studied in isolation or within a limited framework, they are more likely to be misunderstood. Undue emphasis is likely to be given to internal factors such as the characteristics of the

intended curriculum. A second way in which social studies research could be enhanced is through recognition of the complexity of the movement or change effort itself (Warwick's proximate environment). Omission of consideration of the range of potential, immediate, context factors leads to a partial view and misleading conclusions (e.g., that teachers' observed resistance to change is a function of personal characteristics).

Social Context From a Critical Perspective

In his formulation of the social context of classroom practice and change, Popkewitz (1981) treated the school and its surrounding community as context from a critical perspective. Whereas Warwick (1980) treated context to the national level, Popkewitz treated context at the level of the school and its community. Rather than focusing on teacher characteristics or behavior, individually or in the aggregate, as would be the inclination of empirical-analytic researchers, Popkewitz examined the collective school culture and organization. His purpose was not merely to describe, but also to probe beyond surface appearances and stated intentions, in an attempt to account for substantial differences in the learning opportunities made available to students in the schools he studied. This purpose distinguishes his work from that of interpretive researchers.

Popkewitz (1981) drew empirical support for his delineation of social context from a field study of six elementary schools that had been identified as exemplary implementors of the IGE (Individually Guided Education) curriculum model (Popkewitz, Tabachnick, Wehlage, 1982). That study was linked conceptually to prior work in the sociology of school knowledge in which "the interplay among classroom practices, professional ideologies and social and cultural interests" had been examined (Popkewitz, 1981, p. 189).

In the IGE study, Popkewitz et al. (1982) found that personnel in the six exemplary IGE schools used the IGE reform program in different ways. They did not simply adapt the IGE program to reach a common goal; they adapted both the IGE technology and its stated goals in ways that helped to conserve the differing prior conditions in the schools. The explanation of the differences among the schools, in Popkewitz's (1981) analysis, lay in the interrelated social contexts of the schools. He distinguished a pedagogical context, an occupational context of teaching, and a social/cultural context.

Pedagogical context consists of "the daily practices and discourse of classroom life and the patterns of this activity which produce conceptions of school work and knowledge" (Popkewitz, 1981, p. 190). What are the underlying assumptions and routine operating procedures that define what counts as worthwhile knowledge or learning and what constitutes appropriate classroom tasks? The IGE study clearly revealed different answers to this question in the six schools. The authors characterized the differing conditions of schooling that they observed as constructive, technical, and illusory.

Constructive schooling (found in one school) referred to an emphasis on "multiple ways by which children can come to know about the world . . . how knowledge is created . . . Knowledge is treated as permeable and provisional, ideas as tentative, and often ambiguous" (Popkewitz, 1981, pp. 193–194). In technical schooling (found in three schools), procedures were emphasized to enhance efficiency. "Knowledge was standardized; all important ideas and skills were measurable and expressed in a discrete, sequenced form . . . technologies and procedures rose to the status of values" (p. 193). In illusory schooling (found in two schools), little academic or subject-matter knowledge was provided.

Children and teachers engage in the rituals and ceremonies of reading, writing, and arithmetic, but in practice the lessons contain many instances in which the substance of teaching is not carried through. What occurs is an emphasis on form *as* substance . . . The discourse of schooling emphasizes cooperation, hard work, respect for property, and delay of gratification—qualities that teachers in illusory schools believe are not taught at home and have to be built into the school before any "real academic" learning can take place. (p. 194)

For example, students in illusory schools might recite the Pledge of Allegiance daily, but they rarely, if ever, engage in examination of the concepts of republic, liberty, or justice.

Popkewitz (1981) defined occupational context as the "social community which maintains ideologies and mechanisms of legitimacy" (p. 190) with respect to teaching as an occupation. For example, beliefs about how young people develop and learn, about how best to teach various skills and subjects, and about how to adapt teaching to the perceived needs of different student groups are part of a shared occupational context. Occupational context, with shapes pedagogical context, is shaped in turn by social/cultural context.

Social/cultural context refers to the community in which a school is located and "the manner in which a community's social/cultural and economic orientations, sensibilities, and awarenesses affect school practices" (Popkewitz, 1981, p. 190). Also included are "social demands which reflect both local concerns and larger social and cultural issues" (p. 198). In all six schools, the teachers' and administrators' perceptions of community life-styles, occupation, values, and expectations influenced their adaptation of the IGE reform. According to Popkewitz,

In two of the three technical schools, for example, there was an emphasis on teaching the functional skills, responsibility, and discipline that teachers believed would enable the children to succeed in the blue-collar or low-status service occupations of their parents. The intellectual and social point of view in the constructive school responded to the professional, social, and cultural orientation of a community in which interpersonal control, facility with language, and responsiveness to the subtle nuances of interpersonal situations are important. The illusory schools, located in poor communities, reflected the pedagogical ideology of pathology and therapy [i.e., the belief that the problems these students brought to school made academic teaching and learning impossible]. (p. 200)

Although differences among the schools were related to socioeconomic variations among the six communities, the schools did not simply mirror the economic situation of their locations. In addition to SES, religion, geographic location, and community continuity or stability also appeared to be influential aspects of social/cultural context that shaped the conditions of schooling. Technical schools, for example, were found in a poor rural community, in a working, middle-class suburb, and in an affluent, business-oriented community.

Use of a formulation of the social context of classroom practice and change such as that employed by Popkewitz (1981) could enhance social studies classroom research by sensitizing researchers and readers to the ways in which context shapes practice to the benefit of some students and to the disadvantage of others. Critical attention to social context not only increases the explanatory power of classroom and school research but also points to the interrelated changes needed for substantial improvement of social studies teaching and learning.

Structural and Sociocultural Context From a Critical Perspective

A third conceptualization of context relevant to social studies research takes curriculum practice and change as its focus and encompasses both structural and sociocultural context factors (Cornbleth, 1988, 1990). It can be used to frame curriculum studies from the classroom to the national level. This formulation has been influenced by the work of Popkewitz (1981, 1984) and developed in conjunction with studies of educational policy and planning (Adams & Cornbleth, in press; Cornbleth & Adams, 1987). It reflects a critical perspective insofar as the purpose is to account for the substance and distribution of learning opportunities made available to students and their individual and societal, social and political, and pedagogical origins and implications.

Understanding this approach to context requires at least a brief description of the conception of curriculum associated with it (Cornbleth, 1985a, 1988). Curriculum is viewed as a contextualized social process—the day-to-day interactions of students, teachers, knowledge, and milieu. From this view, curriculum construction and change become an ongoing social activity shaped by various contextual influences within and beyond the classroom. A tangible product, usually a document or plan (e.g., a curriculum guide), is one aspect of the context that shapes curriculum practice. If curriculum is constructed and reconstructed in situated practice, then curricular change or stability involves an interplay of biographical (personal and professional), structural, and sociocultural factors over time. Curricular practice and change reflect and respond to their immediate and more distant contexts, as has been illustrated in several recent field studies (e.g., Cornbleth, 1985b; McNeil, 1986; Popkewitz, et al., 1982). One implication of this view is that curricular change is largely a matter of contextual change.

Distinguishing between structural and sociocultural contexts makes context more manageable. Even more important, the distinction calls attention to the educational system as part of the context of curriculum, which tends to be overlooked in curriculum discourse and taken for granted in curriculum practice, particularly in the United States. In critical theoretical work, for example, curriculum is typically treated in relation to larger sociocultural dynamics such as economic and gender relations, but the more immediate setting is neglected. In effect, the intervening structural context of curricula is bypassed. Educational systems are not simply conduits that convey or reflect and, thus, reproduce larger societal patterns. Structural context is important because it both mediates extrasystemic sociocultural influences and generates curriculum practice.

Structural Context. The educational system as structural context includes established roles and relationships including operating procedures, shared beliefs, and the norms that shape them (i.e., tradition, culture). The structure of an educational system conditions outsiders' interaction(s) with it and participants' interaction(s) within it (Archer, 1984). Typically, a national educational system is comprised of several interrelated and, often, nested subsystems. For example, social studies classrooms and the elementary and secondary schools that house them constitute subsystems of the U.S. educational system. As subsystems, social studies classrooms and their curricula are subject to the structural conditioning and social interaction of the larger system (e.g., school, district, nation), as well as to their own internal dynamics. Viewing the educational system as the structural context of curriculum thus directs attention to the roles, relationships, patterns of activity, and culture of interacting system components. Example of structural-context influences are offered to illustrate how they operate and how they might be studied.

In *Contradictions of Control,* McNeil (1986) examined links between school organization and priorities, that is, structural context, on the one hand, and selection, organization, and treatment of social studies classroom knowledge, on the other. Drawing on her field studies of four U.S. high schools, she argued that school knowledge is a function of school organization and administrative emphasis on either controlling students or educating them. What McNeil characterized as "defensive teaching" was more common at the two schools where administrators distanced themselves from curricular concerns, providing little academic support for teachers, and gave priority to controls on students and, less overtly, on teachers.

Defensive teaching, in which students are controlled by controlling classroom knowledge, is characterized by (a) fragmentation or reduction of information, such as New Deal programs, to lists; (b) mystification, or the presentation of a complex or controversial topic such as the Federal Reserve System or socialism as important but unknowable; (c) omission, for example, of contemporary events in U.S. history; and (d) defensive simplification, that is, seeking "students' compliance on a lesson by promising that it will not be difficult and will not go into any depth" (p. 174). In short, there is a "ritual of seeming to deal with the topic" (p. 175).

McNeil found that defensive teaching "cut across differences in teachers' individual political and pedagogical philosophies and across formal definitions of variations in student abilities" (p. 178), suggesting that its occurrence was more a function of school context than individual style. According to McNeil, when

administrative personnel expend most of the staff's time, meetings and resources on discussions of hall order, discipline and numbers of course credits earned, teachers respond wth overt but usually reluctant compliance on those goals, but reduce effort and aim for only minimal standards in their actual teaching. (p. 160)

In such structural contexts McNeil found that teachers

choose to simplify content and reduce demands on students in return for classroom order and minimal student compliance on assignments . . . they teach "defensively," choosing methods of presentation and evaluation that they hope will make their workload more efficient and create as little student resistance as possible. (p. 158)

Thus, analysis of relationships between school organization or administrative context and the occurrence of defensive teaching revealed "a parallel between administrators' attempts to gain minimal compliance from teachers and teachers' settling for minimal compliance from students" (p. 177).

In contrast, at the one of the four schools where administrators most supported teaching and provided incentives for instructional quality,

teachers responded by demanding more of themselves in the presentation and preparation of lessons. They felt, and demonstrated, less of a wall between their personal knowledge and the "official" knowledge of the classroom. They developed entire courses, used original handouts and continually collected and re-designed materials. They used fewer lists and provided more extended descriptions, more opportunities for student discussion, more varieties of learning experiences. (p. 177)

McNeil highlighted an important irony: Efforts to improve schooling by means of regulation or control have the opposite effect. They encourage defensive teaching and minimize meaningful learning. Her account of the school organizational and administrative aspects of the structural context of social studies curriculum vividly illustrates their influence on what students have an opportunity to learn in their social studies classes. Further research along these lines, that is, social studies classroom research that attends to structural context, could extend understanding of curriculum practice and inform social studies curriculum reform efforts.

Consistent with McNeil's (1986) findings regarding the influence of structural context on social studies teaching, McCarthy and Schrag (1988) observed that differences between social studies department chair and school principal leadership were associated with the extent of higher-order thinking in social studies classes. Their conclusions were based on 165 social studies classroom observations and interviews with teachers, department chairs, students, and principals in five very different high schools in which the social studies departments were identified as emphasizing higher order thinking. Ratings of the thoughtfulness observed in each class showed school differences not attributable to individual teachers or differences in the socioeconomic or racial makeup of the student bodies.

The schools that received the highest thoughtfulness ratings had strong departmental leadership and principals who actively supported the department chair's efforts. These department chairs were described as "dynamic leaders who inspire commitment . . . [and] work energetically to improve the quality of thinking in their department's classes" (McCarthy & Schrag, 1988, pp. 17–18). In the top three schools, "principals were very active in working closely with department heads, but in neither of the bottom two did this occur" (p. 18). In addition, success in promoting thoughtfulness was found to be related to a "culture of collegiality which involves consistent, focused discussion of teaching and curriculum within the department" (p. 18). McCarthy and Schrag concluded that "the institutional [i.e., structural] context does make a difference. Collegial school culture and pedagogical leadership from department heads and principals help teachers promote higher order thinking in their classrooms" (p. 18).

How schools as organizations influence teachers and teaching is further illustrated by Zeichner, Tabachnick, and Densmore's (1987) 2-year field study of prospective and beginning elementary teachers. The teachers' perspectives and teaching were found to be shaped not only by their personal characteristics, dispositions, and abilities but also by school organizational controls and cultures. With respect to organizational controls, Edwards's (1979) distinctions among personal, bureaucratic, and technical forms of organizational control were found to be helpful "in understanding how the first-year teachers learned what was expected of them, how desired behaviors were reinforced, and how organizational sanctions were applied" (Zeichner, et al., 1987, p. 53).

Personal control involves direct, personal supervision of teachers' activities by superordinates such as department chairs, principals, or supervisors whose close monitoring increases the likelihood that the teachers "comply with organizational norms" (p. 53). Bureaucratic control is embedded in the school's organization or social structure and "enforced through impersonal bureaucratic rules and hierarchical social relations. Sanctions and rewards . . . are dictated by officially approved policies to which . . . role groups, are held responsible" (p. 53). Technical control, in contrast, is embedded in the physical organization or "structure of the labor process, and jobs are designed in such a way as to minimize the need to rely on workers' compliance with impersonal bureaucratic rules" (p. 53) or organizational norms. In teaching, direction of work tasks, evaluation of work, and reward or discipline can be accomplished technically by adoption of instructional packages or by team teaching arrangements.

Zeichner et al. (1987) found little evidence of personal control of the first-year teachers by their principals. Only one principal attempted to obtain compliance by directly monitoring teacher classroom behavior. Bureaucratic control was widespread but unevenly enforced. Although

there were numerous bureaucratic rules and regulations in each school that attempted to dictate to teachers how and what to teach, procedures for managing pupil behavior . . . and such general activities as when teachers could leave the school buildings . . . the first-year teachers were frequently able to ignore or even to openly violate bureaucratic rules when they wanted to do so. The self-contained classrooms in three of the four schools together with the minimal amount of personal supervision by principals in these three schools weakened the controlling effects of a bureaucratic organization. (p. 53)

The most pervasive and powerful form of organizational control in these four schools was technical. Technical control "was exerted through the timing of instruction, the [written] curriculum and curriculum materials, and the architecture of the schools" (p. 54). It was particularly evident in the one school with a team-teaching arrangement, "where the pace and form of instruction, the open architectural plan, the precise time schedules, and the performance-based curriculum [and pre-set tests] all made deviation from the preferred patterns of teaching very difficult" (p. 54). Technical control, however, was neither absolute nor irresistible. Zeichner et al. (1987) observed that teachers could avoid or redirect aspects of technical control that conflicted with strongly held personal goals if they had the requisite political skills.

In addition to these formal organizational controls over teaching, Zeichner et al. (1987) pointed to the often powerful, but tacit, informal teacher, student, and school cultures that communicate school ethos, tradition, and expectations:

There was usually one formal school culture, but there were several different and often conflicting versions of the informal school culture within a single school; one or more of these informal school cultures were often in conflict with the officially sanctioned one. It was the interaction of these formal and informal cultures rather than the presence or absence of any particular control mechanism by itself that determined the institutional [i.e., structural] constraints and opportunities presented to each teacher. (pp. 54–55)

Aspects of structural context beyond the individual school also have been found to shape classroom and teaching practice. Evidence of the impact of school district and state policies not only suggests that researchers look beyond the school for relevant structural context influences but also that school improvement efforts must extend beyond school walls if they are to be successful. In a year-long field study of the meanings that 19 teachers who were voluntarily participating in a districtwide critical-thinking pilot project gave to critical thinking in their talk and social studies classroom practice, I found that teachers' interpretations of critical thinking were shaped less by project documents and activities than by their preexisting beliefs and practices, the conditions of classroom teaching, and the school district's goals and policies (Cornbleth, 1985b).

Across grade levels (5th, 8th, 11th) and schools, the teachers' interpretations of critical thinking were characterized by fragmentation, mechanization, and a product orientation. Critical thinking was fragmented into skills and elements of essay writing. (In this project, critical thinking was assessed through student essay writing.) *Mechanization* refers to the highly structured and teacher-directed nature of observed critical-thinking tasks and to the teachers' tendency not to pursue student questions. Production orientation was evidenced in the emphasis teachers placed on student production of coherent essays (i.e., written responses to a given question that were well organized and contained the following elements: a topic statement, evidence and examples, an explanation, a conclusion).

Whereas fragmentation and mechanization of critical thinking appeared to be related to teachers' preexisting beliefs and practices and to the conditions and demands of classroom teaching, the product orientation was clearly related to school district goals and policies. A major district goal over the past several years had been to improve student achievement, as measured by commercial and teacher-developed tests. Considerable class time was spent in testing, and school-level test scores were widely publicized, on the assumption that the importance attached to test scores would focus and improve teaching, which in turn would improve student achievement. The teacher-developed, critical-thinking, essay tests were part of the district's testing program. Although intended to be diagnostic, they seemed to be viewed by teachers as achievement measures that could be used against themselves and their students. There was widespread teacher concern that students perform well on the tests and, to this end, most teachers provided more classroom opportunity, support, and instruction for essay writing than for critical thought or dialogue. Scoring of the essay tests was standardized, with scores based on the presence and quality of each of the prescribed elements. The teachers' interpretations of critical thinking and teaching for critical thinking can be seen to make sense in this structural context.

Farrar's (1988) analysis of the structural and sociocultural contexts of school-based reform efforts highlights the often competing perspectives and interests of classroom teachers, school and school district administrators, state policymakers, and the courts. On the basis of a year-long field study of school-based improvement and effective teaching programs in five urban high schools across the U.S., she concluded that, in addition to cultures and organization "antithetical to the purposes of school-based improvement programs" (p. 4), urban high schools operate within an environment that limits their capacity to improve teaching and learning.

State mandates, district policies and procedures, court requirements in de-segregation cases, the interests of bargaining units and the claims of diverse interest groups with a voice in education compete and interact such as to supersede, countermand or undermine school authority. Decentralizing authority to the schools was considered key to the success of school-based programs, but the formal as well as informal authority of external groups and organizations has had the effect of re-centralizing responsibility [and control] to the district or state level. (pp. 5–6)

As a result, the schools have little discretion for self-improvement but increasing accountability for externally imposed improvement outcomes. They are made "responsible for the effective implementation of policies established by others—a top-down reform strategy whose failure helped promote current ideas that reforms should be developed at the school level" (p. 6).

One example of external structural context influences on school-based improvement efforts described by Farrar was that of a teacher-designed, cross-disciplinary, team-teaching and counseling program being superseded by a citywide curriculum and testing program. The teachers regretted the time they had spent on the innovative program, and the school's improvement program stalled.

The just-cited studies are instructive on at least two counts. They illustrate the influence of structural context factors on social studies education, thus supporting the argument that social studies research ought to be contextualized. Second, they illustrate how context can be studied, that is, how contextual questions can be addressed in social studies research. As a group, these studies reflect an interpretive, more than a critical, paradigm. However, the procedures they employed could serve critical purposes in future field studies.

Sociocultural Context. The sociocultural context of social studies education consists of those extrasystemic demographic, social, political, and economic conditions; traditions and ideologies; and events that influence social studies teaching and learning and teacher education. Sociocultural context can be considered at several levels, from the local neighborhood or community (e.g., Popkewitz's, 1981, social/cultural context) to the nation or the world community. Influence can be direct or indirect. The latter may involve the education system as mediator. That is, extrasystemic pressures for educational change often are filtered and modified by educational policymakers and practitioners. The history of the New Social Studies provides a case in point.

The sociocultural context usually provides the impetus for change (e.g., computer literacy). The U.S. educational system's seemingly greater responsiveness to external expectations and demands than to those of its clients or participants (e.g., students and teachers) may be a function of "the external legitimation, definition, and control of their [schools'] internal processes" (Meyer, 1983, p. 269). In addition, with a few notable exceptions, it appears that the sociocultural context is less conservative (or at least more heterogeneous and turbulent) than the structural context. As a result, external demands for change are often moderated within the system. Acknowledged problems and desired but difficult to obtain goals may be redefined and acted upon in ways that are system maintaining rather than reformist (e.g., Cornbleth & Adams, 1987; Popkewitz, 1982). For example, calls for more attention to critical or higher order thinking in social studies often are translated into lists of presumably discrete skills to be mastered. This translation occurs, in part, because a skills approach is more easily incorporated into existing social studies programs and classroom practices than an approach emphasizing substantive verbal or written discourse.

Sociocultural context has been treated only briefly in this chapter, and several components are explored in other chapters in this section. In addition, sociocultural context seems to be more widely recognized by social studies educators and researchers than is structural context. However, the impact of sociocultural context has not been systematically explored in social studies research. A notable exception is Anyon's (1981) study of differences in the social studies and other knowledge made available to students in elementary schools located in different SES communities. Yet even this study sheds little light on how SES differences come to be translated into differential learning opportunities. In the future, social studies researchers might attend, not only to relations between sociocultural factors and social studies education experience or outcomes, but also to the means by which sociocultural factors affect social studies classroom practice either directly or indirectly through one or more layers of the educational system.

CONCLUSIONS

Exploration of the meanings of context from different paradigmatic perspectives, examination of different ways of addressing context, and excerpts from illustrative studies have been offered as argument and evidence in support of the value and feasibility of contextualizing social studies research. In 1982, I noted that "Of the social studies classroom research published in the last five years (fewer than 30 studies were located), a majority of the studies tend toward the asocial on all three dimensions [contextualization, interactive/dynamic, sensitivity to participant conceptions]" (Cornbleth, 1982, p. 7). A similar (unpublished) review of the empirical studies reported in *Theory and Research in Social Education* in the years 1986–1988, revealed little change. The large majority were acontextual. Beyond brief description of samples or settings, there was little attention to structural or sociocultural context. Context tended not to be studied or considered in accounting for findings.

Contextualization of social studies research might take at least two directions regardless of the paradigm adopted. One is research on social studies education in context, in which aspects of the context of the phenomena of interest are examined and considered in interpreting findings and suggesting generalizability. The second is research on aspects of the context of social studies education, for example, on interrelated structural, sociocultural, or other factors (e.g., school, family, peers) that appear to influence social studies classroom practice or mediate its effects. Context is background in the former and foreground in the latter. In neither case is social studies or context studied in isolation.

References

Adams, D., & Cornbleth, C. (in press). *Planning Educational Change*. London: Falmer.

Anyon, J. (1981). Social class and school knowledge. *Curriculum Inquiry, 11,* 3–42.

Archer, M. S. (1984). *Social origins of educational systems*. London: Sage.

Bredo, E., & Feinberg, W. (1982). *Knowledge & values in social & educational research*. Philadelphia: Temple University Press.

Cornbleth, C. (1982). On the social study of social studies. *Theory and Research in Social Education, 10*(4), 1–16.

Cornbleth, C. (1985a). Reconsidering social studies curriculum. *Theory and Research in Social Education, 13*(2), 31–45.

Cornbleth, C. (1985b, April). *Socioecology of critical thinking*. Paper presented at the meeting of the American Educational Research Association, Chicago.

Cornbleth, C. (1988). Curriculum in and out of context. *Journal of Curriculum and Supervision, 3*(2), 85–96.

Cornbleth, C. (1990). *Curriculum in Context*. London: Falmer Press.

Cornbleth, C., & Adams, D. (1987). The drunkard's streetlamp? Contexts of policy change in U.S. teacher education. In Higher Education Group (Ed.), *Governments and higher education: The legitimacy of intervention* (pp. 314–344). Toronto: Ontario Institute for Studies in Education.

Edwards, R. (1979). *Contested terrain: The transformation of the American workplace in the 20th century*. New York: Basic Books.

Farrar, E. (1988, April). *Environmental contexts and the implementation of teacher and school-based reforms: Competing interests*. Paper presented at the meeting of the American Educational Research Association, New Orleans.

Goffman, E. (1964). The neglected situation. *American Anthropologist, 66,* 133–136.

Habermas, J. (1972). *Knowledge and human interests* (2nd ed.). London: Heinemann.

McCarthy, C., & Schrag, F. (1988). Department and principal leadership in promoting higher order thinking. In F. M. Newmann (Ed.), *Higher order thinking in high school social studies: An analysis of classrooms, teachers, students, and leadership* (chap. VII). Madison, WI: University of Wisconsin, National Center on Effective Secondary Schools.

McNeil, L. M. (1986). *Contradictions of control: School structure and school knowledge*. New York: Routledge and Kegan Paul.

Meyer, J. W. (1983). Conclusion: Institutionalization and the rationality of formal organizational structure. In J. W. Meyer & W. R. Scott (Eds.), *Organizational environments* (pp. 261–282). Beverly Hills, CA: Sage.

Mills, C. W. (1959). *The sociological imagination*. New York: Oxford University Press.

Mishler, E. G. (1979). Meaning in context: Is there any other kind? *Harvard Educational Review, 49,* 1–19.

Popkewitz, T. S. (1981). The social contexts of schooling, change, and educational research. *Journal of Curriculum Studies, 13,* 189–206.

Popkewitz, T. S. (1982). Educational reform as the organization of ritual: Stability as change. *Journal of Education, 164,* 5–29.

Popkewitz, T. S. (1984). *Paradigm and ideology in educational research*. London: Falmer Press.

Popkewitz, T. S. (1986). Paradigm and purpose. In C. Cornbleth (Ed.), *An invitation to research in social education* (pp. 10–27). Washington, DC: National Council for the Social Studies.

Popkewitz, T. S., Tabachnick, B. R., & Wehlage, G. (1982). *The myth of educational reform*. Madison, WI: University of Wisconsin Press.

Shaver, J. P. (1982). Reappraising the theoretical goals of research in social education. *Theory and Research in Social Education, 9*(4), 1–16.

Warwick, D. (1980). Integrating planning and implementation: A transactional approach. In R. Davis (Ed.), *Planning education for development, Vol. 1* (pp. 379–411). Cambridge, MA: Harvard University Press.

Wineburg, S. S., & Wilson, S. M. (1988). Models of wisdom in the teaching of history. *Phi Delta Kappan, 70*(1), 50–58.

Zeichner, K. M., Tabachnick, B. R., & Densmore, K. (1987). Individual, institutional, and cultural influences on the development of teachers' craft knowledge. In J. Calderhead (Ed.), *Exploring teachers' thinking* (pp. 21–59). London: Cassell.

·22·

STUDENT GROUPS AND SCHOOL STRUCTURE

Philip A. Cusick
MICHIGAN STATE UNIVERSITY

The purpose of this chapter is to examine data from several descriptive studies to describe informal student groups as they operate within the school structure and influence what students learn in school about citizenship. The chapter is grounded in three ideas. The first is *citizenship education,* which, as Shaver (1987) said, is "that part of the elementary and secondary school curriculum that is specifically concerned with . . . transmitting values, teaching social science and history. . . . and encouraging the development of competencies in decision making and participation" (p. 115). As the argument goes, schools teach citizenship because our representative democracy is dependent on citizen participation. The major purpose of such education is to legitimate government to students, to teach them to transcend the personal in favor of communal interests, and to teach them to think of the nation-state as a community and themselves as members of that community.

The second basic idea is *school structure* or, because schools are social institutions, the *social structure of the school.* Defined, structure is the "constellation of linked and articulated role sets" (Merton, 1957, p. 261). In both their peer groups and the formal school, students have certain roles that contain notions of appropriate behavior, responsibility, and distributive justice. These roles also encourage certain values, modes of participation, and ways of making decisions. In the chapter, the roles that students play within both their groups and the formal school are examined to determine where these separate roles link and articulate with one another and where they oppose or conflict with one another. The chapter includes a discussion of how group roles and formal school roles combine to articulate notions of citizenship, in the school and in the larger society.

The third, and major, idea is *group.* For purposes of this chapter, the term means the informal peer or ad hoc groups that students develop among themselves. Defined, group is "a number of persons who communicate with one another often over a span of time, and who are few enough so that each per-

son is able to communicate with all the others . . . face to face" (Homans, 1957, p. 1). Along with frequent face-to-face interaction, groups share activities, routines, patterns of communication, and leadership. They make decisions and take action. Within groups, individuals cooperate, reciprocate, and transcend the personal in favor of group interests. The existence of such groups among students and in school is widely acknowledged. Also acknowledged is that groups frequently emerge prior to adolescence and are capable of devouring large amounts of students' time and energy, influencing teachers, affecting curriculum, and harboring resistance to legitimate authority.

In a sense, groups exist the way representative governments ought to exist; by the willing consent and active participation of their members. The idea of teaching students to think and behave toward school as they do toward their groups, a normed community with common attitudes, values, and beliefs, and then using the community to bind disparate students together and prepare them for participation in the nation-state is appealing to school staff, interested in both improving student behavior and performance and in citizenship education. The successful joining of school groups with the school community is frequently cited as a reason for the reputed success of private schools; and the inability to make that joining, the reason for the lack of success of public schools (Grant, 1988). There is the general perception that, if intelligible articulation between peer groups, school structure, and the nation-state could be attained, then the ends of citizenship education could also be attained.

The barrier is the students' groups. They are elusive, very difficult to influence from without, and, frequently, more strongly normed than the schools in which they operate. They are characterized not only by similarity in the members' age, sex, and, frequently, race, but also by the members' common social class, the most parochial views of which the members may reflect. These groups may lend themselves to the general

Reviewers were Gerald Grant, Syracuse University; Robert Hampel, University of Delaware; Stephen Thornton, University of Delaware.

goals of the school and the goals of citizenship education, but more often they do not. As the following descriptions show, students frequently remain within their groups, rather than entering the larger school community, and many keep the groups between themselves and the school community. Or, they may participate in the larger school only to the degree permitted by the group. It is argued in this chapter that reluctance to leave the group may be one of the main reasons that schools are structured to deemphasize the normed community and encourage individual students to be responsible for their own behavior and their own learning.

THE STUDIES

The data come from several well-regarded and credible descriptive studies of students in schools. Some were specifically intended to describe group behavior (Cusick, 1973; Everhart, 1983; Willis, 1977). Everhart's study took place in a junior high school; Cusick's, in a senior high school; and Willis's, in a working-class high school in England. Others described student behavior but did not use groups as the central focus. Hollingshead (1949) analyzed social class; the Lynds (Lynd & Lynd, 1929), the community; McNeil (1986), social studies curricula; Powell, Farrar, and Cohen (1985), the modern high school; Grant (1988), the school "ethos"; Johnson (1985), socialization; and Cusick (1983), efforts to improve equality. Some additional studies are referred to: Jackson's (1968) study of elementary school classrooms, Lightfoot's (1983) examination of "good" schools, Cusick and Wheeler's (1987) study of 1980s' reforms, and Metz's (1978) study of two junior high schools. A few other works are cited to fill out the argument.

Each of the major studies cited in the chapter was done with field methods to describe small numbers of students behaving and acting in one or another school settings. The settings are quite diverse. In addition to description, each report also contains some overall thesis; but the works were chosen for their descriptions, not their theses. However, several of the theses are relevant to the topic of citizenship education because they involve the examination of student behavior in terms of students' responsibility to the school, the community, and, in McNeil and Johnson's case, the nation-state. Theses from those works are discussed.

The studies were done over several years, from the 1920s (the Lynds's *Middletown*) to the 1980s (Grant's *Hamilton High*), and they cover students' ages from elementary school (Johnson, 1985) to junior high (Everhart, 1983; Metz, 1978), to senior high (Grant, 1988; McNeil, 1986). Of course, there are differences among the schools. The most interesting for present purposes is that the schools described by the Lynds (1929) and Hollingshead (1949) reflected a community class structure, and Hollingshead in particular described the school's reinforcement of that structure. Later studies, such as Grant (1988) and Powell et al. (1985), were done in schools that, following the government's policy of using education to transfer income to the poor, were consolidated, integrated, and quite diversified. The latter schools represented educators' efforts to widen the concept of equality, break down class barriers, and provide increased op-

portunities to the disadvantaged. Hence, in these later schools, there were different opportunities for peer groups and for citizenship education. But it is argued that, despite differences, group behavior in the schools of the 1980s is very similar to that in the schools of the 1920s. As this slow-motion perspective demonstrates, the enduring realities of student group behavior persist, both across the years and in different settings.

STUDENT GROUPS

There are some basic characteristics of school groups, of which the major one is universality. "Everybody knows that teenagers love being with each other—that they crave conversation with friends, in person or on the phone, almost more than they crave food" (Czikszentmihalyi & Larson, 1984, p. 155). The press to have some friends and some friends to carry on with in school is universal, and everyone who closely examines secondary school life finds that students carry on group activities all the time. As Hollingshead (1949) noted,

This school is full of cliques. You go into the hall, or the commons room [between classes or at noon] and you will find the same kids together day after day. Walk up Freedom Street at noon, or in the evening you'll see them again. The kids run in bunches just like their parents. This town is full of cliques, and you can't expect the kids to be any different from their parents. (p. 151)

For adolescents, in school with hosts of other adolescents, the importance of these "intimate groups human beings demand" (Lynd & Lynd, 1929, p. 214) cannot be exaggerated. For students who cannot, or for whatever reason do not, have these primary affiliations, school can be an intimidating and lonely place. Ken, a student in Cusick's (1973) study, summed it up this way:

When I first came, I hated it. I didn't know anyone. You know, Phil, I skipped fifty-eight days last year because I couldn't stand to come to school, because I didn't know anyone, and when I would try to talk to someone, we would just exchange small talk, we never got down to anything. I felt like a real outsider. And it's bad when you don't know anyone. You just walk around by yourself and feel that the other kids are talking about you. (p. 124)

Not only are these peer groups important, but they also "consume most of the interest, time and activities of the adolescents" (Hollingshead, 1949, p. 152). Cusick (1973) recounted how the groups he studied spent up to two thirds of their school day carrying on their repertoire of behaviors, centered around the members' common interests and extended to out-of-school activities.

The activities, of course, varied. Willis (1977) and Everhart (1983) reported deviance as their groups' major activity; Cusick (1973) reported sports, music, motorcycles, school activities, and hunting as major activities; Grant (1988) reported drugs, sports, extracurricular activities, political activism, and added academic achievement as major common interests among some groups. Along with common interests, time, and interaction come a strong sense of group identity, well-defined roles, acknowledged leadership, and orderly patterns of communication and decision making. Those who study student groups find that they are formed in the early years and, in them, members learn to take on important roles, share confidences, reciprocate obligations, and develop loyalties.

These groups arrange themselves along sexual, racial, and class lines. "In all the high schools I visited, I was struck by the rigid definition of student groups and their internal homogeneity" (Lightfoot, 1983, p. 352). Sexual lines are understandable. Girls with girls, boys with boys is the way of adolescents. Cusick (1973) found that only among the more involved and ambitious students, the ones who controlled the school's extracurriculur activities, were females and males together in one group. Otherwise, the groups were sexually segregated, with each member careful to stay away from other group members when he or she was with his girlfriend or her boyfriend.

In biracial schools, in addition to barriers of gender, class, and background, most students are divided along racial lines. Grant (1988), who studied biracial schools in the 1970s, found wariness and hostility between African-Americans and Whites, save in well-run classes and adult-supervised activities, where students put aside their differences and concentrated on attaining formal goals. Otherwise, more militant African-Americans did not allow others of their race to affiliate with Whites, who themselves were quite uninterested in affiliating with African-Americans. But that divisiveness has diminished and will continue to diminish as geographical and social class differences between the races decrease. As Grant's story of Hamilton High progressed into the later 1970s and the 1980s, he reported the breaking down of barriers and the emergence of biracial dating, friendships, and groups.

We cannot, however, given the dropout or school rejection rate among African-American and lower-class males, simply blame problems with school on class and money. It may be that those who study biracial schools concentrate too much on racial antagonism and not enough on the diversity of students' perspectives toward school. Johnson (1985) reported, from his study of an elementary school, that African-American males combined in groups to defy the classroom's principal norm that each individual would work quietly by herself or himself. He asserted that the referent for these boys was not the school or the classroom, but their own peer group.

Black males continually attempt to dominate the classrooms. These students however, are not merely being rambunctious; they are rebelling and attacking the value system of the classroom culture. They attack books, literacy, and work, and they consciously interrupt the activities of other students. They attack the social system of the classroom. Autonomy, for example, is a core classroom social norm attacked by those Black males whose orientation and interactional frame of reference are toward their own peer group rather than toward the teacher (pp. 206–207).

Johnson went on to compare the behavior of the African-American males with the behavior of the adolescent Sioux males studied by Rosalie Wax (1967). She reported that those students' orientation was toward one another and their own culture, not to the culture of the classroom or the majority culture the classroom represented. Johnson suggested that the African-American males in his study behaved as did those Sioux, "so as to gain status with their peer group rather than with respect to the teacher" (Wax, 1967, p. 46).

The responses of teachers in Johnson's classrooms were to attempt to break up the African-American male groups and enforce the norm of quiet individual work. Johnson (1985) reported that "extensive efforts are made in early and lower grades to break up peer bonding tendencies among children, both Black and White" (pp. 206–207). Failing to break up their groups or to enforce classroom norms on these students, the teachers defined the African-American males as "slow" and treated them accordingly. But, as Johnson stressed, the boys were not slow at all; rather they were, in their groups, exercising their own, and rejecting the teacher's and the school's, alien culture.

Cultural and, subsequently, class characteristics among groups are not limited to African-American males. They are the major definers of student peer groups and the characteristics pursued in this chapter because social classes are essential to learning about and exercising social participation. There is the matter of what it takes to belong to the more prestigious groups. In some respects, it does not seem to take much. As a young lady told the Lynds (1929), "Being good looking, a good dancer, and your family owning a car all help" (p. 216). Cusick (1973), who found that what it took to join a motorcycle gang was a motorcycle, pursued "what it took" to be in a prestigious group by asking Debbie, the school's yearbook editor. "Well, like Alice got in because she's a friend of Dotty's, and Barbara is a friend of the twins and they are in with Sally and Kathy, the two leaders" (pp. 153–154).

However random Debbie made these associations appear, they reflected parents' resources and social standing, particularly in that school, in which most students were middle class. As Coleman (1961/1981) noted: "The leading crowd of the school, and thus the norms which that crowd sets, is more than merely a reflection of the student body, with extra middle-class students thrown in. The leading crowd tends to accentuate those very background characteristics already dominant.... A boy or girl in such a system finds it governed by an elite whose backgrounds exemplify, in the extreme, those of the dominant population group. Hence, a working class boy or girl will be mostly left out in an upper middle class school" (p. 109).

Several writers have reported the embarrassment of students without resources. James Agee and Walker Evans (1936), in their study of southern sharecropping families, heard a young girl say,

"My mother made me the prettiest kind of dress, all fresh for school; I wore it the first day, and everyone laughed and poked fun at me; it wasn't like other dresses, neither the cloth nor the way it was cut and I never" [and the mother] "I made her such a pretty dress and she wore it once, and she never wore it away from home again" (p. 74).

And as a number of mothers who said their children had left Middletown high school explained to the Lynds (1929),

"We couldn't dress him like we ought to and he felt out of it," or "The two boys and the oldest girl all quit because they hated Central High School. They all loved the Junior High School down here, but up there they're so snobbish. If you don't dress right, you haven't any friends." "My two girls and oldest boy have all stopped school," said another mother. "My oldest girl stopped because we couldn't give her no money for the right kind of clothes ... now the youngest girl has left 10B this year. She was doing just fine, but she was too proud to go to school unless she could have clothes like the other girls." (p. 186)

It is not merely appearance. The class lines that students carry into school are real. Explaining class as social consciousness accompanied by common traits, the Lynds (1929) referred to the "adult world upon which the world of this intermediate generation is modeled" (p. 215), and Hollingshead (1949) described students of similar class and background forming groups and "clique ties (that were) strongly associated with an adolescent's position in the [community's] class structure" (p. 156). In Elmtown, where he divided the city into five distinct social classes, Hollingshead found "a corrected coefficient of contingency of .86 for the boys and .90 for the girls ... when the clique relations of each sex were correlated with class" (p. 156). Class I adolescents in their groups aped the behaviors of their privileged parents. They had the clothes, the cars, the ready money, and the access to their parents' country club and life-style. They assumed they would be going on to universities and, further, that they would inherit their parents' privileged place in the community, just as they had inherited a privileged place in the school.

Among groups there was some mobility, but it was limited to moving up or down only one class. Hollingshead (1949) found groups, usually of five students, in which there were three or four Class IIs and one or two Class IIIs, but never a Class II–III group with anyone from Class IV and Class V. In fact, of the lowest on the socioeconomic scale, Class V students, those who were left in school maintained primary affiliations with students outside the school whom they expected to join soon.

These divisions by class make sense. To attain membership in an elite group takes a certain amount of financial resources, and adolescents are very aware of who does and who does not have them, certainly as aware as are their parents. Higher class adolescents in Elmtown enforced class consciousness rigidly, and students without the necessary resources and background were simply excluded. Hollingshead (1949) recorded the perceptions that accompanied this enforcement:

The Polish kids live across the tracks and have bad reps. Everything is wrong with the kids May runs with. First, they live down by the old tannery. They're not clean. They don't dress well. Their hair isn't fixed right. Then May can't live her sisters' reps down. (p. 163)

Not only did students enforce class distinctions, but also the parents, particularly of more privileged students, expected and pressured teachers and administrators to defer to their children just as they did to the parents. Expectations of deference went with being upper class in a small town. In fact, the two "community studies" included in our list, *Middletown* and *Elmtown's Youth,* both described towns with fairly rigid class lines that the school was expected to protect and maintain. As a Class I parent said to Hollingshead (1949) concerning the teachers, "They are such fine teachers. They know the background of each child and teach accordingly" (p. 92). Upper-class parents used their influence in such ways as to assure that a girl from the "prominent families" (p. 138) received an academic award she did not deserve, and they demanded privileges such as that their son or daughter be excused from inconvenient school rules. On the other hand, the school's treatment of lower-class students was frankly unpleasant. The principal, after releasing from detention an upper-class boy whose father had complained, was quoted as saying with regard to a lower-class boy,

Now there's a hot one. He's one of our wise guys. He thinks he's a hotshot. His old man is a laborer out at the fertilizer plant, and he thinks he's something, umph. He'll be on relief twenty years from now. There's one guy I'm going to see put in detention. (p. 140)

Parents even made personal decisions on the basis of their child's position in the social structure. The Lynds (1929) described, in the days before car ownership was universal, the "persistent rumours of the buying of a car by local families to help their children's social standing in high school" (p. 137). Supported by parents, class lines among groups and cliques were encouraged and persisted in school.

Just as the upper classes expected a great deal from the Elmtown schools, including deference, the lower classes expected little. In a discussion of who influenced Elmtown's school, Hollingshead (1949) reported that "Class IV, as a whole, believed that nothing could be done to challenge the position of the 'inner ring' ... Class V people were almost entirely disinterested in the question" (p. 105). The disinterest and/or sense of resignation to whatever would occur in school and perhaps in life was reflected by one of Willis's (1977) students in his account of his parents' attitude toward his education and his future.

I asked the old lady ... "Ain't you ... bothered what I become, don't you worry about it like?" Her never said "What do you want to be?" Nor the old man never said anything. But she answered it in a nutshell. She said "What difference would it make if I ... said anything?" Her said, "You'll still be what you want to be." So I thought, "Oh Well" (p. 75).

It isn't just parental expectations and influence. Hollingshead (1949) described middle- and lower-class students as frequently obligated to work and, thus, prevented from having the time to participate in activities. Also it is difficult for lower-class students to aspire to higher status in school. The patterns and perspectives that students learn or inherit from their parents are very strong, and, in fact, class biases and prejudices seem stronger among adolescents than among adults.

So far the argument is that peer groups are universal, strongly normed, tightly bound, and reflect students' social class and culture and maintain boundaries coterminous with the larger society's class and cultural lines. Parents actively encourage this class structure by watching their children to see that they are learning and exercising the parents values. The descriptions indicate that student groups are not as friendly, fluid, and ad hoc as they can appear. They are serious business and, from the evidence cited, the structure for teaching, learning, and reinforcing inherited patterns of social awareness, participation, and discrimination.

This is particularly evident among lower-class students, whose resistance and antagonism heightens the differences between their own and the society's and the school's norms. Willis's (1977) "lads" and Everhart's (1983) miscreants not only came from the same lower social classes but, according to the authors, were recreating their working-class culture within their groups. As have others who studied working- or lower-class students, these authors noted students' noninvolvement in the academic side of school and their decision to spend school time meeting with friends to carry on group activities. In response to a question about what school had done for him, one of the lads replied (Willis, 1977):

I don't think school does . . . anything to you . . . It never has had much effect on anybody I don't think [after] you've learnt the basics. I mean school, it's . . . four hours a day. But it ain't the teachers who mould you, it's the . . . kids you meet. You'm only with the teachers 30 per cent of the time in school, the other . . . two-thirds are just talking, . . . pickin' an argument, messing about. (p. 26)

Furthermore, the school's efforts to break these patterns avail little partly because these students' perspective toward authority is one of resistance. Willis (1977) noted that, like Johnson's African-American males, the members of his group had devised a modus operandi toward school. They had

adopted and developed to a fine degree in their school counter-culture specific working class themes: resistance; subversion of authority; informal penetration of the weaknesses and fallibilities of the formal; and an independent ability to create diversion and enjoyment. (p. 84)

This group was able to combine its resistance to authority with its propensity to create diversion and enjoyment. Willis (1977) gave an example in an interview with one of his students:

Willis:: What's the last time you've done some writing?
Fuzz: Oh are, last time was in careers, 'cos I writ 'yes on a piece of paper, that broke me heart.
Willis: Why did it break your heart?
Fuzz: 'Cos I was going to try and go through the term without writing anything. 'Cos since we've cum back, I ain't dun nothing. [It was half way through the term] (p. 27)

Everhart (1983) described similar behavior among his junior high school students who spent their in-school time baiting teachers, picking on the weaker students, carrying on in-jokes, smoking, and in general defying authority at every turn. Following Willis (1977), Everhart related his students' behavior to their social class and to the status they would occupy as adults, a status that, according to both authors, was overtly encouraged by the schools and the class-divided society that sponsored the schools.

A similar view of that phenomenon was put forth by Stinchcombe (1964), who suggested that, among working-class adolescent males, defiance of authority, demand for immediate gratification, and appropriation of adult status were related to their inability to articulate in-school activities with their later lives. "High school rebellion, and expressive alienation, occur when future status is not clearly related to present performance" (p. 5). These patterns of rebellion and resistance may be much more visible with the lower-class or "tougher" students, but they are not limited to them. They are equally widespread, however less overt and visible, among adolescents deemed blue-collar.

Cusick (1973) found his working-class "athletes" at Horatio Gates High to be quite compliant with the rules and friendly with and tolerant of teachers. Unlike Willis's (1977) and Everhart's (1983) students, they were not rebellious, hostile, or teacher baiting. But like Willis's and Everhart's students, their relation to the intellectual aspects of schools was almost nonexistent. They agreed that one "needed an education" and that school had something to do with their life plans. They did not study, did not consider prestige careers or upward mobility, and did not articulate a relation between attainment of academic excellence and their later lives. Put another way, they understood the market value of a high school education and were content to stay in school. But they did not understand the merit idea of individual attainment in a competitive world. They did not understand a basic premise of the school: that "individual differences in ability, motivation, and character define varying degrees of individual worth or merit . . . [and] those with the most merit should receive the largest share of social rewards" (Labaree, 1988, p. 23).

Therefore, they were quite content to stay in school, but primarily as members of their peer groups. While in school they remained within their groups and entered into academic endeavors only so far as group norms allowed. If they did their assignments at all, they copied from one another or had their girlfriends do them. They approached class assignments just as did Johnson's African-American males, Willis's lads, and Everhart's miscreants. They kept their groups between themselves and the academic requirements, and they turned academic assignments into opportunities for group interaction. One of Everhart's students explained this latter practice:

We've got this deal, John, me, Mike, and a couple other guys, like when one says something the other guy backs him up, helps him so he doesn't get into a lot of trouble. That's why the rabbit story was so neat. I was able to help John out by asking questions so he could finish his report. He hadn't even started it until we talked about it in class. (p. 175)

Johnson's (1985) African-American males, Wax's (1967) adolescent Sioux, Willis's (1977) working-class lads, Everhart's (1983) junior high school friends, Hollingshead's (1949) Class IVs and Vs, and Cusick's (1973) blue-collar athletes were more attuned to the norms of their peer groups, norms that reflected their class and cultural origins, than they were to the academic side of the school, with its assumption of individual merit and subsequent upward social mobility. The latter was foreign to them. Academic requirements, then, were filtered through the group, and the group defined the members' involvement with the school's formal goals.

Such attitudes toward academic achievement were not limited to lower-class students, although they were easier to observe with those students because their behavior was frequently contrary to school rules and expectations. Both Hollingshead (1949) and the Lynds (1929) described top groups in which academic efforts were as minimal as if they were among the lower classes. Cusick's (1973) music drama group, who "ran" Horatio Gates High, included some who bragged about doing almost nothing academic. The "doers" in Grant's (1988) Hamilton High were not noted for academic excellence but for political activism.

Some of these groups included academic achievers who believed in the merit value of education or the value of education or the value of status attainment within the school and who worked hard. But they made their academic efforts as individuals outside their groups. Otherwise they, too, stayed within their class- and culture-bound groups and away from students unlike themselves.

On the other hand, there are groups that center their activities around academic achievement. Cusick and Wheeler (1987) found several such student groups, Wheeler in the "magnet" programs of his urban school and Cusick in the "honors" track of his suburban school. Grant (1988) also found them at Hamilton High. But both types of students, those whose groups centered around academic achievement and those whose groups did not, within their peer groups were exercising similar attitudes toward those different from themselves and similar modes of social participation. For both academic achievers and academic nonachievers, the groups performed similar opportunities for social training. This idea of group identity and its relation to academic and citizenship goals is pursued next in an examination of differences among groups and the way those differences are maintained.

RELATIONS AMONG PEER GROUPS

Basic to citizenship education is the idea of encouraging students to comingle with others from different backgrounds and, thus, learn to participate in a democracy. Indeed, James Conant, whose *the American High School Today* (1959) spurred the continuation and growth of comprehensive secondary schools, argued that, in addition to providing increased academic opportunities, such schools would "prepare all the pupils as future citizens of a democracy" (p. 15). The school goal of promoting democracy has continued as schools have become more comprehensive, with increasingly diversified and differentiated student bodies.

However, promoting understanding among varied students is difficult. Often students, rather than opening themselves to those of different background and cultures, stay with their like-minded friends and reinforce extant class and cultural lines. It is difficult for students to extend themselves beyond their group norms, and those who do so risk censure from friends. The studies indicate that this is true in both the more homogeneous schools and the schools where the children of several social classes comingle. Lightfoot (1983) noted in her study of Brookline High School that

The distinctions of Black, White, and Asian were visible markers of group identification. A more discerning eye could pick out the Irish Catholic kids from High Point, the working-class enclave in Brookline, and distinguish them from the upper middle-class Jewish students. In this case, the divisions of religion, ethnicity, and class seemed to be more harshly drawn than the more obvious categories of race . . . Many students, for example, spoke of the divisions between the "indigenous" upper middle-class Brookline Blacks, and the "interlopers" from inner city Boston. Social class was a powerful divider and close friendships between these two [Black] groups were rare. (pp. 352–353)

Cusick (1983) found a biracial, urban, working-class school, in theory a hothouse for nurturing tolerance and participation, actually riddled with class and color antagonisms.

The Blacks disparaged both those whom they called the "rich kikes" and the boys in the auto shop, whom they called "white trash." Some of those called "rich kikes" also referred to the boys in the auto shop as "white trash." The boys in the auto shop talked of the "niggers and spades" while they, along with other whites, were referred to as "honkies" by militant blacks, who reserved a special hatred of those whom they called the "colored," the "toms," and the "white girl lovers." Moderate blacks referred to the militants as "back biting ———" and most of the students scorned the drug users. (p. 22)

It was in that school that one of the school leaders, a White girl, said, totally without guile, "Sure there's a lot of racism here but that's because there's a lot of white trash."

At Grant's (1988) Hamilton High, there were several designations of differences. Grant mapped this typology of subcultures based on seating preferences in the cafeteria:

Black

White

Black and white (mixed)

Preps (preppies, senior popular people, haughty people, rich cool seniors)

Druggies (burnouts, outcasts, people of all grades who play guitar or drums, smoke pot, drink and are violent)

Brains (geeks, weirdos, very intelligent seniors, honor society, smart people, ultra intelligent, computer people)

Losers (people without a group, loners and underclass misfits)

Breakers (break dancers)

Homeboys (downtown people, south side, the boys, poor blacks)

Theater people (chorus, dance, artistic types)

ESL (foreign kids, Asians, Koreans, Chinese, Japanese, Latin American, Hispanics, Spanish speaking)

Poor whites

Special ed (autistic, retards, wheelchairs, handicapped, "slow people"—not retarded but not right)

Jocks (athletes) (p. 96)

Such distinctions among groups, often accompanied by suspicion and hostility, are common. Hollingshead's (1949) students were very careful about protecting class lines that were often marked by open antagonism. Willis (1977) recorded the scorn with which his students regarded those who, in general, did as the school authorities asked.

I mean what will they remember of their school life? What will they have to look back on? Sittin in a classroom sweating their bollocks off, you know, while we've been . . . I mean look at the things we can look back on, fighting on the Pakis, fighting on the JA's (i.e., Jamaicans). Some of the things we've done of teachers, it'll be a laff when we look back on it. (p. 14)

Although these class and cultural barriers persist among the groups, schools do contain opportunities for social mobility and awareness of different backgrounds. For those who can break out of their peer group roles, opportunities in school activities are open to those with the energy, interest, and intelligence. Cusick's (1973) "music-drama" group controlled the plays, publications, musical events, and some of the elections and represented the school to the administrators. Common intellectual and political interests drew them together even while they retained strong affiliations with friends whom they had known for years. But the formation of this group and the opportunity to join it had opened and closed quickly in the first year of high school. Once formed, the group maintained rigid lines, and when outsiders tried to enter, they were rebuffed. An instance of this occurred when a nonmember auditioned for a part in *West Side Story*.

[She] asked Dick if she could try out for the show. He apparently said it would be all right because she got up and started singing "There's A Place for Us" . . . I thought she was better than any solo singer I heard in that school, far better, in fact, than the two popular girls who took the lead parts in the humanities production . . . But the other students started giggling and tittering. Joan and Dick were grimacing at each other. Jim and Doug started burping and the twins started giggling. The further she went, the worse it got . . . [and Dick] called to her. "Marion, can you come tomorrow night? We have a lot to do tonight and really can't spare the time." (p. 170)

Athletics are a source of mobility across groups. Even in class-conscious Elmtown, a good athlete was likely to be valued. But it was not automatic. Hollingshead (1949) described a lower-class boy who made the football team but, after several in-practice "muggings" by his higher class teammates, retired from participation. And Lightfoot (1983) noted that the social mobility enjoyed by athletes may be seasonal.

Students pointed to the Black "jocks" and their similarity in dress and style to the White jocks. Their preoccupation with athletics becomes more powerful than racial affiliation. This group identification tends to be seasonal and shifts when football fades into basketball season. A different configuration emerges and many athletes may return to their old racial or ethnic groups in the off season. (p. 353)

Intramurals are also a source of mobility. In their study of an integrated suburban school, Cusick and Wheeler (1987) reported an upper-class student who had already been accepted to Princeton saying

You know what makes this school? It's the [intramural basketball] league. Everybody plays two nights a week and then we go to someone's house to talk. I meet kids I would never meet. I have four friends from [the projects]. I won't see kids like that when I get to Princeton. (p. 41)

There are other opportunities for social mobility. Grant (1988) described several that were open to students in the

Hamilton High of the 1970s. The drug culture was easily accessible to one who would participate.

I met this girl. We were sitting down just having a cigarette, because you're allowed to smoke out back, behind the doors. It's not a rule that you can't. You can. And this girl comes out, and we were just sitting by each other, and then she started introducing me to all of her friends, and then we just started partying. It was like I was one of the gang. (p. 90)

Grant (1988) also described the protesters, a group of 80 students or so that included both drug-using countercultural freaks and political activists. "They published the underground newspaper, organized a Vietnam moritorium day" (p. 60). They also monitored the staff for violations of students' rights. However, Grant noted that many of these students were encouraged by their university-based, Vietnam war–protesting, rights-advocating, and, sometimes, dope-smoking parents who backed their children in disputes with the school (p. 61). As one of these students said, "There are only two ways the school can control me—through my parents or through suspending me. My parents agree with me so the school can't use that method" (p. 61).

Another opportunity for social mobility was less voluntary and more coercive, but certainly a chance to break away from one's background. Grant (1988) described middle-class African-Americans who, to maintain their status with lower-class African-Americans adopted a militant political perspective and ceased interactions with middle-class Whites.

What has been described, then, is a difficult situation in which to conduct citizenship education. Students enter school with formed and/or still forming class and cultural perspectives and behaviors, and with groups of like-minded friends with whom they practice and reinforce these perspectives and behaviors. In school there are opportunities, certainly more than one would normally find in society, for learning about and participating with people from different classes and cultures. But the informal groups, supported by neighborhood affiliations, parental expectations, family resources, and a differentiated school organization that places students in tracks with others like themselves, make the school goal of teaching democracy difficult to achieve.

Working Students

Another factor that decreases opportunities for students to move across groups and increase their social options is work. Many students obtain jobs in their third or fourth year of high school and are unavailable for school-based opportunities. Cusick (1983) reported that half the juniors and two thirds of the seniors left school after fourth period to go to work. To the dismay of the teachers, students would not come for the extra activities through which they might have developed relations outside their groups. As a discouraged teacher explained,

One time they tried to raise money for a booster club for the school, we went out and sold hot dogs and pop and candy at the games, and when we had money we wanted to have a dinner for the athletes at the end of the year. But so few people came it was embarrassing. OK, so you don't want to have a dinner, we'll have a trip. So more preparation and only a few people came there. Then we tried a canoeing trip up north, and there were more coaches and helpers than kids. Finally, I gave that stuff up. I don't know what they want ... these are the less affluent kids, we can't get them away from working and into school. (p. 69)

From the working- or lower-class students' point of view, that is very reasonable. After all, it is students who spend the time in school and forgo income and, thus, bear the major cost of an education. For those who either need the money or do not see the value of increased education, working, rather than attending school, makes sense.

Time

Time is a related factor. The years when students might break out of their childhood and early adolescent groups and open themselves to participation with students who are socially and culturally different from themselves passes quickly. As the perceptive vice-principal of Horatio Gates commented, "High school's only two years long. After that it's a car, a girl, a job, that takes up their life" (Cusick, 1973, p. 25). Given the barriers and the brevity, it is much easier to stay in one's peer group and participate in the school through it.

That is not to deny the opportunities for social mobility and cross-group interaction, but they are mostly open to those who, at an early age, demonstrate some talent and energy and who see involvement in school as somehow rewarding. The good athlete, the student on the way to Princeton, the talented musician, the attractive girl or boy or those who simply understand the merit value of individual effort, can either escape their groups or bridge to other groups. But for the less talented and/or ambitious—the "boys in the auto shop" or the "lads," the angry African-American males, or the poor girls with shabby clothes—who themselves see little possibility of changing their status within or without the institution, there are few opportunities and little time for social broadening. It is easier for those students to stay in their groups where their status is secure, their attitudes and behaviors (and prejudices) unquestioned, and their social lines drawn, maintained, and solidified.

Summary

Whatever the criticisms one can bring against schools' efforts at citizenship education, one has to admit that fostering democratic ideals is an uphill fight with class- and culture-bound groups and their limited views of school and of those different from themselves. One can understand the accusation by Johnson (1985), Willis (1977), and Everhart (1983) that the schools collude with the extant social structure and encourage and maintain the already formed class lines. But the descriptions indicate that the class and cultural differences brought in and exercised in school through the peer groups are very formidible. It is questionable whether publicly funded and community-operated schools can much alter basic social patterns. But so far in this chapter, only group behavior has been described. To take this issue further, the structure of schools has to be described and explained. The question pursued next is, "To what degree do schools enable students to move from their class and culture base and open themselves to broader modes of social participation and increased opportunity for learning about and practicing the goals of citizenship education?"

PEER GROUPS AND SCHOOL STRUCTURE

The argument has been made that adolescent groups exist in schools, that they follow their members' class and culture, and that they are an important part of student life. Further, these peer groups do what citizenship education should do: "transmit values, teach social science ... encourage the development of competencies in decision making and participation" (Shaver, 1987, p. 115). This line of thinking must be extended to explain how the school structure affects and is affected by peer groups and their attendant cultures.

The descriptions indicate that, from Middletown in the 1920s to Hamilton High in the 1980s, there were few school-imposed barriers to the continuation of group life in school. That is not unreasonable. Students' personal lives, it can be argued, are really not the formal business of the school. Others might contend that the tacit approval of peer groups and, consequently, of continued class lines in school, however unintentional, frustrates rather than encourages the teaching of democratic principles. To a third group, the continuation of these groups in school, with their class and cultural differences, demonstrates that the schools' overt purpose is to condition children to extant "stratified social and cultural relationships" (Johnson, 1985, p. 633) or, more bluntly, to assure the upper classes that the lower classes will stay where they are. Not only do groups preserve and transmit class and cultural differences in school but also, it is argued, they do so with purposeful assistance and encouragement from the school structure.

Whatever the view, it is plain that the school structure is important to the way groups operate and therefore important to citizenship education. In this section, then, the school structure and the roles within the structure are described, followed by analysis of the descriptions and functions of groups in terms of that structure.

The Structure

Schools in our society are large differentiated organizations. Their size and differentiation stem from two basic characteristics, universalism and egalitarianism. Combined, these obligate school staff to take and provide each student with opportunities for social, political, and economic equality. The universalism and egalitarianism have been strengthened in recent years with increased numbers of children in school and the government's policy of using education to transfer income to the poor. Schools of today include all young people, even the unable and the unwilling, those who in former times might not have come or stayed if they had come.

The extra increment of universalism has increased the differentiation within the school. The more types of students the schools take and the more functions the schools take on, the more they have to provide separate and different opportunities and categories of specialists. Busing, integration, students' rights, special education, vocational and career education, and the recent wave of school reform, which has fostered honors and magnet programs and private-like academies, all serve to further specialize, bureaucratize, and differentiate the schools.

That makes organizational sense. As Thompson (1967) pointed out, complex organizations accommodate change by further specializing functions and personnel. Such differentiation serves an additional purpose. It allows the schools to implement high quality for those (frequently influential) few who desire it for their children without upsetting the mass of people who are not interested in the effort that high quality requires. As Powell et al. (1985) argued, "the differentiated curriculum made it possible for secondary schools to accommodate demands for improvement at the top while still continuing the older, massive commitment to a weaker curriculum for everyone else" (p. 288).

In sum, schools are complex and differentiated, and getting more so. They are large and offer specialized experiences with varying sets of offerings for different groups of students. Consequently, they are also very dense, with a great many activities and people crammed into very limited amounts of space and time.

Ability Grouping. A structural element that strongly supports peer groups in the school is ability grouping, the assumption that "students learn best in company with others like themselves" (Oakes, 1985, p. 4). As Johnson (1985) described, it can begin as early as kindergarten.

At Westhaven the garden aspects of this grade are muted by the emergence of a new principle of school and classroom organization: stratification, the division of a social group into internally defined inferior and superior subgroups. Termed "tracking" at West Haven the homogeneous preschool student group is ranked, divided, then placed in different kindergarten rooms. (pp. 55–56)

Such ability grouping continues all through school, and its use is presently increasing, particularly for the lower achieving students, with widespread use of state-administered graduation tests. As an administrator of those tests explained, We'll have to

segment off large numbers of kids who have trouble passing the tests. The kids at the low ends will have to study for some terms, or maybe years before they can pass them and that separates them out from the rest of the school. (Cusick & Wheeler, 1987, p. 16)

On the other end of the ability scale, that same school had implemented an honors program to assure their remaining upper-class parents that, in this increasingly integrated school, their children would have the opportunities to enter the best colleges. That program further isolated students by social class and encouraged the continuation of peer groups along those same lines. Cusick and Wheeler (1987) described a remedial English class in that school in which the teacher told the primarily African-American students about some of their schoolmates

who had won the academic bowl game on TV the previous Sunday. A girl in the back raised her hand: "I saw that program. I never saw those kids before. Do they go to this school?" (p. 28).

Summing Up. The result of these characteristics, from universalism and egalitarianism to differentiation, complexity, and density, is that schools are severely differentiated, place great emphasis on maintaining their procedures, and at times put procedures ahead of people. It is not only as Callahan (1957) suggested, that schools have to present a business-like efficiency to satisfy public expectations. It is also that, with their size, differentiation, and many more subordinates than superordinates, schools have to run smoothly in order to run at all and are, therefore, heavily reliant on a bureaucratic structure. The activities of hundreds of young people engaged in separate activities in separate locations cannot be left to chance, even for a few hours. The schedule has to be planned and ordered; the routine has to be respected and maintained.

Compliance

For the purpose of this chapter, this differentiated, bureaucratic structure and the maintenance it demands has two results. First, one of the schools' most important lessons for students is compliance with this demanding organization. Johnson's (1985) West Haven was not characterized by teachers teaching and students learning academic material but by the constant enforcement and reinforcement of "proper" social behavior. The main lessons from kindergarten on were "work quietly," "work by yourself," "raise your hand," "line up," "stand still," "control yourself," "obey the teacher . . . the aides . . . the rules." Whatever the content, the instruction was pervaded by an endless series of these directives. The pervasiveness argues that teaching young children obedience to authority and compliance with organizational directives are major school goals. They combine with and reinforce another major organizational goal, that the mode of production is to be a single individual working quietly by himself or herself. It was to such directives that Johnson's (1985) African-American males refused to adapt and so were judged "slow" and relegated to the bottom track.

McNeil (1986) asserted that, in the schools she studied, bureaucratic control was the curriculum, with actual content reduced to work sheets, lists, short-answer tests, "brief 'right' answers, easily transmitted, easily answered, easily graded" (p. 157). She argued that, for both more and less academically inclined students, teachers engaged in instructional techniques that served the end of control, not the ends of instruction. Metz (1978) noted the inordinate amount of class time devoted to maintenance procedures that accompanied structured written work and suggested that compliance with procedures was sufficient to ensure one's successful passage through school. She also suggested that it was primarily in the lower-achieving classes that "teachers used structured written work as a device to quiet a class or to keep it calm" p. 103).

Whatever the interpretation of the descriptions— whether that the bureaucracy is logistically necessary, that control has unintentionally become the curriculum (McNeil, 1986), or that the schools are engaged in an overt plot to keep the lower classes in their place by denying them knowledge (Everhart, 1983; Johnson, 1985; Willis, 1977)—it cannot be denied that the bureaucracy absorbs a great deal of the students' time and that teaching students to operate in a bureaucracy is a major school goal.

Limited Demands

Compliance with the bureaucracy is not demanding, however, and that brings us to the second result of the bureaucratic structure. The bureaucracy absorbs students' time, not their energy, and for students in the midst of the differentiated and dense routine, there is a great deal of waiting around with little to do. Schools are similar to peacetime armies, prisons, and labor unions. They demand attendance, passive compliance, and limited attention but frequently not a lot more. Adding up the time spent on receiving announcements and assignments, coming and going, eating, waiting, watching, and otherwise complying with procedural demands, one sees a great deal of empty space in the day. As one of Willis's (1977) students, quoted earlier, said, "You'm only with teachers 30 per cent of the time in school, the other two-thirds are just talking, ... pickin' an argument, messing about" (p. 26). This phenomenon is not limited to comprehensive secondary schools. It also occurs in elementary schools. Jackson (1968) referred to the "delay, denial and interruption" that characterize life in elementary classrooms:

Thus in several ways students in elementary classrooms are required to wait their turn and to delay their actions. No one knows for certain how much of the average student's time is spent in neutral, as it were, but for many students in many classrooms it must be a memorable portion. (p. 15)

Most of the authors (e.g., Cusick, 1973; Grant, 1988; Hollingshead, 1949; Johnson, 1985; Willis, 1977) described students filling out the day's empty spaces with peer interactions. Indeed, why not? The opportunity is available and, as Czikszentmihalyi and Larson (1984) demonstrated in their study of the internal states of adolescents, "friends can induce psychic negentropy-intrinsic motivation, feelings of freedom, happiness and excitement—at least in the immediate present" (p. 156). Friends offer intensity and exhilaration that not only fills in the empty spaces but offsets the tedium of the routine. For students the dead time magnifies the importance of having a group and helps one understand Ken's statement that he "couldn't stand to come to school because he didn't know anyone" (Cusick, 1973, p. 124).

In fact, it was suggested earlier that the existence of these groups actually encourages schools to deemphasize the normed community and to motivate each student to take care of himself or herself. The fact is that, for most students, adult-guided, academic endeavors are not sufficiently attractive to offset the intensity and exhilaration offered by the ever-present student groups. The group, or frequently a best friend, or simply a friend is usually present in class, and, in an idle moment or when the teacher's attention is distracted or an interruption occurs, a glance can bring contact. Then, the whole net of shared perceptions, jokes, and interests is awakened and the student can slide easily from class activity into group activity. Teacher efforts at group learning and cooperative projects frequently fail because, as soon as students come together, there is, of necessity, some maintenance time and, subsequently, some slack time when extant group norms and behaviors can usurp academic endeavors. Without sufficient intrinsic appeal to offset the attractiveness and appeal of groups, it is easier and simpler for the content teacher to use a combination of lecture and students' individual work and so discourage the emergence of groups in classes. The result is stronger emphasis on individual effort and achievement.

Group Order

On the other hand, that same structure allows students outside of class and outside of the realm of direct instruction a great deal of free time. That students continue their group associations and activities in this free time is seldom regarded as a problem because peer groups impose behavioral norms on their otherwise uninvolved members. Within their groups, students are reasonably orderly, and so the order imposed by group norms and the order imposed by the bureaucracy are intermingled and mutually supportive. For the most part, the groups support the bureaucracy's need for order. Some groups' interactions may be disruptive, as when Everhart's (1983) miscreants shot and threw things and punched friends around. But more often even these students were not primarily interested in causing trouble, or at least not in causing trouble to the extent of getting sent to the office and perhaps thrown out of school and so out of the group, but in having someone to talk to. Even the worst were careful about how far they went: "You have to know just how much you can push a teacher if you don't want to get sent to the office" (p. 186).

Cusick (1973) reported that, within the groups he studied, the students themselves often handled matters of compliance with the bureaucracy. They exchanged information about bureaucratic requirements and monitored their members to see that they stayed, not out of trouble, but out of excessive trouble, which would have excluded them from school and, hence, the group.

The Overall Effect

In sum, the bureaucracy, with its rules, regulations, and differentiation, supports and is supported by a peer group system that is strongly normed along class and cultural lines. Even while individual teachers may be trying to draw students out of their class- and culture-bound attitudes and perspectives, the school structure is inadvertently encouraging students to stay within them. The roles required by the strongly normed bureaucracy and the roles required by the strongly normed peer groups are mutually supportive.

On the other hand, the academic side of the school is much less strongly normed than either the peer groups or the bureaucracy, and it is particularly weak relative to the combined peer groups and bureaucracy. Every one of our authors—the Lynds (1929) and Hollingshead (1949) years ago and, more recently, Willis (1977), Grant (1988), Everhart (1983), Cusick (1973), and Lightfoot (1983)—described schools as fairly undemanding academically. Comparing schools to consumer-oriented shopping malls, Powell et al. (1985) observed that

The mall works well because it is so exclusively governed by consumer choice. Learning is voluntary: it is one among many things for sale. The mall's central qualities—variety of offerings, choice among them, and neutrality about their value—have succeeded in holding most teenagers on terms they and their teachers can live with. (p. 309)

Powell et al. (1985) noted that the Lynds in Middletown "found that even straight A students in this small Indiana city didn't work hard at their classes, [and] . . . while most students did very little homework, they got through school quite nicely—even in the top academic courses" (p. 237). Twenty years later it was no different in Elmtown, where "the high school load is so light that very few students have to study more than an hour or two a week outside of school hours" (Hollingshead, 1949, p. 199). And nearly 50 years later, Grant (1988) recorded a confirming interview:

Questioner: Describe a typical day for me.
    Student: I get up, go downstairs, and eat, at about seven. Watch TV, smoke about half a pack of cigarettes. Go to school. Probably goof around all day.
Questioner: How do you get to school . . .?
    Student: Walk. Probably smoke the other half a pack walking to school. Um, I go to school, probably goof off. Skip school, go out and smoke some reefer, and then, go back in school. Goof around a little more (p. 91)

One would wonder how such a student managed his classes, but the evidence presented in all the descriptive studies indicates that, when a student has some friends to talk to and does not flagrantly abuse the rules, he can survive in school with minimal compliance. He can even "goof around" and "um . . . goof around a little more" and remain in good standing. Our universal, comprehensive, and bureaucratic schools do not compel learning for those not so inclined. And relatively few are so inclined. As Powell et al. (1985) pointed out, "Whatever the reasons most students had for coming to high school, a hunger for academic learning was not high on the list" (p. 237).

That is not to say that all students "goof around" or that a good education is not to be had in the schools. But it is to say that the strongest norms operating within the schools are those of mutually supporting peer groups and the bureaucracy. Neither alone nor in combination do they compel academic effort. Rather, they encourage students to remain in their groups, where academic effort, because it is individual, competitive, and merit-oriented, mostly opposes the norms held by working- or lower-class students as those students practice and learn modes of social participation, not from the school, but from their groups. Johnson's (1985) African-American males, Cusick's (1973) blue-collar athletes, and Willis's (1977) and Everhart's (1983) friends indicated they were quite unwilling to leave their groups and enter that individualistic, competitive, meritocratic world. They preferred to abide by the cultural norms and they had learned at home and enter into the larger school only marginally, resisting the blandishments of learning, intellectual pleasure, and upward mobility.

What students learn in school, then, is that the cultural perspectives they bring—their modes of decision making and participation, their values and attitudes—are not only sufficient to carry them through school but are also themselves quite legitimate and reasonable. The school structure legitimates extant social and cultural patterns that are practiced in peer groups and that include important lessons of citizenship education.

Academic Achievement

Of course, schools encourage serious academic effort, but as Powell et al. (1985) said, "it is voluntary" (p. 309) and, therefore, limited to those who see the opportunities that accrue to the more educated or who articulate the relation between individual achievement and a future state.

Students who come from ambitious and successful parents have distinct advantages. They enter school open to the opportunities and attuned to "proper" social behavior. As Johnson (1985) pointed out, those students are judged "worthy" even from the earliest grades and are moved into the higher tracks, where, he observed, there is greater opportunity for social and emotional interaction with teachers.

In other words, there are two possibilities for academic achievement. One may simply abide by the school's chief norm, that one should work quietly by herself or himself and, as an individual, obtain what each wants from the school. Or there is the possibility of students and teachers creating positive relations around academic content, relations that can draw students out of their peer groups and into the purposive academic activities. Those who are selected for special academic programs can even find peer groups centered around academic achievement.

Powell et al. (1985) described such positive teacher–student relations in what they termed the schools' "speciality tracks," the top academic, special education, and serious vocational and technical lines. These tracks are selective, they receive increased resources, their classes are smaller, and their teachers give evidence of a certain elan because of their association with something "special." Consequently, both teachers and students increase their efforts. In such tracks students and teachers do not "bargain" down the curriculum, nor do they make treaties to just endure the endeavor. Rather, they combine to create a normative society that elicits increased effort and subsequent learning.

These speciality shops are for a minority, except for special education, a self-selected minority. But for the unspecial majority who lack incentive and whom the school does not incite to academic individual efforts or who do not have positive relations with teachers, and who find themselves sorted to the classes with students similar to themselves, the peer groups that have only marginal affiliation with the academic requirements become increasingly attractive.

In this way, the school's structure teaches all students a powerful lesson about citizenship; Rewards are available for only a few, and for those few, the impetus comes primarily from the individual, not the school. Students who come to school without the correct orientation are likely to either remain without the rewards or have to defy their group norms to obtain them. It is these few who form alternative communities with teachers and, thus, engage in learning. Others simply abide by the schools' chief norm, that one should work quietly alone and as an individual obtain what he or she wants from the school's academic side. The problem is that so many want so little.

Can Schools Change?

The question that Grant (1988) asked was "Can schools develop a community that offsets group norms of nonachievement and the class and cultural barriers that groups represent?" He contended that the present system, with its "corrosive individualism" (p. 1), at best encourages minimal compliance and, at worst, discourages academic effort by leaving each student and each teacher to herself or himself. At Hamilton High, Grant watched "students forge excuses, copy homework, cheat on tests, skip classes and regularly lie to staff members" (p. 107). Similarly, he watched teachers retreat from commitment, character training, and personal example. He traced those problems to the school's individual merit orientation.

Based on his study, Grant argued that the contemporary school structure is a "minimalist contractual model lodged in a bureaucratic hierarchy" (p. 1), insufficient either to encourage academic effort in those not already inclined or to teach good citizenship. It is not enough, he argued, to open the school to individual opportunities: Too few take advantage of the opportunities and too many take advantage of the system.

Grant advocated a purposive school "ethos" to offset the peer groups, one that would call students out of their class- and culture-bound groups into a moral learning community. Then all students could share the opportunities of students in private schools or in the "special" reaches of the public schools. He wanted to see schools develop as pedagogical entities with strong mores, ethos, and communal norms, so that they could teach a responsible social morality and there could be some basis for teaching the ideals of citizenship, using the school as the training ground. He advocated two reforms: the first, building-based control, and the second, teacher autonomy in establishing norms and standards. He argued that, with those characteristics as the basis of the organizational structure, school personnel could establish a communal ethos that would offset the attractiveness of peer groups that reflect students' class and cultural lines.

Grant's (1988) argument is powerful, buttressed as it is by examples from both private and public schools. But, except for the speciality tracks described by Powell et al. (1985), the schools he advocated would be a radical departure from our highly politicized, universal, and publicly supported schools that have to take and retain everyone. It could be argued that class- and culture-based peer groups, with their norms and values, may be simply too much for the school to counter effectively. Grant admitted this, saying that the "minimalist bureaucratic model" that, ostensibly at least, treats the individual as the important unit may be the only model a "new rules" culture can sustain (p. 195). The effort it would take to draw Willis's (1977) and Everhart's (1983) students, or Cusick's (1973, 1983) working-class kids away from their groups, or Grant's (1988) friend from his "um ... goofing off" and into a tightly normed school community where they would be expected to participate might be too much.

Furthermore, building community and using it for pedagogical ends is a very difficult task and carries no guarantee of success. It requires ongoing analysis that borders on criticism. Lightfoot's (1983) Milton Academy is an example of a school facing itself and its educational ideals.

> The philosophical ideals of humanism invited tough self criticism, persistant complaints and nagging disappointments. Among students, faculty, and administrators, there was a clear recognition of the unevenness and weaknesses of their school. Criticism was legitimized, even encouraged. The stark visibility of their institutional vulnerabilities was related ... to a deeply rooted tolerance for conflict, idealism and to feelings of security. (p. 309)

But our universal, locally controlled, and publicly funded schools generate few feelings of security or "tolerance for conflict." Internal criticism is not encouraged. The school's mandated universalism and equality already stretch the public's tolerance for schools and the schools' tolerance for disorder, probably about as far as they can go. Public school administrators rarely feel sufficiently secure to encourage internal criticism. If such ideals were difficult in the private, selective, and highly regarded Milton Academy, they are probably out of the question in public schools. In public schools, it is easier and politically wiser to let individual students select their modes of participation, let class and cultural differences alone, and let the groups serve as training areas for social participation.

This functional explanation can be extended to the relationship between the school and capitalism, which encourages individual attainment but which underneath, according to Heilbroner (1985), has no "organizing moral force."

> It is part of the nature of capitalism that the circuit of capital has no intrinsic moral dimension, no vision of art or idea aside from the commodity form in which it is embodied. In this setting, ideas thrive but morality languishes, and the regime of capital becomes the breeding ground for an explosion of ideational and esthetic creations that conceal beneath their brilliance the absence of an organizing moral force. (p. 140)

But this is perhaps too functional an explanation. It sounds as though what makes such good sense must also be educationally worthwhile. Ignored is the fact that functional relationships can serve disfunctional ends.

The combination of peer group and school structure creates certain problems. It prevents the creation of a school community that might be used to teach broader social values and attitudes, and it discourages students, particularly those without a merit approach to education, from moving beyond their groups. It can actively discourage students from participation in academics and negatively influence the broad goals of citizenship education. It can encourage, rather than discourage, the more unpleasant aspects of class and cultural bias, as well as the more unpleasant aspects of capitalism. Finally, school staff can delude themselves into thinking of the students as orderly when their members are in fact perfecting low-level anarchy, which they will use for the rest of their lives in their relations with larger political structures.

On the other hand, perhaps this sometimes uncomfortable and sometimes inconsistent alliance between small groups and the larger school is just what is needed for a successful school, a successful society, and successful citizenship education. Perhaps this dualism is quite healthy and natural and is just what is needed for a complete education.

To prosper, man . . . needs to function on two levels at once. At the small group level, he treasures virtue such as loyalty and selflessness; in the extended order, he depends on narrow self interest and the profit motive. So be it. The trouble is that man has often made the mistake of finding this apparent inconsistency uncomfortable. Hence his many attempts to stretch small group virtues over society at large. ("Why socialism," 1988, p. 85)

SUMMARY

The argument presented in this chapter is that peer groups, as they operate in school, strongly reflect the social and cultural differences that students bring to school and limit the way their members interact with the school. The school's differentiated bureaucracy has a functional relationship with the groups. It supports them and is supported by them. Just as the bureaucracy creates time for students to interact, so the groups solve a problem of order that might occur if the students were not involved in groups during that time.

But groups not only take up time, they also do a considerable amount of teaching. If we take a simple definition of learning as acquiring certain habits and attitudes, we may conclude from the descriptions that, in their school groups, students learn certain things related to citizenship. They learn to practice social attitudes and modes of participation, make judgments, exercise values, and refine social practices they will use later in society. They learn the benefits of associating in small primary groups and the opprobrium associated with violating group norms. They learn to express collective judgments about those outside the group, judgments that are frequently class- and culture-based. They learn to limit trust and involvement in formal structures while cultivating a personal affective realm. They learn that groups are difficult to penetrate and often treat outsiders cruelly. They learn that the school, and by extension the world, is competitive; that formal rewards are limited; and that certain students are, early on, advantaged in the competition. They learn that those advantages include not only ability and daring, but inherited social and economic status. They learn that those most favored by circumstances of birth or talent are most likely to identify with the larger formal structure.

Students also learn and practice within their groups a certain disinterest in affairs outside the group; and the less likely they are to succeed in competition for formal rewards, the more they practice that disinterest. In groups, the lower-class students and those with few prospects gather to defend themselves against the perjorative judgments expressed by schools. Students also learn about the subtle and not-so-subtle ways that formal authorities select and groom the more talented, able, and advantaged individuals. As several of the authors described, the lack of interest can easily turn to hostility and resistance.

Students learn to differentiate formal structures from personal associations, but they also learn the limits of personal associations and that they may leave these associations to extend themselves as individuals and to expand their interests. Extracurricular activities are replete with such groups, and speciality tracks are also examples. In those, students may learn about the limits of their adolescent groups, and those with talent and energy can learn to move beyond their peer groups into larger arenas.

But more related to citizenship education, students are unlikely, according the studies presented in this chapter, ever to learn to think of larger social and political structures as "a community" and themselves as members of the community. Rather, they learn to guard their cooperation, to avoid transcending personal interests, and to limit their involvement in larger structures. By those interested in extending the power of the larger social structure over the individual, this is regarded as a problem, because it denies to the larger structure the influence it could wield if its members were affectively committed. In fact, it is from the combination of school structure and peer groups that students learn how society actually works.

SOME POSSIBILITIES FOR FUTURE RESEARCH

There are some issues raised in this chapter that warrant further consideration. One is the collusion of school and group structures, a collusion that goes generally unrecognized in studies of either school structure or classroom interaction. On one hand, the attractiveness of groups to the students and the immediacy of groups in the classroom encourage the teachers to use instructional methods that discourage student interaction because, if given an opportunity, students drift into their groups. While they are working individually, they are much less likely to do so. On the other hand, the groups take care of huge amounts of adolescent interest and energy that, if left unchanneled, could seriously disrupt the schools' bureaucratic routine. It seems that the school structure and the group structure both need and oppose each other. Where these two entities join may be where the most important lessons of citizenship, to take care of both personal affect and one's obligations to the larger society, are learned. The larger society does not need love and affection, but competence and clarity. It would be worthwhile to further examine the collusion and opposition of peer groups and school structures.

A second issue that warrants consideration is the place of the capitalistic ideology as it permeates the image of success that schools present. Schools model the capitalist's individual, material, and competitive society; in schools, as in capitalism, secular prizes go to the successful individual achievers. In fact, the most recent wave of secondary school reform, which its emphasis on scores (which further differentiate students), achieving (which is what capitalists are supposed to do), and skill orientation (which further commodifies education) strengthens the capitalistic ideology's hold on schools.

But the groups are a refuge for many students, those from cultures that do not emphasize accumulation, those who are not particularly competitive and might not be successful if they were, those who do believe that "wolfish" is a compliment. Such students need some wall, some barrier to hold between them and the schools' incessant and overwhelming message that competitive, secular, and materialistic individuals are good, the less so, less good. The group is the ideal barrier. It preserves the students' own cultures and protects them from the negative judgments the school passes upon them for being the way they are.

Related to that is the inconsistency between the school and citizenship education. At the same time that the schools promise secular rewards for individual effort, they preach the virtues of community, cooperation, and personal transcendence in pursuit of collective good. This inconsistency seems quite unrecognized, save by students who quietly and intuitively keep their class- and culture-bound groups between themselves and the school and by some critics who have decided the school's public posture is a sham, that the real interest is in preserving the regime of capital for those who are good at it.

Thus there are several lines of potential inquiry about the collusion between peer groups and school structure. All begin with the argument that student groups are an important part of the school's structure.

References

Agee, J., & Evans, W. (1936). *Let us now praise famous men.* Boston: Houghton Mifflin.

Callahan, R. (1962). *Education and the cult of efficiency.* Chicago: University of Chicago Press.

Coleman, J. S. (1981). *Adolescent society: the social life of the teenager and its impact on education.* Westport, CT: Greenwood. (original work published in 1961)

Conant, J. (1959). *The American high school today.* New York: McGraw-Hill.

Conant, J. (1962). *The adolescent society.* Glencoe, IL: Free Press.

Cusick, P. A. (1973). *Inside high school: The students' world.* New York: Holt, Rinehart & Winston.

Cusick, P. A. (1983) *The egalitarian ideal and the American high school.* New York: Longman.

Cusick, P. A., & Wheeler, C. (1987). Improving education through organizational change (No. 400-83-0052). Washington, DC: National Institute of Education. Also, (1988) as Organizational morality and school reform. *American Review of Education, 96*(2), 231–255.

Czikszentmihalyi, M., & Larson, R. (1984). *Being adolescent.* New York: Basic Books.

Everhart, R. (1983) *Reading, writing and resistance: Adolescence and labor in a junior high school.* Boston: Routledge and Kegan Paul.

Grant, G. (1988). *The world we created at Hamilton High.* Cambridge, MA: Harvard University Press.

Heilbroner, R. (1985). *The nature and logic of capitalism.* New York: W. W. Norton.

Hollingshead, A. (1949). *Elmtown's youth.* New York: John Wiley & Sons.

Homans, G. (1950). *The human group.* New York: Harcourt, Brace and World.

Jackson, P. (1968). *Life in classrooms,* New York: Holt, Rinehart & Winston.

Johnson, N. (1985). *Westhaven: Classroom culture and society in a rural elementary school.* Chapel Hill, NC: University of North Carolina Press.

Labaree, D. (1988). *The making of an American high school.* New Haven, CT: Yale University Press.

Lightfoot, S. (1983). *The good high school.* New York: Basic Books.

Lynd, R., & Lynd, H. (1929) *Middletown.* New York: Harcourt Brace.

McNeil, L. (1986). *Contradictions of control: School structure and school knowledge.* New York: Routledge and Kegan Paul.

Merton, R. (1965). The role set: Problems in sociological theory. In A. Ullman (Ed.), *Sociocultural foundations of personality* (pp. 261–271). Boston: Houghton Mifflin.

Metz, M. (1978) *Classrooms and corridors.* Berkeley, CA: University of California Press.

Oakes, J. (1985). *Keeping track: How schools structure inequality.* New Haven, CT: Yale University Press.

Powell, A., Farrar, E., & Cohen, D. (1985). *The shopping mall high school: Winners and losers in the educational marketplace.* Boston: Houghton Mifflin.

Shaver, J. P. (1987). Implications from research: What should be taught in social studies? In V. Richardson-Koehler (Ed.), *Educators' handbook: A research perspective* (pp. 112–138). New York: Longman.

Stinchcombe, A. (1964). *Rebellion in a high school.* Chicago: Quadrangle.

Thompson, J. (1967). *Complex organizations.* New York: Scott, Foresman.

Wax, R. (1967) The warrier dropouts. *Transactions, 4,* 40–46.

Willis P. (1977). *Learning to labour: How working class kids get working class jobs.* Aldershot, Hampshire, England: Gower.

Why socialism will never work. (1988). [Review of *The fatal conceit: The errors of socialism*] *The Economist, 310*(7587), 85.

·23·

THE INFLUENCE OF THE HOME ON SOCIAL STUDIES

Cynthia Szymanski Sunal

UNIVERSITY OF ALABAMA, TUSCALOOSA

Parents, siblings, and the environment they create are usually the child's first teachers. That teaching continues throughout childhood and adolescence. The home's effects on the attainment of commonly sought social studies goals and implications for social studies programs are examined in this chapter.

Citizenship education is the focus of social studies programs (National Council for the Social Studies, 1983). Citizenship involves understanding and fully participating in one's society. It also involves understanding human interrelationships and how the environment affects them. In the home, children learn to be citizens of their society. When they enter school they have already developed an understanding of their roles in their families, in relation to peers, and as citizens of their society. The home has been the primary influence on children's understanding of these interrelated roles, varying in intensity and importance with the age of the child. These relationships change throughout childhood and adolescence. As they change, the influence of the home is strong, although mediated somewhat by the influence of the school, the media, and other factors. At home children learn how to achieve; to relate to other people; to initiate and maintain social relationships; to relate to others who differ from their families racially, economically, or culturally; to live as moral persons; and to participate in the governance of their society. It is imperative that social studies educators recognize and consider the strong and continuing influence of parents, siblings, and the environment they create on children's conception of their role as citizens.

In considering the influence of home factors on children, this chapter begins with an examination of the home's effect on children's motivation for achievement in school. Then the development of social competence in children is discussed, a matter of prime importance as schools work to help students understand and function successfully in their social world. Socially competent students are often good at seeing situations from another's perspective, an important element in moral development. Moral development is considered next, as the home's role in fostering the growth of the child into a morally mature individual is explored. Morality influences politics, although it is not always identified with politics. Children's political socialization by the home is examined next. The media, particularly television, have impacts on all areas discussed in the chapter. How the home strengthens and weakens the influence of television is examined next. Finally, the home's role in developing racial attitudes and, by extension, attitudes toward other groups of people is considered.

DEVELOPMENT OF MOTIVATION FOR ACHIEVEMENT

Research on the home's effect on children's academic performance indicates that it not only directly teaches the child, but it also affects the child's achievement in school. As a consequence, the home has a strong influence on children's responses to the teaching that occurs at school. Home effects are seen early in life. By the time they are 6 months old, children show individual differences in both how ready they are to explore their environment and how they attempt to assert control over aspects of that environment including objects, situations, and people's actions (Yarrow, Waxler, & Scott, 1971). These early differences can be used to predict intellectual performance by 2 1/2 years of age (Messer et al., 1986). Children who are inquisitive and in control of a situation generally demon-

Reviewers were Helen Carlson, University of Minnesota, Duluth; Barbara Hatcher, Southwest Texas State University.

strate higher intellectual abilities than passive youngsters (Messer et al., 1986).

Attachment to an Adult

Children's exploration of their environment, particularly as demonstrated by the curiosity and the problem-solving behavior displayed, is affected by their social experiences. A social experience of particular importance is a clear attachment by 12- to 18-months to a responsible adult. In kindergarten, children who had a positive, early, clear attachment to an adult have more confidence in exploring their environment while away from an adult and are more likely to demonstrate curiosity, self-reliance, and problem solving abilities (Arend, Gove, & Sroufe, 1979); Cassidy, 1986). These three characteristics relate to school achievement and suggest that a clear attachment to a responsible adult may facilitate achievement.

Home Environment

The home environment is another factor that appears to affect achievement. In a longitudinal study, Van Doornick, Caldwell, Wright, and Frankenberg (1981) rated as stimulating or unstimulating the home environments of 50 lower-class children aged 12 months, using the Home Observation for Measurement of the Environment (HOME) Inventory. The standardized achievement test scores and school grades of the children were analyzed between 5 and 9 years later. It was found that 65 % of those whose home environment had been rated as stimulating were doing well in school, whereas 70% of those from unstimulating environments were performing poorly. The study indicated that information about an infant's home environment can be used to predict later school achievement. An unstimulating home environment provides few opportunities for exploration or problem solving, both of which are the basis for later academic achievement in school.

What makes a home stimulating? *First,* the attachment of the child to a responsible and responsive adult is important. *Second,* the variety of stimulation the child receives and the appropriateness of play materials used by the child play a role (Stevens & Bakeman, 1985). These factors are subscales on the HOME instrument and have been found to be strong predictors of young children's first-grade academic performance. Play materials that encourage exploration and problem solving, such as clay, paint, water, and sand, present children with a stimulating environment.

In addition, parental expectation of early independence and their warm reinforcement of attempts to be self-reliant are other factors related to high achievement motivation (Winterbottom, 1959). Additional factors include direct achievement training in which high standards are set, concern about the quality of the child's performance, and immediate praise for the child (Rosen & D'Andrade, 1959). High-achieving students enjoy mastering tasks with family members who are not overly critical of occasional failures. Independence, achievement motivation, and achievement behavior are related and seem to develop best when children are encouraged to do things on their own and to do them well (Shaffer, 1988).

Parenting Style and Parental Expectations

A major factor that can affect achievement is overall parenting style. Children with high achievement motivation and the self-reliance related to such motivation are likely to have authoritative parents. These parents exert some control over their children's activities but do not impose severe restrictions. Extremes in parental control, reflected in authoritarian and permissive parenting styles, tend to be associated with children who are somewhat immature and aimless, and who have little achievement motivation (Baumrind, 1977).

The differential responses of parents to male and female children are another factor that has been identified as affecting achievement (Dweck, Davidson, Nelson, & Enna, 1978; Parsons, Kaczala, & Meese, 1982). During the elementary school years girls show higher achievement than boys. Girls' relatively higher achievement tends to decline in junior and senior high school. Among the contributors to this decline are adult attitudes toward girls' and boys' achievement. Girls are higher achievers than boys during the elementary school years, but they underestimate their achievement, capabilities, and future accomplishments, whereas boys overestimate theirs. Some parents establish and reinforce these inaccurate estimations by modeling different roles for their children, having higher expectations of sons and attributing sons' successes to ability and daughters' successes to effort.

Implications

Each of the factors influencing achievement motivation has implications for social studies teaching. Teachers cannot easily overcome the lack of an early attachment to a responsible caring adult. However, the teacher can be supportive of students and establish a stable environment that provides a measure of security.

Home factors can foster high achievement. And the reverse of each factor can result in low achievement. For example, research results suggest that teachers and parents foster low achievement by frequently informing a student that he or she has not done well on a task because of poor problem-solving skills. After a while such students may give up trying because they are convinced that they don't have the ability to accomplish the problems given to them (Kathowsky, Crandall, & Good, 1967). Because the homes from which any class of students come vary widely, students bring with them a huge range of parental expectations. School personnel need to expect the best, in order to reinforce homes in which the best is also expected and counter the low expectations of other homes. Awareness of the early, strong, and continuing impact of home factors on children's achievement in school is vital.

There is little research describing the interaction of parental and teacher expectations and the effects of such interactions on achievement. There is also little research analyzing the extent to which teachers can overcome low expectations for the child by those in the home or parenting styles that foster low motivation for achievement. It is evident, though, that home factors strongly affect children's motivation for achievement. This suggests that the school may not be a powerful factor. The extent to which teachers and the school environment can enhance or reduce the effects of home factors is not clear. Investigation of school–home interaction is needed to determine how social studies educators can best work to achieve their goals.

DEVELOPMENT OF SOCIAL COMPETENCE

The discussion thus far has centered around achievement. This is certainly an important element in the social world of the child and the adolescent, but it is by no means the only major element. The development of social competence is also important, in part because it influences achievement. Socially competent children may have more prerequisite skills and energy to spend on achievement than less competent children. Social studies teachers can assist students in developing competence in social relationships as an important part of living in the social world.

Early Development of Sociability

Sociability develops early, about age 2, and appears to remain relatively stable thereafter. Bronson (1985) found inconsistency in sociability at age 12 months. He also found that measures of sociability at age 2 were correlated with sociability at age 3 1/2. Videotaped observations of play groups of 38 toddlers from middle-income families were examined for differences in the stability of individual reactions in the first versus the third trimester of their second year. Subsequent assessments of these children's behavior in nursery school at age 3 1/2 indicated a significant increase in their consistency, as well as in their range of reactions to the play groups, and there was a marked end-of-year increase in the researcher's ability to predict later functioning.

Bronson's work supported Schaefer and Bayley's (1963) earlier finding that sociability remains fairly stable over time. Schaefer and Bayley used a sample of 27 boys and 27 girls on whom extensive data from the Berkeley Growth Study were available for the first few years of life. These data were supplemented by child behavior ratings from observations of overt behavior in a test situation. Maternal behavior was also observed during the children's first 3 years. Mothers remaining in the study were interviewed 9 to 14 years later. Based on patterns of high correlation, Schaefer and Bayley concluded that a friendly and outgoing preschooler is likely to be a friendly and outgoing adolescent.

Children who are overly shy, uncomfortable, or aggressive with peers may need intervention, because these characteristics of sociability tend to be stable over time. Research results have indicated the early formation of patterns of sociability and their stability throughout time. What role do parents play in the formation of their children's patterns of sociability?

Parental Role

Warm and supportive parents who require their children to follow certain rules of social etiquette such as "take your turn," "share," and "talk about a problem before fighting about it" are more likely to have children who relate well to both adults and peers (Baumrind, 1971). Permissive parents who set few standards and exert little control over their children often raise children who are aggressive and unpopular with peers and who may resist or rebel against rules set by other adults, for example, teachers. Authoritarian parents who set rigid standards and exert heavy control often raise aggressive and unpopular children. Parental support, responsiveness, and insistence on following reasonable rules are three factors affecting children's social competence (Baumrind, 1971).

As described earlier, clear attachment to a responsible adult is related not only to higher achievement in children but also to greater social competence, as demonstrated by outgoing, popular children. Sensitive, responsive care giving produces clear attachment that, in turn, assists in the development of sociability.

In an effort to relate parental interactions and children's sociability, MacDonald and Parke (1984) studied 13 boys and 14 girls, ages 3 and 4 years, and their parents. Children were videotaped while playing with each parent separately for 20 min in their homes. Children's social competence with their peers was independently evaluated using three measures: (a) teacher rankings of popularity with peers, (b) teacher Q-sort ratings of the children's social competence, and (c) assessments of social interaction with three different peers on separate occasions.

MacDonald and Parke hypothesized that the character of playful interactions between parents and their children is significant in the development of sociability because parents are social partners during play. Parents' style of interacting with their children influences the ways in which children react to other playmates. The researchers found that, if fathers physically played a lot with their sons and mothers talked a lot with them, the sons tended to be socially competent, comfortable, and relaxed with peers. If parents were commanding and often gave orders, sons were less likely to be socially competent and were often aggressive toward peers.

The effects of parental interactions with girls were slightly different. If fathers talked extensively with their daughters and showed interest in their activities, the daughters were socially competent; if fathers involved girls in highly physical play and mothers were commanding, the daughters were less socially competent and were negative toward their peers. Opportunities for learning to regulate affect were suggested as contributors to the relationships that were found. Linkages between family and peer social systems were illustrated by the study.

Some methodological questions can be raised about the researchers' use of teacher ratings and observations. There appear to be some discrepancies between teacher ratings and observed peer interactions, especially for girls. High popularity ratings for girls were associated with fathers' use of physical modes of play, which were observed as dominating and abrasive forms of interaction. More assertive play styles were rated positively by teachers, but it is not known whether peers responded positively to them. Other means of measuring peer competence need to be investigated. The direction of affect in parent–peer relationships is also unclear. It may be that socially skillful children are able to direct play with their parents more effectively, requiring less direction by the parents.

Further longitudinal and experimental studies are needed of the parenting processes explored in the McDonald and Parke study. Included should be an examination of parental provision of opportunities for peer interaction, as well as a detailed study of how parents manage peer–peer interactions when supervising these activities. Family and peer systems are linked in a variety of ways. The assessment of the relative importance of these interactions between mothers and fathers and across children at different ages merits attention.

Implications

Sociability is an early developing trait. It is central to the development of social competence. There is evidence that parents do affect children's interactions with their peers. Studies with young children have suggested that authoritative parents have more sociable children than do authoritarian parents. More research is needed to determine the extent of parental effects, the direction of parent–peer effects on children's interactions with each, and how much control children exert on their interactions with peers. Longitudinal studies to examine parental effects through adolescence are needed. Comparisons of teacher and peer evaluation of social competence are also needed.

The evidently powerful influence of home factors on social competence suggests a limited role for school factors. There has been little research, however, to investigate the relative weights of home and school. Longitudinal research, perhaps ethnographic in methodology, with small samples of children studied in depth, might begin to reveal the extent of the impact of school factors on children's social competence.

MORAL DEVELOPMENT

Peer interactions often require children to consider their conceptions of right and wrong, to regulate their own behavior, and to decide whether to conform to socially accepted standards. A socially competent individual may not also be a moral individual. Yet social interaction does have an impact on moral development.

Growing up involves learning how to satisfy one's own needs and desires while accepting limitations and restrictions imposed by society. As children mature, society's demands become more complex. Young children, for example, are expected to say "please" and to be quiet in restaurants. Older children must follow a list of school rules and do chores at home. Adolescents are expected to understand complex social skills, follow laws regulating how they drive, and not drink alcohol until a specified age.

The expectations for appropriate behavior that adults set require even elementary school children to exercise self-control, work toward exemplary conduct, feel guilty over transgressions, and reward themselves only when they attain the highest standards set. To attain these standards, children must often delay gratification.

In later childhood, children are expected to understand the need for rules, why the rules of their society are in force, and

that rules are not necessarily arbitrary impositions by authority figures but may be based on considerations of mutual respect and reciprocity among human beings. Most children do accomplish all of these expectations, internalizing them.

Morality

Morality is sometimes seen as having three aspects (Shaffer, 1988). The cognitive aspect is moral reasoning, understanding the difference between right and wrong. The affective aspect is moral self-evaluation, and includes such emotions as pride, guilt, and shame. Self-evaluation often involves emotions such as guilt following transgressions and pride following doing what one thinks is right. The behavioral aspect is resistance to deviation, which involves reactions to situations in which the person is tempted to behave in a manner he or she knows to be incorrect. Each of these is a facet of morality that cannot easily be separated from the other. Together they result in morality.

Moral Reasoning

Moral reasoning differs from child to child, even when they are equally aware of social rules. How does the home influence the moral reasoning of children? The development of moral reasoning, self-evaluation, and resistance to deviation seems to be best fostered in homes where inductive reasoning is used as a disciplinary strategy. Neither the withdrawal of love nor the assertion of power by adults in the home seems to promote moral development. Instead, these actions produce children who are morally immature (Hoffman, 1970). When reasoning is used, the adult gives the child explanations or reasons for requiring that a behavior be changed or maintained. Along with using reasoning, parents who foster moral development also point out the likely consequences of the child's behavior, for example, injury to another or sadness at being called a name. An additional strategy is also used. This involves appealing to the child's desire to be grown up and to be thought of by others as mature (Hoffman, 1970).

The children of parents who use reasoning and regularly stress concern for others' needs and emotions have been found to have the highest levels of moral development. Parpal and Maccoby (1985) found that children who resisted deviation, exhibited self-control, and usually tried to comply with rules had mothers who preferred to discipline by using explanations combined with voiced displeasure. Only occasionally did these mothers use limited power assertion.

The researchers contrasted the effects of three modes of mother–child interaction on children's subsequent compliance with maternal directives. Subjects were 39 lower-middle-class children, ranging in age from 3.2 to 4.6 years. Teachers identified each sample child as compliant or noncompliant. Mothers and children were in one of the following conditions: responsive play—child encouraged to direct the action (mother trained); free play—mother positive, but that she should comply with child directions is not taught or stressed (mother untrained); or noninteractive. Children played with their mothers for 15 minutes; then their compliance was tested by telling them that they must soon leave and so must do some things the mother asked. Thirty commands relating to cleanup were issued.

Both the responsive play and the noninteractive conditions produced higher levels of child compliance than the untrained free-play condition. However, noninteractive and responsive play conditions may affect individual children differently. More research is needed on the effects of responsive parenting on the development of compliance in children.

Hoffman (1970) gave several explanations for the effectiveness of reasoning in raising morally mature children. *First,* adults who reason inductively provide cognitive standards or rationales that children can use in self-evaluations of their own behavior and activities. Children are generally asked to consider how others feel in any situation in which others are involved, as part of the rationales provided. Such consideration encourages them to be empathetic and to put themselves in another's place. These behaviors contribute to the development of moral reasoning, the cognitive aspect of morality. *Second,* inductive reasoning encourages adults to talk about self-evaluation and the emotions related to it such as pride, guilt, or shame. Thus, the affective aspect of morality is approached. *Third,* adults can explain what behaviors would have helped children resist deviation and what they could now do to make up for the deviation. The behavioral aspect of morality is also addressed. Reasoning utilizes all three aspects of morality and may help the individual to integrate them (Hoffman, 1970).

Children and adolescents, ages 4–18, have been found to evaluate inductive reasoning as the most appropriate form of discipline, with physical punishment second (Siegal & Cowan 1984). One hundred children divided into 5 groups of 10 boys and 10 girls each were asked to evaluate the disciplinary techniques used by mothers over a range of situations in which someone was described as having transgressed. The maternal child-rearing strategies consisted of inductive reasoning, physical punishment, love withdrawal, and permissiveness. The children tended to demonstrate a preference for authoritative parenting, expressing strong approval for inductive reasoning, accompanied by mild approval for physical punishment. Although favorable ratings of physical punishment generally declined with age and ratings of inductive reasoning increased, there were no age differences in evaluations of inductive reasoning in some situations.

Further research is needed in which children are presented with very subtle reasoning techniques. Other techniques of power assertion besides physical punishment might also be examined. Evaluations of fathers' disciplinary behavior are also needed. And older children may evaluate disciplinary methods differently, depending on the gender of the transgressor.

Perspective Taking

Selman (1971, 1976) found that learning to take the perspective of others increases children's ability to make mature moral judgments. Among children of the same age and level of general intelligence, Selman found that children who had reached the higher levels of perspective taking on his scale were more

likely to have reached the higher levels of moral reasoning when discussing Kohlberg's (1963) dilemmas. However, although individuals at the highest level of morality, the postconventional level, were almost all skillful perspective takers, individuals with excellent perspective-taking abilities were not necessarily highly moral. Knowing what others want, feel, and believe is not enough to make individuals behave considerately and in a prosocial way. Without such knowledge, however, an individual cannot develop a mature understanding of mutual rights and obligations.

To explore the relationship in middle childhood between two social-cognitive processes, role-taking ability and moral reasoning, 60 middle-class children were administered Kohlberg's (1963) moral-judgment measure, two role-taking tasks, and the Peabody Picture Vocabulary Test, a conventional measure of intelligence (Selman, 1971). Among these 8- to 10-year-old students, with intelligence controlled, the development of reciprocal role-taking skills was positively related to the development of conventional moral judgment. One year later, 10 subjects whose role-taking and moral-judgment levels had been low in the original study were reexamined. The results supported the hypothesis that the development of the ability to understand the reciprocal nature of interpersonal relations is a necessary but insufficient condition for the development of conventional moral thought.

Parents who foster their children's perspective-taking skills help them to develop morally. Bearison and Cassel (1975) investigated the kinds of discussions parents had with their children when disciplinary issues arose. They then examined the relationship of these discussions to the children's perspective-taking ability in a communication game. Children whose mothers used person-oriented appeals were more skillful in adjusting their communication styles to the states of their listeners.

When parents frequently call attention to and explain other people's perspectives, children learn to be sensitive to these perspectives. On the basis of Selman's (1971) work, we can infer that children with person-oriented mothers are more advanced than their peers in ability to make moral judgments.

Implications

Morality has three facets that social studies programs should be aimed at developing: cognitive, affective, and behavioral. Research on the role of the home in moral development has indicated that the parent's use of inductive reasoning with children fosters moral maturity. Inductive reasoning has a role in the development of sensitivity to the perspectives of others. Perspective taking appears to be related to moral development. It can be inferred from those research results that social studies teachers should utilize inductive reasoning and foster perspective taking to promote moral development in students.

Researchers should investigate the effects of both parents' and teachers' use of inductive reasoning with children on adolescent reciprocal role-taking skills. Does lack of congruity between parent and teacher approaches create confusion in students? How do students from homes where inductive reasoning is used respond to classrooms where it is not used, and vice versa? To what extent, and in what situations, do adolescents use reciprocal role taking? To what extent do parents adapt their strategies as children mature? What differences are found between teachers of different ages of children? Do parent and teacher strategies change and, if so, to what extent, depending on varying crises in which the student might be involved.

CHILDREN'S POLITICAL SOCIALIZATION

Political socialization involves how children come to understand political processes and structure within their own and other cultures and how they conceive of their role as citizens. Some aspects of moral development, such as resistance to deviation, are related to political socialization. A student who has been socialized to the national political culture understands that certain types of behavior on the part of citizens will be evaluated as deviant, whereas others will be deemed acceptable. The student will evaluate her or his own personal behavior partly in terms of the political arena. Finally, high-level moral reasoning involves evaluation of the categories of acceptable and unacceptable behavior in the political arena. Moral reasoning may eventually place the student in conflict with the political culture or may reaffirm most of the evaluations of behavior embedded in cultural norms. The home influences moral development. What do we know of its influence on political socialization?

Research on the family's role in the development of children's political awareness has been limited. Most researchers have examined children's knowledge at different points in their development, usually in late elementary school and in secondary school. Some of the research, however, gives insights into the role of the family in the political socialization of the younger child.

Easton and Hess (1962) observed that there is strong evidence that the formative years in political socialization are between the ages of 3 and 14. However, little research has been done with preschool and primary grades children, so information on younger children is not well substantiated. The youngest children in the studies of Hess and Torney (1967) were second graders; and those in Andrain's (1971) study, fifth graders. These researchers used children who could respond to a written questionnaire. Studies are probably rarely done with younger children because they require observation and interviewing.

Adelson and O'Neil (1966) found that many adolescents experience a political awakening. Political socialization occurs over a long time, but political awareness is likely to occur first during adolescence. Many students first feel a commitment to a political ideology and are active in support of that ideology during adolescence. Adelson and O'Neil (1966) cited cognitive and moral development as responsible for these events in political socialization. Specifically, formal operational reasoning incorporating causal and hypothetical-deductive thinking and higher stages of moral reasoning have been identified as supporting the political activity seen during adolescence (Connell, 1971; Furth, 1980; Merelman, 1971). Cognitive and moral development enable adolescents to understand the causes of social

problems, to imagine a better society, and to see how their own activity could contribute to the construction of such a society.

Middle adolescents have been found to have a realistic, complex understanding of the political system (Connell, 1971; Furth, 1980; Merelman, 1971). The family affects the political choices students make (Merelman, 1971). Other factors influencing political choices in middle adolescence are the peer group, the opportunities for political activity in the community, and the personality of the pupil. The home has a role, in that some differences in political socialization appear to be age related, whereas others appear to be related to home factors. For example, that some adolescents can cite the multiple effects of poverty and can see that it has multiple and related causes, while others attribute it to a single cause, may be related to their families' understanding and discussion of social problems such as poverty.

Parental Effects on Adolescents' Political Socialization

A major influence on political socialization, and the focus of many political socialization studies, is the political values and behavior of the adolescent's parents. Generally, researchers have found modest positive correlations between parental political beliefs and the political beliefs of their adolescents (Connell, 1972; Hess & Torney, 1967; Hyman, 1959; Jennings & Niemi, 1968). Often adolescents agree with their parents' general political orientation, for example, whether they are conservative or liberal, and the belief system arising from this orientation. However, adolescents may disagree with their parents on specific issues such as drinking laws. Because of these disagreements, if appears that parents do not transmit their political values directly to their children. Correlations between the political beliefs of siblings are positive but low, suggesting again that parents do not directly transmit political values (Hess & Torney, 1967). The home indirectly influences political values toward a general orientation. Parental values cannot be used to predict the specific political behavior of their children.

Although the influence of the home on political behavior is indirect, researchers have identified home factors associated with adolescent political behavior (Chaffee, 1977; Chaffee, McLeod, & Wackman, 1973; Stone & Chaffee, 1970). Adolescents from homes where open discussion of political ideas was encouraged were most likely to engage in political action. The greater the amount of discussion in the home, the more likely that the adolescents were highly informed and accepted civic responsibility.

Parental Effects on Younger Children's Political Socialization

To better understand political socialization among younger children, a longitudinal study was conducted by Moore, Lare, and Wagner (1985). In 1974 they interviewed kindergarteners in five suburban California school districts, then followed them through the fourth grade, interviewing them near the end of each school year. The sample of 243 lower- and middle-class children included 119 boys and 124 girls and was 81.5% Anglo and 18.5% non-Anglo. The researchers found that the comments of the family—especially those of the parents concerning candidates, issues, and governmental processes—had the greatest influence on political interest and information during the first years of elementary school. The impact of the media, particularly television, was dependent on parental interest in it and on their discussion of what was reported in the media.

Moore et al. (1985) reported that their subjects were very sensitive to the role of the law and seemed to have strong potential for lawlessness. The researchers noted that these children were exposed, particularly via the media, to much striving for rights by minorities and nonmainstream groups. They also were exposed to law-related themes on television programs dealing with traffic tickets, murder, divorce, adoption, and the personal and professional lives of lawyers. Finally, some of these children's parents had participated in the civil rights or other movements and were likely to pass on to their children their concerns about, dedication to, and rationale for conflict with the law. These children's exposure to litigation and law-related themes resulted in both sensitivity to the law and ability to build a rationale for lawlessness, particularly because lawlessness is not always punished when depicted in the media. Moore et al. suggested that the demographic, economic, sociological, and psychic forces contributing to young people's consciousness of law cannot be precisely sorted out, but the consequences are clear (pp. 163–164).

Although parents passed on their political consciousness and struggles, generally they avoided discussion of political tensions and conflicts. Moore et al. (1985) postulated that to promote order and unity, parents delayed introducing discussion of divisions in policymaking responsibility and sources of political tension or conflict. This postponement is seen as ultimately detrimental to the proper functioning of a vital, participatory democracy (p. 221). Although their study added much to our knowledge of the early political socialization of children by the home, Moore et al. suggested that more longitudinal research is needed to investigate the parent–child relationship. This might be done best through interviews of parents and their children every 2 years, beginning when the children are 3 or 4 years old.

Implications

The research on the home's influence on political socialization suggests that social studies programs might best foster children's development through discussion of political personages, issues, and concerns. Open discussion at home does appear to foster children's political socialization. Because parents may delay making children aware of political conflict, school personnel may have to make additional efforts to introduce discussion of conflict. Such discussion could begin with the later primary grades, because Moore et al.'s (1985) study indicated that the parents are not yet initiating discussion of political conflicts at that age, even though the media are introducing children to conflicts. Social studies professionals should be aware of the potential for media to cause children to think about political conflicts even though the home is not responding to that likelihood.

Much of the research on political socialization has not involved the use of interview methodology. Multiple interviews with students and their families, both longitudinally and with cross-sectional samples, could yield much information if they were begun at the earliest levels, with 3-year-olds, and continued through late adolescence.

TELEVISION'S EFFECTS ON SOCIAL LEARNING

Media have an effect on the development of children. Television has the largest impact. It is a major vehicle through which children learn about the social world. Television informs children about people—what their characteristics are, who they are, where they live, and what they want out of life. Using the information they glean from television, can children construct an accurate understanding of the social world?

Television viewing starts early; 6-month-old children often spend 1 to 2 hours daily in front of the television (Hollenbeck & Slaby, 1979). Television viewing time increases to 4 hours daily during ages 2–12 but drops to 3 hours daily during adolescence (McCall, Parke, & Kavanaugh, 1977). It is evident that 6-month-old children do not attend to much of what is on the television or imitate it, but, by age 2, they are imitating what they see (McCall et al., 1977). Children's parents initiate them early into television viewing and do not discourage the increase in viewing time that begins at age 2.

Television viewing has reduced the amount of time parents and children spend together in other leisure activities. The amount of time children spend reading or playing with friends, however, has remained the same (Johnson, 1967).

Violence and Aggression on Television

Television suggests that violence and aggression are commonly accepted means of solving problems (Eron, Huesmann, Brice, Fischer, & Mermelstein, 1983; Slaby & Quarforth, 1980). Specifically, television violence may (a) teach children how to threaten and hurt, (b) make the use of aggression more likely by children and adolescents, (c) create a fear of violence directed against oneself, (d) create a disregard for following rules of reasonable conduct when adults are not present, and (e) develop less emotional support for those who have suffered violence. These effects are likely to be compounded as children who prefer and watch a lot of television violence become adults who are more violent than their peers who watched less violent television (Eron, Lefkowitz, Huesmann, & Walder, 1972).

In homes where adults watch television with children and adolescents and criticize aggression when it is depicted, children and adolescents display less aggressive behavior (Grusec, 1973). Moreover, television can have positive effects. Children can learn about cultures far away and different from theirs. Programs can help children develop prosocial behaviors. Programs such as *Mister Rogers' Neighborhood* contain segments that depict helping friends, valuing a person for inner qualities rather than appearance, understanding another's feelings, and paying attention to safety rules and signs. Children who regularly view Mr. Rogers develop many prosocial behaviors, including cooperation, sharing, understanding others' feelings, verbalizing one's own feelings, delay of gratification, persisting at a difficult task in order to do it well, acceptance of rules, and the tendency to engage in imaginative play (Slaby & Quarforth, 1980). Television programming has the potential to foster both cognitive and prosocial development.

Implications

Parents can control the television viewing of their children by turning off the television, arbitrating selection of what is watched, and discussing what is watched. Parents can have a tremendous influence over the substantial effects that television has on children.

Social studies teachers should recognize the positive and negative effects of television programming. Teachers can provide viewing or study guides to students and their parents and can encourage discussion of programs at home. Certainly discussion of programs should occur at school. Because television has a continuing impact on children, the social studies program should include continuing discussion of the positive and negative aspects of what is viewed. Further research should be done to attempt to establish why many homes appear to support violent television programming and why many adults do not yet believe that viewing violence on television increases children's level of aggressive behavior even though there is strong and much-publicized research evidence indicating that these relationships occur.

RACIAL ATTITUDES

One of the most obvious differences between people is race. Media such as television do convey messages concerning race. The most obvious source of individual differences in children's racial attitudes, however, is parents. Children's racial attitudes and behavior often show close similarity to those of their parents (Allport & Kramer, 1946; Gough, Harris, Martin, & Edwards, 1950a; McCandless & Hoyt, 1961).

Authoritarian home backgrounds tend to produce children who hold racial prejudices (Gough et al., 1950a, 1950b). Milner (1983) has suggested that authoritarian parents, who have been found to be more prejudiced than nonauthoritarian parents, tend to raise prejudiced children through both direct and indirect teaching. They also develop prejudiced attitudes through child-bearing beliefs and practices that create authoritarian structures in their children. These authoritarian structures, in turn, make children more receptive to learning their parents' and other peoples' prejudices. The cycle is hypothetical, but research has established that authoritarian home backgrounds do tend to produce children who are disposed to prejudice.

Children's awareness of racial differences and attitudes to-

ward others begins in early childhood and increases through middle childhood. There is evidence of strong own-race preference and other-race rejection from as early as 4 years of age, peaking between 6 and 8, and tapering off somewhat toward adolescence (Milner, 1983). Pushkin (1967) in a British study, found Caucasian children's preferences for their own group among nursery school children that increased with age, frequently with increased hostility at age 6. He found no relation between the children's attitudes and the child-rearing practices of their mothers. However a substantial proportion of the racially hostile children had mothers who were also rated as very hostile. The greatest hostility among both children and mothers was found in an area where there had been marked racial tension. Pushkin concluded that his results indicated that young children imitate their mother's strong ethnic attitudes. He also concluded that local attitudes affect attitude formation in young children.

Horowitz and Horowitz (1938), in an intensive study of a rural Tennessee community in the 1930s, found direct instruction of children by parents to be important in the formation of racial attitudes. Parents specifically told their children not to play with children from other races. Sometimes these prohibitions were reinforced with spanking when the child did not obey them. Horowitz and Horowitz also found that attitudes were conveyed through subtler means such as comparisons of types of clothing worn and forms of leisure activity enjoyed. More indirect instruction also occurs as children model, often unconsciously, aspects of adult behavior including attitudes.

More recently, research has indicated that society, through parents, teachers, peers, and the media, provides children with both direct experience and observation of prejudice (Stein & Friedrich, 1975; Williams & Moreland, 1979). Several studies have explored methods of reducing prejudice. Methods reported to have been somewhat successful include provision of positive contacts between children of different races (Stephan, 1978) and teaching children to discriminate among other-race faces (Katz & Zalk, 1978).

Implications

Racial attitudes—and by extension, other stereotypes, such as those toward the elderly and the overweight—are formed through direct and indirect instruction in the home. As a result, children are likely to enter elementary school with well-formed attitudes. When stereotyping is evidenced, the social studies program must work to reduce it. The best vehicles for moderating prejudice appear to be authoritative classrooms in which guidance is provided, discussion is encouraged, opportunities to work with others are frequent, and exploration of the cultures of ethnic groups within and outside of the country occurs.

The extent to which the school can moderate racial or other prejudices is unclear. Because much teaching of prejudice is indirect, such as comparisons of clothing, it is difficult to pinpoint many of the characteristics identified as negative about a group toward whom the prejudice is directed. Can social studies teachers identify many of the subtler comparisons used at home to produce prejudice? With the limited time available, on what elements of prejudiced attitudes should social studies programs be focused? Can social studies teachers work actively to combat prejudices in the local community without seriously alienating the community and, thereby, generally lowering the effectiveness of the school in other areas? Finally, how many prejudices do teachers and parents share in common in varying types of communities?

CONCLUSIONS

Social studies education does begin at home and continues in the home throughout the school years. Home factors have a tremendous influence on children and adolescents. Varieties of effective teaching methods are used in the home and often differ from classroom methods. Research results indicate that teaching in the home includes modeling, direct instruction, coaching, simulations, making comparisons, interactive play, supervision, and indirect instruction through setting predispositions.

Social studies educators must recognize the home's impact on students. Programs must be based on a recognition of the home's role, or they may be unsuccessful because the underlying assumptions are not realistic. The strong influence of the home suggests a limited role for the school. It is as yet, however, unclear how powerful these limitations are. Research is needed to examine home–school interactions. An appropriate school social studies program should include the positive behaviors that parents and others in the home use to build children's competencies and attitudes for the social world. Research results do suggest that a social studies program in which the most positive parenting strategies are incorporated will be an authoritative program in which inductive reasoning is used to build self-reliance, high standards are set, and achievement of the high standards is rewarded.

References

Adelson, J., & O'Neil, R. (1966). Growth of political ideas in adolescence: The sense of community. *Journal of Personality and Social Psychology, 4,* 295–306.

Allport, G. W., & Kramer, B. M. (1946). Some roots of prejudice. *Journal of Psychology, 22,* 9–39.

Andrain, C., (1971). *Children and civic awareness.* Columbus, OH: Charles E. Merrill.

Arend, A., Gove, F. L., & Sroufe, L. A. (1979). Continuity of individual adaptation from infancy to kindergarten: A predictive study of ego-resiliency and curiosity in preschoolers. *Child Development, 150,* 950–959.

Baumrind, D. (1971). Current patterns of parental authority. *Developmental Psychology Monographs, 4* (No. 1, Pt. 2).

Baumrind, D. (1977, March). *Socialization determinants of personal agency.* Paper presented at the meeting of the Society for Research in Child Development, New Orleans.

Bearison, D. J., & Cassel, T. Z. (1975). Cognitive decentration and social codes: Communication effectiveness in young children from differing family contexts. *Developmental Psychology, 11,* 29–36.

Bronson, W. C. (1985). Growth in the organization of behavior over the second year of life. *Developmental Psychology 21,* 108–117.

Cassidy, J. (1986). The ability to negotiate the environment: An aspect of infant competence as related to quality of attachment. *Child Development, 57,* 331–337.

Chaffe, S. H. (1977). Mass communication in political socialization. In S. A. Renshon (Ed.), *Handbook of political socialization: Theory and research* (pp. 171–216). New York: Free Press.

Chaffee, S. H., McLeod, J. M., & Wackman, D. B. (1973). Family communication patterns and adolescent political participation. In J. Dennis (Ed.), *Socialization to politics* (pp. 89–112). New York: John Wiley and Sons.

Connell, R. W. (1971). *The child's construction of politics.* Carlton, Australia: Melbourne University Press.

Connell, R. W. (1972). Political socialization in the American family: The evidence reexamined. *Public Opinion Quarterly 36,* 323–333.

Dweck, C. S., Davidson, W., Nelson, S., & Enna, B. (1978). Sex differences in learned helplessness: II. The contingencies of evaluative feedback in the classroom, and III. An experimental analysis. *Developmental Psychology, 14,* 268–276.

Easton, D., & Hess, R. D. (1962). The child's political world. *Midwest Journal of Political Science, 6,* 235–236.

Eron, L. D. Huesmann, L. R., Brice, P., Fischer, P., & Mermelstein, R. (1983). Age trends in the development of aggression, sex-typing, and related television habits. *Developmental Psychology, 19,* 71–77.

Eron, L. D., Lefkowitz, M. M., Huesmann, L. R., & Walder, L. O. (1972). Does television violence cause aggression? *American Psychologist, 27* 253–263.

Furth, H., (1980). *The world of adults.* New York: Elsevier Science.

Gough, H. G., Harris, D. B., Martin, W. E., & Edwards, M. (1950a). Children's ethnic attitudes (I): Relationship to certain personality factors. *Child Development, 21,* 83–91.

Gough, H. G., Harris, D. B., Martin, W. E., Edwards, M. (1950b). Children's ethnic attitudes (II): Relationship to parental beliefs concerning child training. *Child Development, 21,* 169–181.

Grusec, J. (1973). Effects of co-observer evaluations on imitation: A developmental study. *Developmental Psychology, 8,* 141.

Hess, R., & Torney, J. (1967). *The development of political attitudes in children.* Garden City, NY: Doubleday.

Hoffman, M. L. (1970). Moral development. In P. H. Mussen (Ed.), *Carmichael's manual of child psychology.* New York: John Wiley and Sons.

Hollenbeck, A. R., & Slaby, R. G. (1979). Infant visual and vocal responses to television. *Child Development, 50,* 41–45.

Horowitz, E. L., & Horowitz, R. E. (1938). Development of social attitudes in children. *Sociometry, 1,* 307–338.

Hyman, H. (1959). *Political socialization: A study in the psychology of political behavior.* Glencoe, IL: Free Press.

Jennings, M., & Niemi, R. (1968). The transmission of political values from parent to child. *American Political Science Review, 62,* 169–184.

Johnson, N. (1967.) *How to talk back to your television.* Boston: Little, Brown.

Katkovsky, W., Crandall, V. C., & Goods, S. (1967). Parental antecedents of children's beliefs in internal–external control of reinforcements in intellectual achievment situations. *Child Development, 38,* 765–776.

Katz, D. A., & Zalk, S. R. (1978). Modification of children's racial attitudes. *Developmental Psychology, 14,* 135–144.

Kohlberg, L. (1963). The development of children's orientations toward a moral order: I. Sequence in the development of human thought. *Vita Humana, 6,* 11–33.

MacDonald, K., & Parke, R. D. (1984). Bridging the gap: Parent–child play interaction and peer interactive competence. *Child Development, 55,* 1265–1277.

McCall, R. B., Parke, R. D., & Kavanaugh, R. D. (1977). Imitation of live and televised models by children one to three years of age. *Monographs of the Society for Research in Child Development, 42*(5, Serial No. 173).

McCandless, B. R., & Hoyt, J. J. (1961). Sex, ethnicity and play preference of pre-school children. *Journal of Abnormal and Social Psychology, 62,* 683–685.

Merelman, R. (1971). The development of policy thinking in adolescents. *American Political Science Review, 65,* 1033–1047.

Messer, D. J., McCarthy, M. E., McQuiston, S., MacTurk, R. H., Yarrow, L. W., & Vietze, P. M. (1986). Relation between mastery behavior in infancy and competence in early childhood. *Developmental Psychology, 22,* 366–372.

Milner, D. (1983). *Children & race.* Beverly Hills, CA: Sage.

Moore, S. W., Lare, J., & Wagner, K. A. (1985). *The child's political world: A longitudinal perspective.* New York: Praeger.

National Council for the Social Studies. (1983). In search of scope and sequence for social studies. Report of the task Force on Scope and Sequence. *Social Education, 48,* 249–262.

Parpal, M., & Maccoby, E. E. (1985). Maternal responsiveness and subsequent child compliance. *Child Development, 56,* 1326–1334.

Parsons, J. E., Kaczala, c. M., & Meese, J. L. (1982). Socialization of achievement attitudes and beliefs: Classroom influences. *Child Development, 53,* 322–329.

Pushkin, I. (1967). *A study of ethnic choice in the play of young children in three London districts.* Unpublished doctoral dissertation, University of London.

Rosen, B. C., & D'Andrade, R. (1959). The psychosocial origins of achievement motivation. *Sociometry, 22,* 185–218.

Schaefer, E. S., & Bayley, N. (1963). Maternal behavior, child behavior, and their intercorrelations from infancy through adolescence. *Monographs of the Society for Research in Child Development, 28* (Serial No. 94).

Selman, R. L. (1971). The relation of role-taking to the development of moral judgment in children. *Child Development, 42,* 79–92.

Selman, R. L. (1976). Social-cognitive understanding: A guide to educational and clinical practice. In T. Lickona (Ed.), *Moral development and behavior: theory, research, and social issues* (pp. 299–316). New York: Holt, Rinehart & Winston.

Shaffer, D. R. (1988). *Social and personality development.* Pacific Grove, Ca: Brooks/Cole.

Siegal, M., & Cowen, J. (1984). Appraisals of intervention: The mother's versus the culprit's behavior as determinants of children's evaluations of discipline techniques. *Child Development, 55,* 1760–1766.

Slaby, R. G., & Quarfoth, G. R. (1980). Effects of television on the developing child. In B. W. Camp (Ed.), *Advances in behavioral pediatrics* (Vol. 1, pp. 40–78). Greenwich, CI: Johnson Associates.

Stein, A. H., & Friedrich, L. K. (1975). Impact of television on children, youth. In E. M. Hetherington (Ed.), *Review of child development research.* (Vol. 5, pp. 2–61). Chicago: University of Chicago Press.

Stephan, W. G. (1978). School desegregation: An evaluation of predictions made in Brown vs. Board of Education. *Psychological Bulletin, 85,* 217–238.

Stevens, J. H. Jr., & Bakeman, R. (1985). A factor analytic study of the HOME scale for infants. *Developmental Psychology, 21,* 1196–1203.

Stone, V., & Chaffee, S. H. (1970). Family communication patterns and source-message orientation. *Journalism Quarterly, 47,* 239–246.

Van Doornick, W. J., Caldwell, B. M., Wright, C., & Frankenberg, W. K. (1981). The relationship between twelve-month home stimulation and school achievement. *Child Development, 52,* 1080–1083.

Williams, J. E., & Moreland, J. K. (1979). Comment on Bank's "White preference in blocks: A paradigm in search of a phenomenon." *Psychological Bulletin, 86,* 28–32.

Winterbottom, M. (1959). Motivation reconsidered: The concept of competence. *Psychological Review, 66,* 297–333.

Yarrow, M. R., Waxler, C. Z., & Scott, P. M. (1971). Child effects on adult behavior. *Developmental Psychology, 5,* 300–311.

THE MASS MEDIA AS AN INFLUENCE ON SOCIAL STUDIES

John E. Splaine
UNIVERSITY OF MARYLAND, COLLEGE PARK

The *1989 Roper Report* (Television Information Office, 1989) indicated that 65% of Americans used television as their main source for news and 44% used television as their only source for news. In 1987, only 16% of the American people said they used two or more sources in order to get news, as compared with 42% in 1959 (Television Information Office, 1987).

For the *1989 Roper Report,* people were asked what they looked forward to in a day. Forty-three percent of the respondents said they looked forward to talking with friends, neighbors, and co-workers. Twenty percent said they looked forward to watching television. Reading was not among the respondents' top six choices, a matter of concern to social studies educators who consider reading as necessary to being an informed citizen.

Nielsen Media Research (1989) estimated that the average person watches 4 to 5 hours of television per day. Those under 18 watch slightly less. More specifically, on the average, children 2 to 5 years old spend nearly 25 hours a week watching television, and children 6 to 11 spend slightly over 23 hours. Male teenagers watch about 22.5 hours, and female teenagers a little over 21.3 hours. Before entering school, a child will have watched approximately 6,000 hours of television, and about 23,000 hours by high school graduation. Of the homes in the United States, excluding Alaska and Hawaii, 98% have at least one television set. The average time a television is turned on in the approximately 90.4 million television homes is 6 hours and 55 minutes per day.

The level of television viewing suggests an increasing influence for this medium and decreased use and influence for other mass media—radio, magazines, newspapers, and books. Certainly, television is omnipresent in American society, and the potential influence on the teaching of the social studies is profound. The research summary that follows reflects some of that influence. The mass media literature is massive, and the summary of research relevant to social studies is by necessity selective.

SELECTED RESEARCH

The statistics cited above identify television as a medium of potential power and considerable influence. Yet, the influence may be growing even greater. With the advent of cable television and the video cassette recorder, children may be viewing even more television in the future than they do now. Singer and Singer (1986) contended:

Children in the United States are growing in a new kind of environment. From their earliest years they are exposed daily to television and its special properties: its representation of places and people rarely encountered in "real life"; its extensive use of fantasy characters, such as those in cartoons; its rapid pacing and sequencing as well as its combination of visual, spoken, and musical stimulation. (p. 107)

What then is the available research on the televised environment in which children grow up? Specifically, what substantive messages do the mass media send and how do the messages get sent? What effects do the messages and the medium have? A discussion of selected studies on the mass media's effects on socialization follows.

Socialization Studies

Walling (1976) found in his study of 30 first- and second-grade students that television does affect the socialization pro-

---

Reviewers were: John D. Haas, University of Colorado, Boulder; Richard Luker, Temple University.

cess of children. Television informs children about their social roles and trains their perceptions. It does this by identifying what is important and setting the social agenda. In his study, Walling asked the students: "Who is your favorite person in the whole world?" Twenty-five percent identified a television actor or television character. He also asked: "If you could change into anyone in the whole world right now, who would you change into?" Forty-five percent of the students named a television actor or character. And to the question, "Do you like to watch television?", 100% of the young people answered that they do (pp. 19–20). What they like about television, what it teaches them, and how they learn from television will have an impact on what happens in the social studies classroom. Such potential influence and its consequences need to be studied systematically. Television communicates examples of people working, family interactions, and other acts of interpersonal communication. All have possible positive or negative effects on children, and can lead to prosocial or antisocial behavior (Desmond, 1978; Williams, 1981).

Sexual stereotyping is a continuing problem in the television age. Silverman-Watkins, Levi, and Klein (1986) argued that both genders should be represented in televised public affairs stories and both genders should be involved in delivering the stories. This is especially so for young viewers who are developing their perceptions regarding gender roles and their own participation in society. Women in the mass media argue that their efforts to gain full participation continue to be difficult even though some apparent improvements are occurring on the national networks (Castro, 1988; Ferri, 1988). The lack of full participation makes it difficult for children to see a variety of role models.

Indeed, gender portrayals and stereotyping can affect public perceptions of the roles of men and women:

Television content may present general, subtle, and unconscious evaluations of various groups and actions. For example, it is no secret that women have been devalued by society. The few women who appear on television are rarely in positions of respect or prestige. Thus, while not deliberately attempting to reflect a devaluation of women, their relative exclusion and unflattering portrayal may be considered an accurate reflection of this devaluation. (Leifer, Gordon, & Graves, 1974, p. 221)

Furthermore, Frueh and McGhee (1975) discovered that television programming may have reinforced male and female stereotypes in the early 1970s. In a study of 80 boys and girls (kindergarten and Grades 2, 4, and 6), children who watched more than 25 hours of television per week were more likely to believe in traditional stereotyped roles for males and females than those who watched less than 10 hours per week. The stereotyped views were not related to age.

Belief, of course, is one thing, behavior another. In three studies, McArthur and Eisen (1976) attempted to determine the influence of television programming, not only on belief but on sex-stereotyped behavior. They determined that in television programming males and females played different roles, showed different degrees of expertise, behaved differently, were treated differently for that behavior, and appeared in disproportionate numbers. Boys in one of the studies imitated televised male

role behavior and girls imitated female behavior. Male behavior on television was more aggressive and more discordant, whereas female behavior was more concordant and less aggressive. The authors concluded that females came out less favorably as far as roles, expertise, behavior, punishment, and frequency of appearance were concerned.

Additionally, Greenberg (1980) determined that those portrayed on television in the 1970s were primarily white males and generally 35 to 45 years old. He found it nearly impossible to find Hispanic female roles on television. Older women were also portrayed less frequently and were given fewer roles. Greenberg argued that the impact of televised images accumulated over time and that these images contribute to how people see the world and how they behave. Such televised accumulation also affects the agenda-setting function of the news (Salwen, 1988). Add to this the accumulated impact of the other mass media and the effects can be profound.

In the broader areas of socialization, Chesebro (1986) examined the kinds of human relationships that were most frequently portrayed in popular television series and how human problems were resolved in those series. He studied the series over an 11-year period in an attempt to identify the values communicated through each series, arguing that televised messages and images that are meant to be entertaining also persuasively convey a set of values. He claimed that "these persuasive messages are patterned rather than random; they selectively reinforce certain types of communication rather than others" (p. 510). For the television year 1984–1985, Chesebro found that 75% of all the series broadcast communicated two values, individuality and authority. These values were consistently repeated over time in exotic and elegant settings, like those in the series *Dallas* and *Dynasty*. The actors and programs were attractive to the public and were "likely to leave [their] influence, if not overtly change our attitudes, beliefs, and actions" (p. 510).

The mass media also affect perceptions of minorities. Newspapers are written for upper-middle-class readers and, as a result, the coverage of minorities is limited (Gutierrez & Wilson, 1979). Furthermore, Wilson and Gutierrez (1985) claimed the news media reflect a "distorted sense of news values held by majority news professionals. Traditional reporting procedures have defined news from a White majority perspective" (p. 148). Such narrowing of perspective has implications for the larger society. Wilson and Gutierrez contended that "the coupling of biased portrayals with the social and psychological power of mass entertainment threatens the maturation of American society" (p. 103). That, they suggested, is one reason that advances in minority-group integration and acceptance since World War II have been nowhere near that needed so that a society for which cultural diversity is an ideal will accept diversity in fact.

Of particular concern, African-American and Hispanic children tend to watch more television, have less access to reading materials, and have less opportunity to use computers than whites (Blosser, 1988). Thus, for members of minorities the potential effects of televised communication are intensified, and they have fewer chances to develop computer and print literacies.

The mass media also define social roles and related behavior. Beer advertisements are an example. According to Postman,

Nystrom, Strate, and Weingartner (1987), beer is associated in TV commercials with themes and myths, "the frontier, the common man, the American dream. Through such repeated associations, beer and beer drinking become part of the myths in which they are embedded, and invoke the same feelings, beliefs, and values" (p. 40). Based on their analysis, Postman et al. (1987) concluded that "beer commercials do promote an association between drinking and driving, and it is an association that reflects and propagates values and attitudes implicated in drunk driving" (p. 49). Before they are old enough to drive, American children view an estimated 100,000 TV commercials that promote the consumption of beer. Postman et al. (1987) asserted, "images and ideals of masculinity . . . link the product to the intended purchaser" (p. 47). The hypothesized effects of advertising on drinking and driving need to be explored further.

Thus, women, racial groups, social classes, and acceptable social behavior are all depicted in television programs. Research indicates that there are at least tenuous effects. The influence on viewers of televised portrayals of minority characters is a research concern (Wilson & Gutierrez, 1985), as is mass media's impact on other areas of socialization. Correlations are suggestive, but research on the causal effects of the media, including the effects on cognitive development, is difficult (Anderson & Collins, 1988).

Political Information-Processing Studies

Political issues are also conveyed through television and the other mass media with varying degrees of influence. For example, Graber and Kim (1977) found that the televised presidential debates of 1976 stimulated interest among viewers, with attendant gains in knowledge but not necessarily changed voting behavior. However, the debates were only one of the events that influenced their sample, illustrating the difficulty in tracing communications causation.

In contrast with the *Roper Report,* cited at the beginning of the chapter, Graber's (1988) respondents indicated that 48% of the information they received was from printed sources, 27% from television, and 25% from other sources. The difference may be explained in part by the higher level of education of Graber's sample. Graber concluded that her sample "did not make judgments based on a single ideology or the recommendations of a single source" (p. 266). Yet, the subjects in her sample made judgments based on the available information. When the information was not available, their ability to draw from other sources and ideologies was limited. With the mass media the primary means of communication, the sources and ideologies that drive those sources will tend to determine information access. Further studies are needed to determine the effects on voter interest, knowledge, and behavior of televised political events.

An important issue for social studies educators is: What political messages are conveyed through the media? This question is crucial because, as Graber (1988) noted, "for many areas of public life, average Americans are totally dependent on media

information. . . . the individual must form schemata from whatever is presented" (p. 264). Voters receive much of their information through a news funnel. The problem is illustrated by a study by Paletz and Guthrie (1987). Based on their analysis of the coverage of President Reagan by the *New York Times,* CBS, and ABC, they contended that in none of the news outlets were the complexities of the office presented in context. "It is this apparent inability of the mass media to capture President Reagan beyond the cliches, in all his complexity and contradictions, that must be our abiding concern" (p. 22).

Another media coverage issue is the compression of media information. According to Jamieson (1988), for example, until about 1940 political candidates purchased, on the average, an hour for radio speeches. From 1940 to 1952, political speeches on radio were about 30 minutes long. By 1956, advertising time was purchased in 5-minute blocks for presidential candidates. Contemporary political commercials are as brief as 15 and 30 seconds, often without the candidate speaking. Such brief periods of time limit the candidate to simple messages and prohibit the explication of issues (Jamieson, 1988).

Communication distortion studies are particularly troublesome. Any news delivery is potentially distorted. For instance, consistent with continuing criticism of the media, Gans (1979) concluded that to be known (like the president or a violator of the law), unusual (e.g., protests, disasters, scandals), or involved in violence (as a victim or a perpetrator) invites media coverage. Even assuming that a given news event could be accurately reconstructed for reporting, the very act of producing the reported story "would constitute a distortion of that reality. Thus, objective or absolute non-distortion is impossible" (Gans, 1979, p. 305). How can the effects of distortion be understood and reduced through social studies education?

Lack of time to completely research or verify a story presents special problems to journalists. Gans (1979) compared the methodologies of social scientists and journalists and found journalists to be at a disadvantage in terms of time allowed for completion of a report. Social scientists have more time and are able to focus more intensively on specific topics than are journalists. The methods of both social scientists and journalists are designed to inform. A major difference is that social scientists seek to explain and predict, whereas journalists seek to describe. Journalists have little time to verify when news deadlines encroach upon them. Understanding this difference is important to citizenship behavior, and how to teach students to comprehend the difference is an important research topic.

The advent of cable television has opened alternative news sources. The effects on citizenship information are yet to be determined. The Cable Satellite Public Affairs Network (C-SPAN), founded in 1979 as a nonprofit cooperative sponsored by the cable industry, telecasts the proceedings of the United States House of Representatives and the United States Senate, along with public-affairs conferences. C-SPAN's telecasts are mostly unedited and without commercial interruption. The University of Maryland Survey Research Center (Lamb, 1988) conducted a national survey to determine the composition of the 42.5 million C-SPAN subscribers. The findings indicated that those who chose to watch C-SPAN are better educated, more interested in politics and the news, and more likely to vote. The implications of C-SPAN for voter and citizenship education have not yet been studied longitudinally, and such studies are needed for C-SPAN's possibilities for the social studies classroom and citizenship education to be determined (Lamb, Splaine, & Tampio, 1987).

Print Versus Video Studies

A number of factors affect how much and what children learn from television newscasts or from television in general. The pictures that accompany a narrative can affect understanding. The visuals can reinforce the narrative, and visuals attract children's attention (Drew & Reese, 1984). However, Postman (1985) concluded in a review of the literature that "television viewing does not significantly increase learning, is inferior and less likely than print to cultivate higher-order, inferential thinking" (p. 152). Similarly, researchers have concluded that reading leads to more inferential and knowledge-based meanings than those produced by television, which are more concrete and detached from previous knowledge (Cohen & Salomon, 1979; Salomon, 1984).

In one study, Salomon (1984) tested 124 sixth graders and found that the children perceived televised messages to be easier to grasp than print. In addition, the students believed that print required them to work harder for the information (Salomon & Leigh, 1984). Salomon concluded that the students developed more and better inferences through reading than when television was used as their information source.

Wright, Watkins, and Huston-Stein (1978) speculated that the simplicity of most television programming is the reason that children learn little from it. A program's simplicity allows children who have experience in watching television programs to quickly grasp the central idea. There is often little else to be gained from the program.

Gadberry (1980) found, not surprisingly, that those children who were restricted in their viewing did do more reading. In her study, 30 six-year-old, middle-class children were assigned to two groups with one group restricted in the amount of television viewing and one unrestricted. The mothers of both groups talked with their children for 20 minutes a day about their television viewing. Those who viewed more television read less regardless of the mother-and-child interaction.

In an intriguing study, Hawkins, Ibok, and Pingree (1983) found only a weak correlation between viewers' attentiveness when viewing programs and the amount of learning. The authors conjectured that those who were more attentive to programs had both their visual and auditory channels occupied and did not think about program messages. Those who looked away from the television program and did something else may have been thinking about the program's content while looking away, or they may have concentrated more when they looked back at the program. In any event, those who looked away learned as much from the program as those fully attentive. Conceivably, the programs offered little substance, and full attention was not necessary.

In a study with similar implications, Lorch, Anderson, and Levin (1979) found that children who were doing something else while watching television comprehended the program as well as children who were only attending to the programs. Even though the program, *Sesame Street,* was supposed to be educational, the results of this study of 72 five-year-old children suggested that television requires less mental effort than other activities and that full attention is not necessary.

Television viewing also affects young viewers' reading in other cultures. Hornik (1978) reported that when television was introduced to a group of junior high school students in El Salvador who had little previous exposure to television, there was a negative association between increased viewing of television and reading skills. The author inferred that the additional time spent viewing television left less time for reading.

Moreover, Morgan (1980) administered questionnaires to 200 students who attended the sixth through the ninth grades in a New Jersey public school. He also conducted structured interviews and submitted questionnaires to the students' parents over a 3-year period. He found that heavy viewers of television initially read more than lighter viewers. By the end of the third year, however, this relationship between heavy viewing and reading did not continue. He found that heavy viewers consistently had poorer reading comprehension than lighter viewers. Morgan also discussed the quality of the reading that heavy and light viewers did. Heavy viewers were more likely to read stories about celebrities, love relationships, and families. Lighter viewers read more general nonfiction, mysteries, and science fiction. Whether the reading of more substantive material might lead to less television viewing merits further research.

Violence and Aggression Studies

Leifer et al. (1974) concluded that "research supports the conclusion that television can influence children's social behavior and attitudes" (p. 213). Television programming affects some children's disposition toward aggression, which is socially valued by some people. It can also affect attitudes toward socially valued behavior that is not aggressive. Indeed, television influences the socialization of viewers from a variety of age groups. What then does the research have to say about the correlation between television viewing and violence and aggression? What about television's effects on prosocial behavior?

Desmond (1978) reported that children use television programming as a source for play activities. In addition, children use the conversations and actions they hear and see as a basis for fantasies. Whether playing the roles affects behavior has been difficult to determine.

Gerbner, Gross, Signorielli, Morgan, and Jackson-Beeck (1979) reported that "heavy viewers in both the New York and New Jersey schools are more likely than light viewers to overestimate the number of people involved in violence and the proportion of people who commit serious crimes" (p. 190). Presumably, such overestimations will affect views of public policies on violence. People with overexaggerated fears might be willing to trade freedom for security. Viewers may advocate solutions to problems that primarily exist in the world of television.

The potential effects of televised violence are acute and pervasive.

TV violence is a dramatic demonstration of power which communicates much about social norms and relationships, about goals and means, about winners and losers, about the risks of life and the price for transgressions of society's rules. Violence laden drama shows who gets away with what, when, why, how and against whom. (Gerbner & Gross, 1976, p. 178)

Clearly, the effects of televised violence are important to discern. Gerbner and Gross further observed that "with all the violence, the leading causes of real life injury and death—industrial and traffic accidents—are hardly ever depicted" (p. 179). Rather, what is presented is the kind of violence that evokes fear of others and might affect public policy decisions.

Televised symbols are most effective in communicating assumptions when the viewer has no direct experience with the subject matter. Television is also effective in communicating ideas that do not contradict a person's beliefs or ideology. Viewers ignorant of the subject are particularly susceptible to manipulation, especially when appeals are made to fear and ignorance. Additionally, if Gerbner and Gross (1976) are correct, then the following assertion has profound implications for American society: "Many times a day, seven days a week, the dramatic pattern defines situations and cultivates premises about society, people, and issues." And what is shown has potential to make an imprint on the viewers, with "about three-quarters of all leading characters are male, American, middle- and upper-class, and in the prime of life" (p. 183). Not only do Americans learn about violence through televised portrayals, but they learn the lessons from a carefully selected cast. Televised reality is so powerful that Gerbner and Gross (1976) reported heavy viewers of television give more "television answers" even when they do considerable reading and are well educated (p. 192).

Singer and Singer (1986) concluded that television viewing may contribute to a whole host of children's problems: restlessness, dysphoria, fears, and aggression. "Watching television trains children to 'take the easy way' and simply to watch even more" (p. 122). Parents who are heavy viewers contribute to the effect. Children adopt the behaviors they know, and televised fantasy may further amplify emotional instability and aggressive behavior. For example, in a study of 5- and 10-year-olds, Messaris (1986) found that when parents indicated they approved of a specific television behavior, the children were more likely to imitate it.

Earlier, Messaris (1986) had studied 119 mothers and their children in the Philadelphia area. He asked the mothers to help their children differentiate between the real and the unreal in television programming, to help their children understand the program's content and intent, and to tell their children which behaviors were appropriate and which were not. Messaris found that parental intervention did help the children distinguish between the real and the unreal and that what a parent says to a child will have an effect on what a child understands from a television program and on whether the child will imitate actions seen on the program.

Aggressive behavior can be stimulated by the form of a program as well as by the content. Form means not only the rapidity of images and the consequent effect on attention spans, but the elements of novelty and surprise. This, added to the enticing elements of uncertainty in dramatic and comedy sequences, can lead to aggressive behavior in the viewers because of physiological arousal (Watt & Krull, 1977). Furthermore, Singer and Singer (1983) suggested that "the rapid pace of presentation of material with constant intercutting, interruption, and shifts in sound levels" (p. 827) has an influence on how one learns and will learn in the future. Additionally, the constant shifting, loud sound, and technically advanced graphics intensify and effectively communicate a violent message. Thus, the mode of communicating reinforces the message. This phenomenon is new in child rearing and is part of living in the television era.

Indeed, young people develop their attitudes toward aggressive behavior from their parents and through their observations of the world. Television provides one window through which to observe. And on television "there is an emphasis on most action/adventure shows on physical action, car chases, shoot-outs, fist fights" (Singer, 1985, p. 808). For that reason, Singer argued that schools should begin to teach children to be aware of the pervasive influence of television: "Teachers may want to use some of the many published curricula that have been prepared by researchers and educators in order to teach children how to become more critical consumers of television" (pp. 809–810). The influence of television on young people may depend in large part on how educators and parents help children think about the viewing experience. Research along those lines is badly needed.

Programs like *Mister Rogers' Neighborhood* and *Sesame Street* can influence prosocial behavior (Coates, Pusser, & Goodman, 1976; Paulson, 1974). Educators speculate that in order to increase positive effects there must be opportunity for reflection after the viewing experience (Mukerji, 1977). Others argue for another approach. Some of the efforts at studying the development of critical viewing and thinking are discussed next.

Critical Viewing and Thinking Efforts

Braverman (1982) recommended that educational researchers work "to enrich the television-viewing experience for children by encouraging deeper, more involved processing and elaboration of recorded material—in short, getting children to think more while they're watching, whether in critical, integrative, or creative modes" (p. 25). The potential for social studies classrooms as places to promote critical viewing and thinking is an area of needed research.

Paul (1985) emphasized the importance of activities and exercises to help students detect propaganda and to be critical as they view and listen to media. One emphasis could be on helping students understand how the media affect their beliefs and values. But research is needed on how the critical viewing process occurs, how it can be taught, and what results can be expected (Leifer et al., 1974).

Nevertheless, some research is available. For example, Salomon (1973) found that parents from lower socioeconomic backgrounds can help their children gain understanding from television. Mothers who watched *Sesame Street* with their 5-year-old children helped them understand and enjoy the programs. Corder-Bolz (1980) obtained similar results with teacher's aides and children who watched *Electric Company*. Corder-Bolz and O'Bryant (1978) reported that adult interpretive intervention helped preschool 4- and 5-year-olds gain more information from television than those who did not experience adult intervention. They also concluded that a significant adult can greatly influence what a young child learns from programs designed to entertain. "Both the amount and the accuracy of the information the child acquires and the nature of the attitudes that the child develops are affected" (p. 103).

There is further research evidence available. Corder-Bolz (1980) reported a study involving 75 boys and girls, aged 5 to 10 years, who watched an episode of *Batman*. A posttest revealed that the children who were told by an adult that violence was unacceptable were less likely to believe that hitting and stealing were appropriate behaviors. In another study of 56 boys and girls, 5 to 11 years old, two 60-second mediation spots were inserted into a *Batman* episode. One spot explained that Batman was not real, and the other that one should not imitate what Batman does during the program. In the groups where the mediation spots were used, the young people were less likely to believe that the characters' antisocial behaviors—hitting, hurting, and stealing—were acceptable.

Secondary social agents, who do not have the power of reward and punishment, can, then, influence the outcomes of television viewing by providing information that helps young people understand what they are viewing. The implication is that social studies educators can help students to view critically what they see in the mass media. How social studies teachers can work with parents to help children develop critical viewing and listening skills is a major research challenge.

One study indicates that a way to help students to learn critical viewing concepts and skills is to get them experientially involved in the process. In a study involving 176 kindergarten, first-grade, and second-grade public school students, it was concluded that children could learn to discern advertising intent and identify persuasive techniques in commercial programming. The most effective technique was role playing in which the students assumed the role of producers and created their own commercials. Less effective was the use of audio-visual demonstrations with student-teacher interaction. Least effective was lecture as the primary teaching method (Desmond & Jeffries-Fox, 1983).

Summary

From this selected review of research, the following tentative conclusions are warranted:

1. The mass media, particularly television, are pervasive in American society.

2. The mass media affect socialization.
3. Inaccurate portrayals of gender and minority roles in society are frequently communicated through the mass media.
4. Television has influenced the conduct and content of political communications.
5. Some individuals rely more on the mass media for information than do other people.
6. Social studies educators need to examine what students learn from the mass media, specifically television.
7. Print learning appears to require more abstract thought than does learning from television, although the use of visuals improves student recall.
8. Televised violence appears to have an effect on viewers. Causation, however, has yet to be proved.
9. Educators and parents can teach young people how to critically view and think about television and can mitigate some of the negative influences of television. Parental and educator influence can also enhance the positive impacts of television.

SIGNIFICANT RESEARCH QUESTIONS

The findings and conclusions cited in the previous section need further verification through systematic research, including replications. In this section, additional research tasks and questions are identified.

Some research findings appear to conflict with the inferences drawn earlier in this chapter. For example, Desmond (1978) reported that preschool and early elementary school children can learn complex behaviors from film and television. If the programming is designed to also include reinforcement at intervals, then learning is retained over a longer period of time. This seemingly contradicts the findings of other researchers (e.g., Cohen & Salomon, 1979; Salomon, 1984) who claimed that little inferential learning is gained from television, especially when children do not perceive the need to invest effort in viewing television. Consequently, further research is needed to determine the variables that are related to differential learning from television.

Desmond found that children are able to predict a given character's behavior but are less able to infer the reasons for the behavior. He observed that the children imitated behavior from programs they liked and were less prone to do so from programs they found less interesting. Desmond's focus was on behavior and its potential for imitation. On the other hand, Salomon (1984) was concerned with cognitive processes. Behavior and cognitive processes may be linked, and research needs to be conducted to determine if they are linked (Anderson & Collins, 1988).

Another important area of inquiry is the structural components of the mass media and their impact. Nystrom (1975) identified the structure of the media as the hidden curriculum. Similarly, Postman (1979) called television the "First Curriculum." Nystrom (1975) identified some issues concerning how television producers organize time, how their sensory biases affect production, how they organize space, and how those factors affect televised messages. The issues of structure are nebulous and measuring their effects is complex, but examination is necessary nonetheless.

Indeed, the way television programs are produced, what is presented to viewers and how viewers perceive the programs need to be analyzed (Silverstone, 1988). What images does the television producer use? How does the producer convey the images? What voice? What text? What is the rhetoric of television (Welch & Watt, 1982)? How do these elements add up to have an effect? The answers to these questions have important social studies implications.

For example, Drew and Reese (1984) argued that those who understand how television news is put together learn more from it, and they advocated that teachers help students learn to view television news. How to do that is still an important question. Underlying that research question is the need for further study of the effects of studio sets, sound tracks, program complexity, and visual activity (Levin & Anderson, 1976; Lorch et al., 1979).

Others have studied the effects of media structure. Paletz and Guthrie (1987) contended that print and broadcast professionals differ in the ways they cover the news, specifically in their coverage of the president and where the media is vulnerable to manipulation. Thus, the differences between print and broadcast news and their respective structures and modes of delivery need to be studied. If citizens receive most of their news from television, they should know how that news is constructed. New technologies may increase the impact of information packaging.

Additional issues have emerged. Diem (1985) recommended that the elementary school curriculum should include discussion of the ethical and social issues related to the adoption and uses of new technologies. The new technologies will not disappear, and their adoption raises important public issues. How best to handle discussions of those issues in the context of the continuing influence of the media and the fundamental issues of free speech and a free press presents difficult challenges to researchers of social studies education.

The effects of social class on media impact also merit more research. Gans (1979) illustrated that readers are generally more affluent, have better jobs, and are better educated than heavy television viewers. If lower-class people are more frequent users of television and rely little on print media for information, then issues of print and visual literacy become central for social studies educators. If television viewers are less informed, the correlation between TV viewing and socioeconomic status becomes more important, with pervasive implications for research on the promotion of intelligent citizen participation.

In general, people's sources of information are of concern in social studies. Gans (1979) found that "some people get the news from several media; and researchers have often found that regular users of one news medium are particularly likely to use others as well. Many television news viewers, however, do not patronize other news media" (p. 224). This latter finding has importance for research in teaching social studies. If many students and adults do not get information from a variety of sources, what are the implications for teaching about social and political issues?

The impact of television on perceptions of reality is another crucial citizenship-education research issue. Viewers, especially children, imbue television programs with qualities of reality (Nikken & Peeters, 1988). However, even television news is a story or narrative about reality, and not reality itself (Bird & Dardenne, 1988). How do citizens decide what is real and what is not? Furthermore, Gans (1979) claimed that "journalists transmit the only nonfiction that most Americans see, hear, or read" (p. 298). If this is so, then what is being transmitted, how is it being transmitted, and to what effect? What stories are Americans being told and how are the stories being told (Newcomb, 1988)? And what will be the effects of the use of news reenactments, a presentation technique accentuated in 1989?

What are the effects of television on attention to complex matters? MacNeil (1987) cited the average American's short attention span as a problem with profound economic, political, and social implications that ought to be studied (p. 23). He stated, "This society is being force-fed with trivial fare with only dimly perceived effects on our habits of mind, our language, our tolerance for effort, and our appetite for complexity" (p. 23). Systematic research needs to be conducted to see if the effects of this forced-feeding are as MacNeil asserted and, if so, to determine if citizenship education can counteract them.

A related public issue is media ownership. Gans (1979) questioned whether the majority ownership of the media should be in the hands of commercial interests. Is there a "media monopoly" (Bagdikian, 1987)? Can a society be well served when its news media are controlled by a few individuals or corporations? Do the media set the political and social agenda? If the media set the agenda, then is the agenda one that presents the most important issues to the American people (Behr & Iyengar, 1985)? What implications does all this have for the social studies classroom?

Another research issue, which Merton (1968) identified two decades ago, was whether economic and military interests determine what researchers measure and for what intended effects the measurements are made. The large amounts of money spent for military and industrial research can be used to control what will be studied, which questions will be asked, and for whose benefit. Such possible narrowing of the issues raises a number of structural research questions about who controls research and of what use the results will be made. Similarly, Gans (1979) was not so concerned with whether facts can be tested and verified, but rather, which facts are tested and verified. He argued that "when concepts—or methods—differ, so do the resulting facts" (p. 306). Thus, what is chosen to be studied influences the outcome or the direction of the outcome. The identification of the important issues will determine the research agenda and what results from that agenda.

As technological innovations occur, new research issues will emerge. For example, the advent of the video cassette recorder (VCR) raises the prospect of even greater media influence through entertainment-program and movie viewing at home. However, Levy (1987) found that VCR users' perceptions of reality are little affected by video viewing, perhaps because the extra effort to secure a video, bring it home, and put it into a VCR makes the fictional elements more apparent than when a television set is simply switched on. With the growing number of VCRs in American homes, questions about the influence and instructional use of the VCR, as well as VCR impact on TV programming (Kim, Baran, & Massey, 1988), will be viable research topics.

Children usually accept the new technologies with which they grow up as normal parts of their environment. Consequently, there is a tendency for them to accept broadcast and cable television, VCRs, computers, and interactive videodisks as if they have always been here. Children do not critically examine the social implications of the various media, because they assume that inasmuch as the media are here, they must be here for a reason and their existence must implicitly be approved by adults. Diem (1985) concluded, based on his study of children's reactions and attitudes toward the new technologies, that "most participants simply accepted computers and robots as part of their daily life" (p. 320). Certainly, children accept television and compact discs, and assume that the ever-changing media environment is a normal phenomenon. Researchers need to determine the effects of that evolving electronic media environment on social studies education and later citizenship behavior. Further, social studies researchers need to examine how the electronic media should be studied in the curriculum so that as adults the students will be aware of the media's social and political implications.

EPISTEMOLOGICAL AND METHODOLOGICAL ISSUES

There are a number of epistemological and methodological issues in studying the mass media that social studies researchers must face. In this section, some promising methodologies are discussed as well as some recurring problems.

Focused interviews, as proposed by Merton, Fiske, and Kendall (1956) as a technique useful in studying social issues, offer research potential in communication studies. Based on his study of VCR use, Levy (1987) recommended that focused interviews be used to gather more valid data on the subtleties of "selective perception and message decoding" (p. 274).

Another methodological suggestion comes from Levin and Anderson (1976) who argued that researchers must determine what children watch on television and when, before the effects of viewing can be isolated. They videotaped children watching TV in order to determine the frequency and duration of viewing. While presenting challenging logistical problems, this methodology may yield more accurate data on the frequency and duration of viewing than retrospective reports by children and parents.

The content analysis of media measured against established baselines is also an important precursor to determining effects and implications for social studies. For example, Banks (1977) analyzed the televised portrayal of African-Americans as a basis for curricular recommendations. Greenberg (1980) emphasized the importance of replication of content-analysis studies to determine whether changes in program content occur. For example, in regard to the portrayals of African-Americans since the late 1960s, Greenberg concluded:

From an immodest beginning of "Amos and Andy" roles, a steady influx of black actors was detailed in several content analyses. From a level of 3 or 4 percent of the television population, blacks rose to 10 percent

within a five-year period, then tapered off, and have remained there for about a decade. But there was change and it was documented because a baseline had been established against which subsequent information could be assessed. (pp. 185–186)

Participant observation is also a promising methodology. Thorburn (1988) contended that participant observers will be able to ferret out more of the intricacies of the media. Participants can experience media effects while at the same time being observers. The use of participant observers raises potential research problems, however. The most obvious one is: "How can one be a participant and at the same time be an observer?" Journalists and social scientists must also remember that as observers they are still members of social, economic, and political institutions (Merton, 1968). The institutional perspectives that they invariably bring to the task affect their perspectives as observers. Observers can control for those perspectives, but cannot disregard them nor claim that those perspectives do not exist (Gans, 1979). Journalists, who by necessity work on shorter time frames, and social scientists, who should have more time, must both realize that neither can claim total objectivity.

Graber (1980) identified another recurring epistemological concern: "the difficulty of isolating media influence when it is one of many factors in a complex environment" (p. 137). It is virtually impossible to control the communication of political information for research purposes, making the study of effects on attitudes, feelings, and behaviors extremely difficult. Graber argued: "Until we can trace an individual's mental processes and isolate the components that interact and combine to form mental images and reactions to these images, we cannot fully assess the impact of media" (p. 137). Thus, Graber identified the most pervasive problem in communication research—how to measure the unobservable. Graber recounted an experiment in which respondents were not able to immediately recall information but were able to at a later time. She concluded: "At times, information recall is delayed. . . . We do not know how commonly such sleeper effects occur and how much learning remains unmeasured as a consequence" (p. 137).

Communication researchers cannot focus on simple cause-and-effect relationships. The total environment in which a child receives television must be studied. At best, causation is the result of a complex interweaving of forces on a child (Walling, 1976). Schramm (1973) made a similar point:

It is not a simple relationship; the participants in an act of communication behave with their whole personalities so that the message is always more than words. It is a tenuous relationship, because each participant brings to it the cognitive map of his own cultural experience, and one's meanings are never entirely like another's; consequently every communication relationship is truly an intercultural one. (p. 291)

Because of the complexity, Walling (1976) suggested that television studies should be done in a naturalistic setting rather than in a laboratory. In addition, there should be a "delay period" between viewing and testing. Most testing is done within a few hours of viewing, and this may be misleading. Researchers may be missing more important, long-term effects that delayed testing would yield (Graber, 1988; Katz, 1987).

Graber's concern with assessment issues has surfaced in another research report—her study (1988) of how people process political information they obtain through the mass media. Studying such information processing is a complex, multifaceted, and interrelated task, and Graber bemoaned the frequent use of self-reports in short-term change studies as the only source of data in political information-processing studies. Schramm (1973) had commented, "Communication researchers . . . have to face up to the need of studying quiet continuing effects that, in perspective, overshadow the more spectacular and more easily measurable ones" (p. 233). Because bias and error inevitably affect self-reports, methods are needed for examining actual behaviors to verify self-reports.

Signorielli (1986) cited a similar problem peculiar to most television research. "Much of the research on selective exposure focuses primarily upon what people do, or say they do (which may not be the same thing) in regard to television viewing" (p. 65). Thus, those who view television programming about which they are embarrassed may not tell researchers what they have actually viewed. Similarly, when viewers are asked to state their motivation for viewing television, they may report what they believe the researchers wish to hear.

The results of surveys that request self-reports are likely to be tenuous at best. Pulliam (n.d.) contended that:

Surveys show that people do not read what they say they read nor view what they say they would like to view. Intellectuals even lie about how much television they view because they recognize its anti-intellectual character. We must now make serious studies of the mass media and gather real data about their impact. Speculation must be replaced with information and sound theory. (p. 16)

A related assessment problem is the use in surveys of closed-ended questions that signal the responses that the researcher hopes to obtain (Graber, 1988). Graber advocated the greater use of open-ended questions, despite the difficulties in coding and interpretation (Geer, 1988). Self-reporting invariably is problematic and alternative techniques need to be used to verify self-reports of behavior or attitudes.

One of the most vexing research problems is how visual representations and images affect perceptions of reality. "How then does one measure the contributions made by visual learning and how does one evaluate them as contributions to informed citizenship? The answers are as important as they are elusive" (Graber, 1988, pp. 264–265). Questions of measurement remain among the most vexing issues for communications and social studies researchers.

References

Anderson, D. R., & Collins, P. A. (1988), *The Impact on Children's Education: Television's Influence on Cognitive Development* (Office of Research Working Paper No. 2). Washington, DC: U.S. Department of Education Office of Educational Research and Improvement.

Bagdikian, B. H. (1987). *The media monopoly* (2nd ed.). Boston: Beacon Press.

Banks, C. A. M. (1977). A content analysis of the treatment of Black Americans on television. *Social Education, 41*(4), 336–339, 344.

Behr, R. L., & Iyengar, S. (1985). Television news, real-world cues, and changes in the public agenda. *Public Opinion Quarterly, 49,* 38–57.

Bird, S. E., & Dardenne, R. W. (1988). Myth, chronicle and story: Exploring the narrative qualities of news. In J. W. Carey (Ed.), *Media, myths, and narratives: Television and the press* (pp. 67–86). Beverly Hills, CA: Sage.

Blosser, B. J. (1988). Ethnic differences in children's media use. *Journal of Broadcasting and Electronic Media, 32*(4), 453–470.

Braverman, M. (1982). *Aptitude and ATI in television comprehension.* Northwest Regional Educational Laboratory. (ERIC Document Reproduction Service No. ED 217 875)

Castro, J. (1988, January). Women in television: An uphill battle. *Channels,* pp. 42–52.

Chesebro, J. W. (1986). Communication, values, and popular television series—An eleven-year assessment. In G. Gumpert & R. Cathcart (Eds.), *Intermedia: Interpersonal communication in a media world* (3rd ed., pp. 477–512). New York: Oxford University Press.

Coates, B., Pusser, H. E., & Goodman, I. (1976). The influence of "Sesame Street" and "Mister Rogers' Neighborhood" on children's social behavior in the preschool. *Child Development, 47,* 138–144.

Cohen, A. A., & Salomon, G. (1979). Children's literate television viewing: Surprises and possible explanations. *Journal of Communication, 29,* 156–163.

Corder-Bolz, C. R. (1980). Mediation: The role of significant others. *Journal of Communication, 30*(3), 106–118.

Corder-Bolz, C. R., & O'Bryant, S. (1978). Teacher vs. program. *Journal of Communication, 28,*(1), 97–103.

Desmond, R. J. (1978). Cognitive development and television comprehension. *Communication Research, 5*(2), 202–220.

Desmond, R. J., & Jeffries-Fox, S. (1983). Elevating children's awareness of television advertising: the effects of a critical viewing program. *Communication Education, 32*(1), 107–115.

Diem, R. A. (1985). A study of children's attitudes and reactions to the new technology. *Social Education, 49*(4), 318–320.

Drew, D. G., & Reese, S. D. (1984). Children's learning from a television newscast. *Journalism Quarterly, 61*(1), 83–88.

Ferri, A. J. (1988). Perceived career barriers of men and women television news anchors. *Journalism Quarterly, 65*(3), 661–667, 732.

Frueh, T., & McGhee, P. E. (1975). Traditional sex role development and amount of time spent watching television. *Developmental Psychology, 11*(1), 109.

Gadberry, S. (1980). Effects of restricting first graders' TV-viewing on leisure time use, IQ change, and cognitive style. *Journal of Applied Developmental Psychology, 1,* 45–57.

Gans, H. J. (1979). *Deciding what's news: A study of CBS evening news, NBC nightly news, Newsweek & Time.* New York: Pantheon Books.

Geer, J. G. (1988). What do open-ended questions measure? *Public Opinion Quarterly, 52*(3), 365–371.

Gerbner, G., & Gross, L. (1976). Living with television: The violence profile. *Journal of Communication, 26,* 173–199.

Gerbner, G., Gross, L., Signorielli, N., Morgan, M., & Jackson-Beeck, M. (1979). The demonstration of power: Violence profile no. 10. *Journal of Communication, 29,* 177–196.

Graber, D. A. (1980). *Mass media and American politics.* Washington, DC: Congressional Quarterly Press.

Graber, D. A. (1988). *Processing the news: How people tame the information tide* (2nd ed.). New York: Longman.

Graber, D. A., & Kim, Y. Y. (1977). *The 1976 presidential debates and patterns of political learning.* Chicago: University of Illinois at Chicago Circle. (ERIC Document Reproduction Service No. ED 147 830)

Greenberg, B. S. (1980). *Life on television: Content analyses of U.S. TV drama.* Norwood, NJ: Ablex.

Gutierrez, F., & Wilson, C. C., II. (1979). The demographic dilemma. *Columbia Journalism Review, 53–55.*

Hawkins, R. P., Ibok, E., & Pingree, S. (1983). *Survey measurement of cognitive activity during television viewing.* Madison: University of Wisconsin. (ERIC Document Reproduction Service No. ED 240 650)

Hornik, R. C. (1978). Television access and the slowing of cognitive growth. *American Educational Research Journal, 15*(1), 1–15.

Jamieson, K. H. (1988). *Eloquence in an electronic age: The transformation of political speechmaking.* New York: Oxford University Press.

Katz, E. (1987). Communications research since Lazersfeld. *Public Opinion Quarterly, 51* (Supplement No. 4), S25–S45.

Kim, W. Y., Baran, S. J., & Massey, K. K. (1988). Impact of the VCR on control of television viewing. *Journal of Broadcasting and Electronic Media, 32*(3), 351–358.

Lamb, B. (1988). *C-SPAN, America's town hall.* Washington, DC: Acropolis.

Lamb, B., Splaine, J. E., & Tampio, C. (1987). Research possibilities: C-SPAN in the classroom. *Media Management Journal, 6*(3), 29–32.

Leifer, A. D., Gordon, N. J., & Graves, S. B. (1974). Children's television more than mere entertainment. *Harvard Educational Review, 44*(2), 213–245.

Levin, S. R., & Anderson, D. R. (1976). The development of attention. *Journal of Communication, 26,* 126–135.

Levy, M. R. (1987). VCR use and concept of audience activity. *Communications Quarterly, 35*(3), 267–275.

Lorch, E. P., Anderson, D. R., & Levin, S. R. (1979). The relationship of visual attention to children's comprehension of television. *Child Development, 50,* 722–727.

MacNeil, R. (1987). Is television shortening our attention span? *National Forum,* 21–23.

McArthur, L. Z., & Eisen, S. V. (1976). Television and sex-role stereotyping. *Journal of Applied Social Psychology, 6*(4), 329–351.

Merton, R. K. (1968). *Social theory and social structure.* New York: Macmillan.

Merton, R. K., Fiske., M., & Kendall, P. L. (1956). *The focused interview.* Glencoe, IL: Free Press.

Messaris, P. (1986). Parents, children, and television. In G. Gumpert & R. Cathcart (Eds.), *Intermedia, interpersonal communication in a media world* (3rd ed., pp. 519–536). New York: Oxford University Press.

Morgan, M. (1980). Television viewing and reading: Does more equal better? *Journal of Communication, 30,* 159–165.

Mukerji, R. (1977). *What effect is TV having on the young learner?* New York: Brooklyn College. (ERIC Document Reproduction Service No. ED 138 589)

Newcomb, H. M. (1988). One night of prime time: An analysis of television's multiple voices. In J. W. Carey (Ed.), *Media, myths, and narratives: Television and the press* (pp. 88–112). Beverly Hills, CA: Sage.

Nielsen Media Research. (1989). *Nielsen report on television 1989.* Northbrook, IL: Author.

Nikken, P., & Peeters, A. L., (1988). Children's perceptions of television reality. *Journal of Broadcasting and Electronic Media, 32*(4), 441–452.

Nystrom, C. L. (1975). Mass media: The hidden curriculum. *Educational Leadership,* 89–92.

Paletz, D. L., & Guthrie, K. K. (1987). The three faces of Ronald Reagan. *Journal of Communication, 37*(4), 7–23.

Paul, R. W. (1985). Critical thinking research: A response to Stephen Norris. *Educational Leadership, 42*(8), 46.

Paulson, F. L. (1974). Teaching cooperation on television: an evaluation of Sesame Street social goals programs. *AV Communication Review, 22*(3), 229–246.

Postman, N. (1979). *Teaching as a conserving activity.* New York: Delacorte Press.

Postman, N. (1985). *Amusing ourselves to death: Public discourse in the age of show business.* New York: Penguin Books.

Postman, N., Nystrom, C. Strate, L., & Weingartner, C. (1987). *Myths, men, and beer: An analysis of beer commercials on broadcast television.* Washington, DC: AAA Foundation for Traffic Safety.

Pulliam, J. D. (n.d.). *Mass media values and the future of education.* Norman: University of Oklahoma. (ERIC Document Reproduction Service No. ED 180 901)

Salomon, G. (1973). *Effects of encouraging Israeli mothers to co-observe Sesame Street with their five-year-olds.* Jerusalem. Israel: Hebrew University. (ERIC Document Reproduction Service No. ED 086 174)

Salomon, G. (1984). Television is "easy" and print is "tough": The differential investment of mental effort in learning as a function of perceptions and attributions. *Journal of Educational Psychology, 76*(4), 647–658.

Salomon, G., & Leigh, T. (1984). Predispositions about learning from print and television. *Journal of Communication,* 119–135.

Salwen, M. B. (1988). Effect of accumulation of coverage on issue salience in agenda setting. *Journalism Quarterly, 65*(1), 141–147, 240.

Schramm, W. (1973). *Men, messages, and media: A look at Human communication.* New York: Harper & Row.

Signorielli, N. (1986). Selective television viewing: A limited possibility. *Journal of Communication, 36*(3), 64–76.

Silverman-Watkins, L. T., Levi, S. C., & Klein, M. A. (1986). Sex-stereotyping as factor in children's comprehension of television news. *Journalism Quarterly, 63*(1), 3–11.

Silverstone, R. (1988). Television myth and culture. In J. W. Carey (Ed.), *Media, myths, and narratives: Television and the press* (pp. 20–47). Beverley Hills, CA: Sage.

Singer, D. G. (1985). Does violent television produce aggressive children? *Pediatric Annuals, 14*(12), 804, 807–810.

Singer, J. L., & Singer, D. G. (1983). Psychologists look at television: Cognitive, developmental, personality, and social policy implications. *American Psychologist,* 826–834.

Singer, J. L., & Singer, D. G. (1986). Family experiences and television viewing as predictors of children's imagination, restlessness, and aggression. *Journal of Social Issues, 42*(3), 107–124.

Television Information Office. (1987). *America's watching: Public attitudes toward television.* New York: Author.

Television Information Office. (1989). *America's watching: The 1989 TIO/Roper Report.* Washington, DC: Author.

Thorburn, D. (1988). Television as an aesthetic medium. In J. W. Carey (Ed.), *Media, myths, and narratives: Television and the press* (pp. 48–66). Beverly Hills, CA: Sage.

Walling, J. I. (1976). The effect of parental interaction on learning from television. *Communication Education, 25,* 16–24.

Watt, J. H., Jr., & Krull, R. (1977). An examination of three models of television viewing and aggression. *Human Communication Research, 3,* 99–112.

Welch, A. J., & Watt, J. H., Jr. (1982). Visual complexity and young children's learning from television. *Human Communication Research, 8*(2), 133–145.

Williams, T. M. (1981). How and what do children learn from television? *Human Communication Research, 7*(2), 180–192.

Wilson, C. C. II., & Gutierrez, F. (1985). *Minorities and media: diversity and the end of mass communication.* Beverly Hills, CA: Sage.

Wright, J. C., Watkins, B. A., & Huston-Stein, A. (1978). *Active vs. passive television viewing: A model of the development of television information processing by children.* Lawrence: University of Kansas. (ERIC Document Reproduction Service No. ED 184 521)

·25·

TESTING AS CONTEXT FOR SOCIAL EDUCATION

Dana G. Kurfman

PRINCE GEORGE'S COUNTY PUBLIC SCHOOLS, MARYLAND

The effects of testing on individual students have long been recognized. For example, teacher tests help determine whether elementary students move from one grade to the next. Passing tests contributes to the high school course credits necessary for graduation. And for many students, minimum college admission scores are needed for selection to college and for financial support after they are admitted.

Only since the mid 1970s have the effects of testing on schools received the serious attention of educators. The potential effects of minimum competency testing programs on the curriculum have been a concern. And for many schools such programs have become the basis for public perceptions of their educational effectiveness. Standardized test scores, once used only as aids in grouping individual students, have become a means of evaluating the performance of school staffs as well.

In this chapter, the primary emphasis is on research dealing with the influences of testing on student achievement, on school curricula and instructional practices, and on the professional status of teachers. The existing research has been focused primarily on the effects of minimum competency testing on attainment of such basic skills as reading and arithmetic, with some attention also given to tests of writing. Reports of the consequences of such testing provide the basis for drawing some implications for social studies. Even more important in social studies are the issues raised by research related to such questions as whether it is appropriate to use test results to rate school effectiveness, who should decide what will be taught, and whether there is too exclusive a reliance on easily scoreable multiple-choice tests to measure outcomes more complex than minimum skills.

There has been far more argumentation about test effects than there has been actual research. Such journals as the *Phi Delta Kappan* and *Educational Leadership* have published numerous articles in the past decade on testing as a part of educational reform. Popham (1987b) and Bracey (1987), in arguing the merits of measurement-driven instruction, illustrated the hopes and concerns of educators with respect to test effects. A helpful summary of test-related issues and the limited research until about 1980 has been provided by Kellaghan, Madaus, and Airasian (1982).

A search of the literature since 1980 confirmed the lack of research on test effects. Volumes of *Education Index* and *Current Index to Journals in Education* from 1980 through 1988 were reviewed using the headings of tests and testing. Curriculum and instruction, secondary education, social sciences, and tests and measurements in the education section of *Dissertation Abstracts International* were examined for the same period. ERIC searches were conducted using the following descriptors: effects of testing, using test results to improve instruction, test interpretation, test results, and minimum competency testing.

STUDIES OF TEST EFFECTS BEFORE 1980

Early research on testing was focused almost exclusively on the use of test data and not on the effects of using test data. Hastings, Runkel, Damrin, Kane, and Larson (1960) examined teacher use of test information in Illinois. Goslin (1967) examined the amount of testing and public attitudes toward testing on a national scale. Burry, Catterall, Choppin, and Dorr-Bremme (1982) conducted a broader-based study of test use which included curriculum embedded tests, district, state, and teacher-made tests, as well as norm-referenced and criterion-referenced standardized tests. Goslin provided an apt summation of the findings of this early test-use research: "While on the one hand, it is somewhat reassuring to learn that teachers are

Reviewers were: Gerald Bracey, Cherry Creek Schools, Englewood, CO; Jean Fair, Professor Emeritus, Wayne State University.

not blindly teaching children how to take tests, it is just a bit disconcerting to find that so little modification of courses is taking place" (p. 138). Such concerns and hopes continued to be expressed in the discourse about testing in educational journals during the 1980s.

Kellaghan et al. (1982) conducted an ambitious longitudinal study of test effects in elementary schools between 1973 and 1977. This study of standardized tests, conceived in the 1960s, was influenced in large part by concern with the potential effects that test results could have on teacher expectations of student capabilities. Because of the widespread use of standardized tests in the United States, the authors thought this country would be a poor setting in which to find a comparison group. Thus, the study was located in Ireland.

Some school staffs received test information, while others did not. The researchers investigated the effects of information from standardized tests on (a) the grouping of students for instruction, (b) student achievement and student self-perceptions, (c) teacher expectations of their students, and (d) the instructional practices of teachers.

Schools were randomly selected and randomly assigned to four major groups. There were two control groups; one had no testing, while testing was done in the other, but no results were provided to teachers. There were also two experimental school groups: Tests were administered to both, but one group received norm-referenced test results only, whereas the second group received norm-referenced results and more detailed test performance information based on specified skills and content, such as language comprehension, drawing inferences, identifying main ideas, spelling, and the addition-subtraction of fractions. Teacher and student questionnaires were administered in all four groups of schools.

Teachers in the experimental groups were provided information about the test performance of their pupils on test-score report forms. Additional materials were sent to teachers in both experimental groups to assist them in understanding and interpreting results, including detailed explanations of each information item on the report forms. A brief description of ways in which test results might be used was included, as well. Field workers also visited schools to explain the results and the material that came with the results.

The major conclusion of the researchers was that testing alone did not have a great deal of impact on the grouping of pupils for instructional purposes, on levels of pupil achievement, or on the perceptions and teaching practices of teachers (p. 127). They noted that "while the cooperation of teachers in administering the test program was good, their commitment to using test results, even on their own admission, was not great" (Kellaghan et al., 1982, p. 128).

In this extended study, then, knowledge of the results of standardized testing had neither positive nor negative effects. That conclusion may only be valid, however, when teachers and administrators feel little pressure to have students do well on tests. The authors acknowledged the lack of generalizability of their results to the contemporary American test setting, noting that "our findings do not relate to the controversial use of tests for accountability purposes" (Kellaghan et al., 1982, p.

18). This relatively new "high stakes" test setting is addressed next.

HIGH STAKES TESTS

As Popham (1987a), Madaus (1988), and Airasian (1988) have described them, *high stakes tests* have been around for some time. Popham referred to high stakes tests as "examinations that are associated with important consequences for examinees" and "examinations whose scores are seen as reflections of instructional quality" (p. 680). They are tests whose results are used to make decisions that students, teachers, or the general public consider to affect them in an immediate, important way. Traditionally, such tests have been the ones used to help determine which students will be promoted and, eventually, which students will get high school diplomas, in addition to their use as admission examinations for college-bound students.

Most of the standardized, norm-referenced tests administered by schools until the late 1970s could not be considered to be high stakes tests. In fact, no one seemed to pay much attention to them. As late as 1981, following interviews of staff in 18 western Pennsylvania school systems, Sproull and Zubrow (1981) reported that central office personnel had little use themselves for the results of the standardized tests they administered; they assumed that the results would be used by the district teachers. In the same study, however, Salmon-Cox (1981) noted that teachers did not find much use for the test results either but assumed that someone else did. Salmon-Cox reported no curricular use of test scores by school administrators. Sproull and Zubrow could report only one: a superintendent who asked his teachers to emphasize geographic terminology after noting low map scores from a standardized test battery.

Madaus (1981) noted that the teachers in both the Irish and Pennsylvania studies worked in circumstances that lacked the sanctions and rewards associated with contemporary test use. He cited the experience of Western European countries that when test results become a critical factor in important decisions, "administrators, teachers, and pupils take the results seriously and modify their behavior and attitude accordingly" (p. 635). Airasian (1987b), a participant in the Irish study of the effects of standardized testing, concluded that "the rise of policy oriented test uses has changed the context of educational testing in America" (p. 409). Koretz (1988) summarized the shift in test use from indicators of achievement to measures for accountability. That is, "tests are increasingly used, not only to show how well students do, but also to judge the competence of the educational enterprise and to hold the participants—students, teachers, principals, superintendents—accountable" (p. 8).

Minimum Competency Tests

When state-mandated minimum competency testing began in a few states in 1975 and 1976, it became clear that external testing programs would become a more influential part of school life than had been the case earlier. Since then, reports have varied on how widespread such state assessments have become. In 1978, Pipho reported that 33 states had taken some type of action to mandate the setting of minimum competency standards for students. As of 1984 (Airasian, 1987a), 29 states required students to take competency tests at some point. Medina and Neill (1988) indicated that 24 states included success on tests as graduation requirements, 12 states had promotion requirements based on tests, and 42 had some form of state assessment program. The State Education Performance Chart provided by the U.S. Department of Education (1989) showed 23 states with graduation assessment requirements. The first graduating class to be assessed was in 1976. Sixteen states had their first graduating class assessments in the 1980s, and three states are scheduled for the 1990s.

Modern high stakes tests are exemplified by the tests used in state minimum competency testing programs where promotion between grades or high school graduation depends on test success. Madaus (1988) noted that in such testing programs "policymakers have mandated that the results be used *automatically* to make such decisions" (p. 87). That is, students who do not reach the level of competence that has been set simply are not promoted or do not graduate. For Madaus, this is the major defining characteristic of modern high stakes tests. Airasian (1988) added that "high stakes" is a relative rather than an absolute concept. The stakes vary depending on the context in which testing takes place. For Airasian, a major influence on the stakes associated with test results is the difficulty of the test for most of the students taking it. Thus, a fifth-grade reading test with competency set at 75% correct should not be difficult for most high school seniors. Airasian maintained that this would be a relatively low stakes test for most high schools. This may help explain why schools with students who usually perform well academically pay less attention to minimum competency tests than schools with students who are generally less successful on achievement tests.

School Results

Publicized comparisons of school results are another major factor contributing to high stakes testing. The significance of achievement tests for school personnel changes when test results are reported by the media in the form of school averages. Madaus (1988) cited the Kentucky Essential Skills Test as a test that had no formal consequences directly linked to test performance. Yet, because state newspapers ranked school districts on the basis of these test results, the results assumed high stakes significance for local educators. Koretz (1988) underlined the importance of publicized school comparisons as an increasing source of pressure on schools:

The stakes have risen for teachers and administrators too, as test scores have increasingly been used to hold them accountable as well. This shift ... forced attention to the average scores of groups—schools, districts, and states—rather than just the scores of individual students. (p. 12)

Research

Research on test effects in the high stakes testing environment of the 1980s has been limited. However, Mathison (1988) conducted a major case study of three school systems in which the "power" of testing programs was the major variable. She defined power as "a function of the sanctions and rewards that are attached to performance on standardized tests ... determined by the uses to which testing and test results are put" (p. 177). Thus, Mathison considered high-powered testing programs to be virtually identical to high stakes testing programs.

Mathison used interviews of teachers and administrators in three school systems to determine whether the effects of tests were different in school systems where tests were taken more seriously than in those where tests were regarded lightly. All three systems were bound by the legal administrative framework of the same midwestern state. All used some standardized tests.

One school district was chosen because it had a minimal amount of testing with no noticeable use of test results. A second, medium power, school system was chosen because more testing was done and the results were intended for such uses as student placement and indirect evaluation of curricula. A third school system was chosen for its high power testing program in which "the results of the testing were used for purposes that would have significant consequences; for example, curriculum evaluation, grade-to-grade promotion, teacher or principal evaluation, and funding allocation" (p. 39).

In Mathison's school systems with low and medium powered testing programs, standardized testing seemed to have little impact on teachers or curricula. The school system with the high powered testing program was another matter, especially with the arrival of a new superintendent who emphasized test scores. Even before his appointment, SRA test score results were reported to the school board and published in the local newspaper. Curricular adjustments were made where there were discrepancies between curriculum and test objectives. The new superintendent reinforced this emphasis on tests by meeting annually with all principals after the testing was completed to review, in detail, their building test results. At this meeting, principals were expected to explain low scores and to have a plan to improve them. As might be expected, "the pressure perceived by teachers resulted in a heightened awareness of the test content" (p. 156). Mathison concluded that where the power of testing is high, there is a very noticeable impact on curriculum and instruction.

The contrast of the Mathison study with the earlier Irish study of test effects illustrates the difference between low stakes and high stakes testing. Because much modern testing is used to hold administrators and teachers accountable for the results students attain, both curricular and instructional efforts are likely to be directed to achieve the objectives that are implicit or explicit in the tests. When test scores are used to assess the effectiveness of school staffs, the tests receive careful attention from school personnel. Research on the effects of tests clearly must take into account the extent to which test results are considered important by the school administrators and teachers.

SOCIAL STUDIES TESTS AND WHAT THEY MEASURE

Clearly, tests have come to mean a great deal for schools as well as students. Though most high stakes testing is directed to the basic skills of reading and computation, some of the tests include social studies components; and as high stakes testing becomes a part of all school programs, social studies is bound to be even more affected.

An examination of standardized achievement test batteries indicates relatively little attention to social studies. Test descriptions in the *Eighth* and *Ninth Mental Measurements Yearbooks* (Buros, 1978; Mitchell, 1985) include social studies subtests in the Iowa Test of Basic Skills, the Iowa Tests of Educational Development, the Metropolitan Achievement Tests, the Science Research Associates Achievement Series, the Sequential Tests of Educational Progress, and the Stanford Achievement Test Series, but not in the California Achievement Tests. Schools may order some, but not necessarily all, of the subtests in a series.

When social studies is not included in a school testing program, the curriculum impact could be negative. Heightened attention to tests of reading and computation could mean less attention to social studies. There is evidence (Weiss, 1978) that social studies receives relatively little time in the elementary curriculum, but no serious studies have been undertaken to determine whether testing programs have influenced time allotments for elementary social studies.

Social studies is included in a number of national testing programs. NAEP included social studies and/or citizenship in assessments undertaken in 1969–1970, 1971–1972, 1974–1975, and 1981–1982. NAEP also conducted the 1986 assessment of history and literature described by Ravitch and Finn (1987). The College Entrance Examination Board (CEEB) has two achievement tests, one dealing with American history and social studies and the other with European history and world cultures. In addition, the CEEB's Advanced Placement (AP) program includes examinations in American history, European history, government, and economics for college-level courses offered in many high schools. Although AP tests affect only a minority of students, over 100,000 students take the history and social science tests annually (CEEB, 1988). There are also a number of nationally standardized social studies achievement tests for each of the major secondary school social studies subjects.

Several state testing programs include a social studies component. Fox, Williams, and Winters (1979) reported that social studies was included in 15 statewide testing programs. Rudman (1987) estimated that in 18% of the states mandating the testing of minimum competencies social studies was included in some way. A few states include social studies in tests of citizenship, for example, Maryland (Maryland State Department of Education, 1988) and Oregon (Fox et al., 1979).

Another source of test effects could be locally developed criterion-referenced tests (CRTs) composed of several sets of test items, each measuring a well-described skill or knowledge domain. Williams and Moore (1980) recommended CRT development for local social studies programs so that achievement of school-level objectives would be assessed. However, Popham (1987a), an early proponent of local CRT development, concluded that local school districts lacked the expertise to develop their own tests for important assessment purposes.

Elements in Testing Programs

Research on social studies test effects must include careful descriptions of the objectives for testing programs, as well as how results are obtained and reported. Such descriptions should answer at least three questions: (a) What objectives do the test designers say the test will measure? (b) Do the test specifications and the different forms of the test modify these objectives in any significant way? and (c) Does the way in which test results are obtained and reported have an impact on objectives? Issues related to each of these questions are discussed next.

Objectives

The most critical feature of any test is the objectives it measures, both the objectives the test designers say they intend to assess and what the test actually measures, because social studies curricula and instruction may be directed to their attainment at the expense of alternative objectives. Although the designers of tests usually intend to measure student attainment of significant skill and/or content objectives, the correspondence between the test designers' statements about the objectives assessed and the objectives which schools, teachers, and/or professional organizations espouse is a crucial issue. For example, Chapin (1974) pointed out, "An important question to social studies educators is the extent to which the NAEP exercises are compatible with the NCSS Social Studies Curriculum Guidelines" (p. 413).

Equally important is the match between the test and the designers' stated objectives. Ideally, the purported objectives and those actually addressed by a test would be highly congruent. To determine whether a test measures what it is purported to measure, the stated objectives and the implicit objectives derived from examining test items must be compared. For example, a test can typically measure only a sample of the universe of objectives and reviews of items may indicate a pattern of inclusion and exclusion that does not correspond with the stated objectives.

Linn (1983) pointed out the importance of the match of intended objectives and actual assessment when considering the potential effects of tests on instruction. If the match is poor and school personnel rely only on the statements of test objectives reported in the test manuals, they may fail to direct their curricular and instructional efforts to the actual objectives measured in the test. Conversely, if they rely only on the objectives inferred from the test forms, they may direct their educational efforts to a narrowly conceived version of the subject. In either case, they may direct instruction to but a part of the objectives they ought to address.

A common criticism of social studies tests is the failure to measure student attainment of more complex, higher-order thinking skills. Larkins (1981), for example, expressed concern about the mechanistic-reductionist view of education fostered by minimum competency tests. More recently, Koretz (1988), Madaus (1988), and Airasian (1988) have suggested that multiple-choice testing focuses attention on narrow, basic objectives at the expense of high-order objectives.

A perusal of social studies standardized tests indicates the widespread use of multiple-choice questions. Frederiksen (1984) maintained that economical machine-scoreable, multiple-choice tests have driven out other types of examinations. Among existing standardized testing programs with a social studies component, only NAEP exercises and AP examinations provide examples of alternative ways of measuring student attainment of social studies objectives.

Koretz (1988) acknowledged the value of multiple-choice tests for efficiently measuring attainment of basic skills, but emphasized that they are valid for a fairly narrow range of tasks, such as recognizing right and wrong answers as contrasted with writing a coherent and well-reasoned passage or explaining why answers differ in their correctness. Frederiksen (1984) noted that "anyone who has prepared a multiple-choice test for a class realizes that it is indeed much easier . . . to write factual items than items that require inference, analysis, interpretation or application of a principle" (p. 195). The difficulty of devising multiple-choice items that measure higher order cognitive skills often results in an emphasis on factual knowledge.

The concern that the use of objective test questions might narrow the scope of the cognitive objectives to which instruction is addressed has surfaced with respect to measuring writing achievement. Suhor (1985) emphasized that English teachers have serious questions about the desirability of relying on multiple-choice tests and that research has established the feasibility of scoring writing samples objectively. After indicating that empirical studies of the effects of testing on instruction in writing are rare, he noted that the findings support the overwhelming testimony of teachers that "objective, norm referenced and criterion referenced competency tests discourage writing instruction . . ., while tests that include writing samples generally result in more teaching of writing" (p. 636).

Certainly, if there is truth in the adage that "what gets tested gets taught", multiple-choice measures of writing are likely to have serious consequences for the amount of actual writing teachers ask students to do. Social studies teachers often express the same reservations about the validity of multiple-choice questions as measures of the higher-order thought processes involved in a meaningful understanding of history and the social sciences.

Reports of Results

Another key factor in the potential effects of tests on curricula is the way scores are reported (Mathison, 1988). Only when test results are reported in a manner that allows comparisons among teachers, schools, school districts, or states are they important for accountability purposes. Reports of test results for individual students can often have high stakes for the individual, but the likelihood of such reports having high stakes for schools is small.

Test results can be reported in a number of ways for groups of students. One is the percentage of students reaching a standard of competence or mastery. Another is the average percent right on a test or the subsections of a test. A third is the percent gain for a group of students between a pretest administration and testing at the conclusion of instruction.

Each of these ways of reporting test results could have different effects on instruction. Minimum standards tend to direct teacher attention to students who are least successful on the test, discouraging the extension of learning by more academically able students. Reporting only average percentages places emphasis on improving all students, even if the less academically able students are ignored. Gain score reporting could lead to the encouragement of low scores at the pretest administration, even for more academically advanced students.

NAEP

Questions about the adequacy of the objectives on which a test is based, the match of objectives with test questions, and the way results are reported provide a basis for examining the major national effort, under the auspices of NAEP, to provide information about student attainment of a broad range of social studies objectives. NAEP social studies and citizenship tests administered in the past 20 years have been of considerable interest to social studies educators. In 1974, a special issue of *Social Education,* the official journal of the National Council for the Social Studies (NCSS), addressed the 1969–70 citizenship and the 1971–72 social studies assessments. Most of the issue was directed to the exercises or test questions used in the assessments, as well as to the results on these exercises, but the objectives and modes of reporting were addressed as well. A NCSS Bulletin (Williams & Moore, 1980) also reflected the interest of social studies educators in NAEP social studies and citizenship assessments.

Fair (1974), the chairperson of an NCSS committee that examined NAEP efforts, supported NAEP's commitment to formulate a broad range of objectives, rather than focusing only on basic skills and information. The broad scope and complexity of the NAEP objectives are evident in the first set of citizenship objectives (NAEP, 1969) and the first set of social studies objectives (NAEP, 1970). Commenting on the subsequent 1981–82 NAEP citizenship and social studies objectives, Carlson (1986) noted: "With 255 people suggesting the objectives, it would have been surprising if anything of substance had been left out. The concern is not with the quality of the objectives, but rather with their sheer quantity" (p. 10).

The 10 major 1969 citizenship objectives included a vast range of desired behaviors, attitudes and knowledge. Behaviors and attitudes, such as showing "concern for the welfare and dignity of others", "community improvement through active, democratic participation", and "rationality in communication, thought, and action" dominated the objectives. Only 2 of the 10 objectives emphasized knowledge: knowing "the main structure and functions of our governments" and understanding "problems of international relations." Each objective was supported by 2 to 7 subobjectives, which totaled 46 in number. Each subobjective was given further meaning by the specification of illustrative behaviors for young people at the age of 9, 13, and 17.

There were only 5 social studies objectives for the 1970 assessment, with 25 subobjectives; but the coverage included attitudes and skills, as well as content knowledge: (a) curiosity about human affairs, (b) using analytic-scientific procedures effectively, (c) sensitivity to creative-intuitive methods of explaining the human condition, (d) knowledge relevant to the major ideas and concerns of social scientists, and (e) reasoned commitment to the values that sustain a free society.

Reviewers of the 1969–1970 assessments found it difficult to fault the scope of the NAEP social studies and citizenship objectives. The major question concerned the degree to which the assessment exercises measured the objectives. Hunkins (1974) addressed this content validity problem by asking, "Are these exercises doing what they are purported to do in relation to the objectives of NAEP" (p. 415)? Hunkins and three social studies specialists concluded that 85% of 194 1971–1972 social studies exercises had content validity in that they constituted direct measures of the objectives. However, only 61% of 152 1971–1972 citizenship exercises were judged to have such content validity. In his examination of NAEP exercises, Hunkins also pointed out that several objectives and subobjectives were not represented by any exercises, whereas some of the tested objectives had considerably more exercises than other objectives. "For example, emphasis on the fourth citizenship objective, which deals with the main structure and function of our government, suggests that citizenship is considered to be primarily political, whereas the overall objectives would suggest a broader interpretation of citizenship" (p. 416).

Carlson's (1986) examination of the 1981–1982 social studies objectives and the exercises released to the public resulted in concerns similar to those expressed by Hunkins. His analysis of only about one-fourth of the exercises revealed omissions and overemphases similar to those noted by Hunkins. Carlson observed that in the 1981–1982 assessment there was a marked overemphasis on American history, in contrast with Hunkins' identification of an overemphasis on the structure of American government.

Though a number of multiple-choice questions were included, NAEP exercises were not limited to this mode of testing. Students were often asked to write responses. Even more unusual were the number of performance exercises. Fair (1974) described the NAEP testing exercises as "sometimes ordinary, sometimes exemplary and even ingenious" (p. 401). Different exercises required students to engage in interviews, participate in discussion groups, analyze cartoons, and even respond to music.

NAEP's testing strategy was also considered important (Larkins, 1974; Taylor, 1974). Confronted with an enormous number of complex objectives, more exercises were needed than could be put into one test administration. So NAEP put together several sets of exercises and administered each set to different samples of students. Larkins (1974) described how this strategy could be used by social studies teachers to assess attainment of a large number of objectives in a short time.

For two decades after the first NAEP assessment in 1969, the reporting of data that could be used to compare state levels of achievement was carefully avoided. Martin (1979), in describing the goals for NAEP activities, included the aim of making data available for research on educational issues, "while protecting the privacy of both state and local units" (p. 46). Only regional (northeast, southeast, central, and west) data were provided. The National Governors Association's (NGA) statement that states should "assume greater responsibility for setting educational goals and defining outcome standards" (Honetschlager & Cohen, 1988, p. 43) resulted in an NGA recommendation that NAEP include state-by-state data on student performance.

The 1990 NAEP assessment in mathematics will be the first for which results will be reported by states (Seldon, 1988). State school officials are expected to provide input on what is to be tested, with the understanding that the tests will measure more than minimum competencies. If such a plan is implemented, it can be expected that state resources will be directed toward improving achievement on the objectives assessed by NAEP. As Honetschlager and Cohen (1988) noted, when school districts consistently perform poorly, this is where "proposals for state takeover or academic bankruptcy come in." Thus, the stakes that NAEP social studies test results might have for local schools could be raised to a marked degree. Research into the factors that influence the effects of these tests could make important contributions, especially in light of the scarcity of such studies.

EFFECTS OF TESTING ON ACHIEVEMENT

Three important aspects of the effects of testing on achievement merit attention. The first is whether test scores do improve in schools where test results are considered important. The reverse side of this coin is whether test scores decline for objectives and/or school subjects not included on the tests considered to be critical. A second achievement-related topic is the extent to which there have been decreases in the performance gap between minority and majority students. A third and far more difficult question for researchers concerns the validity of test scores as evidence of actual achievement.

Effects on Test Scores

Improved test scores in high stakes testing programs of basic skills are a widespread phenomenon. Frederiksen (1984) noted that mean scores on competency tests have been on the rise. He cited the increased scores reported on New Jersey's Minimum Basic Skills tests. Gabrys (1988) reported steady gains, from 61% up to 68% of ninth graders passing the Maryland Functional Mathematics Test between 1983 and 1987. The gains on the Maryland Writing Test were even more striking: from 51% passing in 1984 to 82% passing in 1988. Only reading showed no gain: 93% of the ninth graders passed in 1983 and 93% in 1987. Another example, cited in a report on a National Institute of Education conference on testing (1979), was improved achievement in first-year algebra from a 54% level to an 88% level after implementation of a mastery learning program of minimum essentials. Airasian (1987a) reported that 36% of the students failed to qualify for a Florida high school diploma in 1977, but the failure rate was less than 2% in 1983.

Popham, Cruse, Rankin, Sandifer, and Williams (1985) described measurement-driven instructional programs in Detroit, South Carolina, Maryland, and Texas. Popham (1987b) followed with a report of score improvement gains of up to 25% for seven school systems. Improvement in the three R's was cited for Alabama (1–13% over a 5-year period for students in Grades 3, 6, 9, and 11), Connecticut (6–16% over a 2-year period for students in Grade 9), Detroit (19% over a 5-year period for students in Grade 12), and Maryland (13–25% over a 6-year period for students in Grade 9). Improvements of from 7% to 20% were also noted in reading and math for New Jersey, South Carolina, and Texas.

Clearly, there is evidence to suggest that scores will improve when testing programs direct the attention of school personnel to basics. With few exceptions, there is a lack of information on achievement results for social studies. One exception is Maryland's Test of Citizenship Skills. The Maryland State Department of Education (MSDE, 1988) technical report indicated that only 42% of 9th and 10th graders passed the 1984 administration when performance did not affect graduation. When required for graduation, performance increased each year to the point that 73% passed in 1987 and 71% in 1988. This instance of social studies minimum competency testing supports the conclusion that high stakes testing leads to improved test scores there, too.

A number of testing researchers are concerned about the effects of these concentrated efforts to improve basic skills and content achievement scores. Frederiksen (1984) noted the influence of time and effort on school achievement and expressed the concern that "reliance on objective tests to provide evidence of improvement may have contributed to a bias in education that decreases effort to teach other important abilities" (p. 195). Rudman (1987) indicated a similar concern. After acknowledging slow but steady gains in basic skills among low-achieving students, he concluded that this had been accomplished at the expense of average- or high-achieving students. Research is needed on the effects of time and effort directed to improving basic skills at the possible expense of higher-level skills and more sophisticated concepts in social studies. For example, are improved scores in the basics of government as assessed on citizenship tests achieved at the expense of achievement in geography and history?

Minority Test Scores

A major concern of many educators seeking to improve test scores is the discrepancy between the scores of some ethnic minority groups and White children. Airasian (1987a) noted that a disproportionate percentage of students failing in graduation testing programs were from ethnic or language minority groups. He cited 1983 Florida results which showed that African-Americans, who represented 20% of the high school seniors, constituted 57% of those who failed the graduation exam. And, in 1982, the percentage of first-time test takers who passed both the reading and math parts of the Virginia state graduation test was 83 for African-American students and 96 for White students.

However, most reported pass rates disaggregated by race show a closing of the gap between white and African-American students. For example, Airasian (1987b) reported that Virginia's 25% disparity in 1979 had dropped to 13% in 1982. He commented that "the initial disparity between majority and minority passing rates decreases with time" (p. 60). Popham (1987a) supported this view by stating: "It is particularly gratifying that measurement-driven instruction is apparently reducing the performance gap between majority and minority students" (p. 682).

Reductions in ethnic group discrepancies may be an inevitable outcome of raising the percentage of students attaining minimum competence or mastery. If one group has had an average mastery attainment of 80% and another group of 60%, any significant overall improvement that occurs is most likely due to gains from the second group. If minority-majority discrepancies did *not* narrow as overall scores improved, this would indeed be a matter of great concern.

Validity of Test Scores

The last question to be addressed with respect to student achievement is perhaps the most critical: "To what extent do test scores truly represent the achievement they are purported to measure?" Or, put differently, "Do improved scores really indicate improvement in student capabilities, or are they spurious gains due to the teachers' increasing familiarity with the test?"

Initial public concerns about the effectiveness of schools in maximizing or at least maintaining student achievement derive in large part from the reporting of test scores. When schools initiate programs to improve student achievement, results from the first tests administered usually confirm apprehensions about school inadequacy. In a review of Detroit's minimum competency testing program, Popham et al. (1985) reported considerable public concern that only 55% of the students reached competency in writing and 49% in mathematics on the first testing. Similarly, the results of the first year of Maryland's functional testing program indicated only 50% of students attaining competency (Popham, 1987a).

The question is, do the extensive subsequent test score gains represent real gains in achievement? Cannell's (1988) review of his two earlier "Lake Wobegon" reports highlighted this question. These reports earned their nickname from Garrison Keillor's mythical community where "the women are strong, the men are good looking, and all the children are above average." Cannell pointed out that standardized test results seemed to show that the children in every state were above average. While acknowledging some exaggerations in Cannell's work, Koretz (1988) concluded that current norm-referenced tests do indeed overstate achievement levels, often to a great extent. Koretz reminded his readers that test scores are not equivalent to achievement, but "merely incomplete and fallible indicators of achievement" (p. 46) and "when a test is used as a prod to raise achievement, its value as an indicator of achievement is compromised." He noted, as well, the lack of evidence as to whether gains in test scores are generalizable beyond the particular test form to which students have responded.

Haertel (1986) used the concept of intrinsic validity in discussing the relationship of test scores to the abilities they are purported to measure. He maintained that the validity of educational statistics, including test results, was likely to be influenced by a shift from improving school quality to improving a school's statistics. Thus, test results, as indicators of quality, may be compromised by direct attempts to improve them.

Cannell (1988) and Koretz (1988) cited questionable school practices by which test scores may be improved without actual improvements in skill and concept attainment. For example, Cannell attributed the gains in elementary achievement scores in the 1980s to the use of the same test questions year after year. He asserted that "American elementary schools often 'integrate' the unchanging questions of standardized commercial achievement tests into elementary curriculum" (p. 14). Koretz emphasized some of the consequences when schools control the storage and administration of achievement tests. He cited examples of outright cheating by schools, including the use of actual test questions in exercises preparing students to take a test. Clearly, such practices can be a major contributor to a lack of validity in achievement test scores.

The validity of test scores as indicators of achievement should be a major topic for social studies research. Part of the test score-achievement problem is the lack of corroborative studies of test score validity, using closely related tests as well as teacher observations of student performance. Moreover, for the major objectives of social studies, retesting-retention studies are needed to determine whether achievement as evidenced by a test score is maintained over time.

EFFECTS OF TESTING ON CURRICULUM AND INSTRUCTION

The effects of testing on curriculum and instruction begin when school leaders become concerned about test results as indicators of what students are learning. This concern leads to efforts by teachers and administrators to determine what these critical tests measure. Once the objectives assessed by a test are identified, the next step is to realign the curriculum and modify instructional practices to address the test's objectives and test-taking skills. Subsequently, test results are examined for evidence of improved achievement. This simplified description suggests what is meant by measurement-driven instruction.

These steps, to the extent they take place, represent a significant shift in the traditional relationship of curriculum, instruction, and evaluation. Tyler (1950) identified four questions to be addressed by curriculum developers: (a) What educational purposes (objectives) should schools seek? (b) What educational experiences can be provided which are likely to attain these purposes? (c) How can these experiences be most effec-

tively organized? and (d) How can we determine whether these purposes are being attained? Dressel (1965) described curriculum planning as a similar four-step process from curricular objectives, to learning experiences, to organization of these learning experiences, to evaluation of their impact on students. In this final step, "we must evaluate the achievement . . . of students as a result of the curriculum experience. In the light of our findings, we may need to modify objectives and to select new learning experiences, or to reorganize them" (p. 7).

Thus, from the perspective of this traditional view of curriculum development and evaluation, measurement-driven instruction has the tail wagging the dog. Instead of evaluation serving and refining the other elements in curriculum development, it becomes the driving force, in effect the determiner of curriculum and instruction. In illogical circularity, the test provides both direction to the curriculum and the measure of success for curriculum and instruction.

The effects of recent state accountability programs suggest that many American schools have reached the point where high stakes testing will have the kind of curricular-instructional impact with which European schools have been long familiar. Unfortunately, in some recent discussion of test effects, the Irish and Pennsylvania studies of the 1970s are used to question the axiom that "what gets tested gets taught." For example, Porter (1988) cited those studies of low stakes testing to support the view that educational indicators (test results) will probably not become important mechanisms of school control. To the contrary, if anything, the new era of publicized test results promises to make tests even more dominant in controlling the behavior of principals and teachers.

Diagnostic Use

There is little research evidence on one potentially positive instructional effect of testing: the diagnostic use of test results by teachers to modify their teaching practices to provide remediation for students who need it. The diagnostic use of test results was of interest in both the Pennsylvania and Irish studies cited above. However, the researchers found no such test effect. In contrast, in a study of a small group of Michigan elementary school math teachers (Kuhs et al., 1985), it was found that the only tests that consistently affected teacher practice were those used in mastery learning where objectives were specified and progress regularly monitored through tests tied to objectives. Such "curriculum imbedded" tests, the researchers concluded, have far more promise of being used diagnostically than standardized tests.

Needed Research

Discussions of the curricular-instructional effects of tests in the high stakes climate of the 1980s were most often based on personal experience and analysis. For example, McNeil (1988), in a report on a Texas study, referred to science and social studies as being transformed into factual fragments and jargon as a result of competency testing. She noted, also, that "proficiency based curricula . . . in fact overwhelmed class time" (p. 483).

Bracey (1987), arguing against measurement-driven instruction, referred to the following negative outcomes which "inevitably occur in practice": (a) fragmentation and narrowing of the curriculum, as learning is broken into discrete pieces to be treated in isolation, (b) deflection of the curriculum from important aspects of subjects to the single-minded pursuit of limited objectives, and (c) discouragement of teachers from teaching for transfer. Stedman (1988) argued for changes in the effective schools formula by claiming that teachers have neglected many liberal arts subjects and higher-order thinking skills because they have concentrated on the lower-order reading and math skills measured on most standardized tests. However, research describing such effects is difficult to find for tests of the three Rs, let alone for social studies tests.

Case Studies. More research like Mathison's (1988) case studies is needed for a better understanding of the effects of tests on curriculum and instruction. Although her case studies were limited to three midwestern school systems, in one of which test results were taken seriously, Mathison's conclusions suggest the types of test effects that might be investigated in future research.

Mathison separated test effects into those related to course content and those related to instruction. She found course content to be affected by standardized test results in the following ways: A significant social studies curriculum change was attributed, in part, to relatively low scores on the social studies section of the American College Testing Program; a new language arts textbook was chosen, in part, to improve reading performance; concepts and skills already being taught that appeared in the standardized test received additional attention, while those not appearing on the test were deemphasized. In addition, teachers started teaching concepts and skills on the test that were not typically part of the curriculum; for example, a vocabulary unit was introduced in many English classes.

Mathison also found several instances in which student performance on tests led to instructional changes. One was increased teacher use of multiple-choice testing as a way of providing students with experiences relevant to the standardized test format. Teachers also responded to poor student test performance by providing more ongoing reviews pertinent to the skills and concepts on the test and by having concentrated reviews just before the time of testing. Moreover, the sequencing of concepts and skills was changed to match the time at which they were to be tested.

Studying State Reports. In addition to case studies, another possible direction for future research is the study of state reports that describe mandated tests, test results, and the ways in which local school districts might comply with mandated testing regulations. Most state-mandated graduation competency programs, especially following the 1981 Debra P. v. Turlington case in Florida (Pullen, 1983), require that schools provide relevant preparatory programs for students who must demonstrate competency to graduate (Airasian & Madaus, 1983). As Airasian and Madaus noted: "In short, the ruling by the Fifth Circuit means that a test used as a graduation requirement must cover material actually taught pupils" (p. 110).

Because its minimum competency graduation program includes a social studies component, Maryland provides an appropriate illustration of the curricular implications of state testing programs. In addition to assessments of reading, mathematics, and writing, the Maryland Functional Testing Program included the Maryland Test of Citizenship Skills (MTCS). This test (Maryland State Department of Education, 1988) was designed to assess mastery of certain functional citizenship skills.

Functional citizenship was defined by the Maryland State Department of Education (MSDE, 1980) as the application of knowledge and attitudes in five areas reminiscent of the NAEP citizenship objectives: responsibilities; law and justice; rights; governmental form, function, and process; and civic participation at the local, state, national, and international levels. Six competencies were formulated, with each competency supported by several objectives. There were a total of 26 citizenship objectives. Each objective subsequently was defined in an outline of instructional content and vocabulary eligible for testing. The MSDE (1985b) provided Maryland teachers with outlines of the content eligible for testing, relevant vocabulary, illustrative test questions, sample teaching activities, and worksheets. Thus, there was very little question about the content to be tested and the way it would be tested.

For students who failed the test, schools were required to provide "appropriate assistance" before they could take the test again, and the form that such assistance would take had to be specified (MSDE, 1985a). A few examples indicate the types of curricular change resulting from the Maryland citizenship test:

A reorganized social studies program is being implemented in order to provide instruction in the citizenship objectives in grades 7–8. . . . Built into the (9th-grade) geography class is a special unit on citizenship taught before the spring testing dates (p. 175).

The information published in *Maryland Test of Citizenship Skills: Instructional Content Domains* has been included in the first half of the United States History curriculum guide (p. 154).

Tenth grade students who fail the test as ninth graders work with specially developed (citizenship) materials . . . for four weeks prior to retesting. This necessitates some modification of the grade 10 World History course (p. 143).

The failure of over 25% of Maryland's students to pass the mandated citizenship test graduation requirement in the first years of high school thus had curricular implications for social studies in each of the remaining high school years. The analysis of other state reports might suggest similar implications.

Test-Taking Skills. Besides changes in the established curriculum, concern about test results can lead to the allocation of instructional time to test-taking skills. How much school time is so directed can have a major impact on the total time available for the attainment of other skills and content. Relatively little is actually known about the amount of instructional time devoted to improving "test-wiseness". Most attention has been directed to the effectiveness of such training (e.g., Scruggs, Bennion, & White, 1986) or to its possible nature. Prell and Prell (1986), for example, suggested proper use of time, avoidance of errors, guessing, and deductive reasoning as aspects of test-wiseness, and concluded that 10 hours of instruction would be an appropriate time investment, with additional time for annual reviews just prior to each subsequent test administration. Of course, in addition to such general test-taking instruction, considerably more time is likely to be directed to skills (e.g., identifying the main point of a passage) or content (e.g., vocabulary) likely to appear on the test. Preparation of the latter sort is likely to involve social studies teachers, as well as other teachers, in the weeks preceding administration of high stakes standardized tests.

Effects of Multiple-Choice Testing. Another area of research interest is the extent to which greater specification of objectives and the use of multiple-choice questions to measure their attainment affects basic instructional strategies. For example, inquiry modes of instruction, simulated decision making, and field experiences are inherently time consuming and likely to have several difficult-to-assess outcomes. An important research question for social studies educators is whether specific objectives and multiple-choice tests lead to greater emphasis on drill as an instructional strategy.

EFFECTS OF TESTING ON THE PROFESSIONAL STATUS OF TEACHERS

It would be inappropriate to conclude a discussion of the effects of testing on schools without reference to the possible effects of high stakes testing on teacher perceptions of themselves and their profession. These effects may be greater for social studies teachers than for teachers of some other subjects. Social studies shares with English an affinity with the liberal arts and the humanities. The conception of citizenship education underlying social studies is broad and complex rather than narrow and simplistic. Social studies teachers, as a group, are likely to be at the forefront of those who are wary of the specifying and focusing effects of the modern testing movement.

Wise (1988) noted particularly important factors for consideration by researchers interested in the effects of the modern testing movement on teachers:

In effect, mandates say to many elementary school teachers: don't teach everything, just teach the basics; don't teach children to read, just teach reading skills; don't teach children to write, just teach them to fill in the blanks; don't teach them to think, just teach them to give the right answers. (p. 330)

Such directions for teachers may result in ethical conflict and consequent disillusionment with education as a profession.

Koretz (1988) addressed the question of professional behavior with respect to test security and "teaching to the test". He referred to "the vast gray area of teaching to the test [that] stretches from frank cheating at one extreme to appropriate remediation and instruction at the other" (p. 46). In the new world of high stakes testing, social studies educators need to reach consensus on acceptable and unacceptable professional behavior in the "vast gray area" of teaching to the test.

Madaus (1988) spoke of the difference between external tests developed outside local school systems and the internal tests developed by school districts and individual teachers. He noted that external tests surely diminish the role of teachers in deciding what is most worth teaching. An even more professionally threatening practice is the preparation of "teacher proof" instructional packages designed to help students be successful on a particular test.

Benveniste (1986) summarized some of the dangers of school accountability testing programs for the professional status of teachers. He maintained that such programs can decrease the discretion of teachers in determining educational objectives and setting performance standards, as well as in deciding what educational experiences will help students to learn what is required of them.

To the research needed on how testing affects student achievement, curriculum, and instruction must be added the need for research about the effects of testing on the professional status of social studies teachers.

References

Airasian, P. W. (1987a). The consequences of high school graduation testing programs. *NASSP Bulletin, 71,* 54–68.

Airasian, P. W. (1987b). State mandated testing and educational reform: Context and consequences. *American Journal of Education, 95,* 393–412.

Airasian, P. W. (1988). Measurement driven instruction: A closer look. *Educational Measurement: Issues and Practice, 7,* 6–11.

Airasian, P. W., & Madaus, G. F. (1983). Linking testing and instruction: Policy issues. *Journal of Educational Measurement, 20,* 103–118.

Benveniste, G. (1986). School accountability and the professionalization of teaching. *Education and Urban Society, 18,* 271–286.

Bracey, G. W. (1987). Measurement-driven instruction: Catchy phrase, dangerous practice. *Phi Delta Kappan, 68,* 683–686.

Buros, O. K. (Ed.). (1978). *The eighth mental measurements yearbook.* Highland Park, NJ: Gryphon Press.

Burry, J., Catterall, J., Choppin, B., & Dorr-Bremme, D. (1982). *Testing in the nation's schools and districts: How much? What kinds? To what ends? At what costs?* (CSE Report No. 194). Los Angeles: Center for the Study of Evaluation, University of California, Los Angeles.

Cannell, J. (1988, Summer). Nationally normed elementary achievement testing in America's public schools: How all 50 states are above the national average. *Educational Measurement: Issues and Practices, 7,* 5–9.

Carlson, K. (1986). *The national assessment of educational progress in social studies.* Paper prepared for the Study Group on the National Assessment of Student Achievement. (ERIC Document Reproduction Service No. ED 279 665)

Chapin, J. (1974). Using the NAEP exercises. *Social Education, 38,* 412–414.

College Entrance Examination Board (CEEB). (1988). *1988 Advanced Placement Program national summary reports.* New York: Author.

Dressel, P. L. (1965). The role of evaluation in teaching and learning. In

H. D. Berg (Ed.), *Evaluation in Social Studies* (pp. 1–20). Washington, DC: The National Council for the Social Studies.

Fair, J. (1974). What is national assessment and what does it say to us? *Social Education, 38,* 398–403.

Fox, K., Williams, P., & Winters, L. (1979). Graduation competency testing in the social studies: A position statement of the National Council for the Social Studies. *Social Education, 43,* 367–372.

Frederiksen, N. (1984). The real test bias: Influences of testing on teaching and learning. *American Psychologist, 39,* 193–202.

Gabrys, R. E. (1988). *Maryland functional testing program overview and charts related to program impact on curriculum and instruction.* Paper presented to the National Council of States on Inservice Education.

Goslin, D. A. (1967). *Teachers and Testing.* New York: Russell Sage Foundation.

Haertel, E. (1986). Measuring school performance to improve school practice. *Education and Urban Society, 18,* 326–325.

Hastings, J. T., Runkel, P. J., Damrin, D. E., Kane, R. B., & Larson, G. L. (1960). *The use of test results.* Urbana: Bureau of Educational Research, University of Illinois.

Honetschlager, D., & Cohen, M. (1988). The governors restructure schools. *Educational Leadership, 42,* 42–43.

Hunkins, F. P. (1974). Exercises to assess social studies and citizenship: How good are they? *Social Education, 38,* 415–421.

Kellaghan, T., Madaus, G. F., & Airasian, P. (1982). *The effects of standardized testing.* Boston: Kluwer-Nijhoff.

Koretz, D. (1988, Summer). Arriving in Lake Wobegon: Are standardized tests exaggerating achievement and distorting instruction? *American Educator, 12,* 8–15, 46–52.

Kuhs, T., Porter, A., Floden, R., Freemen, D., Schmidt, W., & Schwille, J. (1985). Differences among teachers in their use of curriculum-embedded tests. *The Elementary School Journal, 86,* 141–153.

Larkins, A. G. (1974). NAEP procedures and small scale assessment: Applications to some local problems. *Social Education, 38,* 425–427.

Larkins, A. G. (1981). Minimum competency tests: A negative view. In H. D. Mehlinger and O. L. Davis, Jr. (Eds.), *The social studies.* 80th Yearbook of the National Society for the Study of Education (pp. 126–150). Chicago: University of Chicago Press.

Linn, R. L. (1983). Testing and instruction: Links and distinctions. *Journal of Educational Measurement, 20,* 179–190.

Madaus, G. F. (1981). Reactions to the "Pittsburgh papers." *Phi Delta Kappan, 62,* 634–636.

Madaus, G. F. (1988). The influence of testing on the curriculum. In L. N. Tanner, (Ed.), *Critical issues in curriculum.* 87th yearbook of the National Society for the Study of Education (pp. 83–121). Chicago: University of Chicago Press.

Martin, W. H. (1979). National Assessment of Educational Progress. *New Directions for Testing and Measurement, 2,* 45–67.

Maryland State Department of Education. (1980). *Declared competencies index.* Baltimore: Author.

Maryland State Department of Education. (1985a). *Appropriate assistance programs in Maryland schools for reading, writing, mathematics, citizenship.* Baltimore: Author.

Maryland State Department of Education. (1985b). *Project basic instructional guide, Citizenship supplement.* Baltimore: Author.

Maryland State Department of Education. (1988). *Technical report: Maryland test of citizenship skills.* Baltimore: Author.

Mathison, S. M. (1988). The perceived effects of standardized testing on teaching and curricula. *Dissertation Abstracts International, 49*(1), 35-A. (University Microfilms No. DA8803130)

McNeil, M. (1988). Contradictions of control, Part 3: Contradictions of reform. *Phi Delta Kappan, 69,* 478–485.

Medina, N., & Neill, D. M. (1988). *Fallout from the testing explosion: How 100 million standardized exams undermine equity and excellence in America's public schools.* Cambridge, MA: National Center for Fair and Open Testing.

Mitchell, J. V. (Ed.). (1985). *The ninth mental measurements yearbook.* Lincoln: University of Nebraska Press.

National Assessment of Education Progress. (1969). *Citizenship objectives.* Ann Arbor, MI: Committee on Assessing the Progress of Education.

National Assessment of Educational Progress. (1970). *Social studies objectives.* Denver: Education Commission of the States.

National Institute of Education. (1979). *Testing, teaching and learning: Report of a conference on research and testing.* Washington DC: U.S. Department of Health, Education and Welfare.

Pipho, C. (1978). Minimum competency testing in 1978: A look at state standards. *Phi Delta Kappan, 59,* 585–588.

Popham, W. J. (1987a). Can high-stakes tests be developed at the local level? *NASSP Bulletin, 71,* 77–84.

Popham, W. J. (1987b). The merits of measurement-driven instruction. *Phi Delta Kappan, 68,* 679–682.

Popham, W. J., Cruser, K. L., Rankin, S. C., Sandifer, P. S., & Williams, P. L. (1985). Measurement-driven instruction: It's on the road. *Phi Delta Kappan, 66,* 628–634.

Porter, A. (1988). Indicators: Objective data or political tool? *Phi Delta Kappan, 69,* 503–508.

Prell, J. M., & Prell, P. A. (1986). Improving test scores—teaching test-wiseness, a review of the literature. *Research Bulletin.* Bloomington, IN: Phi Delta Kappan.

Pullen, D. (1983). Debra P. v. Turlington: Judicial standards for assessing the validity of minimum competency tests. In G. F. Madaus (Ed.), *The courts, validity, and minimum competency testing* (pp. 3–19). Boston: Kluwer. Nizhoff.

Ravitch, D., & Finn, C. E. (1987). *What do our 17-year-olds know?* New York: Harper & Row.

Rudman, H. C. (1987). Classroom instruction and tests: What do we really know about the link? *NASSP Bulletin, 71,* 3–22.

Salmon-Cox, L. (1981). Teachers and standardized achievement tests: What's really happening. *Phi Delta Kappan, 62,* 631–634.

Scruggs, T. E., Bennion K., & White, K. R. (1986). Teaching test-taking skills to elementary-grade students: A meta-analysis. *The Elementary School Journal, 87,* 69–82.

Selden, R. W. (1988). Missing data: A progress report from the states. *Phi Delta Kappan, 69,* 492–494.

Sproull, L., & Zubrow, D. (1981). Standardized testing from the administrative perspective. *Phi Delta Kappan, 62,* 628–630.

Stedman, L. C. (1988). It's time we changed the effective schools formula. *Phi Delta Kappan, 69,* 215–224.

Suhor, C. (1985). Objective tests and writing samples: How do they affect instruction in composition? *Phi Delta Kappan, 66,* 635–639.

Taylor, B. L. (1974). Implications of the national assessment model for curriculum development and accountability. *Social Education, 38,* 404–408.

Tyler, R. W. (1950). *Basic principles of curriculum and instruction.* Chicago: University of Chicago Press.

United States Department of Education. (1989, May 10). State of Education Performance Chart, 1982 and 1988. *Education Week, 8,* 16–17.

Weiss, I. R. (1978). *National survey of science, mathematics, and social studies education.* Research Triangle Park, NC: Center for Educational Research and Evaluation.

Williams, P. L., & Moore, J. R. (Eds.). (1980). *Criterion-referenced testing for the social studies.* Washington DC: National Council for the Social Studies.

Wise, A. (1988). Legislated learning revisited. *Phi Delta Kappan, 69,* 328–333.

SCOPE AND SEQUENCE, GOALS, AND OBJECTIVES: EFFECTS ON SOCIAL STUDIES

William W. Joyce, Timothy H. Little, and Stanley P. Wronski

MICHIGAN STATE UNIVERSITY

What social studies subject matter should be taught in school? In what order should the knowledge, skills, and values of the subject matter be presented to students? This chapter explores various responses to these questions of scope and sequence as reported by social studies researchers.

Significant issues and practices regarding scope and sequence, goals and objectives have not been thoroughly researched. Indeed, as Ehman and Hahn (1981) allege, "We know little or nothing about whether the current scope and sequence is appropriate both to the logical development of the subject and to the psychological development of children" (p. 223). Despite this allegation, there are a variety of philosophical, historical, and conceptual writings that add an important qualitative dimension to an understanding of scope and sequence, goals, and objectives in social studies.

SCOPE AND SEQUENCE IN HISTORICAL PERSPECTIVE

The term *scope and sequence* is of relatively recent origin, having emerged prominently in the educational literature after World War II. But the idea of selecting subject matter for inclusion in a school curriculum and then placing it at successive grade levels has been an integral part of curriculum construction for all formal educational systems.

With respect to social studies instruction, the term *scope* "refers to the range of substantive content, values, skills, and/or learner experiences to be included in the social studies program" (Jarolimek, 1984, p. 252). *Sequence* refers to the order in which these elements occur in the curriculum. The relationship of scope and sequence to goals and objectives has been treated extensively in the social studies literature (Dynneson & Gross, 1986; Wesley & Wronski, 1973). The general consensus is that the determination of goals and objectives should precede and influence the selection of scope and sequence in deriving a social studies curriculum.

Research on scope and sequence is thus constrained by its dependent relationship to the subjective area of goals and objectives. There is no universally agreed upon frame of reference for determining the goals of social studies instruction (Beard, 1934). At the turn of the last century, the implicit goal of social studies instruction—mainly consisting of history, geography and civics—was to transmit knowledge (National Educational Association, 1894; American Historical Association, 1899, 1909). Beginning with the report of the Committee on Social Studies of the National Education Association (NEA, 1916), citizenship education has emerged as a major goal, and some argue the preeminent goal (Engle & Ochoa, 1986; Shaver & Knight, 1986), of social studies instruction. Concomitant with the citizenship emphasis there has emerged a third frame of reference stressing reflective inquiry (Fenton, 1966; Hullfish & Smith, 1961; Hunt & Metcalf, 1968). The historical roots of these three frames of reference have been examined by Barth and Shermis (1980a, 1980b).

The literature dealing with goals and objectives has been rooted in differing conceptual schemata, and the research emerging from these different schemata has not been congruent. For example, Peterson, Marx, and Clark (1978) found that teachers have varying perceptions of the *importance* of objec-

Reviewers were: O. L. Davis, Jr., University of Texas, Austin; Jean Fair, Professor Emeritus, Wayne State University. Lynn Siemsen assisted with the literature review.

tives and that they "rarely consider educational objectives" (p. 418). Nevertheless, with respect to the *effects* of objectives on student achievement, O'Brien, Meszaros, and Pulliam (1985) reported that "teacher uses of objectives during instruction were statistically significant predictors of student achievement" (p. 57).

Influential Committee and Commission Reports

Although its authors did not employ the term *scope and sequence,* the first significant, influential study dealing with this topic appeared in the late 19th century (NEA, 1894). The National Education Association's Committee of Ten organized a series of nine conferences, each of which dealt with some aspect of the total school curriculum from elementary through secondary grades, with the emphasis on Grades 5–12. The recommendation of the Conference on Physical Geography, Geology, and Meteorology reinforced the existing emphasis on physical geography in the school curriculum. The Conference on History, Civil Government, and Political Economy, which included the young Princeton professor Woodrow Wilson, made recommendations that were broader in scope and more influential on the curriculum. The following scope and sequence was proposed for Grades 5–12: Grade 5—biography and mythology; Grade 6—biography and mythology; Grade 7—American history and civil government; Grade 8—Greek and Roman history; Grade 9—French history as an approach to medieval and modern history; Grade 10—English history as an approach to medieval and modern history; Grade 11—American history; Grade 12—a special period of history selected for intensive study; civil government. The Committee of Ten did not make specific recommendations for subjects at the early elementary grade level, but it did suggest that civil government be taught at those grade levels by oral lessons.

The overall impact of the committee's report has been extensive and durable. The emphasis on Greek and Roman history at Grade 8, for example, later evolved into the more inclusive ancient history course that was a stable part of the curriculum well into the 20th century. More recently, in 1987, the revised social studies curriculum guidelines for the State of California (California State Department of Education, 1987) reinstated a heavy emphasis on biography and mythology at the elementary level. In the same year, the authors of the National Endowment for the Humanities *Report on the Humanities in the Nation's Public Schools* (Cheney, 1987) wrote rather wistfully and nostalgically about the report of the Committee of Ten and urged a similar curriculum, rich in biography and mythology, for contemporary schools.

For a quarter of a century after the appearance of the Committee of Ten report, the influence of the National Education Association was overshadowed by reports emanating from the American Historical Association. The most influential report, published in 1899 under the auspices of its Committee of Seven, dealt mainly with secondary schools, but the recommendations included Grade 3 and up at the elementary level. All subjects were to be taught in chronological order. From Grades 3 through 12 they included: stories from literature and legends; biographies of historical characters; Greek and Roman history to 800 A.D.; medieval and modern history; English history; American history; ancient history; medieval and modern European history from 800 to the present; English history and American history (including government).

Because the Committee of Seven did not address the full elementary program, in 1905 the American Historical Association appointed a Committee of Eight to make recommendations for the elementary grades that would be in harmony with the Committee of Seven's recommended secondary school program. The recommendations, published in 1909, included the following for both Grades 1 and 2: Indian life, Thanksgiving, Washington's birthday, local events.

The most significant scope and sequence report to affect the social studies curriculum in American schools appeared in 1916. It was prepared by the Committee on Social Studies of the NEA Commission on the Reorganization of Secondary Education. Among the Committee's salient characteristics were these: (a) Of its 21 members, 13 were employed as public school teachers or administrators. (b) It gave prominence and currency to the term *social studies.* (c) It asserted the radical notion that the social studies curriculum should be concerned with community problems as well as history. (d) It greatly loosened the almost exclusive hold that college academicians had over the school curriculum, thus challenging the idea that school subjects should be small-scale reproductions of their parent academic disciplines.

Again, the emphasis of this committee's report was on the secondary school curriculum, but it indirectly affected the elementary curriculum by stressing the cycle plan of organizing subject matter in which the junior and senior high schools would repeat subject matters areas that had supposedly been covered at the elementary level. Its specific recommendations for the junior high school were: Grade 7—geography, European history, civics; Grade 8—geography, American history, civics; Grade 9—civics, economic and vocational; economic history.

Provisions were also made in the report for flexibility and alternatives. For example, it was assumed that, at Grade 7, geography and European history would be taught for approximately one semester each, with civics introduced or infused once or twice a week. An alternative suggestion provided for European history as the core subject around which geography and civics would be correlated or integrated. Similar suggested alternatives were possible for Grades 8 and 9.

For the senior high school, the following recommendations were made: Grade 10—European history to 1700; Grades 11 and 12—European history since 1700 (a semester or a year); American history (one or a half year); problems of American democracy (a semester or a year).

The introduction of the course on problems of American democracy was a radical curricular innovation. The course was to deal with significant, on-going, contemporary social issues. Such courses became a part of the social studies curriculum in a substantial number of school systems until well into the 1950s.

More importantly, they provided a rough framework for the inquiry or problems-approach rationale (see Fenton, 1966) underlying many of the experimental programs of the New Social Studies in the 1960s and 1970s.

The reports of the various committees and commissions referred to above dealt with *both* the scope and sequence of the social studies curriculum. In the 1930s, the Commission on the Social Studies appointed by the American Historical Association examined extensively the *scope,* but not the sequence, of social studies in the schools. Its 16-volume report was the most extensive treatment to date of the symbiotic relationship between the social studies curriculum and the society of which it is a part.

The New Social Studies

In the late 1960s and early 1970s, over 100 experimental and innovative social studies programs were initiated. Many were subsidized by grants from the U.S. Office of Education and private foundations. Most did not speak to scope and sequence because they dealt with only one segment of the total curriculum either by virtue of a subject matter, grade level, or teaching method emphasis. One program (Capron, 1972) that did address scope and sequence was the University of Minnesota Project Social Studies. The sequence proposed was: Kindergarten—the earth as the home of man; Grades 1 and 2—families around the world; Grades 3 and 4—communities around the world; Grade 5—regional studies; Grade 6—United States history: from community to society; Grade 7—man and society; Grade 8—our political system; Grade 9—our economic system; Grade 10—American history; Grade 11—area studies; Grade 12—value conflicts and policy decisions.

The elementary (Grades 1 through 5) portion of the Minnesota Project Social Studies has been the subject of research studies. Implemented in the schools under the generic title, "The Family of Man," Grades 1–3 were studied by Mitsakos (1978) and Grades 1–5 by Skeel (1980). As for the overall topic of scope and sequence and its relation to goals and objectives, Mitsakos (1978) concluded, "An organized social studies curriculum that has well-defined objectives, specific materials, and some sequence achieves better results than a social studies program that is not well-defined or structured" (p. 13). The Skeel study (1980) confirmed the general findings of Mitsakos.

The Role of the National Council for the Social Studies

By the mid-1970s, the impact of the New Social Studies was beginning to subside (Haas, 1977). Reacting in part to "disappointment over the new social studies movement [and] dissatisfaction with and confusion over the back-to-basics movement" (Superka, Hawke, & Morrissett, 1980, p. 362), the National Council for the Social Studies in 1982 established a Task Force on Scope and Sequence. Their report, in which a "*holistic–interactive* approach to the selection and placement of content"

(Jarolimek, 1984, p. 253), was recommended, can be summarized as follows: Kindergarten—awareness of self in a social setting; Grade 1—the individual in primary social groups: understanding school and family life; Grade 2—meeting basic needs in nearby social groups: the neighborhood; Grade 3—sharing earth-space with others: the community; Grade 4—human life in varied environments: the region; Grade 5—people of the Americas: the United States and its close neighbors; grade 6—people and culture: the Eastern hemisphere; Grade 7—a changing world of many nations: a global view; Grade 8—building a strong and free nation: the United States; Grade 9—systems that make a democratic society work: law, justice, and economics; Grade 10—origins of major cultures: a world history; Grade 11—the maturing of America: United States history; Grade 12—one-year course or courses required; selections to be made from the following: issues and problems of modern society; introduction to the social sciences; the arts in human society; international area studies; social science elective courses: anthropology, economics, government, psychology, sociology; supervised experience in community affairs; local options.

The members of the task force stressed that their report was only preliminary and *illustrative,* that it dealt only with subject matter *content* and not skills, and that it was offered only as a *guide* for curriculum builders (*Jarolimek,* 1984, p. 253). Nevertheless, the report evoked considerable divergence of opinion. The NCSS Board of Directors "was reluctant to endorse a single scope-and-sequence that many thought controversial" (NCSS, 1989a, p. 375).

In response to continuing requests from teachers, administrators, publishers, and curriculum specialists that the National Council not abandon the quest for scope and sequence, a special issue of *Social Education* (November/December, 1986) was devoted to the topic. Rather than advocating a single or preferred scope and sequence the editor of the issue, Donald Bragaw, presented five alternative constructs. The central focus of each may be summarized as follows:

1. Time, space, and culture—with history and cultural geography providing the main integrative ingredient to the social studies curriculum (Downey, 1986).
2. Education for democratic citizenship—based on the assumption that the "key to a curriculum purporting to prepare citizens of a democracy is its capacity to encourage young citizens to think about and make considered decisions" (Engle & Ochoa, 1986, p. 514).
3. Social education for social transformation—with social transformation defined as "the continuing improvement of the society by applying social criticism and ethical decision making to social issues, and using the values of justice and equality as grounds for assessing the direction of social change that should be pursued" (Stanley & Nelson, 1986, p. 530).
4. Social studies within a global education—with the main conceptual themes of interdependence, change, culture, scarcity, and conflict (Kniep, 1986).
5. A social studies curriculum "based upon the assumption that specific scope and sequence decisions should be made by

local curriculum committees and teachers" (Hartoonian & Laughlin, 1986, p. 502).

Presentation of these five alternatives evoked additional discussion in the NCSS House of Delegates. In 1987, the House adopted a resolution requesting the NCSS Board of Directors to "carefully review existing NCSS statements of scope and sequence and endorse three alternative models" (NCSS, 1989a, p. 375). The board responded by establishing an Ad Hoc Committee on Scope and Sequence which published its report in October 1989. Unlike previously reported NCSS scope and sequence studies, the Ad Hoc Committee included a detailed list of 24 criteria that an ideal scope and sequence should meet. Although some of the criteria are generic to all areas of instruction (e.g., "recognize that learning is cumulative" and "be consistent with current research pertaining to how children learn"), others relate more specifically to social studies (e.g., "reflect a balance of local, national, and global content" and "emphasizing concepts from history and the social sciences") (NCSS, 1989a, pp. 375–376). Noticeably lacking from the criteria was any reference to the availability to the schools of instructional materials to implement the selected scope and sequence.

Even though they were more outlines for consideration than complete scope and sequences, three models were recommended by the NCSS Ad Hoc Committee: (a) the Task Force Model (NCSS, 1989b, pp. 376–387), a revision of Jarolimek (1984); (b) the Kniep (1989) model, emphasizing global education; and (c) the Hartoonian-Laughlin (1989) model. None of the models has been implemented in schools, so there are no research data on the effectiveness of any as a complete schema. That the NCSS Board of Directors could not agree on one model reflects the diversity of opinion among social studies educators on a desirable scope and sequence in social studies instruction.

THE EXPANDING COMMUNITIES APPROACH

The previous discussion underscores the stability of social studies curricula in U.S. schools, despite the proliferation of proposals for change. Hanna's expanding communities (1963) has been the prevailing scope and sequence design used in the vast majority of our nation's elementary grade social studies classes. Basic to this approach, alternatively referred to as "expanding environments" or "expanding horizons," is the premise that "children usually learn better about real things and life around them than about abstract topics that they cannot see or feel" (Chapin & Messick, 1989, p. 23).

The immediate world of children is the focal point of the expanding communities. In the primary grades, family, neighborhood, and local communities are studied in succession. As children grow older, they continue to study increasingly remote, abstract communities: the home state in Grade 4, the United States in Grade 5, and the Western or Eastern hemisphere or world cultures in Grade 6 or 7. Several studies report a trend toward using more urban illustrations when the United States is taught and adding content on the teaching of families

and communities in other nations (Ehman & Hahn, 1981; Wiley, 1977).

The scope of the expanding communities approach has been subjected to extensive analysis. Naylor and Diem (1987) questioned the underlying assumption that children are most familiar with their immediate environment and that their frames of reference are confined to it. They contended that such an assumption fails to consider, for example, the impact of television and other media on the lives of children.

Criticisms have also been directed at the sequence of the expanding communities model. It has been criticized for being too age-grade-oriented (Baskerville & Sesow, 1976), for failing to provide for the teaching of issues of immediate concern to children (Joyce & Alleman-Brooks, 1982), and for its philosophical grounding in developmental psychology (Akenson, 1989; Ravitch, 1987). Welton and Mallan (1981) claimed that the model stresses the logic of adults, not of children. They contended that the home state is as complex an abstraction for children as the nation and questioned why children should be required to study their state before their nation.

As the expanding communities model continues to dominate the elementary social studies curriculum, so also U.S. history in Grade 8, civics in Grade 9, world history in Grade 10, U.S. history in Grade 11, and government in Grade 12 continue to constitute the prevailing secondary pattern. Textbooks have contributed to the domination of the expanding communities model as well as these secondary school subjects. The power of textbooks is illustrated by a summary of National Science Foundation studies (Shaver, Davis, & Helburn, 1978) in which they are referred to as "the central instrument of instruction" (p. 151). Schneider and VanSickle's survey of publishers (1979) documented the longevity of the topics presented in textbooks and approaches used in teaching social studies throughout the United States.

THE SOCIAL ROLES MODEL

The New Social Studies movement of the 1960s and 1970s spawned a variety of projects intended to revitalize the social studies (Sanders & Tanck, 1970). Most of these efforts focused on one or several grade levels and so did not speak directly to issues of scope and sequence. Two projects with a grades K–12 emphasis were the Minnesota Social Studies Project (described earlier in this chapter) and the later Social Roles Model (Superka & Hawke, 1982).

Created under the auspices of the Social Science Education Consortium in the late 1970s, the Social Roles Model stressed social participation by students. Basic to this K–12 curriculum design are seven roles that people perform throughout their lives: citizen, worker, consumer, family member, friend, member of various social groups, and self. According to Stanley (1985), proponents of the social roles model claim that compared to other models, this design is more relevant and motivating for students (presumably because the seven social roles relate to and are intended to be taught within the context of the experiences of students), provides a basis for content selection and enhancing instructional practices, and provides a coherent way of organizing the curriculum by synthesizing the best of extant rationales in a manner congruent with the culture of the school. Further, they claim that this synthesis should strengthen public support for schools because of its appeal to liberals and conservatives.

Though the social roles model has been praised for its blend of various curricular orientations into a feasible conception of social studies (Patrick, 1980), it has been vigorously challenged. Shaver (1980) claimed that this construct was deficient on two counts: It was merely a restatement of the life adjustment curriculum of the 1950s and it did not clarify the citizenship role of the social studies. Helburn (1980) attacked the universality of the seven roles and the ideology behind them. In Helburn's opinion, the roles apply to industrial society, not to the many subsistence-level economies found in today's world. Also, she questioned whether the seven social roles will dominate the lives of people in the future. Unfortunately, the program lacks a research base.

AN OVERVIEW OF RESEARCH ON SCOPE IN THE SOCIAL STUDIES

Matters of topical content and pattern have received considerable attention in several surveys (Gross, 1977; Hahn, 1985; Morrissett, 1986; Superka et al., 1980). Herman (1988) found that some 66 percent of a sample of members of the Social Studies Supervisors Association reported that they had a "well defined and organized K–12 scope and sequence, 32 percent gave a negative response, and 2 percent did not complete the item". Results from the same study indicated that "the chief focus was content (73 percent), skills (13 percent), and affective domain (4 percent)". Given the emphasis on content instruction identified by Herman, questions of optimal scope in social studies instruction loom large on the educational agenda. In addition, specialized studies on the various forces which operate to shape the scope of social studies instruction appear with some frequency (Akenson & Neufeldt, 1986; Mehaffy, 1987; Nelson, 1986). Many of these narrowly focused studies will be treated individually in a later portion of this chapter.

A decade ago, Shaver (1979) asserted that "research to date is not a particularly useful source of prescriptions for schooling practices in social studies" (p. 40). Given the current state of controversy over the purposes of, and direction for, social studies (Brophy, 1988), it would be appropriate if more tightly focused research attention were aimed at scope/premise questions in social studies.

The Big Picture: Surveys of Scope in the Social Studies

In a 1980 report Superka, Hawke, and Morrissett reported the dominant scope and sequence pattern in American social studies to be: K—self, school, community, home; Grade 1—families; Grade 2—neighborhoods; Grade 3—communities; Grade 4—state history, geographic regions; Grade 5—U.S. history; Grade 6—world cultures, western hemisphere; Grade 7—world geography or history; Grade 8—American history; Grade

9—civics or world cultures; Grade 10—world history; Grade 11—American history; Grade 12—American government.

The above pattern of topical content may be seen as a remarkably resilient rock of tradition. Against this rock, in the recent past, have broken a series of reform movements such as the inquiry movement and the law-related education movement. While leaders of these movements have commonly called for a change in the topical content of the social studies, often the changes called for stem from alternate frames of reference and/or ideological assumptions about the purposes of social studies instruction. For example, the leaders of the law-related education movement tended to favor an increased emphasis in social studies instruction upon purveying commitment to values embedded within the law, most notably the Bill of Rights. That is, the new topical material called for by the reform leaders has been advocated not only for its intrinsic worth as knowledge, but also because these new materials have carried with them a cluster of political values. Research regarding the degree to which such waves of reform have eroded or affected the "rock of tradition" scope in the social studies curriculum is the focus of the remainder of this section.

If one considers the model of social studies scope and sequence cited by Superka, Hawke, and Morrissett (1980) as an archetype, what does research suggest about the trends and currents that might have affected that model? Gross (1977) reported that social studies as a field of study was in sharp decline in the primary grades. This suggests that one trend regarding the scope of social studies is its deemphasis or omission from the curriculum in the lower elementary grades.

Based on a survey of members of the Council of State Social Studies Specialists (CS4), Hahn (1985) indicated that "most advocates for change called for 'infusion' into existing courses rather than the substitution of one course for another.... The themes most often appearing were law studies, ethnic studies, and global studies" (p. 220). The same study revealed that "The biggest change since 1977 is that law programs are now in wider use than any of the 'new social studies' projects" (p. 221). Of major significance for this chapter, Hahn also found that "The most frequently mentioned concern was for revision of the social studies curriculum.... Some specifically called for guidance on scope and sequence" (p. 223).

Morrissett (1986) reported that "The dominant characteristic of social studies in the U.S. today—as is probably true of other areas of pre-college education—is prescriptive.... There are prescripts about what teachers must do and what students must do, and, to a lesser extent, what courses must do or be" (p. 304). Based upon a sample of CS4 members, Morrissett found that the "hot topics" being discussed by the education profession, legislators, and the public included: (a) global or international education, (b) world history, (c) economic education, (d) religion, creationism, or humanism, (e) geography, (f) nuclear questions, (g) environmental education, (h) peace education, (i) values and ethics, and (j) law-related education.

Only 2 out of the 10 topics cited by Morrissett as hot topics were included in the "rock of tradition" curriculum (history and geography) cited earlier. Each of the remaining topics has been, at one time or another, the subject of controversy and challenge. The explication and examination of the values and premises underlying the differing positions on each topic deserve further attention from researchers. The profiles of those who are advocating these prescriptions ought to be made the subject of research as well. Moreover, there has been little research as to the overall social agendas of the current generation of social studies "prescribers." The need to systematically examine the nature of the forces driving this new prescriptive era in social studies is dramatically underscored by the Morrissett finding that "the factor mentioned most frequently—by 13 states—as causing change at the local level is action to meet new requirements about courses or standards—mostly state standards (often but not always required) but also standards set locally" (p. 306).

Forces at Work Shaping the Scope of School Social Studies

There is a hazard in attempting to reduce the process by which social studies scope has been determined to be the sum of the forces identified as acting upon it. The social studies are likely to be more than the aggregate of discrete social, political, and economic forces that have influenced the curriculum. Such a mechanistic orientation can lead to an oversimplification of the development of patterns of scope in the social studies and to underplaying the role played by individual thinkers in its creation.

Despite the above disclaimer, it is still apparent that the scope of social studies in the 1980s has been influenced by a variety of forces acting independently and/or in concert. What are some of these forces, and what does research indicate about the role played by these alternate forces?

The Power of the Status Quo. Morrissett (1986) found some "moderate departures from the dominant pattern . . . of scope but found that . . . most patterns are still fairly close to the long-familiar pattern" (p. 306). Why? One hypothesis for the resistance to change that marks the social studies can be found in the inertia of textbook publishers, teachers, school districts, and the National Council for the Social Studies itself.

Social Studies as a Second-Tier Priority Subject Field. Another hypothesis to explain the continued entrenchment of the traditional model of social studies emanates from the second-class status attached to the subject field itself. Without the institutional imperatives and initiatives associated with front-line subjects such as reading and mathematics, there is little momentum to reexamine the social studies curriculum in general and its scope in particular. Collateral support for this explanation was provided by Akenson and Neufeldt (1986) in their study of adult schools in the South during the early quarter of the 20th century. They observed, "The role of social studies instruction within the southern literacy campaign proved secondary to primary objectives related to reading, computation, and a modernized South. Good citizenship, be it cleanliness or knowledge of government, played second fiddle to the overall purpose of bringing adults into the twentieth century" (p. 198). Simply put, the field of social studies has typically not had a

sufficiently high priority in the public eye to make imperative massive efforts at upgrading.

Societal Events and Trends as Shapers of the Scope of Social Studies. It can be argued that just as the U.S. Supreme Court is rumored to read the election results, social studies educators allow the contents of daily newspapers to creep into their thinking about the desired scope of the social studies. Certainly recent societal events and trends such as the civil rights movement of the 1960s, the emergence of an environmental protection lobby, and the back-to-basics movement have had some impact upon the way in which social studies teachers think about their craft and its scope. For example, *Social Education,* the official journal of the National Council for the Social Studies, commonly runs thematic issues in which subjects of general societal concern and debate are treated while featuring articles that describe or exhort efforts to infuse these topics into the social studies curriculum. The October 1986 issue of *Social Education,* featuring "Global Education: The Road Ahead", is an example of such efforts.

Mehaffy (1987) and Nelson (1986), in their respective studies of the impact of World War I and World War II upon the scope of the social studies curriculum, provided fascinating documentation of the manner in which compelling outside events can, by the very nature of their significance to the larger society, lead teachers to change the topical nature of social studies, albeit often temporarily.

Ideological Underpinnings of the Scope of Social Studies. The title of an article by Kickbusch (1985), "Ideological Innocence and Dialogue: A Critical Perspective on Discourse in the Social Studies," suggests a force in the determination of the scope of social studies that is infrequently addressed in the research literature: the dominant ideological assumptions of those who choose the topics to be taught and the fashion in which these topics will be treated. Put another way, Kickbusch argued that "Discourse about social studies education, then, has an ideological dimension, a dimension which relates the beliefs and attitudes expressed in that discourse to the material world" (p. 46).

The Role of Preservice Education in Fostering Change in the Scope of Social Studies Instruction. Jantz, Weaver, Cirrincione, and Farrell (1985) argued that one of the factors that contributed to the demise of the inquiry movement in social studies was a lack of adequate preservice teacher training in its use. They also suggested that preservice education limited as well as shaped the scope of social studies. Newly minted teachers may limit their conception of the proper scope of social studies instruction to those topics legitimated by their preservice courses and student teaching. This hypothesis clearly warrants research.

The Role of State Textbook Adoptions in the Determination of the Scope of Social Studies. "Twenty-three states adopt textbooks on a statewide basis. Texas and California, with Florida a close third, have more to do with what will be taught in a given subject area at a given level than any of the other 47 states' " (Schomburg, 1986, p. 58, quoting English, 1980). Given the above, understanding the role of state adoptions as determinants of scope within social studies is critical. Schomburg went on to note that the players involved in setting the criteria for textbook selection in Texas have included the state legislature, textbook companies, professional associations, advocates of a wide variety of organized social interest groups, and the appointed textbook committee itself. That the scope of the national social studies curriculum may be in large measure shaped by such a process represents an hypothesis worthy of major investigation.

The Academy Critique of Current Scope in Social Studies. Gagnon (1988), a professor of history, lauded the recent reforms of the California History-Social Science Framework by saying:

It restores history and geography to the center of the social studies program, where they belong. It more than doubles the time now spent on them in most American schools, so that vital ideas and events may be taught engagingly and in depth. (p. 36)

Critiques such as that by Gagnon suggest that the issues in conflict have as much to do with values as they do with the topics treated. In this case, the struggle is over more than how much history will be taught; the issue goes to the central purposes of social studies instruction in the schools. Critics of the "rock of tradition" scope and sequence pattern in social studies are interested in more than clock hours expended upon a given topic. The topics selected for study are important as much for the disciplinary frame of reference and attendant values that they carry with them as for their intrinsic knowledge base. For example, much of the impetus for expansion of the historical component within the social studies comes from the those who view the school as a purveyor of a common cultural heritage. However, the quest for cultural literacy quickly becomes mired in the matter of whose culture(s) and what kind of literacy. Research regarding the premises for social studies held by the various camps within the profession is clearly warranted if curriculum makers are to make informed choices about desired scopes for social studies curricula.

Thornton (1988) in an insightful review of another academic critique, that by Hirsch in his book, *Cultural Literacy: What Every American Needs to Know* (1987), made a key point regarding the willingness of the larger public to accept and to support external critiques of the status quo in social studies:

His [Hirsch's] argument, in broad outline, is persuasive, even difficult to dispute. Yet broad arguments can be all the more persuasive precisely because they provide apparently straightforward answers to long-standing and complex issues. (p. 244)

Ironically, perhaps, Thornton has targeted an area of weakness within the profession itself. As many social studies educators struggle to nurture their tree of specialization within the field (for example, law-related education), perhaps the forest of social studies scope and purpose has become clouded in the public mind. Rather than more studies on the efficacy of a third-

grade unit on community, what is needed are forest-level analyses, widely publicized, regarding the central purposes to which social studies should be dedicated in the 1990s. Prescriptions for the fine tuning of the social studies "rock of tradition" scope and sequence are frequent within the literature. As noted above, practically nonexistent are research-based calls for reconsideration and reform of social studies through the examination of premises and practices.

There appear to be at least three levels of criticism of the broad definition of scope for the social studies curriculum. At the first level are critiques such as the oft-quoted Tot Sociology analyses by Ravitch (1987). Such critics find current social studies content all too frequently topically vacuous and redundant. The proposed relief from this situation is commonly the substitution of another content base for the currently flawed scope and content.

A second level of criticism is provided by those who seek to factor out the variables that appear to interact within social studies instruction. The FitzGerald work, *America Revised* (1979), serves as a popular example of that effort. In this vein, Egan (1980) began an article on John Dewey and social studies instruction with the admonition:

The Social Studies curriculum does not work. It does not work conceptually, and it is not working in practice. Conceptually it lacks the logical and psychological principles necessary to give it a coherent structure. In practice, surveys consistently show it to be the least popular subject with students, and show, among school leavers and college freshmen, massive ignorance of even its most basic subject matter. (p. 37)

At this level, what is called for is investigation of the interplay of topical content (scope), format of presentation, and principles of learning in the successful teaching of social studies.

There is a third level of scope-related criticism by social studies professionals, exemplified by Kickbusch's (1985) observation that:

Critical theory, recognizing the ideological dimensions of schooling, illuminates the contradictions and tensions among the idealized goals of social studies education and the socializing functions of social studies classrooms (p. 45).

Social studies researchers at this level tend to focus upon the tendency for choices, from scope to presentation format, to be political acts. Indeed, Kickbusch argued that:

Current discourse about the qualitative state of social studies education has continued the traditional, largely apolitical pattern of dialogue which has characterized such work in the past . . . an ideological innocence pervades the work. (p. 53)

Analyses such as Kickbusch's suggest the need for investigations of the degree to which politicization has explicitly or, more likely, implicitly influenced decisions about scope in the social studies.

SEQUENCE AND HISTORY TEACHING

Typically, social studies sequences reflect a sense of logical progression: from near to far, familiar to unfamiliar, simple to complex. According to Akenson (1989), an early discernible view of sequence in social studies was embodied in the recapitualization theory of the Herbartians. The theory held that childhood developed through a series of cultural epochs; as children matured, they passed through stages comparable to the evolution of the human species. Young children were usually taught about Indian and African cultures and other groups believed to be simple and uncomplicated. Older children studied American and European cultures believed to be far more complex and sophisticated. Thus the complexity of the culture studied was believed to be congruent with the child's stage of maturation. The cultural epoch theory, though supplanted by later psychological and philosophical conceptions of sequence, was an important precursor of the expanding communities sequence (Akenson, 1989).

Other conceptions of sequence can be identified. Selecting fewer topics for instruction and teaching them in greater depth was a common element in the New Social Studies projects. This idea, often called "postholing" was used by Taba (1967), who advocated teaching basic concepts such as interdependence by spiraling them on successively higher levels of abstraction throughout the elementary and middle school. This approach is not without its weaknesses. Chapin and Messick (1989) alleged that teachers should ensure "that students actually are spiraling through higher levels of abstraction and not just repeating topics such as 'community workers' or 'food' " (p. 24).

Mandates for Practice

Proponents of various sequential frameworks have drawn on psychological theory and research in explicating their views on social studies instruction and curriculum development. But are these educators justified in relying on such knowledge as prescribers of practice? Shaver (1979) alleged that empirical knowledge and theory provide a tenuous mandate for practice. He cited the tendency of educators to misapply Piaget's research to moving children through the cognitive stages as quickly as possible, in an effort to accelerate the learning of conservation concepts. In a second example, he criticized an attempt to link deficits in children's knowledge of political institutions with prescriptions for sequencing. These caveats reiterate the importance of carefully reviewing the prescriptive implications of research findings before applying them to practice.

The problem of using research and theory to mandate practice is illustrated by the current debate on the teaching of history in our schools. The role of history in the curriculum, when this subject should be taught, and how historical subject matter should be organized and taught have been addressed by critics representing disparate views, including the Bradley Commission (1988), Ravitch and Finn (1987), Newmann (1988), and Downey (1986).

The Development of Historical Thinking

Theory and research on the teaching of history in our schools reflect conflicting views on when history should be taught purposefully to students. One view—essentially Piage-

tian—holds that overall cognitive development is the prime determiner of historical understanding. This view is represented by Hallam's research (1970, 1979), from which he reported that children are limited in their historical reasoning prior to reaching Piaget's formal operations stage (about age 12 or 13). It is significant to note that though this British researcher sought to apply Piagetian theory to the learning of history, his subjects attained the stages of concrete operations five to six years later than Piaget's subjects. Similarly, Hallam's subjects reached the formal operations stage at about age 16, or four years later than Piaget's subjects. Hallam's efforts to accelerate the cognitive development of children met with mixed results (Downey & Levstik, 1988).

Hallam is only one of many advocates of developmental approaches to the teaching and learning of history. Booth (cited in Downey & Levstik, 1980) claimed that no fewer than 24 theses and dissertations applying Piagetian theory to history learning were completed in Great Britain between 1955 and 1980. But more remarkable, these and other studies of historical learning have been based on Piagetian research on student learning *in mathematics and science, not in social studies.*

Other educators have examined issues of sequence regarding the teaching of history and other elements of the social studies. Sleeper (1975), basing his views on the work of Erik Erikson, claimed that adolescence is the best time to begin history instruction. He argued that, as adolescents examine events of their past in terms of the present and future, they develop a sense of identity embracing their own personal histories. Presumably this is the time when students are more sensitive to serious study of historical issues.

Kennedy (1983) claimed that information-processing theory helps to explain historical reasoning. Others have questioned the applicability of universal cognitive theories in general and advocated the cognitive structures specific to the discipline (Downey & Levstik, 1988). Shulman (1974) and Ehman and Hahn (1981) stressed the importance of learning hierarchies. "We need to know . . . which concepts are prerequisite to other concepts in learning sequences and whether certain inquiry skills are prerequisite to other inquiry skills" (p. 77). Armento (1986) asserted that the structure of the discipline approach to organizing subject matter (popularized by the New Social Studies) is being questioned by economics educators, who favor a child development approach.

Downey and Levstik (1988) advocated history teaching based on both a developmental and a history-based, domain-specific approach. In their opinion, courses are needed in which sufficient time is devoted to a particular topic or period to establish an adequate context for the learning of history. The nonsurvey or "discontinuous syllabus" of the Schools Council History 13–16 Project in Great Britain is among the more carefully researched attempts to achieve this goal. This curriculum consisted of an introductory course on the nature of history as a discipline, a course on modern issues, an in-depth course on a single historical period, a topical survey course on the history of human medicine and a local history course (Downey & Levstik, 1988). Shemilt (1980) reported that students enrolled in the 13–16 Project favored the new curriculum over the traditional one by a wide margin. The students "saw history as an explanation seeking discipline that had great personal relevance to them. They also judged it to be a more difficult subject than mathematics" (Shemilt, quoted by Downey & Levstik, 1988, p. 340).

Despite the encouraging reports on the 13–16 Project, it is important to bear in mind that empirical evidence gleaned from this and other projects may not provide a defensible mandate for practice. The California History-Social Science Framework (1987) provides a singularly relevant illustration. If there is any dominant, overarching theme in this curriculum design, it is the pervasive influence of history. Starting in kindergarten, children are to be taught to develop a "beginning sense of historical empathy" by learning about events in the past. In Grade 1 they learn about cultural diversity now and long ago, and in Grade 2 they pursue comparative studies drawn from the past as they learn of the domestication of wild grasses in early Mesopotamia and are inducted into the historical method. Much of this early instruction in history is to be presented by fairy tales and folk tales, fables, legends, biographies, poetry, and stories.

Using children's literature as a vehicle to induct very young children into the study of history may, indeed, have merit. Yet in the absence of relevant research attesting to the value of this approach, one is compelled to question whether it deserves to be followed in our public schools. Indeed, even such researchers as Downey and Levstik (1988), who claimed that children know more about time concepts and history than had previously been thought and who advocated earlier experience with history, have urged educators to proceed with caution.

PROMISING AREAS OF RESEARCH

A number of areas of research pertaining to scope and sequence appear to hold promise for future investigation:

1. How responsive have social studies educators been, when planning curricular innovations, to external events within the general society?

2. To what degree do state adoptions of textbooks shape social studies scope and sequence? How are state textbook adoption decisions made?

3. To what degree do, or will, state-level achievement tests control the scope and sequence of the social studies? What training and/or experience in teaching the social studies do the test developers possess?

4. If some social studies critics are correct in their assertion that battles over scope and sequence are subsets of larger struggles over ideology, are there models of successful mediation of such controversies that maintain the opportunity for intellectual as well as cultural pluralism?

5. Given the current attention to the inclusion of women and minorities in the social studies, to what degree has this attention been manifested in institutionalized changes in scope and/or sequence?

6. To what extent do "thought police," representing a wide spectrum of special interest groups, limit the ideas available in the social studies by virtue of their power over the nature of textbooks and mandated curricula?

7. What are the value proclivities of the various proposed models of scope for the social studies? To what extent are the values contained therein at variance with those of "the rock of tradition" scope and sequence?

8. What evidence exists in the child development literature that might offer guidance in the development of future, or the validation of current, social studies scope-and-sequence plans?

9. What does research suggest about conscious efforts to develop a discrete values strand in the social studies curriculum?

10. What conditions must be met in order for the research on a given approach to scope and sequence to be regarded as a legitimate mandate for practice?

11. When is the most desirable time for students to begin the study of history? How should important concepts and skills be sequenced?

References

Akenson, J. E. (1989). The expanding environments and elementary education: A critical perspective. *Theory and Research in Social Education, 17,* 33–52.

Akenson, J. E., & Neufeldt, H. G. (1986). The social studies component of the southern literacy campaign: 1915–1930. *Theory and Research in Social Education, 14* (3), 187–200.

American Historical Association (1899). *The study of history in schools: Report to the American Historical Association by the Committee of Seven.* New York: Macmillan.

American Historical Association. (1909). *The study of history in elementary schools: Report to the American Historical Association by the Committee of Eight.* New York: Scribner.

Armento, B. J. (1986). Promoting economic literacy. In S. P. Wronski and D. M. Bragaw (Eds.), *Social studies and social sciences: A fifty year perspective,* Bulletin No. 78 (pp. 97–110). Washington, DC: National Council for the Social Studies.

Barth, J. L., & Shermis, S. (1980a). Nineteenth century origins of the social studies movement: Understanding the continuity between older and contemporary civic and U.S. history textbooks. *Theory and Research in Social Education, 8*(3), 29–50.

Barth, J. L., & Shermis, S. S. (1980b). Social studies goals: The historical perspective. *Theory and Research and Development in Education, 13*(2), 1–11.

Baskerville, R. A., & Sesow, F. W. (1976). In defense of Hanna and the "expanding communities" approach to social studies. *Theory and Research in Social Education, 4*(1), 20–32.

Beard, C. A. (1934). *The nature of the social sciences in relation to objectives of instruction.* New York: Scribners.

The Bradley Commission on History in the Schools. (1988). *Resolutions of the commission; Steps towards excellence in the social history curriculum.* Westlake, OH: Author.

Brophy, J. (1988). *Higher order thinking and problem solving in social studies.* Institute for Research on Teaching, Michigan State University, East Lansing.

California State Department of Education. (1987). *History-social science framework*. Sacramento, CA: Author.

Capron, B. J. (1972). University of Minnesota Project Social Studies. *Social Education, 36,* 758–759.

Chapin, J. R., & Messick, R. G. (1989). *Elementary social studies.* New York: Longman.

Cheney, L. V. (1987). *American memory: A report on the humanities in the nation's public schools.* Washington, DC: National Endowment for the Humanities.

Downey, M. T. (1986). Time, space and culture. *Social Education, 50,* 490–501.

Downey, M. T., & Levstik, L. S. (1988). Teaching and learning history: The research base. *Social Education, 52,* 336–342.

Dynneson, T. L., & Gross, R. E. (1986). A century of encounter. *Social Education, 50,* 486–488.

Egan, K. (1980). John Dewey and the social studies curriculum. *Theory and Research in Social Education. 8,* 37–55.

Ehman, L. J., & Hahn, C. L. (1981). Contributions of research to social studies education. In H. D. Mehlinger and O. L. Davis, Jr., (Eds.), *The social studies.* Eightieth yearbook of the National Society for the Study of Education, Part II (pp. 60–81). Chicago: University of Chicago Press.

Engle, S. H., & Ochoa, A. (1986). A curriculum for democratic citizenship. *Social Education, 50,* 514–524.

Fenton, E. F. (1966). *Teaching the new social studies: An inductive approach.* New York: Holt, Rinehart & Winston.

FitzGerald, F. (1979). *America revised.* Boston: Little, Brown.

Gagnon, P. (1988). A look at the new California framework: Turning point for social studies reform? *American Educator, 12,* 36–38.

English, R. (1980). The politics of textbook adoption. *Phi Delta Kappan, 61,* 275–278.

Gross, R. E. (1977). The status of the social studies in the public schools of the United States: Facts and impressions of a national survey. *Social Education, 41*(3) 194–200.

Haas, J. D. (1977). *The era of the new social studies.* Boulder, CO: Social Science Education Consortium.

Hahn, C. E. (1985). The status of the social studies in the public schools of the United States: Another look. *Social Education, 49*(3), 220–223.

Hallam, R. N. (1970). Piaget and thinking in history. In M. Ballard (Ed.), *New movements in the study and teaching of history.* Bloomington: Indiana University Press.

Hallam, R. N. (1979). Attempting to improve logical thinking in school history. *Research in Education, 21,* 1–24.

Hanna, P. R. (1963). Revising the social studies: What is needed. *Social Education, 27,* 190–196.

Hartoonian, H. M., & Laughlin, M. A. (1986). Designing a scope and sequence. *Social Education, 50,* 502–512.

Hartoonian, H. M., & Laughlin, M. A. (1989). Designing a social studies scope and sequence for the 21st century. *Social Education, 53,* 385, 388–398.

Helburn, S. W. (1980). Reactions. *Social Education, 44,* 592, 652–653.

Herman, W. L., Jr. (1988). Development of scope and sequence: A survey of school districts. *Social Education, 52,* 385–388.

Hirsch, E. D., Jr. (1987). *Cultural literacy: What every American needs to know.* Boston: Houghton Mifflin.

Hullfish, H. G., & Smith, P. G. (1961). *Reflective thinking: The method of education.* New York: Dodd, Mead.

Hunt, M. P., & Metcalf, L. E. (1968). *Teaching high school social studies: Problems in reflective thinking and social understanding* (2nd ed.). New York: Harper & Row.

Jantz, R. K., Weaver, V. P., Cirrincione, J. M., & Farrell, R. T. (1985). Inquiry and curriculum change: Perceptions of school and college/ university faculty. *Theory and Research in Social Education, 13*(2), 61–72.

Jarolimek, J. (1984). In search of a scope and sequence for social studies: Report of the National Council for the Social Studies Task Force on Scope and Sequence. *Social Education, 48,* 249–262.

Joyce, W. W., & Alleman-Brooks, J. E. (1982). The child's world. *Social Education, 46,* 538–541.

Kennedy, K. (1983). Assessing the relationship between information processing capacity and historical understanding. *Theory and Research in Social Education, 11,* 5, 16.

Kickbusch, K. W. (1985). Ideological innocence and dialogue: A critical perspective on discourse in the social studies. *Theory and Research in Social Education, 13*(3), 45–56.

Kniep, W. M. (1986). Social studies within a global education. *Social Education, 50,* 536–542.

Kniep, W. M. (1989). Social studies within a global education. *Social Education, 53,* 385, 399–403.

Mehaffy, G. L. (1987). Social studies in World War I: A period of transition. *Theory and Research in Social Education, 15*(1), 23–52.

Mehlinger, H. D. (1981). Social studies: Some gulfs and priorities. In H. D. Mehlinger & O. L. Davis, Jr. (Eds.), *The social studies.* 80th Yearbook of the National Society for the Study of Education (Part II, pp. 19–35). Chicago: University of Chicago Press.

Mitsakos, C. L. (1978). A global education program can make a difference. *Theory and Research in Social Education, 6*(1), 1–15.

Morrissett, I. (1986). Status of social studies: The mid-1980s. *Social Education, 50*(4), 303–310.

National Council for the Social Studies. (1989a). Report of the Ad Hoc Committee On Scope and Sequence. *Social Education, 53,* 375–376.

National Council for the Social Studies. (1989b). In search of a scope and sequence for social studies: Report of the Task Force on Scope and Sequence. *Social Education, 53,* 376–387.

National Education Association. (1894). *Report of the Committee of Ten.* New York: American Book Company.

National Education Association Commission on the Reorganization of Secondary Education. (1916). *The social studies in secondary education.* Washington, DC: U.S. Bureau of Education Bulletin, 28.

Naylor, D. T., & Diem, R. H. (1987). *Elementary and middle school social studies.* New York: Random House.

Nelson, M. R. (1986). Some possible effects of World War II on the social studies curriculum. *Theory and Research in Social Education, 14*(4), 267–275.

Newmann, F. M. (1988). Can depth replace coverage in the high school curriculum? *Phi Delta Kappan, 69,* 345–348.

O'Brien, L. M., Meszaros, B., & Pulliam, W. E. (1985). Effects of teachers' use of objectives on student achievement in social studies. *Theory and Research in Social Education, 13*(3), 57–65.

Patrick, J. J. (1980). Reactions. *Social Education, 44,* 588–589.

Peterson, P. L., Marx, R. W., & Clark, C. M. (1978). Teacher planning, teacher behavior, and student achievement. *American Educational Research Journal, 15*(3), 417–432.

Ravitch, D. (1987). Tot sociology or what happened to history in the grade schools. *American Scholar, 56,* 343–353.

Ravitch, D., & Finn, C. E. (1987). *What do our 17-year-olds know?* New York: Harper & Row.

Sanders, N. M., and Tanck, M. L. (1970). A critical appraisal of twenty-six national social studies projects. *Social Education, 34,* 338–449.

Schneider, D. O., & VanSickle, R. L. (1979). The status of the social studies: The publishers' perspective. *Social Education, 43,* 461–465.

Schomberg, C. E. (1986). Texas and social studies texts. *Social Education, 50,* 58–60.

Shaver, J. P. (1979). The usefulness of educational research in curricular/instructional decision making in social studies. *Theory and Research in Social Education, 7*(3), 21–46.

Shaver, J. P. (1980). Reactions. *Social Education, 44,* 590–591.

Shaver, J. P., Davis, O. L., Jr., & Helburn, S. W. (1978). *An interpretive report on the status of pre-college social studies education based on three NSF-funded studies.* Washington, DC: National Council for the Social Studies. (ERIC Document Reproduction Service No. ED 164 363)

Shaver, J. P., & Knight, R. S. (1986). Civics and government in citizenship education. In Wronski, S. P., and Bragaw, D. H. (Eds.), *Social studies and social sciences: A fifty year perspective.* Bulletin No. 78 (pp. 124–138). Washington, DC: National Council for the Social Studies.

Shemilt, D. (1980). *History 13–16: Evaluation study.* Edinburgh: Holmes McDougall.

Shulman, L. S. (1974). The psychology of school subjects: A premature obituary. *Journal of Research in Science Teaching, 11,* 319–339.

Skeel, D. J. (1980). *Final report presented to the Department of Education, Tennessee State Network Project for Cultural Understandings for Global Citizens.* Nashville: Department of Education.

Sleeper, M. E. (1975). A developmental framework for history education in adolescence. *School Review, 84,* 91–107.

Stanley, W. B. (1985). Recent research in the foundations of social education: 1976–1983. In W. B. Stanley (Ed.), *Review of research in social studies education: 1976–1983* (pp. 310–399). Washington, DC: National Council for the Social Studies.

Stanley, W. B., & Nelson, T. (1986). Social education for social transformation. *Social Education, 50,* 528–533.

Superka, D. P., & Hawke, S. (1982). *Social roles: A focus for social studies in the 1980s.* Boulder, CO: Social Science Education Consortium.

Superka, D. P., Hawke, S., & Morrissett, I. (1980). The current and future status of social studies. *Social Education, 44,* 362–369.

Taba, H. (1967). *Teachers' handbook for elementary social studies.* Reading, MA: Addison-Wesley.

Thornton, S. J. (1988). Review of *Cultural literacy: What every American needs to know. Theory and Research in Social Education, 16*(3), 244–248.

Welton, D., & Mallan, J. (1981). *Children and their world.* Boston: Houghton Mifflin.

Wesley, E. B., & Wronski, S. P. (1973). *Teaching secondary social studies in a world society* (6th ed.), Lexington, MA: Heath.

Wiley, K. B. (1977). *Social science education: Vol. 3 of The status pre-college science, mathematics, and social science education: 1955–1975.* Report to the National Science Foundation. Boulder, CO: Social Science Education Consortium.

·27·

COMMUNITIES, LOCAL TO NATIONAL, AS INFLUENCES ON SOCIAL STUDIES EDUCATION

Jack L. Nelson

RUTGERS UNIVERSITY

Social education, the broader purpose of social studies instruction in schools, is especially sensitive to community interests and influence. Communities are the subject of social studies inquiry, as well as the locations where social studies is taught. The positive value of community is expressed in social studies education, but critical and conflicting community values are also explored in social studies. Historical disputes, contemporary issues, and debates over the future of all forms of community are part of social studies, as are community concepts of knowledge, values, skills, behaviors, myth, and critique.

Social education has the dual, and often contradictory, purposes of transmitting socially approved ideas and of developing critical thinking and reasoned decision-making. Competing community interests encourage both the social criticism necessary for progress and the social pressure to preserve community traditions. Social studies is, therefore, controversial and subject to efforts to influence it (Engle & Ochoa, 1988; Fraenkel, 1973; Hunt & Metcalf, 1968; Nelson & Carlson, 1981; Nelson & Michaelis, 1980; Oliver & Shaver, 1966/1974; Rugg, 1937). Social studies education is a matter of great community concern because of its centrality in the development and testing of cultural, ideological, and political knowledge (Gilbert, 1984).

The controversial nature of social studies makes it a target for those who want to influence the knowledge, values, and behaviors of the young. Citizenship, one of the oft-stated goals for social studies, is "part of a historical tradition that represents a terrain of struggle over the forms of knowledge, social practices and values that constitute the critical elements of that tradition." (Giroux, 1988a, p. 5)

NORMATIVE PURPOSES OF SOCIAL EDUCATION

Social education is often justified in schools as a means for producing "good" citizens, referring to acceptable student behaviors and values that support social norms. Many community efforts to influence social studies instruction follow from these normative purposes and are aimed at controlling the ideas provided in the curriculum, textbooks, teacher presentations, and other materials.

Theoretical grounds for the social studies, whether stated by those identified as traditionalists or progressives, incorporate normative intention (Beard, 1932; Engle & Ochoa, 1988; Leming, 1985, 1987; Newmann, 1975, Shaver, 1977; Stanley, 1981). The normative ideas used in social studies, however, are often in conflict. There are efforts to instill nationalistic patriotism while developing multicultural and global perspectives, to encourage participation in the reconstruction of society while developing support for stable traditions, to emancipate people from social oppression while teaching them to fit in, to develop acceptable conforming attitudes of character while stimulating critical and independent thinking. There is considerable dispute over what norms ought to be taught and whose interests are to be served in social education. The normative intentions of various communities lead to an ideologically based selection of values, data, and behaviors to be expressed or suppressed in social studies instruction. Social education is the site of contests for a variety of communities (Apple, 1979; Aronowitz & Giroux, 1985; Cherryholmes, 1978; Giroux, 1988a, 1988b; Stanley, 1981).

Reviewers were: Kenneth Carlson, Rutgers University; Stuart B. Palonsky, University of Missouri, Columbia.

COMMUNITY, IDEOLOGY, AND INFLUENCE

Cohen (1985) suggested that "the concept of community has been one of the most compelling and attractive themes in modern social science, and at the same time one of the most elusive to define" (p. 7). Community includes political and cultural geography as well as such characteristics as size and valence (Eggleston, 1977; Giroux, 1983; Mills, 1956; Oliver, 1976). Community can involve territorial and political structures such as neighborhood, village, city, and nation, as well as human relations structures without reference to a particular location, such as suggested in a "community of scholars" (Gustfield, 1975). Communities have boundaries, on maps or in the mind, within which there are differing cultural factors such as language, rituals, ceremonies, ideologies, and symbols.

Communities can vary in size from a global community to a two-person community of dialogue, and can be ascribed positive or negative valence. A community can be viewed as positive in social studies when it is seen as a valuable resource for instruction (Schug & Beery, 1984), or when a sense of community exists among teachers and students in a school (Dewey, 1916). Community can be seen as negative when community members or groups exert control over or attempt to censor what is taught (Beale, 1936; Nelson & Ochoa, 1987). The idea of "lost community," where individualism, alienation, and isolation have destroyed shared social values, presumes the positive valence of community as a preferred state; school is expected to restore community (Oliver, 1976; Popkewitz, 1984).

Communities are changing environments that affect schools and schooling, including the internal community of the school itself, as ethnographic and case studies in schools demonstrate (Cusick, 1973; Jackson 1968; Palonsky 1986). These environments are ideological, involving language, behaviors, and symbols; and they include individuals and groups involved in the use and distribution of power (Kamenka, 1982). This definition of community, although vague and complex, reflects the dynamic and often disparate means and ends involved in community attempts to influence what is included in or excluded from social education.

Ideology includes shared beliefs resulting from membership in communities based on attributes such as social class, gender, race or national origin, and age. Ideology is also an element of interest groups such as labor unions, the American Medical Association, a taxpayers league, the American Civil Liberties Union, and the American Manufacturers Association. Groups of historians, social scientists, social education scholars, or social studies teachers represent other communities that want to influence the content or methodology of social studies toward their beliefs. Another community includes those involved in critical education, expressing such ideas as the neo-Marxist concept of "collective commitment" (Apple, 1979), the emancipatory vision of "communities of resistance" to oppressive forces in the society (Giroux, 1988a, 1988b), and the idea of discourse as dialectical communication that can lead toward community (Cherryholmes, 1982).

Not only are the purposes, content, and approach of instruction in social studies subject to influence, the study of influence is itself a social studies topic. Banfield (1961) provided a standard definition of influence as the "ability to get others to act, think or feel as one intends." (p. 3). Social studies includes the examination of influence through study of politics, leadership and group dynamics, propaganda analysis, and free speech. Attempts to influence social education can themselves be studied as social studies content. Some social studies scholars advocate extension of this work to the development of "environmental competence" (Newmann, 1975), with students to be taught the means to influence their communities.

Influence may be either overt or covert. Among the overt forms of community influence on social studies instruction are legal regulation and public acts of political pressure, persuasion, censorship, and threat. Covert means can involve the weight of tradition, economic and social pressures, teacher self-censorship, and ostracism. Influence can also be categorized in terms of intentions: imposition, those efforts to insert certain ideas into social education, and exclusion, those efforts to censor or restrict certain ideas from being included in social education. And influence, like community, has a valence; it is perceived as positive or negative depending on the circumstances and the agency of influence (Deutsch & Gerard, 1955; Kaplan & Miller, 1987).

Influence and the Impact of Social Studies on Students

Efforts by communities to influence social education would not be sensible if social studies had no impact on students. Litt (1963), however, found that students who had taken civics courses were more likely to endorse democratic ideals and less likely to hold chauvinistic political sentiments than students who did not have formal education in civics. This suggests that formal social education has some measurable impact on students' political views.

Early research on political socialization seemed to indicate that there was virtually no impact of the civics curriculum on the political knowledge and attitudes of students (Greenstein, 1965; Hess & Torney, 1967; Jennings & Neimi, 1981; Langton & Jennings, 1968). These studies were based largely on gross analyses of large-scale questionnaire surveys and were criticized for having serious methodological and theoretical defects (Button, 1974; Ehman 1969, 1980; Goldenson, 1978; Hepburn, 1980). If this line of research had been confirmed in more sophisticated experimental and longitudinal studies, efforts at community influence would have no great purpose; but that did not occur, and this remains an area open to further and improved scholarship.

Contexts of Community Influence

Community influence on social studies exists within a cultural and ideological context. Culture, including language and social education, includes elements that derive from communities based on such factors as social class, gender, race, and nationality.

Litt (1963) examined civic education textbooks, interviewed key influential people in schools and the community, and surveyed students in civics classes in three Boston secondary schools in three different socioeconomic communities. He found differences among the communities in the political attitudes and beliefs expressed in civic education and expected by community leaders. More active and participatory decision-making was stressed in the schools of the more affluent areas than in the schools in the working-class area. Anyon's (1978) study of six elementary schools in an urban area also showed that social class differences in communities surrounding the schools were reflected in differences in social studies content, pedagogy, and teacher expectations.

Labov (1966, 1972, 1987), in linguistic studies of speech patterns in urban areas, found that social polarities are expressed in the language used and the concept of literacy adopted by the school. These polarities included: White versus African-American, middle class versus working class, female versus male, high versus popular culture, and submission to authority versus resistance. Ogbu (1982, 1987) identified "oppositional identity" and "oppositional cultural frames of reference" among minority youth as emerging from cultural and linguistic divergence, complicating the forms and perceptions of social education. Bernstein (1976), in studies of language use in England, found class-based differences with language used as a form of social control. Graff (1979) traced the history of literacy movements in Canada and the United States and documented the imposition of a dominant social morality through the influence of religious and political communities. He found that differences in class, age, sex, and ethnicity provided contradictory definitions of, access to, and expectations for literacy. Soltow and Stevens (1981), in tracing literacy in 19th-century American schools, identified social class ideology as the basis for the proposed reforms. Other studies of schooling in Great Britain, Australia, New Zealand, and the United States have also shown disparate educational treatment for women and members of differing social classes (Walker & Barton, 1983).

These illustrative studies suggest the cultural context of community influence on social education, indicate some lines of potential research on gender, class, race, and nationality in social education, and outline a large area in which more specific social studies research is needed. Wexler (1985), in a critique of current studies of social education, suggested the use of new concepts in communication theory to further scholarly insight into ideological factors that influence social education.

Within the cultural and linguistic contexts are the social and political situations in which social studies is taught. As Merriam (1931) noted, in a comprehensive comparative study of civic education in several industrialized nations, "the full understanding of systems of civic education will not be reached unless they are taken as a part of a total social situation, in the midst of which they are set and as a part of which they function" (p. 11). Merriam found that complexity, conflicting loyalties, and fragile social cohesiveness surrounded civic (social) education. Socioeconomic class, ethnic background, religion, and geographic regional differences were found to result in ideological differences in the civic training programs investigated in all nations. There were also national variations in the extent to which governmental ideology could be criticized in schools: no criticism was possible in Russia and Italy, more was possible in Germany and France, and limited criticism was allowed in England and the United States.

Beale (1936) conducted a large-scale study that showed severe limitations on teacher freedom. He noted the relation of social forces in the community to that freedom:

No understanding of the problem of freedom can be attained without thorough knowledge of the forces that dominate the schools and form the public opinion in which the schools must operate. Even the fundamental purposes of education are inextricably bound up with the problem of freedom. (p. x)

For democratic societies, there are diverse agents of influence with varying degrees of power (Almond & Verba, 1963; Bellah, Madsen, Sullivan, Swidler, & Tipton, 1985; Dewey, 1916; Tocqueville, 1848/1969). Dominant groups in a democracy can exert significant control over the means and agents of influence, but there is some opportunity for debate. Among the protections against unwanted or undue influence in a democracy are academic freedom, the relatively open nature of the society, and the threat of public exposure and public debate by partisans.

Ideologies and Community Influence: Hidden Curricula

At its most basic level, community influence can be studied in terms of ideologies and their impacts on schooling. Apple (1979) provided a philosophical analysis of the relation of school knowledge to ideology, following critical scholarship in the sociology of knowledge. Social studies and science are subjects Apple identified as ideologically dominated by a hidden curriculum that limits students to a conservative normative view of the world. Giroux and Penna (1979) defined the hidden curriculum in social studies as "the unstated norms, values and beliefs that are transmitted to students through the underlying structure of meaning" (p. 22). Evidence of the hidden curriculum and its influence on ideologically normative purposes has been provided in studies of: (a) school settings (Dreeben, 1968; Jackson, 1968; Lamperes & Penna, 1978; Metzger & Barr, 1978; Palonsky, 1986; Siegel 1977, 1978); (b) textbooks (Anyon, 1978, 1979a, 1979b; Bagenstos, 1977; Burstyn & Corrigan, 1975; Romanish, 1983; Shaver, 1979); (c) economics (Bowles & Gintis, 1976; Carnoy, 1975; Carnoy & Levin, 1985); (d) social policy (Spring, 1976); (e) teacher education (Kickbush, 1987; Palonsky & Nelson, 1980); (f) curricular structure (Cherryholmes, 1978; Eggleston, 1977); (g) gender and class issues (Arnot, 1981; O'Donnell, 1973; Walker & Barton, 1983); (h) language form (Bernstein, 1976); and (i) the nature of knowledge (Popkewitz, 1984; Young, 1971).

Gilbert (1984) studied the history and current status of pervasive hidden influences on the social subjects in English secondary schools. He noted the disparity between the expressed aims of social education for "participatory and egalitarian concerns for human welfare" and the deterministic and powerless images of individual and society that are actually conveyed in the curriculum and in textbooks. He found that social studies instruction provided no examination of the ideological bases for the subjects studied. There was a lack of treatment of social conflict; a presumption of satisfaction with the government and the current economic system; acceptance of geographic determinism; a general sense of powerlessness for individuals; and imposition of a structuralist-functionalist view of the social world, which was not criticized. He concluded that "the analysis has demonstrated the connections between the images and the political order which has produced them" (p. 225).

Gilbert's results were consistent with findings from studies of social studies in America and other nations (Billington, 1966; Hayes, 1960; Kalinin, 1953; Key, 1961; Merriam, 1931; Murthy, 1973; Nelson, 1978; Peake, 1932; Ridley, Godwin, & Doolin, 1971). These authors argued that social and political education is aimed at imposing the views of dominant groups in the community, inculcating selected governmental and economic ideologies, and restricting conflicting views from examination.

Overt Influence: Formal Agencies of Communities

The major formal influences on school curriculum policies were identified by Kirst (1984) as: (a) legislative, (b) executive, (c) administrative-school, (d) bureaucratic, (e) professional association, and (f) private interests.

Legislative influence includes state requirements in American history or economics and mandated credit hours in history for teacher-credential candidates. An example of executive influence is a public statement from a governor that students do not know enough about history or government or geography. An administrative-school example of influence is a school principal's request that a teacher restrict the treatment of a controversial issue. Bureaucratic influence includes the complexity of a system for obtaining a new textbook or bringing in a speaker. Use of the NCSS curriculum guidelines by a regional accreditation visiting team exemplifies professional association influence. Private interests include a virtually unlimited number of groups and individuals who wish to influence social studies, such as the Daughters of the American Revolution, the National Geographic Society, the state historical association, the oil companies, Earthwatch, the Italian-American Defense League, the World Bank, the Anti-Defamation League, anti-abortion groups, Planned Parenthood, local newspapers, a group of parents, and a vocal participant at a school board meeting.

Legislative and regulatory influence on the curriculum have been examined in a number of studies. Schools, from colonial times, have been the focus of policies and enactments by governments with the intent of producing proper citizens, eliminating social evils, improving individual behavior, making people employable, and instilling values considered appropriate to the community (Callahan, 1962; Cremin, 1961; Curti, 1935; Katz, 1968; Rugg, 1936; Spring, 1976).

Educational historians disagree in their interpretations of the values, ideologies, and intentions of governmental interventions in social education, and on the positive or negative valence of those influences. For example, Katz (1968) determined that the public and governmental movement for educational reform led by Horace Mann was not as altruistic as traditional historians had suggested; instead, Katz argued that Mann had a central aim of making more efficient the social control that the dominant parts of the community imposed on others to make them orderly and moral. Spring (1976) analyzed national education policy since World War II and identified the major influential elements as federal legislation (e.g., National Defense Education Act, National Science Foundation), national organizations concerned with education (e.g., National Education Association, American Federation of Teachers, Educational Testing Service), publishers, courts, and foundations. He argued that educational policy has been "directed toward the creation of a rationalized and controlled labor market through the sorting function of the public schools and the control of social conflict arising from racial discrimination and inequalities in the distribution of income." (p. 262) Karier (1973), studied corporate foundations and standardized testing, finding that the influence of foundations, "amounted to the development of a fourth branch of government, one that effectively represented the interest of American corporate wealth." (p. 110)

Nationalistic Influences on Social Studies

Nelson (1968) examined statutory law and written regulations that governed social studies instruction regarding controversial topics such as religion, sex, patriotism, and economics. Virtually every state had statutory or regulatory documents that imposed or limited what could be taught. The most common requirements in state laws were nationalistic treatment of history, government economics, and other social sciences, and restriction in the teaching of contending ideas, such as communism and socialism. Two forms of nationalistic education were identified: (a) instruction to inculcate loyalty to the nation, and (b) instruction to create a negative view of ideas considered contranational. In later analyses, nationalistic education was shown to conflict with rationales for global education (Nelson, 1978) and with those for thoughtful moral education (Nelson, 1980).

Attempts by national and local organizations to exert influence on social education have been a topic of research for a long period of time. Studies by Pierce (1933) and Raup (1936) showed, through document analysis and interviews, that a variety of patriotic organizations were heavily engaged in attempts to influence the teaching of social studies in schools. Gellerman (1938) studied the American Legion's efforts through its Americanism Program, what Gellerman described as the "war against 'subversive elements'," including advocacy for state-required loyalty oaths for teachers, attempts to rid the schools of those who teach "radical internationalism," and willingness to assist school boards in purging communist and socialist influences from the schools. Gellerman documented the Legion's activities to foster Americanism in schools, including the establishment of American Education Week, patriotic essay contests, flag education, required observance of national holidays and patriotic exercises, and civics instruction using an American history textbook prepared by the Legion.

Naylor (1973, 1974), using a situational research instrument on nationalistic education sent to a random statewide sample of social studies teachers, found that public school educators recognized that schools conform to perceptions of restrictive community influences. He concluded that the public school is "not particularly hospitable to open inquiry in areas of nationalism and patriotism." (1973, p. 69)

Business Influences on School and Social Studies

Influence from dominant communities of interest has an impact upon the general mentality of the school, as well as on formal instruction in social studies. Callahan (1962), in an historical study, showed how business influenced the ideas of school superintendents about the organization and operation of schools in the early 20th century and left a residual idea that a traditional business efficiency should be the basis for education. Callahan concluded that the influence of business was a "tragedy" for education.

Earlier, Veblen (1918/1957), had published a philosophic treatise with numerous examples of the intrusion of business into higher education. He concluded:

The underlying business-like presumption accordingly appears to be that learning is a merchantable commodity, to be produced and sold by standard units, measured, counted and reduced to staple equivalence by impersonal, mechanical tests. [It] conduces to perfunctory and mediocre work throughout, and acts to deter both students and teachers from a free pursuit of knowledge. (p. 163)

Following a two-year field study of public schools, with extensive interviews of teachers in many states, Sinclair (1924) documented corporate influence on schools. He cited specific examples of efforts by industrialists and such groups as the National Association of Manufacturers, the National Chamber of Commerce, and the American Bankers Association to limit and control the operation of schools and the way in which certain subjects such as labor unions are taught in elementary and secondary school. Sinclair's forcefully stated views are less temperate than standard scholarly works, but the data he presented have not been challenged in court or in scholarship despite the fact that he identified by name very influential people in business and schools. Callahan's study provided the extensive documentation and scholarly analysis that lent credibility to the positions taken by Veblen and Sinclair.

A contrasting viewpoint, holding that anti–business and anti-capitalist ideas are predominant influences in schools, was presented by Hayek (1944) and Simon (1978). Well-financed efforts to combat this anti–business bias in schools and colleges produced endowed chairs in free enterprise at universities and state requirements that schools teach free enterprise rather than the more neutral study of economics (Hechinger, 1978).

The influence of the business community on social studies instructional materials has also been studied. Harty (1980) identified economic bias and ideological positions in teaching materials prepared by various industries and distributed to schools and teachers. Labor unions have produced teaching materials for their members and for schools, but several studies have indicated that unions do not fare well in standard textbooks and other teaching materials (Carlson, 1969; Doherty, 1964; Linton, 1965; Scoggins, 1966).

The treatment of economics, a subject of considerable controversy and community interest, has been examined in terms of content, presentation, and consequence. Romanish (1983), in a content-analysis study of contemporary secondary school economics texts, found ideological biases. His operational definition for bias was that a text presented only one economic perspective on a major topic (such as economic systems, labor, roles of government, and environment), when other legitimate perspectives could have been presented. Romanish found the biases to include the presentation of free enterprise to the exclusion of other ideas and the representation that "classical economic theory" is the American model without variation.

Walstad and Watts (1984), responding to Romanish, argued that bias was not demonstrated, that the categories selected were "arbitrary and inconsistent," and that his methodology was flawed because a panel of readers was not used. Romanish (1984) rebutted that the criticisms were nit-picking and that the critics did not deny the central point that there is bias in the texts.

In a comparative study of textbooks and teacher perceptions in economics education in Japan and the United States, Ellington and Uozumi (1988) found that American teachers and texts were more concerned with defending ideological aspects of free enterprise than were the Japanese. Leming (1987) argued that social studies teachers should engage in deliberate and direct normative education in economics to assure that the current political and economic system in the United States is preserved and strengthened.

That social education is involved in imparting normative knowledge, belief, and behaviors is not debated; the issue is what those norms should be and who should determine them. That is the prime subject of community influence.

Censorship as a Means of Exerting Influence

Attempts by communities to restrict the flow of information and ideas have been a part of Western civilization since its earliest time. There is considerable dispute on the value, purpose, and use of censorship (Hart, 1971). Censorship is not only controversial, it is also a proper subject for examination in social studies classrooms because it represents efforts to control the society's values and beliefs.

Censorship includes the deliberate acts of officials to prohibit ideas from being expressed, the political and psychological pressure to hinder the expression of certain ideas, and the control of communication to keep some ideas from being given credible treatment. A school board's decision to prohibit a book from use in school is an example of the first; vocal protests by a group against certain teaching materials or ideas is an illustration of the second; and ideological pressure that results in publishers filtering out or ridiculing divergent ideas in textbooks and other media use in school is an example of the third. In addition to direct efforts to censor, there is self-censorship by teachers.

There is considerable evidence of censorship of each type in schools and libraries. Studies identified earlier (Beale, 1936, 1941; Gellerman, 1938; Merriam, 1931; Pierce, 1926, 1933; Raup, 1936; Sinclair, 1924) provide many examples of official censorship of teachers and community pressure to censor teachers, topics, and teaching materials. Other works document the censorship activities of government agencies, political and economic organizations, religious groups, and other pressure groups (Blanshard, 1955; Breasted, 1970; Davis, 1955; Forster, 1950; LaHaye, 1983; Luthin, 1954; Nelson & Roberts, 1963; Rugg, 1951). Proposing an expansion of scholarly interest in this area, Bennett (1988) stated: "The existing body of theory and knowledge is weak, and in particular adequate research has not been conducted related to the suppression of information by governments" (p. 28).

O'Neil (1981), in one of the most comprehensive examinations of court decisions on school censorship and teacher freedom, determined that there is little legal clarity in some domains. Court decisions have generally given duly constituted school boards and administrators considerable legal authority over curriculum decisions, but less control over teacher actions and texts. U.S. Supreme Court decisions on such matters as the unconstitutionality of teacher loyalty oaths (*Keyishian v. Board,* 1967), curricular restrictions on teacher rights (*Meyer v. Nebraska,* 1923), and student rights to free expression (*Tinker v. Des Moines,* 1969), are helpful in defining some of the issues in academic freedom and censorship. Decisions in lower courts have been a confusing mixture of protection for the acts of boards and administrators to restrict knowledge and protection for the rights of teachers and students to inquire and know.

Analyses of more recent U.S. Supreme Court decisions that determined school authorities' rights to censor textbooks (*Board of Education, Island Trees Union Free School District No. 26 v. Pico,* 1982), to limit and punish lewd speech by students (*Bethel v. Fraser,* 1986), and to control student newspapers (*Hazelwood v. Kuhlmeier,* 1988), suggest a more precise and limited right of expression (Schimmel, 1988).

In the *Island Trees* case, a school board, rejecting recommendations from a board-appointed committee of parents and staff, removed library books they considered filthy, anti-American, anti-Christian, or anti-Semitic. The Supreme Court decided that the board had legal, but not unfettered, authority over curriculum and could remove the books. Faaborg (1985) argued that this case established a test of intention on such board actions; if a board intends to deny students access to opposing ideas, then the action would be unconstitutional.

In the *Bethel* case, involving a student speech of six sentences that included sexual double entendres, Chief Justice Burger wrote the majority opinion that lewd speech in school may be punished because students must be taught "manners of civility" and "the boundaries of socially approved behavior"; but he acknowledged the political rights of students established in the *Tinker* case in 1978 (Schimmel, 1986, p. 1001).

In the *Hazelwood* case, the Supreme Court ruled that school authorities could censor student publications that are part of the school-sponsored curriculum. Schimmel (1988) concluded that the broader student freedom presumed in the *Tinker* case is limited when the means of expression is school sponsored, and he noted that the *Hazelwood* decision left several unre-

solved issues in censorship of student expression, including any application to higher education and any limits on the control of nonschool-sponsored student press. Avery and Simpson (1987), prior to the *Hazelwood* decision, examined student-publication cases at several levels of courts and reported a confusing array of decisions and tests of legality in actions of prior restraint, censorship, and punishment by school officials.

Censorship, Self-censorship, and Academic Freedom. School censorship court cases are obvious evidence of community influence on social studies in schools, but only the rare case goes to court. Censorship has increased in recent years (People for the American Way, 1988) and is frequently reported in journals *(Intellectual Freedom Newsletter of the American Library Association; The Index of Censorship),* but these actions are not often pursued to court.

Overt censorship by outside agencies, publishers, school boards, and school administrators is widely known, but there are other forms of restriction on controversial topics that reflect community influence. Self-censorship by teachers results from the teacher's acceptance of community norms, the conformist traditions of schooling, and the chilling effects that notoriety for dealing with controversy can bring to a teacher and faculty.

Beale (1936), following an extensive study of teacher freedom, stated:

Few teachers have had sufficient training or have done enough thinking to grow out of conventional community opinions and to realize that there is a problem of freedom at all. One of the most striking revelations of the study was the small number of teachers even aware that they would not be free to differ from community views. . . . Many [teachers] do not know they are not free and will be happier never to discover it. . . . Perhaps the greatest difficulty has arisen from the fears of teachers and administrators alike. Many refused to talk at all. (pp. x, xii, xiii)

Palonsky and Nelson (1980), in interviews of college seniors who had completed student teaching in social studies during a 5-year period at one university, found substantial evidence of self-censorship of controversial issues in social studies classrooms. Nelson (1983) interviewed teachers in secondary schools in two states, categorizing the forms of self-censorship as: (a) personal, as when the teacher feels uncomfortable on the topic; (b) professional, as when the teacher believes the particular classroom situation would not be educationally suitable for discussion of the topic; and (c) political, as when the teacher thinks that parents or administrators would complain. Political self-censorship was found to be the most predominant form expressed in interviews. Self-censoring teachers report influence by, or fear of influence from, an administrator or members of the community in dealing with topics of controversy even though these teachers admitted that such topics were pertinent to social studies instruction. Shaver, Davis, and Helburn (1980), summarizing results from case studies of social studies teachers conducted for the National Science Foundation, noted that teachers were very sensitive to the communities in which they taught and had little difficulty avoiding controversy. This coincides with the view expressed by Boyd (1979) that schools have a "zone of tolerance" within which teachers are expected to stay, and that avoiding conflict and controversy, defined differently in differing communities, is in the interest of school administrators and social studies teachers.

Academic freedom for teachers and students is under continual challenge in the schools but is crucial to the maintenance of open inquiry and as a counter to censorship (American Association of University Professors, 1986; Dewey, 1936; National Council for the Social Studies, 1975; Nelson & Ochoa, 1987; Stanley & Nelson, 1985). Carlson (1987) identified the direct relation between community influence and academic freedom, citing research conducted by Daly (1986) and Heintjes (1986) and arguing that "academic freedom dies from abandonment in local communities; it atrophies because teachers fail to exercise it for fear of being penalized" (p. 430).

Based on data from the General Social Surveys from 1972 to 1983, White (1986) suggested that the majority of the American public opposed censorship and supported intellectual freedom but that censorship is a local matter subject to the influence of special interest groups. Violas (1971) examined the rationales offered in several hundred articles on academic freedom for teachers, 1930 to 1960, finding these rationales to be mainly a response to fears and anxieties in the public, a reflection of community influence.

AREAS OF NEEDED RESEARCH AND THEORY DEVELOPMENT

Community influences on social studies instruction are of great significance to education and society and merit substantially more research and theory development in social education scholarship. Research efforts have emphasized historical and philosophical studies, with some researchers using survey, case study, and interview techniques. Few experimental and quasi-experimental studies have been done, probably because complex educational phenomena do not adapt well to the restrictions of traditional experimental designs. Further, there is legitimate dispute over the value of positivistic research paradigms, the role of specific research methods in knowledge development, and the criteria for quality research in social studies education (Feinberg & Bredo, 1982; Fraenkel, 1987; Nelson & Shaver, 1987; Popkewitz, 1984; Wallen & Fraenkel, 1988).

A more serious concern is that few longitudinal, replicable, or comprehensive ethnographic studies have been done on community influences. Theoretical groundings for knowledge in this area have not been sufficiently examined over a period of time using common and repeatable techniques. Consequently, theory is ill-tested and often no more than opinion or perception. The body of literature available in the humanities and social sciences on such topics as culture and language, the political dynamics of communities, persuasion and influence, and censorship can help to inform research and theory on social studies and community influence.

Proposed Research and Theory Development Topics

Some valuable topics for research and theory development are:

1. The status of academic freedom and censorship in a variety of communities, to update such research as that by Pierce (1926, 1930), Beale (1936, 1941), Sinclair (1924), and Gellerman (1938).
2. The ideological roots of differing communities, including social class, gender, racial, and national factors related to community influence in social studies.
3. The relative importance, dynamics, and potential consequences for social studies of factors of community influence, for example, special interest groups, regulations, administrators, legal cases, norms, language.
4. The identification and analysis of techniques of community influence on social studies instruction in different nations.
5. The impact of differing forms of community influence on students, teachers, curriculum, teaching materials, and the school setting.
6. The effects of community influences on the way knowledge is defined and the implications for social studies classrooms.
7. The political, economic, linguistic, and geographic socialization of students as advocated by various communities of interest.
8. The relation of social studies teacher education and professional socialization to the teaching of controversy, academic freedom, views of social education, and responses to community influence.
9. The use of functionalist, Marxist, neo-Marxist, and critical theory perspectives to examine community and social studies instruction.
10. Censorship and self-censorship, treatment of controversy, community norms, teacher self-perception, textbook bias, and other separable factors related to community influence.

Community influence is a subject of special interest in social studies education because it is central to the question of what kind of person and society schools should attempt to produce. The dominant curriculum and pedagogy in social studies are the result of community influence on some level at some time. Social studies researchers should direct more attention to that influence.

References

Almond, G. A., & Verba, S. (1963). *Civic culture: Political attitudes and democracy in five nations*. Princeton, NJ: Princeton University Press.

American Association of University Professors. (1986). *Liberty and learning in the schools*. Washington, DC: Author.

Anyon, J. (1978). Elementary social studies textbooks and legitimating knowledge. *Theory and Research in Social Education, 6,* 40–54.

Anyon, J. (1979a). Education, social structure' and the power of individuals. *Theory and Research in Social Education, 7,* 49–59.

Anyon, J. (1979b). Ideology and U.S. history textbooks. *Harvard Educational Review, 3,* 361–386.

Apple, M. (1979). Ideology and curriculum. London: Routledge & Kegan Paul.

Arnot, M. (1982). Male hegemony, social class and women's education, *Journal of Education, 164,* 64–89.

Aronowitz, S., & Giroux, H. (1985). *Education under siege.* South Hadley, MA: Bergin & Garvey.

Avery, K. B. & Simpson, R. J. (1987). The constitution and student publications. *Journal of Law and Education, 16,* 1–61.

Bagenstos, N. (1977). Social reconstruction: The controversy of the textbooks of Harold Rugg. *Theory and Research in Social Education. 5,* 22–38.

Banfield, E. (1961). *Political influence.* Glencoe, IL: Free Press.

Beale, H. K. (1936). *Are American teachers free?.* New York: Charles Scribner's Sons.

Beale, H. K. (1941). *A history of freedom of teaching in American schools.* New York: Charles Scribner's Sons.

Beard, C. A. (1932). *A charter for the social sciences in the schools.* New York: Charles Scribner's Sons.

Bellah, R. N., Madsen, R., Sullivan, W. M., Swidler, A. & Tipton, S. M. (1985). *Habits of the heart: Individualism and commitment in American life.* Berkeley: University of California Press.

Bennett, J. R. (1988). Censorship by the Reagan administration. *Index on Censorship, 17,* 28–32.

Bernstein, B. (1976). *Class, codes and control.* London: Routledge and Kegan Paul.

Bethel School District No. 403 v. Fraser, 106 S.Ct. 3159 (1986).

Billington, R. A. (1966). *The historians' contribution to Anglo-American misunderstanding: Report of a committee on national bias in Anglo-American history textbooks.* New York: Hobbs, Dorman.

Blanshard, P. (1955). *The right to read.* Boston: Beacon.

Board of Education, Island Trees Union Free School District v. Pico, 457 U.S. 853 (1982).

Bowles, S., & Gintis, H. (1976). *Schooling in capitalist America.* New York: Basic Books.

Boyd, W. L. (1979). The politics of curriculum change and stability. *Educational Researcher, 8*(2), 12–18.

Breasted, M. (1970). *Oh! Sex education.* New York: Praeger.

Burstyn, J., & Corrigan, R. (1975). Images of women in textbooks. *Teachers College Record, 76,* 431–440.

Button, C. B. (1974). Political education for minority groups. In Niemi, R. G. (Ed.), *The Politics of Future Citizens.* San Francisco: Jossey-Bass.

Callahan, R. (1962). *Education and the cult of efficiency.* Chicago: University of Chicago Press.

Carlson, K. (1969). A sociological study of the educational activities of four trade union locals. (Doctoral Dissertation, State University of New York, Buffalo). *American Doctoral Dissertations,* 1969–70, p. 118.

Carlson, K. (1987). Academic freedom in hard times. *Social Education. 51,* 429–430.

Carnoy, M. (1975). *Schooling in a corporate society.* 2d ed., New York: McKay.

Carnoy, M., & Levin, H. (1985). *Schooling and work in the democratic state.* Stanford, CA: Stanford University Press.

Cherryholmes, C. (1978). Curriculum design as a political act. *Theory and Research in Social Education, 6,*(4), 60–82.

Cherryholmes, C. (1982). Discourse and criticism in the social studies classroom. *Theory and Research in Social Education, 9*(4), 57–73.

Cohen, A. P. (1985). *The symbolic construction of community.* London: Tavistock.

Cremin, L. (1961). *The transformation of the school.* New York: Alfred Knopf

Curti, M. (1935). *The social ideas of American educators.* New York: Charles Scribner's Sons.

Cusick, P. (1973). *Inside high school.* New York: Holt, Rinehart & Winston.

Daly, J. (1987). Patterns and perceptions of censorship among secondary educators (Doctoral dissertation, Rutgers University) *Dissertation Abstracts International, 48,* 2303-A.

Davis, W. E. (1955). *Patriotism on parade.* Cambridge, MA: Harvard University Press.

Deutsch, M., & Gerard, H. G. (1955). A study of normative and informational social influences on individual judgment. *Journal of Abnormal and Social Psychology, 51,* 629–636.

Dewey, J. (1916). *Democracy and education.* New York: Macmillan.

Dewey, J. (1936). The social significance of academic freedom. *The Social Frontier, 2,* 136.

Doherty, R. (1964). *Teaching industrial relations in high schools: A survey.* Ithaca: New York State School of Industrial and Labor Relations.

Dreeben, R. (1968). *On what is learned in schools.* Reading, MA: Addison Wesley.

Eggleston, J. (1977). *The sociology of the school curriculum.* London: Routledge & Kegan Paul.

Ehman, L. (1969). An analysis of the relationship of selected educational variables with the political socialization of high school students. *American Educational Research Journal, 6,* 559–580.

Ehman, L. (1980). The American school in the political socialization process. *Review of Educational Research, 50,* 99–119.

Ellington, J. L., & Uozumi, T. (1988). Economic education in Japanese and American secondary schools. *Theory and Research in Social Education, 16,* 103–114.

Engle, S., & Ochoa, A. (1988). *Education for democratic citizenship.* New York: Teachers College Press.

Faaborg, K. K. (1985). High school play censorship. *Journal of Law and Education, 14,* 575–594.

Feinberg, W., & Bredo, E. (Eds.). (1982). *Knowledge and values in social and educational research.* New York: Falmer.

Forster, A. (1950). *A measure of freedom.* New York: Doubleday.

Fraenkel, J. (1973). *Helping students think and value.* Englewood Cliffs, NJ: Prentice-Hall.

Fraenkel, J. (1987). Toward improving research in social studies education. *Theory and Research in Social Education. 15,* 203–222.

Gellerman, W. (1938). *The American legion as educator.* New York: Teachers College Press

Gilbert, R. (1984). *The impotent image: Reflections of ideology in the secondary school curriculum.* London: Falmer.

Giroux, H. (1983). *Ideology, culture, and the process of schooling.* Philadelphia: Temple University Press.

Giroux, H. (1988a). *Schooling and the struggle for public life.* Minneapolis: University of Minnesota Press.

Giroux, H. (1988b). *Teachers as intellectuals.* Granby, MA. Bergin and Garvey.

Giroux, H., & Penna, A. (1979). Social education in the classroom: The dynamics of the hidden curriculum. *Theory and Research in Social Education, 7,* 21–42.

Goldenson, D. (1978). An alternative view about the role of the secondary school in political socialization: A field-experimental study of the development of civil liberties attitudes. *Theory and Research in Social Education, 6,* 44–72.

Graff, H. J. (1979). *The literacy myth: Literacy and social structure in the nineteenth-century city.* New York: Academic Press.

Greenstein, F. (1965). *Children and politics.* New Haven: Yale University Press.

Gustfield, J. R. (1975). *Community: A critical response.* New York: Harper & Row.

Hart, H. (Ed.). (1971). *Censorship: For and against.* New York: Hart.

Harty, S. (1980). *Hucksters in the classroom.* Washington, DC: Center for Responsive Legislation.

Hayek, F. (1944). *The road to serfdom.* Chicago: University of Chicago Press.

Hayes, C. J. H. (1960). *Nationalism: A religion.* New York: Macmillan.

Hazelwood School District v. Kuhlmeier, 433 U.S. 299 (1988).

Hechinger, F. (1978). The corporation in the classroom. *Saturday Review, 5,* 14,15.

Heintjes, J. (1986). Censorship in New Jersey schools (Doctoral dissertation, Rutgers University), *Dissertation Abstracts International, 48,* 98-A.

Hepburn, M. A. (1980). How do they know what they know? *Teaching Political Science, 7,* 425–438.

Hess, R., & Torney, J. (1967). *The development of political attitudes in children.* Chicago: Aldine.

Hunt, M., & Metcalf, L. (1968). *Teaching high school social studies* (2nd ed.) New York: Harper.

Jackson, P. (1968). *Life in classrooms.* New York: Holt, Rinehart & Winston.

Jennings, M. K., & Neimi, R. (1981). *Generations and politics.* Princeton, NJ: Princeton University Press.

Kalinin, M. I. (1953). *On communist education.* Moscow: Foreign Language Publishing House.

Kamenka, E. (Ed.). (1982). *Community as a social ideal.* New York: St. Martin's Press.

Kaplan, M. F., & Miller, C. E. (1987). Group decision making and normative versus informational influence. *Journal of Personality and Social Psychology, 53,* 206–313.

Karier, C. J. (1973). Testing for order and control in the corporate liberal state. In Karier, C., Violas, P. C., & Spring, J. (Eds.), *Roots of crisis* (pp. 108–137). Chicago: Rand McNally.

Katz, M. (1968). *The irony of early school reform.* Boston: Beacon.

Key, V. O. (1961). *Public opinion and American democracy.* New York: Knopf.

Keyishian v. Board of Regents, 385 U.S. 589 (1967).

Kickbush, K. (1987). Civic education and preservice educators: Extending the boundaries of discourse. *Theory and Research in Social Education, 15,* 173–188.

Kirst, M. (1984). *Who controls our schools?* New York: Freeman.

Labov, W. (1966). *The social stratification of English in New York City.* Washington, DC: Center for Applied Linguistics.

Labov, W. (1972). *Sociolinguistic patterns.* Philadelphia: University of Pennsylvania Press.

Labov, W. (1987). The community as educator. In J. A. Langer (Ed.), *Language, literacy, and culture: Issues of society and schooling* (pp. 129–146). Norwood, NJ: Ablex.

LaHaye, T. (1983). *The battle for the public schools.* Old Tappan, NJ: Fleming, Revell.

Lamperes, B., & Penna, A. (1978). Critique of Michael E. Siegel's "Citizenship Education in Five Massachusetts High Schools." *Theory and Research in Social Education, 6*(2), 80–84.

Langton, K. P., & Jennings, M. K. (1968). Political socialization and the high school civics curriculum in the United States. *American Political Science Review, 62,* 852–867.

Leming, J. S (1985). Research on social studies curriculum and instruction: Interventions and outcomes in the socio-moral domain. In W. B. Stanley (Ed.), *Review of research in social studies education: 1976–1983* (pp. 123–213). Washington, DC: National Council for the social studies.

Leming, J. S. (1987). On the normative foundations of economic education. *Theory and Research in Social Education, 15,* 63–76.

Linton, T. L. (1965). *An historical examination of the purposes and practices of the United Automobile Workers.* Unpublished doctoral dissertation, University of Michigan.

Litt, E. (1963). Civic education, community norms, and political indoctrination. *American Sociological Review, 28,* 69–75.

Luthin, R. H. (1954). *American demagogues.* Boston: Beacon.

Merriam, C. F. (1931). *The making of citizens.* Chicago: University of Chicago Press.

Metzger, D. J. & Barr, R. D. (1978). The impact of school political systems on student political attitudes. *Theory and Research in Social Education, 6,* 48–79.

Meyer v. Nebraska, 262 U.S. 390 (1923).

Mills, C. W. (1956). *The power elite.* London: Oxford University Press.

Murthy, P. A. N. (1973). *The rise of modern nationalism in Japan.* New Delhi: Askajanak.

National Council for the Social Studies. (1975). *Position statement on the freedom to teach and the freedom to learn.* Washington, DC: Author.

Naylor, D. (1973). A study of the perceptions of New Jersey educators regarding nationalistic instruction, *Theory and Research in Social Education, 1,* 59–73.

Naylor, D. (1974). An in-depth study of the perceptions of public school educators and other significant school-related groups concerning aspects of nationalistic education, (Doctoral dissertation, Rutgers University). *Dissertation abstracts international, 36,* 687A.

Nelson, J. H., & Roberts, G. (1963). *The censors and the schools.* Boston: Little, Brown.

Nelson, J. L. (1968). Nationalism and education. *Studies in International Conflict. SUNY Buffalo Studies, 4,* 113–132.

Nelson, J. L. (1978). Nationalistic political education: An examination of traditions and potentials. *Cambridge Journal of Education, 8,* 142–151.

Nelson, J. L. (1980). The uncomfortable relationship between moral education and citizenship instruction. In R. Wilson & G. Schochet (Eds.), *Moral development and politics* (pp 124–157). New York: Praeger.

Nelson, J. L. (1983, Sept.). Teacher self-censorship and academic freedom. *The Social Studies Professional,* pp. 1, 2.

Nelson, J. L., & Carlson, K. (1981). Ideology and economic education. In S. S. Symmes (Ed.), *Economic education: Links to the social studies* (pp. 83–97). Washington, DC: National Council for the Social Studies.

Nelson, J. L., & Michaelis, J. (1980). *Secondary social studies: Instruction, curriculum, evaluation.* Englewood Cliffs, NJ: Prentice-Hall.

Nelson, J. L., & Ochoa, A. (1987). Academic freedom, censorship and the social studies. *Social Education, 51,* 424–427.

Nelson, J. L., & Shaver, J. P. (1987). On research in social education. In W. B. Stanley (Ed.), *Review of research in social studies, 1976–1983* (pp. 401–433). Washington, DC: National Council for the Social Studies.

Newmann, F. (1975). *Education for citizen action.* Berkeley, CA: McCutchan.

Ogbu, J. O. (1982). Cultural discontinuities and schooling. *Anthropology and Education Quarterly, 13,* 290–307.

Ogbu, J. O. (1987). Opportunity structure, cultural boundaries, and literacy. In J. A. Langer (Ed.), *Language, literacy and culture: Issues of society and schooling* (pp. 149–177). Norwood, NJ: Ablex.

O'Donnell, R. W. (1973). Sex bias in primary social studies textbooks. *Educational Leadership, 31,* 137–41.

Oliver, D. W. (1976) *Education and community.* Berkeley, CA: McCutchan.

Oliver, D. W., & Shaver, J. P. (1974). *Teaching public issues in the high school.* Logan, UT: Utah State University Press. (original work published 1966)

O'Neil. R. (1981). *Crisis in the classroom.* Bloomington: Indiana University Press.

Palonsky, S. (1986). *900 shows a year: A look at teaching from a teacher's side of the desk.* New York: Random House.

Palonsky, S., & Nelson, J. L. (1980). Political restraint in the socialization of student teachers. *Theory and Research in Social Education, 7,* 19–34.

Peake, C. (1932). *Nationalism and education in modern China.* New York: Columbia University Press.

People for the American Way. (1988). *Attacks on the freedom to learn, 1987–1988*. Sixth annual survey. Washington, DC: Author.

Pierce, B. (1926). *Public opinion and the teaching of history*. New York: Appleton-Century-Crofts.

Pierce, B. (1930). *Civic attitudes in American school textbooks*. Chicago: University of Chicago Press.

Pierce, B. (1933). *Citizens' organizations and the civic training of youth*. New York: Charles Scribners' Sons.

Popkewitz, T. (1984). *Paradigm and ideology in educational research*. Philadelphia: Falmer.

Raup, B. (1936). *Education and organized interests in America*. New York: G. P. Putnam.

Ridley, C. P., Godwin, P. H., Doolin, D. (1971). *The making of a model citizen in communist China*. Stanford, CA: Hoover Institution Press.

Romanish, B. A. (1983). Modern secondary economics textbooks and ideological bias. *Theory and Research in Social Education, 11*, 1–24.

Romanish, B. A. (1984). A brief response to Watts and Walstad. *Theory and Research in Social Education, 12*, 49–51.

Rugg, H. (1936). *American life and the school curriculum*. Boston: Ginn.

Rugg, H. (1937). *Education, democracy and the curriculum*. Third Yearbook, John Dewey Society. New York: Appleton-Century-Crofts.

Rugg, H. (1951). *That men may understand*. New York: Doubleday.

Schimmel, D. (1986) Lewd language not protected: Bethel School District v. Fraser. *Education Law Reporter, 33*, 999–1005.

Schimmel, D. (1988). School censorship of curricular publications: Hazelwood School District v. Kuhlmeier. *Education Law Reporter, 45*, 941–950.

Schug, M. C., & Beery, R. (1984). *Community study: Applications and opportunities*. Washington, DC: National Council for the Social Studies.

Scoggins, W. (1966). *Labor in learning*. Los Angeles: UCLA Center for Labor Research and Education.

Shaver, J. P. (Ed.). (1977). *Building rationales for citizenship education*. Arlington, VA: National Council for the Social Studies.

Shaver, J. P. (1979). Political and economic socialization in elementary school social studies textbooks: A reaction. *Theory and Research in Social Education, 7*, 43–48.

Shaver, J. P., Davis, O. L., & Helburn, S. M. (1980). An interpretive report on the status of precollege social studies education based on three NSF-funded studies. In *What are the needs in precollege science, mathematics, and social science education?: Views from the field*. Washington, DC: National Science Foundation.

Siegel, M. E. (1977). Citizenship education in five Massachusetts high schools. *Theory and Research in Social Education, 5*, 31–55.

Siegel, M. E. (1978). Citizenship education and the high schools: A rejoinder. *Theory and Research in Social Education. 6*, 4, 83.

Simon, W. (1978). *A time for truth*. New York: McGraw-Hill.

Sinclair, U. (1924). *The goslings: A study of the American schools*. Pasadena, CA: Sinclair.

Soltow, L., & Stevens, E. (1981). *The rise of literacy and the common school in the United States*. Chicago: University of Chicago Press.

Spring, J. (1976). *The sorting machine*. New York: David McKay.

Stanley, W. B. (1981). Toward a reconstruction of social education. *Theory and Research in Social Education, 9*, 67–89.

Stanley, W. B., & Nelson J. L. (1985). Academic freedom in social studies: Fifty years standing still. *Social Education, 49*, 662–664.

Tinker v. Des Moines School District, 393 U.S. 503 (1969).

Tocqueville, A. de. (1969). *Democracy in America*. (G. Lawrence, Trans.) New York: Harper & Row. (Original work published 1848)

Veblen, T. (1957) *Higher learning in America: A memorandum on the conduct of universities by business men*. New York: Sagamore Press. (Original work published 1918)

Violas, P. C. (1971). Academic freedom and the public school teacher, 1930–1960. *Educational Theory, 21*, 70–80.

Walker, S., & Barton, L. (Eds.). (1983). *Gender class and education*. Sussex: Falmer.

Wallen, N. E., & Fraenkel, J. (1988). An analysis of social studies research over an eight year period. *Theory and Research in Social Education, 16*, 1–22.

Walstad, W. B., & Watts, M. W. (1984). A response to Romanish: Ideological bias in secondary economics textbooks. *Theory and Research in Social Education, 11*, 25–35.

Wexler, P. (1985). Social change and the practice of social education. *Social Education, 49*, 390–394.

White, H. D. (1986). Majorities for censorship. *Library Journal, 111*, 31–38.

Young, W. F. D. (Ed.). (1971). *Knowledge and control*. London: Collier-Macmillan.

TEACHING FOR AND LEARNING SOCIAL STUDIES OUTCOMES

ACHIEVING THINKING AND DECISION-MAKING OBJECTIVES IN SOCIAL STUDIES

Walter C. Parker

UNIVERSITY OF WASHINGTON, SEATTLE

Specifying thinking and decision-making objectives, planning for their achievement, lamenting their absence in practice, and exhorting teachers to devote themselves to the task are together a time-honored tradition in social studies. No other objectives have been espoused so persistently or with such enthusiasm for their anticipated effects on students and society alike. And perhaps no others have been so consistently underachieved (Goodlad, 1984; Shaver, Davis, & Helburn, 1978).

As early as 1899, the Committee of Seven (1900) of the American Historical Association was criticizing the tradition of rote learning in that subject:

For some unaccountable reason, it has been held that boys and girls must not think about historical material or be taught to reason or be led to approach events with the historical spirit.... Fortunately, the number of persons who argue in this way has decreased and is decreasing, and we may well leave those that remain to the intelligent teachers of history throughout the land who are awake to the possibilities of their subject. (pp. 88–89)

Four decades later, Anderson (1942) opened the 13th Yearbook of the National Council for the Social Studies (NCSS) with the complaint that social studies teachers had "accepted critical thinking in principle without bothering to define the term precisely or to do much by way of direct instruction to see that this goal was achieved" (p. v). Twenty-five years later, Taba (1967) pointed to a number of obstacles to achieving this objective in social studies, among which she considered haziness about what is meant by *thinking* to be the most serious.

There was no more consensus on definitions of thinking then than now. Consider the contemporary clatter of terms: critical thinking, creative thinking, problem solving, decision making, divergent and convergent thinking, metacognition, schema, domain-specific and general thinking skills, dispositions, everyday reasoning, and, simply, higher-order thinking. Numerous schemes have been put forward for making sense of these (Ennis, 1987; Marzano et al., 1988; Nickerson, 1988; Presseisen, 1986; Schrag, 1988; Sternberg, 1985).

As this chapter's title attests, it is particularly important to social studies educators that decision making be distinguished from the more general and, in typical treatments, exclusively cognitive matter of thinking. Special attention to decision making is required by the common rationale for social studies education—the preparation of democratic citizens. At the heart of democratic citizenship is not only the acquisition of information and construction of knowledge related to social life and public policy but, even more pointed and ambitious than these, ethical decision-making on public and private matters of social concern (Engle, 1960, p. 302; also Dewey, 1933; Kurfman, 1977; Metcalf, 1971; Newmann & Oliver, 1970; Oliver & Shaver, 1966/1974; Shaver, 1980; Shaver & Larkins, 1973). Of course, decision making includes thinking—for example, comparing alternative courses of action. But, because the terrain of social knowledge is political and ethical, decision making also is shot through with value commitments, dispositions, and emotions.

The purpose of this review is to make a reasoned pass through this quagmire, concentrating not on the taxonomies that try to order it, but on a limited number of empirical works that have advanced the literature on teaching thinking and decision making in social studies. Roughly four programs of empirical work are treated: the propaganda resistance studies (1932 to 1941), the Harvard Social Studies Project (1956 to

---

Reviewers were: Ronald W. Evans, San Diego State University; Fred M. Newmann, University of Wisconsin, Madison.

1970), Taba's cognitive task studies (1964 to 1971), and the in-progress work of Newmann and associates (Newmann, 1988b in press). The review is followed by a summary and criticism, and a conclusion. Throughout, special attention is paid to three themes: (a) the integration and application of knowledge, skill, and disposition in the act of thinking; (b) the persistent debate over teaching effective thinking directly rather than assuming it will emerge as a by-product of in-depth study within particular content domains; and (c) the linking of thinking and decision-making objectives to the discourse of political democracy.

THE PROPAGANDA-RESISTANCE STUDIES

Research on thinking and decision making in social studies had its first programmatic expression in the propaganda-resistance studies of the 1930s. In an early review of methods and materials used for developing "critical thinking" in students, Ellis (1942) lamented the paucity of such resources, then praised the new emphasis on the analysis of propaganda. He noted Biddle's promising work, *Propaganda and Education* (1932), the Seventh Yearbook of the National Council for the Social Studies, *Education Against Propaganda* (Ellis, 1937), and the numerous teaching aids developed by the Institute for Propaganda Analysis. The latter included the periodical, *Propaganda Analysis*. All of these figured prominently in the empirical work of the period.

Research conducted in the 1930s suggested that student opinions on public controversies could be shifted by propaganda and that such shifts persisted. Bateman and Remmers (1936) conducted four experiments to determine whether shifts in the attitudes of four classrooms of 12th-grade social studies students could be brought about by exposure to propaganda. In the first, a measure of student attitudes toward divorce preceded a two-week unit of instruction on that issue. No effort was made in the unit to influence students' attitudes one way or another. Posttest scores indicated no change from initial student attitudes. The second, third, and fourth experiments assessed initial student attitudes on an issue, then engaged students in a unit of study designed to cause a shift in attitude in a predetermined direction (e.g., from unfavorable to favorable or from somewhat favorable to highly favorable). In each case, the unit had a statistically significant effect (standardized mean difference [SMD] = .64, .79, and 1.5). Numerous factors went uncontrolled.

Osborn (1939) was more careful in testing the attitude shift conclusion. His study featured an experimental unit of instruction designed to help students resist propaganda. Resisting propaganda was understood as the ability to detect attempts to alter one's opinion and "to hold one's opinions and actions in abeyance until the desirability of the proposed opinion or action from one's own point of view is determined" (p. 2). Subjects were students in 20 pairs of 11th- and 12th-grade social studies classes. Each pair was taught by one teacher; one class was experimental, the other was the control. Students in the experimental class studied the forms and techniques of propaganda

for six days; controls were engaged in the usual curriculum. Afterward, the students' knowledge and attitudes on capital punishment were assesed. Then, on the same day, they read a piece of propaganda, "Why Capital Punishment is Necessary." They were administered a parallel measure of attitudes toward the issue immediately after the reading and again two weeks later. Osborn found in *both* groups an immediate and statistically significant shift toward more favorable attitudes on capital punishment: from $\overline{X}$ = 5.87 to 7.12 in the control group, and from $\overline{X}$ = 5.82 to 7.16 in the experimental group (S.D. not given). The difference between the two groups in degree of shift was not statistically significant (SMD = .14). For both groups, the change in attitude persisted to the delayed attitude measurement, and again the difference between the groups was negligible (SMD = .03).

Osborn concluded that the instructional unit was ineffective in developing resistance to propaganda. Forshadowing the present debate over general versus content-specific instruction on thinking skills (McPeck, 1981; Perkins, 1985), Osborn noted that his experimental unit emphasized general instruction on meaning and methods of propaganda without embedding it in a particular social issue. It was this general, or content-free, approach to propaganda resistance, Osborn argued, that proved ineffective. He recommended experimentation on units of instruction "designed for use in developing the spirit of criticism with respect to social issues contemporaneously with the original study of such issues" (p. 16). (The reader will see this articulation of content and skill training later in the Harvard projects.)

In an experiment at the elementary level, Arnold (1938) tested an experimental curriculum designed to develop students' ability to think critically. This was defined as the ability to use data—"to recognize relevance, dependability, bias in sources, and adequacy of data in regard to a particular question or conclusion" (p. 257)—operations then thought improbable before the senior high school years. Arnold's subjects were 173 fifth- and sixth-grade students in one school. Three experimental classes studied 25 vignettes over a 3-month period. Controls studied the usual curriculum. Teachers of the experimental classes read the vignettes, one at a time, to students. Then three conclusions were presented to students, and they were asked to select the best conclusion. For example:

In a discussion about the Japanese, one pupil said "I think they are all warlike. I read in a newspaper that they were building a big army and navy as fast as they can." Another pupil said, "I heard an American speak who had been in Japan for about three months visiting some schools. This American said the Japanese she knew were kindly and peaceful. I think they are peace loving."

1. Which one is giving the best reasons?
2. Can both be right?
3. Can both be wrong? (Arnold, 1938, p. 259)

On a measure designed by Arnold, the experimental group outperformed the control group. Using pretest data from the control group, a regression equation was calculated to predict posttest scores. The experimental group's scores exceeded the prediction to a degree that was statistically significant (SMD not available). Arnold argued that the experimental instruction on critical thinking had caused students to develop in three months a level of ability that would otherwise have required a full year.

Glaser (1941), like Osborn and Arnold, measured the effectiveness of a unit of study that featured direct instruction on critical thinking. Its goal was to teach 12th-grade English students key concepts of critical thinking. Glaser's definition of critical thinking was more encompassing: (a) an attitude of being disposed to consider in a thoughtful way the problems and subjects that come within the range of one's experiences, (b) knowledge of the methods of logical inquiry and reasoning, and (c) some skill in applying those methods (pp. 5–6).

Glaser designed eight lessons to be taught over an 8-week period by the regular teachers of four experimental classes. The lessons relied on materials from the Institute for Propaganda Analysis—for example, "Logic and the Weight of Evidence," and "Prejudice as a Factor Making for Crooked Thinking." Experimental and control classes had one important similarity: instruction for both had as an objective the development of student ability to think critically. Students in the four control classes studied, also for 8 weeks, the usual English curriculum—the literature of Macauley, Bacon, Morley, Addison, Steele, and Stevenson, and a study of newspapers.

Both groups of students were pre- and posttested on an early form of what was to become the Watson-Glaser Critical Thinking Appraisal (1980). Analysis indicated that the experimental groups gained significantly in critical thinking over the control groups (*SMD* = .54). Glaser concluded that direct instruction on critical thinking was an effective intervention for stimulating growth in high school students' ability to think critically and that this ability has a general character: More a disposition than a skill or set of skills, critical thinking is at heart the inclination to consider problems in a thoughtful way—for example, to want evidence for beliefs. It is this general disposition, he reasoned, that is most subject to improvement and to general transfer from the domain(s) of its acquisition to novel situations.

Two additional studies conducted in the 1940s and 1950s cannot be placed in the propaganda resistance era, but are included to show that between the propaganda era and the Harvard projects that followed, there was a turning away from social outcomes to a concern for teaching techniques and logical analysis. As well, they spanned the elementary, junior, and senior high school grades and displayed the resilience of Glaser's conclusion on the need for direct instruction on thinking skills.

An experiment reported in 1944 (Anderson, Marcham, & Dunn), this time located in social studies, began with Glaser's conclusion about direct instruction on thinking and his characterization of critical thinking as mainly a disposition. Despite this initial attention to disposition, however, Anderson et al. assumed that pupils develop skill in critical thinking by mastering discrete subskills—for example, selecting facts and making inferences from facts and trends. This study compared two methods for teaching critical thinking. Five problems centering on

geography were developed for use in 14 pairs of seventh-grade social studies classes. Five other problems drawn from world history were developed for use in 12 pairs of 10th-grade social studies classes. Generally, one teacher taught each pair of classes, and each pair was located in a different school. The study of each problem required three class sessions, and the five problems were spread across the school year. Student materials for each problem were developed in two forms: In one form, "telling," a reading selection was provided along with a detailed description of how an expert would analyze it. In the other form, "doing," the same reading selection was provided but students "were left comparatively free to study and analyze this content as they saw fit" (p. 242).

The dependent measure had two scales, one to assess abstracting and organizing information, the other to assess drawing conclusions. In a pretest, posttest design, the differences in group gains between the two methods were negligible. In the seventh grade, the mean gain for the "doing" group was 13.64 compared to 13.63 for the "telling" group. In the 10th grade, the mean gains were 9.32 and 10.33, respectively.

Like Osborn (1939), Glaser (1941), and Anderson et al. (1944), Hyram (1957) justified an experiment on critical thinking by referring to democratic citizenship. He defined critical thinking as "application of the rules of logic to factual data in order to arrive at valid as well as true conclusions" (p. 125). Citing Piaget (1928) and Anderson et al. (1944), Hyram hypothesized that children in the "upper grades" of elementary school were capable of learning and applying the rules of logic and that the best teaching methods allowed students to discover the rules for themselves and formulate generalizations about their use. On the latter, Hyram relied on a then-current hypothesis that "the most meaningful learnings as well as the most transferable ones are those acquired through self-discovery on the part of the learner" (p. 126). Accordingly, Hyram's experimental unit of instruction, which lasted for four months at 250 minutes per week, was centered on the "Socratic method." This was characterized as well-phrased and ordered questions on simple problems leading to the discovery of patterns across them. Unfortunately, the reader is not told more about the experimental instruction.

Subjects were two groups of 33 "upper grade" children equated on measures of intelligence, reading, language, and reasoning ability. The control group was taught the usual curriculum. The difference between the two groups on a logical reasoning test developed by Hyram was statistically significant (*SMD* = 3.9). Hyram's experiment therefore helped to substantiate Glaser's conclusion favoring the direct teaching of critical thinking while also advancing the argument, developed later by Taba (1963), that discovery learning has a unique role in instruction on thinking.

THE HARVARD SOCIAL STUDIES PROJECT

In 1966, Oliver and Shaver reported on the first comprehensive experimental curriculum project to attempt to develop student thinking and decision making in a way that fit logically the content selected for study. Conducted from 1956 to 1961, this was the first phase of the Harvard Social Studies Project. Building their work on the literature to date, Oliver and Shaver reasoned that prior studies warranted three conclusions. First, thinking abilities were not likely to be achieved indirectly as by-products of the regular course of study, but had to be taught directly. Second, inadequacies in research design had yielded fragmented and questionable results. Third, and most important, the role of ethics in sociopolitical decision making had not yet been explored; rather, a formal, scientized version of decision making had held the attention of curriculum developers.

The project involved two years of planning and pretesting and two years of implementation and evaluation of a 10-unit experimental curriculum. Contrary to the popular structure of the disciplines approach, on which the Taba projects were to draw, the Harvard Project curriculum was derived from an analysis of the needs of society. Pervading the units was the legal-ethical or jurisprudential framework. It "allows the teacher—and the student—to focus on a limited number of important questions whenever issues of public policy arise" (Oliver & Shaver, 1966/1974, p. 14).

The experimental setting was a two-year U.S. history sequence in a suburban junior high school. Experimental units were taught within a chronological history framework. Four units were taught in the seventh grade, and six were taught the following year in 20 weeks to the same students, now in the eighth grade ($N = 109$; five classrooms). Experimental teachers were four investigators with the project who also held teaching appointments at the experimental school. Control groups were located in three other schools where students were exposed to the usual seventh and eighth-grade social studies curriculum.

In addition to evaluating the efffectiveness of the experimental curriculum, two discussion-leadership procedures were compared within it. One emphasized a socratic interchange between teachers and students, the other emphasized recitation: teacher questions and student responses based on information provided earlier by the teacher. For comparison, the five experimental classes were divided into two discussion groups each, and each was exposed to a different leadership style.

On two standardized tests of critical thinking (one used parts of the Watson-Glaser, the other was the social studies interpretation subtest of the Iowa Test of Educational Development), the investigators found no statistically significant differences between the experimental and control groups ($SMDs = .15$ and $.13$). However, on four investigator-constructed measures of "analytic competence" (two paper-and-pencil tests, one structured interview, and a content analysis of student-led discussions), generally positive results were obtained. On all but the fourth, the experimental group significantly outperformed the controls ($SMDs = 1.2, .49,$ and 1.9). On three measures of social studies content knowledge, the experimental group did as well as controls, and student interest in public policy issues generally was enhanced. On all these measures, the two experimental subgroups (socratic and recitation) performed similarly. To account for that finding, the investigators cited the literature to date that indicated that no one teaching style was generally superior.

The study's key strength was its comprehensiveness: philosophical premises were laid out for social studies curriculum development in a democratic society, an experimental curriculum was developed accordingly, and its effectiveness was evaluated in several ways. The authors made clear their position that the jurisprudential approach, implemented here in a junior high school, could be translated into materials and instruction for other grades. In a second phase of the Harvard project, that approach was taken to the senior high school.

That phase was reported by Newmann and Oliver (1970) and Levin, Newmann, and Oliver (1969). Located in a suburban senior high school noted for innovation, an experimental social studies curriculum was implemented and evaluated over a 3-year period. Subjects were 50 students in two 10th-grade classrooms who moved with the experimental curriculum through the subsequent two grades. At least two teachers were assigned to each classroom. This "overstaffing" permitted unconventional interactions such as two teachers modeling dialogue skills for the class, and small group discussions by five or six students supervised by two teachers. There were three comparison groups: other "average" students at the same high school who were also taught with project materials, although by their regular classroom teachers, and two groups of students in another high school—one "average" and the other "honors."

The goal of the experimental curriculum was to teach high school students of average ability "to clarify and justify their positions on public issues" (Levin, Newmann, & Oliver, 1969, p. 31). As in a conventional high school social studies curriculum, an array of historical and social science knowledge was introduced. However, discussion and value conflict were emphasized. The focus of the curriculum was on case studies that were thought likely to serve as "springboards for lively and sustained discussions." The teacher's role as "listener, questioner, and clarifier" was emphasized over and above his or her role as "truthgiver" (pp. 112–113).

The investigators emphasized that the major purpose of the study was materials development and evaluation in a clinical setting, not the design of innovative teaching procedures. Accordingly, the latter was guided by the former. Procedures that emerged included (a) audiotaped discussions in which a small group of students intentionally unloaded their opinions on issues without responding to one another, and then tried to improve the same discussion; and (b) discussion reviews, in which each student was asked to trace the main ideas that emerged in a discussion and evaluate the quality of the discussion.

The scope of the experimental curriculum centered on five problem areas: use and control of violence, standard of living, priorities and privileges, dissent and change, and the tension between civic life and privacy. The sequence of study was designed to engage students first in brief and relatively well-structured case material and then in increasingly broad and complex case material.

Two kinds of dependent measures were administered to the experimental and control groups at the end of the 12th grade. Those in the first category assessed knowledge of academic content (e.g., the American Revolution, the New Deal, monopoly and competition); those in the second assessed knowledge of discussion-analysis concepts and discussion-process skills.

Measures in the first category were a standardized problems of democracy test and an open-ended American history recall test developed by the investigators. Measures in the second were three paper-and-pencil measures. One was a multiple-choice test of students' knowledge of discussion analysis concepts, one was a multiple-choice dialogue-analysis test, and the third was "open-ended." The last presented students with short dialogues and asked questions about the discussion process of each. Also in the second category were two instruments developed to measure student ability in actual discussions with their peers.

On the problems of democracy measure, the experimental group did not score significantly higher than the two average control groups groups ($SMDs = .11$ and $.17$), and it scored significantly lower than the honors group ($SMD = .67$). On the American history test, the experimental group outperformed the average group at the same school ($SMD = .39$). In the second category, there was no significant difference between the experimental and honors groups on knowledge of discussion-analysis concepts, but the experimental group scored significantly higher than the two average groups ($SMDs = .38$ and $.44$). The honors group scored the same as the experimental group on the multiple-choice discussion-analysis test, but the experimental group scored significantly higher than the two average groups ($SMDs = .65$ and $.76$). On the open-ended analysis of the short dialogues, the experimental group significantly outperformed the two average groups ($SMDs = .98$ and $.93$) and the honors group ($SMD = .90$). On the first of the two measures used to assess student ability in actual discussions, the experimental group scored significantly higher than the average group in the same school ($SMD = .76$), but not significantly higher than the second average group ($SMD = .38$). It scored significantly lower than the honors group. On the second of these measures, the experimental group did not score significantly higher than the two average groups ($SMDs = .15$ and $.29$) and, again, scored significantly lower than the honors group.

THE TABA PROJECTS

A unique, though not unrelated, program of research was conducted in the same decade by Taba and her associates at San Francisco State College (Taba 1963, 1966, 1967; Taba, Levine, & Elzey, 1964; Taba, Durkin, Fraenkel, & McNaughton, 1971). The Taba curriculum experiments shared a number of attributes with those at Harvard. First, the description and development of student reasoning processes were central concerns, and the reasoning processes of interest in both projects were matched to the selection and organization of content in the experimental curriculum. Put differently, student reasoning was a primary concern in both, and in both it was content-dependent. In prior studies, riding the wave of direct skill instruction that began with Osborn's study and swelled with those by Glaser and Anderson et al., researchers had not been concerned to fit reasoning processes to the content at hand. Rebuilding this juncture was the most important contribution of the Harvard and Taba projects. Second, both were comprehensive. The experimental curriculum in each was grounded in a theory of curriculum development, built carefully on the literature to date, and was evaluated with measures that were logically related to the curriculum theory. Third, neither dismissed the critical role of values in building social studies knowledge. While the Harvard projects went further, emphasizing value commitments and conflict as the foundation of democratic life and, thus, of the analysis of public in a democracy, Taba considered three value tasks as integral to the social studies curriculum: exploring feelings, considering approaches to solving disputes among persons and groups, and analyzing values. Fourth, both endeavored to capitalize on the heterogeneity of the public school classroom. For Oliver, Shaver, Newmann, and Levin, the diversity of the classroom mirrored the heterogeneity of civic life and, thus, made the former an appropriate training ground for the latter. For Taba, heterogeneity in classrooms caused the products of thinking and valuing to be richer and more powerful than otherwise would be possible. Finally, both sets of projects anticipated the cognitive movement in psychology (Wittrock, 1978) by regarding learning as essentially a constructive activity rather than merely a responsive one. As a constructive activity, learning is a function of the sense-making activity of the learners themselves as they endeavor to derive meaning from experience. While this view is clear in the rationale provided for the jurisprudential approach, Taba went further. She was the first curriculum scholar to elaborate the constructive approach (what she called discovery learning, 1963) for social studies. This was an important moment in the literature on thinking and decision making in social studies, for here we see for the first time a cognitive analysis of the curriculum—an explication of the rationale and procedures for embedding instruction on thinking processes within instruction on content objectives.

The study reported in 1964 began with the identification of three barriers to the implementation in social studies of the longstanding "critical thinking" objective. First, thinking remained poorly and variously defined: Thinking meant anything and everything that happened in the head. Second, the common misconception that higher-order thinking cannot occur until a sufficient body of information has been gathered had fueled superficial coverage of a wide array of facts, actually inhibiting learning. Third, another misconception held that good thinking is an automatic by-product of studying certain subjects. This was wrong on two counts. First, on constructivist grounds, children do not learn ideas by memorizing them as already formed end-products of someone else's constructive thinking but by discovering them themselves. Piaget (1959) had been saying this in terms of accommodation versus assimilation. Dewey (1902) had been saying it in terms of "psychologizing" the subject matter for the learners rather than imposing on them the already digested world of adults. Second, the assumption is spurious because it requires one to accept on faith that memorizing Latin or the steps in math processes constitutes better intellectual training than "memorizing cake recipies, even though both may be learned in the same manner and call for the same mental process" (Taba, Levine, & Elzey, 1964, p. 2).

The study's purpose was to examine the thinking of elementary school children under what Taba considered the optimal conditions of learning: (a) a curriculum designed for the development of thought, (b) teaching strategies focused explicitly on the mastery of the necessary cognitive skills, and (c) a sufficient time span to permit a developmental sequence in training (Taba, Levine, & Elzey, 1964, p. 27, summarized in Taba & Elzey, 1964). Taba reasoned that these conditions required a curriculum that emphasized depth and breadth on a limited number of basic ideas rather than "overburdening the students' minds with disconnected descriptive detail" (Taba, Levine, & Elzey, p. 60). Such a curriculum required that curriculum developers and teachers understand the "structure" of the subject matter—especially the relationship between a concept and the variety of examples and information that can be "sampled" and brought to bear on its formation. Also required was the identification of basic "cognitive tasks" required of learners if social studies knowledge was to be constructed. Three cognitive tasks identified by Taba were concept formation, interpretation of data and inference, and application of principles. Each was broken down into its constituent thinking processes or "operations." For example, concept formation included data gathering, grouping, and labeling.

Students in 20 classrooms in 16 elementary schools in nine school districts in Contra Costa County, California were engaged in a curriculum centered on a limited number of basic ideas drawn from history and the social sciences. It included a sequence of learning activities designed to promote the "spiral" development of these ideas along with steady progress on the requisite thinking processes. Twenty classroom teachers were given five days of inservice training in August before school opened, and 10 half-day sessions throughout the year. The inservice program involved (a) analysis of content sampling and organization (which, the reader is told, teachers had a difficult time understanding), (b) analysis of the cognitive demands of the curriculum, and (c) training in the teaching strategies considered likely to elicit and support the student thinking needed to achieve that curriculum.

To measure growth in student thinking, The Social Science Inference Test was developed. Students were given four scores for Grades 3 through 6: inference, discrimination, caution, and overgeneralization. Identical forms of the test were administered to students at the beginning and end of the year. Statistically significant gains were reported at all grade levels on ability to infer (mean $SMD = .66$) and at the fifth- and sixth-grades on ability to discriminate relevant from irrelevant information ($SMDs = .46$ and $.51$). There were also statistically significant reductions at all grade levels on being overly cautious (mean $SMD = .36$). No statistically significant reduction was found in students' tendency to overgeneralize. A second pre-post measure was a social studies achievement test. At all grade levels, scores increased significantly over the year (mean $SMD = .63$). The investigators took this, despite the lack of controls, to be an indication that the emphasis on depth in the curriculum had not affected general achievement adversely. "Training in thought processes," they concluded, "may compensate for lack of coverage" (p. 99).

As in the Harvard projects, Taba also analyzed classroom interaction. Four discussions audiotaped in each of the 20 classrooms were analyzed. The investigators identified seven teaching functions that they believed influenced student thinking and, depending on their use, facilitated or undermined performance on the cognitive tasks. These functions were focusing student thought, changing the focus, refocusing, deviating from the focus, extending thought at the same level, lifting thought to a higher level, and controlling thought. By tracing the interaction of student thinking and these teaching acts, Taba was able to identify more and less effective strategies for guiding student thought. In the ideal, student thinking is lifted from one level to another appropriately—that is, as required by the cognitive task at hand (e.g., in concept formation, from gathering and recording information to grouping it, and then to labeling these groups)—but sustained at one level long enough and in such a way that depth of processing is encouraged, student participation is distributed widely, and success at the next level made likely.

In a second study, Taba (1966) extended and refined the theoretical constructs and findings of the first. The research design was stronger: One experimental and three control groups were involved; modifications were made both in the inference measure and the scheme for analyzing classroom transactions; a third measure was added for the third cognitive task, application of principles; qualitative data were also gathered; and model teaching strategies identified in the first study were incorporated into the inservice training in the second. The findings generally underscored those of the first: Focused attention by teachers and curriculum developers on helping students perform successfully the cognitive tasks needed to construct understandings of the subject matter considerably influenced "students' facility to transform raw data into useable concepts, generalizations, hypotheses, and theories" (p. 221).

This is the only well-reported set of projects at the elementary level in social studies to date in which objectives concerning student cognitive growth were carefully articulated with objectives concerning student mastery of a limited number of ideas in the curriculum. It is against this dual focus—what Taba called multiple objectives—that the recent tendency to lift thinking away from its content domains (McPeck, 1984; Schrag, 1988) must be seen.

THE NEWMANN PROJECT

Newmann (1988b) has mounted the most important study of higher-order thinking in social studies since the Harvard and Taba Projects. Though the full study has not yet been completed, a portion of it has been reported. Already, an impressive set of theoretical constructs, assessment measures, and findings have been produced. The study is addressing three questions: (a) To what extent can higher order thinking actually find a prominent place in high school social studies departments that are conventionally organized? (b) Why is higher-order thinking so difficult to promote? (c) Why have some schools made successful movement toward this goal, and what have they done to overcome some of the barriers?

Newmann and his associates first worked out a broad and practical conception of higher-order thinking. Newmann reasoned that practitioners and scholars alike do not agree on a single, narrow conception of teaching, be it critical thinking, dialectical thinking, divergent, convergent, or moral reasoning. Little would be gained by promoting a conception of higher-order thinking that only a few in the field would accept. Moreover, research indicates that the problem in schools is hardly diversity in approaches to thinking and decision-making objectives; rather, it is the pervasive absence of *any* approach—the general absence of intellectual challenge. Furthermore, a broad framework likely would have some ecological validity: It would not require a revamping of the school curriculum or the school day, nor would it require the replacement of the present teaching force. So, a broader conception of higher-order thinking is, at least at this time, prudent. The conception offered emphasizes novelty:

Higher order thinking is a challenge that requires the person to go beyond the information given; that is, to interpret, analyze, or manipulate information because a question or a problem to be solved cannot be resolved through the routine application of previously learned knowledge. In contrast, lower-order thinking demands only routine, mechanistic application of previously acquired knowledge.... (Newmann, 1988b, p. II–2)

Succeeding at novel tasks, in Newmann's view, is not simply a matter of having and using well a set of thinking skills. Just as important are two additional components of higher-order thinking: in-depth knowledge of relevant subject matter and dispositions (habits of mind).

How might higher-order thinking, thus conceived, be assessed and promoted? Newmann chose to focus the study on the social studies classroom, examining individual lessons rather than individual students. After all, novelty is relative to student background—a novel task for one student might be a routine matter for another. Furthermore, few observers have argued that the problem in social studies is the lack of thinking by individual *students*. Rather, the problem is the mindlessness, the low level of thoughtfulness, that plagues social studies *lessons*.

Five diverse high school social studies departments participated in the study. The chief criteria for selection were a department-wide emphasis on higher-order thinking, a required social studies course that emphasized in-depth study of a limited number of topics, a view of knowledge as dynamic and problematic, and student involvement in reasoning. In each of the departments, five courses (each taught by a different teacher) were observed from one to nine times over the 1986 to 1987 school year ($n = 30$ teachers, 160 lessons). Also, the teachers, three students from each of the five classes, the social studies department chair, and the school principal completed interviews and questionnaires.

The assessment instrument developed for classroom observations was composed of 17 dimensions of thoughtfulness, each scored once on a 5 point scale for each class session. Scales 1–3 pertain to general characteristics of the lesson. A low score on any of these was presumed to "undermine the disposition to think things through systematically and deliberately" (Newmann, 1988b, p. II–5). Scales 4–10 concern teacher behavior,

and 11–17 focus on student behavior. Six scales were selected as minimal indicators of classroom thoughtfulness:

1. Sustained examination of a few topics rather than superficial coverage of many.
2. Lesson displayed substantive coherence and continuity.
3. Students were given an appropriate amount of time to think—that is, to prepare responses to questions.
4. Teacher asked challenging questions and/or structured challenging tasks (given the ability level and preparation of the students).
10. Teacher was a model of thoughtfulness.
11. Students offered explanations and reasons for their conclusions.

The criterion by which these six scales were selected was this: Based on the conception of higher-order thinking outlined earlier, could a lesson conceivably score low on this scale, yet still be considered a highly thoughtful lesson? If the answer was "no," the scale was judged to be critical for assessing classroom thoughtfulness. Inter-rater reliability was high across all 17 scales ($r = .85$).

The results of this phase of the study only can be sketched here. The most important contribution of the project is development of a general framework of higher-order thinking that is applicable to instruction on a wide variety of topics, that embraces diverse approaches to the teaching of thinking, and that has been defined operationally with an instrument that can be used reliably for assessing the level of thoughtfulness in social studies lessons.

Teachers of both high- and low-scoring lessons believed that key barriers to promoting student thinking are large class size and total student load. The teachers of high-scoring lessons considered the development of student thinking as their chief mission, rather than just one of many concerns; they displayed greater willingness to reduce content coverage as a means toward this end. Indeed, high-scoring teachers differed from low scorers on the first scale (few topics) by one standard deviation. As well, high-scoring teachers were able to articulate more coherent and more elaborate conceptions of thinking than low scorers.

Students in the project departments nominated social studies more often than any other subject as the most intellectually challenging class taken in high school. And, most students indicated that the most challenging class was also their most engaging. Three in four students reported that they had to "think hard" to be successful in social studies, and a majority identified individual writing completed outside class as an example of a challenging task. They reported that writing a longer paper was especially challenging because so much information had to be gathered. In contrast to lecture and recitation, teacher-led discussions were more likely to challenge students to go beyond the information given, as was reading primary documents in contrast to textbook reading. Turning from challenge to engagement, a majority of the students said that the subject matter was intrinsically interesting. Others indicated they were engaged by the opportunity to contribute their own ideas and opinions on the topic at hand. Only a few students attributed their engagement to their teacher.

Newmann conducted a multiple regression on the six critical dimensions and found institutional effects. About 26% of the variance in classroom thoughtfulness was associated with differences among the five departments. The department with the highest composite score on the six critical dimensions of classroom thoughtfulness differed from the lowest by 1.7 standard deviations. Three high-scoring departments had a systematic, department-based, higher-order thinking program. The other two did not. The three high-scoring departments were distinguished by strong leadership from both the department head and the principal, as well as by a departmental culture of collegiality. There was consistent and focused discussion on teaching and curriculum within each of the three departments.

Newmann recognizes that there is yet much to learn. The relationship of classroom thoughtfulness to student achievement and to actual higher-order thinking by students was not examined, as of this writing, nor were these select social studies departments compared to a more representative group or to a select group that had modified the organizational structure in an attempt to overcome institutional barriers to higher-order thinking. The comparisons are being made in subsequent phases of the project.

SUMMARY AND CRITIQUE

Eleven studies in roughly four programs of research were reviewed: The propaganda studies (1936 to 1941), the Harvard jurisprudential studies (1966 to 1970), Taba's cognitive task studies (1964 to 1966), and Newmann's classroom thoughtfulness study (1988 to present). The propaganda studies investigated "critical thinking," defined by some researchers as the ability to withstand pressure to shift one's attitude on a public controversy and by others as knowledge of the rules of logical inquiry or argument analysis. The relevance of these studies to the social studies curriculum was tangential at best, although rationales for them often coincided with the chief rationale for the social studies: democratic citizenship. Generally, the researchers concluded that direct instruction on critical thinking is more likely to improve critical thinking than is instruction on regular course content.

Building on this general conclusion, the Harvard Social Studies Project in both phases broke with the earlier generic conception of critical thinking. The key advance here was the endeavor to consider first the nature of society, then the curriculum question—what knowledge is of most worth in such a society—and then to match thinking to that curriculum. Because public controversies are by nature value-laden and open to wide-ranging interpretations and resolutions, some better and some worse, depending on the criteria used, generic rules of argument will not do. To the contrary, flexible analytic and discussion skills, coupled with ample knowledge, are required as reasoners work their way to decisions on the issue. The experimental curricula of the Harvard projects emphasized precisely this.

Taba also was concerned with the match of student thinking to the cognitive demands of the curriculum. This required a cognitive analysis of the curriculum, on which Taba remains unsurpassed in the social studies field. But Taba was less concerned to fit the social studies curriculum to the needs of a society organized under the democratic ideal. She fit it instead to the structure of the disciplines. Nevertheless, both the Harvard and Taba projects emphasized content-specific thinking and decision making, and this emphasis led, perhaps inevitably, to an interest in depth over superficial coverage. In the Harvard projects, the curriculum was limited to analysis and discussion of select public controversies set within the U.S. history curriculum. The spiral curriculum for Grades 1 through 8 that emerged from the Taba studies was limited to from 3 to 8 main ideas per grade level and 11 concepts throughout. This concern for depth as a condition for enhancing higher-order thinking in social studies was moved to center stage in the study by Newmann and his associates (1988b), where "sustained examination of a few topics rather than superficial coverage of many" was the first of six constituent dimensions for assessing classroom thoughtfulness.

A second important development in the literature is the shift from particularistic to general conceptions of higher-order thinking. In his broad, novel-challenge conception, Newmann recognized that the central persistent problem in social studies education is not that students are engaged in different kinds of higher-order thinking as they go from one social studies classroom to another, but that they are not likely to be engaged, in any sustained way, in any kind of higher-order thinking in their social studies classrooms.

Other important advances found in Newmann's study are the attention to organizational variables—to the contexts that promote and frustrate thoughtfulness—and to recent literature in cognitive psychology and philosophy regarding the nature of thinking and its variations across types of problems. Newmann's emphasis on novel challenges and his reluctance to reduce thinking to the sum of discrete skills are welcome moves (Chipman, Segal, & Glaser, 1985; Nickerson, 1988; Resnick, 1987; Schrag, 1988; Voss, in press). On the other hand, Newmann's withdrawal from the democratic discourse of the Harvard projects and the propaganda studies deserves scrutiny. The retreat may be warranted on the grounds that a foundation of thoughtfulness in social studies classrooms must be laid before work on an even more ambitious project, curriculum and instruction for ethical decision-making, can begin in earnest. Viewed in this way, the creation of thoughtful classrooms is an enormously helpful step, albeit an intermediate one between mindless social studies lessons on the one hand and the vision of social studies classrooms as laboratories of democracy on the other.

Depth Over Breadth of Coverage

The fate of thinking and decision-making objectives in social studies, or the possibility of their ever making the trip from paper to practice, very well may rest on the matter of depth versus breadth of content coverage. It appears to be a sort of lever on which a surprising number of facets of the problem of mindless lessons are forced into consideration: educators' conceptions of higher-order thinking, institutional barriers to its development, student engagement and challenge, teacher education, state and district education policies, and the central curriculum question: "What knowledge is of most worth?"

One position on the matter, which we might call the deep content view, undergirds the Newmann (1988b) project. It holds that thinking and decision-making objectives are best achieved by immersing students in limited content (Cornbleth, 1985; McPeck, 1981, 1984; Newmann, 1988b; Schrag, 1988; Scriven, 1972; Voss, in press). On this analysis, steeping oneself in the facts, concepts, history, and methods necessary to comprehend and reflect well on public policy issues (or whatever the subject matter) delivers more analytic power and brings one closer to a thorough understanding of the issue than does isolated training in general thinking skills. Most helpful for the cultivation of thoughtfulness is not skills training alone—not pedantry on the syntax of thought—but the struggle to understand issues and problems in all their complicated dimensions. Such understanding does not come easily, of course, but it is made all but impossible when too many topics are covered and when concentrated study is dissipated by general skills training.

At the opposite pole is a position taken by educators who are interested less in the problem of mindless lessons than in the problem of student inability to think skillfully. These are distinct but often confused discourses. The discourse of thinking skills, as against the discourse of thoughtful learning, is captured in a surge of current literature: Presseisen (1986), Chance (1986), Costa (1985), deBono (1983), Perkins (1987), and Sternberg (1986). The theme here is to teach thinking, construed to be a set of skills, directly rather than trying to embed it in the curriculum. The rationales for the approach generally address what are considered to be the extraordinary information-processing demands in a postindustrial society. Because the particular information needed cannot be predicted, the emphasis shifts from the content per se to the ability to gather and work with content, whatever it may be. For example:

In a society facing the twenty-first century, where change may be the only constant, the ability to formulate problems, resolve issues, determine the most effective decisions, and create new solutions is a prerequisite of success—for life as well as schooling. The time has come to seriously consider thinking as a major goal for teaching and learning at all levels of education. (Presseisen, 1986, p. 5)

This view was laid out for social studies by Beyer (1985, 1988). He noted that educators have for years attempted to teach thinking, but generally without success. Among several factors responsible, the main culprit has been inexplicit instructional practices. "Instead of providing instruction on how to engage in thinking, teachers generally put students into situations where they must engage in thinking to whatever degree they can" (1988, pp. 28–29). This charge could be leveled at the deep-content approach. The error, on this analysis, is assuming that providing students with higher-order challenges is sufficient. It is not. The higher-order challenge approach alone is not really instruction at all, but blind training (Brown, Campione, & Day, 1981). It skips over the enabling instruction on higher-order thinking. At best, for already-able students, such

challenges provide stimulating opportunities to apply current knowledge to unfamiliar problems; at worst, they test students and leave frustrated those who are not already able to think in the ways needed to be successful at the task.

The remedy, Beyer argued, lies in defining the thinking skills we want students to learn and then teaching those skills to the point of mastery rather than hiding them away in instruction on content and hoping that they will spontaneously develop. In asserting this argument, Beyer is hardly out of touch with the social studies literature. Rather, he is building on the conclusions of Glaser (1941), Anderson et al. (1944), Hyram (1957), and Shaver (1962), and the assumption of the Harvard projects. Nevertheless, it should be clear that he is opposed generally to the deep-content view, with what he sees as its avoidance of direct instruction on skills and its naive hope that thinking will develop as a by-product of content immersion.

Note that this direct-instruction-on-thinking-skills approach is attacked not only by deep-content advocates but by social studies critics who charge that the skills emphasis in social studies diverts teachers and students from content learning, deep or otherwise (Cheney, 1987; Hirsch, 1988; Ravitch, 1985). Cheney, who assessed school learning for the National Endowment for the Humanities and found knowledge of history particularly wanting, laid blame directly on the skills emphasis—"the belief that we can teach our children how to think without troubling them to learn anything worth thinking about . . . that we can teach them how to understand the world in which they live without conveying to them the events and ideas that have brought it into existence" (p. 5).

A Middle Way

Between the deep-content and direct-teaching-of-skills approaches can be discerned a modest, middle way. From this perspective, the predominant concern, as in the deep-content view, is thoughtful learning on a limited number of topics. However, interest in the meaningful learning of selected content is paired with an interest in the learning of strategies that can be used to construct and operate on knowledge. This pairing is more ambitious than promoting just one or the other: it promises to enable more students to benefit from the deep-content approach, and it addresses more explicitly than either extreme the problem of transfer.

Let us assume for a moment that, not unlike the Harvard projects, the secondary social studies curriculum was centered on sustained public policy analysis concerning select cases drawn from United States history and government. Our objectives are student understanding of the case knowledge as well as student understanding of the analytic tools with which they explore or process those cases and the discussions that ensue. Meanwhile, our goal is transfer—that both the case knowledge and the analytic tools will be used, strengthened, and elaborated in subsequent public policy controversies that are studied as part of the curriculum, as well as in the more or less novel controversies that arise incessantly in civic life, both in and out of school. With this goal in mind, it would be wise to avoid the lopsided deep-content approach, because the tools might never be taught, or they would be only introduced and then drowned out by the content immersion; hence, they would be less available for use later in novel challenges. As well, we would avoid the other lopsided approach, the direct teaching of general thinking skills, fearing that it would lead us to trivialize thought into discrete subunits while, making matters worse, never quite getting to the application of the skills to the thoughtful learning of substantive content. This lack-of-application threat should particularly concern us since, contrary to the spirit of depth over breadth, thinking skills in the direct approach easily become yet another add-on to the already jammed curriculum. Opting for the middle way, students would be engaged in the study of select cases (per the deep-content approach) *and* they would be guided systematically to reflect upon that study with the intention of building awareness of the tools of learning and analysis that were employed.

The benefits of metacognitive reflection are the subject of a burgeoning literature in cognitive psychology and well may be the principal contribution of that field to social studies educators concerned with the advancement of thinking and decision making. Among the central concepts of metacognition is strategy. Like a skill, but goal directed, strategies are "processes (or sequences of processes) that, when matched to the requirements of tasks, facilitate performance" (Pressley, Goodchild, Fleet, Zajchowski, & Evans, 1989). Reasoners who are good strategy users know the strategies that help accomplish important learning goals, know when and how to use those strategies, can compare and contrast the benefits of alternative strategies when adopting a particular goal, and use strategies in connection with (not instead of) a rich understanding of the matter at hand (Pressley, Borkowski, and Schneider, 1987).

Among the methods that might be used to teach the attributes of good strategy use are explicit explanation of strategies and their appropriate use (O'Sullivan & Pressley, 1984); reciprocal teaching, in which teacher and students take turns attempting the strategies being taught (Palinscar & Brown, 1984); and metacognitive reflection on prior attempts at strategy use (Parker, McDaniel, & Valencia, in press). The last method was developed for an experimental 6th-grade social studies curriculum in which students were taught to reason dialectically (i.e., to explore all sides) on public policy controversies. Other studies in social studies have indicated that a minimal degree of metacognitive guidance can provoke reasonably successful dialectical reasoning on public controversies by 12th-grade students (Parker, Mueller, & Wendling, 1989).

The advantages of a metacognitive middle way are twofold. First, the pitfalls of either extreme might be avoided: the loss of substantive content knowledge and goal-directed skill use in the direct skills approach, and the loss of enabling, metacognitive instruction in the deep-content approach. Second, depth of coverage and novel challenge (Newmann, 1988b) are maintained as the guiding lights of lesson planning.

Reviewing the literature in this light, we can see that, except for Bateman and Remmers (1936) and Osborn (1939), the propaganda studies were unconcerned with social studies learning, much less depth. Most of these were skills experiments, and—though several of the authors expressed a concern for transfer—none appears to have included metacognitive instruction.

The Taba, Harvard, and Newmann projects all have been more or less dedicated to depth, and all could have been strengthened had they considered more carefully the role of metacognitive awareness. Newmann (1988b) distinguished thoughtful, in-depth lessons from shallow coverage but did not include metacognitive instruction among the 17 criteria for a thoughtful lesson. The metacognitive middle way, in which reflection upon the strategies used to acquire, construct, and manipulate knowledge pervades in-depth study of a few important topics, may provide an avenue for grappling with the twin objectives in social studies of knowledge and skill learning.

CONCLUSION

Social studies educators have exhorted one another to take seriously the teaching of thinking and decision making. Recent advocates of these objectives from outside the field (e.g., de-Bono, 1983; Presseisen, 1986) have provided largely technocratic rationales that emphasized the information-processing demands being brought to bear on the labor force as the century turns. Social studies educators typically have offered rationales grounded in democratic theory, the best examples of which are found in the Harvard Social Studies Project. Despite all the exhortations on the matter, however, these objectives are today still more wish than practice.

It is a curious phenomenon that the wish has remained so fervent yet so unrealized. Newmann and his associates (1988b) have undertaken the first research program to deal soberly with this phenomenon, using it as their starting point. This is an important development and signals a critical shift in theory and research on these objectives. If subsequent studies are to be helpful, researchers must not ignore this shift.

In general, researchers should help spell out the connections between thinking and decision making on the one hand and limited content objectives on the other. So as not to promote a false dichotomy between depth and breadth, the effects on student thinking of various combinations and degrees of these should be explored. Such research will involve building a base of theory and findings that refines the field's conception of thoughtfulness in social studies lessons and describes the variation of thoughtfulness under diverse conditions—*curricular, instructional,* and *institutional.*

On the curricular front, work is needed that clarifies the relationship between content selection and organization on the one hand and the cultivation of thoughtfulness on the other. Which topics in which grades most warrant higher-order thought by students, and which of these topics best promote it? By what criteria ought these content selection decisions be made? (Newmann, 1988a, has named a few.)

Turning to instruction, rich case knowledge is needed that answers three questions. First, What are the varieties of thoughtful lessons on important social studies topics? (It will not be helpful to know the varieties of thoughtful lessons on topics that are unlikely to be treated in considerable depth; that is, curriculum and instruction should not be pulled apart.) Second, What are the effects of thoughtful lessons on students' higher-order thinking as well as on the subject-matter understandings they construct as a consequence? Third, What metacognitive strategies are particularly germane to the construction of key social studies understandings, and how can those strategies best be taught?

Turning to institutional variation, work is needed on the social contexts of thoughtfulness. Newmann's (1988b) finding that 26% of the variance in classroom thoughtfulness was associated with school differences is striking, particularly when we recall (a) the sameness that characterizes public schools (Goodlad, 1984), and (b) the fact that Newmann chose schools that were similar in their relatively strong commitment to higher-order thinking. Newmann's characterization of high- and low-scoring departments is a helpful point of departure for inquiry on the relationship between school organization and management on the one hand and thoughtful forms of social studies education on the other.

An array of studies is needed on this relationship. McNeil's (1986) multiple case study of secondary social studies showed how the tension between order and education can be expressed in ways that clearly undermine thoughtful learning. For example, content is trivialized into lists (e.g., the three causes of the Civil War; the five crops of Argentina). This is done not as a strategy for increasing student understanding but for maintaining classroom order and student cooperation. To what extent is such mindlessness indigenous to present school organization? To what extent are sustainable alternatives possible in setting where 150 students per day, per teacher, are herded through a smorgasbord curriculum managed by officials intent on keeping things running smoothly? Schrag (1988) examined organizational barriers to thoughtful learning and suggested alternative settings to schools (e.g., museums) where thoughtfulness might better thrive.

Looking beyond the school to political and economic institutions in the broader society, the point is essentially the same: educators undermine thinking and decision-making objectives when they overlook the intersection of intellectual development and social setting. Democratic theory emphasizes that deliberation on public policy is not an individual act but a shared social practice that is bound up in shared public meanings, or what Tocqueville (1969) called habits of the heart. Without this sort of social fabric, what reason is there to expect that deliberation can properly proceed or that it can result in policy that serves well the common good (Parker, 1988)? Moreover, critical theory emphasizes the contradiction between a political democracy that is intent on justice and equality and a political economy that is intent on reproducing current arrangements of power and wealth (Carnoy & Levin, 1985). To the extent that schools are influenced by this contradiction, how successfully can they go about distributing higher-order thinking to *all* students?

In the main, research conducted to date on teaching thinking and decision making in social studies has emphasized instruction over curriculum, and curriculum and instruction over institutional context. Needed now are studies that bring the three into focus together.

References

Anderson, H. C., Marcham, F. C., & Dunn, S. B. (1944). An experiment in teaching certain skills of critical thinking. *The Journal of Educational Research, 38,* 241–251.

Anderson, H. R., (Ed.). *Teaching critical thinking in the social studies,* Thirteenth yearbook. Washington, DC: National Council for the Social Studies.

Arnold, O. L. (1938). Testing ability to use data in the fifth and sixth grades. *Educational Research Bulletin, 17,* 255–259, 278.

Bateman, R. M., & Remmers, H. H. (1936). The relationship of pupil attitudes toward social topics before and after studying the subjects. *Bulletin of Purdue University, 37,* 27–42.

Beyer, B. K. (1985). Critical thinking: What is it? *Social Education, 49,* 270–276.

Beyer, B. K. (1988). *Developing a thinking skills program.* Boston: Allyn and Bacon.

Biddle, W. W. (1932). *Propaganda and education.* New York: Teachers College, Columbia University.

Brown, A. L., Campione, J. C., & Day, J. D. (1981). Learning to learn: On training students to learn from texts. *Educational Researcher, 10,* 15.

Carnoy, M., & Levin, H. M. (1985). *Schooling and work in the democratic state.* Stanford, CA: Stanford University Press.

Chance, P. (1986). *Thinking in the classroom: A survey of programs.* New York: Teachers College Press.

Cheney, L. V. (1987). *The American memory: A report on the humanities in the nation's public schools.* Washington, DC: National Endowment for the Humanities.

Chipman, S. F., Segal, J. W., & Glaser, R. (Eds.). (1985). *Thinking and learning skills: Vol. 2. Research and open questions.* Hillsdale, NJ: Erlbaum.

Committee of Seven. (1900). *The study of history in schools: Report to the American Historical Association.* New York: Macmillan.

Cornbleth, C. (1985). Critical thinking and cognitive processes. In W. B. Stanley (Ed.), *Review of research in social studies education: 1976–1983.* Bulletin No. 75 (pp. 11–63). Washington, DC: National Council for the Social Studies.

Costa, A. L. (1985). *Developing minds.* Alexandria, VA: Association for Supervision and Curriculum Development.

de Bono, E. (1983). The direct teaching of thinking as a skill. *Phi Delta Kappan, 64,* 703–708.

Dewey, J. (1902). *The child and the curriculum.* Chicago: University of Chicago Press.

Dewey, J. (1933). *How we think.* Boston: D. C. Heath.

Ellis, E. (Ed.). (1937). *Education against propaganda: Developing skills in the use of sources of information about public affairs.* Seventh yearbook. Washington, DC: National Council for the Social Studies.

Ellis, E. (1942). Methods and materials for developing skill in critical thinking. In H. R. Anderson (Ed.), *Teaching critical thinking in the social studies.* 13th yearbook (pp. 49–92). Washington, DC: National Council for the Social Studies.

Engle, S. H. (1960). Decision making: The heart of social studies instruction. *Social Education, 24,* 301–304, 306.

Ennis, R. H. (1987). A taxonomy of critical thinking dispositions and abilities. In J. B. Baron & R. J. Sternberg (Eds.), *Teaching thinking skills: Theory and practice* (pp. 9–26). New York: W. H. Freeman.

Glaser, E. M. (1941). *An experiment in the development of critical thinking.* New York: Teachers College.

Goodlad, J. I. (1984). *A place called school.* New York: McGraw-Hill.

Hirsch, E. D., Jr. (1988). *Cultural literacy.* New York: Vintage.

Hyram, G. H. (1957). An experiment in developing critical thinking in children. *Journal of Experimental Education, 26,* 125–132.

Kurfman, D. G. (Ed.). (1977). *Developing decision-making skills,* Forty-seventh yearbook. Washington, DC: National Council for the Social Studies.

Levin, M., Newmann, F. M., & Oliver, D. W. (1969). *A law and social science curriculum based on the analysis of public issues* (Final report). Unpublished manuscript, Graduate School of Education, Harvard University, Cambridge, MA.

Marzano, R. J., Brandt, R. S., Hughes, C. S., Jones, B. F., Presseisen, B. Z., Rankin, S. C., & Suhor, C. (1988). *Dimensions of thinking: A framework for curriculum and instruction.* Alexandria, VA: Association for Supervision and Curriculum Development.

McNeil, L. M. (1986). *Contradictions of control.* New York: Routledge.

McPeck, J. E. (1981). *Critical thinking and education.* New York: St. Martins.

McPeck, J. E. (1984). Stalking beasts, but swatting flies: The teaching of critical thinking. *Canadian Journal of Education, 9,* 28–44.

Metcalf, L. E. (Ed.). (1971). *Values education: Rationales, strategies, procedures.* 41st yearbook. Washington, DC: National Council for the Social Studies.

Newmann, F. M. (1988a). Can depth replace coverage in the high school curriculum? *Phi Delta Kappan, 69,* 345–348.

Newmann, F. M. (1988b). *Higher order thinking in high school social studies: An analysis of classrooms, teachers, students and leadership* (Report). Unpublished manuscript, National Center on Effective Secondary Schools, University of Wisconsin.

Newmann, F. M. (in press). Higher order thinking in the teaching of social studies: Connections between theory and practice. In D. Perkins, J. Segal, and J. Voss (Eds.), *Informal reasoning in education.* Hillsdale, NJ: Erlbaum.

Newmann, F. M., & Oliver, D. W. (1970). *Clarifying public controversy.* Boston: Little, Brown.

Nickerson, R. S. (1988). On improving thinking through instruction. *Review of Research in Education, 15,* 3–57. Washington, DC: American Educational Research Association.

Oliver, D. W., & Shaver, J. P. (1974). *Teaching public issues in the high school.* Logan, UT: Utah State University Press. (original work published 1966)

Osborn, W. W. (1939). An experiment in teaching resistance to propaganda. *Journal of Experimental Education, 8,* 1–17.

O'Sullivan, J. T., & Pressley, M. (1984). Completeness of instruction and strategy transfer. *Journal of Experimental Child Psychology, 38,* 275–288.

Palinscar, A. M., & Brown, A. L. (1984). Reciprocal teaching of comprehension-fostering and monitoring activities. *Cognition and Instruction, 1,* 117–175.

Parker, W. C. (1988). Thinking and its contexts. *Social Education, 52,* 495–499.

Parker, W. C., McDaniel, J. E., & Valencia, S. (in press). Helping students think about public issues: Instruction versus prompting. *Social Education.*

Parker, W. C., Mueller, M., & Wendling, L. (1989). Critical reasoning on civic issues. *Theory and Research in Social Education, 17,* 7–32.

Perkins, D. N. (1985). General cognitive skills: Why not? In S. F. Chipman, J. W. Segal, & R. Glaser (Eds.), *Thinking and learning skills: Vol. 2. Research and open questions* (pp. 339–363). Hillsdale, NJ: Earlbaum.

Perkins, D. N. (1987). Thinking frames. In J. B. Baron & R. J. Sternberg (Eds.), *Teaching thinking skills* (pp. 41–61). New York: W. H. Freeman.

Piaget, J. (1928). *Judgment and reasoning in the child.* New York: Harcourt, Brace.

Piaget, J. (1959). *The psychology of intelligence.* London: Routledge and Kegan Paul.

Presseisen, B. Z. (1986). *Thinking skills: Research and practice.* Washington, DC: National Education Association.

Pressley, M., Borkowski, J. G., & Schneider, W. (1987). Cognitive strategies: Good strategy users coordinate metacognition and knowledge. In R. Vasta & G. Whitehurst (Eds.), *Annals of Child Development* (vol. 5, pp. 89–129). New York: JAI Press.

Pressley, M., Goodchild, F., Fleet, J., Zajchowski, R., & Evans, E. D. (1989). Challenges of classroom strategy instruction. *Elementary School Journal, 89,* 301–342.

Ravitch, D. (1985). *The schools we deserve.* New York: Basic Books.

Resnick, L. B. (1987). *Education and learning to think.* Washington, DC: National Academy Press.

Schrag, F. (1988). *Thinking in school and society.* New York: Routledge & Kegan Paul.

Scriven, M. (1972). Education for survival. In D. E. Purpel & M. Berlanger (Eds.), *Curriculum and the cultural revolution.* Berkeley, CA: McCutchan.

Shaver, J. P. (1962). Educational research and instruction for critical thinking. *Social Education, 22,* 13–16.

Shaver, J. P. (1980). Toward the twenty-first century: Social studies goals for decision-making and research skills. *Journal of Research and Development in Education, 13,* 36–46.

Shaver, J. P., Davis, O. L., Jr., & Helburn, S. W. (1978). *An interpretive report on the status of pre-collegiate social studies education based on three NSF-funded studies* (Report to the National Science Foundation). Washington, DC: National Council for the Social Studies. (ERIC Document Reproduction Service No. ED 164 363)

Shaver, J. P., & Larkins, A. G. (1973). *Decision-making in a democracy.* Boston: Houghton Mifflin.

Sternberg, R. J. (1985). *Beyond IQ: A triarchic theory of human intelligence.* New York: Cambridge University Press.

Sternberg, R. J. (1986). *Intelligence applied.* San Diego: Harcourt Brace Jovanovich.

Taba, H. (1963). Learning by discovery: Psychological and educational rationale. *Elementary School Journal, 63,* 308–316.

Taba, H. (1966). *Teaching strategies and cognitive functioning in elementary school children* (Cooperative Research Project No. 2404). San Francisco: San Francisco State College.

Taba, H. (1967). Implementing thinking as an objective in social studies. In J. Fair & F. R. Shaftel (Eds.), *Effective thinking in the social studies,* 37th yearbook (pp. 25–49). Washington, DC: National Council for the Social Studies.

Taba, H., Durkin, M., Fraenkel, J., & McNaughton, A. (1971). *A teacher's handbook to elementary social studies: An inductive approach* (2nd ed.). Reading, MA: Addison-Wesley.

Taba, H., & Elzey, F. (1964). Teaching strategies and thought processes. *Teachers College Record, 65,* 524–534.

Taba, H., Levine, S., & Elzey, F. F. (1964). *Thinking in elementary school children* (Cooperative Research Project No. 1574). San Francisco: San Francisco State College.

Tocqueville, A. de. (1969). *Democracy in America* (J. P. Mayer, Ed.; G. Lawrence, Trans.). New York: Doubleday.

Voss, J. F. (in press). Problem solving and the educational process. In R. Glaser & A. Lesgold (Eds.), *Handbook of psychology and education.* Hillsdale, NJ: Erlbaum.

Watson, G., & Glaser E. (1980). *Watson-Glaser critical thinking appraisal.* San Antonio, TX: Psychological Corporation.

Wittrock, M. C. (1978). The cognitive movement in instruction. *Educational Psychologist, 13,* 15–29.

·29·

ACHIEVING SOCIAL STUDIES AFFECTIVE AIMS: VALUES, EMPATHY, AND MORAL DEVELOPMENT

Kathryn P. Scott

FLORIDA STATE UNIVERSITY

The purpose of this chapter is to review research in three areas of social studies education that incorporates affective processes and aims: values education, empathy and prosocial education, and moral development. Researchers from a variety of perspectives have examined affective behavior, the expression of feelings or emotions. The field is a challenging one because of limited knowledge and understanding of affective processes, the difficulties in measuring affect, and the overlap between affective and cognitive processes. The problems of conducting research in the area of affective development and the limited findings directly related to social studies instruction have been cited by others (Leming 1986; Wallen & Fraenkel, 1988). Yet research on affective outcomes in social studies holds promise for at least two reasons.

First, there has been increased public interest in the topic. Goals of schooling have typically emphasized cognitive rather than affective outcomes. In social studies in particular, academic achievement and skill development have been the pervasive curricular aims. Nevertheless, there is evidence that parents believe that the social and emotional development of students is also a highly desirable goal of schooling. In a recent poll, parents ranked personal and social growth second only to academic subjects in importance (Freeman, Cusick, & Houang, 1985). During the Reagan presidential era, public interest was galvanized by the widely publicized calls of Secretary of Education William Bennett (1980) for a return to character education that has as its goal the inculcation of democratic values and moral virtues. Though these views may be viewed by many as contradictory to the goals of democratic citizenship education, which include reflective thinking and decision making as central, the publicity provides an opportunity for further research and deliberation to address areas of mutual concern.

Second, there is a wealth of theoretical and research investigation in areas where affective processes are relevant, as well as new findings regarding the integrative role of affect. Moral development and moral education are the subjects of voluminous studies. Some newer work on moral development examines affective as well as cognitive variables (Rest, 1983). In current models of human behavior, individuals are viewed as systems where considerable overlap and interaction occur among processes that have traditionally been viewed as distinct domains, i.e. cognitive, affective, and behavioral. For example, there is a growing research literature by development psychologists who are taking a closer look at the development of empathy, its affective, cognitive, and behavioral characteristics.

For many reasons, there is far less research on affective processes than on cognitive processes. The first of these is the difficulty of observing affective processes. Because such emotions as guilt, sympathy, or compassion exist as internal states, they are not easily open to scrutiny by researchers. Second, affective processes are viewed as less important to schooling than cognitive processes, for which the link to achievement outcomes is presumed to be more direct. Therefore, curricular objectives rarely include affective processes as specific outcomes, though processes with an affective component, such as values or attitudes, may be cited. As a consequence, little research is available that directly examines social studies teaching and learning related to affective objectives.

Included in this review of social studies-related research are a brief treatment of values education and related phenomena, character development and education; a discussion of empathy and its role in education, and an extended analysis of moral development and moral education research. A discussion of im-

Reviewers were: Alan L. Lockwood, University of Wisconsin; Pearl Oliner, Humboldt State University.

plications of research for social studies education and for future researchers concludes the chapter.

VALUES, CHARACTER, AND EDUCATION

Values underlie all that humans do. During the late 1960s and 1970s, there was a renewal of interest among social studies educators in questions about what values should be included in the curriculum and the preparation of students to deal with value issues. Of the numerous approaches developed, values clarification (e.g., Kirschenbaum, 1977; Raths, Harmin, & Simon, 1978; Simon, Howe, & Kirschenbaum, 1972) has been the focus of more research studies than any other approach. However, many of the claims for the validity and effectiveness of values clarification have not been supported by this research. In the 1980s, popular interest has championed the goal of building character through character education curricula. Though widely discussed in the media and professional journals, few researchers have undertaken studies to examine curricular implementation or effects.

Major concerns about the values-clarification approach include the following: (a) an inadequate definitional and theoretical base, (b) an implicit ethical relativism, (c) a seemingly haphazard conception and application of curricular interventions, (d) the preponderance of empirical evidence that did not support the effectiveness of recommended teaching strategies, and (e) ahistorical research efforts (Hersh, Miller, & Fielding, 1980; Lockwood, 1978; Leming, 1981, 1985; Shaver & Strong, 1982). For instance, in a review of 42 studies (screened from a pool of 75, with those not conducted in typical K–12 educational settings or that lacked a control group eliminated), Leming (1985) found that only 20% of the 17 reports of student changes in values and 33% of the 9 reports of changes in value-related behavior indicated statistically significant positive effects for the values-clarification intervention.

There remain, however, important questions regarding students' values and effective strategies for influencing them. Broadly defined, values are "standards and principles for judging worth" (Shaver & Strong, 1982, p. 17.) They can be either moral or nonmoral, can affect decision making by both individuals and groups, and are relevant to personal concerns as well as to the resolution of societal issues. Although values pervade the school curriculum in a variety of ways, including social studies instruction, it has been difficult for researchers to isolate and measure meaningfully the effects of instruction on value outcomes (Leming, 1985; 1986).

From efforts to develop other models for values education have come a number worthy approaches to understanding the importance of values in social studies curricula and implications for teaching. Approaches of interest include value analysis (Banks, 1973; Fraenkel, 1977; Metcalf, 1971), the social action model (Hedin, 1984; Newmann, 1975; Newmann, Bertocci, & Landsness, 1977), and the rationale-building model (Shaver & Strong, 1982). However, the advocates of none of the approaches have an ample body of research upon which to ground their assumptions and implications (Hersh et al., 1980; Leming, 1985).

As part of the inquiry for this chapter, I conducted a search for research on values education since the 1985 Leming review using the databases of ERIC, *Dissertation Abstracts,* and *Psychological Abstracts.* The search resulted in very few studies dealing with values education. (Those cited that were social studies-related included Beem & Brugman, 1986; Falikowski, 1984; Hahn & Avery, 1985; Lockwood, 1985; McNamee, 1984.) Most research efforts dealt with moral education, which is treated separately in this review, and a few examined character education.

Character Education

A phenomenon of the last decade has been the increased popular interest in character education as an antidote for the problems of school and society (e.g., Bennett, 1980; Wynne, 1979, 1982, 1986, 1988). The term *character* has been used as an umbrella term to encompass such virtues as responsibility, loyalty, and punctuality. In the popular view, character education is linked with the return of teacher authority, the instilling of moral virtues, and obedience from children and youth. It is believed that if schools and teachers become more directive in teaching moral virtues, hold students accountable to stricter behavior standards, and restrict opportunities for student decision-making, then students will become more responsible citizens. Such a view has precedents in the history of schooling and roots in conservative religion but is counter to most of the available research on moral development and behavior, particularly for students above the primary grades (Damon, 1988). Nonetheless, the character education movement has sparked considerable controversy regarding the legitimacy of its goals and implications for educational policy and research.

In many instances, however, those who write about character development and character education actually refer to approaches that are similar to the moral-development and education approaches described in a subsequent section of this chapter (see Lickona, 1987; Pritchard, 1988; Ryan & McLean, 1987). For example, the *Character Education Curriculum* published by the American Institute for Character Education combines directive instruction on basic values with recommendations to assist students in developing the ability to "make decisions and solve problems through the recognition and understanding of alternatives and consequences" (Mulkey, 1986, p. 1). Hence, many of the implications from research using other definitions of morality and its development cited later in this review are applicable to character development and character education.

EMPATHY AND PROSOCIAL DEVELOPMENT

Because of its presumed link with prosocial behavior and with thoughtful ethical decision-making, empathy has been singled out as a significant characteristic in the development of children and has received considerable attention by researchers, particularly among developmental psychologists. Empathy is has been defined in different ways by different researchers (see Goldstein & Michaels, 1985, and Eisenberg, 1986, for comprehensive reviews). Current views suggest that empathy encompasses three components: affective, cognitive, and communicative. Its affective component refers to an individual's capacity to experience the emotional state of another (Feshbach, 1982a; Hoffman, 1976, 1982; Rogers, 1975). Its cognitive component refers to an individual's capacity to discriminate the affective state of another and to comprehend the perspective of another in order to understand the situation from another's point of view (Feshbach, 1982a).

The third aspect of empathy, communication of empathetic feelings, has received little research attention with children and youth. There is evidence that among adults communicating empathic understanding to others, as in the psychotherapeutic process between counselor and client, contributes to their capacity to handle a problem without further action (Goldstein & Michaels, 1985).

There are at least two reasons for the omission of research on the communication component of empathy in children. One is the difficulty of observing such communication in young children whose communication skills are rudimentary. The second is the preponderance of studies to investigate the development of altruism and other forms of prosocial behaviors (Radke-Yarrow, Zahn-Waxler, & Chapman, 1983). In these studies, the emphasis has been on actions to relieve others' distress rather than on the capacity to communicate understanding of another's situation. Such communication may be particularly amenable to development during the adolescent years, when students begin to be capable of adult empathic communication (Goldstein & Michaels, 1985).

Researchers have documented a positive relationship between empathy and prosocial behavior, a relationship that strengthens as children mature (Eisenberg, 1986; Radke-Yarrow et al., 1983). Few studies of classroom teaching and learning have dealt directly with empathy, however. In one study, Feshbach (1979, 1982a, 1982b) conducted an empathy-training project for children in Grades 3 through 5 from multiethnic public school settings in an effort to promote prosocial values and behaviors and to reduce aggression and antisocial behaviors. Her training exercises were focused on three aspects of empathy: affect identification, perspective taking, and emotional responsiveness. Her findings indicated that children in the empathy-training group displayed more frequent daily prosocial behaviors than the problem-solving control group and increased their mean number of prosocial behaviors over the 15 weeks of the intervention. However, there were no differences between the empathy-training and the problem-solving groups in aggressive behaviors; both groups decreased aggressive behaviors.

The development of prosocial behavior in children has been studied extensively, primarily in laboratory or naturalistic, non-school settings and with children 12 years or younger. Though it is beyond the scope of this chapter to review the large number of experimental and correlational studies available, several generalizations are warranted (Eisenberg, 1982, 1986; Radke-Yarrow et al., 1983; Staub, 1979). First, modeling of prosocial behavior increases children's prosocial behavior, especially

when the adult models are perceived as nurturing, verbalize their feelings of concern, point out what actions they took to improve a situation, express their pleasure or relief at the outcome, and label their behavior as helpful to others. Second, though less powerful than adults, other modeling agents such as peers and television, can influence prosocial behavior, especially role models with whom children strongly identify or who have high prestige. Third, adults use of reasoning instead of power assertion to settle disputes or make decisions affecting children is correlated with greater expression of prosocial behavior. Fourth, high expectations for responsibility for self and others promotes children's prosocial behaviors. Finally, reinforcement of prosocial behaviors, especially when accompanied by an explanation of who did what for whom, increases the likelihood of children's prosocial responses beyond the period of reinforcement.

One educational model based on research findings on the development of prosocial behavior is the Child Development Project, a longitudinal study of interventions in 37 classrooms from several elementary schools (Battistich, Watson, Solomon, Schaps, & Solomon, in press; Solomon et al., 1985). The goal for the Child Development Project was to enhance the social and moral development of elementary students through systematic changes the classroom, school, and home environments for the first five years of elementary school.

The components implemented in this longitudinal study were cooperative learning, developmental discipline, promoting social understanding of norms, building a sense of community, highlighting prosocial values, and helping activities (standardized mean difference [SMD] for total implementation = .44) (Battistich, Solomon, Watson, Solomon, & Schaps, in press). After five years of the project, student behavior indices indicated that program students were slightly more likely to engage in spontaneous prosocial behavior (*SMD* = .18), show greater perspective-taking skills, show more consideration of other person's needs as well as their own in problem situations, and select more prosocial and cooperative strategies than were comparison students (Battistich, Solomon, Watson, Solomon, & Schaps, in press; Battistich, Watson, Solomon, Schaps, & Solomon, in press; Solomon, Watson, Delucchi, Schaps, & Battistich, 1988). However, these findings have not yet been validated through assessments of students in situations and activities outside the classroom. They also come from a sample of primarily white, middle-class students.

Research on empathy and the development of prosocial behaviors suggests promising directions for fostering social responsibility in youth. If what is known about empathy and the development of prosocial behavior were incorporated into social studies programs, then teachers could expect that providing prosocial models from the school or community as well as case studies from history, diverse cultures, literature, and current events would have an impact (Oliner, 1983). Classroom strategies such as cooperative learning, highlighting prosocial values, and encouraging responsibility norms hold promise (Battistich, Watson, Solomon, Schaps, & Solomon, in press). Expanded opportunities for prosocial behaviors could be provided through class- or school-sponsored community service programs (Hedin, 1984; Newmann & Rutter, 1983).

MORAL DEVELOPMENT AND MORAL EDUCATION

Moral development and moral education have attracted considerable interest from researchers in psychology, education, and related areas during the past 30 years. Lawrence Kohlberg's cognitive-developmental theory and its implications for education have dominated research in the area (Colby, Kohlberg, Gibbs, & Lieberman, 1983; Kohlberg, 1976, 1978, 1979, 1981; Kohlberg, Levine, & Hewer, 1985). Developed from the observations of Jean Piaget (1965) earlier in the century, his theory and research are based on a view of morality in which moral reasoning and universal ethical principles are central. Major findings related to Kohlberg's work include the following: (a) Individuals progress through five sequential stages as validated by longitudinal studies (Colby et al., 1983); (b) moral behavior by individuals is weakly correlated with moral stage development (Blasi, 1980); (c) students who participate in teacher-led discussions about moral dilemmas demonstrate small but steady upward progression through the developmental stages, with progress increasing with the length of intervention (Leming, 1985; Rest, 1983; Schlaefli, Rest & Thoma, 1985); (d) students who are part of "just communities" in schools where peer-group interactions and collective norms are fostered also experience upward stage development (Kohlberg et al., 1985); and (e) students who participate in classroom discussions of moral dilemmas in which the major focus is on content-oriented curricula, including social studies content, often do not demonstrate stage development of moral reasoning (Leming, 1985).

While Kohlberg's work no doubt holds a unique and important place in the history of the research on moral development and has been an impetus for a considerable body of research, the preeminence of his theory has made it difficult for competing perspectives to flourish or to gain comparable attention. A central question is one of definition: What is morality? While there is a general consensus among scholars that moral reasoning is an age-related development with maturation occurring as a result of human experiences, there is by no means a consensus among scholars on other aspects of morality, including the characteristics of moral behavior. A recent conference on "Moral Education and Character," sponsored by the U. S. Office of Education, highlighted the need for a better conceptualization of moral behavior, including multiple research perspectives (Pritchard, 1988).

Numerous reviews and critiques have already been published on Kohlberg's cognitive-developmental theory of moral development and its implementation in educational settings, and comprehensive treatments are readily available (e.g., Ehman, 1977; Enright, Lapsley, & Levy, 1983; Johnson, 1983; Kohlberg et al., 1985; Kurtines & Gewirtz, 1984; Leming, 1981, 1985; Lockwood, 1978; Mosher, 1980; Nucci, 1982; Rest, 1983; Schlaeffi et al., 1985).

In this review, other perspectives on moral development are examined. There is considerable overlap among these views as well as some contradictions that have conflicting implications for the goals and processes of moral education. Each of these perspectives is either a significant expansion of Kohlberg's definition of morality or the result of focusing on an inconsistency or contradiction in Kohlberg's approach. Research on the concept of morality, its developmental characteristics, and the effects of interventions is discussed for each of the following perspectives on moral development: (a) children's positive justice development (Damon, 1975, 1980); (b) social convention reasoning (Nucci, 1982; Turiel, 1983); (c) caring as a moral orientation (Gilligan, 1982); (d) an integrated component model (Rest, 1983); and (e) moral discourse (Oser, 1986).

Positive Justice Reasoning

In contrast to Kohlberg's interview dilemmas, which were focused on the negative side of justice (i.e., choices between two or more undesirable outcomes), Damon (1975, 1980) investigated problems of positive justice, such as distribution of wealth, ownership rights, and responsibility for another's welfare. He conducted extensive interviews with children 4 to 12 years of age to understand their ideas about sharing. As with Kohlberg's and Piaget's theories, it is hypothesized that development of positive justice reasoning and behaviors occurs as a result of experiences among peers and growth in the ability to take the perspective of others (Damon & Killen, 1982; Youniss, 1981).

Six levels of positive justice reasoning have been identified by Damon (1975, 1980). At the lowest level, ages 4 and under, children typically make choices based on their desires of the moment as sufficient justification for action. At the next level, choices are based on physical characteristics of individuals, such as their size, age, or sex, as well as on egoistic desires. At subsequent levels, children move from being self-oriented to being considerate of others. Eventually they are able to take into account others' special needs and circumstances.

Enright and his colleagues have developed a standardized instrument, the Distributive Justice Scale (DJS), to measure positive justice (Enright, Enright, & Lapsley, 1981). They have reported no differences in children by sex or cross-culturally, but they have identified variables other than age that influence scores on measures of development. These include the context of the situation requiring a decision, the children's social competence, and children's social class. For example, problems of fair distribution were solved at higher levels in family situations than in peer situations (Enright, Bjerstedt, Enright, Levey, Lapsley, Buss, Harwell, & Zindler, 1984). Differences based on social class were noted in positive justice decisions among kindergarten and third-grade, lower-class and middle-class pupils in integrated schools (Enright, Enright, & Lapsley, 1981; Enright, Enright, Manheim, & Harris, 1980). In these two studies, Enright and his colleagues hypothesized that inequities in the economic and social structure of society are reproduced in schools and in the interactions of children, contributing to lower levels of positive justice reasoning by lower-class children.

Several successful educational interventions to improve positive justice reasoning in elementary school classrooms have been reported (Enright, 1981; Krogh, 1985; Krogh & Lamme, 1985). For example, Enright developed an intervention based on an information processing model as well as developmental stage theory. He trained first-grade teachers to respond to troublesome behavior individually by (a) asking the child to reflect on his or her behavior, (b) challenging the child to think about more complex behavioral alternatives, (c) highlighting discrepancies between the child's words and actions, and (d) encouraging the child to try out new alternatives. In comparison to pupils in a control group ($\overline{X} = .03$), pupils in the treatment group ($\overline{X} = .19$) for 11 weeks made statistically significant gains in distributive justice reasoning on the DJS.

Social Conventional Reasoning

Another approach to understanding morality grows out of efforts to distinguish the concept of morality from that of social convention (Nucci, 1982). In this view, morality centers on issues of justice and fairness, whereas social convention relates to values arrived at by social consensus. Social conventions determined within each social system coordinate the actions of individuals in that system. Based on group acceptance, social conventions maintain social order and have an arbitrary dimension while morality is based on universal concerns that are not arbitrary. Though moral values and actions may overlap those of social convention, they are not determined by social rules or consensus.

Evidence suggests that even young children make distinctions between actions in violation of a social convention (such as breaking a school rule) and actions in violation of a moral principle (such as hitting or stealing), which cause pain to victims (Nucci & Nucci, 1982; Smetana, 1983; Turiel, 1983). In a review of research, Nucci (1982) cited evidence to support the view that children ages 3 to 20 distinguish between situations of convention, where norms relative to a particular social context apply, and situations of morality, where intrinsic moral guidelines apply.

Turiel (1983) hypothesized that children construct concepts about social conventions in age-related, developmental stages. He proposed a model containing seven levels of convention, in which individuals oscillate between affirmation and negation of concepts of convention and social structure as follows: *Level 1* (ages 6–7), convention as descriptive of social uniformity; *Level 2* (ages 8–9), negation of convention as descriptive of social uniformity; *Level 3* (ages 10–11), convention as affirmation of rule system; *Level 4* (ages 12–13), negation of convention as part of a rule system; *Level 5* (ages 14–16), convention as mediated by social system; *Level 6* (ages 17–18), negation of convention as societal standards; and *Level 7* (ages 18–25), convention as coordination of social interactions.

Nucci (1982; 1989) raised the concern that in much of moral education, distinctions have not been made between the domains of social convention and that of morality. If the domains are separate, then experiences necessary for children to develop an understanding of social convention would be different from those that facilitate an understanding or morality. For instance, in resolving moral issues, students need to understand the effects of particular actions on the rights and well-being of others. However, for the development of concepts about social conventions, students need to understand the social function of customs, traditions, and roles in maintaining social systems. Nucci (1982) recommended that the educational approaches advocated by Kohlberg and the cognitive developmentists are apropos to developing concepts of social convention as well, though the content and reasoning would be qualitatively different.

Two alternative explanations regarding children's development of the concept of social convention bear scrutiny. First, Kohlberg maintained that moral or principled reasoning is developed only at the later stages that he called postconventional (Kohlberg et al., 1985). Second, Shweder, Mahapatra, and Miller (1987) have presented numerous examples where principles of morality (such as not hurting or killing others) from one culture contradict normative social values in another culture. Such considerations bear further investigation. Nevertheless, efforts to distinguish concepts of convention and morality provide a useful approach for social educators and researchers in addressing social aims of learning and instruction.

Moral Orientation of Care

Carol Gilligan (1977, 1982) has presented a view of morality that has sparked controversy and received considerable scrutiny. In taking issue with the universality of Kohlberg's justice model, she asserted that "the moral problem arises from conflicting responsibilities rather than from competing rights" (1982, p.19). This approach is based on a view of humanity as most essential in its connections or relationships among individuals and groups. Therefore, responsibility for others and responsiveness is the central moral problem.

Gilligan's theory is rooted in the universal human experiences of attachment with others and love for them (Gilligan & Wiggins, 1987). These experiences begin at very early ages and have a profound effect on children's ideas about how they should act toward others and their knowledge about human feelings. The moral implications of attachment relationships generally are not included in theories of moral development because (a) children are seen as more passive than active in these relationships and (b) development of the self is linked with the ability to separate and detach oneself from others rather than the ability to relate to and love others.

In contrast, Kohlberg's theory of a morality of justice is grounded in the universal experience of inequality encountered by children in their relationship with adults due to their being generally smaller, less capable, and less powerful (Kohlberg, 1981; Piaget, 1965). Through interactions with others, especially with peers, where inequality is reduced, children have opportunities to experience what is fair and equitable in human relationships.

Gilligan argued that these childhood experiences of inequality and attachment may be related to gender. Because of traditional sex roles and cultural expectations, girls may experience greater attachment with their mothers and be less overwhelmed by their experiences of inequality than boys. In contrast, boys may have a greater desire to overcome their feelings of inequality and not be as concerned as girls about detachment or exclusion. Hence, males may be less likely than females to view situations in terms of attachment issues and more likely to view situations from the perspective of fairness and equality issues. Historically, the possibility that Piaget and Kohlberg would develop a morality of care rooted in the universal experience of attachment was precluded by the methods they used to examine moral thinking. Gilligan noted that though Piaget (1965) observed girls as well as boys resolving conflicts while playing marbles, he did not take seriously girls' interactions when they differed from the dominant pattern of the boys. Interestingly, he reported without further investigation that girls were more willing to make exceptions to rules, more tolerant of others, more innovative in solving conflicts, and less concerned with legal ramifications than were boys.

In Kohlberg's initial study, Gilligan pointed out, he examined moral judgment by using males' responses to hypothetical situations where the moral problem was already defined and the number of options to resolve the dilemma were limited. As a consequence, despite the numerous refinements to his theory over the years and adjustments in the instruments used for measuring moral development, the question remains as to whether Kohlberg has captured an adequate representation of moral thinking. At issue is how moral problems are defined and what questions are raised.

In Gilligan's (1987) approach to moral development, what is viewed as a moral problem and how it is framed is as important as the response to the problem:

From a justice perspective, the self as moral agent stands as the figure against a ground of social relationships, judging the conflicting claims of self and others against a standard of equality or equal respect (the Categorical Imperative, the Golden Rule). From a care perspective, the relationship becomes the figure, defining self and others. Within the context of relationship, the self as a moral agent perceives and responds to the perception of need. The shift in moral perspective is manifest by a change in the moral question from "What is just?" to "How to respond?" (p. 23)

For example, when teenagers are asked to describe a moral dilemma, they often cite difficulties in resisting pressure from peers or family to compromise their own point of view. A teenager who views the dilemma from a justice perspective may say that "We both have a right to our own political point of view, even if we disagree." However, if the same dilemma is viewed from an orientation of attachment and relationship with others, the concern becomes one of maintaining or strengthening connections with family or friends, such as, "I can see why my ideas may be threatening, but I wish my parents (or friends) could listen to me and try to understand my beliefs" (Gilligan, 1987).

Gilligan and others are not challenging the validity of moral reasoning as elucidated by Kohlberg's dilemmas. One major problem with Kohlberg's morality of justice is an inadequate definition of what constitutes a moral problem and the limited range of alternatives for responding. Thus, the need is to provide a more complete understanding of human experience, one that includes a perspective of responsibility for self and others as well as the rights of self and others.

Research Evidence. A growing body of research supports the reality of caring as a moral orientation. First are the early studies by Holstein (1976) and Gilligan (1977, 1982), who examined adolescent and adult women's thinking about whether to seek an abortion for their unplanned pregnancies. From her interviews, Gilligan noted the variety of ways that women constructed their dilemma and the predominance of concern about care for others and not harming anyone. Gilligan also interviewed a matched sample of males and females, aged 6 to 60, regarding their own life experiences and the difficult choices they had made. From these extensive interviews, Gilligan (1982) proposed a sequence of perspectives and transitions that individuals experience in developing an ethic of care, "each perspective representing a more complex understanding of the relationship between self and other and each transition involving a critical reinterpretation of the conflict between selfishness and responsibility" (p. 105).

Following Gilligan's work, Lyons (1983, 1987) conducted an analysis of open-ended interviews with 36 educationally advantaged North American individuals, two females and two males at each of nine ages between 8 and 60 years. Modes of self-definition and moral choice regarding real-life dilemmas were ascertained and correlations between them examined. Women were more likely than men to characterize themselves as predominately "connected" to others (69%), while men were more likely than women to describe themselves as separate and objective (79%). She found that 75% of the females in her sample considered responsiveness or care in constructing and resolving moral conflicts, whereas 79% of the males used considerations of rights or justice. Only one subject, a male, used both types of consideration.

Furthermore, Lyons found a significant relationship, regardless of sex, between modes of self-definition and modes of moral choice. Individuals who characterized themselves predominantly in terms of connection with others considered responsiveness or care more frequently in making moral choices than did the individuals who characterized themselves predominantly in separate/objective terms and used considerations of rights more frequently ($\chi^2 = 15.77$, p < .005). Langdale (1983, reported in Gilligan & Wiggins, 1987) examined males' and females' responses to hypothetical dilemmas focused on either justice issues or care issues. She found that hypothetical justice-reasoning dilemmas elicited a greater proportion of justice considerations from both males and females, though females responded with a greater proportion of care considerations overall than men.

The research findings of Johnston (1985) suggest that males and females are equally capable of understanding the two orientations of justice and care for resolving moral conflicts, though they prefer one orientation over the other. Johnston created a measure for assessing spontaneous moral orientation and moral orientation preferences. She asked 60 children, ages 11 and 15, to identify the moral problems posed by two of Aesop's fables and to suggest solutions. The majority of children (92%) framed the problem for each story either as an issue of justice or one of care. If they identified the key problem as conflicting rights or duties, then they used a rule or principle to resolve the conflicting claims. If they identified the key problems in terms of care for all fable characters, then they created a solution that was responsive to all of their needs. When asked whether there was another way to think about the problem in the fable, approximately half of the children were able to switch orientations and give an alternate response. Similar to Lyons' findings, girls (82% of their responses) were much more likely than boys to see the fables as problems of response and prefer care solutions, while boys (63% of their responses) saw the fables as problems of justice and preferred justice solutions.

Considerably more empirical evidence is needed to substantiate fully Gilligan's theoretical claims for a moral orientation of care. To date, no studies have been undertaken to validate the developmental levels that Gilligan has hypothesized for this moral orientation.

Critique of Moral Orientation of Care. Numerous critiques of this approach to moral thinking have been published. Kohlberg asserted that a morality of care is a subset of a morality of justice (Kohlberg et al., 1985). Others have found the theory lacking either in empirical evidence or in the adequacy of its philosophic assumptions, or both (see Brabeck, 1983, for a comprehensive review; also Nunner-Winkler, 1984; Sichel, 1985; Walker, de Vries, & Trevethan, 1987).

One issue that has generated a significant amount of debate is related to the view that a morality of care can be subsumed in a morality of justice as encompassed by Kohlberg's stages of moral development. The issue is gender differences in Kohlberg's stages of moral development. Because of the evidence that females tend to use a morality of care to frame and solve problems and that males more frequently use a morality of justice, one might expect that females would not receive as high scores as males when problem solutions are coded according to the justice reasoning of Kohlberg's stages.

Most studies, however, have not shown gender differences in structural stage development (Brabeck, 1983; Colby et. al, 1983; Gibbs, Arnold, & Burkhart, 1984; Walker, 1984, 1986). Walker (1984), for example, reached that conclusion based on an analysis of 50 studies. His review of the research has been challenged, however. Critics argue that because he averaged differences in studies across age groups, his methodology was not sufficiently sensitive to relatively moderate differences, that he assumed no difference to compute an effect size whenever a nonsignificant difference was reported, and that he included studies with different scoring systems as Kohlberg's measures underwent revisions (Thoma, 1986; Baumraud, 1986). One of the critics (Thoma, 1986) conducted a meta-analysis from a sample of 56 studies in which comparable male and female samples were included and responses were obtained to the Defining Issues Test (Rest, 1979). Thoma (1986) found that females' scores were statistically significantly higher than males ($SMD = -.207$) and the difference increased with age. Less than 50% of the variance was accounted for by gender differences.

Unfortunately, the debate over gender differences in moral development has overshadowed Gilligan's primary criticism of a justice approach to moral reasoning and the substance of her alternate theory. As evidenced in Johnson's study (1985), individuals have the ability to reason using either orientation, regardless of gender, even though they may prefer one orientation over another after considering both options.

The moral orientation of care is a major theoretical construct that has been the focus of numerous theoreticians and researchers. Recent volumes, such as a special issue of the *Journal of Moral Education* (Brabeck, 1987) and *Women and Moral Theory* (Kittay & Meyers, 1987), illustrate the number and variety of scholars pursuing this area. Although implications for education in general and social studies education in particular have not been delineated as precisely as in the areas of empathy and prosocial development or moral education, several directions are noteworthy. Noddings (1984, 1987) proposed a feminine/feminist distinction in understanding caring and detailed an approach to caring to be adopted by teachers. Martin (1985, 1986, 1987) has argued that in order to have moral education that focuses on an ethic of care, education itself must be redefined and transformed. She has called for redefining the basics of education as the three Cs: care, concern, and connection.

Four-Component Model of Morality

Very often when researchers and practitioners discuss morality, they consider three aspects as distinct and necessary: thinking (cognition), feeling (emotions), and action (behavior). Rest (1983, 1984) has found these divisions to be inadequate for several reasons. First, the three subdivisions are not empirically distinct categories. Moral cognitions are no more highly correlated than are thoughts and feelings. Furthermore, thoughts rarely exist without emotions; actions rarely exist without thoughts and emotions. Therefore, Rest has argued, to treat these three areas as separate categories is to misrepresent the varied, multidimensional interrelationships among aspects of morality. He has proposed an integrated model that portrays morality as a series of distinct processes, each involving thoughts, feelings, and action. Four components are identified as follows (Rest, 1983):

1. Interpreting the situation in terms of how one's actions affect the welfare of others (moral sensitivity),
2. Figuring out what would be a moral course of action and the moral ideal for a specific situation (moral judgment),
3. Selecting among competing ideals and deciding whether to try to fulfill one's moral ideal (moral decision making), and
4. Executing and implementing what one intends to do (moral action).

This integrated model expands the definition of morality, making research from a variety of disciplines pertinent to the processes involved in each component and opening avenues for future research. Although the components are sequenced in a logical order, they are also interactive. A person's judgment on the morally ideal course of action can influence his or her interpretation of the situation, or attempting to implement a decison might affect one's choice of an ideal course of action. Furthermore, no one component of morality stands alone in isolation from the other three. The four components are discussed below: moral sensitivity, moral judgment, moral decision-making, and moral action.

Moral Sensitivity. Before moral thinking or action can take place, the person must recognize that a situation exists in which actions could have a meaningful impact. As demonstrated by the research of Gilligan and others, situations can be construed in a variety of ways. Thus sensitivity to other people and the ability to perceive situations where moral action is warranted play a significant role in morality. Rest (1983) reported that many individuals find it difficult to comprehend even relatively simple situations and differ markedly in their sensitivity to the needs and well-being of others. Both cognitive and affective capacities are part of identifying and interpreting situations where moral action may have a role. Research on social cognition (Shantz, 1983) has indicated that, as they mature, individuals are better able to take the perspectives of other people. Emotional factors such as empathy also play a key role and often interact with cognition to influence how individuals perceive a situation where others' welfare is at stake.

Moral Judgment. Most of the focus of moral development and moral education research to date has converged on the moral judgment component. Kohlberg's developmental model, Damon's positive justice reasoning, and Turiel's social convention model concentrate on the moral ideal: "What is right?" "What *ought* I do?" Though an individual's reasoning about justice or social conventions may bear a relationship to the other three components, it remains only one aspect of morality in Rest's model.

Moral Decision-Making. Evidence is lacking that the components discussed so far, recognition of situations needing moral action and moral judgment, are sufficient to predict moral decision making or moral action (Blasi, 1980; 1983). Formulating a course of action involves a broader consideration of values, motivations, and possible outcomes. Unfortunately, very little research exists to suggest how moral decision-making takes place. Models of decision-making proposed for social education may be useful in developing this component of Rest's theory (e.g., Hurst, Kinney, & Weiss, 1983).

Behavioral decision theory suggests that individuals attempt to optimize their actions by considering their value to self and to others as well as the probability of occurrences for the consequences of each possible alternative (Pomazal & Jaccard, 1976, as cited in Rest, 1983). When they realize the costs of a moral decision, people will sometimes rationalize and reassess the situation (component 1). However, given the complexity of most moral decisions and quickness of many human responses, it is questionable that most people actually carry out systematic calculations of probabilities. Individuals sometimes respond to situations out of a sense of duty or feelings of good will, not because of rational calculations.

Theories of motivation present a number of explanations for the moral decision-making of individuals or groups, though conclusive supporting evidence is lacking (Rest, 1983). Traditional views of motivation suggest that people make decisions

regarding moral concerns based on (a) basic human nature, which has a drive to help other humans, (b) a sense of conscience—that is, avoiding guilt and shame, (c) rewards expected, as those learned through social experience (social learning theory), (d) social knowledge that suggests a rational course of action (cognition theory), or (e) a self-concept as a moral being (Blasi, 1985). Newer theories include Hoffman's (1976) depiction of moral internalization, in which several perspectives on motivation are combined to account for the development of children's internalization of societal norms and values. Finally, the work of Gilligan (1982) and Rawls (1971) and the just community approach of Kohlberg (1985) suggest that a sense of connection with another or others motivates moral decision-making.

Moral Action. However well intended, moral decisions do not always result in moral acts. Considerable effort, perseverance, and competence are often necessary to complete actions. This final component in Rest's integrated view is the most difficult to substantiate by empirical research. Ego strength, social assertiveness, delay of gratification, adventurousness are characteristics that may be related to moral action (Rest, 1983).

Implications for Research and Moral Education. In proposing this integrated model of morality, Rest implies that moral development is a process of gaining understanding and proficiency in all four components. Within each component, both cognitive and affective capacities, developmental and nondevelopmental characteristics, and individual and group processes need to be considered. As indicated previously, most researchers on moral education have dealt only with the second component, moral reasoning and judgment. The first and fourth components encompass processes that are essential to morality but are not uniquely moral. Some research related to social studies instruction has focused on aspects of the third and fourth components (e.g., Newmann & Rutter, 1983, as cited in Leming, 1985; Hedin, 1984). Additional research is needed to provide social educators a better understanding of the processes within and between each component.

Moral Education as Moral Discourse

As indicated by the variety of approaches to defining morality, there is no consensus about how morality develops. Likewise, despite the high level of interest in moral education, there is no comprehensive model of moral learning to guide moral education efforts. As a consequence, there is no organizing theory to explain the relationships among the variety of strategies that have been implemented under the names of moral education and values education (see, e.g., Hersh et al., 1980; Scott, 1987).

In the recent edition of the *Handbook of Research on Teaching,* Oser (1986) presented the concept of *moral discourse* as an organizer for the various approaches to moral education. He started with the assumption that classroom interaction, or discussion, is a critical variable in moral education. He outlined a model of moral discourse that draws on research and incorporates seven elements of discourse pedagogy, or classroom discussion. Each element central to moral education is briefly described below.

Moral Conflict. Moral discourse is, first, directed to moral conflict and to the stimulation of a higher level of moral judgment. Identifying a moral conflict that engages students in thinking about possible alternatives and rationales for choosing among them is a central aspect of Kohlberg's model. Research evidence indicates a relationship between exposure to one-stage higher reasoning and the development of higher stages of reasoning, though it may be one of several characteristics of effective moral discussion (Nucci, 1982).

In another line of research, Berkowitz and Gibbs (1983) have identified elements of discussion called *transacts,* characterized as listeners' efforts to integrate the speaker's statements into their own framework before generating a response. They identified 18 kinds of transacts, such as refinement, comparison, contradiction, and integration. From a sample of 5 discussions for each of 30 dyads of adolescents, Berkowitz (1985) found a greater number of transacts among individuals who demonstrated subsequent stage transformation than among individuals who did not. Furthermore, Berkowitz has reported that interactions that contain transacts are more likely to occur in discussions among peers than with teachers. More inquiry on the interactive process during discussions of moral issues is a promising research direction (Lapsley & Quintana, 1985; Oser, 1986).

Moral Role Taking and Moral Empathy. Moral discourse is directed towards moral role taking and moral empathy. To fully understand a moral conflict, one must be able to take the point of view of others. Many of the researchers mentioned above have explored this dimension, including Selman (1980) on social role taking, Hoffman (1982) on empathy, and Kohlberg (1981) on moral stages that include social-perspective development. From this perspective, a key element for further research in moral education comprises the factors that affect the development of role-taking abilities and sensitivity to others.

Moral Choice and Action. Third, moral discourse is oriented to moral choice and action. As with the work of Rest (1983) emphasizing moral action as a distinct component of morality, Oser (1986) suggested that moral educators need to address moral actions as well as reasoning and awareness of others. He outlined features of discourse that take into account making decisions about particular situations and implementing action, drawing on research from diverse perspectives. Included are Gilligan's (1982), Lyons's (1983), and Johnston's (1985) work on defining actions based on a moral response of caring, studies on prosocial behavior (e.g., Eisenberg, 1982, 1986; Solomon, Watson, Delucci, Schaps, & Battistich, in press; Staub, 1984), and the competencies needed to implement action (Rest, 1983).

Shared Norms. The discourse is, fourth, directed towards shared norms and a moral community. Recognition that individuals' thoughts and actions are shaped by the social context has contributed to an emerging research interest in classrooms as

communities. Kohlberg's (1985) development of the just community, the Child Development Project discussed earlier, and other investigations (e.g., Lickona, 1987; Power, 1985) are examples of this focus.

Analysis. The fifth element of moral discourse is the analysis of moral situations and value systems as exemplified by people in history, literature, and diverse cultures. To the extent that narratives and analysis of other people provide an opportunity to clarify one's moral beliefs and ideals as well as to gain perspective on others' morality, such a curriculum can be expected to have an impact on student learning. Given the frequent concern of social studies educators with people's decision making in political, social, economic, religious, and/or cultural contexts, how classroom discussion of these decisions and actions can lead to greater student understanding is an important unanswered research question (Leming, 1985).

Meta-Reflection. Sixth, moral discourse is oriented towards the student's own reasoning through meta-reflection. One perspective on morality suggests that self-observation and reflection, or meta-reflection, contributes to increased understanding and is a condition for change in moral beliefs or actions. As yet, few researchers have addressed these processes (Edelstein, 1985; Oser, 1986), especially as part of classroom discourse.

Theoretical Moral Knowledge. Finally, moral discourse is oriented toward the student's theoretical moral knowledge. There is little documentation to substantiate the view that knowledge about moral theory will enhance morality, broadly defined (Oser, 1986). Furthermore, some researchers report the opposite effect. That is, awareness of Kohlberg's stages by students may create a climate of one-upmanship that is detrimental to community building (Rest, 1983).

Oser's model of moral discourse provides a useful framework for viewing moral education approaches and is compatible with Rest's four-component model of morality. Both models suggest the complexity of morality and moral education and the need for research that takes into account multiple perspectives and influences.

IMPLICATIONS FOR SOCIAL STUDIES EDUCATORS AND RESEARCHERS

In this review, findings from research in three areas have been examined: values and character education, prosocial behavior and empathy, and moral development. While none of these areas is the sole responsibility of social studies educators, all are a part of a vision of social education that is aimed at creating caring, reflective, and proactive adults. The challenge to develop the emotional capacities of children and youth as well as their intellectual capacities should not be overlooked by social studies educators.

Our findings suggest no panaceas for educational aims that involve affective processes. However, they point the way toward new ways of conceptualizing this quest. Foremost is the effort to view affective, cognitive, and behavioral capacities as interactive. Meaningful development in one area cannot occur without consideration of the other two. Therefore, educators and researchers are cautioned from viewing students' cognitive processes in isolation from affective processes or behavioral indices. However, until educators and researchers depart from the time-honored emphases on precise, measurable objectives, implemention of such a shift in conceptualization remains distant.

Second, the major part of this review has focused on moral development, not because it has been researched as a primarily affective process, but because so many researchers have attempted to conceptualize moral development and the influencing factors, including affect. Given the finding that no one influence is paramount, there is evidence to suggest that the creation of learning environments where there is a focus on promoting morally sensitive interactions and prosocial behaviors will prove beneficial. For instance, the growing body of research that indicates cooperative learning is associated with increased academic achievement, as well as with increased prosocial and cooperative actions, suggests a promising direction (Slavin, 1988; Solomon et al., 1985). However, for such practices to have sufficient impact to influence long-term, cognitive, affective, and behavioral outcomes, they may need to be adopted comprehensively on at least a schoolwide basis—an issue that should be addressed by researchers.

Several other directions for research are recommended. One useful line of inquiry is the work underway by the developmental psychologists who are investigating the development of emotions, moral thinking, and prosocial behavior in children and adults. The results of this inquiry will have implications for how social educators view students and understand the influences that shape their development.

A second line of inquiry is further investigation of classrooms and schools as communities that influence students' development in ways as significant, if not more so, than the formal curriculum, with its emphasis on measurable cognitive outcomes. One way of addressing the need for more research in which both the influence of schools as communities and affective and behavioral outcomes of social studies education are considered is through the application of alternative research perspectives. Traditionally, research on schooling has been focused on quantified outcomes, using experimental or quasi-experimental methods drawn from a positivistic, behavioristic psychology (Shulman, 1986). The assumption is made that, if only educators knew more about the process-product relationships between what teachers do in the classroom (process) and what happens to their students (products), then they could improve instruction and learning. The very nature of behavioristic models, if considered at all, underplays the political and social context of learning. Therefore, results often are not truly generalizable or educationally meaningful.

Educational researchers are becoming increasingly influenced by paradigm shifts in the social science disciplines, including anthropology, sociology, and the humanities, where ethnographic and other qualitative approaches are increasingly commonplace. As this trend continues, new perspectives for framing educational questions, creating knowledge, and shaping educational approaches will become possible (see Bloch, 1986; Cornbleth, 1985; Shulman, 1986). These new perspectives will be especially important for the investigation of classrooms and schools as communities of learning, as well as for attaining a deeper understanding of the role of affect in the goals and outcomes of social studies education.

References

Banks, J. (1973). *Teaching strategies for social studies: Inquiry, valuing, and decision-making*. Reading, MA: Addison-Wesley.

Battistich, V., Solomon, D., Watson, M., Solomon, J., & Schaps, E. (in press). Effects of an elementary school program to enhance prosocial behavior on children's cognitive social problem-solving skills and strategies. *Journal of Applied Developmental Psychology*.

Battistich, V., Watson M., Solomon, D., Schaps, E., & Solomon, J. (in press). The Child Development Project: A comprehensive program for the development of prosocial character. In W. M. Kurtines & J. L. Gerwirtz (Eds.). *Moral behavior and development: Advances in theory, research, and application* (Vol. I). Hillsdale, NJ: Erlbaum.

Baumrind, D. (1986). Sex differences in moral reasoning: Response to Walker's (1984) conclusion that there are none. *Child Development, 57*, 511–521.

Beem, A., & Brugman, D. (1986). The effects of values development lessons on pupils' well-being, pleasure in school, mutual relationships, and on pupils' valuational behavior during classroom dialogues. *Theory and Research in Social Education, 14*(2), 97–112.

Bennett, B. J. (1980). The teacher, the curriculum and values education. In *New Directions for Higher Education, 8*, 27–34.

Berkowitz, M. W. (1985). The role of discussion in moral education. In M. W. Berkowitz & F. Oser (Eds.), *Moral education: Theory and application*. (pp. 197–218). Hillsdale, NJ: Erlbaum.

Berkowitz, M. W., & Gibbs, J. C. (1983). Measuring the developmental features of moral discussion. *Merrill-Palmer Quarterly, 29*, 399–410.

Blasi, A. (1980). Bridging moral cognition and moral action: A critical review of the literature. *Psychological Bulletin, 88*, 1–45.

Blasi, A. (1983). Moral cognition and moral action: A theoretical perspective. *Developmental Review, 3*, 178–210.

Blasi, A. (1985). The moral personality: Reflections for social science and education. In M. W. Berkowitz & F. Oser (Eds.), *Moral education: Theory and application* (pp. 433–444). Hillsdale, NJ: Erlbaum.

Bloch, M. N. (1986). Social education of young children. In C. Cornbleth, (Ed.), *An invitation to research in social education*. Washington, DC: National Council for the Social Studies.

Brabeck, M. (1983). Moral judgment: Theory and research on differences between males and females. *Developmental Review, 3*, 274–291.

Brabeck, M. (Ed.). (1987). Feminist perspectives on moral education and development. Special issue of *Journal of Moral Education, 16*(3).

Colby, A., Kohlberg, L., Gibbs, J., & Lieberman, M. (1983). *A longitudinal study of moral judgment*. Chicago: University of Chicago Press.

Cornbleth, C. (1985). Reconsidering social studies curriculum. *Theory and Research in Social Education, 13*(2), 31–46.

Damon, W. (1975). Early conceptions of positive justice as related to the development of logical operations. *Child Development, 46*, 301–312.

Damon, W. (1980). Patterns of change in children's social reasoning: A two-year longitudinal study. *Child Development, 51,* 1010–1017.

Damon, W. (1988). *The moral child.* New York: Free Press.

Damon, W., & Killen, M. (1982). Peer interaction and the process of change in children's moral reasoning. *Merrill-Palmer Quarterly, 28,* 347–367.

Edelstein, W. (1985). Moral intervention: A skeptical note. In M. W. Berkowitz & F. Oser (Eds.), *Moral education: Theory and application* (pp. 387–401). Hillsdale, NJ: Erlbaum.

Ehman, L. (1977). Research on social studies curriculum and instruction: Values. In Hunkins, F. et.al. (Eds.), *Review of research in social studies education: 1970–75* (pp. 55–95). Washington, DC: National Council for the Social Studies.

Eisenberg, N. (Ed.), (1982). *The development of prosocial behavior.* New York: Academic Press.

Eisenberg, N. (1986). *Altruistic emotion, cognition, and behavior.* Hillsdale, NJ: Erlbaum.

Enright, R. (1981). A classroom discipline model for promoting social cognitive development in early childhood. *Journal of Moral Education, 11,* 47–60.

Enright, R. Bjerstedt, A., Enright, W., Levey, V., Lapsley, D., Buss, R., Harwell, M., & Zindler, M. (1984). Distributive justice development: Cross-cultural, contextual, and longitudinal evaluations. *Child Development, 55,* 1737–1745.

Enright, R., Enright, W., & Lapsley, D. (1981). Distributive justice development and social class: A replication. *Developmental Psychology, 17,* 826–832.

Enright, R., Enright, W., Manheim, L., & Harris, B. E. (1980). Distributive justice development and social class. *Developmental Psychology, 17,* 826–832.

Enright, R., Lapsley, D., & Levy, V. (1983). Moral education strategies. In M. Pressley & J. Levin (Eds.), *Cognitive strategy research: Educational Applications* (pp. 43–83). New York: Springer-Verlag.

Falikowski, A. (1984). Moral and values education: A philosophical appraisal. Unpublished doctoral dissertation, University of Toronto, Canada.

Feshbach, N. D. (1979). Empathy training: A field study in affective education. In S. Feshbach & A. Fraczek (Eds.), *Aggression and behavior change* (pp. 234–249). New York: Praeger.

Feshbach, N. D. (1982a). Empathy training and the regulation of aggression: Potentialities and limitations. *Academic Psychology Bulletin, 4*(3), 399–413.

Feshbach, N. D. (1982b). Sex differences in empathy and social behavior in children. In N. Eisenberg (Ed.), *The development of prosocial behavior* (pp. 315–338). New York: Academic Press.

Fraenkel, J. (1977). *How to teach about values: An analytic approach.* Englewood Cliffs, NJ: Prentice Hall.

Freeman, D. J., Cusick, P. A., & Houang, R. F. (1985). *Public response to proposals for raising academic standards in secondary schools.* Washington, DC: National Institute of Education.

Gibbs, J., Arnold, K., & Burkhart, J. (1984). Sex differences in the expression of moral judgment. *Child Development, 55,* 1040–1043.

Gilligan, C. (1977). In a different voice: Women's conceptions of the self and of morality. *Harvard Educational Review, 47,* 481–517.

Gilligan, C. (1982). *In a different voice: Psychological theory and women's development.* Cambridge, MA: Harvard University.

Gilligan, C. (1987). Moral orientation and moral development. In E. F. Kittay & D. T. Meyers (Eds.), *Women and moral theory* (pp. 19–36). Towata, NJ: Rowman & Littlefield.

Gilligan, C., & Wiggins, G. (1987). The origins of morality in early childhood relationships. In J. Kagan & S. Lamb (Eds.), *The emergence of morality in young children* (pp. 277–305). Chicago: University of Chicago Press.

Goldstein, A., & Michaels, G. (1985). *Empathy: Development, training, and consequences.* Hillsdale, NJ: Erlbaum.

Hahn, C., & Avery, P. (1985). Effect of value analysis discussions on students' political attitudes and reading comprehension. *Theory and Research in Social Education, 13*(2), 47–60.

Hedin, D. (1984). Developing values through community service. In Schug, M., & Beery, R. (Eds.), *Community study: Applications and opportunities* (pp. 92–106). Washington, DC: National Council for the Social Studies.

Hersh, R., Miller, J., & Fielding, G. (1980). *Models of moral education: An appraisal.* New York: Longman.

Hoffman, M. L. (1976). Empathy, role-taking, guilt, and development of altruistic motives. In T. Lickona (Ed.), *Moral development and behavior: Theory, research, and social issues* (pp. 124–143). New York: Holt, Rinehart & Winston.

Hoffman, M. L. (1982). Development of prosocial motivation: Empathy and guilt. In N. Eisenberg (Ed.), *The development of prosocial behavior* (pp. 281–313). New York: Academic Press.

Holstein, C. (1976). Development of moral judgment: A longitudinal study of males and females. *Child Development, 47,* 51–61.

Hurst, J., Kinney, M., & Weiss, S. (1983). The decision-making process. *Theory and Research in Social Education, 11*(3), 17–44.

Johnson, H. C. (1983). Moral education. In H. E. Mitzel (Ed.), *Encyclopedia of Educational Research. Vol. 3* (5th ed., pp. 1237–1256). New York: Free Press.

Johnston, K. (1985). *Two moral orientations—Two problem-solving strategies: Adolescents solutions to dilemmas in fables.* Unpublished doctoral dissertation, Harvard University.

Kirschenbaum, H. (1977). *Advanced value clarification.* La Jolla, CA: University Associates.

Kittay, E., & Meyers, D. (Eds.). (1987). *Women and moral theory.* Towata, NJ: Rowman & Littlefield.

Kohlberg, L. (1976). Moral stages and moralization: The cognitive-developmental approach. In T. Lickona (Ed.), *Moral development and behavior: Theory, research, and social issues.* (pp. 29–53). San Francisco: Jossey-Bass.

Kohlberg, L. (1978). Revisions in the theory and practice of moral development. In W. Damon (Ed.), *New directions for child development: Moral development* (pp. 83–88). San Francisco: Jossey-Bass.

Kohlberg, L. (1979). *The meaning and measurement of moral development.* Worcester, MA: Clark University.

Kohlberg, L. (1981). *Essays on moral development: Vol I. The philosophy of moral development.* San Francisco: Harper Row.

Kohlberg, L. (1985). The just community approach to moral education in theory and practice. In M. Berkowitz & F. Oser (Eds.), *Moral education: Theory and application* (pp. 27–87). Hillsdale, NJ: Erlbaum.

Kohlberg, L., Levine, C., & Hewer, A. (1985). *Moral stages: A current formulation and a response to critics.* New York: Karger.

Krogh, S. L. (1985). Encouraging positive justice reasoning and perspective taking skills. *Journal of Moral Development, 14,* 102–110.

Krogh, S. L., & Lamme, L. (1985). Distributive justice and the moral development curriculum. *Social Education, 49,* 616–621.

Kurtines, W., & Gewirtz, J. (Eds.). (1984). *Morality, moral behavior, and moral development.* New York: John Wiley.

Langdale, C. (1983). Moral orientation and moral development: The analysis of care and justice reasoning across different dilemmas in females and males from childhood through adulthood. Unpublished doctoral dissertation, Harvard University.

Lapsley, D. K., & Quintana, S. M. (1985). Recent approaches to the moral and social education of children. *Elementary School Guidance and Counseling, 19*(4), 246–259.

Leming, J. S. (1981). Curricular effectiveness in moral/values education: A review of research. *Journal of moral education, 10*(3), 147–164.

Leming, J. S. (1985). Research on social studies curriculum and instruction: Interventions and outcomes in the socio-moral domain. In W. B. Stanley (Ed.), *Review of research in social studies education: 1976–83* (pp. 123–213). Washington, DC: National Council for the Social Studies.

Leming, J. (1986). Rethinking social studies research and the goals of social education. *Theory and Research in Social Education, 14*(2), 139–152.

Lickona, T. (1987). Character development in the elementary school classroom. In K. Ryan & G. McLean (Eds.), *Character development in schools and beyond* (pp. 177–205). New York: Praeger.

Lockwood, A. L. (1978). The effects of values clarification and moral development curricula on school-age subjects: A critical review of recent research. *Review of Educational Research, 48,* 325–364.

Lockwood, A. L. (1985). A place for ethical reasoning in social studies curriculum. *Social Studies, 76*(6), 264–68.

Lyons, N. P. (1983). Two perspectives: On self, relationships, and morality. *Harvard Educational Review, 53* 125–145.

Lyons, N. P. (1987). Ways of knowing, learning and making moral choices. *Journal of Moral Education, 16*(3), 226–239.

Martin, J. R. (1985). *Reclaiming a conversation.* New Haven, CT: Yale University Press.

Martin, J. R. (1986). Redefining the educated person: Rethinking the significance of gender. *Educational Researcher, 6,* 6–10.

Martin, J. R. (1987). Transforming moral education. *Journal of Moral Education, 16*(3), 204–213.

McNamee, S. (1984). Curriculum review: Reflecting on values (grades 1–6) and Values and Living (grades 7 & 8). *Moral Education Forum, 9*(1), 11–14.

Metcalf, L. (1971). *Values education: Rationale, strategies, and procedures.* Washington, DC: National Council for the Social Studies.

Mosher, R. L. (1980). *Moral education: A first generation of research and development.* New York: Praeger.

Mulkey, Y. J. (1986). *The character education curriculum: An evaluation with principals and teachers.* San Antonio, TX: American Institute for Character Education.

Newmann, F. (1975). *Education for citizen action: Challenge for secondary curriculum.* Berkeley, CA: McCutchan.

Newmann, F., Bertocci, T., Landsness, R. (1977). *Skills in citizen action.* Skokie, IL: National Textbook.

Newmann, F., & Rutter, R., (1983). *Effects of High School Community Service Programs on Students' Social Development.* Final Report to the National Institute of Education (Grant No. NIE-G-81-0009). Madison, WI: Wisconsin Center for Educational Research.

Noddings, N. (1984). *Caring: A feminine approach to ethics and moral education.* Berkeley, CA: University of California Press.

Noddings, N. (1987). Do we really want to produce good people? *Journal of Moral Education, 16*(3), 177–188.

Nucci, L. P. (1982). Conceptual development in the moral and conventional domains: Implications for values education. *Review of Educational Research, 52*(1), 93–122.

Nucci, L. (1989). Knowledge of the learner: The development of children's concepts of self, morality, and societal convention. In M. Reynolds (Ed.), *Knowledge base for the beginning teacher* (pp. 117–127). Oxford: Pergamon Press.

Nucci, L., & Nucci, M. (1982). Children's responses to moral and social conventional transgressions in free-play settings. *Child Development, 53,* 1337–1342.

Nunner-Winkler, G. (1984). Two moralities? A critical discussion of an ethic of care and responsibility versus an ethic of rights and justice. In W. Kurtines & J. Gewirtz (Eds.), *Morality, moral behavior, and moral development* (pp. 348–361). New York: Wiley.

Oliner, P. (1983). Putting "community" into citizenship education: The need for prosociality. *Theory and Research in Social Education, 11*(2), 65–81.

Oser, F. K. (1986). Moral education and values education: The discourse perspective. In M. Wittrock (Ed.), *Handbook of research on teaching* (3rd ed., pp. 917–941). New York: Macmillan.

Piaget, J. (1985). *The moral judgment of the child.* New York: Free Press.

Pomazal, R., & Jaccard, J. (1976). An informational approach to altruistic behavior. *Journal of Personality and Social Psychology, 33,* 317–327.

Power, C. (1985). Democratic moral education in the large public high school. In M. W. Berkowitz & F. Oser (Eds.). *Moral education: Theory and application* (pp. 219–238). Hillsdale, NJ: Erlbaum.

Pritchard, I. (1988). *Moral education and character.* Washington, DC: U.S. Department of Education.

Radke-Yarrow, M., Zahn-Waxler, C., & Chapman, M. (1983). Children's prosocial dispositions and behavior. In P. Mussen (Ed.), *Handbook of child psychology* (vol 3, pp. 469–545). New York: Wiley.

Raths, L. E. Harmon, M., & Simon, S. B. (1978). *Values and teaching* (2nd ed.). Columbus, OH: Charles E. Merrill.

Rawls, J. (1971). *A theory of justice.* Cambridge, MA: Harvard University Press.

Rest, J. (1983). Morality. In P. Mussen (Ed.), *Handbook of child psychology* (vol. 3, pp. 470–545). New York: Wiley.

Rest, J. (1984). The major components of morality. In W. M. Kurtines & J. L. Gewirtz (Eds.), *Morality, moral behavior, and moral development* (pp. 24–40). New York: Wiley.

Rogers, C. (1975). Empathetic: An unappreciated way of being. *Counseling Psychologist, 5,* 2–10.

Ryan, K., & McLean, G. F. (Eds.). (1987). *Character development in schools and beyond.* New York: Praeger.

Schaefli, A., Rest, J., & Thoma, S. (1985). Does moral education improve moral judgment? A meta-analysis of intervention studies using the Defining Issues Test. *Review of Educational Research, 55,* 319–352.

Scott, K. P. (1987). Missing developmental perspectives in moral education. *Theory and Research in Social Education, 15*(4), 257–273.

Selman, R. (1980). *The growth of interpersonal understanding.* New York: Academic Press.

Shantz, C. (1983). Social cognition. In P. Mussen (Ed.), *Handbook of child psychology* (Vol. 3, 4th ed., pp. 495–555). New York: Wiley.

Shaver, J. P., & Strong, W. (1982). *Facing value decisions: Rationale-building for teachers.* New York: Teachers College Press.

Shulman, L. E. (1986). Paradigms and research programs in the study of teaching: A contemporary perspective. In M. Wittrock, (Ed.), *Handbook of research on teaching* (3rd ed., pp. 3–36). New York: Macmillan.

Shweder, R., Mahapatra, M. & Miller, J. (1987). Culture and moral development. In J. Kagan & S. Lamb (Eds.), *The emergence of morality in young children* (pp. 1–82). Chicago: University of Chicago Press.

Sichel, B. (1985). Women's moral development in search of philosophical assumptions. *Journal of Moral Education, 14*(3), 149–161.

Simon, S. B., Howe, L. W, Kirschenbaum, H. (1972). *Values clarification: A handbook of practical strategies for teachers and students.* New York: Hart.

Slavin, R. (1988). Cooperative learning and school achievement. *Educational Leadership, 46*(2), 31–33.

Smetana, J. (1983). Social cognition development: Domain distinctions and coordinations. *Developmental Review, 3,* 131–147.

Solomon, D., Watson, M., Battistich, V., Schaps, E., Tuck, P. Solomon, J., Cooper, C., & Ritchey, W. (1985). A program to promote interpersonal consideration and cooperation in children. In R. Slavin, S. Sharan, S. Kagan, R. H. Lazarowitz, C. Webb, & R. Schmuck (Eds.), *Learning to cooperate, cooperating to learn* (pp. 371–403). New York: Plenum.

Solomon, D., Watson, M., Delucchi, K., Schaps, E., & Battistich, V. (1988). Enhancing children's prosocial behavior in the classroom. *American Educational Research Journal, 25,* 527–554

Staub, E. (1979). *Positive social behavior and morality: Socialization and development.* Vol. 2. New York: Academic Press.

Staub, E. (1984). Steps toward a comprehensive theory of moral conduct: goal orientation, social behavior, kindness, and cruelty. In W. M. Kurtines & J. L. Gewirtz (Eds.), *Morality, moral behavior, and moral development* (pp. 241–260). New York: Wiley.

Thoma, S. J. (1986). Estimating gender differences in the comprehension and preference of moral issues. *Developmental Review, 6,* 165–180.

Turiel, E. (1983). *The development of social knowledge: Morality and convention.* Cambridge: Cambridge University Press.

Walker, L. J. (1984). Sex differences in the development of moral reasoning: A critical review of the literature. *Child Development, 55,* 677–691.

Walker, L. J. (1986). Sex differences in the development of moral reasoning: A rejoinder to Baumrind. *Child Development, 57,* 522–526.

Walker, L. J., de Vries, B., & Trevethan, S. D. (1987). Moral stages and moral orientations in real-life and hypothetical dilemmas. *Child Development, 58,* 842–858.

Wallen, N., & Fraenkel, J. (1988). An analysis of social studies research over an eight year period. *Theory and Research in Social Education, 16,*(1), 1–22.

Wynne, E. (1979). The declining character of American youth. *American Educator, 3,* 29–32.

Wynne, E. (1982). *Character policy: An emerging issue.* Washington, DC: University Press of America.

Wynne, E. (1986). The great tradition in education: Transmitting moral values. *Educational Leadership, 43,*(4), 4–9.

Wynne, E. (1988). Balancing character development and academics in the elementary school. *Phi Delta Kappan, 69,*(6), 424–426.

Youniss, J. (1981). Moral development through a theory of social construction: An analysis. *Merrill-Palmer Quarterly, 27,* 385–403.

30

KNOWLEDGE AND CONCEPT DEVELOPMENT IN SOCIAL STUDIES

Peter H. Martorella

NORTH CAROLINA STATE UNIVERSITY

Knowledge is the fabric of social studies instruction. Woven into it are the facts, generalizations, skills, hypotheses, beliefs, attitudes, values, and theories that students and teachers construct in social education programs. The threads from which the rich and intricate patterns are spun are concepts.

Although the acquisition of knowledge is often regarded as predominantly a "cognitve" activity, its constituent parts embrace all aspects of human learning: cognitive, affective, and psychomotor. Functional knowledge construction in social studies classes involves some mix of the head, the heart, and the hand. Knowledge in practice at any given time may involve remembering and relating, feeling, and doing.

Cognitive processes are generally how individuals confront, encode, reflect upon, transform, and store information. In contrast, *metacognitive* processes refer to self-conscious actions in which the individual's own knowledge, mental states, or thought processes become the object of reflection (Yussen, 1985). As Yussen observed, use of the term *metacognition* is highly variable in the theory and research literature.

Flavell (1971), one of the earliest investigators to use the term, focused on the domain of memory. However, the term *meta-cognition* has been applied broadly to other areas of investigation, especially as they relate to reading processes (see, e.g., Baker & Brown, 1984; Brown, Bransford, Ferara, & Campione, 1983). Metacognition involves self-monitoring, regulating, and questioning. It entails individuals developing responsibility for reviewing their own thinking processes (Solomon, 1987).

In this chapter, the process of knowledge acquisition generally is addressed, focusing on the cognitive and metacognitive processes involved and paying particular attention to the fundamental building blocks of cognition: concepts.

KNOWLEDGE ACQUISITION IN THE SOCIAL STUDIES

Writing over 2 decades ago, M. P. Hunt and Metcalf (1968) observed that "Content assumes an emergent character. From the standpoint of the learner, it comes into existence as it is needed, it does not have a life independent of his own" (pp. 281–282).

Knowledge Versus Subject Matter in the Social Studies

Viewed from the perspective of Hunt and Metcalf, content derives its identity, significance, and vitality from what it can contribute to the cognitive needs of a learner. Content and method in teaching are inseparable (Dewey, 1916). Similarly, it follows that subject matter that is synthesized and organized by instructors or authors in isolation from the cognitive and affective needs of students must be transformed if it is to have potential as knowledge to be acquired (Engle & Ochoa, 1988; Shaver, 1977).

The subject matter addressed in social studies classes, as constructed from students' reflective encounters with the organized work of social scientists and other scholars, results in knowledge (Berger & Luckmann, 1966). In this sense knowledge does not exist independent of learning. It arises from students' interactions with others and their larger social milieu (Resnick, 1981; Stanley & Mathews, 1985). Resnick (1983) stated the matter directly:

Instruction cannot simply put knowledge and skill into people's heads. Instead, effective instruction must aim to place learners in situations

---

Reviewers were Milton Kleg, University of Colorado, Denver; C. Warren McKinney, Oklahoma State University.

where the constructions that they naturally and inevitably make as they try to make sense of their worlds are *correct* as well as sensible ones. (pp. 30–31)

In this interactive process, culture is also an important determinant of how students filter and structure knowledge (R. C. Anderson, 1984).

The process of knowledge acquisition also transcends the disciplinary boundaries established by scholars. In unusually harsh and strident terms, over a half century ago John Dewey (1933) attacked the dualism that isolates the concerns of scholars for their disciplines from the cognitive and affective needs of learners.

The gullibility of specialized scholars when out of their own lines, their extravagant habits of inference and speech, their ineptness in reaching conclusions in practical matters, their egotistical engrossments in their own subjects, are extreme examples of the bad effects of severing studies completely from their ordinary connections in life. (p. 62)

Disciplinary parameters, which are definitional and often arbitrary, normally do not parallel the patterns of data construction that learners employ in their knowledge acquisition. In solving a problem, a student is less likely to be concerned about whether the relevant data are drawn, let us say, from the discipline of history than about whether they contribute to a solution, whatever the source. Further, disciplines themselves are in a constant state of flux, with shifting parameters.

Knowledge Acquisition and Research- and Theory-Based Instruction

Instruction, as opposed to teaching, is focused on the nature and behavior of the learner and what is to be learned (Gagne, Briggs, & Wager, 1988). It is designed for the fundamental purpose of facilitating learning under optimal conditions. In turn, *instructional strategies* are those structured conditions within which mediators facilitate the learning of specific objectives. Various mediators, including teachers, can provide the means to take into account variables within and external to the learner that affect learning. Gagne and others have referred to this general multifaceted context as the *conditions of learning* (Gagne, 1985; Gagne et al., 1988).

This perspective shifts the focus from the teacher to instructional mediators in general. These include printed and text materials, computers, self-direction, peers and mentors, and various other media. This frame of reference also moves the focal point of instruction from teacher behaviors to the creation of optimal learning conditions, whatever the format of mediation (see Gagne et al., 1988).

Research Relating to Knowledge Acquisition

Which body of educational research is of most worth in shedding light on cognitive processes in teaching and learning social studies? In the late 1980s, a number of investigators called attention to the scarcity of cumulative, integrated, and productive research in all areas related to social education (Armento,

1986; Brophy, 1990; Shaver, 1979, 1987; Wallen & Fraenkel, 1988). The criticisms of the existing body of social education research have been summarized by Wallen and Fraenkel (1988) as follows: "Social studies research has been criticized for insignificance in the questions it pursues, sampling bias, inappropriate methodologies, incorrect or inappropriate use of statistics, weak or ill-defined treatments, and/or lack of replication" (p. 1).

The limitations of the existing social education research suggest that we look more broadly to all areas of research in education and psychology for guidance in the matter of knowledge acquisition (Armento, 1986). As a practical matter, relatively few studies are available that specifically address social education. In addition, it would be inappropriate to ignore results that appear to be generalizable across all subject areas. Although it is arguable that in some respects the subject matter of social studies presents unique instructional problems when compared to other areas of the curriculum such as mathematics, a useful starting point in applying research may be to assume commonalities in the absence of contrary evidence.

THEORIES OF KNOWLEDGE CONSTRUCTION

One of the early philosophical dialogues concerning how knowledge is acquired occurs in the *Meno.* Therein, Plato proposed an either–or solution: Either all knowledge has been acquired at birth and, therefore, requires only *recognition,* or it has not and, therefore, cannot be recognized. Beyond these extreme alternatives, investigators over the centuries have searched for adequate and grounded explanations of how knowledge is acquired.

Cognitive developmental theorists regard assimilation and accommodation regulated by equilibration as the fundamental processes through which cognitive structures are formed and knowledge is constructed (Piaget, 1980). Assimilation involves blending new knowledge with prior knowledge. In accommodation, prior knowledge is changed or reconstructed. From the developmental perspective, it is also assumed that interaction among children around structured activities stimulates the construction of knowledge (Vygotsky, 1962).

In addition, Piagetian theorists posit four stages, or periods, of cognitive development through which individuals pass. Bruner (1973) contended that during these stages knowledge is acquired through these three basic forms: enactive, iconic, and symbolic. He suggested that individuals, as they pass through developmental stages, are more dependent on one form than another for processing information.

A number of investigators have attempted to examine historical thinking in children using Piaget's stages (Hallam, 1969; Jurd, 1973; Kennedy, 1983; Levstik, 1986; Lovell, 1961; Peel, 1960). The cumulative results of these efforts suggest that the nature of the relationship between children's developmental stages and their historical understanding is still unclear. Based on their review of the research on teaching and learning history, Downey and Levstik (1988) concluded, "there is no evidence that delaying instruction in history is developmentally appropriate. Even if more mature historical understanding requires formal operations in the Piagetian sense, there is no evidence that the development of historical understanding begins at that stage" (p. 340).

In contrast with cognitive developmental perspectives, information-processing theorists focus on how individuals perceive, structure, keep in memory, and modify information in their environment (Bell-Gredler, 1986). Within this framework, knowledge can be represented as *procedural* or *declarative,* or knowing how and knowing that. Procedural knowledge refers to actions or skills, for example, knowing how to determine the latitude and longitude of a place. Declarative knowledge refers to information in memory, independent of the use made of it. Brophy (1990) contended that one distinction between the social studies and other school subjects is that in social studies the two types of knowledge are not linked in any particular way. Consequently, he argued, much of the information learned by students is perceived as static and unrelated to their real-world social experiences.

Cognitive theorists contend that knowledge is organized into structures known as *schemata* (or schemas). Schema theory posits that the form and content of all new knowledge is in some way shaped by our prior knowledge (Brewer & Nakamura, 1984). The term *schema,* first used by Bartlett (1932) in describing learning, has more recently been defined generally as a mental structure that represents some set of related information (R. C. Anderson, 1984; Howard, 1987; Rummelhart, 1980; Rummelhart & Ortony, 1977). Students, for example, bring their map schemata to the study of spatial issues. They have certain expectations concerning the kinds of information a map contains and the types of questions a map can answer.

Schemata as elements of our prior knowledge are activated when we are provided with clues that elicit them. Perkins (1986) offered an example of how the date 1492 can serve as an important cognitive peg for analysis of parallel historical events. He suggested that such key dates in American history provide a structure for placing intermediate events. In this way dates are not merely facts but also tools for collecting and remembering information.

Our individual collections of schemata comprise our store of prior knowledge that we bring to each new knowledge-acquisition task. Schemata provide the basis for comprehending, remembering, and learning information. Fundamental schemata at the top of our hierarchy of knowledge aid us in processing and interpreting lower level data (Rummelhart, 1984).

Rummelhart and Norman (1981) regarded schemata as specialized cognitive networks that have been accumulated through experience and are used to cope with daily tasks. New schemata come into existence through comparisons with prior ones and through modifications that reflect our current experiences. For example, we acquire some new experiences with native Italians from the northern part of Italy. From these situations, we build a new schema that accommodates our novel perceptions that are at variance with our earlier data on Italians in general. When our prior knowledge conflicts with new data, restructuring of schemata may occur. On the other hand, firmly embedded prior knowledge may be resistant to transformation

and require skillful challenging by a teacher (Marzano et al., 1988).

CONCEPT FORMATION AND THE ELEMENTS OF KNOWLEDGE

Schemata are comprised of various elements of knowledge. In establishing curriculum objectives and learning activities for students, the elements of knowledge identified often include the following: concepts, facts, generalizations, and hypotheses. As suggested earlier, what we regard as an individual's *knowledge* consists of a complex, interrelated web, or network, of these various elements. But all thinking and action involves concepts, the building blocks of knowledge.

Nature of Concepts

In their simplest form, concepts may be regarded as *categories into which we group phenomena within our experience.* Phenomena are sorted into concept categories as the individual discerns their basic or distinguishing characteristics. Individuals may check these characteristics against their memories of past examples or against prototypes that represent their notion of a typical case of the concept. The interrelated collection of characteristics comprises the *criterial attributes* of the concept. If an item of information meets the criteria for a concept category, an individual has created, he or she connects the concept *name* with the phenomenon. Then the person begins to relate it to prior knowledge, thus forming a network or web of ideas.

However, the categories into which individuals sort their experiences have more than names and mental images of phenomena. They contain all of the personal associations that have been constructed by the individual in relation to the concept. Also, as C. W. Anderson and Smith (1987) observed, "An individual's conceptions serve as the organizing and interpretive framework for new information" (p. 94). An individual's concept of money, as an illustration, encompasses more than a category including checks, bank drafts, currency, and credit cards. The concept is also attached to economic goals, perceptions of financial issues, and many other personal associations with money that make an individual's concept unique. However naive these personal conceptions are, they constitute the starting point for concept instruction (C. W. Anderson & Smith, 1987; Bransford & Vye, 1989).

Cross-Cultural Influences on Concept Learning

Considerable evidence demonstrates that culture influences the process of categorization (Cole & Scribner, 1974; Heider, 1972; E. B. Hunt & Banaji, 1988; Pick, 1980; Whorf, 1956). Some investigators, the most prominent of whom was Whorf (1956), have also argued that language influences categorization. The flavor of the Whorfian hypothesis is presented in the statement "users of markedly different grammars are pointed by their grammars toward different types of observations and different evaluations of externally similar acts of observation, and hence are not equivalent as observers but must arrive at somewhat different views of the world" (p. 221).

Modifying Whorf's hypothesis, E. B. Hunt and Banaji (1988) drew a distinction between thought as a process of internal symbol manipulation, which they regarded as following culture-free rules, and the content of the information acquired, which they regard as culture specific. In applying this perspective to concept formation, they contended that a concept has three dimensions: the categorization rule, a definition in relation to some other set of concepts that is meaningful in a particular situation; and an identification function, that is, a rule stating when use of the concept label is appropriate. When cross-cultural information exchanges occur, the *recipient* group can observe the identification functions of an applied concept, but its meaning can only really be explained in terms that are specific to the *transmitting* culture (E. B. Hunt & Banaji, 1988). Put another way, our existing schemata, which are culturally influenced, affect cross-cultural knowledge acquisition.

Instructional Strategies for Concept Learning

A number of general reviews of empirical research on concept formation have been reported in recent years (Jassal & Tennyson, 1982; Tennyson & Cocchiarella, 1986; Tennyson & Park, 1980). The net effect has been to provide a sophisticated, empirically based set of instructional guidelines for aiding students in learning concepts (see Howard, 1987; Klausmeier, 1980; Martorella, 1990; Tennyson & Cocchiarella, 1986; Wilson, 1985).

In a review of recent research on concept learning specifically in social education, Stanley and Mathews (1985) developed a number of implications for instruction. They contended that most methodological discussions of teaching social studies draw primarily upon what Smith and Medin have characterized as the "classical" view of concepts; namely, the notion that concepts are defined exclusively by their shared common properties and that learning of a concept involves repeated hypothesis testing to determine the properties (Smith & Medin, 1981; Medin & Smith, 1984). Kleg's (1986, 1987) instructional materials for teaching the concepts of terrorism and genocide offer two clear and detailed examples of how this perspective on concept learning can be applied in the classroom.

Stanley and Mathews argued that the classical notion is inadequate to address the variety and complexity of concepts in social studies instruction. They pointed to the work of a number of investigators (e.g., Millward, 1980; Rosch & Mervis, 1975; Smith & Medin, 1981; Wittgenstein, 1953) showing that the defining features of most concepts are complex and hard to specify; that category boundaries often are not clear cut (e.g., Was U.S. involvement in Korea a *war* or a police *action?*); and that individuals tend to view concepts holistically, in terms of "best examples," "prototypes," or "family resemblances," especially when the concepts have fuzzy boundaries. Concept learning in

this perspective is a search for central tendencies of patterns rather than for specific exclusive properties (Medin & Smith, 1984; Smith & Medin, 1981).

Rosch and Mervis (1975) built upon Wittgenstein's (1953) idea of family resemblances among word referents as a way to construct natural language classes. They established empirically that the category members considered most prototypical are those with the most attributes in common with other members of the category. Medin and Smith (1984), however, summarized some of the important limitations of prototype theory, including our relative ignorance of how prototype concepts are formed. Drawing on the work of Armstrong, Gleitman, and Gleitman (1983), they implied that instruction could include strategies based upon both classical and prototype theories of concept learning.

More recently, synthesizing the findings of earlier studies of concept learning, Tennyson and Cocchiarella (1986) developed an empirically based instructional design theory for teaching concepts. They postulated that two cognitive operations occur in learning a concept, one resulting in *conceptual knowledge,* which involves the formation of a prototype and a schema, and another resulting in *procedural knowledge,* which involves the classification skills of generalizing to and discriminating among concepts (p. 44). In their theory, they further suggest that any concept has two basic content structural qualities; its relational structure to other concepts and the degree of variability in its attribute characteristics (p. 42).

They contend that each structural quality in turn has two possible levels: the relational structure of the concept to other concepts may be *coordinate* or *successive,* and the attribute characteristics may be *constant* or *variable.* Coordinate concepts are those dependent upon one another for understanding; successive concepts are those for which learning is limited to generalization only within a specific class (p. 54). The attribute characteristics of constant-dimension concepts remain stable across contexts, but those of variable-dimension concepts vary or change.

Working from this theoretical base, Tennyson and Cocchiarella (1986) offered a multidimensional analysis of concept instruction: "Concept teaching is not a system composed of a single set of instructional variables, but rather a system composed of variables brought into use only after consulting well-defined selection procedures and criteria" (pp. 64–65). They suggested four alternative instructional designs matched with different concept content structures. Variations among the four designs are based on the ways in which expository examples and attributes are presented and the degree of context and strategy information provided. Commonalities among the designs are the use of labels and definitions, best examples, expository examples, interrogatory examples, and embedded refreshment (p. 43). Best examples are cases that clearly represent the classes from which the concept is drawn. Expository examples include all other cases. Interrogatory examples are those that cause the learner to attend to the relevant features of the best example by answering a series of questions about the attributes of new cases. Embedded refreshment refers to the review or overview of material related to the concept to be learned.

In addition to the commonalities across all four strategies, Tennyson and Cocchiarella (1986) recommended that for teaching successive-constant concepts, expository examples be presented one after another. The recommended strategy for teaching coordinate-constant concepts is the simultaneous presentation of expository examples and elaboration of attributes. To teach successive-variable concepts, expository examples should be presented one after another, a context should be provided in which the new concept is linked to prior knowledge, and strategy information on the processing of expository and interrogatory examples should be included. The most difficult type of concept to teach, coordinate-variable concepts, requires a context, simultaneous presentation of expository examples, elaboration of attributes, and strategy information.

Tennyson and his associates concluded that their own research findings and those of others "indicate that a best example and an expository presentation establish conceptual knowledge of a concept in memory, whereas the interrogatory format facilitates development of procedural knowledge" (p. 51). They noted further,

Apparently, learners do not store in memory a list of attributes, hypotheses about the attributes, or many specific instances. Instead, they initially form in memory an abstraction of a typical category member, then, with practice, they elaborate on the meaningful dimensions of the prototype (abstraction) as classification skill develops. (p. 51)

In a number of studies specifically dealing with social studies, researchers have examined various aspects of the general instructional models developed by Gagne (1985), Klausmeier (1980), Merrill and Tennyson (1977), and Tennyson and Cocchiarella (1986). In an ambitious series of studies, McKinney and his associates examined the effects of methods of teaching, teacher enthusiasm, recycling and response sensitivity, nonexamples, critical attributes, and prototypes with differing age-level students. Their results validated aspects of the model for concept teaching developed by Merrill and Tennyson (McKinney, Larkins, Ford, & Davis, 1983); showed inconclusive results with respect to the effects of enthusiasm (Burts, McKinney, & Burts, 1985; McKinney, Larkins & Burts, 1984); found no support for recycling missed instances in concept instruction or varying the order of examples on the basis of student responses (Ford & McKinney, 1986); affirmed the importance of ordinary nonexamples in instruction involving certain classes of concepts (McKinney, Burts, Ford, & Gilmore, 1987); and were mixed with respect to the effects of the presentation of critical attributes and best examples on concept formation (McKinney, Gilmore, Peddicord, & McCallum, 1987; McKinney, Gilmore, Larkins, & McKinney, 1987).

In the case of the last finding, McKinney and his associates obtained different results in two studies with respect to the effects of best examples on concept learning. In one study (McKinney, Gilmore, Peddicord, & McCallum, 1987), 103 undergraduates were assigned to one of four treatment groups and taught the concept, transfer propaganda, through the use of slides. Treatments were expository examples only, best exam-

ples only, critical attributes and expository examples, and critical attributes only. Posttests were administered immediately and retention tests were given 2 weeks later. Sets of mean achievement scores on the immediate and on the retention posttests were nearly identical.

In another study (McKinney, Gilmore, Larkins, & McKinney, 1987), 54 fifth-graders were assigned to one of four treatment groups: critical attributes only, critical attributes plus a definition, best example only, and best example and a definition. Treatments were administered through a self-instructional booklet. A posttest was administered immediately following each lesson, and a retention test was given 2 weeks later. Only for the retention test were statistically significant differences reported; the mean for the group taught with the best example only differed significantly from the group taught with critical attributes only. Also, the mean for the group taught with critical attributes and a definition differed significantly from the group taught with critical attributes only. Further, when all other treatments were compared with the critical-attributes-only treatment on the retention test, they yielded standardized mean differences (SMDs) ranging from .82 to 1.09.

The preceding study findings regarding the effects of best examples supported the earlier work of Yoho (1986). In a study involving 147 ninth-grade social studies students in six classes, he compared the effects of four concept-teaching strategies on the learning of four political science concepts. The treatments were carried out over a 2-day period and consisted of a control group and four concept-teaching strategies as follows: Strategy 1—presentation of and stress on critical attributes and the use of examples; Strategy 2—presentation of and stress on a best example and the use of examples; Strategy 3—the same as 1, except nonexamples were included; and Strategy 4—the same as 2, except nonexamples were included. Students in the control group were instructed to read relevant sections of their textbooks. Treatments were administered through a self-instructional booklet. A posttest was administered immediately following each lesson and a retention test was given 1 week later.

All four treatment groups scored substantially higher than the control group on the posttest and the retention test. Strategy 2 produced the highest mean score on both the posttest and the retention test. Further analysis of Yoho's data yielded SMDs for the four treatments that ranged from .83 (Strategy 3) to 1.44 (Strategy 2) on the posttest and from .40 (Strategy 3) to 1.01 (Strategy 2) on the retention test.

A review of the series of concept-learning studies in the area of social studies reveals some anomalies, as well as some patterns. For example, there was a discrepancy between the findings of Yoho (1986) and those of McKinney, Burts, Ford, and Gilmore (1987) in regard to the value of nonexamples in learning. Reasons for the discrepancies in these and other studies may include the variability in concept structures (e.g., whether successive or coordinate concepts were used in the study), the differing ages of students, the difficulty and lack of operational specificity in identifying best examples (i.e., determining what is a clear case) for many concepts, the different ways in which nonexamples were actually used in instruction, and the variability in measure sensitivity (for example, McKinney, Gilmore, Larkins, & McKinney, 1987, used yes–no discrimination items, but Yoho, 1986, employed multiple-choice achievement items). In future research, these and other related procedural issues should be addressed.

Guidelines for Instruction. With some reservations, clear guidelines for social studies instruction emerge as cumulative implications from the extensive body of research on concept learning. Although there is a growing body of evidence to indicate that the structure of individual concepts is a significant variable to be addressed in selecting alternative modes of instruction, a general instructional model for many concepts can be inferred:

1. Identify the set of examples and place them in some logical order for presentation. Include at least one example that best or most clearly illustrates an ideal type of the concept.
2. Include in the materials or oral instructions a set of cues, directions, questions, and student activities that draw attention to the critical attributes and the similarities and differences in the examples and nonexamples used.
3. Direct students to compare all illustrations with the best example and provide feedback on the adequacy of their comparisons.
4. If critical attributes cannot be clearly identified or are ambiguous, focus attention on a few best examples of the concept and help students remember their salient features.
5. Where a clear definition of a concept exists, elicit or state it at some point in the instruction in terms meaningful to the students.
6. Through discussion, place the concept in context with other related concepts that are part of the students' prior knowledge.
7. First assess concept mastery at a minimal level, namely, whether students can correctly discriminate between new examples and nonexamples.
8. Then assess concept mastery at a more advanced level; for example, ask students to generate new exemplars or apply the concept to new situations.

Concept Hierarchies

Often it is helpful for both the teaching and the learning of concepts to order a series of concepts into a *hierarchy*. The work of Novak and Gowin (1984) with what they identify as *concept mapping* illustrates the application of hierarchies. Developing hierarchies of concepts involves placing them in context in an organized way through identifying the most all-encompassing concept in a set and then relating all of the others to it in a logical sequence or diagram. Consider the set of concepts as follows: sea level, rivers, transportation, mountains, oceans, islands, lakes, earth, land areas, continents, and bodies of water. The example in Figure 30–1 depicts a concept map

that organizes these concepts in a logical sequence according to their relationship to one another.

METAPHORS AND OTHER FIGURES OF SPEECH

One of the complex dimensions of concepts is the way they function in *figures of speech.* Both social studies textbooks and classroom discussions frequently employ figures of speech that force students to go beyond the literal meaning of each concept in a statement to fathom the intent of the author (Mahood, 1987; Martorella, 1988). Consider the news commentary, "The facts floated on a sea of innuendo." Even for those who have acquired all of the concepts in the statement, literal decoding does not suffice to interpret it. The metaphorical power of the sentence comes into play when a reader is prepared to go beyond the literal meaning of each word. Interpreting, applying and relating figures of speech to other social studies knowledge appears to require a distinctive set of information-processing strategies. Evidence also suggests that these vary as individuals move from one developmental stage to another (Silberstein, Gardner, Phelps, & Winner, 1982; Vosniadou, Ortony, Reynolds, & Wilson, 1984) and across cultural groups (Readence, Baldwin, Martin, & O'Brien, 1984).

Among the most common figures of speech that students encounter in social studies discussions are *metaphors* and *similes*. A metaphor is a phrase in which something that is well known is used to explain or expand the meaning of something that is less well known; for example, "Television is chewing gum for the mind," or "Reagan was the Teflon president." Similes are used similarly to compare unlike sets of items, but the terms *like* or *as* are used: "SDT, the 'star wars' defense system, will be like the Maginot line."

Due to space limitations, the following analysis of the usage of figures of speech is confined to metaphors. There are only limited, although increasing, empirical data concerning how individuals recognize, comprehend, and produce metaphors, but a considerable body of theory has evolved spanning the fields of philosophy, literature, linguistics, rhetoric, and pyschology.

Theories Concerning the Nature of Metaphors

There are four basic theories concerning the nature of metaphors:

Comparison Theory: Metaphors are implicit comparisons of two domains of concepts. The comparison involves one term that bears a nonliteral resemblance to the other (Ortony, 1975, 1979, 1984; Tversky, 1977).

Anomaly Theory: Metaphors are defined by the dissimilarities between the two sets of concepts and the anomaly that results when they are linked together (Guenther, 1975; Van Dijk, 1975).

Interaction Theory: Metaphors are seen as new ways of viewing and expressing concepts (Black, 1962, 1979; Richards, 1971).

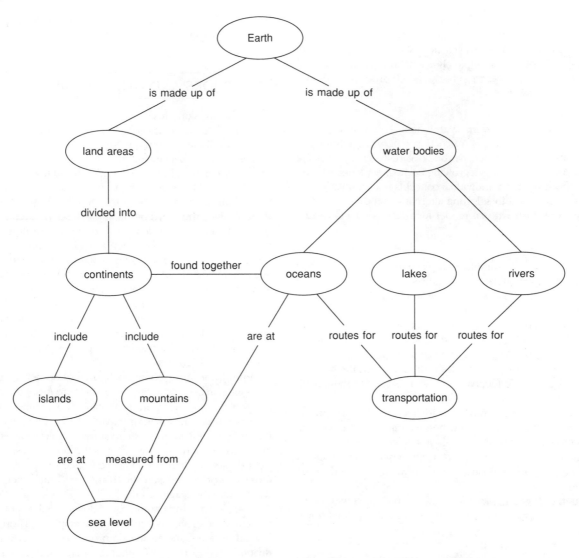

FIGURE 30–1. Concept map. *Note.* From "Teaching Concepts" by Peter H. Martorella. In *Classroom Teaching Skills* (4th ed.) by James M. Cooper (Ed.), 1990. Reprinted by permission.

Domains-Interaction Theory: Metaphors involve viewing in a new light, not only two sets of concepts, but also the domains to which they belong (Tourangeau & Sternberg, 1982).

Ortony (1975, 1979) has argued that metaphors serve us in several ways. One is by transferring elements of experience from well-known to less well-known contexts. Another is by permitting a more memorable learning experience as a result of the imagery involved in metaphors. A third function of metaphors, Ortony (1975) argued, is to supply us with meanings that we otherwise typically might not be able to encode in language. Witness the current references to the "Star Wars" defense policy as metaphorical shorthand for a host of complex ideas.

Ortony, Reynolds, and Arter (1978) have constructed a theory of *salience imbalance* to explain in part what is involved in the analysis of metaphors with simple structures. The two basic elements of a metaphorical statement are the *vehicle,* the more familiar term that serves as the clarifying element, and the *topic,* or *tenor,* the item to be clarified or amplified in the metaphor. The other elements of a metaphorical statement are the *ground,* or *attribute,* the feature shared by the two items, and the *tension,* the cognitive state created by the dissimilarity of the two items. Ortony (1979, 1984) and Tversky (1977) contended that a person understands a metaphor when experiences with the known vehicle are somehow compared with those associated with the unknown topic. Several empirical studies have supported this position (Baldwin, Luce, & Readance, 1982; Readance, Baldwin, & Head, 1986; Readance et al., 1984).

To apply Ortony's theory, consider the metaphorical statement, "The United States is the breadbasket of the world." The term to be clarified, *the United States,* is the topic, and the second term, *breadbasket of the world,* is the vehicle. The matching characteristic between the topic and the vehicle, the ground, is that both "have grain foodstuffs." This attribute is not of equal prominence or salience in both the topic and the vehicle. It is relatively insignificant, or *low,* on the list of criteria that characterize the topic, but *high* on the vehicle list, reflecting a salience imbalance. Moving from topic to vehicle, the directional relationship of the imbalance is from low to high, a condition that produces an effective metaphor. If the direction of the salience imbalance were reversed from high to low, as in "The breadbasket of the world is the United States," the metaphor would appear confusing or silly. Within this framework, grasping a metaphor requires an individual to identify a statement as nonliteral, recognize the matching attribute, and move the attribute from low to high salience in the topic (Readance et al., 1984).

Sticht (1979) observed that to comprehend a metaphor, a person must first infer that she or he must shift from a mode of cognition in which two domains of ideas are being fitted to an existing knowledge structure to a metaphorical mode. In this new mode, the individual constructs a third knowledge structure consisting of the inferred relations between the two domains involved in the metaphor. In this way, the analysis of metaphors can be both *comparative,* in the sense that a topic is clarified by a vehicle, and *interactive,* in the sense that new information is created through the dynamic analysis of the metaphorical statement.

Thompson (1986) explained that, in a metaphor, an individual usually "seeks to eliminate the incompatibility with the vehicle and the topic by comparing the experiences associated with each, searching for possible matches" (p. 106). He noted further that "Actual matches occur when high value experiences from the vehicle become linked with congruent experiences from the topic. The effect is a 'new' topic" (p. 106). Black (1962, 1979) regarded this as the interactive feature of metaphors that allows the creation of new insights.

Instructional Strategies for Analyzing Metaphors

Metaphors apparently can serve as cognitive anomalies that motivate students to find some basis for the similarity between sets of concepts. For a satisfactory cognitive resolution to occur in processing a metaphor, however, the teacher needs to insure that there is a match between the students' prior knowledge of the matching attribute and what is to be learned, as well as suggest conceptual strategies for resolving the anomaly (Petrie, 1979). Howard (1987) observed that metaphors can be used to either clarify points or define a concept in a lesson; for example, "A revolution is an exploding volcano." Lakeoff and Johnson (1980) pointed out also that it may be necessary to use a cluster of metaphors rather than a single one to make comparisons with complex concepts such as "self-concept."

Metaphors apparently function as cognitive stimulants to generate new knowledge. That is, the learner reflects upon old forms to create new ones and finds ways to tie existing conceptual networks to fresh subject matter. When a metaphor passes into common usage, such as "He was out like a light," it produces no anomaly and we regard it as *dead* or, in effect, no longer a true metaphor except for someone who has never before heard the expression.

According to Ortony (1979), helping individuals to dismantle metaphors involves a four-step process: (a) alert students to the anomaly, (b) create the tension implicit in a metaphor by noting that a nonliteral interpretation is required, (c) identify the appropriate matching salient attribute, and (d) increase the salience of the attribute. Petrie (1979, p. 461) offered a general instructional model that is similar to Ortony's: (a) create an anomalous situation in presenting the metaphor; (b) allow students to act upon the anomaly through reflection, dialogue, or some form of analysis; and (c) provide students with feedback that permits corrections in drawing tentative conclusions.

Based on their research, Readance et al. (1984), proposed a more detailed version of Ortony's model:

1. Draw the learner's attention to the nonliteral meaning of the metaphorical statement.
2. Assume initially that the topic precedes the vehicle.
3. Search for matching attributes with low/high salience condition.
4. Disregard matching attributes that are trivial or that lead to contextually inappropriate interpretations.
5. Assist the learner in focusing upon the appropriate salient attributes.
6. If Steps 2, 3, and 4 fail to resolve the metaphor, transpose topic and vehicle and try Steps 3 and 4 again.
7. If Step 6 fails to resolve the metaphor, select any available matching attribute and state it as a literal comparison. (p. 666)

GENERAL INSTRUCTIONAL STRATEGIES FOR FACILITATING KNOWLEDGE ACQUISITION

To the extent that textbook authors and instructors systematically organize data for more efficient remembering, they assist students in creating schemata and referencing, activating, and applying prior knowledge. One of the more useful theoretical constructs that can be applied to social studies instruction, *generative learning,* has been provided by Wittrock (1974, 1986). Wittrock proposed that both memory and comprehension are facilitated when learners relate new information to their prior knowledge and experiences and generate a representation of the relationship between the two domains.

One application of Wittrock's model to social studies instruction was provided by Mackenzie and White (1982). In a study that involved the learning of geography information by ninth-grade students, they used three treatments. In one, based on Wittrock's theory, they incorporated fieldwork, experiences that stimulated active student generation of information, and opportunities to link the events to geographic subject matter. In the second, traditional fieldwork experiences were provided and in the third, conventional classroom instruction was supplied.

The first group retained 90% of the material learned, compared to 58% for the second group and 51% for the third.

Memory Strategies

Social educators have often shunned the issue of how individuals store and retrieve knowledge, that is, *memory,* as an unimportant instructional issue. Memory has suffered from association with the rote learning of nonfunctional information. In reality, students are frequently required in social studies classes to remember a great number of names, places, events, and dates, as well as a great deal of general descriptive information, in order to clarify and link new knowledge in functionally meaningful ways.

A number of specific memory strategies or mnemonics exist for social studies applications, some dating back to the early Greeks and Romans (Bellezza, 1981; Wittrock, 1986). Mnemonics involve either imagery or verbal devices or some combination of the two. Simple schemes that have produced significant memory retention in studies include mediators such as the *first-letter technique,* which is taking the first letter of each word to be remembered and composing a word or sentence from these letters; *chunking,* which is combining small units into larger ones (Miller, 1956); *organization of material into hierarchies;* and the *narrative technique,* which involves constructing narrative stories to link together words to be remembered.

Keyword Mnemonics. Another mnemonic device, the *keyword technique,* initially used for learning foreign language vocabulary (Atkinson, 1975), has been applied to a variety of types of information. In recent years a significant body of research has established the efficacy of the keyword technique, which involves first identifying a word to be related to the one to be remembered and then generating an interactive image between the two words (Levin & Pressley, 1985).

One illustration of the keyword technique that has application to social studies instruction can be found in the work of Levin, Shriberg, and Berry (1983). Subjects in two studies were 178 eighth-graders; four classes participated in the first study and four in the second. In each study, students were asked to examine lists of 10 fictitious town names and lists of 20 corresponding attributes. In the first study, 10 passages were used with two attributes per town (i.e., short narrative passages concerning town name, plus attributes such as *growing* and *affluent*); in the second study, 5 four-attribute-per-town passages were used. The same four conditions were used in each study: control, with subjects given a sheet with name and attribute information; a *separate picture,* with a drawing replacing written descriptions of each attribute; an *organized picture,* with the pictorial representations of attributes integrated into a single drawing; and an *organized keyword picture,* with a keyword accompanying each town's name (e.g., Planeville = plane) incorporated into the scene of the organized picture condition.

The treatments were administered through booklets, and the total task administration time was approximately 30 minutes. Dependent measures required students to match a list of the town names with the set of attributes associated with the

towns. In the study involving two attributes per town, students who received the organized-keyword-picture treatment scored almost twice as high on the posttest as those receiving the other three conditions. In the study involving four attributes per town, the organized-keyword-picture treatment also produced the highest mean performance scores.

These results supported the earlier findings of Jones and Hall (1982); Levin, Shriberg, Miller, McCormick, and Levin (1980); Pressley and Dennis-Rounds (1980); and Shriberg, Levin, McCormick, and Pressley (1982) that the keyword technique can be effective in remembering certain kinds of social studies data. Based on their extensive review of the related research, Pressley, Levin, and Delaney (1982) concluded that "The evidence is overwhelming that use of the keyword method, as applied to recall of vocabulary definitions, greatly facilitates performance... In short, keyword method effects are pervasive and of impressive magnitude" (pp. 70–71). Their conclusion was based on the positive outcomes of studies in which both concrete and abstract words were the learning tasks and the subjects were of varying ages. Some caution, however, is appropriate in interpreting these and other such studies, because the researchers generally did not address the *retention* effects of mnemonic instructional devices.

Imagery and Memory. A number of researchers have concluded that imagery, especially pictures, facilitates memory (Bower, 1972; Richardson, 1980; Wittrock, 1986). In an extensive review of 23 studies, Levie and Lentz (1982) concluded that drawings and pictures have a powerful effect on learning from printed instructional materials. In all but one study, students learned more from materials that included related illustrations or pictures than from materials without them.

One of the issues that must be taken into account in interpreting such studies, however, is the developmental level of the students. For example, Bull and Wittrock (1973) found that 10-year-olds who read each word and its definition, wrote the word, and then constructed a picture based on the word, retained more vocabulary words than did a group given comparable instructions and a ready-made picture. Wittrock and Goldberg (1975) concluded that although children younger than 8 or 9 are able to use imagery effectively to assist in remembering information, they are incapable of constructing their own imagery devices.

Nonliteral Images and Memory. Other forms of illustration that are nonliteral images, such as maps, graphic organizers, and diagrams, have also been demonstrated to affect memory. Reviews of the research relating to the impact of maps show that spatial information may be learned more effectively from maps than from verbal descriptions and that maps improve memory for related prose (Dean & Kulhavy, 1981; Levie & Lentz, 1982; Phillips, 1979; Potash, 1977; Schwartz & Kulhavy, 1981). Abel and Kulhavy (1986) further clarified the effects of different types of maps by establishing that those with pictorial features specifically organized according to spatial referents in adjoining text passages greatly increase the learning of pertinent subject matter.

Although maps have been found to improve students' memory of related subject matter, it is not clear how they specifically affect learning. Abel and Kulhavy (1986), for example, contended that maps serve a mnemonic-like function for encoding information in memory. Levie and Lentz (1982) suggested that learners often lack experience in effectively processing nonliteral representations, such as maps, in comparison with pictures and drawings, which may require less interpretation. Students may ignore illustrations unless they are prompted or required to study them in order to complete a task (Carr, Bachrach, & Mehner, 1977; Dean & Kulhavy, 1981; Jahoda, Cheyne, Deregowski, Sinha, & Collingbourne, 1976).

Advance Organizers

The term *advance organizers* was introduced by Ausubel in 1960 to characterize higher order abstractions that are more inclusive than the new information to be presented. In the original sense in which Ausubel used the term, it implied an awareness of the learner's existing knowledge structure so that new information could be linked to prior knowledge. As currently employed, the construct *advance organizers* may be regarded as any device used to provide a preview of material to be learned in order to help the learner organize, remember, and relate prior knowledge to new information to be learned. Borich (1988) suggested that "An advance organizer identifies the highest level of behavior resulting from a sequence of lessons and to which the outcome of the present day's lesson is to contribute" (p. 171).

Advance organizers include simple verbal instructions, charts, diagrams, and semantic maps. For example, in an American history class a teacher might begin a discussion of New Deal programs by first overviewing the ways in which the Roosevelt administration constituted a departure from past administrations. A government class could be given a chart outlining the structure of the executive branch before examining each of the major units. The concept map in Figure 30–1 could serve a similar purpose in a geography lesson.

In a meta-analysis of over 100 studies, Stone (1983) confirmed the earlier findings of the meta-analysis by Luiten, Ames, and Ackerman (1980) that advance organizers facilitate both learning and retention. Mayer (1979) had confirmed in an earlier review that the effects of advance organizers were especially strong when the material to be learned was poorly organized.

A special type of advance organizer that has direct application to social studies instruction, the *structural organizer,* was developed by Slater, Graves, and Piche (1985). In a study involving 224 ninth-grade students and passages from a social studies history text, they found that an organizer, which consisted of structured information on the organization of a text passage, could facilitate comprehension and recall of the material in the passage. Two types of structural organizers were used as treatments in the study: (a) A set of written materials that called the students' attention to the author's organization of material and how it could be used to learn the material, and (b) the written materials plus a structured outline to be completed as the students read the passage. In addition, there were two control conditions: instructions to read passages in the text and instructions to read the passages and take detailed notes. Dependent measures were written recall protocols and a multiple-choice comprehension test.

Students who used the structural organizer that included completion of an outline received the highest mean scores on recall and comprehension tests. Compared to students in the control conditions, those with the structural organizer plus outline recalled 77% more information (SMD = 1.66) and scored 19% higher on the comprehension test (SMD = .89).

Perhaps the most surprising and unintended finding of the study concerned the control condition in which brief instructions were given to take detailed notes while reading the passages. This group had the second highest set of mean scores. Compared to students in the other control condition, students with instructions to take notes recalled 45% more information (SMD = .98) and scored 18% higher on the comprehension test (SMD = .87). Given the costs (small) of encouraging students to take notes, in relationship to the apparent benefits (great), this finding bears further investigation.

Instructional Materials Organization

Beyond the application of advance organizers, what other techniques have been found effective in facilitating knowledge acquisition through the use of instructional materials? These devices can be incorporated in all forms of expository instructional materials including texts, computer software, and workbooks. There is strong evidence for the conclusion that manipulation of the organization and design of instructional materials can greatly facilitate learners' recall and comprehension of information (Armbruster, 1984; Calfee & Drum, 1986; Meyer, 1984).

An extensive body of research evidence documents the limitations of existing social studies text materials from a variety of perspectives (Anderson, Armbruster, & Kantor, 1980; Beck & Mckeown, 1988; Cheyney, 1987; Gagnon, 1987; Martorella, 1982; Sewall, 1987; Siler, 1987). From a cognitive perspective, one major criticism of social studies textbooks, especially history texts, is that they compartmentalize information and fail to aid students in linking passages. Bean, Sorter, Singer, and Frazer (1986) observed, for example, that students may move from a study of the colonial revolution as it unfolded in England and America to a discussion of the French Revolution of 1790s without any linkage to the concept of revolution or any development of a revolution schema. Textbooks and reading in social studies are considered further in the chapters by Beck and McKeown and Camperell and Knight in this *Handbook.*

Direct Instruction

In recent years, in the wake of interest in *effective teaching,* a category of instructional strategies has emerged labeled *direct instruction.* According to Rosenshine (1987), "The terms explicit teaching or direct instruction ... refer to a systematic method of teaching with emphasis on proceeding in small steps, checking for student understanding, and achieving active and successful participation by all students" (p. 34). Findings on the effects of direct instruction have come primarily from studies involving urban elementary and junior high school students in mathematics and reading, and many of them include instruction over short periods of time.

Direct instruction involves both a high degree of teacher control over the instructional process and a high percentage of student on-task behavior. Typically, direct instruction involves considerable lecturing, demonstrating, drill-and-practice, low-level questioning, monitoring of student behavior, and immediate feedback to insure that instructional time is used efficiently (Ross & Kyle, 1987). Research findings on direct instruction may be summarized as suggesting the following teaching procedures (see Rosenshine, 1987):

1. Initiate a lesson with a statement of objectives and a review of previous learning.
2. Introduce new material in small steps, giving clear and explicit directions and providing opportunities for practice after each step.
3. Guide the practice sessions, providing feedback and corrective information.
4. Supervise independent practice.
5. Provide for review and testing over spaced periods of time.

Generalization of these findings to K–12 social studies instruction must be approached with caution. Research findings on direct instruction seem most applicable to teaching for low-level cognitive objectives, especially in mathematics and reading with low socioeconomic students (Soar & Soar, 1983). Rosenshine and Stevens (1986) suggested that the findings can be applied to those area of social studies that relate to the learning of skills and factual information; in sum, objectives that can be achieved by breaking instruction into small parts. However, Rosenshine (1987) cautioned, "These procedures seem less applicable to areas that cannot be broken into smaller parts such as analysis of literature or discussion of social science issues" (p. 34).

CONCLUSION

Much remains unknown about the process of knowledge acquisition in social studies instruction, posing challenges for future researchers. At the same time, there is a critical mass of grounded theory and research, drawn primarily from the framework of cognitive psychology and from fields outside of the social studies, upon which to build. Beyond researchers, social educators in general have at their disposal a repertoire of validated principles and guidelines for assisting students in acquiring various elements of knowledge.

A number of clear and explicit guidelines exist for teaching the most fundamental elements of social studies knowledge, concepts. These include procedures for developing both concepts that have clearly defined properties and those that have fuzzy boundaries; for linking coordinate, supraordinate, and subordinate concepts; and for relating them within and between schemata. Given the complexity and variety of the types of concepts that emerge during social studies instruction, some

significant hypotheses also exist concerning how teachers and students might analyze concept groupings when they appear in forms such as metaphors.

In addition, a number of general instructional strategies that apply to the efficient acquisition of all elements of knowledge have been identified. These range from mnemonic devices, imagery techniques, advance organizers, to organizing principles for making instructional materials more comprehensible. Although such strategies can be useful when employed as discrete activities, they can be more meaningfully applied within the framework of an integrative instructional theory that is sensitive to students' prior knowledge. One example is Wittrock's generative learning model, which emphasizes relating new information to prior knowledge and experiences and the generation of a representation of the relationship between the two domains.

As a general instructional strategy, direct-instruction techniques probably have a limited role in knowledge acquisition in social studies. Their most effective applications would seem to be to those areas of the curriculum that emphasize declarative knowledge comprised of discrete facts that need not be retained in memory for long periods of time.

To apply and add substantially to our accumulated body of information in systematic and meaningful ways, practitioners and researchers must shift their attention from teacher behaviors to the broader framework of instruction within which learning can be optimized. Functional knowledge construction in social studies occurs in many forms, through assorted media and under a variety of instructional conditions. With respect to specific avenues of future research in social education, a critical, basic agenda item is to address how instruction can most effectively aid students in acquiring different elements of knowledge, both procedural and declarative, in a holistic pattern or integrated network. Concepts, facts, generalizations, hypotheses, and other forms of knowledge in social studies can neither exist nor be formed in isolation from one another. At the same time, existing instructional strategies do not very effectively address the problem of how different elements can be taught concurrently or even sequentially for efficient and meaningful learning. Similarly, an important pragmatic instructional question is how unique individual student schemata can be linked effectively to a holistic pattern of instruction. As an illustration, consider the problem of introducing Allport's (1954) theory of prejudice, which incorporates a wealth of concepts, generalizations, facts, and hypotheses, to an integrated class of seniors whose prejudice-related experiences and general backgrounds typically would be varied both cognitively and affectively.

A further agenda item is the expansion of our understanding of concept teaching across all categories of concepts. A great deal is already known regarding effective strategies for teaching concepts, but the recent emergence of significant research findings concerning the constructs of prototypes and best examples raises some important new questions for social studies, because the field has so many concepts that lend themselves to prototype, rather than attribute, analysis. Issues that remain include how to determine what constitutes a best example for an individual learner, how prototypes actually are formed, which concepts are most efficiently learned through prototype formation, and how cross-cultural differences affect concept formation.

Other fruitful areas for further investigation involve topics that already have a solid base of evidence but about which important questions remain. These areas include how figures of speech are produced and processed in social studies discussions and what the optimal instructional strategies are for learning types such as metaphors. Although some useful hypotheses exist to guide instructional practice in analyzing metaphors, little is known about how students *produce* metaphors and figures of speech generally. Another area for examination is the effects on learning of general instructional strategies such as imagery, maps, and special structural organizers including outlines, diagrams, and note-taking.

It is likely that for some time the base of grounded theory and research concerning knowledge development in the social studies will continue to come from the larger body of growing and significant work in the general field of cognitive psychology. Although this is both a desirable and an efficient way to build a systematic base of instructional information and applications, social studies researchers must contribute to a more direct theory and research base for social studies instruction. Apart from the areas of concept formation and selected areas of general instructional strategies, few studies related to the focus of this chapter could be found that dealt specifically with social studies instruction. In contrast, mathematics, science, and reading as subjects in the school curriculum were far better represented in the literature. Given the structure of the subject matter of the social studies in comparison with other subjects, the hypothesis that this field raises a unique set of issues related to knowledge acquisition needs to be more adequately tested.

References

Abel, R. R., & Kulhavy, R. W. (1986). Maps, mode of text presentation, and children's prose learning. *American Educational Research Journal, 23,* 263–274.

Anderson, C. W., & Smith, E. L. (1987). Teaching science. In V. Richardson-Koehler (Ed.), *Educators' handbook: A research perspective* (pp. 84–111). New York: Longman.

Anderson, R. C. (1984). Some reflections on the acquisition of knowledge. *Educational Researcher, 13,* 5–10.

Anderson, T. H., & Armbruster, B. B. (1984). Content area textbooks. In R. C. Anderson, J. Osborn, & R. T. Tierney (Eds.), *Learning to read in American schools: Basal readers and content texts* (pp. 193–224). Hillsdale, NJ: Lawrence Erlbaum.

Anderson, T. H., Armbruster, B. B., & Kantor, R. N. (1980). *How clearly written are children's textbooks?: Or of bladderworts and alfa.* Reading Education Report No. 16. Urbana, IL: University of Illinois, Center for the Study of Reading. (ERIC Document No. ED 192 275).

Armbruster, B. B. (1984). The problems of "inconsiderate" text. In G. G. Duffy, L. R. Roehler, & J. Mason (Eds.), *Comprehension instruction: Perspectives and suggestions* (pp. 202–217). New York: Longman.

Armento, B. J. (1986). Research on teaching social studies. In M. C. Wittrock (Ed.), *Handbook of research on teaching* (3rd ed., pp. 942–951). New York: Macmillan.

Armstrong, S. E., Gleitman, L. R., & Gleitman, H. (1983). What some concepts might not be. *Cognition, 13,* 263–308.

Atkinson, R. C. (1975). Mnemonotechnics in second language learning. *American Psychologist, 30,* 821–828.

Ausubel, D. P. (1960). The use of advance organizers in the learning and retention of meaningful verbal material. *Journal of Educational Psychology, 51,* 267–272.

Baker, L., & Brown, A. L. (1984). Cognitive monitoring in reading. In J. Flood (Ed.), *Understanding reading comprehension* (pp. 21–44). Newark, DE: International Reading Association.

Baldwin, R. S., Luce, T. S., & Readance, J. E. (1982). The impact of subschemata on metaphorical processing. *Reading Research Quarterly, 4,* 528–543.

Bartlett, F. C. (1932). *Remembering.* Cambridge: Cambridge University Press.

Bean, T. W., Sorter, J., Singer, H. G., & Frazer, C. (1986). Teaching students how to make predictions about events in history with a graphic organizer plus options guide. *Journal of Reading, 29,* 739–745.

Beck, I. L., & McKeown, M. G. (1988). Toward meaningful accounts in history texts for young learners. *Educational Researcher, 17,* 31–39.

Bellezza, F. S. (1981). Mnemonic devices: Classification, characteristics, and criteria. *Review of Educational Research, 51,* 247–275.

Bell-Gredler, M. E. (1986). *Learning and instruction: Theory into practice.* New York: Macmillan.

Berger, P. L., & Luckmann, T. (1966). *The social construction of reality: A treatise in the sociology of knowledge.* Garden City, NY: Doubleday.

Black, M. (1962). *Models and metaphors: Studies in language and philosophy.* Ithaca, NY: Cornell University Press.

Black, M. (1979). *More about metaphor.* In A. Ortony (Ed.), *Metaphor and thought* (pp. 19–43). New York: Cambridge University Press.

Borich, G. (1988). *Effective teaching methods.* Columbus, OH: Merrill.

Bower, G. H. (1972). *Human memory: Basic processes.* New York: Academic Press.

Bransford, J. D., & Vye, N. J. (1989). Cognitive research and its implications for instruction. In L. B. Resnick & L. E. Klopfer (Eds.), *Toward the thinking curriculum: Current cognitive research* (pp. 173–205) (1989 Yearbook of the Association for Supervision and Curriculum Development). Alexandria, VA: Association for Supervision and Curriculum Development.

Brewer, W. F., & Nakamura, G. V. (1984). *The nature and function of schemas* (Tech. Rep. No. 325). Cambridge, MA: Bolt, Beranek and Newman. (ERIC Document Reproduction Service No. ED 248 291)

Brophy, J. (1990). *Higher order thinking and problem solving in social studies.* East Lansing, MI: Center for the Learning and Teaching of Elementary Subjects.

Brown, A. L., Bransford, J. D., Ferara, R. A., & Campione, J. C. (1983). Learning, remembering, and understanding. In J. H. Flavell & E. M. Markman (Eds.), *Handbook of child psychology: Cognitive development* (Vol. 3, pp. 77–126). New York: John Wiley & Sons.

Bruner, J. (1973). *Beyond the information given.* New York: W. W. Norton.

Bull, B. L., & Wittrock, M. (1973). Imagery in the learning of verbal definitions. *British Journal of Educational Psychology, 43,* 289–293.

Burts, D. C., McKinney, C. W., & Burts, B. L. (1985). Effects of teacher enthusiasm on three- and four-year-old children's acquisition of four concepts. *Theory and Research in Social Education, 13,* 19–29.

Calfee, R., & Drum, P. (1986). Research on teaching reading. In M. C. Wittrock (Ed.), *Handbook of research on teaching* (3rd ed., pp. 804–849). New York: Macmillan.

Carr, T. H., Bachrach, V. R., & Mehner, D. S. (1977). Preparing children to look at pictures: Advance descriptions direct attention and facilitate active processing. *Child Development, 48,* 22–29.

Cheyney, L. V. (1987). *American memory: A report on the humanities in the nation's public schools.* Washington, DC: National Endowment for the Humanities.

Cole, M., & Scribner, S. (1974). *Culture and thought.* New York: John Wiley & Sons.

Dean, R. S., & Kulhavy, R. W. (1981). Influence of spatial organization in prose learning. *Journal of Educational Psychology, 73,* 57–64.

Dewey, J. (1916). *Democracy and education.* New York: Macmillan.

Dewey, J. (1933). *How we think.* Boston: D. C. Heath.

Downey, M. T., & Levstik, L. S. (1988). Teaching and learning history: The research base. *Social Education, 52,* 336–342.

Engle, S., & Ochoa, A. (1988). *Education for democratic citizenship: Decision making in the social studies.* New York: Teachers College Press.

Flavell, J. H. (1971). First discussant's comments: What is memory development the development of? *Human Development, 14,* 272–278.

Ford, M. J., & McKinney, C. W. (1986). The effects of recycling and response sensitivity on the acquisition of social studies concepts. *Theory and Research in Social Education, 14,* 21–33.

Gagne, R. (1985). *The conditions of learning* (4th ed.). New York: Holt, Rinehart & Winston.

Gagne, R., Briggs, L., & Wager, W. (1988). *Principles of instructional design* (3rd ed.). New York: Holt, Rinehart & Winston.

Gagnon, P. (1987). *Democracy's untold story: What world history textbooks neglect.* Washington, DC: American Federation of Teachers.

Guenther, F. (1975). On the semantics of metaphor. *Poetics, 4,* 199–200.

Hallam, R. (1969). Piaget and the teaching of history. *Educational Research, 12,* 3–12.

Heider, E. R. (1972). Universals in color naming and memory. *Journal of Experimental Psychology, 93,* 10–20.

Howard, R. W. (1987). *Concepts and schemata: An introduction.* Philadelphia: Cassell.

Hunt, E. B., & Banaji, M. R. (1988). The Whorfian hypothesis revisited: A cognitive science view of linguistic and cultural effects on thought. In J. W. Berry, S. H. Irvine, & E. B. Hunt (Eds.), *Indigenous cognition: Functioning in context* (pp. 57–84). Norwell, MA: Kluwer.

Hunt, M. P., & Metcalf, L. E. (1968). *Teaching high school social studies: Problems in reflective thinking and social understanding* (2nd ed.). New York: Harper & Row.

Jahoda, G., Cheyne, W. M., Deregowski, J. B., Sinha, D., & Collingbourne, R. (1976). Utilization of pictorial information in classroom learning: A cross-cultural study. *AV Communications Review, 24,* 295–315.

Jassal, R. S., & Tennyson, R. D. (1982). Application of concept learning research in the design of instructional systems. *International Journal of Instructional Media, 9,* 185–205.

Jones, B. F., & Hall, J. W. (1982). School applications of the mnemonic keyword method as a study strategy by eighth graders. *Journal of Educational Psychology, 74,* 230–237.

Jurd, M. (1973). Adolescent thinking in history-type material. *Australian Journal of Education, 17,* 2–17.

Kennedy, K. J. (1983). Assessing the relationship between information processing capacity and historical understanding. *Theory and Research in Social Education, 11,* 1–22.

Klausmeier, H. (1980). Instructional design and the teaching of concepts. In J. R. Levin & V. L. Allen (Eds.), *Cognitive learning in children: Theories and strategies* (pp. 191–217). New York: Academic Press.

Kleg, M. (1986). Teaching about terrorism: A conceptual approach. *Social Science Record, 24,* 31–39.

Kleg, M. (1987). Genocide: A concept action model. *Social Science Record, 24,* 68–73.

Lakeoff, G., & Johnson, M. (1980). *Metaphors we live by.* Chicago: University of Chicago Press.

Levie, W. H., & Lentz, R. (1982). Effects of text illustrations: A review of research. *Educational Communication and Technology Journal, 30,* 195–232.

Levin, J. R., & Pressley, M. (1985). Mnemonic vocabulary instruction: What's fact, what's fiction. In R. F. Dillion (Ed.), *Individual differences in cognition* (Vol. 2, pp. 145–172). New York: Academic.

Levin, J. R., & Shriberg, L. K., Miller, G. E., McCormick, C. B., & Levin, B. B. (1980). The keyword method in the classroom: How to remember the states and their capitols. *Elementary School Journal, 80,* 185–191.

Levin, J. R., Shriberg, L. K., & Berny, J. K. (1983). A concrete strategy for remembering abstract prose. *American Educational Research Journal, 20,* 277–290.

Levstik, L. S. (1986). The relationship between historical response and narrative in a sixth-grade classroom. *Theory and Research in Social Education, 14* 1–15.

Lovell, K. (1961). A follow-up study of Inhelder's and Piaget's "The growth of logical thinking." *British Journal of Psychology, 52,* 143–153.

Luiten, J., Ames, W. A., & Ackerson, G. (1980). A meta-analysis of the advance organizers on learning and retention. *American Educational Research Journal, 17,* 211–218.

Mackenzie, A. W., & White, R. T. (1982). Fieldwork in geography and long-term memory structures. *American Educational Research Journal, 19,* 623–632.

Mahood, W. (1987). Metaphors in social studies instruction. *Theory and Research in Social Education, 15,* 285–297.

Martorella, P. H. (1982). Cognition research: Some implications for the design of social studies instructional materials. *Theory and Research in Social Education, 10*(3), 1–16.

Martorella, P. H. (1988). Students' understanding of metaphorical concepts in international relations. *Social Science Record, 25,* 46–49.

Martorella, P. H. (1990). Teaching concepts. In J. M. Cooper (Ed.), *Classroom teaching skills* (4th ed.). Lexington, MA: D. C. Heath.

Marzano, R. J., Brandt, R. S., Hughes, C. S., Jones, B. F., Preseissen, B. S., Rankin, S. C., & Suhor, C. (1988). *Dimensions of thinking: A framework for curriculum and instruction.* Alexandria, VA: Association for Supervision and Curriculum Development.

Mayer, R. E. (1979). Can advance organizers influence meaningful learning? *Review of Educational Research, 49,* 371–383.

McKinney, C. W., Burts, D. C., Ford, M. J., & Gilmore, A. C. (1987). The effects of ordinary and coordinate concept nonexamples on first-grade students' acquisitions of three coordinate concepts. *Theory and Research in Social Education, 15,* 45–50.

McKinney, C. W., Gilmore, A. C., Larkins, A. G., & McKinney, K. C. (1987). *Effects of critical attributes and a best example on fifth-grade students' concept and prototype formation.* Paper presented at the meeting of the College/University Faculty Association of the National Council for the Social Studies, Dallas.

McKinney, C. W., Gilmore, A. C., Peddicord, H. Q., & McCallum, R. S. (1987). Effects of a best example and critical attributes on prototype formation in the acquisition of a concept. *Theory and Research in Social Education, 15,* 189–201.

McKinney, C. W., Larkins, A. G., & Burts, D. C. (1984). Effects of overt teacher enthusiasm on first-grade students' acquisition on three concepts. *Theory and Research in Social Education, 11,* 15–24.

McKinney, C. W., Larkins, A. G., Ford, M. J., & Davis, J. C. (1983). The effectiveness of three methods of teaching social studies concepts to fourth-grade students: An aptitude-treatment interaction study. *American Educational Research Journal, 20,* 663–670.

Medin, D. L., & Smith, E. E. (1984). Concepts and concept formation. *Annual Review of Psychology, 35.* 113–138.

Merrill, M. D., & Tennyson, R. (1977). *Teaching concepts: An instructional design guide.* Englewood Cliffs, NJ: Educational Technology.

Meyer, B. J. F. (1984). Organizational aspects of text: Effects on reading comprehension and applications for the classroom. In J. Flood (Ed.), *Promoting reading comprehension* (pp. 113–138). Newark, DE: International Reading Association.

Miller, G. A. (1956). The magical number seven, plus or minus two: Some limits on our capacity for processing information. *Psychological Review, 63,* 81–97.

Millward, R. B. (1980). Models of concept formation. In R. E. Snow, P. Federico, & W. E. Montague (Eds.), *Aptitude, learning, and instruction: Cognitive process analysis of learning and problem solving Vol. 2* (pp. 245–275). Hillsdale, NJ: Lawrence Erlbaum.

Novak, J., & Gowin, D. B. (1984). *Learning how to learn.* Cambridge, Eng.: Cambridge University Press.

Ortony, A. (1975). Why metaphors are necessary and not just nice. *Educational Theory, 25,* 45–53.

Ortony, A. (Ed.). (1979). *Metaphor and thought.* New York: Cambridge University Press.

Ortony, A. (1984). Understanding figurative language. In P. D. Pearson (Ed.), *Handbook of reading research* (pp. 453–470). New York: Longman.

Ortony, A., Reynolds, R. E., & Arter, J. A. (1978). Metaphor: Theoretical and empirical research. *Psychology Bulletin, 85,* 919–943.

Peel, E. A. (1960). *The pupil's thinking.* London: Oldbourne Press.

Perkins, D. N. (1986). *Knowledge as design.* Hillsdale, NJ: Lawrence Erlbaum.

Petrie, H. (1979). Metaphor and learning. In A. Ortony (Ed.), *Metaphor and thought* (pp. 438–461). New York: Cambridge University Press.

Phillips, R. J. (1979). Making maps easy to read: A summary of research. In P. A. Koler, M. E. Wrolstad, & H. Bouma (Eds.), *Processing of visible language. Vol. 1* (pp. 165–174). New York: Plenum.

Piaget, J. (1980). *Adaptation and intelligence: Organic selection and phenocopy.* Chicago: University of Chicago Press.

Pick, A. D. (1980). Cognition: Psychological perspectives. In H. C. Triandis & W. Lonner (Eds.), *Handbook of cross-cultural psychology* (Vol. 3, pp. 117–153). Boston: Allyn & Bacon.

Potash, L. M. (1977). Design of maps and map-related research. *Human Factors, 19,* 139–150.

Pressley, M., & Dennis-Rounds, J. D. (1980). Transfer of a mnemonic keyword strategy at two age levels. *Journal of Educational Psychology, 72,* 575–582.

Pressley, M., Levin, J. R., & Delaney, H. D. (1982). The mnemonic keyword method. *Review of Educational Research, 52,* 61–91.

Readence, J. E., Baldwin, R. S., & Head, M. H. (1986). Direct instruction in processing metaphors. *Journal of Reading Behavior, 18,* 325–340.

Readence, J. E., Baldwin, R. S., Martin, M. A., & O'Brien, D. G. (1984). Metaphorical interpretation. An investigation of salience imbalance hypothesis. *Journal of Educational Psychology, 76,* 659–667.

Resnick, L. (1981). Instructional psychology. *Annual Review of Psychology, 32,* 659–704.

Resnick, L. (1983). Toward a cognitive theory of instruction. In S. G. Paris, G. M. Olson, & H. W. Stevenson (Eds.), *Comprehension instruction: Perspectives and suggestions* (pp. 202–217). New York: Longman.

Richards, I. (1971). *The philosophy of rhetoric.* Oxford: Oxford University Press.

Richardson, J. T. E. (1980). *Mental imagery and human memory.* London: Macmillan.

Rosch, E. R., & Mervis, C. B. (1975). Family resemblances: Studies in the internal structure of categories. *Cognitive Psychology, 7,* 573–605.

Rosenshine, B. (1987). Explicit teaching and teacher training. *Journal of Teacher Education, 38,* 34–36.

Rosenshine, B., & Stevens, R. (1986). Teaching functions. In M. C. Wittrock (Ed.), *Handbook of research on teaching* (3rd ed.), (pp. 376–391). New York: Macmillan.

Ross, D. D., & Kyle, D. W. (1987). Helping preservice teachers learn to use teacher effectiveness research. *Journal of Teacher Education, 38,* 40–44.

Rummelhart, D. E. (1980). Schemata: The building blocks of cognition. In R. J. Spiro, B. C. Bruce, & W. F. Brewer (Eds.), *Theoretical issues in reading comprehension* (pp. 33–58). Hillsdale, NJ: Lawrence Erlbaum.

Rummelhart, D. E. (1984). Understanding understanding. In J. Flood (Ed.), *Understanding reading comprehension* (pp. 1–20). Newark, DE: International Reading Association.

Rummelhart, D. E., & Norman, D. A. (1981). Analogical reasoning processes in learning. In J. R. Anderson (Ed.), *Cognitive skills and their acquisition* (pp. 335–385). Hillsdale, NJ: Lawrence Erlbaum.

Rummelhart, D. E., & Ortony, A. (1977). The representation of knowledge in memory. In R. C. Anderson, R. J. Spiro, & W. E. Montague (Eds.), *Schooling and the acquisition of knowledge* (pp. 99–135). Hillsdale, NJ: Erlbaum.

Schwartz, N. H., & Kulhavy, R. W. (1981). Map features and the recall of discourse. *Contemporary Educational Psychology, 6,* 151–158.

Sewall, G. T. (1987). *American history textbooks: An assessment of quality.* New York: Educational Excellence Network.

Shaver, J. P. (1977). Needed: A Deweyean rationale for teaching social studies. *The High School Journal, 58,* 345–352.

Shaver, J. P. (1979). The usefulness of educational research in curricular/instructional decision-making in social studiess. *Theory and Research in Social Education, 7,* 21–46.

Shaver, J. P. (1987). Implications from research: What should be taught in social studies? In V. Richardson-Koehler (Ed.), *Educators' handbook: A research perspective* (pp. 112–138). New York: Longman.

Shriberg, L. K., Levin, J. R., McCormick, C. B., & Pressley, M. (1982). Learning about "famous people" via the keyword method. *Journal of Educational Psychology, 74,* 238–247.

Silberstein, L., Gardner, H., Phelps, E., & Winner, E. (1982). Autumn leaves and old photographs: The development of metaphor preferences. *Journal of Experimental Child Psychology, 34,* 135–150.

Siler, C. R. (1987). Content analysis: A process for textbook analysis and evaluation. *International Journal of Social Education, 1,* 78–99.

Slater, W. H., Graves, M. F., & Piche, G. L. (1985). Effects of structural organizers on ninth grade students' comprehension and recall of four patterns of expository text. *Reading Research Quarterly, 20,* 189–202.

Smith, E. E., & Medin, D. L. (1981). *Categories and concepts.* Cambridge, MA: Harvard University Press.

Soar, R. S., & Soar, R. M. (1983). Context effects in the teaching learning process. In D. C. Smith (Ed.), *Essential knowledge for beginning educators* (pp. 65–75). Washington, DC: American Association of Colleges for Teacher Education.

Stanley, W. B., & Mathews, R. C. (1985). Recent research on concept learning: Implications for social education. *Theory and Research in Social Education, 12,* 57–74.

Sticht, T. G. (1979). Educational users of metaphor. In A. Ortony (Ed.), *Metaphor and thought.* New York: Cambridge University Press.

Stone, C. L. (1983). A meta-analysis of advance organizer studies. *Journal of Experimental Education, 51,* 194–199.

Tennyson, R. D., & Cocchiarella, M. J. (1986). An empirically based instructional design theory for teaching concepts. *Review of Educational Research, 56,* 40–71.

Tennyson, R. D., & Park, O. (1980). The teaching of concepts: A review of instructional design research literature. *Review of Educational Research, 50,* 55–70.

Thompson, S. J. (1986). Teaching metaphoric language: An instructional strategy. *Journal of Reading, 30,* 105–109.

Tourangeau, R., & Sternberg, R. J. (1982). Understanding and appreciating metaphors. *Cognition, 11,* 203–244.

Tversky, A. (1977). Features of similarity. *Psychological Review, 84,* 327–352.

Van Dijk, T. (1975). Formal semantics of metaphorical discourse. *Poetics, 4,* 173–198.

Vosniadu, S., Ortony, A., Reynolds, R. E., & Wilson, P. T. (1984). Sources of difficulty in the young child's understanding of metaphorical language. *Child Development, 55,* 1588–1606.

Vygotsky, L. S. (1962). *Thought and language* (E. Hanfmann & G. Vakar, Eds. and Trans.). Cambridge, MA: MIT Press.

Wallen, N. E., & Fraenkel, J. R. (1988). An analysis of social education research over an eight year period. *Theory and Research in Social Education, 16,* 1–22.

Whorf, B. (1956). *Language, thought and reality.* (J. B. Carroll, Ed.). Cambridge, MA: MIT Press.

Wilson, B. G. (1985). What is a concept? Concept teaching and cognitive psychology. *Performance and Instruction, 25,* 16–18.

Wittgenstein, L. (1953). *Philosophical investigations.* New York: Macmillan.

Wittrock, M. C. (1974). Learning as a generative process. *Educational Psychologist, 11,* 87–95.

Wittrock, M. C. (1986). Students' thought processes. In M. C. Wittrock (Ed.), *Handbook of research on teaching* (3rd ed.), (pp. 297–314). New York: Macmillan.

Wittrock, M. C., & Goldberg, S. G. (1975). Imagery and meaningfulness in free recall: Word attributes and instructional sets. *Journal of General Psychology, 92,* 137–151.

Yoho, R. F. (1986). Effectiveness of four concept teaching strategies on social studies concept acquisition and retention. *Theory and Research in Social Education, 14,* 211–223.

Yussen, S. (1985). The role of metacognition in contemporary theories of cognitive development. In D. L. Forrest-Pressley, G. E. MacKinnon, & T. G. Waller (Eds.), *Metacognition, cognition, and human performance* (Vol. 1, pp. 253–283). Orlando, FL: Academic Press.

31

IMPACTS ON SOCIAL AND POLITICAL PARTICIPATION

Patrick Ferguson
THE UNIVERSITY OF ALABAMA

As phrased in the curriculum guidelines of the National Council for the Social Studies (NCSS), "the basic goal of social studies education is to prepare young people to become rational, participating citizens . . ." (NCSS, 1979, p. 262). Assuming that this statement has broad support within the profession (Barr, Barth, & Shermis, 1977; Bragaw & Hartoonian, 1988; Crabtree, 1983; Dynneson, Gross, & Nickel, 1988; NCSS, 1979; Parker, 1989; Parker & Jarolimek, 1984; Shaver, 1977; Wood, 1988), it follows that the success or failure of the social studies may be gauged by the extent to which the citizenry takes a reflective and active part in the political and social life of the community. A review of the research on the impact of the social studies on civil participation should be instrumental in determining whether the profession is accomplishing its central purpose.

In this review, an effort is made to answer two questions. *First,* what evidence is there that the social studies curriculum influences social and political participation? *Second,* what research is needed to improve the effectiveness of the social studies in educating for civic action? The chapter begins with a definition of participation, followed by an overview of the research on current levels of civic activity. The theoretical and empirical literature relating civics instruction to participation is examined next, and the chapter closes with a discussion of needed research on the influence of the social studies on participatory behavior.

PARTICIPATION DEFINED

Given that social studies goals related to participation are usually stated in terms of educating for various forms of politi-

cal action and that the research is focused almost exclusively on this domain, this review is centered on participation in the political arena. Because social studies educators have called for a broader definition of participation (Newmann, 1989; Parker & Jarolimek, 1984; Remy, 1980), consideration is given to an expanded view of civic activity in the section on recommendations for future research.

For political scientists, participation is narrowly defined as the acts of private citizens aimed at influencing the selection of government personnel and the actions they take (Milbrath & Goel, 1977; Verba Nie & Kim 1978). Stated more succinctly, political participation involves attempts, successful or otherwise, by individuals to influence the government. However, many social studies educators prefer an expanded definition that includes a host of seemingly nonpolitical acts such as work with community organizations, charitable and church-related activities, volunteer work with agencies, and presentations to organizations and youth groups (Clark, 1989; Newmann, 1975; Parker & Jarolimek, 1984; Rutter & Newmann, 1989).

Political researchers share most of the following assumptions concerning participation: (1) the activity must be voluntary, not coerced; (2) the action must have some relationship to the selection of rulers and the making of public policies; (3) there must be the possibility of action to challenge existing policies of the government and to replace that government through open and competitive elections; and (4) the activity must be a matter of right, not privilege. Political activity that is involuntary, or exercised because it is expected or coerced, has held minor interest for participation researchers. In terms of measurement, the most valid empirical measures of political participation are considered to be those that assess action, not

---

Reviewers were William Fernekes, Hunterdon Central Regional High School, Flemington, NJ; Dennie L. Smith, Memphis State University.

merely attitudes and feelings (LaPalambara, 1978; Verba et al., 1978).

Political researchers distinguish between individual and group-motivated participation (Verba, et al., 1978). Group-based political mobilization derives from membership in a particular social group and is primarily motivated by economic position, race, ethnicity, religion, sex, language, region, or other group-based factors. In light of the interest of political behaviorists in voluntary participation, the lion's share of the research has involved the study of individual, rather than group-motivated, forms of action. To intersect the mainstream research on political participation with the conventional goals of the social studies, usually phrased in terms of educating for personally responsible civic action, this review is focused on studies of voluntary, individually motivated forms of participation.

Earlier investigators took a unidimensional view of participation (Milbrath, 1965). Political action was gauged in terms of general levels of civic activity, without regard for the nature of the participation. For example, in Milbrath's (1965) early work, participants were ranged along a single dimension, from those who took a fully active role (the gladiators), through those who were passive participants (the spectators), to those who were uninvolved (the apathetics). This hierarchy was based on the assumption that activists participate indiscriminately in all forms of civic activity included below their level of classification. Also, participation in school, labor union, community, religious, and other "nongovernmental" organizations, as well as activities that might disrupt or call for fundamental change in the government, were excluded.

In the more recent literature, participation is treated as a considerably more complex, multidimensional variable, with civic activity measured in terms of more extensive and intricate participatory modes (Sigel & Hoskin, 1981) and with finer distinctions made among types of activists (LaPalambara, 1978; Parker & Jarolimek, 1984; Remy, 1980; Verba, et al., 1978). Verba, et al.'s multimodal approach to participation is described more fully later in this chapter.

Most studies of democratic civic participation divide political action into two modes: electoral and nonelectoral. Electoral actions are those associated with voting, campaigning, and running for political office. Nonelectoral behaviors include such actions as taking part in community interest associations, organizing and leading political action groups, initiating contacts with government officials, taking part in social protests, and pursuing aggressive, radical action for change. Out of necessity, the focus of this research review is on conventional political participation, although some evidence concerning nonpolitical participation is also included.

RESEARCH ON CURRENT LEVELS OF PARTICIPATION

Critics contend that the social studies curriculum has been ineffective in producing an active, civic-minded citizenry. An examination of the evidence concerning levels and patterns of citizen participation may be instructive about the accuracy of this assertion.

TABLE 31–1. Percentage Engaging in Twelve Different Acts of Political Participation

Type of Participation	Percentage
1. Report regularly voting in Presidential elections	72
2. Report always voting in local elections	47
3. Active in at least one organization involved in community problems	32
4. Have worked with others in trying to solve some community problems	30
5. Have attempted to persuade others to vote as they were	28
6. Have ever worked actively for a party or candidate during an election	26
7. Have ever contacted a local government official about some issue or problem	20
8. Have attended at least one political meeting or rally in the last three years.	19
9. Have ever contacted a state or national government official about some issue or problem	18
10. Have ever formed a group or organization to solve some local community problem	14
11. Have ever given money to a party or candidate during an election campaign	13
12. Presently a member of a political club or organization	8

Note. From *Participation in America: Political Democracy and Social Equality* (p. 31) by S. Verba and N. Nie, 1972, New York: Harper & Row. Copyright 1972 by Harper & Row. Reprinted by permission.

Table 31–1 presents the findings of a landmark study by Verba and Nie (1972) in which they found relatively high levels of participation in election-related activities but infrequent participation in other participatory modes. This pattern of civic activity has been confirmed through subsequent investigation and is generally accepted as an accurate portrayal of civic behavior in the United States (Dalton, 1988).

Although the data reported in Table 31–1 are informative, simple frequency distributions may obscure as much as they reveal, for they do not give us information on the overlap and distribution of various political activities. For example, it would be incorrect to conclude from the evidence presented in Table 31–1 that 70% to 80% of the citizenry engage in no activity beyond voting or that 20% to 30% perform all of the more active types of participation.

To construct a more precise representation, Verba and Nie cluster analyzed their data and were able to identify six internally homogenous categories of civic participation. Assignment to one of these categories meant that the respondent had an inclination to concentrate on that type of activity to the exclusion of other forms of participation. Table 31–2 shows the six participatory types that emerged, as indicated by the figures in the last column: voting specialists (21%), community activists (20%), campaigners (15%), parochial participants (those who contact officials on personal matters) (4%), complete activists (11%), and inactivists (22%). By identifying both the types of activists, and the proportion of the citizenry falling into each type, Verba and Nie were able to account for the kinds of activities citizens perform in more sophisticated ways. Their findings

TABLE 31–2. Participatory Profiles of the American Citizenry

Groups produced by cluster analysis	Scores on participation scales for				
	Voting	Campaign activity	Communal activity	Particularized contacting	Percent of sample in type
1. Inactive	37	9	3	0	22
2. Voting specialists	94	5	3	0	21
3. Parochial participants	73	13	3	100	4
4. Communalists	92	16	69	12	20
5. Campaigners	95	70	16	13	15
6. Complete activists	98	93	92	15	11
					93
Unclassifiable					7
					100%
Population means on the participation scales	76	29	28	14	

Note. From *Participation in America: Political Democracy and Social Equality* (p. 79) by S. Verba and N. Nie, 1972, New York: Harper & Row. Copyright 1972 by Harper & Row. Reprinted by permission.

challenged the previous assumption that civic activity could be viewed as hierarchical and cumulative along a single dimension.

Although subsequent investigations supported the participatory model of Verba and Nie (Dalton, 1988), some researchers questioned whether individuals freely ranged from one mode to another as circumstances warranted. Using Verba and Nie's modal categories, Dalton (1988) conducted a cross-national study and found that people do, in fact, specialize in the mode that matches their own personal motivations and goals, reinforcing the idea that modes of participation are not used interchangeably according to immediate circumstances (Dalton, 1988). Lawrence (1981), although acknowledging the validity of the Verba and Nie model, criticized it for focusing on who participates, not on why. He designed an alternative model that included the attitudinal variables of interest, sense of civic duty, and sense of efficacy as mediating influences. His research showed that more of the variance in voting and campaign activity is explained when these intervening variables are accounted for than when they are not.

Types of Activity

Recent trends in voter activity have concerned many social studies educators. In the United States, voting activity appears to be waning. Voter turnout figures for the 1988 presidential election were nearly 20% below voter participation numbers in 1960. The decline has been even more dramatic in nonpresidential elections. The percentage of participation in the 1986 congressional elections was the lowest recorded for the American electorate since 1942 (Powell, 1986). Social studies educators are especially sensitive to the erosion in participation among the youngest age cohorts. In 1984 only half of the 18- to 30-year-olds were registered to vote, and only 16.6% of the eligible voters in the 18–24 age group voted in the 1986 elections (Powell, 1986).

Using a much broader definition of participation that included many nongovernmental forms of activity, Sigel (Sigel & Hoskin, 1981) investigated the participation of adolescents and found that almost half of those surveyed were active in the community and that many had already begun to participate in direct political affairs. As with adults, adolescents favored highly conventional activities requiring little effort.

Cross-national studies of participation help put the U.S. experience into perspective. For example, the declines in electoral participation in the United States have not occurred in other democratic countries. From 1972 through 1980, the average voter turnout for national elections in the United States was 54% whereas in 29 other countries it averaged 80%. Although voter turnout declined by 20%, it remained stable elsewhere. Furthermore, recent studies of American voters reveal an interesting paradox: U.S. voters appear to be more politically aware and involved in other ways than citizens in other democracies, but voter turnout in the United States is substantially below the average for other democratic nations (Powell, 1986; Verba, et al., 1978).

Although participating in campaigning, contacting public officials, and joining and participating in organizations is not extensive among U.S. citizens, it is higher than in other democratic countries. In one study, community participation rates for Britain, West Germany, and France were found to be less than half that for the United States (Dalton, 1988). Furthermore, the United States contained the largest number of complete activists (those who take part in all forms of political activity) of the four countries. Dalton (1988) has concluded that, despite the fact that election participation is lower in the U.S., when all forms of participation are taken into account, U.S. citizens are more politically involved.

The critic of social studies can point to the evidence that 20% of the U.S. citizenry takes no active part in political life. This percentage is somewhat higher than in Britain (18%) and considerably above the figure for West Germany (7%); overall, however, the percentage of inactive citizens is not above the percentage for the other democracies studied by Dalton (1988).

The United States also contains the largest proportion of *complete activists,* those who participate with great frequency in all the types of political activity. Comparison of participation data for four democracies—West Germany, France, Britain, and the United States—revealed that, although all have relatively high voting rates, more U.S. citizens (about 1 in 3) take part in the more demanding forms of campaign activity and community activity. By way of contrast, only 1 in 4 Britains is actively involved in these activities (Dalton, 1988). In their cross-national study of participation, Verba and colleagues (1978) concluded that citizens in each country have a wide repertory of ways in which they can participate and, under similar circumstances, choose different ways to take civic action. They therefore cautioned researchers against making overly simple generalizations about political participation on the basis of cross-national data.

With reference to more aggressive modes of political activity—such as participation in illegal strikes, membership in groups seeking to dislodge the government, battles with other demonstrators—it is not possible to report meaningful figures on levels of participation. It has been estimated that, on the average, less than 17% of the population was participating in these forms of political activity in the 1970s (Verba et al., 1978).

Declines in voting percentages may not necessarily indicate a diminution in civic interest but may be attributed in part to changes in the nature of participation. Dalton (1988) observed that an increasingly sophisticated and cognitively mobilized electorate does not rely on voting and campaign activity as the primary means of expanding its involvement in politics. Increasingly, activists prefer referendums over elections and community activity over campaign work. Dalton (1988) cited evidence showing that citizen lobbies, single-issue groups, and citizen action groups are increasing in all western democracies. The implication is that citizen participation is becoming more closely linked to direct efforts at influence.

From a cross-cultural perspective, activists in other nations and in certain groups within the United States have been found to prefer group-based, rather than personal, approaches to political participation. For example, group-based forms of participation have been found to be the preferred modes of political action in Japan and within certain groups in the United States (Almond & Verba, 1963; Verba et al., 1978). The current focus on private forms of action, such as voting and citizen-initiated contacting, may not be the most effective means of educating and assessing participation for these populations.

Implications

How should one interpret all this evidence concerning civic activity with reference to conducting social studies research designed to expand civic participation? It depends on one's perceptions and beliefs concerning the goals of civic education. There is nearly virtually unanimous support among social studies educators for the belief that educating for universal participation is a self-evident good. However, some have questioned the goal of producing an entire population of rational, activist citizens (Dahl, 1971; Leming, 1986).

Leming (1986), for example, has argued that increasing participation knowledge and skills equally across all socioeconomic levels of society could exacerbate existing social and economic inequalities, because higher status groups, in possession of greater resources and power, would be in a position to exercise their newfound political expertise to the disadvantage of lower status groups. Nor can it be assumed that increasing participation skills would result in a more liberal and enlightened society. Increasing participation among those who do not hold democratic attitudes, who wish to achieve influence for the purpose of invoking repressive policies, or who would do injury to others to achieve their goals would hardly advance the cause of democracy. Finally, producing entire populations of rational activists who engage in high levels of civic activity could disrupt present democratic systems that function on the basis of a system whereby nonelites choose a select group of governing elites to act on their behalf (Dahl, 1961; Leming, 1986). This is not to suggest that social studies researchers abandon experiments to increase and improve levels of rational civic activity, only that careful thought be given to the social consequences of experiments designed to educate for extended social participation.

The recent research has established that participation is a much more complex, multidimensional, and contextually determined phenomenon than is reflected in the current social studies literature. Social studies practitioners and researchers need to move in the direction of this more refined definition if they hope to provide better insight into the influence of the social studies on social and political participation.

THE RESEARCH ON EDUCATION, SCHOOLING, AND CURRICULAR EFFECTS

The intricate mix of interrelated social, historical, and situational variables influencing an individual's decision to take political action greatly obscures the task of conducting tightly controlled causal studies designed to measure the influence of solitary factors. This problem has not deterred researchers from undertaking research to assess the singular influence of educationally related experiences on civic participation. That body of research is reviewed in this section.

To make the review task manageable, only studies examining the relationship between educationally related variables and participation are included. As in Ehman's (1980) earlier review, purely descriptive studies, single-variable investigations, and theoretical or prescriptive works have been excluded. The review is presented under four headings according to the variables investigated: (a) educational attainment, (b) school activities, (c) social studies curriculum, and (d) classroom-level factors. Generalizations derived from this research are presented at the end of the section.

The Influence of Education

There is abundant evidence for the existence of a strong positive relationship between educational attainment and civic participation (Dalton, 1988; Nie, Powell & Prewitt, 1969; Powell, 1986; Verba, et al., 1978). In these investigations *education* is defined as simply the number of years of schooling completed, and years of schooling have generally been found to be positively associated with level of political activity (Kamens, 1988). The relative size of the impact of education is in question. For example, Burn and Konrad (1987) found that education was less important than stress, job autonomy, income, and contact with political organizations in predicting political activity. Comparative investigations have shown that the positive relationship between education and political activity holds across cultures. It is important to indicate that this research has been almost exclusively conducted within the community of developed nations. (Almond & Verba, 1963; Barnes & Kaase, 1979).

Close scrutiny of the literature also suggests that educational expansion may have an impact on aggregate political participation in ways other than through individual socialization. For example, Krassa (1985) found that, whatever levels of education individuals possessed, their information on and interest and activity in politics were closely related to the aggregate level of education in the neighborhood where they resided. Alford and Lee (1968), in their analysis of correlational studies on the subject, concluded that, among certain urban populations, higher levels of education were negatively related to voter turnout but positively associated with other forms of political activity. Convincing evidence on the contextual influence of education comes from the comparative participation research of Igra (1976). He examined both individual and group data for six nations in a covariance design and found that, although education had a general positive effect on political activity for individuals, participation was actually lower in some countries with higher GNPs per capita. Overall, the findings in this area of the research suggest that higher levels of educational attainment are associated with increased civic activity but that contextual factors may exert an important mediating effect.

The lion's share of the political science research employing education as an independent variable has peripheral relevance for social studies practitioners because education is defined simply in terms of years of schooling and is utilized merely as a convenient measure of social status or as a coarse indicator of the level of intellectual achievement of the population under investigation. In the light of this restricted use, only the body of research examining the direct relationship between school-related factors and political participation is treated for the balance of the chapter.

School Activities

In their review of the research literature on the relationships between extracurricular participation and adolescent development, Holland and Andre (1987) found that school activity correlated with high levels of self-esteem, improved race relations, academic ability and grades in males, educational aspirations, feelings of control over one's life, lower delinquency, and involvement in political and social activity in young adulthood. Congruent with Barker's theory of behavior settings (Barker & Gump, 1964; Schoggen, in press), researchers have consistently found that students in smaller schools receive greater social

and developmental benefits as a consequence of having taking part in a greater variety and number of activities than students in larger schools (Cornbleth, 1982; Holland & Andre, 1987; Schoggen & Schoggen, 1988).

Studies of participation in school governance and extracurricular activities have supported Milbrath's hypothesis that active participation in one setting is likely to be transferred to new political situations (Milbrath & Goel, 1977). In their classic study of civic behavior in five nations, Almond and Verba (1963) found that political activity was higher among respondents who remembered that they had participated in school decisions. Researchers conducting parallel research at about the same time also found that reported school activity correlated with subsequent community involvement (Barker & Gump, 1964; Bennet, 1956). Both Lewis (1962) and Trenfield (1965) found a higher expectation of future political participation among those who took part in extracurricular activities.

In a more recent path analysis study, Hanks (1981), using data collected from a representative national sample of 1,200 high school seniors for the National High School Longitudinal Study of 1972 (Fetters, 1974), found a statistically significant positive relationship between high school activity and involvement in political activities 2 years after leaving high school, regardless of SES, academic achievement, and self-concept. Analyzing the same data base, Lindsay (1984) found that, of various predictor variables, extracurricular participation had the strongest relationship to involvement in a variety of adult activities—political, youth, union or professional, social or hobby, religious, sports, literary or art, educational service, and community organized volunteer work. Years of schooling and sociability were the second and third strongest predictors.

Beck and Jennings (1982), using a data base of more than 1,000 students drawn from the 1965–73 National Socialization Study (Jennings & Niemi, 1981), conducted a path analysis to investigate the effect of high school activity on later adult participation. The high school activities used as independent variables were voting in school elections, helping with campaigns, running for office, belonging to extracurricular organizations, working on school publications, joining clubs, and participating in service and community groups. Of the four causal models tested, parent socioeconomic status (total effect, .24) and high school activity (total effect, .17) were the most statistically significant predictors of later political participation. Based on these findings, Beck and Jennings concluded that, although school activities were often nonpolitical and frequently represented contrived "shadow politics," they did appear to help young people develop skills and orientations that could be transferred to the political world. They also concluded that school experiences calling for activity were somewhat more effective in promoting a positive orientation toward participation than those that merely called for knowledge and cognitive thought processes.

Not all studies have reported a positive effect for school involvement. Ziblatt (1965) found that extracurricular participation had no relationship to attitudes toward politics. Merelman (1980) reported that school variables, including student decision-making, were not related to political participation. Jones (1974) found that even participation experiences specifically designed to involve students in school-related political activities had limited impact on political attitudes, including political efficacy.

Sigel's study of adolescent participation (Sigel & Hoskin, 1981) showed that most adolescents were active in school activities and that level of school involvement was positively correlated with political cognition and political affect. On the basis of her findings, Sigel credited school experiences with a positive effect on participation. Supporting Sigel's hypothesis, Eyler's (1982) path analysis study of 3,087 students in 13 high schools revealed that students with more positive attitudes toward the political system generalized those attitudes to the school as a surrogate political system and were more inclined to take part in extracurricular and school governance activities.

Both studies underscore the need to exercise caution in assuming that there is a direct cause-and-effect relationship between participation in school activities and later adult civic activity. Eyler inferred that, if educators wish to increase student political competence, they cannot simply provide opportunities for voluntary school participation, because that merely ensures that the interested and competent students become even more so, while students already lacking in political interest remain deficient. A more systematic approach involving planned governance and course-related experiences for all students is necessary if political skills and participation rates are to be substantially increased for the citizenry at large.

In summary, although the research has shown that positive correlations exist between participation in school activities and a host of desirable personality and social characteristics, including increased civic activity in later adult life (Cornbleth, 1982), it has not demonstrated that school participation causes such desirable outcomes (Holland & Andre, 1987).

The Social Studies Curriculum

There is limited empirical support for the assumption that social studies courses exert a positive influence on participation-related attitudes and knowledge. Levenson (1972) discovered that civics courses were positively associated with students' tendency to define good citizenship in participatory terms. Ehman (1972) reported that the number of semesters of social studies classes taken was positively related to feelings of political efficacy, and Rockler (1969) found that a junior high school political behavior course had a positive effect on attitudes toward efficacy and participation.

Other studies have shown that civics courses had a greater effect on African-Americans and youngsters from lower socioeconomic status groups (Jennings, Langton, & Niemi, 1974). Hulbury (1972) found that ethnic studies courses were linked to increased orientation toward political activity among minority students. Button (1974) reported that attitudes toward participation were more positive among minority students following a 4-month experimental government course in which students were taught to think about the use of political strategies for bringing about political and social change. It has been hypothesized that the impact of course experiences is greater on minority and lower SES students because they receive so little information about the political process at home and in the community (Button, 1974; Jennings et al., 1974). Interestingly, it

has also been found that although teachers' views of citizenship seem to have little effect on Whites, they do inculcate in African-Americans the notion that a good citizen is a loyal citizen rather than an active one (Jennings et al., 1974).

These investigations notwithstanding, Beck and Jennings (1982), Cornbleth (1982), Ehman (1980), and Jennings, et al. (1974) have all noted the dearth of empirical evidence supporting the conventional assumption that civics courses have an effect on later adult participation. Through a regression analysis of the High School and Beyond and National Longitudinal Study data collected from a sample of 35,000 high school seniors, Miller (1985) was able to verify the findings of earlier researchers that formal course exposure has a limited relationship with participation. In support of Button's (1974) research results, Miller also found that the relationship was considerably higher for minority students.

Whatever is overall effect may be, the civics curriculum appears to be more instrumental in contributing to the acquisition of political knowledge than in shaping the dispositions and skills related to political participation (Ehman, 1980; Litt, 1963). Although most of the major curriculum development projects have not been subjected to rigorous investigation, there is some evidence to suggest that even the best received programs have had little effect. Patrick's (1972) summative study of one major high school civics curriculum, *American Political Behavior*, yielded no better gains in political efficacy for experimental over control groups after a year-long course.

Although the effect on lower SES and minority students appears to be greater, Litt (1963) found that lower SES students tended to be exposed to a more passive and idealistic-consensual political education, possibly causing them to perceive political activity in more mechanistic and harmonious terms. More recent evidence on the effect of civics instruction on minorities since the civil rights movement began is not available.

Community Activity

In 1982, the Report of the Council for the Advancement of Citizenship stated that the best preparation for full participation in society involved exposure to real-life experiences outside of the classroom and recommended that all citizen education courses include hands-on, practical components. Is there evidence that courses involving students in community civic activities make a difference?

There have only been a few studies of this approach and the findings are not conclusive. Marsh (1973) and Jones (1974) found that social studies courses that included community involvement increased students' predispositions to act over those that did not. However, in a study of eight exemplary community service programs, Newmann and Rutter (1983) reported that participation in high school community service programs had no appreciable effect on students' anticipated community involvement of future political participation. In a subsequent study, in which they analyzed the 1984 High School and Beyond Supplemental Community Service Data, Newmann and Rutter (1986) estimated that 900,000 students were enrolled in community service programs and that approximately 27% of high schools offered some form of community service program.

They concluded, however, that although such programs appeared to have some positive effect on personal development, they had little effect on students' sense of civic responsibility. Only miniscule gains were found for students' attitudes toward future political participation. Although descriptions of a number of experiments involving community-based social studies courses have appeared in the literature, there is no published research on their effects on later adult participation. Other investigations of the influence of social studies course work on a wide range of related political knowledge and attitudes are reported elsewhere in this volume, and the reader is referred to those chapters for an analysis of the findings.

Summary

There is no recent evidence to refute Ehman's (1980) earlier conclusion that the formal curriculum has little impact on students' inclination toward participation. Where an impact has been demonstrated, the main effect has been on lower SES and minority groups, although the effect has been in terms of increased political knowledge rather than participation-related attitudes or behaviors (Ehman, 1980; Leming, 1986). Although Beck and Jennings (1982) hypothesized that the failure of the formal curriculum to register an impact is most likely due to the fact that passive, classroom-bound instruction, however stimulating, bears little resemblance to the realities of participation in the political world, the reasons for this lack of a demonstrated effect remain unclear.

Classroom-level Factors

Practitioners will be disappointed to learn that the research provides little insight into the most effective methods for teaching civic participation. This is largely due to the fact that relatively few studies involving participation-related dependent variables have been conducted at the classroom level. Those that have been conducted are dated and have poor generalizability.

There is some empirical confirmation for the conviction that inquiry-oriented teaching is more effective than expository instruction in furthering participation-related attitudes and knowledge (Cornbleth, 1982). Almond and Verba (1963) reported that students who remembered participating in classroom political discussions and debates in school had higher levels of civic competence. In a 2 year longitudinal study, Ehman (1972) found that, in classrooms where above-average proportions of time were spent in a normative mode (teachers and students engaged in the expression of opinions and judgments), students had lower political cynicism, although their feelings of efficacy remained at the same level. In her path analysis investigation, Guyton (1988) determined that, among college students, critical thinking had an indirect, positive effect on self-reported levels of political participation, implying that inquiry-oriented instruction may have a positive influence on participatory behavior. However, Ferguson (1989) found that teachers who took a reflective approach to instruction were only slightly more likely to have students who were more posi-

tively inclined to be "complete activists" following a full-year course of study.

There is evidence to suggest that the teacher's role is pivotal in promoting political participation; however, teachers' conceptions of citizenship are often at odds with the idealized views of citizen behavior promoted in the literature (Bricker, 1989). In contrast with the views of many social educators who believe that the most effective citizens are those who critically scrutinize institutions, public officials, and political operations (Cherryholmes, 1980; Engle & Ochoa, 1988; Giroux, 1980; Shaver, 1977), Levenson (1972) found that most teachers defined *good citizen* in terms of obedience, loyalty, conformity, avoidance of controversy, and restraint from criticism of government officials and that their students were not inclined to conceive of citizenship in broad participatory terms (Levenson, 1972). However, Ferguson (1989) found little relationship between teachers' own civic attitudes and activities and their students' attitudes toward participation (Phi coefficients were .11 and lower).

Other studies are relevant. Sherry (1976) found that fifth graders' participation-related knowledge and attitudes were increased through a 2 week experiment consisting of lessons on voting behavior, political parties, and politicians. Boocock (1968) concluded from her research that active role taking in classroom simulations changed students' inclination to take personal action, whereas Livingston and Kidder (1972) found that simulation experiences actually decreased students willingness to take action. Glenn (1972) found that elementary students who had more positive feelings about their opportunities for classroom participation had a higher sense of political efficacy. Button (1974) reported that attitudes toward participation were more positive among minority students following a 4-month experimental government course in which students were taught to think about the use of political strategies for bringing about political and social change. No common independent variables could be identified across these studies that might provide insight into effective teaching for participation, pointing out the need for greater coordination and replication of research in this area.

In view of the small number of classroom-related investigations, and given the eclectic nature of the research conducted, little can be generalized concerning the relative effectiveness of different approaches to teaching for participation. There is some evidence to suggest that activity-oriented, inquiry-based teaching methods have a positive effect on broadening participatory attitudes. The fact that teachers are inclined to promote conventional and passive forms of participation puts them at odds with the current citizenship literature on the subject and indicates that a wide chasm may exist between theory and classroom practice.

Summary

The following generalizations have been derived from the research reviewed in this section. More extensive and rigorous investigation is needed before they can be accepted with a high degree of confidence.

1. Students who take part in extracurricular and school governance activities are more likely to become civically active as

adults. (It has not been demonstrated that this is a cause-and-effect relationship; the correlation may simply be the result of the shared influence of other variables.)

2. The formal social studies curriculum has little appreciable effect on civic attitudes and behavior.

3. In cases where there is an effect, social studies instruction is more instrumental in promoting knowledge of the political system than in advancing participatory attitudes and skills.

4. The social studies curriculum has more influence on the participatory attitudes and knowledge of minorities and lower socioeconomic status groups than on other groups of students.

5. An inquiry-based, activity-oriented approach to instruction is somewhat more effective in promoting participatory attitudes and skills than are expository, didactic teaching methods.

6. Teachers are inclined to socialize students toward passive, conventional forms of civic action and to avoid discussion of the more personally responsible, active modes of participation.

7. Socialization for participation within the school is largely an academic experience, occurring almost exclusively within the walls of the civics classroom. Few opportunities are provided to learn through hands-on school and community civic activities.

8. There is no evidence to either support or challenge the conviction that community and school-related participation experiences are more effective than traditional, classroom-bound methods of instruction.

THE IMPROVEMENT OF THEORY AND RESEARCH ON PARTICIPATION

In conducting research on participation as a dependent variable, most social studies investigators have been satisfied to investigate relationships between static independent variables, rather than to undertake controlled investigations of the contextual variables that might bring about changes in participatory behavior. Thus, the majority of the research is of the type showing, for example, that adults who graduated from academic high school programs were more likely to be politically active than those who attended vocational schools, or that students who participated in extracurricular activities had more positive attitudes toward voting than those who did not. These sorts of findings, although acceptable to dissertation committees and publishable in the journals of the field, make no serious theoretical contribution and are of little use to social studies practitioners. Clearly, a change in the present approach to theory and research is needed.

The key to extending our insight into the impact of social studies on participation is to increase the explanatory power of the existing knowledge base. The notion of increasing the explanatory power of knowledge in the social sciences comes from the work of George Homans (1967), who called on social scientists to move beyond merely identifying and verifying the existence of phenomena to investigating the factors that explain their existence, that is, to devoting more attention to explaining

the *why* rather than the *what* of human behavior. Ebel (1982) reflected this sentiment when he called for research aimed not merely at discovering how the process of education for participation works, but also at creative ways to make education for participation work better. Recommendations for improving the explanatory power and usefulness of theory and of research on the impact of social studies on participation are presented next.

The Improvement of Theory

It is generally held that the central purpose of scholarly activity is to develop grounded theory (Armento, 1986); however, not all scholars agree that this is the most important goal of research in the social studies (Popkewitz, 1978; Shaver, 1979, 1982). The controversy over the theoretical significance of social studies research has particular relevance for participation-related inquiry because, ostensibly, it is directed toward the practical goal of improving the quality and quantity of civic behavior. What about the theories of participation currently in vogue?

Existing Theories of Participation

The flagship theories of civic participation are found in the literature of political science. The theoretical models developed by Beck and Jennings (1982), Milbrath and Goel (1977), and Verba and Nie (1972) are those most frequently referenced in the literature. They are presented because they have commanded widespread respect among political scientists and a number of social studies researchers.

In their causal model, Beck and Jennings (Figure 31–1) predicted the influence of a number of variables, including high school activity, on young adult participation. The model is organized from top to bottom. The key presage variable at the top of the diagram is parent SES and the outcome variable at the bottom is young adult participation. The other elements in the diagram are intervening variables predicted to moderate the relationship between SES and participation. The variables are presented in sequence from top to bottom in the order of their estimated influence. The numbers represent regression coefficients indicating the strength of the relationship between variables. Direct and indirect paths of influence are indicated by the connecting arrows showing unidirectional relationships between the variables. For example, civic orientation is always interpreted as influencing participation, never the reverse. The validity of this unidirectional model has been called into question by Ehman and Eyler (1982), who, in their reanalysis of Beck and Jennings's data, found an inverse relationship between civic attitudes and participation.

The participation paradigms of Milbrath and of Verba and Nie were described earlier, and a more detailed presentation of these models does not fall within the scope of this chapter. Both paradigms acknowledge education as an important variable; however, neither deals explicitly with school or curriculum-related factors.

Four efforts to develop and test causal models of civic participation have been reported in the social studies literature. Us-

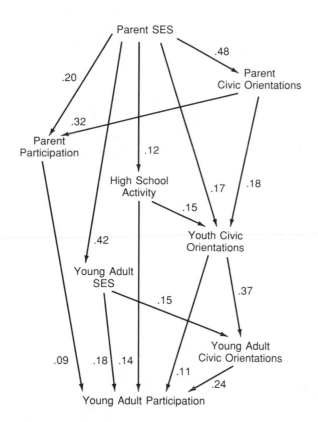

FIGURE 31-1. Pathways to Participation: The Combined Model. *Note*. From "Pathways to Participation" by P. A. Beck and M. K. Jennings, 1982, *American Political Science Review* 76, p. 104. Reprinted by permission.

ing an available sample of adults attending college, Guyton (1988) tested a model of the effects of critical thinking on political participation that has implications for classroom instruction (pp. 44–45). The diagram in Figure 31–2 displays the segment of her final path diagram that emerged as the best representation of the effects of critical thinking on participation. Her analysis showed that, although critical thinking ability does not independently influence participatory attitudes, a significant relationship emerges when the effect is mediated by personality variables such as self-esteem, personal control, and political efficacy. The limitation of this model is indicated by Guyton's estimate that 75% of the variance in participation was accounted for by variables not posited in her theory. In support of her argument of the need for more systematic, sustained, and sophisticated efforts to develop scientifically grounded theory in the field, Armento (1986) cited Guyton's path analysis study as exemplary of the kind of research needed to generate holistic theory in the social studies. However, although Guyton's methodology (path analysis) is a preferred method of analysis over previous correlational research, her theory has very limited explanatory power and yields information that is of limited use to the practitioner.

In a similar vein, Eyler (1982) tested a path analysis model (Figure 31–3) of sociopolitical attitudes as predictors of participation in high school extracurricular activities. The values of

the coefficients in Figure 31–3 indicate that the empirically derived path model approximated the predicted model, allowing Eyler to conclude that positive attitudes generalize to the school as a political system and are predictors of participation in extracurricular activities, particularly in governance groups. Eyler concluded that high school thus provides an arena in which predispositions can be expressed in activities that, in turn, are expected to increase political competence. It should be noted that political skills as such were not assessed in the model. Eyler also concluded that grade level and gender have only a negligible impact on extracurricular participation. Eyler discussed the implications for theory and further research but made no mention of the model's relevance for immediate practice.

Ehman and Eyler (1982), using path analysis and least squares regression, replicated Beck and Jennings's (1982) study and obtained similar results. However, as mentioned earlier, it was found that the direction of the relationship between attitudes and participation was not positive as predicted, but slightly negative. In the least squares analysis, the differences between their findings and Beck and Jennings's results were not trivial, causing Eyler and Ehman to seriously question the validity of the Beck and Jennings paradigm.

Miller (1985), working with data on 35,000 students from the 1972 National Longitudinal and the 1980 High School and Beyond studies, used a multivariate regression model to test the effect of social studies course exposure on participation, controlling for level of participation in extracurricular activities, type of high school program, SES, and race. He concluded that the primary factor influencing level of actual participation was parental SES, in this case supporting the relationship predicted in the earlier Beck and Jennings model. Miller verified the findings of earlier researchers that formal course exposure has a limited impact in general (Beck & Jennings, 1982) but a considerably higher impact on minority students (Button, 1974).

As interesting as these regression models are from a methodological perspective, none makes a theoretical contribution that can be translated into meaningful practice. We must, therefore, consider new approaches to the development and verification of theories that will lead to more powerful and usable knowledge.

Improving Theory

In discussing her findings, Guyton (1988) noted that only about 25% of the variance in participation could be accounted for by the variables included in her model. Similar estimates of the variance accounted for apply to most of the other path analysis models in the literature, pointing to their failure to assess the direct and interactive effects of the numerous variables that influence participatory behavior. Eyler (1982) pointed out that although the empirically derived path models approximated her predicted model, there are other models that might yield plausible results. Improving on such theories would require the blueprinting of more refined models to account for the portion of missing variance that is attributable to programmatic, instructional, and curricular influences.

Holland and Andre's (1987) recommendations for improv-

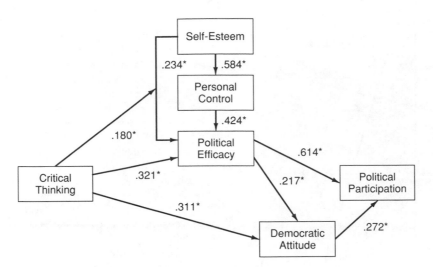

FIGURE 31–2. Final Path Diagram Showing The Indirect Effects of Critical Thinking Through Personal Control, Political Efficacy, and Democratic Attitude On Political Participation. *Note.* From "Critical Thinking Political Participation: Development and Assessment of a Causal Model" by E. M. Guyton, 1988, *Theory and Research in Social Education*, 16, p. 41. Reprinted by permission.

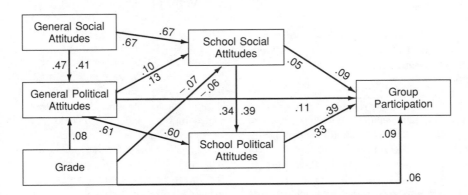

FIGURE 31–3. Empirically Derived Path Model Relating Socio-Political Attitudes to Participation in the High School Political Arena—Females above or to the left of line, males below. *Note.* From "A Test of a Model Relating Political Attitudes to Participation in High School Activities" by J. Eyler, 1982, *Theory and Research in Social Education*, 10, (1) p. 54.

ing research on extracurricular participation, suggested by the previous work of Dunkin and Biddle (1974), provide insight into how social studies researchers can develop more relevant and cohesive theories by constructing paradigms in which presage variables (e.g., SES, family, ethnic group, sex), contextual variables (e.g., community, school size), process variables (e.g., curriculum, teaching methods, programs, materials), and outcome variables (social and political participation) are interrelated. Holland and Andre (1987), proposed the following approach to planning for improved theory-based research: (a) identify and define the outcome variables, (b) specify the pro-

cess variables likely to influence the outcome variables, (c) identify the presage variables likely to influence both process and outcome variables, and (d) identify the contextual variables likely to influence process and outcome variables. Attention to all four types of variables is necessary for stronger theory-related research.

Although it seems reasonable to assume that following this strategy would strengthen the theoretical foundation of participation-oriented research, using it merely to improve upon theories of the type developed by Beck and Jennings, Eyler, Guyton, and Miller will not yield knowledge of practical and immediate use to curriculum developers and practitioners. Nelson and Shaver (1985) have expressed the urgent need for social studies researchers to undertake studies more directly concerned with applied problems in social studies instruction and curriculum. In his call to improve the research in political socialization, Patrick (1977) urged research on political learning in schools to guide curriculum developers in the design of more efficient instructional materials and producers. The key to developing and testing theories with improved explanatory power and usefulness to practitioners rests with applying the Holland and Andre approach to the development of midrange or nomothetic models that connect presage, contextual, and process variables with community and school-based curricular and instructional strategies.

A final suggestion for the improvement of theory concerns the call for new theories based on a revised definition of participation. Newmann (1989) and others have suggested that the dominant conception of citizenship conveyed in teaching civics and government—that democratic citizens are persons who advance their own personal interests through rational, critical-minded activities—is flawed. Newmann has advocated a redefinition of participation in terms of the need for public-minded citizens to work in pursuit of the general welfare. Refocusing participation in terms of commitment to the public good would call for the reformulation of existing theories predicated solely on the definition of participation as th pursuit of narrow private interests.

Improving Research

The paucity of reliable evidence on the effects of social studies on participation cannot be solely attributed to faulty theory. The fact that much of the research is methodologically flawed also hinders the accretion of reliable and useful knowledge. All of the many weaknesses that have been attributed to research in the field at large (Armento, 1986; Leming, 1986; Shaver, 1982; Stanley, 1985; Wallen & Fraenkel, 1988) apply to the research on participation as an outcome. The following recommendations for improving and expanding the scope of the research are offered in the interest of rectifying this condition.

The need for the development and verification of nomothetic models assimilating presage, contextual, process, and outcome variables requires more researchers to shift their attention to causal-experimental and longitudinal designs. To be of practical value, experimental studies must be designed to test for the effects of specific programs, instructional strategies, and curricula on participatory behavior.

This recommendation reflects Ebel's (1982) call for operational research: not research that is aimed merely at discovering how the process of education for participation works but, rather, research on creative ways to make education for participation work better (Armento, 1986). In operational research, hypotheses are derived from experience and previous research. These hypotheses can lead to the development of creative approaches that hold some likelihood of being effective. The outcomes of such programs must be assessed in terms of measured

changes in participatory knowledge, skills, and behaviors. For example, Newmann, Bertocci, and Landsness's (1977) skills-based, community-activity model, developed in the Civic Participation Curriculum Project, could be tested for its validity and effectiveness in many different community settings.

Also needed, to provide insights into the sequential and cumulative influence of curricula over time, are longitudinal studies that are initiated in elementary school or before, and continued through secondary school and on into adult life. The existence of *critical development periods* in the process of socialization for participation could be investigated as a key to targeting programs at particular age and grade levels. Palonsky (1987) argued that the elementary grades represent one such critical period and recommended that researchers undertake child-centered studies to gain insight into the development of political thinking in the early grades. Longitudinal studies would also permit researchers to make direct connections between school-related and developmental experiences and later adult action.

With reference to improving internal validity, future researchers must develop better operational definitions and utilize more refined measures of participation. Earlier researchers often relied upon simplistic attitudinal measures in which the respondents were asked to simply report on their anticipated or past behaviors. Questionnaire items, such as those used in the National Assessment of Educational Progress (NAEP) citizenship assessments—which merely ask respondents to indicate whether they ever intend to vote, might consider running for office, or anticipate becoming active in community affairs—are subject to response bias and are poor predictors of later civic activity (Carlson, 1986). More comprehensive and accurate measures of the various modes of participation need to be developed and validated for use in educational investigations. The instrument developed by Verba and Nie (1972), described earlier in this chapter, represents one point of departure for future scale developers. Better assessment would insure a broader perspective on participation through the collection of data on the nonelectoral, communal, particularistic modes of behavior. There is also a need to develop and validate measures of the apolitical components of participation, including community service, voluntary group efforts, and church- and school-related extracurricular modes of participation.

There is a need for better designed sociological investigations into the contextual and ecological factors that influence efforts to educate for participation. Metzger and Barr (1978) concluded that from their review of research that the school environment in general and the school political system in particular have significant influences on student social and political attitudes associated with effective citizenship. They noted, however, that there were serious weaknesses in the internal and external validity of most of the studies they reviewed. More specifically, Murray (1986) has suggested that it might be important to know whether the current effective-schools movement, with its increased emphasis on the maintenance of an orderly environment and reliance on the achievement of standardized goals, reduces the opportunities for democratic participation, thereby constraining the growth of participation-related knowledge, skills, and values. The comparative study of schools and communities in different ecological settings may be instrumental in determining the effects of different social climates and contextual factors on the implementation of programs designed to promote participation. Cross-cultural and comparative studies of the influence of social studies on participation would be an important element in such research.

Related to the study of contextual factors is Palonsky's (1987) recommendation that, instead of using positivist research paradigms to measure responses to predetermined questions coming out of the investigator's view of participation, researchers should focus more on ways that individual students appropriate information from home, community, and school experiences and combine it into a personal political reality. This would require the use of open-ended data-collection methods rather than rigorously controlled research produces utilizing scientifically validated measures.

Sociological studies would also be instrumental in helping social studies educators delineate more definite objectives for their programs in terms of specific behavioral outcomes. Presently there is no empirically based knowledge of the kinds of attitudes, knowledge, skills, and behaviors that distinguish active from inactive citizens. Nor is it known if the attributes possessed by activists vary across the different modes of participation. Generating this knowledge would require field-based research in which case study, ethnographic, observational, and interview methods were used to study the attributes and behaviors of citizens who are complete activists, who engage in certain forms of participation but not others, who are apathetic, or who are alienated from participation. These field-validated attributes could then be used to conduct research on the effectiveness of participation-oriented citizenship education programs with reference to specific behavioral outcomes.

In making recommendations for future research, Cornbleth (1982) identified the need for intensive case studies of school and classroom events that seem to influence politically relevant learning. However, investigations conducted with samples of typical social studies classrooms will probably not yield productive data. Instead, researchers should choose to consciously avoid the ordinary and focus on classroom, school, and community settings where effective approaches to educating for participation are known to be taking place. For example, using the observation and interview methods utilized in the "wisdom of practice studies" conducted through the Teacher Assessment Project at Stanford University (Shulman, 1987), investigators could determine why those programs and practices work so effectively. The findings would be useful for ordinary practice.

There is a need to extend the research on participation beyond the confines of the classroom to the school at large and on into the community (Cornbleth, 1982; Rutter & Newmann, 1989). It has been more than a decade since Remy (1978) called for an expansion of civic education beyond the confines of the elementary and secondary curriculum. Since then, there have been only a few efforts, most notably those by Newmann and Rutter (1983, 1986), to study the development of civic participation outside the walls of the school. Further research investigating the effects of interlaced classroom, school, and community

experiences, as well as programs initiated out in the community, are needed. For example, a study might be conducted to assess the impact of a program designed to educate citizens on how to contact government officials over a local community problem; or an investigation of the knowledge, skills, and attitudes acquired by high school students in working with community residents to take action on a community issue might be undertaken. In keeping with Cornbleth's (1982) earlier recommendation, expanding the research on participation education beyond the classroom into the school and the community may be one means of overcoming the demonstrated ineffectiveness of the traditional social studies curriculum.

In closing, it may be useful to cite some of the kinds of research that should probably be assigned a low priority for the future. There is little need to continue investigation into the overall impact of the conventional social studies curriculum on participation. It has been more than adequately demonstrated that the present curriculum has very little effect on civic participation. Researchers would be better advised to move on to studies that investigate ways of improving current practice. Neither does it seem productive to study programs introducing only minor adjustments to existing social studies courses (e.g., solitary lessons or units of instruction). Continuing the present trend of utilizing sophisticated correlational techniques to ferret out quasi-causal relationships among static variables does not appear to be efficacious, particularly when the findings have little bearing on educational practice. Perhaps more innovative and practical uses of regression analysis would yield more useful findings. Finally, the recent recommendation that social studies researchers use some of the new combinatorial statistical techniques, such as meta-analysis, to derive new insights from existing studies (Armento, 1986) holds little promise for research on the impact of the social studies on participation because the body of research is small, fragmented, and methodologically weak.

CONCLUSION: FOCUS AND PURPOSE FOR FUTURE RESEARCH

In contrast with the recommendations of Armento (1986) and others for the field at large, the most urgent need in participation-related research is not for the development of holistic, scientifically grounded theory but for field-based research that will inform practice. There is an urgent need for research that will validate the participatory components of existing citizenship education curricula and assess innovative school and community-based programs such as the five-mode, community-based model for citizenship participation developed by Conrad and Hedin (1977). Giving priority to developing knowledge that will be of immediate use to practitioners does not preclude the development of nomothetic theory in the near future and perhaps even macrotheory in the long run. Nonetheless, the goal of achieving a unified theory of education for civic participation seems illusive, if not unattainable, and social studies researchers would be better advised to devote their efforts to more immediate and pressing concerns.

References

Abramson, P. R., & Aldrich, J. H. (1982). The decline of electoral participation in America. *American Political Science Review, 76,* 502–521.

Alford, R., & Lee, E. (1968). Voting turnout in American cities. *American Political Science Review, 62,* 796–813.

Almond, G. A., & Verba, S. (1963). *The civic culture: Political attitudes and democracy in five nations.* Princeton, NJ: Princeton University Press.

Almond, G. A., & Verba, S. (1980). *The civic culture revisited.* Boston, Little, Brown.

Armento, B. J. (1986). Research on teaching social studies. In M. C. Wittrock (Ed.), *Handbook of research on teaching* (3rd ed., pp. 942–951). New York: Macmillan.

Barker, R. G., & Gump, P. V. (1964). *Big school, small school: High school size and student behavior.* Stanford, CA: Stanford University Press.

Barnes, S. H., & Kaase, M. (1979). *Political action: Mass participation in five western democracies.* Bevery Hills, CA: Sage.

Barr, R. D., Barth, J. L., & Shermis, S. S. (1977). *Defining the social studies.* Arlington, VA: National Council for the Social Studies.

Beck, P. A., & Jennings, M. K. (1979). Political periods and political participation. *American Political Science Review, 73,* 737–751.

Beck, P. A., & Jennings, M. K. (1982). Pathways to participation. *American Political Science Review, 76,* 94–108.

Bennet, F. (1956). *The relationship between participation in student activities in central New York state high schools and later civic participation.* Unpublished doctoral dissertation, Cornell University.

Boocock, S. S. (1968). An experimental study of the learning effects of two games with simulated environments. In S. S. Boocock & E. O. Schild (Eds.), *Simulation games in learning* (pp. 107–133). Beverly Hills, CA: Sage.

Bragaw, D. H. (1989). New York's experiment: Participation in government. *Social Education, 53,* 364.

Bragaw, D. H., & Hartoonian, H. M. (1988). Social studies: The study of people in a society. In R. Brandt (Ed.), *Content of the curriculum* (pp. 9–29). Arlington, VA: Association for Supervision and Curriculum Department.

Bricker, D. C. (1989). *Classroom life as civic education: Individual achievement and student cooperation in schools.* New York: Teachers College Press.

Burn, S. M., & Konrad, A. M. (1987). Political participation: A matter of community, stress, job autonomy, and contact by political organizations. *Political Psychology, 8,* 125–138.

Button, C. B. (1974). Political education for minority groups. In R. G. Niemi & Associates (Eds.), *The politics of future citizens* (pp. 167–198). San Francisco: Jossey-Bass.

Carlson, K. (1986). *The National Assessment in Social studies.* Princeton, NJ: National Assessment for Educational Progress. (ERIC Reproduction Services Document No. ED 279 665)

Cherryholmes, C. H. (1980). Social knowledge and citizenship education: Two views of truth and criticism. *Curriculum Inquiry, 10,* 115–141.

Clark, T. (1989). Youth community service. *Social Education, 53,* 367–368.

Conrad, D., & Hedin, D. (1977). Learning and earning citizenship through participation. In J. P. Shaver (Ed.), *Building rationales for citizenship education* (pp. 48–73). Arlington, VA: National Council for the Social Studies.

Cornbleth, C. (1982). Citizenship education. In H. E. Mitzel (Ed.), *Encyclopedia of educational research* (pp. 259–265). New York: Free Press.

Council for the Advancement of Citizenship. (1982). *Citizenship and the new federalism: New roles for citizens on the '80s?* Arlington, VA: Council for the Advancement of Citizenship.

Crabtree, C. (1983). A common curriculum in the social studies. In G. D. Fenstermacher & J. I. Goodlad (Eds.), *Individual differences and the common curriculum.* 82nd yearbook of the National Society for the Study of Education (pp. 248–281). Chicago: University of Illinois Press.

Dahl, R. A. (1971). *Polyarchy, participation and opposition.* New Haven, CT: Yale University Press.

Dalton, R. J. (1988). *Citizen politics in western democracies.* Chatham, NJ: Chatham House.

Dunkin, M. J., & Biddle, B. J. (1974). *The study of teaching.* New York: Holt, Rinehart & Winston.

Dynneson, T. L., Gross, R. E., & Nickel, J. A. (1988). *An exploratory survey of CUFA members' opinions and practices pertaining to citizenship education in the social studies, 1985–86.* Stanford, CA: Stanford University, Center for Educational Research.

Ebel, R. (1982). The future of educational research. *Educational Researcher, 11,* 18–19.

Ehman, L. H. (1972). Political efficacy and the high school social studies curriculum. In B. G. Massialas (Ed.), *Political youth, traditional schools: National and international perspectives* (pp. 90–102). Englewood Cliffs, NJ: Prentice-Hall.

Ehman, L. H. (1980). The American school in the political socialization process. *Review of Educational Research, 50,* 99–119.

Ehman, L. H., & Eyler, J. (1982, November). *Exploring alternative casual hypotheses with across-time political attitudes and participation data.* Paper presented at the annual meeting of the National Council for the Social Studies, Boston. (ERIC Reproduction Service Document No. ED 224 758)

Engle, S., & Ochoa, A. (1988). *Education for democratic citizenship: Decision making in the social studies.* New York: Teachers College Press.

Eyler, J. (1982). Test of a model relating political attitudes to participation in high school activities. *Theory and Research in Social Education, 10,* 43–62.

Ferguson, P. (1989, March). *Promoting political participation: Teacher attitudes and instructional practices.* Paper presented at the annual meeting of the American Educational Research Association, San Francisco.

Fetters, W. B. (1974). *National Longitudinal Study of the High School class of 1972.* Washington, DC: National Center for Education Statistics.

Giroux, H. A. (1980). Critical theory and rationality in citizenship education. *Curriculum Inquiry, 10,* 329–366.

Glenn, A. D. (1972). Elementary school children's attitudes toward politics. In B. G. Massialas (Ed.), *Political youth, traditional schools: National and international perspectives* (pp. 51–63). Englewood Cliffs, NJ: Prentice-Hall.

Guyton, E. M. (1988). Critical thinking and participation: Development and assessment of a causal model. *Theory and Research in Social Education, 16*(1)23–50.

Hanks, M. (1981). Youth, voluntary associations and political socialization. *Social Forces, 60,* 211–223.

Hawley, K. E., & Nichols, M. L. (1982). A contextual approach to modeling the decision to participate in a political issue. *Administrative Science Quarterly, 27,* 105–119.

Holland, A., & Andre, T. (1987). Participation in extracurricular activities in secondary school: What is known, what needs to be known. *Review of Educational Research, 57,* 437–466.

Homans, G. (1967). *The nature of social science.* New York: Harcourt, Brace and World.

Hulbury, W. E. (1972). *Adolescent political self images and political involvement: The relative effects of high school black studies courses and prior socialization.* Unpublished doctoral dissertation, University of Iowa.

Igra, A. (1976). *Social mobilization, political participation and economic development.* Unpublished doctoral dissertation, Stanford University, Stanford.

Jennings, M. K., Langton, K. P., & Niemi, R. G. (1974). Effects of the high school civics curriculum. In M. K. Jennings & R. G. Niemi (Eds.), *The political character of adolescence* (pp. 181–206). Princeton, NJ: Princeton University Press.

Jennings, M. K., & Niemi, R. G. (1974). *The political power of adolescence.* Princeton, NJ: Princeton University Press.

Jennings, M. K., & Niemi, R. G. (1981). *Generations and Politics.* Princeton, NJ: Princeton University Press.

Jones, R. (1974). Changing student attitudes: The impact of community participation. *Social Science Quarterly, 55,* 439–450.

Kamens, D. (1988). Education and democracy: A comparative institutional analysis. *Sociology of Education, 61,* 114–127.

Krassa, M. (1985). *Contextually conditioned political interactions.* Unpublished doctoral dissertation, Washington University, St. Louis.

LaPalambara, J. (1978). Political participation as an analytical concept in comparative politics. In S. Verba & L. W. Pye (Eds.), *The citizen and politics: A comparative perspective* (pp. 167–194). Stamford, CT: Greylock Press.

Lawrence, D. G. (1981). Towards an attitudinal theory of political participation. *Polity, 14,* 332–346.

Leming, J. S. (1986). Rethinking social studies research and the goals of social education. *Theory and Research in Social Education, 14,* 139–152.

Levenson, G. (1972). The school's contribution to the learning of participatory responsibility. In B. G. Massialas (Ed.), *Political youth, traditional schools: National and international perspectives* (pp. 123–136). Englewood Cliffs, NJ: Prentice-Hall.

Lewis, H. (1962). The teenage joiner and his orientations toward public affairs: A test of two multiple group membership hypothesis. Unpublished doctoral dissertation, Michigan State University, East Lansing.

Lindsay, P. (1984). High school size, participation in activities, and young adult social participation: Some enduring effects of schooling. *Educational Evaluation and Policy Analysis, 6,* 73–83.

Litt, E. A. (1963). Civics education, community norms and political indoctrination. *American Sociological Review, 29,* 69–75.

Livingston, S. A., & Kidder, J. J. (1972). Effects of a legislative game on the political attitudes of junior high school students. *Simulation and Games, 3,* 41–51.

Marsh, D. (1973). *Education for political involvement: A pilot study of twelfth graders.* Unpublished doctoral dissertation, University of Wisconsin, Madison.

Massiala, B., & Simone, M. (1977, April). *Decision-making in the school: A participatory model.* Paper presented at the annual meeting of the American Educational Research Association, New York. (ERIC Reproduction Service Document No. ED 141 203)

Merelman, R. M. (1980). Democratic politics and the culture of American education. *American Political Science Review, 74,* 319–332.

Merelman, R. M., & King, G. (1986). The development of political activists: Towards a model of early learning. *Social Science Quarterly, 67,* 473–90.

Metzger, D. J., & Barr, R. D. (1978). The impact of school political systems on student political attitudes. *Theory and Research in Social Education, 6,* 48–79.

Milbrath, L. W. (1965). *Political participation.* Chicago: Rand McNally.

Milbrath, L. W., & Goel, M. L. (1977). *Political participation: How and why people get involved in politics.* Chicago: Rand McNally.

Milbrath, L. W., & Klein, W. W. (1974). Personality correlates of political participation. In G. J. Di Renzo (Ed.), *Personality and Politics* (pp. 67–89). Garden City, NY: Doubleday Anchor Press.

Miller J. D. (1985, April). *The influence of high school social studies courses on political participation by young adults.* Paper presented at the meeting of the American Educational Research Association, Chicago. (ERIC Reproduction Service Document No. ED 265 086)

Morrisett, I., & Williams, A. M. (Ed.). (1981). *Social and political education in three countries: Britain, West Germany and the United States.* Boulder, CO: Social Science Education Consortium. (ERIC Document Reproduction Service No. ED 201 558)

Muller, E. N. (1982). An explanatory model of differing types of participation. *European Journal of Political Research, 10,* 1–16.

Muller, E. N., Seligson, M. A., & Turan, I. (1987). Education, participation and support for democratic norms. *Comparative Politics, 20,* 19–33.

Murray, P. V. (1986). Educating for participatory democracy in the effective school. *Education, 106,* 409–412.

National Assessment of Educational Progress. (1978). *Changes in political attitudes and knowledge, 1969–76.* Denver, CO: Education Commission of the States. (ERIC Reproduction Services Document No. ED 166 123)

National Assessment of Educational Progress. (1983). *Citizenship and social studies achievement of young Americans: 1981–1982. Performance and changes between 1976 and 1982.* Denver, CO: Education Commission of the States.

National Assessment of Educational Progress. (1987). *Civics, United States government and politics objectives: The 1988 assessment.* Princeton, NJ: Author.

National Council for the Social Studies. (1979). Revision of the NCSS social studies curriculum guidelines. *Social Education, 43,* 261–273.

Nelson, J. L., & Shaver, J. P. (1985). On research in social education. In W. B. Stanley (Ed.), *Review of research in social studies education: 1976–1983* (pp. 401–433). Washington, DC: National Council for the Social Studies.

Newmann, F. M. (1975). *Education for citizen action: Challenge for secondary curriculum.* Berkeley, CA: McCutchan.

Newmann, F. M. (1989). Reflective civic participation. *Social Education, 53,* 357–360.

Newmann, F. M., Bertocci, T. A. & Landsness, R. M. (1977). *Skills for citizen action.* Madison, WI: University of Wisconsin.

Newmann, F. M., & Rutter, R. A. (1983). *The effects of high school community service programs on students' social development* (Final report to the National Institute of Education, Grant No. NIE-G-81-0009). Madison, WI: Wisconsin Center for Educational Research.

Newmann, F. M., & Rutter, R. A. (1986). A profile of high school community service programs. *Educational Leadership, 43,* 64–71.

Nie, N. H., Powell, B., & Prewitt, K. (1969). Social structure and political participation. *American Political Science Review, 63,* 361–378, 808–832.

Palonsky, S. (1987). Political socialization in elementary schools. *Elementary School Journal, 87,* 493–505.

Parker, W. C. (1989). Participatory citizenship: Civics in the strong sense. *Social Education, 53,* 353–354.

Parker, W. C., & Jarolimek, J. (1984). *Citizenship and the critical role of the social studies.* Washington, DC: National Council for the Social Studies.

Patrick, J. J. (1972). The impact of an experimental course, "American Political Behavior," on the knowledge, skills and attitudes of secondary school students. *Social Education, 36,* 168–179.

Patrick, J. J. (1977). Political socialization and political education in the schools. In S. A. Renshon (Ed.), *Handbook of political socialization: Theory and research* (pp. 190–222). New York: Free Press.

Popkewitz, T. (1978). Educational research: Values and visions of social order. *Theory and Research in Social Education, 6*(4), 20–35.

Powell, G. B. (1986). American voter turnout in comparative perspective. *American Political Science Review, 80,* 36–43.

Remy, R. C. (1980). *Handbook of basic citizenship competencies.* Alexandria, VA: Association for Supervision and Curriculum Development.

Remy, R. C. (1978). Social studies and citizenship education: Elements of a changing relationship. *Theory and Research in Social Education, 6,* 40–59.

Rockler, M. J. (1969). *The effects of a junior high school course on political socialization.* Unpublished doctoral dissertation, University of Minnesota, St. Paul.

Roos, M. H. (1986). Female political participation: A cross-cultural explanation. *American Anthropologist, 88,* 843–858.

Rutter, R. A., & Newmann, F. M. (1989). The potential of community service to enhance civic responsibility. *Social Education, 53,* 371–374.

Schoggen, P. (in press). *Behavior settings: A revision of Barker's ecological psychology.* Stanford, CA: Stanford University Press.

Schoggen, P., & Schoggen, M. (1988). Student voluntary participation and high school size. *Journal of Educational Research, 81,* 288–293.

Shaver, J. P. (Ed.). (1977). *Building rationales for citizenship education.* Washington, DC: National Council for the Social Studies.

Shaver, J. P. (1979). The usefulness of educational research in curricular/instructional decision-making in social studies. *Theory and Research in Social Education, 7,* 21–46.

Shaver, J. P. (1982). Reappraising the theoretical goals of research in social studies education. *Theory and Research in Social Education, 9,* 1–16.

Sherry, F. T. (1976). *A study of the effect of lessons in political science on fifth grade children.* Unpublished doctoral dissertation, Boston University.

Shulman, L. (1987). Assessment for teaching: An initiative for the profession. *Phi Delta Kappan, 69,* 38–44.

Sigel, R., & Hoskin, M. (1981). *The political involvement of adolescents.* New Brunswick, NJ: Rutgers University Press.

Stanley, W. B. (Ed.). (1985). *Review of research in social studies education, 1976–1983.* Washington, DC: National Council for the Social Studies.

Stentz, M., & Lambert, H. D. (1977). An empirical reformulation of political efficacy. *Theory and Research in Social Education, 5,* 61–85.

Trenfield, W. G. (1965). An analysis of the relationship between selected factors and the civics interests of high school students. *Journal of Educational Research, 58,* 460–462.

Verba, S., & Nie, N. (1972). *Participation in America: Political democracy and social equality.* New York: Harper & Row.

Verba, S., Nie, N., & Kim, J. (1978). *Participation and political equality: A seven-nation comparison.* New York: Cambridge University Press.

Wallen, N. E., & Fraenkel, J. R. (1988). An analysis of social studies research over an eight year period. *Theory and Research in Social Education, 16,* 1–22.

Wood, G. H. (1988). Civic education for participatory democracy. In S. D. Franzosa (Ed.), *Civic education: Its limits and conditions* (pp. 68–98). Ann Arbor, MI: Prakken.

Ziblatt, D. (1965). High school extracurricular activities and political socialization. *Annals of the American Academy of Political and Social Science, 361,* 20–31.

·32·

TEACHING AND LEARNING HISTORY

Matthew T. Downey
UNIVERSITY OF CALIFORNIA, BERKELEY

Linda S. Levstik
UNIVERSITY OF KENTUCKY

The research base for the teaching and learning of history is thin and uneven. Much of the professional literature about history teaching consists of either descriptions of exemplary practices, usually reports from the teachers who developed the approach or the method or untried prescriptions for effective teaching. Claims for the exemplary nature of the methods being recommended are seldom supported by evidence of what or how much student learning took place.

There is a dearth of research on history teaching, in large part because little of the research on teaching and learning within the social studies has been discipline centered. As Tucker (1977) noted, most of the research undertaken during the discipline-based New Social Studies movement of the 1960s and 1970s was directed by social scientists who were mainly concerned about areas other than history. Consequently, most of the systematic research that has been done in history education is of relatively recent origin. A number of areas of critical importance to the field still remain largely unexplored. Nevertheless, there are areas in which substantial and significant research has been undertaken. In this chapter, we review that modest, but important and growing, body of research literature and offer suggestions for future research.

CHILDREN'S CONCEPTION OF TIME

By its very nature, history is linked to time and chronology. It seems obvious, then, that children's concepts of time must be connected to the development of historical understanding.

Yet we know relatively little about that connection. To begin with, there are many different aspects of time, including past, present, and future; conventional clock and calendar time; duration of physical processes; historical succession and duration (Friedman, 1978, 1982). Some of these aspects appear to be more related to historical cognition than others. For example, children's ability to distinguish between past, present, and future; their understanding of conventional notions of calendar time; and their grasp of historical duration might be presumed to be relevant to conceptual change in history.

As Thornton and Vukelich (1988) pointed out, however, the connections between children's conceptions of time and their ability to think historically have gone largely unresearched. Instead, children's perceptions of physical time—duration, order, succession, and velocity—have been assumed to constrain historical thinking. Studies of physical time concepts have described slowly acquired concepts linked to a linear time scale and a Western conception of the nature of time (Fraisse, 1963; Lello, 1980; Piaget, 1969). Yet this may not be the time sense most relevant to historical thinking.

John Poster (1973) postulated that there are different times within a single cultural context: social time, literary time, personal or interior time, physical or clock time, and historical time. Historical time, he suggested, requires a "sense of existing in the past as well as the present, a feeling of being in history rather than standing apart from it" (p. 589) and may be constrained as much by lack of reinforcement as by developmental levels. These cultural influences may mean that some societies are heavily influenced by the past in terms of what they think and talk about (Harner, 1982). Others, including most Western

Reviewers were Douglas Adler, Dixie College; Jere Brophy, Michigan State University; Wayne Dumas, University of Missouri, Columbia; Samuel Wineburg, University of Washington.

societies, do not reward increased sophistication in understanding historical time concepts. In those societies, not only do physical time concepts develop slowly, but also the important sense of historical time is impeded by cultural disinterest (Poster, 1973).

A closer look at the research, however, warrants a somewhat different reading of the development of time concepts. Studies indicate that young children can and do understand historical time in a variety of ways. Children see patterns and sequences in real events, though some of these patterns may be general and imprecise. In Levstik and Pappas's (1987) study, for instance, children in grades 2, 4, and 6 linked history to chronology. Young children were able to use broad time categories in describing times past (e.g., "cave times" or "before Mom and Dad were born"). Older children used more elaborate categories and identified more specific historical eras, including "the time of empires" or "the American Revolution." By ages 8 and 9, children are able to estimate how long ago events took place, to place events in sequence, and to associate dates with particular people and events (Bradley, 1947; Friedman, 1978; Oakden & Sturt, 1922).

Spatio-Temporal Relations

Another promising body of research in cognitive psychology suggests the presence of a mode of conceptual organization based on spatio-temporal relations (Gelman & Baillargeon, 1983; Nelson, 1986). The fundamental units in this type of organization are schemata, rather than categories. Schemata might be conceived of as "scripts" or a set of optional and obligatory activities related to an event. On a very simple level, for instance, a child might have a "script" for birthday parties that includes a particular sequence of events: First there is cake and ice-cream, then presents are opened, and, finally, games are played. The elements in the script might include making a wish and blowing out the candles or playing pin-the-tail-on-the-donkey, but the child has learned the sequence of events and actions, the appropriate sites, and the relationships among these elements. Significantly, even very young children appear to be sensitive to, and use, conceptual organization that emphasizes spatial and temporal relations over taxonomic or hierarchical schemes.

In recent studies, children have shown an understanding of a range of logical relationships, including causal and temporal relations, much earlier than previously thought (e.g., Piaget, 1969). Thus, they can discuss a range of logical relationships when those relationships are embedded in a script or schema that is familiar to them (Nelson, 1986; Shank & Abelson, 1977). Indeed, by the time children are 5 to 7 years old they appear to be able to use spatio-temporal knowledge flexibly and explicitly (Fivush & Slackman, 1986; Friedman, 1978; Harner, 1982; R. N. Smith & Tomilson, 1977).

Time and Causation: The Narrative Connection

There is further evidence that the form of discourse may influence the formation of time concepts. As has already been noted, time concepts are bound to the linguistic forms (before, after, soon, previously, upcoming, lately) for temporal references (Harner, 1982; Wells, 1981, 1985). In addition, the larger discursive context may be equally significant. Narrative, for instance, has been particularly related to the development of time and causation concepts (Rabinowitz, 1987). In this view, narrative provides a representation of events that allows experience, both one's own and others', to be internalized (Van Dongen, 1987). More specifically, the structure of narrative generally shows the relationship of events through time and causality (Applebee, 1978).

The term *narrative* is problematic, to say the least. For purposes of discussion in this chapter, it refers to writing that is shaped as a story. It flows on a chain of cause and effect and has a narrator who takes an aesthetic stance in regard to the elements of the narration. Narrative can be found in fiction and nonfiction. It appears to be the story shape that is the important element in differentiating narrative from other forms of discourse, at least in regard to the studies reported in this chapter.

Bruner (1986) noted that narrative, like history, deals with intention and action, with the particular: not any person, but this person, at this time and place, and given this set of circumstances. White (1980) described the way in which narrative transforms a list of events "into a discourse about the events considered as a totality evolving in time" (p. 19). The conventions of narrative also include the "rule of temporal causation" in which "it is appropriate to assume that temporally connected events are causally connected unless there is a signal to the contrary" (Rabinowitz, 1987, p. 108). In this sense, narrative can provide a temporal scaffolding that makes some degree of historical understanding accessible even to quite young children.

There is evidence, then, that historical time concepts are not beyond the understanding of young children, though the level of understanding may be constrained by the form of instruction and by children's prior experiences. These constraints, however, do not appear to justify delaying the introduction of history until mature time concepts appear. As Thornton and Vukelich (1988) noted, "increasingly, the new time terms learned . . . are derived from the subject matter of history. This suggests that their development is crucially dependent upon instruction" (p. 74). Therefore, the important question is how to involve children most effectively in making the connections between their developing time concepts and historical understanding. Considerably more basic research is needed on the connections between spatio-temporal thinking and historical understanding, and on the forms of discourse and methods of instruction that support concept development.

Historical Understanding and Developmental Theory

Understanding and interpreting history is essentially a cognitive process. For this reason, many studies of the development of historical understanding have been designed to investigate its connection to Piagetian stages of development. Although Piaget's work was based on learning in mathematics and science, E. A. Peel (1965, 1967), a British psychologist, concluded that developmental stages could be identified in the learning of other subjects including history. A great deal of work has been done, mainly in Britain, that elaborates on Peel's findings. According to one report (Booth, 1980), no fewer than 24 theses and dissertations were completed between 1955 and 1980 in the United Kingdom in which Piagetian theory was applied to historical learning (p. 245).

The work of Roy W. Hallam is the most widely reported and best known of this research. Hallam (1966, 1967, 1972) determined levels of operational thinking in history by having 100 students, aged 11 to 16, respond to questions about short historical narratives. He found that the students in his sample reached the concrete and formal operational stages of thought in historical thinking considerably later than had Piaget's students in science and mathematics. Concrete operational thinking by Hallam's history students began at a chronological and a mental age of from 12.4 to 13.2 years, compared with ages 7 and 8 for Piaget's students. Formal operational thinking began at a chronological age of 16.2 to 16.8 and a mental age of 16.8 to 18.2 years, compared with ages 11 and 12 for Piaget's subjects. Subsequent studies by Stokes (1970), Lodwick (1972), and others supported Hallam's conclusion that adolescents find it more difficult to think hypothetically and deductively in history than in other disciplines. In later research, Hallam (1975, 1979) found that the development of formal operational thinking could be accelerated to some extent through effective teaching, especially with young students.

Criticism of the Piaget-Peel-Hallam Model

The findings about historical learning derived from the Piaget-Peel-Hallam model of developmental research have come under sharp criticism. Booth (1980, 1984) has criticized Hallam's work for both its excessively narrow view of historical thinking and the weaknesses in his research design. Hallam's emphasis on hypothetical-deductive thinking is inappropriate, Booth has argued that, as the logic of historical thought is not primarily deductive, "The historian has much of the creative artist in him. He aims to recreate in words the most credible account of the world we have lost. [David Hackett] Fischer describes such thinking as 'adductive' " (1984, p. 104). Booth also found fault with Hallam's use of narrative texts to the exclusion of other kinds of historical materials and with the kind of questions that he asked.

What, for example were children meant to make of the following questions on a short "text book" about Mary Tudor: "Mary Tudor thought that God wanted her to take England back to the Catholic church. (a) What would God have thought of her methods? (b) Can you think of any reasons why Mary Tudor should use such methods to make people follow her religion?" (1984, p. 106)

It should also be noted that Hallam's (1972) criteria for identifying cognitive stages of historical thinking call for a rather sophisticated kind of historical analysis. Only one of his 100 student subjects showed a consistent ability "to oppose, balance and compensate variables in an historical context," which was his definition of fully developed formal operational thought.

"Only one other subject of the hundred was able even to approach such a developed level of thinking" (p. 340).

Underlying the controversy over Hallam's work are concerns about its curricular implications. "If British students can be considered representative," noted Laville and Rosenzweig (1982), "these findings suggest that young people cannot grasp history until well beyond the time when they usually encounter it in school" (p. 55). However, Hallam (1966) did not conclude that the discipline of history is inherently too abstract for students at any level. He recognized the value of teaching history to students younger than age 16, so long as the instruction is selected so that it " 'matches' the pupil's schemata" (p. 238). Although his findings do not support instruction that depends upon hypothetical-deductive thinking at the lower grades, they do not rule out other kinds of historical thinking and learning.

Alternative Approaches to Evaluating Historical Understanding

Dissatisfied with the Piaget-Peel-Hallam model, Martin Booth (1980) devised an alternative approach to evaluating historical thinking. His subjects, students enrolled in a 2-year world history course in a comprehensive secondary school in the south of England, were taught with a variety of instructional materials, including primary sources, photographs, and films. They were tested on their ability to exhibit "adductive historical thought," as determined by their performance in grouping pictures and short quotations from historical documents into sets and explaining why the items belonged together. The sets created by the students were judged to be either *concrete* (based on evidence immediately apparent in the pictures or quotes) or *abstract* (based on inferred qualities or ideas).

Booth found that the students taking the course made "marked and significant gains" in their ability to think abstractedly over the 2-year period of the study. He concluded that "adductive historical thinking does appear to be attainable by pupils of a range of abilities in the fourth and fifth years of the secondary school" (p. 255). He argued that comparison with a control group demonstrated that the improvement was the result of teaching, rather than of maturation.

Important aspects of historical learning in the courses developed under the sponsorship of the Schools Council History 13–16 Project in Britain did not fit neatly into the Piagetian framework. The staff of this project created a 3-year, evidence-based history curriculum using a nonsurvey, or "discontinuous syllabus," approach designed to develop historical understanding. The 3-year sequence of courses included an introductory course on the nature of history as a discipline, a course on modern issues viewed historically, an in-depth course focused on a single historical period, a topical survey course (the history of medicine), and a course on local history (Boddington, 1984; Rosenzweig & Weinland, 1986; Samec, 1979).

In his report evaluating the new curriculum, Shemilt (1980) found that compared to a control group that took traditional history courses, the students enrolled in the project were

more accustomed to giving and seeking explanations, see more problems and puzzles in History, proliferate ideas more readily, frequently—if implicitly—arrange these ideas into the germ of what deserves to be called a 'theory of History,' and are generally more bold and vigorous in their thinking. (pp. 13–14)

The students taking the new courses saw history as an "explanation seeking discipline" that had a great deal of personal relevance to them. They also judged history to be a more difficult subject than mathematics. Shemilt concluded that although the students did not attain a fully mature appreciation of history in Piagetian terms, *"Children ... can still develop and refine their understanding of History to a considerable degree..."* (p. 44).

Other studies have focused on the kind of reasoning that is demonstrated in children's use of historical evidence. In a study similar to Booth's, Blake (1981) used documentary sources as the primary instructional materials in an extended unit on Victorian England for a group of 9- to 11-year-olds. A control group was taught with more traditional secondary accounts and work cards. Fewer of the students in the experimental group were able to reason as abstractly as had Booth's 14-year-olds when grouping items into sets, but the instruction produced a striking qualitative difference in the way they thought about the past. Although their knowledge of the period was less comprehensive than that of the control group and they knew fewer dates, they acquired a sharper awareness of how we know about people who lived in the past and a much deeper understanding of the problems those people faced. Drake (1986) also found that the use of primary source materials in history instruction made high school students more sensitive to the interpretive nature of history.

Other Challenges to a Piagetian Model of Historical Cognition

Other scholars have also questioned whether the Piagetian system is an appropriate cognitive model for describing historical learning. Kennedy (1983), for instance, explored the relationships among developmental level, information-processing capacity, and historical understanding. His study included three main types of assessment: a Backward Digit Span task to assess information-processing capacity, a group measure of developmental levels adapted from Tisher and Dale (1975), and two measures of historical understanding: a test/interview (Lunzer, Wilkinson, & Dolan, 1976) and a multiple-choice test. Kennedy reported statistically significant, but weak, correlations between scores on the two measures of historical understanding (.14, f *[sic]* < .001), between scores on the measures of historical understanding and information-processing capacity (.14; p < .01), and between historical understanding scores and scores on measures of developmental level (.16, f *[sic]* < .01). These results, Kennedy suggested, indicated that developmental measures and traditional historical understanding measures may have been assessing different constructs. Previous research on the development of historical understanding had been largely premised on the assumed relationship between performance on such measures of developmental levels and levels of historical understanding.

Kennedy has not been alone in suggesting that logical structures from one domain such as science or mathematics may not have analogies in history. Booth's (1984) characterization of the historian as creative artist was noted earlier. Jurd (1973) argued that the search in science and mathematics for evidence to construct laws is not characteristic of history. Instead, evidence in history is particularistic, and interpretation is dependent on the historian's perspective. Louis O. Mink (1966), a philosopher of history, claimed that historical thinking is different from either scientific or commonsense thinking in that it cultivates a specialized habit of "seeing-things-together" (p. 40). This perspective

is at least in part a claim that for the historical understanding of an event one must know its consequences as well as its antecedents; that the historian must look before and after.... Not infrequently we ask "and then what happened?" not merely out of curiosity but in order to understand what we have already been told. (p. 43)

For Mink, such understanding requires both intuition and empathy.

Domain-specific Cognition and Historical Understanding

More recent challenges to Piagetian theory stem from current knowledge-based conceptions of human cognition that emphasize the role of prior knowledge in learning and thinking (Carey, 1985a, 1985b; Gelman & Baillargeon, 1983; Mandler, 1983). Called into question is the notion that general stages of learning apply across domains. Instead, learning may be domain specific. The topic or conceptual domain in which the child is involved may directly influence his or her cognition.

According to this interpretation of cognition, there may be some general principles of learning to which everyone appeals when faced with an area out of their range of experience; but, it may be that only the novice resorts to these principles. Keil (1984), for instance, suggested that, whenever possible, children resort to some underlying theory to explain their world. They show a marked inclination to move beyond surface features—the concrete representations characteristic of Piagetian stage theory—and search for "chains" that lead them back to an object's origin. It appears that learners assume, and look for, the presence of underlying structures that are causal in nature and that, as they beome more knowledgeable in a domain, they become increasingly dissatisfied with the notion that meaning (or a concept) is merely a set of characteristic features that happens to be associated with a class of things. Thus, in Keil's (1984) study, children presented with photographs of the transformation of one common object into another (a change of surface features) tended to insist that the original identity remained, despite outward appearances, and referred to ideas about origin and causation to defend their stance.

Cognitive development, in this view, is dependent on the acquisition of specific concepts and integrations of these concepts (Novak, 1977). In the domain of history, this type of theory generation is found as children deal with how something becomes history (Levstik & Pappas, 1987). In Levstik and Pappas's study, second-grade and some fourth-grade children used "pastness" as a characteristic features of history, whereas the sixth graders generated a different theory having to do with change and significance. For these older students, something became history if it was important or caused change to occur.

Younger children's difficulty in areas such as time and history have, in the past, been seen as the result of developmental or global stage constraints. More recent research indicates that it may be a result of an absence of expertise in the relevant domain (e.g., Chi, Glaser, & Rees, 1982; Voss, Greene, Post, & Penner, 1983). According to this perspective, the knowledge of novices and experts is organized differently. Experts' conceptual systems or schemata include more and different relations among concepts than do those of novices. The knowledge of novices tends to be organized around the specific objects at hand, whereas the knowledge of experts is organized in terms of principles or abstractions that subsume objects (Glaser, 1984). Thus, the problem-solving difficulties of novices are not the result of their processing capabilities per se but are attributable to the inadequacies of their knowledge bases.

Some reformers have taken the research in domain-specific cognition to mean that all that children need to develop more mature concepts is to acquire information in the given domain by memorizing it. Yet studies of domain-specific cognition suggest that the core of concept attainment may be the comprehension of causal relationships. Meaning seems to be derived from notions of cause and explanation, with the result that concepts need to be embedded in causal theories to have power for the learner. Causal relationships empower the learner to make inductions and draw analogies. They provide coherence to the elements that make up a concept and bind together the features of a concept that occur together (Bruner, 1986; Nelson, 1986).

It is at this point that theories of narrative have particular relevance for historical understanding. In traditional research on historical understanding, students have generally been required to use and understand a particular form of discourse, such as the analytical essay, not familiar to younger children (Wishart & Smith, 1983). Yet children do have recourse to a narrative, or story, framework that remains powerful well into adolescence and is part of many children's cultural milieu (Meek, Warlow, & Barton, 1978). Levstik (1986) and Blake (1981) found that history embedded in literary narrative elicited strong interest among students and could be used to encourage study using more traditional sources. In a later study, Levstik (1989) found that reading and discussing literary narratives such as historical fiction and biography could encourage a student's interpretation and analysis of textbook versions of history. In Levstik and Pappas's (1987) study of second, fourth, and sixth graders, children as young as 7 and 8 were able to respond to history in a literary narrative, had concepts for *history* and *the past,* and were able to distinguish between history and the past on the basis of significance (i.e., history is that part of the past designated as important).

These studies suggest that historical narrative may help children generate causal theories with which to interpret historical information from other sources. As White (1980) noted, "the historical account endows ... reality with form ... imposing upon its processes the formal coherency that only stories possess" (p. 23). Bruner (1986) described the crucial process of reader engagement with narrative as a "triggering of presuppositions" or creation of implicit meanings. Well-written narrative

contextualizes history, in this view, and presents it as a human construction open to interpretation, in fact demanding interpretation (Iser, 1978).

The power of narrative to create context is not without problems. As Kermode (1980) explained, stories, especially first-person narratives, give "eye-witness credibility and the authority of the spoken voice" (p. 91). As children have been found to be generally uncritical of narrative sources, critical analysis needs to be part of instruction. Children do not appear to use the causal theories generated by narrative to critique that narrative unless specifically led to do so (Levstik, 1986, 1989).

CLASSROOM METHODOLOGY

Most of the research studies on the teaching of history published during recent decades have focused on the methods that history teachers use in the classroom. The most extensive of these studies is the Report of the 1977 National Survey of Science, Mathematics and Social Studies Education sponsored by the National Science Foundation (Weiss, 1978). Although the report did not distinguish between the teaching of history and other social studies subjects, the reporting of the data by grade levels (K–3, 4–6, 7–9, and 10–12) permits some differentiation. At grades 10–12, where United States and world history account for the majority of social studies enrollments, the teaching methods most commonly used were class discussions, lectures, and periodic tests and quizzes (Appendix B-67).

Weiss's finding is supported by the results of several less extensive studies conducted during the period 1950–1975, reviewed by Wiley (1977) in the literature review component of the study sponsored by the National Science Foundation. For example, in a 1951 study, Gross (1952) found that group discussion, supervised study, recitation, and teacher-made guide sheets or syllabi were the teaching methods most commonly used by teachers of American history in 100 junior and senior high schools in California. In a survey of 420 high school social studies teachers in Missouri, Wood (1966) found that the most commonly used instructional methods were "teacher-centered, i.e., question-answer recitation, teacher-led class discussion, and lecture" (Abstract).

The more recent study of high schools by Goodlad (1984) indicates that the pattern persists. He reported that the preponderance of activity in social studies classrooms involved "listening [which presumably includes listening to discussions as well as to lectures], reading textbooks, completing workbooks and worksheets, and taking quizzes" (p. 213). English-language journals occasionally contain reports on the status of history in countries other than the United States, some of which include observations on teaching methods. Dumas and Lee (1976), for example, found that student recitation in response to teacher questions was the basic method used in German schools, augmented by fairly frequent field trips into the community at the lower *Grundschule* and middle *Haupschule* levels.

Limitations of Survey Research

Surveys based on questionnaires that ask teachers about the methods they most commonly use have a number of limitations. In the first place, they contain little or no information about how teachers use these methods. The survey sponsored by the National Science Foundation included frequency of use (daily, weekly, monthly, or never) but not the amount of time the teacher used the technique during each class period (Hertzberg, 1985). There was no indication whether lectures took up entire class periods or only small portions of them. The questionnaires also did not ask whether class discussions were open and free-flowing exchanges or tightly controlled question-and-answer recitations.

Moreover, the methods reported by the teachers may not always correspond to what they actually do in their classrooms. Gross (1977) found studies in which teachers claimed to be using the methods associated with the New Social Studies. However, the teachers admitted that they paid little attention to the teaching of skills, which was the purpose the methods were designed to accomplish. These same teachers also said that they seldomly used the materials produced by the New Social Studies Projects.

A survey of teachers in independent schools by Rulon and Lubick (1982) indicated similar discrepancies. Teachers in this study acknowledged that they relied heavily upon such traditional methods as lectures and lengthy term paper assignments, but they also gave a high ranking to inquiry, role playing, and simulation gaming. However, only 2 of the 40 respondents included games among the materials they used to supplement the textbook, and none reported using inquiry materials such as those developed by the Carnegie-Mellon Social Studies Curriculum Project (pp. 249–250).

It is possible that these teachers were using standard textbooks for inquiry-oriented teaching. Fetsko (1978) found that United States and world history textbooks and teacher's manuals published in the 1970s had incorporated many of the characteristics of the New Social Studies. But the more likely explanation is that teachers tend to adopt the terminology currently in vogue to describe what they do, whether or not they have altered their teaching methods. Many teachers at least adopted the terminology of the New Social Studies.

Survey research also tends to mask the great diversity of methods and approaches that characterize the teaching of history in the schools (Fancett & Hawke, 1982). It focuses attention on central tendencies, on what most teachers do most frequently. The great diversity of teaching styles and methods emerges more clearly in ethnographic studies based on sustained classroom observation. Such studies also provide a much clearer picture of the dynamics of teacher–student interaction in history classrooms.

The pioneering ethnographic study of history-social studies education was the third component, or case studies part, of the 1977 NSF-sponsored study (Stake & Easley, 1978). The case studies were conducted at 11 school *clusters* (a high school and some of its feeder schools) in widely dispersed geographical locations in the United States. Although the Stake and Easley case studies described some of the varied ways history was taught in the schools, the reports are difficult to interpret. The field observers were given a great deal of autonomy and approached their task in quite different ways.

The study of history teaching in four midwestern high schools by McNeil (1986, 1988a, 1988b, 1988c) is a more promising model for future ethnographic research. Through year-long observations in classrooms in the four schools, McNeil found that the way history was taught and the quality of history teaching varied widely among the schools and among teachers within each school.

McNeil's intensive studies also yielded significant insights into the internal dynamics of history classrooms and into how the interaction among school administrators, teachers, and students influenced the way history was taught in the schools. How and how well history is taught, McNeil concluded, is shaped by the tension between the contradictory goals of educating and of processing, or credentialing, students. The school administrators in her study who emphasized order-keeping and credentialing goals did not merely fail to encourage good history teaching, they actively promoted teaching that was boring and mechanical when such teaching promoted order in the classroom. The teachers in these schools had little incentive to draw upon the store of historical and pedagogical knowledge at their command. They, in turn, developed teaching strategies that had negative effects on students and the value they placed on historical study. More such painstaking and sustained classroom observations of the teaching of history are needed for an adequate understanding of what is happening in history classrooms.

Importance of Teacher Knowledge

How history gets taught in the schools also depends upon how and how well history teachers know their subject. Focusing on the knowledge base of teaching, researchers in Stanford University's Teacher Assessment Project and Knowledge Growth in a Profession Project have studied both novice and expert history teachers (Gudmundsdottir, Carey, & Wilson, 1985; Shulman, 1986; Wilson, Shulman, & Rickert, 1987; Wineburg & Wilson, in press).

Knowledge in the content disciplines is only one aspect of a teacher's professional knowledge, but the Stanford projects found it to be a critical ingredient in teacher performance (Wineburg & Wilson, in press). Not only did expert history teachers have a large store of information at their command, they also had a "vision of history," a perception of the discipline "as a human construction, an enterprise in which people try to solve a puzzle" (p. 41). Novice teachers who were history or American studies majors tended to have a perception of the discipline like that of the expert teachers. They were more sensitive to the role of interpretation, to multiple causation, and to the importance of seeing events in a broad context than were nonmajors. The nonmajors did not necessarily become better history teachers by acquiring a larger store of factual knowledge, as "their naive and, at times, distorted conceptions of history acted as powerful sieves through which new information was filtered" (Wilson & Wineburg, 1988, p. 537). Evans (1988) also examined teachers' conceptions of history, looking especially at how their differing perceptions of the discipline affected what and how they taught. The research on teacher knowledge and perceptions of history has significant implications for the undergraduate training of future history teachers.

Role of Textbooks in History Instruction

Much of the concern in recent years about how history is taught in the schools has been focused on the role of textbooks in history instruction. It is widely assumed that textbooks dominate history and social studies instruction (Shaver, Davis, & Helburn, 1980; Wiley, 1977; Stake & Easley, 1978; Wineburg & Wilson, in press). A 1977 report by the Educational Products Information Exchange Institute concluded that 90% of classroom time involved the use of curricular materials, two thirds of this time being spent on commercially produced materials, mainly textbooks (Fancett & Hawke, 1982). A more recent report by the National Assessment of Educational Progress found a similar pattern of textbook use in history classes in secondary schools (Ravitch & Finn, 1987). Nearly 60% of the students surveyed reported using a textbook daily. Another 21% used textbooks 2 or 3 times a week (p. 191).

However, two recent ethnographic studies raise questions about the extent of textbook use in history instruction. Observations in middle school and high school social studies classrooms by F. R. Smith and Feathers (1983) found little reading of any kind taking place, with textbooks employed mainly as occasionally used reference books. McNeil (1986) found history teaching to be teacher, rather than textbook, driven. Torn between the conflicting needs of delivering information and imposing limits on classroom discussion, most of the teachers observed by McNeil resolved the tension "by maintaining tight control over course content, eliminating almost all reading assignments or written work" (p. 166).

Frequency of textbook use was not investigated in the 1977 NSF-sponsored study. The research literature review component of that study (Wiley, 1977) reported only on content analysis research on social studies textbooks. All of this suggests that there is still a need for research on how and how extensively textbooks are actually used in history classrooms, especially in the elementary and middle school grades where very little research has been done.

Student Attitudes Toward History

History and social studies are widely thought to be one of the least popular of school subjects, in part because of the use of teaching methods and materials that kill student interest in the subject. Goodlad (1984), for example, found that upper elementary school students liked social studies less than any other subject, with secondary students finding the subject less popular than English and mathematics but on a par with science (p. 212).

There is some support in the research literature for the assumption that student attitudes toward history are a reflection of the way the subject is taught. Shemilt found that the British Schools Council History 13–16 Project (1980), in which history was presented as an explanation-seeking discipline through in-depth study, was consistently successful in modifying the students' image of the subject. Students in the project courses were less likely to find history tedious and boring than students in the control group, who were enrolled in traditional history courses. However, the project students were more likely to complain of overwork and of being overwhelmed by masses of historical data. A new seventh-grade history program developed by the Israeli Curriculum Center that emphasized the analysis

of historical evidence was found to develop more positive student attitudes toward learning the subject (Lewy, Wolff, & Shavit, 1974).

THE STATUS OF HISTORY IN THE SCHOOLS

There is a widespread perception that history has lost ground in elementary and secondary schools in the United States during the past several decades (Bradley Commission, 1988; Howard & Mendenhall, 1982). After surveying history educators in several states, Kirkendall (1975) concluded that history was in a state of crisis and was in serious danger of being displaced from the curriculum, primarily by other social studies subjects. To what extent is this perception supported by research on the status of history in the curriculum?

In a review of the research literature on the status of history in the public schools, Downey (1985) found that the perception of decline was valid for some areas of the history curriculum. Drawing upon studies of course offerings and enrollments by H. R. Anderson (1949), Moreland (1962), Anderson et al. (1964), Osterndorf and Horn (1976), and Weiss (1978) and on studies of state curriculum requirements by Sutton (1976) and H. L. Smith et al. (1983), Downey found that offerings and enrollments had declined in eighth-grade United States history and in high school European and world history courses during the past several decades. However, there had been substantial gains in enrollments in the 11th-grade United States history course since the 1930s. By the 1950s, United States history was the most widely required and most commonly offered course in the social studies curriculum. Although fewer states required a year of United States history for high school graduation in 1983 than in 1954 (Cartwright, 1954; H. L. Smith et al., 1983), the removal of state mandates did not greatly affect offerings or enrollments in that course. Weiss (1978) found that United States history was still a required subject in 81% of the nation's school districts, was offered in 93% of them and was probably included in courses listed as "social studies" in the remaining 7% (pp. 26, 54). Although Weiss reported the average number of minutes per day devoted to social studies in grades K–6, she did not report the time devoted specifically to history.

In a more recent national study by the National Center for Education Statistics, West, Diodato, and Sanberg (1984) found little change in the pattern of history offerings and enrollments previously described. There was a small decline in history enrollments during the period 1972–1973 and 1981–1982, with high school history enrollments declining from 47% to 45% of the total number of students enrolled in high schools. Most of the decline was in European and world history course enrollments. American history enrollments (including United States, state, local, and other American history courses) increased as a percentage of all history enrollments from 65% to 68% during that 10-year period. The most striking decreases in United States history enrollments were in ethnic history courses, with enrollments in Afro-American and American Indian history courses dropping off sharply. These findings lend further support to Downey and Levstik's (1988) observation that, despite the decline in the number of states requiring history for high school graduation, the high school United States history course "has more than held its own. To take a somewhat longer perspective, United States history has been gaining ground in the high schools since the 1930s, partly at the expense of European history" (p. 336).

Although history experienced some decline in public high schools in recent decades, a 1979 survey of history instruction in private secondary schools (Rulon & Lubick, 1982) found that history "had experienced no identifiable decline in enrollments or in prestige over the last decade" (p. 251). History graduation requirements in independent secondary schools were similar to those in the public schools, with most private schools requiring only one year of United States history, but the vast majority of schools surveyed reported that their students took three or four history courses.

A number of studies published from the mid-1970s to the mid-1980s included information on the status of history teaching in other nations. Among them are reports by Dumas and Lee (1976, 1978, 1985) on the teaching of history and social science subjects in the schools of West Germany and France, by Rosenzweig (1984) and Avery (1974) on history education in Great Britain, and by Adejunmobi (1975) on Nigeria, and by Kiigi (n.d.) on Kenya. For the most part, these reports describe history curricula but provide only impressionistic evidence about enrollments. Although they are grounded in part on classroom observations, few incorporate survey data. The reports clearly indicate that the concern about the status of history in the schools and its relevance to students is widespread and is not a condition peculiar to the United States.

CONCLUSIONS AND RECOMMENDATIONS

Although the current reform movement has drawn attention to the history that children do not know, presumably after instruction, there has been a disturbing lack of attention to what children do know and to how they came to learn what they know. The research in both these areas is slim, especially when compared with research in such areas as literacy and language acquisition. However, there is a growing body of work that might provide a sounder basis for decision making than the field has had in the past. Even given a limited body of research, some conclusions can be drawn.

First, there is no evidence that delaying instruction in history is developmentally appropriate. Even if mature historical understanding requires formal operations in the Piagetian sense, there is no evidence that the development of historical understanding begins at that stage. More significantly, global-stage theory appears to have limited explanatory power in historical thinking. Research in domain-specific cognition suggests that children know more about time and history than has been thought and that they are capable of more mature thinking when they possess adequate background knowledge. These results argue for an early introduction to historical study rather than delay.

Second, the value of a shallow "cultural literacy" approach to concept development in history is brought into serious question by the research. Instead, studies link cognition to context

and to a framework of experience rich enough to provide more than surface features of concepts. Sustained study of significant material appears more likely to develop the habits of mind relevant to the domain of history and more likely to precipitate the learner's shift from novice to expert thinking.

Third, the current subject-matter-versus-pedagogy debate deflects attention from the more important issue of linking content and method to facilitate the learner's construction of meaning. The research on domain-specific cognition indicates that content knowledge is crucial to mature thinking. The intellectual scaffolding for historical thinking is historical data. Teachers need content knowledge to build an appropriate framework for learning, and students need it to construct adequate schemata and causal theories. But subject-matter expertise is not a sufficient condition for effective teaching. The research literature indicates that content and process count. How one learns influences what one learns.

Fourth, there is an inadequate body of research on instruction in history. We know little about how interactions among students, teachers, and others whose influence is felt in the classroom affect how history is taught and learned.

Fifth, the research based on both Piagetian and domain-specific theories has implications for the history curriculum. Courses that emphasize coverage and memorization are probably not useful settings for the development of either hypothetical-deductive thinking or autonomous historical reasoning. For these purposes, courses should devote sufficient time to a particular topic or period to establish an adequate historical context. Apparently, students need to see how particular information fits into the larger domain of historical knowledge. They certainly need historical topics rich enough to support sustained study. The Schools Council History 13–16 Project in Britain emphasizes in-depth study of this kind. Students in the project's courses were capable of arranging ideas into what Shemilt (1980) described as "the germ of what deserves to be called a 'theory of history'" (pp. 13–14). By building such germs of theories, by seeking and providing explanations, students are constructing the frameworks, or schemas, with which to develop more mature understandings of history. The research suggests that the Schools Council curriculum is a promising approach.

NEEDED RESEARCH

The Pedagogy of History

Few of our most common assumptions about how history is and should be taught have been tested empirically, including the notion that textbooks have a dominant influence in history instruction. Many history teachers make regular use of historical fiction, biography, journals, letters, and diaries. There needs to be more research on the value of such narrative accounts in motivating historical interest, in providing temporal and causal frames for historical learning, and in helping children recognize the interpretive nature of history.

More research is also needed on how teachers introduce concepts of historical time and on whether current practice contributes to, rather than eases, the difficulties children have in this area. There is also a need for continued development and testing of curricula based on new research. The expanding environments K–6 social studies curriculum is held in place more by tradition than by a rationale grounded in research. Are there other arrangements more likely to tap children's potential for historical learning? What is the best context for the development of historical understanding? There is also need for further research focused on the effective teaching that is being done in the schools.

Post-Piagetian Models of Cognition

The preceding examination of the research on domain-specific cognition suggests several directions for further research. *First,* if knowledge acquisition is domain specific, how should knowledge in the domain of history be studied, by both students and researchers? Further research is necessary if we are to know whether some of history's subdomains (e.g., social history, political history, economic history) are more appropriate than others for study by students of various ages.

Second, the research on the need for context to enable children to build causal theories suggests that historical understanding may not develop except where there is sufficient depth of study, rather than broad surveys of history, to support theory generation. Important research questions include how both depth and coverage can be defined and assessed, how much depth is necessary, and how much coverage is detrimental.

Third, the impact on children's historical understanding of different genres of historical literature (fiction, primary sources, secondary narratives) needs to be researched if we are adequately to understand the use of historical narrative.

Finally, John Poster's (1973) argument that historical understanding is culturally constrained remains to be researched. What impact does the larger society's uses of history have on the development of historical understanding? Further research, including cross-cultural studies, is needed to shed light on the impact of the cultural uses of history on the development of historical understanding.

Noncognitive Aspects of Development

Much of the newer research concentrates on the cognitive aspects of the development of historical understanding. How do other aspects of development bear upon the teaching and learning of history? In his 1973 study drawing on Erik Erikson's work, Martin Sleeper posited that young people are interested in the past as part of their concern with their own newly emerging sense of identity and "as a way of validating the perceived directions of their own lives" (p. 261). He found that the majority of the high school seniors in his study tended to judge the significance of historical events by either their impact on the present or their effect on the students' own lives and families. However, for most students the strands of formal history and autobiography remained compartmentalized, yet to be woven together into an integrated personal–cultural history. The challenge for the teacher, Sleeper concluded, remains

one of connecting the two categories of autobiography and history... Only through such a link is the adolescent likely to emerge from his study of history with a sense of the past in which he has woven his own existence into the mainstream of societal history. (p. 274)

How to build such links is another research challenge.

Status of History in the Schools

The research indicates that history is not the beleaguered part of the curriculum that it is sometimes claimed to be. Nevertheless, its status in the schools should be closely monitored. Should history lose ground in the curriculum, it is important to know at what grades it is vulnerable and why. It is equally important to know at what places in the curriculum it remains strongly entrenched and for what reasons. This monitoring should indicate how particular courses are faring, not just in relation to other social studies offerings but also in the context of the larger school curriculum.

Finally, it must be kept in mind that research can only help schools decide when it is possible to teach history. Whether history should be introduced at a particular grade level or how much history should be taught are questions of a different order. The answers to these questions must also reflect the values and sense of priorities of the larger society. However, it is the duty of educators concerned about the kind and quality of history taught in the schools to see that policymaking is informed by research.

References

Adejunmobi, S. A. (1975). Objectives of history teaching in Western Nigeria high schools. *The History Teacher, 8,* 424–436.

Anderson, H. R. (1949). *Teaching of United States history in public high schools: An inquiry into offerings and registrations, 1946–1947* (Bulletin, 1949, No. 7). Washington, DC: Federal Security Agency, Office of Education.

Anderson, S. B., et al. (1964). *Social studies in secondary schools: A survey of courses and practices.* Princeton, NJ: Educational Testing Service.

Applebee, A. N. (1978). *The child's concept of story.* Chicago: University of Chicago Press.

Avery, R. (1974). American studies in British classrooms. *The History Teacher, 7,* 564–573.

Blake, D. W. (1981). Observing children learning history. *The History Teacher, 14,* 533–549.

Boddington, T. (1984). The Schools Council history 13–16 project. *The History and Social Science Teacher, 19,* 129–137.

Booth, M. (1980). A modern world history course and the thinking of adolescent pupils. *Educational Review, 32,* 245–257.

Booth, M. (1984). Skills, concepts, and attitudes: The development of adolescent children's historical thinking. *History and Theory, 22,* 101–117.

Bradley Commission on History in Schools. (1988). *Resolutions of the commission: Steps toward excellence in the school history curriculum*. Westlake, OH: Author.

Bradley, N. C. (1947). The growth of the knowledge of time in children of school-age. *British Journal of Psychology, 38,* 67–68.

Bruner, J. (1986). *Actual minds, possible worlds*. Cambridge, MA: Harvard University Press.

Carey, S. (1985a). Are children fundamentally different kinds of thinkers and learners than adults? In S. F. Chipman, J. W. Segal, & R. Glaser (Eds.), *Thinking and learning skills: Research and open questions* (Vol. 2, pp. 485–517). Hillsdale, NJ: Lawrence Erlbaum.

Carey, S. (1985b). *Conceptual change in childhood*. Cambridge, MA: MIT Press.

Cartwright, W. H. (1954). What is happening in the social studies. *Social Education, 18,* 77–79.

Chi, M., Glaser, R., & Rees, E. (1982). Expertise in problem solving. In R. Sternberg (Ed.), *Advances in the psychology of human intelligence* (Vol. 1, pp. 7–75). Hillsdale, NJ: Lawrence Erlbaum.

Downey, M. T. (1985). The status of history in the schools. In M. T. Downey (Ed.), *History in the Schools* (pp. 1–12). Washington, DC: National Council for the Social Studies.

Downey, M. T., & Levstik, L. S. (1988). Teaching and learning history: The research base. *Social Education, 52,* 336–342.

Drake, F. D. (1986). Using primary sources and historians' interpretations in the classroom. *Teaching History: A Journal of Methods, 11,* 50–61.

Dumas, W., & Lee, W. B. (1976). Politische bildung: The social studies in West Germany. *The History Teacher, 9,* 228–243.

Dumas, W., & Lee, W. B. (1978). Social studies in French schools. *The History Teacher, 11,* 401–411.

Dumas, W., & Lee, W. B. (1985). Joan of what? The history crisis in French schools. *The History Teacher, 18,* 543–553.

Evans, R. W. (1988). Lessons from history: Teacher and student conceptions of the meaning of history. *Theory and Research in Social Education, 16,* 203–225.

Fancett, V. S., & Hawke, S. (1982). Instructional practices in social studies. In Project SPAN staff and associates (Ed.), *The current state of social studies: A report of Project SPAN* (pp. 207–263.) Boulder, CO: Social Science Education Consortium.

Fetsko, W. J. (1978). *An analysis of selected social studies textbooks to determine the impact of the "new social studies" on publishers materials*. Unpublished doctoral dissertation, School of Education, University of Colorado, Boulder.

Fivush, R., & Slackman, E. (1986). The acquisition and development of scripts. In K. Nelson (Ed.), *Event knowledge: Structure and function in development* (pp. 71–96). Hillsdale, NJ: Lawrence Erlbaum.

Fraisse, P. (1963). *The psychology of time*. New York: Harper & Row.

Friedman, W. J. (1978). Development of time concepts in children. In H. W. Lipsett (Ed.), *Advances in child development and behavior* (Vol. 12, pp. 267–298). New York: Academic Press.

Friedman, W. J. (1982). Introduction. In W. J. Friedman (Ed.), *The developmental psychology of time* (pp. 1–11). New York: Academic Press.

Gelman, R., & Baillargeon, R. (1983). A review of some Piagetian concepts. In J. H. Flavell & E. M. Markman (Eds.), *Handbook of child psychology: Vol. 3. Cognitive development* (pp. 167–230). New York: John Wiley & Sons.

Glaser, R. (1984). Education and thinking: The role of knowledge. *American Psychologist, 39,* 93–104.

Goodlad, J. (1984). *A place called school*. New York: McGraw-Hill.

Gross, R. E. (1952). What's wrong with American history? *Social Education, 16,* 157–161.

Gross, R. E. (1977). The status of the social studies in the public schools of the United States: Facts and impressions of a national survey. *Social Education, 41,* 194–200, 205.

Gudmundsdottir, S., Carey, N., & Wilson, S. (1985). *The role of subject-matter knowledge in learning to teach social studies* (Knowledge Growth in a Profession Project Tech. Rep. No. CC-05). Stanford, CA: Stanford University, School of Education.

Hallam, R. N. (1966). An investigation into some aspects of the historical thinking of children and adolescents. Unpublished master's thesis, University of Leeds, Yorkshire, England.

Hallam, R. N. (1967). Logical thinking in history. *Educational Review, 19,* 183–202.

Hallam, R. N. (1972). Thinking and learning in history. *Teaching History, 2,* 337–346.

Hallam, R. N. (1975). *A study of the effect of teaching method on the growth of logical thought with special reference to the teaching of history*. Unpublished doctoral dissertation thesis, University of Leeds, Yorkshire, England.

Hallam, R. N. (1979). Attempting to improve logical thinking in school history. *Research in Education, 21,* 1–24.

Harner, L. (1982). Talking about the past and future. In W. J. Friedman (Ed.), *The development of time* (pp. 141–169). New York: Academic Press.

Hertzberg, H. W. (1985). Students, methods and materials of instruction. In M. T. Downey (Ed.), *History in the schools* (pp. 25–40). Washington, DC: National Council for the Social Studies.

Howard, J., & Mendenhall, T. (1982). *Making history come alive: The place of history in the schools*. Washington, DC: Council for Basic Education.

Iser, W. (1978). *The act of reading*. Baltimore: Johns Hopkins University Press.

Jurd, M. (1973). Adolescent thinking in history-type material. *Australian Journal of Education, 17,* 2–17.

Keil, F. C. (1984). Mechanisms of cognitive development and the structure of knowledge. In W. Demopoulos & A. Marras (Eds.), *Language learning and concept acquisition* (pp. 81–99). Norwood, NJ: Ablex.

Kennedy, K. J. (1983). Assessing the relationship between information processing capacity and historical understanding. *Theory and Research in Social Education, 11,* 1–22.

Kermode, F. (1980). Secrets and narrative sequence. *Critical Inquiry, 7*(1), 83–101.

Kiigi, E. N. (n.d.). *An examination of the problems in history teaching at secondary school level in Kenya*. Thesis submitted for postgraduate diploma in curriculum development, University of Nairobi.

Kirkendall, R. S. (1975). The status of history in the schools. *The Journal of American History, 62,* 557–570.

Laville, C., & Rosenzweig, L. W. (1982). Teaching and learning history: Developmental dimensions. In L. W. Rosenzweig (Ed.), *Developmental perspectives on the social studies* (pp. 54–66). Washington, DC: National Council for the Social Studies.

Lello, J. (1980). The concept of time, the teaching of history, and school organization. *The History Teacher, 13,* 341–350.

Levstik, L. S. (1986). The relationship between historical response and narrative in a sixth-grade classroom. *Theory and Research in Social Education, 14,* 1–19.

Levstik, L. S. (1989). Historical narrative and the young reader. *Theory Into Practice, 28,* 114–119.

Levstik, L. S., & Pappas, C. C. (1987). Exploring the development of historical understanding. *Journal of Research and Development in Education, 21,* 1–5.

Lewy, A., Wolff, J., & Shavit, S. (1974). Students' and teachers' perceptions of studying history. *The History Teacher, 8,* 73–80.

Lodwick, A. R. (1972). *The development of children's reasoning in relation to mathematical, scientific and historical problems*. Unpublished master's thesis, University of Manchester.

Lunzer, E., Wilkinson, J., & Dolan, T. (1976). The distinctiveness of operativity as a measure of cognitive functioning in five year old children. *British Journal of Educatioinal Psychology, 46,* 280–294.

Mandler, J. M. (1983). Representation. In J. H. Flavell & E. M. Markman (Eds.), *Handbook of child psychology*, Vol. 3. *Cognitive development* (pp. 420–494). New York: John Wiley & Sons.

McNeil, L. A. (1986). *Contradictions of control: School structure and school knowledge*. New York: Routledge & Kegan Paul.

McNeil, L. A. (1988a). Contradictions of control: Part 1. Administrators and teachers. *Phi Delta Kappan, 69,* 333–339.

McNeil, L. A. (1988b). Contradictions of control: Part 2. Teachers, students, and curriculum. *Phi Delta Kappan, 69,* 432–438.

McNeil, L. A. (1988c). Contradictions of control: Part 3. Contradictions of reform. *Phi Delta Kappan, 69,* 478–485.

Meek, M., Warlow, A., & Barton, G. (Eds.). (1978). *The cool web*. New York: Atheneum.

Mink, L. O. (1966). The autonomy of historical understanding. *History and theory: Studies in the philosophy of history, 15,* 24–47.

Moreland, W. D. (1962). Curriculum trends in the social studies. *Social Education, 26,* 73–76.

Nelson, K. (1986). *Event knowledge: Structure and function in development*. Hillsdale, NJ: Lawrence Erlbaum.

Novak, J. D. (1977). An alternative to Piagetian psychology for science and mathematics education. *Science Education, 61,* 453–477.

Oakden, E. C., & Sturt, M. (1922). The development of knowledge of time in children. *British Journal of Psychology, 12,* 309–336.

Osterndorf, L. C., & Horn, P. J. (1976). *Course offerings, enrollments, and curriculum practices in public secondary schools, 1972–73*. Washington, DC: National Center for Education Statistics.

Peel, E. A. (1965). Intellectual growth during adolescence. *Educational Review, 17,* 169–180.

Peel, E. A. (1967). Some problems in the psychology of history teaching. In W. H. Burston and D. Thompson (Eds.), *Studies in the nature and teaching of history* (pp. 159–190). New York: Humanities Press.

Piaget, J. (1969). *The child's conception of time*. London: Routledge & Kegan Paul.

Poster, J. (1973). The birth of the past: Children's perceptions of historical time. *The History Teacher, 6,* 587–598.

Rabinowitz, P. J. (1987). *Before reading: Narrative conventions and the politics of interpretation*. Ithaca, NY: Cornell University Press.

Raven, R. (1977). Test of Piaget's operative comprehension. *Science Education, 61,* 271–278.

Ravitch, D., & Finn, C. E. (1987). *What do our 17-year-olds know?* New York: Harper & Row.

Rosenzweig, L. W. (1984). Perspectives on history education in England. *The History Teacher, 17,* 169–190.

Rosenzweig, L. W., & Weinland, T. P. (1986). New directions for the history curriculum: A challenge for the 1980s. *The History Teacher, 19,* 263–275.

Rulon, P. R., & Lubick, D. C. (1982). The status of history in American independent secondary schools: A survey. *The History Teacher, 15,* 243–254.

Samec, C. E. (1979). Teaching for historical understanding in British schools. *The History Teacher, 13,* 61–69.

Shank, R. C., & Abelson, R. P. (1977). *Scripts, plans, goals, and understanding: An inquiry into human knowledge structures*. Hillsdale, NJ: Lawrence Erlbaum.

Shaver, J. P., Davis, O. L., Jr., & Helburn, S. W. (1980). An interpretive report on the status of precollege social studies education based on three NSF-funded studies. In *What are the needs in precollege science, views from the field, mathematics, and social science education?* Washington, DC: National Science Foundation.

Shemilt, D. (1980). *History 13–16 evaluation study*. Edinburgh, Scotland: Holmes McDougall.

Shulman, L. S. (1986). Those who understand: Knowledge growth in teaching. *Educational Researcher, 15,* 4–14.

Sleeper, M. (1973). The uses of history in adolescence. *Youth & Society, 4,* 259–274.

Smith, F. R., & Feathers, K. M. (1983). Teacher and student perceptions of content area reading. *Journal of Reading,* 348–354.

Smith, H. L., et al. (1983). *Humanities and state education agencies: Policies, perspectives and prospects*. Washington, DC: Council of Chief State School Officers.

Smith, R. N., & Tomilson, P. (1977). The development of children's construction of historical duration: A new approach and some findings. *Educational Research, 19,* 163–170.

Stake, R. E., & Easley, J. A. (1978). *Case studies in science education*. Urbana, IL: University of Illinois, Center for Instructional Research and Curriculum Evaluation.

Stokes, A. B. G. (1970). *An investigation into the presence of logical thinking in a group of 18-year-olds in historical and related study*. Unpublished master's thesis, University of Leeds, Yorkshire, England.

Sutton, J. (1976). *National survey, social studies education, kindergarten–grade twelve*. Richmond, VA: Virginia Department of Education.

Thornton, S. J., & Vukelich, R. (1988). Effects of children's understanding of time concepts on historical understanding. *Theory and Research in Social Education, 15,* 69–82.

Tisher, R., & Dale, L. (1975). *Understanding in science test*. Victoria, Australia: Australian Council for Educational Research.

Tucker, J. (1977). Research on social studies teaching and teacher education. In, *Review of research in social studies in education, 1970–1975* (pp. 97–136). Washington, DC: National Council for the Social Studies.

Van Dongen, R. (1987). Children's narrative thought at home and at school. *Language Arts, 64,* 79–87.

Voss, J. F., Green, T. R., Post, T. A., & Penner, B. C. (1983). Problems solving skill in the social sciences. In G. H. Bower (Ed.), *The psychology of learning and motivation: Advances in research and theory* (Vol. 17, pp. 165–213). New York: Academic Press.

Weiss, I. R. (1978). *Report of the 1977 national survey of science, mathematics, and social studies education*. Research Triangle Park, NC: Center for Educational Research and Evaluation.

Wells, G. (1981). *Learning through interaction: The study of language development*. Cambridge, England: Cambridge University Press.

Wells, G. (1985). *Language development in the pre-school years*. Cambridge, England: Cambridge University Press.

West, J., Diodato, L., & Sanberg, N. (1984). *A trend study of high school offerings and enrollments: 1972–73 and 1981–82*. Washington, DC: National Center for Education Statistics.

White, H. (1980). The value of narrativity in the representation of reality. *Critical Inquiry, 7*(1), 5–27.

Wiley, K. B. (1977). *The status of pre-college science, mathematics, and social science education: 1955–1975: Vol. 3. Social science education*. Boulder, CO: Social Science Education Consortium.

Wilson, S. M., Shulman, L. S., & Rickert, A. E. (1987). 150 different ways of knowing: Representations of knowledge in teaching. In J. Calderhead (Ed.), *Exploring teachers' thinking,* (pp. 104–124). London, England: Cassell.

Wilson, S. M., & Wineburg, S. S. (1988). Peering at history through different lenses: The role of disciplinary perspectives in teaching of American history. *Teachers College Record, 89,* 525–539.

Wineburg, S. S., & Wilson, S. M. (in press). Subject matter knowledge in the teaching of history. In J. E. Brophy (Ed.), *Advances in research on teaching*. Greenwich, CT: JAI Press.

Wishart, E., & Smith, J. L. (1983). Understanding the logical connections in history. *Australian Journal of Reading, 6,* 19–29.

Wood, F. H. (1966). *A study of social studies education in the rural, urban, and suburban high schools of Missouri*. Unpublished doctoral dissertation, University of Missouri, Columbia.

·33·

TEACHING AND LEARNING ECONOMICS

Mark C. Schug
UNIVERSITY OF WISCONSIN–MILWAUKEE

William B. Walstad
UNIVERSITY OF NEBRASKA–LINCOLN

A compelling case can be made for economic literacy. There are at least two basic reasons why economic understanding is important (Stigler, 1970). *First,* we are a nation of people who want to think and talk about economic issues. These issues affect us in our roles as consumers, workers, producers, and citizens. Individuals and the nation benefit from education in the concepts, method, and logic that help in the analysis of economic issues. *Second,* economic decisions are made on a daily basis. In our society, the ability to apply an economic perspective to public and private concerns is an essential skill for all citizens.

If there is a case for economic literacy, then education about the world of economics must begin in the schools. But then questions arise. What economics concepts should be taught to students? Should economics be introduced to students at early grades? Which instructional practices improve economic understanding? What level of performance can we expect from students graduating from high school? Answers to such questions depend on scholarly reflection and research. Fortunately, the quantity of research in economic education has increased since the late 1960s. There is now a large body of work for social studies researchers and practitioners interested in economic education. (For those researchers who want a source of current information on research articles, there exists a microcomputer file, Research in Economic Education Database [REED], available for purchase from the Joint Council on Economic Education [432 Park Avenue South, New York, NY 10016]. REED contains detailed abstracts of most of the journal articles that have been published since 1969 and can be searched across key descriptors.)

Four considerations guided the preparation of this review

of research. *First,* the review presents a summary of the major topics in the economic education literature. The risk of oversimplifying complex issues was overshadowed by the importance of a review that would improve communication among researchers on substantive issues. *Second,* the studies reviewed are primarily those easily accessible to researchers in the field. Research in economic education has improved to the point where it is not necessary to depend on obscure references or sources that are difficult to obtain. *Third,* although much research in economic education has been focused on teaching at the college level, this review, consistent with the proposed scope of the *Handbook,* is concentrated on economic education at the elementary and secondary levels. *Fourth,* we limited the critical analysis of research methods and concentrated on findings and implications, because comprehensive reviews are available of research methods in economic education (Becker, 1983a, 1983b, 1983c; Becker, Greene, & Rosen, 1990) and of social studies research (Fraenkel, 1987; Wallen & Fraenkel, 1988). The main goals of this review are to offer valid generalizations and to suggest ideas for new studies of the teaching and learning of economics at the precollegiate level.

ECONOMIC IDEAS THAT ARE WORTH TEACHING

Major work by economists and educators to describe the economics content that should be taught in schools began with the publication of the report by a national task force on economic education (Bach et al., 1961). This report described the "minimum understanding of economic essential for good citi-

---

Reviewer was Donald R. Wentworth, Pacific Lutheran University.

zenship and attainable by high school students" (p. 4). It was succeeded by the *Framework for Teaching Economics* (Hansen, Bach, Calderwood, & Saunders, 1977). The *Framework* reduced the task force statement to a set of 24 economic content categories and became the guide for numerous curriculum development efforts.

The *Framework* was revised in 1984 (Saunders, Bach, Calderwood, & Hansen, 1984) to incorporate changes in the discipline of economics and to reorganize the set of economic concepts. It, along with similar proposals for the content of the precollegiate economics curriculum (e.g., Becker & Reinke, 1975; Schur, 1985), covers basic concepts in the fundamental, microeconomic, macroeconomic, and international economic clusters.

Although influential, the *Framework* has had its critics. The Joint Council on Economic Education, for example, sponsored a 1986 conference to reexamine economics at the precollegiate level as reflected in the *Framework*. The critics identified problems with the *Framework* such as the weak treatment of ideology (Heilbroner, 1987), the omission of significant microeconomic theory (Strober, 1987), an unrealistic view of international trade (Culbertson, 1987), the fractured presentation of macroeconomics (Galbraith, 1987), and the limitations of the evaluation of economic policy (Thurow, 1987). Perhaps the strongest defense of the *Framework* was published in a later article by Baumol (1988).

An alternative to the more conceptual approach in the *Framework* was proposed by Wentworth (1987), drawing on the work of Fuchs (1983) and Heyne (1987). Wentworth argued that economic instruction is too often characterized by emphasis on discrete economic concepts. Instead, the goal of economic education should be to help students learn and apply the logic of economics. Development of an economic way of thinking should be given priority over coverage of economic content. Economic concepts should be presented to elaborate key economic assumptions and to help students understand and anticipate economic behavior. The premise is that, if students are taught the logic of economics, they will analyze economic events more clearly, long before they know much formal economic content. Wentworth and Western (1990) present the following statements as examples of economic assumptions to guide logic:

1. Scarcity forces people to choose.
2. People choose purposefully among alternatives.
3. All choices involve alternatives; therefore, there are no cost-free choices.
4. Producers and consumers respond in predictable ways to incentives.
5. Individual incentives are influenced by the actions of others and by the rules of the economic system.
6. Voluntary trade creates wealth.
7. The consequences of choice lie in the future.

Although this approach has not been widely discussed, the focus on economic reasoning makes it an appealing topic for further study.

In addition to the identification of what economics is worth

teaching, work has been done to develop a sequence for the presentation of economic ideas to students in the K–12 curriculum. *Economics: What and Where* (Gilliard, Caldwell, Dalgaard, Reinke, & Watts, 1988) was built on the outline of the *Framework,* providing more detailed content statements and describing concepts in student language. Also recommended were the grade levels at which the economic concepts and generalizations should be introduced and developed. Scope and sequence efforts were guided in part by survey studies (Watts, 1987b, 1989) in which teachers, principals, economic educators, and social studies coordinators were asked to judge the minimum grade levels at which each of the content areas could be feasibly taught. More research, however, on student performance within grade levels and across grades is needed to establish the validity of this scope and sequence.

THE STATUS OF ECONOMICS IN THE CURRICULUM

State and national surveys have been conducted to examine the status of economic education in the curriculum. There have not, however, been reports of direct investigations of the behaviors of teachers, including their use of textbooks and supplemental materials in the classroom.

State Department of Education Surveys

Many state legislatures have taken actions to require the teaching of economics in the curriculum. These state mandates offer insights into the current status of economics in the curriculum. Highsmith (1989) updated an earlier survey of state mandates by Brennan and Banaszak (1981). Questionnaires were mailed to state social studies supervisors in all 50 states. Follow-up telephone interviews and contacts with the state councils on economic education were also used to obtain information. Highsmith found that in 28 states some form of instruction in economics is mandated. Most state mandates call for economics to be taught at the secondary level. In 16 states, students are required to complete a semester course in economics for high school graduation.

These survey data are frequently cited as evidence that instruction in economics is increasing. This appears to be the case if changing graduation requirements are examined. Brennan and Banaszak (1981) reported that a semester or yearlong course in economics was required for high school graduation in seven states. By 1989, nine more states had such a requirement. However, state reports often contain vague information about economic education. For example, several states report infusing economics into the social studies curriculum but do not report how this is done.

School Surveys

A study conducted by Yankelovich, Skelly, and White (1981) provided evidence that economic education was becoming well established in the school curriculum. The random sampling procedures used in this study represented a significant improvement over most prior surveys based on nonrandom samples. The primary purpose of the study was to determine the status of economics in the school curriculum through the perceptions of teachers. Included in the survey were nearly 800 teachers in 510 randomly selected school districts, from 357 senior high schools and 153 junior high schools. Over 500 personal interviews were conducted; the remaining teachers completed self-administered questionnaires. The results reported from this study were that most teachers said that economics was introduced relatively early in their schools. Two-thirds said that economics was available in the sixth or seventh grades. Moreover, nearly half of the teachers reported that economics was a required subject in their schools.

The results of the Yankelovich, Skelly, and White, Inc. (1981) study should be considered in light of related work by Walstad and Watts (1985). Wary of the optimistic results from the earlier study, Walstad and Watts reviewed 15 state surveys of the status of economic education and reached somewhat different conclusions. They found that the dominant method for including economics in the curriculum was the infusion approach, in which economic content is taught in other courses such as U.S. history. They identified several weaknesses in integrating economics into other courses, including lack of teacher confidence in teaching economic concepts, poor teacher preparation in economics, superficial instruction, weak persentation of economic ideas in the curricular materials, and the limited time available for economics in the curriculum. Their examination of the state surveys suggested that separate high school economics courses reach far fewer students than had been indicated by the Yankelovich, Skelly, and White, Inc. study.

More national studies are needed on the status of economics in the curriculum. Moreover, state or local studies that included visits to schools and observations of teachers would help to sharpen our understanding of what economic education is in practice. In addition, it would be worthwhile knowing if there is a difference between the performance of students who take economics in states where the subject is mandated and that of students who take economics in states where it is an elective. Are mandates an effective strategy for improving economic understanding among students?

TEACHER EDUCATION

In 1985 the Joint Council on Economic Education issued a report calling for more formal preparation of teachers to teach economics. The council recommended that all elementary and secondary school teachers be required to take one basic course in economics, that all secondary social studies teachers be required to take at least nine semester hours of economics, and that teachers of advanced placement economics courses be required to earn an academic major in economics. Moreover, the inclusion of economics content in teaching methods courses and in clinical experiences was strongly endorsed.

Current training practices do not fulfill these recommenda-

tions. Walstad and Watts (1985) investigated the quantity of the economics courses that teachers have taken. Their analysis of 15 state surveys suggested that teachers had limited course work or inservice training in economics. They found, for example, that about half of elementary teachers had taken no courses in economics, and another 25% had taken only one course. For secondary social studies teachers, about 10% to 20% had taken no course, about 25% had taken one course, and about 30% had taken two courses. Teachers with this level of course work would probably not be very confident in the adequacy of their knowledge for teaching economics.

Inservice education has been suggested as one way to correct the deficiencies in the economic understanding of teachers and students. This topic has received considerable attention, including studies at the secondary level by Highsmith (1974); Thorton and Vredeveld (1977); Schober (1984); Weaver, Deaton, and Reach (1987); and Walstad and Soper (1988a) and studies at the elementary level by Walstad (1979, 1980), Chizmar and Halsinski (1983), and Chizmar and McCarney (1984).

The in-service studies have been similar in design. The work of Schober (1984) exemplifies the general line of investigation. Schober's study involved 247 teachers; 150 were participants in an economic education workshop and 97 were not. Over 600 students were involved in the study. The treatment group consisted of 219 students enrolled in the economics classes of the seven economics teachers who were workshop participants. The comparison group of 432 were students enrolled in the economics classes of nonparticipants. Pretest and posttest scores were obtained on a test of economic learning and on an attitude survey administered to the teachers and students. Two-stage least squares regression analysis indicated a statistically significant relationship between teacher participation and the posttest achievement scores of teachers and students. Among other things, Schober concluded that participation in an inservice workshop had a positive impact on teachers' economic knowledge and a positive impact on the economics achievement and economics attitudes of their students. The report did not contain adequate information to compute effect sizes, other investigators of the effectiveness of inservice programs at both the elementary and secondary level have reported improved achievement for the teachers and their students. Thus, although the real magnitude of these findings is unclear, taken together the studies offer evidence of the positive influence of economic education workshops and courses on teachers and students.

THE DEVELOPMENT OF ECONOMIC THINKING IN CHILDREN

A small but growing body of research has been focused on how children's thinking about economic ideas develops and changes over time. These studies follow a similar pattern. The investigator poses to children situations or problems that illustrate economic ideas; then he or she interviews them about their understanding or explanation of the situation. The interviews are often accompanied by props to help stimulate the children's thinking, such as dollar bills and play scores. The interviews are usually transcribed, and the coded data are analyzed using descriptive and nonparametric statistics. Another characteristic of these studies is their non-American origin. In about half, the samples are European children.

About 25 studies have been completed since the 1950s on how children think about economic problems. The studies track the economic thinking of young people; usually their thinking is described as proceeding through a series of levels or stages similar to those described by Jean Piaget. Examples of work in this area include that by Berti and Bombi (1988); Berti, Bombi, and Lis (1982); Danziger (1958); Furth (1978); Jahoda (1979, 1981); Kourilsky and Graff (1986); Schug and Birkey (1985); Strauss (1952); and Tan and Stacy (1981).

The following account of one study illustrates the nature of this line of research. Jahoda's 1981 study followed up on earlier work (Jahoda, 1979); both studies were focused on how and at what age children achieve a simple understanding of the idea of profit. The 1979 study was focused on the profit that might be earned by a shopkeeper, particularly the understanding that a shopkeeper would usually have to charge customers a higher price on products than the price he or she had paid to the supplier. In the 1981 study, Jahoda extended this simple notion of profit to banking. He interviewed 96 children, aged 11 through 15, in schools classified as working-class or middle-class. Based on the interview data, Jahoda identified five levels of thinking.

1. *No knowledge of interest.* The children reasoned that money placed in the bank neither increased or decreased. The bank was a safe place for people to store their money. People got back precisely what they deposited.
2. *Interest paid on deposits only.* The responses here suggested that, if people left their money in the bank for a period of time, they could earn interest. Some children began to understand that the bank uses income from deposits in various ways; some children also connected these used to the interest that banks charge.
3. *Interest paid on both loans and deposits* (but deposits stressed). Responses in this level suggested some recognition that the same principle that applied to the bank (paying interest on deposits) also applied to the bank customers (paying interest on loans).
4. *Interest the same on deposits and loans.* Children at this level began to realize that, to be successful, the bank needed to make a profit. Children at this level were close to understanding that banks make a profit on loans.
5. *More interest charged for loans than for deposits.* Here the children understood that banks must charge more money for the use of loans than they pay on customers' deposits. In other words, the simple idea of a bank's making a profit was present.

Jahoda concluded that at first children tend to view the principles regulating bank transactions as the same as those between friends. If you borrow something, you return the same. Anything else would not be "fair." Only gradually do young people begin to recognize the need for a bank to make a profit. He noted further that these findings illustrate how difficult it

may be for children to begin to distinguish between personal arrangements such as those between friends and the more impersonal arrangements of society.

The studies of economic thinking suggest two important conclusions. *First,* children's economic ideas tend to follow a developmental sequence. Their thinking becomes more abstract and flexible with age. *Second,* although economic thinking shows a gradual improvement with age, mature reasoning appears more quickly for some concepts than for others. A concept like profit, for example, which is central to understanding how a market economy runs, may not emerge until about age 11. A concept like scarcity may be understood in a very simple form by children about age 6 (Schug & Birkey, 1985).

The reports of economic thinking can be criticized for being long on descriptions of how children think about economic problems but short on explanations of instructional implications. What, if anything, do the developmental studies tell us about how teachers should teach economics?

Consider the same question as it has been raised in science education. Eaton, Anderson, and Smith (1984) stressed that children's conceptions of the world are often misconceptions, quite different from the scientific explanations offered in school, that interfere with learning. In the teaching of economics, it is easy to imagine similar dysfunctional misconceptions, such as a youngster quietly listening to the teachers' explanation of what interest rates are but persisting in the belief that banks are merely places where people store their money. Unless teachers deliberately recognize and correct the confusions young people are likely to have, misunderstandings probably will persist even after textbook definitions are memorized successfully and test questions answered correctly. Moreover, failure to correct students' misconceptions may get them off to a false start in learning economics and prevent them from learning new ideas correctly. The value of developmental studies in economic education is that they can alert teachers to the confusions young people are likely to possess about common economic ideas.

STUDIES OF ECONOMIC KNOWLEDGE AND ATTITUDES

The development of national standardized tests for elementary through high school grades has improved our knowledge of what economics children know. At the elementary level, for example, Chizmar and Halinski (1981) developed the Basic Economics Test (BET). Walstad and Robson (1990) recently completed a revision of the BET. The test was designed to measure understanding of economic concepts as outlined in the second edition of the *Framework for Teaching Economics* (Saunders et al., 1984). The items were classified into three cognitive levels: knowledge, understanding, and application.

Data from the 1990 BET standardization sample provided an indication of the ability of elementary students to learn economics. The mean scores on the 29-item BET for students without formal economic instruction were 15.84 on Form A of the test and 17.32 on Form B. Mean scores for students with economic instruction were 18.48 on Form A and 18.88 on Form B.

Walstad and Soper (1988c) used the norming data of the

Test of Economic Literacy (TEL) to provide an assessment of the economic understanding of U.S. high school students. The TEL was administered as a pretest to 6,570 students at the beginning of a school semester. Another 8,205 students took the TEL as a posttest at the end of the school semester. Of that total national sample, 3,031 students had taken the TEL as both a pretest and a posttest. Half of the students had been enrolled in economics courses; the others were enrolled in either a consumer economics course or a social studies course, such as government or U.S. history, in which either the teacher reported including economics or no economic instruction was reported.

Examination of the pretest scores provided evidence of student understanding of economics prior to taking separate courses in economics or other social studies courses. Students in economics courses scored 44.9% correct on all items on the pretest, students in social studies courses in which the teacher included economics scored 47.7% on the average, students in social studies courses in which the teacher did not include economics scored 37.4% on all items, and students in consumer economics classes scored 40.3% correct. Students performed the best on items related to microeconomics and fundamental economics and the worst on items measuring understanding of macroeconomics and international economics. The posttest results were essentially the same as the pretest results for students in social studies courses with or without reported economics content, and for students in consumer economics courses. Only for students taking a separate economics course was there a gain from pretest to posttest (44.9% to 52.4%).

The results from this study and related studies (Soper & Walstad, 1988b; Walstad & Soper, 1989) raise questions about the teaching of economics at the K–12 level and suggest areas for further study. *First,* students about to graduate from high school had relatively limited knowledge of economics. The reason for this level of performance is not completely clear, but it may stem from inadequate K–12 instruction in economics. More longitudinal studies of the type undertaken by Buckles and Freeman (1983) might shed light on the development of student economic understanding over time. *Second,* more emphasis is needed on the improvement of instruction in macroeconomics and international economics. New instructional materials and new measures to assess level of understanding are needed to improve knowledge in particular areas of economics. *Finally,* including economics in general social studies courses appears to add little to student knowledge, whereas separate courses in economics appear to contribute to improved achievement. This result raises doubts about using infusion as a strategy for teaching economics. Infusion may make a valuable contribution to economic understanding, but we need to know how and under what circumstances.

Gender Effects

MacDowell, Senn, and Soper (1977) initially phrased the question, "Does sex really matter in understanding economics?" From a research perspective, the answer is yes and no. Yes, sex matters because it has been found that, at any point in time, males tend to score higher than females on economics tests (Siegfried, 1979). This finding holds true in terms of both simple mean comparisons of scores on tests and regression studies that control for other variables. The results are fairly consistent in studies with multiple-choice tests at the elementary, secondary, and college levels; all other things being equal, males appear to know more economics than females. The differences in test scores are usually small but statistically significant; whether they are of practical significance is open to debate (see Ladd, 1977).

The no answer to the question comes from research in which a flow model was used. With the flow model, initial economic knowledge is controlled and the researcher attempts to explain performance at the end of the course. In studies that have been used this design at the college level, Seigfried (1979) reported, two-thirds showed no difference in male and female performance. In other words, males and females appear to learn economics at the same rate. Women may enter a class with slightly less understanding, but they seem to learn the same amount as men during the course. Recent findings at the high school level are more mixed. Watts (1987a) reported statistically significant higher mean gain scores for males in the 11th grade but not in the 12th grade. Walstad and Soper (1988b) also found that males had higher mean gains. Whether there are differences in economic knowledge and learning and, if so, what produces them remains unknown.

Recent research from Great Britain, however, suggests one possible answer. Lumsden and Scott (1987) found that males tended to show some slight superiority on multiple-choice examinations but that females did substantially better on essay examinations. The psychological literature suggests that females mature earlier and have higher verbal skills than males. Because essay exams tap verbal skills more than multiple-choice exams do, it is reasonable to expect females to be better on them. Whether the type of test is the factor contributing to a gender differential in economic knowledge at the high school level is a topic for further study.

Economic Attitudes

The development of economic attitudes has been a long-standing interest in economic education (Dawson, 1980). Although little research has been done in this area, some valuable work has been reported from national studies based on survey instruments for which information on measurement reliability and validity is available. For example, the *Survey of Economic Attitudes* (Walstad & Soper, 1983) measures attitudes toward economics as a subject and economic attitude sophistication. It was re-normed in 1986 with 6,000–7,000 senior high school students (Soper & Walstad, 1988a).

To study the emerging attitudes of early adolescents, O'Brien and Ingels (1987) collected data with the Economic Values Inventory they had developed. The 850 junior high school students in their sample expressed

strong support for the economic system;
slight agreement with statements expressing trust in business;
mild support for a strong government role in maintaining social welfare;
neutral feelings about government price controls;

mild disagreement with the idea that workers receive fair treatment;

mild agreement with the idea that there is a need for changes toward greater equality in our economic system.

Researchers have investigated the relationship between economic knowledge and attitude toward the economic system at the high school level. In their study of over 1,000 high school students in Hawaii, Jackstadt and Brennan (1983) found that student attitudes toward the economic system were related to many variables, including economic knowledge, grade level, parental occupation, media attention, and parental membership in a labor union. Jackstadt and Brennan also highlighted the importance of age. They found, for example, that adolescents became more cynical in their attitudes toward economic institutions as they grew older; however, their attitudes became more positive after they took an economics course.

Walstad and Soper (1983) followed a somewhat different approach in their use of the Survey on Economic Attitudes with high school students. Rather than study attitudes toward the economic system, which is a difficult construct to measure with any degree of reliability or validity, they built on earlier work by Mann and Fusfeld (1970) to develop a measure of "economic sophistication." Economic sophistication refers to the extent to which reported opinions on economic issues are in agreement with the current knowledge or consensus views of economists. Walstad and Soper (1989) reported results from a replication of an earlier study with 1,630 students (Walstad & Soper, 1982). In both studies, economic understanding and IQ scores had significant positive relationships with economic attitude sophistication. In other words, the more students knew about economics, the more sophisticated their views on economic issues.

Such attitude studies offer a basis for understanding young people's economic attitudes. In the middle grades, young people continue to have a generally supportive view of the economic system, although they increasingly express a sense of perceived economic injustice. By high school, many students seem to have accepted many of the basic values of the economic system, although expressions of cynicism also increase. Finally, economic understanding appears to be related to student attitudes toward the economic system and to the degree of sophistication in assessing economic issues.

A related topic of study has been attitudes toward economics as a subject. In fact, for a long time the belief has been that economics achievement and attitudes toward economics as a subject are related. That is, if students like economics, they will learn more, and if they learn more, their attitude toward the subject will improve. Most of the early research on this conjecture, however, was conducted with single-equation models using ordinary least squares regression. When estimated with two-stage least squares in simultaneous equation models, the results of the elementary, secondary, and college levels suggest that there may be a one-way relationship (Schober, 1984; Walstad, 1979, 1980, 1987). If students learn more economics, over and above what they knew before they took the course, they will like the subject more. In contrast, liking the subject more does not necessarily mean they will learn more economics.

INSTRUCTIONAL PRACTICES SEEM EFFECTIVE

No studies could be located of formal observations of how economics is taught at the elementary or secondary school levels. Economics instruction is probably similar to other social studies instruction. Shaver, Davis, and Helburn (1979), for example, found that printed curricular materials are the basic tools of instruction in social studies classes. Textbooks are used as the primary source of knowledge, reflecting the belief of many teachers that students do learn from textbooks. Social studies teachers also depend heavily on lecture and class discussion. Although lecture and discussion predominate, teachers reported using other practices such as student reports, library work, role playing, and simulations. Elementary teachers tend to use a wider variety of teaching methods than secondary teachers.

Numerous authors have made the case for beginning economic instruction in the elementary grades (Kourilsky, 1977, 1987; Ramsett, 1977; Schug & Armento, 1985; Smith, 1988). These authors stress the idea that economic education is too important to be left out of the elementary curriculum. In fact, several eary curricula have been shown to have improved student learning.

Lawrence Senesh was a pioneer in the development of instructional materials for teaching economics at the elementary level. Larkins and Shaver's study (1969) of Senesh's *Our Working World* (1963) materials tended to confirm his optimism that economics is an intellectually appropriate subject for elementary students. This study included four experiments of differing levels of sophistication with 393 first graders in five experimental groups and 349 students in four control groups from urban areas, small cities, suburbs, and semirural towns. The means on economic achievement tests were repeatedly and consistently higher than for uninstructed students. The preponderance of evidence from this and other studies (e.g., Sulkin & Pranis, 1969) supports the idea that economics can be learned at the elementary level.

Perhaps the most widely noted and researched programs for the elementary level have been the mini-society and the kinder-economy simulations developed by Marilyn Kourilsky. The purpose of these programs is to have children experience economic concepts in a concrete and direct way. In the mini-society, for example, students establish their own simulated economy and earn money by becoming entrepreneurs and by selling goods (such as wallets) or services (such as needlepoint lessons). They can choose to become salaried workers in the simulated private sector or in the civil service sector. The mini-society approach affords active student participation, real economic experiences, and decision making wherein individuals learn the consequences of their decisions.

The results from a study of the kinder-economy by Kourilsky (1977) tended to support its effectiveness. She found that 96 children in five kindergartens learned such concepts as scarcity, supply and demand, and opportunity cost after participating in economic activities 30 min per day for a semester. The preponderance of evidence from this and other studies (e.g., Cassuto, 1980) supports the effectiveness of the mini-society approach.

Televised instruction can also be an effective way of teaching economics at the elementary level. Walstad (1980) and Chizmar and Halsinski (1983) investigated students' performance on tests of economic knowledge after viewing the Trade-Offs television series produced by the Agency for Instructional Technology. Trade-Offs was a series of fifteen 20-minute television and film programs in economics. It was designed for children aged 9 to 13 years of age. Walstad (1980) found in his study of 563 students that those who viewed the Trade-Offs series had a statistically significant higher economics test mean than that of the students in the control groups who did not view the series. Chizmar and Halsinski's (1983) study involved 56 school classrooms in 23 states. Increased instruction with Trade-offs was associated with improved student performance. Students' performance with instruction of 13 weeks or more improved by more than three-quarters of a standard deviation. Results from both studies suggested that training teachers in the use of the materials improved their students' economic learning.

Instruction in economics at the secondary level has received less attention from researchers. One factor about which little is known is the influence of the textbook on economics learning in junior and senior high schools. Miller (1988) provided a detailed review of studies evaluating textbooks on the basis of the quality and quantity of economic content. There is only one controlled study of the effects of selected textbooks or the different uses of textbooks by teachers on student economic knowledge or attitude in junior and senior high schools (Walstad & Van Scyoc, 1990).

There are some studies of effective teaching approaches at the secondary level. Morton (1987) described in detail the instructional practices used to teach economics in his high school. The teachers followed a four-step model that involved teaching the basic principles, reinforcing the basic principles, applying economic logic, and applying economic reasoning. Test results for the program indicated that students of low, middle, and high ability can make large gains in economic understanding as compared with national forms. The failure, however, to report standard deviations made it impossible to compute effect sizes. As with textbooks, there is a need for more study of effective teaching practices.

A number of studies have been focused on the Developmental Economic Education Project (DEEP) sponsored by the Joint Council on Economic Education (Walstad & Soper, in press). School districts that participate in DEEP agree to include economics in the K–12 curriculum and to train teachers in the teaching of economics. The results of recent studies (e.g., Walstad & Soper, 1982, 1988a) indicate that students in DEEP districts have statistically significant higher mean scores than students in non-DEEP districts, even after controlling for the influence of other major factors. The positive results for DEEP, however, are not without controversy. Questions remain about the definition of a DEEP school district (Brenneke, Highsmith, Soper, Walstad, & Watts, 1988), the size of the effects (Luker, 1984), and the possibility that sample selection bias has influenced the results (Becker & Walstad, 1990).

CONCLUSIONS

Research in economic education shares many of the same methodological and design problems as research in social studies education generally (Fraenkel, 1987; Wallen & Fraenkel, 1988). These criticisms aside, some have argued that the overall quality of the research work is strong because of the use of economic theory to influence the design of studies and the application of sophisticated statistical analyses including the widespread use of regression analyses (Becker, 1983a, 1983b, 1983c; Becker & Walstad, 1987; Becker et al., 1990).

The major conclusions from this review of research are:

1. Researchers have developed useful measures of economic knowledge and attitude that have been normed using large national samples. Examples of tests include the Test of Economic Literacy, the Test of Economic Knowledge, and the Basic Economics Test. Attitude measures include the Survey on Economic Attitudes and the Economic Values Inventory.

2. The results of several studies indicate that economic education in-service programs result in gains in teacher and student scores on tests of economic knowledge. Although the gains have not always been impressive, the preponderance of the research evidence supports the effectiveness of in-service programs.

3. Research in economic education has provided a glimpse of how children reason about economic problems without the benefit of formal instruction. This line of investigation should help curriculum leaders to refine scope and sequence guidelines, alert teachers to the type of confusion that students are likely to have about particular economic concepts, and assist curriculum developers in writing age-appropriate instructional materials.

The following are recommendations for future research:

1. The debate continues over what economic content will best improve student understanding. Suggestions from the *Framework for Teaching Economics* have tended to stress instruction based on categories of concepts. Others have argued in behalf of teaching the logic of economics (Wentworth & Western, 1990). Additional research is necessary to determine which emphasis in instruction is most effective.

2. More studies to determine effective instructional practices are necessary. For example, almost nothing is known about which instructional approaches are most effective for teaching particular economic ideas. How can the concept of demand be best demonstrated to sixth graders? What analogies best illustrate the concept of GNP to students at Grade 11? Researchers might begin by observing the teaching of expert teachers to identify exemplars and sound instructional practices (Berliner, 1986).

3. Although studies have been completed on how children reason about various economic concepts, additional work remains to be done. Many economic concepts are missing from this literature. For example, there are no studies on how students reason about macroeconomic ideas.

4. Researchers should reduce reliance on reports from state departments of education and self-reports from teachers and curriculum leaders about what is going on in the classroom. More effort should be devoted to observing actual instruction and examining the effectiveness of instructional materials and practices.

References

Bach, G. L., Bellack, A. A., Chandler, L. V., Frankel, M. L., Gordon, R. A., Lewis, B. W., Samuelson, P. A., & Bond, F. A. (1961). *Economic education in the schools.* New York: Committee on Economic Development.

Baumol, W. (1988). Economic education and the critics of mainstream economics. *Journal of Economic Education, 19*(4), 323–330.

Becker, W. E. (1983a). Economic education research: Part I. Questions. *Journal of Economic Education, 14*(1), 10–17.

Becker, W. E. (1983b). Economic education research: Part II. New directions in theoretical model building. *Journal of Economic Education, 14*(2), 4–10.

Becker, W. E. (1983c). Economic education research: Part III. Statistical estimation methods. *Journal of Economic Education, 14*(3), 4–15.

Becker, W. E., Greene, W., & Rosen, S. (1990). Research on high school economic education. *Journal of Economic Education, 21*(3), 231–245.

Becker, W. E., & Reinke, R. W. (1975). What economics should the educator know? *The Social Studies, 66*(5), 195–204.

Becker, W. E., & Walstad, W. B. (Eds.). (1987). *Econometric modeling in economic education research.* Boston: Kluwer-Nijhoff.

Becker, W. E., & Walstad, W. B. (1990). Data loss from pretest to posttest as a sample selection problem. *Review of Economics and Statistics, 72*(1), 184–188.

Berliner, D. C. (1986). In pursuit of the expert pedagogue. *Educational Researcher, 15*(7), 5–13.

Berti, A. E., & Bombi, A. S. (1988). *The child's construction of economics.* Cambridge: Cambridge University Press.

Berti, A. E., Bombi, A. S., & Lis, A. (1982). The child's conceptions about means of production and their owners. *European Journal of Social Psychology, 12,* 221–239.

Brennan, D. C., & Banaszak, R. A. (1981). *A survey of state mandates and competencies for economic education.* Stockton, CA: University of the Pacific, Center for the Development of Economic Education.

Brenneke, J. S., Highsmith, R. J., Soper, J. C., Walstad, W. B., & Watts, M. W. (1988). A research and evaluation agenda for DEEP and precollege economic education. *Journal of Economic Education, 19*(1), 5–13.

Buckles, S., & Freeman, V. (1983). A longitudinal analysis of a developmental economics education program. *Journal of Economic Education, 15*(1), 5–10.

Cassuto, A. E. (1980). The effectiveness of the elementary school mini-society program. *Journal of Economic Education, 7*(2), 59–61.

Chizmar, J. F., & Halinski, R. S. (1981). *Basic Economics Test: Examiner's manual.* New York: Joint Council on Economic Education.

Chizmar, J. F., & Halinski, R. S. (1983). Performance in the Basic Economics Test (BET) and Trade-Offs. *Journal of Economic Education, 14*(1), 18–29.

Chizmar, J. F., & McCarney, B. J. (1984). An evaluation of a Trade-Offs implementation using canonical estimation of joint educational production functions. *Journal of Economic Education, 15*(1), 11–20.

Culbertson, J. M. (1987). A realist international economics. *Journal of Economic Education, 18*(2), 161–176.

Danziger, K. (1958). Children's earliest conceptions of economic relationships (Australia). *Journal of Social Psychology, 47,* 231–240.

Dawson, G. G. (1980). *Attitudes and opinions on economic issues: Research in economic education, report 2.* Old Westbury, NY: Empire State College.

Eaton, J. F., Anderson, C. W., & Smith, E. L. (1984). Students' misconceptions interfere with science learning: Case studies of fifth-grade students. *Elementary School Journal, 84*(4), 365–379.

Fraenkel, J. R. (1987). Toward improving research in social studies education. *Theory and Research in Social Studies Education, 15*(3), 203–222.

Fuchs, V. R. (1983). *How we live.* Cambridge, MA: Harvard University Press.

Furth, H. G. (1978). Young children's understanding of society. In H. McGurk (Ed.), *Issues in childhood social development* (pp. 228–256). Cambridge: Cambridge University Press.

Galbraith, J. K. (1987). On teaching a fractured macroeconomics. *Journal of Economic Education, 18*(2), 213–226.

Gilliard, J. V., Caldwell, J., Dalgaard, B. R., Reinke, R. W., & Watts, M. (1988). *Economics: What and when: Scope and sequence guidelines, K–12.* New York: Joint Council on Economic Education.

Hansen, W. L., Bach, G. L., Calderwood, J. D., & Saunders, P. (1977). *A framework for teaching economics: Basic concepts.* New York: Joint Council on Economic Education.

Heilbroner, R. L. (1987). Fundamental economic concepts: Another perspective. *Journal of Economic Education, 18*(2), 111–120.

Heyne, P. (1987). *The economic way of thinking* (5th ed.). Chicago: Science Research Associates.

Highsmith, R. J. (1974). A study to measure the impact of in-service institutes on the students of teachers who have participated. *Journal of Economic Education, 5*(2), 77–88.

Highsmith, R. J. (1989). *A survey of state mandates for economics instruction.* New York: Joint Council on Economic Education.

Jackstadt, S. L., & Brennan, J. M. (1983). Economic knowledge and high school student attitudes toward the American economic system, business, and labor union. *Theory and Research in Social Education, 11*(3), 1–15.

Jahoda, G. (1979). The construction of economic reality by some Glaswegian children. *European Journal of Social Psychology, 19,* 115–127.

Jahoda, G. (1981). The development of thinking about economic institutions: The bank. *Cahiers de Psychologie Cognitive, 1*(1), 55–73.

Joint Council on Economic Education. (1985). *Economic education for future elementary and secondary teachers: Basic recommendations.* New York: Author.

Kourilsky, M. (1977). The kinder-economy: A case study of kindergarten pupils' acquisition of economic concepts. *Elementary School Journal, 77*(3), 182–191.

Kourilsky, M. (1987). Children's learning of economics: The imperative and the hurdles. *Theory Into Practice, 26*(3), 198–205.

Kourilsky, M., & Graff, E. (1986). Children's use of cost-benefit analysis: Developmental or non-existent. In S. Hodkinson & D. Whitehead (Eds.), *Economic education: Research and developmental issues* (pp. 127–129). Essex, England: Longman.

Ladd, H. F. (1977). Male–female differences in precollege economic education. In D. R. Wentworth, W. L. Hansen, & S. H. Hanke (Eds.), *Perspectives in economic education* (pp. 145–155). New York: Joint Council on Economic Education.

Larkins, A. G., & Shaver, J. P. (1969). Economics learning in grade one: The USU assessment studies. *Social Education, 33,* 955–963.

Luker, W. (1984). DEEP Revisited. *Journal of Economic Education, 15*(2), 111–118.

Lumsden, K. G., & Scott, A. (1987). The economics student reexamined: Male–female differences in comprehension. *Journal of Economic Education, 18*(4), 365–375.

MacDowell, M. A., Senn, P. R., & Soper, J. C. (1977). Does sex really matter? *Journal of Economic Education, 9*(1), 28–33.

Mann, W. R., & Fusfeld, D. R. (1970). Attitude sophistication and effective teaching in economics. *Journal of Economic Education, 1*(2), 111–129.

Miller, S. L. (1988). *Economic education for citizenship.* Bloomington, IN: Foundation for Teaching Economics.

Morton, J. (1987). The high school economics course comes of age. *Theory Into Practice, 26*(3), 206–210.

O'Brien, M. U., & Ingels, S. J. (1987). The economics values inventory. *Journal of Economic Education, 18*(1), 7–18.

Ramsett, D. E. (1977). Toward improving economic education in the elementary grades. *Journal of Economic Education, 4*(1), 30–35.

Saunders, P., Bach, G. L., Calderwood, J. D., & Hansen, W. L. (1984). *A framework for teaching economics: Basic concepts* (2nd ed.). New York: Joint Council on Economic Education.

Schober, H. M. (1984). An analysis of the impact of teacher training in economics. *Theory and Research in Social Education, 12*(1), 1–12.

Schug, M. C., & Armento, B. J. (1985). Teaching economics to children. In M. C. Schug (Ed.), *Economics in the school curriculum, K–12* (pp. 33–43). Washington, DC: Joint Council on Economic Education and the National Education Association.

Schug, M., & Birkey, C. J. (1985). The development of children's economic reasoning. *Theory and Research in Social Education, 13*(1), 31–42.

Schur, L. (1985). What economics is worth teaching? In M. C. Schug (Ed.), *Economics in the school curriculum, K–12* (pp. 21–32). Washington, DC: Joint Council on Economic Education and the National Education Association.

Senesh, L. (1963). *Our working world: Families at work.* Chicago: Science Research Associates.

Shaver, J. P., Davis, O. L. Jr., & Helburn, S. W. (1979). The status of social studies education: Impressions from three NSF studies. *Social Education, 43*(2), 150–153.

Siegried, J. J. (1979). Male female differences in economic education: A survey. *Journal of Economic Education, 10*(2), 1–11.

Smith, D. (1988). Industry and the primary school curriculum. In D. Smith (Ed.), *Industry in the primary school curriculum* (pp. 3–20). London: Falmer Press.

Soper, J. C., & Walstad, W. B. (1987). *The test of economic literacy examiner's manual* (2nd Ed.). New York: Joint Council on Economic Education.

Soper, J. C., & Walstad, W. B. (1988a). The economic attitudes of U.S. high school students: New norms for the Survey on Economic Attitudes. *Theory and Research in Social Education, 16*(4), 295–312.

Soper, J. C., & Walstad, W. B. (1988b). The reality of high school economics: The teacher's perspective. *Journal of Private Enterprise, 4*(3), 85–96.

Soper, J. C., & Walstad, W. B. (1988c). What is high school economics? Posttest knowledge, attitudes, and course content. *Journal of Economic Education, 19*(1), 37–51.

Stigler, G. J. (1970). The case, if any, for economic education. *Journal of Economic Education, 1*(2), 77–84.

Strober, M. H. (1987). The scope of microeconomics: Implications for economic education. *Journal of Economic Education, 18*(2), 135–149.

Strauss, A. L. (1952). The development and transformation of monetary meanings in the child. *American Sociological Review, 17,* 275–284.

Sulkin, H. A., & Pranis, R. W. (1969). Evaluation of an elementary school social studies program. *Educational Leadership, 27*(3), 271–276.

Tan, H., & Stacy, B. G. (1981). The understanding of socioeconomic concepts in Malaysian Chinese school children. *Child Study Journal, 2*(1), 33–49.

Thorton, D. L., & Vredeveld, G. M. (1977). Inservice education and its effect on secondary students: A new approach. *Journal of Economic Education, 8*(2), 93–99.

Thurow, L. C. (1987). Evaluating economic performance and policies. *Journal of Economic Education, 18*(2), 237–245.

Wallen, N. E., & Fraenkel, J. R. (1988). An analysis of social studies research over an eight year period. *Theory and Research in Social Education, 16*(1), 1–22.

Walstad, W. B. (1979). Effectiveness of USMES in-service economic education program for elementary school teachers. *Journal of Economic Education, 11*(1), 1–12.

Walstad, W. B. (1980). The impact of Trade-Offs and teacher training on economic understanding and attitudes. *Journal of Economic Education, 12*(1), 41–48.

Walstad, W. B. (1987). Applying two stage least squares. In W. E. Becker & W. B. Walstad (Eds.), *Econometric modeling in economic education research* (pp. 111–134). Hingham, MA: Kluwer Nijhoff.

Walstad, W. B., & Robson, D. (1990). *The Basic Economics Test: Examiner's manual* (2nd ed.). New York: Joint Council on Economic Education.

Walstad, W. B., & Soper, J. C. (1982). A model of economics learning in the high schools. *Journal of Economic Education, 13*(1), 40–54.

Walstad, W. B., & Soper, J. C. (1983). Measuring economic attitudes in high school. *Theory and Research in Social Education, 9*(1), 41–54.

Walstad, W. B., & Soper, J. C. (1988a). High school economics: Implications for college instruction. *American Economic Review, 78*(2), 251–256.

Walstad, W. B., & Soper, J. C. (1988b). What is high school economics? TEL revision and pretest results. *Journal of Economic Education, 19*(1), 24–35.

Walstad, W. B., & Soper, J. C. (1989). What is high school economics? Factors contributing to student achievement and attitudes. *Journal of Economic Education, 20*(1), 53–68.

Walstad, W. B., & Soper, J. C. (Eds.). (in press). *Effective economic education in the schools.* Washington, DC: National Education Association.

Walstad, W. B., & Van Scyoc, L. (1990). The effects of textbooks on economics understanding and attitudes in high school economics courses. *Journal of Research and Development in Education, 24*(1), 46–54

Walstad, W. B., & Watts, M. (1985). Teaching economics in the schools: A review of survey findings. *Journal of Economic Education, 16*(2), 135–146.

Watts, M. (1987a). Student gender and school district differences affecting stock and flow of economic knowledge. *Review of Economics and Statistics, 69,* 561–566.

Watts, M. (1987b). Survey data on precollege scope-and-sequence issues. *Journal of Economic Education, 18*(1), 71–91.

Watts, M. (1989). Social studies coordinators and the economics curriculum. *Theory and Research in Social Education, 17*(1), 53–68.

Weaver, A. M., Deaton, W. L., & Reach, S. A. (1987). The effect of economic summer institutes for teachers on the achievement of their students. *Journal of Educational Research, 80*(5), 296–300.

Wentworth, D. R. (1987). Economic reasoning: Turning myth into reality. *Theory Into Practice, 26*(3), 170–175.

Wentworth, D. R., & Western, R. D. (1990). High school economics: The new reasoning imperative. *Social Education, 54,* 78–80.

Yankelovich, Skelly, & White, Inc. (1981). *National survey of economic education 1981.* New York: Playback Associates.

TEACHING ANTHROPOLOGY, SOCIOLOGY, AND PSYCHOLOGY

Murry R. Nelson

THE PENNSYLVANIA STATE UNIVERSITY

Robert J. Stahl

ARIZONA STATE UNIVERSITY

The three social sciences, anthropology, sociology, and psychology, are often linked because their respective contents overlap or impact on one another. In the field of social studies education, they are linked by their consignment to relatively minor roles in the greater schema of social studies and by the commensurately lesser emphasis on them as academic specialties on the part of social studies educators.

In the narrowest of views, these social sciences, those closest to human growth and interaction, are seen as unsupportive of, if not impediments to, citizenship. The concepts of culture, group, and self (the keys of anthropology, sociology and psychology) do not lend themselves as immediately to nationalistic goals. Barber (1989) observed that citizenship has often been viewed as entailing "merely voting and overseeing representatives" (p. 355). And Engle and Ochoa (1988) referred to the classic sense of citizen as one who is "patriotic, loyal and obedient to state" (p. 3). Obviously, there is a definitional problem in directly linking citizenship with nationalism; the implication is that the nation-state is the only possible instrument of citizenship. This is a reductionist view, but nevertheless, is prevalent among many social studies educators.

A clearer, more expansive definition of citizenship would provide support for including anthropology, sociology, and psychology in the curriculum as possible abettors of good citizenship. Citizenship should foster the pluralism basic to a democratic society, and these social sciences provide conceptual foundations that promote the understanding and appreciation of pluralism. Remy (1980) noted that "citizenship education involves learning and instruction related to the development of citizen competence" (p. 1). Accentuating the role of citizens in a group or culture would serve to foster a more conceptual approach to citizenship, though not necessarily nationalism. As long as the definition of citizenship is limited to roles in the nation-state, the political-historical view will only provide for the well-being of history and political science in the schools.

In this chapter, the research is examined in these three content areas within social studies education. That research is surprisingly thin in two respects. First, the number of studies conducted in classrooms is small; and, second, the depth of the research is usually shallow, often relying on description alone.

The three social science areas are addressed separately, but the research is generally similar. Research on psychology in social studies is dominated by status studies with little known about actual classroom behavior or the effects on learning. Anthropology in schools is addressed in many anecdotal "testimonies" that we hesitate to call research; a few status studies have been reported. Studies of the teaching of both anthropology and sociology in schools have largely been the result of the use of the New Social Studies materials. This is far less so in psychology.

Except for an occasional article or issue in professional journals like *Social Education* and *The Social Studies* during the era of the New Social Studies, little attention has been paid to

Reviewers were James Matiya, Carl Sandburg High School, Orland Park, IL; H. Wells Singleton, University of Wyoming; Thomas J. Switzer, University of Northern Iowa.

the place of anthropology, sociology, and psychology in the school curriculum. Not student enrollments, the number of teachers who teach a particular course, or the percentage of schools that offer a particular course for credit has had any direct relationship to the extent to which the subject area involved has received attention by the social studies profession or researchers investigating the social studies on the precollege level. Yet for precollege psychology, for example, survey reports and reviews constitute nearly 90% of all reported research. Results from such studies are interesting to some, but they do not provide important details regarding programs, actual instruction, and student learning. Thus, such status studies are discussed only in passing in this chapter.

This is a review of the research on the teaching of and learning in anthropology, sociology, and psychology as separate, self-contained units and courses of study in the precollege curriculum. We did not include studies in which the teaching of particular concepts, principles, or generalizations from these disciplines were investigated. Researchers in those areas are more often concerned with testing the efficacy of a particular teaching strategy or method than with the content used. In some cases, the nature of a concept itself makes uncertain its exact discipline: For example, does research on teaching the concept of "conflict" or "power" belong in psychology, sociology, political science, or history, or all? Questions like these will *not* be considered.

ANTHROPOLOGY

In 1973, anthropology was offered as a course to approximately 89,000 students (National Center for Education Statistics [NCES], 1984) in fewer than 9% of the secondary schools in the United States. Nine years later, the percentage had grown only slightly to 11.7%, but the number of students had remained stable. Dynneson (1986) "attempted to measure the status of precollegiate anthropology at both elementary and secondary levels in all 50 states." However, his data were sparse, inconclusive, and largely anecdotal (e.g., Pennsylvania Department of Education, 1969).

Research in anthropology has generally been confined to three areas: (a) the place of anthropology in the schools, often reported as descriptions or status studies; (b) the teaching and learning of anthropology, particularly anthropological concepts; and (c) the use of materials in anthropology. As noted above, the studies in the first category will not be reviewed.

Teaching and Learning Anthropology

One of the most famous (or infamous) of the New Social Studies projects was Man: A Course of Study (MACOS), the focus of great controversy in the 1970s. There is surprisingly little research on MACOS, although an internal team did some evaluations of MACOS in the late 1960s (Hanley, Whitta, Moo, & Walter, 1970). Much of the data is qualitative, from interviews and observations. The evaluators noted that "children seemed to become much more aware of similarities between humans and other animals than they did of differences . . ." (p. 18). They also

concluded that "where basic similarities in human behavior have been grasped, children demonstrate verbally that the unit is having positive effects in creating a sense of the family of man, i.e., reducing ethnocentrism" (p. 40). The evaluation was not rigorous, despite the fact that descriptions of the evaluation sample and methodology in the appendix of the report indicate that responses from over 3,000 students in more than 150 classrooms were analyzed (p. 53). No instruments were reported, nor were data broken out into subsets. Most of the report is anecdotal.

Barnes, Stallings, and Rivner (1981) investigated whether MACOS affected the attitudes of children toward six practices: cruelty to animals, divorce, cannibalism, murder, senilicide, and female infanticide. Two experimental classes of fourth graders taught with MACOS and two control classes of fourth graders taught with the regular social studies curriculum were given an attitudinal inventory before and after seven weeks of study. The researchers concluded that MACOS produced no statistically significant attitudinal change towards the six practices.

The Anthropology Curriculum Project (ACP), funded by the United States Office of Education (USOE) in 1961, was located in the Department of Social Science Education of the University of Georgia. After USOE funding expired, the University of Georgia kept the project alive until the mid-1970s. Hunt (1969/1970) used project-developed tests to examine the anthropology achievement of 160 normal and disadvantaged kindergarten youngsters who had studied ACP-developed lesson materials on the methodology of anthropologists and the development of the concepts of cultural universals, cultural variation, and enculturation. Hunt concluded that both groups learned anthropology concepts, that neither gender nor socioeconomic status had a statistically significant association with anthropology achievement, and that mental age was more important than chronological age in learning anthropology.

In another dissertation, Clawson (1972/1973) sought to determine the effects of conceptual organizers on the learning of the ACP concepts by third graders. He concluded that "the study was unable to produce evidence . . . that either pre or post organizers facilitate [the] learning of structured anthropology materials at the third grade level" (p. 4788). Barnes (1972/1973), in a study using sixth graders, reached the same conclusion.

The effects of the ACP materials on the ethnocentrism of fourth-grade students were studied by Frech (1973/1974). He concluded that students in classes in which the materials had been used had lower mean ethnocentrism scores than did students who had used regular social studies materials on a posttest and a delayed posttest administered two to three weeks later. The higher the class mean achievement score for anthropology, the lower the mean ethnocentrism score.

There have been studies of anthropology instruction in which New Social Studies materials were not used. In most cases, the researcher was the teacher. Feer (1976), for example, described a one-semester class in general anthropology taught by him in a Massachusetts high school in the spring of 1972. Feer made an important point regarding generalizability: "Another limiting factor is the fact that all the programs . . . are taught by one teacher" (p. 6). If the teacher leaves, so does the program.

Dacanay (1977) described an elective anthropology course for eighth graders that he taught in a junior high school in Stockton, California, with an emphasis on physical anthropology and archaeology, including laboratory and field methods. In a crude evaluation, two-thirds of the students rated the course as good or excellent. Dacanay recommended more such courses, but noted that the key to success was a "properly trained teacher."

Also in the 1970s, Mattson and Abshire-Walker (1976) offered a series of anthropology workshops for public school teachers in California. Their workshop evaluations raised a common dilemma for subject matter specialists who work with teachers, that is, "Do we teach anthropology to the teachers or do we teach how to teach anthropology?" (p. 22).

Use of Anthropology Materials

Dynneson (1981) characterized the entire period before World War II in noting, "Instructional materials were ... the single most serious barrier to teaching anthropology in elementary and secondary schools" (p. 304). This lack of materials continues to restrict the teaching of anthropology in the schools.

Lanouette (1985) examined and analyzed high school anthropology textbooks in an attempt to determine why they were so unpopular. Like others before her (Dynneson, 1981), she found a dearth of appropriate, stimulating classroom materials. She interviewed 15 teachers in the District of Columbia area who also taught a semester anthropology class for students in grades 11 and 12, and she analyzed three high school textbooks. Insights gained from her own teaching and the interviews, combined with her personal experience with the National Science Foundation Anthropology for Teachers Program (1978–1982), led her to conclude that anthropology textbooks were inadequate. A number of teachers used college-level anthropology textbooks. Although some schools still used the Anthropology Curriculum Study Project materials, *Patterns in Human History,* judged to be stimulating and useful, the kits were difficult to procure.

Reflections on the Research

Research on anthropology in social studies classrooms is rare and shallow. Dwyer-Shick's (1976, 1977) bibliographies have enhanced the historical foundations of the area, but there is no evidence to indicate that subsequent researchers have relied on, consulted, or even been aware of her work. Dynneson's willingness to work nearly alone in this field is to be commended. However, his research has been shallow, often inconclusive survey studies resulting in few suggestions, implications of consequence, or conclusions.

Frech's (1973/1974) promising work suggested that the knowledge and appreciation of cultural diversity gained through the study of anthropology can reduce ethnocentrism. Not only are follow-up studies needed, but it should be determined whether reduced ethnocentrism leads to a reduction in acts of prejudice. For example, a qualitative study of the effects of an anthropology course in a school or classroom with racial discord would be an important contribution.

Few relationships have been drawn between anthropology and citizenship education. How do they relate? Should they? Can they? Research on teaching and learning anthropology in school is nearly nonexistent.

SOCIOLOGY

The earliest years of sociology were characterized by a concern for social welfare, particularly at the University of Chicago where sociology first flourished as a discipline. A number of sociologists were members of the 1916 Committee on the Social Studies, and the report of that committee reflects a greater emphasis on social problems than before (Lybarger, 1980). However, relatively little direct sociology instruction was recommended. The American Sociological Association (ASA) (which succeeded the American Sociological Society) has since 1919 (except for the period 1934 to 1944) had some committee concerned with sociology in secondary schools (Grier, 1972). Nevertheless, Switzer (1986) argued there is "general disinterest in precollegiate education by professionals in the field of sociology" (p. 124).

Considerable growth in student interest in sociology has been evident over the past 10 years. In 1973, 582,000 students were enrolled in sociology courses (4.9% of total student enrollment) in U.S. high schools (NCES, 1984). Nine years later, that number had nearly tripled, with 1,602,000 students (12.7% of total secondary enrollment) enrolled in sociology classes. However, in a study of the utilization of New Social Studies curriculum programs, Turner and Haley (1977) found that "only 89 of the 980 responding social studies teachers indicated that they were teaching sociology" and of those 89, only 32 were using materials from the Sociological Resources for the Social Studies (SRSS) new social studies projects (p. 72). Switzer (1986) claimed that "very little from the formal discipline of sociology is usually taught in K–12 classrooms in the U.S." (p. 134). Generally, textbooks deal with either problems of communities and societies or problems of persons and small groups (p. 128).

Grier (1972), in an historical analysis of sociology courses in American secondary schools, described seven objectives or values that sociology had promoted in its 50-year history. Based on his research, he stated that the potential impact of sociology was great, but not as taught. Changes in content during 50 years of sociology teaching included a decline in treatments of heredity, immigration, poverty, and "defectives." Grier concluded that sociology courses overemphasized social problems and that the teachers were poorly prepared.

The research on sociology in social studies education, much like that on anthropology, can be divided into three areas: (a) status studies—of little interest in this review, (b) studies on the teaching and learning of the content of sociology, and (c) problems or issues related to materials' use or teacher training.

Teaching and Learning Sociology

The research in the teaching of sociology has been largely investigations of SRSS, one of the New Social Studies projects of the 1960s and 1970s. A few other studies on sociology instruction were located. SRSS was developed by the 1961 Committee on Social Studies in the Schools of the American Sociological Association. The project was funded in 1964 and continued until 1971 (Switzer, 1986). Descriptions are available of SRSS (Switzer & Wilson, 1969), the development of the materials (Switzer 1986), the decline of SRSS (Angell, 1981), and an evaluation of the project (Haley, 1972). Problems that Switzer and Wilson (1969) saw in the SRSS materials were: (a) rigidity in structure and sequence, (b) a pretense of an inductive mode but actually being manipulative, and (c) variations in teacher competence (pp. 348–349).

In 1972, Haley noted that no evaluative data were available on SRSS. She viewed the project materials as having a high level of affective content, scientifically solid cognitive content, and excellent sociological skill development. She noted, however, that "careful preparation and skillful handling by the teacher is necessary to convince students of the importance of dealing scientifically with issues that are often highly personal and affective" (p. 766).

Research on Materials Usage

Smith (1980) performed a content analysis on sociology materials in use before, during, and following the period of the New Social Studies. Directing special attention to SRSS, he concluded those curriculum materials had little lasting influence, directly or indirectly, on the teaching materials used in sociology in high schools.

Robert Angell (1981), a sociologist who had helped develop the SRSS materials, suggested that the decline of their use was directly linked to: (a) a lack of further funding for development; (b) tight money in schools, and (c) the lack of continued contact between teachers and sociologists (p. 41). Switzer (1986) suggested that social studies methods instructors were unaware of SRSS and thus failed to expose preservice teachers to the new curricular materials (p. 136). In a 1974 study of social studies teachers in five states (Michigan, Ohio, Illinois, Indiana, and Wisconsin), Switzer, Lowther, Hanna, and Kidder (1977) found that only 30% of 252 social studies teachers had heard of the SRSS materials. In a 1977 study, Switzer, Walker, and Mitchell (1981) reported that of 301 undergraduate social studies methods instructors in 13 states, only 60% had heard of SRSS, and only 45% of those told their students about the project materials.

Earlier, Switzer (1974) had noted the inadequate preparation of teachers in sociology and in teaching techniques appropriate for sociology. However, he posited three factors that should make SRSS acceptable to teachers: (a) ease of modifying the course to fit specific teaching situations, (b) ease of modifying the course to fit the school schedule, and (c) student interest.

PSYCHOLOGY

Psychology emerged during the 1830s as a separate course of study in American secondary schools and academies (Louttit, 1956; Noland, 1966). By 1981–1982, 656,000 students were enrolled in psychology courses offered in 58.7% of U.S. high schools, a figure less than sociology (81.6%, but more than anthropology (11.7%) (NCES, 1984). This growth from 140,377 in 1961 represented an increase of 367%. The growth in the number of schools offering psychology courses and students enrolled in these courses was steadily linear from the 1930s through the early 1980s (Bare, 1986; Ostendorf, 1976). Of special note, during the period from 1961 to 1981, psychology was the fastest growing elective course for social studies credit in U.S. secondary schools (Stahl & Matiya, 1981).

The research on psychology as a school subject can be divided into three major categories: (a) the characteristics of psychology courses in schools, (b) the characteristics of psychology teachers and students, and (c) teaching and learning in psychology classes. Only the last is discussed here.

Teaching and Learning in Psychology Courses

Although psychology is among the courses most often taken for social studies credit, it is among the least researched courses in the precollege curriculum. Over the years, two basic and seemingly divergent approaches to the teaching of psychology on the precollege level have existed. The first of these to emerge historically was the discipline-centered or "scientific" approach aimed at preparing students for college courses; the second is "humanistically" and personal adjustment-oriented, designed to be more relevant and practical to a broad spectrum of adolescents (Goldman, 1983; Kasschau & Werheimer, 1974). Within the past decade, the academic, discipline-oriented approach has prevailed, partly due to a decline in the humanistic and affective focus in many school programs and to the back-to-basics movement, in which content is stressed over personal adjustment as a primary focus of school efforts.

In the past two decades, studies have been conducted to measure the effects of numerous affectively oriented psychology curricula. Working alone and with various associates, Sprinthall, a leading proponent of deliberate psychological education within the precollege curriculum, proposed that psychology be taught as personal development (e.g., Mosher & Sprinthall, 1970; Sprinthall & Erickson, 1974). Data from efforts to implement this type of course led to revisions in the academic content, teaching methods, and learning activities. Working with the Minneapolis Public Schools, Sprinthall and his associates at the University of Minnesota implemented a seminar-practicum format to teach psychology (Chiosso, 1976; Erickson, 1977; Fink, 1973). In a review of the findings from efforts to develop and implement this approach to helping students personalize psychology, Sprinthall (1980) criticized the content-acquisition model of teaching psychology. He reported that on two psychological growth variables, ego development and moral maturity, adolescents who had deliberate psychological education improved more than did randomized control groups.

Attempts to evaluate effectiveness were included in the majority of the affective education secondary level courses and programs in which psychology was used as the vehicle (Goldman, 1983). Dependent variables were such constructs as self-concept, moral maturity, risk taking, and interpersonal skills. Small groups of students were assessed following often indirect, low-potency intervention for a few hours a week over a maximum of 18 weeks. The researchers reported minimal change or growth, rare instances of statistically significant changes, no statistically significant changes, or some of all three on the different dependent measures (e.g., Graff & Beggs, 1974; Hoffman, 1973; Rappaport & Sorenson, 1971; Rustad & Rogers, 1975; Sprinthall, 1980). These findings supported the conclusion of Kasschau and Wertheimer (1974), reiterated by Rest (1977), that although the teaching of psychology to encourage students' personal adjustment and development has many strong advocates, research on programs in developmental psychology designed to implement this approach have not furnished adequate evidence of impact.

In 1970, the American Psychological Association (APA) received a National Science Foundation (NSF) grant for the Human Behavior Curriculum Project (HBCP), for which John Bare served as project director. The developers of HBCP stressed the application of principles of behavior to their lives by students. The curriculum materials were developed by a team consisting of a psychologist, two teachers, and two students. A two- to three-week module format was used, with teachers selecting the number and sequence of modules they would use. Besides being tested locally by the development teams and the project leaders and revised as necessary, the modules were field tested nationally by teacher volunteers. In 1981, Teachers College Press published the 8 finished modules of the 30 that had originally been planned. Although data were collected to meet NSF guidelines, the results were never published. Even though social studies teachers were involved in this project at different levels, the extent to which the modules were tried out and worked or did not work in psychology-for-social-studies-credit classrooms was not reported in the literature.

No reports were found of research on the effects on student academic achievement and affect variables of teaching particular psychological concepts and principles, of using particular teaching methods, or of teaching specific content or material as part of a discipline- and scientific-oriented course in psychology. This is not to suggest that such courses do not exist or that students are not provided opportunities to learn extensive psychological information using a wide range of methods, activities, and approaches. There are, however, few available data about what is actually occurring and what students are learning in such classes. In three studies of long-term impact, students who took a high school psychology course had essentially the same mean score on the final exam in a freshman introductory psychology course as students who did not have psychology in high school (Carstens & Beck, 1986; Dambrot & Popplestone, 1975; Federici & Schuerger, 1976). Students who had the course in high school did have a higher pretest mean score although not at a statistically significant level. In short, there is little research evidence on psychology on the precollege level, regardless of the approach taken by the curriculum or teacher.

Conclusions

While abundant survey data about the characteristics of psychology courses, teachers, and students are available, findings on actual classroom instruction and learning outcomes are virtually nonexistent. Meanwhile, the APA and commercial publishers continue to advocate materials and activities that ought to work to improve the curriculum and instruction. Research on the effects of psychology instruction is badly needed.

CLOSING COMMENTS

A review of the research revealed very little about the teaching and learning of anthropology, sociology, and psychology in precollege courses. There are extensive survey studies in the area of psychology; however, well-constructed studies of attempts to implement K–12 curriculum and instruction in these areas are virtually nonexistent.

One of the reasons for the lack of research by social studies educators may be the obvious and long-standing disinterest in the teaching of anthropology, sociology, and psychology on the part of many social studies professionals. For instance, major efforts to rethink the social studies scope and sequence over the past decade, such as the Bradley Commission (1988) report on history in the schools, and James Madison High School developed by then Secretary of Education William Bennett (1987), have stressed the traditional history orientation with provision for geography and political science (i.e., civics and the Constitution), with economics receiving some attention. Concepts, objectives, and topics that are specifically anthropological, sociological, or psychological in nature have not been of prime concern to these decision makers.

It may be a mistake to view the research that has been reported as being "research in the social studies." The only thing "social studies" about many of these studies is that the courses were taught by teachers assigned to a social studies department and given social studies credit, or that the materials were, in nearly every instance, assumed to fit into or replace existing social studies units, materials, or topics. In other words, are anthropology, sociology, and psychology courses, units, and materials generally thought to be a part of social studies, or are they accepted only by particular teachers in particular situations? As a frequent conductor of status surveys of precollege psychology, one of the coauthors of this chapter, Stahl, has found that teachers of these courses rarely mention objectives, goals, or topics that indicate they considered, planned, or perceived their course in light of objectives posited by the National Council for the Social Studies or even their local district or state social studies curriculum guides.

Needed Research

Research is needed to determine if citizenship knowledge, understanding, or practice are enhanced, diminished, or unaffected by participation in anthropology, sociology, or psychology courses. Much would be added to our understanding of these courses if more qualitative, naturalistic research techniques were utilized. The use of ethnography as a research technique has grown dramatically in the past 10 years. This type of research study applied to the school teaching of anthropology, sociology, and psychology would give social studies educators a much better picture of how these social studies areas are taught. Recent dissertation studies at Stanford University have provided ideas of how teachers think about their social studies teaching (Gudmundsdottir & Shulman, 1987), but the focus of such observational work must be broadened.

Questions to be addressed include whether students in anthropology are involved in ethnographic studies, or do they only read about them? Are these same students evaluated using ethnographic techniques? If students only engage in read-lecture-discuss work in anthropology, is the meaningfulness of the work in the discipline implicitly questioned or disparaged, with the result lack of respect for the field? So, too, with sociology. Is field study a part of sociology courses? Do sociology courses ease (or seek to ease) role conflict in schools or among youngsters? Is there really assessment of the socialization process; or is this, too, just mentioned in lectures? Regarding psychology: Is it taught using clinical case data and analysis; or is this subject, too, predominantly addressed in a lecture-read-discussion format? What are the purposes that teachers have in teaching psychology, and are those purposes actually met or even addressed? Clearly, the role of these social sciences in the social studies curriculum merits examination with high-quality research.

References

Angell, R. C. (1981). Reflections on the project, Sociological Resources for the Social Studies. *The American Sociologist, 16,* 41–43.

Barber, B. R. (1989). Public talk and civic action: Education for participation in a strong democracy. *Social Education, 53,* 355–356, 370.

Bare, J. K. (1986). Teaching psychology in the high schools. In S. P. Wronski and D. H. Bragaw (Eds.), *Social studies and social sciences: A fifty-year perspective.* (pp. 179–188). Washington, DC: National Council for the Social Studies.

Barnes, B. (1973). The effects of the position of organizers to facilitate learning of structured anthropology materials in the sixth grade (Doctoral dissertation, University of Georgia, 1971). *Dissertation Abstracts International, 33,* 5027A–5028A.

Barnes, B., Stallings, W., & Rivner, R. (1981). Are the critics right about MACOS? *Theory and Research in Social Education, 9*(1), 35–44.

Bennett, W. J. (1987). *James Madison High School: A curriculum for American students.* Washington, DC: U.S. Department of Education.

Bradley Commission on History in the Schools (1988). *Building a curriculum: Guidelines for teaching history in the schools.* Washington, DC: Educational Excellence Network.

Carstens, C. B., & Beck, H. P. (1986). The relationship of high school psychology and natural science courses to performance in a college introductory psychology course. *Teaching of Psychology, 13*(3), 116–118.

Chiosso, E. T. (1976). A high school curriculum in interpersonal relations: A deliberate psychological education intervention (Doctoral dissertation, University of Minnesota, 1976). *Dissertation Abstracts International, 37,* 3372A.

Clawson, E. (1973). A comparison of the effects of organizers on the learning of structured anthropology materials in the third grade (Doctoral dissertation, University of Georgia, 1972). *Dissertation Abstracts International, 33,* 4788A.

Dacanay, A., Jr. (1977). Teaching anthropology as science at the junior high school level. *Anthropology and Education Quarterly, 8*(1), 19–22.

Dambrot, F. H., & Popplestone, J. A. (1975). High school psychology revisited: Student performance in a college-level psychology course. *Journal of School Psychology, 13,* 129–133.

Dwyer-Shick, S. (1976). *The study and teaching of anthropology: An annotated bibliography.* Athens, GA: Anthropology Curriculum Project, University of Georgia.

Dwyer-Shick, S. (1977). The development of the academic study and teaching of anthropology. *Anthropology and Education Quarterly, 8*(1), 1–7.

Dynneson, T. (1981). The status of pre-collegiate anthropology: Progress or peril. *Anthropology and Education Quarterly, 12*(4), 304–309.

Dynneson, T. (1986). Trends in precollegiate anthropology. In S. Wronski and D. Bragaw (Eds.), *Social studies and social sciences: A fifty year perspective* (pp. 153–163). Washington, DC: National Council for the Social Studies.

Engle, S., & Ochoa, A. (1988). *Education for democratic citizenship.* New York: Teachers College Press.

Erickson, V. A. (1977). Deliberate psychological education for women. *Counseling Psychologist, 6*(4), 25–29.

Federici, L., & Schuerger, J. M. (1976). High school psychology students versus non-high school psychology students in a college introductory class. *Teaching of Psychology, 3*(4), 172–174.

Feer, M. (1976). Anthroplogy at Lincoln-Sudbury Regional High School. *Anthropology and Education Quarterly, 7*(1), 4–6.

Fink, A. M. (1973). Application of social learning principles to a high school psychology of adjustment curriculum: Effects of extra-classroom behavior (Doctoral dissertation, University of Minnesota, 1973). *Dissertation Abstracts International, 34,* 2302B.

Frech, W. (1974). An analysis of the effect of the anthropology curriculum project material, *The Concept of Culture,* on the ethnocentric attitudes of fourth grade students (Doctoral dissertation, University of Georgia, 1973). *Dissertation Abstracts International, 34,* 3830A-3831A.

Goldman, J. J. (1983). Recent trends in secondary school psychology: The decade from Oberlin to the HBCP. *Psychological Documents, 13*(2), MS 2529.

Graff, R. W., & Beggs, D. L. (1974). Personal and vocational development in high school students. *Journal of School Psychology, 12,* 17–23.

Grier, W. (1972). The history of the teaching of sociology in the secondary school. (Doctoral dissertation, Duke University, 1971). *Dissertation Abstracts International, 34,* 5580A.

Gudmundsdottir, S., & Shulman, L. (1987). Pedagogical content knowledge in social studies. *Scandinavian Journal of Educational Research, 31,* 59–70.

Haley, F. (1972). Sociological Resources for the Social Studies. *Social Education, 36,* 765–767.

Hanley, J. P., Whitta, D. K., Moo, E. W., & Walter, A. S. (1970). *Curiosity, competence, community—Man: A Course of Study, an evaluation.* Cambridge, MA: Education Development Center.

Hoffman, D. (1973). Teaching self-understanding for productive living. *NASSP Bulletin, 57*(370), 74–79.

Hunt, A. (1970). Anthropology achievement of normal and disadvantaged kindergarten youngsters (Doctoral dissertation, University of Georgia, 1969). *Dissertation Abstracts International, 30,* 5166A.

Kasschau, R. A., & Wertheimer, M. (1974). *Teaching psychology in secondary schools.* Washington, DC: American Psychological Association; Boulder, CO: ERIC Clearinghouse for Social Studies/Social Science Education.

Lanouette, J. (1985). High school anthropology texts: Sound the alarm! *Anthropology and Education Quarterly, 16*(4), 331–336.

Louttit, C. M. (1956). Psychology in nineteenth century high schools. *American Psychologist, 11,* 717.

Lybarger, M. (1980). The political context of the social studies: Creating a constituency for municipal reform. *Theory and Research in Social Education, 8*(8), 1–28.

Mattson, P. H., & Abshire-Walker, T. (1976). An experiment in education: Anthropology workshops for public school teachers. *Anthropology and Education Quarterly, 7*(1), 22–24.

Mosher, R. A., & Sprinthall, N. A. (1970). Psychological education in secondary schools: A program to promote individual and human development. *American Psychologist, 25,* 911–924.

National Center for Education Statistics. (1984). *A trend study for high school offerings and enrollments: 1972–73 and 1981–82* (Document No. ED 1.115H53/5). Washington, DC: U.S. Government Printing Office.

Noland, R. L. (1966). A century of psychology in American secondary schools. *Journal of Secondary Education, 41,* 247–254.

Ostendorf, L. (1976). *Summary of offerings and enrollments in public secondary schools 1972–73* (Document No. HE 19.334, 1972–73: NCES 76-150). Washington, DC: National Center for Education Statistics.

Pennsylvania Department of Education. (1969). *The concept of culture.* Harrisburg, PA: Author.

Rappaport, J., & Sorensen, J. (1971). Teaching psychology to "disadvantaged" youth: Enhancing the relevance of psychology through public education. *Journal of School Psychology, 9,* 120–126.

Remy, R. C. (1980). *Handbook of citizenship competencies.* Alexandria, VA: Association for Supervision and Development.

Rest, J. E. (1977). Comments on the Deliberate Psychological Education Program and the Toronto Moral Education Programs in secondary education. *Counseling Psychologist, 6*(4), 32–34.

Rustad, K., & Rogers, C. (1975). Promoting psychological growth in a high school class. *Counselor Education and Supervision, 14,* 277–285.

Smith, D. W. (1980). Assessing the impact of the "new social studies" upon school curriculum: A case study of high school sociology (Doctoral dissertation, Northwestern University, 1979). *Dissertation Abstracts International, 40,* 5393A-5394A.

Sprinthall, N. A. (1980). Psychology for the secondary schools. The saber-tooth curriculum revisited? *American Psychologist, 35,* 336–347.

Sprinthall, N. A., & Erickson, V. L. (1974). Learning psychology by doing psychology: Guidance through the curriculum. *Personnel and Guidance Journal, 52,* 396–405.

Stahl, R. J., & Matiya, J. C. (1981). Teaching psychology in the high school: Does area of certification translate into different types of teachers and courses? *Theory and Research in Social Education, 9*(2), 172–174.

Switzer, T. (1974). Factors associated with adoption and rejection of the course, *Inquiries in Sociology* by teachers who participated in its classroom evaluation (Doctoral dissertation, University of Michigan, 1973). *Dissertation Abstracts International, 34,* 4720A-4721A.

Switzer, T. (1986). Teaching sociology in K–12 classrooms. In S. Wronski and D. Bragaw (Eds.), *Social studies and social sciences: A fifty year perspective* (pp. 124–138). Washington, DC: National Council for the Social Studies.

Switzer, T., Lowther, M., Hannah, W., & Kidder, R. (1977). Dissemination and implementation of social studies materials. In C. Hahn, G. Marker, T. Switzer, & M. J. Turner (Eds.), *Three studies on perception and utilization of "New Social Studies" materials.* Boulder, CO: Social Science Education Consortium.

Switzer, T., Walker, E., & Mitchell, G. (1981). Undergraduate social studies methods instructors knowledge and use of new curricular materials. *Journal of Social Studies Research,* (5), 9–18.

Switzer, T., & Wilson, E. K. (1969, February). Nobody knows the trouble we've seen: Launching a high school sociology course. *Phi Delta Kappan, 50,* 346–350.

Turner, M. J., & Haley, F. (1977). Utilization of "new social studies" curriculum programs. In C. Hahn, G. Marker, T. Switzer, & M. J. Turner (Eds.), *Three studies on perception and utilization of "New Social Studies" materials.* Boulder, CO: Social Science Education Consortium.

·35·

TEACHING GOVERNMENT, CIVICS, AND LAW

John J. Patrick

INDIANA UNIVERSITY

John D. Hoge

UNIVERSITY OF GEORGIA

Teaching government in schools has been important in the United States since the founding of the republic. President George Washington reflected the views of his era when he endorsed

the education of our Youth in the science of Government. In a Republic, what species of knowledge can be equally important? And what duty more pressing on the Legislature, than to patronize a plan for communicating it to those, who are to be the future guardians of the liberties of the Country. (Eighth Annual Address to Congress, December 7, 1796)

From Washington's time to our own, schools have had the mission of inducting "future guardians of the liberties of the Country" into the civic culture. In line with this tradition, elementary and secondary schools have educated students in the interrelated subjects of government, civics (citizenship), and law. Teachers have used these three subjects separately and conjunctively to give students alternative and overlapping views of the institutions, principles, and values of constitutional democracy in the United States.

What does the scholarly literature reveal about the teaching and learning of government, civics, and law today—almost 200 years after President Washington's advice to Congress and the American people on "the education of our Youth"? This chapter provides a synthesis of findings on (a) curriculum patterns, (b) contents of the curriculum as indicated by widely used textbooks, (c) patterns of student learning, and (d) effects of schools on what students learn.

CURRICULUM PATTERNS IN GOVERNMENT, CIVICS, AND LAW

Expectations about teaching and learning are revealed by curriculum patterns and trends. What has been the place of government, civics, and law among our educational priorities of the past and present? What is the current status of these subjects in the school curriculum?

Curriculum Patterns in Historical Perspective

The ancestry of today's secondary school courses in civics and government can be traced directly to activities of the American Political Science Association (APSA) and the National Education Association (NEA) during the early years of this century. The APSA, founded in 1903, quickly became concerned about the teaching of government and civics and established three different committees in 1908, 1916, and 1921 to study the curriculum and make recommendations for improving it. The NEA organized the Commission on the Reorganization of Secondary Education in 1913, which included a Committee on Social Studies. Unlike the APSA committees, the NEA worked for comprehensive curriculum reform, including civics and government (Tryon, 1935, pp. 5–49).

In its 1916 report, *The Social Studies in Secondary Education,* the NEA Committee argued that the overriding goal of social studies is education for citizenship, and courses in civics, government, and problems of democracy should be keystones

Reviewers were Richard C. Remy, The Ohio State University; Mary Jane Turner, Close Up Foundation.

of the new curriculum. These new courses were supposed to be "concerned less with constitutional questions and remote governmental functions and should direct attention to social agencies close at hand and to the informal activities of daily life that regard and seek the common good" (Committee on Social Studies, 1916, p. 52).

The American Political Science Association's Committee of Seven (1916) issued a report, *The Teaching of Government*, which declared its commitment to "education for citizenship and public service and . . . to personal participation in public affairs" (p. 2). This APSA report reinforced the NEA recommendations, and these two reports shaped the scope and sequence of the emerging government-civics curriculum. The report of the 1921 APSA Committee on Civics Instruction in High School generally supported the work of its predecessors, but it also urged substantial treatment of the institutions of constitutional government in concert with studies of citizenship in local communities (Tryon, 1935, pp. 46–49).

During the 1920s, educators throughout the United States established junior high school courses in civics (usually at the 8th or 9th grades) and in government (usually at the 12th grade) that tended to follow the NEA and APSA guidelines, including those of the 1921 APSA committee (Quillen, 1966, pp. 255–256; Tryon, 1935, p. 49). Courses in civics emphasized the rights and responsibilities of citizens and their relationships to one another and to the government. Courses in government treated the political and legal institutions and constitutional principles of the United States. Public issues and social trends were emphasized in schools that combined the study of American government with problems of democracy (Tryon, 1935, pp. 242–281).

The curriculum patterns of the 1920s persisted into the 1950s, as evidenced by a report of the American Political Science Association that proclaimed development of democratic citizenship the predominant goal of education in political science and government (APSA, 1951). Different ideas, however, took shape during the 1960s and 1970s—the so-called "era of the New Social Studies"—which temporarily brought the illusion of profound curriculum reform (Haas, 1977).

A new APSA Committee on Pre-Collegiate Education (1971) recommended "political science education in elementary and secondary schools" that would emphasize (a) "knowledge about political behavior and processes", (b) "skill in the process of social science inquiry", and (c) "skills needed to participate effectively and democratically in the life of the society" (pp. 4–5). New courses in American political behavior and comparative political systems were developed through federally-funded projects and implemented widely, for a brief time (Hertzberg, 1981, pp. 126–142). However, use of the New Social Studies materials in government and politics declined near the end of the 1970s. Many teachers who had moved away from the dominant approaches to teaching government or civics returned to them.

As the New Social Studies moved out of favor, a new curricular force gained momentum—law-related education (LRE). The American Bar Association had established committees on citizenship education in the 1920s, which promoted education about the U.S. Constitution (Tryon, 1935, pp. 58–64). However, the current LRE movement is rooted in the 1970s and a broad view of its mission. According to its founders, law-related education is "those organized learning experiences that provide students and educators with opportunities to develop the knowledge and understanding, skills, attitudes and appreciations necessary to respond effectively to the law and legal issues in our complex and changing society" (Study Group on Law-Related Education, 1978, p. 50). The overriding goal of the LRE leaders has been education for citizenship in a constitutional democracy, not specialized legal education.

For the most part, LRE has entered the curriculum through infusion into standard units of instruction in elementary social studies (grades K–6) and in such secondary school courses as civics, government, and American history. Elective courses in law-related education also have been developed for secondary school students (Gallagher, 1987).

Curriculum Patterns of the 1980s

A nationwide survey of state social studies specialists (Hahn, 1985) revealed that, since 1975, LRE had been added to the curriculum in more than half of the respondents. 46 states. LRE was mentioned more frequently than other topics as having been added to the social studies curriculum since 1975. The state specialists also ranked LRE 4th as a priority in social studies education in 1985; it had ranked 11th in 1975. The results of a recent national curriculum survey (Council of State Social Studies Specialists, 1986) indicated that courses in LRE are offered widely as electives in about 40% of the 50 states plus the District of Columbia. As of 1988, in no state had an LRE course been mandated as a requirement for graduation from high school.

The study of government or civics, however, is required for graduation from high school in about 70% of the 50 states plus the District of Columbia (Council of State Social Studies Specialists, 1986; Eckenrod, 1987, pp. 3–8). In addition, courses in civics or government tend to be offered as electives in the school districts of states that do not require them for graduation; and in many schools of these states, these courses are required (Council of State Social Studies Specialists, 1986; Eckenrod, 1987).

During the 1980s, the high school government or civics course (mostly offered at grade 12) has maintained the secure place gained in the curriculum during the 1920s and 1930s. By contrast, civics has fallen from the prominent position it occupied in Grades 7 to 9 from the 1920s through the 1950s. A seventh-, eighth-, or ninth-grade civics course is required in only about 20% of the 50 states, and it is a prevalent elective in less than 30% of them (Council of State Social Studies Specialists, 1986; Eckenrod, 1987, pp. 8–11). Less than 40% of U.S. students in Grades 7 to 9 are enrolled annually in civics courses (Eckenrod, 1987, p. 12).

Ideas and facts in government, civics, and law are woven into the multisubject social studies curricula of elementary schools. Attention to these subjects has increased at the expense of content in the social and behavioral sciences (Council of State Social Studies Specialists, 1986).

Current curriculum patterns indicate a secure place for government, civics, and law in elementary and secondary schools. These subjects invariably have been included in the core curriculum recommendations of the 1980s educational reform reports. Curriculum reformers of the 1980s have emphatically argued for core content, essential subjects that all students should learn. For example, Ernest Boyer stated a widely-shared position in his 1983 report on secondary education in the United States: "A core of common learning is essential. The basic curriculum should be a study of those consequential ideas, experiences, and traditions common to all of us" (p. 302). Boyer recommended that the high school core curriculum include a one-year course in American government (pp. 104–105).

Other major curriculum reform reports of the 1980s have supported a required high school course in government and promoted infusion of content in government, civics, and law throughout the social studies curricula of elementary and secondary schools, especially in units and courses on history and geography (Bennett, 1986, 1987; Butts, 1980, 1988; History-Social Science Curriculum Framework and Criteria Committee, 1988). William J. Bennett's (1987) model curriculum for high schools includes a one-semester course in "Principles of American Democracy" and a one-semester course in "American Democracy and the World" (pp. 19–20). Bennett's (1986) model elementary school curriculum in the social studies is organized around the interrelated subjects of civics, geography, and history (pp. 28–29).

The Education for Democracy Project (1987) of the American Federation of Teachers has been especially concerned about the infusion of civics into the study of American history and world history (p. 7). There is an emphatic call for teaching the civic values of a constitutional democracy at all grades of elementary and secondary schools. A course in American government is also proposed for the high school core curriculum (p. 20).

The 1980s curriculum reform literature also includes exciting proposals and examples of school-based programs for civic learning through participation in the community outside the school. Although reminiscent of progressive education in the 1920s and 1930s, these experiential education programs fit 1980s thinking about learning through participation in concert with solid academic foundations. They seem to avoid an excessive emphasis on social utility at the expense of intellectual development (Boyer, 1983, pp. 306–307; Janowitz, 1983, pp. 170–191).

In 1988, two major projects were launched: (a) *CIVITAS,* the civics curriculum framework project of the Council for the Advancement of Citizenship and the Center for Civic Education, and (b) *Our Democracy: How America Works,* the civics curriculum development project of the Foundation for Teaching Economics and the Constitutional Rights Foundation. These projects suggest that the teaching of government, civics, and law in schools is likely to remain at the top of the curriculum improvement agenda in the near future.

TEXTBOOK CONTENT IN GOVERNMENT, CIVICS, AND LAW

Curriculum reform reports and guides reveal expectations about teaching government, civics, and law in schools. Widely used textbooks, however, are the best indicators of what is taught in the typical classroom (Patrick & Hawke, 1982, pp. 39–40).

This discussion of textbook contents is based on selected studies of elementary and secondary school textbooks, and reviews of such studies, conducted from the 1960s through the 1980s (Anyon, 1978; Carrol et al., 1987; Harrington, 1980; Janowitz, 1983; Joyce, 1967; Katz, 1985; Larkins, Hawkins & Gilmore, 1987; Massialas, 1967; Patrick & Hawke, 1982; Price, 1966; Remy, 1981; Shaver, 1965; Smith & Patrick, 1967; Taylor & Birchell, 1983). The findings in these studies are indicative of what is, and is not, emphasized in the teaching of government, civics, and law in elementary and secondary schools and how the textbooks of today compare to those of the 1960s.

General Content Characteristics

Widely used textbooks reflect national curriculum patterns as indicated by state-level curriculum guides. Thus, publishers produce textbooks on American government for older high school students and on civics for use in the eighth or ninth grades (Patrick & Hawke, 1982, p. 44).

Widely used elementary school textbooks from different publishers are remarkably similar. The textbooks and teacher's guides are filled with statements about civic traditions, norms, patriotic rituals, conformity to rules and laws, and other facets of dutiful social behavior. Prescriptions about good citizenship are emphasized to the point of redundancy (Larkins, et al., 1987).

Secondary school textbooks in government and civics are largely compendiums of information about institutions of American government, political processes, and the rights and responsibilities of citizenship. Core principles of constitutional government in the United States are included, such as federalism, separation of powers, checks and balances, and representative democracy. Differences in these books are slight, more degrees of variation than distinctions in types of subject-matter treatments (Carroll et al., 1987).

Elementary and secondary school textbooks are designed for passive learning, transmission of facts and ideas rather than active involvement of learners in the pursuit of knowledge. Many topics, terms, and facts are mentioned, but few, if any, are developed in detail. Superficial survey of subject matter, not in-depth treatment of critical issues or key ideas, is the prevailing style (Carroll et al., 1987; Larkins et al., 1987).

The textbooks at all levels of schooling tend to be supportive of the status quo. Critical or alternative views of government and civic traditions in the United States tend to be missing from elementary textbooks and downplayed in secondary materials. Bland, matter-of-fact presentations of content and the absence of controversy are hallmarks of treatments of government, civics, and law in schoolbooks (Carroll et al., 1987; Larkins et al., 1987).

General Criticisms of Widely Used Textbooks

A 1966 review of textbooks began with the statement that "the entire teaching profession is presently being assaulted by an avalanche of criticism particularly related to the quality of textbooks being used in the schools" (Price, 1966, p. 21). Common criticisms of high school civics and government textbooks pertained to (a) superficial and simplistic coverage of material, (b) abstract or lifeless treatment of ideas and events, (c) idealistic and unrealistic presentations of society, (d) fragmentation of subject matter, (e) avoidance of controversial topics or issues, (f) emphasis on low-level cognition in questions and activities for learners, (g) unattractive format and design, and (h) misrepresentation or avoidance of content on ethnic and racial minorities and women in the civic life of the United States.

These common criticisms of the 1960s texts have tended to be repeated in the 1980s, with two exceptions. First, textbooks today tend to be much more attractive in format and design, especially in use of graphics. Second, textbooks of the 1980s are more likely to reflect the ethnic and racial diversity and social pluralism of the United States. However, some critics have judged 1980s textbooks to be excessive in their emphasis on social pluralism and cultural diversity and deficient in their treatments of national unity and the common good (Glazer & Ueda, 1983, pp. 57–64; Harrington 1980; Janowitz 1983, pp. 91–105).

Civics content in the typical 1980s elementary social studies series has been judged to be too thin, too supportive of the status quo, and deficient in treatments of democratic values. Widely used texts focus mainly on respect for rules, laws, and authorities, almost to the exclusion of democratic rights and liberties (Harrington, 1980; Larkins et al., 1987; Taylor & Birchell, 1983).

Secondary school textbooks in civics and government were roundly criticized in a comprehensive 1987 study sponsored by the People for the American Way (Carroll et al., 1987). The reviewers castigated widely used textbooks for their mediocre content. In particular, they faulted most of the books for lacking a sound sequence of topics and ideas, covering too much information, avoiding in-depth discussions of important ideas and events, glossing over or omitting controversial topics, and failing to emphasize the crucial role of citizen participation in a democracy. The biggest criticism, however, was dull presentation of subject matter. In the judgment of these reviewers, inherently interesting subjects—politics, applications of law to daily life, public issues, governmental decision making, citizen action in community affairs—were shorn of drama and excitement by tedious and simplistic prose presented in rigid formats.

Criticisms of Treatments of Specific Topics or Themes

Textbook studies focusing on particular topics or themes have shed additional light on weaknesses of content in typical secondary school courses in civics and government. Two valuable studies of textbook treatments of the U.S. Constitution were done in recognition of the Bicentennial (Katz, 1985; Remy, 1981).

Katz reported that the five high school government texts in his study included mostly "dry institutional descriptions" with only slight attention to political processes, ideas, and issues. Federalism, for example, was treated mainly as a set of legal relationships with scant attention to federal-state relationships

and little discussion of the theory underlying this core principle of the Constitution.

Remy's study of 10 textbooks (5 ninth-grade civics texts and 5 high school government books) revealed such common weaknesses as superficial treatment of Supreme Court decisions, failure to show how the Constitution influences or limits actions of government officials, and shallow discussion of core constitutional principles. Remy concluded that the texts were virtually devoid of detailed treatments of fundamental ideas, such as constitutional government, federalism, and democracy.

Treatments of limits to growth issues were examined in 63 secondary school textbooks, including 5 civics texts (Newitt, 1983). Newitt concluded that the texts presented one-sided discussions of population growth, worldwide production and distribution of food, use of energy resources, pollution of the environment, and industrial development. In general, the textbooks emphasized arguments for government policies that would limit economic growth and excluded or deemphasized alternative positions on the economic future of the United States and other areas of the world.

Most civics and government textbooks have been criticized for failure to attend systematicaly to development of higher-order cognitive processes and skills, such as decision making and critical thinking. These criticisms have been highlighted in studies conducted in the 1960s and 1980s (Carroll et al., 1987; Shaver, 1965; Smith & Patrick, 1967). In 1965, Shaver found—in an exhaustive review of virtually all available civics and government texts—that the books lacked clear and systematic models to guide development of reflective thinking and provided few, if any, opportunities for the exercise of reflective or critical capacities. Most books relied on simple exhortations to think critically rather than provision of learning activites to develop the intellectual capacities needed to respond thoughtfully to public issues. Weak textbook treatments of critical thinking and other higher-level cognitive processes have persisted through the 1980s (Carroll et al., 1987).

The preceding synthesis of textbook studies highlights major weaknesses in the contents of government, civics, and law in the curricula of schools. Are these weaknesses in presentation of subject matter reflected in studies of students' knowledge, attitudes, values, and skills?

CIVIC LEARNING: KNOWLEDGE, ATTITUDES AND VALUES, SKILLS

Civic learning refers to knowledge, attitudes and values, and skills (cognitive and participatory) about government, civics, and law. What are the achievements of students in these categories of civic learning?

This discussion of civic learning is based on the following sources: (a) the most recent and relevant reports of NAEP—the National Assessment of Educational Progress (1976, 1983, 1987); (b) nationwide surveys conducted by the Center for Civic Education [CCE] (1987), the Hearst Corporation (1987), and the National Assessment of Secondary School Principals [NASSP] (1984); (c) international studies involving representative samples of American youth (Dalton, 1988; Torney, Oppenheim, & Farnen, 1975); and (d) selected smaller-scale studies (Avery, 1988; Elam, 1984; Hastings, 1986; Hepburn, 1985; Hess & Torney, 1967; McCloskey & Brill, 1983; Miller, 1985; Moore, Lare, & Wagner, 1985; Remmers & Franklin, 1963; Sigel & Hoskin, 1981; Zellman, 1975). Findings about the civic learning of upper-level high school students and adults are emphasized, because these findings suggest what is, and is not, learned and retained about government, civics, and law following exposure to most, or all, of the elementary and secondary school curriculum.

Knowledge About Government, Civics, and Law

Citizens of a constitutional democracy are expected to know principles and facts necessary for meaningful participation in government and public affairs, and civic educators endeavor to transmit this knowledge to learners in elementary and secondary schools. To what extent do American adolescents and adults satisfy the knowledge requirement of democratic citizenship?

Most 17-year-olds (more than 60%) have general and superficial knowledge of governmental institutions and officials. For example, they tend to know that Congress is composed of two houses; the power of public officials is limited by law; certain public officials are elected to office and others are appointed; powers of government are separated among three branches of government; and powers and duties of government are divided between the federal and state governments. Most older adolescents recognize the need for government and laws and can state positive purposes served by law. They can at least identify purposes and functions of constitutional rights and liberties, such as freedom of expression, freedom of religion, protection against unreasonable searches and seizures, right to trial by jury, and protection against double jeopardy for a crime (NAEP, 1976, 1983).

Most high school students and adults, however, lack detailed knowledge and understanding of institutions, principles, and processes of government, law, and politics in the United States. More than half of student and adult respondents in national assessments and surveys have revealed serious misconceptions about the powers and duties of the president and the federal judiciary. They also tend to have shallow or confounded conceptions of core principles, such as constitutionalism, democracy, and federalism (CCE, 1987, pp. 3–5; Hearst Corporation, 1987, pp. 16–26; NAEP, 1983, pp. 14–16; Sigel & Hoskin, 1981). And they tend to have very limited knowledge about how to participate in public affairs (beyond voting in elections) to influence the decisions of government officials (Miller, 1985, pp. 6–11; NAEP, 1983, p. 17).

A national sample of 17-year-olds performed dismally on a 19-item set of questions on the U.S. Constitution that was included in a 1987 NAEP study: the average score was 54.4% correct (Ravitch & Finn, 1987, pp. 55–58). Less than half of the respondents correctly answered questions about the *Federalist Papers,* landmark decisions of the Supreme Court, and major events in constitutional history. Only 60% demonstrated knowledge of a core constitutional principle, separation of powers (Ravitch & Finn, 1987, pp. 55–58). Another 1987 study (CCE) revealed similar shortcomings in student knowledge of constitutional principles and history, as did the Hearst Corporation survey of adults (1987, pp. 12–36).

A major objective in teaching government, civics, and law in schools has been to transmit knowledge. However, assessments of the knowledge of older adolescents and adults suggest only modest success in this important dimension of education in schools. However, critics argue that the NAEP-type tests of knowledge do not provide an accurate picture of what students really know. Respondents are required to answer multiple-choice questions that emphasize recall of discrete information and do not measure higher-level learning of a subject. Thus the critics say that poor performances on these tests are not necessarily an indicator of the respondents' ignorance (Torney-Purta 1988, pp. 16–18).

Defenders of these knowledge surveys admit the limitations of the tests and argue that they still are useful in revealing whether the respondents have the knowledge that educators believe they should learn in school. They also contend that acquisition of a minimum knowledge base is a prerequisite to higher-order thinking in government, civics, and law, or other academic subjects (Ravitch & Finn, 1987, pp. 21–28).

Civic Attitudes and Values

Education in government, civics, and law is heavily weighted with attitudes and values associated with constitutional democracy in the United States. To what extent have students formed commitments to standards (values) associated with the Constitution and system of government in the United States? To what extent have they developed postive orientations (attitudes)—based on their values and other beliefs—toward constitutional democracy in the United States?

Adolescents and adults tend to have favorable attitudes toward and values about their Constitution, system of government, and nation (Dalton, 1988, pp. 119–120; Hepburn, 1985; Kammen, 1986, pp. 3–43). These positive and supportive feelings and beliefs emerge at an early age, and they are well developed among youngsters in the upper-elementary and middle school grades. Most children appear to develop these positive attitudes without solid knowledge of their government or civic heritage (Hess & Torney, 1967; Moore et al., 1985). High school students are more likely than preadolescents to express criticism and cynicism about government and politics; this was especially so during and immediately after the era of the Vietnam War and the Watergate scandal (Hastings, 1986, p. 455; Hepburn, 1985, p. 673). High school students are also likely to agree that a "good citizen" can be loyal to the United States and its Constitution and strongly disagree with or dislike government leaders and policies (NASSP, 1984, p. 46). Despite criticisms or doubts about particulars, American adolescents tend to have positive general feelings toward their country and its system of government (NASSP, 1984; Sigel & Hoskin, 1981; Torney et al., 1975).

Attitudes toward constitutional democracy are generally positive. Students express support for majority rule and minority rights. But support for certain liberties and rights tends to decline when they are applied to unpopular minority groups or individuals (Avery, 1988; Hastings, 1986; Hepburn, 1985; McCloskey & Brill, 1983; Sigel & Hoskin, 1981).

The Purdue Youth Opinion Polls of the 1950s showed that a large proportion of adolescents were "authoritarian" in their attitudes toward the Bill of Rights; they tended to oppose application of certain rights and liberties to African-Americans, communists, atheists, and other unpopular minority groups or individuals (Remmers & Franklin, 1963). Adolescents of the 1980s were given the same statements about the Bill of Rights as used in the 1950s Purdue polls. In a few responses, the 1980s adolescents were more democratic than their counterparts of the 1950s. But a larger percentage of the 1980s high school students were willing to allow a police search without a warrant, to deny legal counsel to criminals, and to accept restrictions on religious freedom (Elam, 1984).

There has been persistent misunderstanding and lack of commitment to the values inherent in the central paradox of a constitutional democracy: majority rule and minority rights. In the abstract, students express support for constitutional democracy; but they also tend to hold simplistic conceptions that do not take into account the inherent tensions of majority rule with minority rights (CCE, 1987; NAEP, 1976; Sigel & Hoskin, 1981). Furthermore, students tend to understand and value the majority-rule facet of democracy more than the minority-rights facet (Kammen, 1986, pp. 336–356; Zellman, 1975).

The majoritarian sentiments of students are revealed in their generally favorable views of political participation, especially voting and taking part in an election campaign (NAEP, 1983, p. 14). However, most students express rather low levels of political interest and efficacy. Socioeconomic status—and the values and opportunities that accompany it—are directly associated with levels and amounts of political interest, efficacy, and activity: the higher the individual's socioeconomic status the more likely he/she is to have higher levels of political interest, efficacy, and inclinations to participate (Jennings & Niemi, 1974; Miller, 1985, pp. 25–28).

Students' tendencies to express some antidemocratic attitudes and values may be related to the poor quality of textbook treatments of the core concepts of democracy and constitutionalism. It is very possible that students' misconceptions or shallow understanding of core concepts affects their learning of attitudes associated with these concepts (Sigel & Hoskin, 1981).

Skills in Cognitive Processes and Participation

Education for citizenship in a constitutional democracy implies development of students' capabilities to make and judge civic decisions (Remy, 1976). It also denotes ability to act on civic decisions, to influence and implement them. To what extent do adolescents demonstrate the high-level cognitive capacities for making rational civic decisions and taking effective civic action?

In contrast to the domains of civic knowledge and attitudes/values, there is a paucity of data about cognitive- and participa-

tion-skill learning directly associated with civic education. The limited data suggest that more than 60% of 17-year-olds have certain middle-range cognitive skills, such as the ability to interpret political information in a graph or a brief written statement and to formulate questions to guide the search for data. The majority of these students also demonstrate ability to generate reasonable alternatives and to connect choices with consequences in making civic decisions. Furthermore, most 17-year-olds can distinguish factual statements from value judgments (NAEP, 1983, pp. 5–11).

However, most adolescents are not prepared to use the full range of cognitive skills needed to define, analyze, and evaluate public issues and to make rational decisions about them, because they lack knowledge about these issues (Ravitch & Finn, 1987, pp. 55–58). For example, if students cannot recognize and comprehend their rights in the U.S. Constitution, then they certainly will not be able to reflect cogently upon public issues associated with these rights. In their 1987 report on the National Assessment of History, Ravitch and Finn concluded:

Many of the most profound issues of contemporary society ... have their origins and their defining events in the evolving drama of the Constitution. Yet our youngsters do not know enough about that drama, either in general or in specific terms, to reflect on or think critically about its meaning. (p. 58)

Lack of knowledge about how to participate in civic affairs may also account for low levels of participation and limited development of participation skills among a majority of adolescents and adults (Miller, 1985, pp. 28–29).

Another reason for low levels of cognitive and participation skills among adolescents is lack of emphasis in the classroom on this dimension of civic learning. Goodlad's (1984) nationwide study of schooling found little evidence of critical thinking and concluded that "preoccupation with the lower intellectual processes pervades social studies and science as well" (p. 236). Studies of civics and government textbooks have revealed slight and unsystematic treatments of cognitive and participation skills in the learning activites of these books (Carroll et al., 1987).

Effects of the Classroom and School on Civic Learning

Strengths and weaknesses in civic learning are likely to be associated with the quality of the content and pedagogy to which students are exposed. After all, the learning of students in schools depends to a great extent upon the substance, design, and manner of presentation of their lessons. Furthermore, the organization, operation, and culture of the school may shape important aspects of students' civic learning.

Classroom-level Effects. Civic knowledge of elementary and secondary school students is increased through direct classroom instruction. Students' achievement of civic knowledge is related to the number of courses taken, the regularity of well-organized and detailed learning activities that students are required to complete, and the amount of time spent on lessons in the classroom and on homework. The more engaged learning time that students experience, the more likely they are to increase their learning of civic knowledge (Mullis, 1979; Parker & Kaltsounis, 1986; Patrick, 1972). Students in systematic and extensive law-related education programs have increased their knowledge of the purposes and types of law, state and federal judicial institutions, and rights and responsibilities of citizenship (Johnson & Hunter, 1987).

Direct teaching of civic attitudes and values does not have an independent effect on students' learning; nor does extensive instruction in civic knowledge have a discernible effect on the learning of civic attitudes (Ehman, 1980; Leming, 1985; Patrick, 1972). Positive attitudes and values about patriotism, support for the common good, and various civic virtues are developed among children and adolescents through mutually supportive experiences in the family, church, peer groups, and school and in their exposure to the mass media (Hess & Torney, 1967; Moore et al., 1985). However, evidence from a large study of high school students in Western Europe and the United States indicates than an overemphasis on direct teaching of patriotic attitudes and values in school is associated with lower scores on tests of civic knowledge and diminished support for democratic values (Torney et al., 1975).

The classroom climate established by the teacher is one key to the development of civic attitudes through formal instruction. Another key is regular and systematic teaching about issues. Teachers who emphasize analysis and appraisal of controversial public issues in an "open" classroom environment, where students feel free and secure in their expression of ideas and information, are likely to enhance learning of democratic attitudes, such as political interest, sense of political efficacy, political trust, and respect for the rights of other persons (Ehman, 1980; Goldenson, 1978; Leming, 1985; Torney et al., 1975). Furthermore, teachers increase their students' potential for development of democratic attitudes and values when they provide systematic instruction in critical thinking about public issues and create classroom conditions conducive to the free and open exchange of viewpoints (Guyton, 1988; Hahn, 1988). However, overuse of controversy and one-sided teaching about issues in a "closed" or authoritarian classroom can produce negative effects, such as passivity, disinterest, and civic intolerance (Hahn, 1988).

Evaluators of law-related education programs have claimed that when properly implemented, these programs lead to increased knowledge about the justice system and citizenship rights and responsibilities. These programs also have been touted as contributors to development of positive attitudes toward the law and judicial institutions (Hunter, 1987; Hunter & Turner, 1981; Johnson, 1984; Johnson & Hunter, 1987).

In many LRE programs, analysis of issues and critical thinking in "open" classroom environments have been emphasized. Teaching strategies have involved coopeative learning, higher-order cognition involving critical thinking and decision making, and free exchanges of ideas—all of which have been associated with the development of positive attitudes in various studies of classroom-level effects on learning in the social studies (Cornbleth, 1985; Leming, 1985).

An additional claim for law-related education programs is that they deter juvenile delinquency (Hunter & Turner, 1981). In a thorough critique of LRE evaluation studies, Shaver (1984) disputed this claim, because of serious flaws in the methodology of the study from which it was made, such as the (a) absence of a sound experimental design, (b) reliance on self-report data, and (c) use of correlational data to make cause-effect statements.

Studies of the teaching and learning of higher-order cognitive processes and skills, such as critical thinking and decision making, indicate that students' capabilities are likely to be increased if they practice skills in concert with their learning of specific subject matter, such as content in government or law. Effective instruction in critical thinking interrelates content and cognitive processes because in order to carry out higher-order cognitive operations, the student must know concepts and facts related fundamentally to the question under consideration. A successful critical thinker is also aware of differences in the criteria and evidence used to justify propositions in different subjects, such as history, political science, and law (Cornbleth, 1985).

The formal curriculum and classroom instruction have little or no effect on the political participation of American youth and adults. In particular, data from longitudinal studies indicate that exposure to social studies courses in high school is not related to the kind or quantity of political participation by the students as adults (Jennings & Niemi, 1974; Miller, 1985).

School-level Effects. In addition to teaching and learning in classrooms, educators must be concerned about how the school is organized and managed, about the climate or ethos of the place (Grant, 1981, 1988; Pritchard, 1988). Civic learning results from the interplay of academic experiences in the classroom and practical experiences within the school. So nonclassroom attributes of schools, such as style of administration, executive organization, school governance, peer interactions, and extracurricular programs, are likely to affect profoundly the civic learning of students (Ehman, 1980; Pritchard, 1988).

It is generally accepted that student participation in extracurricular activities of the school is positively related to the development of political efficacy and propensities for participation in civil life outside the school. And it seems that these student activities are much more influential than formal study of academic content in the classroom in the development of postive values and attitudes about participation in public affairs (Ehman, 1980; Jennings & Niemi, 1974).

There may be a positive relationship between "a democratic school climate" and the development of democratic civic attitudes and behavior among students (Ehman, 1980, pp. 110–114; Leming, 1985, pp. 156–163). One experienced researcher (Ehman, 1980) has claimed: "School organizational and governance climate is related to political attitudes of students. More participant and less authoritarian climates are linked to more positive [democratic] political attitudes and behavior of students" (p. 113). Some civic educators have used this "democratic school climate" research to propose active student involvement in decisions about school rules and policies (Hepburn, 1983).

There is, however, another way to look at school-level effects on civic learning; it is based on a growing body of research on school climates and character education that suggests the utility of authoritative leadership by administrators and teachers in achieving democratic citizenship goals (Grant, 1981, 1988; Rutter, Maughan, Mortimore, Ouston, & Smith, 1979). Some educators have used this research to argue against conceiving of the school as a microdemocracy, which mimics the political processes of the local, state, and national governmental system. Rather, they propose school climates in which adults authoritatively and unambiguously support core values of the community as standards for responsible behavior in the school and as preparation for democratic citizenship by students after leaving the school (Grant, 1981, p. 13; Pritchard, 1988, pp. 10–14).

There is obvious agreement in the research literature about the importance of school climate in the development of civic values, attitudes, and behavior for responsible citizenship in a democracy. There is also confusion and contradiction about the meaning of key terms—such as *democratic schooling*—and about the relationships between school-level practices and desired effects of civic education.

CONCLUDING COMMENTS ABOUT PROBLEMS AND NEEDS

There is ample room for improvement in the teaching and learning of government, civics, and law in American schools. For example, the discussion in a preceding section of this chapter indicated that at least half of the graduates from high school have only superficial knowledge of the institutions, principles, and processes of their constitutional democracy. And more than half of the students appear to have weak orientations toward some core values of their civic heritage, such as the civil rights and liberties of unpopular individuals or minority groups. They also tend to have underdeveloped capacities for making rational civic decisions and taking effective action to advance interests related to their choices. Finally, they are more inclined to be mere spectators and supporters than reflective, interested, and efficacious participants in their political system.

Research on the teaching of government, civics, and law suggests some remedies for deficiencies in students' learning of knowledge and attitudes. For example, a generally accepted conclusion of the literature discussed in the preceding section is that students' learning of democratic attitudes is enhanced by regular and systematic discussions of controversial issues in "open" classroom climates. Another established theme in the literature is that students' achievement of civic knowledge is advanced by increasing their exposure to subject matter through systematic and detailed assignments that compel their attention and commitment.

There also is consensus in the research literature about major deficiencies in the contents of textbooks that are relied upon to convey knowledge of government, civics, and law in classrooms. An implication of these textbook studies is that improvements in students' learning of civic knowledge would be a likely outcome of improvements in the selection and presentation of subject matter in widely used textbooks.

Research discussed in this chapter offers rather limited help to practitioners. The solid findings are too few and unrelated to help practitioners make a powerful difference in how they teach government, civics, and law, and in what their students learn from them. Improvements in research are greatly needed before practitioners can confidently look to it for keys to vastly improved civic learning in schools.

Most studies in this field have been conducted discretely, with little or no gounding in conceptual frameworks or theories that might tie them together. Thus, studies tend to stand alone, which limits their meaning and utility.

Some studies have methodological flaws, which diminish their credibility. Claims about practice made from these studies are of questionable value, and practitioners should be very cautious in using them as guides to teaching and learning. Shaver (1984), for example, has been critical of strong and seemingly unwarranted claims about the effectiveness of law-related education programs in reducing juvenile delinquency and developing positive attitudes toward the law and the judicial system. Cause-effect relationships have been incorrectly based on correlational data, faulty generalizations have been made from unrepresentative samples of respondents, and flawed comparisons have been made of nonequivalent treatment and control groups. Leming (1985) has also issued warnings about recommendations to practitioners based on the democratic school-climate research, because it "both reflects the paucity of evidence available as well as the eclectic interpretations of democratic education in the literature" (p. 158).

There is a great need for more and better research to assist practitioners—teachers, curriculum developers, and textbook authors. New studies are needed to substantiate or repudiate claims about the effectiveness of law-related education programs. Shaver's critical review (1984) is a useful source of ideas for designers of new LRE studies.

New and improved studies, based on precise use of key concepts and with multiple means of gathering data, are also needed to determine the relative validity of competing interpretations of school-level effects on civic learning. Grant's (1988) methods of on-site observation and participation to gather data about a school's climate and its effects on learning provide a model for other researchers.

Research is needed about how to improve the delivery of subject matter to learners via textbooks and other media of instruction. Researchers need to move beyond mere assessments of textbook contents to studies of how textbooks are used in classrooms and the various effects on civic learning of different uses of textbooks in teaching. Practitioners also need research about the effects on civic learning of different ways of organizing and presenting subject matter in textbooks, video programs, and computer software. Furthermore, practitioners need help from researchers to guide their decisions about how to vary their packaging and delivering of content to learners of varying backgrounds and abilities.

Curriculum patterns and trends in elementary and secondary schools indicate that government, civics, and law will continue to be mainstays of formal education in the social studies. The teaching and learning of these interrelated subjects—keystones in school programs to educate students for effective citizenship in our constitutional democracy—can be enhanced by more and better research designed to provide dependable findings and recommendations to practitioners.

References

American Political Science Association Committee for the Advancement of Teaching. (1951). *Goals for political science.* New York: William Sloane.

American Political Science Association Committee on Pre-Collegiate Education. (1971). *Political education in the public schools: The challenge for political science.* Washington, DC: American Political Science Association.

American Political Science Association Committee of Seven. (1916). *The teaching of government.* New York: Macmillan.

Anyon, J. (1978). Elementary social studies textbooks and legitimating knowledge. *Theory and Research in Social Education, 6*(3), 40–55.

Avery, P. G. (1988). Political tolerance among adolescents. *Theory and Research in Social Education, 16*(3), 183–201.

Bennett, W. J. (1986). *First lessons: A report on elementary education in America.* Washington, DC: U.S. Department of Education.

Bennett, W. J. (1987). *James Madison High School: A curriculum for American students.* Washington, DC: U.S. Department of Education.

Boyer, E. L. (1983). *High school: A report on secondary education in America.* New York: Harper & Row.

Butts, R. F. (1980). *The revival of civic learning: A rationale for citizenship education in American schools.* Bloomington, IN: Phi Delta Kappa.

Butts, R. F. (1988). *The morality of democratic citizenship: Goals for civic education in the republic's third century.* Calabasas, CA: Center for Civic Education.

Carroll, J. D., Broadnax, W. D., Contreras, G., Mann, T. E., Ornstein, N. J., & Stiehm, J. (1987). *We the people: A review of U.S. government and civics textbooks.* Washington, DC: People for The American Way.

Center for Civic Education. (1987). *Preliminary report on high school students' knowledge and understanding of the history and principles of the United States Constitution and Bill of Rights.* Calabasas, CA: Author.

Committee on Social Studies of the Commission on the Reorganization of Secondary Education of the National Education Association. (1916). *The social studies in secondary education.* Washington, DC: U.S. Government Printing Office.

Cornbleth, C. (1985). Critical thinking and cognitive process. In W. B. Stanley (Ed.), *Review of research in social studies education: 1976–1983* (pp. 51–63). Washington, DC: National Council for the Social Studies.

Council of State Social Studies Specialists. (1986). *National survey: Social studies education, kindergarten–grade 12.* Richmond: Virginia Department of Education.

Dalton, R. J. (1988). *Citizen politics in Western democracies.* Chatham, NJ: Chatham House Publishers.

Eckenrod, J. S. (1987). *Our democracy: How America works: Program marketing research.* San Francisco: Foundation for Teaching Economics.

Education for Democracy Project. (1987). *Education for democracy: A statement of principles.* Washington, DC: American Federation of Teachers, Educational Excellence Network and Freedom House.

Ehman, L. H. (1980). The American school in the political socialization process. *Review of Educational Research, 50*(1), 99–119.

Elam, S. M. (1984). Anti-democratic attitudes of high school seniors in the Orwell year. *Phi Delta Kappan, 65,* 327–332.

Gallagher, A. F. (1987). How law-related education fits into the curriculum. *The International Journal of Social Education, 2*(2), 37–44.

Glazer, N., & Ueda, R. (1983). *Ethnic groups in history textbooks.* Washington, DC: Ethics and Public Policy Center.

Goldenson, D. R. (1978). An alternative view about the role of the secondary school in political socialization: A field-experimental study of the development of civil liberties attitudes. *Theory and Research in Social Education, 6,* 44–72.

Goodlad, J. I. (1984). *A Place Called School.* New York: McGraw-Hill.

Grant, G. (1981). *Education, character, and American schools.* Washington, DC: Ethics and Public Policy Center.

Grant, G. (1988). *The world we created at Hamilton High.* Cambridge, MA: Harvard University Press.

Guyton, E. M. (1988). Critical thinking and political participation: Development and assessment. *Theory and Research in Social Education, 16*(1), 23–49.

Haas, J. D. (1977). *The era of the New Social Studies.* Boulder, CO: Social Science Education Consortium and ERIC Clearinghouse for Social Studies/Social Science Education.

Hahn, C. L. (1985). The status of the social studies in public schools of the United States: Another look. *Social Education, 49*(3), 220–223.

Hahn, C. L. (1988). *The effects of the school, media and family on the civic values and behaviors of youth.* Paper prepared for the International Conference on the Development of Civic Responsibility Among Youth, University of Urbino, Italy. (ERIC Document Reproduction Service No. ED 314 291)

Harrington, C. (1980). Textbooks and political socialization. *Teaching Political Science 7*(2), 481–500.

Hastings, W. L. (1986). Political socialization themes in the post-Watergate era. *Social Education, 50*(6), 453–457.

Hearst Corporation. (1987). *The American public's knowledge of the U.S. Constitution: A national survey of public awareness and personal opinion.* New York: Author.

Hepburn, M. A. (1983). Can schools, teachers, and administrators make a difference? The research evidence. In M. A. Hepburn (Ed.), *Democratic education in schools and classrooms* (pp. 5–30). Washington, DC: National Council for the Social Studies.

Hepburn, M. A. (1985). What is our youth thinking? Social-political attitudes of the 1980s. *Social Education, 49*(8), 671–677.

Hertzberg, H. W. (1981). *Social studies reform, 1880–1980.* Boulder, CO: Social Science Education Consortium.

Hess, R., & Torney, J. (1967). *The development of political attitudes in children.* Chicago: Aldine.

History-Social Science Curriculum Framework and Criteria Committee. (1988). *History-social science framework for California public schools.* Sacramento: California State Department of Education.

Hunter, R. M. (1987). Law-related educational practice and delinquency theory. *The International Journal of Social Education, 2*(2), 52–64.

Hunter, R. M., & Turner, M. J. (1981). *Law-related education evaluation project: Final report.* Boulder, CO: Social Science Education Consortium and Center for Action Research.

Janowitz, M. (1983). *The reconstruction of patriotism: Education for civic consciousness.* Chicago: University of Chicago Press.

Jennings, M. K., & Neimi, R. (1974). *The political character of adolescence.* Princeton, NJ: Princeton University Press.

Johnson, G. (1984, April). *When law-related education is a deterrent to delinquency: Evaluation methods and findings.* Paper prepared for the Rocky Mountain Regional Conference of the National Council for the Social Studies, Phoenix. (ERIC Document Reproduction Service No. ED 252 459)

Johnson, G., & Hunter, R. M. (1987). *Using school-based programs to improve students' citizenship in Colorado: A report to Colorado educators.* Denver: Colorado Juvenile Justice and Delinquency Prevention Council.

Joyce, B. (1967). The primary grades: A review of textbook materials. In C. B. Cox & B. G. Massialas (Eds.), *Social studies in the United States: A critical appraisal* (pp. 15–36). New York: Harcourt, Brace & World.

Kammen, M. (1986). *A machine that would go of itself: The Constitution in American culture.* New York: Alfred A. Knopf.

Katz, E. (1985). Federalism in secondary school American history and government textbooks. In S. L. Schecter (Ed.), *Teaching about American federal democracy* (pp. 91–98). Philadelphia: Center for the Study of Federalism at Temple University.

Larkins, A. G., Hawkins, M. L., & Gilmore, A. (1987). Trivial and noninformative content of elementary social studies: A review of primary texts in four series. *Theory and Research in Social Education, 15*(4), 299–311.

Leming, J. S. (1985). Research on social studies curriculum and instruction: Interventions and outcomes in the socio-moral domain. In W. B. Stanley (Ed.), *Review of research in social studies education: 1976–1983,* (pp. 65–121). Washington, DC: National Council for the Social Studies.

Massialas, B. G. (1967). American government: We are the greatest! In C. B. Cox & B. G. Massialas (Eds), *Social studies in the United States: A critical appraisal,* (pp. 167–195). New York: Harcourt, Brace & World.

McCloskey, H., & Brill, A. (1983). *Dimensions of tolerance: What Americans believe about civil liberties.* (New York: Russell Sage Foundation.

Miller, J. D. (1985, June). *Effective participation: A standard for social science education.* Paper presented at the meeting of the Social Science Education Consortium, Racine, WI. (ERIC Document Reproduction Service No. ED 265 083)

Moore, S., Lare, J., & Wagner, K. (1985). *The child's political world: A longitudinal perspective.* New York: Praeger.

Mullis, I. V. S. (1979). *Effects of home and school on learning mathematics, political knowledge and political attitudes.* Denver: Education Commission of the States, National Assessment of Educational Progress.

National Assessment of Educational Progress. (1976). *Education for citizenship: A bicentennial survey.* Denver: Education Commission of the States.

National Assessment of Educational Progress. (1983). *Citizenship and social studies achievement of young Americans: 1981–1982 performance and changes between 1976 and 1982.* Denver: Education Commission of the States.

National Assessment of Educational Progress. (1987). *Civics: United States government & politics objectives, 1988 assessment.* Princeton, NJ: Educational Testing Service.

National Association of Secondary School Principals. (1984). *The mood of American youth.* Reston, VA: Author.

Newitt, J. (1983). *The treatment of limits to growth issues in U.S. high school textbooks.* Croton-on-Hudson, NY: The Hudson Institute.

Parker, W. C., & Kaltsounis, T. (1986). Citizenship and law-related education. In V. A. Atwood (Ed.), *Elementary school social studies: Research as a guide to practice* (pp. 14–33). Washington, DC: National Council for the Social Studies.

Patrick, J. J. (1972). The impact of an experimental course, "American Political Behavior," on the knowledge, skills, and attitudes of secondary school students. *Social Education, 36*(2), 168–179.

Patrick, J. J., & Hawke, S. D. (1982). Curriculum materials. In I. Morrissett (Ed.), *Social Studies in the 1980s: A report of Project SPAN* (pp. 39–50). Arlington, VA: Association for Supervision and Curriculum Development.

Price, R. D. (1966). Textbook dilemma in the social studies. *The Social Studies 57,* 21–27.

Pritchard, I. (1988). *Character education: Research prospects and problems.* Washington, DC: U.S. Department of Education.

Quillen, I. J. (1966). Government-oriented courses in the secondary school curriculum. In D. H. Riddle & R. S. Cleary (Eds.), *Political science in the social studies* (pp. 254–272). Washington, DC: National Council for the Social Studies.

Ravitch, D., & Finn, C. E., Jr., (1987). *What do our 17-year-olds know? A report of the first national assessment of history and literature.* New York: Harper & Row.

Remmers, H. H., & Franklin, R. D. (1963). Sweet land of liberty. In H. H. Remmers (Eds.), *Anti-democratic attitudes in American schools* (pp. 61–72). Evanston, IL: Northwestern University Press.

Remy, R. C. (1976). Making, judging and influencing political decisions: A focus for citizen education. *Social Education, 40*(6), 360–365.

Remy, R. C. (1981). Treatment of the Constitution in civics and government textbooks. In H. D. Mehlinger (Ed.), *Teaching about the Constitution in American secondary schools* (pp. 107–128). Washington, DC: Project '87 of the American Historical Association and the American Political Science Association.

Rutter, M., Maughan, B., Mortimore, P., Ouston, J., with Smith, A. (1979). *Fifteen thousand hours: Secondary schools and their effects on children.* Cambridge, MA: Harvard University Press.

Shaver, J. P. (1965). Reflective thinking, values, and social studies. *School Review 73,* 226–257.

Shaver, J. P. (1984, April). *The law-related education evaluation project: A methodological critique of the "impacts on students" findings.* Paper prepared for the Rocky Mountain Regional Conference of the National Council for the Social Studies. (ERIC Document Reproduction Service No. ED 252 459)

Sigel, R., & Hoskin, M. B. (1981). *The political involvement of adolescents.* New Brunswick, NJ: Rutgers University Press.

Smith, F. R., & Patrick, J. J. (1967). Relating social study to social reality. In C. B. Cox & B. G. Massialas (Eds.), *Social studies in the United States: A critical appraisal,* (pp. 105–127). New York: Harcourt, Brace & World.

Study Group on Law-Related Education. (1978). *Final report of the U.S. Office of Education Study Group on Law-related Education.* Washington, DC: U.S. Government Printing Office. (ERIC Document Reproduction Service No. ED 175 737)

Taylor, B. L., & Birchell, G. R. (1983, November). *Has the "back-to-basics" movement influenced elementary social studies textbooks?* Paper presented at the National Council for the Social Studies Annual Conference, San Francisco. (ERIC Document Reproduction Service No. ED 237 432)

Torney, J., Oppenhim, A., & Farnen, R. (1975). *Civic education in ten countries.* New York: John Wiley & Sons.

Torney-Purta, J. (1988, October). *Political socialization.* Paper prepared for the National Conference on the Future of Civic Education, Washington, DC. (ERIC Document Reproduction Service No. ED 307 186)

Tryon, R. M. (1935). *The social sciences as school subjects.* New York: Charles Scribner's Sons.

Washington, G. (1948). Eighth annual address to congress. In S. Commins (Ed.), *Basic writings of George Washington,* (pp. 644–652). New York: Random House.

Zellman, G. (1975). Antidemocratic beliefs: A survey and some explanations. *Journal of Social Issues, 31*(1), 31–53.

RESEARCH ON GEOGRAPHY TEACHING

Joseph P. Stoltman

WESTERN MICHIGAN UNIVERSITY

The development of geography teaching within the K–12 curriculum has been discussed in numerous publications (James, 1969; Kohn, 1982; Libbee & Stoltman, 1988; Winston, 1986). Since 1960, several bibliographies on geographic education (Anderzohn, 1963; Ball, 1969), reviews of research in the social studies (Hunkins, 1977; Stanley, 1985), and research reviews by individual scholars (Rice & Cobb, 1978; Saveland & Pannell, 1978) have addressed research issues.

Dissertations have been the source of most research on geography teaching. The number of dissertation studies that were investigations of geography teaching, as compared to all of the social studies doctoral dissertations research reported from 1932 to 1982, is presented in Table 36–1. As can be seen in Table 36–1: (a) geography teaching has generally been a minor topic within social studies education research; (b) the period from 1969 to 1973 was the most productive of any comparable period; and (c) research on geography teaching has lost ground relative to all social studies research.

TEACHING GEOGRAPHY AS A SUBJECT

Research on teaching geography as a subject falls into four main categories: (a) K–12 geography teaching, subdivided into elementary and secondary instruction; (b) the use of maps in geography teaching; (c) children's spatial/cognitive development; and (d) geography's status as a school subject.

Geography Teaching—Grades K–12

The perusal of the research literature on geography teaching indicated two pervasive topics at both the K–6 and 7–12 levels: (a) content and concept validity studies, and (b) empirical studies directed towards learning outcomes.

Content and Concept Validity Studies, Grades K–6. The selection of geographic content and the validity of concepts selected for instruction at different grade levels has been a consistent focus of researchers. The validity of the technical terms that students encounter as terminology in textual materials has been examined (Ritter, 1941). Geography textbooks on statewide adoption lists in Alabama (Berry, 1961) and Texas (Schomburg, 1966) have been analyzed in order to develop models for validating both the content and concepts presented.

Peters (1969) pursued the question of validity by comparing the importance assigned to seven key geographic concepts by 40 geography teachers, 40 social studies teachers, and 20 professional geographers randomly selected from membership lists of social studies and geography education societies in Minnesota. Two tests were used to identify key geographic concepts: (a) a free association test and (b) a similarity-judgment test. The mean scores of professional geographers were statistically significantly different from those of social studies teachers on both tests ($p < .01$). There was no statistically significant difference between the mean scores of professional geographers and geography teachers on the free association test, but there was a statistically significant difference ($p < .05$) for mean scores on the similarity-judgement test.

The educational significance of the research was revealed by the analysis of verbal response patterns among the groups. Social studies teachers had a view of geography that entailed only the description of spatial distributions. Professional geographers and geography teachers had response patterns that reflected the interactions between and among spatial distributions, a perspective consistent with current geographic thought. The data suggested that the social studies teachers had a narrower view of the discipline and of geographic inquiry than did the other groups.

Reviewers were Sarah W. Bednarz, Texas A & M University; Marilyn Brown, University of Western Ontario; Nicholas Helburn, University of Colorado, Boulder; Barbara B. Petchenik, R. R. Donnelly and Sons Company, Chicago; Barbara J. Winston, Northeastern Illinois University.

TABLE 36–1. Geography Teaching Dissertations Reported in Summaries of Social Studies Research: 1934 to 1982

Year of Report	Total		Percent of Total
	Geography	Dissertations	
1934–62	52	566	9.2
1963–69	8	216	3.7
1969–73	30	417	7.2
1973–76	12	322	3.7
1977–82	23	394	5.8

Note: Information is from Chapin, 1974; Gross & de la Cruz, 1971; Hepburn & Dahler, 1983; McPhie, 1964; Wrubel & Ratliff, 1978.

Content and Concept Validity Studies, Grades 7–12. Research on the inclusion of geographic generalizations in secondary social studies textbooks has been carried out by Langhans (1961) and Cross (1981). Farrell and Cirrincione (1988, 1989) studied the responses of social studies teachers to the fundamental themes of geography as proposed by the Joint Committee for Geographic Education (1984). A survey was mailed to a national stratified random sample (middle through high school) of 1,138 social studies teachers asking them to rate the relative importance of five fundamental themes of geography education. A 5-category Likert scale was used. The data from the 576 usable responses suggested the following: there were no statistically significant differences between the importance assigned to each of the five themes by the teachers; region was identified as the least important theme, with a mean of 3.96 (SD = .92) and movement was considered the most important theme, with a mean of 4.33 (SD = .81).

There were no statistically significant differences in the mean ratings of the fundamental themes by groups of teachers in the sample classified by classroom assignment, but history and geography teachers displayed slightly greater agreement regarding the importance of the fundamental themes than did civics and social studies teachers. Similarly, there were no statistically significant differences between the teachers' mean ratings of the fundamental themes when classified by middle, junior high, and high school level teaching assignment.

The mean scores on the Likert-type instrument were greater than 3.9, above the 2.5 midpoint on a 5-point scale. The instrument may not have provided response options that adequately sampled the full range of beliefs about the fundamental themes of geography, and thus lacked discriminatory power. Despite that weakness, the favorable responses by teachers to the fundamental themes were educationally significant.

Empirical Studies of Learning Outcomes, Grades K–6. Empirical studies of geography teaching have included observational and experimental research designed to determine changes in students, usually as a result of some special treatment or experience. A few research studies comparing different ways of teaching geography were carried out in the early and middle periods of the 20th century, but from the late 1960s to the early 1970s was the period of major research activity. A nucleus of empirical research on geography teaching was conducted as part of the Georgia Geography Curriculum Project.

That research had two major dimensions: (a) systematic, conceptually based geographic content was used, and (b) theories of mastery learning and advance organizers were tested. The Georgia researchers used the pretest-posttest research design, relied upon samples of convenience (usually intact classroom groups which preempted random selection of subjects) in Georgia or the Southeast, and employed analysis of variance and correlation statistical procedures. Research data were collected using researcher-designed instruments and standardized tests. The research reports, when examined chronologically, reflect an impressive growth in research using materials design as the instructional variable. As pointed out by Tucker (1977), the Georgia studies provide an example of investigating the effects of classroom materials based upon theories of learning.

In his research, Steinbrink (1970) examined the use of advance organizers with 77 African American, rural, disadvantaged students in the fifth and sixth grades. The researcher concluded that educationally significant learning outcomes resulted from the use of advance organizers. The studies by Fagan (1975) and Contreras (1975) were investigations of the relationships between mastery learning and aptitude. The conclusions from both studies were that aptitude as measured by standardized tests was a more important variable in geography learning than were the effects of the mastery learning procedures designed within the experimental classroom materials.

Collectively, the Georgia Project studies have considerable educational significance since they provided information about instructional approaches that did not bring about changes in geography achievement as well as those that did.

The use of computers to assist in geography teaching has been part of the general increase in computer usage in social studies. A review of computer-based education in social studies (Ehman & Glenn, 1987) included several citations to geography teaching. One researcher examined the effects of using a computer adventure game and specially designed maps to teach place-location information (Forsyth, 1986). The study included random assignment of 120 fourth- and fifth-grade subjects, control of the experimental treatment through the computer program, and a posttest and delayed test to measure the effects of the treatment. Two experimental variables were examined: gender and map design. Statistically significant differences ($p < .05$) in posttest mean scores indicated that place-location recall was greater for the three treatment groups, each of which used a different map design, than for the no-map control group. The posttest mean scores for Treatment Groups 1 through 3 were 12.83, 12.83, and 7.9, respectively, as contrasted with the no-map control group's mean score of 1.33. As an estimate of the effects of treatment, the researcher reported that 42% of the variation on the posttest was associated with the type of map used. The main effects of gender were not statistically significant. Mean scores on the place-location recall posttest two weeks following the treatment were 70.1% as high as the posttest mean scores, suggesting that much of the place location knowledge was retained for that period.

Forsyth's research has educational significance because it suggests that computer use in conjunction with maps may be more effective. Teachers using computers for instruction may find that supplemental instructional materials in the form of paper and pencil activities provide an enhanced learning opportunity over the use of computers only. No comparable studies of the effectiveness of computers in geography teaching for secondary school students were found.

Empirical Studies of Learning Outcomes, Grades 7–12. Most studies of secondary school geography teaching have been focused on materials designed for geographic content delivery. In some instances, geography content has been used in research on a specific instructional methodology. The effects of repeated recall on learning and remembering geographic information (McKenzie & Sawyer, 1986; Tiedeman, 1941), the effects of directed study (Ramsauer, 1955), and programmed instruction (Fraenkel, 1966; Wood, 1962) have been researched.

Using a posttest-only, control-group design, Fraenkel (1966) investigated the effects of programmed geography instruction administered in different time sequences on the geography learning of 231 ninth-grade students divided randomly into five groups. A control group used case studies. A standardized unit test was administered following 160 minutes of instruction over eight days. The difference among mean test scores was statistically significant ($p < .001$), with the programmed instruction experimental groups having higher means than the control group.

Curriculum projects often provide opportunities for empirical studies using classroom trials of materials. The High School Geography Project (HSGP) was the major curriculum development effort in secondary school geography during the past 25 years. Among seven research studies on HSGP, only Womack (1969) used an experimental design to investigate the effectiveness of the inquiry-oriented HSGP materials with junior high school students. Classrooms with a total of 900 ninth-grade students in six schools were assigned to three groups: (a) no geography instruction; (b) traditional instruction in urban geography; and (c) instruction using the HSGP inquiry-oriented urban geography materials. An HSGP-developed test on the growth of cities was used as the dependent variable. The Spearman-Brown corrected reliability coefficient for the scores on the HSGP test was .72. The test was administered as a pretest, posttest, and as a retention test six months after treatment. The mean scores on the pre-, post-, and retention tests for the (a), (b), and (c) groups above were, respectively: 14.28, 14.6, 15.55; 16.11, 18.97, 19.51; 14.9, 18.26, 18.33. The differences between the pre- and the posttest mean scores and the pretest and the retention test mean scores for the experimental groups were statistically significant ($p < .05$). In terms of educational significance, the small differences between the pretest mean scores and the posttest and retention test mean scores for the experimental groups suggested no difference in the effectiveness of the instructional approaches.

Research on Maps in Geography Teaching

Map making and map usage skills have a long tradition in geography teaching and research. Research was located on the identification and development of map skills learning sequences, as well as on the teaching and learning of world images and mental maps.

Maps Skills Sequencing. In several of the earliest studies on geography teaching, the effectiveness of instructional programs for teaching map skills was investigated and student abilities in reading maps surveyed (Forsyth, 1949; French, 1932; Rushdoony, 1961; Starr, 1954). Sabaroff (1957) investigated not only how students learn map skills, but also proposed sequences in which they developed the skills. After completing an extensive review of the psychological and geographical literature, she identified 10 groups of map skills and proposed a map skills sequence for Grades 1 through 3.

Since the late 1960s, map skills researchers have investigated the effects of different map designs on student map reading. One study was a comparison of 868 fifth- and sixth-grade students' ability to read simplified maps such as are commonly found in classroom materials and conventional maps containing more words and symbols (Duhon, 1970). A researcher-designed, 30-item, multiple-choice map test yielded a reliability coefficient of .72 for the students' scores. The researcher concluded that: (a) most sixth-grade students are able to read conventional maps as well as simplified maps; (b) fifth-grade students are better able to read simplified maps than conventional maps; and (c) there was not a statistically significant difference in the mean map-reading test scores for boys and girls in either grade.

In another study, approximately 1000 children aged 9 to 14 years were interviewed individually to determine how they decoded information on maps (Bartz, 1971). When asked to determine distance on a map with a graphic scale, only 40 percent of the 9-year-old children responded correctly. However, by 13-years-of-age, 90% of the children responded with the correct answer. The data from the study were used to propose five stages in the development of graphic scale use by children.

Several researchers have applied theory from cognitive and perceptual psychology to map skills development (Beilin, 1970). Frye (1973) investigated the relationship between ability to interpret the symbolic representation on maps and the ability to classify objects. A stratified, random sample of 30 males and 30 females in Grades 3 through 8 completed four mapping and two classification tasks. There were no statistically significant mean differences between males and females on the mapping tasks. It was of educational significance that the children were able to differentiate form and shape more readily than color on maps. This is important when considering the large number of multicolored and color-shaded maps used in teaching geography.

The effects on map interpretation of the shape, size, and color of symbols have also been examined by Phillips (1973). A stratified sample of 984 students in Grades 1 through 6 was tested on the use of simple to complex maps with pictorial, semipictorial, and abstract symbols. Two types of assessment were used: (a) map symbol interpretation, and (b) route-tracing tasks. No reliability or validity data were reported. The researcher concluded: (a) the more abstract the map symbol, the less often it was identified correctly; (b) symbol identification and task performance were better with semipictorial than with abstract symbols; (c) the greatest improvement in test scores occurred at Grade 4; and (d) test performance was cyclic, with progressively better scores in grades two, four, and six.

Piaget's theories of spatial and cognitive development have also influenced research on map skills. Piagetian tasks, such as the three-mountain scene, were used in research comparing perspective ability and map-reading readiness (Cobb & Stoltman, 1974). Cooke (1978) researched spatial cognitive development levels and the achievement of map skills and concepts. A sample of 75 fourth-grade students was administered the Iowa Test of Basic Skills, Grade 4, map skills subtest, and three spatial tasks. The reliability of the Iowa subtest scores was .82, but reliability coefficients were not reported for the spatial tasks. It was found that achievement on spatial tasks was positively correlated with map skill achievement. Of practical significance was the finding that the achievement of certain spatial tasks preceded achievement of the most complex map skills test items.

The applications of the research results to curriculum development have been summarized in two publications. In the first, a sequence was proposed for developing skills in reading different types of maps, ranging from basic outline maps, showing shapes, through complex topographic maps (Rushdoony, 1968). In the second, a synthesis of information from research reports was presented and a map and globe skills sequence for grades K–8 proposed (Winston, 1984).

Maps and Images of the World. Maps have served a special function in research on mental images and cognitive mapping. Research using sketch maps, mental maps, and cognitive maps has been common in geography (Downs & Stea, 1977; Gould & White, 1974). In research on geography teaching, Wilson (1980) used sketch maps drawn by students from memory to study the reasoning skills of 196 pupils in the third, fifth, and seventh grades. The study revealed that proportion was the most difficult map element for students to sketch, followed by arrangement (location), abstraction (symbolization), and perspective (orthogonal view).

Bosowski (1981) studied the sketch maps of the world drawn and labeled by 2,255 students in Grades K–12 to determine if there was a progression in the formation of map images. Both the quantity and variety of information included on the sketch maps increased with age. Progressively greater amounts of information on the maps appeared from subjects in Grades 3, 6, and 9. Not surprisingly, the major geographic unit that the students included on their sketch maps was the United States. Next in order was Canada, followed by the continents of South America and Africa.

Criticisms of sketch mapping as a data-collection technique include the lack of standard criteria for evaluating maps, that map drawing skills rather than spatial information are being assessed, and the mental map may be only a copy of a map viewed regularly in school. The research has also been criticized for lack of random sampling. Despite those criticisms, the mental mapping research has revealed that children have major distortions in meaning and misconceptions about the world in mapped form, a finding that has practical significance for geography teaching.

Spatial and Cognitive Development

Geography is recognized as the spatial science concerned with the location of elements on the earth's surface and their relationship to each other. Researchers have addressed the way that spatial thinking develops and how it affects the way space on the earth is viewed (Almy, 1967; Eliot, 1970; Miller, 1967).

Spatial Development. Several researchers have investigated the ways that students learn and perform spatial tasks in geography (Massey, 1971; Rand & Towler, 1974; Satanek, 1971; Stoltman, 1971). In only one of these studies (Satanek, 1971) were the effects of instruction researched. Nine geography lessons with an emphasis on spatial orientation were taught to 60 fourth-grade subjects as the experimental treatment. A control group with the same number of subject was taught similar lessons but without the emphasis on spatial orientation. Subjects were not randomly selected, and IQ scores were used as a covariate to adjust for the effects of ability. A 32-item, researcher-designed, objective test was used in a pretest, treatment, post-test design. A reliability coefficient of .74 was reported for the geography test scores. Reliability estimates were not reported for the four Piagetian subtests used to assess children's spatial orientation.

The experimental group had a statistically significant ($p <$ .05) higher mean score on the geography posttest. Mean scores for the experimental and control groups were 25.77 and 23.67, respectively. The researcher concluded that the nine lessons in spatial orientation concepts had a positive effect upon student geography learning. However, the control group had the higher posttest mean score on the Piagetian subtests. The composite mean scores for the experimental and control groups were 3.96 and 4.27, respectively.

Massey (1971), Stoltman (1971), and Rand and Towler (1974) investigated the spatial development of students ranging from 5 to 10 or 12 years of age, using tests designed for the assessment of Piaget's theory of spatial development (Piaget & Weil, 1951; Piaget & Inhelder, 1967). They all reported similar results for their samples: (a) spatial concepts followed a near-by to far-away pattern of development; (b) descriptions of spatial settings became more definite as children's ages increased; (c) subjects considered more than one political unit or classification for spatial inclusion only after about 10 years of age; and (d) the sequence of stages proposed by Piaget for spatial development was verified, but the ages at which children made the transition from one stage to another varied depending upon socioeconomic status and ability.

In designing studies to replicate Piaget's research and test cognitive and spatial theories of development, the researchers faced several difficulties: (a) Piaget did not use widely accepted sampling and analytical techniques; (b) his reporting of results was limited; (c) the samples in the United States were diverse compared to the homogeneous samples used by Piaget; and (d) it was difficult to account for the effects of intervening variables, such as television and the space program, on children's spatial development.

The research by Downs, Liben, and Daggs (1988) continued

the interest in the applications of Piaget's theories to geography teaching. They reported relationships between class inclusion and transivity, both classical Piagetian tasks, and the concept of geographic hierarchy, with 78 children in the first through third grades. Performance, as indicated by mean scores on six tasks designed to measure geographic hierarchy, improved with each grade. Statistically significant ($p < .01$) relationships ranging from .25 to .42 were reported between the verbal and graphic versions of the geographic hierarchy test and measures of class inclusion and transitivity. An important finding from the study was that children's understanding of geographic hierarchy reflected cognitive development rather than merely the fact that older children knew more information.

The Status of Geography in the Curriculum

Status studies of geography teaching are numerous, having been completed for New York City (Becker, 1954), several states (Gandy, 1960; Hubbard & Stoddard, 1979; Sarkez, 1986), larger regions (Anderson, 1962), and the country (Mayo, 1964; McAulay, 1948; National Council of Geography Teachers, 1956; Salyer, 1975; Stowers, 1962). The status studies chronicle the changes that have occurred in geography teaching since 1892, a period of major change in education in general. Such studies provide the basis for important monitoring of geography, both as a separate subject and as a component of the social studies curriculum. They serve an important function by (a) providing baseline data that documents the study of geography in different locations at specific times and (b) providing the basis for designing future replication studies of the development, trends, and status of geography teaching.

GEOGRAPHY TEACHING AS SOCIAL STUDIES

Research on geography teaching in the social studies has included investigations of specific content or concept attainment with different instructional strategies (Libbee & Stoltman, 1988). Studies of values and attitudes, and critical thinking in geography as a social study were also found.

Grades K–6

Different instructional models from the social studies have been researched using geographic content. For example, Crabtree (1968) investigated the effects of a curriculum organized around the structure of the discipline. Two 16-week instructional sequences were used. One was based on a core of organizing concepts and analytic methods of the discipline; the second was based on a core of geographical generalizations. Students in first-, second-, and third-grade classrooms were randomly assigned to one of the treatment groups. A control group was not used. Prior to and at the conclusion of the treatment, the sample of 303 students was administered a researcher-designed, criterion-based test consisting of three subtests. The reliability estimates for scores on the subtests ranged from .52 to

.95. For second-grade children, the group that used the concept/analytic process to study geography had a statistically significant ($p < .05$) higher mean score on the posttest. Statistically significant differences were not observed between the treatment groups for either first or third graders. It was of practical significance that the mean scores for all grades in both treatment groups were higher than the chance score on the criterion measure. Both the concept/analytic- and generalization-based treatments were judged educationally effective by the researcher.

In another investigation, the effects of two social studies teaching strategies on learning strategic concepts and generalizations were investigated using third-grade students (Lahnston, 1972). Two models of instruction in social studies education, the deductive-expository and the inductive-discovery, were used to design the treatments. Twenty-four subjects were classified in high and low intelligence groups and then randomly assigned to a treatment group. Instructional time was held constant, with instruction on a one-to-one basis for five consecutive school days. Subjects were tested on the sixth day, and a delayed test was given two weeks later. The researcher designed five outcome tests. No reliability coefficient for subtest scores was higher than .43, partly a result of each subtest having only 10 items. The students who received the deductive-expository mode of instruction had a significantly higher mean score ($p < .01$) than did the group that received the inductive-discovery treatment. On the delayed posttest, however, there was no statistically significant difference between the mean scores for the groups. The lack of a difference on the delayed assessment suggested that, in practicality, both strategies were equally effective for high- and low-intelligence subjects when content and time were held constant.

Grades 7–12

The effects of presenting seventh-grade students with behavioral and nonbehavioral objectives to guide their learning of geographic content were examined by Lapolla (1983). The 194 subjects in the study were all white and upper middle class. The students were in nine classrooms to which three treatments were randomly assigned: (a) in four, the students received behavioral objectives; (b) in three, they received general, nonbehavioral objectives; and (c) in two, no objectives were provided. Time and content, a four-day study of New Zealand, were constant for all classes. A posttest, with the reliability for scores reported as .71, was administered at the conclusion of the treatment. The validity of the posttest relative to the behavioral objectives was assessed and judged appropriate by two experienced social studies teachers. Adjusted for IQ differences, the mean score on the posttest for the classes receiving the behavioral objectives (13.38) was significantly higher ($p < .05$) than the means for the groups receiving nonbehavioral objectives (12.45), or no objectives (11.65). The researcher concluded that positive learning effects were attained by informing students of the behavioral objectives prior to instruction. However, the small differences between mean scores suggest that the results had little practical significance. The practical significance of the results must also be judged in terms of the additional time the teachers expended in preparing the preinstructional materials.

The relevancy of the content of secondary school geography curriculum materials to African American students has also been studied (Davis, 1972). The literature from psychology, sociology, and education was reviewed to determine how geography could be made more inviting to African-American students, and four criteria were identified to guide content selection: (a) spatial significance to the African-American community; (b) presentation of real social and political problems; (c) examination of ethnic hostilities and conflicts; and (d) inclusion of positive aspects of the African-American experience. Four high school geography textbooks and the High School Geography Project were evaluated using the criteria. The researcher found that three of the four textbooks failed to include meaningful elements for African-American students. One book presented a positive image of African-American people and their achievements. The High School Geography Project materials used several social and political problems relevant to the African-American community. The researcher concluded that the materials were not an adequate basis for teachers to identify and develop issues in which the spatial attributes of geography and the African-American perspective merged.

Geography has also been a content area in research on attitudes, images, and cross-cultural understanding in relation to knowledge. Research on secondary school students' images and knowledge of Africa were studied by Beyer and Hicks (1969). The research revealed that secondary students had stereotyped images and either little or quite inaccurate information about Africa.

Currin (1973) researched the relationships between knowledge of, image of, and attitudes toward Africa and the conceptual level of 104 10th-grade students. Correlations between scores on the measures for 11 of 22 variables were statistically significant ($p < .05$), but only ranged from $-.12$ to $.38$. The researcher concluded that the data were of no educational significance in regard to attitudes, images, and conceptual level. Knight (1982) reached a similar conclusion based on his research. Both researchers raised important questions about the relationship between geographic knowledge and attitudes toward other countries of the world and how teaching about other countries should be approached in the social studies.

Results from another research study suggested that social studies textbooks may be, in part, the reason that students develop and maintain certain attitudes and stereotypical images of other peoples and nations (Stalker, 1985). An analysis of social studies textbook treatments of Central America indicated that people of the region were often presented in stereotypical roles.

Critical thinking has often been advocated as a major goal of the social studies. Only one research study on critical thinking and geography within the social studies was found (Wilson, 1972). In that research, critical thinking as measured by the Watson-Glaser Critical Thinking Appraisal was the dependent variable. The reliability coefficient for scores on the Watson-Glaser was .85. No validity coefficients were reported. The Ge-

ography Achievement Test from the National Council for Geographic Education, published in 1964, was used as the achievement measure. No reliability data were presented for the test scores. From a population of 166 ninth-grade students enrolled in one school, a sample was selected made up of students who had scores from the S.R.A. Achievement Test in social studies and the Lorge-Thornkike Intelligence Test in their cumulative record. A total of 117 students in six classes were invited to participate in the study; complete data were available for 97 students.

The treatment was a unit on Asian geography that lasted for 25 instructional periods. Six additional periods were used for pretesting and posttesting. Of the 25 periods, 15 were spent with the teachers leading similar learning activities for all six classes. The remaining 10 periods were spent in one of three instructional strategies: (a) discussion, which served as the control group, (b) peer teaching, and (c) independent study. There were no statistically significant differences in the mean scores ($p > .05$) for critical-thinking skills or geography achievement among the groups. Students with higher IQ scores achieved significantly greater gains ($p < .05$) on the critical-thinking skills and the geography achievement tests for all three instructional strategies. Older students made greater gains on the critical-thinking test than did younger students, but there were no statistically significant differences in geographic achievement test scores between age groups. There were no statistically significant differences between the means of males and females on the critical-thinking or geography achievement tests. The educational significance of this study was in the relationships between IQ and the development of critical-thinking skills. High-ability students gained in critical thinking with each of the different teaching strategies, but none of the strategies had the desired effect on students of lower ability.

The examination of values has been an important aspect of social studies research in general, but within the teaching of geography only one study was located. Cirrincione (1970) used a schema based upon the categorization of outcomes in the affective domain (Krathwohl, Bloom, & Masia, 1964) to identify and analyze affective elements in the research literature on geography and in the literature on geography education. He concluded that despite some research on values in geography education, geographic eductors had demonstrated little concern for values as outcomes. The lack of attention to values was attributed to: (a) lack of clarity regarding the terminology of the affective domain; (b) lack of a clearly defined rationale for incorporating values-related topics into geography; and (c) a subject-matter framework that did not distinguish between value-based and scientific judgments.

The Geography Strand of Social Studies

Research on the geography strand within the social studies has focused mainly on instructional sequences, time allocations, or topics taught (Bemis, 1966; Cowan, 1950). Only one study was found in which the role of geography as an integrated element of the social studies was investigated. Douglass (1954) was concerned with the ways in which the human-to-environment and human-to-human relationships that are of major concern to geographers might serve as guides in developing the geography strand of a social studies curriculum. Through an extensive review of the geography literature, he identified 824 discrete statements of relationships between people and the environment. He organized the statements into a perspective on modern geography and the implications for assessing instructional objectives, training teachers, and selecting curricular content. Douglass's study was significant because: (a) He identified the strengths of geography as an integrating discipline within the broadly based social studies curriculum and (b) there has been no similar analysis of geography's role within the broader social studies curriculum since 1954.

SUMMARY

Research on the teaching of geography began and has continued as a diverse field of inquiry. Fraenkel and Wallen's (1988) analysis of research in social studies provided guidelines for the following summary of the research on geography teaching and learning.

Topics Investigated

Concept and knowledge acquisition, map skills development and sequence, and status studies of geography teaching were consistent research topics from the 1940s until 1980. Research into specific types of teaching methods or techniques have also been of concern to researchers, but they have received less attention. Even less attention has been devoted to students' spatial and cognitive development.

The role of geography in citizenship education has been ignored almost entirely in the research on geography teaching. There have been only a few studies of the effects of geography study on the attitudes students have toward other ethnic and cultural groups. Cross-cultural and international comparisons using case studies from other countries could make major contributions to our knowledge about the effects of geography instruction on such attitudes. Values and critical thinking are also topics that have received little attention from researchers of geography teaching.

Attention has been given to gender in numerous studies, but generally as a variable of convenience that could be readily correlated with outcomes or used as a criterion for classification as the basis for an analysis of variance. Only in the studies by Forsyth (1986) and Frye (1973) was gender utilized in designing the research. Among the research studies on geography teaching in which differences in learning were analyzed by gender, most reported no statistically significant differences between females and males.

Only two research studies addressing the teaching of geography to minority and ethnic populations were found. Only Steinbrink (1970) employed a theory-based, experimental design. The study by Davis (1972)—although it provided educationally pertinent information regarding how geography might be viewed by African-American students—was an examination of professional literature and curriculum documents rather than a study of African-American students in the geography classroom.

Methodology

A major proportion of the research on geography teaching has been completed as doctoral dissertations, with experimental, survey, or historical research methodologies largely used. Outside the dissertation research category, the studies reported have been mainly experimental and survey research. More recently, several researchers have used naturalistic research methods to analyze the ways that people respond to their immediate environment. In those studies—usually classified as research on spatial cognition, mental mapping, or mental images of the world—correlation procedures have been used to detect observed patterns of relationships. Those researchers also have compared freehand-sketch maps drawn by students to determine how they differ from standard maps.

Although subjects were randomly selected for a number of studies, samples of convenience were often used. The effects of the size of the sample in analyzing data were rarely considered, and statistically significant results may often have had little practical significance.

Testing Theories of Learning

Several of the research studies reviewed were designed to test a particular theory of learning. Most notable were studies of Piaget's theory of spatial development (Piaget & Weil, 1951; Piaget & Inhelder, 1967), but there were also studies of programmed and demonstration-discovery models of instruction, mastery learning, and the principle of advance organizers. The examination of a single theory through a series of dissertations was absent, with the exception of the research completed as part of the Georgia Geography Curriculum Project. There were few connections made between studies. Such connections were often not possible because of the concurrent development of research projects. However, lack of coordination also resulted from oversight and hindered the building of a coordinated body of theory-based research knowledge regarding the learning of geography.

Replication

There are some examples of replication studies within research on geography teaching but not many. The emphasis upon doctoral research encourages the asking of new questions and the design of new experiments rather than the replication of studies to validate earlier research and reinvestigate the questions raised by that research. Replication studies in which a controlled experimental treatment was repeated were not found. Studies designed to test Piaget's theories of spatial development were the only replications located, but they tended to be quasi-replicative at best, due to the unique aspects of Piagetian research cited earlier in this chapter.

RECOMMENDATIONS FOR FUTURE RESEARCH

Recommendations for research initiatives are not new in the literature on geography teaching. Four prior sources of recommendations for research (Bacon & Kennamer, 1967; National Council for Geographic Education, 1972; Pike & Barrows, 1979; Saveland & Pannell, 1978) together suggest nearly 100 topics. While suggestions for research in those publications are worthy of consideration and should be reviewed by researchers contemplating projects, they perhaps encourage greater diversity than the field can afford. Following are four main recommendations for future research on geography teaching, with several questions to provide specific foci.

Learning Outcomes

Adequate attention to persistent questions about the effects of teaching on the learning of geography will require a continued and concerted research focus. Research is needed on geography's role in students' development of a world image that is spatially accurate and intellectually attuned to values, attitudes, and perceptions of one's own country and of other countries and other peoples.

1. How do both in- and out-of-school experiences with geographic content affect the student's knowledge of and attitude towards the world's nations and cultures, and what experiences result in spatially accurate mental images of the world?
2. What are the effects of duration of treatment upon short-term and long-term retention of learning in geography?
3. What content from geography works best for students of differing ability, gender, and ethnic identity?
4. What teaching and learning strategies work best for students of differing ability, gender, and ethnic identity?

New Technology

The effectiveness of classroom technologies for teaching geography—including computer-assisted instruction, interactive videodisc, images of the earth from space, and geographic databases—should be studied.

1. Which of the new technologies are being used in geography teaching? How are the new technologies being used?
2. What instructional designs for using the new technologies best enhance teaching and learning of geography for different ability and gender groups?

New Initiatives

The effects on the curriculum of initiatives in geography by professional organizations and societies should be a matter of continued examination.

1. How have the geographic initiatives of the 1980s altered the status of geography as a school subject?
2. What changes in the way geography is presented in textbooks and other materials can be attributed to initiatives by special-interest groups?
3. Has the geographic literacy of the school population improved as a result of initiatives by special-interest groups?

New Approaches to Teaching

Map skills research is well established within the literature. However, it has been proposed that geographic skills are much more comprehensive than map skills alone (Joint Committee on Geographic Education, 1984). Research is needed on how to help students use geographic information to promote problem solving, decision making, and critical thinking.

1. What is the range of skills that can be taught through geography?
2. How can geography skills that result in higher-level thinking by students be incorporated in curriculum materials?
3. What instructional methodologies work best for teaching geographic skills to students of different ability and gender?

A persistent question that arises when geography teaching is considered within the broader social studies curriculum is the importance and role of geographic knowledge and skills in preparing informed citizens. Researchers of geography teaching need eventually to address the question: Is the spatial learning experience significant educationally in developing citizens who are competent in knowing about, responding to, and dealing with an increasingly interdependent world.

References

Almy, M. (1967). The psychologist looks at spatial concept formation: Children's concepts of space and time. In P. Bacon & L. Kennamer Jr. *Research needs in geographic education* (pp. 23–40). Normal, IL: National Council for Geographic Education.

Anderson, R. (1962). *Secondary school geography and its status in the North Central Region 1962–1963*. Emporia: Kansas State Teachers College.

Anderzohn, M. L. (1963). *A selected bibliography of geography education for curriculum committees*. Normal, IL: National Council for Geographic Education.

Bacon, P., & Kennamer, L., Jr. (Eds.). (1967). *Research needs in geographic education*. Normal, IL: National Council for Geographic Education.

Ball, J. M. (1969). *A bibliography for geographic education*. Athens: Geography Curriculum Project, University of Georgia. (ERIC Document Reproduction Service No. ED 092 436)

Bartz, B. S. (1971). Designing maps for children. In B. V. Gutsell (Ed.), *Cartographia* (pp. 35–40). Toronto: York University Department of Geography.

Becker, C. F. (1954). A history of the development of the course of study of geography in the New York City high schools, 1898–1953. *Dissertation Abstracts, 15,* 220–221. (University Microfilms No. 10,656)

Beilin, L. A. (1970). An analytical-empirical study of sequence in curriculum development. *Dissertation Abstracts International, 31,* 3329A. (University Microfilms Order No. 70-26,762)

Bemis, J. R. (1966). Geography in the elementary school social studies program. *Dissertation Abstracts International, 27,* 989A–990A. (University Microfilms No. 66-10,527)

Berry, M. T. (1961). *A study of the vocabulary load of Geography of Many Lands, an Alabama state adopted text for the fourth grade.* Unpublished doctoral dissertation, University of Alabama.

Beyer, B. K., & Hicks, E. P. (1969). *Images of Africa: A report on what American secondary school students know and believe about Africa south of the Sahara.* (ERIC Document Reproduction Service No. ED 023 693)

Bosowski, E. F. (1981). The formation of cognitive images of the world: An analysis of sketch maps. *Dissertation Abstracts International, 42,* 3542A–3543A. (University Microfilms Order No. 8200786)

Chapin, J. R. (1974). *Social studies dissertations: 1969–1973.* Boulder, CO: Social Science Education Consortium. (ERIC Document Reproduction Service No. ED 098 085)

Cirrincione, J. M. (1970). The role of values in the teaching of geography. *Dissertation Abstracts International, 31,* 4377A. (University Microfilms No. 71-7424)

Cobb, R. L., & Stoltman, J. P. (1974). *Perspective ability and map conceptualization in elementary school children.* (ERIC Document Reproduction Service No. ED 086 615)

Contreras, G. (1975). Mastery learning: The relation of different criterion levels and aptitude to achievement, retention, and attitude in a seventh grade geography unit. *Dissertation Abstracts International, 36,* 5979A. (University Microfilms No. 76-6389)

Cooke, K. G. (1978). The relationship between spatial cognitive developmental levels and the achievement of map skills and concepts. *Dissertation Abstracts International, 39,* 2023A. (University Microfilms No. 7818169)

Cowan, A. W. (1950). *Elementary school social studies: A research guide to sequence.* Unpublished doctoral dissertation, Stanford University.

Crabtree, C. A. (1968). *Teaching geography in grades one through three: Effects of instruction in the core concept of geographic theory.* (ERIC Document Reproduction Service No. ED 021 869)

Cross, K. C., Jr. (1981). The status of future orientation in selected secondary geography textbooks. *Dissertation Abstracts International, 42,* 2465A. (University Microfilms No. 8127483)

Currin, C. B. (1973). American secondary school students and foreign culture areas: An analysis of the interrelationships of knowledge, attitude, image, and conceptual level using Africa as a case study. *Dissertation Abstracts International, 34,* 6864A. (University Microfilms No. 74-10,141)

Davis, G. A. (1972). Secondary school geography: Its relevancy to black students. *Dissertation Abstracts International, 33,* 1315A. (University Microfilms No. 72-26,996)

Douglass, M. P. (1954). Interrelationships between man and the natural environment for use in the geographic strand of the social studies curriculum. *Dissertation Abstracts, 14,* 2237–2238. (University Microfilms No. 10,349)

Downs, R. M., Liben, L. S., & Daggs, D. G. (1988). On education and geographers: The role of cognitive developmental theory in geographic education. *Annals of the Association of American Geographers, 78*(4), 680–700.

Downs, R. M., & Stea, D. (1977). *Maps in minds: Reflections on cognitive mapping.* New York: Harper & Row.

Duhon, J. M. (1970). The value of simplified maps in selected fifth and sixth grades. *Dissertation Abstracts International, 31,* 1999A. (University Microfilms No. 70-20,707)

Ehman, L. H., & Glenn, A. D. (1987). *Computer-based education in the social studies.* Bloomington, IN: Social Studies Development Center-ERIC Clearinghouse for Social Studies/Social Science Education.

Eliot, J. (1970). Children's spatial visualization. In P. Bacon (Ed.), *Focus Upon Geography: Key Concepts and Teaching Strategies* (pp. 263–290). Washington, DC: National Council for the Social Studies.

Fagan, J. S. (1975). Mastery learning: The relationship of mastery procedures and aptitude to the achievement and retention of transportation-environmental concepts by seventh grade students. *Dissertation Abstracts International, 36,* 5981A. (University Microfilms No. 76-6402)

Farrell, R. T., & Cirricione, J. M. (1988). Teachers assess the five fundamental themes of geography. In S. J. Natoli (Ed.) *Strengthening Geography In the Social Studies* (pp. 119–122). Washington, DC: National Council for the Social Studies.

Farrell, R. T., & Cirricione, J. M. (1989). The content of the geography curriculum—A teacher's perspective. *Social Education, 53*(2), 105–108.

Forsyth, A. S., Jr. (1986). A computer adventure game and place location learning: Effects of map type and player gender. *Dissertation Abstracts International, 47,* 2131A. (University Microfilms No. DA8619409)

Forsyth, E. (1949). *Experiment in the teaching of certain map reading skills at the junior high school level.* Unpublished doctoral dissertation, Cornell University.

Fraenkel, J. R. (1966). The effect of variations in sequencing programmed instruction in secondary school geography. *Dissertation Abstracts, 27,* 2097A-2098A. (University Microfilms No. 66-14,665)

Fraenkel, J. R., & Wallen, N. E. (1988). *Toward improving research in social studies education.* Boulder, CO: Social Science Education Consortium.

French, L. C. (1932). *The effect of specific training in vocabulary, reading of maps, graphs, and tables, and organization on achievement in geography.* Unpublished doctoral dissertatin, University of Pittsburgh.

Frye, M. (1973). The development of map-reading abilities in nine to fourteen year old children. *Dissertation Abstracts International, 33,* 6646A. (University Microfilms No. 73-14,253)

Gandy, W. (1960). The status of geography in the public senior high schools of California. *Dissertation Abstracts, 20,* 4347. (University Microfilms No. 60-1347)

Gould, P., & White, R. (1974). *Mental maps.* Harmondsworth, England: Penguin Books.

Gross, R., & de la Cruz, L. (1971). *Social studies dissertations, 1963–1969.* Boulder, CO: ERIC Clearinghouse for Social Studies/Social Science Education. (ERIC Document Reproduction Service No. ED 054 999)

Hepburn, M. A., & Dahler, A. (1983). *Social studies dissertations, 1977–1982.* Boulder, CO: ERIC Clearinghouse for Social Studies/Social Science Education and Social Science Education Consortium. (ERIC Document Reproduction Service No. ED 245 970)

Hubbard, R., & Stoddard, R. H. (1979). High school students' images of geography: An exploratory analysis. *Journal of Geography, 78*(5), 188–194.

Hunkins, F. P. (1977). Research, criticism, and dialogue. In F. P. Hunkins, L. H. Ehman, C. L. Hahn, P. H. Martorella, & J. L. Tucker (Eds.), *Review of research in social studies education: 1970–1975* (pp. 1–13). Washington, DC: National Council for the Social Studies.

James, P. E. (1969). The significance of geography in American education. *Journal of Geography, 68,* 473–483.

Joint Committee on Geographic Education. (1984). *Guidelines for geographic education: Elementary and secondary schools.* Washington,

DC: Association of American Geographers and National Council for Geographic Education.

Knight, C. L. (1982). An international study of relationships between geographic knowledge of students and their attitude to other nationalities. *Dissertation Abstracts International, 43,* 3562A. (University Microfilms No. DA8308184)

Kohn, C. (1982). Looking back; working ahead. *Journal of Geography, 81*(2), 44–46.

Krathwohl, D. R., Bloom, B. S., & Masia, B. B. (1964). *Taxonomy of educational objectives—Handbook II: Affective domain.* New York: David McKay Company.

Lahnston, A. T. (1972). A comparison of directed discovery and demonstration strategies for teaching geographic concepts and generalizations. *Dissertation Abstracts International, 33,* 4064A. (University Microfilms No. 73-3740)

Langhans, E. J. (1961). An analysis of current social study texts, grades seven through twelve, in terms of inclusion of geographic generalizations. *Dissertation Abstracts, 22,* 3043. (University Microfilms No. 62-1250)

Lapolla, L. L., Jr. (1983). The effects of instructional objectives on achievement of knowledge by seventh grade social studies classes. *Dissertation Abstracts International, 45,* 2744A. (University Microfilms No. DA8429333)

Libbee, M., & Stoltman, J. P. (1988). Geography within the social studies curriculum. In S. J. Natoli (Ed.), *Strengthening geography in the social studies* (pp. 22–41). Washington, DC: National Council for the Social Studies.

Massey, D. L. (1971). A study of children's spatial and temporal concepts. *Dissertation Abstracts International, 32,* 3007A-3008A. (University Microfilms No. 7127178)

Mayo, W. L. (1964). The development of secondary school geography as an independent subject in the United States and Canada. *Dissertation Abstracts, 25,* 7027-7028. (University Microfilms No. 65-5349)

McAulay, J. D. (1948). *Trends in elementary school geography, 1928–1948.* Unpublished doctoral dissertation, Stanford University.

McKenzie, G. R., & Sawyer, J. (1986). Effects of text-like practice and mnemonics on learning geographic facts. *Theory and Research in Social Education, 14*(3), 201–209.

McPhie, W. E. (1964). *Dissertations in social studies education: A comprehensive guide.* Washington, DC: National Council for the Social Studies.

Miller, J. M. (1967). Measuring perspective ability. *Journal of Geography, 66,* 167–171.

National Council for Geographic Education. (1972). Special issue on geographic learning. *Journal of Geography, 71*(4).

National Council of Geography Teachers. (1956). *The status of geography in the secondary schools of the United States.* Normal, IL: National Council of Geography Teachers.

Peters, W. (1969). Perceptual agreement of social studies teachers and professional geographers on aspects of a cognitive geographic paradigm. *Dissertation Abstracts International, 31,* 937A. (University Microfilms No. 70-15,785)

Phillips, W. F. (1973). *A study of symbol design for elementary school maps.* Unpublished doctoral dissertation, University of Kansas.

Piaget, J., & Inhelder, B. (1967). *The child's conception of space.* London: Routledge and Kegan Paul.

Piaget, J., & Weil, A. (1951). The development in children of the idea of homeland and of relations with other countries. *International Social Science Bulletin, 3,* 561–578.

Pike, L. W., & Barrows, T. S. (1979). *Other nations other peoples.* Washington, DC: U.S. Government Printing Office.

Ramsauer, R. T. (1955). *Directed exercises in the political geography of Europe and the Near East.* Unpublished doctoral dissertation, Teachers College of Columbia University.

Rand, D. C., & Towler, J. O. (1974). *Piaget's spatial stages: An examination of their relationship to elementary children's classification-class inclusion abilities.* (ERIC Document Reproduction Service No. ED 086 616)

Rice, M. J., & Cobb, R. L. (1978). *What can children learn in geography: A review of research.* Boulder, CO: Social Science Education Consortium. (ERIC Document Reproduction Service No. ED 166 088)

Ritter, O. P. (1941). *Repetition, spread, and meanings of unusual, difficult, and technical terms in fourth grade geography texts.* Unpublished doctoral dissertation, State University of Iowa.

Rushdoony, H. A. (1961). *A study of relationships between achievement in map-reading and selected factors.* Unpublished doctoral dissertation, University of California.

Rushdoony, H. A. (1968). A child's ability to read maps: Summary of the research. *Journal of Geography, 67*(April), 213–222.

Sabaroff, R. E. (1957). A framework for developing map skills in primary grade social studies. *Dissertation Abstracts, 18,* 534. (University Microfilms No. 25,358)

Salyer, G. M. (1975). Geography in the elementary school as portrayed by the *Journal of Geography. Dissertation Abstracts International, 36,* 1279A. (University Microfilms No. 75-19,281)

Sarkez, A. O. (1986). A survey of the status of geography education in Colorado senior high schools. *Dissertation Abstracts International, 47,* 1594A. (University Microfilms No. DA8617678)

Satanek, M. C. (1971). An application of selected Piagetian spatial tasks to geographic education. *Dissertation Abstracts International, 32,* 4429A. (University Microfilms No. 72-6332)

Saveland, R. N., & Pannell, C. W. (1978). *Some aspects of the study and teaching of geography in the United States: A review of research, 1965–1975.* Sheffield, England: The Geographical Association. (ERIC Document Reproduction Service No. ED 204 204)

Schomburg, C. E. (1966). A study of the presentation and reenforcement of geographic concepts found in selected geography textbooks in adoption in the State of Texas during 1964–1965. *Dissertation Abstracts, 27,* 2752A. (University Microfilms No. 67-2020)

Stalker, S. W. (1985). The portrayal of Central America in selected contemporary social studies textbooks. *Dissertation Abstracts International, 46,* 2911A. (University Microfilms No. DA8527036)

Stanley, W. B. (Ed.). (1985). *Review of research in social studies education: 1976–1983.* Washington, DC: National Council for the Social Studies.

Starr, J. W. (1954). *A comparison of two methods of teaching map reading skills at the intermediate grade levels.* Unpublished doctoral dissertation, Colorado State College of Education.

Steinbrink, J. E. (1970). The effectiveness of advance organizers for teaching geography to disadvantaged rural black elementary students. *Dissertation Abstracts International, 31,* 5949A. (University Microfilms No. 71-13,133)

Stoltman, J. P. (1971). Children's conception of territory: A study of Piaget's spatial stages. *Dissertation Abstracts International, 32,* 5623A. (University Microfilms No. 72-11,047)

Stowers, D. M. (1962). Geography in American schools, 1882–1935: Textbooks and reports of national committees. *Dissertation Abstracts, 23,* 146–147. (University Microfilms No. 62-2220)

Tiedeman, H. R. (1941). *A study of retention in geography.* Unpublished doctoral dissertation, University of Iowa.

Tucker, J. L. (1977). Research on social studies teaching and teacher education. In F. P. Hunkins, L. H. Ehman, C. L. Hahn, P. H. Martorella, & J. L. Tucker (Eds.), *Review of Research in Social Studies Education: 1970–1975* (pp. 97–135). Washington, DC: National Council for the Social Studies.

Wilson, J. W. (1972). The effects of three instructional designs: Small groups, peer-teaching and independent study on ninth grade geography students' ability to think critically. *Dissertation Abstracts International, 33,* 2000A. (University Microfilms No. 72-30,533)

Wilson, P. S. (1980). The map reasoning development of pupils in years three, five, and seven as revealed in free recall sketch maps. *Dissertation Abstracts International, 41,* 4355A. (University Microfilms No. 8107412)

Winston, B. J. (1984). *Map and globe skills: K–8 teaching guide.* Macomb, IL: National Council for Geographic Education.

Winston, B. J. (1986). Teaching and learning in geography. In S. P. Wronski & D. H. Bragaw (Eds.), *Social studies and the social sciences: A fifty-year perspective* (pp. 43–58). Washington, DC: National Council for the Social Studies.

Womack, J. A. (1969). An analysis of inquiry-oriented High School Geography Project urban materials. *Dissertation Abstracts International, 30,* 3869A. (University Microfilms No. 69-19,824)

Wood, L. A. (1962). Programmed textual material as a partial substitute of teacher-led classroom procedures in geography. *Dissertation Abstracts, 23,* 2037. (University Microfilms No. 62-5451)

Wrubel, P. R., & Ratliff, R. (1978). *Social studies dissertations: 1973–1976.* Boulder, CO: Social Studies Education Consortium.

·37·

EDUCATION FOR INTERNATIONAL UNDERSTANDING

Byron G. Massialas

FLORIDA STATE UNIVERSITY

In a world of continuous conflict among sovereign states, many educators are trying to promote international understanding through school programs that engage students in activities to enhance their understanding of other countries and promote active participation in the solution of world problems. How successful have educators been in their quest to bring about international understanding and involvement? What qualities characterize students who develop global understanding and concern? What are the significant gaps in the research on international education, and what is a meaningful research agenda for the future? These questions were the parameters for the review of literature in this chapter.

THE QUEST FOR A CONCEPTUAL FRAMEWORK

The profession's interest in global understanding is exemplified by such historical works as Day's (1988) study of the images of the world conveyed in the official organ of the National Council for the Social Studies, *Social Education*. Day concluded that although there were some image fluctuations during certain historical periods (e.g., wars and economic depressions), the global perspective remained pervasive in the journal over the entire 43-year period, 1937 to 1979.

In a similar study, Stomfay-Stitz (1984) analyzed primary sources and articles written by educators to trace the development of peace education in the United States from 1828 to 1983. She identified major themes in the literature: "awareness for the global perspective," "the value of studying history," and "the role of the military." Key agencies in the development

and evaluation of peace education included peace societies (e.g., the American School Peace League, 1909 to 1976), peace educators (educators who believed that peace education "could bring about a transformation in the individual and society" [p. 1633]), and members of the Quaker movement. In the 1980s, peace education took the form of "nuclear war or disarmament education," "global education," and "community education."

The development of a conceptual framework to guide research and study in the area of teaching for international understanding has, however, only recently been the focus of researchers in the field. In many of the studies reviewed here, the researchers sought primarily to improve practice—of students, of teachers, of administrators—in the area of international understanding. Indirectly, however, some of them have attempted to clarify the phenomenon under study. For example, Horton (1981) sought to develop a set of guidelines on "global education"—a program of formal school studies that contributes to international understanding—for teacher-educators and teachers. In doing so, he provided some basis for delimiting the field. Through an analysis of literature published between 1970 and 1980, he established that "ecological systems and associated environmental issues" constituted key themes in the literature in the early part of the decade, whereas "citizenship, interdependence, and human rights" constituted the foci for the latter part of the decade. Horton concluded that contributors to the literature were quite enthusiastic about the prospects for education in this field, but failed to come to grips with the substantive issues underlying the concepts they advanced (p. 2064).

In another study aimed at developing guidelines for school

Reviewers were Buckley R. Barnes, Georgia State University; John J. Cogan, University of Minnesota; Judith Torney-Purta, University of Maryland, College Park.

administrators, Corkle (1983) not only failed to provide a conceptual framework that would generate further systematic research but did not help to clarify the field. The practical type of guidelines he developed (through a review of literature and a questionnaire) for "identifying teachers and administrators who have an interest in the concept," have limited usefulness for establishing specific school programs and systematically assessing and evaluating their effects on students' international understanding. A study by Morrow (1983) was hampered by the same constraints, although an effort was made to present behavioral objectives for teachers to use in measuring the presumed cognitive, affective, and psychomotor outcomes of a curriculum in Afro-Asian civilizations.

In both of the above studies historical methods were employed, but systematic content analysis was not. A combination of those methods might have produced more powerful results through attention to general patterns and trends and to detail expressed in quantitative terms.

Gualdoni (1980) sought to define global education as a program of studies leading to international understanding through a questionnaire administered to directors of Title IV-C global education projects (innovative projects supported by federal funds) in Michigan. The Delphi technique was used to construct the questionnaire. Interviews with the project directors yielded additional information on their views of the scope of global education. There was general agreement that global education should develop students' knowledge, skills, and attitudes vis-a-vis a global society. For instance, on a scale of 0–5, with 5 indicating highest agreement, the questionnaire statement, "Global education should make students conscious of the natural resources distribution throughout the world," received a mean rating of 4.75. Understanding world interdependence as an outcome of instruction was the prevailing theme stressed by the respondents.

Although Gualdoni aimed his study at defining the field, his questionnaire did not ask the respondents to specify the concrete behaviors that might exemplify a "globally minded person." Based on a review of the literature, an "operational definition" of global education was proposed: "education that helps people to develop the knowledge, skills, and understanding needed for responsible, intelligent participation in a global society" (p. 141). This definition is not operational, however, because it does not include specific measures in the cognitive, affective, or participatory domains.

Gualdoni found that project directors considered global education not to be a separate discipline or content but rather an approach that could be included in any subject or level of instruction. Olson (1981), who also reviewed the literature and interviewed leaders in global education in Michigan, found that global education was perceived as involving most, if not all, areas of the curriculum including bilingual and multicultural education. Although he offered some practical suggestions for developing global education programs, Olson also failed to provide an adequate definition for systematic research. Other studies (e.g., Terrill, 1982) have offered little in the way of conceptual clarity as a basis for developing and conducting studies of global education and its effects on students.

Studies of international understanding on the part of practitioners have also not produced clear definitions of global education. Elementary school principals in Pennsylvania had a difficult time explaining the concept of global education (Sidemaker, 1984). Furthermore, a low priority was given to global education as a curriculum topic, notwithstanding the fact that the Pennsylvania Board of Education had given the program a high priority. Top priority was given by the principals to such areas as computer education and aeronautic/space education.

Vocke (1985) canvassed Iowa secondary school social studies teachers attending global education conferences in the state and a second sample of social studies teachers paired on the basis of location, size of school district, and grade level. Neither sample was considered to be representative of Iowa social studies teachers. Responses from both samples indicated that instruction was not based on a clear definition of the concept of global education. Very few of the teachers could explain different conceptions of global education, that is, global education as (a) foreign policy/world affairs and world culture/area studies, (b) a world-centered-studies approach, (c) a world-order-studies approach, and (d) a single-issue approach.

The need for a defensible conceptual framework in education for international understanding has not been met by those who specialize in the field, either. The debate among these specialists (e.g., Becker 1979; Jacobson, Reardon, & Sloan, 1983; Mendlovitz, Metcalf, & Washburn, 1977) as to which approach to global education is appropriate has not given the social studies researchers a theoretical basis for their studies.

Beginnings of promising frameworks have intermittently appeared in the literature. Anderson (1968), for example, proposed the development of a conceptual framework to guide research based on the nature of *competence* in world citizenship and on the obstacles hindering development of that competence. In developing such a model, he suggested, we should ask:

What do individuals need to possess in the way of cognitive abilities, values, motivations, and information in order to function competently as observers, analysts, evaluators, and judges or critics of events, decisions, trends, or developments occurring in the international dimensions of their social environment? (p. 90)

Lamy (1983) reviewed the literature on different approaches to global education and the corresponding world views. The paradigms upon which global education is based include images of the world cast in idealistic or realistic terms. Regardless of a particular world perspective, however, Lamy asserted, "Global education is expected to develop an understanding of the necessity for global cooperation together with individual activism and participation in order to change the existing international system" (p. 18). Global education should prompt students to find creative solutions to international problems. Lamy recognized the difficulty in defining global education in a particular way, given the varieties of world perspectives. However, his proposal that educators "recognize the pluralism of world views that exists in this area of study" (p. 19) implies a particular view and does not, in itself, create a solid basis for a theoretical framework to guide research in the field. Nor does his suggestion of student outcomes for global education provide enough specificity for development of the competencies of "world citizenship" for which Anderson (1968) called.

A more comprehensive conceptualization was provided by Hughes (1983), who distinguished between intercultural education and training on one hand and international education on the other, the former emphasizing process and the latter, content. International education is intended to enhance knowledge about international problems and posit possible solutions, whereas intercultural education is aimed at improving relations and interactions among people of different cultures based on an accurate interpretation of others and the development of "'third culture' patterns of interaction that accommodate each others' differences" (p. 42). Hughes's shift from the traditional emphasis on concepts primarily from political science and world studies (e.g., power, conflict) to concepts based on social psychology and cultural anthropology (e.g., social and subjective culture) in developing a concept of global education is promising.

RESEARCH ON IN-SCHOOL FACTORS THAT INFLUENCE INTERNATIONAL UNDERSTANDING

Classifying studies in international understanding under logical rubrics is an extremely difficult task, in part because a clear conceptual framework has not guided the research. As noted above, the student attitudinal or behavioral outcomes that are to issue from exposure to global education or similar programs are rarely specified. Typically, no theoretical basis is presented for developing hypotheses and linking them to a defensible study design.

Curriculum Effects

Mitsakos (1978) investigated the effects of a social studies program, "Family of Man," on children's view of foreign peoples. The experimental group included 21 intact third-grade classes comprised of a total of 509 students. Two control groups were used: One "included 233 third-grade children who had worked with some other well-defined or continuous social studies program for three years." The other "included 220 third-grade children who had not been exposed to a well-defined or formal continuous social studies program for three years." (p. 5) No details were given to indicate how the samples were selected to meet the investigator's goal of having "a cross-section of community locations and sizes" and "diversity in each group."

Three posttest measures were used to tap children's views of other people, in addition to the STEP II social studies test of general knowledge. The data were analyzed using one-way of variance. No statistically significant differences ($\chi = .05$) among the three groups were found on the STEP II test. On the People Pictures test, an instrument intended to measure per-

ceptions of foreign people, however, children in the experimental group had "a more favorable view of foreign people" as compared to the control groups. Children in the experimental group "used statistically significantly fewer unfavorable evaluative descriptions, such as 'mean,' 'stupid,' or 'unfriendly' to describe the four reference peoples (Americans, Chinese, Germans, and Kenyans)" (p. 9). On the Describing Nations test, an instrument that was also purported to tap children's perceptions and understanding of foreign people, there were statistically significant differences among the groups, favoring the experimental group "in the use of 15 of the 22 adjectives" such as "peaceful," "friendly," and "happy." Application of the Duncan multiple-range test "indicated that the experimental group had the highest means on 12 of these descriptives," while Control Group 2 performed "at a rate significantly below that of the other two groups on 14 of the variables on which there were significant differences" (p. 9). Mitsakos concluded that social studies programs, if carefully designed, can have a positive effect on children's understanding and views of other nations and peoples.

Further analysis of the data suggests that Mitsakos may have been overly optimistic in his claims. Standardized mean differences (*SMD*s) were computed for the statistically significant People Pictures results by dividing a pooled control group standard deviation of 8.74 (from Mitsakos's Table 3) into the differences between the experimental group and the two control group means. The SMDs were were only .21 and .04, respectively. Cohen (1977), for example, suggested criteria of .20, .50, and .80 for small, medium, and large SMD. Although like the .05 level of statistical significance, such criteria are arbitrary they do provide an initial guideline. The *SMD*s of .21 and .03 are especially small considering that they are overestimates due to the standard deviation used. Mitsakos apparently conducted his analysis using the means of the intact classes (21 in the experimental group and probably 10 in Control Group 1 and 9 in Control Group 2), rather than the scores of the students as data points, as indicated by the 2/39 degrees of freedom reported in Table 3. The standard deviations Mitsakos reported are, therefore, an underestimate of variability among the students; the variability among group means is always less than that among the scores upon which the means are based.

*SMD*s were also calculated for this chapter based on the data Mitsakos presented in Table 4 reporting on the Describing Nations test results (see Table 37–1). Although all of the differences were statistically significant, it is apparent from the *SMD*s in Table 1 that the magnitude of differences between the means for treatment group and Control Group 1 are educationally trivial, while those for the treatment group and Control Group 2 are small.

As a whole, Mitsakos's claims about the effects of the Family of Man program on the performance of students on dimensions of international understanding must be viewed with caution. Moreover, the importance of calculating effect sizes in determining the magnitude of results in social studies research is demonstrated clearly.

The results from a study by Hamilton (1982) of the effects

TABLE 37–1. Standardized Mean Differences (SMDs) for Mitsakos' (1978) Describing Nation's Test Results

Adjectives	SMDs	
	E and C_1	E and C_2
Peaceful	.12	.27
Are like us	.06	.36
Friendly	.06	.26
Warm weather	.20	.38
Happy	.06	.35
Small	−.006	.23
Many farms	.034	.28
Many people	.04	.31

TABLE 37–2. Standardized Mean Differences (SMDs) for Hamilton's (1982) Mean Gain Results

Table	Group		SMD
1 (p. 56)			
	E_1	1.1/9.36 =	.12
	E_2	1.4/9.36 =	.15
	E_3	.2/9.36 =	.02
	C_1	.3/9.36 =	.03
4 (p. 59)			
	E_1	−0.12/10.75 =	−.01
	E_2	−1.14/10.75 =	−.11
	E_3	1.25/10.75 =	.12
	C_1	3.62/10.75 =	.30
7 (p. 62)			
	E_1	−.56/8.98 =	−.06
	E_2	−2.78/8.98 =	.11
	E_3	1.00/8.98 =	.32
	C_1	2.87/8.98 =	.32
10 (p. 66)			
	E_1	5.8/7.34 =	.79
	E_2	3.4/7.34 =	.46
	E_3	6.3/7.34 =	.86
	C_1	1.9/7.34 =	.26

of three courses on high school students' attitudes toward and knowledge of global education further confirmed some of the concerns above. A purposive sample consisting of a total of 57 students enrolled in three 12-week courses with a global focus (i.e., "Internatinal Communications," "The American Way of Life," and "Atlanta and the World") comprised the three experimental groups. No group representativeness was claimed. In fact, the school "was selected because of its unique course offerings in global education" (p. 41). The comparison group was composed of 27 students with attributes similar to the experimental students (in terms of age, grade level, gender, and ethnic background.) Pre- and posttests were administered to determine mean gains. The Newark, Delaware, Global Attitude Scale (GAS), was used to measure such attitudes as reciprocity, acceptance, and international cooperation; the Educational Testing Service's Global Measures for Understanding (GMU) was used for measuring knowledge.

Analysis of variance "revealed no significant differences at the .05 level in attitude and knowledge scores between the experimental and control groups" (Hamilton, 1982, Abstract, p. 2). However, different results were suggested when effect sizes were calculated. Based on information obtained in Hamilton's Tables 1, 4, 7, and 10, corresponding tables of SMDs are presented in Table 37–2.

The trivial SMDs for the data in Hamilton's Table 1 confirm her rejection of the hypothesis that "students who participate in a global education course will show a more positive attitude towards reciprocity than similar students who do not participate in such a course" (p. 55). The data for the second hypothesis concerning student performance on the dimension of acceptance (Hamilton's Table 4) also yielded trivial SMDs for the three experimental groups but a small SMD (.30) for the control group. A similar pattern prevailed for the data for the hypothesis on attitudes towards international cooperation (Table 7). On the test of global knowledge, however, Hamilton's (Table 10) SMDs are large for the first and third experimental group and about medium for the second experimental group.

Again calculating effect sizes gives a more comprehensive and accurate picture of the results of social studies research. Aside from the limited research design, the author correctly identified other limitations such as the utilization of intact classes, the relatively small size of the three experimental

groups (ns of 18, 13, and 11, respectively), the influences of the larger social environment (an "international city") that could not be controlled, and the lack of observation of the classes to determine whether there were significant content differences among them.

Evaluating the effects of different global education programs on high school students' knowledge of and concern toward the world was the focus of Torney-Purta (1986). The instruments used in the study were a shortened version of the Educational Testing Service's Global Awareness Survey Instrument, developed as a measure of college students' knowledge and beliefs (Barrows, Klein, and Clark 1981) and a 10-item scale developed to measure "concern for world problems and interest in people from other cultures." A reliability coefficient (alpha) of .70 was reported for the scores of the high school sample on the first instrument. No reliability coefficient was reported for scores on the second instrument. The sample was a purposive sample of students in programs known for their global content—international high schools, instructional baccalaureate schools, and federally funded "603" projects. While a comparison group of students was sought in each school, one was not obtained in several of the schools. Many differences in the demographic and academic characteristics of students made it virtually "impossible to have a perfectly balanced design" (p. 10).

Given Torney-Purta's admitted difficulty in controlling all of the important variables, caution should be exercised in interpreting her results. It was found, for example, that when the mean scores of groups of students enrolled in specific global education programs, such as the 603 federally financed programs, were contrasted (holding grades constant) with those of students in the same school who were not in such programs, there were for the most part no statistically significant differences. Statistically significant differences were obtained for the group that participated in "extra-curricular global" activities. On the Global Awareness test the extra-curricular global group obtained a mean score of 16.69 ($n = 28$) as contrasted to a score of 11.48 ($n = 27$) in the comparison group, a difference statistically significant at the .0001 level. On the Global Concern test, the difference was statistically significant at the .05 level. A separate analysis of variance on the group means indicated (without further elaboration) that there were "highly significant between-group differences (probability less than .0001)" (p. 15). The differences that were found, it was conjectured, might in part be explained by "the intensive and highly selective programs enrolling able students ... especially those which combine curricular and extra-curricular activities" (p. 18).

Step-wise multiple regression analyses were also performed to establish which variables had predictive validity in terms of student scores on the Global Awareness and Global Concerns tests. Grade point average was the best predictor on the Global Awareness test (Beta = $-.284$ *[sic]*, significant at the .0001 level); the higher the students' GPA the higher their performance on the test. Other statistically significant predictors included "reading the international views in the newspaper," gender (boys tended to have higher scores), enrollment in social studies courses in all four years of the high school, "watching the news on TV," and "visiting another country." (Overall, $N = 987$ and $R = .503$.) Variables such as "years of foreign language study, extracurricular activity, perceived foreign language fluency, reading newspaper daily, discussion of world problems in class, grade [level] in school" did not make a statistically significant contribution when entered in the regression equation (p. 21). Another regression analysis indicated that having taken courses such as international relations, world geography, and Western Europe were statistically significant sensitive predictors of global awareness scores. Having taken world history, however, made a "significant negative contribution" (p. 21). There was no statistically significant relationship between student awareness scores and enrollment in courses entitled World Cultures, Latin American Studies, and Current Events.

Similar analyses were performed for the test of Global Concern "Reading international news", "watching news on TV," and GPA were, as in the previous analysis, statistically significant predictors. There were also sex differences with regard to global concern, but in this case girls tended to have higher scores. Also statistically significant were participation in extracurricular activities with an international focus, foreign language fluency, and number of years of foreign language study.

Although there was some congruence in statistically significant predictors on the Global Awareness and the Global Concern tests, there were also some differences that merit further examination. The role of foreign language study is a case in point—this type of study contributed to predictions of global concern scores, but it did not make any significant contribution to predictions of global knowledge scores. As Torney-Purta pointed out, given the lack of detailed information on the nature of the courses or programs in which the students were enrolled and the inability to control many background variables, the findings of the study should be used as a source of hypotheses for further research.

A follow-up study was conducted in the spring of 1984 in selected Bay area (California) high schools (Torney-Purta & Lansdale, 1986). Two student subsamples were selected, the first based on criteria such as location (inner city versus suburban high schools) and the second based on participation in a global education program, SES, and grade level. The first sample included 757 and the second 200 students. Multiple regression analyses on both samples confirmed the earlier predictors of global awareness scores (Torney-Purta, 1986); in this case, scores on the test of Knowledge in International Economics, grade point average, gender (males tended to have higher scores), and reading international news were statistically significant predictors. Additional statistically significant predictors were found, for example, whether students came from more educated families, whether they were born in the United States, and whether they were beginning high school students or were in the higher grade levels. With a few exceptions, the same variables were statistically significant predictors of scores on the test of International Security Knowledge. In one of the samples, whether students perceived they could engage freely in classroom discussions and the extent of teacher interest in international issues were significant predictors of student performance on both tests.

On a Global Perception Scale, measuring "interest," "kinship," and "concern," "girls showed more concern in their perception of the international community than boys" and those born outside the U.S. had scores indicating a higher sense of understanding and kinship (empathy toward people from other cultures) (p. 22). Unlike the earlier study (Torney-Purta, 1986), foreign language study was not a significant predictor. Classroom observational data generally corroborated the findings above, especially those involving student perceptions of opportunity to engage freely in discussions of international issues. The investigators concluded that "it is not primarily the frequency with which international issues are discussed in the classroom which influences knowledge and attitudes, but how that discussion is framed" (p. 27).

The Effects of Teachers

There are virtually no studies in which the direct effects of teachers on students' international understanding are examined in depth. In some studies, teacher influences are examined along with a host of other in-school and out-of-school variables (e.g., Torney-Purta & Lansdale, 1986). What has been mostly reported in the literature are studies on the effects of in-service training, graduate/undergraduate education, or study-abroad programs on teachers' knowledge of and attitudes toward the world (e.g., Barnes & Curlette, 1985; Swift, 1983; Tarolli, 1984; Wieber, 1982).

Social Studies Textbooks and International Understanding

There have been some attempts to critically review textbooks and other materials to determine the images they convey about other peoples (e.g., Cox & Massialas, 1967). Underlying all of the reviews is the assumption that school materials will have an impact on students' knowledge about and attitude toward the world. This assumption is rarely been put to a test in social studies research.

Examples of studies employing a "subjective" approach in analyzing textbooks are those conducted by Goldstein (1972) and Fleming (1983). In the first study, textbooks and curriculum guides used in Grades 4 to 6 were reviewed for their treatment of foreign countries and peoples. It was found that implicitly or explicitly other nations were judged in accordance with the standards of "industrialization and democracy," always similar to those employed to characterize the United States; thus countries that did not meet these standards were looked down upon. The people of the nonindustrialized Third World who did not meet these standards were "viewed as technologically backward, poor, uneducated, etc. They rarely, if ever, receive praise for their personal qualities" (pp. 26–27). Books and curriculum guides on Russia and Eastern-bloc countries gave extremely narrow views of the people and their social institutions. Goldstein concluded that "the material on foreign countries and people includes both some rewriting of history and a distinctly ethnocentric viewpoint." (p. 30)

The review by Fleming (1983) of world and U.S. history texts revealed that war and arms limitation were given "scant attention" (p. 483). "Six of the ten [U.S. history texts] failed to make any note of the radiation effects of the atomic bomb and only one gave more than superficial coverage to the results of the bombing and the threat of nuclear war" (p. 483).

Another work (Glickman, 1976), in which explicit criteria were not used in reviewing curriculum materials, confirmed the ethnocentric biases in these materials. The reviewer found that 43% of the materials "present a negative and/or stereotypic view of peoples and countries of Africa, Asia and Latin America. They convey little value for people of preindustrial countries, viewing them as passive and backward" (p. 108). In the remaining 57% of the materials, a global perspective was excluded completely. For the most part, the materials did not provide a context within which students could feel themselves to be potential participants in the problems and the solutions of the world community.

Examples of the application of systematic techniques of content analysis are the studies by Kasambira (1980) and Jarrar (1976). Kasambira selected 24 secondary school geography textbooks published since 1945 on the basis of a questionnaire sent to those generally involved in textbook adoptions. He used Pratt's Evaluation Coefficient Analysis (ECO Analysis)—a method of content analysis focusing on the number of evaluative terms in a text that are classified as "favorable" or "unfavorable"—to analyze the textbooks and found that Africans were generally viewed in unfavorable terms. Terms such as "primitive," "natives," "warlike," were characteristic of those used with Africans. The total number of unfavorable terms depicting Africans in all the textbooks was 453, with only 92 favorable terms.

Jarrar (1976) also applied ECO analysis to the examination of textbooks used in social studies (general), world history, geography and world affairs, and problems of American democracy courses in grades 7 through 12. He sought to identify the images of Arabs presented in these texts. More negative than positive images of the Arabs were found in his sample of textbooks from state adoption lists. On a coefficient scale of 0 to 100 established through the ECO analysis, geography texts were found to be the most unfavorable to the Arabs with a coefficient of 17.7. The combined coefficient for all the textbooks was 25.5. The "general" social studies textbooks were the least unfavorable with a coefficient of 32.8. Factual errors and stereotypes were found in abundance. The Arabs, much like the Africans in the Kasambira study, were depicted as being "primitive nomads," "war loving," "terrorists," and the like.

The ECO analysis system provides a systematic method for analyzing the content of textbooks. The major constraint, however, is the possibility that the emphasis on evaluative terms might lead to judging terms out of context. This problem was considered by Jarrar, who conducted a judgmental analysis of the textbooks using a modified version of the Evaluation Criteria Checklist (Kane, 1970) in addition to the ECO analysis. The checklist included such criteria as validity, balance, concreteness, realism, and inconsistency in a rather subjective way, "to pinpoint sources of bias not covered by the ECO analysis" (Jarrar, 1976, p. 55).

The Content of Student International Knowledge and Attitudes

The work of the Survey Research Center of the Institute for Social Research, University of Michigan, holds promise for periodic assessments of preuniversity students' international knowledge and attitudes. Beginning in 1975, the Center has conducted an annual national survey of high school seniors (e.g., Bachman, Johnston, & O'Malley, 1980). A multistage, nationwide sample was administered, a detailed instrument covering such broad topics as work and leisure, drugs, sex roles and family, politics, and social problems.

The sample stages included selection procedures based on (a) *geographic areas,* with the United States divided on the basis of population into 74 primary areas; (b) *schools,* with high schools drawn in such a way "that the probability of drawing a school is proportionate to the size of its senior class (the larger the senior class, according to recent records, the higher the selection probability assigned to the high school)" (p. 3); and (c) *students,* with all students included from small schools (under 400 seniors), and from large schools, "a subset of seniors is selected either by randomly sampling classrooms or by some other random method that is convenient for the school and judged to be unbiased" (p. 3). One limitations in sample selection was that the study did not tap an estimated 15% to 20% of the corresponding age group who dropped out of school before graduation.

Although global concern did not constitute a separate "measurement content area" on the list of topics to be studied in depth, questions about global issues were interspersed throughout the questionnaire. For example, 23.9% of the total sample stated that in their opinion "there was no such thing as a 'necessary' war." Among the females, 29.3% responded this way, whereas 18% of the males did. Other items on the questionnaire dealt with the likelihood of nuclear or biological annihilation, the inevitability of the human race going through rough times, whether or not life was purposeful given the present world situation, potential money contributions to international relief organizations, and the frequency of thinking about social problems of the nation and the world. To the statement, "My guess is that this country will be caught up in a major world upheaval in the next 10 years," 33.8% of the respondents mostly agreed or agreed. More than one-third, 35.1%, of the respondents neither agreed nor disagreed with the statement (p. 158).

Although the survey yielded only descriptive data, social studies education researchers can utilize the data for their research interests. Data on the characteristic of American youth over a period of years allows for the systematic analysis of important changes taking place within this population. Many demographic and personality variables, such as where and when born, ethnic background, parents' education, and religion might provide the basis for explaining a good portion of the response variances. It was, in fact, an intent of the investigators to examine "what causes these young people to be as they are" (p. 1). Path analysis and multiple regression could presumably be used to make sense of the vast data in the series of volumes.

For those who see war and peace issues as part of education for international understanding, a recent review of research on children's understanding of nuclear war (Tizard, 1984) will be of interest. Students' concerns about the threat of nuclear war, as well as their misinformation about the use of nuclear weapons in a war, are matters of importance for those concerned with preparing students to participate in the resolution of critical social issues (Wood, 1985). Much of the research on children's understanding of nuclear issues have been conducted by psychiatrists. This is an important topic for social studies education researchers, especially in regard to the role of the classroom teacher. Tizard (1984) identified four major areas of needed research, including the "ways teachers approach the task of nuclear education" and the impact of various methodologies and approaches on children (p. 21).

RESEARCH ON OUT-OF-SCHOOL FACTORS THAT INFLUENCE INTERNATIONAL UNDERSTANDING

There have been investigations of the influences of such agencies or factors as the family, peer groups, media, general cultural conditions, and personality and demographic antecedents on international understanding. A major piece of research was the IEA study conducted in 1971 in nine countries (Federal Republic of Germany, Finland, Ireland, Israel, Italy, the Netherlands, New Zealand, Sweden, and the United States) (Torney, Oppenheim, & Farnen, 1975). Attitudinal scales were developed and validated during 1970 and 1971 with a sample of 30,000 students in the nine countries in which the study was conducted. Two-stage probability sampling was used. First, "schools were selected from a nationally stratified frame with a probability proportional to their student-body size." Second, "students were selected randomly from within the chosen schools inversely proportional to the size of the school" (Torney, 1977, p. 8). School size, region served, and type of school were factors considered in selecting the original school sample. The sampling technique could not be followed in all of its detail, in all of the targeted countries, thus producing "somewhat less adequate samples" (p. 7).

On global issues, of all the countries studied in the IEA project, the U.S. 14-year-olds were the least interested in discussing international politics with parents and peers while more interested in discussing national affairs. In Israel and Italy, more than twice as many 14-year-old students than in the U.S. "reported discussion of other countries at least once a week" (Torney, 1977, p. 10). A similar pattern of response characterized preuniversity students (Torney, 1979). The lower level of interest in international politics among U.S. students may be because U.S. teachers consider the discussion of national problems to be more important than international ones (Torney, 1977, p. 10).

On a test of knowledge of international institutions and processes, the 14-year-old Americans also scored relatively low, ranking seventh among the eight countries (p. 14). Conversely, Americans scored relatively high on knowledge of national political affairs and demonstrated relatively high support for their national government.

Although teachers may influence student knowledge and attitudes toward international matters, the national environment in which students operate might be the most pervasive factor. On an "index of foreign contact" established by the IEA study, the United States in 1971 scored the lowest in the proportion of its GNP entering world trade (e.g., 6% of the total GNP in the United States as opposed to 40% in the Netherlands). On volume of imported films and textbooks, and international mail and telephone calls, the United States also placed the lowest. Torney (1977) concluded:

These data may be interpreted either as indicating that the national systems vary in their demand for given levels of international knowledge among citizens or that the degree to which everyday life in a nation includes foreign contact, influences the acquisition of such knowledge. (p. 15)

It seems apparent that students living in an "isolationist" or "parochial" environment will be less likely than those in a "cosmopolitan" environment to enter into discussions about and be active in global issues. In this type of social environment, the school can have only a limited influence. As suggested by Torney, more research is needed on the relationship between a country's total sociopolitical environment and student level of international understanding. Attention should be given "to compensatory international political education in countries where naturally occurring contact with international matters is not part of students' life" (Torney, 1977, p. 19).

The IEA findings were confirmed in part by data reported by Cogan, Torney-Purta, and Anderson (1988) from two surveys, one conducted in the United States by ETS (Barrows, Klein, & Clark, 1981) and one conducted in Japan by Cogan, Torney-Purta, and Anderson (1988) during 1982 to 1983. The survey in the United States was based on a probability sample using a two-stage, stratified design. In the first stage, 185 tertiary or postsecondary institutions with undergraduate programs were identified; in the second stage, 3,000 students were randomly selected—freshmen and seniors in four-year college programs and students in two-year colleges. The survey in Japan was based on a stratified random sample of "the total population of national universities throughout Japan involved in the training of teachers and educational leaders" (Cogan et al., 1988, p. 286). From out of the 15 universities identified—14 national and 1 private—a random sample of 50 freshmen and 50 seniors was selected. The 1,436 valid questionnaires constituted a 90% response rate. The original ETS instrument, developed by a panel of experts in such areas as international economics and world history, included 101 items on the previous background and experiences of the respondents, their foreign language study, and their sources of information. "Adequate reliability" was established (Cogan et al., 1988, p. 283). The Japanese version was a 93-item test translated and slightly modified from the ETS instrument, with a back-translation "to ensure accuracy of the Japanese version before dissemination and administration" (p. 285).

The data indicated that Americans about to enter college were less knowledgeable about global issues than their Japanese counterparts, but there was no difference for college seniors. For the U.S. students, mean scores on the subtest of knowledge of global issues were as follows: freshmen, 37.87, seniors, 46.13. For the Japanese they were: freshmen, 44.54, seniors, 46.29. Standard deviations were given only for the Japanese data, about 8.00.

Other analyses indicated that Americans "were much more positive about the value of foreign language study for themselves than were the Japanese" (pp. 291–292). On foreign language study, Cogan et al. (1988) entered a caveat (acknowledged by others writing in the field as well) that while students exposed to foreign language study seem to be more concerned with global issues, "it is not clear whether such interest and concern leads to language study, or the reverse" (p. 296).

The Media

Researchers as a rule report that children learn to dislike countries and people as part of their political socialization experience, that is, they learn to dislike those disliked by the adults with whom they come in contact—for example, in the 1970s, Russia was normally disliked in the United States but Canada was not (Remy, Nathan, Becker, & Torney, 1975). Earlier studies established similar patterns of international political socialization (Lambert & Klineberg, 1967).

Sources of information for children's views on foreign peoples vary with age. Six-year-olds seem to rely on parents, television, and movies, whereas the 10- and 14-year-olds rely on media and general reading material (Lambert & Klineberg, 1967, p. 213). The results of other studies indicate that children learn about the world at an early age and these learnings are cumulative (Remy et al., 1975, pp. 39–40). Middle childhood is crucial in international education, because the children's likes and dislikes have not been irretrievably impacted. During this period,

mass media are important sources of international political learning (Remy et al., 1975, p. 40).

The potential influence of the media in international political socialization is suggested by Tolley's (1973) finding that children learned more about the Vietnam War from television than from any other source. Parents and the school also "contribute jointly to a child's outlook on war . . ." (p. 120). Parents have more influence than teachers, but for children "whose parents rarely discuss the war, school exercises the greater influence" (p. 120).

SUMMARY

In this chapter, the research in the last 10 to 15 years on education for global or international understanding was critically examined. The critical review revealed the following:

1. Conceptually, the research leaves much to be desired. Conceptualization studies have generally failed to provide frameworks that adequately define the field, delimit the scope of work, and provide a basis for generating meaningful hypotheses. The literature is still dominated by arguments over whether educators should be concerned with global education, nuclear education, human rights education, peace education, world order education, and the like.

Developing curriculum guidelines based on educators' perceptions of global education is the primary activity reported in the social studies education literature. Numerous articles have been written, especially by social studies educators, to justify global or international education in the curriculum. The assumption, however, that such education actually contributes to international understanding has rarely been put to a test.

There has been little specification of the particular competencies or characteristics that constitute worldmindedness and international understanding or the types of instruments available or needed to measure these competencies and characteristics. International understanding is stressed, but there is little mention of actual participation in international decision-making. In general, there is a nontheoretical trend to the research, especially among those studies conducted by social studies educators. Social scientists, on the other hand, have usually operated from some theoretical framework—for example, socialization or enculturation theory, theory of personality, theory of cognitive or moral development, or intercultural communication theory.

2. There are serious methodological problems in the research, especially in the research conducted by social studies educators. In studies in which experimental designs were used to compare the effectiveness of instructional approaches (e.g., a "global education" approach versus a "traditional" approach) only statistical significance was typically used as the criterion for the importance of results. Other flaws in carrying out the research include (a) the failure to match experimental and control groups on salient student characteristics; (b) the failure to identify significant variables, contextual or environmental, that may have affected student learning; (c) inadequate sample size; (d) inadequate sample selection procedures, with convenience

samples the norm; (e) treatments too brief to be effective; (f) low statistical power, either as a function of the level of statistical significance applied or the sample size used; and (g) lack of reports of effect sizes.

Social science researchers, on the other hand, mostly sociologists or psychologists, usually employed more adequate techniques both in drawing samples and in analyzing data. The IEA cross-cultural research in civic education (Torney, 1977) is exemplary in this regard, especially the efforts to establish links among a host of variables.

3. The content focus of most of the studies conducted by social studies educators has been, monotonously, on the effects of formal school efforts to promote global or international understanding or worldmindedness. What has rarely received attention is the effect of the "implicit" or "hidden" curriculum. For example, the SES, gender, and ethnicity of teachers and students, as well as community mores and expectations (Anyon, 1988; Spener, 1988), are known to affect the teaching-learning process, the way the formal curriculum is delivered, the selection of textbooks, the implementation of reward systems, and the attendant values formed by students. Yet these factors were not included in many of the studies reviewed here or, when included, they were treated as being much less important than the formal school programs. The persistence on studying only formal programs has left unexplained most of the variance in student scores on relevant tests of global knowledge and attitudes.

The failure to establish substantial effects of formal programs on student global understanding may explain, in part, why every study is focused on a *new program,* with different measures of student performance. Studies have rarely been replications or extensions of other studies. Consequently, the research has not been cumulative.

4. Most of the studies on global understanding by social studies educators have been conducted with students in the United States. It is, indeed, paradoxical to place an emphasis on the global or international while excluding from the studies students in other countries. In this regard, it is seldom (exceptions: Massialas, 1965; Shafer, 1981) that social studies educators have shown an interest in how social studies is taught in other lands. This omission places severe limitations on the quest to establish the impact of national or cultural forces on global understanding. It goes without saying that cross-national data would enable investigators to explain better why students in different countries perform differently on tests of international understanding. The IEA studies (Torney, 1977) are exemplary in this regard, especially the attempt to relate countries' indices of cosmopolitanism to students' global understanding.

The Research Agenda

Given the deficiencies in the field unearthed by this review, the following suggestions are made:

1. Researchers should develop conceptual frameworks for education for global/international understanding and participation that are comprehensive (i.e., include relevant factors in and out of school) and draw systematically from theories in the so-cial, behavioral, and pedagogical sciences. Of particular interest to those studying global understanding should be socialization/enculturation theories and theories of moral or cognitive development. The work of psychiatrists on theories concerning attitude formation by young children toward war and peace should also be considered.

2. There is a need for conceptual specificity on the phenomenon called global/international understanding or worldmindedness. Included should be specification of competencies and the development of tests, observation schedules, questionnaires, and interview schedules validated for the particular program to be evaluated (Torney-Purta, 1989). Relevant cross-cultural instruments should be developed for use with samples drawn from different cultural settings.

3. In studies utilizing an experimental design, effect sizes should be reported. Survey research of the type reported here should also be utilized more by social studies educators, preferably in longitudinal designs, to assess the performance of various student populations and relate this performance to relevant background variables. Ethnographic research methods and case studies should be utilized more extensively so that the full range of environmental effects on students' and teachers' international beliefs and knowledge, including the propensity to participate directly in international decision-making, can be better understood. Systematic observation methods (e.g., Massialas, Sprague, & Hurst, 1975), which were almost nonexistent in the research reviewed, should also be applied to identify variables, such as classroom climate, that may be related to test results. Content analysis of textbooks and materials should be used in research to determine whether different materials do have different or any effects on students' knowledge, values, and participatory behavior.

4. The research focus should be changed from formal programs to the relationship of the hidden or implicit curriculum to student global understanding and involvement. National educational policies, informal community norms, and economic considerations are areas that need to be investigated thoroughly as they relate to school conditions that promote or restrict the development of worldmindedness.

5. Social agencies and processes need to be included formally in the study design. There is dire need to investigate the influence of family, peer groups, media, teachers, and other socialization agents on students' learning about the world. The role of mediating factors—such as age, personality, or gender of the student—in the process of attitude formation should also be studied.

6. Studies dealing with the development of global understanding ought to be conducted cross-culturally. While the effort would be greater than for a national study, investigators could establish the importance of the effects of prevailing cultural conditions on international understanding.

In sum, the research agenda calls for a radical redirection of the effort expanded in studies on education for international understanding: away from a limiting focus on formal programs and the use of narrow experimental designs. Unless there is concentration on the societal forces that impact on students, future studies will continue to produce insignificant or trivial results.

References

Anderson, L. F. (1968). Education and social science in the context of an emerging global society. In J. M. Becker & H. D. Mehlinger (Eds.), *International dimensions in the social studies*. 38th Yearbook. (pp. 78–97). Washington, DC: National Council for the Social Studies.

Anyon, J. (1988). Social class and the hidden curriculum of women. In J. R. Gress (Ed.), *Curriculum: An introduction to the field* (pp. 306–389). Berkeley, CA: McCutchan.

Bachman, J. G., Johnston, L. D., & O'Malley, P. M. (1980). *Monitoring the future: Questionnaire responses from the nation's high school seniors, 1978*. Ann Arbor: Institute for Social Research, University of Michigan.

Barnes, B. R., & Curlette, W. L. (1985). Effects of instruction on teachers' global mindedness and patriotism. *Theory and Research in Social Education, 13*(1), 43–49.

Barrows, T. S., Klein, S. F., & Clark, L. D. (1981). *College students' knowledge and beliefs: A survey of global understanding*. New Rochelle, NY: Change Magazine Press.

Becker, J. M. (1979). *Schooling for a global use*. New York: McGraw Hill.

Cogan, J., Torney-Purta, J., & Anderson, D. (1988). Knowledge and attitudes toward global issues: Students in Japan and the United States. *Comparative Education Review, 32* 282–297.

Cohen, J. (1977). *Statistical power analysis for the behavioral sciences*. (rev. ed.) New York: Academic Press.

Corkle, M. A. (1983). Guidelines for the implementation of a global education program in a K–12 school district (K–12) (Doctoral dissertation, University of Nebraska). *Dissertation Abstracts International, 44/04A*, 925.

Cox, C. B., & Massialas, B. G. (Eds.). (1967). *Social studies in the United States: A critical appraisal*. New York: Harcourt, Brace & World.

Day, B. A. (1986). *An examination of the continuity and change of images of the world in the journal "Social Education" 1937–1979*. Unpublished doctoral dissertation, New York University.

Fleming, D. B. (1983). Nuclear war: What do high school history textbooks tell us? *Social Education, 47*, 480–484.

Glickman, A. (Ed.). (1976). *Growth implications and the earth's future: a study of curriculum materials and student views*. Newton, MA: Education Development Center.

Goldstein, R. J. (1972). Elementary school curriculum and political socialization. In B. G. Massialas (Ed.), *Political youth, traditional schools: National and international perspectives* (pp. 14–33). Englewood Cliffs, NJ: Prentice-Hall.

Gualdoni, M. A. (1980). *Global education: A genetic identification based on a natural delphi and practical application within the state of Michigan*. Unpublished doctoral dissertation, Wayne State University.

Hamilton, B. S. (1982). *Assessing the effects of planned curricular interventions on high school students' attitudes toward and knowledge of global education*. Unpublished doctoral dissertation, Georgia State University.

Horton, J. S. (1981). A global perspective in education: Toward a clearer understanding. (Doctoral dissertation, Ohio State University) *Dissertation Abstracts International, 42/05A*, 2064.

Hughes, G. (1983). Intercultural education in elementary and secondary schools. In D. Landon and R. W. Brislin (Eds.), *Handbook of intercultural training: Vol. III. Area studies in intercultural training* (pp. 21–54). New York: Pergamon.

Jacobson, W., Reardon, B., & Sloan, D. (1983). A conceptual framework for teaching about nuclear weapons. *Social Education, 47*, 475–479.

Jarrar, S. A. (1976). *Images of the Arabs in United States secondary school social studies textbooks: A content analysis and a unit development*. Unpublished doctoral dissertation, Florida State University.

Kane, M. B. (1970). *Minorities in textbooks*. Chicago: Anti-Defamation League.

Kasambira, T. S. (1980). An analysis of the treatment of Africa and Africans in American secondary school geography textbooks. (Doctoral dissertation, Kent State University). *Dissertation Abstracts International, 41/09A*, 3858.

Lambert, W. E., & Klineberg, O. (1967). *Children's views of foreign peoples*. New York: Appleton-Century-Crofts.

Lamy, S. L. (1983). Defining global education. *Educational Research Quarterly 8*(1), 9–20.

Massialas, B. G. (1965). Social studies instruction in world perspective. In B. G. Massialas & F. R. Smith (Eds.), *New challenges in the social studies: Implications of research for teaching* (pp. 191–234). Belmont, CA: Wadsworth.

Massialas, B. G., Sprague, N. F., & Hurst, J. B. (1975). *Social issues through inquiry: Coping in an age of crises*. Englewood Cliffs, NJ: Prentice-Hall.

Mendlovitz, S. H., Metcalf, L., & Washburn, M. (1977). The crisis of global transformation, interdependence, and the schools. In B. F. Brown (Ed.), *Education for responsible citizenship: The report of the National Task Force on Citizenship Education* (pp. 189–212). New York: McGraw Hill.

Mitsakos, C. L. (1978). A global education program can make a difference. *Theory and Research in Social Education 6*(1), 1–15.

Morrow, S. R. (1983). The development of a curriculum guide for Afro-Asian history in secondary social studies education. (Doctoral dissertation, Ball State University). *Dissertation Abstracts International, 44/10A*, 3029.

Olson, W. D. (1981). The development of global education in Michigan. (Doctoral dissertation, Michigan State University) *Dissertation Abstracts International, 42/08A*, 3420.

Remy, R. C., Nathan, J. A., Becker, J. M., & Torney, J. V. (1975). *International learning and international education for a global age*. Washington, DC: National Council for the Social Studies, Bulletin 47.

Shafer, S. M. (1981). Social studies in other nations. In H. D. Mehlinger & O. L. Davis Jr. (Eds.), *The social studies*. 80th Yearbook of the National Council for the Study of Education (pp. 81–101). Chicago: University of Chicago Press.

Sidemaker, M. S. (1984). Global education as viewed by elementary school principals in Pennsylvania: A descriptive study. (Doctoral dissertation, Pennsylvania State University) *Dissertation Abstracts International, 45/07A*, 1985.

Spener, D. (1988). Transitional bilingual education and the socialization of immigrants. *Harvard Educational Review, 58*, 133–153.

Stomfay-Stitz, A. M. (1984). *Peace education, 1828–1983: Historical perspectives*. Unpublished doctoral dissertation, Northern Illinois University.

Swift, J. (1983). An investigation of the rationale, construction, operation and evaluation of an interdisciplinary high school curriculum in global education. (Doctoral dissertation, Michigan State University) *Dissertation Abstracts International, 44/09A*, 2672.

Tarolli, F. F. (1984). The effect of a global education workshop on intern teachers' attitudes and perceptions of global issues and goals. (Doctoral dissertation, Syracuse University) *Dissertation Abstracts International, 46/01A*, 42.

Terrill, M. M. (1982). The rationale for and the design of an interdisciplinary semester course with a global perspective: Intercultural communication for eighth and ninth grade students. (Doctoral dissertation, University of Akron) *Dissertation Abstracts International, 43/02A*, 357.

Tizard, B. (1984). Problematic aspects of nuclear education. *Harvard Educational Review, 54*(3), 271–281.

Tolley, H., Jr. (1973). *Children and war.* New York: Teachers College Press.

Torney, J. V. (1977). The international attitudes and knowledge of adolescents in nine countries: The IEA civic education survey. *International Journal of Political Education, 1,* 3–20.

Torney, J. V. (1979). Psychological and institutional obstacles to the global perspective in education. In J. M. Becker (Ed.), *Schooling for a global age* (pp. 59–93). New York: McGraw-Hill.

Torney, J. V., Oppenheim, A. N., & Farnen, R. F. (1975). *Civic education in ten countries: An empirical study.* New York: John Wiley & Sons.

Torney-Purta, J. (1986). *Predictors of global awareness and concern among secondary school students.* Columbus: The Mershon Center, Ohio State University. (ERIC Document Reproduction Service No. ED 271 364)

Torney-Purta, J. (1989). Measuring the effectiveness of world studies courses. In R. B. Woyach and R. C. Remy (Eds.), *Approaches to world studies: A handbook for planners* (pp. 209–247). Boston: Allyn & Bacon.

Torney-Purta, J., & Schwille, J. (1986). Civic values learned in school: Policy and practice in industrialized nations. *Comparative Education Review, 30*(1), 30–49.

Vocke, D. E. (1985). Selected populations of secondary social studies teachers' perceptions of global education in Iowa. (Doctoral dissertation, University of Iowa). *Dissertation Abstracts International, 46/01A,* 3313.

Wieber, D. L. (1982). An assessment of global knowledge of K–12 teachers in an American-sponsored overseas school. (Doctoral dissertation, Michigan State University) *Dissertation Abstracts International, 43/12A,* 3806.

Wood, G. H. (1985). Education for democratic participation: Democratic values and the nuclear freeze campaign. *Theory and Research in Social Education, 12*(4), 39–56.

·38·

MULTICULTURAL EDUCATION: ITS EFFECTS ON STUDENTS' RACIAL AND GENDER ROLE ATTITUDES

James A. Banks

UNIVERSITY OF WASHINGTON, SEATTLE

Consensus does not exist about the scope and boundaries of multicultural education (Sleeter & Grant, 1987). Some writers use the term to refer only to education related to ethnic groups (Baker, 1983; Bennett, 1986), a common usage in the schools. Other writers define the term to include educational issues that focus on race/ethnicity, social class, gender, and exceptionality (Gollnick & Chinn, 1986; Grant & Sleeter, 1986a). In this chapter, *multicultural education* is used in this more inclusive way (Banks & Banks, 1989), with *multiethnic education* used to denote education related to race and ethnicity (Banks, 1988). The scope of this chapter is limited to only two of the major variables of multicultural education: race and gender, so that the major variables of multicultural education discussed in it can be treated with sufficient depth and comprehensiveness.

The major goal of this chapter is to describe the research on the effects of materials and other curricular experiences related to race and gender (i.e., knowledge and structured educational experiences such as courses, and units) on the perceptions, attitudes, and beliefs of students in grades kindergarten through 12. The review of the literature and research is broad in scope and is not limited to courses called *social studies*. This was done for several reasons. A few significant experimental studies that describe the effects of curricular materials on students' racial and gender attitudes and perceptions were not conducted in social studies classes (e.g., Flerx, Fidler, & Rogers, 1976; Litcher & Johnson, 1969). These studies, however, have important implications for teaching social studies content and courses. There is a paucity of research that describes the effects of materials

and courses related to race and gender. A broad conceptualization of studies is needed to provide guidelines for further research and to improve practice.

THE ROLE OF MULTICULTURAL CONTENT IN THE SOCIAL STUDIES

This chapter is on the effects of multicultural content on students' perceptions, beliefs, and attitudes toward racial and ethnic groups and females and males. However, it is important for readers to realize that the justification for the inclusion of multicultural content in the social studies curriculum is not grounded in the empirical demonstration of the effects of such materials on student behavior and attitudes, but rather on two other important grounds: (a) the need for historical accuracy and (b) the national commitment to a democratic society (Myrdal, with Sterner & Rose, 1944).

A study of the American Revolution is included in the social studies curriculum primarily because social studies educators believe that it is necessary to give students an accurate depiction of the development of U.S. society and culture. Content about people of color, women, and disabled persons should be included in the curriculum for the same reason: to give students an accurate view of U.S. society and culture. Multicultural content should also be included in the social studies curriculum because of the nation's commitment to fostering a democratic society (Myrdal, with Sterner & Rose, 1944). A pluralistic demo-

Reviewers were Gloria Contreras, University of North Texas; Carlos E. Cortés, University of California, Riverside; Christine E. Sleeter, University of Wisconsin, Parkside; Roberta Woolever, University of North Carolina, Chapel Hill.

cratic society functions best when its diverse groups believe they are an integral part of its institutions and social structure. When groups within a democratic society feel excluded and experience anomie and alienation, ethnic polarization develops (Patterson, 1977). Thus, schools in a pluralistic democratic society, in order to promote the structural inclusion of diverse groups and help them to develop a commitment to the national ethos and ideology, should structure a social studies curriculum that reflects the perspectives and experiences of the diverse groups that constitute the nation-state.

Even though there are important historical and philosophical reasons for including multicultural content in the social studies curriculum, it is also important to determine the effects of such content on students' attitudes, perceptions, and beliefs. This knowledge can help us to design curricular interventions that will help students to develop attitudes and beliefs consistent with a democratic ideology (Clark, 1955; Gabelko & Michaelis, 1981; Katz, 1976). It can also contribute to the developing theory in multicultural education and intergroup relations (Allport, 1954; Banks, 1988; Sleeter & Grant, 1987).

MODIFICATION OF STUDENTS' RACIAL ATTITUDES

Social scientists have been interested since at least the 1920s in the racial and ethnic attitudes expressed by children. Lasker's (1929) pioneering research on children's racial attitudes indicated that young children are aware of racial differences. Lasker also described some of the emotional components that accompany racial prejudice. An early study by Minard (1931) also indicated that children's racial attitudes are formed during the earliest years of life. Since the seminal research by Lasker and Minard, a number of other researchers have studied race awareness and self-identifications of young children. This research has generally confirmed Lasker's early findings (e.g., Clark, 1955; Goodman, 1952; Milner, 1983; Porter, 1971; Williams & Morland, 1976; Wilson, 1987). Most of the research on children's racial attitudes has focused on children in preschool and kindergarten. Comparatively little research has been done on the racial attitudes of adolescent youths. An exception is the important study by Glock, Wuthnow, Piliavin, and Spencer (1975).

While there is a rich literature describing the racial attitudes and racial self-identifications made by children, there is a paucity of studies that describe the results of interventions designed to change students' racial attitudes. Reviews of prior research have been undertaken by Cook (1947), Proshansky (1966), Katz (1976), and Stephan (1985). These reviews, except for the ones by Cook (1947) and Katz (1976), were focused on studies dealing with adults rather than with children. Those studies on the modification of children's racial attitudes shared several problems. In most, the effects of short-term interventions were examined and the researchers failed to determine their long-range effects. The interventions were usually not defined in sufficient detail for other researchers to replicate the studies or for readers to determine the precise nature of the interventions. Different measures were usually used in various studies and intercorrelations of racial attitude measures tend to be low, making comparisons of results from different studies problematic. Scores on racial attitudes measures are often influenced by the students' knowledge of the socially acceptable responses; this makes it difficult to assess their attitudes and beliefs accurately.

Measures of behavior were not included in most of the studies. Determining the relationship between attitudes and behavior is a major problem in race relations research. Another problem is that the intervention studies were usually not grounded in a theoretical or conceptual framework. Theories developed by social scientists such as Adorno, Frenkel-Brunswik, Levinson, and Sanford (1950) and Allport (1954) have been used frequently in studies of adult prejudice, but have been used rarely in studies dealing with curriculum interventions with students. Reinforcement studies, perceptual differentiation studies, and contact studies of attempts to modify children's racial attitudes are more theoretically grounded than studies that examine the effects of courses and curriculum. Stephan (1985) pointed out that few of the intervention studies in educational settings involve comparisons of alternative approaches and thus provide little information about which approaches are the most effective. He also noted that in most of the studies White prejudice toward African Americans is examined, limiting the generalization of the findings to other racial and ethnic groups.

Since at least the 1940s, a number of researchers have investigated the effects of educational and curricular experiences on students' racial and ethnic attitudes and beliefs. These studies have had encouraging but mixed results. They reveal that students' racial attitudes can be affected by curriculum interventions, but that the results of such interventions are inconsistent, complex, and probably influenced by many different factors, including the nature and structure of the intervention, its duration, student characteristics, the characteristics of the school environment (e.g., whether cooperative or competitive), and the characteristics of the community in which the school is located. Logic and wisdom of practice suggest that teacher characteristics are also an important mediating variable in curriculum intervention studies. It is surprising that only a few of the studies reviewed in this chapter examine the teacher in any detail or treat the teacher as a variable.

TYPES OF RACIAL ATTITUDE MODIFICATION STUDIES

Several major types of racial attitude modification studies exist: (a) studies in which the effects of courses, curriculum content, and units are examined (e.g., Litcher & Johnson, 1969; Trager & Yarrow, 1952); (b) studies of the effects of reinforcement techniques (e.g., McAdoo, 1985; Parish, Shirazi, & Lambert, 1976; Williams & Edwards, 1969); (c) perceptual differentiation studies (e.g., Katz, 1973; Katz, Sohn, & Zalk, 1975; Katz & Zalk 1978); and (d) studies of the effects of cooperative classroom and school environments (e.g., Slavin, 1985; Slavin & Madden, 1979).

The richest and most productive work has been done on reinforcement techniques, perceptual approaches, and the effects of cooperative learning environments. The research using these approaches has also resulted in rather consistent positive findings. In one such study, Katz and Zalk (1978) compared the effects of four short-term intervention techniques on the racial attitudes of high-prejudice White students in the second and fifth grades. They assessed attitudes after two weeks and again four to six months later. The four techniques were: (a) increased positive racial contact, (b) vicarious interracial contact, (c) reinforcement of the color black, and (d) perceptual differentiation of minority group faces. All of the experimental groups experienced a short-term reduction in mean prejudice scores on combined measures. However, the reductions were greater for the vicarious contact and perceptual groups than for the racial contact and reinforcement groups. The treatment effects were less pronounced in the long-term assessment. However, some experimental gains were maintained by the vicarious contact and perceptual differentiation groups. Each experimental treatment in the Katz and Zalk study lasted only 15 minutes. It is remarkable that the treatments resulted in a reduction in prejudice and even more remarkable that some effects were still in evidence four to six months later.

The results from cooperative learning studies have rather consistently indicated that students from different ethnic groups develop more positive racial attitudes when they participate in cooperative learning activities (Aronson & Gonzalez, 1988; Slavin, 1985; Slavin & Madden, 1979). These studies have involved African-American and White students as well as White students and Mexican-American students. Students not only develop more positive racial attitudes in cooperative learning situations, but ethnic minority students tend to experience academic achievement gains. The achievement of White students tends to be about the same in cooperative and competitive learning environments.

INTERGROUP EDUCATION IN THE 1940S AND 1950S

Race relations research, like all research, has reflected the dominant ideologies, trends, and concerns of the times. It has ebbed and flowed with dominant social concerns. The intergroup education movement emerged during the World War II period when African Americans began their exodus to northern cities and racial conflict erupted in major U.S. cities (Cook, 1947; Taba, Brady, & Robinson, 1952). Studies such as those by Trager and Yarrow (1952) and Hayes and Conklin (1953) were part of the intergroup education movement of the 1940s and 1950s. Intergroup education had become a low national priority by the late 1950s. New initiatives in race relations would not command national attention again until the civil rights movement of the 1960s and 1970s.

A number of researchers examined the effects of curriculum materials on students' racial attitudes during the 1940s and 1950s. In studies by Jackson (1944) and Agnes (1947), stu-

dents who read materials about African Americans expressed more positive racial attitudes than students who did not read such materials. However, in the Jackson study, the experimental gains disappeared after two weeks. The serious limitations of the Agnes study make it impossible to generalize its findings.

Trager and Yarrow (1952) studied the effects of a democratic and a nondemocratic curriculum on the racial attitudes of first- and second-grade students. The curriculum interventions in this study consisted of reading materials, activities, and teachers who role-played democratic and nondemocratic teaching styles. After the interventions, the students who participated in the democratic intervention expressed more positive racial attitudes and behaviors than the students who participated in the intervention that taught the prevailing views and attitudes in U.S. society. The teachers also expressed more positive racial attitudes after the interventions.

The effects of a variety of curriculum interventions were examined by Hayes and Conklin (1953) in a two-year project implemented in nine schools. Each teacher selected a different technique to use with an experimental class. The use of biographies of ethnic scientists, lectures on "The Growth of Democracy," direct contact with another ethnic group, and vicarious experience with another ethnic group were some of the techniques used by teachers in the two-year project. The researchers concluded that the students in the experimental groups developed more positive racial attitudes than did the students in the control groups in each of the two years, and that vicarious experiences were more effective than direct experiences in helping students to develop more positive racial attitudes. The findings of this study, however, should be interpreted with caution. The curricular interventions were diverse and unique from school to school, consequently, it is difficult to determine exactly what experiences were compared and almost impossible to replicate the study. However, the strengths of the study are that each intervention continued for three weeks and a multiple-intervention strategy was used.

RACIAL MODIFICATION STUDIES SINCE THE 1960S

The civil rights movement of the 1960s focused the nation's attention on serious problems in race and ethnic relations. Such deepened national concern about racial and ethnic problems had not been witnessed since the intergroup education movement of the 1940s. During the 1960s and 1970s, renewed attention was given to race relations research and children's racial attitudes. These studies can be grouped into four categories: (a) curriculum units and courses, (b) curriculum materials, (c) reinforcement studies, and (d) teaching methods.

Curriculum Units and Courses

A number of researchers have studied the effects of units and courses on students' racial attitudes, including Johnson

(1966), Roth (1969) and Leslie and Leslie (1972). Johnson found that an African and African-American history course in a freedom school had a positive effect on African-American students' attitudes and beliefs. The students became more convinced that African Americans and Whites were equal. The course was only marginally effective with girls.

African-American fifth-grade students who studied African-American history integrated into the regular social studies curriculum developed more positive attitudes toward African Americans in the Roth (1969) study. The self-concept of the students in the experimental groups did not change as a result of the intervention.

The effects of an experimental three-month unit about Africa and African Americans on the racial attitudes of White sixth-grade students and their peers were examined by Leslie and Leslie (1972). Each student in the experimental groups also tutored and interacted with a second-grade minority child from a central–city school. The experimental students also attempted to influence the racial attitudes of control group students with montly class presentations. The mean racial attitude score of the students in both the experimental and control groups became more positive after the unit. Peer influence was as effective in changing attitudes as were the curricular-tutorial interventions.

The effects of selected multiethnic social studies readings with historical, cultural, and social content about African Americans on White children's attitudes toward African Americans in rural and urban settings were investigated by Yawkey (1973). The experimental treatment consisted of the teacher reading and leading a discussion of six books that dealt with African-American history and culture. The intervention had a positive effect on the students' attitudes toward African-Americans in both the rural and urban settings.

Intermediate-grade students experienced statistically significant growth in their academic achievement but not in self-concept scores in a study by Yee and Fruth (1973) in which social studies units that integrated the African-American experience were studied. Yawkey and Blackwell (1974) found that two interventions had a statistically positive effect on the racial attitudes of 4-year-old African-American students: (a) listening to and discussing multiethnic social studies materials; and (b) listening to and discussing multiethnic social studies materials combined with taking field trips related to the readings.

An eight-week intergroup relations unit examined by Lessing and Clarke (1976) included multiethnic readings, guest speakers, and the preparation of reports. There was not a measurable effect on the racial attitudes of a sample of junior high school students in a nearly all-White suburban school. One problem with this study is that students were allowed to select the books they read about each of five ethnic groups. The investigators hypothesized that the intervention did not help the students to develop more positive racial attitudes because of unfavorable race relations in the community in which the school was located and because the books the students read about ethnic groups may have reinforced negative feelings about ethnic minorities.

Shirley (1988) investigated the effects of integrating multicultural activities into the English, social studies, and reading curricula on the self-concept, racial attitudes, and achievement of students in racially integrated fifth- and sixth-grade classes. The teachers who taught the students in the experimental groups attended weekly training sessions. There were no statistically significant changes in the self-concept and achievement means of African-American students in the experimental groups. However, the racial attitudes of the White students in the experimental groups became more positive than the racial attitudes of the White students in the control groups.

Curriculum Materials

The effects of reading six stories about American Indians on the racial attitudes of fifth-grade students was examined by Fisher (1966). The groups in the study were: a reading-only group, a group that read and discussed the stories, and a control group that had no exposure to the stories. Both reading the stories only and reading and discussing them resulted in more positive attitudes toward American Indians. However, reading and discussing the stories resulted in more attitude change than merely reading them. In a related study, Tauran (1967) found that positive and negative literary materials influenced the attitudes of third-grade students toward Eskimos in the expected directions. The ethics of this intervention are questionable because the students in one of the treatment groups were taught unfavorable information about Eskimos.

The effects of multiethnic readers on the attitudes toward African Americans of second-grade White students in a midwestern city were examined by Litcher and Johnson (1969). For four months, the children in the experimental groups used a multiethnic reader that included characters from several different racial and ethnic groups. The students in the control groups used a reader that included only White characters. The students who read the multiethnic raders had more positive posttest racial attitude mean scores than did the control groups. The Litcher and Johnson study in one of the most carefully designed and implemented and, consequently, one of the most important studies of the effects of curriculum materials on students' racial attitudes.

In a study related to the earlier Litcher and Johnson (1969) study, Litcher, Johnson, and Ryan (1973) examined the effects of pictures of multiethnic interactions on the racial attitudes of White second-grade students. This intervention had no measurable effects on the students' racial attitudes. The authors posited reasons for the different findings from Litcher and Johnson (1969). The duration of the latter study was shorter (1 month compared to 4). The students in the latter study lived in the suburb of a metropolitan area that had a considerably higher African-American population than the city in which the earlier study was conducted. Consequently, their attitudes may have been more firmly rooted or extreme and thus harder to change.

The effects of reading stories about Mexican Americans on students' racial attitudes was examined by Howell (1973). The investigator varied the length of the intervention in the two experimental groups: one group read 10 stories over a period of 10 weeks; the other group read 5 stories over a 9-week period. A control group received no treatment. The 10-week group showed statistically significant differences on three of the four measures used in the study; the 5-week group showed statistically significant differences on only one of the measures. A strength of this study is that the length of the treatment varied and four different indices were used to measure attitude change. Racial attitude scales are not highly correlated (Katz, 1976). Katz interpreted this to mean that prejudice is a highly complex variable, involving perceptual, attitudinal, and cognitive components. Consequently, carefully designed studies of curriculum interventions to modify racial attitudes will include several scales.

The effects on social distance scores of a minority literature program integrated into the social studies, reading, and language arts curricula were examined by Kimoto (1974). Fifth- and sixth-grade students were involved in this three-month intervention. At the end of the intervention, the experimental and the control groups had means on two of the social distance scales that were statistically different, that is, the students in the experimental group had more empathy and understanding of minority groups as measured by these two scales. However, experimental and control group means did not differ on one of the social distant scales and on the total scale.

Koeller (1977) studied the effects of reading excerpts from stories about Mexican Americans on the racial attitudes and self-concepts of sixth-grade students attending racially integrated schools. The experimental group students listened to excerpts from six stories with ethnic themes over a six-week period. Control group students heard excerpts from stories with non-ethnic themes. There was not a statistically significant difference in the racial attitudes mean scores of the students. However, the investigator concluded that the treatment had a positive effect on the attitudes of the boys and a reverse effect on the girls' attitudes.

Reinforcement Studies

Reinforcement techniques to help students develop more positive associations with the color black, and consequently more positive attitudes toward African Americans, were developed by Williams and his colleagues (Williams & Robertson, 1967). In a series of studies with preschool and kindergarten children, the use of these reinforcement techniques resulted in more positive associations with the color black and with African-American people (Williams & Morland, 1976). However, Shanahan (1972) and Collins (1972) failed to obtain statistically significant attitude changes using the techniques.

Most of the attitude modification studies in which reinforcement has been investigated have been conducted in the laboratory rather than the classroom. An exception was Yancey's (1972) study. He developed a curriculum based on the Williams reinforcement techniques to help White first-graders develop less bias toward the color white and toward Whites. The curriculum intervention lasted 30 minutes each day and was conducted for 30 consecutive school days. The curriculum included stories and filmstrips that depicted African Americans positively and a game designed to develop positive associations with a black box. The investigator was also the teacher. After the

curriculum intervention, the students expressed more positive racial attitudes.

In an investigation by McAdoo (1970), an 18-session "Black consciousness" curriculum had no measurable effects on the racial attitudes of African American preschool children. The effects of a 6-week curriculum in which African American and White kindergarten children listened to stories that depicted African Americans favorably or described African Americans and Whites interacting positively were examined by Walker (1971). The students did not develop more positive racial attitudes during the intervention.

Teaching Method

Few researchers have examined teaching method or approach as a variable or the relative effects of different instructional techniques in modifying students' racial attitudes. Greenberg, Pierson, and Sherman (1957) found that none of three methods—a debate, a lecture, and a discussion related to prejudice and racial integration—had any statistically significant effects on the racial attitudes of students enrolled in four different sections of an introductory college psychology class. The fourth group was a control. The changes that did occur in the means were in the direction of improved attitudes for the discussion group. This study is limited because each treatment was given in only one class session.

The effects of teaching a semester unit on Africa in two different ways on students' attitudes toward African Americans and Africa was examined by Gezi and Johnson (1970). The students who participated in the study ranged in age from 8 to 11. The control group students studied the unit in a traditional way— e.g., lectures stressing factual information and book assignments. The students in the experimental group studied the unit by participating in first-hand experiences and learning about Africa vicariously through such activities as viewing slides, movies, pictures, and writing letters. The experimental-group students developed more positive attitudes toward African Americans and Africans. Gray and Ashmore (1975) examined the effects of informational, role-playing, and value-discrepancy treatments on the racial attitudes of college students. The three treatments were equally effective in developing more positive racial attitudes, as compared to the control group results. When the students were tested eight weeks after the intervention, the experimental-group students were still lower in prejudice, although the difference was not statistically significant.

Jane Elliott's use of arbitrary discrimination to help third-grade students in Riceville, Iowa, to understand discrimination has been widely publicized in two films about her teaching and consultant work, *The Eye of the Storm* and *A Class Divided* (Peters, 1987). During the first day of the intervention, brown-eyed children were declared "superior" and treated as such. The next day the roles were reversed and the blue-eyed children were declared and treated as "superior." Weiner and Wright (1973), in an intervention similar to the one implemented by Elliott, divided a third-grade class randomly into Orange and Green people. On the first day, the Orange children were "superior"; the Green children were "superior" on the second day.

The experimental class was significantly more likely to want to picnic with a group of African-American children and held less-prejudiced beliefs when compared to the control group on Day 3 as well as two weeks later.

The affects of a teaching method called *principle-testing* on the attitudes of high school students were investigated by Kehoe and Rogers (1978) in a city in British Columbia (Canada). In this teaching method, students are given the facts of a discrimination case and are asked to state what should be done. They are then asked a series of questions to determine the consistency with which they apply the principles implicit in their decisions. The investigators examined the effects of principle testing on the students' attitudes toward women, the physically handicapped, and an ethnic minority group, East Indians. The students who participated in the principle-testing discussions developed more positive attitudes toward the physically handicapped. However, the intervention had no measureable effects on the students' attitudes toward women and East Indians.

Summary

The studies reviewed above indicate that curriculum interventions can help students to develop more positive racial attitudes but that the effects of such interventions are likely not to be consistent. The conflicting findings from the careful studies by Litcher and Johnson (1969) and Litcher, Johnson, and Ryan (1973) attest to the difficulties of curriculum intervention studies. The inconsistencies may be due in part to the use of different measures to assess attitude change and because the duration of the interventions has varied widely. The duration of the intervention has rarely been varied to determine the effects.

The inconsistent results from curriculum intervention studies may also be partly due to the variety in the social settings and contexts in which the studies took place. The racial, ethnic, and social class characteristics of the students participating in the studies also vary considerably. Lessing and Clarke (1976) believed that the racial climate of the community influenced the results of their study. The community context may have also affected the results of the Litcher, Johnson, and Ryan (1973) study. These variables must be systematically varied and examined in curriculum intervention studies before we can understand what factors are essential for such interventions to help students acquire democratic racial attitudes and values. Although the results of curriculum intervention studies are not always consistent, they do indicate that materials and curriculum interventions can have a positive influence on students' racial attitudes and beliefs (Katz & Zalk, 1978; Litcher & Johnson, 1969; Tager & Yarrow, 1952).

GENDER AND TEACHING MATERIALS

Research indicates that sex role attitudes and gender associations develop early and that teaching materials, the mass media, and society at large often reinforce sex role stereotyping (Guttentag & Bray, 1976; Katz, 1986; Klein, 1985; McGhee & Frueh; 1980; Weitzman, 1972). A number of researchers have investigated the ways in which small-scale curriculum interventions, such as stories, vocational information, and television, influence sex role attitudes. However, there is a paucity of studies that examine the effects of curriculum units and courses on children's sex role attitudes and gender associations.

The research on the effects of curricular interventions on students' sex role attitudes and gender associations shares many of the problems with the research on racial attitudes and curricular interventions described above. The studies tend to be short-term interventions, to have measurement problems, and rarely to be examinations of the relationships between expressed attitudes and behavior. In hardly any of the studies was the role of the teacher examined, the teacher treated as a variable, or the effects of teacher training on the teacher's ability to help students to develop less-stereotyped gender role conceptions examined.

Inservice Education and Materials

One of the few studies that examined the effects of both teacher training and curriculum materials on students' gender attitudes was conducted by Tetreault (1979). She compared the gender attitudes of students following participation in three experimental conditions: (a) having a teacher who completed a 26-hour course on the inclusion of women in U.S. history and who used a classroom set of materials on women's history; (b) having a teacher who only had the inservice training; and (c) having a teacher who only used the materials on women's history. The teachers of control group classes neither participated in the inservice training nor used the curriculum materials on women's history.

Students in the experimental classes taught by teachers who participated in the inservice course and used the curriculum materials developed less-stereotyped attitudes about males and females. However, the sex role attitudes of the teachers who participated in the inservice program and used the curriculum materials were no different from the attitudes of the teachers in the other two experimental groups and in the control group. Most of the teachers who participated in the inservice training program, however, used three times more women's history materials than did teachers who received the materials but were not trained.

This study is important for several reasons. It is one of the few studies on gender attitudes in which an intervention that lasted for an entire academic year was examined. The study also had a large sample: 1,074 students in 55 classrooms. By defining inservice training and materials as separate variables, the investigator was able to determine their separate and combined effects. The two variables were effective when combined and less effective when used alone. The results of this study underscore the need to undergird curriculum interventions designed to change sex role attitudes with teacher inservice education.

No data were reported on the attitudes of students who were members of different racial and ethnic groups. Likewise, few of the studies of racial attitudes reviewed above analyzed data by gender. Future studies will contribute more to knowledge development if data are analyzed for the main effects of both race and gender (Grant & Sleeter, 1986b) as well as for their interactions with the treatment. The results of the Tetreault (1979) intervention, for example, may have been different for African-American and White students.

Teachers who participated in several workshops that gave them access to curriculum materials designed to promote gender equity made little use of these materials in an intervention by Woolever (1976). However, there was a statistically significant positive correlation between the amount of teacher intervention and pupil attitude changes for grades kindergarten through two. This finding, however, did not hold for Grades 3 through 6.

The Effects of Reading Materials

A number of researchers have examined the effects of fiction and factual readings on the gender role attitudes and perceptions of students in various grades. These interventions are usually short term and their long-term effects are rarely determined.

The effects of egalitarian books and stories on the sex-type attitudes of 3-, 4-, and 5-year-old White students enrolled in a kindergarten were examined by Flerx, Fidler, and Rogers (1976). Two experiments were reported. In the first experiment, the students in the experimental group were read egalitarian stories and shown pictures illustrating the stories in which males and females pursued careers and shared household duties. Another group heard stories that described men and women in traditional stereotyped roles and occupations. In the second experiment, a third treatment was added, a film condition in which egalitarian acts were modeled by males and females in the film. The students who participated in the egalitarian book and film groups developed more-egalitarian and less-stereotyping sex role attitudes.

There was some evidence that the boys were not as strongly affected by the treatment as were the girls and that the film had a more enduring influence than the picture books. The results of this study are encouraging because of the short duration of the treatment—2.5 hours for Experiment 1, and 2 hours for Experiment 2.

Other researchers have also found that stories can influence gender role attitudes and sex role choices. Three hundred preschool boys and girls participated in a study by Lutes-Dunckley (1978). One group heard a story that depicted traditional sex-role behavior; another group heard a story in which all sex roles were reversed. A control group heard no story at all. The children who heard the story in which all sex roles were reversed made more nontraditional choices when asked to indicate which of two things they would rather do or which they liked better. There were no differences in the choices made by students who heard the traditional story and those who heard no story. Berg-Cross and Berg-Cross (1978) found that listening to four books had a positive effect on students' social attitudes, including their attitudes toward boys who play with dolls, as assessed by responses to open-ended questions. Evidence of the reliability and validity of the assessment was not presented; consequently, its results should be interpreted with caution.

However, the results of this study are consistent with the findings of other studies reviewed in this chapter.

The effects on children's sex role perceptions and story evaluations of stories that portrayed a female main character in a traditionally male role were examined by Scott and Feldman-Summers (1979). Male characters were replaced with female main characters in several stories. The third- and fourth-grade students read two stories a week for four weeks. The three experimental conditions were the combination of male and female main chararcters in the stories; (a) female-majority, (b) male-majority, and (c) equal proportions. Students who read stories with females in nontraditional roles increased their perceptions of the number of girls who can engage in these same activities. However, their perceptions of sex role activities not presented in the stories were not affected.

In a study with 4th-, 7th-, and 11th-grade students, Scott (1986) confirmed the results of the Scott and Feldman-Summers (1979) investigation. She found that students who read narratives that showed females and males in nontraditional roles were more likely to think that both males and females should and could do the activity of the main character than were students who read traditional narratives. Scott also found that neither comprehension nor interest was diminished by the use of sex-fair materials. However, Kropp and Halverson (1983) found that preschool children tended to prefer stories whose main characters were of the same sex and who engaged in stereotypic activities. Jennings (1975) had obtained similar results with preschool students, but they did recall better stories in which the character's sex role was atypical.

The reading of a picture book to preschool children can influence the kinds of toys they choose (Ashton, 1983). The children were observed playing with toys for two minutes. They were then read a picture book that presented a character of the same sex playing with a stereotypic or nonstereotypic toy. Next, the children were given an opportunity to play with experimental toys for two more minutes. The children who heard a nonstereotypic story more often chose a nonstereotypic toy after the intervention. The reverse was the case for the children who heard a stereotypic story.

Vocational Choices and Expectations

A number of investigators have examined the effects of curriculum interventions on male and female students' vocational choices and expectations. In general, these interventions have had statistically significant effects. Barclay (1974) examined the effects on the gender role attitudes of suburban and inner-city kindergarten children of reading books about women working and general career information without reference to sex. The three treatments were: (a) reading and discussing three books dealing with working women, (b) reading and discussing a career information pamplet, and (c) viewing a flannelboard demonstration of the story of the Gingerbread Man, with later discussion (a nonrelated control treatment). The treatment in each group lasted 15 minutes for three days. The boys and girls exposed to the books dealing with working women increased the number of jobs they considered appropriate for females. The general career information enabled girls, but not boys, to see women in a greater number of vocational roles.

The choices made by high school juniors on the basis of sex stereotypes or lack of knowledge of probability of success in a given occupation can be influenced by vocational information that describes new opportunities for women (Hurwitz & White, 1977). The attitudes of ninth graders toward sex-typed careers can also be changed by career information that describes nontraditional role models. After reading such materials, the students in a study by Greene, Sullivan, and Beyard-Tyler (1982) thought that more of the jobs they had read about were appropriate for both females and males. The females in the study had less-sex-typed attitudes about sex-appropriateness of careers then males. Both males and females thought that it was more appropriate for females than males to enter nontraditional sex-typed occupations. These latter two findings are consistent with those of most other investigators who have investigated the gender role attitudes of females and males; females tend to have more flexible gender role attitudes and perceptions than males.

The effects of an innovative economics curriculum project, Mini-Society, on students' perceptions of entrepreneurship and occupational sex stereotyping were investigated by Kourilsky and Campbell (1984). Among the strengths of the study were its large sample (938 children in Grades three through six), its geographic scope (students from three cities in different states), and its ethnic mix. The duration of the intervention is also noteworthy; it lasted 10 weeks, longer than most of the interventions reviewed in this chapter. Like the Tetreault (1979) study, this intervention had a teacher inservice education component, a 24-hour workshop that took place over a four-week period. Another strength of the study is that it was an investigation of an actual school curriculum, rather than of merely reading a story or viewing a film, as was the case in most of the studies of gender attitudes reported in this chapter.

The most serious limitation of the study was the lack of a control group; a preexperimental, single-group, pretest-posttest design (Campbell & Stanley, 1963) was used. Consequently, causal inferences about the intervention are difficult. On the pretest, the students viewed entrepreneurial roles as primarily a male domain. After participation in the Mini-Society curriculum, both boys and girls placed more females in entrepreneurial positions on the posttest. However, the change for boys was not statistically significant; the boys still saw entrepreneurship as predominantly a male domain. The interaction effects of race and gender were also examined. Most of the girls, except the African-American girls, did not initially attempt entrepreneurship in the early phase of the Mini-Society curriculum.

The Effects of TV and Films

Some investigators have studied the effects of television and films on children's gender role attitudes and perceptions. Di-Leo, Moely, and Sulzer (1979) investigated the effects, on the sex-typed behavior of toy choices and game preferences of nursery school, kindergarten, and first-grade children of a film showing a model choosing non-sex-typed toys. Before the intervention, the children evidenced high levels of sex-typing in their choice of toys. After viewing the film, the students in the experimental groups made fewer sex-typed toy choices. On both the pre- and posttests, males and older children made more highly sex-typed choices than did females and younger children.

The effects of television cartoons on the sex-role stereotypes of kindergarten girls was investigated by Davidson, Yasuna, and Tower (1979). The girls viewed one of three television network cartoons: high stereotype, low stereotype, or neutral. After the intervention, they were tested for sex-role stereotyping. The children who viewed the low-stereotyped television cartoon scored significantly lower on the sex-role stereotype measure than did the girls who viewed the high-stereotyped or neutral cartoons. The scores of the girls who reviewed the high-stereotyped and neutral cartoons did not differ.

The findings by DiLeo, Moely, and Sulzer (1979) and by Davidson, Yasuna, and Tower (1979) were not confirmed by Drabman et al. (1981). They found that preschool, first-, and fourth-grade students maintained their sex-role stereotypes after viewing a videotape that depicted a male nurse working with a female physician. After viewing the videotape, the students were asked to identify photographs or names of the physician and the nurse. The students in preschool, first-, and fourth-grade selected male names or pictures for the physician and female names or pictures for the nurse. The seventh-grade students correctly identified the names of the nurse and the physician.

The investigators conducted three different experiments in order to strengthen various aspects of the study. The findings were essentially the same in the first experiment and in the two replications. The investigators concluded that the responses of the students in preschool, first, and fourth grades were influenced more strongly by their stereotypes than by the film they viewed. The nature of the experiment, the visual presentation, the social setting, and the region might be among the reasons that the findings of this study failed to confirm the two previous ones.

Summary

Although the findings are not totally consistent, the studies reviewed above indicate that different kinds of curriculum interventions can help students to develop less-stereotypic gender role attitudes. The inconsistent results may have resulted from varied interventions, pupil ages, duration of interventions, social settings, and teacher attitudes and behavior. The research reviewed also indicates that students' conceptions of gender-appropriate occupations can be modified with curriculum interventions. While the studies are, on the whole, encouraging to social studies educators, they do share several problems. Only a few have examined the relationship between attitudes and behavior, the duration of treatment as a variable, or have been designed to modify the attitudes and behavior of teachers.

IMPLICATIONS FOR RESEARCH AND PRACTICE

Research Implications

More studies on the effects of curriculum interventions on racial and gender roles attitudes are needed. Both ERIC and

Psychological Abstracts were searched for studies in these areas. None of the studies on the effects of curriculum intervention on racial attitudes was published in the 1980s; most were published in the 1960s and 1970s. Most of the studies on gender role attitudes examined in this chapter were also conducted in the 1970s. It appears that intervention research on racial and gender role attitudes nearly halted at the end of the 1970s. This probably indicates that the United States has entered another phase in its history in which racial and social concerns have taken a backseat in a neoconservative national atmosphere (Schlesinger, 1986). If future projections can be based on past trends (which is always risky), national attention will again focus on racial and gender issues when the nation faces a social crisis, as in the World War II period when intergroup education emerged and in the 1960s when the Black-studies and women's-studies movements arose as a part of the civil rights movement.

Because funding for race relations and gender–related studies is likely to be scarce for the foreseeable future, there is not likely to be a rash of such studies soon. Thus any implications for research stated here should be tempered by reality.

Social studies university educators face many demands, not all of which are consistent. They are expected to interpret research for practitioners, teach methods courses, become involved with schools, and write student materials. They are also expected to do research. Research, however, often becomes the lowest priority in their day-to-day involvement with practice and practitioners. It is noteworthy that not one of the studies reviewed in this chapter was published in a National Council for the Social Studies publication. This is not because the council is not concerned with issues related to race and gender—quite the contrary. The council has published many excellent publications related to race and gender designed to help the practitioners who constitute the bulk of its membership (e.g., Banks, 1973; Grambs, 1976; Simms & Contreras, 1980). Social studies educators should be encouraged to conduct research on race and gender curriculum interventions. They can conduct small-scale descriptive studies while doing their daily chores, such as supervising student teachers, working with doctoral candidates, and consulting with school districts.

One of the major problems with existing studies is that they are not characterized by what Geertz (1973) called "thick description." They do not contain sufficient detail about the nature of interventions, the behavior of the students and the teachers, and the interactions that took place between students and materials. By working with student teachers and the schools in which they do their practice teaching, social studies educators could conduct ethnographic and case studies of the use of units and courses designed to modify the racial and gender attitudes of students. The ethnographic studies of social studies teachers being conducted at Stanford by Shulman (1987) and his students exemplify the kind of research needed.

Social studies educators could make several important contributions to the research on racial and gender role attitude modification. They could examine ways in which such variables as race, gender, and social class interact to influence students' behavior and attitudes. Very few of the studies reviewed in this chapter included the examination of the interaction effects of race and gender. Grant and Sleeter (1986b) have pointed out why it is important to describe interaction effects. Research by social studies educators and their graduate students should also be focused on in-depth examinations of teacher characteristics and their role in multicultural education, as well as on documentation of the relationships between attitudes and behavior.

Implications for Practice

That a 15-minute intervention influenced the racial attitudes of second- and fifth-grade children from four to six months later (Katz & Zalk, 1978) is the most striking finding of this research review. Most of the studies reviewed in this chapter consist of interventions of rather short duration. If a 15-minute intervention can influence students' racial attitudes, we can only surmise that the impact of a teacher and a curriculum with which a student interacts for over 180 days must be tremendous. This is cause for both hope and concern. This situation is hopeful if the teacher and the curriculum are democratic, but a cause for deep concern if the teacher or the curriculum is status-quo-oriented, biased, or nondemocratic.

An important implication of this research review for practice is that teachers must be provided with training and opportunities that will enable them to examine their feelings, attitudes, and values, and helped to develop attitudes consistent with a democratic society (Tetreault, 1979; Trager & Yarrow, 1952). Another important implication is that students must be helped to acquire more democratic attitudes and behavior. Research findings substantiate media reports of racial discrimination and violence; many students have negative racial and gender attitudes (Glock et al., 1975; Klein, 1985; Milner, 1983). Research findings also indicate that student attitudes can be changed by curricular interventions. The precise conditions that will consistently lead to attitude change are, however, not yet clear. Interventions appear to be most successful with young children, particularly preschoolers and kindergartners (Williams & Morland, 1976; Williams & Roberson, 1967). These findings suggest that if the twig is going to be straightened (Katz, 1976), we must start as early as possible. In general, girls are more influenced than boys in intervention studies related to gender issues. Studies should be undertaken to help explain this difference and to develop more effective intervention methods for boys. Efforts must also be made to ensure that teaching materials are multicultural and gender-fair. Materials apparently influence students' racial and gender role attitudes even when they are never discussed.

The changing demographics of U.S. society and the world—one out of three people in the United States will be a member of an ethnic minority by 2000 (The Commission on Minority Participation in Education and American Life, 1988)—require that social studies educators act now and act decisively to create a more humane and caring world. Multicultural education is a road rarely taken. If taken properly, it might make a major difference. More carefully designed research is needed to help provide the direction. In the meantime, we should use the guidelines derived from the research reviewed in this chapter to help create a more caring and humane nation.

References

Adorno, T. W., Frenkel-Brunswik, E., Levinson, D. J., & Sanford, R. N. *The authoritarian personality.* New York: W. W. Norton, 1950.

Agnes, M. (1947). Influences of reading on the racial attitudes of adolescent girls. *Catholic Educational Review, 45,* 415–420.

Allport, G. (1954). *The nature of prejudice.* Reading, MA: Addison-Wesley.

Aronson, E., & Gonzalez, A. (1988). Desegregation, jigsaw, and the Mexican-American experience. In P. A. Katz and D. A. Taylor (Eds.), *Eliminating racism: Profiles in controversy.* New York: Plenum Press.

Ashton, E. (1983). Measures of play behavior: The influence of sex-role stereotyped children's books. *Sex Roles, 9,* 43–47.

Baker, G. (1983). *Planning and organizing for multicultural instruction.* Reading, MA: Addison-Wesley.

Banks, J. A. (Ed.). (1973). *Teaching ethnic studies: Concepts and strategies.* Washington, DC: National Council for the Social Studies.

Banks, J. A. (1988). *Multiethnic education: Theory and practice* (2nd ed.). Boston: Allyn and Bacon.

Banks, J. A., & Banks, C. A. M. (Eds.). (1989). *Multicultural education: Issues and perspectives.* Boston: Allyn and Bacon.

Barclay, L. K. (1974). The emergence of vocational expectations in preschool children. *Journal of Vocational Behavior, 4,* 1–14.

Bennett, C. I. (1986). *Comprehensive multicultural education: Theory and practice.* Boston: Allyn and Bacon.

Berg-Cross, L., & Berg-Cross, G. (1978). Listening to stories may change children's social attitudes. *The Reading Teacher, 31,* 659–663.

Campbell, D. T., & Stanley, J. C. (1963). *Experimental and quasi-experimental designs for research.* Chicago: Rand McNally.

Clark, K. B. (1955). *Prejudice and your child.* Boston: Beacon Press.

Collins, J. (1972). *The effect of differential frequency of color adjective pairings on the subsequent rating of color meaning and racial attitude in preschool children.* Unpublished master's thesis, East Tennessee State University, Johnson City.

The Commission on Minority Participation in Education and American Life. (1988). *One-third of a nation.* Washington, DC: American Council on Education.

Cook, L. A. (1947). Intergroup education. *Review of Educational Research, 17,* 266–278.

Davidson, E. S., Yasuna, A., & Tower, A. (1979). The effects of television cartoons on sex-role stereotyping in young girls. *Child Development, 50,* 597–600.

DiLeo, J. C., Moely, B. E., & Sulzer, J. L. (1979). Frequency and modifiability of children's preferences for sex-typed toys, games, and occupations. *Child Study Journal, 9,* 141–159.

Drabman, R. S., Robertson, S. J., Patterson, J. N., Jarvie, G. J., Hammer, D., & Cordua, G. (1981). Children's perception of media-portrayed sex roles. *Sex Roles, 7,* 379–389.

Fisher, F. (1965). *The influence of reading and discussion on the attitudes of fifth graders toward American Indians.* Unpublished doctoral dissertation, University of California, Berkeley.

Flerx, V. C., Fidler, D. S., & Rogers, R. W. (1976). Sex role stereotypes: Developmental aspects and early intervention. *Child Development, 47,* 998–1007.

Gabelko, N. H., & Michaelis, J. U. (1981). *Reducing adolescent prejudice.* New York: Teachers College Press.

Geertz, C. (1973). *The interpretation of cultures.* New York: Basic Books.

Gezi, K. I., & Johnson, B. (1979). Enhancing racial attitudes through the study of black heritage. *Childhood Education, 46,* 397–399.

Glock, C. Y., Wuthnow, R., Piliavin, J. A., & Spencer, M. (1975). *Adolescent prejudice.* New York: Harper & Row.

Gollnick, D. M., & Chinn, P. C. (1986). *Multicultural education in a pluralistic society* (2nd ed.). Columbus, OH: Merrill.

Goodman, M. E. (1952). *Race awareness in young children.* New York: Macmillan.

Grambs, J. D. (Ed.). (1976). *Teaching about women in the social studies: Concepts, methods, and materials.* Washington, DC: National Council for the Social Studies.

Grant, C. A., & Sleeter, C. E. (1986a). *After the school bell rings.* Philadelphia: Falmer.

Grant, C. A., & Sleeter, C. E. (1986b). Race, class, and gender in education research: An argument for integrative analysis. *Review of Educational Research, 56,* 195–211.

Gray, D. E., & Ashmore, R. D. (1975). Comparing the effects of informational, role-playing, and value-discrepancy treatments on racial attitudes. *Journal of Applied Social Psychology, 5,* 262–281.

Greene, L. A., Sullivan, H. J., & Beyard-Tyler, K. (1982). Attitudinal effects of the use of role models in information about sex-typed careers. *Journal of Educational Psychology, 74,* 393–398.

Greenberg, H., Pierson, J., & Sherman, S. (1957). The effects of single-session education techniques on prejudice attitudes. *Journal of Educational Sociology, 31,* 82–86.

Guttentag, M., & Bray, H. (1976). *Undoing sex stereotypes: Research and resources for educators.* New York: McGraw-Hill.

Hayes, M. L., & Conklin, M. E. (1953). Intergroup attitudes and experimental change. *Journal of Experimental Education, 22,* 19–36.

Howell, M. (1973). *A study of the effects of reading upon the attitudes of fifth graders toward Mexican Americans.* Unpublished doctoral dissertation, Southern Illinois University, Carbondale.

Hurwitz, R. E., & White, M. A. (1977). Effect of sex-linked vocational information on reported occupational choices of high school juniors. *Psychology of Women Quarterly, 2,* 149–154.

Jackson, E. P. (1944). Effects of reading upon attitudes toward the Negro race. *The Library Quarterly, 14,* 47–54.

Jennings, S. A. (1975). Effects of sex typing in children's stories on preference and recall. *Child Development, 46,* 220–223.

Johnson, D. W. (1966). Freedom school effectiveness: Changes in attitudes of Negro children. *The Journal of Applied Behavioral Science, 2,* 325–330.

Katz, P. A. (1973). Perception of racial cues in preschool children: A new look. *Developmental Psychology, 8,* 295–299.

Katz, P. A. (Ed.). (1976). *Towards the elimination of racism.* New York: Pergamon Press.

Katz, P. A. (1986). Modification of children's gender-stereotyped behavior: General issues and research considerations. *Sex Roles, 14,* 591–602.

Katz, P. A., Sohn, M., & Zalk, S. R. (1975). Perceptual concomitants of racial attitudes in urban grade-school children. *Developmental Psychology, 11,* 135–144.

Katz, P. A., & Zalk, S. R. (1978). Modification of children's racial attitudes. *Developmental Psychology, 14,* 447–461.

Kehoe, J. W., & Rogers, W. T. (1978). The effects of principle-testing discussions on student attitudes towards selected groups subjected to discrimination. *Canadian Journal of Education, 3,* 73–80.

Kimoto, C. K. (1974). *The effects of a juvenile literature based program on minority group attitudes toward Black Americans.* Unpublished doctoral dissertation, Washington State University, Pullman.

Klein, S. S. (Ed.). (1985). *Handbook of achieving sex equity through education.* Baltimore: John Hopkins University Press.

Koeller, S. (1977). The effect of listening to excerpts from children's stories about Mexican-Americans on the attitudes of sixth graders. *Journal of Educational Research, 70,* 329–334.

Kourilsky, M., & Campbell, M. (1984). Sex differences in a simulated classroom economy: Children's beliefs about entrepreneurship. *Sex Roles, 10,* 53–65.

Kropp, J. J., & Halverson, C. F. (1983). Preschool children's preferences and recall for stereotyped versus nonstereotyped stories. *Sex Roles, 8,* 261–272.

Lasker, G. (1929). *Race attitudes in children.* New York: Henry Holt.

Leslie, L. L., & Leslie, J. W. (1972). The effects of a student centered special curriculum upon the racial attitudes of sixth graders. *The Journal of Experimental Education, 41,* 63–67.

Lessing, E. E., & Clarke, C. (1976). An attempt to reduce ethnic prejudice and assess its correlates. *Educational Research Quarterly, 1,* 3–16.

Litcher, J. H., & Johnson, D. W. (1969). Changes in attitudes toward Negroes of White elementary school students after use of multiethnic readers. *Journal of Educational Psychology, 60,* 148–152.

Litcher, J. H., Johnson, D. W., & Ryan, F. L. (1973). Use of pictures of multiethnic interaction to change attitudes of white elementary school students toward Blacks. *Psychological Reports, 33,* 367–372.

Lutes-Dunckley, C. J. (1978). Sex-role stereotypes as a function of sex of storyteller and story content. *The Journal of Psychology, 100,* 151–158.

McAdoo, J. L. (1970). *An exploratory study of racial attitude change in Black preschool children using differential treatments.* Unpublished doctoral dissertation, University of Michigan, Ann Arbor.

McAdoo, J. L. (1985). Modification of racial attitudes and preferences in young black children. In H. P. McAdoo & J. L. McAdoo (Eds.), *Black children: Social, educational, and parental environments.* Beverly Hills, CA: Sage.

McGhee, P. E., & Frueh, T. (1980). Television viewing and the learning of sex-role stereotypes. *Sex Roles, 6,* 179–188.

Mercer, J. R. (1973). *Labeling the mentally retarded.* Berkeley: University of California Press.

Milner, D. (1983). *Children and race.* Beverly Hills, CA: Sage.

Minard, R. D. (1931). Race attitudes of Iowa Children. *University of Iowa, Studies in Character, 4,*(2).

Myrdal, G., with Sterner, R., & Rose, A. (1944). *An American dilemma: The Negro problem and modern democracy* (Vols. 1 and 2). New York: Harper & Brothers.

Parish, T. S., Shirazi, A., & Lambert, F. (1976). Conditioning away prejudicial attitudes in children. *Perceptual and Motor Skills, 43,* 907–912.

Patterson, O. (1977). *Ethnic chauvinism: The reactionary impulse.* New York: Stein & Day.

Peters, W. (1987). *A class divided: Then and now* (expanded ed.). New Haven, CT: Yale University Press.

Porter, J. D. R. (1971). *Black child, white child: The development of racial attitudes.* Cambridge, MA: Harvard University Press.

Proshansky, H. (1966). The development of intergroup attitudes. In I. W. Hoffman & M. L. Hoffman (Eds.), *Review of child development research* (Vol. 2, pp. 311–371). New York: Russell Sage Foundation.

Roth, R. W. (1969). The effects of "Black Studies" on Negro fifth grade students. *The Journal of Negro Education, 38,* 435–439.

Schlesinger, A. M., Jr. (1986). *The cycles of American history.* Boston: Houghton Mifflin.

Scott, K. P. (1986). Effects of sex-fair reading materials on pupils' attitudes, comprehension, and interest. *American Educational Research Journal, 28,* 105–116.

Scott, K. P., & Feldman-Summers, S. (1979). Children's reactions to textbook stories in which females are portrayed in traditionally male roles. *Journal of Educational Psychology, 71,* 396–402.

Shananhan, J. K. (1972). *The effects of modifying black-white attitudes of black and white first grade subjects upon two measures of racial attitudes.* Unpublished doctoral dissertation, University of Washington, Seattle.

Shirley, O. L. B. (1988). *The impact of multicultural education on self-concept, racial attitude, and student achievement of black and white fifth and sixth graders.* Unpublished doctoral dissertation, University of Mississippi.

Shulman, L. (1987). Knowledge and teaching: Foundations of the new reform. *Harvard Educational Review, 57,* 1–22.

Simms, R. L., & Contreras, G. (Eds.). (1980). *Racism and sexism: Responding to the challenge.* Washington, DC: National Council for the Social Studies.

Slavin, R. E. (1985). Cooperative learning: Applying contact theory in desegregated schools. *Journal of Social Issues, 41,* 45–62.

Slavin, R. E. & Madden, N. A. (1979). School practices that improve race relations. *American Educational Research Journal, 16,* 169–180.

Sleeter, C. E., & Grant, C. A. (1987). An analysis of multicultural education in the United States. *Harvard Educational Review, 57,* 421–444.

Stephan, W. G. (1985). Intergroup relations. In G. Lindzey & E. Aronson (Eds.), *The handbook of social psychology* (pp. 599–658). New York: Random House.

Taba, H., Brady, E. H., & Robinson, J. T. (1952). *Intergroup education in public schools.* Washington, DC: American Council on Education.

Tauran, R. H. (1967). *The influences of reading on the attitudes of third graders toward Eskimos.* Unpublished doctoral dissertation, University of Maryland, College Park.

Tetreault, M. K. T. (1979). *The inclusion of women in the United States history curriculum and adolescent attitudes toward sex-appropriate behavior.* Unpublished doctoral dissertation, Boston University School of Education, Boston.

Trager, H. G., & Yarrow, M. R. (1952). *They learn what they live.* New York: Harper.

Walker, P. A. (1971). *The effects of hearing selected children's stories that portray blacks in a favorable manner on the racial attitudes of groups of black and white kindergarten children.* Unpublished doctoral dissertation, University of Michigan, Ann Arbor.

Weiner, M. J., & Wright, F. E. (1973). Effects of undergoing arbitrary discrimination upon subsequent attitudes toward a minority group. *Journal of Applied Social Psychology, 3,* 94–102.

Weitzman, L. J. (1972). Sex-role socialization in picture books for preschool children. *American Journal of Sociology, 77,* 1125–1150.

Williams, J. E., & Edwards, C. D. (1969). An exploratory study of the modification of color and racial concept attitudes in preschool children. *Child Development, 40,* 737–750.

Williams, J. E., & Morland, J. K. (1976). *Race, color and the young child.* Chapel Hill: University of North Carolina Press.

Williams, J. E., & Roberson, J. K. (1967). A method of assessing racial attitudes in preschool children. *Educational and Psychological Measurement, 27,* 671–689.

Wilson, A. (1987). *Mixed race children: A study of identity.* Boston: Allen & Unwin.

Woolever, R. (1976). *Expanding elementary pupils' occupational and social role perceptions: An examination of teacher attitudes and behavior and pupil attitude change.* Unpublished doctoral dissertation, University of Washington, Seattle.

Yancey, A. V. (1972). *A study of attitudes in white first grade children.* Unpublished paper, Pennsylvania State University, University Park.

Yawkey, T. D. (1973). Attitudes towards black Americans held by rural and urban white early childhood subjects based upon multi-ethnic social studies materials. *The Journal of Negro Education, 42,* 164–169.

Yawkey, T. D., & Blackwell, J. (1974). Attitudes of 4-year old urban Black children toward themselves and Whites based upon multi-ethnic social studies materials and experiences. *Journal of Educational Research, 67,* 373–377.

Yee, A. H., & Fruth, M. J. (1973). Do Black studies make a difference in ghetto children's achievement and attitudes? *The Journal of Negro Education, 42,* 33–38.

·39·

CONTROVERSIAL ISSUES IN SOCIAL STUDIES

Carole L. Hahn

EMORY UNIVERSITY

Social studies educators have long asserted that studying and discussing issues is important to democracy. The rationale for including controversial issues in social studies instruction rests on the necessity of preparing citizens to participate in the democratic decision-making processes within a pluralistic society. Empirical evidence gathered over the past 25 years, although meager and often coming from nonrepresentative samples, consistently supports the position that positive citizenship outcomes are associated with giving students opportunities to explore controversial issues in an open, supportive classroom atmosphere. This chapter begins with the philosophic underpinnings of the controversial-issues tradition in democratic education. Studies of relationships between the exploration of controversial issues and student attitudes and knowledge are reviewed, along with research on teacher and student attitudes toward such instruction. Finally, needed lines of research related to controversial issues and social studies are identified.

For years the National Council for the Social Studies (NCSS) has advocated using controversial issues as an instructional strategy (Cox, 1977; Gross, 1952; Muessig, 1975). The reasoning that underlies such advocacy is that in a democracy, discussion is the means by which differing solutions to public problems are deliberated. Because the free discussion of current issues is at the heart of the democratic process, an NCSS policy statement adopted in 1951 asserts:

It follows that education for citizenship in a democracy must emphasize the study and discussion of controversial issues and must teach the skills needed for this study and discussion.... [for that reason] ... the National Council for the Social Studies recommends that it be the explicit policy of the nation's public schools to encourage and maintain the study of the unsolved problems and the current, controversial is-

sues of our society. Only through this study can children develop the abilities they will need as citizens of a democracy (NCSS, 1977, p. 26).

John Dewey's emphasis on the importance of the examination of social problems to education in a democracy has been applied specifically to social studies instruction by a number of scholars (Engle & Ochoa, 1988; Griffin, 1942; Hunt & Metcalf, 1968; Newmann, 1970; Oliver & Shaver, 1966/1974). For example, Hunt and Metcalf (1968) argued that the exploration of controversial issues should be the focus of high school social studies instruction because citizens in a pluralistic society need to be able to resolve interpersonal and intrapersonal conflict; setting off some subjects as taboo for investigation is a totalitarian practice inconsistent with democratic ideals; and it is only through resolving problems contained in controversial issues that meaningful, lasting learning will occur.

In the United States in the 1960s, several social studies curriculum projects and methods textbooks sought to implement the controversial-issues philosophy (Hunt & Metcalf, 1968; Newmann, 1970; Oliver & Shaver, 1966/1974, Shaver & Larkins, 1973). The centrality of controversial issues to social studies is not, however, unique to the U.S. scene. For example, in the United Kingdom, Stenhouse's 1970s Humanities Project was based on the principle that controversial issues should be discussed in the classroom by adolescents (Rudduck, 1983). Also in the United Kingdom, the Programme for Political Literacy advocated that British students examine issues of conflict at the school, community, national, and international levels (Crick & Lister, 1979) and Stradling, Noctor, and Baines (1984) began *Teaching Controversial Issues* with the premise that "controversial issues are now an integral and inescapable part of the secondary school curriculum" in the United Kingdom.

Reviewers were Ann Angell, Emory University; Beverly Armento, Georgia State University; Patricia Avery, University of Minnesota, St. Paul; Glen Blankenship, Gwinnett County Schools, GA; Gerald Marker, Indiana University; Mary Mason, Gwinnett County Schools, GA; Fred M. Newmann, University of Wisconsin, Madison; Anna Ochoa, Indiana University; Jack Zevin, Queens College.

Similar emphasis on teaching controversial issues can be found in other Western democracies as well. For example, in Denmark all students in Grades 7–9 are required to take a course in contemporary studies to gain insights into the problems and conflicts of contemporary society (Ministry of Education, 1986). In the Netherlands, 14- to 16-year-old students are required to take a course in social and political education to help them cope with current social and political problems (Hooghoff, 1988).

Is this advocacy of controversial-issues exploration supported by empirical evidence of the benefits of such an approach? A number of researchers have sought to demonstrate that the investigation of controversial issues is associated with positive citizenship outcomes. Other researchers have measured student and teacher attitudes toward the inclusion of controversial issues.

Before examining that research, it should be emphasized that findings from a series of early studies suggested that social studies courses without controversial issues had little or no effect on students' political interest or orientation towards participation (Langton & Jennings, 1968; Litt, 1963). It was suggested in a major review of political socialization research (Patrick, 1967) that "perhaps high school political education programs would have a greater influence upon the formation of 'democratic' attitudes if they were conducted in an atmosphere more conducive to inquiry and openmindedness" (p. 45). This statement is the key to the review of research into the relationships between discussions of controversial issues and students' political attitudes.

CONTROVERSIAL ISSUES DISCUSSION AND AMERICAN HIGH SCHOOL STUDENTS' POLITICAL ATTITUDES

Growing out of the tradition of political socialization research, a series of studies was conducted primarily in the midwestern United States in the decade, 1965 to 1975. Ehman's (1969, 1970a, 1970b, 1972) study of a randomly stratified sample of 334 10th- to 12th-grade students in a Detroit high school began the search for empirical evidence on the connection between discussions of controversial issues in social studies classes and attitudinal outcomes. Ehman's questionnaire included scales developed at the University of Michigan's Survey Research Center (SRC) to measure political cynicism, political efficacy, political participation (participation in political discussions and rallies), and sense of citizen duty. To those measures Ehman added a Classroom Climate Scale in which students were asked whether most of their teachers dealt with social problems, discussed both sides of issues, and took a neutral position, and whether students felt free to express their opinions (the reliability coefficients for scores on the cynicism, efficacy, participation, citizen duty, and climate scales were .87, .91, .90, .93, and .86, respectively). Ehman (1969) found that students who had experienced more social studies courses, who reported higher degrees of controversial-issues exposure, and

whose responses on the Classroom Climate Scale were highest, exhibited lower levels of cynicism, higher levels of sense of citizen duty, increased participation, and increased levels of political efficacy. But, the magnitude of the relationships were "quite low indeed"—the highest Eta and Beta coefficients were .25 and .21 for political participation and classroom climate.

Taking the analysis one step further, Ehman divided his sample into "closed-" and "open- climate" subgroups and looked at the political attitudes of African-American and White students separately within each subgroup (Ehman, 1969). In the closed-climate group, (for African-American and White students, respectively) more reported exposure to controversial issues had a negative correlation with sense of citizen duty (− .39, − .52), efficacy (− 20, − .32), and participation (− .30, − .66). For White students in the closed-climate group there was also a positive correlation between exposure to controversial issues and cynicism (+ .45), whereas there was no significant correlation (− .05) for African-Americans. Controversial content presented in a biased and closed atmosphere evidently was related to negative outcomes.

On the other hand, in the open-climate group, exposure to controversial issues for African-American students was positively correlated with sense of citizen duty (+ .13), sense of political efficacy (+ .29), and participation (+ .43), and inversely correlated with cynicism (− .28). For White students in the open-climate group, exposure to controversial issues was positively correlated with sense of citizen duty (+ .24). There was virtually no relationship with the other variable for White students in the open-climate group.

Ehman supplemented his survey data on the Detroit high school seniors' political attitudes with observations of social studies classes in the school (Ehman, 1970a, 1970b). From the observational data, Ehman (1970b) determined the amount of time each teacher's class spent in the "normative mode." That is, he recorded the amount of class time during which the teacher or students made value-laden statements or asked value-oriented questions (characterized by "shoulds," "oughts," "goods," "bads," and the like). The observational data were then related to the attitude change scores of students who had been exposed to particular teachers. Ehman concluded that the teachers of students at or above the median in increased political cynicism generated more than twice as much total class time in the normative mode. That is, students exposed to teachers who were observed encouraging more value-laden comments and questions became slightly more cynical over the two-year period, as compared to their peers who were exposed to teachers whose classes were less normative. This finding suggested that if controversial-issues discussions are characterized by normative evaluations on the part of students and teachers, high school students may move away from an idealistic, trusting (some would say naive) view of government officials toward skepticism or moderate levels of cynicism.

Additionally, in the Detroit study, exposure to teachers whose classes were more normative had a slight positive relationship with students' sense of political efficacy, but Ehman emphasized the relationship was too small to be considered meaningful (Ehman, 1970b). Unfortunately, no other research has substantiated or discredited Ehman's findings related to the possible effects of normative discourse. Several researchers have, however, explored the relationships between controversial-issues discussions, open climate, and student political attitudes.

In a three-year longitudinal study of 339 students from nine Midwestern high schools, Ehman (1977) once again investigated the effects of discussion of controversial issues on students' political development. Ehman measured students' perceptions of classroom climate and the extent to which they recalled that controversial issues had been discussed in their high school social studies classes. Responses to the Classroom Climate Scale were correlated with measures of student attitudes that had referents in society in general and with student attitudes toward school-level phenomena.

It was clear from the responses for all three years that more reported exposure to controversial issues was associated with positive changes in attitudes at the societal level—increased levels of political interest, political confidence, and social integration (the reverse of alienation). (In the 1977 report, all findings related to political confidence were reported to be negative, but in later correspondence, Ehman said that he had originally erred by not accounting for the direction of negatively stated items and the relationships with political confidence were positive.) School attitudes were also positively related to scores on the controversial-issues variable. Students reporting more frequent issues exposure showed increasingly positive attitudes over the three years on measures of trust in other students, trust in school adults, integration in school culture, school political confidence, and school political interest than did students without such exposure.

Ehman (1977) also found that the range of views that students perceived to have been considered in their classroom was positively related to the dependent variables. The students who recalled a wider range of views having been considered in their classrooms were more trusting in society, more socially integrated, more politically confident, more politically interested, more trusting of other students and school adults, more politically confident in regard to school decision-making, and more interested in school-level politics.

Finally, in regard to students' reported feelings of freedom to express their opinions during controversial-issues discussions, the results were substantial. Attitudes were considerably more positive for students who felt free, rather than hesitant, to express their views. Ehman concluded that this variable was the strongest predictor of positive attitudinal outcomes in regard to both school and society. To summarize, in this longitudinal study in nine high schools, all climate variables were positively associated with all student outcome variables, thus suggesting the benefits of controversial-issues discussion in an open, supportive environment.

Ehman was not the only researcher to explore the impact of teaching controversial issues on students' attitudes. Long and Long (1975) administered surveys to 588 secondary school students in three Illinois communities. Relevant here was the inclusion in the questionnaire of a two-item Controversial Discussion Index on which students were asked how frequently controversial matters were discussed in their social studies classes and how willing they thought their social studies teachers were to have controversial opinions advocated or discussed in the classroom.

Findings from the Illinois study at first glance seemed to contradict some of the findings from Ehman's Detroit study in regard to political efficacy and cynicism. In particular, the researchers found negative correlations between controversial-issues discussion and a sense of political efficacy (Gamma = −.24 for junior high school students and −.27 for senior high school students). They also found slightly positive relationships between reported participation in controversial issues discussion and political cynicism (gamma = .08 for junior high school and .13 for senior high school students). Although not consistent with the results from Ehman's total sample, the findings were consistent with those from his closed-climate subsample. Unfortunately, Long and Long did not measure whether students perceived their teachers as maintaining neutral or objective positions or whether students felt comfortable expressing their opinions. As a result, one cannot be certain that their findings come from controversial-issues discussions conducted in a closed or open climate.

The study seemed to enhance, however, Ehman's argument that including controversial-issues discussions in social studies classes is not alone sufficient to produce positive student attitudes of efficacy and trust; evidently an open, supportive classroom climate also is necessary. Long and Long suggested themselves that the controversial content of a topic may not be the salient variable, but rather verbalization in the normative mode, as was found by Ehman (1970b).

Additionally, Long and Long (1975) measured student political activity. Reported frequency of discussions of political matters with friends and family, following current events in the media, and participation in extracurricular activities (clubs, sports, and student government) were all positively correlated with reported controversial-issues discussions. The relationships were the strongest for junior high school students' media use (Gamma = .60) and senior high school students' frequency of political discussions with friends and family (Gamma = .40); all other correlations were between .10 and .31 for those reports of behaviors and controversial discussions. Thus, it appeared that controversial-issues discussions in social studies were associated with benefits beyond those previously identified.

In the 1979–80 school year, Zevin (1983) conducted a small-scale investigation of the relationship between classroom interaction patterns believed to be related to openness of climate, student feelings about classroom political discussions, and student political attitudes. The sample consisted of 10 11th-grade United States history classes in five New York high schools. The classes were selected from 24 classes after they were observed twice, using Flander's Interaction Analysis system. Based on the Flanders analysis, the five most "open" (student-oriented) and the five most "closed" (teacher-oriented) classrooms were selected for the study.

The 10 classrooms were visited three times during the year by an observer who had been trained in the use of Flander's Interaction Analysis system. Some classrooms exhibited seven or eight times the amount of student involvement as others.

The students in the sample classrooms were administered a questionnaire adapted from one used by Ehman (1969) to measure political trust and political efficacy. The climate variable was measured by items such as "My social studies class often discusses politics" and "We almost never debate issues in my social studies class." Although, "controversial issues" were not specifically mentioned, Zevin's concern for student perceptions of involvement in discussion was similar to the climate variable that was measured in other studies. To analyze the data, Zevin used the means on the trust, efficacy, and climate scales as the dependent variables in a standard regression matrix. The student-initiated to teacher-initiated (SI:TI) talk and student talk to teacher talk (ST:TT) ratios were the independent variables.

Corroborating the findings of other studies in which climate had an inverse relationship with trust, Zevin found that students' attitudes of political trust were inversely related to his measures of classroom openness (− .16 with ST:TT and − .46 with SI:TI). Zevin postulated that greater discussion of politics may result in frank expressions of negative feelings, which reinforce each other in a more open setting.

Also supporting earlier studies, Zevin found a positive relationship between feelings of efficacy and higher levels of student-initiated discourse in social studies classes (.37 with ST:TT and .49 with SI:TI). Zevin concluded that more discussion, particularly when initiated by students, was correlated with belief that people can successfully affect their political system.

Controversial Issues Discussion and Civil Libertarian Attitudes

Knowledge about the relationship of controversial-issues discussion and classroom climate to civic attitudes was further extended by several researchers to include other attitudes valued in democracies, such as toleration of dissent and support for civil liberties. Grossman (1975/1976) administered questionnaires to 1,312 secondary school students in 58 classrooms in nine San Francisco Bay Area high schools. The questionnaire included a 10-item scale to measure open/closed school environment. Only 2 of the 10 items dealt with controversial issues ("even when we disagree with a teacher, students are allowed to freely express their opinions in class" and "values and value conflicts in American society are discussed in the classroom"). Other items on the scale had to do with the relaxed nature of the class, student input into school decision-making, and students' liking of the school. In addition to the School Environment Scale, other discrete items measured number of controversial-issues-oriented classes taken, amount of time in a particular social studies class devoted to controversial issues, and the students' willingness to express themselves freely in the classroom. Dissent toleration was measured by subscales of support for free speech, perceived legitimacy of dissent, and range of protest and violence considered acceptable.

Grossman used a multiple regression analysis to explore the relationship of 28 independent variables to the dependent variable, toleration of dissent. The number of controversial-issues courses taken was found to be related to dissent toleration scores (Beta = .11) as well as to student participation in dissent

activities, such as protests. Another statistically significant—but only slight—relationship was that between students' perceptions of freedom to express their views in class and tolerance scores (Beta = .07). Responses to the School Environment Scale were not clearly related to toleration of dissent, but because classroom discussion of controversial issues was only one of several dimensions of school environment measured with the scale, it is not possible to draw any conclusions from this study about the relationship between student views of controversial issues discussions and toleration of dissent.

Like Grossman, Long and Long (1975) also found that time reportedly spent on controversial issues was not related to support for dissent. In their Illinois study, they reported frequency of discussion and perceived willingness of teachers to permit controversial discussions had a low negative correlation with scores on their Civic Tolerance Scale (which included items about free speech for atheists and communists' right to hold office) for the junior high school respondents (Gamma = − .15); for the senior high school students, no relationship was found between civic tolerance scores and reported frequency of discussion and teacher willingness to permit discussions (Gamma = .02). It appears there is not a simple relationship between exposure to controversial issues and tolerance of dissent.

Baughman (1975) was interested in whether a "participatory classroom" (identical to open-climate classrooms) was related to civic tolerance and student support of procedural rights and civil liberties guaranteed by the Bill of Rights. To explore that relationship, Baughman administered a questionnaire to 672 students enrolled in ninth-grade civics courses in three communities. The questionnaire contained Ehman's (1969) Classroom Climate Scale and scales to measure political interest, efficacy, and trust. Baughman also measured support for free speech, free press, and free assembly, and procedural rights, such as those related to search warrants, right to a lawyer, and being informed of charges.

Consistent with earlier studies, the students in Baughman's sample who reported that their class was "high participatory" were more likely to report a higher sense of political efficacy and interest than students who perceived that they were in a low-participatory (closed climate) classroom. Also consistent with earlier studies, those students who indicated they were in a high-participatory classroom indicated less political trust than did students who perceived a medium amount of participation. But, interestingly, the findings in regard to political efficacy, interest, and trust were found before the civics course began, as well as at its conclusion. This suggests that students with high levels of political interest and efficacy and low levels of trust may be more attuned to the attributes of a high-participatory or open-climate classroom.

Moreover, those students who perceived their classrooms to be more participatory exhibited higher levels of support for rights guaranteed by the Bill of Rights. Again, the difference was observed at the beginning of the civics course as well as afterward; the two groups experienced similar amounts of change over the period of the course.

Further research is needed to establish the specific conditions under which controversial-issues exposure is related to civic tolerance, as well as to political attitudes. More studies like those by Ehman (1970a, 1970b) and Zevin (1983) that include the observation of classroom processes are needed. Moreover, studies are needed that go beyond establishing correlations to determining which processes cause particular outcomes.

Experimental Treatments and Students' Attitudes

Studies that measure the outcomes of experimental curriculum projects provide some insight into the effects of controversial-issues discussions on students. The most extensive such studies were the evaluations of the Harvard Social Studies Project in which students were taught to use a "jurisprudential approach" to analyze controversial public policy issues (Levin, Newmann, & Oliver, 1969; Oliver & Shaver, 1966/1974). The project operated for four years in a junior high school and for three years in a senior high school in middle-class Boston suburbs.

The evaluation of the junior high school version of the project as reported by Oliver and Shaver, (1966/1974) will be discussed first. Over a two-year period, experimental curriculum units were taught by specially selected teachers who had been involved in the development of the units. The experimental materials were used for approximately half of the social studies instructional time; during the remaining time, more traditional approaches to U.S. history, geography, and current events were used. A standard control group design was used to test the hypothesis that "It is possible to teach adolescent students to use an abstract conceptual model for analzying and clarifying public controversy" (p. 257). Control groups in three other schools were used to compare the gains of the experimental group.

In order to measure the effects of the junior high school experimental program, four types of measures were used: standardized critical thinking tests, Social Issues Analysis Tests (SIAT) developed by the project staff, a measure of interest in current events, and standardized measures of factual social studies content. The tests of critical thinking and social studies content yielded no statistically significant differences between the experimental and control groups, leading the researchers to conclude that the public-issues curriculum did not affect general reasoning ability (critical thinking) nor did the time spent in the analysis of controversial issues reduce the amount of traditional content learned. On the measure of interest in societal issues, experimental-group students, in comparison with control-group students, showed less gain in topics they studied intensively; perhaps saturation had occurred. However, experimental students showed greater gain in regard to issues they had not studied than did control students.

Most importantly, junior high school students who were exposed to the public issues curriculum showed statistically significant gains over the control group on the tests designed to measure students' thinking in the abstract conceptual modes that were the basis of the curriculum project. The experimental-group students were better able than control-group students to analyze argumentative dialogues.

In the senior high school portion of the Harvard Public Issues Project, the experimental treatment consisted of using a set of curriculum units focused on controversies arising from enduring problem areas such as equality, morality/responsibility, and welfare/security (Levin et al., 1969). The project used fictional and historical cases to generate discussion about conflicting values. It emphasized the role of the teacher as listener, questioner, and clarifier in a dialogue. Experimental-group students were exposed to the curriculum for three years—in their 10th-, 11th-, and 12th-grade social studies classes. Two experimental classes were taught by project staff. Comparison-group classes in the same academic track in the same school and at another school in the same track and in an honors track were taught by the regular teachers. To determine the effects of the project, several instruments were administered to the four groups in the 12th grade: a Concept Application Test, a structured Dialogue Analysis Test (adapted from the junior high school project), an open-ended Dialogue Analysis Test (DAT), an open-ended factual recall test of topics in American history, and a standardized high school Problems of Democracy (POD) test. In addition to those five written tests, students also discussed a case similar to the ones used in project instruction.

Although the honors group scored higher than all other groups on the POD test, the project group did as well as the other comparison groups on that test—suggesting that project students were not at a disadvantage on the standardized content test compared to students of similar ability. The honors class and the project class scored higher on the Concept Application Test than did standard level students not taught by project staff. On the structured DAT, the honors class and the project class did better than the other two groups. In the open-ended DAT, the project group scored substantially higher than all other groups (mean-48.6; s.d.-13.6 compared to means of 34.8 to 37.9 for the other three groups). Students who used the project materials did less well on the test of American history facts than did students in both the honors and standard class who took a traditional, chronological course. A complex analysis of the discussion measure suggested that project students did better than students in the other groups, but "the bulk of the dialogues (for all groups) were undistinguished either in terms of discussion skill or intellectual substance" (p. 173).

Whereas the Harvard Project findings focused on knowledge, skills, and interest, other evaluation studies explored attitudinal outcomes associated with controversial-issues curriculum and instruction. For example, Goldenson's (1978) study of the impact of a specially designed unit of instruction on students' attitudes toward civil liberties contributed further to the research on the discussion of controversial issues and civic tolerance. He collected data in the context of a field experiment at two high schools in working-class communities near Minneapolis. The three-week curriculum unit was designed to expose students to a series of controversial topics that involved the application of abstract constitutional principles to concrete situations. Group research projects on topics related to freedom of religion, search and seizure, freedom of expression, and due process of law were the focus of the unit. Students contacted community members such as lawyers, police, and representatives of the American Civil Liberties Union to hear conflicting perspectives on their topics. Goldenson emphasized that it was probably the teaching methods more than the materials that affected students.

To measure attitude change, Goldenson asked students to respond to brief case studies in terms of the degree to which they agreed with a decision and the degree to which they were concerned about an issue. At the end of the treatment, 20% more of the experimental group students than of the comparison group students exhibited attitude changes in the direction of greater support for civil liberties. Moreover, the students who participated in the controversial-issues investigation of civil liberties topics were also more likely to have both a change in attitudes and an increased level of concern for the issues presented in the case studies.

Looking at finer distinctions in the treatment's effect, Goldenson noted that almost half (45%) of the experimental students whose attitudes changed toward greater support for civil liberties (12% of the experimental group) showed dramatic changes—greater than 50% of the possible range of attitude scores. None of the control students showed changes of that magnitude. That a relatively brief social studies unit could have such an impact suggests the potential power of incorporating the investigation of controversial issues in the curriculum.

Although no measure was taken of students' perception of classroom climate, there was some indication that the tone the teacher set was important. The teacher's influence on the process of attitude change was attested to by the findings in regard to teacher "credibility." Credibility was operationally defined as the degree to which students rated their teacher as fair, knowledgeable, concerned, interesting, and understandable. Experimental group students who rated their teachers high on the Credibility Index were even more likely to have undergone supportive attitude change in regard to civil liberties than were other experimental group students. Indeed, experimental group students who rated their teachers low in credibility were more likely than corresponding control group students to change their opinions in an anti-civil-libertarian direction (Goldenson, 1978). Those results reinforce Ehman's (1969) conclusion from the Detroit study that "controversial content presented in a biased and closed atmosphere can apparently be related to negative outcomes" (p. 578) and thus be counterproductive.

Another study of the effects of a unit of instruction incorporating active student research into a controversial issue had similarly positive effects on student outcomes. Curtis and Shaver (1980) measured the impact of a study of housing problems on slow learners in British Columbia, Canada. In an extensive unit, newspaper articles, booklets, and a community survey of attitudes toward the local housing situation were used. Experimental-group students, as compared to control-group students, showed increased self-esteem, decreased dogmatism, increased interest in housing and other social issues, and increased scores on a test of critical thinking. Furthermore, in response to open-ended questions, experimental group students were more likely to express beliefs that citizens could make a difference in improving conditions. There were, however, no differences between the experimental and control groups on the Fundamental Freedoms Scale, which measured support for civil liberties, apparently contradicting Goldenson's (1978) and Grossman's (1975/1976) findings, but supporting the results of Long and Long (1975).

Summary

Findings from evaluations of experimental curricula may be influenced by the Hawthorne effect and by the use of volunteer teachers, some of whom were involved in the curriculum development. Nevertheless, the findings from several separate projects together suggest hypotheses worthy of further study. Students who have the opportunity to investigate controversial issues in social studies as compared to students without such opportunities seem likely to learn as much traditional content, develop an interest in the issues studied and in other societal problems, become supportive of civil liberties, acquire the ability to analyze arguments, improve in self-esteem, and become less dogmatic.

CROSS-NATIONAL RESEARCH ON CONTROVERSIAL ISSUES DISCUSSIONS

The apparent benefits of students discussing controversial issues in open, supportive classroom climates are not limited to social studies classes in the United States. In Almond and Verba's (1963) classic cross-national study of democratic cultures, adults with the highest levels of political efficacy were those who remembered discussing and debating social and political issues in school. That was especially true for adults from the United States and United Kingdom; to a lesser extent the generalization also applied to citizens in the other nations studied—West Germany, Mexico, Italy. In all five countries, the relationship between political efficacy and recall of controversial issues discussions was the greatest for the adults who completed secondary school.

In a major cross-national study of civic education, the International Association for the Evaluation of Educational Achievement (IEA) administered a survey to over 30,000 students ages 10, 14, and pre-university level. The sample was selected with a two-step stratified random sampling technique (students within schools), yielding a representative sample of the school population at the three age levels in nine nations (Torney, Oppenheim, & Farnen, 1975). The IEA researchers concluded that students who said they had the opportunity to participate regularly in classroom discussions in which they were encouraged to express their opinions were more politically knowledgeable, more politically interested, and less authoritarian than students who did not recall such discussions. The reverse was true for the students who said they primarily received their civics instruction in the form of lectures, recitation, and patriotic rituals; they were less politically interested and more authoritarian than the students who said they expressed their opinions in discussions.

In a study which used nonrepresentative samples from five nations, Hahn, Tocci, and Angell (1988) examined several of the relationships explored in the IEA study and in the earlier American studies reported above. Surveys were administered to 1,459 secondary school students in social studies classes in 21 schools in the United States ($n = 375$), the United Kingdom ($n = 344$), West Germany ($n = 148$), Denmark ($n = 314$), and the Netherlands ($n = 279$). The Classroom Climate Scale, based on the IEA study, included items about frequency of controversial-issues discussions and perceptions of the teachers' encouragement of student expression of opinions. It did not measure the number of "controversial-issues courses" to which students had been exposed, the number of sides presented in discussions, or the normative nature of the lessons as had some of the assessments used in earlier research. Measures of political efficacy, trust, confidence, and interest were the same as those used in Ehman's (1969, 1970, 1977) research. A Freedom of Expression Scale was similar to the scales used to measure civic tolerance and toleration of dissent, except that it was focused on free speech and free press for extremist groups on the right and the left in the various countries. Reliability coefficients for the efficacy, trust, confidence, interest, free expression, and climate scales were .64, .78, .69, .85, .59, and .58, respectively. Small but positive correlations were found between scores on the Climate Scale and on all of the attitude scales except for Free Expression. The correlations were: .20 with Political Efficacy, .21 with Political Trust, .16 with Political Confidence, .21 with Political Interest, and .02 with Free Expression.

Taken together, research findings from the United States and other Western democracies suggest that when secondary school students discuss controversial issues in an open, supportive environment, there are often positive outcomes in terms of political interest, efficacy, confidence, and trust. Moreover, controversial-issues teaching in a closed climate appears to be negatively correlated with those outcomes. Some studies have found a positive correlation between open climate and civic tolerance or support for civil liberties, but most have found no relationship. Because the findings are based on survey data and correlational analysis, causal possibilities cannot yet be assumed to exist. That is, students who initially have high levels of political interest, confidence, and efficacy may be attuned to controversial-issues discussions and thus be more likely to recall (when later responding to a questionnaire) that they participated in such discussions than are their less politically oriented classmates. The study by Baughman (1975) suggests that such may indeed be the case. Longitudinal studies are needed in which classroom observations are combined with student interviews to determine whether controversial-issues discussions in an open environment foster positive civic attitudes in students.

In the meantime, researchers and policy makers have reason to be concerned with the extent to which teachers, students, and community members support the principle advocated by social studies professionals that schools in a democracy should model citizen examination of controversial public policy issues. For that reason, the research on student and teacher attitudes toward including controversial issues in the social studies curriculum is relevant.

STUDENT PERCEPTIONS OF AND ATTITUDES TOWARD CONTROVERSIAL ISSUES IN SOCIAL STUDIES

The results from student surveys indicate that secondary school students are receptive to the inclusion of controversial issues in social studies courses (Long & Long, 1975; Remy, 1972). In the Illinois study described earlier, Long and Long (1975) found that students who reported more controversial-issues discussions had positive feelings toward social studies courses, textbooks, and teachers. Indeed, Gamma coefficients for the correlations between responses on the Controversial Discussion Index and attitudes toward social studies courses were .70 for junior high school respondents and .65 for senior high school respondents (Long & Long, 1975, p. 292).

It is interesting that in three different surveys of American high school student samples, about 70% of the respondents reported that in their social studies classes, controversial issues were discussed often; fewer than 10% said they were never discussed (Ehman, 1969, Hahn, Angell, & Tocci, 1987; Torney-Purta & Lansdale, 1986). In regard to how free students felt to express their opinions when they differed from the teachers', however, only half of the students said they felt free most of the time (Ehman, 1969; Hahn, Angell, & Tocci, 1987; Torney-Purta & Landsdale, 1986).

The reports from students in the United States can, to a limited extent, be put in cross-national context. In the large-scale study of civic education in nine nations, the IEA researchers asked 10-year-old, 14-year-old, and pre-university students how much they had been encouraged to express independent opinions in their classes. Finnish students reported low levels of encouragement of expression, as did Dutch students (at ages 10 and 14; not pre-university). Students in West Germany, Ireland, New Zealand, and the United States reported high levels of encouragement (Torney et al., 1975).

Similar to the IEA researchers' findings, Hahn, Tocci, and Angell (1988) found students in West Germany, Denmark, and the United States to have perceived more discussion of controversial issues in their classes than did sample students from the United Kingdom and the Netherlands. In the samples from all five countries, the majority of students thought that teachers respected their opinions and encouraged them to express their views in class. Students in Denmark and West Germany were most likely to report that they expressed their opinion even when it differed from that of the teacher and other students; U.K. students were the least likely to say they did so.

In summary, the data on high school students' perceptions suggest that most students in the 1970s and 1980s believed that there were some opportunities to discuss controversial issues in their classes. Furthermore, students expressed a desire to study controversial issues; and when such issues were explored, students said they liked social studies classes more. It is probable that with more discussions of controversial issues fewer students would feel that social studies is dull and irrelevant to the real world, as is so often reported in surveys of students attitudes towards social studies. Moreover, the findings presented earlier in regard to political attitudes suggest that students' interests are compatible with the classroom practices that seem to foster positive civic outcomes.

Students, however, are not the ones who determine what is studied in social studies or how topics will be presented. It is the teachers who make such decisions within the parameters set by school systems in the United States. Therefore, teachers' attitudes toward controversial issues are important to understanding the extent to which controversial issues are explored in social studies classes.

TEACHERS' ATTITUDES TOWARD CONTROVERSIAL ISSUES DISCUSSIONS

To what extent do social studies teachers want to include controversial issues in their courses? The findings over the last 25 years of research suggest a willingness on the part of teachers to deal with most, but not all, controversial issues. Moreover, although students report spending class time exploring controversial issues, teachers' reports suggest that time devoted to such issues is a small percentage of total instructional time.

The most systematic study of teachers' perceptions of controversial issues in classrooms was the one conducted by Massialas, Sprague, and Sweeney (1970). Questionnaires were sent to the social studies, biology, and English teachers in a random sample of Michigan high schools. Questionnaires were returned by 73% (493) of the teachers in the sample. Only 16% of the social studies teachers who responded reported that they spent as much as 25% of their class time discussing controversial social issues. The English and biology teachers reported less time. Teachers were given a list of topics and asked to identify whether or not they were controversial and appropriate for classroom discussion. At least 80% of the teachers of the three subject areas were willing to discuss 10 of the 13 issues presented. Some issues perceived by teachers as highly controversial, such as race relations and Vietnam, were considered appropriate topics for classroom discussion by the majority of teachers; sex-related topics, however, were more often identified as taboo classroom topics. More male than female teachers would discuss all issues in the classroom; the women were particularly less willing to discuss the sex-related issues. Overall, teachers with more experience were less willing than newer teachers to discuss controversial issues, but even new teachers were unwilling to discuss some issues.

The more experienced teachers were also less likely than novice teachers to agree that students should be encouraged to express their opinions frequently in class discussions. However, they were no less likely to believe that teachers should express their positions in class discussions. The social studies teachers were considerably more supportive of student expression than were the biology or English teachers. Moreover, teachers who reported the highest levels of belief in student expression (BSE) devoted more class time to discussion of issues than did low-BSE teachers. High-BSE teachers were also more willing to discuss all issues than were low-BSE teachers. Finally, high-BSE teachers used more types of instructional materials than did low-BSE teachers. They were more likely to use pamphlets written from various perspectives, primary sources, and materials published outside of the United States.

No other studies were located that used representative samples of teachers to measure teacher attitudes toward student expression or percent of class time devoted to classroom discussion of controversial issues. The results of several surveys of nonrandom samples of teachers and supervisors suggest that although there may have been a greater willingness to deal with controversial issues in social studies in the 1970s than there was in the earlier Michigan study, there appeared to be a swing back to greater hesitancy in the 1980s (Gross, 1977; Hahn, 1985; Mol-

nar, 1983; Morrisett, 1975). Other surveys found, as Massialas et al. (1970) did, that teachers were most likely to avoid sex-related topics such as abortion and homosexuality (Morrisett, 1975; Stradling et al., 1984).

Only one study was identified that dealt with training teachers to handle controversial issues in social studies (Guyton & Hoffman, 1983). The instructors of a course titled "Teaching Controversial Issues in Social Studies," sent a survey to 98 students who had taken the course over a three-year period. With a low return rate of 49% and no data from comparable teachers who did not take the course, it is not possible to attribute conclusively the respondents' reported attitudes and behavior to the course. Moreover, it is likely that self-selection occurred, as individuals who enrolled in the course probably already believed in teaching about controversial issues. Nevertheless, despite the limitations, Guyton and Hoffman's findings reinforce the generalization that a considerable number of teachers do support the inclusion of controversial issues in social studies. Indeed, 95% of the teachers responding to the survey agreed that "students need to study controversial issues." Furthermore, only 2% agreed that "middle grades and high school social studies texts deal adequately with controversial issues." Of the respondents, 16% said that they taught about controversial issues as frequently as weekly, which is comparable to the findings of Massialas et al. (1970). More (29%) taught about such issues two to three times a month or once a month (36%). Nearly half (46%) said that they taught about controversial issues more after taking the course than they had before (another 22% said they thought they taught about such issues as frequently after the course as before).

Guyton and Hoffman did not measure teacher attitudes toward student expression of beliefs, which Massialas et al. (1970) suggested could be important. Teacher training that develops teachers' ability to conduct classroom discussions characterized by openness (as suggested by earlier sections of this review) and in which the value of encouraging students to express their opinions freely is demonstrated may be the key to fostering democratic attitudes. Research is clearly needed on the impact of teacher training on classroom practice. However, in many cases, training may have little effect on deeply rooted aspects of personality that prevent some teachers from conducting open discussions of controversial issues (Marker, 1970).

PROMISING LINES OF FUTURE RESEARCH

Returning to the rationale for including controversial issues in social studies, it is clear that we do not yet know much about the connections between instructional practices and civic outcomes. We are not yet able to state conclusively that examining and discussing controversial public policy issues in an open, supportive climate causes young people to possess the attitudes and skills necessary to participate effectively in the public discourse of democratic societies. Nor are we yet able to describe the elements of a teacher-education program that is effective in producing teachers who can teach in a manner that prepares students for the tasks of democratic citizenship. Researchers are, however, well on the way to such a point. As suggested earlier in this chapter, it is time to build on the cumulative quantitative data from surveys, correlational studies, and curricular evaluations with richer, deeper qualitative descriptions of classroom interaction, students' perceptions, and teachers' thinking.

Consistent with the contemporary emphasis in educational research, Ochoa (1986) noted the particular need for qualitative research on the role of controversial issues in social studies classes. Such methodology has the potential for providing insights into the meanings that the participants—students and teachers—have of controversial issues. For example, Ochoa's (1986) interviews with teachers demonstrate the complexity of the decision-making process when social studies teachers approach controversial issues. The recent studies by Lee Shulman's students at Stanford University on "content pedagogical knowledge" and the "wisdom of practice" and other case studies offer a method that can help to explicate the complexity of teaching controversial issues in social studies (McGraw, 1987; Stradling et al., 1984; Wineburg & Wilson, 1988).

Other contemporary research emphases are equally relevant to controversial issues in social studies. For example, in a summary of research on the role of classroom controversy in fostering learning, Johnson and Johnson (1979) linked cooperative learning, controversy, and learning. Their findings confirmed the points Hunt and Metcalf (1968) put forward two decades earlier when they advocated that social studies classes investigate the "closed areas" of society. Johnson and Johnson (1979) emphasized that the positive outcomes identified in their review occurred only when teachers structure learning activities cooperatively, ensure that the cooperative groups are heterogeneous, teach perspective-taking skills, show students how to affirm one another's personal competence while disagreeing with each other's position, and emphasize rational argument. As the cooperative learning movement appears to be picking up adherents, many of whom are social studies educators, there will be increasing numbers of opportunities to study the effects on students of examining controversial issues under cooperative conditions. The earlier research on controversial-issues discussions in social studies suggests that expected outcomes might include positive citizenship attitudes as well as the increased knowledge, perspective-taking ability, and levels of moral reasoning identified by Johnson and Johnson (1979).

A third line of research that promises to be fruitful is on how different subgroups of students think about controversial issues. Some studies suggest that age, gender, race, and class may be important variables affecting how diverse student populations perceive controversial issues.

As regards age, Merelman's (1971) interviews with 8th and 12th graders suggested that there is a developmental nature to policy thinking, that would be relevant to how young people think about controversial public policy issues. Merelman's theoretical model ought to receive extensive testing by asking groups of students at various ages to think aloud about controversial public policy issues. Current research on novice and expert problem solvers is also relevant to understanding the qualitative nature of student's thinking about controversial issues.

Recent research on gender and thinking also has implications for understanding how students think about controversial issues (Belenky, Clinchy, Goldberger, & Tarule, 1986; Wormald, 1983). For example, Nell Noddings' (1984) research on an ethic of caring that develops from female socialization suggests that male and female students may reason differently about controversial issues—from abortion to environmental problems. Gilligan's (1982) distinctions between female reasoning, based on concern for relationships, and male reasoning, based on concern for rights and responsibilities, similarly might be applicable to classroom discussions about controversial public policy issues.

So far those doing research on gender differences in thinking have relied on interviews with college students and adults. The theoretical work should now be tested with empirical studies of elementary and secondary classes. Observations of classroom discussions of controversial issues and indepth interviews with students might yield insights. Analyzing teacher interviews by gender might also prove fruitful. For example, the results from the one study identified here that contained some analysis by gender (Massialas et al., 1970) suggested that male and female teachers may approach controversial issues differently. Because most social studies researchers and high school social studies teachers are the products of male socialization, it is possible that "the different voice" of female students and teachers has not been heard in arriving at descriptions of and prescriptions for controversial-issues discussions. Until such gender-sensitive research is undertaken, we cannot be certain that gender is not a relevant variable.

The few studies in which race and class were considered as variables affecting civic outcomes suggest that they, too, should be considered as researchers focus on variations among subgroups of students (Ehman, 1969; Greenberg, 1970; Hess & Torney, 1967; Langton & Jennings, 1968; Lyons, 1970; Vaillancourt, 1972). Moreover, the work of researchers in multicultural education who are examining differences in the learning styles of students from various ethnic groups is applicable to understanding student perceptions of controversial issues in increasingly diverse classrooms. Classroom discussions can provide a microcosm of democratic discourse in a pluralistic society.

Other needed lines of research include, for example, the following questions: Does exposure to controversial issues contribute to moral reasoning? What impact do students' discussions of controversial public policies with their parents have on the development of civic attitudes? How do mass media presentations interact with school studies of controversy to influence student learning?

There is much yet to be learned about controversial issues in social studies and, given the longstanding commitment of the profession to teaching controversial issues, this topic warrants a top priority in our collective research agenda. Social studies teachers tell our youth that the United States has held out to the world a vision of democracy in which dialogue in the "free marketplace of ideas", public participation in decision making, and respect for diversity in a pluralistic society are ensured. It is time now that as researchers we ask our colleagues in other western democracies to join with us in inquiry into how civic and social education can pass that dialogue, participation, and diversity on to tomorrow's citizens.

References

Almond, G., & Verba, S. (1963). *The civic culture*. Princeton, NJ: Princeton University Press.

Baughman, J. E. (1975). An investigation of the impact of civics on political attitudes of adolescents (Doctoral dissertation, University of Maryland, 1975). *Dissertation Abstracts International, 36,* 3974A.

Belenky, M., Clinchy, B., Goldberger, N., & Tarule, J. (1986). *Women's ways of knowing: The development of self, voice, and mind*. New York: Basic Books.

Cox, B. (1977). *The censorship game and how to play it*. Washington, DC: National Council for the Social Studies.

Crick, B., & Lister, I. (1979). Political literacy, the centrality of the concept. *International Journal of Political Education, 2,* 83–92.

Curtis, C. K., & Shaver, J. P. (1980). Slow learners and the study of contemporary problems. *Social Education, 44,* 302–309.

Ehman, L. H. (1969). An analysis of the relationships of selected educational variables with the political socialization of high school students. *American Educational Research Journal, 6,* 559–580.

Ehman, L. H. (1970a). *A comparison of three sources of classroom data: Teachers, students and systematic observation*. Paper presented at the annual meeting of the American Educational Research Association, Minneapolis.

Ehman, L. H. (1970b). Normative discourse and attitude change in the social studies classroom. *The High School Journal, 54,* 76–83.

Ehman, L. H. (1972). Political efficacy and the high school social studies curriculum. In B. G. Massialas (Ed.), *Political youth, traditional schools: National and international perspectives* (pp. 90–102). Englewood Cliffs, NJ: Prentice Hall.

Ehman, L. H. (1977, April). *Social studies instructional factors causing change in high school students' sociopolitical attitudes over a two-year period*. Paper presented at the annual meeting of the American Educational Research Association, New York.

Engle, S. H., & Ochoa, A. S. (1988). *Education for democratic citizenship: Decision making in the social studies*. New York: Teachers College Press.

Gilligan, C. (1982). *In a different voice: Psychological theory and women's development*. Cambridge, MA: Harvard University Press.

Goldenson, D. R. (1978). An alternative view about the role of the secondary school in political socialization: A field experimental study of the development of civil liberties attitudes. *Theory and Research in Social Education. 6*(1), 44–72.

Greenberg, E. (1970). *Political socialization*. Chicago: Aldine Atherton.

Griffin, A. F. (1942). *A philosophic approach to the subject matter preparation of teachers of history*. Unpublished doctoral dissertation, Ohio State University, Columbus.

Gross, R. E. (1952). *How to handle controversial issues* Washington, DC: National Council for the Social Studies.

Gross, R. E. (1977). The status of the social studies in the public schools of the United States: Facts and impressions of a national survey. *Social Education, 41,* 194–200.

Grossman, D. L. (1976). Educational climates and attitudes toward dissent: A study of political socialization of conflict norms in adolescents (Doctoral dissertation, Stanford University, 1975). *Dissertation Abstracts International, 36,* 7980.

Guyton, E., & Hoffman, A. (1983, November). *Teaching controversial issues in social studies*. Paper presented at the annual meeting of the National Council for the Social Studies, San Francisco. (ERIC Document Reproduction Service No. ED 242 625)

Hahn, C. L. (1985). The status of the social studies in the public schools of the United States: Another look. *Social Education, 49,* 220–223.

Hahn, C. L., Angell, A., & Tocci, C. (1987, November). *Civic attitudes in five nations*. Paper presented at the annual meeting of the National Council for the Social Studies, Dallas.

Hahn, C. L., Tocci, C., & Angell, A. (1988, June). *Civic attitudes and controversial issues discussions in five nations*. Paper presented at the International meeting of the Social Studies, Vancouver, British Columbia, Canada.

Hess, R. D., & Torney, J. V. (1967). *The development of political attitudes in children*. Chicago: Aldine Press.

Hooghoff, H. (1988). *Curriculum development in political education particularly the international dimension*. Paper presented at the 14th World Congress of the International Political Science Association, Washington, DC.

Hunt, M. P., & Metcalf, L. E. (1968). *Teaching high school social studies: Problems in reflective thinking and social understanding* (2nd ed). New York: Harper & Brothers.

Johnson, D. W., & Johnson, R. T. (1979). Conflict in the classroom: Controversy and learning. *Review of Educational Research, 49,* 51–70.

Langton, K. P., & Jennings, M. K. (1968). Political socialization and the high school civics curriculum in the United States. *American Political Science Review, 62,* 852–869.

Levin, M., Newmann, F. M., & Oliver, D. W. (1969). A law and social science curriculum based on the analysis of public issues (Final Report Project No. HS-058, Grant No. OE310142). Washington, DC: U.S. Department of Health, Education, and Welfare, Office of Education.

Litt, E. (1963). Civic education, community norms, and political indoctrination. *American Sociological Review, 28,* 69–75.

Long, S., & Long, R. (1975). Controversy in the classroom: Student viewpoint and educational outcome. *Teaching Political Science, 2,* 275–299.

Lyons, S. L. (1970). The political socialization of ghetto children: Efficacy and cynicism. *Journal of Politics, 32,* 288–304.

Marker, G. W. (1970). Teacher dogmatism and its impact upon the political attitudes of students (Doctoral dissertation, Indiana University, 1970). *Dissertation Abstracts International, 31,* 2775A.

Massialas, B. G., Sprague, N. F., & Sweeney, J. A. C. (1970). *Structure and process of inquiry into social issues in secondary schools. Inquiry into social issues. Vol. 1*. Ann Arbor: MI: The University of Michigan.

McGraw, L. (1987, March). *The anthropologist in the classroom, Chris: A case study of a beginning teacher*. Unpublished manuscript. Knowledge, Growth, and Teaching Project, Stanford University, Stanford, CA.

Merelman, R. M. (1971). The development of policy thinking in adolescence. *American Political Science Review 65,* 1033–1047.

Ministry of Education. (1986). *The aims of the subjects taught in the Folkeskole in Denmark*. Copenhagen, Denmark: Author.

Molnar, A. (1983). Are the issues studied in school the important issues facing humankind? *Social Education, 47,* 305–307.

Morrisett, I. (1975). Curriculum information network fourth report: Controversies in the classroom. *Social Education, 39,* 246–252.

Muessig, R. H. (1975). *Controversial issues in the social studies: A contemporary perspective*. Washington, DC: National Council for the Social Studies.

National Council for the Social Studies. (1977). The treatment of controversial issues in the schools. In B. Cox, *The censorship game and how to play it* (pp. 26–30). Washington, DC: The National Council for the Social Studies.

Newmann, F. M. (1970). *Clarifying public controversy: An approach to teaching social studies*. Boston: Little, Brown.

Noddings, N. (1984). *Caring*. Berkeley: University of California Press.

Ochoa, A. (1986, November). *Academic freedom: A call for research*.

Paper presented at the annual meeting of the National Council for the Social Studies, New York.

Oliver, D. W., & Shaver, J. P. (1974). *Teaching public issues in the high school*. Logan, UT: Utah State University Press. (original work published 1966)

Patrick, J. J. (1967). *Political socialization of American youth: Implications for secondary school social studies*. National Council for the Social Studies, Washington, DC.

Remy, R. C. (1972). High school seniors attitudes toward their civics and government instruction. *Social Education, 36,* 590–597, 622.

Rudduck, J. (1983). *The Humanities Curriculum Project: An introduction*. Norwich, U.K.: School of Education, University of East Anglia.

Shaver, J. P., & Larkins, A. G. (1973). *Decision-making in a democracy*. Boston: Houghton Mifflin Co.

Stradling, R., Noctor, M., & Baines, B. (1984). *Teaching controversial issues*. London: Edward Arnold.

Torney, J. V., Oppenheim, A. N., & Farnen, R. F. (1975). *Civic education in ten countries: An empirical study*. New York: John Wiley & Sons.

Torney-Purta, J., & Lansdale, D. (1986). *Classroom climate and process in international studies: Qualitative and quantitative evidence from the American schools and the world project*. Paper presented at the American Educational Research Association annual meeting, San Francisco.

Vaillancourt, P. M. (1972). *The political socialization of young people: A panel survey of youngsters in the San Francisco Bay area*. Unpublished doctoral dissertation, University of California, Berkeley.

Wineburg, S., & Wilson, S. (1988). Models of wisdom and the teaching of history. *Phi Delta Kappan, 70,* 50–58.

Wormald, E. (1983). Apolitical women: The myth of early socialization. *International Journal of Political Education, 6,* 43–64.

Zevin, J. (1983). Future citizens: Children and politics. *Teaching Political Science, 10,* 119–126.

COMPONENTS OF
INSTRUCTION

INTERACTION AND DISCOURSE IN SOCIAL STUDIES CLASSROOMS

William W. Wilen
KENT STATE UNIVERSITY

Jane J. White
UNIVERSITY OF MARYLAND, BALTIMORE COUNTY

Discourse is language that is generated naturally as people interact (Stubbs, 1983). This chapter is limited to a review of research on spoken discourse because classroom talk is considered "the medium by which much teaching takes place and during which students demonstrate to teachers much of what they have learned" (Cazden, 1986, p. 432).

Educational researchers originally assumed that classroom language was a "transparent" medium that could be ignored as one studied classroom instruction (Cazden, 1988; Edwards & Westgate, 1987). However, over the last two decades researchers have found that the forms of the language used in the classroom both reflect and shape the types of academic knowledge produced there (Stodolsky, 1988).

The two major forms of discourse in social studies classrooms are recitation and discussion. In this chapter, research studies are reviewed in terms of how the interactional patterns of recitation and discussion facilitate or constrain students' acquisition of social studies knowledge. The persistence of recitation is explained in an analysis of its interactional pattern. Teachers' questions and questioning techniques receive considerable attention because of the influence they have on students' thinking, involvement, and learning. Discussion is analyzed in terms of how its definition, purpose, structure, and occurrence differ from recitation. Nonquestioning techniques, student questioning, and forms of teacher feedback are emphasized. Different forms of discussion that have been popular during the last 30 years—including inquiry, critical thinking about social issues, exploratory talk, and, most recently, responsive teach-ing—are reviewed. Conclusions and recommendations are drawn from the contrasts between these two forms of interaction.

Research studies from both the quantitative and interpretive traditions are reviewed in this chapter. Although different underlying assumptions resulted in different questions, types of data, and validation procedures, research findings from both traditions are beginning to show a surprising amount of overlap and consensus. Although the actual "doing" of research may remain distinct, those who conduct research in either tradition can no longer afford to ignore the knowledge being produced by the other.

RECITATION

Both quantitative and interpretative researchers have found recitation to be the predominant form of discourse in classrooms (Cazden, 1986; Hoetker & Ahlbrand, 1969; Mehan, 1978; Stodolsky, 1988). From preschool through the university, the typical recitation pattern is teacher initiation–student response–teacher feedback (Bellack, Kliebard, Hyman, & Smith, 1966). As Cazden (1988) noted, "seemingly invulnerable to repeated criticisms, the recitation-type lesson has had a long and hardy life through many decades of formal, Western-type schooling" (p. 30). In her 1912 study of verbal behavior in secondary schools, Stevens found that teachers talked 64% of the time: They asked questions that called for rote memory or superficial

Reviewers were Virginia Atwood, University of Kentucky; Allan Brandhorst, University of North Carolina.

comprehension at the average rate of two per minute. Hoetker and Ahlbrand (1969) concluded that recitation was both prevalent and persistent in their historical review of early classroom observation studies.

The Persistence of Recitation

Recitation persists in social studies classrooms because of three contextual features. First, there are differences in the power relationships between the teacher and the students. The social context for discourse in the classroom is vastly asymmetrical with the teacher holding most of the basic speaking rights:

Teachers have the right to speak at any time and to any person; they can fill any silence or interrupt any speaker; they can speak to a student anywhere in the room and in any volume or tone of voice. And no one has any right to object. (Cazden, 1988, p. 54)

While conversation is defined as "talk between equals in which no participant has special rights allocated in advance," teacher talk is a language of control (Edwards & Westgate, 1987, p. 25).

Secondly, talk in school is constrained because schools are "extremely crowded environments in which attendance is compulsory" (Cazden, 1979, p. 146). Rather than the one-to-one interactions which characterize most spontaneous, natural conversations, teachers are responsible for managing a flow of talk with a 1-to-30 ratio and with fellow participants who may not be willing to talk voluntarily, particularly about the topic selected by the teacher (Cazden, 1988; Shuy, 1988).

Finally, a crucial difference between classroom talk and ordinary informal conversation is that teachers react to what students say by rating it positively or negatively. Cazden (1988, p. 30) illustrated the difference:

Conversation	*Classroom Talk*
What time is it, Sarah?	What time is it, Sarah?
Half-past two.	Half-past two.
Thanks.	Right.

In fact, "the deep groves along which most classroom talk seems to run" (Edwards & Westgage, 1987, p. 27) are so institutionalized that any young child playing teacher can easily reproduce the role by "standing in front of a group of relatively passive onlookers, doing most of the talking, asking questions to which they already know the answers, and evaluating the responses by passing judgments" (Simon & Boyer, 1970, p. 2).

Since the dominant role normally taken by teachers "imposes severe situational constraints on the communicative options available to pupils," researchers and practitioners need to be particularly attentive to "the often limited and limiting quality of language experience which schools offer children" (Edwards & Westgate, 1987, p. 5).

The Structure of the Basic Recitation Pattern of Interaction

In an extensive three-year investigation of the linguistic behavior of teachers and students, Bellack et al. (1966) analyzed 60 social studies lessons from a unit on international trade taught to 10th- and 12th-graders by 15 teachers in a major urban center. They found that classroom discourse consisted of a teacher solicitation–student response–teacher reaction cycle and that teachers dominated the discourse. Within this cycle, the students' primary responsibility was to respond to the teacher's solicitations. Other researchers have consistently found this underlying exchange structure in classroom discourse. Sinclair and Coulthard (1975) described it as teacher initiation–pupil response–teacher feedback (IRF). Mehan (1978, 1979, 1982) described it as teacher initiation–student response–teacher evaluation (IRE).

Poole (1988) described how the IRE pattern was used during a quiz review on the U.S. Constitution in an East Los Angeles eighth-grade social studies class. In terms of topic development, she found that each initiation move "constitutes a *test-question*, i.e., one to which the answer is already known" (p. 23). Poole argued that:

Test question and answer sequences comprise single propositions that span utterances by more than one speaker. Such sequences allow novice and expert to participate in the co-construction of the same proposition, so that the following initiate–reply sequence:

T: When was the Constitution written and signed?
(Maria raises hand; T recognizes her)
Maria: 1787

can be viewed as constituting the single but overtly co-constructed proposition A: The Constitution was written and signed in 1787. (p. 23)

The structure of the recitation pattern allowed this teacher to simultaneously accomplish important managerial as well as academic functions. When she asked the question, "When was the Constitution written and signed?", the teacher also signaled that it was time for the students to pay attention, physically directed the students to look at the quiz in front of them, and established the topic for discussion. When the student replied, she transmitted both academic and social messages; she not only informed the class of the correct answer, but also displayed that she got the correct answer on the test.

Poole found the teacher's closing feedback move depended on the students' performance on the test. When most of the students answered the item correctly, there was no closing frame. However, when the students performed poorly on a question, the teacher reiterated the correct answer and made certain aspects of it more explicit.

The Acquisition of the Recitation Pattern. Bremme and Erickson (1977) found that in order for students to be able to participate in school, they had to be able both to speak to the topic and speak within the initiation–response–feedback discourse pattern. For example, to be able to talk in class, primary students had to (a) have something relevant to say and (b) know how and when to raise their hand, catch the teacher's eye, and be acknowledged by the teacher just prior to "student time." Mehan (1982) found that over the course of a school year, the primary-grade children he studied became more sophisticated and learned how to speak within the format of the recitation pattern. By the end of the year, there were fewer inappropriate attempts by students to speak and a significant increase in student initiations that were incorporated into lessons.

At higher grade levels, however, students typically ask few questions during recitation. In a study of 27 10-minute, randomly selected segments of social studies and religion classrooms from six parochial high schools, Dillon (1988) observed a total of 11 questions from 8 students out of a possible 721 students engaged in classroom discussions. While questions accounted for less than 1% of students' talk, over 60% of the teachers' talk was questions. In an earlier study, Dillon (1981b) found that student teachers, responding to questionnaire surveys, reported that their pupils were reluctant to ask questions because of negative reactions from teachers and other students.

Occurrence and Purpose of Recitation. In a two-year study of 28 elementary social studies classes in the greater Chicago region, Stodolsky, Ferguson, and Wimpelberg (1981) identified three general purposes for which teachers conducted social studies recitations. Review accounted for 21%, and introducing new ideas accounted for over half of the segments coded (56%). Checking understanding or clarifying (which occurred after reviewing or introducing material) accounted for 14% of the social studies recitations. Stodolsky et al. also found that recitations occurred more frequently in lower SES schools than in high-SES schools.

Farrar (1984) offered several reasons why recitation is so ingrained in teachers' instructional styles: Teachers can diagnose students' comprehension of the content, control the topic through questioning, and control students' behavior more easily through the question-answer format. Weil and Murphy (1982) in their review of research concluded "For learning factual material, this pattern may be the most effective method available" (p. 911).

The Production of Lower-Level Thinking and Knowledge Through Questioning

Stevens (1912), in her early study on questioning, demonstrated that teachers have emphasized the recall of facts requiring memory-level thinking. This finding has been particularly evident in social studies at both the elementary and secondary levels and has persisted through today. Haynes (1935), in his study of sixth-grade history classes, reported that 77% of the teachers' questions were solicitations of factual information, whereas only 17% could be classified as requiring students to think.

Bellack et al. (1966), in the report of their study, noted that "by far the largest proportion of the discourse involved empirical (i.e., factual) meanings" (p. 85). Gall and Gall (1976) also characterized the teacher-student interaction pattern of a recitation as emphasizing lower-cognitive level questions, asked for the purpose of recalling information.

In three studies conducted in intermediate and junior high social studies classes during the late 1960s, it was found that the major emphasis was on lower-cognitive-level questions that required recall of content (Crump, 1970; Godbold, 1969; Sch-

reiber, 1967). Two other studies conducted during this time also found that secondary social studies student teachers asked memory-level questions in their classrooms (Davis & Tinsley, 1967) and planned memory level questions to guide their class discussions (Tinsley & Davis, 1971). Based on his review of research, Gall (1970) generalized that 60% of teachers' questions require students to recall facts, 20% require thinking, and 20% are procedural in nature. An updated review of research by Gall (1984) yielded the same conclusion.

Questions and Achievement. Is there a relationship between the cognitive levels of the questions that social studies teachers ask and their students' gains in achievement? Research findings are inconclusive. In studies conducted at the University of Washington, the relationship between the cognitive levels of social studies teachers' oral questions and students' achievement was examined. Using second-grade teachers and students, Buggey (1971) found statistically significantly greater achievement ($p < .05$) by the treatment group whose teachers asked 70% higher-level questions and 30% knowledge questions, as compared to a treatment group with 70% knowledge and 30% higher-level questions and a control group. In a replication of this study with fifth-graders, however, Savage (1972) found no differences in achievement between the two questioning treatments. Also using fifth-graders in social studies, Kniep (1974) found that treatment groups of teachers using high-level questions at least 70% of the time, fostered students' ability to recall content and their ability to respond to high-level questions.

Gall et al. (1978) exposed sixth-grade students to three types of recitation based on different percentages of low and high cognitive levels of questions asked by teachers during a unit on ecology. Students in the experimental groups of 25%, 50%, and 75% higher cognitive questions achieved more information recall than the no-recitation control group students on measures containing low- and high-cognitive-level questions. Ryan (1973) and Dunkin (1978) also found that higher-order questions influenced the achievement of the fifth- and sixth-grade students in the social studies classes comprising their samples. On the other hand, Armento (1977) found that student achievement was not correlated with high and low cognitive questions in her study of third- through fifth-grade preservice and inservice social studies teachers. Not surprisingly, then, in several major reviews of correlational and experimental studies not limited to social studies, contradictory conclusions have been drawn regarding the effects of higher- and lower-cognitive-level questions on students' achievement (Redfield & Rousseau, 1981; Rosenshine, 1976; Samson, Strykowski, Weinstein, & Walberg, 1987; Winne, 1979).

In his review of research on questioning, Gall (1987) suggested several reasons why these studies yielded different results: the researchers used different definitions of higher-cognitive-level questions and different question-classification systems; teachers primarily ask lower cognitive questions and find it more difficult to implement instruction based on higher cognitive questions; and, higher cognitive questions are more difficult for many students to respond to, thereby having differential influence on learning and performance on tests. He recommended that teachers ask lower-level cognitive questions to enhance students' learning of basic facts and skills and higher cognitive questions to develop their thinking ability and skills.

Student Responses to Questions. The relationship between the cognitive levels of teachers' questions and students' responses is low. Dillon (1982), in an investigation of secondary social studies and religion classes, found that only 50% (approximately) of pupils' responses were identical to the levels of teachers' questions. Mills, Rice, Berliner, and Rousseau (1980) found a similar percentage of lack of congruence using three different question-classification systems to classify teachers' questions and students' responses. Higher-level questions did not necessarily lead to correspondingly higher levels of student thinking as indicated by their responses.

In their review of research, Winne and Marx (1979) suggested that students' perceptions regarding higher cognitive questions may not be the same as the teacher's, and this may lead to the lack of congruence between questions and responses. Klinzing, Klinzing-Eurich, and Tisher (1985) trained a group of 29 primary teachers in a West German school district on techniques for asking questions. Results showed a statistically significant increase ($p < .01$) in the proportion of higher cognitive questions asked by teachers and in the proportion of correspondence between the cognitive levels of teachers' questions and students' responses. Another possibility is to acquaint students with the relationship of questions to thinking and train them to respond to the levels of questions (Mills et al., 1980).

One important exception to the findings of a low relationship between the level of teachers' questions and students' responses is Gallagher and Aschner's (1963) study of gifted social studies students. They found that a 5% increase in the frequency of higher-cognitive-level questions resulted in as much as a 40% increase in the number of corresponding higher-level responses.

Questioning Techniques That Result in Student Learning Gains

Question Frequency. Teachers ask a high frequency of questions at all grade levels and in all subject areas (Wilen, in press). Over 75 years ago, Stevens (1912) recorded a mean of 395 questions per day during recitations in high school social studies and English classes. More recently, Schreiber (1967) reported that 14 5th-grade teachers asked an average of 64 questions each during 30-minute social studies lessons. In a four-year study of 36 teachers of secondary pupils (11 to 12 years of age) in England, Kerry (1987) found that, on average, teachers asked 43.7 questions per hour, with language teachers asking the most (76.5 per hour) and social studies teachers asking the least (22.5 per hour). Godbold (1969) found that elementary school social studies teachers asked statistically significantly more ($p < .05$) questions than junior high social studies teachers and that experienced teachers asked more than inexperienced teachers at the secondary level. In their review of effective-teaching research, Levin and Long (1981) concluded that teachers generally ask between 300 and 400 questions per day.

Process-product researchers have reported that the frequency of questions asked by teachers is positively related to student learning. Several reviewers of research have found that teachers who maximize student achievement ask high frequencies of low-cognitive-level questions, particularly with low-SES students in elementary settings (Berliner, 1984; Brophy & Good, 1986; Weil & Murphy, 1982).

Clarity. Clearly phrased questions communicate response expectations to students. Two major sources of ambiguity are vague and run-on questions. Question clarity increases the probability of precise and accurate responses from students (Wilen, 1987a; Wilen & Clegg, 1986). In several reviews of research on effective teaching behaviors, question clarity has been identified as a strong correlate of student achievement (Berliner, 1984; Brophy & Good, 1986).

Probing. A probe is a follow-up question to a student's initial response to the teacher's question. Probes generally serve the purpose of encouraging students to clarify or expand their responses, support a point of view, or extend their thinking to a higher level. When students are not accustomed to thinking and responding at higher cognitive levels, probing can encourage them to go beyond their initial incomplete, superficial, or ambiguous responses (Wilen, 1987a; Wilen & Clegg, 1986). Reviewers of research have concluded that probing is correlated with students' achievement (Brophy & Good, 1986; Weil & Murphy, 1982). On the other hand, Gall et al. (1978) found that probing during recitations did not assist sixth-grade students to in learn factual knowledge or gain higher-level understandings.

Redirection. Redirecting questions to other students communicates the desire for student participation. Studies have demonstrated that this questioning technique is correlated with student achievement (Evertson, Anderson, Anderson, & Brophy, 1980; Riley, 1981; Wright & Nuthall, 1970). However, Gall et al. (1978) found that redirecting questions during recitations with sixth-graders did not contribute to achievement gains. Smith (1980) found mixed results in a study involving high school social studies students. In two reviews of research, support was found for redirection (Brophy & Good, 1986; Weil & Murphy, 1982).

Volunteers and Nonvolunteers. Student participation and learning are enhanced if the contributions of volunteering students are balanced with those of nonvolunteering students. Nonvolunteers should be brought into recitations and discussions when the teacher knows a high probability exists that they know the answer or have a contribution to make (Wilen & Clegg, 1986; Wilen, 1987a). In his study on solicitation patterns of 11th- and 12th-grade social studies teachers and students, Smith (1980) found that teachers who used an unpredictable pattern of calling on nonvolunteering students maintained their intellectual involvement. In their review of research, Brophy and Good (1986) concluded that balancing the contributions of volunteers and nonvolunteers is a positive correlate of student achievement.

Wait Time. Wait time can occur at two points during interaction with students: immediately after a teacher asks a question and before a student responds, and immediately after the student responds before the teacher or another student reacts. Teachers typically wait one second after asking a question (Rowe, 1974). After Rowe (1974) trained teachers to increase wait time to 3 to 5 seconds, the quantity and quality of students' responses improved dramatically: length increased, responses reflected higher level thought, failures to respond decreased, and the frequency of student questions increased. In their reviews of research on wait time, Rowe (1987) and Tobin (1987) concluded that a wait time of 3 to 5 seconds is positively correlated with higher-cognitive-level achievement. Several other reviewers of effective teaching practices have come to the same conclusion (Berliner, 1984; Brophy & Good, 1986).

Teacher Feedback. Often teachers use acknowledgement and/or praise following an acceptable student response, anticipating that it will serve as encouragement of further participation. Praise, or positive reinforcement, has been found to be an effective form of feedback. Dunkin (1978) found the percentage of positive teacher reactions (praise) to sixth-grade students' responses during social studies lessons was positively correlated, although at low levels, with achievement (three measures, r = .15, .19, .31). Gage (1978) concluded in his review of research on the use of Flanders Interaction Analysis System that teacher acceptance and use of student ideas are positively correlated with achievement.

For the most part, though, teachers tend to use praise when a simple verbal or nonverbal acknowledgement to a student's answer or contribution is all that is necessary. In their review of research on effective teaching practices, Brophy and Good (1986) concluded that teachers should provide feedback to students in the form of acknowledgement for correct answers or portions of answers, and assist students in getting an improved response. Praise is more effective when used sparingly and specifically.

DEVELOPMENT OF KNOWLEDGE AND HIGHER-LEVEL THINKING

Not all recitations emphasize lower-cognitive-level thinking. After having junior high students review information about public issues, a method labeled "recitation-analysis" was used to encourage in-depth examination of public issues in a study conducted by Oliver and Shaver (1966/1974). In her investigation of elementary social studies classes, Stodolsky (1988) found that the more complex questions within recitations at the application, analysis, and synthesis levels elicited higher levels of student attention and involvement.

In a recitation that Secretary Bennett conducted with a class of Banneker High School social studies students in Washington, DC, Shuy (1986) found that two-thirds of the 99 questions Bennett asked were higher-order questions. Shuy noted that Bennett's question-asking strategy is an excellent model for other teachers. Bennett began with higher-order "why?" questions that encouraged the student to "generalize, infer or develop cause and effect relationships." If a student was unable to do this, Bennett then probed and asked for specification with a factual recall "when, where, who, or how?" question. If this did not provide a basis for a generalization or inference, Bennett then moved to a "yes/no" question prior to moving back up to a "why?" question (p. 318).

Constraints on Development of Knowledge and Higher-Level Thinking

Several studies have shown, however, that there tend to be constraints on development of knowledge and higher-level thinking when a recitation format is used in the classroom. Several researchers (Klinzing & Klinzing-Eurich, 1988; Wood & Wood, 1988) who were part of an extensive multidisciplinary research study on discussion and questioning concluded that many of the teachers controlled classroom interaction excessively. Klinzing and Klinzing-Eurich (1988) suggested that more student involvement could have been stimulated by asking a few key questions, rather than frequent questions, and by not reacting to every student response. Wood and Wood (1988) analyzed the degree of control teachers exhibited through their encouragement or restriction of students' opportunity to participate. Teacher "power" scores were computed based on the extent students were allowed to take initiative in discussions by asking questions or making comments other than those specifically requested by the teacher. High power characterized the recitation lessons because the students displayed low initiative. The authors concluded that teachers' questions can stifle student initiative since they serve the purpose of group control. In a review of these and other research studies, Wilen (1988) recommended that teachers need a full repertoire of questioning skills in order to encourage students to think, participate, and assume responsibility for discussion.

In a study of six elementary classrooms, Shuy (1988) also found that the teachers focused on the management rather than the content of lessons. Several teachers repeatedly asked the same type of question. For example, five straight "how?" questions or seven consecutive "yes-no" questions were asked rather than an open-ended "why?" question followed by probing questions. Shuy argued that superficial lessons resulted from the high degree of classroom control. He also found that academic ideas would be more fully developed if teachers sometimes asked several probing questions of one student rather than calling on a different student for each turn.

White (1989b) also found that teachers' high status and power limited the modes of discourse that they could use with students and constrained the development of substantial academic knowledge. In her ethnographic study of a social studies lesson in a kindergarten, White found that the teacher used politeness strategies such as compliments, exaggeration, and deference to lessen the status inequity and to invite young students to participate and to exchange information. However, the politeness strategies that invited student participation also limited the types of knowledge that were constructed in the classroom. Politeness extended to the construction of ideas resulted, for example, in only admirable traits of Native Americans being mentioned; exploratory talk, questions, and differences of opinion were constrained.

Differential Treatment of Students

Some researchers have found that teachers' expectations for students of differing abilities do influence the students' behaviors. In their study of the interaction between social studies student teachers and seven classes of high school students, Cornbleth, Davis, and Button (1974) found that the student teachers treated differently students they ranked low or high achievers. Among the findings, the teachers interacted more with high-expectancy students, both in the classroom and privately, asked these students more questions, and gave more extended responses to their questions and comments. Jeter's (1973) study of 10 fourth-grade social studies teachers yielded similar results. Herman (1977) found that fifth-grade teachers of above-average and average classes involved their students in teacher question–pupil answer activities twice to four times as often as teachers of below-average classes. Loring (1987), in contrast, found that 20 sixth-grade teachers used similar low-level questions in a recitation format with both skilled and unskilled readers who were primarily African-American and Hispanic.

Wilcox (1982) described how a primary teacher in a working-class school responded to student narratives with a low-level question or praise, whereas a primary teacher in a high-SES school responded to students' narratives by connecting the child's experience to subject matter in class discussions. Calling this technique "teacher uptake," Collins (1982) also found that teachers follow-up on and use ideas from the high-group children significantly more often than from the low-group children.

Nystrand (1987), in his study of eighth- and ninth-grade social studies and English classes found that teachers conducted different discussions for classes of high- and low-ability students. In addition to having discussions nearly twice as often, students in high-ability classes were asked to express their opinions 2 1/2 times as often. They were also asked "authentic" questions, those questions for which the teacher doesn't have the answer, four times as often.

Another way that teachers can discriminate in their interactions with students is in terms of gender. Although Jeter (1973) found in her study that fourth-grade teachers did not differentially interact with boys and girls, Scott (1985) concluded, upon her review of research on peer interaction, that interaction among peers is sex-segregated. She recommended that teachers teach cross-sex–interaction skills to help students develop the social skills and confidence to interact with peers of both sexes on an equal basis. Sadker and Sadker (1986) concluded that male students were given more time to talk in classrooms and received more remediation, praise, and criticism than female students. The Sadkers also found that inservice training can make teachers more aware of the impact that their discriminatory practices have on their students, thereby reducing or eliminating the gender bias in classroom interactions.

Shuy (1986) also found sharp differences in how male and female students responded to higher-order questions during Bennett's lesson. Males participated during peak periods of Bennett's "why?" questions much more than females did. Shuy argued that further study is needed to explain why females have fewer turns of talk, have fewer words per turn, are more likely to respond to "yes/no" and "when, where, who, and how?" questions than "why?" questions, and contibute fewer generalizations, cause-and-effect conclusions, or inferences (p. 319).

Ethnographic researchers have found that students from cultures other than the majority culture often have great difficulty participating within the standard-recitation IRE structure. For example, Native American and Hawaiian students are not comfortable responding in a context in which the teacher is the central authority or in which the teacher spotlights or calls on individual students by name to publicly give the correct answers at a rapid pace. Classroom interactions are more successful when teachers address questions to the entire group, when they slow down the number and pace of questions that they ask, and when they share the authority and responsibility for a lesson with the students by being active listeners more than 50% of the time (Erickson & Mohatt, 1982; Jordan, 1985; Philips, 1972, 1973; Vogt, Jordan, & Tharp, 1987). Additional research on culturally diverse students is explored in the handbook chapter by Gay. Also see White (1990).

Summary

Recitation as characterized by the interactional pattern of teacher initiation–student response–teacher evaluation has dominated social studies classrooms for more than 80 years. Teachers use recitation for review, for introducing new ideas, for checking to see if students understand material, and most often for the recall of facts requiring memory-level thinking. Student achievement can be enhanced by teachers who ask lower-level questions and use techniques such as increased wait time, probing, and redirection. Higher-cognitive-level questions are sometimes asked during recitation but do not always lead to corresponding levels of student responses.

Recitation has persisted because it allows teachers to simultaneously accomplish both academic and managerial functions. The IRE pattern is useful because it allows teachers to control the development of the topic, to allocate turn taking with large numbers of students, and to evaluate student responses. However, a steady diet of teachers asking questions to which they already know the answers also results in extremely limited opportunities for students to use language to explore ideas in the classroom.

It is troublesome that recitation-type interactions are used more frequently in low-SES classrooms and in classrooms where students are perceived as low achievers. It is also of concern that males are apparently given more time to talk in classrooms and receive more remediation, praise, and criticism than do females. The IRE recitation structure also presents difficulties for students from cultures different than the majority culture.

In order for social studies teachers to accomplish the wide range of citizenship objectives for which they are responsible, they need to develop a repertoire of discourse strategies that includes more than recitation. Alternative forms of discourse that incorporate more of the characteristics of conversational dialogue offer much potential for achieving social studies goals.

DISCUSSION

As Cazden (1988) noted, "IRE is the 'default' pattern—what happens unless deliberate action is taken to achieve some alternative" (p. 53). However, unvarying use of the recitation pattern of IRE results in the classroom becoming a place where students display knowledge but do not acquire it (Stevens, 1912). Tharp and Gallimore (1988) contend that, "In American classrooms, now and since the 19th century, teachers generally act as if students are supposed to learn on their own" (p. 3). But can the IRE pattern of classroom interaction be modified so that students are freed from the necessity of producing answers anticipated by the teacher? Are there forms of classroom interaction that will enable students to acquire new academic knowledge and connect it in meaningful ways to bodies of formal and informal knowledge that they already possess? Tharp and Gallimore (1988) argued that if teachers are to help students gain access to "accumulated knowledge and important facts of our civilization and the world's cultures," they need to change their relationships with their students and engage in conversations in which they assume that the students have more to say than the answers already known by the adult (p. 18).

Definitions and Purpose of Discussion

Discussion is a term often used indiscriminately. For example, in his review of research Dillon (1984) found that many researchers labeled any teacher-student interaction, including recitation, as discussion. In this chapter, discussion is used to refer to a specific form of discourse that does not include recitation.

Gage (1969) defined discussion as a teacher's engagement of "two or more learners in a cooperative examination and comparison of views in order to illuminate an issue and contribute to the learners' understanding" (p. 1454). Stodolsky et al.(1981) distinguished discussion from recitation in a similar manner: "Discussion segments usually involve longer exchanges between teacher and students and among students than do recitations. Furthermore, the teacher is often trying to build to some idea and may solicit opinions and thoughts, not just 'right' answers from children" (p. 123). Wilen (1990) further distinguished discussion from recitation by defining it as an educative and structured group conversation between teacher and students about subject matter at the higher cognitive levels. A key word is *conversation,* which suggests that the interaction pattern is informal, involving the exchange of thoughts and feelings.

Bridges's (1979) philosophical rationale for the use of discussion is that it is compatible with democratic values and processes including rationality; decision making; commitment to fairness; and respect for others' opinions, feelings, and interests. The primary attributes of a discussion are that understanding and judgment of the issue under consideration are developed, more than one point of view is offered, and participants are open to differing points of view (Bridges, 1987).

Bridges (1987) suggested that teachers might engage students in a subject-matter discussion for several purposes: to have them learn information from others in the group, to introduce them to differing points of view, and to stimulate and expand ideas and refine opinions through criticism. Gall and Gall (1976) and Gall (1985), in their reviews of research, found that discussion was generally effective in promoting higher-level thinking, changing students' attitudes, advancing students' capability for moral reasoning, and engaging students in group problem solving—important citizenship-education goals.

The Occurrence and Structure of Discussion

Discussions physically look and sound different from recitations. During discussions, the pace slows. Both teacher and student utterances become longer. The intonation and pitch drop to a quieter, more intimate tone and there are more pauses (Cazden, 1988; Farrar, 1988). There are shifts in the turn taking from T–S–T to, for example, T–S–S–T–S–S–S–T.

In the real world of the social studies classroom, many lessons are not pure forms of recitation or discussion. As Cazden (1988) noted, "Purposes can . . . change . . . , not just from hour to hour but from minute to minute. And interactions that have some features of discussions may erupt briefly within other events" (p. 62). Cazden (1988) has described "temporary eruptions of discussions with younger children" that are "a fine line between order and chaos" and "that are—to both teacher and observers—the intellectual high point of the lesson" (p. 62).

White (1985) observed a sixth-grade teacher in a White, blue-collar school in which a discussion briefly erupted in the midst of a recitation. In a lesson on ancient Greece, there was minimal pupil engagement as the teacher asked a series of questions straight from the textbook, such as, "What was the Delian League?" However, when the teacher asked a hypothetical question about how the students would make meaning out of the situation—for example, "How would you feel if you were living in a city state and you had to ask Athens for permission . . . to trade with someone else?" (p. 61)—the interaction immediately switched into a discussion format. Students sat up straight, made long declarative statements, asked a series of questions, and began speaking directly to one another without the teacher intervening at each turn. The discussion format ended just as rapidly as it began when the teacher answered a student question by saying that the answer was in the textbook and then assigning a page to read.

In the third grade at the same school, White (1989a) also found a discussion that was initiated with a "what-if" question at the conclusion of a social studies recitation. After watching a filmstrip about Pittsburgh's role in the industrial revolution, Mrs. Kay asked, "What if they came and put a steel-making factory here? What would happen to Glentown?" The students responded with a series of causal "if, then" statements: "If a steel mill was built, then Glentown would get bigger" and there would be, "More houses." "More stores." "More cars." "More factories." "More food." "More hospitals and more doctors."

Mrs. Kay structured the conversation so that students could use their personal knowledge of their community to elaborate on and give meaning to the academic concept of industrialization.

It should be noted, however, that all classroom interactions that are not recitations are not automatically discussions. For example, Farrar (1988) described a secondary high school lesson on smoking and senior privileges that met some but not all of the criteria for discussion. The teacher began the lesson with an open-ended question, "Does anybody have any strong feelings about. . .?" There were more student-initiated exchanges than teacher-initiated exchanges, and the students raised questions, responded to one another, and expressed feelings, opinions, and observations. Nevertheless, Roby (1988) classified this lesson as a "bull session." He claimed that it was not a discussion, because the students and teacher merely argued about the "rightness" of each of their ideas rather than thoughtfully "entertain(ing)" the validity of more than one idea" (p. 171).

Instructional Techniques for Discussion

Teachers have traditionally relied on different types of questions and a variety of questioning techniques to encourage discussion. The role of questions in stimulating student participation, thinking, and learning has rarely been challenged.

Nonquestioning as an Instructional Technique for Discussion. Only within the past decade have nonquestioning alternatives been seriously considered and debated in the literature. The use of questions as a means for teachers to encourage discussion may not be as essential as their use in recitation. Dillon (1981a) studied 26 parochial junior and high school social studies and religion discussions. An in-depth analysis of five of these discussions, primarily centered around history, sociology, and psychology content, indicated that nonquestioning alternatives, including statements and wait time, resulted in more student participation and talk, more student–student interaction, and more student questions. In 1983, Dillon argued again that using questions is detrimental to achieving the goals of discussion and that the use of a variety of statement forms, pausing, and student questions are more conducive to stimulating student participation and thinking.

The Role of Student Questions. Little research has been conducted on the use of student questions within discussion. In her review of research, Cornbleth (1975) concluded that students can learn to ask particular types of questions and that there is a positive relationship between student question-asking and achievement. Based on his research, Dillon (1988) advocated that teachers use student-generated questions as a basis for recitations and a component of discussions. The role of student questions as a means to encourage involvement and thinking has been comprehensively developed by Hunkins (1976, 1985).

The Development of Higher-Level Thinking and Knowledge

During the "New Social Studies" movement in the late 1960s and early 1970s, researchers focused on the development of higher-level thinking and knowledge in different types of classroom discussions. They described how teachers and students used processes from the social sciences such as inquiry and critical thinking to construct key concepts and generalizations from the social science disciplines.

Recently, researchers from cognitive psychology as well as ethnography and linguistics have been asking questions remarkably similar to those raised almost three decades ago. Newcomers to the field of social studies education should first become acquainted with some of the earlier studies (e.g., Barnes, 1976; Massialas & Zevin, 1967; Newmann & Oliver, 1970) that contain rich descriptions and insightful analyses of classroom discourse still relevant today. More than 20 years ago, Taba (1966) developed models sequencing questions so as to "lift" students to develop concepts and generalizations. Also, Kohlberg (1973, 1976) developed a model for discussions to shift students' reasoning from lower to higher moral stages. The current focus on critical thinking, problem solving, and responsive teaching, in which students are enabled to "lift" their levels of thinking should be seen as continuations of this earlier tradition.

Many forms of discussion have been proposed and described in the research literature, ranging from inquiry to critical thinking about social issues, exploratory talk, and responsive teaching. These forms are not mutually exclusive.

Inquiry. The purpose of inquiry teaching is to engage students in the analysis of societal issues and problems in a logical and systematic fashion. A problem is identified and clarified, solutions or explanations in the form of hypotheses are offered, and information is gathered and analyzed to test the hypotheses. In the final phase, conclusions are drawn that result in acceptance, rejection, or modification of each of the hypotheses (Hunt & Metcalf, 1968; Massialas & Cox, 1966).

Massialas and Zevin (1967) described an inquiry lesson in which a class of high school sophomores themselves developed and then tested generalizations about the conditions under which violent secret societies were likely to form. Once the teacher had selected and presented the primary texts for the students to study, the role of the teacher shifted to being that of a collaborator, a "fellow inquirer who has no final and absolute answers to give out" (Massialias & Zevin, 1967, p. 250).

Inquiry has generally been found to be as effective as other approaches, such as lecture, to teaching content (Ponder & Davis, 1982). Martorella (1977) in his review of research did not find inquiry to be superior over other methods in influencing students' achievement, and Ponder and Davis (1982) concluded that the findings on inquiry and the learning of higher cognitive skills are inconsistent.

Critical Thinking About Social Issues. One important goal of citizenship education is critical thinking (National Council for the Social Studies, 1979). A critical thinker is a rational thinker, one who can demonstrate reasoning by supporting and justifying arguments and conclusions (Common, 1985). Classroom discourse can stimulate critical thinking, as the teacher and students move beyond background information to the careful examination of beliefs through teacher and student questions (Cherryholmes, 1985). The questions teachers ask within an atmosphere of critical classroom discourse serve the additional role of establishing expectations for student thinking and learning (Nystrand, 1987).

Teachers using the jurisprudential strategy (Newmann & Oliver, 1970; Oliver & Shaver, 1966/1974) would have as their purpose encouraging students to think systematically about controversial societal issues. Teachers might use both recitation and socratic methods to encourage students to examine the legal, ethical, and factual substance of issues and examine their own personal knowledge and values in relation to the issues. The "recitation-analytic" style was used in the Harvard Project to review students' substantive understanding of information related to a public issue, and to clarify and examine value dimensions of the issue. With the "socratic-analytic" style, students were encouraged to take a position on an issue. The teacher then used probing questions to force the students to examine the clarity, relevancy, and consistency of their positions. The socratic-analytic style is clearly adversarial in nature.

Oliver and Shaver (1966/1974) conducted a two-year study of students as they progressed through a seventh- and eighth-grade U.S. history program. The experimental jurisprudential program was found to be more effective than the conventional history curriculum in promoting thinking and discussion skills and just as effective in terms of learning knowledge of American history.

Exploratory Talk. In Great Britain, Barnes, Britten, and Rosen (1969) argued that pupils needed more opportunities than were observable in most classrooms to "find their own solutions to the problems posed, to follow a sustained argument and discuss it afterwards and to ask questions as well as answer them" (Edwards & Westgate, 1987, p. 10). Barnes (1976) developed the notion of "exploratory talk" as a way to describe the type of discussion in which students first begin to explore an idea and make the first tentative connections between concepts that are learned in school and their private experiential knowledge. Barnes contrasted "exploratory talk" with a more polished "final draft" talk in which students confirm and revise their ideas. Central to this distinction is Barnes's differentiation between open and closed approaches to tasks. Open tasks are characterized by use of the hypothetical mode:

The pupils ask ruminative questions of themselves, and their statements are tentative, exploratory, inviting elaboration by others. They freely find new questions to ask of one another, and see further possibilities in the materials beyond what the task explicitly requires. They persevere in trying to organize their ideas . . . , make frequent use of one another's contributions by extending or modifying them . . . , [and] deal with disagreement in open discussion. (p. 67)

Barnes argued that in exploratory talk the students begin with background information that they already have acquired from personal experiences and earlier social studies lessons. They "talk their way into insights" by connecting and relating their old knowledge with new information presented in the text and in class.

Responsive Teaching. Responsive teaching is aimed at supporting student thinking and stretching or "scaffolding" students so that they can develop higher levels of thinking. The purpose is to assist students to reach the upper limits of their "zone of proximal development" (Vygotsky, 1978). In a zone of proximal development, the student has "only partially mastered a skill but can successfully employ it and internalize it with the assistance and supervision of an adult" (Tharp & Gallimore, 1988, p. 7). It is assumed that individuals develop higher-order mental functions only after these functions have first appeared in social interactions, so students must experience a cognitive activity before they acquire it. In later phases of learning, students take over their own performance, develop an automatic performance, and de-automatize performance (Tharp & Gallimore, pp. 33–40).

Proponents of responsive teaching argue that discussions should be "contextualized in the child's experience, previous knowledge, and schemata" (Tharp & Gallimore, 1989, p. 356). For example, in the KEEP Project in Hawaii, the teachers began by asking the students to speak about their relevant personal experiences prior to the introduction of new text material. The level of cognitive functioning was then lifted when the teacher asked questions that enabled students to explore relationships between their experiences and the text (Au, 1980). Tharp and Gallimore (1989) point out that the paradox of starting with contextualization to achieve decontextualization: "The literacy goals of school—verbal, analytic, and abstract knowledge and cognition are better achieved in everyday culturally meaningful contexts" (p. 356).

To assist students in reaching higher levels of comprehension, the teacher often structures and models the desired task. Rather than simplifying the task if students cannot do it, the teacher sometimes performs the students' role until they can accomplish it unassisted.

In responsive teaching, teachers can use feedback to identify and describe what their students have done (Mehan, 1982, pp. 77–78; White, 1986). Heath (1987) calls this "talk about the talk" or meta-language. In a 10-year study of how children used language in three Appalachian communities (rural African-American, rural White, and townspeople), Heath (1983, 1987) described how elementary teachers helped low-achieving rural African-American and White children raise their test scores dramatically by immersing them in many different types of talk and by helping the children learn how to identify the different types of talk. For an entire year, classes of children became language "detectives" or ethnographers who analyzed the questions and language they heard at home, at school, and used by different workers in their community.

Palinscar, Brown, and Campione (1989) described how first-grade teachers successfully used meta-language to assist a group of "at-risk" first-graders improve their comprehension skills. As they read stories and discussed how, for example, animals protected themselves from their enemies, four strategies—questioning, summarizing, clarifying, and predicting—were modeled and labeled by the teachers. The first-graders then began to use the meta-language as entrees for their own contributions in the class conversation, for example, "This is my question . . ." (p. 10).

The Continuing Search for Higher-Order Thinking. Despite the potential benefits, the research literature clearly demonstrates that discussion is used infrequently and with uneven results by teachers. Gall (1985) concluded that discussion is used infrequently because teachers lack training in discussion leadership skills, they fear relinquishing their control to students, the acquisition of facts is emphasized, and classes are too large to allow meaningful discussions.

In a recent study at the secondary level, Newmann (1988) conducted a national search for social studies departments in which the teachers promoted discourse characterized by higher-order thinking. Higher-order thinking was defined as interpreting, analyzing, or manipulating information. Five departments were selected from 60 nominated. Forty-five teachers in those schools were observed during 160 lessons using a 17-point scale of aspects of thoughtful discourse. The teachers and 45 of their students also completed at least two questionnaires and were interviewed extensively. Teachers in the classes identified as less thoughtful relied more on lecture, recitation, and the textbook. However, the dominant practice in classes identified as more thoughtful was teacher-directed discussion, during which the teacher pushed students to explain their ideas and encouraged a high degree of student interaction.

Summary

Discussion is structured conversation in which the participants work cooperatively to present, examine, compare, and understand often diverse views about an academic topic or issue. Discussion more closely approximates natural conversation than recitation because it is slower paced and not driven by the questions or evaluations of one person. Discussion can be used to accomplish purposes that might not be easily achieved with recitation, including introducing students to differing points of view, encouraging the exploration of student ideas, critical thinking, and engaging students in group problem-solving. Different forms of discussion have been developed over time. In inquiry and exploratory talk, the power inequity between the teacher and students is lessened, the discussions are driven by questions initiated by the students, and the answers to the questions are not known in advance. The teacher's relationship with the students shifts toward being a collaborator rather than an evaluator. In critical thinking about social issues and responsive teaching, students are encouraged to find their own solutions to the problems posed and to develop sustained arguments. In responsive teaching, the use of meta-language or talk about the talk becomes an important tool in allowing students to become aware of how the forms of language they produce affects their own learning.

CONCLUSIONS

The recitation pattern of teacher initiation–student response–teacher evaluation is the primary form of discourse used in social studies classrooms. Teachers persist in using questions to recall factual information for purposes of review, to introduce new information, and to evaluate student knowledge. Teachers' use of these low-level questions with probing,

wait time, and redirection is positively related to gains in student achievement. Although recitation enables teachers to control the quantity and quality of student participation, it often results in limiting students' use of language to making meaning out of the academic material. Alternative forms of discussion are characterized by students participating at higher cognitive levels to construct more complex forms of social studies knowledge. However, teachers use forms of discussion infrequently in social studies classrooms.

IMPLICATIONS AND RECOMMENDATIONS

1. Both quantitative and interpretative researchers need to study why, given the oft-proclaimed advantages of discussion and disadvantages of recitation, teachers persist in conducting recitations to the exclusion of discussion in their social studies classes. Long-term case studies are needed to describe the sequencing and mix of recitation and discussion type interactions. For example, do episodes of discussions erupt at the end of lessons or units? How do the patterns of use vary in different situations, and why are recitations more prevalent in lower-SES situations? Studies similar to Newmann's (1988) are needed to analyze why as well as how specific types of social studies classroom interactions may promote thought more than others. Descriptions are needed of teachers as they change from reliance on recitation to the use of more diverse forms of discussion. Social studies theorists need to develop a better understanding of the contexts and constraints that shape teachers' preferences for different types of classroom discourse.

2. There is a need to study how the use of teacher power, authority, and control affects the level of student thinking, student initiative, and the types of knowledge that are produced. How can leadership and responsibility for classroom discourse be shared in a way that is productive and comfortable for both teacher and students?

3. How different classroom participants make meaning out of classroom discourse should be studied. Quantitative research (Dillon, 1982; Mills et al., 1980) has shown that there is approximately 50% congruence between the teacher's intended cognitive level for a question and the cognitive level at which a student responds. Interpretative researchers (Barnes, 1976) have also described how higher-level questions asked by teachers are redefined at lower levels by students. In the future, researchers should use complete exchange between teachers and students as the basic unit of analysis rather than only coding teacher questions.

4. There is a need to study how teachers and students can be trained in instructional techniques that encourage interaction patterns appropriate for discussions. Although research has shown that teachers can develop and apply questioning skills associated with recitation and discussion (Wilen, 1984, 1987b), more studies need to be conducted on, for example, how teachers might learn to use the alternative, nonquestioning techniques advocated by Dillon (1983).

5. The forms and levels of thinking cannot be studied in isolation from the academic content in which they are embedded. As Shulman (1986) argued, one of the most serious faults

of current research "has been the tendency to ignore the *substance* of classroom life, the specific curriculum content and subject matter being studied" (p. 22). The greatest paucity of research is in the area of how new information is introduced and developed in classroom discourse. How do teachers connect academic topics with formal and informal student knowledge, lift cognitive levels within the discussion of a topic, and develop decontextualized disciplinary concepts through a series of tasks within a lesson, across a unit, and across a semester or school year? In-depth and long-term studies are needed of how diverse classroom groups use language to construct different types of social studies knowledge. Researchers have just begun to understand the complexity of social studies classroom discourse.

References

Armento, B. J. (1977). Teacher behaviors related to student achievement on a social science concept test. *Journal of Teacher Education, 28,* 46–52.

Au, K. (1980). Participation structures in a reading lesson with Hawaiian children: Analysis of a culturally appropriate instructional event. *Anthropology and Education Quarterly, 11,* 91–115.

Barnes, D. (1976). *From communication to curriculum.* London: Penguin.

Barnes, D., Britton, J., & Rosen, H. (1969). *Language, the learner and the school.* Harmondsworth, England: Penguin.

Bellack, A. A., Kliebard, H. M., Hyman, R. T., & Smith, F. L., Jr. (1966). *The language of the classroom.* New York: Teachers College Press.

Berliner, D. (1984). The half-filled glass: A review of research on teaching. In P. Hosford (Ed.), *Using what we know about teaching* (pp. 51–77). Washington, DC: Association for Supervision and Curriculum Development.

Bremme, D., & Erickson, F. (1977). Relationships among verbal and nonverbal classroom behaviors. *Theory into Practice, 5*(3), 153–161.

Bridges, D. (1979). *Education, democracy and discussion.* Windsor, England: NFER.

Bridges, D. (1987). Discussion and questioning. *Questioning Exchange, 1,* 34–37.

Brophy, J., & Good, T. L. (1986). Teacher behavior and student achievement. In M. C. Wittrock (Ed.), *Handbook of research on teaching* (3rd ed., pp. 328–375). New York: Macmillan.

Buggey, L. J. (1971). A study of the relationship of classroom questions and social studies achievement of second grade children (Doctoral dissertation, University of Washington, 1971). *Dissertation Abstracts International, 32,* 2543A.

Cazden, C. (1979). Language in education: Variation in the teacher-talk register. In J. Alatis & R. Rucker (Eds.), *Language in public life* (pp. 144–162). Washington, DC: Georgetown University Round Table on Languages and Linguistics.

Cazden, C. (1986). Classroom discourse. In M. C. Wittrock (Ed.), *Handbook of research on teaching* (3rd ed., pp. 432–463). New York: Macmillan.

Cazden, C. (1988). *Classroom discourse.* Portsmouth, NH: Heinemann.

Cherryholmes, C. H. (1985). Language and discourse in social studies. *Social Education, 49,* 395–399.

Collins, J. P. (1982). Discourse style, classroom interaction and differential treatment. *Journal of Reading Behavior, 14,* 429–437.

Common, D. L. (1985). Teacher authority in the social studies classroom: Erosion of barren ground. *Theory and Research in Social Education, 12,* 25–38.

Cornbleth, C. (1975). Student questioning as a learning strategy. *Educational Leadership, 33,* 219–222.

Cornbleth, C., Davis, O., & Button, C. (1974). Expectations for pupil achievement and teacher-pupil interaction. *Social Education, 38,* 54–58.

Crump, C. D. (1970). Self-instruction in the art of questioning in intermediate grade social studies. (Doctoral dissertation, Indiana University, 1969). *Dissertation Abstracts International, 31,* 259A.

Davis, O. L., Jr., & Tinsley, D. C. (1967). Cognitive objectives revealed by classroom questions asked by social studies student teachers. *Peabody Journal of Education, 45,* 21–26.

Dillon, J. T. (1981a). Duration of response to teacher questions and statements. *Contemporary Educational Psychology, 6,* 1–11.

Dillon, J. T. (1981b). A norm against student questions. *Clearing House, 55,* 136–139.

Dillon, J. T. (1982). Cognitive correspondence between question/statement and response. *American Educational Research Journal, 19,* 540–551.

Dillon, J. T. (1983). *Teaching and the art of questioning.* Fastback Series No. 194. Bloomington, IN: Phi Delta Kappa.

Dillon, J. T. (1984). Research on questioning and discussion. *Educational Leadership, 41,* 50–56.

Dillon, J. T. (1988). The remedial status of student questioning. *Journal of Curriculum Studies, 20,* 197–210.

Dunkin, M. (1978). Student characteristics, classroom processes, and student achievement. *Journal of Educational Psychology, 70,* 998–1009.

Edwards, A. D., & Westgate, D. P. G. (1987). *Investigating classroom talk.* Philadelphia: Falmer.

Erickson, F., & Mohatt, G. (1982). Cultural organization of participation structure in two classrooms of Indian students. In G. Spindler (Ed.), *Doing the ethnography of schooling: Educational anthropology in action* (pp. 132–174). New York: Holt, Rinehart & Winston.

Evertson, C., Anderson, C., Anderson, L., & Brophy, J. (1980). Relationships between classroom behaviors and student outcomes in junior high mathematics and English classes. *American Education Research Journal, 17,* 43–60.

Farrar, M. T. (1984). Why do we ask comprehension questions? A new conception of comprehension instruction. *The Reading Teacher, 37,* 452–456.

Farrar, M. T. (1988). A sociolinguistic analysis of discussion. In J. T. Dillon (Ed.), *Questioning and discussion: A multidisciplinary study* (pp. 29–73). Norwood, NJ: Ablex.

Gage, N. L. (1969). Teaching methods. In R. L. Ebel (Ed.), *Encyclopedia of educational research* (4th ed., pp. 1446–1458). London: Macmillan.

Gage, N. L. (1978). *The scientific basis of the art of teaching.* New York: Teachers College Press.

Gall, M. D. (1970). The use of questions in teaching. *Review of Educational Research, 40,* 707–721.

Gall, M. D. (1984). Synthesis of research on teachers' questioning. *Educational Leadership, 41,* 40–47.

Gall, M. D. (1985). Discussion methods of teaching. In T. Husen & T. N. Postlethwaite (Eds.), *International encyclopedia of education* (Vol. 3, pp. 1423–1427). Oxford: Pergamon Press.

Gall, M. D. (1987). Review of research on questioning techniques. In

W. Wilen (Ed.), *Questions, questioning techniques, and effective teaching* (pp. 23–48). Washington, DC: National Education Association.

Gall, M. D., & Gall, J. P. (1976). In N. L. Gage (Ed.), *The psychology of teaching methods*, 75th Yearbook of the National Society for the Study of Education, (pp. 166–216). Chicago: University of Chicago Press.

Gall, M. D., Ward, B. A., Berliner, D. C., Cahen, L. S., Winne, P. H., Elashoff, J. D., & Stanton, G. S. (1978). Effects of questioning techniques and recitation on student learning. *American Educational Research Journal, 15,* 175–199.

Gallagher, J. J., & Aschner, M. J. (1963). Preliminary report on analyses of classroom interaction. *Merrill Palmer Quarterly, 9,* 183–194.

Godbold, J. V. (1969). Oral questioning practices of teachers in social studies classes (Doctoral dissertation, University of Florida, 1968). *Dissertation Abstracts International, 30,* 1912A.

Haynes, H. C. (1935). Relation of teacher intelligence, teacher experience, and type of school to types of questions (Doctoral dissertation, George Peabody College for Teachers, 1934). *Dissertation Abstracts International,* p. 63.

Heath, S. B. (1983). *Ways with words: Language, life and work in communities and classrooms.* Cambridge: Cambridge University Press.

Heath, S. B. (1987). A lot of talk about nothing. In D. Goswami & P. Stillman (Eds.), *Reclaiming the classroom: Teacher research as an agency for change* (pp. 39–48). Upper Montclair, NY: Boynton/Cook.

Herman, W. (1977). Teacher behavior in the elementary school social studies. *Theory and Research in Social Education, 5,* 39–63.

Hoetker, J., & Ahlbrand, W. P., Jr. (1969). The persistence of the recitation. *American Educational Research Journal, 6,* 145–167.

Hunkins, F. P. (1976). *Involving students in questioning.* Boston: Allyn & Bacon.

Hunkins, F. P. (1985). Helping students ask their own questions. *Social Education, 49,* 293–296.

Hunt, M. P., & Metcalf, L. E. (1968). *Teaching high school social studies: Problems in reflective thinking and social understanding* (2nd ed.). New York: Harper & Row.

Jeter, J. T. (1973). Elementary social studies teachers differential classroom behavior with children as a function of differential expectations of pupil achievement (Doctoral dissertation, University of Texas at Austin, 1972). *Dissertation Abstracts International, 33,* 4680A.

Jordan, C. (1985). Translating culture: From ethnographic information to educational program. *Anthropology & Education, 16,* 105–123.

Kerry, T. (1987). Classroom questions in England. *Questioning Exchange, 1,* 32–33.

Klinzing, H., Klinzing-Eurich, G., & Tisher, R. (1985). Cognitive behaviors in classroom discourse: Congruences between teachers' questions and pupils' responses. *Australian Journal of Education, 29,* 63–75.

Klinzing, H. G., & Klinzing-Eurich, G. (1988). Questions, responses, and reactions. In J. T. Dillon (Ed.), *Questioning and discussion: A multidisciplinary study* (pp. 212–239). Norwood, NJ: Ablex.

Kniep, W. M. (1974). A study of the effect of social studies achievement of high level questions with conditions of prior training and positive reinforcement (Doctoral dissertation, University of Minnesota, 1974). *Dissertation Abstracts International, 35,* 941A.

Kohlberg, L. (1973). *Collected papers on moral development and moral education.* Cambridge, MA: Harvard University Laboratory for Human Development.

Kohlberg, L. (1976). This special section in perspective. *Social Education, 40,* 213–215.

Levin, T., & Long, R. (1981). *Effective instruction.* Washington, DC: Association for Supervision and Curriculum Development.

Loring, R. M. (1987). Questions used by teachers with skilled and less skilled readers (Doctoral dissertation, North Texas State University, 1986). *Dissertation Abstracts International, 47,* 2974A.

Martorella, P. H. (1977). Research on social studies learning and instruction: Cognition. In F. Hunkins (Ed.), *Review of research in social studies: 1970–1975* (pp. 15–53). Washington, DC: National Council for the Social Studies.

Massialas, B. G., & Cox, C. B. (1966). *Inquiry in social studies.* New York: McGraw-Hill.

Massialas, B. G., & Zevin, J. (1967). *Creative encounters in the classroom.* New York: Wiley.

Mehan, H. (1978). Structuring school structure. *Harvard Educational Review, 48*(1), 32–64.

Mehan, H. (1979). *Learning lessons: Social organization in the classroom.* Cambridge, MA: Harvard University Press.

Mehan, H. (1982). The structure of classroom events and their consequences for student performance. In P. Gilmore & A. Glatthorn (Eds.), *Children in and out of school: Ethnography and education* (pp. 59–87). Washington, DC: Center for Applied Linguistics.

Mills, S., Rice, C. T., Berliner, D. C., & Rousseau, E. W. (1980). The correspondence between teacher questions and student answers in classroom discourse. *Journal of Experimental Education, 48,* 194–204.

National Council for the Social Studies (1979). NCSS curriculum guidelines. *Social Education, 43,* 261–178.

Newmann, F. M. (1988). *Higher order thinking in high school social studies: An analysis of classrooms, teachers, students and leadership* (Report by the National Center on Effective Secondary Schools). Madison: University of Wisconsin, Madison.

Newmann, F. M., & Oliver, D. W. (1970). *Clarifying public controversy.* Boston: Little, Brown.

Nystrand, M. (1987, April). *A framework for assessing the role of instructional discourse in high school English and social studies.* Paper presented at the meeting of the American Education Research Association, Washington, DC.

Oliver, D. W., & Shaver, J. P. (1974). *Teaching public issues in the high school.* Logan, UT: Utah State University Press. (work first published 1966)

Palincsar, A. S., Brown, A., & Campione, J. (1989, March). Discourse as a mechanism for acquiring process and knowledge. In *Extending Vygotskian theory: Discourse and interaction in the classroom.* Annual Meeting of the American Educational Research Association, San Francisco.

Philips, S. (1972). Participant structures and communicative competence: Warm Springs children in community and classroom. In C. Cazden, V. John, & D. Hymes (Eds.), *Functions of language in the classroom* (pp. 370–394). New York: Teachers College Press.

Philips, S. (1973). *The invisible culture: Communication in the classroom and community on the Warm Springs Indian Reservation.* White Plains, NY: Longman.

Ponder, G., & Davis, O. L., Jr. (1982). Social studies education. In H. Mitzel (Ed.), *Encyclopedia of educational research* (5th ed., pp. 1723–1732).

Poole, D. (1988, November). Contextualizing IRE in an eighth grade quiz review. In Y. Moses (Chair), *Classroom discourse and spatial cognition: Learning in a classroom context.* Symposium given at the American Anthropological Association Annual Meeting, Phoenix, AZ.

Redfield, D. L., & Rousseau, E. W. (1981). Meta-analysis of experimental research on teacher questioning behavior. *Review of Educational Research, 51,* 237–245.

Riley, J. P. (1981). The effects of preservice teachers' cognitive questioning level and redirecting on student science achievement. *Journal of Research in Science Teaching, 18,* 303–309.

Roby, T. W. (1988). Models of discussion. In J. T. Dillon (Ed.), *Questioning and discussion: A multidisciplinary study* (pp. 163–191). Norwood, NJ: Ablex.

Rosenshine, B. (1976). Classroom instruction. In N. L. Gage (Ed.), *The psychology of teaching methods.* 75th Yearbook of the National Society for the Study of Education (pp. 335–371). Chicago: University of Chicago Press.

Rowe, M. B. (1974). Relation of wait time and rewards to the development of language, logic, and fate control: Part one-wait time. *Journal of Research in Science Teaching, 11,* 81–94.

Rowe, M. B. (1987). Using wait time to stimulate inquiry. In W. Wilen (Ed.), *Questions, questioning techniques, and effective teaching* (pp. 95–106). Washington, DC: National Education Association.

Ryan, F. L. (1973). Differentiated effects of levels of questioning on student achievement. *Journal of Experimental Education, 41,* 63–67.

Sadker, M., & Sadker, D. (1986). Sexism in the classroom. *Phi Delta Kappan, 67,* 512–515.

Samson, G. E., Strykowski, B., Weinstein, T., & Walberg, H. J. (1987). The effects of teacher questioning levels on students' achievement: A quantitative synthesis. *Journal of Educational Research, 80,* 290–295.

Savage, T. (1972). A study of the relationship of classroom questions and social studies achievement of fifth-grade children (Doctoral dissertation, University of Washington, 1972). *Dissertation Abstracts International, 33,* 2245A.

Schreiber, J. E. (1967). Teachers' question-asking techniques in social studies (Doctoral dissertation, University of Iowa, 1967). *Dissertation Abstracts International, 28,* 523A.

Scott, K. (1985). Social interaction skills: Perspectives on teaching cross-sex communication. *Social Education, 49,* 610–615.

Shulman, L. S. (1986). Paradigms and research programs in the study of teaching: A contemporary perspective. In M. C. Wittrock (Ed.), *Handbook of research on teaching* (3rd ed., pp. 3–36). New York: Macmillan.

Shuy, R. (1986). Secretary Bennett's teaching: An argument for responsive teaching. *Teaching & Teacher Education, 2*(4), 315–323.

Shuy, R. (1988). Identifying dimensions of classroom language. In J. Green & J. Harker (Eds.), *Multiple perspective analyses of classroom discourse* (pp. 115–134). Norwood, NJ: Ablex.

Simon, A., & Boyer, G. (Eds.). (1970). *Mirrors for behavior: An anthology of classroom observation instruments.* Philadelphia: Research for Better Schools, Inc.

Sinclair, J., & Coulthard, M. (1975). *Towards an analysis of discourse: The language of teachers and pupils.* London: Oxford University Press.

Smith, B. D. (1980). Influence of solicitation pattern, type of practice example, and student response on pupil behavior, commitment to discussion and concept attainment. *Theory and Research in Social Education, 17,* 1–17.

Stevens, R. (1912). *The question as a measure of efficiency in instruction: A critical study of classroom practice.* New York: Columbia University, Teachers College.

Stodolsky, S. (1988). *The subject matters.* Chicago: University of Chicago Press.

Stodolsky, S., Ferguson, T., & Wimpelberg, K. (1981). The recitation persists, but what does it look like? *Journal of Curriculum Studies, 13*(2), 121–130.

Stubbs, M. (1983). *Discourse analysis: The sociolinguistic analysis of natural language.* Chicago: University of Chicago Press.

Taba, H. (1966). *Teaching strategies and cognitive functioning in elementary school children.* San Francisco: San Francisco State University.

Tharp, R., & Gallimore, R. (1988). *Rousing minds to life: Teaching, learning and schooling in social context.* Cambridge: Cambridge University Press.

Tharp, R., & Gallimore, R. (1989). Rousing schools to life. *American Educator, 13*(2), 20–25, 46–52.

Tinsley, D. C., & Davis, O. L., Jr. (1971). Questions used by secondary student teachers to guide discussion and testing in social studies: A study in planning. *Journal of Teacher Education, 22,* 59–65.

Tobin, K. (1987). The role of wait time in higher cognitive level learning. *Review of Educational Research, 57,* 69–95.

Vogt, L., Jordan, C. & Tharp, R. (1987). Explaining school failure, producing school success: Two cases. *Anthropology & Education Quarterly, 18,* 276–286.

Vygotsky, L. S. (1978). *Thought and language.* Cambridge, MA: MIT Press.

Weil, M. L., & Murphy, J. (1982). Instructional processes. In H. Mitzel (Ed.), *Encyclopedia of educational research* (5th ed., pp. 890–917). New York: Macmillan.

White, J. J. (1985). An ethnographic approach. In C. Cornbleth (Ed.), *Invitation to research in social education* (pp. 51–77). Washington, DC: National Council for the Social Studies.

White, J. J. (1986). Decision-making within an integrative curriculum. *Childhood Education, 62,* 337–343.

White, J. J. (1989a). The construction of substantial knowledge in social studies lessons. Paper presented at the annual meeting of the American Educational Research Association, San Francisco.

White, J. J. (1989b). The power of politeness in the classroom: Cultural codes that create and constrain curriculum construction. *Journal of Curriculum and Supervision, 4,* 289–321.

White, J. J. (1990). Involving different social and cultural groups in discussion. In W. Wilen (Ed.), *Teaching and learning through discussion: The theory, research and practice of the discussion method* (pp. 147–174). Springfield, IL: Charles C. Thomas.

Wilcox, K. (1982). Differential socialization in the classroom: Implications for equal opportunity. In G. Spindler (Ed.), *Doing the ethnography of schooling: Educational anthropology in action* (pp. 268–309). New York: Holt, Rinehart & Winston.

Wilen, W. W. (1984). Implications of research on questioning for the teacher educator. *Journal of Research and Development in Education, 17,* 31–35.

Wilen, W. W. (1987a). Effective questions and questioning: A classroom application. In W. Wilen (Ed.), *Questions, questioning techniques, and effective teaching* (pp. 107–134). Washington, DC: National Education Association.

Wilen, W. W. (1987b). Improving teachers' questions and questioning: Research informs practice. In W. Wilen (Ed.), *Questions, questioning techniques, and effective teaching* (pp. 173–200). Washington, DC: National Education Association.

Wilen, W. W. (1988). Review of pedagogical perspectives. In J. T. Dillon (Ed.), *Questions and questioning: A multidisciplinary study* (pp. 306–314). Norwood, NJ: Ablex.

Wilen, W. W. (1990). Forms and phases of discussion. In W. W. Wilen (Ed.), *Teaching and learning through discussion: The theory, research and practice of the discussion method* (pp. 3–24). Springfield, IL: Charles C. Thomas.

Wilen, W. W. (in press). *Questioning skills, for teachers* (3rd ed.). Washington, DC: National Education Association.

Wilen, W. W., & Clegg, A. A., Jr. (1986). Effective questions and questioning: A research review. *Theory and Research in Social Education, 14,* 153–161.

Winne, P. H. (1979). Experiments relating teachers' use of higher cognitive questions to student achievement. *Review of Educational Research, 49,* 13–50.

Winne, P. H., & Marx, R. W. (1979). Perceptual problem solving. In P. Peterson & H. Walberg (Eds.), *Research in teaching: Concepts, findings, and implications* (pp. 210–230). Berkeley, CA: McCutchan.

Wood, D., & Wood, H. (1988). Questioning vs. student initiative. In J. T. Dillon (Ed.), *Questioning and discussion: A multidisciplinary study* (pp. 280–305). Norwood, NJ: Ablex.

Wright, C. J., & Nuthall, G. (1970). Relationship between teacher behaviors and pupil achievement in three elementary science lessons. *American Education Research Journal, 7,* 477–493.

·41·

SUBSTANTIVE AND METHODOLOGICAL CONSIDERATIONS FOR PRODUCTIVE TEXTBOOK ANALYSIS

Isabel L. Beck and Margaret G. McKeown

UNIVERSITY OF PITTSBURGH

The centrality of textbooks is a well-accepted starting point for discussions of social studies instruction and a key motivation for the analysis of textbooks. The evaluation of textbooks as generally inadequate also seems to be a well-accepted theme in the social studies literature. Moreover, the reports that have been written, over time, about social studies textbooks contain similar observations and conclusions about the problematic characteristics of textbooks across at least 3 decades of textbook analyses.

Many of the same criticisms that are presently being launched were made in earlier work. For example, in 1960 Alexander found history textbooks to be dull and lifeless, and lacking in critical interpretation and representation of different points of view. Palmer had similar complaints in 1967, citing the absence of "the analyses, the interpretation, the explanatory hypotheses and conflicting points of view" (p. 141). Twelve years later, FitzGerald (1979) saw textbooks as demonstrating "a fairly consistent level of dullness" (p. 150), lacking in explanation of ideas and "written without conflicts" (p. 155). Similar themes were sounded in 1988 by Sewall, who found texts to be drained of "voice, drama, and coherence" (p. 554) and devoid of explanations of the facts presented. White (1988) summed up the attributes of textbooks taken from a decade of reviews in *Theory and Research in Social Education* with the words "biased, bland, superficial, and dull" (p. 115).

SUBSTANTIVE CONSIDERATIONS FOR TEXTBOOK ANALYSIS

The congruence of criticisms across the decades indicates that there is much agreement about the problems with textbooks. The approach taken in this chapter is not to review the various critiques, but to try to understand the textual features that contribute to the negative evaluations of textbooks and the effects these features might have on student learning. To do so, a perspective on text analysis will be offered that is drawn from recent cognitive research on text processing.

The cognitive orientation to reading research has brought much progress in understanding the ways that readers interact with texts. In investigations of the reading process, emphasis is now placed on understanding the mental activities involved in reading (that is, what the reader does while reading) rather than being confined to the products of reading (that is, what the reader remembers from reading). Insights gained from the cognitive perspective have also yielded understanding of how the reader's execution and coordination of the processes involved during reading affect the products of reading (see, e.g., Just & Carpenter, 1987; Perfetti, 1985). The understandings gained from this research have much to offer to textbook analysis work. Particularly fruitful is the inherent focus on learning,

Reviewer was Dan Fleming, Virginia Polytechnic Institute and State University.

The preparation of this chapter was supported by a grant from the A. W. Mellon Foundation to the Learning Research and Development Center, University of Pittsburgh. The opinions expressed do not necessarily reflect the position or policy of the Mellon Foundation, and no official endorsement should be inferred.

which could open the way for understanding how the characteristics of texts affect learning.

As reading researchers, our work has been profoundly influenced by the new understandings of complex cognitive processes that have been gained from "the cognitive revolution" (Gardner, 1987). Over the last several years our research with texts has moved from materials used to teach reading to the study and analysis of social studies textbooks (Beck & McKeown, 1988; Beck, McKeown, & Gromoll, 1988, 1989). Work with social studies textbooks seems a natural continuation of a line of research directed toward the improvement of instructional practices associated with comprehension and learning from text. Previously, the objects of our analyses were basal reading programs, that is, the graded student textbook anthologies and accompanying teachers' manuals so ubiquitous in elementary and middle school reading instruction (see, e.g., Beck, 1981; Beck & McKeown, 1989; Beck, McKeown, McCaslin, & Burkes, 1979).

A major finding from the analysis of reading programs emphasized the importance of students' prior knowledge in understanding even seemingly simple narratives. But selections in basal reading programs tend to be a smorgasbord of content, with frequent, often daily, changes in topic. What students read about is chosen from the multitude of topics in the world. This situation precludes both an in-depth treatment of any given topic and the kind of introduction and sequential development needed to understand many topics in various subject-matter domains. In contrast, the social studies curriculum is arranged around extensive treatment of broad topic areas. There are long chapters and topic-specific units that are meant to be covered in weeks rather than in days, in contrast with basal reading texts. This makes social studies textbooks particularly appropriate objects of examination for considering the role of background knowledge on comprehension and learning.

Relevant Research

Two areas of research particularly pertinent to text analysis research involve recent understandings about the nature of the reading process and its interaction with a reader's knowledge, and characteristics of texts that promote or impede comprehension. The current information-processing view of reading emphasizes that it is a complex process, consisting of a set of subprocesses operating concurrently. The reading process is seen as constructive, because the meaning of a text is constructed from the interaction between a reader and what is printed on the page. In the course of reading, readers must call upon perceptual, linguistic, and conceptual operations, from encoding letters within words to establishing referents, while following the structure of the text (Beck & Carpenter, 1986; Perfetti, 1985). Readers also need to apply their knowledge of the world and integrate it with text information (Bransford & Johnson, 1972; Brown, Smiley, Day, Townsend, & Lawton, 1977).

Recent research results emphasize that, not only does lack of knowledge about a topic impede comprehension, but also the extent and depth of knowledge influence the quality of understanding derived from a text. Voss and his colleagues (Chiesi, Spilich, & Voss 1979; Spilich, Vesonder, Chiesi, & Voss, 1979) showed how the quality of text recall differed between people with high and low knowledge of a topic. High-knowledge people were more likely to recall the sequence of events that developed the theme of the text and to integrate events to construct a representation of the text. Low-knowledge people were more likely to recall information peripheral to the main ideas of the text. Similarly, Pearson, Hansen, and Gordon (1979) showed that children with high knowledge of a topic were better able to answer questions about a text that required inferences to be drawn.

An important feature of knowledge is that it is organized; knowledge of a topic is conceptualized as a schema, or framework, containing slots to be filled by incoming information (R. C. Anderson, Spiro, & Anderson, 1978; Minsky, 1975; Rumelhart, 1980; Schank & Abelson, 1977; Thorndyke & Yekovich, 1980). Schemata help a reader create expectations about the information in a text, which then allow the reader to draw relationships within the information and integrate it with what is already known, in order to develop a representation of what is being read (Anderson, 1977; Kieras, 1985).

Readers also have expectations about how categories of information in particular kinds of texts are organized. Even young children know the typical structure of a story narrative; it begins with a setting, introduces a problem or conflict followed by a plan to solve it, presents attempts to solve the problem, and, finally, resolves the problem (Mandler, 1978; N. L. Stein & Trabasso, 1982). Narrative structure has been shown to affect comprehension in that, if an element of the structure is omitted or if elements are presented in scrambled order, comprehension suffers (Mandler, 1978; N. L. Stein & Glenn, 1978).

In addition to a reader's prior knowledge, the way a text is written can help him or her organize information, bring appropriate knowledge to bear, and draw relationships. Texts that assist readers in these ways are often discussed in terms of coherence or considerateness. *Coherence* refers to the extent to which the sequence of ideas or events in a text makes sense and the extent to which the text makes the nature of events and ideas and their relationships apparent (Beck, McKeown, Omanson, & Pople, 1984). A considerate text is one designed to maximize the possibility for a reader to gain information and establish relationships among concepts (T. H. Anderson & Armbruster, 1984). A number of textual elements related to coherence or considerateness that influence comprehension have been identified. Among those elements that affect comprehension negatively are the use of references that are ambiguous (Frederiksen, 1981), distant (Cirilo, 1981; Lesgold, Roth, & Curtis, 1979), or indirect (Haviland & Clark, 1974; Just & Carpenter, 1978); the inclusion of concepts for which the reader lacks requisite background (Chiesi et al., 1979; Pearson et al., 1979); the lack of clear relationships between events (Black & Bern, 1981; Kintsch, Mandel, & Kozminsky, 1977; N. L. Stein & Nezworski, 1978); and the inclusion of events or ideas irrelevant to the rest of the text (Schank, 1975; Trabasso, Secco, & van den Broek, 1984).

Much has been written about the importance of making

texts coherent, or considerate. But one key factor has not been well emphasized in discussions of applying these ideas to the creation of texts: That is, coherence must arise from the content that is to be communicated; coherence is not something separate from the content that can be applied in a piecemeal way. For example, using headings and supplying syntactic connections are sometimes discussed as ways to improve coherence. But the mere placement of these devices in a text does not affect coherence unless their use helps to clarify or explain content in terms of whatever understanding is the goal of the text.

In a similar vein, the notion of making information explicit, which is an important factor in coherence, should not be interpreted in too egalitarian a way. Merely making all information more explicit is not the point. What is needed is explication of the meaning of important information in a way that makes apparent its role in the event or concept being developed. The creation of coherent text means figuring out what information needs to be made explicit in order to develop an adequate explanation of an event, concept, or phenomenon.

A demonstration of what might be called content-mediated use of text devices, versus a more structural use is provided in Bransford's work on elaboration (Franks et al., 1982; B. S. Stein, Bransford, Franks, Vye, & Perfetto, 1982). Bransford and his associates showed that elaborations that make information more memorable are those that help explain some connection within the content. For example, elaborating the sentence "The man bought the crackers" as "The bald man bought the crackers that were on sale" would not make the information more memorable. However, the elaboration "The tall man bought the crackers that were on the top shelf" would improve memory because, although there is nothing that relates a bald man to crackers on sale, there might be a reason for a tall man to purchase crackers from a top shelf.

What has been learned from research on the reading process and characteristics of texts that affect readers' processing can provide a productive basis for textbook analyses. Research on textbooks that is conducted from a cognitive perspective holds the promise of greater understanding of what it is about textbooks that has caused so much adverse reaction.

In a recent study, we used the research just discussed as a backdrop against which to examine the textbooks for grades 4 through 7 of four widely used elementary social studies programs (Beck & McKeown, 1988; Beck et al., 1988, 1989). The programs used in the analysis were *Heath Social Studies* (Heath, 1985); *Macmillan Social Studies* (Macmillan, 1985); *Scott, Foresman Social Studies* (Scott, Foresman, 1983); and *The World and its People* (Silver Burdett, 1985). The programs are referred to as Programs, or Textbooks A, B, C, and D. The research backdrop was used to develop a qualitative, content-driven approach to analyzing textbooks. Just as cognitive psychology is concerned with "getting inside" the process of learning, rather than observing the outward manifestations of performance, the concern of the analysis was with getting inside the textual presentations so that what was found could be considered in relation to the learning process.

In the following section, examples of the analysis are presented. In a later section of the chapter, the kind of analysis suggested by the cognitive perspective is drawn on to raise some issues about the conducting and reporting of textbook analyses that would contribute to a greater understanding of textbook characteristics.

Cognitive-based Textbook Analysis: An Example

How can textbook presentations, viewed in relationship to the research just discussed, be analyzed in terms of what students are likely to learn? The approach to analysis was to identify a content goal and examine how text content was developed in service of that goal. Content goals were conceptualized as the understanding that students were intended to develop about a particular topic in the textbook. To analyze a section of text, a determination was made of the goal of a unit of content, which could range in length from a paragraph to a chapter. The determination of a goal involved either what the goal appeared to be upon reading the text or a goal that could be reasonably expected for the topic being presented. The text was then evaluated as to whether the goal was likely to be met for target-aged readers. For this step it was necessary to hypothesize the understanding that seemed likely for students of the target age, based on judgments of the background knowledge that could be expected of them and consideration of the effects of limited background knowledge and characteristics of text that might cause the reading process to break down.

The examples that are discussed are drawn from one textbook's fourth-grade unit on desert regions. Given the focus on world regions of the fourth-grade curriculum, a reasonable goal seemed to be that students develop a concept of the regions studied that would contribute to an understanding of each region's characteristics and their consequences for life there. For the acquisition of such a concept, the content that students encounter needs to go beyond, for example, a description of deserts as dry or prairies as grassy; the text must communicate a sense of the extent to which such features create a distinct environment and must emphasize the implications of such features for life in the region. To do so, relationships need to be drawn among such factors as climate, topography, vegetation, and the way people live. The kind of presentation envisioned here could be likened to a framework for a particular type of region.

The notion of a framework, or schema, stems from the organized nature of knowledge (R. C. Anderson et al., 1978; Minsky, 1975; Rumelhart, 1980; Schank & Abelson, 1977; Thorndyke & Yekovich, 1980). If information about an area's physical characteristics can be set in a framework that exposes relationships among factors such as climate and commerce, it will likely be more meaningful and more memorable (R. C. Anderson, 1977; Bransford & Johnson, 1972). If students are thereby helped to establish a framework for deserts, for example, they could call upon that framework to interpret information presented in later learning about various desert areas of the world.

Of the four textbook presentations on desert regions that were examined, the goal of establishing the general concept, desert, was implicit in three of them. To provide a sense of the raw material from which students are expected to construct a

TABLE 41–1. Commentary on Program B's Nile River Discussion

Text Discussion	Commentary
Each year for thousands of years, the Nile has flooded.	The implication here is that the Nile still floods, information that will be contradicted in a few sentences.
When this happened, the farmers had water for crops.	This is a rather obscure reference to a situation of severe overabundance or lack of water.
But it happened only once a year.	Students are left to surmise the problems this caused for farmers.
Then dams were built to control the water.	When? Shouldn't young students be alerted to the fact that this is a relatively new situation?
As you know, lakes are formed behind dams. Today the Nile does not flood.	The assumption that fourth graders would be able to infer the connections between these two sentences (i.e., the lakes behind dams hold excess water, and, thus, water is not available to cause floods and the Nile no longer floods) borders on the ludicrous. Incidentally, the "as you know" refers to information students were given 75 pages earlier.
The water from the lakes behind dams is used to water crops all year. The water of the Nile is carefully guided to the crops.	Young students must infer that "water from the lakes" and "water of the Nile" refer to the same water. And they are not told for two sentences just how water is "carefully guided."
This is called irrigation. Irrigation supplies the ground with water, using ditches or pipes. (p. 148)	Finally, readers are told how irrigation occurs. But, they must infer that "crops" and "the ground" are the same.

representation of a region, the full reports of the analysis (Beck et al., 1988, 1989) contain a running commentary of Textbook C's entire desert presentation, stressing issues of content and presentation that are relevant to comprehension and learning. In this chapter, selected issues from that commentary are discussed to illustrate the approach to text analysis. The first example discussed here is a 400-word passage that describes the Nile River area.

A Close Look at a Problematic Discussion. The passage occurs in the midst of a discussion of oases and begins with some description of the fertile land in this area of Egypt. The text then moves to a rather confusing discussion of the effects of modern dams on farming. The purpose of this discussion, we inferred, was to tell young readers about flooding and damming along the Nile River. The background needed to understand this situation, but not presented, includes knowledge that a river flows through Egypt and, thus, the area near it is saved from being a desert; that the Nile has a cyclical annual flood that has created a water feast-or-famine situation; and that, in modern times, dams have been built so that water can be saved and distributed throughout the year as needed. The discussion as presented in the textbook portends confusion for its young readers as a result of assumed background knowledge and unclear relationships among sentences. The problem can best be illustrated by providing a sentence-by-sentence commentary, as in Table 41–1. Not only does understanding of this textbook's description require a great deal of background knowledge and some hefty inference making, but the description also fails to make clear the water feast-or-famine and the water saved-and-distributed points suggested as important to a discussion of the Nile.

Too Many Concepts. Research has shown that, when texts of equal length are compared, those in which the ideas are more dense are harder for readers to comprehend (Kintsch & Keenan, 1973). Relatedly, a text that says a little about many things appears more difficult to comprehend than one that says a lot about a few things (Kintsch, Kozminsky, Streby, McKoon, & Keenan, 1975). In all four of the textbook programs analyzed there were numerous instances of presentations in which too many concepts were introduced in too few words. A particularly worrisome example of this problem was found in a short section on desert climate in Textbook C (pp. 125–126). It is worrisome because information about climate involves a large number of scientific concepts that require sophisticated background knowledge.

As illustration, consider the number of major concepts found in the discussion of desert temperature. In 200 words, the text describes the effect of humidity on the heating and cooling of air, the influence of cloud cover on heat retention, the relationship between proximity to the equator and direct sunlight, and the influence of direct sunlight on temperature. Moreover, the section concludes with the information that there are cold deserts and gives the Gobi as an example.

In considering this temperature discussion, the difficulty of making sense of this amount of information in just 200 words needs to be recognized. The complexity of content and brevity of text allow little room for elaboration. Adult readers may not need elabortion to understand a statement such as, "But there is no cloud cover to act like a blanket, so nights are cold." That is because they probably already understand the relationship between clouds and heat retention. However, young students who encounter the statement on cloud cover without background knowledge of the phenomenon may well wonder what cloud cover is and how it acts like a blanket. Thus, not only are a large number of concepts presented in a few words, but also each of those concepts requires a significant amount of elaboration to be meaningful to young students. This is an instance in which the extent of a learner's prior knowledge deserves especially serious attention (Chiesi, et al., 1979; Spilich, et al., 1979). The text seems intended to explain concepts related to desert temperature and humidity but evidences little consideration of the knowledge needed to understand the ideas that make up that explanation.

What's the Point? A frequent problem found in the textbooks was that the point of text passages was not made explicit and, indeed, was often difficult to infer. One example occurs early in Textbook C in a brief section in the desert unit, in conjunction with a map, on the locations of desert regions around the world. The purpose of this section, it would seem, is to impart the notion that deserts are found throughout the world. However, the point is never stated, and this is a problem because, as readers begin a text, they expect the topic to be established (Kieras, 1985). Instead, the text is simply a series of unconnected statements and questions such as: "Over 30 countries are at least part desert... Some deserts are in the middle of continents... [Some] deserts take up a large part of a continent... Which deserts are on a coast?" (p. 127). Without any indication of the point these statements and questions are supporting, it is unlikely that most fourth graders will either infer the point that deserts are found throughout the world or remember the details.

Another vivid example of the lack of a higher order statement is found in a section about the natural resources to be found in the desert. Although the information is presented as prose, it reads like a list of discrete items. The section begins, "Many minerals are found in the desert," and ends, "Copper comes from the Atacama Desert in Northern Chile" (p. 127), with an enumeration of natural resources (e.g., oil, natural gas, diamonds) sandwiched in between. Certainly a useful point about deserts is that, despite their apparently barren topography, they contain things of commercial value. But a higher order statement that would explicate the concept that comprises the individual examples is never made. Without it, young readers simply are presented with an unmemorable list of natural resources.

The example of natural resources was characterized as having a list-like quality, a feature common throughout the textbooks' presentations. But, a quintessential example of list-like presentation of information occurs in the following discussion about the people in the Sahara:

Some of the people of the Sahara are Berbers. Some are called Tuaregs. Another group is the Tedas. Many of these people are Arabs.

Some Berbers live in the northwestern part of the Sahara. The Tuaregs live in the area of the Ahaggar Mountains. The Tedas live in the Tibesti Mountains. (p. 137)

These chopped-off sentences are examples of the kind of writing that results when readability formulas are applied, limiting sentence length. Recently, much has been written about the inadequacies of these formulas to control comprehensibility and the problems their use produces (Beck et al., 1984; Davison, 1984; Rubin, 1985). In this application, a typical result is demonstrated; the chopping of information—the names of tribal groups—into separate sentences requires readers to infer a relationship. Studies have shown that longer sentences that make relationships explicit yield better comprehension (Marshall & Glock, 1978–79; Pearson, 1974–75).

Asides That Overwhelm the Purpose. There were additional textual features, beyond omissions of statements of conceptual intent and presentations of ideas in lists, that made it difficult to understand the purposes of discussions. For example, the Sahara is first introduced in a 200-word passage whose purpose, we inferred, was to describe the size and location of that desert region. Appropriately, the passage begins by directing students to find the Sahara on a map on which desert areas are shaded and notes that "The Sahara is almost as large as the United States," a comparison that makes sense in that students are likely to have some idea of the size of the United States. The section also notes that another desert, the Kalahari, is located on the continent of Africa. Given that students are looking at a map that denotes desert areas and their attention has been directed to Africa, it is reasonable that other deserts on the same continent be mentioned. But it is more than a mention; a full paragraph of about 40 words is devoted to aspects of the Kalahari, which, in a 200-word section, is rather long for a side focus.

The third paragraph in the section is a 50-word presentation of the fact that Sahara is the Arabic word for desert, another instance of an aside that overwhelms the purpose of the text. Rather than simply introducing this fact, the text describes Arabic as "the language of a large group of people in North Africa and the Middle East," labels these people "Arabs," states that they used the word "Sahara" to describe the desert in North Africa, that *Sahara* and *desert* mean the same thing, and that, therefore, it is incorrect to say "Sahara Desert."

The implication is not that students should never be told about a word's derivation or about some interesting side issues. Perhaps the point is best made by noting that the Kalahari and Arabic asides combined take up 40% of a scant 200–word section discussing size and location of the Sahara. Such lengthy deviations may well overwhelm, and thus distract young readers from, the purpose of the passage. Support for this conclusion comes from the work of Schank (1975); Stein and Trabasso (1982); Bradshaw and Anderson (1982); and Mohr, Glover, and Ronning (1984), which showed that the presence of irrelevant passages within a text interferes with comprehension.

Inadequate Examples and Comparisons. The textbooks' authors often tried to use well-accepted instructional strategies to make concepts clear, for instance by presenting examples and drawing comparisons. But the implementation of these strategies was often less than successful. An instance occurs following the two paragraphs of asides when, in the text just dealt with, the discussion returns to the location and size of the Sahara. In locating the Sahara, the text mentions that it is part of many countries and gives one example, the Sudan. The usefulness of thoughtful examples cannot be overestimated, as much recent evidence points to the importance of examples in learning (Chi, Bassock, Lewis, Reimann, & Glaser, 1989; Klausmeier, Ghatala, & Frayer, 1974; Merrill & Tennyson, 1977). However, in the discussion of that example, the sole information given is, "Parts of the Sudan get 40 inches of rain a year." Certainly, if only one example is to be given, it makes no sense to use one that is at odds with the desert context.

A use of comparison occurs in the initial discussion of the

desert unit, in which deserts are described as dry places that get less than 10 in. of rain a year. In an effort to give significance to "less than 10 inches," the author implies a comparison by stating that average rainfall on earth is 20–60 in. The usefulness of this comparison for students is dubious, for what do 10 in. or 20–60 in. of rainfall mean to a fourth grader? A comparison that might be useful would utilize a known benchmark, for example, by asking students to find out the amount of rainfall in their towns and compare it with that of the desert. However, as presented, the first defining characteristic offered for deserts is unlikely to be usable in building a desert concept for fourth graders.

Cause Without Consequence. Consider the impediment to students' understanding of stating the cause of a phenomenon without satisfactorily describing its consequence. For example, in the textbook's section about water on the desert, the point is made that, when rain does fall in a desert, little water soaks in, and, therefore, running water can cut into the land and "change it." But the nature of those changes, such as canyons and dryriver beds, is not mentioned, despite the fact that formations like dryriver beds are distinctive aspects of desert topography. Instead, the text goes on to a new concept, that of rapid water evaporation in the desert. Clearly, "change it" is a highly nebulous description of the consequence of running water on desert land. If young students are not told what the land is changed to, it is unlikely that they will find this allusion to a desert phenomenon memorable.

No Sense of Time. There is ample evidence to indicate that young students have difficulty establishing a sense of time (e.g., Harrison, 1934; Jahoda, 1962; Lello, 1980). But this difficulty did not seem to be considered in many places in the textbooks that were examined. For example, in the textbook under consideration, early in the chapter about the Sahara there is a description of the region as it existed thousands of years ago, a fertile environment of farmlands and forests with many people living there. "But then," the text notes, "the climate began to change."

The text fails to make the important point that such a sweeping climatic change was gradual, occurring over thousands and thousands of years. No such sense of time is provided. Consider the statement, "The climate turned dry and windy." Overnight? Similarly, consider the statements, "Plants died... Streams and lakes dried up... Then farmers began to leave." The time lapse of these events could be days or eons, but the students are not told. A reasonable goal for this section would seem to be to impart some sense of the sweeping, long-term nature of a change in ecosystem. Yet there was only one vague mention of passing time in the statement, "Through the years the Sahara spread."

Poorly Ordered Components of an Explanation. Several types of problems in the explanation of concepts were found. One was that the components of an explanation were sometimes presented in illogical order. An instance of this situation was found in a discussion about how the changed ecosystem resulted in a nomadic culture. Given that the explanation is in the form of a problem–solution relationship, the ordering is problematic, in that the statement of the problem appears at the end of the sequence. The text presents the explanation as (a) Many people became nomads, (b) nomads are people who move from place to place to find grazing land for their animals, (c) the nomads of the Sahara began to move about the desert, (d) they had to find food for their sheep, goats, and camels.

Reversing the order of the sentences provides a more logical sequence, in which, with only slight rewording, the problem of finding food initiates the sequence: (a) The people of the Sahara needed to find food for their sheep, goats, and camels; (b) so they began to move about the desert; (c) people who move from place to place to find grazing land for their animals are called *nomads;* (d) many people of the Sahara became nomads. The work of Mandler (1978) and N. L. Stein and Glenn (1978) has illustrated that comprehension difficulties are caused by misordered components in narratives. In their studies, scrambled order disrupted narrative comprehension when the type of presentation was usually familiar; illogical order is at least as likely to interfere with the comprehension of new information.

Inadequate Explanations. Another problematic explanation involved the following discussion of why camels are one of the few animals able to survive in the desert:

Camels have humps on their backs. They store fat in these humps. The fat gives them energy. Because camels do not store water, fat helps produce water when camels move through the dry desert. They can go for several months without water. Camels eat grass to get moisture.

Several issues are raised by this explanation. One is that, if the decision is made to include an explanation of camel physiology (a decision that will be discussed later), it needs to be presented in a way that considers the prior knowledge of the target audience of 9-year-olds. Part of that consideration should be to present the components of the explanation in a logical order. That is, the text ought to start with the explanation that camels can go for a long time without water and then discuss why that is the case: Camels have humps that store fat, and they are able to use this fat to produce water for their bodies.

We suspect that the text's explanation has been confounded by an attempt to debunk the camels-store-water-in-humps myth. Note the phrases, "They [camels] store fat in these humps" and "Because camels do not store water..." The myth debunking could have been achieved directly and with less potential for confusing young readers by the simple statement that the myth is not true: "Camels don't store water in their humps, as many people think. Instead, the humps store fat, and camels use this fat to..."

In regard to whether to include an explanation of how the camel's adaptions function, a writer has at least two obvious options. One is simply to state that the ability exists (e.g., "Camels can go long distances in the desert without food or water"). A second option is to explain what those adaptations are and how they function. The point here is that information on camel physiology is not the linchpin for building an understanding of the Sahara or of the fact that camels can survive for long times in the desert. So, inclusion of information on how the camel survives is not mandatory. Moreover, to say "Because camels do not store water, fat helps produce water" is to present a non sequitur that provides no explanation at best, and is likely to be confusing at worst.

This instance of a problematic explanation illustrates that oftentimes certain textual information is not needed to achieve the general goal of a passage. When considering whether to include an aspect of a topic that might be difficult for target-aged learners, thought should be given to the complexities it might add to the text and how that might add to the information-processing load. The camel discussion also illustrates the confusion that can occur when a text attempts to do too many things at one time.

Understated Presentation of Important Information. Textbook presentations often fail to emphasize the most important ideas. This problem is exemplified in a section the purpose of which seems to be to describe the importance of oil and natural gas to countries of the Sahara. In terms of this content, consider the significant geopolitical and socioeconomic implications of the region's natural resources. Yet the short two-paragraph section on the topic of oil resources contains only two sentences that touch on these issues, "This [oil and natural gas] is very important to people who live there [the Sahara] and to others around the world. It provides many jobs and money." These two sentences, we suggest, do little to establish the significance of oil resources to this region and to global political and economic issues, and even less to establish the cultural change that has occurred in the area as a result of an oil economy.

Some Comments. The overall goal for the textbook's desert unit appeared to be the establishment of the concept *desert,* comprising characteristics of a desert and the phenomena underlying them. Yet the text presentation leaves the impression that it was not based on a plan for communicating this information. There does not seem to be consideration of the main concepts to be established and how to arrange information so that those concepts are explained and the most important ideas are emphasized. Rather, the text presents a broad variety of brief topics; frequently misorders or omits components of sequences of information such as explanations, causal chains, and hierarchies of ideas; and fails to make relationships among concepts explicit. The result is that the text presentation resembles a tossing forth of ideas associated with a topic. Implications of the notion that knowledge is organized and that its organization is necessary to building understanding (Anderson et al., 1978; Minsky, 1975; Rumelhart, 1980; Schank & Abelson, 1977; Thorndyke & Yekovitch, 1980) are ignored. Little help is offered learners in drawing relationships to organize information and develop meaningful representations of a topic. As noted earlier, the problems discussed came from one textbook; however, they were found to lesser or greater degrees in all four programs examined in the analysis.

METHODOLOGICAL CONSIDERATIONS FOR TEXTBOOK ANALYSIS

In the commentaries on social studies textbooks across the years, as mentioned at the outset of this chapter, there has been consensus about their adequacy—or inadequacy. Although we would venture that most of the conclusions have been quite valid, validity is not enough. Often missing from the reports are levels of analysis that provide a strong sense of what the texts are like and of whether they would function as intended for student learning. The generality of the reporting of analyses inhibits their usefulness both for educators interested in refining instructional practice and for further research. What needs to be exposed are the details that allowed the formation of conclusions about the textbooks; general statements alone do not promote understanding of the issues. The focus of this section, then, is the distinction between an observation that the skilled eye of an expert can detect from casual scrutiny and the analysis and subsequent reporting of factors that contributed to that observation.

When writers express themselves in generalizations, they can well omit "the detail that would give these generalities meaning" (Metcalf, 1963). As Metcalf explained in regard to textbooks, such vagueness violates a law posited by one of the founders of modern psychology, William James, that "no one sees further into a generalization than his knowledge of detail extends" (p. 953). These notions about generalizations mirror the situation referred to as missing levels of analysis in research on textbooks. To illustrate some of the issues involved, aspects of various social studies textbook examinations are analyzed in terms of how far the level of detail provided allows one to see into the generalizations made. In the following section, then, the scholarship on social studies textbook analyses is scrutinized. The section might be considered an analysis of the analyses of social studies textbooks, including some of the present authors' work.

Three Dimensions of Textbook Analysis

Three dimensions are integral to providing the detail that would give deeper meaning to some prevalent generalizations about textbooks. The three dimensions are *first,* a situation model that is a thoughtful analysis of the situation being presented in the text in terms of the information a learner would need to construct adequate understanding; *second,* extensive examples of the textbooks' presentations of the situation; and *third,* a commentary in which the investigator explains why the various textbook treatments have been judged likely to be adequate or inadequate for enabling the learner to understand the situation.

The Situation Model. The term *situation model* comes from a significant recent focus in research on text processing. It is proposed that readers, in coming to understand a text, construct a multilevel representation of it (Johnson-Laird, 1983; Just & Carpenter, 1987; Perfetti, in press; van Dijk & Kintsch, 1983). First, at a surface level, the reader constructs a restricted, or literal, sense of meaning. At a second level, the reader uses background knowledge to elaborate text statements and draw relationships among ideas, in order to develop an interpretation of the text. The distinction between these two levels is demonstrated in Kintsch's (1986) assertion that being able to learn effectively from a text differs from being able to comprehend and remember it; to learn effectively, a reader needs to understand the situation described by the text. Or, in Kintsch's (1986) words, "If the goal of instruction is to enable students to learn some subject matter on the basis of a text, it becomes necessary to consider how the student can construct from the text a mental model of the situation" (p. 108).

The term *situation model,* as applied to text analysis, is intended to mean the set of ideas and their relationships that a researcher believes would constitute student understanding about a specific topic. The situation model that a researcher establishes can derive from either the researcher's beliefs about what is important in learning about a topic or the researcher's interpretation of what students are intended to learn from a textbook presentation.

When an investigator launches a critique of textbooks, the presumption is that she or he has some notions about a situation that learners ought to understand. One of the researcher's primary responsibilities should be to make the elements of that situation public so they can be scrutinized by others. To some extent, the situation model for a text is the premise from which the rest of the analysis follows. As such, making this premise public is crucial if others are to have an adequate basis for agreeing or disagreeing with the analysis, perhaps even arguing that the situation model should have been different.

An example of such a situation model comes from Miller and Rose's (1983) examination of the treatment of the causes of the Great Depression in high school history books. Miller and Rose provided enough detail about the situation they wanted textbooks to convey to students for others to understand what they believed to be the causes of the Great Depression and to take specific issue with their analysis if they disagreed. This level of detail allows a productive dialogue. Let us look at Miller and Rose's analysis of the situation.

The motivation for Miller and Rose's stated purpose for examination of the treatment of causes of the Great Depression in high school American history textbooks was to determine whether previous criticisms and current economic scholarship were finding their way into texts. They characterized these criticisms by suggesting that it is incorrect to describe the Great Depression as if it were an enormous forest fire—dry timber suddenly blazing out of control—that the smoke jumpers (government) could not put out. The inappropriate forest fire analogy became the theme for their analysis of the situation. That is, the Great Depression was not a sudden, single event; rather, the economy took nearly 4 years to reach bottom, with much happening along the way. Thus, "an accurate analysis must examine how the fire spread and, in particular, what the smoke jumpers did" (p. 26).

A major factor in an accurate analysis, according to Miller and Rose, was the role of the discretionary macroeconomic policy of the government. The authors explained what this policy was, and sketched its role in creating and prolonging the depression by discussing areas of agreement and disagreement about these issues among economists. For example, they stated that the "consensus conclusion seems to be that fiscal and especially monetary policies prevented an earlier recovery and, indeed, were major causes of the Depression" (p. 27). Miller and Rose then made the point that modern macroeconomic theory called for "increased government spending or tax decreases or

both" to fight a recession and that government actions were in contrast to that prescription. For example, monetary policy was "sharply contractionary through 1934," and tax cuts were eliminated in favor of a large tax increase.

Miller and Rose's explanations of events surrounding the Great Depression and their citation of support for the validity of these explanations yield a clear portrayal of the situation these authors wanted students to understand. Their situation model became a template from which they could examine textbook treatments of the Great Depression and against which they could make judgments about the adequacy of various treatments. That their interpretation was made public serves an important purpose: It permits others to scrutinize and criticize the premises underlying their analysis.

The general judgment of Miller and Rose was that the textbooks they reviewed were woefully inadequate because they did not match the situation model proposed. That judgment appears to be well–founded. However, Miller and Rose said what the texts did or did not do, but they rarely provided actual examples from the 16 textbooks they examined, to let the reader understand the inadequacies cited. The few examples included in their article were mostly isolated sentences. Specifically, from the 16 economics textbooks they analyzed, they presented 2 one-sentence examples; 2 two-sentence examples; and 1 three-sentence example.

The Need for Extensive Examples. Most of us have had the experience of reading about an unfamiliar phenomenon and having the light bulb go on when the author provided us with an example of it, so the value of examples is intuitively compelling. Beyond that, much research evidence points to the importance of examples in understanding and learning (Chi et al., 1987; Klausmeier et al., 1974; Merrill & Tennyson, 1977). It is our contention that, to enhance the productivity of textbook analyses, abundant examples must be provided of the treatment of whatever situation and features an investigator is examining. Such examples are the detail that gives meaning to an analyst's generalizations about what is good, or just okay, or downright poor about how certain situations were handled.

In the case of Miller and Rose, the reader is left with only the authors' generalizations. Some individuals who understood the authors' premise may not necessarily recognize subsequent text presentations as instances of what Miller and Rose would classify as inappropriate. Following is some detail to support that contention.

Miller and Rose made the point that important concepts and information about the causes of the Great Depression were not emphasized: "Authors of recent textbooks have not recognized the importance of fiscal and particularly monetary policies" (p. 30). Moreover, they went on to say that the presentations of causes were deeply flawed: "Many of the factors cited in the texts have been rejected by economists or did not operate in the way the textbooks recount" (p. 30). Next Miller and Rose presented some elaboration.

Chief among those factors is the stock market crash. While a few texts recognized that the crash and the Depression are not synonymous, some continued to leave the impression that the crash was the pivotal event, explicitly or by virtue of the amount and placement of copy devoted to the crash. Others carefully stated that the crash was only one factor. A few noted that the market collapse intensified a recession that already had begun. (p. 30)

These descriptive generalizations by Miller and Rose, based on their observations, are not adequate to help others see what they saw; excerpts from the text are needed. For instance, providing an excerpt from a text that discussed the "crash and the Depression synonymously" and another excerpt from a text that "recognized that the crash and the Depression are not synonymous" would enable readers to compare the differences. What is it that textbooks do that "leaves the impression that the crash was the pivotal event?" When they leave the impression "explicitly," do they actually say the crash and the Depression are the same thing?

When the impression about the crash is made more subtly, "by virtue of the amount and placement of copy devoted to the crash," how much copy? One thousand words in a 2,000-word section devoted to the Great Depression, or, if preferable, approximately 80% of a 20-page section on the Great Depression? It would be even more enlightening if the actual amount of text devoted to the crash from a textbook in which the crash was overemphasized had been compared with the amount of text devoted to the crash in a textbook that recognized that it was not "the pivotal event." Moreover, what was it about the "placement of copy devoted to the crash" that contributed to "the impression that the crash was [so] pivotal"? Was it that such copy was presented first? Was copy about the importance of the crash frequently interwoven with other topics?

Additional questions could be asked about just this one paragraph of Miller and Rose's discursive description of problematic features. Many other questions came to mind as we studied the authors' characterizations of what textbooks do. However, all the questions boil down to one large request: Show us. That is, real examples are needed of various textual presentations that the investigators saw as doing or not doing what they thought should be done.

But examples in and of themselves are not necessarily enough. This leads to the third dimension noted earlier as important for providing deeper meaning to generalizations about textbooks, that is, commentaries in which the investigators explain what it is that they saw in various text treatments that caused them to develop their generalizations.

The Need for Commentaries. Those who investigate and write about various topics have particular interest in, and usually extensive knowledge about, those topics. But the knowledge that allows one to make astute observations and to analyze texts at greater depth than less-skilled observers also plays a role in the need for commentaries. An investigator needs to pull apart his or her thinking about why a particular text treatment demonstrates an issue and make that thinking explicit for the audience. This can be difficult because often the knowledge that allows an investigator to recognize problems in a text is so automatically applied that he or she is not aware of the process.

Examples of the difficulty in sorting out one's knowledge from text information are not hard to find in research reports. Researchers have found that readers with high knowledge of a topic, when asked to recall or recognize sentences from a text, often assert that the text contained statements that are congruent with the topic but which did not appear in the text (see e.g., R. C. Anderson & Pichert, 1978; Bartlett, 1932; Bransford & Johnson, 1972; Dooling & Lachman, 1971). Hence, to communicate with readers less knowledgeable about a topic, investigators need to analyze their thinking about what it was in a text that caused them to make certain judgments and then spell out their reasoning. An example from Miller and Rose's article can be used to illustrate the importance of commentary about a text example to understanding what it shows or how it is an example of something.

Miller and Rose's major concern was that students would come away from texts about the Great Depression with "erroneous conclusions." They then elaborated this worry as follows:

The texts can leave the impression that unionization, equality of income and subsidization of ailing industries are necessary to eliminate depressions. Furthermore, questions posed at the end of the chapters and at various points in the teacher's editions compound the damage. One book suggests that the teacher "Explain the differences between the 'trickle-down' theory with the opposing theory of spreading the wealth around. Ask: which theory did Hoover seem to hold?" (p. 32)

After reading that example, the expectation was that the authors would tell how the suggestion to the teacher of what to explain and the specific question to ask were instances of "compounding the damage." Instead, the authors followed with, "Of considerably more importance are questions that were not asked: how macroeconomic policy is made and conducted and whether following policy rules or permitting discretion gives the greater chance of stability" (p. 32).

Although this comment suggesting what should be included in textbooks is useful because it elaborates the analysts' situation model, it does not reveal the features of the text example that "compound the damage." In an attempt to understand that point, a reader could study the example thoughtfully and make some inferences, but she or he could not know if the inferences were correct. Hence, for a reader to understand an example as an instance of something, it is frequently necessary for an investigator to provide a commentary that explains how and why the example illustrates what the investigator says it does. Otherwise, the point may remain opaque.

In a short section at the end of their article, Miller and Rose point to "several possible remedies for textbook *bias* and inaccuracy [italics added]." Although this was the only actual use of the term bias, aspects of bias were implicit throughout their discussions. This is hardly surprising, given the interpretive nature of the social sciences. Next, two examples from an article that was concerned with various bias-related issues are presented to further elaborate the importance of commentaries.

In a discussion of how textbooks present the effects of modernization on African nations, Crofts (1986) provided commentaries on two text passages, one of which illustrates the ingredients for a successful commentary, the other of which has some missing ingredients. First, consider the latter instance.

Crofts described a theory of modernization held by Westerners to which she believes the texts ascribe. Within this theory is the implicit belief that technological and material development are major indicators of how good or advanced a culture is. Crofts stated that "textbooks frequently suggest that Africans could 'develop' if they really tried, or if they were willing to give up the 'old ways' and accept the 'new' " (p. 349). She then offered the following text excerpt to support her assessment:

Although urban Africans are learning new customs, they often feel the tug of their old, traditional ways. It is difficult to be a part of city life and still follow the ways of village elders who may have never seen a town. (p. 349)

Crofts's remarks about this excerpt seem to be a less than effective commentary because she has not made clear how it displays the attitude that Africans *should* be willing to give up the "old ways" and "develop." One reading of the excerpt could be that the author is simply saying that the juxtaposition of old and new ways can be difficult to deal with. This is not to say that the attitude Crofts described was not present in the textbooks; but her brief comments in setting up the excerpt did not reveal why she saw what she saw in the excerpt, what in the text gave her the message she described?

In contrast, consider Crofts's discussion of a notion related to the modernization theory that she said texts often use in presentations about African culture:

The reverse of the modernization theory is the "noble savage" theory. In some instances, the "simplicity" of people is equated with virtues admired by the author and presented in a "would-you-believe-it" manner: "Some of the most thoughtful and honest people I ever met could carry everything they owned on their backs, and they often did." (p. 349)

Crofts's introduction to the textbook example acts to alert the reader that it is inappropriate. But what if a reader does not make that inference and views the statement as reasonable, thinking that the author has only offered admiration for the individuals encountered? Crofts quickly took the reader beyond this naive interpretation with comments that made transparent what she saw in the text statement:

One could ask if people with fewer possessions are basically more honest or thoughtful, or conversely, are dishonesty and thoughtlessness functions of personal wealth? What is the purpose of this confusing mixture of moral qualities and material possessions? (p. 349)

Crofts then went on to elaborate on her commentary, indicating what she saw as the effects that such texts may have on students:

This oversimplification of the lifestyle of certain African societies encourages students to develop an attitude that these are strange, simple people, resistant to technological benefits to life. Such an attitude of condescension toward less technologically advanced societies does not promote understanding and open-mindedness. (p. 359)

Because many of the conditions that produce bias are very subtle, it is especially important that those who observe it in their areas of expertise provide commentaries for less keen observers, to explain what it is about a text's treatment that

shows bias. Researchers need to provide the details that give meaning to discussions of textbook content judged to be biased. To say that an account is biased is worlds away from explaining why it is a biased account.

The Three Dimensions and the Analysis of History Textbooks. History, as contrasted with economics and world cultures, the textbook topics covered in the discussion thus far, is likely viewed by most citizens as a more familiar and accessible area of knowledge. Asked which they understand better, most Americans would probably answer "history." This situation belies a problem in the teaching of history, a problem that was aptly described by Metcalf (1963) as "easy familiarity." Metcalf pointed out that, because history contains few technical terms, scientific concepts, or formulas, a reader may find it easy to comprehend and, therefore, more readily accept any account of historical events without critical examination.

SOME EXAMPLES AND COMMENTARY IN HISTORY.

Social studies educators have long been concerned that history instruction encourage critical examination and that historical material be presented in ways that promote student inquiry. In 1967, Palmer examined high school history books to see whether, and to what extent, the material was presented to promote student inquiry. For the most part, Palmer concluded that the way the content was presented rarely encouraged students to apply the process of inquiry. But Palmer did discuss one text in which he believed the authors often invited inquiry by "mak[ing] their own position and the reasoning behind it quite clear" (p. 142). He then presented an example from the text in a way that illustrates why an investigator needs to provide commentary that clues a reader in to his thinking. Palmer introduced the textbook example as follows: "The authors' distinctive interpretation of the Neutrality Act of 1937 and its consequences . . . invites the reader to question or even disagree" (p. 142). Then the example was presented:

This new law swept away the old principle of freedom of the seas for neutral trade. Thus it gave up the very rights for which we had fought in 1917. More important, it stopped the most powerful nation in the world, the United States, from contributing to collective security. As President Roosevelt said later, "Our arms embargo played right into the hands of aggressive nations." (p. 142)

Two issues come to mind about the way this example is presented. First, Palmer seems to have assumed that readers would share his basic familiarity with the Neutrality Act. A reader who knew nothing of the act and its consequences could not even hope to grasp Palmer's point. For readers who might not have known as much as he did about the act or the usual interpretations of its consequences, Palmer needed to explain why this interpretation is distinctive. (Having consulted several college texts about the Neutrality Act and related events, we are puzzled as to why Palmer referred to this excerpt as representing a distinctive interpretation, as it coincides with what we learned. But perhaps in 1967 most texts carried quite different information on this historical episode.)

Second, how does this discussion of the Neutrality Act invite one to disagree? Why would a student not be as likely to accept this discussion as an accurate, objective account as to question and disagree? Palmer ought to have explained what he found inviting here, or perhaps provided a counterexample from a text that seemed not to issue such an invitation. Part of the problem in trying to understand how Palmer reached his assessment of the text passage may be that Palmer did not provide enough text, nor did he provide a description of the context in which the passage occurred. Providing more of the setting for the passage might have helped readers understand why Palmer believed this example revealed "the authors'... own position and the reasoning behind it" (p. 142).

ELEMENTARY SCHOOL HISTORY TEXTS: ANATOMY OF AN ANALYSIS.

To this point, our discussion of the three dimensions of textbook analysis—situation models, extensive examples, and commentary—has been mostly in the context of high school material. Now we will move to the elementary school level, with further discussion of the cognitive-based analysis presented earlier (Beck et al., 1988, 1989). Examples from a portion of the analysis dealing with fifth-grade history will be used to make two points in particular. One is that the developmental level of target learners is an essential consideration in an investigator's proposed situation model. Simply, how much of the complexity inherent in social science content does an investigator propose be presented when discussing, for example, a given historical episode for 5th graders, 8th graders, 11th graders?

The other point is that textbook analysts should communicate to their audience a sense of the wholeness of the way a topic has been treated. A portion of the analysis is used to illustrate ways in which an investigator might communicate to readers the essence of the treatment of a topic in a textbook. Beck et al.'s approach to analysis of the textbooks was to consider extensive sequences of text on single topics, rather than to examine examples of text problems isolated from the context in which they occurred. The use of extensive content sequences allowed consideration of the learning that might develop as students move through a sequence. This approach also provided the wholeness of examples that enabled communication of a sense of the raw material from which young students were intended to build an understanding of a topic.

Toward creating a situation model, the broad goal that we conceived for fifth-graders' study of topics in history was the development of an understanding of a historical chain of events. An important aspect to consider in creating a situation model to represent this understanding is that young learners need to be presented with more than simply the elements of a chain of events; they need to know how these elements are related to each other. Here a critical distinction needs to be made between presenting elements of an episode, for example, the cause, event, and consequence of a chain of events, and explaining why *a* caused *b* and why *b* led to *c*. Explaining the meaning of those elements and how they fit together is the key to making instructional content meaningful. This notion comes from a large body of research about causal sequences that suggests that the construction of a coherent interpretation requires making connective inferences, assisted by stated connections (e.g., Graesser, 1981; Kintsch & van Dijk, 1978; Lehnert, 1978, 1982; Trabasso & Sperry, 1985; Trabasso & van den Broek, 1985).

One of the topic sequences examined was the presentation of events leading to the American Revolution, from the French and Indian War to Lexington and Concord, in 4 fifth-grade social studies texts. In considering how texts could best communicate this topic to fifth-graders, a first question was, what content should be presented? That is, what content would build an understanding of how a chain of events led to the Revolution? Our decisions about content selection were based on the focus of our analysis of elementary social studies texts, which was the presumed effect of content on student learning.

Clearly, there is a range of issues in regard to how students learn. For instance, in the case of history, to mention just a few, should content be covered chronologically or organized around themes and concepts? How much sensitivity should there be to the place of women and minorities in the events? To what extent should the interpretative nature of history be emphasized? However, prior to dealing with such important questions, a basic issue is, what can students learn about whatever is presented, in terms of the way it is presented in a textbook?

The historical elements considered in the analysis represent a causal sequence of eight episodes and events for which there was consensus across three of the four textbooks examined. That is, the events were selected precisely because they were the events around which the textbook presentations were structured. Specifically, that sequence is colonial development, the French and Indian War, taxation without representation, the Committees of Correspondence/Sons of Liberty, the Boston Tea Party, the Intolerable Acts, the First Continental Congress, and the Battles of Lexington and Concord. Although the particular sequence is a reasonable representation of the causal chain, the adequacy of a textbook presentation based on the sequence is highly dependent upon the specific information included about each element.

An excerpt from the analysis (Beck et al., 1989) illustrates the development of a situation model, the use of extensive text examples, and the level of commentary on those examples as one way to provide the detail that allows deeper understanding of certain textual presentations. The segment presents a discussion of the Intolerable Acts, the punishing laws passed by Britain following the Boston Tea Party. First, as part of the development of a situation model, the role of the Intolerable Acts in the revolutionary chain of events is assessed. A proposal is offered for how that information might be presented to facilitate young students' understanding of the effect of the acts on the rapidly crystallizing anti-British feelings among the colonists. Then, examples from the texts and commentary on those examples are provided as part of an evaluation of the extent to which the programs' presentations are likely to lead students to understand how this episode contributed to the causal sequence that led to revolution.

The first of the following excerpts outlines the situation that the texts seemed to be intended to teach, and the second paragraph presents aspects of the content that should be emphasized in order for students to develop a mental representation of the situation (Beck et al., 1989).

[The Intolerable Acts were a] direct result of the Boston Tea Party. Britain's anger over the tea dumping resulted in a punishing set of laws aimed at the Massachusetts colony. Colonists dubbed these laws the

TABLE 41–2. Textbook's Descriptions of the Intolerable Acts

Textbook A	Textbook B
When news of the Boston Tea Party reached London, members of Parliament were furious. They decided to punish the people of Boston. They closed Boston Harbor to all trade until the colonists paid for the tea. In addition, Parliament made the head of the British army in the colonies governor of Massachusetts. Massachusetts was no longer allowed to govern itself. Committees of Correspondence throughout the colony went to work. They sent letters out to all the other colonies. Before long, rice, corn, flour, meat, and money poured into Boston from other colonies. (p. 175)	Parliament was very angry, and passed a number of new acts to punish the citizens of Boston. One act closed the port of Boston. No ships were allowed to enter or leave Boston harbor. The city now faced being short of food. Another act placed the people of Massachusetts under a British governor instead of their local governments. Still another act ordered the colonists to supply housing and food for 10,000 British troops. Shocked Americans called these harsh acts the "Intolerable Acts." The colonists joined in smuggling food and other supplies to the people of Boston. The colonists also began to unite against British rule. Many Americans said that the colonies should gain independence from Britain. (p. 86)

Textbook C	Textbook D
The Boston Tea Party, as this event was called, delighted Americans who wanted to break away from England. The English government saw things differently. In 1774, England passed laws meant to punish the colonists in Massachusetts. More soldiers were sent to keep the peace. The colonists were ordered to feed and house them. (p. 48)	The British were very angry! Within a few months, they passed what the colonists called the Intolerable Acts. Intolerable means "unbearable." These acts were meant to punish the people of Boston. The Port of Boston was closed. No self-government was allowed in Massachusetts. British troops had to be housed and fed by the Massachusetts colonists. The Committees of Correspondence acted quickly—letters were sent telling what happened in Boston. Other colonies sent help and supplies. People wondered if their colony would be the next to feel the anger of Great Britain. (p. 109)

Intolerable Acts. The punishment they carried was severe. Boston Harbor was closed, causing a shortage of food and supplies. Self-government was suspended. British troops were sent, and the colonists were forced to house and feed them. Boston took on the atmosphere of an "armed camp" (Garraty & McCaughey, 1987). The result of these laws was that other colonies rallied to the aid of Massachusetts out of sympathy for the plight of those colonists and fear that Britain might react similarly against them. They sent food and supplies to ease the shortages.

The first important point to communicate to students about this chain of events is the severity of the punishment. This allows understanding of how desperately colonists in Massachusetts needed help. Second, the assistance of other colonies represented a united stand against Britain, another instance of the growth of colonial identity and unity. This is particularly so because other colonies could have used the hardships of Massachusetts to their advantage. That is, ships that could no longer dock in Boston could have gone on to another colonial port. In fact, this is what Britain had expected would happen.

Full excerpts of the discussion of the Intolerable Acts in the four textbooks shown in Table 41–2, are then provided in the report, followed by a discussion of how likely the texts are to promote students' understanding of this episode. In particular, it is emphasized that, in judging whether a text is likely to enable students to develop an appropriate model of a situation, particular attention must be given to the explanatory material used to develop specific concepts within general topics and themes. An important issue is whether concepts that support a text topic are explained in a way that assists readers to see the connections necessary to understand the topic.

In commentary about the excerpts (Beck et al., 1989), some of the specific content included in the textbooks was examined and judged as to whether it conveyed the severity of punishment imposed by Britain and its consequences for colonial unity:

Textbooks A, B, and D include the information that Boston Harbor was closed. But only Program B follows that up by explaining that this meant no ships could enter or leave the harbor, which resulted in a food shortage. This kind of explanation seems necessary, for it is not clear that today's 10-year-olds will immediately infer the consequences of closing a harbor.

Textbooks A, B, and D also take up the issue of the banning of self-government in Massachusetts. Programs A and D simply state that no self-government was allowed. Because American 10-year-olds do not have a strong non-example of self-government in their experience, students may well wonder what "no self-government" means; what will there be instead? A factor that compounds this problem is that the notion that the colonists had some self-government and that it was important to them has not been well-established in previous text.

Another aspect of the punishing laws, the colonists were forced to house and feed British soldiers, is presented by all four programs. But none of the programs explains what that meant, that is, colonists had to take soldiers into their homes and give them food that was already in short supply.

None of the programs adequately portrays the help of the other colonists and its implications of unity against Britain. Programs A, B, and D state that help and supplies were sent, but Programs A and D had never established a need for assistance! These three programs all make some attempt to address the unity issue. But in our judgment the treatment is not particularly effective because it is not presented as integral to the chain of events. For example, Program D states, as the final sentence about the Intolerable Acts, "people wondered if their colony would be the next to feel the anger of Great Britain." Thus stated and placed, it seems like a random musing rather than a strong motivation for drawing the colonies together.

In the full analysis, Textbook C is discussed in terms of some unique aspects of its presentation, but that material is not useful to the present discussion. Finally, a summary evaluation of the textbook presentations is offered:

Overall, [the programs] do not provide a unified presentation of the textbook chain of events related to the Intolerable Acts. Rather, the text passages seem but series of facts related to the events. Relationships among ideas, motivations, and consequences are for the most part poorly portrayed or completely lacking.

It may have become apparent that the situation model was based on one point of view, perhaps what might be called "a traditional American point of view." Although the development of multiple points of view is a serious and important issue in learning history, it was outside the purpose of the analysis. The analysis was based on the goals inferred from the texts themselves. Thus, our focus was on explicating what the goals seemed to be and examining whether they were met. The question that drove the analysis was whether much would likely be learned about the topic from the content presented, given the way it was presented. Even at the fifth-grade level, however, it is possible to write textbooks that make students aware of other views, even if direct attention is not afforded the alternatives. This tone could be conveyed by using phrases such as "Some people believed," "The leaders in Boston saw this as," and "They thought Britain was trying to." Although the analysis was not focused on the use of such language, which could set the stage for students to understand that history is interpretive, we saw little of it.

Review of Dimensions of Text Analysis. The discussion has been focused on three dimensions of text analysis that could be useful in bringing deeper meaning to the analysis of social studies textbooks and making that work of greater utility for educators trying to bring about changes in instruction. These three dimensions—situation model, extensive examples, and commentary on examples—have been characterized as missing levels of analysis because they do not appear in the reports of the analyses with the explicitness and consistency that is needed to go beyond the level of sharing generalities.

In this section, the three dimensions are reviewed. Some summary comments are made and some points are expanded on that have only been alluded to in the discussion thus far. A major consideration is that the three dimensions are not independent; they interact and are often interwoven. Rarely is it possible, or even desirable, to present a complete situation model followed by examples followed by commentary. The three can be interwoven so that, for instance, the examples provide the detail needed to "see into" the situation model that the investigator is trying to establish. Or commentary may be made by way of contrast of what is in a text with what should be in a text, thereby virtually blending into a situation model.

Situation Model. A situation model can rarely be presented as a whole; rather, some of its characteristics must be outlined early on, and then it becomes enriched and elaborated as examples and commentary show the differences in what the investigator proposes and what exists in the textbooks under consideration. In addition, positive examples in the textbooks can also serve as illustrations of aspects of the situation model. An investigator can use such devices as description, comparison, contrast, and exemplification to present and flesh out the situation model.

Use of Extensive Examples. The discussion of the use of examples in reporting textbook analyses has been focused on excerpts from texts. However, it is not always feasible or practical to present extensive excerpts in a report to illustrate text treatment of a topic; discursive descriptions of text content can also provide a faithful portrayal of a text presentation, particularly if they are liberally salted with some direct quotes. The following account from Beck et al. (1988) provides an illustration. The account comes from a section on how eight texts for sixth and seventh graders gave an overview of geographical features of the Soviet Union. Specifically, this exerpt is focused on how one text provides a sense of the Soviet Union as a flat, open land and considers implications of this geography.

[Textbook A] emphasizes the USSR's vast expanse of land and its few barriers to movement. The text attempts to set up an image for students by describing the USSR as "a rolling plain that sweeps from Eastern Europe to the Pacific Ocean," and the Ural Mountains dividing Europe and Asia as "no more than a wrinkle in the great, flat land." The text then uses this image to point to the influence of the country's geography on its history, stating that because there were no natural barriers, the USSR was open to invasion from all sides when it was weak, and could expand in all directions when it was strong. (p. 89)

Another point about text examples is that providing a range of examples can make for a much richer picture for the reader. That is, several examples from different texts on the same issue can show different ways in which problems can be manifested or varying degrees of problematic features. Again, an illustration is provided from a discussion of the Soviet Union (Beck et al., 1988). This section concerns the general location of the USSR:

[Textbook A]'s attempt to locate the USSR includes information that the country spreads across Europe and Asia, and that it borders 12 countries, but names none of them. Although there is a map on the page, it shows only the USSR and identifies no bordering countries.... The presentation in [Textbook B] includes reference points that may be familiar to young students, such as Western Europe and the Pacific Ocean, and other reference points that students may have heard of because of their significance in current events.... As for the remaining six textbooks, one gave mostly less familiar reference points such as the Caucasus Mountains and the Caspian and Black Seas; three gave very sketchy location details, such as merely stating the USSR was "high in the northern latitudes"; one textbook made no attempt to provide general location information; and one gave only a pre–World War I description of the location of the Russian Empire. (pp. 85–86)

Providing examples of how topics are treated differently in different textbook accounts can be valuable to understanding because of the inherent contrast. The importance of such examples is supported by models of concept teaching in which an important part of developing a concept is the presentation of examples and nonexamples (see, e.g., Klausmeier et al., 1974; Merrill & Tennyson, 1977). Contrasting examples highlight the salient features of the target concept. White (1988) used this technique in her article on substantial knowledge in social studies texts. She presented three example narratives about the Industrial Revolution in the United States and discussed the extent to which each met the criteria she set forth for substantial knowledge.

Commentary. The degree to which examples illustrate an analyst's point is typically dependent on the commentary provided. The level of commentary that is appropriate to get ideas across depends upon factors such as the complexity of the example and how many features contributed to an investigator's judgment about the text. Conversely, text examples that are particularly transparent need little comment. Instances of transparent, easily communicated examples appear in Larkins, Hawkins, and Gilmore's (1987) article on primary grade social studies texts. They discussed what they labeled "superfluous information" (p. 305), that is, information that they believed did not need instructional attention because children would learn it in the natural course of living in society. Larkins et al. provided examples and commentary in the following way:

Will our society suffer if [Textbook A] does not teach third-grade children that cities such as Memphis have radio stations, television stations, and newspapers? Is it really necessary for [Textbook B] to teach third-graders that children go to school, or that parents sometimes have a car wash for the P.T.A.?

Little elaboration is needed; it does not take a trained eye to understand what is meant by superfluous information.

In conclusion, the message of this section of the chapter is a call for more conscious attention to the kind and extent of information a reader needs to understand what the investigator has judged to be adequacies and inadequacies of the texts examined.

SOME FINAL COMMENTS

Some features of text analysis implied in our earlier discussion should be examined further because they entail decisions that must be made in developing one's approach to the analysis of text. One important decision is how much to deal with. Studies have been reported in which anywhere from 3 to 43 textbooks have been analyzed (Wiley, 1977). The level of analysis that researchers can undertake if they deal with 43 textbooks is almost certainly different from that which they can undertake with three textbooks. The kind of detail recommended in the discussion of the three dimensions of analysis is typically not possible unless the number of textbooks to be analyzed is limited. Although studies in which a wide number of texts are analyzed are useful for establishing general perspectives, the approach presented in this chapter emphasizes the productivity of information that can be gained by doing more with less. As such, this approach to text analysis is analogous to Newmann's notions about social studies content, that is, "go for depth" (1988a, 1988b).

A textbook analyst must make major decisions about research method. Much of the discussion about research method in text analysis is related to the differences in quantitative and qualitative approaches. In this regard, there are some lingering effects of the quantitative–qualitative dichotomy that Holsti (1969) characterized as, "if you can't count it, it doesn't count" versus "if you can count it, that ain't it" (p. 11). For example, Larkins, Hawkins, and Gilmore (1987) declared themselves, "simply not interested in quantitative content analysis" and "convinced . . . that qualitative reviews of text are more informative" (p. 302).

Although we are in basic agreement with the sentiments of Larkins and his coauthors, we are not as ready to reject quantitative analyses. Indeed, as noted earlier, in our discussion of Miller and Rose (1983), their analysis of how the textbooks treated the stock market crash would have been more informative had they given some quantitative information about the "amount and placement of copy devoted to the crash" (p. 30). In addition, the reader of their report could have formed a better representation of the extent to which problems occurred in the 16 textbooks they analyzed if Miller and Rose had specified what constituted *most, generally,* and *largely* in their expressions, "most textbooks erred in their explanation of," "the textbooks generally," "the textbooks examined largely ignored," and "most authors [of the textbooks] felt compelled to." The point is simply that quantitative information can enrich qualitative work.

Methodologies for text analysis should not be selected "off the shelf." Rather, they should be selected to enable the researcher to gather the most revealing and productive information about the topics being investigated. This point is related to a variety of concerns voiced in the field about social studies research methodology (Fraenkel, 1987; Nelson & Shaver, 1985; Shaver, Davis, & Helburn, 1980). These researchers call for fresh approaches and more flexibility in how various approaches are applied to research problems. Our position in regard to such concerns can best be explained by discussing several points Fraenkel (1987) made in an article about improving social studies research.

After characterizing the field as dominated by "too narrow a vision of research" (p. 204) and suggesting that it lacked systematic effort "to build a cumulative base of knowledge" (p. 205), Fraenkel made specific suggestions for improving the quality of research in seven research paradigms: experimental, survey, content analysis, correlational, observational, ethnographic, and historical. The suggestions Fraenkel made across the seven paradigms are pertinent to concerns raised in this chapter about text analyses. A sampling of his recommendations that are particularly applicable to text analysis is discussed next.

In regard to experimental research, Fraenkel recommended that investigators "concentrate on description and explanation" and provide "more details, described as vividly as possible" (p. 210). These notions are at the heart of our call for researchers to expose for the reader the conditions that led to a particular evaluation of texts. Fraenkel also recommended that experimental researchers incorporate several dependent variables. He gave the example of a researcher whose main focus is achievement data but who also collects data on student attitudes. This corresponds to the point that quantitative information can be useful in qualitative work; various types of information that cross traditional methodological lines can help a researcher paint a richer picture.

Within observational research, Fraenkel warned against using an "observation form with too many categories" (p. 216). A related caution directed toward textbook analysts might be that attempting to deal with too many topics or too many textbooks in one analysis is problematic. The result can be that only superficial information is revealed.

Of the suggestions Fraenkel made for content analyses, one is arguable. It is that analysts should "be sure to select a random sample of the material to be analyzed." A random sample implies a quantitative approach to content analysis, an approach that may be very limiting. Correspondingly, a random sample is an ill fit to qualitative approaches. The kind of analysis argued for in this chapter does not require a random sample, but rather a careful selection of instructional sequences based on an explicit rationale. For example, the Beck et al. (1988) analysis focused on a sequence on a geographical region to represent the fourth-grade curriculum, a historical period to represent the fifth-grade curriculum, and an introduction of an area of the world to represent the sixth- and seventh-grade curriculum.

Interestingly, our view of random samples for textbook analysis is in concert with Fraenkel's view of random samples for experimental research, which is, "forget about random samples" (p. 210). The alternative he offered is to describe the relevant demographics of the sample in detail, to create a fuller picture. Indeed, detailed description of characteristics toward creating a full picture is precisely the recommendation made for text analysis researchers in this chapter.

Fraenkel made a recommendation for content analysis that deserves to be underscored, that is, that a researcher should analyze latent as well as manifest content and report the feelings and impressions obtained from reading the texts. This notion is closely related to the recommendation that analysts report and explain what they perceive in a text by developing a commentary. The importance of latent content was also expressed in FitzGerald's (1979) view that "what sticks to the memory from textbooks is not particular series of facts but an atmosphere, an impression, a tone. And this impression may be the more influential just because one cannot remember the facts and the arguments that create it" (p. 4). In the context of the view of text analysis presented in this chapter, the importance of FitzGerald's statement is that a book's tenor is created by a variety of textual features, and texts must be explored deeply enough, with sufficiently detailed descriptions, to make evident the features that contribute to the tenor.

One more decision is how to place one's research in the context of previous research. Nelson and Shaver (1985) and Fraenkel (1987) have asserted that too often researchers in social studies do not take advantage of the work that has preceded them. A corollary takes us back to an issue presented at the outset of this chapter; that is, recent cognitive research has uncovered much rich information about the reading process and the characteristics of learners and texts that affect comprehension and learning. Cognitive research is focused on getting inside the process of learning, rather than examining outward manifestations of performance. As such, this body of research provides a natural backdrop for textbook analysis, one that will enhance our understanding of the instructional adequacy of textbooks by centering attention on how textbooks might affect student learning.

There are two ways in which the understanding of text effects on learning may lead to better instructional practice. The obvious implication is that these considerations be more prominently used in the development of textbooks. But under the best of circumstances that would take a long time. However, the kind of problematic textual features that were derived from the analyses presented here could alert teachers to the need to formulate ways to promote students' understanding of what the textbooks intend to present. That is, teachers can help students overcome some of the inadequacies of textbook presentations by, for example, providing background knowledge and extensive explanations.

Although findings from text analyses imply ways to improve social studies instructional materials, descriptive analytic work is hypothetical in nature. When the improvement of instruction is the goal, textbook analysis can only be viewed as an initial step. Specific suggestions and demonstrations of more effective ways of presenting social studies content must be based on empirical research.

References

Alexander, A. (1960). The gray flannel cover on the American history textbook. *Social Education, 24,* 11–14.

Anderson, R. C. (1977). *Schema-directed processes in language comprehension* (Tech. Rep. No. 50). Urbana, IL: University of Illinois, Center for the Study of Reading.

Anderson, R. C., & Pichert, J. W. (1978). Recall of previously unrecallable information following a shift in perspective. *Journal of Verbal Learning and Verbal Behavior, 17,* 1–12.

Anderson, R. C., Spiro, R. J., & Anderson, M. C. (1978). Schemata as scaffolding for the representation of information in connected discourse. *American Educational Research Journal, 15,* 433–440.

Anderson, T. H., & Armbruster, B. B. (1984). Content area textbooks. In R. C. Anderson, J. Osborn, & R. J. Tierney (Eds.), *Learning to read in American schools: Basal readers and context texts* (pp. 193–224). Hillsdale, NJ: Lawrence Erlbaum.

Bartlett, F. C. (1932). *Remembering.* Cambridge University Press.

Beck, I. L. (1981). Reading problems and instructional practices. In L. B. Resnick & P. Weaver (Eds.), *Reading Research: Advances in Theory and Practice, 2,* 53–94.

Beck, I. L., & Carpenter, P. A. (1986). Cognitive approaches to understanding reading: Implications for instructional practice. *American Psychologist, 41,* 1098–1105.

Beck, I. L., & McKeown, M. G. (1988). Toward meaningful accounts in history texts for young learners. *Educational Researcher, 17*(6), 31–39.

Beck, I. L., & McKeown, M. G. (1989). Expository text for young readers:

The issue of coherence. In L. B. Resnick (Ed.), *Knowing, learning, and instruction: Essays in honor of Robert Glaser* (pp. 47–65). Hillsdale, NJ: Lawrence Erlbaum.

Beck, I. L., McKeown, M. G., & Gromoll, E. W. (1988). *Issues that may affect social studies learning: Examples from four commercial programs.* Pittsburgh: University of Pittsburgh, Center for the Study of Learning. Learning Research and Development Center.

Beck, I. L., McKeown, M. G., & Gromoll, E. W. (1989). Learning from social studies texts. *Cognition and Instruction, 6,* 99–158.

Beck, I. L., McKeown, M. G., McCaslin, E. S., & Burkes, A. M. (1979). *Instructional dimensions that may affect reading comprehension: Examples from two commercial reading programs.* Pittsburgh: University of Pittsburgh, Learning Research and Development Center.

Beck, I. L., McKeown, M. G., Omanson, R. C., & Pople, M. T. (1984). Improving the comprehensibility of stories: The effects of revisions that improve coherence. *Reading Research Quarterly, 19,* 263–277.

Black, J. B., & Bern, H. (1981). Causal coherence and memory for events in narratives. *Journal of Verbal Learning and Verbal Behavior, 11,* 717–726.

Bradshaw, G. L., & Anderson, J. R. (1982). Elaborative encoding as an explanation of levels of processing. *Journal of Verbal Learning and Verbal Behavior, 21,* 165–174.

Bransford, J. D., & Johnson, M. K. (1972). Contextual prerequisites for understanding: Some investigations of comprehension and recall. *Journal of Verbal Learning and Verbal Behavior, 11,* 717–726.

Brown, A. L., Smiley, S. S., Day, J. D., Townsend, M. A., & Lawton, S. C. (1977). Intrusion of a thematic idea in children's recall of prose. *Child Development, 48,* 1454–1466.

Chi, M. T. H., Bassock, M., Lewis, M. W., Reimann, P., & Glaser, R. (1989). Self-explanations: How students study and use examples in learning to solve problems. *Cognitive Science, 13,* 145–182.

Chiesi, H. L., Spilich, G. J., & Voss, J. F. (1979). Acquisition of domain-related information in relation to high and low domain knowledge. *Journal of Verbal Learning and Verbal Behavior, 18,* 275–290.

Cirilo, R. K. (1981). Referential coherence and text structure in story comprehension. *Journal of Verbal Learning and Verbal Behavior, 20,* 358–367.

Crofts, M. (1986). Africa. *Social Education, 50*(5), 345–350.

Davison, A. (1984). Readability-appraising text difficulty. In R. C. Anderson, J. Osborn, & R. J. Tierney (Eds.), *Learning to read in American schools: Basal readers and content texts* (pp. 121–139). Hillsdale, NJ: Lawrence Erlbaum.

Dooling, D. J., & Lachman, R. (1971). Effects of comprehension on retention of prose. *Journal of Experimental Psychology, 88,* 216–222.

FitzGerald, F. (1979). *American revised: What history textbooks have taught our children about their country, and how and why those textbooks have changed in different decades.* New York: Vintage.

Fraenkel, J. R. (1987). Toward improving research in social studies education. *Theory and Research in Social Education, 15*(3), 203–222.

Franks, J. J., Vye, N. J., Auble, P. M., Mezynski, K. J., Perfetto, G. A., & Bransford, J. D. (1982). Learning from explicit versus implicit texts. *Journal of Experimental Psychology: General, 11,* 414–422.

Frederiksen, J. R. (1981). Understanding anaphora: Rules used by readers in assigning pronominal referents. *Discourse Processes, 4,* 323–348.

Gardner, H. (1987). *The mind's new science.* New York: Basic Books.

Garraty, J. A., & McCaughey, R. A. (1987). *The American nation.* New York: Harper & Row.

Graesser, A. C. (1981). *Prose comprehension beyond the word.* New York: Springer-Verlag.

Graves, M. F., & Cooke, C. L. (1980). Effects of previewing difficult short stories for high school students. *Research on Reading in Secondary Schools, 6,* 38–54.

Graves, M. F., & Palmer, R. J. (1981). Validating previewing as a method

of improving fifth- and sixth-grade students' comprehension of short stories. *Michigan Reading Journal, 15,* 1–3.

Hansen, J. (1981). The effects of inference training and practice on young children's reading comprehension. *Reading Research Quarterly, 16,* 391–417.

Harrison, M. L. (1934). The nature and development of concepts of time among young children. *Elementary School Journal, 34,* 507–514.

Haviland, S. C., & Clark, H. H. (1974). What's new? Acquiring new information as a process in comprehension. *Journal of Verbal Learning and Verbal Behavior, 13,* 512–521.

Holsti, O. R. (1969). *Content analysis for the social sciences and humanities.* Reading, MA: Addison-Wesley.

Johnson-Laird, P. N. (1983). *Mental models.* Cambridge, MA: Harvard University Press.

Jahoda, G. (1962). Children's concepts of time and history. *Educational Review, 11,* 89–90.

Just, M. A., & Carpenter, P. A. (1978). Inference processes during reading: Reflections from eye fixations. In J. W. Senders, D. F. Fisher, & R. A. Monty (Eds.), *Eye movements and higher psychological functions* (pp. 157–174). Hillsdale, NJ: Lawrence Erlbaum.

Just, M. A., & Carpenter, P. A. (1987). *The psychology of reading and language comprehension.* Boston: Allyn & Bacon.

Kieras, D. E. (1985). Thematic processes in the comprehension of technical prose. In B. K. Britton & J. B. Black (Eds.), *Understanding expository text: A theoretical and practical handbook for analyzing explanatory text* (pp. 89–107). Hillsdale, NJ: Lawrence Erlbaum.

Kintsch, W. (1986). Learning from text. *Cognition and Instruction, 3*(2), 87–108.

Kintsch, W., & Keenan, J. M. (1973). Reading rate as a function of the number of propositions in the base structure of sentences. *Cognitive Psychology, 5,* 257–274.

Kintsch, W., Kozminsky, E., Streby, W. J., McKoon, G., & Keenan, J. M. (1975). Comprehension and recall of text as a function of content variables. *Journal of Verbal Learning and Verbal Behavior, 14,* 196–214.

Kintsch, W., Mandel, T. S., & Kozminsky, E. (1977). Summarizing scrambled stories. *Memory and Cognition, 5,* 547–552.

Kintsch, W., & van Dijk, T. A. (1978). Toward a model of text comprehension and production. *Psychological Review, 85,* 363–394.

Klausmeier, H. J., Ghatala, E. S., & Frayer, D. A. (1974). *Conceptual learning and development.* New York: Academic Press.

Larkins, A. G., Hawkins, M., & Gilmore, A. (1987). Trivial and noninformative content of elementary social studies: A review of primary texts in four series. *Theory and Research in Social Education, 15,* 299–311.

Lello, J. (1980). The concept of time, the teaching of history, and school organization. *History Teacher, 13,* 341–350.

Lehnert, W. G. (1978). *The process of question answering.* Hillsdale, NJ: Lawrence Erlbaum.

Lehnert, W. G. (1982). Plot units and narrative summarization. *Cognitive Science, 4,* 293–331.

Lesgold, A. M., Roth, S. F., & Curtis, M. E. (1979). Foregrounding effects in discourse comprehension. *Journal of Verbal Learning and Verbal Behavior, 18,* 291–308.

Mandler, J. M. (1978). A code in the node: The use of a story schema in retrieval. *Discourse Processes, 1,* 14–35.

Marshall, N., & Glock, M. D. (1978–1979). Comprehension of connected discourse: A study into the relationship between the structure of text and information recalled. *Reading Research Quarterly, 16,* 10–56.

Merrill, M. D., & Tennyson, R. D. (1977). *Teaching concepts: An instructional design guide.* Englewood Cliffs, NJ: Educational Technology.

Metcalf, L. E. (1963). Research on teaching the social studies. In N. L. Gage (Ed.), *Handbook of research on teaching* (pp. 929–964). Chicago: Rand McNally.

Miller, S., & Rose, S. (1983). The Great Depression: A textbook case of problems with American history textbooks. *Theory and Research in Social Education, 11,* 25–39.

Minsky, M. (1975). A framework for representing knowledge. In P. H. Winston (Ed.), *The psychology of computer vision* (pp. 211–280). New York: McGraw-Hill.

Mohr, P., Glover, J. A., & Ronning, R. R. (1984). The effect of related and unrelated details on the recall of major ideas in prose. *Journal of Reading Behavior, 16,* 97–108.

Nelson, J. L., & Shaver, J. P. (1985). On research in social education. In W. Stanley (Ed.), *Review of research in social studies education: 1955–1975* (pp. 401–433). Washington, DC: National Council for the Social Studies.

Newmann, F. M. (1988a). Can depth replace coverage in the high school curriculum? *Phi Delta Kappan, 69,*(5), 345–348.

Newmann, F. M. (1988b). Another view of cultural literacy: Go for depth. *Social Education, 52*(6), 432–436.

Palmer, J. R. (1967). American history. In C. B. Cox & B. G. Massialas (Eds.), *Social Studies in the United States* (pp. 131–149) New York: Harcourt, Brace and World.

Pearson, P. D. (1974–1975). The effects of grammatical complexity on children's comprehension, recall, and conception of certain semantic relations. *Reading Research Quarterly, 10,* 155–192.

Pearson, P. D., Hansen, J., & Gordon, C. (1979). The effect of background knowledge on young children's comprehension of explicit and implicit information. *Journal of Reading Behavior, 11,* 201–209.

Perfetti, C. A. (1985). *Reading ability.* New York: Oxford University Press.

Perfetti, C. A. (in press). There are generalized abilities and one of them is reading. In L. Resnick (Ed.), *Knowing and learning: Issues for a cognitive science of instruction.* Hillsdale, NJ: Lawrence Erlbaum.

Rubin, A. (1985). How useful are readability formulas? In J. Osborn, P. T. Wilson, & R. C. Anderson (Eds.), *Reading education: Foundations for a literate America.* Boston: D. C. Heath.

Rumelhart, D. E. (1980). Schemata: The building blocks of cognition. In R. J. Spiro, B. C. Bruce, & W. F. Brewer (Eds.), *Theoretical issues in reading comprehension* (pp. 33–58). Hillsdale, NJ: Lawrence Erlbaum.

Rumelhart, D. E., & Ortony, A. (1977). The representation of knowledge in memory. In R. C. Anderson, R. J. Spiro, & W. E. Montague (Eds.), *Schooling and the acquisition of knowledge* (pp. 99–135). Hillsdale, NJ: Lawrence Erlbaum.

Schank, R. C. (1975). The structure of episodes in memory. In D. Bobrow & A. Collins (Eds.), *Representation and understanding: Studies in cognitive science* (pp. 237–272). New York: Academic Press.

Schank, R. C., & Abelson, R. P. (1977). *Scripts, plans, goals, and understanding: An inquiry into human knowledge structures.* Hillsdale, NJ: Lawrence Erlbaum.

Sewall, G. T. (1988). American history textbooks: Where do we go from here? *Phi Delta Kappan, 69*(8), 553–558.

Shaver, J. P., Davis, O. L., Jr. & Helburn, S. M. (1980). *What are the needs in precollege science, mathematics, and social science education? Views from the field.* Washington, DC: National Science Foundation.

Spilich, G. J., Vesonder, G. T., Chiesi, H. L., & Voss, J. F. (1979). Text processing of domain-related information for individuals with high and low domain knowledge. *Journal of Verbal Learning and Verbal Behavior, 18,* 275–290.

Stein, N. L., & Glenn, C. G. (1978). *The role of temporal organization in story comprehension* (Tech. Rep. No. 71). Urbana, IL: University of Illinois, Center for the Study of Reading.

Stein, B. S., Bransford, J. D., Franks, J. J., Vye, N. J., & Perfetto, G. A. (1982). Differences in judgments of learning difficulty. *Journal of Experimental Psychology: General, 111,* 406–415.

Stein, N. L., & Nezworski, T. (1978). The effects of organization and instructional set on story memory. *Discourse Processes, 1,* 177–193.

Stein, N. L., & Trabasso, T. (1982). What's in a story: An approach to comprehension and instruction. In R. Glaser (Ed.), *Advances in instructional psychology, Vol. 2* (213–267). Hillsdale, NJ: Lawrence Erlbaum.

Thorndyke, P. W., & Yekovich, F. R. (1980). A critique of schemata as a theory of human story memory. *Poetics, 9,* 23–49.

Trabasso, T., Secco, T., & van den Broek, P. (1984). Causal cohesion and story coherence. In H. Mandl, N. L. Stein, & T. Trabasso (Eds.), *Learning and comprehension of text* (pp. 83–111). Hillsdale, NJ: Lawrence Erlbaum.

Trabasso, T., & Sperry, L. L. (1985). Causal relatedness and importance of story events. *Journal of Memory and Language, 24,* 595–611.

Trabasso, T., & van den Broek, P. (1985). Causal thinking and the representation of narrative events. *Journal of Memory and Language, 24,* 612–630.

van Dijk, T. A., & Kintsch, W. (1983). *Strategies of discourse comprehension.* New York: Academic Press.

White, J. J. (1988). Searching for substantial knowledge in social studies texts. *Theory and Research in Social Education, 16*(2), 115–140.

Wiley, K. B. (1977). *The status of pre-college science, mathematics, and social science education: 1955–1975: Vol. 3. Social Science Education.* Boulder, CO: Social Science Consortium.

·42·

INTERACTIVE TECHNOLOGY IN SOCIAL STUDIES

Lee H. Ehman

INDIANA UNIVERSITY

Allen D. Glenn

UNIVERSITY OF WASHINGTON, SEATTLE

In this chapter, we review the research related to the use in and impact of interactive technology on social studies education and identify substantive and methodological research issues. The chapter is an effort to provide a foundation for the educator interested in conducting research related to interactive technologies and social studies. It is based in part on our earlier, initial review of the literature (Ehman & Glenn, 1987).

For purposes of this review, *interactive technologies* are computer-controlled programs and associated media such as electronic databases, videodiscs, and compact discs. They are teaching and learning tools that give teacher and learner control over the sequence in which material is accessed and presented. The media used in conjunction with computers differ from more traditional media, such as books, films, photographic slides, and overhead transparencies, in that the latter permit little or no teacher and learner control over access and presentation.

The results presented in this chapter incorporate a review of the general interactive technology literature with special emphasis on studies with social studies content. The effectiveness of interactive technology in American schools has generally been the central question for several national reports (Becker, 1986; Martinez & Mead, 1988; U.S. Congress, 1988). The findings that are social studies related are drawn from primary sources in educational journals, ERIC databases, and *Dissertation Abstracts International.*

APPLICATION OF INTERACTIVE TECHNOLOGIES IN SOCIAL STUDIES

Social studies teachers, as well as other teachers, indicate they want to use interactive technologies, especially computers, in their classrooms (Ross, 1988; Sabir, 1986; U.S. Congress, 1988; White, 1988). They perceive computers as having a significant impact on student enthusiasm, as providing additional learning opportunities for gifted students, and as a means for helping handicapped or learning disabled students (Becker, 1986). They also suggest that using computers leads to personal growth. Some, however, also indicate they are responding to external pressures when suggesting they want to use computers in the classroom (U.S. Congress, 1988, p. 89).

Classroom applications of computers differ between elementary and secondary school. In a series of surveys, Becker (1986) found that most elementary school teachers used the computer for enrichment of traditional classroom activities. At the secondary level, most teachers responded that they used the computer for instructional purposes (Becker, 1986, Issue 2, p. 2).

Computer applications were used in social studies by few teachers in the Becker surveys. He found only 1% of the total use in Grades K–3 was in social studies; 4% at Grades 4 through 8; and 1% at Grades 9 through 12. In social studies, computer use was limited to "simple simulation games in middle school" (Becker, 1986, Issue 3, p. 8).

Becker's findings about the lack of use by social studies teachers are supported by the results from surveys by White (1986a, 1988), Ross (1988), Sabir (1986), Robbat (1984/1985), and Ashley (1983). White (1986a) for example, after two surveys of social studies teachers, concluded that relatively few social studies teachers understood or used computers, with experienced teachers and secondary school teachers least likely to use computers. In a later stratified random sample of 1,200 National Council for the Social Studies members, White (1988) found that 29% of the secondary teachers responded that they used

Reviewers were Alfred S. Forsyth, Jr., Weber State College; Charles S. White, George Mason University.

the computer in the classroom. Sabir's data indicated a similar use pattern. In his survey of 53 history teachers and department chairs in Oregon and Massachusetts, Robbat found that although 50% had used the computer outside of the classroom, only one had used it as part of an instructional sequence in history: a drill and practice program. Ashley's study of United Kingdom teachers yielded similar results.

Similar findings have come from statewide surveys of teacher use of computers in social studies. Percentages of repeated use have ranged from around 2.5% in Idaho, Indiana, and Texas (Green, 1983; Tucker, 1982; Robbat, 1984/1985); through 17% in Louisiana (Louisiana State Department of Education, 1985), to 22% in Massachusetts (Robbat, 1984/1985).

The reasons most often given by social studies teachers for not using the computer in the classroom include lack of knowledge about computers and computer software, limited access to computers, lack of expectations for use in social studies by school leaders, and lack of adequate software (Robbat, 1984/1985; Ross, 1988).

The National Assessment survey of student experiences with technology (Martinez & Mead, 1988) supported the conclusions from teacher surveys. When students in grades 3, 7, and 11 were asked, "Have you used a computer in social studies?" only about 12% of the sample of 3rd graders, 10% of the 7th graders, and 5% of the 11th graders indicated they had (p. 36). When asked how often they used computers in subject areas, 7th and 11th graders did not mention social studies.

Only in White's survey (1988) of a sample of NCSS members were social studies educators asked about other interactive technologies such as interactive videodisc and videoconferencing. The respondents indicated lack of knowledge and need for more training before such technologies could be used in their classrooms (p. 13). Training, according to White, appears to be a critical area.

Social Studies Teachers' Preparation

No published data are available on the extent of preparation of social studies teachers to use technology. Conclusions about preparation must be inferred from the general literature about preservice and in-service teacher preparation. For example, Glenn and Carrier (1987) reviewed the findings from surveys of teacher-training programs and school districts and found that the majority of the teachers in those studies had received less than 10 hours of instruction on how to use the computer. Most of the instruction had been focused on how to operate the computer and run various software packages.

In a survey of preservice teacher education programs by the U.S. Department of Education (1986), it was found that 88% of all schools of education offered some form of technology training. The most commonly reported course was an introductory one in which students were taught the basics of computer use. Additional experience may come during the social studies methods course and during student teaching. However, 42% of the education faculty and 71% of the preservice students surveyed by the American Association of Colleges for Teacher Edu-

cation (1987) thought education students were not ready to teach with computers.

Social studies teachers may receive additional technology training from the school district or state. According to the results of an *Electronic Learning* survey (1987), $25 million was being spent annually on teacher technology training in 25 states. In its survey, the Office of Technology Assessment (U.S. Congress, 1988, p. 209) found that 75% of the states reported sponsoring technology conferences and 50% reported supporting teacher-training through centers and regional organizations.

Specific inservice training in social studies tends to come after other content area needs have been met. Becker's surveys found mathematics, computer science, science, English, and business education to have priority over social studies (1986, Issue 2, p. 8). In the National Association of Educational Progress study, Martinez and Mead (1988, p. 65) found that computer coordinators listed social studies and history at the bottom of subject areas taught with the aid of computers. A recent survey by Ross (1988) established that social studies teachers identify lack of experience and training as a barrier to the integration of computers in social studies.

What can we conclude about the preparation of social studies teachers to use interactive technologies? First, social studies teachers who have graduated since the early 1980s have probably received introductory-level training on how to use the computer. Depending on the institution, the individual may also have received some explicit training on social studies applications. Those individuals who have been in the classroom for an extended period are less likely to have had training. Elementary teachers may have had more training than secondary teachers because of attendance at workshops that focus on all the subject matter taught in the elementary school. Both elementary and secondary social studies teachers believe they need additional training if they are to use interactive technologies effectively in the classroom. These conclusions, however, must be considered tentative because the data for social studies teachers are limited.

Impact on the Social Studies Teacher's Role

Advocates of the use of interactive technologies suggest that these new technologies will change the role of the teacher. The truth, however, is that researchers have little knowledge about the impact of technology on the teacher's role. Few researchers have examined the influence of interactive technologies on how the teacher prepares for, delivers, and evaluates instruction. And no reports of research to examine whether the teacher's work is made easier or harder, or whether the teacher's sense of professionalism and satisfaction is increased or decreased, are available. Our conclusions are based on a series of case studies and three statistical studies.

Wiske and Zodhiates (1988) developed a series of case studies about the impact on teacher role of using computers in the classroom. On the basis of telephone interviews, the researchers concluded that interactive technologies helped the teachers act as facilitators and enabled them to observe more of the learning process. Teachers also reported that students assumed more responsibility for their own work, worked at their own speeds, and cooperated more with each other.

Three studies provided additional insights into the impact of technology on teacher role. Pollak and Breault (1985) examined a study-guide program for social studies teachers in which lesson plans and supporting newspaper materials on contemporary issues were available on an on-line computer system. Teachers had access to the lessons on a 24-hour basis. They could review the lessons on the monitor and then download to their own computer system those lessons that they wanted to use in class. Based on a tally of the number of times lessons were downloaded and a survey of the teachers, the authors found teachers quite willing to access the lesson plans and then to adapt them to their own particular teaching situations. The authors concluded that, when teachers have an accessible computer database, they are quite willing to adapt the materials to their own needs. Unfortunately, no data were collected by the investigators concerning whether the teachers altered their role when using the materials in class.

A study by Germundsen and Glenn (1984) on the difference between using a computer gradebook system and a pencil-and-paper grade-keeping method provided additional insights into the impact of technology on teachers' roles. Studying six junior high school teachers and their students, the researchers found that four of the six teachers thought their students tried harder in class because of the weekly posting of computer-generated grade reports. All six teachers received positive feedback from parents on the computer-generated grade reports they sent home. Parents overwhelmingly liked the reports, and about 90% of the students reported that the system helped them keep track of their work and know their grades in the class.

Teachers reported that entering grades in the computer gradebook took as much or more time than the paper-and-pencil system. They also indicated that they received more telephone calls from parents seeking assistance with their children's work as a result of the computer-generated reports. Although increased parent interest was beneficial, teachers, who did not have easy access to a telephone and who had to make calls after school, found a lot of time was used returning parents' calls. Overall, however, the authors concluded that the computer grade-book system did increase the productivity of the teacher and lead to more positive attitudes by students and parents.

Conclusions from the 1988 report from the Office of Technology Assessment (U.S. Congress, 1988, pp. 96–97), based on the work of Wiske and Zodhiates and other reports, suggest that using interactive technologies affects the manner in which teachers manage their classrooms. Initially the use of interactive technologies makes teaching more difficult because of classroom management issues. Scheduling, additional planning of new materials, and student behavior all take more time and thought. As one teacher noted to an Office of Technologies Assessment interviewer, "Computers give teachers a better opportunity to individualize, but that doesn't mean it's easy. Individualization is difficult to manage" (p. 97). Time appears to be one of the key variables: time to learn new skills, time to develop new materials, and time to plan different instructional strategies.

There are so few studies that bear on the question of the impact of interactive technologies on the social studies teacher's role that it would be presumptuous to conclude that we understand this area. More naturalistic studies utilizing in-depth classroom observations, open-ended interviews with teachers and students, and survey and test data are needed.

INTERACTIVE TECHNOLOGIES AND THE INSTRUCTIONAL PROCESS

The studies reviewed previously suggest that the introduction of interactive technologies affects the classroom environment. Teachers act differently and students are asked to act differently and do different things. Additional research related to social studies provides insights into the impact of interactive technologies on the instructional process.

Several researchers examined the social consequences of using the computer in a social studies classroom. Diem (1987) studied upper elementary classrooms in four schools in Texas. Each classroom was observed weekly over a 9-month period. Diem, like Becker (1986), concluded that teachers used technology as part of their positive reward structure. Students who completed their work used the computer for supplementary learning experiences or learning games.

Diem also found that, while using computers in groups, students took on differentiated roles such as experts, experimenters, and observers. Males tended to dominate the groups, and teachers made little or no effort to change the pattern. These differences between males and females were also found by Becker (1986, Issue 2, pp. 9–11); by Roblyer, Castine, and King (1988, p. 40); by Bracey (1988, p. 36); by Talaiver (1987); and by Sanders (1988). These differences raise implications for social studies teachers interested in equity issues.

Another classroom procedure observed by Diem was the grouping of students according to their prior computer knowledge. Students with more experience and knowledge were often grouped together, and students with less experience and knowledge were grouped together. Such grouping patterns, if widespread, would contribute to widening the gap between the two groups. Girls, students with special learning needs, and minority students often fall into the less experienced group, thus contributing to equity problems.

Grouping patterns in which students are segregated by experience or knowledge are contrary to the research findings of Johnson, Johnson, and Stanne (1985), who studied cooperative grouping and computer use. Using a modification of Tom Snyder Production's *Geography Search* simulation, they found that students in cooperative groups outperformed individualistic and competitive students on factual recognition, application, and problem solving. The cooperative groups were also more task oriented, goal centered, and cooperative.

Weigand (1985) examined teacher and student behavior when computers were used for instruction. In his descriptive study of 12 secondary school geography classrooms, Weigand videotaped teachers and students using six different tutorial programs ranging from demography and economics to consumer behavior and transportation connectivity. Computers were used in three different instructional settings: whole-class instruction using a large TV monitor; a competitive group situation designed to increase student motivation to learn; and a "cafeteria instructional approach," in which a variety of tasks including one using a computer, occurred simultaneously.

Weigand found that teachers kept a very high level of control and directiveness during most computer activities. They acted as gatekeepers, controlled the computers, and determined student access and use. Students were not active learners responsible for their own learning but rather, were "button pushers." Interactive possibilities during which students could explore the computer programs were severely limited.

Controlling behavior on the part of the teacher should not be surprising. Teachers tend to control student behavior during instructional activities and see themselves as the managers of instruction and student behavior. When trying a new instructional technique, teachers often attempt to maintain strict control of the instructional activities and student behavior so that "things don't get out-of-hand." If such teacher behaviors are common, then it would be normal for teachers to want to be in control when using computers as part of instruction. Unfortunately, there are so few studies in teacher management during computer instruction that generalization is impossible.

Impact of Interactive Technologies on Students

Possibly the most prevalent question about interactive technologies is, "Do they make a difference in student learning?" Educators, parents, and citizens want to know if the commitment to technology, especially the computer, is paying off in improved student learning. To answer that question the research literature can be reviewed from two perspectives: computers as teachers' assistants and as students' learning tools. As teachers' assistants, computers can be used to promote students' knowledge and skills through the use of drill and practice software, tutorial programs, and simulations. As students' learning tools, computers can be used to foster critical thinking and problem-solving skills through student use of databases, spread sheets, and electronic networks to access remote databases for analysis.

Computers As Teachers' Assistants. Drill and practice programs dominate the social studies computer software market; however, little research has been done to examine their effects on student learning and attitudes. The research that has been reported points to modest impacts. Kulik, Bangert, and Williams (1983), Bangert-Drowns, Kulik, and Kulik (1985), and Niemiec and Walberg (1985, 1987) all found drill and tutorial programs to have a small but positive impact on achievement and on attitudes toward the subject matter and toward using the computer. They also found that instructional uses of computer programs reduced the amount of time needed to learn materials. For example, Niemiec and Walberg reported a standardized mean difference of .42 for elementary school students involved in computer-assisted instruction, compared to students in a noncomputer instructional program. Assuming a normal distribution, on the average 66% of the students in the computer-

assisted course would outperform the average student in the noncomputer course. They also found a higher SMD for drill and practice programs than for tutorials, with the highest mean SMD for primary students, boys, and special education students. For a latter group, the mean SMD was 1.07 for mentally retarded students, 1.43 for students with visual impairment, and .83 for emotionally disturbed students.

None of the studies reviewed by Kulik et al., Bangert-Drowns et al., and Niemiec and Walberg were research on social studies. But the general conclusions of these researchers provide a basis for the review of the social studies research in the remainder of this section.

The findings from several studies support the claim that drill and practice computer applications and tutorials can have an impact on student outcomes in social studies. Bradley (1983/1984), Marsh (1984/1985, 1986), and Way (1984) found higher mean achievement scores on social studies tests as a result of use of drill and practice and tutorial programs. Bellows (1987) found statistically significant pre- and posttest gains for second graders who used a drill program to reinforce map skills. He also found that students in triads of mixed ability made statistically significantly greater mean achievement gains than did those in homogeneous groups. On the average, females did as well on the tests as did males. Forsyth (Forsyth, 1986a, 1986b; Forsyth & Lancy, 1987) found that a computer program with an adventure game format facilitated recall and retention of geographic information.

Feldhausen (1985/1986), Beltran and deJuarez (1982), and Pedersen (1977/1978) also reported positive findings for computer-assisted instruction. Feldhausen's experimental study involved the use of a computer software program to assist students in the review of materials. He found that the students' mean scores were not statistically different from those of students who used a study guide. The students did report that they liked using the computer and that it helped them learn the material, even though their scores were no better on the average than those of students who had used the study guide.

Beltran and deJuarez (1982) also found positive attitudes among students, parents, and teachers in their study involving bilingual students' study of concepts. Through use of a computer-assisted program to reinforce social studies concepts taught in the seventh and eighth grades, 26 lessons were presented to students in both English and Spanish. Students were tested in groups of two to four during the school year. No statistically significant mean differences were found in general language achievement; however, a 6-month mean increase in vocabulary occurred.

Pedersen (1977/1978) studied Virginia students who were taught for 10 weeks with regular tests from a computer test file. Students using the computerized tests learned more specific knowledge but not more general knowledge.

The results from two studies of interactive computer and video program use suggested the combination of the two technologies can lead to student knowledge gains. Glenn, Kozen, and Pollak (1984) studied the use of an interactive computer and videodisc economics tutorial. They found statistically significant mean gains on knowledge of economic principles. Responding to a survey, students rated the computer–videodisc method of studying economics as interesting and indicated that the technologies were easy to use. Unfortunately, the study was carried out with only 44 students, mostly in the 12th grade, with no comparison group.

Dalton and Hannafin (1987) used a computer-assisted program and a 30-minute videotape on "opportunity costs of buying on credit" in a three-group experiment, to study the effects of knowledge-based, versus contextually based, interactive video strategies on student recall and application-level learning. In the knowledge strategy lesson, the concepts were taught through definitions, examples, and application questions. In the context strategy lesson, concept applications were illustrated without definitions and examples. In both lessons, there were provisions for reteaching and retesting. In the control-group lessons, the videotape was presented in linear fashion, with no interactive tutoring or questions. For recall, there was not a statistically significant difference between the experimental group means, although both were statistically significantly higher than the control group mean. The application-level mean of the context lesson group was significantly higher than those of the knowledge lesson and control groups. The researchers concluded that both types of lessons were effective for teaching low-level factual knowledge using computer-based interactive video but that the knowledge-based strategy was more effective in promoting higher level understanding.

In several studies, the use of computer simulations in the social studies classroom has been examined. Bolton and Mosow (1981) and Weible and McMahon (1983), for example, found that students felt positive about using computer simulations. Hetzner (1972) and Roberts (1976) found that computer-assisted simulations promoted interest, attention to achieving goals, and an enhanced sense of personal control. Talaiver (1987) studied the effects of student work-group size on the outcomes of computer-based simulations. She found no difference in the mean achievement or attitude scores of students working alone, in pairs, or in groups of three on an economic development simulation at the ninth-grade level.

In an impressionistic case study involving a sixth-grade classroom in Massachusetts, Vincent (1986) examined the impact of a simulation entitled "Foreign Policy: The Burden of World Power" from *Decisions, Decisions* by Tom Snyder Productions. Students reported high motivation for studying the topic and increased intellectual curiosity. Vincent also reported, on the basis of informal observations, more persistent questioning and data-seeking behaviors on the part of the students. The findings must be tempered because students not only had prior experience using LOGO, BASIC, and other computer-assisted programs but also had used a similar Tom Snyder simulation entitled "The Other Side." The questioning and data-seeking behaviors reported by Vincent as a result of using the simulation may have been influenced by prior practice.

A few social studies teachers have involved students in the creation of computer-based simulations. Although it is time consuming, some teachers believe that, through the development process, the student gains a better understanding of the theoretical model of the simulation and the interaction among the variables comprising the model. Roessler (1987) reported on his efforts to involve middle school students in the develop-

ment of a computer simulation on the Great Depression. Relying on informal evaluation techniques, he found that students showed a very positive reaction to the development process, even though they thought it to be quite difficult, complained that some students didn't do their jobs, and felt at times the process was boring. Roessler concluded that the motivational impact alone makes this type of learning worth the time and effort.

The general picture that emerges from the review of the research is that computer simulations stimulate affective outcomes such as interest, enjoyment, sense of control, and perseverance. Although the studies are often impressionistic, the results suggest that computer simulations can be important tools for the social studies teacher.

Computers As Student Tools. Proponents of increased use of computers in social studies contend that the power of interactive technologies lies in their use by students to increase their higher level thinking and problem-solving skills. The most frequently mentioned software applications are databases and data analysis tools (Budin, Kendall, & Lengel, 1986; Ehman & Glenn, 1987; Hodges, 1985; Hunter, 1983).

In social studies education, several researchers have studied the use of computer databases. White (1985/1986b, 1987), using an experimental design, studied the impact on 11th-grade students' learning of a computerized database during a 2-week unit in U.S. history. He found that students using computers to retrieve data had a statistically significant higher mean on a test of information-processing skills than did students using a non-computer data-retrieval system. Elder (1988), however, found no mean differences in information-processing skills or geography knowledge between ninth-grade students using an electronic database on world geography and those using the same data in printed form. She used the same information-processing skills test as White, and the length of instruction was 3 weeks, rather than 2.

Rawitsch (1987) compared a computer database and a pencil-and-paper method of analyzing data in a study involving junior high school students in American history courses. He found that students using the computer database took more time to reach their conclusions, but their answers to questions about the data were more accurate than those of students who used the pencil-and-paper methods. Rawitsch also found that students classified as more structured in their learning styles were more efficient, as measured by time using the database to accuracy of response, than students who were classified as more exploratory learners. He, as have most other researchers, found that students preferred using the computer.

In a similar investigation, Rawitsch, Bart, and Earle (1988) found that seventh-grade student use of an *Appleworks* database on the Civil War made no impact on proportional reasoning or hypothetical-deductive reasoning, when compared to student use of the Oregon Trail simulation.

Hawkins and Sheingold (1986) and Cornelius (1985/1986) also studied the use of computer databases. Their findings were less positive. Hawkins and Sheingold found that social studies students had difficulty integrating the use of computer databases into the instructional strategy for developing topic-oriented research projects. The researchers thought that, until databases were significantly larger, they would be difficult for teachers to use in the classroom (p. 47).

Cornelius (1985/1986) examined three different methods of using a database. Thirty-six students in a world cultures class in a Pennsylvania high school were divided into three groups whose task was to find the answers to a series of questions. One group used key words to access a computer database; a second used a linear computer text-searching process; and a third searched the printout from the database. The treatment lasted for only one class period. A retention test given 5 days later showed all groups to have increased their knowledge from a pretest; however, no statistically significant differences were evident across groups in either mean knowledge or overall attitude scores.

Exploration of the effect of instruction using computer databases on information-using and question-asking skills was the purpose of two British studies. Underwood (1985) found that students "may acquire sophisticated and valuable skills" (p. 27). During a 3-week experiment, upper elementary students were taught a classification and retrieval system for entering data in one database and then using another computer program to add information or investigate problems whose answers involved analyzing the database. Based on his observations and analysis of student questions, Underwood concluded that students learned how to ask more precise questions; however, the experience did not lead to more recall of factual information.

The second British study (Ennals, 1985) involved 19th-century trade directories, census records, and other historical data from a school's village. Secondary school students used computers to access and view the data on monitors and printed databases. Relying on informal impressions, the researchers suggested that printed records were good for answering questions about small data sets, but, if students wanted to ask questions that involved more data and several variables, computer databases were better tools.

A pilot study conducted by the Harvard University Educational Technology Center was focused on the effectiveness of an integrated computer instructional package. The researchers used the center's *Irish Immigrant* curriculum package, which included a computer database, to gather data about the Irish; a spread sheet to organize the data; and a word-processing system to record observations and conclusions. Survey data from the students indicated that they liked using such tools. Data from the teachers suggested that a curriculum package utilizing various computer applications could be integrated into a curriculum (Mendrinos & Morrison, 1986; Morrison & Walters, 1986a, 1986b).

Traberman (1983, 1984) had eighth-grade students create their own databases, analysis and presentation programs, using the APL programming language. Although he did not conduct a formal study, Traberman asserted that the students learned facts, as well as concepts, and showed deeper understanding of the concepts and generalizations because they actually manipulated the raw data and developed the presentations.

Rothman (1982) devised a computer program to allow high school students to study the process of political revolution. Working in cooperative groups, students gathered data and en-

tered their findings into the computer program. Rothman observed that students were more motivated, persisted in their study, and cooperated more than they had in the past. Johnson et al. (1985) found similar results 5 years later, in their research involving cooperative groups.

The database studies conducted during the early 1980s provided some insights into their potential for the social studies classroom. As databases become more readily available on the market and teachers begin to use them in their classrooms, opportunities for further study will increase.

RESEARCH ISSUES IN SOCIAL STUDIES AND INTERACTIVE TECHNOLOGIES

Several methodological problems and substantive research issues are suggested by common features of the studies reviewed.

Methodological Problems

The majority of the studies had one or more of the following research design flaws.

Description of the Treatment. In far too many cases the treatment was not clearly defined or described. For example, in Rogers and de Leeuw's study (1986), LOGO was used to teach map concepts and skills over 2 years, and, in another study, students were taught to use a binary classification system to enter data into a computer program (Underwood, 1985). What exactly occurred during either of these treatments is unclear. Better definition and description of treatments are needed if others are to begin to understand the analysis and results. Social studies researchers would be well advised to examine the work of Johnson et al. (1985), Elder (1988), and White (1985a, 1985/1986b, 1987) for examples of treatment definitions and descriptions.

Duration of the Treatment. Teaching students new skills and content requires substantial time and effort. Experiments with one-shot treatments of one or a few hours most often do not lead to practically or statistically significant impacts on student learning. For example, Cornelius (1985/1986) studied three different methods of using a database. The length of the treatment was one hour. Talaiver (1987) had students use two simulations, one for an average of 28 minutes, the other for an average of 18 minutes. Even in better designed studies, such as Johnson, et al.'s (1985), the treatment duration has been only several class periods.

Retention and Transfer Studies. Do students retain the knowledge learned while using interactive technologies? Do problem-solving skills and data analysis skills transfer to other learning situations? Few of the researchers sought to retest students as much as a month later to determine whether they had retained or could transfer their skills to a new setting. Although Rawitsch (1987) and Cornelius (1985/1986) both sought to measure transfer and retention of knowledge, they used very short delays. Rawitsch measured students' ability to analyze a new database 5 days after the original instruction; Cornelius also retested knowledge after 5 days.

Other Design Problems. Sample size, assessment of outcome variables, and subject selection are design problems common to most of the studies reviewed in the chapter. Sample sizes are small; evidence of the reliability and validity of scores from assessment instruments was lacking; subjects were not randomly selected, and designs were often pre-experimental. Glenn, Kozen, and Pollak (1984), for example, included neither a comparison group nor a pre- and posttest assessment of student learning.

More complete reporting of statistical result is needed. Few researchers reported effect sizes for experimental or correlational studies. Effect sizes allow some inferences about the practical significance of results, facilitate comparisons of studies, and are useful in estimating cost-effectiveness ratios. Unfortunately, some authors omitted sufficient information, such as means and standard deviations, to permit others to calculate effect sizes.

Substantive Research Questions Needing Attention

Improved research designs are important if the field is to move forward; however, better designs with the wrong questions will not help. Before outlining several needed areas of research, it is important to note points made about media research generally. Clark (1983) and Clark and Salomon (1983) have pointed out that the common media studies, comparing one medium with another, have been, and will continue to be, fruitless. They assert that instructional variables, content, and novelty factors often confound the results from such comparison research. According to their analysis, there has been a shift in media research toward studies *on* media, aiming at the effects of distinguishable attributes of particular media in combination with learner traits and varying contextual factors. They also traced the impact of cognitive-theory development upon research in this field.

Several categories of research questions could serve to focus and move forward research on interactive technology as applied to social education.

Questions Linking Teacher Effectiveness and Technology Research. Findings from research on process–product relations, teacher and student thought processes, and classroom ecology have built up since the late 1960s. Parallel to the growing research base in pedagogy is that in instructional technology. Researchers in the two fields of inquiry should combine this knowledge.

Process–product classroom researchers have found that high teacher structure, effective classroom management, and task-oriented, business-like behavior are positively related to some types of student learning. It is not surprising, therefore, that Diem (1987) found that teachers maintained tight control during computer instructional activities, even though such con-

trol might negatively affect the learning experience. Teachers who had been taught techniques of effective instruction transferred what they had learned to computer lessons. Unfortunately, few technology researchers have examined the relationship between common pedagogical skills and their applications to instructional uses of technology.

A more positive example of linking important concepts from effective instruction and technology research is the work of Johnson et al. (1985). In their studies of cooperation in the classroom, they have applied basic concepts from social psychology and extended those findings to understanding the effects of different grouping patterns when technology is used. This study provides the best empirical support for cooperative groups. The link between pedagogy and technology use is direct and extends knowledge about effective ways to organize students for a computer learning experience.

Research from the study of student thought processes and the social environment of the classroom can also contribute to a better understanding of the impact of technology on teachers and students. For example, work by Doyle (1983) related to reducing complexity during teaching, which can lead to better student achievement, can be applied directly to the manner in which a teacher structures instruction using databases and simulations. Also, the effects of student learning styles should be examined more carefully. The study by Rawitsch (1987) provided insight into how students with particular orientations approached databases. And research on the social environment related to classroom rules could also be applied to effective technology instruction.

Technology and Positive Student Outcomes. The impact of technology on higher order thinking skills of students has not been adequately researched. Data from the Higher Order Thinking Skills (HOTS) Program developed at the University of Arizona suggest that such outcomes can be attained (U.S. Congress, 1988, p. 47). No systematic studies, however, have been conducted on social studies content. In addition to higher thinking skills, social studies researchers need to explore the impact of varied images, manipulated interactively by the learner during instruction, on concept acquisition and skills application. Also, how do different media interacting in an integrated system impact on student learning?

Cognitive outcomes are important, but they should be examined together with affective outcomes. Many of the researchers reviewed here suggested that students continue after the novelty of computer use has faded. Do differences continue between the attitudes of females and males? Does learning with the computer help students feel more prepared to live and work in a technological society? What impact do telecommunications have on students' understanding of and attitudes toward a global society?

Technology Applications and Instruction and Cost-effectiveness. The question raised here requires comparison of instruction using technology with alternatives without technology, while looking at student outcomes in combination with such practical factors as time required for learning, effort devoted by teachers in preparation and implementation of instruction, and cost. For cost-effectiveness studies, the model of Levin (1984) should be followed. He found that peer and adult tutoring were more cost effective than computer-assisted instruction for elementary students. Reductions in class size and increases in instructional time were less cost effective than the use of computers. Although it did not involve social studies learning, this type of research is critical, given the cost of technology in schools and the ever-present competition for education resources such as money and teachers' time. Educational researchers have not usually framed such questions, but, without evidence of cost-effectiveness, it is unlikely that major additional investments will be made in education technology to support teaching and learning.

Integration of Technology into the Social Studies Curriculum. Indicators of teacher use and inservice training suggest that social studies teachers are unlikely to use interactive technology without increased incentives and decreased inhibitors (Ross, 1988). Ross summarized three major inhibitors to integration. *First,* teachers do not have easy access to computers in their classrooms and schools; when computers are owned by the schools, scheduling their use is difficult. *Second,* perceived inappropriateness of software deters many teachers from adopting it as part of the curriculum. *Third,* lack of training and experience is a barrier. Nevertheless, Ross underscored teachers' desire to increase their use of computers in the social studies classroom.

The challenge to computer educators is to overcome the inhibitors and use the teachers' generally positive attitude to effect change. However, computer coordinators report that they spend little time preparing social studies teachers. And the availability of social studies software usually trails behind that for mathematics, science, and general problem-solving. More knowledge is needed about incentives and factors that inhibit social studies teachers from using computers and related technologies.

A CONCLUDING NOTE

The research reviewed in this chapter falls into two phases. Earlier studies were aimed mostly at comparing computer-assisted instruction with other modes to determine relative effectiveness. In more recent investigations, the tendency is to examine student outcomes after use of computer-based tools such as databases. This trend is a healthy one, because it signals movement away from oversimplified research questions.

In the earlier phase, tutorials and drill and practice programs seemed to have a positive impact on student learning and attitude outcomes. Computer simulations in social studies classes stimulate affective outcomes, but there is scant evidence about their influence on cognitive growth. In a sense, however, the questions addressed in these studies do not enable us to improve teaching and learning unless the policy outcome is mass equipping of social studies classrooms with computers and software. Educationally and practically, this by itself is a very dubious solution to the teaching and learning problems we face.

During the second, more recent, phase, researchers addressed more important questions that could lead to instructional improvement. By studying the use of computer-based tools such as databases, and asking about how to best employ them in situations in which they have a comparative advantage over other media such as texts or films, researchers have begun to follow the trend, pointed out by Clark (1983) and Clark and Salomon (1983), toward research *on* media, rather than comparisons *of* media.

There is low use of interactive technology in social studies classrooms and a very thin knowledge base from research about this use. However, we should not lose sight of the fact that new tools such as databases are now available and that others are being invented, such as hypermedia. These tools could be used by teachers and students to avoid unnecessary effort and to gain access to information and to make meaning of it in ways not possible without interactive technology. It is the task of social studies educators—teachers, supervisors, researchers, teacher trainers—to understand these new possibilities and devise ways to implement them.

References

American Association of Colleges for Teacher Education. (1987). Teaching teachers: Facts and figures. Washington, DC: Author.

Ashley, K. (1983, June). *The impact of the micro on social studies curricula or computer assisted learning (CAL) in economics, history, and geography curricula in England, Wales, and Northern Ireland.* Paper presented at the annual conference of the Social Science Education Consortium, Athens, GA. (ERIC Document Reproduction Service No. ED 231 747)

Bangert-Drowns, R. W., Kulik, J. A., & Kulik, C. C. (1985). Effectiveness of computer-based education in secondary schools. *Journal of Computer-Based Instruction, 12,* 59–68.

Becker, H. J. (1986). *Instructional use of school computers: Reports from the 1985 national survey.* Issues 1–3. Baltimore: Johns Hopkins University.

Bellows, B. P. (1987, April). *What makes a team? The composition of small groups for C.A.I.* Paper presented at the meeting of the American Educational Research Association, Washington, DC. (ERIC Document Reproduction Service No. ED 280 616)

Beltran, M. B., & deJuarez, C. L. (1982). *Computer-assisted Spanish English transition sequence: A developmental research approach for the implementation of educational software* (Research Rep. No. 143). Dallas: Dallas Independent School District. (ERIC Document Reproduction Service No. ED 222 189)

Bolton, H., & Mosow, D. K. (1981). Microcomputers in the classroom: A foot in the door. *Educational Computer, 1,* 34–36.

Bracey, G. W. (1988). The impact of computers. *Phi Delta Kappan, 70,* 70.

Bradley, T. M. (1984). Computer instruction in teaching American history in high school. (Doctoral dissertation, Illinois State University, 1983). *Dissertation Abstracts International, 44,* 2663A.

Budin, H. R., Kendall, D., & Lengel, J. (1986). *Using computers in the social studies.* New York: Teachers College Press.

Clark, R. E. (1983). Reconsidering research on learning from media. *Review of Educational Research, 53,* 445–459.

Clark, R. E., & Salomon, G. (1983). Media in teaching. In M. C. Wittrock (Ed.), *Handbook of Research on Teaching* (3rd ed., pp. 464–478). New York: Macmillan.

Cornelius, C. S. (1986). A comparison of computer-based data base instruction and retrieval strategies with traditional instruction. (Doctoral dissertation, Pennsylvania State University, 1985). *Dissertation Abstracts International, 47,* 68A.

Dalton, D. W., & Hannafin, M. J. (1987). The effects of knowledge-based versus context-based design strategies on information and application learning from interactive video. *Journal of Computer-Based Instruction, 14,* 138–141.

Diem, R. A. (1987). Computers in a school environment: Preliminary report of the social consequences. *Theory and Research in Social Education, 14,* 163–170.

Doyle, W. (1983). Academic work. *Review of Educational Research, 53,* 159–99.

Ehman, L. H., & Glenn, A. D. (1987). *Computer-based education in the social studies.* Bloomington, IN: ERIC Clearinghouse for Social Studies/Social Science Education. (ERIC Document Reproduction Service No. ED 284 825)

Elder, C. L. (1988). *Development of a social studies database with accompanying curriculum materials to enhance information-processing skills and geographic knowledge.* Unpublished doctoral dissertation, George Mason University, Fairfax, VA.

Electronic Learning. (1987). A report on EL's seventh annual survey of the states, 7, 39.

Ennals, R. (1985). Micro-PROLOG and classroom historical research. In I. Reid & J. Rushton (Eds.), *Teachers, computers, and the class room* (pp. 130–137). Manchester, England: Manchester University Press.

Feldhausen, M. W. (1986). The effects of computer review assistance modules (CRAM) on student achievement in United States history. (Doctoral dissertation, University of Nebraska–Lincoln, 1985). *Dissertation Abstracts International, 47,* 68A.

Forsyth, A. S., Jr. (1986a, April). *Applications of microcomputer research-type adventure games in research on spatial orientation, place location, and memory for places.* Paper presented at the meeting of the American Educational Research Association, San Francisco. (ERIC Document Reproduction Service No. ED 273 264)

Forsyth, A. S., Jr. (1986b). A computer adventure game and place location learning: Effects of map type and player gender (Doctoral dissertation, Utah State University, 1986). *Dissertation Abstracts International, 47,* 2132A.

Forsyth, A. S., Jr., & Lancy, D. F. (1987). Simulated travel and place location learning in a computer adventure game. *Journal of Educational Computing Research, 3,* 377–392.

Germundsen, R., & Glenn, A. D. (1984). Computer guidebooks: Implications for teachers. *Computing Teacher, 12,* 13–15.

Glenn, A. D. & Carrier, C. A. (1987). *A review of the status of technology training for teachers* (Final report for the Office of Technology Assessment, Contract No. H3-4590-0) Springfield, VA: U.S. Department of Commerce, National Technical Information Service. (NTIS No. PB88-194766)

Glenn, A. D., Kozen, N. A., & Pollack, R. A. (1984). Teaching economics: Research findings from a microcomputer videodisc project. *Educational Technology, 24,* 30–32.

Green, G. L. (1983). Instructional use of microcomputers in Indiana public high schools. (Doctoral dissertation, Ball State University, 1983). *Dissertation Abstracts International, 44,* 1678A.

Hawkins, J., & Sheingold, K. (1986). The beginning of a story: Computers and the organization of learning in classrooms. In J. A. Culbertson & L. L. Cunningham (Eds.), *Microcomputers and education.* 85th National Society for the Study of Education Yearbook (Part 1, pp. 40–58). Chicago: Chicago University Press.

Hetzner, D. R. (1972). Life decisions: A computer based simulation game for social studies classrooms (Doctoral dissertation, State University of New York at Buffalo, 1972). *Dissertations Abstracts International, 33,* 1078A.

Hodges, J. O. (1985). Using database management to achieve social studies objectives. *Virginia Resolves, 27,* 6–14.

Hunter, B. (1983). Powerful tools for your social studies classroom. *Classroom Computer Learning, 4,* 50–57.

Johnson, R. T., Johnson, D. W., & Stanne, M. B. (1985). *The effects of cooperative, competitive, and individualistic goal structures on computer-assisted instruction.* Unpublished manuscript, University of Minnesota, Minneapolis.

Kulik, J. A., Bangert, R. L., & Williams, G. W. (1983). Effects of computer-based teaching on secondary school students. *Journal of Educational Psychology, 75,* 19–26.

Levin, H. (1984). *Costs and cost-effectiveness of computer-assisted instruction.* Stanford, CA: Stanford University, Institute for Research on Educational Finance and Governance. (ERIC Document Reproduction Service No. ED 252 915)

Louisiana State Department of Education. (1985). *The use of the computer in Louisiana schools* (Fourth annual report. Bulletin No. 1679, rev.). Baton Rouge, LA: Office of Research and Development. (ERIC Document Reproduction Service No. ED 265 829)

Marsh, M. (1985). Computer assisted learning in the social studies: Development and evaluation of a series of computer programs for middle school students (Doctoral dissertation, University of Maryland, 1984). (ERIC Document Reproduction Service No. 46, 884A.

Marsh, M. (1986). Teaching history with microcomputers: A case study. *Social Education, 50,* 134–135.

Martinez, M. E., & Mead, N. A. (1988). *Computer competence: The first national assessment.* Princeton, NJ: Educational Testing Service.

Mendrinos, R. B., & Morrison, D. M. (1986). The Irish immigrant: How the program works. *Classroom Computer Learning, 7,* 42.

Morrison, D. M., & Walters, J. (1986a). IMMIGRANT: A social studies simulation for AppleWorks. In C. Thompson & L. Vaughn (Eds.), *Computers in the Classroom: Experiences teaching with flexible tools* (pp. 70–76). Chelmsford, MA: Northeast Regional Exchange. (ERIC Document Reproduction Service No. ED 268 013)

Morrison, D. M., & Walters, J. (1986b). The Irish immigrant: Origins of the project. *Classroom Computer Learning, 7,* 40–41.

Niemiec, R., & Walberg, H. J. (1985). Computers and achievement in the elementary school. *Journal of Educational Computing Research, 1,* 435–440.

Niemiec, R., & Walberg, H. J. (1987). Comparative effects of computer-assisted instruction: A synthesis of reviews. *Journal of Educational Computing Research, 3,* 19–37.

Pedersen, N. G. (1978). An evaluation of the effect of a computer-assisted testing program on instruction in United States history (Doctoral dissertation, University of Virginia, 1977). *Dissertation Abstracts International, 38,* 3917A.

Pollak, R. A., & Breault, G. (1985). ON-LINE contemporary issues brings today's world to social studies classrooms. *Computing Teacher, 12,* 10–11.

Rawitsch, D. (1987). The computerized database: Not a simple solution. *Computing Teacher, 15,* 34–37.

Rawitsch, D., Bart, W. M., & Earle, J. F. (1988). Using computer database programs to facilitate higher-order thinking skills (*Research Bulletin* No. 1, 7–9). St. Paul, MN: Minnesota Educational Computing Consortium/University of Minnesota Center for the Study of Educational Technology.

Robbat, R. J. (1985). The utilization of computers in high school history education. (Doctoral dissertation, University of Oregon, 1984). *Dissertation Abstracts International, 45,* 3537A.

Roberts, N. (1976). *Simulation gaming: A critical review.* Cambridge, MA: Lesley College, Graduate School of Education, and Massachusetts Institute of Technology. (ERIC Document Reproduction Service No. ED 137 165)

Roblyer, M. D., Castine, W. H., & King, F. J. (1988). Computer applications have 'undeniable value,' research shows. *Electronic Learning, 8,* 38–40.

Roessler, M. (1987). Students design a depression simulation. *Social Education, 51,* 48–51.

Rogers, L., & de Leeuw, G. (1986). Explorations in LOGO mapping with children: An interim report on a longitudinal study. *History and Social Science Teacher, 22,* 15–18.

Ross, E. W. (1988). *Survey of microcomputer use in secondary social studies classrooms.* Paper presented at the meeting of the National Council for the Social Studies, Orlando.

Rothman, M. (1982). Using the microcomputer to study the anatomy of revolution. *Computing Teacher, 10,* 16–20.

Sabir, A. B. (1986). An investigation of social studies teachers' definitional orientation and its relationship with teachers' attitudes toward, knowledge about, and willingness to use computer-based education. (Doctoral dissertation, Pennsylvania State University, 1986). *Dissertation Abstracts International, 47,* 1274A.

Sanders, J. (1988). Computer equity for girls. In A. O. Carelli (Ed.), *Sex Equity in education: Readings and strategies.* Springfield, IL: Charles C Thomas.

Talaiver, M. P. (1987). *Effects of instructional grouping on achievement and attitude toward using social studies simulations.* Unpublished doctoral dissertation, University of Georgia.

Traberman, T. (1983). Using interactive computer techniques to develop global understanding. *Computing Teacher, 11,* 43–70.

Traberman, T. (1984). Using microcomputers to teach global studies. *Social Education, 48,* 130–137.

Tucker, G. B. (1982). Data summary of the use of microcomputers in Idaho public schools. *Computing Teacher, 10,* 54.

Underwood, J. D. M. (1985). Cognitive demand and CAL. In I. Reid & J. Rushton (Eds.), *Teachers, computers, and the classroom* (pp. 25–57). Manchester, England: Manchester University Press.

U.S. Congress Office of Technology Assessment. (1988). *Power on! New tools for teaching and learning.* Washington, DC: Government Printing Office.

U.S. Department of Education. (1986). *Teacher preparation in the use of computers.* Washington, DC: Office of Educational Research and Improvement.

Vincent, B. (1986). Design for decision-making in the classroom. *T.H.E. Journal, 14,* 80–84.

Way, J. W. (1984). *Evaluation of computer assisted instruction.* Kansas City, KS: Kansas City School District. (ERIC Document Reproduction Service No. ED 257 840)

Weible, T. D., & McMahon, J. (1983). Using microcomputers in the Social Studies. In R. Abelson (Ed.), *Using microcomputers in the social studies classroom.* Boulder, CO: ERIC Clearinghouse for Social Studies/Social Science Education. (ERIC Document Reproduction Service No. ED 233 967)

Weigand, P. (1985). CAL in the geography classroom. In I. Reid & J. Rushton (Eds.), *Teachers, computers, and the classroom* (pp. 138–150). Manchester, England: Manchester University Press.

White, C. S. (1986a). Committee surveys teachers about instructional media. *Social Studies Professional, 84,* 4.

White, C. S. (1986b). The impact of structured activities with a computer-based file-management program on selected information-processing skills. (Doctoral dissertation, Indiana University, 1985). *Dissertation Abstracts International, 47,* 513A.

White, C. S. (1987). Developing information-processing skills through structured activities with a computerized file-management program. *Journal of Educational Computing Research, 3,* 355–375.

White, C. S. (1988). *Media and technology use in the social studies: A status report.* Paper presented at the meeting of the National Council for the Social Studies, Orlando.

Wiske, M. S., & Zodhiates, P. (1988). *How technology affects teaching.* Cambridge, MA: Harvard University, Educational Technology Center.

43

GAMES AND SIMULATIONS IN SOCIAL STUDIES EDUCATION

Ambrose A. Clegg, Jr.
KENT STATE UNIVERSITY

Although games and simulations have been used in education for many years, only since the late 1950s have they been used as a major teaching tool. The origins of gaming date back to the 12th century to chess as a war game, played with pieces named for important elements of medieval society: king, queen, bishops, knights, castles, and pawns. More recently, during World War II, the military services used a number of simulation devices, such as the Link Trainer, to improve the speed, effectiveness, and reality of training. Competitive business games were developed during the 1950s for use in training executives in various aspects of business and corporate management (Rausch, 1982). In 1965, a computer-based warfare simulator was developed for training senior naval officers in advanced tactics and strategy and for playing complex war games on a global scale (Allen, 1987). Cherryholmes and Shapiro (1969) demonstrated how a computer program could be used to simulate important political processes such as legislative voting.

By the early 1970s, games and simulations were used in many schools of business management, in university classes, and in elementary and secondary schools for teaching about such varied areas as business decision-making, political activities, environmental issues, and career information. In their extensive reviews, Becker (1980) and Horn and Cleaves (1980) cited several hundred published games and simulations on a wide variety of topics. Greenblat (1987) prepared a comprehensive handbook for designing games and simulations, with more than 70 examples drawn largely from the social sciences.

DEFINITIONS

The terms *game, simulation, simulation games, role playing,* and *computer simulations* are frequently used interchangeably, but somewhat different meanings have developed for each. A *game* is a situation in which an individual or a team of people play or compete against one another with an agreed-upon set of rules, a limited time, and a means of scoring winning or losing actions. The term *game* also implies that the participants will have enjoyment and fun and that they will be highly motivated to play for relatively long periods of time. In contrast, a *simulation* is a special type of game, based upon an abstract, limited model of some real phenomenon, usually a decision-making or conflict-resolution situation, and designed to teach the operation and interaction of principles that operate in the situation. Simulations usually represent the dynamic, interactive character of a system (Greenblat, 1985). The terms *gaming simulation* and *simulation games* are used interchangeably to take into account features of both terms.

Role playing is an important part of games and simulations. In the typical classroom use, the purpose of role playing is to bring out the dramatic quality of a situation, as in the re-creation of a historical setting such as a mock trial or a constitutional convention. In simulations, however, the players act out well-defined roles by interacting with others in a decision-making setting with rules for choosing among designated options or playing out certain constraints (e.g., a governor must decide whether to veto legislation that exceeds the state budget limitations).

Reviewers were Wayne Mahood, State University of New York at Geneseo; Thomas N. Turner, University of Tennessee.

Computer simulations are simulations played largely with computers. In the 1980s, microcomputers were used in simulations to store, retrieve, and sort large amounts of data; to compress the passage of time; and to emulate problem-solving heuristics using artificial intelligence applications (Patterson & Smith, 1986).

GOALS FOR GAMES AND SIMULATIONS

There is no clear agreement on why and how games should be used in social studies. Most writers have emphasized the experience of becoming involved in decision making and learning firsthand the interactions of various factors in the complex problems of business or governmental policy planning (Cherryholmes, 1965, 1966; Greenblat, 1985, Seidner, 1976). Unfortunately, there is little research evidence as to whether those goals are achieved and, if so, under what conditions.

RESEARCH ON GAMES AND SIMULATIONS

Most of the major research on games and simulations since the 1950s has been on the use of business management games conducted at the college or graduate school level (Greenlaw & Wyman, 1973; Wolfe, 1985). Although many games are available for elementary and secondary schools, there have been few studies of their effectiveness in the social studies or other curricular areas. Seidner (1976) reviewed a large number of studies that suggested promising leads for understanding the effects of games and simulations in the school curriculum, but there has been little follow-up of these leads or replication of the studies in subsequent years. Although the advent of the microcomputer in the 1980s markedly changed the potential of games and simulations as classroom tools (Patterson & Smith, 1986), there has been little research on their use.

Of the nearly 800 articles, documents, and books on games and simulations related to K–12 social studies surveyed by this writer for the period 1955–1989, the vast majority are anecdotal reports, descriptions of particular games, handbooks offering guidelines for selecting games, and books dealing with the general theme of using games and simulations. Most of the studies for which research data have been reported fail to meet the elementary standards of design outlined by Campbell and Stanley (1963). In a comprehensive review of studies on games and simulations in social studies programs, VanSickle (1986a) examined nearly 400 articles. He identified only 42 comparative experimental studies done over a 20-year period, 1965– 1985.

Inter-Nation Simulation

The development of games and simulations at the college level had an impact upon curriculum development in the upper elementary and secondary school grades. Using the principles of simulation already developed in business games, Harold Guetzkow (1959, 1962, 1963) and a group of his associates developed a complex simulation game, Inter-Nation, for teaching international relations (Guetzkow & Cherryholmes, 1966).

The Inter-Nation Simulation game was used as the core activity in a 6-week unit in international relations in a college preparatory course in Lawrence, Kansas, high school classes in American government. Over a 2-year period almost 500 high school students were involved in eight separate simulation runs. Using a 12-item attitude questionnaire, Cherryholmes (1963, 1965) found that (a) students like the games, (b) the games were reported to be about as effective for cognitive learning as other methods of teaching but not necessarily any better, and (c) students' attitudes about the way a social system works became more realistic (i.e., more practical and less idealistic) through participation in the games. Although the consistent findings over eight replications cannot be ignored, there was no control or comparison group, and conclusions must be drawn with caution.

Cherryholmes (1966) analyzed six reports of research on classroom simulations in social studies. Four of the studies dealt with Inter-Nation, two with high school students (Cherryholmes, 1963; Garvey & Seiler, 1966) and two with college students (Anderson, 1964; Robinson, Anderson, Herman, & Snyder, 1966). The two other studies were investigations of simulations with high school students, Election Game (Boocock, 1963) and Career Game, Legislative Game, and Disaster Game (Boocock & Coleman, 1966). In five of the six studies, a control group used case studies, recitation or other games.

Cherryholmes (1966) concluded that, when compared to students involved in conventional teaching activities, the students who participated in the simulations (a) reported more interest in the simulation activities, but did not (b) learn significantly more facts or principles, (c) retain more information, (d) gain critical thinking or problem-solving skills, or (e) significantly change their attitudes about the referent social system. He noted that the students did not seem to learn facts or principles based on the structure of the simulation, perhaps because they were presented with the rules of the game as operating procedures, rather than being allowed to discover such processes as decision making, elements of leadership, or bargaining. Cherryholmes inferred that "students do not *discover* structural relationships in the simulate, they *memorize* them" (p. 6).

Cherryholmes (1968) suggested that, because Inter-Nation was an operational model of international politics, researchers should focus upon cognitive dependent variables related to the dynamic qualities of the model, rather than on the facts and principles of a static concept of international politics. In the affective area, he suggested that researchers should investigate whether introducing students to politics through the dynamic aspects of the simulation made them more tolerant of political conflict, less rigid in their ideological stance, less prone to use stereotypes in analyzing political issues, and more likely to favor compromise over dictated solutions to social and political problems. Unfortunately, other investigators have not pursued Cherryholmes's (1966, 1968) suggestions in his pioneering efforts to establish a research framework for simulation games in social studies. Moreover, none of the research on games has been the subject of as extensive evaluation as were his studies of Inter-Nation.

Reviews of Research

Within seven years after the introduction of Inter-Nation Simulation in 1965, Taylor and Walford (1978) listed nearly 300 games and simulations available to social studies teachers. Reports of research on social studies classroom games and simulations began to emerge in the 1960s, but the data were often conflicting.

Boocock and Schild (1968) reviewed nine well-designed research studies done between 1962 and 1968 on social studies topics. In each, randomly assigned or equivalent experimental and control groups were used, sample sizes ranged from 50 to 1,200, and pre- and posttest data were collected using questionnaires, attitude surveys, and tests of knowledge of facts and principles. Five were conducted in high school social studies classes (Barker, 1968; Boocock, 1968; Inbar, 1968; Schild, 1968; Zaltman, 1968), two in elementary schools (Farran, 1968; Wing, 1968), and two in graduate schools of business (McKenney & Dill, 1968; Starbuck & Koslow, 1966). Consistent with Cherryholmes's (1963, 1966) findings, students in the experimental groups (a) enjoyed playing the games and were highly motivated, but (b) did not learn statistically significantly more facts or principles, or (c) change attitudes significantly more than the control groups. Boocock and Schild (1968) suggested that research ought to be done on the learning effects of disadvantaged and gifted students and on the problems of dissemination and in-service training.

Livingston and Stoll (1973) reviewed 26 studies of simulations on social studies topics conducted in elementary, junior, and senior high schools between 1963 and 1972. In each study, randomly assigned or equivalent control-group designs were used with pre- and posttesting, often on several variables. Data came from scores on questionnaires, attitude surveys, and tests of factual knowledge and principles. The dependent variables included (a) knowledge, (b) attitudes, (c) sense of political efficacy, (d) preference for games, and (e) motivation. The performance of low-ability students was also investigated.

The findings were mixed, often contradictory, but some trends were evident. In 8 of 16 studies, students who played the simulations gained in factual knowledge, although in 8 other studies there was either no difference or a negative result. Students' attitudes changed in 8 of 11 studies, most often toward more realistic (and less idealistic) views and toward greater approval of the real-life person whose role they played in the game. But the results were inconsistent in the 7 studies in which students were asked if they had achieved greater belief in their own ability to succeed or to control factors in their environment (political efficacy). The students preferred simulation games to conventional methods in seven studies, and they said the games motivated them to greater participation in related learning activities in five of eight studies.

The findings on whether simulations provided increased opportunity for low-ability students were negative in five studies and inconsistent in five others. Students of low ability usually did much better at learning *to play* the simulation game than at learning *from* the game. Their greatest difficulty was in transferring their understanding of the game to the real-life situation the game represented.

Other studies described by Livingston and Stoll (1973) and Seidner (1976) yielded similar results for knowledge outcomes, attitude change, and student motivation. Most of these early reports, however, contained little information to support statements of statistical significance, making it impossible to calculate effect sizes.

VanSickle (1986a) undertook a meta-analysis of the 42 comparative experimental studies he culled from some 400 studies using rigorous design criteria. Of these 42, only 22 reports included sufficient data to compute effect sizes. VanSickle further subdivided the 22 studies into two subgroups, 6 studies that were simple pre- and posttest studies or no-treatment control groups and 16 studies that compared simulation to an alternative treatment. Using procedures described by Glass, McGaw, and Smith (1981) and Light and Pillemer (1984), VanSickle computed standardized mean differences (SMDs) for eight types of cognitive and affective variables by dividing the difference between the mean of the experimental group and the mean of the control (or comparison group) by the standard deviation of the control group.

VanSickle (1986a) identified three knowledge-dependent measures in the simulation studies: immediate, or short-term, recall; retention; and application of knowledge to analysis or decision making. Overall, he found that simulation games produced greater cognitive learnings, but only to a small degree, as shown in Table 43–1. The SMDs were considerably smaller

TABLE 43–1. Mean Standardized Mean Differences (SMDs) for Knowledge Variables

Groups	Immediate Recall of Knowledge	Retention	Application
Pre/posttest & no treatment	.43 (67% > $\overline{X}_c$) $n = 3$ R = .15 to .78		.27 (60% > $\overline{X}_c$) $n = 4$ R = .10 to .55
Alternative treatments	.12 (55% > $\overline{X}_c$) $n = 9$ R = −.43 to .64	.28 (61% > $\overline{X}_c$) $n = 6$ R = −.34 to .87	.10 (54% > $\overline{X}_c$) $n = 2$ R = .02 to .17

Note. n = number of studies; R = range of SMDs. Figures in parentheses indicate the percentage of subjects in the experimental group who exceeded the control-group mean, assuming normal distributions.

From "A Quantitative Review of Research on Instructional Simulation Gaming: A Twenty-Year Perspective" by R. L. VanSickle, 1986; *Theory and Research in Social Education*, 14, pp. 250–251. Copyright 1986 by the College and University Faculty Assembly of the National Council for the Social Studies. Adapted by permission.

when the simulation group was compared to an alternative treatment, a finding that is consistent with earlier evidence that simulations are generally no more effective than other methods in teaching knowledge.

In the same meta-analysis VanSickle (1986a) also analyzed the data on three attitudinal variables: attitudes toward (a) the subject content of the game and the course involved, (b) the social phenomenon under study, such as presidential elections or environmental policies, and (c) oneself, including a sense of political efficacy or academic self-confidence. Overall, Van-Sickle found that simulation games produced mixed results on changes in attitudes, as shown in Table 43–2. In the set of studies that involved an alternative treatment group, there was a small mean SMD of .16 for attitude toward the subject content, a small negative mean SMD of −.13 for attitudes toward the social phenomenon, and a negligible mean SMD of .01 for attitudes toward self. The SMDs for individual studies ranged from −.66 to .57.

VanSickle's results contrasted sharply with those from the early studies on attitude change reported earlier. Not only were the SMDs small in the group of studies in which simulation was compared to an alternate method of teaching, but the wide range of SMDs indicates a very inconsistent pattern of attitude change. To explain this inconsistency, VanSickel suggested that the degree of student control of the simulation game may be important for attitude development. "It seems likely that the model underlying a political simulation game could promote a sense of political efficacy or undermine it depending upon how much control participants are given over the simulation game outcomes" (p. 252).

Despite the fact that simulation is an experiential kind of learning, very few studies have been conducted dealing with interpersonal relationships during classroom game play. Little is known about the effects of team membership; the role of the group leader; outcomes for experienced, versus novice, players; how goals are set and conflicts are resolved; how the outcomes differ for boys and girls at various stages of play or at different ages; how the teacher can set a positive classroom climate for play over a sustained period of time; and the effects of various roles for the teacher such as coach, mentor, or facilitator of learning.

In the meta-analysis described, VanSickle (1986a) examined four studies on two variables related to interpersonal relationships. In two control-group studies in which social interaction was the dependent variable, the mean SMD was .89; the two individual SMDs were .44 and 1.33. In two other studies with alternative treatment groups, the effects on classroom climate were examined. The two SMDs of −.04 and .64 yielded a small mean SMD of .30. Despite the promising potential for simulation to help students discover how to relate to others and how to develop social interactions, the limited data suggest that there have been only small, inconsistent effects, as compared to alternative treatments.

USING MICROCOMPUTERS FOR GAMES AND SIMULATIONS

Games and simulations continue to be used in the elementary and secondary schools, but with nowhere near the frequency of the years 1965–1975. In a study conducted for the National Science Foundation, Weiss (1978) found that most teachers reported using simulations less than once a month, with one in five teachers indicating that they never used simulations.

The gradual introduction of the microcomputer into elementary and secondary schools in the 1980s provided possibilities for a renaissance in the use of educational games and simulations. Technological capability is far ahead of the computer simulation programs that have been available for school use, but there is potential for games and simulations that involve students more directly in learning and experiencing the processes of decision making and problem solving. One middle school social studies teacher in Michigan, for example, has reported how seventh-grade students created computer simulations on such topics as "The Depression" and "Hard Times in the 1930s" using microcomputers and authoring language problems (Roessler, 1987).

Because the use of computers with simulation games is relatively new, there has been little research on their use. In an early study using a computer-based simulation called *Life Decisions*, Hetzner (1972) found that secondary school students

TABLE 43–2. Mean Standardized Mean Differences (SMDs) for Attitude Variables

Groups	Attitude Toward Content	Attitude Toward Phenomenon	Attitude Toward Self
Pre/post & no treatment	.22 (59% > $\overline{X}_c$) $n = 2$ R = .17 to .27	.80 (79% > $\overline{X}_c$) $n = 5$ R = .15 to 1.76	.29 (61% > $\overline{X}_c$) $n = 2$ R = .11 to .46
Alternative treatments	.16 (56% > $\overline{X}_c$) $n = 4$ R = −.20 to .57	−.13 (44% > $\overline{X}_c$) $n = 11$ R = −.66 to .53	.01 (0% > $\overline{X}_c$) $n = 6$ R = −.20 to .26

Note. n = number of studies; R = range of SMDs. Figures in parentheses indicate the percentage of subjects in the experimental group who exceeded the control group mean, assuming normal distributions.

From "A Quantitative Review of Research on Instructional Simulation Gaming: A Twenty-Year Perspective" by R. L. VanSickle, 1986, *Theory and Research in Social Education*, 14, pp. 250–251. Copyright 1986 by the College and Faculty Assembly of the National Council for the Social Studies. Adapted by permission.

who played the computer simulation had statistically significant higher mean scores on tests of interest, goal-directed behavior, and application of principles related to career development than those students in a conventional class in career information. In one study on the effects of computer simulations on attitudes, sixth-grade students who played a world resources simulation had a statistically significant higher posttest mean on a test sense of personal control over world events than that of students in the control group (Roberts, 1976).

In a more recent case study report, Vincent (1986) used the computer-based simulation *Foreign Policy: The Burdens of World Power* from the *Decisions, Decisions* series (Tom Snyder Productions) with sixth graders in Massachusetts. She reported increased motivation and intellectual curiosity and students engaging in persistent questioning and data-seeking activities. In a field study that might have far-reaching implications, Johnson, Johnson, and Stanne (1985, cited in Ehman & Glenn, 1987) tested the hypothesis that computer-assisted cooperative learning was superior to competitive and individualistic learning. They used a modified version of *Geography Search* (Tom Snyder Productions) that required students to navigate a ship from Europe to America and back in order to accumulate gold. Three randomly assigned groups of about 24 elementary school students each used the simulation in groups of four, either cooperatively, competitively, or individually, for 10 days. The cooperative groups performed statistically significantly better than the competitive or individual students on measures of achievement including factual recognition, application, and problem solving. In terms of group skills, the students in the cooperative groups generated more observed on-task statements and behavior and less off-task socializing and talking to the teacher during computer work times. The students in the cooperative groups were also more goal oriented and cooperative.

Important sex differences emerged in this study. Females did much better in the cooperative and individual modes, whereas males did better in the competitive groups. Females showed more persistence than males in the cooperative groups, but females in the competitive groups liked working with the computers less and had less confidence in using them than did males.

The results of this study suggest the superiority of cooperative strategies over competitive and individual ones in using computer simulations. However, they also suggest important differences in the ways that females differ from males in work patterns and in attitudes toward computers.

In summary, the research on computer simulations is very limited, but some tentative directions are evident. Students using computer simulations demonstrated increases in affective outcomes such as interest, motivation, enjoyment, sense of personal control, and willingness to persevere in completing learning tasks. Cooperative strategies with computer games increased both lower and higher order learning and tended to benefit female students more than males (Ehman & Glenn, 1987). These findings must be taken with caution because most of the studies to date have been largely impressionistic, descriptive, or case study reports, lacking rigorous controls and comparative experimental designs.

PROBLEMS OF RESEARCH DESIGN

As noted, the research designs used to study the various effects of games and simulations leave much to be desired. In few studies were subjects randomly selected or assigned to treatment groups; in most, pre-existing, intact groups were used. Many designs lacked a control or comparison group, and researchers frequently failed to define clearly the "traditional" mode of instruction. In few of the articles were means, standard deviations, or *t* or *F* ratios reported to support reports of statistical significance or to permit calculation of effect sizes. Most of the research reports lacked a clear theoretical or conceptual approach, the authors seemed unaware of previous research studies, and there were no replications to verify previous findings.

Methodological and Theoretical Issues

Researchers should consider the following methodological suggestions to improve research on games and simulations in social studies.

1. Admittedly, random assignments of subjects is difficult in many school settings; but the random assignment of classroom units to experimental and control conditions is often a plausible alternative. When randomization is not possible, every effort should be made to describe fully the samples used and to look for differential effects within the samples.

2. There has been over-reliance on tests of statistical significance (VanSickle 1983, 1986b). Effect sizes, as shown by Van Sickle (1986a), have greater usefulness for understanding the magnitude of the results and for assessing their educational importance.

3. Researchers should define the dependent measures more clearly and describe how data were obtained. Very few researchers made use of standardized tests or reported data on the reliability and validity of test scores. Not a single researcher cited Buro's *Mental Measurements Yearbook,* now in its 10th edition. Scores from locally prepared tests, reported without supporting information, must be considered fragile, suspect data at best.

4. More attention needs to be given to replication studies to determine if reported outcomes are stable with other samples or under modified conditions.

5. No longitudinal studies of simulation have been reported. Games seem to be a one-time-only activity. No researchers have reported exploring the effects on students' decision-making skills in simulation games played in subsequent classes or in later real-life experiences. Except for military war gaming (Allen, 1987), few researchers have dealt with the effect of simulation experiences on real-world decision-making.

Researchers should also address the theoretical basis for studies of the effects of games and simulations.

1. Most games are designed so that teams use a competitive strategy to win. There is, however, a considerable body of research from psychology and organizational development that

indicates that cooperative strategies are more effective in problem solving and team organization. Except for the study by Johnson et al. (1985), there have been no reports of studies of simulations in which cooperative, competitive, and individualistic strategies have been directly compared. Such comparisons should have high priority in future studies.

2. There has been virtually no research on such intervening variables as interpersonal relations, leadership, team membership, and the decision-making process. Although there has been much theory and research in psychology and organizational development on these topics, there has been no carryover into the studies done on simulation in social studies classrooms.

3. Too often debriefing at the end of a game gets only scant attention. In an article entitled "Truth as a Variable," Brooker (1988) raised important questions about the moral implications of pragmatic strategies designed to win regardless of the cost. He suggested that careful discussion and analysis of the issues during the debriefing are as important as playing the game itself. This is particularly true when unethical behaviors such as lying, cheating, or breaking agreements are seen as pragmatic strategies that can win the game.

In short, despite the great educational potential of games and simulations as a tool in social studies classrooms, the research base for making decisions about their use in classroom teaching and learning is inadequate. Theoretical and conceptual frameworks have been ignored, research design has been weak, and important knowledge from related disciplines has not been applied to the study of games and simulations.

References

Allen, T. B. (1987). *War games: The secret world of the creators, players, and policy makers rehearsing World War III today*. New York: McGraw-Hill.

Anderson, L. F. (1964). *Combining simulation and case studies in the teaching of American foreign policy*. Unpublished manuscript, Northwestern University, Evanston, IL.

Baker, E. H. (1968). A pre–civil war simulation for teaching American history. In S. S. Boocock & E. O. Schild (Eds.), *Simulation games in learning* (pp. 135–142). Beverly Hills, CA: Sage.

Becker, H. A. (1980). The emergence of simulation and gaming. *Simulation & Games, 11*, 223–345.

Boocock, S. S. (1963). *Effects of election campaign game in four high school classes* (Rep. No. 1, Research Program in the Effects of Games with Simulated Environments in Secondary Education). Baltimore: Johns Hopkins University.

Boocock, S. S. (1968). An experimental study of the learning effects of two games with simulated environments. In S. S. Boocock & E. O. Schild (Eds.), *Simulation games in learning* (pp. 107–133). Beverly Hills, CA: Sage.

Boocock, S. S., & Coleman, J. S. (1966). Games with simulated environments in learning. *Sociology of Education, 39*, 215–263.

Boocock, S. S., & Schild, E. O. (Eds.). (1968). *Simulation games in learning*. Beverly Hills, CA: Sage.

Brooker, R. G. (1988). Truth as a variable: Teaching political strategy with simulation games. *Simulation & Games, 19*, 43–58.

Campbell, D. T., & Stanley, J. C. (1963). Experimental and quasi-experimental designs for research. In N. L. Gage (Ed.), *Handbook of research on teaching* (pp. 171–246). Chicago: Rand McNally.

Cherryholmes, C. H. (1963). *Developments in simulation of international relations in high school teaching*. Unpublished master's thesis, Kansas State Teachers College, Emporia.

Cherryholmes, C. H. (1965). Developments in simulation of international relations in high school teaching. *Phi Delta Kappan, 47*, 227–231.

Cherryholmes, C. H. (1966). Some current research on effectiveness of educational simulations: Implications for alternative strategies. *American Behavioral Scientist, 10*, 4–7.

Cherryholmes, C. H. (1968). Simulating inter-nation relations in the classroom. In J. M. Becker & H. D. Mehlinger (Eds.), *International dimensions in the social studies* (38th Yearbook, pp. 173–190). Washington, DC: National Council for the Social Studies.

Cherryholmes, C. H., & Shapiro, M. J. (1969). *Representatives and roll calls: A computer simulation of voting in the 88th Congress*. Indianapolis, IN: Bobbs-Merrill.

Ehman, L. H., & Glenn, A. D. (1987). *Computer-based education in the social studies*. Bloomington, IN: ERIC Clearinghouse for Social Studies/Social Science Education.

Farran, D. C. (1968). Competition and learning for underachievers. In S. Boocock and E. Schild (Eds.), *Simulation games in learning* (pp. 191–203). Beverly Hills, CA: Sage.

Garvey, D., & Seiler, W. (1966). *A study of effectiveness of different methods of teaching international relations to high school students*. Emporia, KS: Kansas State Teachers College.

Glass, G. V, McGaw, B., & Smith, M. L. (1981). *Meta-analysis in social research*. Beverly Hills, CA: Sage.

Greenblat, C. S. (1985). Games and simulations. In H. E. Mitzel (Ed.), *Encyclopedia of educational research* (5th ed.) (Vol. 2, pp. 713–716). New York: Macmillan.

Greenblat, C. S. (1987). *Designing games and simulations. An illustrated handbook*. Beverly Hills, CA: Sage.

Greenlaw, P. S., & Wyman, F. P. (1973). The teaching effectiveness of games in collegiate business courses. *Simulation & Games, 4*, 259–294.

Guetzkow, H. (1959). A use of simulation in the study of Inter-Nation relations. *Behavioral Science, 4*, 183–191.

Guetzkow, H. (Ed.). (1962). *Simulation in social sciences: Readings*. Englewood Cliffs, NJ: Prentice-Hall.

Guetzkow, H. (Ed.). (1963). *Simulation in international relations: Developments for research and teaching*. Englewood Cliffs, NJ: Prentice-Hall.

Guetzkow, H., & Cherryholmes, C. H. (1966). *Inter-nation simulation kit*. Chicago: Science Research Associates.

Hetzner, D. R. (1972). *Life decisions: A computer based simulation game for social studies classrooms* (Doctoral dissertation, State University of New York at Buffalo). *Dissertation Abstracts International, 33*, 1078A.

Horn, R., & Cleaves, A. (1980). *The guide to simulations/games for education and training* (4th ed.). Beverly Hills, CA: Sage.

Inbar, M. (1968). Individual and group effects on enjoyment and learning in a game simulating a community disaster. In S. Boocock & E. Schild (Eds.), *Simulation games in learning* (pp. 169–190). Beverly Hills, CA: Sage.

Johnson, R. T., Johnson, D. W., & Stanne, M. B. (1985). *The effects of cooperative, competitive, and individualistic goal structures on computer-assisted instruction.* Unpublished manuscript, University of Minnesota.

Light, R. J., & Pillemer, D. P. (1984). *Summing up: The science of reviewing research.* Cambridge, MA: Harvard University Press.

Livingston, S. A., & Stoll, C. S. (1973). *Simulation games: An introduction for the social studies teacher.* New York: Free Press.

McKenney, J. L., & Dill, W. R. (1968). The effect of team assignment on faculty boards on student attitudes and learning. In S. Boocock & E. Schild (Eds.), *Simulation games in learning* (pp. 217–231). Beverly Hills, CA: Sage.

Patterson, J. H., & Smith, M. S. (1986). The role of computers in higher-order thinking. In J. A. Culbertson & L. L. Cunningham (Eds.), *Microcomputers in education.* 85th Yearbook of the National Society for the Study of Education (Part I, pp. 81–108). Chicago: University of Chicago Press.

Rausch, E. (1982). Management games. In C. Heyel (Ed.), *The encyclopedia of management* (3rd ed., pp. 409–413). New York: Van Nostrand Reinhold.

Roberts, N. (1976). *Simulation gaming: A critical review.* Cambridge, MA: Lesley College, Graduate School of Education, and Massachusetts Institute of Technology. (ERIC Document Reproduction Service No. ED 137 165)

Robinson, J., Anderson, L., Herman, M., & Snyder, R. (1966). Teaching with Inter-Nation simulation and case studies. *American Political Science Review, 60,* 53–66.

Roessler, M. (1987). Students design a depression simulation. *Social Education, 51,* 48–51.

Schild, E. O. (1968). The shaping of strategies. In S. S. Boocock and E. O. Schild (Eds.), *Simulation games in learning* (pp. 143–154). Beverly Hills, CA: Sage.

Seidner, C. J. (1976). Teaching with simulation and games. In N. L. Gage (Ed.), *The psychology of teaching methods.* 75th Yearbook of the National Society for the Study of Education (Part I, pp. 217–251). Chicago: University of Chicago Press.

Starbuck, W. H., & Koslow, E. (1966). The effects of advisors on business game teams. *American Behavioral Scientist, 10,* 28–30.

Taylor, J. L., & Walford, R. (1978). *Learning and the simulation game.* Beverly Hills, CA: Sage.

VanSickle, R. L. (1983). Statistical power and effect size in social educational research. *Journal of Social Studies Research, 7,* 1–17.

VanSickle, R. L. (1986a). A quantitative review of research on instructional simulation gaming: A twenty-year perspective. *Theory and Research in Social Education, 14,* 245–264.

VanSickle, R. L. (1986b). Toward more adequate quantitative instructional research. *Theory and Research in Social Education, 14,* 171–184.

Vincent, B. (1986, November). Design for decision-making in the classroom. *T.H.E. Journal, 14,* 80–84.

Weiss, I. R. (1978). *National survey of science, mathematics and social studies education.* Washington, DC: National Science Foundation.

Wing, Richard L. (1968). Two computer-based economics games for sixth graders. In S. Boocock & E. Schild (Eds.), *Simulation games in learning* (pp. 155–165). Beverly Hills, CA: Sage.

Wolfe, J. (1985). The teaching effectiveness of games in collegiate business courses: A 1973–1983 update. *Simulation & Games, 16,* 251–288.

Zaltman, G. (1968). Degree of participation and learning in a consumer economics game. In S. Boocock & E. Schild (Eds.), *Simulation games and learning* (pp. 205–215). Beverly Hills, CA: Sage.

44

CLASSROOM ORGANIZATION FOR SOCIAL STUDIES

Nancy E. Winitzky

UNIVERSITY OF UTAH

Among the curricular, disciplinary, interpersonal, and other uncertainties teachers daily face are questions like: Should I teach the whole group today or divide the students into small groups? Should I cluster students by ability or heterogeneously? Should I assign seatwork? How a teacher responds to these questions may have impacts on student learning. These are the kinds of problems that researchers in classroom organization seek to illuminate.

The purpose of this chapter is to review the findings of the research literature regarding the effects of classroom organization on academic, affective, and behavioral outcomes in social studies classrooms from kindergarten through high school. Classroom organization refers here to variations in grouping students for instruction; it does not mean classroom management, nor does it refer to units of organization beyond the classroom.

The most recent treatment of research on classroom-organization practices in social studies was by Fancett and Hawke (1982). They summarized the results of three surveys (Stake & Easley, 1978; Weiss, 1978; Wiley, 1977), and were able to paint a clear picture of then-current practice. Most social studies teachers at every grade level used whole-group instruction predominantly, devoting less than 15% of available time to small-group work (Fancett & Hawke, 1982, p. 210). The emphasis on whole-group activities increased with grade level. A substantial amount of time was also spent working with students individually. No information, however, was provided concerning the impact of various organization practices on student outcomes. The goal of the present chapter is to examine research conducted on this relationship since the Fancett and Hawke review.

METHOD

Locating Studies

The literature review began with a computer search of the ERIC database using the descriptors "class organization" and "grouping (instructional purposes)." Thirty-five studies were identified, four of which were germane. Next, prior reviews of social studies instruction (Fancett & Hawke, 1982; Leming, 1985) were combed for appropriate bibliographic leads, adding one article. A handsearch of relevant journals contributed several studies (the journals searched were *Review of Educational Research, American Educational Research Journal, Social Education, Theory and Research in Social Education, Social Studies, Elementary School Journal, Indiana Social Studies Quarterly, High School Journal, Journal of Education, Educational Researcher, American Journal of Education,* and *Journal of Educational Research*). Finally, bibliographies of those studies were examined for further relevant research.

Selection Criteria

Decisions about which studies to include were guided initially by several a priori criteria: Only primary studies published since 1980 that dealt with classroom organization and its effects on student achievement, affect, and behavior in social studies were included for review. Due to the dearth of research in social studies classrooms, however, the search was expanded to other subject areas—namely, reading, language arts, English, and science—similar to social studies in emphasis on academic

---

Reviewer was Richard Arends, University of Maryland.

learning, on learning from print, on evaluating learning through writing, and on complex problem solving.

The three dependent variables of interest—achievement, affect, and behavior—were defined in accordance with the goals for social studies, as described by the National Council for the Social Studies (NCSS, 1984, 1989): mastering facts and concepts and acquiring problem solving and evaluative strategies so that students can become responsible and active citizens. Implicit in the NCSS goal statements are other important objectives such as tolerating diversity in ideas and people and working effectively with others. Dispositions and skills like these are essential to citizenship.

With this framework in mind, student achievement was defined as student performance on either standardized or locally made tests of facts, concepts, or complex problem solving. Affective variables of interest included attitudes toward political participation, self-efficacy, and tolerance of diverse others. Excluded were variables like self-esteem and attitude toward social studies, neither of which is listed by NCSS. For the same reason, the behavioral variables included were prosocial behavior, and interaction with those from different ethnic or other groups, and group interaction skills, for example, but not time-on-task.

After all germane studies had been located, additional criteria were set following Slavin's (1986, 1987) recommendations for a "best evidence" synthesis of research. To bring to the surface this best evidence, after amassing and reading all relevant studies one sets methodological criteria that have a substantive basis. Then the best pieces within that particular literature are included for review and the weakest are disregarded. This procedure, Slavin claimed, minimizes the "noise" that might interfere with drawing clear implications from the research.

Several criteria were established in this way. To ensure a measure of external validity, only studies conducted in field settings were included. No limitations were set on research design; both descriptive and quantitative works were reviewed. However, within experimental designs, evidence of treatment implementation was required. For example, Pierce, Lemke, and Smith (1988) devised and tested an experimental program to enhance critical thinking in secondary students, but they failed to provide evidence that the experimental program had actually been carried out as described. The reader cannot know, then, whether the experimental treatment indeed accounted for the obtained improvement in performance of experimental group subjects. This study was thus excluded.

Theoretical Perspective

Armento (1986) discussed the trend toward understanding social studies classroom processes, teaching, and learning from a cognitive perspective. Although past research focused on relating teacher behavior to student outcomes, current theorists posit that student thought processes are mediating factors (Tobias, 1982; Wittrock, 1986). To the extent that instruction engages students in actively organizing new material and in connecting it with previous knowledge, these researchers believe, students will learn.

The new perspective was used to generate hypotheses about the relationship of classroom organization variables to student outcomes. Following this approach, what forms of classroom organization would (a) allow or encourage students to actively generate idiosyncratic organizations of new material and (b) do it in such a way that the new is mentally intertwined with prior knowledge? It is hypothesized that organizational practices involving small-group work will engender greater learning under varying degrees of teacher control, in which the group members define a problem, study it, and construct a product or a report requiring them to synthesize the material, organize it, and tie it in with what they already know. Teacher-dominated whole-class or individual learning is hypothesized to be less effective, because students would have fewer opportunities to create their own organization of new material and to hook it to their prior knowledge. Does the research on classroom organization bear these hypotheses out? The remainder of the chapter will be devoted to that question.

This chapter is structured around dimensions of classroom organization that emerged from the literature: variables of group size, task/reward structure, group composition, and teacher control. The literature addressing each category is discussed, with the dual goals of theoretical understanding within a cognitive framework and practical application for the improvement of social studies teaching and learning.

GROUP SIZE

Group size is really a misnomer because the condition of students working alone is included, and one is not a group. However, the designation has been retained because it was deemed less cumbersome than other terms. Within-class groupings were the focus, not class-level ones; the many studies on class size were not included (see, e.g., Bangert, Kulik, & Kulik, 1983; Cahen, Filby, McCutcheon, & Kyle, 1983). The independent variable was simply the number of students in a group.

Individual Work

Seatwork and individualized instruction are two ways teachers can organize students to work alone. Some might expect such solitary work to enhance student achievement and other outcomes because, conceivably, it could be better tailored to students' prior knowledge and to the amount of time individual students need to complete assignments. On the other hand, because there is usually no explicit attempt to help students organize knowledge, cognitive theorists do not expect this form of organization to be especially effective. What does the research on individual work in social studies classrooms say?

Unfortunately, no studies were found in social studies that pertained directly to that question. Bangert et al. (1983) did report the results of a meta-analysis comparing individualized with conventional instruction. Fifty-one experimental studies conducted between 1955 and 1983 were examined. The mean achievement standardized mean difference (SMD) for individualized instruction was about .10, a trivial result; and for critical thinking, .26. Only one of the studies had been conducted in a social studies classroom, and the SMD for achievement was −.12 in that case. The results of this meta-analysis support the hypothesis that individual work is not more effective than conventional instruction in social studies.

A descriptive study of seatwork done in first-grade reading groups helps to shed light on when and why individual work might be effective. Anderson, Brubaker, Alleman-Brooks, and Duffy (1985) investigated how low and high achievers differed in their responses to seatwork assignments. Low and high achievers ($N = 23$) were observed during five half-day visits, the teachers' ($N = 6$) explanations of assignments were audiotaped, and students were informally interviewed. At first it appeared that there was an inappropriate match between student ability and task difficulty; low achievers did not persist in the seatwork task, apparently because the material was too difficult. After interviewing the students, though, the investigators found that the low-ability students were poor responders, that is, they did not react to the assignment in ways conducive to learning. The difficulty level of the material was less important than their poor strategies for coping with misunderstanding. Further, the students' overt behavior did not alert teachers to the need to intervene and assist. While teachers worked with one reading group, they monitored those doing seatwork by scanning and looking for obviously off-task or disruptive behavior, which they promptly corrected. The low-achieving students did not give these cues. The researchers concluded that organization for monitoring may need to be changed. The results from this study highlight the mediating effect of student cognitions, in this case comprehension strategy use, thus supporting a cognitive orientation.

Working in Dyads

Several researchers have investigated the effects of student–student tutoring. In this setting, teachers organize students into tutor–tutee pairs for the purpose of having the tutor, usually an older child, help the tutee master some specified topic or skill. In a 1982 meta-analysis, Cohen, Kulik, and Kulik synthesized findings from 65 evaluations of school tutoring programs conducted in a variety of subject areas and at a variety of grade levels. They found an average SMD for tutee's achievement of .40. Tutoring was also found to be beneficial to the tutors.

Researchers since 1982 have arrived at similar findings. Bloom (1984) reported two studies, one using probability as the subject area and the other cartography; in each study, elementary students in the tutoring condition achieved at a level of 2 standard deviations above the conventionally taught students. Top and Osguthorpe (1987) also found positive effects for elementary tutors and tutees, with SMDs for reading achievement in the area of .58 for tutors and .86 for tutees.

Bargh and Schul (1980) wondered why tutoring had beneficial effects on the tutor as well as the tutee, and they postulated that one reason may be the planning, thinking, and structuring of the material that one must do when preparing to teach. The act of organizing material for a tutee, they reasoned, causes tutors' cognitive structures to become more organized. Thus, they learn and remember more. In their experimental study, as hypothesized, students who were told merely to study a passage did not achieve as much as students who were told they would have to teach the passage. The posttest mean score for the experimental group was 8% higher than for the control group, after adjusting for pretest scores ($F(1,151) = 4.69, p < .04$).

Small Groups

Many investigators have studied learning in small groups. Much of this research falls within the lines of study on cooperative learning and ability grouping. The cooperative-learning research is discussed in the section on reward and task structures, and the ability-grouping studies are discussed in the section on group composition.

The small-group research is particularly important because, traditionally, social studies teachers have used small groups more than teachers in other subject areas (Stodolsky, 1981). Graybeal and Stodolsky (1985) examined the use of small groups in fifth-grade mathematics and social studies classrooms. They found distinctive subject-matter differences in both frequency and type of small-group work. More was done in social studies classes, and more was focused on higher cognitive levels, than in the mathematics classes. Further, the nature of interaction differed; mathematics work groups operated under a "help permitted" orientation, but social studies group tasks required more interdependence.

Blumenfeld and Meece (1988) compared the cognitive engagement of students in small groups and whole classes. Working with upper elementary students in two science classes, they made extensive observations of teacher and student behavior. They assessed student cognitive engagement after each observed lesson by asking students to check which of 21 cognitive strategies listed on a questionnaire they had used during the lesson. Students in the whole-class arrangement reported using more cognitive strategies than those in small groups. The investigators attributed this to the teacher's emphasis on cognitive involvement. In contrast, in the small-group classroom, the teacher's emphasis was on following correctly a set of procedures for the lesson, not on thinking about it. As might be expected, cognitive engagement declined when there was less demand for it. The results of this study indicate that teacher interaction patterns can mediate the effects of classroom organization; although small-group work might generally be expected to promote greater learning because of the nature of the interaction that can take place, teacher behavior can negatively affect that by fostering unproductive interaction.

Summary

What can be concluded about the effects of within-class group size on outcomes of interest? Individual work seems not to be relatively effective in producing achievement; its effectiveness may hinge on whether students possess cognitive strategies for the learning task. When students are set up in tutoring dyads, there are consistently positive effects on achievement for both tutor and tutee. Not enough information is available on small groups to warrant any conclusion.

Can these results be explained within a cognitive framework? Traditional individual work does not demand cognitive organization, nor does it necessarily tie in with students' prior knowledge. It is not surprising, then, that individual work was not relatively effective. However, mental strategies were found to be important if students were to execute seatwork successfully. In dyadic teaching situations, tutors must come up with multiple explanations and illustrations, forcing them to expand and elaborate their own cognitive structures. The tutees receive instruction tailored to their prior knowledge. In all cases, then, a cognitive framework can be used to account for results.

TASK AND REWARD STRUCTURES

Task and reward structures refer, respectively, to the degree of interdependence among students to complete learning tasks and to obtain rewards. Researchers (see Slavin, 1983) have described three types of classroom structures: individualistic, competitive, and cooperative. In *individualistic* task structures, each student's ability to complete a task is unrelated to whether other students complete the task. Seatwork is an example of an individualistic task structure. In *competitive* task structures, students are negatively interdependent for the purpose of accomplishing a task; that is, their ability to accomplish the task hinges on other students not being able to do it. One classroom example of a competitive task structure occurs when materials are limited; only a few students can practice with a computerized social studies simulation, say, because only one terminal is available. When students are positively interdependent for a task, that is, their ability to accomplish a task depends on other students working on it too, a *cooperative* task structure is in place. Sports provide many examples of such structures; a baseball game depends on each team member doing his or her part. A group research project in which each group member is responsible for a particular section of the project is a classroom example of a cooperative task structure.

Reward structures are closely related to, but distinct from, task structures. In *individualistic* reward structures, each student is rewarded for her or his own performance, regardless of the rewards that others may receive. An example is individualized learning programs, in which students are evaluated on progress toward personal goals. *Competitive* reward structures obtain when students are negatively interdependent for rewards, that is, one or a few students' rewards preclude others from obtaining them. Grading on a curve is such a structure. Last, *cooperative* reward structures are based on positive interdependence; individuals receive rewards when their group receives rewards. Cooperative learning models provide many academic examples of cooperative reward structures. In the most typical classroom arrangement, an individualistic task structure (students can accomplish learning tasks whether or not others do) is coupled with a competitive reward structure (only a few students can receive high marks) (Slavin, 1983).

The studies on these variables are reported together because, with few exceptions, task and reward structure are con-

founded. This is not a serious problem. It is possible to imagine a factorial design in which, say, a competitive task structure is crossed with a cooperative reward structure; in practice, however, the logistics would be daunting. Results reported in this section, then, come from comparisons of individualistic tasks and rewards, competitive tasks and rewards, and cooperative tasks and rewards. Experimental studies are grouped by outcome—achievement, behavioral, and affective effects—followed by descriptive studies. Table 44–1 summarizes the reviewed research.

Which structures would be more likely to produce positive results, according to the cognitive perspective? As discussed above, forms of classroom organization that encourage students to work together discussing material, producing reports, and studying are hypothesized to promote higher achievement through helping students to forge stronger cognitive links between new knowledge and old. Clearly cooperative task and reward structures, which give students the opportunity to work together and reward them for doing so, should be more effective.

Achievement Effects

In 10 studies, the effects of task and reward structures on achievement were examined. The studies were conducted in a variety of regions, in urban, suburban, and rural settings; with diverse subject matters; and at most grade levels. In 8 studies, the cooperative condition was found to be more effective; in one, the results were mixed between cooperative and competitive conditions; and in one there was no statistically significant difference. Standardized mean differences (SMDs) estimated from t or F statistics (see Glass, McGaw, & Smith, 1981) for seven studies ranged from .30 to 2.5, with a mean SMD of .88.

Achievement was operationalized in a number of ways, from experimenter- and teacher-made tests to standardized tests. D. W. Johnson, Skon, and Johnson (1980), for example, used three measures of problem solving; on each, students' performance in the cooperative condition was statistically significantly higher than in the competitive or individualistic conditions—on a categorization and retrieval task (SMD = 2.5), a spatial reasoning task (SMD = 1.99), and a verbal reasoning task (SMD = .74).

Of particular interest are the five studies that utilized social studies content. In four, statistical significance was achieved for the cooperative condition, with a mean SMD of .76. Johnson, Johnson, and Stanne (1986) used a particularly tight design. They randomly assigned 75 eighth-grade subjects, stratified by sex, handicap, and ability, to three treatment groups. All subjects participated in the same simulation game, *Geography Search,* about the early exploration of the Americas in which a primary aim was to amass as much gold as possible from the New World. Instructional time was balanced across treatments. The teachers received extensive training in each format, worked from scripts, and were rotated across treatments to ensure fidelity of implementation and to minimize teacher effects. Research assistants observed students in each class. Four measures of achievement were collected: number of worksheet

TABLE 44–1. Effect Sizes for Cooperative Task and Reward Structures on Achievement, Behavioral and Affective Outcomes

Study	Location	Grade (N)	Subject Area	SMD for Cooperative Condition
Achievement				
Slavin, 1978	Mid-Atlantic rural	4–5 (252)	Language arts	.3
D. W. Johnson, Skon, & Johnson, 1980	Midwest suburban	1 (45)	Problem solving	.74-2.5; mean SMD = 1.74
Skon, Johnson, & Johnson, 1981	Midwest suburban	1 (86)	Language arts	.62
R. T. Johnson, Tiffany, & Zaidman, 1984	Midwest urban	4 (51)	Science	Intergroup cooperation for minorities = .85; for majority students = .25.
R. T. Johnson, Johnson, & Stanne, 1986	Midwest suburban	8 (75)	Social studies	.36-1.29; mean SMD = .70
Lew, Mesch, Johnson, & Johnson, 1986	Eastern suburban	6 (4)	Vocabulary	1.29
Lew et al., 1983	Eastern suburban	9	Social studies	Cooperative condition favored. SMD not available.
Edwards & DeVries, 1974	Eastern urban	12	Social studies	No difference. SMD not available.
Devries, Edwards, & Wells, 1974	Southern suburban	10–12	Social studies	Cooperative condition favored. SMD not available.
Allen & VanSickle, 1984	Southern rural	9 (51)	Social studies	.94
Behavior				
D. W. Johnson & Johnson, 1982	Midwest urban	4 (76)	Environmental issues (Cross-ethnic interaction)	.09
R. T. Johnson et al., 1984	Midwest urban	4(51)	Science (Cross-ethnic interaction)	Intergroup cooperation SMD for minorities = +.06; SMD for majority students = −.45
D. W. Johnson & Johnson, 1985	Midwest urban	6 (72)	Science (Cross-handicap interaction)	1.06
R. T. Johnson et al., 1986	Midwest suburban	8 (75)	Social studies (Collaborative behavior)	1.13
Lew et al., 1986	Eastern suburban	6 (4)	Vocabulary	1.9
Affect				
R. T. Johnson et al., 1986	Midwest suburban	8 (75)	Social studies (Accepting diverse others)	.44
D. W. Johnson & Johnson, 1982	Midwest urban	4 (76)	Environmental issues (Cooperative attitude, cross-ethnic sociometric)	.23

questions completed, number of worksheet questions answered correctly, results of an achievement test, and amount of gold collected during the simulation. Mean scores for the cooperative condition were statistically significantly higher on all four; the lowest SMD was on the standardized achievement test (.36), and the highest was for gold accumulated (1.29).

Behavioral Effects

In five studies, the behavioral outcomes of varying task and reward structures were examined. Behaviors of interest to the researchers were, for example, cross-ethnic interaction, during both work time and free time, and collaborative behavior. In all but one study, the cooperative condition was statistically favored. SMDs ranged from −.8 to 1.90, with a mean of .27. Overall, cooperative structures engendered more collaborative behavior and interaction between minority and majority students and between handicapped and nonhandicapped students.

Affective Effects

In two studies in social studies classrooms, the researchers examined the impact of task and reward structures on affective outcomes such as acceptance of diverse others, cooperative attitude, and cross-ethnic sociometric nominations. R. T. Johnson, Johnson, and Stanne (1986) found an SMD of .44 for a cooperative task an reward structure on promoting acceptance of others. In their study of fourth graders, D. W. Johnson and Johnson (1982) found SMDs for cooperative structures of .30 for cooperative attitude, .13 for cross-ethnic sociometric nominations during play time, and .26 for cross-ethnic sociometric nominations for helping.

Descriptive Studies

Three studies were uncovered in which the more intangible aspects of task and reward structures, particularly cooperative ones, were probed. Lockheed and Harris (1984) studied gender differences in fourth- and fifth-grade cooperative learning groups. They found that boys' perceptions of their problem-solving and leadership abilities were positively related to cooperative small-group work, whereas girls' perceptions were unrelated. This result may be explained by the fact that interaction in the groups was dominated by males; thus males received more experience and practice with problem solving and leadership. Logan (1986) observed two elementary classes, one fourth grade and one fifth, as the teachers implemented and carried out cooperatively structured lessons in science and mathematics. Logan reported that the children had a great deal of difficulty working cooperatively, despite instruction in how to do so. Tama (1986) looked more specifically at task-related interaction within cooperatively and competitively structured high school social studies discussion groups. The amount of interaction, broken down into the categories of giving information, asking a question, agreeing, and disagreeing, was consistently higher in the competitively structured classroom. Tama cautioned, however, that within-class variation was very high, rendering interpretation of the findings difficult.

Summary

The efficacy of cooperative task and reward structures in promoting achievement, positive behavior, and affective outcomes is strongly supported by the research reported here, a finding consistent with the cognitive theoretical perspective undergirding this chapter. This body of research is especially noteworthy for social studies educators for at least three reasons. First, as noted earlier, social studies teachers have tended to use group work more than other teachers, and this line of research gives teachers practical help in making these activities more effective. Second, the goals of social education, as described by the National Council for the Social Studies (1984; 1989), are highly congruent with the behavioral outcomes associated with cooperative task and reward structures, such as cross-ethnic acceptance and interaction and integration of handicapped students. Finally, the values underlying cooperative structures are also more in alignment with the values promulgated by social studies educators, such as belief in democracy, active participation by citizens, and a global, multicultural perspective.

Many research questions remain to be addressed. The descriptive studies raise disturbing issues about implementation and gender stereotypes. More research is needed, both qualitative and quantitative, on implementing cooperative reward and task structures in the classroom. How long does it take for students to learn how to function effectively within a cooperative structure? Would a sudden, total immersion in the new structures work better, or a slower, incremental approach? Work is also needed on how the possible exacerbation of gender stereotypes can be avoided. Further, researchers should begin to study broader questions such as how these task/reward structures should be orchestrated and sequenced. Should classrooms be organized cooperatively all the time, or would a mixture be better? A related concern is whether the positive effects of cooperative structures could be explained as novelty effects. Most studies lasted about a month; the longest was a semester. If the treatment time was extended, would the magnitude of results be reduced? The cognitive learning theory guiding this chapter would suggest not, but the question remains empirical.

Another problem is the paucity of studies on outcomes of particular interest to social studies educators. What is the effect of cooperative structures on political attitudes, for example? Longitudinal studies would also be helpful. It would be instructive to find out whether cooperative structures engender political activity in adulthood, long a thorny problem for social studies teachers. It seems reasonable that they would, because practice with democratic activities, as experience in cooperative work groups could be construed, ought to result in greater use of democratic skills later in life.

GROUP COMPOSITION

Within-class instructional groups can be either homogeneous or heterogeneous. That is, students of like or unlike ability can be grouped together. In the studies reviewed in this section, the effects of homogeneous and heterogeneous grouping were examined. From a cognitive point of view, organizing students heterogeneously should be more likely to engender positive outcomes than homogeneous grouping, because students of unlike ability would be forced, as they interacted together, to produce multiple and diverse explanations for the material under study. Every time they did so, they would strengthen and elaborate their cognitive structures.

Hallinan and Sorensen conducted a series of studies on homogeneous grouping, often referred to as ability grouping. In their first study, Hallinan and Sorensen (1983) looked at the stability of elementary reading and mathematics groups in 48 classrooms in northern California over a school year. They found groups to be very stable; once a student was placed in a particular group, he or she usually stayed there. They also found that ability grouping increased the class variance in achievement. Further, the greater the within-group homogeneity, the more the class variance increased.

Hallinan and Sorensen (1985) next studied friendship patterns in 32 fourth-, fifth-, and sixth-grade ability-grouped classes. They found that students assigned to the same within-class group were more likely, not surprisingly, to identify other students within that group as best friends. Similarly, the overlap between ability groups and cliques increased over time. It may be inferred, then, that homogeneous grouping reduced cross-ability interaction.

Sorensen and Hallinan (1986) turned next to a study of the effects of ability grouping on growth in academic achievement, using the data set from their 1983 study ($N = 1477$). Multiple regression analysis showed no statistically significant relationship between ability grouping and either spring achievement or growth in achievement over the year. The findings held for students at all ability levels. According to the authors, students are exposed to less instruction in an ability-grouped classroom, because the teacher can spend less time with each group, but students can utilize more of the instruction they do receive. The effects cancel each other out, and the net result is no difference. A disturbing note in this study was the finding that ability grouping exacerbated racial differences in achievement; minority students started the school year at lower achievement levels than majority students, and their position had worsened by year's end.

In a descriptive study, Haskens, Walden, and Ramey (1983) observed teacher and student behavior in high- and low-ability groups. Students in homogeneous low-ability groups were more often off-task and disruptive. Teachers, apparently in response to this behavior, more often used drill, error correction, control statements, and positive reinforcement with them. In contrast, high-ability students were able to work on their own. The authors concluded that differential teacher responses to low- and high-ability students were appropriate because of the students' behavioral differences. However, no evidence was presented that showed low-ability student behavior improved as a result of differential teacher behavior.

Webb and Cullian (1983) reported two studies in which student interaction and achievement were compared in mixed-ability and uniform-ability within-class groups of junior high students ($N = 105$). They found that certain types of student–student interaction were related to achievement. Positively related to achievement were asking questions and receiving answers in response to those questions (Study #1, $r = .24, p < .09$; Study #2, $r = .34, p < .02$). A stronger negative relationship was found between asking a question and receiving no response and achievement (Study #1, $r = -.41, p < .001$; Study #2, $r = -.42, p < .001$). Interestingly, homogeneous groups exhibited more of this undesirable interaction than heterogeneous groups.

Summary

Capsuling this diverse group of studies poses difficulties. Each was designed to answer different questions, so drawing conclusions on the basis of an accumulation of findings is not possible. It is safe to say, however, that homogeneous grouping has no demonstrated advantages, but has demonstrated disadvantages, while heterogeneous grouping shows promise of enhancing achievement via more productive interaction. These tentative conclusions are consistent with cognitively based predictions. A deficiency in the research is that, in many of the ability-grouping studies, homogenous groups were contrasted with ungrouped classes, obscuring effects due to group composition. More research is needed similar to that of Webb and Cullian (1983) specifically comparing small groups of varying composition.

Ability, or homogenous, grouping is used most often in elementary schools, but it is important to acknowledge that de facto ability grouping also occurs at the secondary level in the form of grouping by curriculum when students self-select or are counseled into academic, general, or vocational coursework (Rosenbaum, 1980). Tracking is outside the scope of this chapter, but there is some indication that it, too, may have deleterious effects by reproducing racial and class inequities and by adversely affecting achievement and classroom behavior (Bowles & Gintis, 1976; Rosenbaum, 1980; Veldman & Sanford, 1984).

TEACHER CONTROL

Teacher control refers to the degree of structure teachers impose on their students. A traditional, lecture-recitation setting is typically high in teacher control and is very tightly structured, whereas a genuine open-space classroom is lower in teacher control, with the organization of the class more fluid. Most teachers, including social studies teachers, organize for high teacher control, emphasizing activities like listening, reading textbooks, and completing worksheets or workbooks (Goodlad, 1984). From a cognitive point of view, lower teacher control would give students more opportunity to actively manufacture their own cognitive structures, thus fostering higher achievement.

Even though most teachers construct tightly organized classrooms, there is some variation. In an ethnographic study, Anyon (1980) found class-related organizational differences among social studies classes in schools in a working-class community, a middle-class community, and an affluent, professional community. In the working-class community, classroom organization was highly routinized, and success was measured by how well students followed teacher-prescribed procedures. Classroom organization in the middle-class community, however, involved somewhat more student input; these students were expected to think through their actions a little more, rather than blindly follow a set routine. The students whose parents were affluent professionals experienced the least imposed structure; assignments were more centered on self-expression and logical criteria than on teacher-prescribed criteria.

The forces creating teacher control do not seem to emanate solely from the teacher, however. In two studies (Copeland, 1980; Doyle & Carter, 1984), it was found that students influence teachers in subtle ways, most often in the direction of increasing structure and teacher control. Students behave in ways that elicit teacher behavior consistent with the students' expectation for classroom life.

In numerous studies, researchers have compared the effects of relatively teacher-controlled forms of organization with more student-centered forms on a number of outcome variables. In two studies, negative relationships were found between degrees of teacher control and outcomes (Anderson, Stevens, Prawat, & Nickerson, 1988; Curtis & Shaver, 1980). Anderson et al., for example, found a correlation between teachers' tendency to give students opportunities to direct their own activities within clearly defined limits and students' intrinsic motivation ($r = .61, p < .01$). Curtis and Shaver (1980) determined that an inquiry-oriented program with slow learners, in which students investigated a current social problem and teachers acted as facilitators, fostered critical thinking and other characteristics pertinent to good citizenship. For example, SMDs computed from adjusted posttest mean scores in a nonequivalent control-group design were $-.71$ on the Dogmatism Scale and $.36$ on the Cornell Critical Thinking Test.

Not all studies, however, have supported such relationships. Peterson, Janicki, and Swing (1980) found, for example, that achievement on a multiple-choice test was higher in more structured social studies classrooms. In several studies, researchers either found no statistically significant differences between variations in teacher control or obtained mixed results: Glenn and Ellis (1982) for problem solving; Harrison, Strauss, and Glaubman (1981) for achievement and creativity; and Hayes and Day (1980) for basic skills, self-perceptions, and school attendance.

Summary

Why such mixed results for the effects of teacher control? One possibility is that these studies concerned different kinds of outcomes, and that affective outcomes, such as reduced dogmatism, tend to be enhanced by a less directive teacher, while achievement as measured by multiple-choice tests is advanced by a more directive one. Peterson (1979), in an extensive review of studies conducted in the 1970s comparing direct instruction with open classrooms, found just such a trend. More experimental research is needed in which degree of structure and type of outcome are purposefully varied before conclusions for theory or practice can be drawn.

CONCLUSION

Has the cognitive perspective that guided the review of research for this chapter been confirmed? The answer is a qualified yes. Forms of classroom organization that helped students see the links between new and prior knowledge, and that promoted construction of cognitive structures by students, were in general more effective in producing desired outcomes. Small, heterogeneous groups operating within a cooperative task and reward structure allowed students more of this kind of activity than traditional work, and the result was higher achievement. Gray areas still exist, of course; findings are mixed for individualized study and for teacher control.

What can be recommended, then, as to best practice in classroom organization for social studies? Social studies teachers should continue their practice of using small-group work but should actively incorporate cooperative task and reward structures. They should use heterogeneous grouping, not homogeneous, and they should incorporate some less structured activities.

What about recommendations for research? Certainly more research is needed to understand how classroom organization variables affect student outcomes and to develop practical guidelines for teachers. But a more striking need is the application of a consistent theoretical perspective, framework, or system of research for coherently investigating these variables. The literature has a piecemeal, eclectic quality, despite the post hoc imposition of a cognitive theoretical orientation. Systematizing the research in classroom organization should be a fundamental concern.

Slavin has proposed an approach to educational research

and development called *component building* (1984). With this approach, a particular constellation of instructional elements, the best "package" according to current wisdom, is put together and field tested. Once the total program has been deemed effective, each separable component is tested experimentally by systematically withdrawing it from the package under controlled conditions in the field. At least two advantages accrue with this approach. *One,* the effectiveness of each component can be determined; some components may turn out to be unnecessary or even detrimental. *Two,* by determining the contribution of each separate component, ideas for future research and the development of new programs may be generated. This approach is similar to Ebel's (1982) operational research strategy, advocated by Armento (1986).

A good example of this sort of programmatic research is Slavin's own work on cooperative learning. After determining the effectiveness of a cooperative learning package, he tried to sort out whether the cooperative task structure or cooperative reward structure or both were important for producing the achievement results. In a factorial experiment, he discovered that the cooperative reward structure was the most salient (Slavin, 1978).

How might component building be applied in the area of classroom organization? A constellation of components thought to enhance achievement, behavioral, and affective outcomes must be constructed. Cooperative structures and heterogeneous grouping are clearly prime candidates for the initial package, because these variables have been established as having strong positive impacts on desired outcomes. However, more refined components should be tested. For example, implementation of cooperative groups can sometimes be problematic (Logan, 1986), so it could be argued that the initial package should include both immersion in a cooperative structure and training in constructive interaction within that structure. Further, even though the empirical data are mixed, cognitive theory leads to the prediction that low teacher control will foster active structuring by students and, thus, achievement; so the initial package should also incorporate that element. Care should be taken, however, to utilize appropriate and diverse outcome measures, because multiple-choice tests cannot assess all types of learning validly. The research program should be conducted in social studies classrooms at a variety of grade and socioeconomic levels to maximize external validity.

Other questions of theoretical interest include whether student–student interaction is an important mediating variable between classroom organization and achievement. Webb and her colleagues (see Webb, Ender, & Lewis, 1986), in an interesting line of research in laboratory and non–social studies settings, have examined the effects of such interaction on achievement. An important next step in testing cognitive theory would be to look at interaction, cognitive structure, and achievement together.

Component building and theory testing offer a fruitful approach for researchers interested in understanding the complexity of classroom effects. The gains in knowledge about classroom organization and outcomes would be a boon to social studies teachers and their students.

References

Allen, W. H., & VanSickle, R. L. (1984). Learning teams and low achievers. *Social Education, 48,* 60–64.

Anderson, L. M., Brubaker, N. L., Alleman-Brooks, J., & Duffy, G. (1985). A qualitative study of seatwork in first-grade classrooms. *Elementary School Journal, 86,* 123–140.

Anderson, L. M., Stevens, D. D., Prawat, R. S., & Nickerson, J. (1988). Classroom task environments and students' task related beliefs. *Elementary School Journal, 88,* 281–295.

Anyon, J. (1980). Social class and the hidden curriculum of work. *Journal of Education, 162,* 67–92.

Armento, B. J. (1986). Research on teaching social studies. In M. C. Wittrock (Ed.), *Handbook of research on teaching* (3rd ed., pp. 942–951). New York: Macmillan.

Bangert, R. L., Kulik, J. A., & Kulik, C. L. C. (1983). Individualized systems of instruction in secondary schools. *Review of Educational Research, 53,* 143–158.

Bargh, J. A., & Schul, Y. (1980). On the cognitive benefits of teaching. *Journal of Educational Psychology, 72,* 593–604.

Bloom, B. S. (1984). The 2 sigma problem: The search for methods of group instruction as effective as one-to-one tutoring. *Educational Researcher, 13,* 4–16.

Blumenfield, P. C., & Meece, J. L. (1988). Task factors, teacher behavior, and students' involvement and use of learning strategies in science. *Elementary School Journal, 88,* 235–250.

Bowles, S., & Gintis, H. (1976). *Schooling in capitalist America.* New York: Basic Books.

Cahen, L. S., Filby, N., McCutcheon, G., & Kyle, D. W. (1983). *Class size and instruction.* New York: Longman.

Cohen, P. A., Kulik, J. A., & Kulik, C. L. C. (1982). Educational outcomes of tutoring: A meta-analysis of findings. *American Educational Research Journal, 19,* 237–248.

Copeland, W. D. (1980). Teaching–learning behaviors and the demands of the classroom environment. *Elementary School Journal, 80,* 163–177.

Curtis, C. K., & Shaver, J. P. (1980). Slow learners and the study of contemporary problems. *Social Education, 44,* 302–308.

DeVries, D. L., Edwards, K. J., & Wells, E. H. (1974). *Teams-games-tournament in social studies classrooms: Effects on academic achievement, student attitudes, cognitive beliefs, and classroom climate* (Report No. 173). Baltimore: Johns Hopkins University, Center for Social Organization of Schools.

Doyle, W., & Carter, K. (1984). Academic tasks in classrooms. *Curriculum Inquiry, 14,* 129–149.

Ebel, R. (1982). The future of educational research. *Educational Researcher, 11*(8), 18–19.

Edwards, K. J., & DeVries, D. L. (1974). *The effects of teams-games-tournaments and two structural variations on classroom process, student attitudes, and student achievement* (Report No. 172). Baltimore: Johns Hopkins University, Center for Social Organization of Schools.

Fancett, V. S., & Hawke, S. (1982). Instructional practices in social studies. In I. Morrissett (Ed.), *The current state of social studies:* A report of Project SPAN (pp. 207–263). Boulder, CO: Social Science Education Consortium. (ERIC Document Reproduction Service No. ED 218 199)

Glass, G. V., McGaw, B., & Smith, M. L. (1981). *Meta-analysis in social research.* Beverly Hills, CA: Sage.

Glenn, A. D., & Ellis, A. K. (1982). Direct and indirect methods of teaching problem solving to elementary school children. *Social Education, 46,* 134–136.

Goodlad, J. I. (1984). *A place called school.* New York: McGraw-Hill.

Graybeal, S. S., & Stodolsky, S. S. (1985). Peer work groups in elementary schools. *American Journal of Education, 93,* 409–428.

Hallinan, M. T., & Sorensen, A. B. (1983). The formation and stability of instructional groups. *American Sociological Review, 48,* 838–851.

Hallinan, M. T., & Sorensen, A. B. (1985). Ability grouping and student friendships. *American Educational Research Journal, 22,* 485–499.

Harrison, J., Strauss, H., & Glaubman, R. (1981). The impact of open and traditional classrooms on achievement and creativity: The Israeli case. *Elementary School Journal, 82,* 27–35.

Haskens, R., Walden, T., & Ramey, C. T. (1983). Teacher and student behavior in high- and low-ability groups. *Journal of Educational Psychology, 75,* 865–876.

Hayes, R. K., Jr., & Day, B. D. (1980). Classroom openness and the basic skills, the self-perceptions, and the school-attendance records of third-grade pupils. *Elementary School Journal, 81,* 87–96.

Johnson, D. W., & Johnson, R. (1982). Effects of cooperative, competitive, and individualistic learning experiences on cross-ethnic interaction and friendship. *Journal of Social Psychology, 118,* 47–58.

Johnson, D. W., & Johnson, R. T. (1985). Classroom conflict: Controversy versus debate in learning groups. *American Educational Research Journal, 22,* 237–256.

Johnson, D. W., Skon, L., & Johnson, R. T. (1980). Effects of cooperative, competitive, and individualistic conditions on children's problem-solving performance. *American Educational Research Journal, 17,* 83–93.

Johnson, R. T., Johnson, D. W., & Stanne, M. B. (1986). Comparison of computer-assisted cooperative, competitive, and individualistic learning. *American Educational Research Journal, 23,* 382–392.

Johnson, R. T., Tiffany, M., & Zaidman, B. (1984). Cross-ethnic relationships: The impact of intergroup cooperation and intergroup competition. *Journal of Educational Research, 78,* 75–79.

Leming, J. S. (1985). Research on social studies curriculum and instruction: Interventions and outcomes in the socio-moral domain. In W. B. Stanley (Ed.), *Review of research in social studies education: 1976–1983* (pp. 123–213). Washington, DC: National Council for the Social Studies.

Lew, M., Gangi, D., Orban, D., Spandos, G., Maglio, R., Sullivan, G., & Schimmel, J. (1983, April). *Group contingencies in the secondary school: Some research applications.* Paper presented at the meeting of the American Educational Research Association, Montreal.

Lew, M., Mesch, D., Johnson, D. W., & Johnson, R. T. (1986). Positive interdependence, academic and collaborative-skill group contingencies, and isolated students. *American Educational Research Journal, 23,* 476–488.

Lockheed, M. E., & Harris, A. M. (1984). Cross-sex collaborative learning in elementary classrooms. *American Educational Research Journal, 21,* 275–294.

Logan, T. F. (1986). Cooperative learning: A view from the inside. *Social Studies, 77,* 123–135.

National Council for the Social Studies. (1984). In search of a scope and sequence for social studies. Report of the Task Force on Scope and Sequence. *Social Education, 48,* 249–262.

National Council for the Social Studies, Task Force on Early Childhood/Elementary Social Studies. (1989). Social studies for early childhood and elementary school children: Preparing for the 21st century. *Social Education, 52,* 14–23.

Peterson, P. L. (1979). Direct instruction reconsidered. In P. L. Peterson & H. J. Walberg (Eds.), *Research on teaching: Concepts, findings, and implications* (pp. 57–69). Berkeley, CA: McCutchan.

Peterson, P. L., Janicki, T. C., & Swing, S. R. (1980). Aptitude-treatment interaction effects of three social studies teaching approaches. *American Educational Research Journal, 17,* 339–360.

Pierce, W., Lemke, E., & Smith, R. (1988). Critical thinking and moral development in secondary students. *High School Journal, 71,* 120–126.

Rosenbaum, J. E. (1980). Social implications of educational grouping. In D. C. Berliner (Ed.), *Review of research in education* (Vol. 8, pp. 361–401). Washington, DC: American Educational Research Association.

Skon, L., Johnson, D. W., & Johnson, R. T. (1981). Cooperative peer interaction versus individual competition and individualistic efforts: Effect on the acquisition of cognitive reasoning strategies. *Journal of Educational Psychology, 73,* 83–92.

Slavin, R. E. (1978). Effects of student teams and peer tutoring on academic achievement and time on task. *Journal of Experimental Education, 48,* 252–257.

Slavin, R. E. (1983). *Cooperative learning.* New York: Longman.

Slavin, R. E. (1984). Component building: A strategy for research-based instructional improvement. *Elementary School Journal, 84,* 255–269.

Slavin, R. E. (1986). Best-evidence synthesis: An alternative to meta-analytic and traditional reviews. *Educational Researcher, 15*(8), 5–11.

Slavin, R. E. (1987). Best-evidence synthesis: Why less is more. *Educational Researcher, 16*(4), 15–16.

Sorensen, A. B., & Hallinan, M. T. (1986). Effects of ability grouping on growth in academic achievement. *American Educational Research Journal, 23,* 519–542.

Stake, R. E., & Easley, J. A. (Eds.). (1978). *Case studies in science education.* Urbana, IL: Center for Instructional Research and Curriculum Evaluation, University of Illinois.

Stodolsky, S. S. (1981, April). *Subject matter constraints on the ecology of classroom instruction.* Paper presented at the meeting of the American Educational Research Association, Los Angeles.

Tama, M. C. (1986). How are students responding in discussion groups? *Social Studies, 77,* 133–135.

Tobias, S. (1982). When do instructional methods make a difference? *Educational Researcher, 11*(4), 4–9.

Top, B. L., & Osguthorpe, R. T. (1987). Reverse-role tutoring: The effects of handicapped students tutoring regular class students. *Elementary School Journal, 87,* 413–423.

Veldman, D. J., & Sanford, J. P. (1984). The influence of class ability level on student achievement and classroom behavior. *American Educational Research Journal, 21,* 629–644.

Webb, N. M., & Cullian, L. K. (1983). Group interaction and achievement in small groups: Stability over time. *American Educational Research Journal, 20,* 411–423.

Webb, N. M., Ender, P., & Lewis, S. (1986). Problem-solving strategies and group processes in small groups learning computer programming. *American Educational Research Journal, 23,* 243–261.

Weiss, I. R. (1978). *Report of the 1977 national survey of science, mathematics, and social studies education.* Research Triangle Park, NC: Center for Educational Research and Evaluation.

Wiley, K. B. (1977). *The status of pre-college science, mathematics, and social science education: 1955–1975: Vol. 3. Social Science Education.* Boulder, CO: Social Science Education Consortium.

Wittrock, M. C. (1986). Students' thought processes. In M. C. Wittrock (Ed.), *Handbook of research on teaching* (3rd ed., pp. 297–314). New York: Macmillan.

45

SCHOOL–COMMUNITY PARTICIPATION FOR SOCIAL STUDIES

Dan Conrad

UNIVERSITY OF MINNESOTA AND HOPKINS PUBLIC SCHOOLS, MINNETONKA, MINNESOTA

Social studies teachers face a dilemma. They are charged with imparting to their students a sense of history and an understanding of the complexities of modern society. At the same time, they bear the major responsibility for promoting something that is not essentially a matter of knowledge at all, but a practice, even a habit: active and informed citizenship. The usual way out of the dilemma is to emphasize the academic mission of the social studies, to assert that it constitutes appropriate preparation for citizenship, and to trust that it will translate at some later point into regular and effective citizen action.

Some educators take a different approach. Their solution is to stress that citizenship education ought to include the opportunity for students to actually do the things that good citizens do. Their basic assumptions are that (a) academic content and skills are better learned when acquired and applied in real settings; (b) such experiences are more likely than classroom experiences to develop the personal attributes and social dispositions associated with effective citizenship; and (c) the practice of civic involvement by children and youth will carry over as a habit of adult life. This approach to social studies education is examined in this chapter.

Programs of school–community participation are typically categorized by the type of participation they feature. These include volunteer service (e.g., in a nursing home or food center), school service (especially tutoring), community study (e.g., recording oral histories), community projects (taking on tasks not addressed by existing agencies), internships (such as with a county attorney or local businessperson), and sociopolitical action, in which the goal is to influence public policy.

The distinguishing feature of participatory programs is not the activities per se; it is that the students move from being mere recipients of services into new and more active roles in which they perform significant tasks that (a) both students and community think are worthwhile; (b) involve real consequences, in that others are dependent on their actions; (c) are challenging and stretch and strengthen participants' skills, knowledge, intellect, and values; (d) include the responsibility of making decisions and promote an authentic sense of being in charge; and, (e) are surrounded by opportunities for reflection to think, discuss, and write about what they are doing.

There are many school and youth programs that foster such participation, and they do so for a variety of purposes. The prime focus of this chapter is on those that are explicitly social studies' offerings, but other programs that have citizenship included among their aims are also treated.

Programs featuring participation in the school and community are identified by various labels, the most common of which is *experiential education*. Throughout this chapter the terms *participatory* and *experiential* are used interchangeably. The most commonly used label is *experiential,* because that is the primary identifier for these programs in the major educational reference works such as *Journals in Education* and the ERIC files.

SPECIAL METHODOLOGICAL PROBLEMS

The study of participatory programs involves persistent and unique difficulties that must be considered when interpreting the results of prior research or planning a study of one's own. These difficulties were encountered in each study cited in this chapter; discussing them here lessens the need to add laborious

Reviewers were Steve F. Hamilton, Cornell University; Fred M. Newmann, University of Wisconsin, Madison; Robert D. Shumer, University of California, Los Angeles.

caveats to every reported finding. A further economy can be achieved by acknowledging that this discussion of problems draws heavily on the writings of Steve Hamilton (Hamilton, 1980; Hamilton & Fenzel, 1988).

The fundamental difficulty in assessing participation as an educational method is that the term encompasses a wide variety of practices undertaken for an even wider variety of purposes. The result is a potential for mind-boggling confusion.

1. Some confusion exists over what counts as participation. Touring the state capital with one's civics class would seem, by the usual criteria, not to count, but serving as a legislator's aide would. There are, however, many possibilities in between that are less clear.

2. Even if what counted as participation were clear, there is little reason to assume that every form of participation—volunteering in a day care center, running a consumer action service, or picking up litter—would have the same kind or depth of effect.

3. Given the wide range of plausible outcomes for any participatory experience, it is a challenge to identify the appropriate dependent variables. Newmann (1975, pp. 9–10) laid out nine possible citizenship-related outcomes that could accrue from the same activity featuring direct civic involvement, and he did so without even touching on issues of political efficacy, later civic involvement, factual recall, and self-esteem!

4. Even if the focus is narrowed to one or two outcomes from one particular kind of experience and program, it is unlikely that all participants will do the same things. In putting out a community newsletter, some might do research, others write, and others type or distribute the finished newsletter. Even if all participants did the same things, they would not be likely to experience them in the same way. A night in a homeless shelter may be one experience for a streetwise urban youth aspiring to a business career and quite another for a sheltered suburbanite contemplating social work.

5. The hypothesized outcomes often are changes in very broad and stable personal characteristics (such as self-esteem or level of political efficacy) that are not altered overnight or in ways that are captured using paper-and-pencil questionnaires.

6. Most participatory experiences are relatively brief and isolated departures from classroom study. Thus, there is little opportunity to assess the cumulative effect of a variety of such experiences over a longer period of time (such as when one can examine the impact of 1, 2, or 3 years of American history or 10 years of social studies).

7. The instruments available to researchers are usually borrowed from other research efforts conducted on quite different programs. Often they are not designed to capture the complexity or nuances, let alone serendipity, of participation.

8. The majority of youth-participation programs are voluntary, with the consequences that (a) the sample is atypical and (b) it is difficult to assemble valid control groups. As a consequence, it is difficult to interpret the educational significance of the results or know if they would apply to youth other than those who volunteer for such programs.

9. To this date, nearly all studies of participatory programs have been conducted by advocates of the practice and, in some of these cases, by the operators of the very programs being studied.

Other problems in doing research on participatory programs could be listed. Those just enumerated, however, suffice to illustrate the obstacles faced by the researchers cited in this chapter. They also indicate the challenges facing those who follow in their paths.

ARGUMENTS FOR PARTICIPATION AND RESEARCH FINDINGS

The arguments for experiential education are rooted in concern for the total development of young people—social, psychological, and intellectual. This development is seen as being jeopardized by a social milieu that increasingly isolates young people from the kinds of experiences, encounters, and challenges that form the basis for healthy development and that add purpose and meaning to formal education. In this section, each of the general arguments for participation is briefly sketched and then examined in the light of recent research.

Social Development

Since the mid-1960s, there has been growing public concern over the level of commitment to basic democratic values exhibited by youth. Charges of increased privatism, hedonism, and aimlessness among adolescents have become commonplace, along with findings that they feel powerless in relation to the larger society and have no sense of fulfilling a significant role in it. The educational literature is replete with examples and research data that suggest that life in the schools not only does not counter such attitudes but also is a chief contributor to them.

In a review of the literature on the impact of high school on the development of social competence, Newman and Newman (1987) found mostly negatives: strong norms for conformity, regimentation and blind obedience; role bound, impersonal, and inflexible adult–student relationships; rigid and stereotypical status systems among peers; powerlessness of students and minimal opportunity to help make decisions effecting them; and lack of support, in practice, for the principles of the Bill of Rights.

Social studies has not escaped this critique. Jennings and his associates, for example, have repeatedly reported lack of effects of formal social studies instruction on political knowledge, attitudes and behavior (M. Jennings & Niemi, 1974). Others have taken the social studies to task for fostering passivity (Shermis & Barth, 1982) and for neither engaging nor being engaging to students (Schug, Todd, & Beery, 1984).

Research into efforts to combat these trends and influences through school–community participation has produced results that are promising but far from conclusive. To date, the broadest look at the impact of participation on social development was undertaken by Conrad and Hedin (1981). They studied 27 school-sponsored programs featuring direct participation in the community through community service, community study, career internships, and outdoor adventure. Their general finding was that students in participatory programs did gain in social and personal responsibility as measured by the project-developed Social and Personal Responsibility Scale (SPRS). The greatest gains were recorded on subscales focused on feelings of competence (to be responsible) and respondents' perceptions of themselves as persons who act responsibly. Gains of lesser magnitude were reported on subscales that assessed feelings of responsibility for the welfare of others and of obligation to fulfill personal duties.

Hamilton (Hamilton & Fenzel, 1988) used a slightly modified version of the SPRS with 4-H members in 12 programs featuring either child care or community-improvement projects. He reported gains on the Social Responsibility subscale but not on the Personal Responsibility subscale. He found, further, that girls showed greater gains than did boys, as did persons working in community-improvement projects, versus those in child care.

Another modification of the SPRS was used by Newmann and Rutter (1983) to examine the impact of school-sponsored community service programs in eight diverse school districts. Their overall finding was that community service programs did have a positive impact on students' sense of social responsibility and sense of personal competence, vis-à-vis comparison groups. The advantages, however, were modest, and they were unable to uncover what, if anything, about these programs accounted for the advantages they found.

Stockhaus (1976/1977) investigated the impact of community service performed as part of the 12th-grade social studies requirement in two suburban high schools. He reported gains in participants' sense of social responsibility, community responsibility, and level of altruism, as compared with nonparticipants.

Researchers have investigated several other dimensions of social development. Hamilton (1981) concluded, from data gathered through questionnaires and interviews, that youth paired with mentors outside the school gained more positive attitudes toward, and richer associations with, adults. Conrad and Hedin (1981), using a series of semantic differentials, found that students who participated in the community developed more favorable attitudes toward adults in general and also toward the types of institutions and people with whom they were involved. Luchs (cited in Danzig & Szanton, 1986, pp. 56–57) reported that students involved in community service gained more positive attitudes toward others, along with a greater sense of efficacy, than did nonparticipating comparison students. Herman and Bury (1988) evaluated programs in several Los Angeles high schools in which students planned and implemented after-school service projects. From extensive interviews and direct observation, they concluded that such participation increased students' sense of responsibility and ability to work with others, along with fostering heightened management and leadership skills.

Using Campbell's Scale of Political Efficacy, Wilson (1974/1975) found that students in a community-based alternative school who engaged in political and social action in the school and the wider community gained in political efficacy. Button (1972/1973), employing both an efficacy scale and interviews, found that students who did fieldwork regarding the political structure of their city gained in political efficacy and became more interested in politics. Corbett (1977), however, in a study of a yearlong community service program, did not find gains on standard measures of either political efficacy or social responsibility. Newmann and Rutter (1983) reported no gain in political efficacy in their study of eight high school service programs.

In examining a related phenomenon, Conrad and Hedin (1981) found that young people in experience-based programs showed significant gains in both their evaluation of, and likelihood of, actually "being active in the community." In a longitudinal study of University of Virginia graduates who had participated in the University Year for Action (UYA) while at school, Gansneder and Kingston (1984) found that UYA graduates were significantly more involved in community volunteer activities and more likely to be pursuing careers in human services than were their non-UYA peers. F. M. Newman and Rutter (1983), however, did not get the same result in their study of service programs. Nor did Horenstein (1985/1986) in a follow-up study of college students who were graduates of a high school featuring extensive community-based activity. She found that, while in college, the students volunteered service to their community less frequently than did a sample of students from other schools.

Two of the best and most extensive studies of experience-based programs are those of the Volunteer Work Camps of the American Friends Service Committee (Riecken, 1952) and of the Encampment for Citizenship (Hyman, Wright, & Hopkins, 1963). Both of these programs involved post-high-school-age youth in summer live-in experiences. Nonetheless, the programs' goals were so close to those of citizenship education and the research so sound and creative that the studies deserve attention from other researchers. Among their findings were the following: Participants in both programs became more service oriented in career choice, more aware of and concerned about social problems, more inclined to political participation, more respectful of others, more strongly supportive of basic democratic values, and more self-confident and mature. The study of the Encampment was followed up by another, 10 years later, from which it was concluded that the effects of the experience were lasting ones.

Psychological Development

Psychological development has not traditionally been a formal objective of social studies education. Yet there is ample evidence that many of its traditional aims are, in fact, inextricably linked to such development. Research into citizenship behavior has demonstrated that active participation is linked to such psychological variables as self-esteem (Stockhaus, 1976/1977) and level of moral reasoning (Haan, Smith, & Block, 1968). Studies of altruistic behavior have shown that young persons who engage in prosocial acts are "relatively self confident

. . . [and] advanced in moral reasoning as well as in role-taking skills and empathy" (Mussen & Eisenberg-Berg, 1977, p. 159). In addition to these are the more commonly cited links between psychological health and such variables as academic achievement (Purkey, 1970) and overall adult happiness and accomplishment (Heath, 1977).

An important finding from the research on schools is that studying the formal, academic curriculum does not automatically lead to personal and psychological growth. In fact, there is a substantial body of research documenting that schooling has a largely negative impact on such variables as self-esteem, interest in learning, and personal autonomy (Sprinthall & Sprinthall, 1977). Proponents of experiential education have argued that placing students in challenging situations where the problems and consequences are real is an effective means of promoting personal growth. The research reviewed for this chapter tends to support this assumption. In fact, the most consistent finding of studies of participatory programs is that these experiences do tend to increase self-esteem and promote personal development.

Self-esteem. Self-esteem has been the psychological variable most commonly investigated in research on participation. Not all of the findings have been positive. Stockhaus (1976/1977), for example, found no increase in the self-esteem of high school students involved in community service. Sager (1973/1974), however, found that high school youth who spent a summer as full-time helpers in institutions for mentally retarded persons did gain in self-confidence and self-esteem. Luchs's results (cited in Danzig & Szanton, 1986) were similar in a study of high school students performing 30 hours of community service, as were those of Yul Lee and Challen (1982) in a study of 10th graders who taught in an elementary school. Most studies of tutoring, in fact, have found that moving into the role of teaching others has had a positive impact on the self-esteem of the tutors (Hedin, 1987).

Three other studies of community service also yielded positive results in regard to self-esteem. Newmann and Rutter (1983) reported that students involved in community service projects increased more than comparison students on their measure of social competence. They regarded this as a measure of something very close to self-esteem because respondents were asked such things as how confident they were that others would pay attention to them and how successful they felt they were in persuading adults to take their views seriously. Horenstein (1985/1986) studied graduates of a high school where every student was involved in community-based experiences. As undergraduates in college, these students scored higher than peers from traditional schools on a standardized test of self-confidence and self-confidence in work situations. Conrad and Hedin (1981) reported modest gains in self-esteem in their study of several types of participatory programs. Although there was some gain by students in each type of program, the greatest gains in self-esteem were registered by students in outdoor adventure experiences.

Moral and Ego Development. A more complex framework for assessing psychological impact has been suggested by develop-mental stage theorists such as Jean Piaget (1972), Jane Loevinger (1976), and Lawrence Kohlberg (1981). Psychological theories of development vary in focus, but they share the central concepts of stage, structure, and interaction. It is posited that individuals grow and develop in a series of qualitatively distinct stages. The occurrence of growth depends upon a certain maturity and readiness within the individual and upon the kind and quality of the person's interactions with the environment.

The relationship between experience and development has made the developmental view particularly relevant to participatory education, and vice versa. A number of studies with this perspective have been made of a series of programs united under the label Deliberate Psychological Education. Students in these programs participated actively as interviewers, teachers, tutors, and peer counselors. The typical, though not universal outcome was that the students gained in both moral and ego development (Cognetta & Sprinthall, 1978). One reviewer of the findings of the research on developmental education concluded, *first,* that it is possible to stimulate moral and ego development through educational interventions and, *second,* that the factors critical to moral development include discussion of moral issues, exercise of empathy and role taking, and action on behalf of moral and social goals (Mosher, 1977).

Some of these conclusions were examined by Conrad and Hedin (1981) as part of their study of experiential education. Three groups of students in one high school were all tested in moral reasoning prior to receiving identical instruction, by the same teacher, in Kohlberg's theory of moral development. Two of the groups were simultaneously involved in service activities in the community. Pre- and posttest results from the Defining Issues Test showed that both experimental groups had gained in moral reasoning, while the control group had not. This finding was consistent with the conclusion of Kohlberg (1973) that movement to the highest stages of development demands more than classroom discussion; it "requires some experiences of moral responsibility and independent moral choice" (p. 500). In his last years, Kohlberg's recommendations for moral education increasingly emphasized active and consequential experiences for students, most particularly through the operation of what he referred to as "just communities." The just community integrates curriculum and moral discussion in real, participatory democracy. Evaluations of such schools have revealed a number of problems in their implementation. But research into the impact of the programs on students has consistently yielded positive changes in moral reasoning, concern for fairness of rules and policies, development of a sense of the school as a moral community, and self-perceived moral behavior change (W. S. Jennings & Kohlberg, 1983; Wasserman, 1977/1978).

Alienation. Programs aiming at reducing adolescent alienation frequently include giving youth more decision-making authority and more meaningful participation in the school and community. Calabrese and Schumer (1986) examined the impact of involvement in service projects on the alienation of junior high students enrolled in a program for youth with behavioral problems. They reported finding lower levels of alienation and isolation as measured by the Dean Alienation Scale. The researchers' examination of school records revealed improved attendance,

attendance, fewer discipline problems, and improved grade point averages. Interviews with persons who supervised the projects revealed that the students had won the affection and confidence of the adults with whom they worked in the community. An interesting additional finding was that the reduction in discipline problems lasted only so long as participation in community service continued.

Academic Learning and Intellectual Development

No outcome of experiential programs is more common than participants reporting that they have learned a great deal from their experiences. For example, in a nationwide survey of nearly 4,000 students involved in experiential programs, about 75% reported learning "more" or "much more" in their participation program than in their regular classes (Conrad & Hedin, 1981). Similar findings are regularly reported in other studies. When people feel strongly that they have learned a great deal, they probably have done so, but it is not always possible for them or others to delineate just what they have learned.

The theoretical case for experience as a source of learning is well grounded and persuasive but too complex to spell out in detail here. Suffice it to say that its roots extend back at least to Aristotle and continue through Rousseau and into more modern times through the writings of Dewey (1938), Polanyi (1962), Piaget (1972), Olson and Bruner (1974), Coleman (1977), and Kolb (1984). It does the barest sort of justice to such thinkers to say the essential argument is that real learning and intellectual development occur as the individual interacts with the environment, with experience serving variously as a source and test of knowledge, a stimulus for thought, and a guard against meaningless abstraction. Despite the richness and complexity of the theoretical case, perhaps even because of it, the research evidence for the impact of experiential education on academic learning and intellectual development is neither extensive nor conclusive. Some attempts to investigate the impact of participation on this dimension of development are reported next.

Intellectual Development. Some researchers have focused their efforts on examining the impact of participation on the processes of thinking rather than on the mastery of content or the attainment of skills. Wilson (1974/1975), for example, focused on open-mindedness as measured by the Rokeach Dogmatism Scale. He found that students involved in political and social action in the school and wider community did become more open-minded. Conrad and Hedin (1981) focused on how students analyzed problems. They devised a Problem Solving Inventory to categorize reactions to a series of real-life problems according to the degree of (a) empathy with the key "other" in the simulus story and (b) complexity of their analysis of the problem. Their basic finding was that students who encountered problems similar to those presented in the test *and* who were in programs in which problem solving was a deliberate focus, showed substantially more complex patterns of analysis from the pretest to the posttest. Students in programs in which only one or the other of these features was present showed less change. Students who neither reflected on experiences nor encountered problems similar to those presented showed no more change than students in conventional classrooms.

Of particular interest, perhaps more for the age of the participants than the elegance of the research, is a qualitative study of a group of English 7-year-olds. These children did firsthand research, including field interviews, on the potential impact of a controversial new road to their town. They then presented their views on a televised public inquiry (Carre & Howitt, 1987). From direct observation and from analysis of the students' writing and oral comments, the researchers concluded that the students had increased their ability to weigh arguments, articulate ideas, reflect on their values, and make sound decisions and had become more autonomous in their thinking. It was their further conclusion that it was the realism of the experience that accounted for these gains.

Skills. An approach taken by some researchers has been to focus on the particular skills that are employed in the participation program. The aforementioned Deliberate Psychological Education programs engaged adolescents as teachers, tutors, and counselors of peers and younger children. Studies of these programs have consistently shown that, in addition to growing in psychological maturity and gaining in content knowledge, the adolescents have become highly skilled in classroom management and have often developed counseling skills "higher than those achieved by graduate students in counseling" (Sprinthall & Sprinthall, 1977, p. 580).

Hamilton (Hamilton & Fenzel, 1988) examined several dimensions of learning that might be gained by young people working with children and in various other community projects. Students, and the adults in the community who supervised them, responded to written questionnaires and personal interviews. Both groups of respondents attested to the students having learned about themselves and their community and to their having learned the skills demanded of them in their placements. These ranged from "construction skills" at a building site to "keeping the interest of children" at a child care center.

Gilliland, Hartman, and Jessee (1985) studied a summer program for 10th graders who investigated the quality of the drinking water in rural Alabama and then presented their findings in a public forum. They concluded that the students learned and applied basic social research skills, thought critically about issues, learned about their communities, and gained in self-confidence and ability to work with others.

Academic Learning. Researchers studying experiential programs have tended to steer away from facts and concepts as a focus of inquiry. Standardized tests of factual knowledge are nearly guaranteed to show no effects. A typical example is an evaluation of field courses in secondary economics done for the Institute of Education of London University (Smith, 1985). These courses, which were more like field trips than true examples of participation, were rated as highly enjoyable and worthwhile by both staff and students. Yet those who participated in the courses scored no better or worse on the standard course examinations than those who did not. An almost identical outcome was reported in an extensive study of a series of programs joined under the rubric of the Executive High School Internship Program (Crowe & Walker, 1977). All persons connected with the program judged it a great learning experience, but the test data showed no difference between participants and non-participants on any test of knowledge about government.

Lack of subject-matter learning is not always the result, of course. Button (1972/1973), in a study of students engaged in political and social action, and Hamilton and Zelden (1987), in a study of interns in local government, both found increases in political knowledge. The key is that these researchers used instruments that were focused on the kinds of information students were likely to encounter in their fieldwork.

The best substantiated link between participation and academic learning is found in the extensive literature examining the impact of tutoring. In a meta-analysis of tutoring studies, Hedin (1987) reported that, not only did the students who were tutored have higher mean mathematics and reading test scores than those taught in conventional classrooms (or with computer-assisted instruction), but that the tutors uniformly gained academically as well. In most studies, the tutors' academic gains were more substantial than those of the students they taught.

Summary of Findings From Research

The research on the impact of school–community participation suggests that this approach often does have a positive impact on the social, psychological, and intellectual development of participants. Researchers have consistently reported a heightened sense of social responsibility, more positive attitudes toward adults and others, enhanced self-esteem, growth in moral and ego development, more sophisticated and complex patterns of thought, and greater mastery of skills and content directly related to the experiences of the participants.

On the less positive side, the evidence in regard to the effects on political efficacy and the likelihood of later participation in civic affairs is conflicting. There is also no evidence that participation results in higher scores on standardized tests of knowledge.

All of these findings are subject, of course, to the usual cautions about instrumentation, design, researcher bias, and the like. There is, however, one finding that is not. It is an outcome of every study into the matter. Participants, their teachers, their parents, and their community supervisors overwhelmingly agree that their programs were worthwhile, useful, enjoyable, and powerful learning experiences.

There is an old cartoon in which a philosopher responds to another's article with the comment, "Of course none of the arguments are valid, but, taken collectively, they present a body of evidence too considerable to be disregarded." That might serve as an apt appraisal of the research evidence on the impact of experience-based educational programs. The expectation of impact is solidly grounded in theory, and positive outcomes are uniformly attested to by participants. Formal research has tended to support the conclusion that participation has positive effects, but the results fall short of absolute confirmation. Further research may not resolve the contradictory findings, and surely will not if only conventional instruments, methods, and designs are used. The practice is too varied, too unpredictable, too complex, perhaps even too profound in its effects. Such

concerns lead, appropriately, to a concluding discussion on research questions and methodology.

SUGGESTIONS FOR RESEARCH

The greatest challenge facing researchers interested in experiential education is to develop creative new methods of investigation. That need is considered first, followed by specific questions that need to be addressed through their application.

Methodology

The first and most encompassing recommendation, echoing Hamilton and Fenzel (1988), is to *shift the level of analysis* from the program as a whole to the individual participants. The varied nature of the activities and the idiosyncratic ways they are experienced are enduring parts of the character, even the strength, of experiential education. Analysis on this microlevel would not only better capture the real impact of a given program, but would also document the effects of various experiences on individuals and provide more well-founded hypotheses to guide further research.

Second, the examination of individual effects ought to be guided by clear *links to appropriate theories,* in order to direct the collection, organization, and analysis of data. The theoretical base for experiential education is rich and varied, with less emphasis on how people gather and recall information than on how they grow, change, develop, and mature into healthy and contributing members of adult society. The appropriate theories are often outside those that guide the usual research on classroom instruction.

An excellent model of individual-level analysis and research grounded in theory is provided by a study of college students involved in a variety of field-study and service activities. Hursh and Borzak (1979) gathered qualitative data from pre–post questionnaires and interviews, as well as from student papers. The data were gathered, organized, interpreted, and reported in accordance with theories of learning and development generated by Perry (1970), Loevinger (1976), and Kolb (1984), as well as with the role theory summarized by E. J. Thomas (1968) and the steps of psychological development outlined by Chickering (Chickering, 1969; R. Thomas & Chickering, 1983). This approach enabled the researchers to assign meaning to, and draw compelling conclusions from, what might otherwise have been an interesting but incomprehensible collection of anecdotes.

A third suggestion is that paper-and-pencil pre–post testing be deemphasized, *shifting to richer and more varied sources of data,* with more sophisticated means of gathering and interpreting them and more convincing ways of reporting them. Questionnaires, checklists, interviews, field observations, and other qualitative methods of data collection could become the central focus of research efforts (rather than merely ancillaries) if their use were grounded in theory as suggested. Participants' self-reports ought to be taken more seriously and their meanings analyzed more systematically. Hedin and Conrad (1987) found student journals to be valuable sources of insight into the influences and outcomes of service programs. Such self-reports would be even more valuable if students were prepared with a theoretical perspective for interpreting their own experience and helped to develop language to articulate what they sense occurring.

What students actually do in participation programs deserves to be considered as important in and of itself. In a program designed to enhance social responsibility, for example, the fact that participants actually are being socially responsible in real life (volunteering in a nursing home or petitioning city hall to crack down on polluters) is at least as relevant as how they mark a test of attitudes toward social responsibility.

Research methods that are common in other fields could be applied to educational research. Puckett's (1986) ethnohistory of the Foxfire program contains rich insights into the dynamics, development, and effects of a long-standing experiential program. Moore (1981, 1986), whose work deserves more space than is available here, has used techniques from ethnographic research to develop case studies and "learning narratives." In a sophisticated, even laborious, manner, his work uncovers processes of learning that occur in nonschool settings, pointing to a deeper understanding of how learning takes place generally. Hedin (Hedin & Simon, 1981) has developed a means to collect data through directed discussions of "peer panels" and then to analyze them in ways that could provide rich insight into the dynamics and outcomes of experiential programs.

Other methodological innovations could be cited. These, at the least, point toward addressing in a more insightful manner the kinds of questions listed next.

Research Questions

The list of potentially useful questions is endless. Presented here are questions that reflect broad issues of interest. Selected illustrative questions, relevant to each broad question are also presented.

Who benefits from participation, how, and in what ways?

1. What are the relationships between individual characteristics and the impacts of experience? To what degree are autonomy and maturity, for example, causes or consequences of learning from experience?
2. Are there certain features of age or developmental stage that make different kinds of experiences more appropriate for different students?

3. Are there specific skills and habits that enable a person to learn and grow from experience? If there are, can they be isolated, taught, and learned in the way that skills in learning from symbols (as in reading) have been?
4. Can participatory experiences enhance the traditional academic aims of schooling? If so, how?
5. What is the value to the community and schools of having youth acting as resources, rather than only as recipients, of services?

How should teachers organize and guide participation?

1. What is the potential for, and the differences in impact of, various kinds of experiences such as volunteer service, community study, and internships? What works best for what aims and for whom?
2. What is the impact of, and on, learning style?
3. How does the impact of voluntary participation resemble and differ from that of paid work experiences?
4. If reflection is the key to learning from experience, how can it be effectively encouraged, structured, and guided?
5. How can teachers (or site supervisors) be trained to effectively plan and guide experience-based programs?

What happens in the long run and why?

1. What are the long-term effects of experience-based programs on personal development, citizenship, career choice, and success in life?
2. Do the appeal and power of participation increase (or decrease) with repeated experiences?
3. Why do young people choose to participate? In a time of privatism and civic apathy, who are the activists and why are they active?

What is the impact of policy?

1. How do school rules, procedures, aims, and general climate restrict or encourage meaningful student participation in the school or community?
2. How do state rules or even public opinion restrict or encourage participation?
3. What would it take to make participation a significant element in social studies education locally, statewide, nationally? What is the relative impact of attempts to increase participation through government mandate and support?
4. What is the impact of requiring some kind of community experience versus making it voluntary, or offering it for credit versus as an extracurricular activity?

References

Button, C. (1973). The development of experimental curriculum to effect the political socializations of anglo, black and Mexican-American adolescents (Doctoral dissertation, University of Texas, 1972). *Dissertation Abstracts International, 33,* 4787A–4788A.

Calabrese, R. L., & Schumer, H. (1986). The effects of service activites on adolescent alienation. *Adolescence, 21,* 675–687.

Carre, C., & Howitt, B. (1987). Learning through talking. *Educational Review, 39*(1), 47–54.

Chickering, A. (1969). *Education and identity.* San Francisco: Jossey-Bass.

Cognetta, P. V., & Sprinthall, N. A. (1978). Students as teachers: Role taking as a means of promoting psychological and ethical development during adolescence. In N. A. Sprinthall & R. L. Mosher (Eds.), *Value development as the aim of education* (pp. 53–68). Schenectady, NY: Character Research Press.

Coleman, J. S. (1977). Differences between experiential and classroom learning. In M. T. Keeton (Ed.), *Experiential learning: Rationale, characteristics and assessment* (pp. 49–61). San Francisco: Jossey-Bass.

Conrad, D., & Hedin, D. (1981). *National assessment of experiential education: A final report.* St. Paul: University of Minnesota, Center for Youth Development and Research.

Corbett, F. C. (1977). *The community involvement program: Social service as a factor in adolescent moral and psychological development.* Unpublished doctoral dissertation, University of Toronto.

Crowe, M. R., & Walker, J. P. (1977). *Evaluation of the Executive High School Internship Program: Final report.* Columbus, OH: Ohio State University, Center for Vocational Education.

Danzig, R., & Szanton, P. (1986). *National service: What would it mean?* Lexington, MA: D. C. Heath.

Dewey, J. (1938). *Experience and education.* New York: Collier.

Gansneder, N. J., & Kingston, P. W. (1984). *University year for ACTION interns and their post-graduate career choices: A retrospective study.* Charlottesville, VA: University of Virginia. (Available from National Society for Internships and Experiential Education, 3509 Haworth Dr., Raleigh, NC 27609)

Gilliland, M. J., Hartman, J. A., & Jessee, P. O. (1985). *Teaching social science research: An applied approach using community resources.* Tuscaloosa: Alabama University, University College of Community Health Services. (ERIC Document Reproduction Service No. ED 266 918)

Haan, N., Smith, M. B., & Block, J. (1968). Moral reasoning of young adults: Political-social behavior, family background and personality correlates. *Journal of Personality and Social Psychology, 10,* 183–201.

Hamilton, S. F. (1980). Experiential learning programs for youth. *American Journal of Education, 88,* 179–215.

Hamilton, S. F. (1981). Adolescents in community settings: What is to be learned? *Theory and Research in Social Education, 9*(2), 23–38.

Hamilton, S. F., & Fenzel, L. M. (1988). The impact of volunteer experience on adolescent social development: Evidence of program effects. *Journal of Adolescent Research, 3*(1), 65–80.

Hamilton, S. F., & Zeldin, R. S. (1987). Learning civics in the community. *Curriculum Inquiry, 17,* 407–420.

Heath, D. (1977). *Maturity and competence.* New York: Gardner Press.

Hedin, D. (1987). Students as teachers: A tool for improving school. *Social Policy, 17*(3), 42–47.

Hedin, D., & Conrad, D. (1987). Service: A pathway to knowledge. *Community Education Journal, 15*(1), 10–14.

Hedin, D., & Simon, P. (1981). Listening to young people: The Minnesota Youth Poll. *New Designs for Youth Development, 2*(1), 1–6.

Herman, J. L., & Bury, J. (1987). *Evaluation report of the Constitutional Rights Foundation's Youth Community Service Program.* Unpublished manuscript, University of California, Los Angeles, Graduate School of Education, Center for the Study of Evaluation. (Available from Constitutional Rights Foundation, 601 South Kingsley Drive, Los Angeles, CA 90005)

Horenstein, M. A. (1986). The effects of high school experiential education on career focus and academic achievement in college students (Doctoral dissertation, Rutgers University, 1985). *Dissertation Abstracts International, 46,* 2543A.

Hursh, B. A., & Borzak, L. (1979). Toward cognitive development through field studies. *Journal of Higher Education, 50*(1), 63–78.

Hyman, H. H., Wright, C. R., & Hopkins, T. K. (1963). *Studies in evaluation: A case history of research on the Encampment for Citizenship.* Berkeley: University of California Press.

Jennings, M., & Niemi, R. (1974). *The political character of adolescence: The influence of family and schools.* Princeton, NJ: Princeton University Press.

Jennings, W. S., & Kohlberg, L. (1983). Effects of a just community pro-

gramme on the moral development of youthful offenders. *Journal of Moral Education, 12*(1), 33–50.

Kohlberg, L. (1973). Stages and aging in moral development: Some speculations. *Gerontologist, 13*(4), 497–502.

Kohlberg, L. (1981). *The philosophy of moral development: Moral stages and the idea of justice.* San Francisco: Harper & Row.

Kolb, D. (1984). *Experiential learning: Experience as the source of learning and development.* Englewood Cliffs, NJ: Prentice-Hall.

Loevinger, J. (1976). *Ego development.* San Francisco: Jossey-Bass.

Moore, D. T. (1981). Discovering the pedagogy of experience. *Harvard Educational Review, 51*(2), 286–300.

Moore, D. T. (1986). Learning at work: Case studies in non-school education. *Anthropology and Education Quarterly, 17*(3), 166–184.

Mosher, R. L. (1977). Theory and practice: A new E.R.A? *Theory Into Practice, 16*(2), 81–88.

Mussen, P., & Eisenberg-Berg, N. (1977). *Roots of caring, sharing and helping: The development of prosocial behavior in children.* San Francisco: W. H. Freeman.

Newman, B. M., & Newman, P. R. (1987). The impact of high school on social development. *Adolescence, 22*(87), 525–534.

Newmann, F. M. (1975). *Education for citizen action: Challenge for secondary curriculum.* Berkeley: McCutchan Publishing Corp.

Newmann, F. M., & Rutter, R. A. (1983). *The effects of high school community service programs on students' social development.* Madison, WI: Wisconsin Center for Education Research, University of Wisconsin.

Olson, D., & Bruner, J. (1974). Learning through experience and learning through media. In D. R. Olson (Ed.), *Media and symbols: The forms of expression, communication, and education.* 73rd Yearbook of the National Society for the Study of Education (Part 1, pp. 125–150). Chicago: University of Chicago Press.

Perry, W. G. (1970). *Forms of intellectual and ethical development in the college years.* New York: Holt, Rinehart and Winston.

Piaget, J. (1972). *To understand is to invent: The future of education.* New York: Viking Press.

Polanyi, M. (1962). *Personal knowledge: Towards a post-critical philosophy.* Chicago: University of Chicago Press.

Puckett, J. L. (1986). Foxfire reconsidered: A critical ethnohistory of a twenty-year experiment in progressive education (Doctoral dissertation, University of North Carolina). *Dissertation Abstracts International, 47,* 3652A.

Purkey, W. W. (1970). *Self-concept and school achievement.* Englewood Cliffs, NJ: Prentice-Hall.

Riecken, H. W. (1952). *The Volunteer Work Camp: A psychological investigation.* Cambridge, MA: Addison-Wesley.

Sager, W. G. (1974). A study of changes in attitudes, values, and self-concepts of senior high youth while working as full-time volunteers with institutionalized mentally retarded people (Doctoral dissertation, University of South Dakota, 1973). *Dissertation Abstracts International, 34,* 4760.

Schug, M. C., Todd, R. J. & Beery, R. (1984). Why kids don't like social studies. *Social Education, 48*(5), 382–387.

Shermis, S. S., & Barth, J. L. (1982). Teaching for passive citizenship: A critique of philosophical assumptions. *Theory and Research in Social Education, 10*(4), 17–37.

Smith, P. K. (1985). *An investigation into the effectiveness of field courses in teaching economics.* London: London University, Institute of Education. (ERIC Document Reproduction Service No. ED 257 747)

Sprinthall, R. C., & Sprinthall, N. A. (1977). *Educational psychology: A developmental approach* (2nd ed.). Reading, MA: Addison-Wesley.

Stockhaus, S. H. (1977). The effects of a community involvement program on adolescent students' citizenship attitudes (Doctoral dissertation, University of Minnesota, 1976). *Dissertation Abstracts International, 37,* 3545A.

Thomas, E. J. (1968). Role theory, personality, and the individual. In E. F. Borgatta & W. W. Lambert (Eds.), *Handbook of Personality Theory and Research* (pp. 691–727). Chicago: Rand McNally.

Thomas, R., & Chickering, A. (1983). Education and identity revisited. *Journal of College Student Personnel, 392–399.*

Wasserman, E. R. (1978). The development of an alternative high school based on Kohlberg's just community approach to education (Doc-

toral dissertation, Boston University, 1977). *Dissertation Abstracts International, 38,* 5416A.

Wilson, T. C. (1975). An alternative community based secondary school education program and student political development (Doctoral dissertation, University of Southern California, 1974). *Dissertation Abstracts International, 35,* 5797A.

Yul Lee, D., & Challen, P. (1982). Student-initiated adult-role experience: Its impact on classroom climate and personal growth. *Canadian Counselor, 16*(2), 102–105.

INTERRELATIONS BETWEEN SOCIAL STUDIES AND OTHER CURRICULUM AREAS

46

ART, MUSIC, AND LITERATURE WITHIN SOCIAL STUDIES

Elliot W. Eisner
STANFORD UNIVERSITY

American education is buffeted by two seemingly competing expectations. On the one hand, teachers are expected to increase the disciplinary rigor of the courses they teach so that their students will learn more substantive content. Such critics of American schools as E. D. Hirsch (1987) claim that American students know little because the content they should have learned in school has not been taught; the emphasis of American pedagogues on process has undermined attention to the fact that students need to have meaningful access to the legacies of our culture. What is called for in Hirsch's view is more attention to, indeed, more memorization of the content within individual subjects. Presumably this means teaching historical facts within the context of a history course, economic facts within economics, and the facts and allusions of literature within the field of literature. Rigor is achieved as the unique content of each field is taught by teachers and learned by students from the 1st grade through the 12th.

Another view is that one of the major problems of schooling is the lack of connectedness among the subjects that students study (Boyer, 1983). Departmentalization, which begins in some schools formally at the fourth and fifth grades, isolates subjects; a student can be studying U.S. history and American literature without ever realizing that these fields might have something in common. Even in self-contained elementary school classrooms, where the practical difficulties of relating fields to each other are not so formidable, subjects are often taught in isolation, leaving students with the impression that the boundaries between fields are natural rather than the results of distinctions made by academics who themselves have been professionally socialized to see the world through the lenses of their own disciplines.

Given the former view of what is wrong with American schools and what needs to be remedied, it is not likely that teachers, whether social studies specialists or general classroom teachers, will be inclined to use the arts in their programs as major sources of content. When expectations focus upon feeding students facts, or making sure that the curriculum is covered, or testing students' possession of a narrow range of knowledge, using the arts as a part of a social studies program is likely to be seen as a diversion from substance and as a retreat from rigor. An educational climate driven by expectations that give priority to the model of cultural literacy represented by the content of individual disciplines and measured by tests that are discipline specific is not conducive to the kind of bridge building that many students of American schooling believe schools need.

Thus, diagnoses of the ills of American schools emphasize two very different positions. One group says the patient suffers from a lack of attention to the facts. The other group says the patient suffers from a lack of integration. The former wants more attention paid to the content of each subject. The latter wants connections between the subjects students study to be an intentional aim of curriculum planners and teachers.

Although the integration of subjects is an idea that is likely to fall on receptive ears among most of those who work in the social studies—a field whose very name suggests an integrative attitude—the reasons for relating the arts to the social studies are not self-evident. We can talk about bridge building and connection making, but these are metaphors that imply or suggest rather than explain. Good reasons are needed in the first instance for using the arts within social studies education. These reasons need to support the unique missions of both social

Reviewers were George W. Chilcoat, Brigham Young University; Robert W. Johns, University of Arkansas, Little Rock; Richard S. Knight, Utah State University.

studies and arts education; both missions need to be satisfied. Superceding these reasons are the over-all aims of education as a normative enterprise: What larger aims do both the social studies and the arts serve within the broader goals of education?

THE EPISTEMIC FUNCTIONS OF THE SENSES, LANGUAGE, AND THE ARTS

It will be useful to begin with some general epistemological considerations for deciding what to teach and then to relate the results of that analysis to the relationship of the social studies to the arts. From there, the ways in which the arts might contribute to the aims of the social studies and to the way in which social studies might contribute to arts education will be examined. Consider first the concept of representation.

All cultures possess means through which humans learn to represent the world they have experienced. One source of experience is secured from contact with the phenomenal world. Another is secured through the life of imagination. Although imagination comes into play in ordinary perception, it is useful to distinguish between the perception of the qualities of the world encountered and experience generated in the mind's eye—experience created by our fantasies, reveries, our musing about the future, our visions of new possibilities. These experiences, experiences construed within a dynamic environment, must in some way be given a public status if they are to become a part of public discourse.

The most common, as well as one of the most precise means through which the public articulation of experience occurs is through language. Humans in every culture employ language as a way of sharing ideas and coping with the environment within which they function. But language is not a monolithic enterprise. Language comes in many forms and has a multitude of functions. First, the forms and functions of oral and written language can be distinguished. Even forms of language as general as these have consequences for the content, modes of thought, and circumstances they create.

Written language, for example, requires a degree of specificity and precision that can often be forgone in oral communication (Olson, 1985). Oral communication makes it possible to create a dialectical relationship with others that written text tends to preclude. As a result, there is often a sense of authority ascribed to text that is not quite so present in the dialectic of spoken dialogue. The point here is not to analyze the differences between oral and written language, but the fact that humans have invented means that make the *partial* representation of experience possible. What can be represented is both constrained and made possible by the mode and form employed (Eisner, 1982).

The differences between oral and written language are important, but of equal importance are the forms that languages can take. For example, literal language, a form that finds its apotheosis in mathematics, provides a level of syntactic precision that is not found in poetry or literature. Yet, poetry and literature, forms that exploit connotation, prosody, cadence, and innuendo make possible the public representation of ideas that literal language cannot capture (Langer, 1957). Poetry, ironically, was created to say what words can never say. Slang, the

poetics of the vernacular, performs functions that the literal and precise language of a scientific text cannot.

Language, one of our most important means of communication, takes shape in many forms. Growing up and becoming literate and enculturated means, in part, knowing how to encode and decode experience in the forms of language appropriate to it. Schooling is societies' means for developing such literacies.

Yet, language, as rich and as diversified as it is, does not exhaust the forms of representation that humans have invented to convert personal experience into its public representation. The arts of dance, music, painting, sculpture, architecture, theater, as well as the popular arts are also potent means through which personal experience is transformed and given public status. Meaning requires a form for both its apprehension and its dissemination. The forms of representation within a culture or as some call them, the symbol systems people know how to use, delimit the kind of meanings that they are able to construct and convey.

It should be noted that different forms of representation provide different kinds of meaning. What one is able to convey about a society through a literal or quantitative form of sociology is not the same as what is sayable through a novel. The images of photographer Dorthea Lang display a content pertaining to life in the Great Depression that a poem cannot reveal. Poetry can capture the nuances of life in a way that a measured array of variables cannot. Looked at as conveyors of meaning, each culture cultivates a variety of ways through which different kinds of meaning can be secured and represented. To become culturally literate in the deeper sense means having the skills and schemata through which the legacies of culture can be meaningfully construed.

THE COGNITIVE FUNCTIONS OF REPRESENTATION

What does such a conception of the cognitive functions of different forms of representation mean for social studies education? And what does it mean for the uses of the arts in social studies education? There are two answers to these questions. One pertains to the aim of helping students understand the social world. The other pertains to matters of educational equity and to human learning.

The social world, the world with which social studies educators are primarily concerned, is not primarily a world of text. Our lives and the lives of others are mainly lives of doing and making, of having relationships, of negotiating traffic, of paying bills, shopping, maintaining friendships, raising children, and the like. The social world we are trying to help children understand is in large measure just that life. We want students to develop a critical consciousness of the society that they now take for granted, often do not see, or believe to be a product of nature. We are interested in helping them overcome those forms of social adaptation that encourage the stock response and that dull their own perceptivity.

The development of such consciousness is enhanced by helping students experience the world through a variety of forms so that meanings that will not take the impress of a literal text can be developed in other ways. The understanding of Egyptian civilization is likely to be enhanced by seeing as well as by reading about the Sphinx, the Pyramids, and about Nefertete. To experience these forms requires that at least two conditions be met. First, it requires that nontext forms be a part of the curriculum provided to students and, second, that students can "read" the forms that are made available. Thus, if students are to have a broad and deep understanding of the pre-Civil War period in the American South, text alone will not do. The music of the slaves, the myths and stories that were a part of their lives, their folksay, programs like "Roots," the music and dance of the period, the architecture of their quarters, and those of their masters, are all relevant sources for enlarging understanding (Epstein, 1989). They are relevant because each form tells a different tale, each provides a different kind of content and engenders a different kind of engagement. Text, particularly the text of textbooks as contrasted with literary history, is often so eviscerated of affect that the feel of the period cannot be experienced. A lifeless text about a difficult and painful period in American history is a kind of lie. In this sense, many of the textbooks provided in school lie.

The point here is an epistemological one: What students can learn about a culture, past or present, is both constrained and made possible by the forms of representation to which they have access and are able to "read" (Eisner, 1982). When social studies carries its messages to students mainly or solely through textbooks, it inevitably and severely limits what students are able to learn. Thus, attention to the arts, to music, and to literature in social studies programs is not a way to "gussy-up" the curriculum, it is a way to enlarge human understanding and to make experience in the social studies vivid.

The need to expand the resources through which meaning itself can be broadened is one way to ground or justify the inclusion of the arts in social studies programs. Another justification pertains to matters of educational equity.

TOWARD A MORE GENEROUS VIEW OF MIND

In the past few years, psychologists such as Howard Gardner (1983) and Robert Sternberg (1985) have contributed significantly to a broader, more complex view of human intelligence. The static conception of intelligence as an essentially genetically determined, measurable ability that can be represented by a single IQ score has increasingly given way to a conception of intelligence as much more differentiated and plastic. Gardner, for example, argued that there are at least seven distinct kinds of intelligence, each with its own developmental history and its own location in the brain. These intelligences function in some degree for virtually all humans. Idiot savants, he pointed out, may be inept in all but one form of intelligence. Whatever went wrong did not impair at least one cognitive function; these individuals are able to perform feats in a specific area of competence that are truly impressive. What we see in the idiot savant is an example of the autonomy of brain functions; it is possible to be mentally handicapped in virtually all areas and, at the same time, to be brilliant in one.

The line of argument and the evidence that Gardner mustered are not unknown in research on human aptitude: People have different proclivities, they are more apt to learn when they have opportunities to play to their strengths (Snow, 1986).

One practical implication of these newly developing ideas about mind and intelligence is that social studies programs that constrain what they teach through a restricted array of tasks and highly limited forms of representation are unfair to those whose aptitudes reside in areas neglected in the curriculum. If the sole mediator of the message is the written word, not only will the meanings made available be constrained by what the word can reveal, but the opportunities to learn will be biased towards those whose proclivities reside in the processing of text.

One might look at it another way. How many channels are made available for students to tune into? How diversified are the resources teachers provide in class? The provision of an array of forms through which students can come to know and understand a period in history or their own contemporary culture not only a contributes to the meanings that they have an opportunity to construct, it contributes to the equitable distribution of opportunities to learn in school.

IMPEDIMENTS

There are, of course, a host of practical difficulties in providing the kinds of programs alluded to in this chapter. One of these is that as the content and forms of representation employed in social studies curricula expand, and as students have increased opportunity to take from what is taught that which is most congruent with their aptitudes and intelligences, making comparisons among students becomes increasingly difficult. When all students run the same course (whether or not they started at the same place), the task of determining who crosses the finish line first is relatively simple. But when students pursue different tracks or create outcomes expressed through different forms, commensurability of performance may be impossible to achieve.

While theoretically the virtue of productive incommensurability can be persuasively justified in an *educational* program, in a meritocracy such as ours, the political difficulty in doing so is substantial. Common standards applied objectively to all with an aura of detachment and measured precision obviate the need for judgment. When judgment is required it often smacks of subjectivity and conjures up its own sense of inequity. Procedures that educators have become accustomed to—objective testing, for example—can and do lead to evaluation practices that are believed to provide for another type of equity, even-handedness. In fact, equity is confused with sameness, and there is a failure to recognize that the conventional forms used to teach and assess tap only a small portion of human aptitude, often handicapping students who, had other options been provided, might have done very well indeed.

The assessment problem is not the only problem of significance. The use of nonconventional forms of representation, particularly those used in the arts, requires teachers who themselves know how to read the content that artistically rendered images convey. It requires teachers who can look at a Romanesque church and understand the way in which its forms represent a world view and a way of life. It requires teachers who can see in a postmodern building a return to the sensuous surface and to pattern and fantasy and who are prepared to link these features with the current social scene. "Why now," they need to be able to ask, "are such buildings being built?" "What does such architecture have to tell us about what people seem to need?" "Why hasn't the pristine glass and steel high-rise architecture of the 1950s and 60s been continued?" In short, to use the arts optimally in teaching, one must be able to deal with them meaningfully as art forms. It is the art in the form that has the potential to inform. Thus, the ability to "read" artistic meaning is critical if the teacher is to use art *as art* in social studies programs.

Works of art in any of the forms in which they might appear can be treated in inartistic ways. A work of art, for example, can be treated as an artifact, that is, as a cultural datum for making inferences about a society. Some art educators believe this ought to be art's main educational function (Chalmers, 1981). Yet, a genuine sociological or anthropological treatment *of a work of art* depends, initially at least, on the ability to experience the artistic content of the work. To the extent to which this cannot be done, the significance of using art forms, as contrasted with a host of other forms, evaporates. The point of using the arts is that works of art possess a content that itself is uniquely informative. To gain access to this content one must have the requisite schemata and refined sensibilities. To the artistically illiterate, works of art do not exist—at least experientially.

WHAT MEANING DO THE ARTS CONVEY?

How is it that the arts—music, the visual arts, and literature—convey meaning and enlarge understanding? Through what means are their contributions made? What all of the arts have in common is their capacity to generate emotion, to stimulate and to express the "feel" of a situation, individual, or object. This feeling is achieved by the qualities that make literature literary, art artistic, and music musical. These are qualities of form. All art forms become art by virtue of the way they are formed by those who make them. The way a form is formed is critical to the kind of feelings a reader of that form can experience. Hence, a writer of history may craft language artistically so that the reader can get a feel for the period or situation he or she addresses. A painter can portray a character or a battlefield to enable a viewer to get a sense of what it might be like to have been there. A composer can create a mood that tells us about life in the court of Henry VIII or about the sadness of a dying princess. In this sense, the arts *re*present. They re-present to us by virtue of their form—assuming we know how to read it—how something feels.

Feeling is a part of all human encounters and all situations and objects. When the feeling tone is incongruous with the content described, understanding is diminished. In fact, feeling can "contradict" what is said explicitly. Thus, the artistically rendered novel or history enables the reader to vicariously participate in events. The work stimulates imagination in the service of insight and feeling (Langer, 1957). When artistic qualities are absent, imagination is left dormant and meaning is made factual. Facticity is hardly ever adequate to get a sense for the lives of people.

SOCIAL STUDIES CONTRIBUTIONS TO THE ARTS

Thus far I have emphasized the contributions of the arts to the social studies. That is as it should be in a handbook devoted to research on social studies education. But the relationship ought to be regarded as reciprocal. Social studies has something to contribute to the arts. That contribution is helping students situate works of art within their social, historical, political, and economic contexts. Works of art are not only phenomenologically dense and multilayered forms, they are social as well as individual products. Their form, their content, their iconography, their materials, the techniques employed in their creation are products of culture. To encounter a work of Bernini adequately, the values of the Italian renaissance need to be understood. This means understanding the rise of the Medici, the expansion of trade, the development of commerce, and the influence of Greek philosophy. To appreciate Italian futurism, the growth of Italian nationalism and the influence of the machine, power, and heritage must be taken into account. To understand the reasons underlying the structure of the Gregorian chant, the architecture of the churches and monasteries of the Middle Ages needs to be appreciated. To grasp the meaning of traditional Japanese architecture, an understanding of Taoism's view of the relationship of man to nature is critical. What the social studies can do for the arts is as important as what the arts can do for the social studies. And what the social studies can do is to situate the arts in the human context in which they were created.

This aspect of arts education to which the social studies have such an important contribution to make is rapidly emerging within the arts education community as a major curricular aim. Increasingly, arts educators, particularly those of the visual arts, are recognizing that an adequate arts curriculum ought not only to enable students to develop the creative thinking skills that have traditionally been the focus of such programs, it should also help them to acquire a sensitivity towards visual form and an understanding of the ways in which works of art effect and are affected by culture. In short, the cultural and historical context within which works of art are situated is being increasingly recognized as an important, not a marginal aspect of a sound arts curriculum.

This view of appropriate curricular content in the arts is most clearly articulated in the publications and policies of the J. Paul Getty Center for Education in the Arts and finds its practical manifestations in discipline–based art education (Eisner, 1987). This chapter is not the place to describe the details of this orientation to art education, except to say that there is a growing receptivity among art educators to the contributions that social studies can make to their educational aims. This receptivity can do much to create the kind of integration in which the aims of both social studies and arts education are well served.

ANTECEDENTS OF ART AND SOCIAL STUDIES INTEGRATION

To those familiar with the history of American education, it will come as no surprise that may of the practices and ideas referred to earlier deeply permeated the classrooms and teaching practices of progressive educators in the 1920s and 1930s (Cremin, 1961). To be sure, the theoretical sophistication, particularly the psychological theories that are available today to justify an integrative or multimodal approach to curriculum and instruction, were not available then. And, in any case, when progressive education was practiced, it was practiced by elementary and secondary school teachers; and these teachers were not then, nor are they now, ardent consumers of educational research. Teachers who work daily with children steer their ships by other stars. Many of them, especially elementary school teachers, know in their sinews that it makes educational sense to learn by doing, to use more than text to teach, and to relate the arts and other fields to each other in order to increase their meaningfulness. They know that sensory experience is important for learning and that the distinctions made by academics are formalisms that are less important to children than to those working within the halls of ivy. Progressive curriculum practices fostered curricular integration; stories, music, and murals were a part of what Kilpatrick called "the project method" (1918). Meaning and purpose in such activities were essential, and meaning and purpose were more likely if the materials students worked with in school were not abstracted into oblivion.

Interestingly enough, a model of such practice can still be found in American schools. Its home—kindergarten. Despite pressures on kindergarten teachers to formalize teaching and learning (Elkind, 1988), many still create classrooms that provide an abundance of active and connected learning that is similar in spirit to the progressive education practices or 50 years ago. Kindergartners write stories and illustrate them. They study their community and create plays about what they have discovered. They learn about the care and feeding of living things by caring for animals and plants, measuring their growth, and by reading about them. This orientation to curriculum is predicated on the belief that children need to *get in touch,* to literally feel the experience, and for that experience to be as seamless in quality as possible. It is in the first grade when schooling becomes "serious." With this seriousness often comes the division of subjects, the formalization and the fragmentation that typically characterize the remainder of their public schooling.

In the recent past, an important curriculum development project—one in which Jerome Bruner was involved—exemplified the usefulness of the multimodal approach to social studies curriculum. *Man: A Course of Study* (Macos) does not emphasize the arts, though it does use artifacts from the Netslik culture, and does employ film, slides, and myths to help students create answers to three important questions: What is human about man? How did he get that way? How can he be made more so? These materials reflect a deep awareness of the variety of sources useful for fostering student learning within a social studies context. Despite the political difficulties that it encountered from those who objected to the values they believed the program conveyed, Macos provided an imaginative, indeed, a courageous prototype of what a good curriculum could be.

The importance of providing a wide spectrum of curriculum materials, each designed to elicit different kinds of responses and to convey different types of meaning, is often less appreciated by publishers than by teachers. By comparison, textbooks are a known commodity and their production is routine. They are less costly and more easily marketed and shipped. An array of curriculum materials, many of which are three-dimensional and bulky, pose more complex problems. Unless the profit margins are clear, publishers tend to shy away from producing them. It should also be said that not a few teachers prefer the tidy textbook. It is easier to use and it is familiar. The point is that changes in educational practice in any field require more than a good idea or even several of them; they require changing behavior patterns, those familiar routines that all of us have created to adapt comfortably to the world we inhabit.

CURRICULUM THEORIES RELEVANT TO THE ARTS AND SOCIAL SCIENCES

I now turn to theories of curriculum that pay special attention to the notion of different forms of meaning and to the function of different forms of representation. In the mid-1960s, in *Realms of Meaning* Phenix (1964) classified the distinctive forms of meaning constructed and conveyed by different disciplines. Later, in the early 1970s, English philosopher Paul Hirst (1971) presented a conception of modes of knowing and argued that the selection of curriculum content should be made on the basis of the type of knowledge that each mode provided. Hirst argued that it was neither necessary nor feasible to teach every variety of science or art. What is important is that at least one science be taught; the same principle held for the arts. In this approach, the disciplines are treated as representatives of what might be called an epistemological taxonomy; one does not need to encounter each species of cat to understand the essence of "catness." What should be provided in a school program are the major species of knowledge. Hirst's argument could be extended to social studies, in which case a theme or topic would be studied through particular disciplines. Each *type* of discipline would provide a unique form of knowledge about that theme to students.

In the 1980s, the thesis of my *Cognition and Curriculum: A Basis for Deciding What to Teach* (Eisner, 1982) was that the sensory system is the primary means through which concepts are formulated. Concepts, I argued, are imagic in nature. Even such abstract ideas as *nation, infinity,* and *justice* acquire meaning insofar as an individual can imagine their referents. One important task that humans face is transforming what they have conceptualized into some public form. As noted above, each public form of representation has its own constraints and provides its own opportunities to display meaning. A song about a bird in flight conveys meanings that differ from those made possible through poetry or through a literal or a choreographic form. Pictures provide still other forms of meaning, and a measured trajectory of the flight provides still other meanings.

Because most subject matters are complex, they can be seen from a variety of perspectives. Each form or representation provides its own perspectives. The educational equity and the problems of providing a variety of forms of representation in the curriculum, as well as of giving students opportunities to display what they have learned in the forms of representation in which they are most able, have been discussed above.

The other side of my epistemological argument (Eisner, 1982), as well as those of Hirst (1971), and Phenix (1964) is a psychological one. It has to do with aptitude. Given differences in aptitude among students, the provision of conditions in schools that treat these differences as strengths, not liabilities, is important. It is important not only because such treatment is likely to increase the personal satisfactions that students experience, but because the development of individual aptitude nurtures the society. We learn from each other, and in such learning the differences among us are an asset (Read, 1944). A symphony orchestra with woodwinds, strings, percussion, and brass is in a better position to make interesting music than one with woodwinds alone. Those responsible for educational programs, as contrasted to training programs, have an obligation to cultivate productive idiosyncrasy, even if the achievement of such aims make it difficult to compare students with each other.

What the Research Says

It would be instructive to turn now to a host of studies that provided through careful research and evaluation a set of credible conclusions about the effects of art, music, and literature in social studies education. Yet, it is too much to expect that research in education would provide conclusive or comprehensive answers to questions of practice; education is a field whose problems are too context-specific to lend themselves to the kind of research results applicable to medicine or derived from physics. What is striking in this instance, however, is the virtual absence of research. Literature searches by two doctoral students at Stanford, consultation with a third, and my own search yielded only one relevant research study. The sources investigated include a search since 1979 of Educational Resources Information Center (ERIC), computer database searches of social science research, and a computer search of the Arts and Humanities Citation Index. Although there are many practically focused essays on the use of the arts in social studies, only one research study could be identified.

The single study is a doctoral dissertation completed in the School of Education at Harvard University in 1989. This study investigated the practical application of the theory of literacy elaborated in this chapter to the social studies (Epstein, 1989). In this study, Epstein designed a two-week social studies curriculum to help high school sophomores and juniors learn about the slavery period in America. Television programs, stories, myths, music, visual art, poetry, and other artistic forms were used to try to make the period come to life. Students watched the TV production "Roots," they looked at pictures, they heard music, learned about folk tales and myths; in short, the curricula was designed to help students get into the skins of the slaves.

The processes and effects of the curricula were evaluated through a variety of methods, including the application of educational criticism (Eisner, 1985) to the teaching process. Educational criticisms were prepared both by the teacher and by an independent educational critic. In addition, students' written work and the music that some of them composed at the end of the instructional period were analyzed. The students also completed a questionnaire about their experiences in this curriculum. The evaluation was, therefore, a multimodal effort to secure a wide variety of information that would allow the researcher to draw credible conclusions about the effects of the approach.

The results of the research were promising. Epstein wrote:

Overall, students felt they learned from and liked the materials and methods represented in class and found the approach an improvement over more common social studies practices. Throughout the interviews and questionnaires, students continuously commented that the curriculum gave them a feel or picture of what slavery was really like. As a result, they learned more from it than from a textbook, which they perceived either as an assemblage of facts, one person's views, or an account removed from the reality of the experience.

Most students also enjoyed and learned from the project. They liked not having to memorize facts and appreciated having a choice in evaluation and an opportunity to express their own ideas and feelings. Most felt they would have done a better job if they had spent more time on the project, and if the teacher had given better direction or more class time.

Five students felt the essay test was a fairer measure of their learning. Some of these students might have benefited from more direction and a project. Others simply may feel more comfortable expressing their thoughts in essay form under any circumstances. (pp. 209–210)

Although these results could be due to the Hawthorne effect, the excerpts included in the study of student work in a variety of forms and the observations made by the critic lend credence to the value of using multiple forms of representation in teaching about complex events whose features cannot be reduced to text. The study provides a beginning in the systematic investigation of the uses of the arts and other forms for enriching the experiences of students in social studies and in broadening the array of means students can use to represent what they have gotten out of such experiences.

An Agenda for Research

What kind of research could be undertaken that would be useful to social studies educators? What kinds of questions can be raised? What follows are brief descriptions of five questions, each with a short rationale, that could be used as a focus for research.

First, does increasing the number of forms of representation used in social studies curricula increase the variety of meanings that students secure in studying a topic or problem? *Variety* refers to the meanings individual students secure or to the varieties of meanings that the class as a whole achieves. *Meaning* refers to what students know about a topic or problem—the varieties of knowledge and/or what they are able to convey about a topic or problem by using the various forms of representation. For example, if students were to describe what they had learned about cultural transmission after having studied the great waves of immigration during the last two decades of the 19th century, one might expect that their portrayals of the period through pictures, novels, history, music, drama, poetry, would reveal a broader understanding than if they were restricted to writing literal text. The wider array of options for students might provide a better and fuller picture of what students made of their experiences.

It should be apparent that it is tricky to assess such outcomes. The complexity of using forms of representation for which students have only limited skills should also be apparent: it requires at least some skill for a student to use a form of representation to give expression to a point. Yet, it is precisely this kind of tough problem that needs to be addressed by curriculum planners, teachers, and evaluators if research is to yield more than a narrow, mechanical view of what students have learned and experienced.

A second question has to do with the effects of multimodal curricula on students' theoretical understanding of what they have studied. The previous question focused on the different kinds of meaning that a multimodal curriculum might yield. The second question is predicated on the idea that by diversifying the forms of representation to which students had access, their theoretical understanding of social phenomenon might be enhanced. In other words, integrated curriculum might prove to be instrumental to a better and more robust comprehension of theory.

A third question is focused on the transfer of learning. One major aim of educators is to develop programs and to teach so that students can apply what they learn in school to problems and contexts outside of school. Yet, the way in which problems and tasks are situated in classrooms—their formalized features, their abstract qualities, the absence of the texture of everyday life—often creates insurmountable obstacles for transfer (Greeno, 1989). Much school learning begins and ends in school.

How can transfer be fostered? It is more likely to occur if students engage in curricular activities that require attention to events beyond those provided by text? Might it be, for example, that artistically rendered narrative has the capacity to display life in ways that detached analytic text cannot reveal? Do video programs and other dramatic materials have the power to invest learning with feeling so that its internalization is increased? And might not such internalization increase the likelihood that students will remember and use what they learn? Answers to these questions are as yet unavailable.

One function of fiction and literary history is its capacity to "replicate" the world through its form and content. It seems reasonable to assume that the kind of learning that occurs in situations that approximate those outside of school are more likely to be applied than content learned in contexts far removed from real life situations. The arts have a large potential for contributing to social studies education by making content more relevant to the life students lead after they leave the classroom.

The fourth question deals with matters of integration. How can social studies be taught so that culture is seen from multiple perspectives rather than from a narrow, single view? One of the persistent criticisms of departmentalized schools is their fragmented character. The day is fragmented, the curriculum is fragmented, teaching is fragmented, evaluation is fragmented. Few bridges between subject areas are made available, and most students do not expect that there should or even could be conceptual connections among the subjects they study. Do social studies curricula that employ the arts better foster multiple perspectives? Do students grasp the arts better when they see them as manifestations of social values and cultural technology? Are social studies issues and topics better understood and appreciated when they are examined through the arts? Does the purposeful integration of curriculum content from fields not usually included in social studies foster cognitive integration? Do students more readily see connections between subjects? Do their programs appear to them to be more of a piece, more whole? Research to investigate greater integration in social studies with other areas, such as the arts, could provide valuable information about the relationship between the structure and content of the curriculum and the sense of conceptual unity that students believe they have secured.

A fifth question in some ways essentially reflects a development problem in education. That problem pertains to the creation of assessment procedures for evaluating incommensurable outcomes from the same unit of study of multimodal social studies curricula. What is needed to describe, interpret, and appraise outcomes that differ in content and form and that differ from student to student? What kinds of problems or tasks will reveal different kinds of understandings about social phenomenon? How can students produce stories, texts, pictures, poems, and songs that can be used as data for making valid inferences about what they have learned? How can the processes in which students relate the arts to the social studies be assessed for their educational importance? These and questions like them are crucial if American schools are to free themselves from the limitations of the kind of testing now used to measure student achievement.

The public is entitled to a dependable picture of how well both students and schools are performing. Creating forms of assessment that are congruent with our most deeply held educational values is of critical importance if educators are to have the freedom to build new, more educationally meaningful social studies programs. Such assessment is likely to be a mix of qualitative and quantitative methods. It is likely to involve paying attention not only to outcomes, but to the roads students have taken to get there. It is likely to provide insight not only into what students have achieved, but what their experiences have meant to them.

The aims laid out in this chapter are formidable. Their achievement will require new forms of inquiry, new ways of thinking about knowledge and understanding, and new criteria for appraising what counts as research. But perhaps most of all, their achievement will require intellectual courage and a willingness to take risks. Unless these risks are taken, our grandest visions of education are not likely to be realized, because the research necessary to anchor our programs to the values we cherish is destined to remain absent.

References

Boyer, E. (1983), *High school.* New York: Harper and Row.

Chalmers, G. (1981). Art education as ethnology. *Studies in Art Education, 22*(3), 6–14.

Cremin, L. (1961). *The transformation of the school: Progressivism in American education, 1876–1957.* New York: Alfred A. Knopf.

Eisner, E. W. (1982). *Cognition and curriculum: A basis for deciding what to teach.* New York: Longmans.

Eisner, E. W. (1985). *The educational imagination* (2nd ed.). New York: Macmillan.

Eisner, E. W. (1987). *The role of discipline based art education in America's schools.* Los Angeles: J. Paul Getty Center for Education in the Arts.

Elkind, D. (1988). *The hurried child.* Reading, MA: Addison-Wesley.

Epstein, T. (1989). *An aesthetic approach to the study of teaching and knowing in the social studies.* Unpublished doctoral dissertation, Harvard University, Cambridge, MA.

Gardner, H. (1983). *Frames of mind.* New York: Basic Books.

Greeno, J. (1989). Situations, mental models, and generative knowledge. In D. Kalar & K. Kotousky (Eds.), *Complex information processing: The impact of Herbert A. Simon* (pp. 285–318). Hillsdale, NJ: Erlbaum.

Hirsch, E. D. (1987). *Cultural literacy.* Boston: Houghton-Mifflin.

Hirst, P. (1971). *Knowledge and the curriculum.* Boston: Routledge and Kegan Paul.

Kilpatrick, W. H. (1918). The project method. *Teachers College Record, 19,* 319–335.

Langer, S. K. (1957). *Problems of art.* New York: Charles Scribner's Sons.

Olson, D. R. (1985). *Literacy, language, and cognition.* New York: Cambridge University Press.

Phenix, P. (1964). *Realms of meaning.* New York: McGraw-Hill.

Read, H. (1943). *Education through art.* New York: Panthem Books.

Snow, R. (1986). Individual differences and the design of educational programs. *American Psychologist, 41*(10), 1029–1039.

Sternberg, R. J. (1985). *Beyond I.Q.: A triarchic theory of human intelligence.* New York: Cambridge University Press.

47

THE SCIENCE-TECHNOLOGY-SOCIETY (STS) THEME AND SOCIAL STUDIES EDUCATION

James R. Giese and Lynn Parisi
SOCIAL SCIENCE EDUCATION CONSORTIUM

Rodger W. Bybee
BIOLOGICAL SCIENCES CURRICULUM STUDY

The increased influence of science and technology on individual lives and public policy, combined with widespread concerns about the environment and resources and general reform efforts in curriculum and instruction, have contributed to the emergence of a new educational theme—science-technology-society or STS (Bybee, 1986; Hurd, 1987; Roy, 1985; Rubba, 1987). Because STS is focused on the interrelationships of science and technology in society, the theme naturally encompasses both science and social studies education. The concern in this chapter is with the research related to science and technology in the social studies curriculum, as well as research on STS in science that may have implications for social studies or for collaborative science-social studies efforts.

Social studies education is aimed at enhancing students' personal development and contributing to their ability to function as citizens. To achieve that purpose in this modern age, social studies educators must incorporate scientific and technologic topics in the curriculum. In fact, however, interest in science as an element in the social studies curriculum is not new. Over 30 years ago, the 27th yearbook of the National Council for the Social Studies (NCSS), *Science and the Social Studies* (Cummings, 1956–1957), was based on the premises that the 1950s were the age of science and that science and technology were significant social forces that should be included in social studies programs. In his introductory chapter, Cummings (1956/1957) sounded quite contemporary: "Social studies courses in the past have not been adequate for providing a pupil the knowledge to understand the complexities of a scientific technological society" (p. 5).

This chapter provides both a current assessment of the status of research on STS and suggestions for future investigations. The review is organized into three sections—the intended curriculum, the actual curriculum, and the learned curriculum—an organization used in a recent National Research Council report (Murnane & Raizen, 1988).

THE INTENDED CURRICULUM

Prior to the 1980s, some educators argued that both social studies and science courses should include STS (Benne & Birnbaum, 1978; Charles & Samples, 1978; Hurd, 1975; Zoller & Watson, 1974). Recognizing the importance of the connection between science, technology, and social studies, NCSS established the Science and Society Advisory Committee in 1977. The preamble to the committee charter states:

The impact of science and technology on society, and of society on science and technology, are of increasing and vital importance. Scientific and technological developments often move so rapidly that social institutions are unable to respond effectively. This gives rise to ethical questions and societal problems and creates demands on citizens and on society for new insights and understandings.

In the early 1980s, two policy statements promoted the STS theme in education. In 1982, the National Science Teachers Association (NSTA) published *Science-Technology-Society: Sci-*

Reviewers were Phillip A. Heath, Ohio State University, Lima; Paul D. Hurd, Stanford University *ence Education for the 1980s.* Two of the five goals emphasized in the statement were: "to use the skills and knowledge of science and technology as they apply to personal and social decisions" and "to study the interaction among science-technology-society in the context of science-related societal issues" (NSTA, 1982).

The following year, NCSS published a policy statement on "Guidelines for Teaching Science-Related Social Issues" (NCSS, 1983). The NCSS guidelines included suggestions for selecting study topics, evaluating extant materials, setting educational objectives, and assessing student achievement. Studying science-related social issues was justified as having such beneficial outcomes as preparing "young people to analyze issues and use empirical data . . . to make informed judgments about [science-related social] issues" and providing opportunities for students to "explore value-laden issues, clarify their own values, and use these values as a basis . . . for making personal and social decisions" (p. 1).

In 1987, the Social Science Education Consortium (SSEC), as part of an NSF-funded project to build and enhance support networks for STS education, published a framework for reforming the secondary social studies and science curricula to include STS (Hickman, Patrick, & Bybee, 1987). The framework included not only a rationale for STS education, but a description of knowledge, skill, and attitude objectives for STS and a description of alternatives for the design of STS curricula.

Despite the early involvement of NCSS and subsequent involvement of such other national organizations as the SSEC, studies focused on social studies educators' views of and attitudes toward STS are virtually nonexistent. Molnar (1983) compared a small sample ($N = 89$) of NCSS members with a sample ($N = 186$) of Association for Supervision and Curriculum Development (ASCD) members. Molnar noted that he did not obtain a scientific sample and that the results should be used with caution. The two groups were asked to indicate how significant they considered a variety of socially important topics, including nuclear disarmament, environmental pollution, and genetic engineering. Molnar concluded that:

1. Both groups of respondents were very sensitive to social issues in general.
2. Both groups tended to indicate that the most important issues facing humankind were not the same as the most important social issues studied in school.
3. Both groups thought educators as a group should attempt to formulate positions on social issues (p. 305).

These results suggest that social studies educators who are NCSS members, like their colleagues in supervision and curriculum development, are receptive to greater instructional emphasis on contemporary social issues including STS.

Several surveys completed by Bybee and his colleagues indicate that such receptivity is also present among scientists, engineers, and citizens (Bybee, 1984), college students (Bybee & Najafi, 1986), science teachers and other science educators in the United States (Bybee, 1987; Bybee & Bonnstetter, 1986), and an international population of science educators (Bybee & Mau, 1986).

The international survey (Bybee & Mau, 1986) included 262 science educators from 41 countries; the response rate was 80%. A majority of the respondents thought most global problems related to science and technology (e.g., world hunger and food resources, population growth, air quality and atmosphere) would be worse by the year 2000; a majority also thought that studying global problems in school was either very important or fairly important. Particularly significant for social studies educators is the finding that 73% of the science educator respondents recommended incorporating the science and social studies aspects of STS into one course.

To summarize, in the early 1980s, NCSS and NSTA both developed policy statements supporting the implementation of STS. Findings from several surveys provided additional support for including the STS theme in school programs.

THE ACTUAL CURRICULUM

Although national associations and educational leaders have called for including STS in educational programs, such recommendations are not always implemented. Since the textbook *is* the curriculum in many social studies classes (Weiss, 1978, 1987; Morrissett, 1982), reviews of textbooks can serve as one indicator of the degree to which the STS theme is part of the actual curriculum. Studies of actual classroom practice can serve as another.

Textbook Reviews

In the early 1980s, two content analyses of STS in social studies texts were reported. In his Hudson Institute content analysis of 63 textbooks in American history, world history, geography, civics, and economics, Newitt (1983) focused specifically on textbook treatment of such limits-to-growth issues as population, resources, environmental problems, and economic development. He concluded that "no combination of basal history, geography, civics, and economics texts fully meets this need [to treat the social effects of science and technology]. A great many . . . will repeatedly expose the students to erroneous information" (p. 12).

Patrick and Remy (1984) also reported an analysis of science-related social issues in social studies textbooks. They summarized their results as follows:

An analysis of social studies textbooks, although limited in number and scope, suggests that new goals of citizenship education which pertain to science-technology-society themes and issues have not become prominent in main-line courses—American history, government, civics, geography, world history—where they could be related logically to traditional content. It has become trendy to proclaim these new goals at conferences and in professional journals, but they have not yet become a national trend in the curricula of our schools. (p. 35)

Nor can one conclude from reviews of science textbooks that science courses are filling the gaps found in social studies. A 1984 analysis of the social issues content of high school biology textbooks (Rosenthal, 1984) confirmed earlier study results showing that such texts contain little information about STS issues (Boschmann, Hendrix, & Mertens, 1978; Levin & Lindbeck, 1979). Rosenthal clearly defined social issues, developed 12 categories of social issues based on an extensive review of the literature, had the classification of social issues reviewed by experts, and checked inter-rater reliability in use of the classification scheme. She concluded:

For 22 textbooks published between 1963 and 1983, the percentage of total textbooks dealing with social issues has declined. There is no evidence from this study that textbook authors and publishers have responded to the statements of numerous scientists and science educators' call for a greater emphasis on science and society in high school biology textbooks.

Although the quality of treatment varies from category to category and from textbook to textbook, in general, the treatment of science and society in high school biology textbooks minimizes the controversial aspects, avoids questions of ethics and values, lacks a global perspective, and neglects the interdisciplinary nature of problems. (p. 829)

It is important to note that over 90% of high school biology teachers use one of the textbooks reviewed in this study. Furthermore, high school biology is the last science course the majority of students take (Hurd, Bybee, Kahle, & Yager, 1980).

Hamm and Adams (1987) analyzed 10 sixth- and seventh-grade science textbooks for their treatment of global problems as identified by Bybee and Mau (1986). Less than 2% of the 4,393 pages in these books was devoted to such STS issues as population growth, world hunger, air quality and atmosphere, and water resources.

Since the mid-1980s, two textbooks incorporating the STS theme have been published for use in full-year science courses, *Global Science* (Christensen, 1984) and *CHEMCOM* (American Chemical Society, 1988). No research on the use of these books has been published. No comparable social studies textbooks are currently available.

A variety of supplemental STS curriculum materials is available for use in social studies and science classes. In addition, reviews of extant materials (Jarcho, 1986) and exemplary programs (Penick, 1986) are available, as are collections of model STS lessons (LaRue, 1988; Pearson, 1988). *The STS Reporter,* published by Pennsylvania State University, provides current information on materials.

Studies of Classroom Practice

Very little information is available about what is actually being taught about STS. A 1982 survey of science and social studies teachers (Barman, Harschman, & Rusch) indicated that the majority of teachers supported the integration of science and social studies; 90% of those surveyed supported teaching about STS topics. However, 68% were undecided about their level of commitment to initiate an STS program.

Mitman, Morgandollar, Marchman, and Parker (1987) reported on a study in which 11 seventh-grade life-science teachers were observed teaching two different topics in varied units. Four instruments were used to gather data: a record of class events (including time on topic and activities), a record of STS

items on academic assignments, a survey of student's perceptions of components of instruction, and a student pre-posttest. Eight observers collected the observational data after training sessions and the establishment of satisfactory inter-observer reliability.

The researchers were interested in the extent to which the "teachers . . . made linkages between science content and its societal, reasoning, historical, or attitudinal implications. Such linkages were hypothesized to facilitate students' scientific literacy." The study results showed that:

(a) teachers rarely or never addressed the non-content components of science in their presentations and academic work assignments; (b) students perceived content as the prominent focus of their teachers' instruction; and (c) teachers' references to the non-content components were unrelated to growth on all but one student outcome, where the association was negative. Altogether, the results indicate a large gap between scientific literacy as a normative goal of science instruction and current teaching practice. Furthermore, natural levels of reference to the non-content components may be of such low frequency and quality as to preclude empirical tests of their effectiveness (p. 611).

The results of this study provide a detailed confirmation of what was reported in two national surveys (Weiss, 1978, 1987).

Why don't teachers implement activities and programs based on the STS theme? No direct evidence could be found for social studies teachers, but results of studies involving science teachers may shed some light on this question. Bybee and Bonstetter's 1987 survey of 317 science teachers produced results similar to those of an earlier study by Barman, Harshman, and Rusch (1982). Although 89% of the teachers surveyed had *considered* incorporating STS activities into some aspect of their program, over 90% of the teachers said they *would* incorporate the STS theme *if* materials and instructional strategies were available. Over 70% even suggested a specific way (e.g., short vignettes, single lessons, complete K–12 programs) in which they would incorporate the STS theme.

When asked about the limitations on teaching about STS topics, the teachers in Bybee and Bonstetter's (1987) study ranked the following as the top reasons for not teaching STS: economic (budget for materials, facilities, books, equipment), personal (teacher education, teacher background, abilities, information), and pedagogical (lack of available teaching techniques, new strategies, abilities, lack of goals, rationale).

A study by Barrow and Germann (1987) indicated that availability of materials on STS issues—in this case acid rain—were a key factor in teachers' development of units on the issue. While teachers were interested in the issue and supported its inclusion in the curriculum, they were more likely to cover the issue if specific activities and instructional resources (e.g., films, filmstrips, and readings) were available.

Powell and Wright (1988) also conducted a survey on factors influencing implementation of STS in school science programs. Their survey instrument was validated by a panel of national experts and yielded highly reliable data (alpha = 0.92). Middle school science teachers ($N = 465$) in Kansas were surveyed via the mail. The response rate after a reminder postcard and second letter was 39%, with no statistical difference between early and late respondents. Three factors were reported to have influenced the adoption of STS topics by middle-school teachers: membership in professional organizations, amount of background knowledge, and administrative support. Actual implementation of STS topics was most influenced by time, resources, knowledge, and teaching experience.

A qualitative investigation of 14 secondary science teachers' perceptions of and consequent decisions about the implementation of a model STS program was reported by Mitchener and Anderson (1989). Over a period of six months, clinical interviews and classroom observations were conducted and documents analyzed. Analysis of the three data sources yielded three groups of teachers: those who accepted the STS program, those who accepted and altered the program, and those who rejected the program. Five themes were important to all three groups: (a) concerns over content, (b) discomfort with grouping, (c) uncertainties about evaluation, (d) frustrations about the student population, and (e) confusion about the teacher's role. This study reconfirmed the key place of the teacher in the implementation of a new program.

Summary

Little is known about the actual teaching of STS topics in social studies and science. Most textbooks do not include STS topics, although supplemental curriculum materials are available. The research on science teaching practices indicates little or no recognition of STS themes. A major research question is how to close the gap between policy recommendations and what is actually being taught in social studies and science classes. These findings suggest that the efforts of teachers to implement the STS theme have lacked direction and occurred at a low frequency. The need for greater understanding of systematic implementation—including administrative support, staff development programs, and techniques such as coaching of teachers in new strategies—poses important research problems.

THE LEARNED CURRICULUM

Learned curriculum refers to students' STS knowledge, attitudes, and skills. Here we deal first with national assessments; individual research is summarized in the latter part of the section.

National Assessments

In 1986, the National Endowment for the Humanities funded the first national assessment of 17-year-olds' knowledge of history and literature. The 262-question assessment instrument contained only 10 items on scientific discoveries and technological developments, but students scored well in this area. The mean score of 71.3% was in the passing range, one of only 2 of 16 scales on which a mean score above 70% was achieved (Ravitch and Finn, 1987).

How these results are viewed, however, depends to a great

extent on how important the questions asked are deemed to be. The recall of such facts as who invented the light bulb or telephone or the effect of the cotton gin on slavery in the South may not indicate significant STS knowledge.

None of the National Assessment of Educational Progress (NAEP) tests in social studies and political knowledge have included items on STS topics, but those on science have yielded some relevant information. The 1976–1977 national assessment of science was the first to include items on science and society and to assess awareness of the methods, assumptions, and values of science (NAEP, 1979). Students at ages 9, 13, and 17 were aware of science-related societal problems and were willing to contribute to the amelioration of the problems, but their reported participation in solving problems was low. Students lacked an overall understanding of scientific research methods and did not understand the difference between basic and applied research. In all, the 1976 results were disappointing and a basis for concern about students' understanding and attitudes toward STS topics (Bybee, Harms, Ward, & Yager, 1980).

Results from the 1981–1982 national assessment of science (Hueftle, Rakow, & Welch, 1983) showed a statistically significant increase in elementary students' (9-year-olds) understanding of STS items. Middle and high school students' (13- and 17-year olds, respectively) understanding generally increased, but the increase was not statistically significant. The authors proposed a "media hypothesis" to explain students' awareness of STS issues; that is, those items, or clusters of items, on which there was the largest increase were also those receiving the greatest attention in the media. Acid rain and food shortages are examples cited by the researchers (Hueftle, Rakow, & Welch, 1983).

STS topics were not prominent in the 1986 NAEP assessment items (Mullis & Jenkins, 1988), but several questions on the perceived applications of science were included. In both 1977 and 1986, 17-year-olds were more likely than 13-year-olds to perceive that scientific knowledge could be applied to help resolve national and global problems of the types listed. Students were more likely in 1986 than in 1977 to agree that the applications of science could help to preserve natural resources, reduce air and water pollution, and prevent birth defects. The largest changes across time were the decreases in the percentages of 13- and 17-year-olds who believed that science applications could help to resolve the problems of world starvation.

Mullis and Jenkins (1988) speculated about the reasons for these results:

Although the data cannot shed light on the reasons for this change, perhaps students are becoming more cognizant that multiple conditions—political, economic, and social, as well as agricultural—may contribute to world starvation, and that many of these conditions confound scientific solutions (p. 145).

The trend away from STS items in the NAEP assessments is disappointing. The 1990 national assessment (NAEP, 1989) will include few STS items. Moreover, the international assessment, *Science Achievement in Seventeen Countries* (IEA, 1988), did not include items on STS topics.

Studies by Individual Researchers

Aikenhead, Fleming, and Ryan (1987) assessed Canadian high school graduates' knowledge of STS. A stratified sample of 10,800 students, comprising approximately 5% of all high school graduates, were asked to write argumentative paragraphs on STS topics. Fleming (1987) reported on students' understanding of STS interactions:

In summary, one major interaction between science and society was viewed by students in a rather simplistic fashion: Science (technoscience) should inform society in order to resolve socio-scientific issues, issues which students perceived as technical problems; our society should inform science in terms of science policy as it guides research programs. The formulation of policy for a research program was not perceived as a socio-scientific issue. (p. 185)

Aikenhead (1987) summarized another portion of the results in this manner:

In summary, high school graduates harbored diverse and contradictory beliefs about scientific knowledge. Student paragraphs reflected a belief in certain aspects of authentic science; particularly, the nature of classification schemes, the tentative nature of knowledge, and the social dimensions of knowledge from within the scientific community. On other issues, however, students seemed to be uniformed; for instance, on the nature of scientific models, on the outside influences on scientific knowledge, on the motivations for generating knowledge, and on scientific method. Students generally viewed "the scientific method" as a vague rule of thumb—follow the procedure as given. (p. 485)

Ryan (1987) analyzed the data from the Canadian study to determine the students' beliefs about the characteristics of scientists. The majority of students thought that scientists should be concerned with the potential effects of their discoveries and that scientists are taking responsibility for their actions. Most students felt that scientists should report their results. Students were also able to distinguish between characteristics of honesty and objectivity in scientific work and in other human endeavors. There were very few differences between the attitudes of male and female students relative to scientific work.

An analysis of the Canadian students' responses was also the basis for another assessment instrument, entitled Views on Science-Technology-Society (VOSTS), subsequently validated in a large-scale study (Aikenhead, 1988b) and compared with other means of assessing students' beliefs about STS topics (Aikenhead, 1988a). The VOSTS is claimed to be superior to Likert-type scales, written paragraphs, semistructured interviews, and empirically developed multiple-choice tests.

Although no specific studies on STS outcomes from social studies instruction could be found, the results from two studies of STS-oriented science instruction may indicate both the effectiveness of STS instruction and the potential for collaboration. Zoller and his colleagues (1988) used the VOSTS instrument in a study to assess goal attainment in STS education. Students in an STS course were compared with students in a more traditional science class. The findings indicated that the STS course was effective in improving high school students' viewpoints concerning STS issues.

Yager and his colleagues (Yager, 1988a, b, c; Yager Blunck, Binadji, McComas, & Penick, 1988) assessed the impact on student learning of teacher participation in an STS leadership training program. Over a three-year period (1984 to 1986), 97 exceptional science teachers attended a series of five workshops on STS approaches and materials, followed by a summer institute in which they worked on such projects as developing an STS program. A follow-up study compared student outcomes in the classes of 60 of the teachers with control classes in the same schools; Grades 4-9 were included in the study.

The study focused on student outcomes in five domains—connections and applications of science concepts, attitudes, creativity, understanding of scientific processes, and STS information. Most of the items were from the 1986 NAEP instrument. Results indicated that students in STS programs were better able to apply information to problems, to relate new information to other situations, to act independently, and to make decisions; they also had more favorable attitudes toward science, were more creative, had better process skills, and learned at least as much scientific information as students in comparison classes.

Summary

Evidence at both the national and local levels suggests that students are learning about STS issues and have positive attitudes about studying STS, even though other research indicates there is little being taught about STS in school programs. What students learn about STS is probably related to factors other than social studies and science instruction. More research is needed on the linkages between instruction on STS topics and student outcomes.

THE RESEARCH AGENDA

As indicated above, research on science-technology-society education has been conducted almost exclusively in science education. While social studies educators have contributed to the rationale for STS education, there is virtually no research on how STS is perceived, taught, or learned in social studies. The following section, organized by the major categories of intended, taught, and learned curriculum, explicates our suggestions for developing a research base on STS in social studies.

The Intended Curriculum

Research on social studies educators' views of and attitudes toward science and technology, as well as their definitions of STS education, is clearly needed. Research should focus on three critical groups: STS advocates, including participants in national projects funded specifically to expand and institutionalize the STS innovation; school administrators; and classroom teachers.

STS Advocates. Do leading advocates of STS operate from a common definition of essential knowledge, skills, and attitudes?

For example, do the three national NSF-funded projects to expand STS education at the precollegiate level (i.e., the Science through Science/Technology/Society Project and National STS Network Project, both at Pennsylvania State University, and the Building Support Networks for Enhanced Science/Technology/Society Education Project at the Social Science Education Consortium) share common definitions of STS, so there is a common thrust in efforts to integrate STS innovations into the precollegiate social studies and science curricula?

Administrators and Teachers. To what degree are practitioners aware of, committed to, or able to clearly define STS education? Studies of social studies teachers similar in intent and design to those reported in science by Bybee and his associates (Bybee, 1984, 1987; Bybee & Bonstetter, 1986; Bybee & Mau, 1986; Bybee & Najafi, 1986) and by Molnar (1983) would provide a research foundation for designing and implementing curriculum change.

Similarly, research focused on the degree of consonance between social studies teachers' explicit educational goals and objectives and the goals and objectives of STS education would be helpful in guiding STS awareness and training activities. Such research could take as its point of departure the work of Porter and Brophy (1988) and Brophy and Good (1986), who have begun to look closely at the dynamics of actual teacher behavior. In addition, the exploratory work by Evans (1988) on the self-perceptions of history teachers and the implications of those perceptions for how and what they teach may be instructive in study design.

The Actual Curriculum

One immediate research task is to generate information that will help close the gap between policy and needs statements and what is actually being taught in social studies and science classrooms. As with the intended curriculum, much more is currently known about the teaching of STS in science than in social studies.

Quantitative studies are needed to determine what is occurring with respect to STS in local schools and districts. How many state or local curricula contain STS strands, courses, or units? To what extent have prescribed elements of STS, as defined in the intended curriculum, been implemented in classroom practice? Research is needed to identify the grade levels and courses in which STS is actually taught, the degree of collaboration between social studies and science teachers, and the specific STS content areas and topics addressed. Quantitative studies might also focus on the forms STS education has taken in local districts—that is, have districts created discrete STS courses, infused STS topics into traditional courses, created truly interdisciplinary courses, and so on?

Significant qualitative research might focus on STS as an explicit and implicit curriculum, especially within the social studies. Advocates of STS education generally believe that social studies educators have not "bought into" the relevance and critical need for STS education to the extent that science educators have. However, social studies teachers may more routinely teach about STS topics as they deal with current events, controversial and values issues, decision making, and government policy—all prominent features of the intended STS curriculum. Questions to be pursued include: To what extent are social studies teachers routinely or systematically teaching the knowledge, skills, and attitudes of STS without explicitly defining their teaching as such? To what degree does conscious and explicit instruction based on a defined STS curriculum alter or improve student outcomes?

Further analysis of the STS content of textbooks and supplementary materials is also needed. Of particular importance would be analysis of social studies curriculum materials to complement the prior analyses of science materials.

The processes of adoption, implementation, and institutionalization of STS should also be studied. How do the states or local districts in which STS curricula have been implemented differ from those where implementation has not occurred? Do causal relationships exist between state and district STS implementation and involvement with national or regional STS education projects? What strategies have facilitated or impeded adoption and implementatation at the local level? To what extent has STS required significant changes in teacher behavior and how have these changes been encouraged in local settings? How have districts addressed differing needs for teacher training (e.g., providing social studies teachers with greater scientific background and science teachers with strategies for teaching the skills of decision making and values analysis)?

The Learned Curriculum

A determination of the extent to which STS education can and does achieve such important objectives as developing analytical and decision-making skills, respect for science, and active citizen participation in public policy formation constitutes a valuable research aim. The research on student outcomes is severely limited. STS items have not been prominent in NAEP assessments. Moreover, there has been a trend away from including such items in NAEP.

Several specific research tasks related to student outcomes suggest themselves. U.S. researchers should replicate the studies of Canadian students' STS learning (Aikenhead, 1988a, 1988b; Aikenhead, Fleming, & Ryan, 1987). Such studies could valuably be expanded to examine student attitudes towards STS, as well as their cognitive outcomes. Further research similar to Zoller's study (1988) should be conducted to gauge the effectiveness of STS courses, as well as implicit STS instruction. Further work regarding the "media hypothesis" of Hueftle, Rakow, and Welch (1983) is warranted; such research would contribute to clarifying the origins of student awareness and learning about STS topics and issues. Whether and how teachers use the media appropriately in STS instruction is another important research question.

CONCLUSION

Most of the STS literature has been devoted to advocating STS as a reform in social studies and science education and to discussions of what ought to be included in STS programs. Survey results indicate that teachers, students, and scientists view STS topics as important. Students in STS programs appear to learn STS concepts and skills. Extant research also indicates, however, that little STS is actually being taught in traditional classrooms.

Little research has been done on the effects of STS programs on student learning; this should be a focus of future research efforts. Other major foci for research include what is currently being taught, the degree of collaboration between science and social studies educators, and factors influencing the adoption, implementation, and institutionalization of STS.

References

Aikenhead, G. S. (1987). High school graduates' beliefs about science-technology-society. III. Characteristics and limitations of scientific knowledge. *Science Education, 71*(4), 459–497.

Aikenhead, G. S. (1988a). An analysis of four ways of assessing student beliefs about STS topics. *Journal of Research in Science Teaching, 25*(8), 607–629.

Aikenhead, G. S. (1988b). *A field trial of a new type of assessment instrument. Project report for Saskatchewan Schools.* Saskatoon: University of Saskatchewan.

Aikenhead, G. S., Fleming, R. W., & Ryan, A. G. (1987). High school graduates' beliefs about science-technology-society. I. Methods and issues in monitoring student views. *Science Education, 71*(2), 145–210.

American Chemical Society. (1988). *ChemCom: Chemistry in the community.* Dubuque, IA: Kendall Hunt.

Barman, C., Harshman, R., & Rusch, J. (1982). Attitudes of science and social studies teachers toward interdisciplinary instruction. *The American Biology Teacher, 44*(7), 421–426.

Barrow, L. H., & Germann, P. (1987). Acid rain education and its implications for curricular development: A teacher survey. *Science Education, 71*(1), 15–20.

Benne, K. D., & Birnbaum, M. (1978). *Teaching and learning about science and social policy.* Boulder, CO: ERIC Clearinghouse for Social Studies/Science Education and Social Science Education Consortium.

Boschmann, H., Hendrix, J., & Mertens, T. (1978). Six state-adopted biology textbooks: Do they raise bioethical issues? *Hoosier Science Teacher, 4*(1), 13–20.

Brophy, J., & Good T. L. (1986). Teacher behavior and student efforts. In M. C. Wittrock (Ed.), *Handbook of research on teaching* (3rd ed., pp. 328–375). New York: Macmillan.

Bybee, R. W. (1984). Global problems and science education policy. In R. W. Bybee, J. Carlson, & A. McCormack (Eds.), *Redesigning science and technology education: 1984 NSTA yearbook* (3rd ed., pp. 60–75). Washington, DC: National Science Teachers Association.

Bybee, R. W. (1986). The sisyphean question in science education: What should the scientifically and technologically literate person know, value, and do—As a citizen? In R. W. Bybee (Ed.), *Science-technology-society: 1985 NSTA yearbook,* (pp. 79–93). Washington, DC: National Science Teachers Association.

Bybee, R. W. (1987). Teaching about science-technology-society (STS): Views of science educators in the United States. *School Science and Mathematics, 87*(4), 274–285.

Bybee, R. W., & Bonstetter, R. J. (1986). STS: What do teachers think? In R. W. Bybee (Ed.), *Science-technology-society: 1985 NSTA yearbook* (pp. 117–127). Washington, DC: National Science Teachers Association.

Bybee R. W., & Bonstetter, R. J. (1987). What research says: Implementing the science-technology-society theme in science education: Perceptions of science teachers. *School Science and Mathematics, 87*(2), 144–182.

Bybee R. W., Harms, N., Ward, B., & Yager, R. (1980). Science, society, and science education. *Science Education, 64*(3), 377–385.

Bybee, R. W., & Mau, T. (1986). Science and technology-related global problems: An international survey of science educators. *Journal of Research in Science Teaching, 23*(7), 599–618.

Bybee, R. W., & Najafi, K. (1986). Global problems and college education. *Journal of College Science Teaching, 15*(5), 443–447.

Charles, C., & Samples, R. (Eds.). (1978). *Science and society: Knowing, teaching, and learning.* Washington, DC: National Council for the Social Studies.

Christensen, J. W. (1984). *Global science: Energy, resources, environment.* Dubuque, IA: Kendall Hunt.

Cummings, H. H. (1956/1957). The social studies in a scientific age. In H. H. Cummings (Ed.), *Science and the social studies.* Washington, DC: National Council for the Social Studies.

Evans, R. W. (1988, Summer). Lessons from history: Teacher and student conceptions of the meaning of history. *Theory and Research in Social Education, 16,* 203–225.

Fleming, R. W. (1987). High school graduates' beliefs about science-technology-society. II. The interaction among science, technology and society. *Science Education, 71*(2), 163–186.

Hamm, M., & Adams, D. (1987). *An analysis of global problems and issues in sixth and seventh grade science textbooks.* Columbus, OH: ERIC Clearinghouse for Science, Mathematics, and Environmental Education.

Hickman, F. M., Patrick, J. J., & Bybee, R. W. (1987). *A framework for curriculum reform in secondary school science and social studies.* Boulder, CO: Social Science Education Consortium.

Hueftle, S., Rakow, S., & Welch, W. (1983, June). *Images of science: A summary of results from the 1981–82 national assessment in science.* Minneapolis: University of Minnesota.

Hurd, P. D. (1975). Science, technology, and society: New goals for interdisciplinary science teaching. *The Science Teacher, 42*(2), 27–30.

Hurd, P. D. (1987). A nation reflects: The modernization of science education. *Bulletin of Science, Technology, and Society, 7,* 9–13.

Hurd, P. D., Bybee, R. W., Kahle, J., & Yager, R. (1980). Biology education in secondary schools of the United States. *The American Biology Teacher, 42*(7), 388–410.

International Association for the Evaluation of Educational Achievement (IEA). (1988). *Science achievement in seventeen countries.* New York: Pergamon Press.

Jarcho, I. (1986). Curriculum approaches to teaching STS: A report on units, modules, and courses. In R. W. Bybee (Ed.), *Science-technology-society. 1985 yearbook* (pp. 162–173). Washington, DC: National Science Teachers Association.

LaRue, R. L., Jr. (1988). *Science/technology/society: Model lessons for secondary social studies classes.* Boulder, CO: Social Science Education Consortium.

Levin, F. S., & Lindbeck, J. S. (1979). An analysis of selected biology textbooks for the treatment of controversial issues and biosocial problems. *Journal of Research in Science Teaching, 16*(3), 199–203.

Mitchener, C. P., & Anderson, R. O. (1989). Teachers perspective: Developing and implementing an STS curriculum. *Journal of Research in Science Teaching, 26*(4), 351–369.

Mitman, A. T., Morgandollar, J. R., Marchman, V. A., & Parker, M. J. (1987). Instruction addressing the components of scientific literacy and its relation to student outcomes. *American Educational Research Journal, 24*(4), 611–633.

Molnar, A. (1983). Issues studied in school: The important issues facing mankind. *Social Education, 47*(5), 305–307.

Morrissett, I. (Ed.). (1982). *The current state of social studies: A project SPAN report.* Boulder, CO: Social Science Education Consortium.

Mullis, I., & Jenkins, L. (1988). *The science report card: Properties of failure . . . Elements of recovery. Trends and achievement based on the 1986 national assessment.* Princeton, NJ: National Assessment of Educational Process, Educational Testing Service.

Murnane, R., & Raizen, S. (1988). *Improving indicators of the quality of science and mathematics education in grades K–12.* Washington, DC: National Academy Press.

National Assessment of Educational Progress. (1979). *Attitudes toward science.* Denver: Education Commission of the States.

National Assessment of Educational Progress. (1989, March). *Science objectives: 1990 assessment.* Princeton, NJ: Education Testing Service.

National Council for the Social Studies. (1983). Guidelines for teaching science-related social issues. *Social Education, 47*(4), 258–261.

National Science Teachers Association. (1982). *Science-technology-society: Science education for the 1980s.* Washington, DC: National Science Teachers Association.

Newitt, J. (1983). *The treatment of limits-to-growth issues in U.S. high school textbooks.* Croton-on-Hudson, NY: Hudson Institute.

Patrick, J. J., & Remy, R. C. (1984). *Connecting science, technology, and society in the education of citizens.* Boulder, CO: ERIC Clearinghouse for Social Studies/Science Education and Social Science Education Consortium.

Pearson, J. V. (1988). *Science/technology/society: Model lessons for secondary science classes.* Boulder, CO: Social Science Education Consortium.

Penick, J. (1986). A brief look at some outstanding science, technology, and society programs. In R. W. Bybee (Ed.), *Science-technology-society: 1985 NSTA yearbook* (pp. 158–161). Washington, DC: National Science Teachers Association.

Porter, A. C., & Brophy, J. (1988). Synthesis of research on good teaching: Insights from the work of this industry for research on teaching. *Educational Leadership, 45*(8), 74–85.

Powell, J. C., & Wright, E. T. (1988). *Factors influencing the adoption and implementation of STS themes.* Unpublished paper. Colorado Springs, CO: Biological Sciences Curriculum Study.

Ravitch, D., & Finn, C. J., Jr. (1987). *What do our 17-year-olds know?* New York: Harper and Row.

Rosenthal, D. (1984). Social issues in high school biology textbooks: 1963–1983. *Journal of Research in Science Teaching, 21*(8), 819–831.

Roy, R. (1985). The science/technology/society connection. *Curriculum Review, 24*(3), 12–16.

Rubba, P. (1987). Perspectives on science-technology-society instruction. *School Science and Mathematics, 87*(3), 181–186.

Ryan, A. G. (1987). High school graduates' beliefs about science-technology-society. IV. The characteristics of scientists. *Science Education, 71*(4), 489–510.

Weiss, I. (1978). *Report of the 1977 national survey of science, mathematics, and social studies education.* Triangle Park, NC: Research Triangle Institute.

Weiss, I. (1987, November). *Report of the 1985–86 national survey of science and mathematics education.* Triangle Park, NC: Research Triangle Institute.

Yager, R. (1988a). *Assessing the impact of the Iowa honors workshop on science teachers and students: A final report for NSF.* Iowa City: University of Iowa, Science Education Center.

Yager, R. (1988b). *Science/technology/society: The current focus for achieving useful science.* Unpublished paper. Iowa City: University of Iowa, Science Education Center.

Yager, R. (1988c). S/T/S produces superior student performance. *Chautaugua Notes, 3*(5), 1–3.

Yager, R., Blunck, S., Binadji, A., McComas, W., & Penick, J. (1988). *Assessing impact of S/T/S instruction in 4–9 science in five domains.* Unpublished paper. Iowa City: University of Iowa, Science Education Center.

Zoller, U., Ebenezer, J., Morby, K., Paras, S., Sanberg, V., West, C., Wolthers, T., & Tarr, S. (1988). *Goals attainment in science-technology-society (S/T/S) education: Expectations and reality. A probe into the case of British Columbia.* Manuscript submitted for publication.

Zoller, U., & Watson, F. (1974). Technology education for the nonscience students in secondary school. *Science Education, 58*(1), 105–116.

· 48 ·

READING RESEARCH AND SOCIAL STUDIES

Kay Camperell and Richard S. Knight

UTAH STATE UNIVERSITY

The nature of reading and how to promote its development have been concerns of reading and social studies educators for several decades because most learning in the social studies depends on the medium of print and the processes of reading (Lunstrum, 1976). Shaver, Davis, and Helburn (1980), for example, reported that 80% to 90% of social studies teachers view reading as a prerequisite skill for learning social studies content. Although much has been written about how to teach reading using social studies material (Herber, 1978; Peters & Hayes, 1989; Wade, 1983), little progress has been made in implementing such instruction. Results of survey research (Tixier y Vigil & Dick, 1987) reveal that most secondary social studies teachers do not employ methods they were taught for guiding student learning from textbooks. Moreover, Durkin (1978–1979) found that only 1% of the time in the elementary social studies lessons she observed was spent teaching students how to comprehend their textbooks.

Peters and Hayes (1989) suggested two reasons why social studies teachers ignore the instructional recommendations of reading educators. First, reading educators make instructional recommendations without considering the objectives of social studies teachers and without varying the techniques according to the structure of the different disciplines that comprise the field. Second, reading educators often base their recommendations on skills models of reading that are outmoded because they present a static conception of reading. Specific skills are prescribed without considering that the effectiveness of any reading skill can vary depending upon students' background knowledge, their purpose for reading, the nature of the material they read, and the type of support or guidance teachers provide them (Pearson & Dole, 1987). The specific skills models that dominated reading research and instruction during the 1960s and 1970s are giving way to advances in theory and research that have dramatically influenced reading educators' conceptions of the processes of reading and how to foster their development.

Historically, American schools and instruction have responded to social, economic, and technological changes in society (Scribner & Cole, 1981), and recent changes in our society have led to new expectations about literacy skills needed to function as citizens in a modern, technological society. For example, simple skills that may have been sufficient for most Americans at the end of the 19th century, such as the ability to declaim short texts or comprehend familiar stories, are no longer regarded as adequate.

During World War I, standardized reading tests were developed and administered to military recruits, most of whom were unable to read short passages and answer questions about them. As a result of this testing, literacy came to be defined as the ability to answer questions about short passages on unfamiliar topics. This standard has persisted throughout most of the 20th century and is reflected in the criterion-referenced and norm-referenced tests used in most states to assess reading (Resnick & Resnick, 1977; Valencia, Pearson, Peters, & Wixson, 1989).

As Americans approach the 21st century, simple decoding and comprehension skills are not sufficient to function effectively. The literacy standard has shifted again. Functional literacy is now defined as the ability to apply information gained from reading lengthy, complex texts about unfamiliar topics. Students graduating today are expected to comprehend and learn from reading so that they can draw conclusions, reason critically, and solve problems (Applebee, Langer, & Mullis, 1987). Such skills do not develop through drill and practice on isolated skills but emerge gradually as students learn about different subject-matter domains in school and use what they have learned to reason and solve problems (Glaser, 1984; Resnick, 1987; Voss, 1987). Reading, from this perspective, is not an all-purpose skill which, once acquired, can be transferred and used in all subject-matter areas. Instead, reading consists of a variety of skills that develop gradually and vary widely as a con-

---

Reviewer was Charles W. Peters, Oakland Public Schools, Michigan.

sequence of the tasks students engage in and the knowledge they acquire in school. The research that underpins this view of reading is new and has not yet widely influenced classroom practice. As a result, a gap exists between university professors' and classroom teachers' conceptions about how to teach reading.

A gap also exists between university professors' and classroom teachers' conceptions about how to teach social studies (Shaver, 1981). The journals and conference presentations of university professors who train social studies teachers are filled with exhortations to teach students higher-order reasoning, inquiry, or citizenship skills. Nevertheless, at both the elementary and secondary level, research findings indicate that social studies instruction is dominated by teacher-led recitations that center around remembering textbook content (Shaver et al., 1980). Recent theory and research in reading may provide a way to bridge the gap between those who see social studies instruction as the development of higher-order reasoning skills and the classroom practices of teachers who emphasize remembering textbook content. Results of this research demonstrate that reading is a knowledge-based process and that the strategies students develop to comprehend and learn from written material develop hand in hand with the knowledge they acquire in specific subject-matter domains in school (Bransford, Sherwood, Vye, & Rieser, 1986). While little is known at this stage about the precise role social-studies-domain knowledge plays in reading development (Armento, 1986), some research has been initiated in this area (see Beck & McKeown, this volume) and much more is needed. Familiarity with current reading theory and research can provide social studies educators with new research ideas and methods, as well as new insights to enhance student learning in social studies domains.

The purpose of this chapter is to review current trends and patterns in research on reading and learning from texts as related to teaching and learning in social studies. Much of this research stems from the development of cognitive theories about discourse processing. Against that backdrop, research is discussed to illustrate theoretical developments in reading as well as the implications for social studies. An enormous body of research on reading exists, so this review is selective, focused primarily on research related to understanding and learning from expository texts. The field has become complex, and collaborative efforts are needed to determine how to improve student reading performance in history and social science domains.

The construct of metacognition has had a strong influence in recent research. The notion has gained widespread appeal because it concerns ways students plan, monitor, and control their own learning. The term *metacognition,* however, is used in different ways to refer to a wide variety of behaviors (Brown, 1987; Chi, 1987; Jacobs & Paris, 1987). This tendency has resulted in confusion about what metacognition is, how to measure it, and how it develops. Thus, although metacognitive studies will be integrated whenever appropriate, the term will be avoided and those referring to more specific behaviors, such as comprehension monitoring or conscious and deliberate strategy use, will be employed. Much of the current research has addressed issues related to new conceptions of what makes a

text easy or difficult to read and ways to write comprehensible texts (Beck & McKeown, this volume). In order to delimit the chapter, this literature is not reviewed nor is research on map, graph, and chart skills.

THEORETICAL BACKGROUND

During the 1960s and 1970s a paradigm shift occurred in the field of psychology (Lachman, Lachman, & Butterfield, 1979). Cognitive theories and research strategies replaced those grounded in behaviorism. One of the major reasons for this shift was advanced computer technology that enabled researchers to investigate and model human information processes through computer simulations. Major outcomes of this research were demonstrations that basic processes such as attention, understanding, and remembering depend upon a vast array of knowledge. Once researchers focused on knowledge as a key ingredient of information processing, the nature of that knowledge and how it is organized in people's minds became central research issues and generated the current schema-theoretic approaches which now dominate reading research (Pearson, 1985). A common characteristic of the schema theories discussed next is the assumption that language comprehension is an interactive process in which the characteristics of learners and the activities they engage in are as important as the tasks they perform and the materials they read. When reading researchers and theorists refer to reading as an interactive process, they generally are referring to interactions among what is written, the characteristics of readers, including their knowledge and cognitive processes, and contextual factors.

Relationships Between Reading and Writing

A basic assumption in most theories of reading is that reading and writing are interrelated modes of communication (van Dijk & Kintsch, 1983). Written language differs from speech in that it is a technology, a tool invented to convey ideas, feelings, beliefs, and information over time and space. Social conventions (e.g., customs such as using greetings and closings in business and personal letters) govern both spoken and written language, but writing requires a special knowledge for using the shared language conventions within a society (Scribner & Cole, 1981). Once learned, the conventions become strategies for understanding and learning from written material.

No text ever contains all of the words needed to convey a message; writing and reading would be too cumbersome. Thus, writers make assumptions about what their readers probably know, omit most of that information, and write about what may be new or different to readers. Because of this, much of the meaning of a text is transmitted by implication; writers expect readers to infer the ideas that they have omitted. As several researchers have noted (e.g., Graves & Slater, 1986), many of the social studies textbooks currently used in schools may impede student learning because inappropriate assumptions have been made about students' background knowledge and reading strategies.

Reading as Interactions Among Tests, Readers, and Contexts

The constructs of frames (Minsky, 1975), scripts (Schank & Abelson, 1977), and schemata (Rumelhart & Ortony, 1977; Wilson & Anderson, 1986) come from theories about how knowledge is organized and represented in people's minds and how they use that knowledge to understand, remember, and learn from reading. In these theories, reading ability is assumed to be inextricably intertwined with the life experiences and knowledge of individuals. Learning to read and write involves learning how to deal with linguistic forms and, more importantly, with acquiring the knowledge and experience to understand what the linguistic forms symbolize. What readers understand and remember from a given text depends upon their knowledge, motives, beliefs, and personal experiences, all of which shape their interpretations. Because of this, reading is referred to as a constructive process: Readers use the words and sentences in a text to build (construct) in their minds a representation of the ideas, events, objects, and experiences as conceptual wholes (van Dijk & Kintsch, 1983).

These holistic units are referred to as *macrostructures,* hierarchical representations of the global meaning of a text, ranging from its gist to its topic or theme (van Dijk & Kintsch, 1983). Macrostructures include ideas readers infer or abstract from a text. For example, a reader's memory for the story "Little Red Riding Hood" is an abstraction from the words of the text, and may include a theme or moral (e.g., beware of strangers) never explicitly stated in the story. Because readers differ in prior knowledge and experience, a writer may intend that readers understand a particular point or main idea (e.g., passive resistance as a means of civil disobedience), but the main ideas that readers actually construct (e.g., peace marches or bombing draft centers as a means of civil disobedience) result from the knowledge and purposes they use to process the text.

Jenkins (1978) summarized the interactive nature of learning in an organizational framework in which the characteristics of learners (e.g., background knowledge, motivation, interest) and the strategies they employ (e.g., rehearsal, elaboration, monitoring) interact with variations in the materials they learn from (e.g., expository or narrative texts) and the criterial tasks they perform (e.g., recognition, recall, problem solving). Within this framework, the meaning constructed for any text will vary as a function of interactions among these variables.

Part of the interactions come from what students learn in beginning reading instruction in which they are taught how to pronounce printed words and use the syntax of sentences to decode written material. The strategies students develop from this instruction are referred to as *bottom-up* processes (Adams & Collins, 1985). Once readers begin to encode words and sentence-level information, they can activate background knowledge relevant to the topic of a text, using this knowledge to build a representation of the meaning of the text, a macrostructure. Building knowledge in this way is referred to as *top-down* processes. Bottom-up and top-down processes continuously interact as readers progress through a text. Bottom-up processes affect word identification; top-down processes affect comprehension and generate expectations that influence which infor-

mation readers attend to and select as important, the inferences they make, and subsequently, what they remember after reading.

Perhaps the most controversial area in reading research is whether and how contextual variables are related to strategy development. Can skills such as problem solving, reasoning, or comprehension be developed in isolation from the domains of knowledge in which they are used? Some researchers (e.g., Ennis, 1989; Perkins & Salomon, 1989) argue that these skills can be developed in isolation because they are general processes that operate across content domains. This approach is reflected in many of the commercial materials designed for teaching reading, problem solving, and learning strategies. Other researchers (e.g., Bransford et al., 1986; Chi, 1987) argue that learning, reasoning, and problem-solving skills, as well as the ability to plan, monitor, and evaluate one's own performance, are domain-specific skills that develop as students gradually acquire subject-matter knowledge in school. At this time, most of the research evidence tends to support those who argue that comprehension and higher-order reasoning skills are domain-specific (Resnick, 1987), but much more research is needed.

Current theories of reading have important implications for social studies educators. Social studies content involves events that students have not personally experienced, institutions and values that they did not create, and places and cultural practices that they may never have seen. Textbooks are vehicles for knowledge transmission (Kintsch, 1982), and social studies textbooks present information about sociocultural events, institutions, and actions that members of a society need to know about in order to understand common texts such as newspapers, novels, and magazines. Thus, if current theories are correct, social studies teachers can play a significant role in promoting student reading performance because the knowledge students acquire from social science and history domains will influence the strategies they develop for understanding and learning from texts.

Research Findings

The theory of van Dijk and Kintsch (1983) has been highly influential in reading research because of a model they developed (Kintsch & van Dijk, 1978) that simulates comprehension processes using microcomputers. Studies supporting the validity of the model have been summarized by Kintsch (1979) and Kintsch and Vipond (1979). In most of that research, text variables (e.g., narrative or expository; cohesive or incohesive) and task variables (e.g., recognition, recall, or problem solving) have been manipulated while the age and ability level of subjects have been held constant. Other researchers, however, have varied the age or ability level of subjects and held the task and text variables constant.

Reader Variables. Voss, Fincher-Kiefer, Greene, and Post (1986) referred to research that focuses on reader variables as a contrastive research approach through which individual differences in memory, comprehension, and problem solving are examined. A major finding from this type of research was that many poor readers have adequate decoding skills but fail to comprehend what they read due to differences or deficits in domain-specific knowledge and strategies. Thus, in addition to age and ability differences, knowledge differences often are employed as an independent variable in reading research.

Frequently cited in this area of research are the results from a series of studies conducted by Voss and his associates (Chiesi, Spilich, & Voss, 1979; Spilich, Vesonder, Chiesi, & Voss, 1979) to examine the effects of domain-specific knowledge on text processing. Adult subjects who had equivalent comprehension ability, but differed in the degree of knowledge they had about baseball, read and recalled passages about baseball innings. The domain of baseball was selected because the goal structure of the game (winning) as well as relationships among actions (e.g., stealing a base) and states (e.g., number of outs) are well known. Subjects with a high degree of knowledge about baseball (a) recalled more information over all, (b) recalled more information that was significant to the goal structure of the game, and (c) produced more organized recall. These findings were interpreted as showing that high-knowledge subjects were able to construct a macrostructure for the game that enabled them to integrate and monitor the flow of successive changes in the innings (i.e., to follow the organizational structure of the passage and attend to the most important elements of the text). Low-knowledge subjects, however, were unable to form an adequate macrostructure for the passage and, therefore, were unable to identify important information or determine how different events were related to the goal of the game. The findings have been replicated by Recht and Leslie (1988) with seventh- and eighth-grade students using simplified versions of the same material, suggesting that students may fail to comprehend reading assignments in social studies because they lack domain-specific knowledge.

Task Variables. Task variables are an important element of reading theory and research because how comprehension is taught and how it is assessed are intimately related. For example, current reading instruction involves teaching students how to write summaries, answer questions, and draw inferences (Pearson & Dole, 1987), and these instructional tasks are the same as those employed in research to assess comprehension. Because comprehension is a multifaceted process, different tasks (dependent measures) assess different aspects of comprehension. Commonly employed tasks and the outcomes/processes they measure are listed in Table 48–1.

As can be seen in Table 48–1, an important assessment issue is whether to distinguish between comprehension and memory. Van Dijk and Kintsch (1983), like other researchers (Voss, Tyler, & Bisanz, 1982), do not do so because the processes of comprehension entail some maintenance of information in memory (e.g., memory of preceding text segments is used to interpret incoming information). If readers can remember information, it is assumed that they have comprehended it on some level. Other researchers (e.g., Langer, 1984), however, do distinguish between comprehension and memory (i.e., recall) and use multiple-choice questions that subjects can answer by referring back to the text.

As a basis for scoring subjects' recall and summaries, the text

they are to read may be analyzed into propositions or idea units (i.e., clauses), the relationships among the idea units, and the overall structure using available systems (Meyer, 1985; Tierney & Mosenthal, 1980; Turner & Green, 1977). Or the recall of expert and/or adult subjects after reading the text may be analyzed (e.g., Brown, Day, & Jones, 1983) to develop criteria for judging the adequacy of novice or young subjects' recall.

Scores from standardized reading achievement tests are still used to assign subjects to treatment conditions, but rarely are such scores used as dependent measures because they do not assess comprehension as it is currently defined. Reading educators in some states (Valencia & Pearson, 1988; Wixson & Peters, 1987) have developed achievement tests that reflect recent theory and research, providing models of how wide-scale assessment of reading will be conducted in the future. The tests include measures of prior knowledge as well as measures of student ability to (a) identify and follow the organizational structure of different types of texts, (b) draw inferences and integrate information from different points in a text, and (c) apply information gained from reading.

As noted by Beck and McKeown (this volume), authors should write social studies textbooks so that readers understand the significance and relevance of the situations described in them. However, if readers do not construct in their minds a representation for the situations they read about, they will not understand even the best written texts. Memory tests (i.e., recall or recognition tests) may not adequately assess whether readers understand the significance and relevance of information. A common finding (e.g., Bransford et al., 1986; Resnick, 1987) is that students who pass memory tests cannot use information they remembered to solve problems, draw inferences, or understand other texts. Because of this, to assess understanding, researchers have begun to employ application tests that require inference and problem solving. For example, van Dijk and Kintsch (1983) distinguish three levels of comprehension in their theory and each level is assessed in different ways: Memory for words, phrases, or sentences is assessed with recognition tests; memory for factual content and organizational structure is assessed with immediate and delayed recall/summarization tests; and understanding of the situation (i.e., knowledge domain) referred to in a text is assessed with delayed application or problem-solving tests. Application or problem-solving tests have not been common dependent variables in research on reading instruction but should be used more frequently.

READING INSTRUCTION RESEARCH

The subjects in most of the research in the 1970s on reading were adults. Since then, an enormous amount of research has been conducted (a) to describe (i.e., contrast) the comprehension abilities of students at different age and ability levels and (b) to identify effective techniques for improving student comprehension. Examples of contrastive research are summarized in Table 48–2, and examples of instructional research are summarized in Table 48–3. Trends and issues related to both types of research are discussed in this section.

TABLE 48–1. Frequently Employed Dependent Measures in Reading Research

Outcome/Process Measured	Criterial Task	Unit of Measurement	Scoring
Overall retention of information; memory for important ideas or details; application of summarization rules	Free recall; summary	Ideas	Number of ideas (i.e., propositions, clauses) recalled that correspond to the number of stated ideas in a text; number of ideas that correspond to the most important ideas in a text (see, e.g., Meyer, 1985)
Ability to use prior knowledge to connect related ideas, infer implied ideas, or draw conclusions from a text;	Free recall; summary	Inferences	Number and type (i.e., text explicit or implicit) of inferences (see, e.g., Lipson, 1983)
identification and use of the implied or explicitly signaled organizational structure of a text; organized representation for the meaning of a text		Organization	Extent to which recall corresponds to the organizational structure of a text; type of structure used by subjects to organize recall or summary (see, e.g., Mannes & Kintsch, 1987)
Retention of information when provided prompts from the text; retention of stated or implied main ideas and/or details	Cued, probed recall	Ideas Inferences	Number of ideas recalled; number of inferences constructed or recalled (see, e.g., Beck, Omanson, & McKeown, 1982)
Retention of details	Cloze	Words	Number of exact words recalled from different segments of a text (see, e.g., van Dijk & Kintsch, 1983)
Recognition of stated or implied main ideas and/or details; identification of prior knowledge differences	Recognition	Test item	Number of ideas or inferences correctly identified on multiple-choice or true/false tests and on sorting tasks (see, e.g., Langer, 1984)
Identification of prior knowledge used to interpret a text or a segment of text as inferred from ability to make predictions; identification of prior knowledge differences	Anticipation	Ideas Inferences	Number of correct predictions about upcoming or subsequent ideas and events in a segment of text (see, e.g., Chiesi et al., 1979)
Application or transfer of knowledge gained from reading; conceptual learning	Problem solving	Varies	Accuracy of solutions or predictions based on information from a text, for example, "given a small array of economic data, forecast the inflation rate one year from now" (see, e.g., Bean, Singer, Sorter, & Frazee, 1987)

Much of the contrastive research has been centered on the effects of prior knowledge on recall or on the reading/study strategies employed by subjects of different age or ability levels. As the independent and dependent variables listed in Table 48–3 indicate, few researchers have examined the effects on student comprehension of learning in specific subject-matter domains. Most research on reading/study strategies has been focused on general rather than domain-specific skills, and interactions between knowledge of specific content domains and strategy development have, for the most part, been ignored.

Contrastive Research

As previously noted, a recurrent theme in the theoretical literature on reading is that readers use prior knowledge to understand and remember spoken or written texts, but surpris-

ingly few researchers have examined the influence of prior knowledge on the comprehension of school-aged subjects. Brown et al. (1977) provided children and adults with thematic background information before having them listen to an ambiguous passage about a fictitious tribe. The passages could be interpreted in several ways depending on the information the subjects were given before hearing them. Based on recognition and recall tests, Brown et al. found that children as well as adults interpreted the story using the background information they had been provided, suggesting that children as well as adults rely on prior knowledge to comprehend.

Few other researchers have examined the effects of prior knowledge on student comprehension (e.g., Hayes & Tierney, 1982; Lipson, 1982; Recht & Leslie, 1988), and little is known about how the comprehension, recall, and problem-solving abilities of children may differ from those of adults. More research is needed, because the most straightforward means of

TABLE 48–2. Summary of Selected Contrastive Research

Study	Sample and Independent Variables	Dependent Variables	Findings and Conclusions
Brown, Smiley, Day, Townsend, & Lawton (1977)	Second to seventh graders, adults. Thematic framework for comprehending short stories	Recognition of whether sentences were congruent or incongruent with thematic framework presented prior to reading	No developmental trends were observed. At all grade levels, as with adults, the ideas read and recalled reflected the thematic framework they were given prior to reading. Children as well as adults use prior knowledge to comprehend.
Lipson (1982)	28 third-graders. Reading ability; prior knowledge	Recognition of implicit and explicit information from a variety of short expository texts	Prior knowledge about the topic of a text is a powerful influence on reading comprehension. Average and poor readers were better at correctly recognizing new ideas gained from reading than they were at correcting inaccurate ideas they had prior to reading.
Recht and Leslie (1988)	64 seventh- and eighth-graders. Reading ability; prior knowledge	Recall and summary of a passage about baseball; sorting sentences according to importance levels	Prior knowledge about the topic of a text determined the amount and quality of both good and poor readers' recall. This effect was powerful enough to enable poor readers to compensate for low reading ability. Helping students develop prior knowledge before reading is equally as important as strategy development.
Lipson (1983)	32 fourth and fifth grade, average and above-average readers. Religious affiliation	Reading time; cued recall of a neutral passage, a passage about a first communion, and a passage about a Bar Mitzvah	Students were more likely to comprehend a text when they had culturally appropriate prior knowledge. Cultural knowledge can limit understanding of unfamiliar texts so that recall accuracy diminishes and distortions increase.
Stein, Bramsford, Franks, Vye, & Perfetto (1982)	30 fifth-graders. Reading ability	Cued recall of precisely and imprecisely elaborated facts from sentences; learning of precisely and imprecisely elaborated facts from sentences	Good readers were able to predict accurately the difficulty of learning facts from sentences that had precise elaborations and to vary their study behaviors accordingly. Students with the same degree of prior knowledge differed in use of strategies for elaborating material so that it was more easily remembered.
Brown, Day, & Jones (1983)	67 students from fifth grade through college. Constrained and unconstrained summaries	Use of deletion, construction, generalization, and invention rules for generating a summary	Young and less-effective students summarized texts by copying verbatim and deleting words from a text. Until college, most students are unable to identify or invent topic sentences effectively.

improving students' comprehension may be simply to ensure that they have the appropriate background knowledge prior to reading. Some researchers (e.g., Recht & Leslie, 1988) found that the recall of good and poor readers did not differ if poor readers had prior knowledge about the topic of a text, and they suggested that helping poor readers develop background knowledge before reading might be as effective for improving their reading performance as reading strategy instruction. Other researchers (e.g., Stein et al., 1982), however, found differences in recall due to poor readers' inability to employ effective reading/study strategies. Because of these conflicting results, more research is needed to determine when comprehension instruction should be focused on helping students acquire prior knowledge or on teaching reading/study strategies.

More research on comprehension also is needed because students' preconceptions, attitudes, and beliefs influence comprehension (Voss, Tyler, & Yengo, 1983). Social studies topics are often inherently controversial. Students' strong beliefs and attitudes about the material they are required to read may shape the interpretations they achieve. A few studies have demonstrated (e.g., Lipson, 1983, Maria & MacGinite, 1987) that poor readers and young readers construct interpretations that are consistent with what they already know and believe rather than with the interpretations intended by authors. Nevertheless, there has been little research on how such factors influence comprehension and learning in social studies and history domains.

Several researchers (e.g., Brown, Bransford, Ferrara, & Campione, 1983) have attempted to identify the strategies students

TABLE 48–3. Summary of Selected Instructional Research

Study	Sample and Independent Variables	Dependent Variables	Findings and Conclusions
Beck, Omanson, & McKeown (1982)	48 third-graders. Reading ability; basal directed-reading lesson (DRL); redesigned DRL	Story recall; answers to questions about central, noncentral, or implied story content	Students in the redesigned lesson group achieved higher mean scores on all measures. These findings are significant because daily lessons that consistently improve comprehension of individual stories may lead to the development of general comprehension skills.
Hayes & Tierney (1982)	Eleventh- and twelfth-grade average and above-average readers. Prior knowledge; topic-related or unrelated organizer passages; sequence in which the passages were read	Quantity and quality of recall; discrimination/prediction	Results of multiple-regression analysis indicated that prior provision of an advance organizer text that gave students prior knowledge about a topic explained most of the variance in student's scores. Prior presentation of information about an unfamiliar topic enhances comprehension and learning from texts.
Beck, Perfetti, & McKeown (1982)	Various-sized groups of fourth-graders matched by ability level Intensive, long-term vocabulary instruction or traditional vocabulary instruction; stories containing the vocabulary words	Retention of vocabulary; semantic decision and sentence verification; fluency of access; story recall; Comprehension	Students who received intensive, long-term instruction on a set of vocabulary words achieved higher scores on almost all of the word-knowledge tests as well as the story recall and multiple-choice tests. Results of this study and related studies show that acquiring knowledge of word meanings enhances comprehension of stories containing the words if intensive, long-term instruction is provided.
Nagy, Anderson, & Herman (1987)	352 third-, fourth-, and fifth-graders. Reading ability; expository or narrative texts; word properties; text characteristics	Delayed retention	At all age and ability levels, small but statistically significant gains in knowledge of words encountered in the texts read by students were obtained. Students do learn word meanings from context. Thus, wide regular reading helps students improve their vocabulary knowledge. However, learning word meanings from expository texts is difficult, and teachers can't rely on students acquiring new concepts from a single reading of a textbook passage.
Rinehart et al. (1986)	70 sixth-grade average readers. Training in how to apply summarization rules and identify main ideas	Cued recall of major and minor information from a social studies text; study time; quality of notes; outlining; summary of short paragraphs with implicit or explicit main ideas	Students who received summarization training recalled more major information from the the social studies passage than students in a control group. Trained students also produced better summaries of paragraphs with explicit main ideas. Summarization training appears to improve reading ability by increasing students' awareness of important information in texts.
Armbruster et al. (1987)	82 fifth-grade average and above-average readers. Training to recognize and summarize social studies texts organized in a problem/solution structure; discussion of answers to questions about social studies passages	Answers to a main-idea essay question; summaries of two passages	Training in how to recognize and employ a problem-solution structure to summarize social studies material improved student ability to answer essay questions and write summaries. The instruction appeared to facilitate macrostructure formation. Thus, summarization training may improve comprehension ability.

develop for understanding and learning from expository texts. Most of this research has been focused on determining how students use the organizational structure of expository texts to help them distinguish important from less-important information. Results of this research indicate that even high school students have difficulty identifying and following expository text structures and because of this have difficulty with academic tasks that require them to distinguish main ideas from details, take notes, or write summaries. Summarizing has received more attention recently because (a) summarization rules from the Kintsch and van Dijk (1978) model are being used to teach students how to write summaries (e.g., Rinehart, Stahl, & Erickson, 1986) and (b) the ability to write effective summaries requires conscious and intentional use of strategies (e.g., Brown, Day, & Jones, 1983).

Instructional Research on Comprehension

Most research on reading instruction has been centered on developing more effective methods for helping students use prior knowledge so that they make appropriate inferences as they read, or on methods for teaching particular comprehension and study strategies. Overall, the aim has been to develop techniques that help students acquire general skills and abilities, and only a few researchers (e.g., Armbruster, Anderson & Osterag, 1987; Rinehart et al., 1986), as illustrated in Table 48–3, have examined methods for improving reading instruction in specific social studies domains.

Because of the influence of prior knowledge on comprehension, instructional practices such as advance organizers and prereading discussions have received increased attention. In his extensive review of research, Mayer (1984) concluded that advance organizers are a basic technique teachers can use to help students link what they already know to the content of a text. Much less research has been conducted to determine the effects of prereading discussions. Such discussions traditionally are employed as part of a directed reading lesson (Beck, Omanson, & McKeown, 1982). The aim of the discussions, within a schema-theoretic perspective, is to help students elaborate and connect information for the upcoming reading with prior knowledge. Omanson, Beck, Voss, & McKeown (1984), for example, found that prereading discussions that helped students focus attention on and build connections among ideas relevant to the central content of a text were more effective than prereading discussions that induced students to overrely on prior knowledge or to connect what they read to irrelevant knowledge. The results from the Omanson et al. study are significant because they illustrate how different instructional practices influence the representations students construct and, therefore, their ability to recall and to answer questions about what they read.

A basic assumption in current reading theories is that students' vocabulary knowledge affects comprehension. The results of research on teaching vocabulary (Calfee & Drum, 1986; Graves, 1986) indicate that vocabulary instruction alone usually does not lead to enhanced comprehension. Beck and her associates (Beck, Perfetti, & McKeown, 1982; McKeown, Beck, Omanson, & Perfetti, 1983; McKeown, Beck, Omanson, & Pople,

1985) have found that direct and varied vocabulary instruction accompanied with repeated experience using the words over a long period of time are needed if students are to learn new words well enough to affect comprehension.

Vocabulary instruction in subject-matter disciplines such as social studies is critical because students encounter numerous new words in each discipline and learning new words from expository texts is difficult (Nagy et al., 1987). The results of the research by Beck and her associates suggest, moreover, that simply telling students the meanings of new words or having them memorize words and their definitions may not help students learn them well enough to recognize and understand them in reading assignments. More active instruction, like that provided in concept lessons (e.g., Yoho, 1985) may be an effective method for enhancing student knowledge of vocabulary in social studies if the lessons include opportunities for students to use the words repeatedly over time.

The teachers observed by Durkin (1978–1979) were not teaching their elementary students comprehension strategies. Since then, numerous studies have been conducted to identify effective techniques teachers can use to teach comprehension and study strategies. A direct or explicit lesson format (Pearson & Dole, 1987) has been employed in these studies to teach strategies such as how to locate answers to comprehension questions and how to use the organizational structure of texts to identify main ideas, take notes, or write summaries (Garner, 1987; Calfee & Drum, 1986). Typically, a series of nonsequential texts from a variety of content domains are employed in the studies, and learning is assessed with recognition, recall, or summary tests. Researchers have rarely examined whether learning any particular strategy improves student ability to learn from cumulative texts in a specific content domain like social studies. Such studies are needed because, as noted previously, ability to identify implicit or explicit main ideas, to follow the organizational structure of a passage, or to write effective summaries may be effective means for students to increase their knowledge of a domain.

Reading in the Social Studies

In most studies designed to examine how to improve student reading performance in social studies, classroom textbooks were used as the material for teaching and practicing strategies. For example, Rinehart et al. (1986) used a direct instruction method to teach sixth-graders how to write summaries using social studies texts. The results indicated that the training improved student ability to identify and remember main ideas and supporting details in social studies material.

Generally, conceptual understanding of the social studies concepts and principles students read about during training has not been assessed. An exception of this was a study conducted by Bean et al. (1987) to compare the effects of teaching two different notetaking strategies. Tenth-grade honor students in world history either (a) read a text using traditional outlining or (b) read a text after being trained to construct graphic organizers as a tool for organizing information and then use them to make predictions about historical events they had not studied in class. No differences were found between the groups on any of the unit tests, indicating that both groups remembered text and lesson content equally well. However, students in the graphic-organizer group achieved a higher mean score on a transfer essay test in which they applied knowledge about characteristics of European revolutions to make predictions about the Cuban revolution, which they had not yet studied. These findings indicate that students can be taught reading strategies and content concurrently and that such instruction can lead to improved conceptual understanding of social studies content.

A major aim of social studies education is the development of citizenship and decision-making skills (Shaver, 1969). Critical reading is a foundation skill on which these processes depend, because many of the ideas, events, and issues students are asked to make decisions about are presented to students via written texts. Nevertheless, very few reports of studies of critical reading were located in the current literature. The few found (Hudgins & Edelman, 1988; Patching, Kameenue, Carmine, Gersten, & Colvin, 1983) were focused on teaching general skills, such as how to make deductive inferences, rather than domain-specific skills. Many researchers (e.g., Glaser, 1984; Resnick, 1987) now assume, however, that critical thinking, problem solving, and decision making are knowledge-based processes in which people understand, reason, and think in terms of what they know. These researchers argue that traditional critical-thinking skills, such as the ability to distinguish facts from opinion, recognize the influence of prior knowledge and beliefs on understanding, and analyze arguments and language, may be influenced as much by the content knowledge students acquire as by the reading/thinking skills they develop.

The results of reading research do suggest that success on traditional critical-reading tasks requires readers to have insights about and the ability to reflect on their own thinking processes. Young and poor readers as well as many older readers may lack these insights (Brown, Bransford, Ferrara, & Campione, 1983). Repeatedly, researchers have found that readers distort the meaning of a text to conform to pre-existing knowledge and are unaware of misinterpreting what they read. Many students, moreover, cannot identify and follow the organizational structure of texts, and even college students can fail to identify implied main ideas.

Results of research on comprehension monitoring (Garner, 1987) show that many readers are extremely tolerant of ambiguities, inconsistencies, and untruths in passages they hear or read. Often these difficulties stem from an inability to develop representations of texts that are inconsistent with prior knowledge or beliefs, but they also may stem from instructional practice. As noted by Garner (1987), students may not develop skill at evaluating the internal or external consistency of ideas in texts because they are not expected or taught how to evaluate what they read. The ability to read critically is probably a late-emerging skill which depends on (a) an adequate knowledge base, (b) insights about and control over one's own reading processes, (c) skill at identifying and following the organizational structure of texts, and (d) instruction in how to evaluate information in written material.

An obstacle to developing effective techniques for teaching critical-reading/thinking skills in social studies lies in the nature of social science controversies and problems. Social science problems, unlike those in mathematics and physical science, are ill-structured in that there are few agreed-upon rules, algorithms, or formulas for solving them (Voss, Greene, Post, & Penner, 1984). Generally these problems involve some undesirable state (e.g., a high crime rate) that requires a solution, yet solutions in the field are inherently controversial (e.g., gun control). Skill at solving such problems depends on a high degree of knowledge about relevant issues so that political, social, or economic constraints are considered and a case can be built for any proposed solution.

Voss and his associates (Voss et al., 1983; Voss, Greene, Post, & Penner, 1984) examined problem-solving differences among expert and novice college students in political science and economics. They found that experts could use their knowledge effectively to identify problem constraints and build cases to support proposed solutions. Novices, even though they had passed economics and political science courses, could not. Voss and his associates suggested that the difference in knowledge application occurred because the novices had not been taught how to use the information they acquired in economics and political science courses to reason and solve problems. Except for this research, however, very little is known about knowledge-utilization strategies for effective thinking in history and social science domains. Reading and social studies researchers might focus on what constitutes critical-reading/thinking skills in these domains. If strategies used by effective problem-solvers can be identified, then domain-specific instruction could be designed. A clear example of the potential of this approach is provided in a study by Lundeberg (1987).

Lundeberg employed protocol analysis to examine differences between novices and experts in reading legal case analyses. The purpose of the study was to identify strategies to teach first year law students to read the primary materials used in law instruction. Based on an analysis of experts' reading (practicing lawyers or law professors), Lundeberg identified strategies that she then taught to beginning law students (e.g., how to identify the most important elements in a case, the organizational structure of legal case documents, and the process of judicial reasoning in a case). The effectiveness of the instructional program was then evaluated in four different studies. Results indicated that the instruction was most effective when (a) students had at least two months of course experience in law school and (b) it included training in how to self-monitor and evaluate use of the strategies. Lundeberg's study illustrates that effective, domain-specific instruction in critical reading can be designed once the strategies used by effective readers in a domain are identified.

SUMMARY

New theories and models that emphasize the interactive nature of reading have had a profound impact on reading research in the past decade. A major consequence has been increased concern about how to promote the development of comprehension. A key issue highlighted by the theory and research is the role of prior knowledge and how it interacts with the strategies students develop for understanding and learning from text. The results of this research suggest that both content knowledge and strategies must be developed if students are to become effective readers. Collaborative efforts between reading and social studies researchers are needed to identify strategies that are specific to history and the various social science domains.

Another issue highlighted by the new theory and research is the variable nature of reading processes. Essentially, research findings suggest that instructional approaches and tasks should be identified or developed that reflect differences between the cognitive outcomes of remembering information from texts and understanding the significance and relevance of the information. Research is needed to identify techniques that help students acquire content knowledge and strategies so that they develop cognitive structures they can use to reason and solve problems as they read.

References

Adams, M. J., & Collins, A. (1985). A schema-theoretic view of reading. In H. Singer & R. Ruddel (Eds.), *Theoretical models and processes of reading* (pp. 404–423). Newark, NJ: International Reading Association.

Applebee, A. N., Langer, J. A., & Mullis, I. N. (1987). *Learning to be literate in America: Reading, writing and reasoning.* Princeton, NJ: Educational Testing Service.

Armbruster, B. B., Anderson, T. H., & Osterag, J. (1987). Does text structure/summarization instruction facilitate learning from expository text? *Reading Research Quarterly, 22,* 331–346.

Armento, B. J. (1986). Research in the social studies. In M. J. Wittrock (Ed.), *Handbook of research on teaching* (3rd ed., pp. 942–951). New York: Macmillan.

Bean, T. W., Singer, H., Sorter, J., & Frazee, C. (1987). Acquisition of hierarchically organized knowledge and prediction of events in world history. *Reading Research and Instruction, 26,* 99–114.

Beck, I. L., Omanson, R. C., & McKeown, M. G. (1982). An instructional redsign of reading lessons: Effects on comprehension. *Reading Research Quarterly, 17,* 462–481.

Beck, I. L., Perfetti, C. A., & McKeown, M. G. (1982). Effects of long-term vocabulary instruction on lexical access and reading comprehension. *Journal of Educational Psychology, 74,* 506–521.

Bransford, J. D., Sherwood, R., Vye, N. J., & Rieser, J. (1986). Teaching thinking and problem solving: Research foundations. *American Psychologist, 41,* 1078–1089.

Brown, A. L. (1987). Metacognition, executive control, self-regulation and other more mysterious mechanisms. In F. E. Weinert & R. H. Kluwe (Eds.), *Metacognition, motivation and understanding* (pp. 65–116). Hillsdale, NJ: Erlbaum.

Brown, A. L., Bransford, J. D., Ferrara, R. A., & Campione, J. C. (1983). Learning, remembering and understanding. In J. H. Flavell & E. M. Markman (Eds.), *Handbook of child psychology: Vol. 3. Cognitive development* (pp. 77–166). New York: Wiley.

Brown, A. L., Day, J. D., & Jones, R. S. (1983). The development of plans for summarizing texts. *Child Development, 54,* 968–979.

Brown, A. L., Smiley, S. S., Day, J. D., Townsend, A. R., & Lawton, S. C. (1977). Intrusion of a thematic idea in children's comprehension and retention of stories. *Child Development, 48,* 1454–1456.

Calfee, R., & Drum, P. (1986). Research on teaching reading. In M. C. Wittrock (Ed.), *Handbook of research on teaching* (3rd ed., pp. 804–839). New York: Macmillan.

Chi, M. T. H. (1987). Representing knowledge and metaknowledge: Implications for interpreting metamemory research. In F. E. Weinert & R. H. Kluwe (Eds.), *Metacognition, motivation and understanding* (pp. 239–266). Hillsdale, NJ: Erlbaum.

Chiesi, H. L., Spilich, G. J., & Voss, J. F. (1979). Acquisition of domain-related information in relation to high and low domain knowledge. *Journal of Verbal Learning and Verbal Behavior, 18,* 257–273.

Durkin, D. (1978–1979). What classroom observations reveal about reading comprehension instruction. *Reading Research Quarterly, 15,* 481–533.

Ennis, R. H. (1989). Critical thinking and subject specificity: Clarification and needed research. *Educational Researcher, 18,* 4–10.

Garner, R. (1987). *Metacognition and reading comprehension.* Norwood, NJ: Ablex.

Glaser, R. (1984). Education and thinking: The role of knowledge. *American Psychologist, 39,* 93–104.

Graves, M. F. (1986). Vocabulary learning and instruction. In E. Z. Rothkopf (Ed.), *Review of Research in Education* (Vol. 13, pp. 49–90). Washington DC: American Educational Research Association.

Graves, M. F., & Slater, W. (1986). Could textbooks be better written and would it make a difference? *American Education, 10,* 36–42.

Hayes, D. A., & Tierney, R. J. (1982). Developing readers' knowledge through analogy. *Reading Research Quarterly, 17,* 256–279.

Herber, H. L. (1978). *Teaching reading in the content areas.* Englewood Cliffs, NJ: Prentice Hall.

Hudgins, F. B., & Edelman, S. (1988). Children's self-directed critical thinking. *Journal of Educational Research, 81,* 262–273.

Jacobs, J. E., & Paris, S. G. (1987). Childrens' metacognition about reading: Issues in definition, measurement, and instruction. *Educational Psychologist, 22,* 255–278.

Jenkins, J. J. (1978). Four points to remember. A tetrahedral model of memory experiments. In L. S. Cermak & F. I. M. Craik (Eds.), *Levels of processing in human memory* (pp. 429–446). Hillsdale, NJ: Erlbaum.

Kintsch, W. (1979). On modeling comprehension. *Educational Psychologist, 14,* 3–14.

Kintsch, W. (1982). Text representations. In W. Otto & S. White (Eds.), *Reading expository material* (pp. 87–102). New York: Academic Press.

Kintsch, W., & van Dijk, T. A. (1978). Toward a model of text comprehension and production. *Psychological Review, 85,* 363–394.

Kintsch, W., & Vipond, F. (1979). Reading comprehension and readability in educational practice and psychological theory. In L. G. Nilsson (Ed.), *Perspectives on money research* (pp. 329–365). Hillsdale, NJ: Erlbaum.

Lachman, R., Lachman, J. I., & Butterfield, E. C. (1979). *Cognitive psychology and information processing: An introduction.* Hillsdale, NJ: Erlbaum.

Langer, J. A. (1984). Examining background knowledge and text comprehension. *Reading Research Quarterly, 9,* 469–481.

Lipson, M. Y. (1982). Learning new information from text: The role of prior knowledge and reading ability. *Journal of Reading Behavior, 14,* 243–261.

Lipson, M. Y. (1983). The influence of religious affiliation on children's memory for text information. *Reading Research Quarterly, 18,* 448–457.

Lundeberg, M. A. (1987). Metacognitive aspects of reading comprehension: Studying understanding of legal case analysis. *Reading Research Quarterly, 22,* 407–432.

Lunstrum, J. P. (1976). Reading in the social studies: A preliminary analysis of recent research. *Social Education, 40,* 10–17.

Mannes, S. M., & Kintsch, W. (1987). Knowledge organization and text organization. *Cognition and Instruction, 4,* 91–115.

Maria, K., & MacGinite, W. (1987). Learning from texts that refute the reader's prior knowledge. *Reading, Research and Instruction, 26,* 222–238.

Mayer, R. E. (1984). Aids to text comprehension. *Educational Psychologist, 19,* 30–42.

McKeown, M. C., Beck, I. L., Omanson, R. C., & Perfetti, C. A. (1983). The effects of long-term vocabulary instruction on reading comprehension: A replication. *Journal of Reading Behavior, 15,* 3–18

McKeown, M. C., Beck, I. L., Omanson, R. E., & Pople, M. T. (1985). Some effects of the nature and frequency of vocabulary instruction on the knowledge and use of words. *Reading Research Quarterly, 20,* 522–535.

Meyer, B. J. F. (1985). Prose analysis: Procedures, purposes, and problems. In B. K. Britton & J. Black (Eds.), *Understanding expository text: A theoretical and practical handbook for analyzing explanatory text* (pp. 11–65). Hillsdale, NJ: Erlbaum.

Minsky, M. (1975). A framework for representing knowledge. In P. H. Winstron (Ed.), *The psychology of computer vision.* New York: McGraw-Hill.

Nagy, W. E., Anderson, R. C., & Herman, P. A. (1987). Learning word meanings from context during normal reading. *American Educational Research Journal, 24,* 237–270.

Omanson, R. C., Beck, I. L., Voss, J. F., & McKeown, M. G. (1984). The effects of reading lessons on comprehension: A processing description. *Cognition and Instruction, 1,* 45–67.

Patching, W., Kameenue, E., Carnine, D., Gersten, R., & Colvin, G. (1983). Direct instruction in critical reading skills. *Reading Research Quarterly, 18,* 406–418.

Pearson, P. D. (1985). *The comprehension revolution: A twenty-year history of process and practice related to reading comprehension.* (Reading Education Report No. 57). Urbana, IL: University of Illinois, Center for the Study of Reading.

Pearson, P. D., & Dole, J. A. (1987). Explicit comprehension instruction: A review of research and new conceptualization of instruction. *Elementary School Journal, 88,* 151–165.

Perkins, D. N., & Salomon, G. (1989). Are cognitive skills context-bound? *Educational Researcher, 18,* 16–25.

Peters, C. W., & Hayes, B. (1989). The role of reading instruction in the social studies classroom. In D. Lapp, J. Flood, & N. Farnan (Eds.), *Content area reading and learning* (pp. 152–178). Englewood Cliffs, NJ: Prentice Hall.

Recht, D. R., & Leslie, D. (1988). Effects of prior knowledge of good and poor readers' memory of text. *Journal of Educational Psychology, 80,* 16–20.

Resnick, D. P., & Resnick, L. B. (1977). The nature of literacy: An historical exploration. *Harvard Educational Review, 47,* 370–385.

Resnick, L. B. (1987). *Education and learning to think.* Washington, DC: National Academy Press.

Rinehart, S. D., Stahl, S. A., & Erickson, L. G. (1986). Some effects of summarization training on reading and studying. *Reading Research Quarterly, 21,* 422–438.

Rumelhart, D. E., & Ortony, A. (1977). The representation of knowledge in memory. In R. C. Anderson, R. J. Spiro, & W. E. Montague (Eds.), *Schooling and the acquisition of knowledge* (pp. 99–136). Hillsdale, NJ: Erlbaum.

Schank, R. C., & Abelson, R. P. (1977). *Scripts, plans, goals, and understanding.* Hillsdale, NJ: Erlbaum.

Scribner, S., & Cole, M. (1981). *The psychology of literacy.* Cambridge, MA: Harvard University Press.

Shaver, J. P. (1969). Reading and controversial issues. In R. C. Preston (Ed.), *A new look at reading in the social studies* (pp. 34–49). Newark, DE: International Reading Association.

Shaver, J. P. (1981). Citizenship, values, and morality in social studies. In H. D. Mehlinger & O. L. Davis (Eds.), *The social studies: Eightieth yearbook of the National Society for the Study of Education* (pp. 105–125). Chicago: University of Chicago Press.

Shaver, J. P., Davis, O. L., & Helburn, S. W. (1980). An interpretive report on the status of precollege social studies education based on NSF studies. In *What are the needs in precollege science, mathematics, and social studies education? Views from the field* (pp. 3–18). Washington, DC: National Science Foundation.

Spilich, G. J., Vesonder, G. T., Chiesi, H. L., & Voss, V. F. (1979). Text processing of domain-related information for individuals with high and low domain knowledge. *Journal of Verbal Learning and Verbal Behavior, 18,* 275–290.

Stein, B. S., Bransford, J. D., Franks, J. J., Vye, N. J., & Perfetto, G. A. (1982). Differences in judgments of learning difficulty. *Journal of Experimental Psychology: General, 3,* 406–413.

Tierney, R. J., & Mosenthal, J. (1980). *Discourse comprehension and production: Analyzing text structures and cohesion.* (Technical Report No. 152). Urbana, University of Illinois, Center for the Study of Reading. (ERIC Document Reproduction Service No. ED 179 945)

Tixier y Vigil, T. Y., & Dick, J. (1987). Attitudes toward and perceived use of textbook reading strategies among junior and senior high school social studies teachers. *Theory and Research in Social Education, 15,* 51–59.

Turner, A., & Green, E. (1977). *The construction and use of a propositional text base.* (Technical Report No. 63). Boulder, CO: University of Colorado Institute for the Study of Intellectual Behavior.

Valencia, S. W., & Pearson, D. P. (1988). Principles for classroom comprehension assessment. *Remedial and Special Education, 9,* 26–35.

Valencia, S. W., Pearson, P. D., Peters, C. W., & Wixson, K. K. (1989). Theory and practice in statewide reading assessment: Closing the gap. *Educational Leadership, 46,* 57–63.

van Dijk, T. A., & Kintsch, W. (1983). *Strategies of discourse comprehension.* New York: Academic Press.

Voss, J. F. (1987). Learning and transfer in subject-matter learning: A problem-solving model. *International Journal of Educational Research, 11,* 607–622.

Voss, J. F., Fincher-Kiefer, R. H., Greene, T. T., & Post, T. A. (1986). Individual differences in performance: The contrastive approach to knowledge. In R. J. Sternberg (Ed.), *Advances in the psychology of human intelligence* (pp. 297–334). Hillsdale, NJ: Earlbaum.

Voss, J. F., Greene, T. R., Post, T. A., & Penner, B. C. (1984). Problem-solving skill in the social sciences. In G. Bower (Ed.), *The psychology of learning and motivation: Advances in research and theory* (pp. 165–213). New York: Academic Press.

Voss, J. F., Tyler, S. W., & Bisanz, G. L. (1982). Prose comprehension and memory. In R. Puff (Ed.), *Handbook of research methods in human memory and cognition* (pp. 349–393). New York: Academic Press.

Voss, J. F., Tyler, S. W., & Yengo, L. A. (1983). Individual differences in the solving of social science problems. In R. F. Dillon & R. R. Schmeck (Eds.), *Individual differences in cognition* (pp. 205–232). New York: Academic Press.

Wade, S. F. (1983). A synthesis of the research for improving reading in the social studies. *Review of Educational Research, 53,* 461–497.

Wilson, P. T., & Anderson, R. C. (1986). What they don't know will hurt them: The role of prior knowledge in comprehension. In J. Orasanu (Ed.), *Reading comprehension: From research to practice* (pp. 31–48). Hillsdale, NJ: Erlbaum.

Wixson, K. K., & Peters, C. W. (1987). Comprehension assessment: Implementing an interactive view of reading. *Educational Psychologist, 22,* 333–356.

Yoho, R. F. (1985, April). *Effectiveness of four concept teaching strategies on social studies concept acquisition and retention.* Paper presented at the Annual Meeting, of the American Educational Research Association, Chicago.

49

WRITING FOR THE SOCIAL STUDIES

Robert L. Gilstrap

GEORGE MASON UNIVERSITY

A literate citizenry has been one of the major goals of our democratic society since its beginning. The major emphasis during the earliest days was on reading in order to help our young ones save their souls from "that old deluder Satan." Thomas Jefferson later wrote eloquently of the need for the citizens of the new republic to have a basic education for active participation in a democracy:

Above all things, I hope the education of the common people will be attended to; convinced that on this good sense we may rely with the most security for the preservation of a due degree of liberty. If a nation expects to be ignorant and free in a state of civilization, it expects what never was and never will be.... (Haskew, 1956)

Jefferson's concern for the education of all Americans was made explicit in his bill "For the More General Diffusion of Knowledge," introduced into the legislature of Virginia in 1779. In this bill, the first plan for a statewide public school system in the United States, Jefferson proposed: "At every of those schools shall be taught, reading, writing, and common arithmetick, and the books which shall be used therein for instructing the children to read shall be such as will at the same time make them acquainted with Graecian, Roman, English, and American history."

Literacy has received emphasis during recent years with increased interest at the federal level in the education of our nation's young people. One of the most vocal national spokesmen has been William J. Bennett, former United States Secretary of Education. Responding to the 1986 National Assessment of Educational Progress (NAEP) study, which reported what he considered to be some "awful" findings about children's ability to write, Bennett (1986) said:

Writing should be part of the teaching strategy in every subject, not just "language arts." By the time they reach the upper elementary grades, children should be asked to compose essays about science projects and write biographical sketches of historical figures. They should even be asked to write about how they solve mathematical problems, and to put the solutions to word problems into full sentences. By the end of eighth grade, children should be writing more extended compositions, including some that call upon them to draw information from several sources. They should write and write and write some more, until it becomes second nature to put pencil—or printer—to paper and produce something coherent and expressive. (p. 12)

Writing literacy has an importance that goes beyond being successful in school or being an effective citizen. Vygotsky (1978) pointed out that learning to write involves the acquisition of a particular system of symbols and signs whose mastery heralds a critical turning point in the entire cultural development of the child. Thus, questions about the acquisition of written literacy by children raise fundamental issues about both individual psychological development and membership in the community.

The acquisition of systems of signs and symbols in speaking, reading, and writing provides stunning examples of the interconnections between the growth of the individual and society. Speech, reading, and writing are instances of the use of cultural tools—systems created and passed on in societies in order for the members of those societies to live and work together meaningfully (Florio & Frank, 1982).

The focus of this chapter is on the use of writing in school settings (K–12) to enhance the learning of and thinking about social studies knowledge, skills, and attitudes in preparation for assuming adult responsibilities in our society. First, the two major roles of writing in the social studies will be examined. Since much of the support for using writing comes from the research on written composition, research on the current writing-process approach is reviewed next and the process briefly described. Finally, the limited amount of research specifically on the use of writing in social studies classrooms (K–12) is reviewed and the implications for future research are discussed.

Reviewers were Susan Florio-Ruane, Michigan State University; Joyce Kinkead, Utah State University.

RELATIONSHIP OF WRITING TO LEARNING

The two major roles typically seen for writing in the social studies are as a means for assessing learning and as a tool of learning. In recent articles on writing for social studies, Blackey (1981), Jolliffe (1987), and Welton (1982) focused on writing for both purposes.

Writing as Assessment of Learning

Traditionally, writing has been used to assess learning from social studies activities in both elementary and secondary classrooms. The emphasis is on a final product, usually in the form of a research report or written answers to an examination.

The development of a research report can be a significant integrating experience for a student, with much learned by gathering information—from print and nonprint materials as well as from other sources such as interviews—and organizing these findings in writing. When the emphasis is on the assessment of learning in the social studies, however, the teacher typically provides the students with information about the form in which the paper is to be completed. Very little assistance is provided during the development of the paper except to respond to questions about the preferred way to prepare the final product. The paper is then evaluated and returned to the student with the teacher's suggestions for improvement the *next time* that such a project is done. Little learning takes place through critiques by the teacher and revisions by the students as the paper is being written.

Writing as a Tool of Learning

The use of writing as a tool of learning emerged during the 1970s, stimulated by the Schools Council Writing Across the Curriculum Project, affiliated with the University of London Institute of Education. In that landmark study (Britton, Burgess, Martin, McLeod, & Rosen, 1975), the researchers focused on two questions in examining student compositions: (a) What is the writing for? and (b) Who is it for? The researchers examined a sample of about 2,000 pieces of school writing collected from 65 secondary schools in England in order to describe how writing was used in schools and to provide a basis for defining or tracking any development of writing abilities.

The researchers found that 84% of the writing done in the secondary schools in the study was extremely narrow, usually limited in audience to the teacher as examiner, with the purpose to inform or report. In essence, most writing was for tests and reports, or what the researchers referred to as *transactional* writing.

In the report, detail about the kinds of transactional writing done in history was lumped with information about science classes. Less than 6% was higher-level writing, such as writing to speculate, to hypothesize, or to theorize. Most of the writing was lower level—to report, to record, or to classify—and evaluated by the teacher.

The following year, a report on writing across the curriculum was published from the same project (Martin, D'Arcy, Newton, & Parker, 1976). The theme was not the "teaching of English," but the role of language in learning in all parts of the curriculum. Although the focus was on writing, much was also said about talking, reading, thinking, and learning in school.

The project team had worked with teachers of all subjects to find ways in which pupils' writing could more effectively contribute to their personal development and learning. The book provides many examples of secondary students' meaningful writing about a wide variety of topics.

When the book was published, there was the expectation that it would contribute to a wider discussion of the use of writing across the curriculum, and that goal appears to have been reached more than 10 years later. From 1976 to the present, many books and articles have been written to describe how writing can be used as a tool of learning in all curriculum areas. In spite of all the publications, however, there is still much confusion about cross-curriculum writing.

The confusion about what writing across the curriculum might entail is well described in the humorous introduction to a publication developed for the Virginia Department of Education (Self, 1987). Judy Self explained that in her role with the Virginia Department of Education, she encountered many people who believe that writing across the curriculum means writing *more* reports and essays to be graded by overworked teachers. These people think that transactional writing or product writing is the only kind of writing that students should do in schools.

Self (1987) defined writing across the curriculum as

when all teachers of all subjects give frequent opportunities to use writing in ways that will help students to learn course material and learn to think with that material. This kind of frequent and ungraded writing is called writing to learn. It's the important part of the picture that many educators don't realize is even in the whole picture of writing. (p. 2)

The preface to *Plain Talk* (Self, 1987) was written by Nancy Martin, one of the members of the London research and development team mentioned earlier. She indicated that we still have much to accomplish in our schools to utilize writing as a tool for learning:

In times past, reading was the highly esteemed province of the educated and the powerful; writing was a lowly skill performed by hired scribes for practical purposes only. Much of this view lingers today. People use writing as necessary for the practicalities of daily life. They use it as seldom as possible. To see it as an aspect of thinking is as unbelievable as seeing a genie coming out of a bottle, yet, studies in the last fifty years exploring the relationship of thought to language have shown writing to have a transforming power over thought which is little short of magical. "Thought is born through words" wrote Vygotsky. (p. iii)

WHAT DOES RESEARCH SAY ABOUT WRITING

Before considering the limited amount of research on the use of writing in the social studies, attention must be given to the research that has been done on writing itself. Social studies educators have sometimes drawn from this body of research in designing studies and in modifying curriculum and instruction at both the elementary and secondary levels.

Early Research Focused on Teachers' Methods

Prior to 1971, research on the teaching of writing was guided by the belief that the method used by the teacher should be studied. When Graves (1980) reviewed research on writing in the elementary grades from 1955 to 1972, he found that only 156 studies had been reported. Most of these studies (68%) had been focused on how teachers get children to write, 12% on what students do when they write, and 12% on the correlates of quality writing. In the seven studies that were focused on what students do, the researchers analyzed the products of student writing. Only one researcher (Emig, 1971) broke from the tradition of experimental tests of particular teaching techniques to focus on the process of writing (Freedman, Dyson, Flower, & Chase, 1987).

Emig influenced research methods by demonstrating that the case study is a respectable and informative methodology for studying written language. In addition, she pioneered the think-aloud protocol to study writing, a methodology that gives researchers access to the thinking processes of writers as they compose. Emig used multiple sources of data to inform her conclusions, including interviews with the students about their writing experiences and analyses of the writing they produced.

Writing Researchers Shift Focus

Emig's study with adolescents was soon followed by Graves's (1973) research on the writing processes of seven-year-old children. Together they stimulated a series of studies in the 1970s focused primarily on gaining a better understanding of the major stages of the writing process and how these stages could be addressed in planning curriculum and instruction (e.g., Flower & Hayes, 1977; Graves, 1981; Perl, 1979; Pianko, 1979; Stallard, 1979). As commonly conceptualized, the major stages are: (a) prewriting, (b) writing, (c) rewriting, (d) editing, and (e) sharing. Each stage is viewed as part of an overall process by which a writer can create and produce a piece of writing.

During the 1980s, a third focus for writing research emerged: context. In this line of research, homes, classrooms, and workplaces are examined as critical social contexts in which people learn to write as they interact with their peers and teachers. According to Freedman, Dyson, Flower, & Chafe, (1987), researchers (e.g., Applebee, 1984; Dyson, 1983; Farr, 1985) found that writing is a functional ability that begins to develop well before the school years as stories, messages, and greetings are drawn and written. Moreover, the ways in which young children approach writing are related to the language and literacy tasks to which they have been exposed in their home and community environments. The researchers have also suggested that learning and instruction in writing at all ages can only be understood within the complexities of the natural communicative environments in which those processes occur.

Debate Over Focus and Methodology

Although there has been, since the 1970s, a movement away from experimental studies focused on teachers' methods of teaching writing, studies of this type have not faded from the research scene. When Hillocks (1984) prepared a meta-analysis of experimental studies on teaching composition reported from 1963 to 1983, he discovered 500 published studies, dissertations, studies in the Education Resources Information Center (ERIC), and studies in mimeographed form.

Hillocks's (1984) review of these studies revealed that they were much more carefully designed than those reported in Braddock, Lloyd-Jones, and Schoer's (1963) influential review of research on written composition. He also found that the total number of experimental studies completed in the 20 years covered in his study exceeded the total number of studies included in the Braddock et al. bibliography.

Hillocks's most surprising discovery was that analysis of the studies he categorized as fitting the description of the widely used and praised *natural-process approach* revealed this methodology to be less effective than the one he categorized as *the environmental mode*. In that mode, writing is taught as a process, but the teacher creates structures to guide the student and thereby "brings teacher, student, and materials more nearly into balance and, in effect, takes advantage of all resources of the classroom" (p. 160). Hillocks found the environmental mode to be three times more effective than the natural-process, free-writing approach. He described the latter approach as one in which "the instructor encourages students to write for other students, to receive comments from them, and to revise their drafts in light of comments from both students and the instructor." In his interpretation, with this approach "the instructor does not plan activities to help develop specific strategies of composing" (pp. 159–160).

Proponents of the writing-process approach have responded to Hillocks's research review by pointing out that he appears to be confused about what the writing-process approach really is. Freedman et al. (1987) pointed out that his environmental mode is much like the writing-process approach advocated by Flowers and Hayes (1980), who pioneered much of the research on the writing process and emphasized its problem-solving nature. They suggested that Hillocks found the natural-process approach to be less effective in his review because he was not clear about how that approach has been defined. They also expressed concern that writing process was being studied separately from written products, as well as concern about the danger that classroom contexts would be separated from cognitive processes in research on writing. They argued for an integrative approach to research on writing, with social context and cognition both studied in the same projects. Then, they suggested, the three threads of research history (process, product, and context) could be used to form a cooperative, multidisciplinary perspective that would, in its turn, lead to the building of a social-cognitive theory of writing.

WHAT DOES RESEARCH SAY ABOUT WRITING IN THE SOCIAL STUDIES?

The movement to include more writing in the social studies was enhanced by a special issue of *Social Education* edited by Beyer and Brostoff (1979). The purpose of this issue was "to suggest ways to improve instruction in and learning of the basic skills and process of writing while simultaneously facilitating student subject-matter learning and thinking in social studies classrooms" (p. 176). In reaching this goal, they applied selected research findings on the relationship of writing to cognitive development (e.g., Ausubel, 1968; Haynes, 1978; Katona, 1960; Van Nostrand, 1976).

Some social studies teachers have experimented with a variety of activities as part of the writing across the curriculum movement. The professional literature for both elementary and secondary teachers contains descriptive reports of the classroom use of these activities, ranging from the personal (journals, learning logs, letters, taking notes, outlining, writing local history) to the less personal (essays, research reports, short-answer study questions, essay exams) (e.g., Blackey, 1981; Howard, Hunnicutt, & Draves, 1980; Jolliffe, 1987; Nelms, 1987; Welton, 1982). In many classrooms, students have used computer word-processing programs, some of which were designed to provide assistance in moving through the stages of the writing process more efficiently, such as *WANDA* (now *HBJ Writer*) and *Writer's Workbench* (Wresch, 1984).

As mentioned earlier in this chapter, there has been little research specifically on the use of writing in the social studies. Most of the reports during the past decade have been descriptions of specific writing activities (e.g., Fulwiler & Young, 1982; Gere, 1985; Jenkinson, 1988; Macrorie, 1980; Tchudi, 1984). Although these descriptions may be useful to practitioners, they do not qualify as educational research and so are not included in this chapter. Nine studies, however, were located and will be reviewed according to their primary foci: (a) what kind of writing are students doing in social studies?, (b) what methods of incorporating writing in social studies work best?, (c) can writing be used to improve student learning?, and (d) does the environment influence writing activities?

Two of the nine studies reviewed were experimental in nature. The other seven are primarily descriptive, although Langer and Applebee (1987) included two experimental studies as part of their larger design.

What Kind of Writing Are Students Doing in Social Studies?

Three studies of the status of writing to learn in the social studies were done in the early 1980s. Applebee's (1981) major study was designed to (a) describe the writing that secondary school students were asked to do in six major areas (English, foreign language, math, science, social studies, and business), (b) examine teachers' purposes and techniques in teaching writing, and (c) determine the extent to which the characteristics of these assignments varied with subject area, grade level, and patterns of instruction.

To accomplish their goals, Applebee and his staff conducted year-long observations in two contrasting secondary schools and carried out a national questionnaire survey. The observations, beginning in October 1979, were concentrated on the nature and frequency of the situations in which students were asked to write in the six target subject areas. The individual lesson was the sampling unit, with regular classes randomly selected for observation throughout the academic year. The observers recorded in logs the activities in 259 lessons represent-

ing 13,293 minutes of instruction in 9th- and 11th-grade classes in the two schools. Of the potential sample of teachers, 85% allowed the observations. Teacher and student attitudes toward writing were also assessed using standardized interview schedules.

In the national survey, data were gathered from a larger and more representative sample of teachers than those observed, allowing Applebee to relate specific findings from the observational studies to more general practice in American schools. A two-stage sampling procedure was used. First, principles in a stratified national sample were asked to nominate a good teacher in each of the six target subject areas. *Good* was defined as competence in teaching the subject area, not as special interest in teaching writing. Second, the nominated teachers were asked to complete a questionnaire about writing and related activities in their classrooms.

Eighty-three percent of the principles and 68% of the teachers contacted provided usable responses, resulting in a national sample of 754 teachers, stratified by school size and metropolitan status. According to Applebee, the teachers in the sample had more experience and more supervisory responsibilities than the typical teacher, and students of below-average ability were underrepresented in their classes. The portrait of student writing that emerged from the survey might thus be expected to be a "best case" version of instruction in American schools.

Analysis of the observational data yielded the following about the use of writing in the social studies: (a) The mean percentage of lesson time involving note taking was 39.1, (b) the mean for mechanical uses of writing—such as short-answer responses on study sheets, fill-in-the-blank, and multiple-choice exercises—was 12.3%, (c) the mean for any other writing activity was 5.1%, and (d) the mean for all uses of writing was 56.4%, as compared with the 44% for all uses of writing observed in all of the targeted academic areas. When asked about writing activities in their social studies classes, the students' descriptions paralleled the observers' reports. Informational uses of writing, including note taking, were by far the most prevalent tasks. In the national survey of teachers, note taking was again mentioned by more teachers (67%) than any other activity, followed by multiple-choice exercises or full-in-the-blank responses (55.8%), short answers (51.8%), and paragraph-length writing (36.3%).

Applebee (1981) concluded that a first step to improve the writing of secondary school students would be to provide more situations in which writing served as a tool for learning rather than as a means to display acquired knowledge. To bring this about, he proposed further work in two dimensions: (a) practical descriptions of specific techniques and activities that can be successfully incorporated into the various content areas; (b) systematic investigation of the outcomes of such activities, in terms of both student writing skills and subject-area knowledge. The available research base at the time of Applebee's study contained little evidence about the benefits of writing across the curriculum, but Applebee projected that with adequate research designs, the benefits could be shown to be real and powerful.

Elementary Social Studies. A less extensive and intensive study of writing in social studies was a survey of elementary teachers (K–6) who had participated in the National Writing Project summer institutes. The purpose was to learn how much writing the teachers' pupils were doing in social studies (Gilstrap, 1982). Out of 300 teachers, 64 responded. One of the questions on the questionnaire was: "In general, what kinds of writing projects do you use or plan for your class in the area of social studies (research reports, book reports, interviews, etc.)?" In response, the teachers identified 102 social studies activities that involved writing, with some form of research paper or report the most frequently mentioned (33) and book reports the next highest (14). Receiving five or more responses were letters, poems, paragraphs, short plays, stories, interviews, class notes, diaries, outlines, summaries of materials read, essays, and essay questions. The responses were classified in four basic categories of used or planned writing opportunities: (a) planning and initiating (8 activities), (b) gathering information (39 activities), (c) using and sharing information (43 activities), and (d) culminating and evaluating (9 activities).

Only 5 of the 64 elementary school teachers indicated that they had their students do no or little writing as part of their social studies program. The teachers' responses also indicated considerable variety in their reported use of writing in social studies. However, the survey showed that even a self-selected sample of those teachers sufficiently interested in writing to participate in the National Writing Project did not report using what they had learned about the writing process to its fullest potential. Based on that result, Gilstrap recommended that teachers-in-training be given more opportunities to use writing as a tool for learning in their preservice classes in hopes of carryover to their own teaching.

Ethnographic Findings. Although not focused exclusively on writing for social studies, an ethnographic study by Florio and Clark (1982) is relevant. Social studies was part of the nondepartmentalized, integrated curriculum studied in a two-year effort to describe the writing undertaken in two classrooms and the teacher planning related to that writing. Data were collected in a second/third-grade combination classroom and a sixth-grade classroom, both of which were team taught. Interdisciplinary procedures were used, combining the perspectives of ethnography and cognitive psychology with the insights of experienced practitioners:

1. Ethnographic field notes were taken during extensive participant observation in each classroom.
2. Selected videotapes were made of everyday life in the classroom.
3. Weekly journals were kept by the key informant on each teaching team describing the instruction in general and the teaching of writing in particular.
4. Interviews were conducted with teachers about the content of journals and videotapes.
5. Student written work was analyzed and discussed with students.

The following general functions of writing were identified in the classrooms: (a) writing to participate in community, (b) writing to know oneself and others, (c) writing to occupy free time, and (d) writing to demonstrate academic competence. These four functions were not commented on directly by the children but were inferred from the ethnographic study to be the purposes for which their writing was undertaken.

Florio and Clark (1982) concluded that teachers who understand and are aware of the functions of writing in the classroom can aid students to acquire writing skills by furnishing and taking advantage of meaningful and diverse opportunities for student writing. Although a range of writing opportunities were observed in the classrooms, some aspects of what the researchers found were unsettling—for example, the teachers relieved the students of many important roles and responsibilities in the writing process, such as identifying topics for the children, and the only type of writing that the teachers evaluated was that produced through the use of published educational materials such as workbooks.

Summary. The descriptive studies reviewed in this section provide information on the kinds of writing being done by secondary and elementary students in the early 1980s. Traditional writing opportunities dominated the findings. Other researchers were, however, attempting to determine which activities were most effective in helping students to learn the content of social studies. The three studies reviewed in the next section are examinations of specific teaching methodologies in both elementary and secondary settings. The first two are experimental studies and the third is descriptive.

What Activities Are Most Effective?

The value of precis writing and outlining in learning social studies content was studied by Bromley (1983) in a fifth-grade classroom. She trained two groups of students to apply the mechanics of precis writing or outlining to their social studies readings. After a pretest for content knowledge and attitudes toward the learning strategies being introduced, 24 students received four weeks of training in precis writing and 28 received the same amount of training in outlining. Following a posttest made up of a multiple-choice test, an essay test, and another attitude measure related to the strategy being taught, the treatment was reversed so that students would learn both study aids.

Analysis of variance between mean test scores for the strategies revealed no statistically significant differences in students' social studies knowledge of detail and main ideas, assessed using 30 multiple-choice items and one essay question. Additionally, the lack of statistically significant differences in mean attitude scores indicated that regardless of the activity, the students felt similarly about the amount of material learned, the difficulty of the activity, the help required, and the extent of student participation in lessons. A majority of students reported, however, that outlining was a more helpful study aid than precis writing. The results of the study must be viewed cautiously because no indicators of reliability or validity were reported for the measures of student knowledge and attitudes.

Bromley (1983) concluded that the lack of statistically significant differences in either learning or attitude scores for her fifth-grade students implied that either writing activity could be used, depending on student and teacher preferences.

Reading and Writing. Raphael and Kirschner (1985) investigated how knowledge of text structure affects the reading comprehension and writing production of elementary learners. Specifically, the focus of the study was on the effects of an instructional intervention introducing sixth-grade students to a strategy (scaffold) for gathering and organizing information based on compare-and-contrast text structures.

The three-week intervention integrated research on text structures with instructional research on sensitizing students to sources of information for answering questions. The researchers developed a scaffold that would help students to get information from the text they read and help them organize the information into an appropriate form for writing about it. The scaffold (a) made the students aware of the structure of the texts they read to increase their access to relevant information, (b) helped them to supplement this information by adding relevant background knowledge, (c) gave them a way to organize information, and (d) made the students aware of a structure that they could use to write about the information.

The scaffold was introduced to the 22 sixth-grade students in the treatment group using a process-writing approach. The 23 sixth-grade students in the control group were only posttested. To supplement direct instruction, the researchers prepared student workbooks on the selection of relevant information, the addition of necessary background information, and the imposition of an appropriate organizational pattern. The workbook contained excerpts from social studies texts consisting of compare-contrast passages, related questions, and compare-contrast charts. The three dependent measures were based on free recall, multiple-source summarization, and writing-production tasks.

The results indicated that the use of a scaffold significantly enhanced student ability both to identify and to organize expository writing, improved the students' performances on a free-recall test, and improved their selection and organization of information in a free-writing test. By the second week, students demonstrated that they had internalized the questions guiding information gathering for compare-contrast activities as measured in terms of their written responses to a brief questionnaire.

The connections between reading and writing have received a great deal of attention in recent literature. Raphael and Kirschner (1985) concluded that the importance of their study was that it indicated what instructional materials to provide for specific points in the writing process where students need support. Such materials appear to be particularly important during the planning and revision stages of the writing process.

Writing and Civic Issues. A study focused on writing as an aid in learning social studies content was conducted by Parker, Mueller, and Wending (1987). This was an exploratory study based on the assumption that dialectical reasoning is central to critical thinking about civic matters, and that adolescents' reasoning on civic issues can be improved through instruction. The purpose of this study was to generate hypotheses, not to test them.

The sample was 24 11th-grade students attending a month-long, summer civic-leadership institute in a Pacific Northwest city. The students' dialectical reasoning on civic issues was elicited through essays composed following explicit directions (written scaffolding) for presenting an argument for and against a position on a given issue. The essays were to be organized so that the first paragraph was a summary of what the students knew about the issue, the second paragraph was to be a statement of their position on the issue with the reasons, the third paragraph was to be a counterargument, and the fourth paragraph was to be their conclusion. There were no specific directions beyond these for organizing each paragraph.

The essays were analyzed to identify use of six categories of dialectical reasoning: value claims, lines of support (a reason given to justify the author's position), relevant counterarguments, empathic counterarguments, lines of counterargument, and dialectical conclusions (those in which the writer acknowledged the existence of a counterargument or, beyond that, pointed to some aspect of the counterargument that was worth considering or, going still further, pitted against one another the "my-side" and "other-side" arguments).

Twenty-two of the 24 students produced essays according to the instructions given. Most of the students (a) argued both for and against their position on the issue, (b) summarized what they knew about the issue without apparent interference from their own bias about it, (c) used only one line of reasoning, (d) wrote an empathic paragraph about the other side of the issue, (e) argued against their position using just one line of reasoning, but (f) did *not* show even incipient dialectical reasoning in the concluding paragraph.

The purpose of the study was to develop hypotheses, and the following three were formulated: (a) Dialectical reasoning is more available than one might suspect (inasmuch as it was elicited from 92% of the sample in arguing for and against their own position), although it is rarely seen in secondary and college classrooms. (b) The apparent rarity of dialectical reasoning among adolescents and adults is related more to metacognitive difficulty than to neurophysiological deficiency or cognitive underdevelopment (the problems the writers had in the four paragraphs occurred precisely where explicit metacognitive guidance—scaffolding—was lacking because directions for what to include in each paragraph were not explicit). And (c) appropriate metacognitive guidance (scaffolding), as represented in the explicit directions, can help students acquire the habits of dialectical reasoning. The researchers thought that the most important finding of the study was that a form of dialectical reasoning was elicited from 92% of the sample without benefit of prior instruction and by nothing more clever than a set of clear instructions for writing the essay—even though 54% of the students evidenced no dialectical reasoning in the concluding, unscaffolded paragraph.

Summary. These three studies focused on the effectiveness of writing activities to assist students in learning social studies content were the only ones that could be located. Clearly, the topic has hardly been explored. The findings have some practical implications for classroom teachers and provide a point of departure for researchers interested in this line of investigation. In the next section, investigations of how writing shapes the learning and thinking of students in school settings are reviewed.

Can Writing Be Used to Improve Students' Learning and Thinking?

Langer and Applebee (1987) followed up on the findings in the earlier study by Applebee (1981) which suggested that, in the content areas of secondary schools, writing was rarely used other than to assess knowledge and skills. This study took two forms: (a) a series of studies of *teaching*, in which a total of 23 teachers and their students were studied as the teachers used writing to foster learning in their academic courses, and (b) a series of studies of *learning*, in which they examined the effects of different types of writing tasks on academic learning.

In their studies of *teaching*, Langer and Applebee (1987) first surveyed 18 science and social studies teachers, recommended because they had already incorporated writing into their classrooms, to learn about the types of writing activities they used and the extent to which they thought these activities aided students' learning. Each teacher was interviewed for about three-quarters of an hour and observed for one class period. The survey was followed with a series of in-depth studies of eight classrooms (science, social studies, English, home economics) in one school site. Five other teachers joined the project for the second year of study of classroom work. Data came from field notes and observation schedules, teacher interviews, student interviews, and writing samples.

In this research, the investigators collaborated with experienced teachers who wanted to incorporate additional writing into their instruction as a way to support academic learning. The researchers brought their knowledge of writing tasks and process-oriented writing instruction to the collaboration, and the teachers brought their knowledge of their specific subject areas and their understanding of the needs and interests of their students.

Langer and Applebee (1987) lived as observers in the eight classrooms several days a week for periods ranging from five months to two years. The purpose was to document the effects of introducing new writing tasks intended specifically to further student understanding of new concepts as part of the regular curriculum. The investigators examined instructional planning, classroom activities, and curriculum coverage, as well as students' approaches to the new tasks. Individual students were selected as case-study informants who reported on their interpretations of the lessons, the ways in which they approached their work, their understandings of the teachers' expectations, and their own goals. Case studies were conducted of individual students working on their regular classroom assignments. Think-aloud, self-report techniques were used in conjunction with more traditional tests of learning and recall to examine whether the learning of new content was influenced by relevant background knowledge and by the type of writing task.

Langer and Applebee (1987) also conducted three group-design studies of *learning* (one descriptive and two experimental) as part of their investigation. Passages from social studies textbooks were used for each of the studies. For the first, six volunteer, high school juniors participated in a descriptive study of the ways they approached writing about text and the effects that writing might have on learning what they read. The researchers examined how the students approached three common study tasks: (a) completing short-answer study questions, (b) taking notes, and (c) writing essays.

Next came an experimental study to examine a broader range of tasks and passages and to test the effects over a longer term (one month instead of a few days). For this study, there were two primary purposes: (a) to document the longer-term effects of writing versus not writing (represented by a read-and-study task) and (b) to explore the effects of writing tasks that required the reformulation of new information versus simpler ones that called only for the review of the new information. Teachers (and directions in instructional materials) often ask students to write in conjunction with their textbook reading, and the researchers were interested in the kinds of learning engendered by the two different writing activities.

A final study, also experimental, was conducted on the relationship between what students did during the study task and what they remembered later. They compared the kinds of behaviors and learning that resulted when students engaged in four different kinds of tasks: (a) read and study, but not write, (b) answer comprehension questions (20 short-answer questions), (c) write summaries, and (d) write analyses.

In all, 566 students participated in the project: 326 in experimental studies of writing and learning, 20 in case studies, and the remaining 180 in the eight collaborating classrooms. They represented the typical range of student achievement levels in working- and middle-class suburban communities in the San Francisco Bay area. All 23 teachers had been teaching for at least eight years and wished to develop more effective ways of using writing to foster student learning of course content.

Langer and Applebee (1987) concluded that there was clear evidence across the entire study that all of the activities that involved writing led to better learning than reading and studying only. Different kinds of writing activities led students to focus on different kinds of information, to think about that information in different ways, and in turn to take quantitatively and qualitatively different kinds of knowledge away from their writing experiences. Short-answer study questions, for example, led students to focus on particular items of information either located in the text or implied by it, thus little rethinking of the material took place. In contrast, analytic writing led to a more thoughtful focus on a smaller amount of information, because ideas were linked and understanding construed. Less information is likely to be remembered immediately, but over time this information is longer lived. Although they concluded that writing across the curriculum as defined earlier in this chapter is perhaps too simplistic a concept, Langer and Applebee also concluded that their findings provided support for the assumption that writing tasks have a significant role to play in all areas of academic study.

Elementary School Writing. No study at the elementary level has been as intensive as the one by Langer and Applebee (1987). Rosaen (1990) did, however, examine the role of writing in learning American history in the primary grades. She conducted an ethnographic study during the last 7 weeks of a 12-week American history unit in an early-elementary classroom (Grades 1 through 3). The purposes of the study were to describe how students and teachers interpreted learning activities and to explain how the meanings students assigned to the activities shaped their knowledge development. During the unit, students completed weekly writing assignments on different periods of American history.

As Rosaen examined the development and unfolding of the weekly writing assignments, she discovered important differences in the ways that students interpreted and participated in seemingly similar writing activities. For example, in one writing activity some of the children took a more active role in their learning, taking more responsibility for judging the quality of their work. These differences had important implications for the kinds of learning opportunities available to the students.

Helping students use writing as occasions to understand subject matter knowledge, she concluded, required more than creating a good writing assignment and more than just making sure students have regular opportunities to write. The effective use of writing is a complex undertaking that requires careful consideration of students' current knowledge of the topic, their skills in various thought processes, their knowledge of and ability to produce written forms, and ways to support appropriately the students' knowledge development and writing process. Just having students write about subject-matter content did not guarantee learning.

Rosaen (1990) also concluded that if writing activities are to function as tools for subject-matter learning, teachers must examine the quality of the writing experiences for students in their classrooms before taking on the additional challenge of increasing the frequency with which they provide writing opportunities. Five criteria recommended by Rosaen for this examination are: (a) the duration of the writing activities must be sufficient for linkages to be made in the composing process; (b) the writing activities must arise in the context of real events in the classroom and/or community; (c) the writing activities must be linked thematically over time; (d) the activities must be expressive in nature and involve multiple modes of oral-written expression; and (e) teachers and students must work together, taking on multiple roles in the negotiation of the social and academic goals of the occasion for writing.

Summary. Rosaen's (1990) conclusions and those of Langer and Applebee (1987) reveal clearly the complex nature of investigations of writing to learn; they provide no simple prescriptions for understanding that process. Both studies, however, are encouraging to those who believe that writing has the potential to enhance learning and the development of thinking skills.

How Does the Environment Influence Writing in the Social Studies?

The final study located in the literature search was focused on how the environment influences writing in social studies. Florio and Frank (1982) conducted a case study of the teaching and learning of writing in a second-grade classroom in a small Michigan town. Classroom activities, many of which involved writing, were observed. The researchers got to know the members of the class, provided help when asked, joined in class activities, made videotapes of some lessons, and asked ques-

tions of both the teacher and her students during formal interviews and discussions.

The teacher established a small, classroom community—dubbed by the children "Betterburg"—that included law enforcement, cultural activities, commerce, a bank, social welfare, a library, and a postal system. An opportunity was provided to examine the relationship between literacy and community in the social context of the classroom. The teacher provided a truly integrated social studies experience for the children.

The researchers concluded that learning to read, write, and compute in the context of Betterburg was reinforced for the children in a variety of ways:

1. Letters were written for a purpose, and there were the expectation and, generally, the receipt of a reply, such as when the children wrote the postmaster to ask him about his responsibilities.
2. Many written works were published, either within Betterburg itself or in the wider community. For example, a proclamation written by the students to a local drain commissioner, honoring his efforts in a lake cleanup, was read and presented to the official by citizens of Betterburg at the ceremonies marking the start of the dredging of the lake.
3. All writing was undertaken in the accomplishment of tasks, varying from record keeping for Betterburg's banker to a persuasive letter written to a game manufacturer requesting that the students be allowed to purchase games at wholesale prices for sale in Betterburg stores.

These are just some of the examples of how the environment of Betterburg influenced writing in the social studies. The children soon realized that Betterburg could not exist without literacy. Every job and civic office required it. The researchers concluded that the essential lesson for writing instruction to be drawn for Betterburg is virtually the same lesson that can be drawn from the observation of first language acquisition or from the studies of the acquisition of cognitive skills in traditional societies. The lesson is not that skills are seldom taught directly in such contexts by those already expert in their use, but that even the most rudimentary attempts of novices to use the skills are taken to have social functions. In the community of Betterburg, the most complex of writing activities—and the ones in which the most time is spent—transpired outside of the direct teaching of skills.

IMPLICATIONS FOR FUTURE RESEARCH

Although the "writing across the curriculum" movement has gained in popularity since the 1970s, there has been little systematic inquiry by social studies educators to find out if writing, or particular types of writing, help students better learn the content of the social studies, improve their thinking skills, or provide them with a smoother integration into the society as productive citizens. Applebee (1981), a specialist in the field of English and language arts, concluded when he finished his first study on writing across the curriculum that the available research base did little to demonstrate those benefits, although he believed that they could be shown to be "real and powerful." Six years later, in their study of the ways in which writing works to support learning, he and Langer (1987) gained a better understanding and were convinced of the important, yet complex, role that writing can play in learning in subject areas such as social studies. They also became more aware of the difficulty of getting teachers in non-English content areas to use writing more effectively. They concluded:

If writing is to play a meaningful role in subjects other than English, then the teachers of those subjects will need a conception of writing specific to their disciplines, one that emphasizes what is unique about writing (and thinking) in their subject, rather than one that emphasizes ways in which such activities will foster the work of the English teacher. (p. 150)

As Hillocks (1984) argued, experimental studies designed to compare the effectiveness of one approach over another have value and are needed to fulfill the knowledge-building function of research. Langer and Applebee (1987) included two experimental studies of learning as part of their complex research design. Classroom teachers tend to be skeptical of experimental research, however, because of the diversity of settings and the difficulty of controlling related variables.

The studies of the use of writing in the social studies reviewed for this chapter that are likely to be most useful to the classroom teacher in making more effective use of writing in the social studies are the descriptive ones involving participant-observers in classroom settings, especially those using the ethnographic approach. These studies provide detailed information about the context of writing activity and allow teachers and researchers interested in writing to visualize how the setting compares with the one in which they are or will be teaching or observing. As Langer and Applebee (1987) pointed out, the lack of a clear conceptualization of how writing can be used effectively in the social studies classroom is the greatest obstacle to its use.

The ethnographic approach is appropriate for the research by classroom teachers that has been stimulated by such movements as the National Writing Project (Glaze, 1982; Mohr & MacLean, 1987). Teacher-researchers may be able to provide important links between theory and practice (Goswami & Stillman, 1987). If classroom teachers were involved as collaborators in research on the use of writing in the social studies, the studies would more likely be focused on questions that practitioners see as relevant, and the results would be more likely to have a positive effect on the education of elementary and secondary students.

Conducting any type of research related to writing is not easy, but there are some special problems in using the ethnographic approach to study writing. First of all, the researchers must establish rapport with the teachers and students to be involved in the study. Earning the students' trust is a special challenge in research on writing because pupils are often asked to write about topics that are personal to them. Second, the use of the ethnographic approach, even with a major investment of time in the research setting and a variety of collection techniques, does not automatically ensure insights into processes of thinking and writing. Other approaches may be necessary to assess that which cannot be observed. In writing, as in other areas, ethnographic researchers face problems of objectivity in recording and interpreting observations. Moreover, transcribing audio-tapes is expensive, and the analysis of data is time consuming (Cates, 1985).

In spite of these problems (North, 1987), the ethnographic method has great potential for identifying specific writing techniques and activities that can be successfully incorporated into the diverse settings of elementary and secondary school social studies. Studies during the 1980s have provided a good beginning for developing the knowledge base needed to convince teachers and researchers that this is a field of inquiry worthy of their time and effort.

References

Applebee, A. N. (1981). *Writing in the secondary school: English and the content areas*. Urbana, IL: National Council of Teachers of English.

Applebee, A. N. (1984). Writing and reasoning. *Review of Educational Research, 54*(4), 577–596.

Ausubel, D. P. (1968). *Educational psychology: A cognitive approach.* New York: Holt, Rinehart & Winston.

Bennett, W. J. (1986). A critical look at curriculum goals. *Principal, 66,* 11–15

Beyer, B. K. & Brostoff, A. (1979). Writing to learn in social studies. *Social Education, 43,* 176–197.

Blackey, R. (1981). A guide to the skill of essay construction in history. *Social Education, 45,* 178–182.

Braddock, R., Lloyd-Jones, R., & Schoer, L. (1963). *Research on written composition.* Urbana, IL: National Council of Teachers of English.

Britton, J., Burgess, T., Martin, N., McLeod, A., & Rosen, H. (1975). *The development of writing abilities 11–16.* London: Macmillan.

Bromley, K. D. (1983, October). *Precis writing and outlining: Aids to learning social studies content.* Paper presented at the College Reading Association Conference, Atlanta.

Cates, W. H. (1985). *A practical guide to educational research.* Englewood Cliffs, NJ: Prentice-Hall.

Dyson, A. H. (1983). The role of oral language in early writing processes. *Research in the Teaching of English, 17,* 1–30.

Emig, J. (1971). *The composing processes of twelfth graders.* Urbana, IL: National Council of Teachers of English.

Farr, M. (Ed.). (1985). *Advances in writing research: Vol. I. children's early writing development.* Norwood, NJ: Ablex.

Florio, S., & Clark, C. (1982). The functions of writing in an elementary classroom. *Research in the teaching of English, 16,* 115–129.

Florio, S., & Frank, J. H. (1982). Literacy and community in the classroom: A case study of Betterburg. In B. K. Beyer & R. L. Gilstrap (Eds.), *Writing in elementary school social studies* (pp. 31–42). Boulder, CO: Social Science Education Consortium.

Flower, L., & Hayes, J. R. (1977). Problem-solving strategies and the writing process. *College English, 39,* 449–461.

Freedman, S. W., Dyson, A. H., Flower, L., & Chafe, W. (1987). *Research in writing: Past, present and future.* University of California, Berkeley: Center for Study of Writing.

Fulwiler, T., & Young, A. (Eds.). (1982). *Language connections: Writing and reading across the curriculum.* Urbana, IL: National Council of Teachers of English.

Gere, A. R. (Ed.). (1985). *Roots in the sawdust: Writing to learn across the curriculum.* Urbana, IL: National Council of Teachers of English.

Gilstrap, R. L. (1982). Writing in elementary school social studies: Report of a personal search. In B. K. Beyer & R. L. Gilstrap (Eds.), *Writing in elementary school social studies* (pp. 19–29). Boulder, Colorado: Social Science Education Consortium.

Glaze, B. M. (1982). Role writing to understand the past. In *Research in writing: Reports from a teacher-researcher seminar* (pp. 91–103). Fairfax, VA: The Northern Virginia Writing Project.

Goswami, D., & Stillman, P. R. (Eds.). (1987). *Reclaiming the classroom: Teacher research as an agency for change.* Upper Montclair, NJ: Boynton/Cook.

Graves, D. (1973). *Children's writing: Research directions and hypotheses based upon an examination of the writing processes of seven-year-old children.* Doctoral dissertation, State University of New York at Buffalo, ED 095 586.

Graves, D. (1980). Research update: A new look at writing research. *Language Arts, 57,* 913–991.

Graves, D. (1981). *A case study observing the development of primary children's composing, spelling and motor behaviors during the writing process.* Washington, DC: National Institute of Education.

Haskew, L. (1956). *This is teaching.* Chicago: Scott, Foresman.

Haynes, E. (1978). Using research in preparing to teach writing. *English Journal, 67,* 82–88.

Hillocks, G., Jr. (1984). What works in teaching composition: A meta-analysis of experimental treatment studies. *American Journal of Education, 93,* 133–170.

Howard, D. F., Hunnicutt, H. H., & Draves, D. D. (1980). Writing local history: A new look at old Portsmouth. *Childhood Education, 56,* 264–267.

Jenkinson, E. B. (Ed.). (1988). Writing across the curriculum. *Phi Delta Kappan, 69,* 712–745.

Jolliffe, D. A. (1987). A social educator's guide to teaching writing. *Theory and Research in Social Education, 15,* 89–104.

Katona, G. (1960). *Organizing and memorizing.* New York: Columbia University Press.

Langer, J. A., & Applebee, A. N. (1987). *How writing shapes thinking: A study of teaching and learning.* Urbana, IL: National Council of Teachers of English.

Macrorie, K. (1980). *Searching writing.* Rochelle Park, NJ: Hayden.

Martin, N., D'Arcy, P., Newton, B., & Parker, R. (1976). *Writing and learning across the curriculum 11-16.* London: Ward Lock Educational.

Mohr, M. M., & MacLean, M. S. (1987). *Working together: A guide for teacher-researchers.* Urbana, IL: National Council of Teachers of English.

Nelms, B. F. (1987). Response and responsibility: reading, writing, and social studies. *The Elementary School Journal, 87,* 571–589.

North, S. M. (1987) *The making of knowledge in composition: Portrait of an emerging field.* Portsmouth, NH: Boynton/Cook.

Parker, W. C., Mueller, M., & Wending, L. (1987, April). *Dialectical reasoning on civic issues.* Paper presented at the annual meeting of the American Educational Research Association in Washington, DC.

Perl, S. (1979). The composing processes of unskilled college writers. *Research in the Teaching of English, 13,* 317–336.

Pianko, S. (1979). A description of the composing process of college freshman writers. *Research in the Teaching of English, 13,* 5–22.

Raphael, T., & Kirschner, B. M. (1985). *The effects of instruction in compare/contrast text structure on sixth-grade students' reading comprehension and writing products.* Research series No. 161. East Lansing: Michigan State University, Institute for Research on Teaching.

Rosaen, C. L. (1990). Improving writing opportunities in elementary classrooms. *Elementary School Journal, 90,* 419–434.

Self, J. (Ed.). (1987). *Plain talk about learning and writing across the curriculum.* Richmond: Virginia Department of Education.

Stallard, C. (1979). An analysis of the writing behavior of good writers. *Research in the Teaching of English, 8,* 206–218.

Tchudi, S. (1984). *Writing in the content areas: The NEA inservice training program.* West Haven, CT: National Education Association.

Van Nostrand, A. D. (1976). English I and the measurement of writing. In B. A. Greene, Jr. (Ed.), *Personalized instruction in higher education: Proceedings of the second national conference held by the center for personalized instruction* (pp. 23–27). Washington, DC: The Center for Personalized Instruction.

Vygotsky, L. S. (1978). *Mind in society: The development of higher psychological processes.* Cambridge, MA: Harvard University Press.

Welton, D. A. (1982). Expository writing, pseudowriting, and social studies. *Social Education, 46,* 444–448.

Wresch, W. (Ed.). (1984). *The computer in composition instruction: A writer's tool.* Urbana, IL: National Council of Teachers of English.

Section

·VIII·

INTERNATIONAL PERSPECTIVES ON RESEARCH ON SOCIAL STUDIES

50

CROSS-NATIONAL RESEARCH IN SOCIAL STUDIES

Judith Torney-Purta

UNIVERSITY OF MARYLAND, COLLEGE PARK

Cross-national research relating to social studies can be viewed from several perspectives. The review in this chapter is broadly based. Not only is research explicitly on social studies or civic education included, but also research on political socialization, or the way young people acquire cognitions, attitudes, and skills preparing them for political participation. The major purpose for the chapter is to illustrate the variety of reasons for doing cross-national studies. Therefore, the reviews of research will be organized according to the researcher's purpose and not according to the area of the world in which data were collected or the methodology used.

There is a growing literature on the theoretical foundations of cross-national research (Jahoda, 1986). An earlier review of political socialization cross-nationally focused on political theories (Nathan & Remy, 1977). A less theoretical approach is taken in this chapter in order to address the interests of those who wish to develop criteria for designing and judging cross-national research or who wish to understand the purposes for which it may be used in social studies. The emphasis is on what U.S. educators might learn from research on other countries, especially industrialized countries.

CRITERIA FOR JUDGING CROSS-NATIONAL RESEARCH

Some general principles and associated criteria are especially important for judging research conducted cross-nationally. These criteria can be viewed as responses to the problem of choosing a sample from a larger population or universe. There are three types of such sampling problems: first, sampling respondents from a population of students or teachers; second, sampling measures or items from a universe of possible topics, measures, or items related to society or political institutions; and, third, sampling independent variables to be re-lated to educational performance (either characteristics of individuals or of schools) from a universe of possible influences on the outcomes of social studies education or political socialization.

Sampling of Respondents

The sample of students or teachers utilized in a piece of social studies research is always important. Having a representative sample of respondents is critical if the purpose of the research is to compare estimates of average levels of achievement in one country with levels in another. Thus, carefully developed sampling plans with associated standard errors and response rates usually appear in reports of research conducted for this purpose. Studies in which the intent is not to compare nations' achievement are often conducted with less-representative samples.

An important caveat is not to use data collected on unrepresentative samples to make national comparisons. An example of a poor study in this respect is a survey of geography achievement conducted by a Texas newspaper in the early 1980s. Small samples of student respondents were recruited by individuals ranging from the Prime Minister of Sweden to newspaper reporters in Dallas, Texas, and Bordeaux, France. Broad generalizations were made about the performance of students in these countries based on these inadequate samples (see Torney-Purta, 1984b for a critique).

Differences between countries in the proportion of students who continue in school until late adolescence present a problem when sampling secondary school students cross-nationally. Although European schools have become much more comprehensive during the past two decades, the percentage of 17-year-olds still in school in the United States remains higher than in many countries. If compulsory schooling ends at age 15, students of higher socioeconomic background are more likely to

Reviewers were Derek Heater, Brighton, England; T. Neville Postlethwaite, University of Hamburg; Jack Schwille, Michigan State University.

remain in school, biasing comparisons between high school juniors or seniors in the U.S. and their counterparts abroad.

Not every cross-national study is budgeted at a level to allow a stratified random sample of schools and students within schools, nor can high response rates from sampled schools always be obtained. However, policy makers and practitioners who read research should be wary of overly broad generalizations about national differences based on small or unrepresentative samples and should be attentive to biases that may exist in all samples.

Sampling of Items or Measuring Instruments

The questionnaire or other technique designed to collect data from respondents can also be thought of as a sample from a universe of test items that could have been asked or methods that could have been used.

Postlethwaite (1987) described three approaches to instrument construction in cross-national studies. In the first, a committee of subject-matter experts from several different countries chooses a sample of items measuring content important for mastery by young people of the age to be tested. Experts could also be asked to identify attitudes that are of central importance to democratic citizen participation in several countries. Discussion by a committee of experts familiar with other countries followed by pilot testing is often the best way to accomplish this kind of item sampling.

Postlethwaite identified a second approach, in which a single national curriculum is used as the basis for constructing a test to be used in several nations. When such tests are initiated in the United States, the items may be more suitable for measuring attitudes toward a president and Congress than toward a prime minister and Parliament, or the test may be formulated on the basis of a written Constitution and Bill of Rights, as exists in the United States but not in the United Kingdom or Israel. Generalizations about performance in one country relative to that in another country should be tempered if there are unrepresentative samples of items, just as generalizations ought to be tempered if there are unrepresentative samples of respondents.

A third method of constructing tests is to undertake a detailed content analysis of the intended or published curriculum (and related documents such as textbooks) in the given subject area in each country. The resulting content grid of topics and countries is used in the construction of a measuring instrument. Developing tests using this third process is very difficult for social studies in the United States because of the decentralized nature of decision making and the absence of any national curriculum guidelines. Although organizations like the National Council for the Social Studies suggest sequences of course offerings, these have nothing like the force of guidelines issued by a ministry of education in a centralized system.

This difficulty is illustrated by an ongoing discussion about whether the United States should participate in an extensive cross-national study of education relating to social values and morality. That study's international design requires as a first step an analysis of documents, guidelines, and textbooks for courses in which social values and morality are major topics;

these analyses are intended to be the basis for drawing up a content grid and survey questions to be used cross-nationally. In most Asian and many European countries, such guidelines and textbooks are readily available. No such set of national educational guidelines can easily be identified in the United States. Problems in specifying the intended curriculum of the school in the United States arise even in subject areas like science, but are very serious for cross-national instrument construction in social studies.

A separate but related issue concerns the choice of methods of data collection. For example, how appropriate is a multiple-choice test of knowledge in a country where essay examinations are much more familiar to students? How useful will attitude measures be in a country where there are strong pressures to give positive and socially desirable responses on any questionnaire administered by someone in authority?

These problems are of great concern to individuals doing large-scale cross-national studies. They should also be factored into project planning by individuals attempting more limited studies. Early in a project, the researchers should seek advice on the content of instruments from educators or social scientists in all of the countries where they will be administered, developing the measures collaboratively as much as possible. If an attempt is made to assess the school's effect on knowledge level, it is important to examine the curricular objectives in the countries under study. The process of specifying the major categories of topics or items from which samples will be drawn may clarify differences across countries in the meaning of key concepts such as democracy or citizenship.

It is important to examine carefully the validity of attitude scales developed in one national setting if they are to be used in another, rather than relying on the labeling of a scale as a measure of "political efficacy" or "international understanding." Careful pilot testing of instruments in order to analyze their reliability and validity in different nations may be indicated. If the samples from other nations participating in the study are not native speakers of English, both translation and backtranslation should be used to check equivalance, especially of abstract terms. Readers of cross-national research as well as researchers need to be sensitive to these issues in making judgments of data presentations.

Sampling of Relevant Background or Educational Variables

Many of the most interesting cross-national studies in social studies and political socialization are investigations of relationships between independent variables and achievement or attitude scale scores as dependent variables. The independent variables may be personal characteristics such as gender or type of motivational attribution, or educational variables such as teacher training or classroom climate for discussion. There is a wide range of possible independent variables, and it is useful to think of those chosen for a given study as a sample from that universe.

An independent variable such as socioeconomic status may present hidden problems. For example, in Finland there is no separate category for farmer in socioeconomic status rankings. A farmer who owns a large farm is equivalent to a professional, while a smaller land owner is equivalent to a skilled worker. In a rural area of a developing country, the type of roof on one's house or how many chickens one owns may be the best measure.

In many international studies of science and mathematics there have been attempts to assess the curriculum implemented in the classroom as an independent variable. What the average teacher covers is assessed with what is called an "Opportunity to Learn" measure (Postlethwaite, 1988). Teachers or curriculum coordinators are asked to rate each item included in the students' test according to how much exposure the average student would have in the classroom to the information necessary to answer that item. Many between-country differences in achievement are correlated with differences in students' learning opportunities. Such measures have not been incorporated into social studies research cross-nationally, perhaps because most studies have dealt with attitudes where opportunity to learn does not have the same meaning.

An especially important aspect of the social studies or civic education classroom is the extent of participation by students in discussions of historical trends or current events. The *climate* of the classroom or school is widely recognized as having an important impact on all kinds of learning, but especially in fostering attitudes and skills related to participation in democratic civic life. Some researchers suggest that items such as "Teachers care about our opinions and encourage us to express them" are reasonably powerful measures of an open climate for discussion in the classroom (Ehman, 1980). Because retrospective reports gathered from students are potentially biased, it can also be argued that observations of classrooms, peer interactions, and authority relations should be included in indices of these important educational factors.

Student motivation is increasingly recognized as a potent source of differences in the effectiveness of instruction in different countries. Students in Asia, who excel in international comparisons in mathematics and science, regularly report that they are expending little effort on their studies and not performing as well as they could (Stevenson, 1987). Students in the United States whose actual achievement is much lower in international comparisons, report that they are expending a great deal of effort and performing very well. The level of effort students believe they need to expend and their standards of excellence are important potential explanations of differences between and within countries in subject areas such as mathematics (Holloway, 1988). Items measuring attributions for effort and perceived success should be more widely included in cross-national research on social studies.

In summary, cross-national research can be judged by many of the criteria used to assess research conducted in a single nation. There are also special issues of sampling of students, items or measuring instruments, and background or educational variables that deserve attention in designing and interpreting the findings of cross-national research. No study, even if conducted by a very sophisticated international research organization, can be a perfect study from all of these points of view. Readers of research need to develop criteria based on these

three types of sampling, as well as the usual concerns of internal and external validity.

A REVIEW OF CROSS-NATIONAL RESEARCH ACCORDING TO ITS PURPOSE

The remaining sections of the chapter illustrate the different purposes for which cross-national research has been conducted. Findings of some large-scale studies will be summarized and some existing gaps in research knowledge indicated.

Comparing Political Attitudes or Cognitive Outcomes of Education

The common thread in several studies has been the comparison across nations of levels of political attitudes or students' achievement of the cognitive outcomes of education.

Early Cross-National Studies to Compare Political Culture. The cross-national comparison of political cultures began with attempts to assess differences in "national character," especially personal characteristics associated with authoritarian political systems (Benedict, 1946; Schaffner, 1948).

Almond and Verba (1963) in their book, *The Civic Culture*, pointed to the internalization of aspects of the political system in the cognitions and feelings of a population and related this to the functioning of the macropolitical system. In their survey of adults in Great Britain, the United States, Germany, Italy and Mexico, they asked retrospectively about childhood experiences in the school and family that influenced political socialization.

The Civic Culture stimulated new interest in the comparison of political cultures and in differences across countries in the types of civic obligation and political competence that promoted the stability of democratic regimes. The book set the terms of reference for cross-national comparisons of political culture and political socialization and identified the United States as a participant rather than a passive civic culture. In a second volume, *The Civic Culture Revisited* (Almond & Verba, 1980), political scientists from the five countries of the original study speculated about the validity and durability of the original findings.

More recently there have been some thumb-nail sketches of national differences in orientations toward issues such as human rights. Gallatin (1976), for example, interviewed a convenience sample of 11-, 13-, 15-, and 18-year-olds and reported that American students had the strongest sense of individual rights combined with a sense of political community. British respondents were more pragmatic, seeing government more as a provider of social services than as a protector of individual liberties. German adolescents fell in between, sometimes submissive and authoritarian but generally more concerned than the British about individual rights.

Many social studies programs are intended to transmit aspects of the political culture. Few studies have satisfactorily addressed the sources of national differences in the civic culture as reflected in the educational experiences of youth. Nevertheless, the issues which remain of concern to researchers are closely tied to facets of the political culture, in particular the difference between participant and nonparticipant orientations.

Comparisons of Student Outcomes. Another kind of cross-national comparison also had its roots in the early 1960s, in the founding of the International Association for the Evaluation of Educational Achievement (IEA), a consortium of educational research institutes. Researchers associated with IEA have conducted comparative surveys of the outcomes and processes of education in many subject areas. The major focus has been on understanding the diversity of educational processes in the more than 30 countries that participate, and not on conducting a "cognitive Olympics." However, the bar graphs drawn from IEA studies comparing science or mathematics achievement in different countries regularly make headlines in the press (Postlethwaite, 1988). Some argue that publicized comparisons of educational outcomes are potent in stimulating educational reform within countries whose students perform at low levels; others contend that without careful analysis of the inputs to education, these studies only promote national hand-wringing followed by a search for scapegoats and prescriptions for short-term solutions.

The one study conducted by IEA in civic education (Torney, Oppenheim, & Farnen, 1975) attracted less attention than studies in science and mathematics, perhaps because there was no single bar graph comparing achievement cross-nationally, or because of the lesser attention usually paid to social studies. The civic education questionnaires, composed of about half cognitive and half attitudinal items, were planned and developed by an international committee that derived the kind of content-grid described earlier under the discussion of item sampling. The fact that the large majority of countries who participated in planning the IEA survey shared the Western European tradition meant that many common aims in civic education could be identified. The questionnaires were translated and backtranslated.

The civic education questionnaires were answered in 1971 by 10- and 14-year-olds and by students in the last year of pre-university education. Data were collected in the Federal Republic of Germany, Finland, Ireland, Israel, Italy, Netherlands, New Zealand, Sweden, and the United States. Data collected in Iran were never analyzed because of technical difficulties. In IEA studies, each participant country decides at which age levels they will test, since each is responsible for national research costs; three countries tested 10-year-olds, eight tested 14-year-olds, and seven tested pre-university students (ranging from 17 to 20). The schools were selected from nationally stratified sampling frames, and students were selected randomly within schools. A total of 30,000 students responded to civic education survey instruments; more than 5,000 teachers replied concerning pedagogical practices; and 1,300 principals and headmasters described their schools.

Among the 14-year-olds, students in the Netherlands performed the highest on the cognitive test (a mean of 27.3 items correct out of 47); students in Ireland, the lowest (a mean of 20.8 items). U.S. students, with a mean of 24.7, were fourth-ranked out of the eight countries in which testing took place at this age level. A subsequent analysis of cognitive subscores indicated that American students tended to know relatively more about domestic politics and institutions than about international politics and institutions (Torney, 1977).

The IEA attitude scales were factor-analyzed for each age by country group. Three independent clusters of scales were found across countries: Support for Democratic Values (including scales measuring antiauthoritarianism, support for women's rights, support for civil liberties, and support for equality); Support for National Government (including scales measuring general evaluation of the national government and its responsiveness to citizens and sense of political efficacy); and Civic Interest/Participation (including scales measuring civic activities, political discussion, and interest in current-events television).

The between-nation comparisons on attitude scales indicated a complex picture, which Torney-Purta and Schwille (1986) summarized as follows: "No Western industrialized country has a uniformly high level of success in transmitting civic values, perhaps because subtle incompatibilities exist" (p. 34). In no country did the students score above the international mean on all three of the attitudinal factors. In other words, among 14-year-olds, the countries in which average support for democratic values was above the overall mean for all countries fell below the mean for all countries in average support for national government and civic interest/participation. For example, 14-year-olds in the Netherlands scored high in their support for democratic values and had the highest score on knowledge of civics and politics; their interest in political discussion and their support for national government were both low. In contrast, U.S. students expressed strong positive feelings about their government and had scores on participation that were high relative to those in other countries; yet they scored relatively low on support for democratic values (particularly on support for women's rights).

This is by far the most extensive research on social studies conducted cross-nationally. However, it is limited by reliance on a paper-and-pencil survey. Moreover, the data were collected nearly 20 years ago, before Watergate and the height of the women's movement in the United States. Moves toward more liberal social and political education took place in most European countries in the mid-1970s, followed by a conservative swing in the 1980s (Torney-Purta & Hahn, 1989).

Although between-country comparisons were made in the IEA study, they presented a complex picture. No nation's students were clearly outstanding in civic knowledge and attitudes. The most interesting of the IEA findings had to do with educational processes and the extent to which sex differences in political attitudes were similar in different countries. They will be discussed in later sections.

Student Protest. Several cross-national studies of political attitudes were undertaken to understand the worldwide phenomenon of student protest and to track generational discontinuities. Although little attention was paid to schooling in these studies, it could be argued that in societies undergoing rapid social change, schooling serves to accentuate the differences between the attitudes of parents and their children.

In 1969 to 1970, Klineberg, Zavalloni, Louis-Guerin, and Ben-Brika (1979) conducted research on university students in 11 countries, using what they called a "varied" rather than a representative sample. Sample sizes ranged from 190 in Tunisia to more than 1,000 in the United States and Italy. The instrument was developed in collaboration with social scientists from the participating nations.

The findings of Klineberg et al., like those of IEA, could not be summarized on a single attitudinal dimension, but countries were grouped into three general types. The first set of countries, including Austria, Japan, and Spain, was called "internationalist" because large numbers of students held attitudes favorable to immigration, the elimination of nationalism, and the establishment of a worldwide government. The second set of countries, including Tunisia and Nigeria, was labeled "nationalistic," because large numbers of respondents opposed any limitation of national sovereignty and distrusted supranational organizations. The third set of countries, including the United States, France, Great Britain, Italy, Yugoslavia, and Australia, was called "social protectionist" because respondents reported some hope for the elimination of nationalism along with some distrust of world government and some support for limitations on immigration.

U.S. students were generally more concerned with private than public issues when compared with those in other countries. Comparisons made with data collected in 1977 showed decreasing liberalism on the majority of issues among U.S. students. Students in the United States and Britain, even those toward the left of the political spectrum, often agreed that the realization of an ideal society could be expected through gradual reform. In almost all of the other countries, more radical means of societal change were suggested.

A second cross-national project that also originated with an interest in student protest was conducted in 1974 by Jennings, Allerbeck, and Rosenmayr (1979). As part of a larger, eight-nation study of adult attitudes based on nationally representative samples (the Political Action Project), subsets of adolescents aged 16 through 20 and their parents were interviewed. Adolescents held less materialistic views than their parents, were more accepting of unconventional political behavior, were more positive about the women's liberation movement, expressed more disapproval of repressive techniques applied by government, and were somewhat more liberal in their political and religious beliefs. The size of the generation gap in the aggregate differed from country to country. It was the largest in Germany and the United States; it was smaller in the Netherlands where parents were very liberal and in Austria where adolescents appeared quite moderate; it was smallest in Britain. However, the authors noted that even a large generation gap when country statistics are considered does not necessarily mean conflict within individual families.

Neither of these studies included an investigation of the influence of primary or secondary schooling on propensities to participate in political protest. They all illustrate, however, the multidimensional nature of political attitudes and the difficulties of using simple single indicators to make meaningful general comparisons across countries.

Student Characteristics Related to Political Attitudes or Knowledge

The common thread in the studies reviewed in this section is the examination of the extent to which student characteristics, especially gender, age, and home background, have the same relationship to political attitudes and cognition across nations. Are the same gender differences found in countries with very different types of sex-role differentiations with respect to politics? Do age and cognitive capacities appear to have the same relationship to the understanding of social, political, and economic concepts in different countries? Are children from more disadvantaged family backgrounds likely to show similar patterns of attitudes in different countries?

Age, Gender, and Socioeconomic Background. In the IEA Civic Education Survey previously described, data were gathered on sex, age, and socioeconomic status. Regression analyses were conducted for three criterion variables: cognitive civics achievement, antiauthoritarian attitudes, and participation in political discussion (Torney et al., 1975). The socioeconomic status of the home (assessed by father's occupation and education, mother's education, and number of books in the home) was a moderately powerful predictor of 14-year-olds' scores on the cognitive test of civics and of anti-authoritarian attitudes in all countries. In contrast, socioeconomic background was not a statistically significant predictor of participation in political discussion for 14-year-olds in any country. This suggests that coming from a home of high social and educational level is associated with experiences that influence knowledge and basic democratic values but not with motivation to be an active participant in politics.

The findings for students enrolled in the last year of secondary education before university entry were difficult to interpret because of the reduced range of home background in some countries due to school selectivity. However, students from higher socioeconomic status groups tended to be more knowledgeable and less authoritarian in most countries at this age level as well.

The gender differences for these three criterion variables followed similar patterns across countries. According to the regression analyses, males performed significantly better on the cognitive tests in half of the countries in which 14-year-olds were tested and in all of the countries in which pre-university students were tested.

To examine age and sex differences on a broader range of attitudinal variables, the IEA data from the United States, Finland, and New Zealand were analyzed (Torney-Purta, 1984a). These three countries were chosen because 14-year-olds and pre-university students had been sampled using similar stratification categories. In order to make valid age-group comparisons within countries, controlling for socioeconomic status, matched pairs of students were randomly selected for analysis. Each member of a pair was of the same sex, from the same socioeconomic background, and from the same type of residence area (urban or rural); one member of each pair was a 14-year-old and one a preuniversity student, 17- to- 20 years old. Analyses of variance within each country were performed on this sample of reduced size in which the SES level of the younger and older students had been matched.

There were striking similarities in the patterns of attitudinal differences between age groups in the three countries. In the United States there were statistically significant mean score differences by age on 13 out of 13 attitude scales examined, in Finland on 12 out of 13, and in New Zealand on 11 out of 13. Older students had higher mean scores than younger students on all the scales measuring support for democratic values, had lower mean scores on scales of positive attitude toward both national and local government, and had higher mean scores on a measure of perceived political conflict.

There were statistically significant sex differences on 11 out of 13 of the IEA attitude scales in the United States, on 10 out of 13 in Finland, and on 9 out of 13 in New Zealand. The nature of these differences was also very similar. In all three nations, females were on the average less authoritarian than males and more supportive of equality of rights for all groups. The largest mean differences were on the scale assessing support for women's political rights. Females believed these to be of vital importance; males were much less likely to agree. Females also had mean scores indicating more positive attitudes toward national and local government than did males. In all three nations, males on the average reported more participation in political discussion and perceived more political conflict. Females were somewhat more likely than males to report participation in civic activities such as collecting for charity.

In summary, females were more supportive of government and more concerned about others' rights, while males saw more conflict and participated in more critical dialogue. The similarity of these sex differences in all three countries was of interest because in Finland adult women maintain a much more active political profile than in either the United States or New Zealand.

Fuente and Muñoz-Repiso (1981) administered the IEA questionnaires in Spain to samples drawn by IEA criteria in 1977 to 1980 (six to eight years after the original testing). The sex differences were parallel to those reported above, with males more knowledgeable and more critical of the government.

Differences associated with gender and age were also investigated recently in a bi-national study. Cogan, Torney-Purta, and Anderson (1988) administered a translated and backtranslated version of the ETS survey of global awareness to college freshmen and seniors in Japan (a survey originally used in the United States by Barrows, 1983). The higher mean score achieved by males on the test of knowledge of global issues in the U.S. sample was replicated in Japan; there was, however, not a statistically significant sex difference in the mean scores on attitudes of concern about international problems, a scale on which U.S. females had a higher mean score than U.S. males. There were also much larger differences in knowledge means between col-

lege freshmen and seniors in the U.S. sample than between freshmen and seniors in Japan. It appears that international information is likely to be acquired during secondary school by Japanese and during college by Americans.

Further Focus on Gender Differences. Some evidence about the extent to which gender differences in political attitudes are similar in different countries can be gleaned from other studies. In 1986 Hahn administered a questionnaire that included measures of political interest and confidence, efficacy, and support for women's rights similar to those used in earlier studies (Hahn, Tocci, & Angell, 1988). The sample, of approximately 1,500 students, aged 13 through 18 from 21 schools in the United States, Britain, Denmark, the Netherlands, and the Federal Republic of Germany, was not drawn to be representative. However, observations of classrooms supplemented data from paper- and- pencil surveys. Hahn found no statistically significant gender differences in means on the scales of political efficacy, political trust, and freedom of expression. Males had higher mean scores for political confidence and political interest. These sex differences were similar to those found in the IEA study, including a large sex difference in support for women's rights.

Jennings and Farah (1980) analyzed data from the adult sample collected in the Political Action study for gender differences. Males had a higher mean score on ideological thinking than females in every country. Controlling for level of education caused substantial shrinkage in this difference only in Britain. There were fewer sex differences in younger age groups (the 18- to 27-year-olds, born after World War II). Although many more women than men were classified in the politically nonactive category, women were also more likely to be classified as "dissenters," showing willingness to be mobilized in protest.

Further Focus on Age Differences. Studies of age differences are important primarily as they help to identify common patterns of maturation in young people's thinking about social problems and as they suggest age periods where political topics might be introduced in the school curriculum. The majority of studies concentrated on age differences in political concepts outside the United States have been conducted with interview methods similar to those used by Piaget. Gallatin (1976), in the only such study of more than two countries, reported very similar age trends in British, American, and German adolescents, with the 18-year-old respondents much more able to address problems from a comprehensive view of the social order.

The other studies relevant to cognitive development and its role in political socialization have been conducted in single countries, not cross-nationally. However, Connell (1971), based on his interview study of Australian children and adolescents, and Stevens (1982), based on her study of British children, came to a similar conclusion: there is a spurt at about age 9 or 10 in the child's ability to see political alternatives and to realize that opposing political positions and different interpretations of political situations exist. Stevens concluded that the age of 9 or 10 is a particularly appropriate time to begin political education. These researchers also presented extensive evidence that children construct their own concepts of politics and do not simply incorporate ideas presented by parents or teachers. That is, an active process in which the child is applying newly developed cognitive abilities to political content is hypothesized to lie behind the age trends observed.

Jurd (1978) reviewed a number of studies conducted in Britain and Australia on the role of concrete and formal operational thought in students' understanding of history. The major focus was on differences in the way in which younger and older secondary students applied cognitive processes to historical questions. The data were collected from students in written form as part of a school assignment, unlike the interview studies previously described. Older students were able to focus on several alternative ways of interpreting a historical event, to reconcile conflicting information, and to order events in time. Essay questions asking students to interpret events are more likely to be used in research abroad than in the United States, where multiple-choice tests, which do not allow inferences about cognitive processes, are common.

A further step in research on cognitive differences is represented by studies of the networks of concepts concerning political and economic actors existing in the child's mind. Studies using graphic representations of these concept networks have been undertaken independently in Europe and the United States. Verges (1987) used the idea of representation popularized by Moscovici, a French psychologist, to study the views of a small sample of young people in France and the United Kingdom regarding the connections they saw between concepts such as banks, families, business firms, foreign trade, investment, saving, and government. He also examined the effects of a course in elementary economics, finding in France more connections between concepts after the course.

Torney-Purta (1990) used a similar method but linked it closely to problem-solving methods from cognitive psychology. A small sample of American adolescents was given hypothetical problems in international relations and foreign policy and asked to think aloud in solving them. Their responses were analyzed to produce cognitive maps of each individual's concept networks. More complex concept networks included several international actors, each engaging in several actions, and each responsive to constraints on those actions. Comparison of these concept maps before and after participation in an international computer-assisted simulation, showed changes toward more complex concepts much like Verges's maps of conceptual connections.

The studies of Torney-Purta and Verges illustrate a movement cross-nationally to study cognitive processes as they relate to concepts in the specific domains of politics and economics rather than studying domain-general cognitive processes or stages such as those identified by Piaget.

In summary, cross-national studies conducted with a variety of methodologies have yielded similar differences by sex, age, and socioeconomic background across Western industrialized countries. However, many of these studies were conducted at least 15 years ago and should be replicated to assess possible changes traceable to trends such as the heightened women's movement or increased political conservatism.

Among the most interesting studies are those that have been conducted using open-ended interviews, short essays scored

for cognitive processes, or concept-sorting and problem-solving tasks derived from cognitive psychology applied to the political domain. These approaches have not been used widely to study political concepts in the United States. Although the same general age trends would likely be found in the United States as in other developed countries, the variety of concepts in the political domain and some underlying assumptions about politics might be substantially different. These approaches should be explored.

Educational Processes and Political Attitudes or Knowledge

The common thread in studies reported in this section is the researcher's explicit interest in relating aspects of classroom practice or educational policy to outcomes of social studies or civic education.

Classroom and Teacher Characteristics Relating to Civic Education Outcomes. The IEA Civic Education Study was undertaken with the main purpose of investigating the relationship between characteristics of educational systems or processes and educational outcomes. Regression analyses were used in this study to statistically control home background, age, sex, and type of school and then to assess the extent to which learning conditions were significant predictors of civic education outcomes (Torney et al., 1975).

The IEA findings were remarkably similar cross-nationally. In all countries, the extent to which students reported that teachers encouraged the expressions of opinion in the classroom—a measure of classroom climate—was related to high scores on the cognitive tests and to self-reports of participation in political discussions among 14-year-olds. A high degree of reported openness in classroom climate was also related to less authoritarian attitudes for both 14-year-olds and pre-university students.

Students who reported the frequent practice of patriotic rituals in their schools (ceremonies with the flag or singing patriotic songs) tended to be less knowledgeable and more authoritarian, but also more interested in political discussion than students who spent less time on patriotic observances. This was true of both 14- and 17- to 20-year-olds, and in all countries except Italy and Sweden. The amount of class time spent on printed drill or on memorizing facts and dates was also negatively related to scores on the cognitive test and positively related to authoritarian attitudes in some countries. In a number of countries, being taught by someone who specialized as a civics or social studies teacher was related to learning civics and acquiring anti-authoritarian attitudes.

In general, a reported stress on rote learning and on ritual performance within the classroom tended to be negatively related to civic education outcomes, while the reported opportunity to express an opinion in class had a positive relationship. One cannot infer cause and effect from these correlational analyses. However, the findings are made more credible because the socioeconomic status of the family and the type of school (academic or vocational) were controlled statistically in the regression analysis. Further, these findings were extremely similar across nine Western industrialized countries with different educational and political contexts.

Textbook Comparisons. Textbooks are a major component of school curricula. Multinational research on the depiction of historical events and cultural characteristics of other countries in textbooks began early in the century. Enhanced efforts were organized by UNESCO in the late 1940s. European researchers, often acting under mandates from their governments, have been more active in these studies than researchers in the United States. Existing textbooks are examined and inferences made about their probable effect on students' images rather than more direct study of the impact of different textbooks.

Schissler (1987), in reporting a study comparing history textbooks from Britain and Germany, noted that the British books provided narrative history, focused on promoting respect for the national past through identification with historical personalities, showed distrust of governmental solutions, and presented Britain as separate from Europe. In contrast, German texts were more oriented to social problems that the government was expected to solve, looked at governmental processes and structures, and embedded the study of German history in a European context.

The United States has not been active in multinational textbook studies, an inactivity that Hutton and Mehlinger (1987) attributed to a general preference for bilateral over multilateral international participation dating from the League of Nations, a certain cultural arrogance, poor command of languages other than English, and the control of the textbook content in the United States by market forces rather than by guidelines issued by the federal government.

In the last decade, U.S. researchers have undertaken bi–national textbook studies with researchers in Japan, in USSR, the Netherlands, and the Federal Republic of Germany. Each study was focused on widely used history and geography texts and upon their information about the other country and the relationship between the two countries. Hutton and Mehlinger (1987) concluded from a review of these studies that textbooks tend to give their own leaders the benefit of the doubt while attributing baser motives to other nations and leaders. American textbooks were the best designed and most attractively illustrated but the least demanding and scholarly. An issue not yet addressed is how to encourage studies that move beyond the content of textbooks to research on how they are used in classrooms.

Cross-National Differences in Approaches to Research. In general, educational researchers in the United States have been more comfortable with quantitative approaches to research than with qualitative approaches. However, qualitative research using interviews or unstructured observations has recently experienced a surge of popularity on both sides of the Atlantic. Atkinson, Delmont, and Hammersley (1988), British researchers, argued that in Britain this qualitative research tradition has a somewhat different character than in the United States. Issues such as racial and socioeconomic effects on the classroom fre-

quently arise in ethnographic research. Atkinson and his colleagues noted that a British researcher is likely to explain a nonWhite child's experience of discontinuity between home and school in terms of social class, while an American will explain it as a clash of the pupil's culture with White middle-class American culture. Further, in Britain qualitative research methods have been used to provide teachers with "images of their work and its context that will allow them to generate reflections on it and develop their own practice" (p. 240), through the teacher-as-researcher movement. There has been less use of qualitative methods as part of teacher training or educational improvement in the United States. Cross-national studies conducted with qualitative methods have considerable untapped potential (see Tobin, Wu, & Davidson, 1989).

In summary, a number of different methods—ranging from regression analysis to ethnography and content analysis of textbooks—have been used in research on the effects of educational practices on social studies and citizenship knowledge and attitudes. This remains an area where what is known is much less substantial than what should be known.

Programs Within a Single Country as Naturally Occurring Educational "Experiments"

The common thread in the studies reported in this section is the examination of a country that presents a unique example of a particular aspect of the social or political context of education or of a particular program relating to social studies education that contrasts with social studies education in the United States. The studies cited here are not cross-national research, in the sense that they are not conducted across countries. One way of looking at these countries and programs is as naturally occurring "experiments," situations in which one country may be examined so as to shed light on a principle important to social studies education in other countries. An example of the use of a naturally occurring experiment in one subject area was reported by Easley and Easley (1983). They conducted a detailed study of mathematics teaching in a Tokyo elementary school and implemented some of the methods in an American school. Several publications in this country have reviewed the social studies programs of other nations, asking whether some of these approaches might be useful in the United States (Gross & Dufty, 1980; Mehlinger & Tucker, 1979). Three naturally occurring "experiments" in social studies in other countries are described briefly next.

Political Education in Britain. For centuries, Britain was a culturally homogeneous society with a very selective educational system to train an elite for political leadership. Until relatively recently, there was faith in implicit rather than explicit teaching about democracy through courses in history or through instruction preparatory to an examination on the British Constitution (Stradling, 1981). The lowering of the voting age to 18 (in 1970), the raising of the school-leaving age, and the expanding number of immigrants from former colonies increased pressure to include more political and social education in the secondary curriculum for a wide range of students (Heater, 1977).

A program of publications and teacher workshops was undertaken by a private organization called the Politics Association to promote students becoming politically literate persons who would base their active involvement in politics on commitment to a number of "procedural values." These values included willingness to adopt a critical stance towards political information, willingness to give reasons why one holds a view and to expect similar reasons from others, respect for evidence, and value placed on freedom to choose between political alternatives (Stradling, 1981). Harber (1987) found that the number of British schools providing some form of political education doubled from the mid-1970s to the early 1980s. Survey research has indicated modest positive effects of these programs (Stradling, 1977). However, since the early 1980s there has been a swing toward a more conservative climate in Britain. This includes calls for the inculcation by schools of strict moral codes, patriotism, humble pride, and respect for tradition (Torney-Purta & Hahn, 1989).

The political literacy project is of interest because it was an attempt to move from implicit to explicit citizenship education by identifying a short list of values that guide democratic practice and encouraging the teaching of those values. It also illustrates how an association with a private base can have an impact upon social studies education programs in a country with decentralized educational decision making.

Values Education in Sweden. In Sweden, a country with a highly centralized educational system, the national curriculum guidelines explicitly state values that the school is obliged to teach: "Instruction must help to inculcate in pupils an understanding for other people and their conditions as a foundation for a desire for equality and solidarity" (National Swedish Board of Education, 1980, p. 5). This instruction is also to show pupils how the conditions in which other people live may contribute to antipathies and conflicts between groups. Other values endorsed in the curriculum include tolerance, equal rights, respect for truth, justice, and human dignity. Official Swedish curriculum documents also note that immigrant pupils shall be taught that men and women are equal, "even if this conflicts with the opinion of a certain pupil's family" (Swedish Ministry of Education, 1979, p. 13).

In addition to studying textbook discussions of democracy and conflict, beginning in the first grade pupils hold a weekly formal class-council meeting to discuss problems of national scope as well as school or local problems. Teachers are instructed to discuss in class issues on which conflict exists, the basis for that conflict, and the pupil's role in solidarity with those who experience injustice.

The Swedish program is of interest because of its explicit stress on teaching specific values in school. Englund (1986) reviewed both successes and problems in promoting an understanding of conflict. Although there is little current empirical research, Swedish students in cross-national studies such as IEA, showed very strong support for all democratic values measured on paper-and-pencil instruments, and were especially support-

ive of women's rights (Torney et al., 1975). There is also some evidence that family socialization of an ideologically coherent set of political attitudes contributes to shaping these values in Sweden (Sidanius, Ekehammar, & Brewer, 1986).

Perceptions of Citizenship in Israel. There are several interesting facets of the context for social and political education in Israel. Ichilov (1981) compared the orientations to citizenship among youth raised on a kibbutz and those raised in a city, finding that the youth on the kibbutz were more likely to include both political and nonpolitical aspects in the role of the good citizen and more likely to stress active participation. In the city, in contrast, youth saw the citizen's role limited to a public one. Passive orientations to politics were more common than active ones. In a reversal of the findings cited from many other international studies, Israeli females in both settings were more likely than males to attach importance to the political dimensions of citizenship and to active participation.

Israel is also a society in which political and social conflicts are widely depicted on television as prominent features of everyday life. Cohen, Adoni, & Drori (1983) presented 9th- and 12th-graders, selected to be representative of the school population, with specially constructed segments of television news dealing with a highjacking, a strike at a food factory, and an attempt to prevent the integration of children from socially heterogeneous neighborhoods in the school. The older adolescents perceived the real-world conflicts as more intense, more complex, and more difficult to solve than their TV depictions. Growing up in a society with a high level of conflict or being raised in a communal setting both present a kind of naturally occurring "experiment," which may be of value in understanding political socialization cross-nationally.

Other Natural Experiments. A variety of other examples could be given of processes at work in the political socialization of a particular country or group of countries—for example, the meanings given to nationalism in countries such as Canada or Great Britain (Harvey, Hunter-Harvey, & Vance, 1975; Heater, 1980) and the effect of growing up on the East or West side of the Berlin Wall (Davey, 1987). Other political education programs are described in a publication of the Research Committee on Political Education of the International Political Science Association (1982). To some extent, every country has unique features of political and social education as well as features held in common with other countries. Cross-national research to analyze the uniquenesses as well as the commonalities could have implications for social studies education in the United States as well as other countries.

SUMMARY AND FUTURE RESEARCH DIRECTIONS

The first purpose for this chapter was to review criteria for judging cross-national research in social studies, taking into account the special problems of sampling of respondents, sampling of assessment items, and sampling of influences. Researchers embarking on cross-national studies should attend to sampling issues of all three types and bear in mind caveats against overgeneralization. Collaboration with colleagues in other nations and pilot testing are two ways to deal effectively with many of these problems. It is particularly important that readers of research be sensitive to criteria such as these in judging how seriously findings should be taken.

The majority of the research reviewed in the second part of the chapter met reasonable sampling standards for respondents and items. There is so little research in which the relationships of educational variables have been examined in relation to social studies outcomes that it is difficult to make a statement about the sampling of independent variables.

The second major purpose of this chapter was to review existing cross-national research, especially in civic education and political socialization. Comparisons of overall achievement or attitudes in different countries receive the most public attention. In most cross-national studies of attitudes, conclusions are drawn in terms of multiple dimension or typological categories, suggesting the complexity of this area.

There have been very few cross-national studies of the impact of educational practices upon achievement in civics or social studies, although this type of study has the greatest potential value for educational improvement. Some ambivalence about how much schools ought to try to shape student values may dampen interest in such research. Studies are needed not only of the content of textbooks but of ways in which the differences in textbooks used in different countries influence what children learn in those countries. The IEA finding that reported climate for open discussion in the classroom is positively related to learning and attitudes has been widely replicated and should be more widely known. Teacher practice in this area is difficult to change, but cross-national observational research on classrooms characterized by such discussion should be explored.

There are unique situations and programs for political and civic education that represent naturally occurring "experiments." For example, it would be useful to have studies in which programs such as political education or values inculcation in countries such as Sweden were compared with programs having similar aims in other countries. The effects of program variations and their interaction with cultural differences and societal contexts, such as the prevalence of political tension in Israel, should be investigated.

A coordinated research base describing U.S. children and young people as compared with those in other nations in the 1980s is lacking. There is a particularly large gap in research on children of elementary and junior high age and in research

concentrated on the immigrant and minority groups that exist in many societies. The gender differences that appear so regularly in cross-national studies also deserve further attention. Motivational factors as well as information-processing and problem-solving skills should be further explored as explanations of differential student performance in social studies.

High-quality cross-national research is expensive. U.S. participation in large-scale comparative studies has not always been stable or timely because of the absence of dependable funding. The recent establishment of a Board on Comparative International Studies in Education by the National Research Council of the National Academy of Sciences is an attempt to alleviate some of the impediments to high-quality U.S. participation in cross-national studies.

Because the United States is such a large country, it is expensive to draw and test adequate national samples. Researchers might consider drawing a representative sample of selected U.S. states to compare with other countries. This would follow the lead of some recent IEA studies in which samples have been drawn of a province of Canada and generalizations drawn about that province without an attempt to generalize to Canada as a whole. Educational research specialists at universities in collaboration with state education departments might coordinate the participation of states in cross-national studies. Many states issue social studies curricular guidelines, making the process of test construction through item sampling easier when conducted on these smaller units rather than on a national basis.

Qualitative comparative research on a small scale also could be useful for confirming some types of inferences. Local school districts might cooperate in data collection with equivalent units in another country. Even if the generalizations from these data would be very limited, such collaborative inquiry would serve the function of making U.S. social studies educators more reflective about their own practice, much as qualititative research in the United Kingdom has contributed to teachers' reflections through teacher-researcher programs. Such programs could be especially effective in stimulating connections between the United States, Britain, Canada, Australia, and New Zealand because no foreign language capacities would be required.

Cross-national research can serve many purposes—identifying strengths and weaknesses in educational programs, indicating the extent of gender or age differences across cultures, pointing to effective classroom practices such as open discussion, and identifying underlying educational assumptions. Such research has a potentially important role to play in improving social studies education.

References

Almond, G., & Verba, S. (1963). *The civic culture*. Princeton, NJ: Princeton University Press.

Almond, G., & Verba, S. (1980). *The civic culture revisited*. Boston: Little Brown.

Atkinson, P., Delamont, S., & Hammersley, M. (1988). Qualitative research traditions: A British response to Jacobs. *Review of Educational Research, 58*, 231–250.

Barrows, T. (1983). *College students' knowledge and beliefs: A survey of global understanding*. New Rochelle, NY: Change Magazine Press.

Benedict, R. (1946). *The chrysanthemum and the sword: Patterns of Japanese culture*. Boston: Houghton Miflin.

Cogan, J., Torney-Purta, J. & Anderson, D. (1988). Knowledge and attitudes toward global issues: Students in Japan and the United States. *Comparative Education Review, 32*, 282–297.

Cohen, A., Adoni, H, & Drori, G. (1983). Adolescents' perceptions of social conflicts in television news and social reality. *Human Communication Research, 10,* 203–225.

Connell, R. (1971). *The child's construction of politics.* Carleton, Victoria, Australia: Melbourne University Press.

Davey, T. (1987). *Generation divided.* Durham, NC: Duke University Press.

Easley, J., & Easley, E. (1983). Horizontal mathematics. *Journal of Curriculum Studies, 15,* 429–431.

Ehman, L. (1980). The American school in the political socialization process. *Review of Educational Research, 50,* 99–119.

Englund, T. (1986). *Curriculum as a political problem: Changing educational conceptions with special reference to citizenship education.* Stockholm, Sweden: Almqvist & Wiksell.

Fuente, C., & Muñoz-Repiso, M. (1981). *Preparation for life in democratic society in five countries in Southern Europe.* Strasbourg, France: Council for Cultural Cooperation, Council of Europe.

Gallatin, J. (1976). The conceptualization of rights: Psychological development and cross-national perspectives. In R. Claude (Ed.), *Comparative human rights* (pp. 302–325). Baltimore: Johns Hopkins University Press.

Gross, R. & Dufty, D. (Eds.). (1980). *Learning to live in society.* Boulder, CO: Social Science Education Consortium.

Hahn, C., Tocci, C., & Angell, A. (1988). Five-nation study of civic attitudes and controversial issue discussions. Paper presented at the International Conference on the Social Studies, Vancouver, B.C.

Harber, C. (1987). Political education 14–16. In C. Harber (Ed.), *Political education in Britain* (pp. 25–46). Lewes, East Sussex, England: Falmer Press.

Harvey, T., Hunter-Harvey, S., & Vance, W. (1975). Nationalist sentiment among Canadian adolescents. In E. Zureik & R. Pike (Eds.), *Socialization and values in Canadian society: Political socialization* (pp. 232–280). Toronto: Macmillan of Canada.

Heater, D. (1977). A burgeoning of interest: Political education in Britain. *International Journal of Political Education, 1,* 325–345.

Heater, D. (1980). *World studies.* London: Harrap.

Holloway, S. (1988). Concepts of ability and effort in Japan and the United States. *Review of Educational Research, 58,* 327–345.

Hutton, D., & Mehlinger, H. (1987). International textbook revision: Examples from the United States. In V. Berghahn & H. Schissler (Eds.), *Perceptions of history: International textbook research in Britain, Germany and the United States* (pp. 141–56). Oxford: Berg.

Ichilov, O. (1981). Citizenship orientations of city and kibbutz youth in Israel. *International Journal of Political Education, 4,* 305–17.

International Political Science Association, Research Committee on Political Education. (1983). *Perspectives in political education in 1980s.* Warsaw: RCPE.

Jahoda, G. (1986). Nature, culture, and social psychology. *Journal of Social Psychology, 16,* 17–30.

Jennings, M. K., Allerbeck, K., & Rosenmayr, L. (1979). Generations and families. In S. H. Barnes & M. Kaase (Eds.), *Political action: Mass participation in five Western democracies* (pp. 449–486). Beverly Hills, CA: Sage.

Jennings, M. K., & Farah, B. (1980). Ideology, gender, and political action. *British Journal of Political Science, 10,* 219–240.

Jurd, M. F. (1978). Concrete and formal operational thinking in history. In J. A. Keats, F. K. Collis, & G. S. Halford (Eds.), *Cognitive development.* (pp. 285–348). Chester: Wiley.

Klineberg, O, Zavalloni, M., Louis-Guerin, C., & BenBrika, J. (1979). *Students, values, and politics: A cross-cultural comparison.* New York: Free Press.

Mehlinger, H., & Tucker, J. (Eds.) (1979). *Teaching social studies in other nations.* Washington, DC: National Council for the Social Studies.

Nathan, J., & Remy, R. (1977). Comparative political socialization. In S. Renshon (Ed.), *Handbook of political socialization* (pp. 85–114). New York: Free Press.

National Swedish Board of Education. (1980). *The 1980 compulsory school curriculum.* Stockholm: National Swedish Board of Education.

Postlethwaite, T. N. (1987). *Cross-national convergence of concepts and measurement of educational achievement.* Paper presented at the International Conference on Cross-National Educational Indicators. Washington, DC: National Center for Education Statistics.

Postlethwaite, T. N. (1988). *Science achievement in seventeen countries: A preliminary report.* Oxford: Pergamon Press.

Schaffner, B. (1948). *Fatherland: A study of authoritarianism in the German family.* New York: Columbia University Press.

Schissler, H. (1987). Perceptions of the other and the discovery of the self: What pupils are supposed to learn about each other's history. In V. Berghahn & H. Schissler (Eds.), *Perceptions of history: International textbook research in Britain, Germany and the United States* (pp. 26–37). Oxford: Berg.

Sidanius, J., Ekehammar, B., & Brewer, R. (1986). The political socialization determinants of higher order sociopolitical space: A Swedish example. *Journal of Social Psychology, 126,* 7–22.

Stevens, O. (1982). *Children talking politics.* Oxford: Martin Robertson.

Stevenson, H. (1987). America's math problems. *Educational Leadership, 45,* 4–10.

Stradling, R. (1977). *Political awareness of school leavers.* London: Hansard.

Stradling, R. (1981). Political education: Developments in Britain. In D. Heater & J. Gillespie (Eds.), *Political education in flux* (pp. 81–105). London: Sage.

Swedish Ministry of Education and Cultural Affairs. (1979). *Schooling and upbringing* (R. Tanner, Trans.). Stockholm: Swedish Ministry of Education and Cultural Affairs.

Tobin, J., Wu, D., & Davidson, D. (1989). *Preschool in three cultures.* New Haven: Yale University Press.

Torney, J., Oppenheim, A. N., & Farnen, R. F. (1975). *Civic education in ten countries: An empirical study.* New York: Wiley.

Torney, J. (1977). The international attitudes and knowledge of adolescents in nine countries: The IEA civic education study. *International Journal of Political Education, 1,* 3–20.

Torney-Purta, J. (1984a). Political socialization and policy: The U.S. in a cross-national context. In H. Stevenson & A. Siegel (Eds.), *Child development research and social policy* (Vol. 1, pp. 471–525). Chicago: University of Chicago Press.

Torney-Purta, J. (1984b). *Raising the alarm: The only role for comparative education in the debate on excellence.* Claude Eggertsen Lecture, Comparative International Education Society, Houston, TX.

Torney-Purta, J. (1990). From attitudes to schemata: Expanding the outcomes of political socialization research. In O. Ichilov (Ed.), *Political socialization and citizenship education in democracy* (pp. 98–115). New York: Teachers College Press.

Torney-Purta, J., & Hahn, C. (1989). Values education in the Western European tradition. In W. Cummings & Y. Tomoda (Eds.), *The revival of values education in Asia and the West* (pp. 31–57). Elmsford, NY: Pergamon Press.

Torney-Purta, J., & Schwille, J. (1986). Civic values learned in school: Policy and practice in industrialized countries. *Comparative Education Review, 30,* 30–49.

Verges, P. (1987). A social and cognitive approach to economic representations. In W. Doise & S. Moscovici (Eds.), *Current issues in European social psychology: Vol. 2* (pp. 271–306). Cambridge: Cambridge University Press.

·51·

RESEARCH ON SOCIAL STUDIES AND CITIZENSHIP EDUCATION IN ENGLAND

Ian Lister

UNIVERSITY OF YORK, ENGLAND

In England, unlike in the United States, there is no tradition of explicit citizenship education in the schools. Indeed, civic education has been consistently opposed, by official statements of central government commissions, as a curriculum item (as controversial, dangerous, and likely to be biased and to lead to indoctrination). The dominant curriculum tradition has been based on scholarship, not citizenship (offering academic knowledge rather than preparation for social life [Johnston, 1987]), and for high-status pupils has been mostly history and geography. During the 1960s and the early 1970s, curriculum projects in the social studies were aimed at the "less able," the "non academic," and "the early leaver," and even the most impressive of the projects (such as the Humanities Curriculum Project and Geography for the Young School Leaver) were marginalized by their disassociation from mainstream students.

More recently, the "New Geography" and the "New History" have affected the curriculum for all secondary school pupils. In the New Geography, influenced by social and political geography, the stress has been on the importance of power and decision making in the shaping of human-made environments. In the New History, students have been encouraged to acquire the perspectives, empathy, and skills of the practicing historian. Both the New Geography and the New History have some potential contribution to make to citizenship education, but—as they stand—they too are in the tradition of scholarship, not citizenship. Some research was carried out on the New History (Shemilt, 1980), but the studies were designed to assess academic effectiveness, not citizenship education potential.

From 1974 until 1988—the first the date of the launch of the national Programme for Political Education, the second the date of the central government's Education Reform Act—there were a number of new initiatives in the field of social, political, and civic education, and all of these have been aimed at *all* pupils. These new initiatives were launched under a range of keywords—*political literacy, development, peace, human rights, multiculturalism,* and *environment/ecology.* As these new initiatives promoted not only new content but also "new forms of teaching and learning" (which are "old," in that they would be familiar to Dewey but are "new" in classrooms, where the dominant tradition is oral exposition), they are sometimes referred to as the "new educations." These new educations have been devised and promoted by the avant-garde, referred to by me as "the vanguard educators" (Lister, 1987, p. 47). Sometimes they managed to mobilize the support of key persons in central government, Her Majesty's Inspectorate (who inspect all public sector schools), and in local government (which, until the Education Act of 1988, played the most powerful role in the administration of education, as education was, until then, centrally provided and locally administered). Some of the new educations, though—particularly peace education, development education, and multicultural education—have been questioned and sometimes opposed by central government ministers, and they have been embroiled in a passionate debate, characterized by assertion versus counterassertion, with little appeal to evidence derived from research on actual practice.

However, although the new educations have been *development areas* rather than *research fields,* a number of research studies have been carried out—including surveys of provision, research on children's attitudes and values, and some case-study research on actual practice in real classrooms in real schools. In this chapter, I argue for more research in this field so that the best of the new educations might be identified, analyzed, described, preserved, and extended. This is apposite and vital at a time when the central government has promulgated a

Reviewers were Chris H. Brown, Walsall, England; Clive Harber, The University of Birmingham, England; Derek Heater, Brighton, England.

"National Curriculum" and, through the 1988 Act, given it the force of law. This National Curriculum is made up, mostly, of traditional academic subjects, including history and geography, and is in the tradition of scholarship, not citizenship. Nevertheless, citizenship is to be a "cross-curricular theme" in the National Curriculum—careers, economic awareness, and personal and social education are some of the others—and one current project aims to provide "*global* perspectives for the *National* curriculum" (my emphasis). How the new educations might relate to the current educational reform will need to be worked out in theory and in practice. In this chapter, I will discuss the need to discover what kind of contributions they might make.

RESEARCH AND DEVELOPMENT, DEVELOPMENT AND RESEARCH

In the social studies field in England, the period from the late 1960s until the present has been characterized more by *development* than by *research*. The curriculum development era saw projects like the Humanities Curriculum Project, the General Studies Project, the Geography for the Young School Leaver Project, and the History 13–16 Project. A main activity of all these projects was to produce curriculum materials. The national Programme for Political Education was an exception in that it had a unit (the Political Education Research Unit—PERU) whose task was to research the possibilities and problems of political literacy in action. (The PERU created a line of research activities, and detailed information about them will be recounted later.)

In the 1980s the vanguard educators in the new educations (usually operating under umbrella terms such as *World Studies* or *Global Education*) also opted to make first curriculum development and then teacher development their top priorities. This was partly because their funding agencies—charitable trusts—preferred to finance work that had obvious material outcomes (such as teachers' handbooks and classroom materials) with direct links to practice, than to finance research (which is often protracted and usually suffers from low visibility). A radical change in the funding system for teacher and school development activities, introduced on April 1, 1987, meant that local education authorities became key sponsors of in-service teacher education as well as of much school-based research. These authorities, too, opted for development, rather than research; and those authorities who favored the vanguard educators chose to use them for in-service workshops, courses, and consultancies. Although the vanguard educators do not like Thatcherism (which praises the spirit of enterprise and decries the spirit of globalism) and Thatcherists do not like them, one of the paradoxes of the time is that, generally failing to attract central government funding, they live in "the enterprise culture," living from hand to mouth on soft money from charitable trusts, local authority contracts, earnings from publications, and fees for courses and consultancies.

The nature of central government sponsorship of educational research during the period also left the new initiatives in the social studies field as a developing but underresearched area. At least between October 1976, when Prime Minister Calla-

ghan launched "the Great Debate on Education," and the drafting of the Great Education Reform Bill (GERBIL) in 1987, economics dominated politics, and the economy was the government's prime concern. Thus, governments were far more interested in questions concerning young people and the economy (such as preparation for working life, technical and vocational education, and alternatives to youth unemployment) than in questions concerning young people and the polity. The central government sponsored projects on economic awareness, and the most richly funded project of all in the social area of the school curriculum was the national Technical and Vocational Education Initiative (TVEI), through which technical and vocational elements in the school curriculum were developed for pupils in the 14 to 18 age range. The central government was more interested in schools preparing young people for the work culture than for a civic culture, and it sponsored research on the TVEI programmes. This research was carried out in universities and in research institutes (such as the National Foundation for Education Research). The Economic and Social Research Council (formerly the Social Science Research Council, but renamed because the Minister of Education thought that social research could not be scientific!) funded research in the area of youth studies.

The nature of central government sponsorship of research meant that the document *Current Projects Supported by the Department of Education and Science* and the document *Current Projects of the National Foundation for Educational Research* contained no entries at all relating to the social studies, citizenship, or the new educations. Central government priorities in education are the raising of standards (*quality* is the key word) and the three core subjects—English, mathematics, and science. Thus, "literary" literacy, mathematical literacy, and scientific literacy—but *not social* literacy—are seen as the foundations of an "entitlement curriculum." Some national priority funding is allocated (mainly to *development* work) in mathematics, special needs, and technology.

During this period, there has been a shift to cash-led research and the use of research by the central government to legitimize policy decisions already taken rather than to inform policy as it is made.

At the same time, we have seen two major shifts in the field of applied research in education. The first is the movement of "the teacher as researcher." The second is the growth of case-study research and ethnographic research by professional researchers. The teacher-as-researcher movement began in the 1970s. (The first paper I have with the title "Teacher as Researcher" was presented at a conference at the University of York in 1972, Bartholemew, 1972). Pioneers in this field have included Lawrence Stenhouse, John Elliot and Rob Walker, all at some time at the University of East Anglia—at the Centre for Applied Research in Education (CARE). (Stenhouse, a giant among curriculum reformers in the United Kingdom, died young; Elliot is still at East Anglia; and Walker is now an emigré professor in Australia.) Those in this movement wanted to end the hierarchical gap between professional researchers (the researcher) and practicing teachers (the researchee) and to close the gap between theory and practice in education. This meant that university teachers and schoolteachers needed to work together on cooperative projects. (Previously, university departments of education had been characterized as "centres of actionless thought," and schools had been characterized as "centres of thoughtless action"). Those in the movement criticized quantitative research as a mode and questionnaires as a method. They practiced qualitative research and case-study research (aimed at "illuminative evaluation") based on anthropological models.

In some parts of the country it is now common for teachers to research their own practice, as the movement for "practitioner research" has gathered momentum. With rare exceptions—a study by Parker (1988) on a course on "Inner Ecology" is one such—the research agenda does not touch upon avantgarde courses. The agenda is derived essentially from central government educational reform policy (which tends to be national and even inward-looking). At its best, such teacher research illuminates and informs practice—particularly innovative practice. At its worst, though, such research is introverted and parochial. The researcher is in the cave and gains greater knowledge of the details of the cave without ever getting out of the cave. Citizenship education, social education, and the new educations (like education generally) is about getting out of the cave and away from the world of shadows.

To give some idea of the growth of the phenomenon of the teacher as researcher, I can give the example of the University of York, which is now one of the major centers of the movement. In the Autumn of 1989 around 200 teachers were registered in the Department of Education (mainly on a part-time basis) for higher degrees in the practitioner-research program. People now planning new initiatives in research in the social studies and citizenship need to consider how to recruit teacher-researchers and how to mobilize their interest and expertise.

RESEARCH OF THE PROGRAMME FOR POLITICAL EDUCATION (PPE)

The national Programme for Political Education (PPE) was launched in 1974. It aimed—through its central concept "political literacy"—to introduce some teaching and learning about and for political life into the social area of the secondary school curriculum. It was an attempt to be a pioneering project in several regards. Following one of its directors, Professor Bernard Crick (author of the landmark work *In Defence of Politics,* 1964), the project proposed an *issue-based* approach to political education (in place of the anatomy of constitutions and institutions) and a broad concept of "the political" (to include not only central and local government, but also the politics of school and college, of firm and factory, of the environment, and of everyday life). It stressed the importance of political *skills* (whereas the stress, hitherto, had been on *attitudes* and *knowledge content*). A goal was to promote more activity-based teaching and learning (including discussion and debate, problem-solving exercises, group work, games, and simulations).

There was development *and* research, with some dramatic tension between the two. The main research, carried out by the Political Education Research Unit of the University of York (PERU), was case-study research conducted in six institutions across the country. It was aimed to identify the possibilities, problems, and limitations of the political-literacy approach.

Some impressive courses were found, but it was concluded, as well, that the difficulties of the issue-based approach and the broad concept of "the political" had been seriously underestimated. In particular, when handling issues, teachers rarely invited students to consider more than two sides of a question; highly sensitive issues, such as Northern Ireland, tended to be left out of courses, and local issues—in which the research revealed students had high levels of interest—were evaded. When presenting the broad concept of "the political," teachers constantly came up against the firmly held assumption that politics was a gladiatorial contest between the leaders of the two main political parties and that its location was in London. Interviews revealed that for most students, participation in politics was understood as something in their own futures, and it meant mainly voting in a general election.

The PERU worked in the tradition of qualitative research and illuminative evaluation. The main methods used were classroom observation, semistructured interviews, and informal discussions, both with teachers and with students. The intensive research period was during the school year of 1975 to 1976, when programs were followed through the six institutions.

The focus of the program was political education and not the international and global perspectives developed later by the vanguard educators. In an analysis of the issues that teachers brought into the classroom, the researchers noted that "nearly all of them were present-day issues, and that issues taken from the past or projected for the future were virtually absent," and that "the majority of issues were either national or international" (Allen & Lister, 1975). Among the issues, themes, and topics logged by fieldworkers were the following:

1. Minority rights
2. Terrorism
3. The Third World and poverty and the terms of trade
4. Emerging countries and appropriate forms of government
5. The role of Russia and China in the Third World
6. Soviet influence in Africa
7. The Common Market
8. The Arab-Israeli dispute

In addition, some schools had speakers on Third World issues, on the political system of the United States, and on the People's Republic of China. Environmental issues crossed national boundaries (pollution as a European question, for example), and international questions were used to illustrate general political questions (such as the individual and the state, the advantages and limitations of democracy versus dictatorship versus anarchy as systems of government, and the causes of war). However, although the key document of the program (*Political Literacy: The Centrality of the Concept,* Crick & Lister, 1975) suggested that an awareness of alternatives and an acceptance of the plausibility of other political systems would represent a high level of political literacy, the research team found it rare for teachers to present alternatives to students and there was relatively little reference to examples from history, or from other societies and political systems (Allen & Lister, 1975).

The central concern of the Programme for Political Education was *political education,* not to promote international and global perspectives—which was to be a central concern for the vanguard educators. The focus of the PPE was to encourage students to understand and work on issues in order to promote the acquisition and development of the skills needed for active participation in political life. Some of those issues might be international and global (the hardest to work on because of their distance, inaccessibility, and intractability) and some might be local (the ones that afforded the most opportunities for active participation). Some of the issues were national (but many of these encouraged contemplation rather than participation—politics as a spectator sport).

PERUVIAN RESEARCH RELATED TO THE PPE: 1977 TO 1989

The Political Education Research Unit (PERU) set out an agenda for further research, most of which was carried out by its own members or by close collaborators. The PERU Report of 1977 recommended that more work should be done on identifying the barriers to political education in schools. Tom Brennan (1981) took on that task, analyzing the barriers of the strongly entrenched conservative tradition in education and society, professional barriers, pedagogical barriers, and societal barriers—including "the lack of consensus about the nature and aims of democratic government (e.g., the dominant emphasis on representative forms and the relative neglect of the participatory perspective)." (Brennan, 1981, p. 73).

Robert Stradling and his associates carried out three research projects. The first (Stradling & Noctor, 1981) was a survey of the provision of political education in schools, with particular reference to the strategy employed for introducing it into the curriculum. The three strategies identified were the *exclusive* (whereby there was an actual course called "Political Education"); the *modular* (whereby a module, unit, or minicourse of political education existed in a social studies course, alongside other modules, such as health education); and the *indirect* (whereby political education was infused into existing subjects, most commonly history). Given the nature of the National Curriculum, established by law in 1988, with history and geography as foundation subjects, Stradling's work on the indirect, infusion strategy will take on a renewed importance.

The second project (Stradling, 1977) tested the political awareness of the school leaver (16-year-olds at that time). The results revealed widespread political ignorance. On European affairs, knowledge of the European Economic Community was "fairly sound," but knowledge of communist countries was "considerably lower" (with only 37% $N = 4,027$, of the sample recognizing Hungary as a communist country, and 10% thinking that Austria was a communist country). Thirty-four percent thought that Japan was ruled by a military government that was not elected by the people; 52% did not know that presidential elections in the United States are held every four years; and 44% thought that the IRA was a Protestant organization set up to prevent Ulster from being united with Ireland.

The third project (Stradling, Noctor, & Baines, 1984) was a systematic study, using classroom observation and interviews, of the teaching of controversial issues. Topics researched included teaching about Northern Ireland, nuclear weapons, and Third World issues. On teaching and learning about Third World issues, Stradling et al. noted:

Underlying most of the teaching material and much classroom teaching is a liberal humanist tradition. The emphasis is on international understanding and tolerance, mutual interests and cooperation. The value-position is perhaps epitomised by the widespread use of such phrases as "global village," "one world," and "spaceship earth". (p. 65)

He saw one teaching problem that of "capturing the interest of 14–16-year-olds on issues which they perceive as having no relevance to their own lives, and on topics such as 'The Third World', or 'North-South' which are both geographically and conceptually remote" (p. 75). Even though he argued that "many concepts relating to the Third World and development issues are simply unfamiliar to pupils, rather than highly abstract and demanding" (he cited "neo-colonialism," "diversification," and "gross national product" as being in this category), he added that "some concepts, clearly, are highly abstract and they will always be difficult to teach" (p. 86). Here he cited concepts such as "interdependence," "development," and "structural violence." Stradling identified two major problems in Third World studies—the value package (the liberal humanism of the Green Movement) and the difficult concepts that provide much of the analytical framework.

Stradling's third study was of curriculum territory that is now very much that of the vanguard educators. More recent PERU studies have also been research of that territory. Judy Dyson (1986) conducted case-study research on Third World studies in a secondary school. Such studies in England have often been offered under the umbrella title of "Development Education." Although this always includes issues on Third World development—i.e., "developing countries"—it often also includes questions of how our own societies might develop, of how humanity as a whole might develop, and of how we might develop as individuals. (Thus, such courses might owe something to humanistic psychology, as well as to development economics.) Dyson's project was focused on whether the demands of traditional examinations (with their stress on testing content knowledge within conventional subjects) might be reconciled with the aims of development educators (with their concern for affective learning and their use of nonconventional kinds of knowledge). Her conclusion was not without hope:

There were indications that a minority of exams might offer an opportunity for Development Education, either "by default" through a sufficiently flexible style that put much of the shaping of content and assessment into teachers' hands, or by design and intention of the Examining Board itself. (p. 90).

She recorded teachers' views of some of the problems of development education:

The pupils lack a concept of the scale of the problems and issues. . . . They don't even know the location of the countries. (Teacher 4, p. 64)

The pupils find it boring and too hard. They come with a limited set of stereotypes, and keep them. It's all too distant. (Teacher 5, p. 65)

I'm disappointed that there wasn't more empathy shown for the lot of the people of the Third World. (Teacher 5, p. 65)

Dyson researched pupils' images of other countries and peoples. On the United States, one pupil said, "They speak the same language . . . their way of life is similar, just exaggerated." (Pupil 8, p. 78) On Africa, another pupil said, "They've got a different language. They haven't got towns and cities. Not as civilised as us." (Pupil 3, p. 79) And another said, "They're all starving." (Pupil 10, p. 79) Dyson reported:

In every case of people identified by the pupils as "different from us," with the sole exception of the Chinese, comments on why these people were unlike us revolved around negative perceptions of life in those areas. Africans had a lot of problems. As for Brazilians—"We're more civilised, the way we work." (Pupil 7)

Overall, she thought that

The research into the pupil perspective certainly did not reveal signs of any great success in challenging assumptions about aid, or in reducing the distance that they put between themselves and the peoples of the Third World. . . . However, it did show a predisposition to a "global perspective" which the evidence indicates the course succeeded in building on. (p. 92)

Two of the problems she highlighted were:

the controversial nature of the message of Development Education, as it is characterised by its opponents. It does present a view of history and of current affairs that is not greatly flattering to the West. (p. 92)

During the course of the interviews with the pupils it was clear that there had been little change in their unsophisticated perception of international political and economic forces. (p. 93)

RESEARCH ON PEACE EDUCATION

Some of the difficulties identified by Dyson may have been peculiar to development education, but most of them are equally relevant to other categories of the new educations (such as peace education, teaching about human rights, multiculturalism, and environmental awareness), all of which are based on proposals for wider social and global responsibilities for the modern citizen. Presenting contemporary societies and cultures to young people may pose peculiar difficulties to those teachers who have not visited those societies or experienced those cultures. (This is unlike, for example, teaching about Norman England inasmuch as *no* living teacher "has been there.") Teachers, too, may have unsophisticated images of the Third World, received from charity posters and television newsreels—which show Third World items at times of mass famines. To help overcome some of these problems, a useful project was carried out by Amanda Batchelor of the Center for Global Education at the University of York. She identified people who had lived in other cultures and who were willing to speak to school students about their experience. Names of speakers and details of expe-

rience and topics were published in a register, *Speaking Out* (Batchelor, 1985).

Most of the writing on peace education is theoretical—some speculative (about what might be achieved), some exhortatory (about how good the outcomes would be), and some adversely critical (how peace education—as "one-sided disarmament education"—could lead to the end of Western civilization as we know it). Hicks (1988) affords the best overview of peace education during the period. Marks (1984) and Cox and Scruton (1984) provide the main arguments of the negative critique.

Some limited research on peace education has been carried out. Smoker and Rathenow (1983) carried out a questionnaire survey in which they asked local education authorities about their attitudes toward, and provision in their schools of, peace education. Generally the authorities, regardless of the political color of their local government, were positive in their attitudes toward peace education and claimed to be providing it in their schools. In spite of this, Kevin Green (1986), when carrying out a study of peace education in the United Kingdom, had great difficulty in finding any, in practice, in schools. He reran the Smoker and Rathenow questionnaire and found far fewer authorities claiming to be supportive of peace education and far fewer claiming to provide it in their schools. (The attacks on peace education had grown since the Smoker and Rathenow survey, and Mrs. Thatcher—personally and publicly hostile to peace education—had been reelected to office as prime minister in 1983.)

Stefanie Duczek (1984) carried out some case-study research of the Peace Studies Project at Atlantic College, an international sixth-form (16–19) college located on the south coast of Wales. The college, whose patrons have included Earl Mountbatten and Prince Charles, was founded after World War II, and its aims have included the promotion of international cooperation and understanding and a recognition of the supranational responsibilities of modern citizenship. Among the teachers of peace studies she found two schools of thought—the optimistic liberals who thought that a peaceful future might be secured by reason, persuasion, and the reduction of misunderstanding, and those who believed that the lack of peacefulness was caused by the "structural violence" of the political, social, and economic systems. (The term *structural violence* is a key concept of the peace education theorist, Johan Galtung, 1975.)

Among the students, Duczek found some excellent project work, and an outstanding and informative exhibition on human rights in the world was mounted for the local population by the students. She also found that the study of some of the major issues concerned with peace, development, and human rights could have a depressing and dispiriting effect on students because of their long-term and, apparently, intractable nature.

RESEARCH ON HUMAN RIGHTS EDUCATION

The literature of human rights is also, preponderantly, theoretical. Most of the literature is philosophical and legal (Spurgeon, 1986). There are some handbooks (Heater, 1984; Lister, 1984) and some practical classroom exercises (Selby & Pike, 1988).

Two pieces of case-study research have been carried out—one by Grainger (1986) on the infusion of human rights elements into some courses in a polytechnic (which is a kind of university with a technical and vocational orientation), and one by Cunningham (1986) on a course on human rights in a secondary school. Grainger found that "the housing courses and urban studies courses were the most receptive" to the infusion of human rights. Cunningham's work included an analysis of 12- to 14-year-old students' opinions on human-rights principles at the start of the course. Principles were all positively stated (e.g., "Everyone must be allowed to leave their country and return to it"), and students were invited to agree or disagree with the statements. Some interesting areas of uncertainty and disagreement were revealed. On the statement, "Everyone must have equal pay for equal work," 21% were in the don't-know category, and 7% disagreed with the statement. On the statement, "No-one must be tortured," 26% were in the don't-know category and 26% disagreed with the statement. And on the statement, "No-one must be arrested without being charged," 19% were in the don't-know category and 15% disagreed.

Cunningham (1986) attempted to identify and rate students' interest in particular human-rights issues by using a number of "true stories." These true stories were about four or five lines long and recounted the essentials of some human-rights situations and incidents. Students were invited to tick agreement boxes—ranging from very interested to very uninterested. (Cunningham was also trying to collect data on which to base his understanding of students' interest rather than, as some teachers are wont to do, to assume it. He was also challenging the simplistic position of some social studies teachers—start with the local and the familiar—and the obverse simplistic position of some other social studies teachers—start with the distant and the exotic.) Cunningham found that the students showed highest interest in racism in South Africa, mistreatment in Northern Ireland, racism in Brixton, London, and arbitrary arrest in the USSR. Low-interest stories included some human-rights issues in the school itself.

Cunningham's findings concerning the possibilities and the problems of human-rights courses sometimes echoed those of Dyson, particularly where problems are concerned. Cunningham wrote:

Interviews with those teachers who had been responsible for writing the course ... gave some insights into its deficiencies and successes. The areas touching on torture and personal rights were seen to be very successful, generating discussion, controversy and motivation. Racism was also successful in these terms, but a number of staff were very uneasy about the forces unleashed by open discussion. Some retreated into an attempt to teach attitudes.... A section on culture and religions was seen to be a failure.... A more general criticism was that students felt themselves bombarded with values and problems. Some actually felt guilty at their powerlessness to affect a situation like apartheid in South Africa and had a sense that they were being taught about it "in order to feel responsible for it." Most definitely the course failed to communicate to students the main point that you need to understand your rights and responsibilities in order to appreciate what you can and cannot be held responsible for in a global context. This is a common criticism of this type of course—that far too much time is spent on

problems, without giving students the chance to think what they would *like* to happen in the future. (p. 159)

MULTICULTURAL EDUCATION

At the end of the 20th century, Britain is a multicultural and multifaith society in search of a pluralist approach to civic education that might achieve social coherence and accommodate diversity. Multicultural education has developed in order to promote multicultural awareness among students. It rarely leads to curriculum courses, as such, but multicultural dimensions are contained within school subjects (e.g., history and geography, mathematics and science) and they are stressed in new initiatives, such as teaching about human rights. The literature of multicultural education is largely based on political theory (such as the political theory of multicultural societies, pluralism, and the search for common frameworks), sociology (studies of ethnic cultures), and curriculum theory (the multicultural curriculum). The major official report, *Education for All* (Swann, 1975), affirmed the claims of all future citizens to access to quality education *as an entitlement* and viewed multicultural understanding as an element of modern citizenship:

Pupils from all backgrounds will one day be voting, decision-making citizens whose views will influence public policies which affect people of all cultural backgrounds. All will contribute to the values of society. It is therefore important that all are made aware of the multicultural nature of British society today, and are encouraged in the attitudes of mutual knowledge, understanding and tolerance which alone can make such a multicultural society a successful one. (p. 319)

The report recommended the kind of political-literacy education pioneered by the national Programme for Political Education, and supported the ideal of

the politically literate person [who] is not merely an informed spectator [but who is also] someone capable of active participation ... [and who] while tolerating the views of others, is capable of thinking in terms of change and of methods of achieving change. (p. 335)

However, although there now exists a plethora of policy guidelines, particularly at the local-education-authority level, there is a dearth of applied case-study research, based on observed practices in schools that have made formal policy commitments to practicing multicultural education.

RESEARCH ON ENVIRONMENTAL EDUCATION

The most recent of the new educations is environmental education of the ecological variety (what the Germans call *Ökopädagogik*, Beer, 1984). Through it global educators seek to promote environmental awareness and some global dimensions to the responsibilities of the modern citizen. Of all the new educations it is the one most in vogue at the present time. Environmental issues are now on the national political agenda and all of the major political parties now include "green" elements in their policy statements. However, within the social studies in schools, environmental education is essentially in a practical development stage. The Global Impact Project, for example, has produced theoretical writings and teaching materials and exercises, and has run workshops for teachers. Its publications, to date, include *Earthrights: Education as if the Planet Really Mattered* (Greig, Pike, & Selby, 1987) and *Greenprints for Changing Schools* (Greig, Pike, & Selby, 1988).

The project (which is based at the Centre for Global Education at the University of York) does collect opinions from teachers and learners. For example, in a survey of teacher opinion on issues related to global and environmental education, over 800 teachers responded to a questionnaire. Sixty-nine percent of respondents thought that environmental and development education were relevant to their subject area. Seventy-eight percent thought that development and environmental education were central to achieving an understanding of, and active participation in, the world today. Sixty-seven percent thought that the political aspects of environmental and development education were *not* too controversial to be dealt with in the classroom. And 75% thought that developing an understanding that the world is an interrelated, interdependent system of lands and peoples was very important in the promotion of a global perspective in education. At first sight, these are impressive responses from a large sample ($N = 803$). However, the response rate was only 18.9%.

CONCLUSIONS AND PREDICTIONS

In this chapter, I have tried to recount the recent history of social studies and citizenship education in England. Unlike in the United States, both social studies and citizenship education are highly contested categories—the first, mainly because some claim that social studies are inferior as knowledge systems to conventional subjects like history and geography; and the second, because there is a traditional cry that "politics should be kept out of schools." In the social studies in England, we have seen the growth of new educations, pioneered by vanguard educators, promoting new perspectives (including multicultural, environmental, and global perspectives) in the school curriculum.

There has also been during this period a predominance of development over research. Central government funding has been invested in research on education to prepare young people for the economic culture (technical and vocational education projects and economic awareness programs), but not on education to prepare young people for the civic culture. However, in spite of this, some interesting case-study research has been carried out on some pilot projects— in areas like development education, peace studies, and teaching about human rights—and some of the findings of that research can inform the planning of new programs of civic education.

In England, we are living in a time of major challenges and change in education. The 1988 Education Act has established by law a National Curriculum. We have come a long way since the time when, in 1951, the Minister of Education said that the school curriculum had nothing to do with him. There are calls from some quarters for the teaching of "our heritage"—although we do not, as yet, have a Heritage Foundation. There are calls for the teaching of *English* English, and there are calls for the teaching of British history. The National Curriculum Working Party on the History Curriculum has been told by the Prime Minister, no less, to include more British history in its program. A debate is in progress about what British history might be. It has usually been *English* history. It has usually been the Whig interpretation of history, which celebrated parliamentary government—where freedom broadened (peacefully) from precedent to precedent—as *man*kind's supreme achievement. It may be this kind of collective myth (history as ideology and not as contested and critical accounts of the past) that central governments now seek to promote.

It is not surprising that all of this is happening at a time when there is a fundamental uncertainty about what it is, in the late 20th century, "to be *British*." A *National* Curriculum is produced at a time when it is not clear what the nation is, or which nation it is intended for. The elite private schools, like Eton and Harrow, are excluded from its requirements, and thus, skeptics may argue that Britain is still, in Disraeli's phrase, two nations and that the National Curriculum has been designed by the adults of one nation for the children of the other.

The National Curriculum also has its paradoxical element. The head of the National Curriculum Council is a Scot. He negotiates with the Welsh on how such controversial episodes as how the reign of Edward I should be treated in the curriculum. In parts of London the National Curriculum is taught by teachers from Denmark, Holland, and West Germany to children from Bangladesh.

While the National Curriculum affirms and confirms the primacy and superior status of English, mathematics, and science, and is in the dominant academic curriculum tradition, the schools are nevertheless being asked to educate for nationhood and citizenship. History and geography may have been chosen (and sociology and politics excluded), but both the History and Geography Working Parties have accepted citizenship commitments. The chairman of the Geography Working Group, Sir Leslie Fielding, has said: "It is essential for our survival that children are educated to make them fit citizens of the world" (*quoted in* Waterhouse, 1989, p. 6).

Citizenship is an important cross-curricular theme now being developed by a working party of the National Curriculum Council. The Minister Douglas Hurd is promoting a concept of "active citizenship" (which seems to be voluntary social work by young people) to take the politics out of citizenship, and if not to take the welfare out of politics, at least to reduce the welfare obligations of governments. Prince Charles has a trust that sponsors citizenship initiatives. There is a Speakers' Commission on Citizenship on which the wise and the good (nearly all White, middle-class, middle-aged, and male) devise paper programs. And a citizenship foundation has just been established, its early initiatives arising from law-related education.

In reflecting on the recent history of the social studies in England, as I have recounted it, I am struck by three controversial questions that run through the story as recurring themes:

1. How is social knowledge organized and presented in the schools (and how might it best be presented)?
2. How might all citizens be guaranteed access to socially useful and powerful knowledge (an entitlement curriculum)?
3. What might be the nature, the rights, and responsibilities of modern citizenship (i.e., citizenship appropriate to postin-

dustrial, multicultural, pluralistic society in an interdependent world)?

It is on the last of these questions—the nature of modern citizenship—that much research will be focused during the next 10 years.

References

Allen, G., & Lister, I. (1977). *Report of the Political Education Research Unit on the Programme for Political Education*. York: University of York.

Bartholemew, J. C. (1972). *The teacher as a researcher: A key to innovation and change*. York: University of York.

Batchelor, A. (1984). *Speaking out*. Centre for Global Education. York: University of York.

Beer, W. (1984). *Ökopädagogik*. Weinheim: Beltz.

Brennan, T. (1981). *Education and democracy*. Cambridge: Cambridge University Press.

Cox, C., & Scruton, R. (1984). *Peace Studies: A critical survey*. London: Institute for European Defence and Strategic Studies.

Crick, B. (1964). *In defence of politics*. London: Penguin Books.

Crick, B., & Lister, I. (1975). *Political literacy: The centrality of the concept*. York: University of York.

Cunningham, J. (1986). *Human rights in a secondary school*. York: University of York.

Department of Education and Science. (1988a). *Current projects supported by the DES*. London: Author.

Department of Education and Science. (1988b). *The National Curriculum, 5–16*. London: Author.

Duczek, S. (1984). *The Peace Studies Project: A case study*. York: University of York.

Dyson, J. (1986). *Development education for the 14-16 age group: An exploratory study of theory and practice*. York: University of York.

Galtung, J. (1975) *Strukturelle Gewalt*. Hamburg: Rowohlt.

Grainger, N. (1986). *The possibilities and problems of infusing human rights into law in courses in a polytechnic*. York: University of York.

Green, K. (1986). *Peace education in the UK*. Bradford: University of Bradford.

Greig, S., Pike, G., & Selby, D. (1987). *Earthrights: Education as if the planet really mattered*. London: WWF/Kogan Page.

Greig, S., Pike, G. & Selby, D. (1989). *Greenprints for changing schools*. London: WWF/Kogan Page.

Heater, D. (1984). *Concepts for human rights*. Strasbourg: Council of Europe.

Hicks, D (Ed). (1988). *Education for Peace*. London: Routledge.

Johnston, G. (1987). *Political education: Citizenship versus scholarship?* York: University of York.

Lister, I. (1984). *Teaching and learning about human rights*. Strasbourg: Council of Europe.

Lister, I. (1987). Global and international approaches in political education. In C. Harber (Ed.). *Political education in England* (pp. 47–62). Lewes: Falmer Press.

Marks, J. (1984). *Peace Studies in our schools: Propaganda for defencelessness*. London: Women and Families for Defence.

National Federation for Educational Research. (1989). *Current projects*. Slough, England: Author.

Parker, A (1988). *Towards an inner dimension of teaching and learning: Inner awareness in the classroom*. York: University of York.

Selby, D., & Pike, G. (1988). *Human Rights: An activity file*. London: Mary Glasgow.

Shemilt, D. (1980). *History 13–16: Evaluation study*. London: Holmes McDougall.

Smoker, P. & Rathenow, H-F. (1983). *Peace education in Great Britain*. Munster: Englisch-Amerikanische Studien.

Spurgeon, C. (1986). *A quotational bibliography of human rights*. York: University of York.

Stradling, R. (1977). *The political awareness of the school leaver*. London: Hansard Society.

Stradling, R., & Bennett, E. (1981). *Political education in West Germany*. London: Curriculum Review Unit.

Stradling, R., & Noctor, M. (1981). *The provision of political education in schools: A national survey*. London: Curriculum Review Unit.

Stradling, R., Noctor, M., & Baines, B. (1984). *Teaching controversial issues*. London: Arnold.

Swann, M. (1985). *Education for all*. London: HMSO.

Waterhouse, R. (1989, November 21). Geography lessons should be greener. *The Independent* (No. 972), p. 6.

·52·

RESEARCH ON SOCIAL STUDIES IN EASTERN EUROPE

Péter Szebenyi

NATIONAL INSTITUTE OF EDUCATION, BUDAPEST, HUNGARY

First of all, the title of this chapter requires discussion. What do *Eastern Europe* and *social studies* mean? In relation to the first, Western readers have become used to thinking of socialist countries when they read about Eastern Europe. The term appears in this sense in the title of the chapter. However, the usage can be criticized, with good reason, from the scientific point of view. Geographically, Germany, Czechoslovakia, and Hungary are not eastern, but central, European countries, and, historically, a 1,000-year history connects these countries more to Western than to Eastern Europe.

The other question is, what is meant by *social studies* in this chapter? In the wider sense of that term, any gathering of information about society is called social studies. But in a narrower sense, the teaching and learning of social studies imply educational activities within the school system. It is evident that young people gather information about society from a variety of sources: from national and foreign mass media, from family and friends, and from youth organizations. In many countries the influence of the church and of nonofficial political groups is also significant. Nevertheless, the term is used here in the narrower sense of the word to mean the study of history, social science, and other society-related topics.

THE STATUS OF SOCIAL STUDIES IN EASTERN EUROPE

The most important social studies subject in the Eastern European countries is history, that is, a "knowledge of the past."

"Knowledge of the present" is taught in relatively few lessons under different names, such as civics, economics, social studies, sociology, law, and "the morality and psychology of family life."

Because social studies subjects play an important role in political socialization in these countries, their share in the general education curricula always has been, and still is, important (see Table 52.1). Because students in these countries indicated in the statistics generally have 7,700 lessons during their school career from Grade 1 to Grade 8, and 8% of the lessons are devoted to social studies, these figures illustrate the power of social studies education in Eastern Europe.

Some Common Features

1. In European socialist countries all subjects, including social studies, are taught in accordance with centrally prepared and introduced, unified curricula and textbooks—which, to satisfy state policy, promote the existing social system. Recent curricula distinguish between compulsory and optional material, and there are countries where school personnel are allowed to determine curricula for the optional subjects (e.g., in Estonia and Hungary).
2. Marxism is the theoretical foundation of the social studies curricula. Undoubtedly, there are significant differences in the interpretations of Marxism. But all curricula start from the fundamentals of Marxism, both its structure and interpretation and, thus, describe society as a contradictory but progressive process in which law-like tendencies are dominant.
3. The Marxist conception par excellence favors history, be-

Reviewers were Vratislav Čapek, Charles University, Czechoslovakia; Mary Hepburn, University of Georgia; Czeslaw Majorek, Higher Pedagogical School, Kraków, Poland.
Editor's Note: Work on this chapter was completed prior to the dramatic political developments in Eastern European nations in late 1989 and 1990. It should be read in that context as important background for the changes in social studies education and research likely to occur in those nations.

TABLE 52–1. Percentages of Curricula Devoted to Different Subject Areas

Country	Language and Literature	Aesthetics	Mathematics	Social Studies	Science	Foreign Language	Technics	Physical Education
Bulgaria	26	10	19	8	12	9	8	8
Croatia	22	13	20	9	15	7	4	10
Czechoslovakia	27	9	19	9	15	6	6	9
German Democratic Republic	31	7	19	5	11	7	12	8
Hungary	26	13	18	7	13	6	6	11
Poland	28	9	21	8	14	5	7	8
Rumania	26	11	19	8	13	8	7	8
Serbia	21	11	21	8	11	6	10	12
Soviet Union	30	6	22	7	14	6	8	7
Mean	26	10	20	8	13	7	8	9

Note. The data in this table came from national reports on The Development of Education, 1984–1986, presented to the 40th International Conference on Education, sponsored by the International Bureau of Education, United Nations Educational, Scientific, and Cultural Organization (UNESCO), Geneva, Switzerland, December 2–11, 1986.

cause history is the most useful subject to show the long-course processes of human society.

4. The majority of the nonhistorical social studies subjects, instead of objectively examining the present and introducing the conceptions of different scientific schools, are efforts to justify the Marxist interpretation dominant in a given country and to verify the everyday politics. Recently, there have been some changes in this practice. Sociology, which was prohibited in the Stalinist era, has been revived in the East European countries. Also, there is ongoing economic research and the field of political science has been established. In those countries where these developments are the most conspicuous (Poland, Hungary, and Yugoslavia), their effects can also be seen in the school curriculum.

5. So far as teaching methods are concerned, there is a general persistence of traditional methods in the East European countries. That it is not only because of the strong roots of Herbartism, but also because of the steady efforts of Soviet educators to strengthen the position of educational conservatism. In the Soviet Union, which was an important "social laboratory" of progressive education in the 1920s and where Dewey was honored as the "Darwin of pedagogy," the Stalinist leadership prohibited all sorts of reform pedagogy from the mid-1930s on. After World War II, dogmatic, uniform, educational theory also exerted a strong influence on other Eastern European countries.

The Different Features

The different features of social studies in Eastern European countries can be viewed from several aspects: (a) time, (b) different countries, and (c) political-educational trends.

Differences Over Time. The common features mentioned above have manifested themselves in different ways and intensities since World War II. The late 1940s and early 1950s were characterized by dogmatic Marxism, with the content of curricula selectively chosen to support political objectives. Alternative analyses and differing opinions were missing from both textbooks and teaching practice. Popular teaching techniques were *actualization,* that is, comparing historical phenomena ahistorically with the present; *trans-politicizing,* that is, criticizing the capitalist world and praising the socialist countries; and the *cult of personality,* not only the glorification of Stalin and the party leaders but also unceasing citations *(citatology)* from their works.

After Stalin's death in 1953, and especially after the 20th Congress of the Communist Party of the Soviet Union in 1956, changes were experienced in education as a direct result of the political thawing. The popular movements in Eastern Europe had staggering effects on social studies teachers. Under such circumstances, official criticisms of simplification *(vulgarism)* and actualization became quite natural. But changes in teaching material and style occurred slowly. Reaction against the earlier simplification and cautious disbelief in radical political changes equally strengthened the position of *facticism.* Textbook writers and social studies teachers sought refuge behind facts and tried to delineate unbiased, true pictures of historical and economic-geographical phenomena through providing only data. Facticism reinforced older teaching styles. The children's duty was to learn and recite data. The teacher's task was to render the material.

New developments occurred during the mid-1960s. Experts in educational theory, among them those who dealt with the methodology of social studies, expressed their dissatisfaction with the heavy emphasis on facts in the teaching material and with children's passivity in classrooms. They wished to adjust the teaching material and teaching methods to the students' level of development, and they assumed a point of view in favor of student activities and problem-solving methods. From the 1970s on, these changes in educational theory were reacted to in different ways in almost every socialist country.

Differences Among Countries. Some examples will illustrate the different national reactions to the reforms of the 1960s. In the Soviet Union, for example, by the early 1970s (1972–1973) an attack had been launched against problem-solving methods, on the ground that their use failed to affect students' emotions, so that their education was defective in respect to patriotic loyalty to socialism. Although the representatives of the progressive wing dominated the open debate, they were ignored in practice; citations and political slogans became numerous in periodicals and books again, and the "fight against bourgeois ideology" came to the fore anew. But those who adhered to a more open-minded way of thinking continued their work and had an audience of most enlightened teachers. Gorbachëv's *perestroika* and *glasnost* naturally have strengthened their positions.

Poland and Hungary took a different course in the 1970s and 1980s. In spite of various internal political changes, the dogmatic forces in the methodology of social studies could not regain their earlier positions.

Yugoslavia is another case. Because that country broke off all relations with the Stalinist leadership in 1948, educators could maintain contacts with Western educational movements more easily.

Rumania represents another model. Here, the personality cult has become stronger. Social studies has been forced to serve the aim of this policy.

Political-educational Trends. Not only did different educational trends develop in different countries, but also groups supporting the different approaches gradually formed in the international scene. One of the most important opportunities for group formation was in the history teaching symposia that the socialist countries organized every 2 and, later, 3 years.

There were 11 such symposia between 1965 and 1988. The first was held in East Berlin, with experts from Bulgaria, Czechoslovakia, Yugoslavia, Poland, and Hungary participating. Some conflicts appeared. The head of the Czech delegation, for instance, criticized some papers for their "vulgarism."

At the second symposium, held in Czechoslovakia, different trends began to become clear. It was symptomatic that during the third symposium (in Hungary), two basic topics got sharply isolated. "Patriotic and internationalist education in history teaching" was the title of the first topic, with presentations that were full of political slogans. The other topic was "professional," and it included reports on analyzing the importance of the role of audio-visual aids. The papers delivered on the second topic were usually based on research.

During the fourth symposium, held in Bulgaria in 1971, the group interested in the professional topic succeeded in dividing the next symposium (to be held in the USSR) into three sections. From that time on, ideology dominated the plenary meetings and one of the sections; higher education experts who were interested in the relation between history and history teaching, teacher training, and further education, met in another section; and the "methodological wing," interested in the development of teaching instruments and methods, attended the meetings of the third section. This structure held for the sixth symposium, in Poland, the seventh, in Czechoslovakia, and the eighth, in the German Democratic Republic (East Germany). Members of the different groups often invited each other to conferences organized in their own countries and pub-lished articles jointly. There was, at the same time, little cooperation between members of the different groups.

The last three symposia (Bulgaria, 1981; Hungary, 1984; and Estonia, 1987) represented a new phase. There were debates not only over problems of methodology but also over content and ideological questions. Moreover, the debates over methodology (e.g., possibilities for local curricula, need for differentiation of teaching materials, pluralism in the evaluation of historical phenomena) had ideological aspects. However, the existence of different scientific schools in the countries meant that there were conceptual and political differences on professional issues. An advisory council, called Social Science Education in Schools of Socialist Countries, was established in 1986. Its work has been characterized by rivalry between the diverse groups but also by efforts to compromise. (The member countries in 1989 were Bulgaria, Czechoslovakia, Cuba, the German Democratic Republic, Hungary, the Soviet Union, Poland, and Vietnam).

THE MOST IMPORTANT RESEARCH IN SOCIAL STUDIES: TEACHING AND LEARNING AND THE RESULTS

It is not easy to give a comprehensive picture of the research on social studies teaching and learning because such a topic requires treatment of several subjects, countries, and periods. In addition, educational research is conducted not only at the universities and colleges but also in national and local (county) institutes. For instance, in the Soviet Union alone, the number of researchers in the field of education in the early 1980s was between 20,000 and 30,000. In every Eastern European country, each social science subject has a periodical, usually published every two months. The more significant research results are published in book form, too. So it is difficult to select from this varied material and even more difficult to describe the varied research methods.

It is significant that remarkable empirical research in education began in Eastern Europe in the 1960s, with pertinent reference books appearing then (Itelson, 1964; Schmidt, 1961). (Itelson's book was not published in Hungary and Rumania until 1967 or in Yugoslavia until 1969.) Since then, many books introducing the methodology of mathematical statistics have been published, and the number of empirical research reports in the social sciences has increased. In the late 1960s, Hungary and Poland joined the International Association for the Evaluation of Educational Achievement (IEA) and participated in several studies.

In the second half of the 1980s, as a result of perestroika, there was growing emphasis on "objective methods." In 1987, the Russian Miheev wrote that "without applying mathematical methods in education, it cannot be developed as a science anymore. We need statistical analysis and the modelling of diverse educational, psychological and didactical situations. And it cannot be done without the extensive use of computers" (p. 189). Nevertheless, the study of social science subjects continues to be characterized by theoretical and historical–comparative methods, rather than by quantitative methods, as indicated by the themes of different studies. The most important research is described next.

Issues of Teleology and Epistemology

The study of educational aims, as a result of the Herbartian heritage, has long had an important position in Eastern Europe. The Marxist attitude, following the German classical philosophy, made this role even stronger. But the representatives of diverse educational and political trends, in different times and places, treated the question of aims in different ways and on different levels.

From early the 1940s to the late 1950s, the dominant aim was to serve the everyday policies of the Communist Party. At the beginning, from the early 1930s onward, it could not have been otherwise, because Stalin and his leadership group directly and explicitly interfered in social studies education. Consequently, in-depth analyses of the aims and content of history teaching began to be published in Eastern European countries only in the early 1960s. One of them was the work of A. Bornholtzowa and W. Moszczénska (1964) entitled *History Teaching at School and the Science of History*. In this book appeared the approach that has characterized the best schools of historical methodology ever since: the effort to treat the aspects of epistemology, historiography, and educational psychology together.

The essence of this conception was that cognitive process passes from the concrete to the abstract and from the abstract to the concrete. So, in history teaching, students should pass from the concrete (facts) to the abstract (concepts, connections, law-like generalizations) through the analysis of facts, and then they should apply these generalizations to the analysis of further facts. However, historical facts (the events of the past) cannot be directly observed, so the study of history is a difficult job that requires developed abstract thinking on the part of the student. Teaching can have positive results only if based on the principle of "less but thoroughly" *(non multa multum)*. Learning can be achieved if children are provided with the "totality" of the facts within the framework of pedagogically selected topics, thus grounding the students in historical thinking and teaching them the use of scientific methods in acquiring knowledge.

The question of what to choose was naturally born of the need for content selection. Researchers' answer to this question from the 1960s onward usually was that we do not primarily teach political history topics to serve current political aims (revolutions, wars, movements of independence, workers' movements), but that we should emphasize the history of culture, intellectual history, and ways of life (Balázs, 1970; Balcar, 1965; Cerović, 1972; Petrykowska, 1963; Szabolcs, 1972; Veress, 1968).

In the Soviet Union, the revision of the ossified system of educational aims did not begin with the theoretical examination of objectives. Rather, some experts in educational psychology first pointed out the untenability of dogmatic history teaching by analyzing children's poor knowledge of historical concepts through empirical studies (Redyko, 1961).

Problems of the theory of aims played a less important role in the methodology of other social studies subjects in the 1960s. That was so because these subjects followed the directives of Stalin's *Short History of the Party,* Chapter IV, "Dialectical and Historical Materialism," with some up-to-date politics. There was nothing to study about aims because of the direct dependency on politics.

Owing to its relative independence from politics, geography teaching did not have to face a "crisis of aims." Therefore, the researchers of methodology were less interested in aims than were their colleagues in history teaching. The situation changed only in the 1970s when the theory of objectives entered the period of taxonomies.

This switchover took place in relation to the development of new curricula in the majority of the countries. In Bulgaria, for instance, experts tried to project a system of objectives to be applied in geography teaching during school reform in the mid-1970s. The purpose was to establish optimal relations between (a) students' productive and reproductive activities, (b) education inside and outside the school, and (c) acquisition of knowledge and development of abilities and skills (Vekilska, Lazarev, & Nedelcheva, 1975). At that time, even in the Soviet Union the explanation of subject objectives and tasks was considered to be the most important research work on the methodology of geography teaching (Darinsky, 1975).

In the Soviet Union, a special branch of taxonomical research evolved at the end of the 1960s: the planning and experimental testing of so-called "cognitive exercises." The experiments were implemented in the field of humanities (history, economic geography, language, and literature) under the direction of I. J. Lerner (1972). The exercises were classified into two typical dimensions: on the one hand, according to their inherent problem and, on the other, according to the methods necessary for the solution of the problem. Taking this double typology into consideration, the researchers framed several hundred concrete exercises and tested them with a sample of students.

The analysis of the concept system to be studied by students was the other direction taken by the taxonomical researchers. In this field, the Rumanian experts on methodology, C. Dinu and R. S. Bărbuleanu (1979), played a leading role. Their research had two stages: a fact-finding phase and an experimental one. *First,* they gathered the historical concepts taught in Grades 5–7; *second,* they tried to determine their applicability in practice. As a result of their efforts, an extremely detailed but coherent network of concepts was set up, providing a system of objectives that covered all the concepts to be taught.

The Czech and Hungarian experts relied not only upon research going on in the socialist countries, but also upon Western, taxonomies, especially Bloom's (1956). The direct evidence of the results include, in Hungary, new objectives of geography (Köves & Magirius, 1973) and, in Czechoslovakia, elaboration of a taxonomical system for history teaching work by a team under the direction of V. Čapek (Čapek, Pátek, Faktorová, Michovsky, & Vlčková, 1974).

The taxonomical approach had an invigorating effect on methodological research. The earlier, very narrow, scope of objectives, which involved mainly political socialization, was widened. Taxonomical research has also contributed to the development of empirical studies as a result of the operationalization of general aims as concrete objectives.

The mid-1970s not only saw the development of taxonomical research but also—for example, in the USSR—renewed counterattacks by the "ideological wing" against the "methodological wing." The return of the theory of aims to "ideologism" was only one of the tendencies, and it was not characteristic of every Eastern European country either. In certain countries events took other directions. For example, in Hungary and Poland, a fundamental reassessment of the system of aims, which went beyond taxonomical research, began in the early 1980s in the spirit of "pluralism" (Mátrai, 1982).

History of Teaching and Comparative Studies

Inquiries into the history of teaching began in the period of the Khrushcevian "thaw" in the Soviet Union. L. P. Bushchik (1961) surveyed the history of history teaching from 1917 onward. A. G. Koloskov (1984) did the same in his dissertation more than two decades later, making use of ample archivalia. At the same time, Polish experts went back to the beginning of systematic history teaching in their works based on careful source criticism. L. Mokrzecki (1973) described history teaching in the 17th century through the example of a grammar school in Gdansk. T. Slowikowski (1960) and K. Augustynek (1962) inquired into the history of the subject in the 18th and 19th centuries. J. Maternicki's works (1974, 1978) covered the whole period between 1773 and 1939. In his book, Majorek (1989) traced history teaching in Galicia in the period 1772–1918. Researchers in Hungary have so far examined only particular periods or aspects of history teaching. They have worked out in detail the first half of the 19th and 20th centuries (to 1945) on the evidence of contemporary textbooks (Biró, 1960; Unger, 1976). And they have studied the historical process of the development of objectives, methods, and means from the 17th century until the 1960s (Szebenyi, 1970). In Czechoslovakia, studies have been published on the history of Slovak history teaching (Brťkova, 1971, 1973) and the beginning of the Czech methodological work (Šlik, 1973).

Special attention must be paid to V. Čapek's works (1973, 1976) surveying main trends of the development of history teaching in Europe. Similar inquiries of more or less importance into the history of the subject have been made not only by historians but also by experts in other social studies subjects and in other countries, too (Darinsky, 1955; Udvarhelyi & Göcsei, 1973).

The subject of *comparative studies* initially has not been comparison par excellence but, rather, the study of each other's results and examinations. This meant the translation of Soviet methodological works (Karcov, 1951; Karzow, 1954). The publication of international thematic works and, later, reports on common research were steps forward (Wermes & Gora, 1977). Publications of the material of international conferences also offered possibilities for comparison (Sýkora, 1986).

From the 1970s, comparative studies have served the development of a more open and more differentiated methodology of social studies, including useful foreign experiences, not necessarily only those of Eastern Europe.

The Study of Students' Knowledge

In the Eastern European socialist countries, researchers concentrated their attention first on the examination of students' concepts among other elements of social knowledge. The reasons for this were twofold: On the one hand, Marxist educators attribute great importance to the elaboration of social science concepts. On the other hand, as a consequence of the dogmatic and, thus, too abstract character of the teaching material, grave difficulties arose in establishing clear and meaningful student concepts through educational practice. It was the Soviet researchers who pointed out the shortcomings of history and geography teaching in this respect (Kabanova-Meller, 1950; Redyko, 1950). Assessment of concepts was also started in other socialist countries in the 1960s. Piaget's and Vygotsky's basic works (translated at that time) had considerable effect on the researchers, and their methods were influenced by contemporary research methods and mathematical statistical procedures from applied social psychology.

Following are some characteristic examples of research from the late 1960s and early 1970s. Hunyady (1968) tested 800 children. The study was aimed at discovering the evolution of three concepts—social development, social class, and nation—in the students' thinking between the ages of 10 and 18.

Another study, conducted by G. Eperjessy and P. Szebenyi (1976), involved a wider circle of learners. Their national representative sample included 7,710 Hungarian students from Grades 5, 8, and 12 and a series of experiments in 10 classes. Each student was asked to write an essay on an historical topic. The responses were coded for conceptual level. To clarify the meaning of the quantitative scores, students were also interviewed.

Unlike Eperjessy and Szebenyi, S. Milanović-Nahod (1973) involved only 185 eighth-grade children from six schools. Nevertheless, her study of concepts yielded some interesting findings. She found, using mathematical-statistical methods, that there were important differences in the students' active and passive geographical, historical, and linguistic concepts; that the students' functional levels for the three types of concepts were parallel; and that verbalization did not always imply the successful application of the concept.

Besides examining students' concepts, researchers in the European socialist countries began wide-ranging studies of students' knowledge. In certain countries, testing flooded the schools. Under such circumstances, it was an important duty of researchers to work out highly standardized tests and variable series of test items and test batteries. To do that, principles of test–making had to be established. A team of Czech experts (Michovský, Faktorová, Čapek, & Pátek, 1977), for instance, classified tests in view of whether they measured knowledge, orientation in time and space, ability to gather information, or historical thinking. Hungarian experts (Báthori, Helméczy, & Somogyvári, 1972) invited teachers to categorize items according to whether they examined knowledge of (a) economy and technology, (b) society and politics, (c) culture, (d) chronology, or (e) topography; and whether they required of students (a) recall, (b) grouping and systematizing, (c) comparison, (d) generalization, (e) judgment, or (f) verification.

Examinations in political socialization meant a new phase in the research on students' historical-social knowledge. The task was no less than to find out how society influences children, including the effects of social studies education. The research on political socialization threw light on a profound but, until then, hidden problem of social education. The results of the Hungarian examinations indicated that schools educate children for political passivity and conformism instead of for active political participation, the declared aim of education (Kéri, 1985). In the background lurk young people's "double consciousness" and "double system of values."

A concrete example might illustrate the problem. Researchers in 1982 (Szabó & Csepeli, 1984) asked children ages 10–14 which country they thought was the "happiest." One of the socialist countries was chosen by 67% of the children. But when the question was put, "Where would you live for a year if you could choose?" 78% of them mentioned one of the capitalist countries.

Clearly, the "official" values of the school and the values that students internalize outside of the school exist in parallel, and few conflicts arise even if these values contradict one another. This duality does not cause conflicts but political passivity and conformism. Similar investigations into young people's attitudes have been conducted in Poland, too (Gerula, 1985; Kociecka, 1988), by the Youth Research Institute (established in 1972) in the Ministry of Education and Instruction.

Experiments in the Field of Teaching Aids, Methods, and Organizational Forms

Socialist educators did not refrain from treating questions of methodology in the narrower sense in either the 1930s or 1940s; on the contrary, the reform pedagogy of the 1920s was criticized because it was not "methodological" enough. (It is characteristic that different subject methodological periodicals were first published in the Soviet Union in 1934.)

Visualization and Visual Aids. The first principle of the official Soviet theory of education was *visualization* (Kairov, 1948). Experts from all socialist countries agreed that, without clear conceptualization, social studies subjects could not be taught successfully. In the teaching of history, however, visualization must be secured through demonstration, because historical phenomena cannot generally be observed directly. This is why "vivid historical demonstration" is so important.

Some experts of history teaching in the German Democratic Republic examined thoroughly the optimal possibilities of the application of traditional visual aids. F. Osburg (1962, 1975) dealt with drawings and blackboard sketches, H. J. Fiala (1967) with maps, and A. Krause (1975) with cartoons.

New technology also exerted considerable influence on social studies education. Educational programs have been broadcast on TV since the 1960s. Independent teams of researchers have investigated the influence of the programs and the possibilities of integrating their material into school life. Even more important was J. Rulka's study (1974) in which he found, using mathematical–statistical methods, that young people aged 10–18 gathered the majority of their socio-political information from television, so that such information must be taken into account in instruction. In the mid-1970s, D. I. Poltorak (1976) published a comprehensive work on the methodology of technical aids to be used in social studies subjects. He wrote about slides, overhead projectors, films, TV programs, radio broadcasts, and tapes, stressing that there was much ongoing research with respect to their applications.

The use of video and computers increased in social studies subjects in the 1980s, too. In 1987, an international conference was held in Esztergom, Hungary, on the applicability of video in education. Both Western and Eastern European experts participated, and they voiced more or less the same worries as had been expressed earlier in connection with films and TV. After the experts viewed diverse video-films, a sharp debate evolved on the questions: What is the best application of the video in education? Can videos be used to explain a particular topic like a teacher would do? Can videos be used to help make social-historical phenomena more tangible? Or can video-films be used to direct students' attention to contradictions, thus creating problem situations that would help children learn to treat visual historical sources critically?

There are many uncertainties in relation to the use of computers, too. This was the general impression at two specialists' conferences, one held in Esztergom, Hungary; the other, in Brno, Czechoslovakia. It cannot be denied that computers have become more common in schools. For example, in Hungary there were only 165 computers in schools at different levels of education in 1981, but this figure rose to 13,160 by 1986. It is also evident that computers can and should be used in the teaching of social studies. The first programs, however, were concentrated mainly on the successful acquisition of data, and the possibilities for modeling social alternatives on the basis of substantial social and historical facts have been overlooked so far (Dedinszky & Horányi, 1987).

The requirement of visualization cannot be solely identified with visual and technical instruments. Contemporary social processes can be directly observed in the case of geography and modern social science subjects, and, in the teaching of history, historical evidence and sources play a dominant role. In all of these fields there has been considerable research since the 1960s. In the Soviet Union, for instance, the curriculum of geography introduced in the 1960–1961 school year emphasized that teaching must be based on fieldwork when new concepts are being introduced. This standpoint was shared by experts in geography teaching in other socialist countries, too. Accordingly, a number of publications came out about field trips and student fieldwork.

In respect to the modern social studies subjects, L. N. Bogolubov (1977) studied how newspapers, radio, and TV programs can be integrated into the process of teaching.

On the handling of historical sources, a substantial literature is also available. In Hungary, M. Unger (1958) outlined the possibilities inherent in grammar school history lessons using historical evidence. F. P. Korovkin (Korovkin & Zaporozets, 1970) proved that different historical sources can be successfully used in history lessons in Grades 5 and 6.

Research dealing with visual education and aids became so widespread from the late 1950s on that comprehensive syntheses of previous results appeared from time to time. V. Mejstřik, H. Bartašova, and V. Habětín (1959) published a book on visualization in history teaching. This lengthy work was devoted entirely to showing blackboard sketches, teachers' drawings, and methods of making and using statistical tables, charts, and diagrams. Similar publications have come out.

In contrast, P. V. Gora (1971) worked out a whole system of visual aids and methods for history teaching, distinguishing between means of demonstrating historical phenomena and deeper connections. Suhoński (1987), in a book on methodology of media published in Poland, analyzed methods for use of the following technical aids on a wide experimental basis: tapes, radios, records, slides, episcopes, overhead projectors, films, and videos.

Students' Activity: Problem Solving and Development of Thinking. If visualization was the number one principle of the official Soviet theory of instruction, then *activating* children was the second. This requirement was interpreted in the Stalinist era as meaning that "the profound understanding and firm acquisition of the teaching material can only be achieved through the active students' work under the teacher's direction" (Kairov, 1948, p. 92). However, Party decrees in the 1930s definitely declared that the teacher's explanation is the "proper" teaching method, and students should study from traditional textbooks. Consequently, the principle of student activity was not practiced, but only a requirement: Children should understand what they study and be able to recite textbook readings in their own words. But the students' independence was only appearance; "independent acquisition" meant the acceptance and cramming of *other people's* thoughts from textbooks, the teacher, or obligatory supplementary readings.

A new interpretation of students' activity emerged in the mid-1950s at the beginning of the Khrushcevian era. In this new context, *independence* meant *independent way of thinking*. A student cannot be considered independent if he or she "independently" crams the contents of the textbook at home, but can be if he or she independently solves a problem mentally while listening to the teacher and not saying a word during the whole lesson.

A number of experiments were carried out in this field. The most famous one was by N. G. Dairi (1966), who conducted an extensive and well-documented study of the efficiency of the so-called problem-raising teacher's explanation. The core of this method is that the teacher raises an interesting problem for the children right at the beginning of an explanation, then provides them with ample facts to solve the problem without giving a direct answer to it. Dairi presented the essence and use of this method by analyzing experimental lessons on three topics and related measures of outcomes.

Other researchers, for example, S. E. Levin (1957), focused on students' debates, directed by the teacher's appropriate questions. P. V. Gora (1971) examined the possibilities of students' independent problem solving on the basis of many-sided demonstrations. The most positive results were achieved by A. I. Nazarets (1974), who, in three schools in Moscow, studied whether students' creative work could be developed through a problem-solving method based on analysis of primary historical sources.

Similar developments took place in other Eastern European countries, starting with experiments on problem-solving meth-ods and going on to the elaboration of systems of exercises. In Poland, C. Szybka (1957) described primarily how students should work independently with textbooks, supplementary readings, maps, illustrations, and local history resources. In a book that attracted much attention, A. Bornholtzowa and J. Cent-kowski (1969) stressed unambiguously the importance of problem-solving history teaching. They analyzed the meaning of *problem* and the differences among historical problems, educational problems, and problem situations, and described the theoretical and practical aspects of problem solving.

A few years later, J. Růžičková (1974) gave an account of her similar experimental results, and the Bulgarian, M. Radeva (1975), also published a study on this issue. A book edited by P. Szebenyi (1975) gave a comprehensive view of such efforts in Eastern European countries.

Students' activity and problem-solving education are closely bound up with the problems of the *development of thinking*. As in the previous case, here there are also several approaches and research programs. One approach is to emphasize primarily the content of thinking, that is, the teaching material. How teaching material should be arranged to develop children's thinking is the focus of the research. This point of view was first expounded in scientific depth by the representatives of the so-called "Potsdam School" (B. Gentner, D. Behrendt, & V. Waade, as presented in Gentner, 1967). According to their opinion, the scientific material of history must be transformed into teaching material, in accordance with "cognitive objectives," in such a way that the logical structure of the material would optimally develop students' historical thinking. More complex teaching material supposes, and concurrently develops, more profound and differentiated thinking. According to Gentner, it is important to distinguish between "knowledge of facts" and "interpretative knowledge." To the latter belong all of the key concepts that ground the analysis of facts, their interpretation, and the drawing of conclusions.

Another approach dealt with the formal aspects of thinking, that is, with the operations of thinking. The most notable representative of this approach in Eastern Europe is the so-called "Leipzig School" (H. Wermes, H. Meltzer, S. Müller, and their colleagues, as discussed in Wermes, 1976). Their conception starts from a distinction between knowledge of facts and ability to think. Consequently, knowledge of facts is not a satisfactory condition for the development of thinking. Students' inner "spiritual activities" must be also developed.

Differentiated Organizational Forms. To realize students' independent work, that is, having students learn by thinking, teachers must have suitable organizational forms. Research in this field also began in the 1960s and 1970s.

Students' independent thinking and their work done either individually or in small groups are closely interrelated. In particular, so-called *frontal instruction,* that is, lessons held for large groups of students in whole classes, the predominant organizational form in the 1950s and 1960s, did not encourage students' independence of thought. In this situation, the teacher explained and the students listened (at least they pretended to be doing so), then studied the lesson and, if they were asked to, recited what they had learned. It was difficult to remove this traditional teaching style in Eastern European countries, because, among other factors, Soviet Party decrees of the 1930s sharply criticized the "brigade-teaching" (project work in small groups) endeavors of the reform pedagogy and voiced the importance of frontal instruction. It is thus understandable that experiments with the individualization of instruction and group work were first started in Yugoslavia. Yugoslavians translated the most important Western works (Lustenberger, 1959; Mory, 1950) and conducted research of their own (Švajcer, 1964).

In the late 1950s, there was already research in group work in Poland. In a work cited before, Szybka (1957) devoted a whole chapter to students' work in small groups. In Hungary, a longitudinal experiment, carried out between 1964 and 1968, using tape recordings and sociometric measurements, showed the conditions under which group work could be successfully applied in Grades 5–8 (Szebenyi, 1969). This organizational form also appeared in the theory and practice of social studies education in other Eastern European countries in the 1970s. In Czechoslovakia, for instance, V. Franko (1973) wrote a book on the organizational forms of history teaching. A comprehensive survey of research was rendered by E. Meyer (1972). The gradual introduction of the system of optional courses in the mid-1960s assisted the spread of differentiated organizational forms of instruction in all European socialist countries.

Research in this field began in the Soviet Union in 1966. In history, for instance, 10 different optional programs were developed and tested in several schools. The most useful experiences were published and the results generalized. G. V. Klokova (1973) concluded that, in the first lessons of an optional course, children should study a particular topic first within the framework of frontal instruction guided by the teacher, then work individually (in the school library, a museum, or archives), write accounts of their findings, and, finally, present the results of their studies in joint discussions and seminars. (It is obvious that in the optional courses, the widespread "project method" of the 1920s was revived.)

Syntheses: Handbooks and Curriculum Development

Handbooks (also applied in teacher training and further education) that synthesized the results of the already described research have appeared from time to time. But in practice, curriculum projects make use of research findings in a complex way.

Handbooks. Handbooks on teaching social science subjects have been prepared in every Eastern European country. These works reflect well the researchers' preferences for different approaches during different periods in different countries. Regarding history teaching, between 1960 and 1986, more than 30 handbooks were published in Eastern Europe. What is there behind this figure? *First,* the changing socio-political needs and the accumulation of research findings necessitated new syntheses. The most influential handbook in the early 1960s (Stohr, 1962) was published in a considerably revised edition in 1968, because, as the author argued in the Preface, "the struggle against dogmatic history teaching required it." *Second,* there

are differences of opinion between those who adopt different approaches and schools of methodology. In Poland, for instance, there were two methodological schools of history teaching: one in Warsaw, the other in Krakow. C. Szybka's work (1966) belongs to the former; T. Slowikowski's book (1967) represented the views of the latter. The methodologies of P. S. Leibengrub (1960), A. A. Vagin (1968), and N. V. Andreevskaya, Popova, Speranskaya, and Shabalina (1970) represented different schools, too (see Vagin, 1972, pp. 2–16).

Another reason for the diversity is that some of these works are special handbooks. M. M. Lisenko's books (1970, 1971), for example, gave assistance for the teaching of Ukrainian history, Korovkin and Zaporozets's work (1970) dealt with the methodology of the teaching of ancient times and the Middle Ages in Grades 5–6, and Vinokurova and Dobrinina (1986) worked out a handbook for teaching economic history.

The number of handbooks was also increased by efforts to develop the "Great Methodology" in several countries since the mid-1970s, with the intent of synthesizing all of the relevant research findings. The first of these efforts was published in the German Democratic Republic (Gentner & Kruppa, 1975) and in Bulgaria (Shopov & Georgiev, 1975), then in the Soviet Union (Korovkin & Dairi, 1978). In Czechoslovakia, *Didactics of History Teaching* (Čapek et al., 1985, 1988) and in Poland, *Methodology of History Teaching in the Basic Schools* (Majorek, 1988) were published. Handbooks appeared, not only for history and geography teaching, but also for other social studies subjects, although their number is not so high.

Curriculum Development. If theoretical syntheses of research findings appear primarily in handbooks, their practical synthesis takes shape in new curricula and the experiments that underlie them. Curriculum makers endeavor to make use of research results in practice in the periodically recurring processes of curriculum development. In the optimal case, experiments precede the implementation of the new curricula. This has become customary (though not exclusively so) in Eastern Europe, and several types of curriculum experiments have evolved. These experiments, along with other factors, have contributed to the current curricula by (a) strengthening the position of skill-based, developing instruction and (b) providing better possibilities for curriculum diversification.

As for the development of skill-based instruction, it is by now widely accepted in Eastern Europe that at the center of a curriculum, there should be some taxonomy of educational objectives that outlines in the different areas of the teaching–learning process (views of time and space, communication, operations of thinking) what levels of skills and abilities the students should achieve. Skill-based instruction is also promoted by a taxonomy of basic concepts and a system of law-like generalizations in the curriculum; possibilities for coordination between different subjects are referred to also. In the methodological parts of the curricula, emphasis is placed on student activities, on methods of problem solving and inquiry, on the individual treatment of students, and on the importance of individual and group work.

In respect to curriculum diversification, there are bigger differences between the curricula of particular countries. In Yugoslavia, for example, each republic and autonomous territory has a curriculum of its own (amounting to eight curricula). In addition, the histories of different ethnic groups are studied. In the Soviet Union, a centralized curriculum is obligatory all through the country. Supplementary study of the history and geography of the individual republics is allowed, however.

Optional courses have also been established as a means of curriculum diversification in all European socialist countries. In certain countries (e.g., Hungary and Bulgaria), the teaching material is divided into compulsory material and additional material for the more gifted children. It is also a sign of diversification that in Hungary teachers are free to decide what to do during one-third of the teaching period. Within this time, they can use local curricula to teach.

CONCLUSION

The current curricula, as discussed, are innovative mainly in educational and methodological respects. Less progress has been achieved in issues of content, though there have been changes there, too. However, few are satisfied with the size and speed of developments. What has happened is too much for the conservatives and too little for the members of the progressive wing. But further research will be conducted to advance the learning of students in social studies. Of course, the recent fundamental changes in the political life of Eastern Europe will no doubt influence deeply the features of social studies and research on social studies there.

References

Andreevskaya, N. V., Popova, A. I., Speranskaya, N. V., & Shabalina, T. S. (1970). *Metodika prepodavania istorii v vosemletney skole (Methodology of history teaching in the eight-grade school)*. Moskva: Prosveshchenie.

Augustynek, K. (1962). Wladislawa Smoleńskiego poglady na nauczanie historii (Wladislaw Smolensky's views on history teaching). *Kwartalnik Historyczno—Oswiatowy, 2*.

Balázs, G. (1970). *Korkép kialakitása a történelemtanitásban (History teaching as a perspective on everyday life)*. Budapest: Akadémiai Kiadó.

Balcar, L. (1965). *Kommunista világnézetre nevelés a történelemtanitásban (Developing a communist world view in history teaching)*. Bratislava: Slovanské Pedagogické Nakladatelstvo.

Báthori, F., Helméczy, M., & Somogyvári, S. (1972). *Történelmi témazáró feladatlapok (Summative history teaching tests)*. Budapest: Tankönyvkiadó.

Biró, S. (1960). *Történelemtanitásunk a XIX. század elsö felében a tankönyvirodalom tükrében (Hungarian history teaching at the first part of the 18th century and the textbooks)*. Budapest: Tankönyvkiadó.

Bloom, B. S. (Ed.). (1956). *Taxonomy of educational objectives. The classification of educational goals: Handbook I. Cognitive domain*. New York: David McKay.

Bogolubov, L. N. (1977). *Izuchenie tekushchih sobitiy v kurse noveyshey istorii (Study in current events in a modern history course)*. Moskva: Prosveshchenie.

Bornholtzowa, A., & Centkowski, J. (1969). *O problemowym nauczaniu historii (Problem solving history teaching)*. Warszawa: Państwowe Zaklady Wydawnictw Szkolnych.

Bornholtzowa, A., & Moszczeńska, W. (1964). *Nauczanie historii w szkole a nauka historyczna (History teaching at school and the science of history)*. Warszawa: Państwowe Zaklady Wydawnictw Szkolnych.

Brtková, M. (1971). Príspevok k dejinám vyučovania dejepisu na Slovensku v rokoch 1848–1875 (Contribution to the history of the history teaching in Slovakia during the years 1848–1875). In Zbornik Pedagogickej fakulty UK v Trnave, *História 3*. Bratislava: Slovenské Pedagogické Nakladatelstvo.

Brtková, M. (1973). Vyučovanie dejepisu na Slovenských školách v rokoch 1875–1918 (History teaching in the Slovak schools during the years 1875–1918). In Universitas Comeniana Facultas Paedagogica Tyrnaviensis. Spoločenske vedy, *Historia 4*. Bratislava: Slovenské Pedagogické Nakladatelstvo.

Bushchik, L. P. (1961). *Ocherk razvitia shkolnovo istoricheskovo obrazovania v SSSR (A sketch of the development of historical school education in the USSR)*. Moskva: Akademia Pedagogicheskih Nauk RSFSR.

Čapek, V. (1973). *Pohledy do počátku dějepisneho vyučování v Evropě (A look at the beginnings of European history teaching)*. Praha: Universita Karlova.

Čapek, V. (1976). *Rozvoj dějepisného vyučovani v buržoasní společnosti (Development of history teaching in bourgeois society)*. Praha: Universita Karlova.

Čapek, V., á kolektiv. (1985, 1988). *Didaktika dějepisu I and II (Didactics of history teaching)*. Praha: Státni pedagogické nakladatelství.

Čapek, V., Pátek, J., Faktorová, L., Michovsky, V., & Vlčková, V. (1974). *Cilové struktury v dějepise a jejich prověřovani ve vyučováni (System of objectives in history and its control in teaching)*. Praha: Universita Karlova.

Cerović, L. (Ed.). (1972). *Prvi jugoslovenski simpozijum o nastavi istorije (First Yugoslav symposium on history teaching)*. Novi Sad: Društvo istoričara Vojvodine.

Dairi, N. G. (1966). *Obuchenie istorii v starshih klassah sredney skoli (History teaching in higher classes of the secondary school)*. Moskva: Prosveshchenie.

Darinsky, A. V. (1955). *Ocherki razvitia shkolnoy geografii v dorevolucionnoy Rossii (Sketch of development of school geography until the Russian revolution)*. Leningrad: Uchpedgiz.

Darinsky, A. V. (1975). *Metodika prepodavanie geografii (Methodology of teaching geography)*. Moskva: Prosveshchenie.

Dedinszky, F., & Horányi, I. (1987). *Számitástechnika a történelemtanitásban. (The computer in history teaching)*. Budapest: Novotrade.

Dinu, C., & Bărbuleanu, R. S. (1979). *Formarea sistemului de notiuni la istorie. (Development of the system of historical concepts)*. Bucuresti: Editura didactică si pedagogică.

Eperjessy, G., & Szebenyi, P. (1976). *A tanulók történelmi fogalmainak fejlödése (Development of historical concepts of learners)*. Budapest: Tankönyvkiadó.

Fiala, H. J. (1967). *Die Karte im Geschichtsunterricht. (Maps in history teaching)*. Berlin: Volk und Wissen Volkseigener Verlag.

Franko, V. (1973). *Organizačne formy dejepisného vyučovania (Organisational forms of history teaching)*. Bratislava: Slovenské Pedagogické Nakladatelstvo.

Gentner, B. (Ed.). (1967). *Aktuelle Probleme der Denk- und Erkenntnisarbeit im Geschichtsunterricht (Current problems of thinking and cognitive activity in history teaching)*. Berlin: Volk und Wissen Volkseigener Verlag.

Gentner, B., & Kruppa, R. (Ed.). (1975). *Methodik Geschichtsunterricht*

(Methodology of history teaching). Berlin: Volk und Wissen Volkseigener Verlag.

Gerula, M. (1985). *Świadomość polityczna i prawna mlodziezy. Na podstawie badan w klasach maturalnych z lat 1977–78 (The political and legal consciousness of youth. Based on research in school-leaving examination classes 1977–78)*. Wroclaw: Polska Akádemia Nauk.

Gora, P. V. (1971). *Metodicheskie priomy i sredstva nagladnovo obuchenia istorii v sredney skole (Visual methods and aids of history teaching in the middle school)*. Moskva: Prosveshchenie.

Hunyady, G. (1968). *A tanulók történelmi alapfogalmainak vizsgálata (Study of the basic historical concepts of learners)*. Budapest: Tankönyvkiadó.

Itelson, L. B. (1964). *Matematicheskie i kiberneticheskie metodi v pedagogike (Mathematical and cybernetical methods in the pedagogy)*. Moskva: Prosveshchenie.

Kabanova-Meller, E. N. (1950). *Psichologicheskiy analiz primenenia geograficheskih poniatiy i zakonomernostey (Psychological analysis using geographic concepts and laws)*. Moskva: Akademia Pedagogicheskih Nauk, RSFSR.

Kairov, I. A. (Ed.). (1948). *Pedagogika.* (Pedagogy). Leningrad: Uchpedgiz.

Karcov, V. G. (1951). *A történelemtanitás módszertana (Methodology of history teaching)*. Budapest: Tankönyvkiadó.

Karzow, W. G. (1954). *Beiträge zur Methodik des Geschichtsunterrichts (Contribution to the methodology of history teaching)*. Berlin: Volk un Wissen Volkseigener Verlag.

Kéri, L. (1985). Ifjuság és politikai szocializáció (Youth and political socialization). In F. Bojti (Ed.), *Politizáló fiatalok*. Budapest: Zrinyi Kiadó.

Klokova, G. V. (Ed.). (1973). *Fakultativnie zaniatia po istorii i obshchestvovedeniu (Optional programs of history and social study)*. Moskva: Prosveshchenie.

Kociecka, D. (1988). Mlodziez a przeszlość (Youth and the past). *Studia Socjologiczne, 1,* 327–346.

Koloskov, A. G. (1984). *Stanovlenie i sovershenstvovanie shkolnovo istorichestkovo obrazovania v SSSR (The foundation and improvement of historical school education in the USSR)*. Dissertacia na soiskanie uchonoy stepeni doktora pedagogicheskih nauk, Akademia Pedagogicheskih Nauk SSSR, Moskva.

Korovkin, F. P., & Dairi, N. G. (Ed.). (1978). *Metodika obuchenia istorii v srednej skole (Methodology of history teaching in the secondary school)*. Moskva: Prosveshchenie.

Korovkin, F. P., & Zaporozets, N. I. (Ed.). (1970). *Metodika obuchenia istorii drevnevo mira i srednih vekov v V–VI klassah (Methodology of ancient times and middle-ages history teaching in V–VI grades)*. Moskva: Prosveshchenie.

Köves, J., & Magirius, G. (1973). *A földrajz követelményrendszere (A system of objectives in geography teaching)*. Budapest: Tankönyvkiadó.

Krause, A. (1975). *Die politische Karikatur im Geschichtsunterricht (The political cartoon in history teaching)*. Berlin: Volk und Wissen Volkseigener Verlag.

Leibengrub, P. S. (1960). *Didakticheskie trebovania k uroku istorii v sredney skole (Educational requirements of the history lesson in the secondary school)*. Moskva: Akademia Pedagogicheskih Nauk RSFSR.

Lerner, I. J. (Ed.). (1972). *Poznavatelnie zadachi v obuchenii humanitarnim naukam (Cognitive exercises in the teaching of human sciences)*. Moskva: Pedagogika.

Levin, S. E. (1957). *Rabota uchitela i uchashchihsa na urokah istorii v VIII–X klassah (Teacher's and student's work on the history lessons in VIII–X grades)*. Moskva: Uchpedgiz.

Lisenko, M. M. (1970, 1971). *Metodika vikladannya istorii Ukrainskoi RSR (Methodology of history teaching of Ukrainian SSR)*. Kiev: Radyanska Skola.

Lustenberger, W. (1959). *Shkolski rad po grupama (Group work in the school)*. Beograd: P. D. Srbije.

Majorek, C. (Ed.). (1988). *Metodyka nauczania historii w szkole podstawowej. (Methodology of history teaching in the basic school)*. Warszawa: Wydawnictwa Szkolne i Pedagogiczne.

Majorek, C. (1989). *Szkolna edukacja historyczna w Galicji 1772–1918 (Historical school education in Galicia 1772–1918)*. Warszawa: Pańtswowe Wydawnictwa Naukowe.

Maternicki, J. (1974). *Dydaktyka historii w Polsce 1773–1918 (Didactic of history in Poland 1773–1918.)* Warszawa: Wydawnictwa Szkolne i Pedagogiczne.

Maternicki, J. (1978). *Polska dydaktyka historii 1918–1939. (Polish didactic of history 1918–1939)*. Warszawa: Wydawnictwa Szkolne i Pedagogiczne.

Mátrai, Z. (Ed.). (1982). *Vélemények, elképzelések a társadalmi képzés megujitásáról (Opinions and conceptions about the renewing of social education)*. Budapest: Országos Pedagógiai Intézet.

Mejstřik, V., Bartašova, H., & Habětín, V. (1959). *Názornost při vyučování dějepisu (Visualization in history teaching)*. Praha: Státní Pedagogické Nakladatelství.

Meyer, E. (1972). *Gruppenpädagogik zwischen Moskau und New York (Group work between Moscow and New York)*. Heidelberg: E. Meyer Verlag.

Michovský, F., Faktorová, L., Čapek, V., & Pátek, J. (1977). Didaktiká analýza obsahu vyučování dějepisu a didaktické testy a úkoly na základní a střední kole (Didactic analysis of history teaching content and the didactic tests and exercises in the elementary and secondary schools). In Sborník Pedagogické fakulty University Karlovy, *Historie VI.* Praha: Universita Karlova.

Miheev, V. I. (1987). *Modelirovanie i metodi teorii izmereniy v pedagogike (Modeling and methods of measurement theory in the pedagogy)*. Moskva: Visshaya Skola.

Milanović-Nahod, S. (1973). *Ispitivanje poznavanja osnovnih pojmova iz društvenih nauka kod učenika završnog razreda osnovne škole. (Research on knowledge of basic concepts in social studies by the learners of the finishing classes of the elementary school)*. Beograd: Naučna Knjiga.

Mokrzecki, L. (1973). *Studium z dziejów nauczania historii. Rozwój dydaktyki przedmiotu w Gdańskim Gimnazjum Akademickim do schylku XVII w (A study of the history of history teaching. Development of the subject didactic in the Gdánsky grammar school until the end of the 17th century)*. Gdańsk: Gdańskie Towarzystwo Naukowe.

Mory, F. (1950). *Individualizovana nactava i grupni rad (Individualized teaching and group work)*. Beograd: P. D. Srbije.

Nazarets, A. I. (1974). Formirovanie u uchashchihca VII klassa navikov issledovatelskovo podhoda k izucheniu istoricheskih dokumentov (Development of inquiry skills and attitudes of grade VII pupils in the study of historical documents). In P. V. Gora (Ed.), *Razvitie poznavatelnih vozmoznostey uchashchihsa pri obuchenii istorii.* Moskva: Gosudarstvenny Pedagogichesky Institut imini V. I. Lenina.

Osburg, F. (1962, 1975). *Tafelilder in Geschichtsunterricht (Blackboard drawings in history teaching)*. Berlin: Volk und Wissen Volkseigener Verlag.

Petrykowska, C. (1963). *Elementy kultury materialnej w nauczaniu historii (Elements of material culture in history teaching)*. Warszawa: Państwowe Zaklady Wydawnictw Szkolnych.

Poltorak, D. I. (1976). *Technicheskie sredstva v prepodavanii istorii i obshchestvovedenia (Technical instruments in history and social studies teaching)*. Moskva: Prosveshchenie.

Radeva, M. (1975). Problemt za metodite na obuchenie po istoria i povishavane efektivnostta na uchitelskia trud (Problems in history teaching methods and increasing the efficiency of teachers' work). In G. Georgiev (Ed.), *Problemi na obuchenieto po istoria.* Sofia: Narodna Prosveta.

Redyko, A. Z. (1950). *Usvoenie istoricheskih poniatiy uchashchimica V–VII klassov (Acquire historical concepts by learners in V–VII classes).* Moskva: Akademia Pedagogicheskih Nauk RSFSR.

Redyko, A. Z. (Ed.). (1961). *Psichologia usvoenia istorii uchashchimisa (The psychology of acquisition of history).* Moskva: Akademia Pedagogicheskih Nauk RSFSR.

Rulka, J. (1974). *Recepcja informacji polityczno-spolecznych przez mlodziez szkolna (Socio-political information reception of learners).* Warszawa-Poznań: Państwowe Wydawnictwo Naukowe.

Růžičková, J. (1974). *Problémové vyučování v dějepise (Problem solving in history teaching).* Praha: Státní Pedagogické Nakladatelství.

Schmidt, H. D. (1961). *Empirische Forschungsmethoden der Pädagogik (Empirical research methods of the pedagogy).* Berlin: Volk und Wissen Volkseigener Verlag.

Shopov, J., & Georgiev, G. (1975). *Metodika na obuchenieto po istoria (Methodology of history teaching).* Sofia: Izdatelstvo Nauka i Izkustvo.

Šlik, V. (1973). Z dějin teorie vyučováni dějepisu v českých zemich v 19. století (On the question of the history of the methodology of history teaching in the Czech territory). In Sborník Pedagogické fakulty University Karlovy, *Historie III.* Praha: Universita Karlova.

Slowikowski, T. (1960). *Poglady na nauczanie historii w Polsce w wieku XVIII oraz koncepcja dydaktyczna Joachima Lelewela (Views about history teaching in Poland and the didactic conception of Joachim Lelewel).* Krakow: Polska Akademia Nauk.

Slowikowski, T. (1967). *Metodika nauczania historii. (Methodology of history teaching).* Warszawa: Państwowe Zaklady Wydawnictw Szkolnych.

Stohr, B. (1962). *Methodik des Geschichtsunterrichts (Methodology of history teaching).* Berlin: Volk und Wissen Volkseigener Verlag.

Suhoński, A. (1987). *Środki audiowizualne w nauczaniu i uczeniu sie historii (Audio visual aids in the teaching and learning of history).* Warszawa: Wydawnictwa Szkolne i Pedagogiczne.

Švajcer, V. (1964). *Grupa kao subject obrazovanja (The group as subject of education).* Zagreb: Matica Hrvatska.

Sýkora, J. (1986). *Vyučovací pomůcky jako prostředek modernizace výuky dějepisu. Sborník příspěvků z konference—řijen 1986 (The teaching aid as an instrument of modernization of history learning. Collection of conference materials—October 1986).* Brno: Universita Jana Evangelisty Purkyne, Pedagogická fakulta.

Szabó, I., & Csepeli, G. (1984). *Nemzet és politika a 10–14 éves gyerekek gondolkodásában (Nation and policy in the thinking of 10–14 year-old pupils).* Budapest: Tömegkommunikációs Kutatóközpont.

Szabolcs, O. (Ed.). (1972). *Korszerü történelmi müveltség és az ifjuság (Up-to-date historical culture and youth).* Budapest: Országos Pedagógiai Intézet.

Szebenyi, P. (1969). *Csoportmunka az általános iskolai történelemtanitásban (Group work in elementary school history teaching.)* Budapest: Országos Pedagógiai Intézet.

Szebenyi, P. (1970). *Feladatok-módszerek-eszközök. Visszapillantás a hazai történelemtanitás multjára (Objectives, methods, and means: A look at the past of Hungarian history teaching).* Budapest: Tankönyvkiadó.

Szebenyi, P. (Ed.). (1975). *Gondolkodásra nevelés a történelemtanitásban: Válogatás a szocialista országok metodikai irodalmából (Improvement of thinking in the teaching of history: Collection from the methodological literature of socialist countries).* Budapest: Országos Pedagógiai Intézet.

Szybka, C. (1957). *Samodzielna praca uczniów na lekcjach historii (Learner's independent work in history lessons).* Warszawa: Państwowe Zaklady Wydawnictw Szkolnych.

Szybka, C. (1966). *Metodyka nauczania historii w szkole średniej (Methodology of history teaching in secondary school).* Warszawa: Państwowe Zaklady Wydawnictw Szkolnych.

Udvarhelyi, K., & Göcsei, I. (1973). *Az alsó-és a középfoku földrajztanitás története Magyarországon (History of teaching geography in elementary and secondary schools in Hungary).* Budapest: Tankönyvkiadó.

Unger, M. (1958). *Történelmi forrásfeldolgozó órák a gimnázium III. osztályában (Using primary sources in the third grade of academic secondary school).* Budapest: Tankönyvkiadó.

Unger, M. (1976). *A történelmi tudat alakulása középiskolai történelemtankönyveinkben (Change of the historical consciousness in Hungarian history textbooks).* Budapest: Tankönyvkiadó.

Vagin, A. A. (1968). *Metodika prepodavania istorii v skole (Methodology of history teaching in the secondary school).* Moskva: Prosveshchenie.

Vagin, A. A. (1972). *Metodika obuchenia istorii v skole. (Methodology of history instruction in the school).* Moskva: Prosveshchenie.

Vekilska, P., Lazarev, P., & Nedelcheva, V. (1975). Sostoanie i problemi shkolnoy geografii pri perestroike narodnovo obrazovania v Bolgarii (Situation and problems of school geography in the time of changing public education in Bulgaria). *Geografia v skole, 1,* 63–64.

Veress, J. (1968). *A történelemtanitás módszertanának pedagógiai alapjai (Pedagogical bases of the methodology of history teaching).* Budapest: Tankönyvkiadó.

Vinokurova, M. M., & Dobrinina, Z. I. (1986). *Izuchenie ekonomicheskih voprosov v skolnih kursah istorii (Study of economic issues in school history courses).* Moskva: Prosveshchenie.

Wermes, H. (1976). *Zur Entwicklung des dialektisch-materialistischen Denkens der Schüler (Development of dialectical materialistic thinking of pupils).* Berlin: Volk und Wissen Volkseigener Verlag.

Wermes, H., & Gora, P. V. (1977). *Puti formirovania nauchnovo mirovozrenia na urokah istorii (Ways to form scientific ideology in history lessons).* Moskva: Gosudarstvenny Pedagogichesky Institut imeni V. I. Lenina.

RESEARCH ON SOCIAL STUDIES IN AFRICA

Merry M. Merryfield
THE OHIO STATE UNIVERSITY

Peter Muyanda-Mutebi
AFRICAN SOCIAL STUDIES PROGRAMME

NAIROBI, KENYA

Social studies is a relatively recent innovation in African education. During the late 1950s and early 1960s African peoples increasingly regained their independence from colonial powers. Subsequently, these independent nations sought ways of changing inherited colonial educational systems to make them more suitable to present and future needs. Geography, history, and civics attracted the immediate attention of educators and government leaders, as these subjects were considered to be closely tied to national aspirations and citizenship.

In the 1960s, the integration of social science curricula as social studies was initiated in Africa. The benchmark in the development of social studies was a conference of 11 African nations held in Mombasa, Kenya, in 1968. The participants agreed on broad parameters for social studies that continue to guide the movement today. As set forth by the Mombasa Conference, social studies has four goals: (1) to enable students to understand people's interaction with their cultural, social, and physical environments; (2) to help students appreciate their homes and heritages; (3) to develop skills and attitudes expected of citizens; and (4) to teach students to express their ideas in a variety of ways.

The participants agreed that social studies should integrate the concepts and orientations of all the social science subjects and the humanities. They called for social studies to connect students with their communities and countries, to stress study of the local and immediate before the foreign and remote, and to emphasize skills and attitudes along with factual content. The conferees agreed that skills and attitudes should be developed through inquiry methods by which students would learn to ask and answer questions, raise and solve problems. These characteristics remain the ideal construction of African social studies as advocated by the African Social Studies Programme (ASSP), the pan-African social studies organization that grew out of the Mombasa Conference and provides leadership in social studies today. Currently, member nations include Botswana, Ethiopia, The Gambia, Ghana, Kenya, Lesotho, Liberia, Malawi, Nigeria, Sierra Leone, Somalia, Sudan, Swaziland, Tanzania, Uganda, Zambia, and Zimbabwe.

As African countries initiated social studies programs, they drew from the Mombasa conceptualization. The characteristics most frequently adopted were the integration of history and the social sciences, especially geography, and a focus on connecting students with their local communities and nation. The status of social studies varies from country to country (see Table 53–1). Although other African countries teach social science subjects, they do not necessarily accept or advocate a social studies approach with the characteristics just outlined. This chapter is focused on those 17 nations that accept the goals and characteristics of social studies as set forth by the Mombasa Conference.

THE LIMITATIONS OF THIS REVIEW

There are three sources of research on social studies in Africa. In sheer quantity, the most important source is students seeking degrees. Papers and evaluation reports presented at professional conferences, seminars, and ministries of education are a second source of research. Journals are a third, relatively

Reviewers were James L. Barth, Purdue University; Howard Mehlinger, Indiana University; Cynthia S. Sunal, University of Alabama, Tuscaloosa; Etim Udoh, Ahmadu Bello University, Zaria, Nigeria; Angene Wilson, University of Kentucky.

TABLE 53–1. Status of Social Studies in Selected African Nations

Country	Year Initiated	Status P S T U	Materials Produced
Botswana	1975	x x x	syllabuses, pupil books 1–3; teacher guides 1–7
Ethiopia	1975	x x	pupil books 1–6, teacher education materials
The Gambia	1975	x x x	syllabuses, pupil books 1–6; teacher education materials
Ghana	1969	x x x x	syllabuses, pupil books 1–6; workbooks 4–6; teacher guides for primary; syllabuses for secondary
Kenya	1971	x x x x	syllabuses, textbooks & teacher guides 1–8; syllabuses for teacher education
Liberia	1965	x x	syllabuses 1–12; pupil books 1–6
Lesotho	1978	x	syllabuses and some pupil books
Nigeria	1963	x x x x	syllabuses, many texts, teacher guides, references at each level
Sierra Leone	1964	x x	syllabuses, teacher guides & pupil books for 1–7 & 1–3 secondary
Somalia	1984	x x	pupil books 1–4; 3 books for teacher education
Swaziland	1974	x x	syllabuses, pupil books 3–7, & teacher guides
Uganda	1975	x x	syllabuses, pupil books 4–7, teacher guides
Zambia	1970	x x x	syllabuses and pupil books 3–9 & teacher guides 3–7
Zimbabwe	1975	x x	syllabuses; some pupil and teacher materials

Note. Initiated means *started*, not *institutionalized*. Status: P = primary, S = secondary, T = teacher education, U = university. Malawi, Sudan, and Tanzania are not listed because they continue with the separate subjects of geography, history, and civics.

Source for Botswana. "Report of the Seminar of the Coordinating Committee of the ASSP" by African Social Studies Programme, 1985, author. Data for other countries came from presentations by representatives at Strengthening Social Studies in Africa, an institute held at Indiana University, June 28–August 15, 1987.

miniscule, source. Journals in the West rarely publish African studies, and the few African journals of educational research are usually occupied with larger issues. Thus, the majority of research reviewed in this chapter is unpublished student research or papers presented in professional contexts.

Student Research

With few exceptions, the student studies reviewed are master's theses or doctoral dissertations. Most of the student research is based on relatively simple paper-and-pencil instruments administered to small, localized populations and analyzed by frequency distributions. In a number of studies, interview, observational, and survey data have been triangulated to focus on a particular concern such as instructional methods. The research is limited by the inexperience of the researchers and the one-shot nature of much of the data collection.

Geographic Distribution

The geographic distribution of the research reviewed limits the generalizability of conclusions. As explained above, this review is limited to the 17 member nations of the African Social Studies Program, although one study does include data on Egypt.

Within the ASSP nations there exist disparities in the distribution of social studies research. Several of the countries are only included in cross-national reports published by the ASSP. Either no research exists on social studies in the country (Botswana, for example) or the studies were unavailable for inclusion in this review. Because of the paucity of pan-African indices of research and journals in education, many studies are undoubtedly gathering dust on library shelves or fading with the memories of professional meetings. Although this review includes research on social studies in Botswana, Egypt, Ethiopia,

The Gambia, Ghana, Kenya, Lesotho, Liberia, Malawi, Nigeria, Sierra Leone, Swaziland, Tanzania, Uganda, Zambia and Zimbabwe, over half of the studies reviewed are Nigerian.

Why have Nigerians carried out so much research in social studies, compared to other African countries? Nigeria was the first African nation to initiate social studies (see Table 53–1), so there has been more time for development of social studies programs and concurrent research. Nigeria had a better educational infrastructure in two of its three regions at independence than did most other countries. Nigeria's estimated 100 million people make up one fourth of the population of sub-Saharan Africa and have the largest number of universities and teacher colleges. Nigeria boasts many bachelor and master's degree programs in social studies and has Africa's only PhD program in social studies. As an oil exporter, Nigeria used its *petro-naira* to expand and improve education during the oil boom of the 1970s and early 1980s. Nigeria is known for its freedom of expression and dissent. There have been no despots throughout frequent changes of political power and a civil war. In fact, one result of the civil war in the 1960s was popularization of social studies as a means to national unity through formal education.

The paucity of research from other African countries reflects the newness of the subject (see Table 53–1) and African problems with carrying out research on social studies. In most African countries there are few persons capable of researching social studies, and those persons are constrained by time (a professor may teach 25–30 hours a week) and lack of funding. Africa's economic poverty and high birth rates make building schools and training teachers the education sector's highest priorities.

WHAT HAS BEEN LEARNED ABOUT SOCIAL STUDIES IN AFRICA

The studies reviewed here represent the first 14 years of research on social studies in Africa (1974–1988), and they are examinations of the basic issues of conceptualization, development, and diffusion of social studies as a course of study. Together, they represent the questions, problems, and successes of the social studies movement in its formative years. The studies are organized under generalizations about what has been learned.

Confusion Exists About the Conceptualization of Social Studies

Much has been written about the ambiguous nature of social studies in African countries. There exists an enormous gap between conceptualizations of social studies by ministry staff and the realities of social studies classrooms. The central question—How is social studies different from the subjects it replaced?—is answered many different ways by those who are responsible for its diffusion.

Several studies have been focused on the conceptualization of social studies. In 1975, the social studies staff of Ahmadu Bello University (ABU) in northern Nigeria administered the Barth/Shermis Social Studies Preference Scale (B/SSSPS) to 55 undergraduate social studies students (Barth & Norris, 1976). The B/SSSPS is intended to assess teachers' beliefs according to three social studies traditions: citizenship transmission, social science, and reflective inquiry. The results, as in research in the United States (White, 1982), indicated an eclectic view of social studies. The scores of more than half of the students reflected general agreement, with the purposes and methods of all three traditions, although there was a preference for the content of citizenship transmission.

In 1981, another group of 27 social studies undergraduates at Amadu Bello responded to the B/SSSPS (Barth, 1986). In contrast with 43% in the 1975 sample, over 73% of the 1981 sample chose one tradition. Those choosing reflective inquiry rose from 20% (choice of method) and 2% (choice of content) to 70% and 41%, respectively. Barth (1986) interpreted the results as indicating that graduates in social studies at the university were becoming more sophisticated in their knowledge of social studies and, consequently, less confused over the ambiguity in the purpose, methods, and content of what they would eventually teach.

Barth (1986) also compared the 1981 B/SSSPS responses of the ABU students to the 1982 responses of 96 Egyptian students who were preparing to become social studies teachers. Social studies was a new program in Egypt at the time, and most teacher-training institutions did not have social studies courses. The results for the Egyptians in 1982 were similar to those for the Nigerians in 1975.

Adeyemi used the B/SSSPS in his study of the philosophical orientations of social studies secondary teachers (1985) and university students (1987) in Oyo state in southern Nigeria. He found that the secondary teachers were eclectic, in that they chose characteristics of all three traditions. On the other hand, 80% of the social studies students at Obafemi Awolowo University, formerly the University of Ife, could be classified in one tradition. Over 36% chose reflective inquiry, and 22%, social science combined with reflective inquiry. Adeyemi interpreted the results as evidence of competent instructors and attention

to the National Policy on Education's emphasis on reflective inquiry.

Other studies have been focused on the conceptualization of social studies as citizenship education. Adeyoyin's (1981) sample was students at Lagos State Teacher Training College in Nigeria between 1978 and 1980. The students perceived social studies as an amalgam of subjects unrelated to citizenship education. Orimoloye (1983) examined the perspectives of social studies educators in Oyo state, Nigeria, toward four models of citizenship education: citizenship transmission, social science, reflective inquiry, and social criticism and action. His findings indicated that the respondents approved of all four models. Those with more education, especially teacher educators and inspectors, tended to prefer reflective inquiry and social criticism.

In 1985, Sunal, Gaba, and Osa (1987) administered the Citizenship Education Status Survey to 147 Nigerian social studies teachers. Unlike most of the other African research, this sample contained cross-sections of Nigeria's ethnic, religious, and geographic diversity. The findings indicated that, although teachers' attitudes were generally positive toward citizenship education goals, they did not associate social studies with the content, attitudes, or skills of citizenship education. They perceived their role as that of teaching social science content through teacher-centered, expository methods.

Other studies in Ghana, Kenya, Malawi, Nigeria, and Uganda (Merryfield, 1986b; Odada, 1988; Okoh, 1979; Tamakloe, 1988) have demonstrated that those persons most directly responsible for the implementation of a social studies program, teachers and teacher educators, are not clear about its meaning and how it differs from the separate subjects of geography, history, and civics. This problem undoubtedly constrains the development and diffusion of social studies. There is evidence, however, that clarity can be enhanced by effective preservice and inservice education programs (Adeyemi, 1985; Barth, 1986; Merryfield, 1986b).

Teachers Need to be Educated in the Rationale, Instructional Methods, and Content of Social Studies

One of the most critical problems facing social studies in Africa is the training of teachers. The situation in most African countries could be called the static domino theory of social studies education. If no one in the country has been trained in social studies, who develops materials and teaches courses for teacher educators? If the teacher educators have no background in social studies, how can they prepare social studies teachers? If the social studies teachers have only experienced expository teaching in the separate subjects of geography and history, how can they teach integrated content by inquiry methods? Research documents the severity of the training problem and its possible relationship with attitudes toward social studies, instructional methods, and the status of social studies in schools and teacher colleges.

Uganda. Odada's research in Uganda (1988) vividly demonstrates the basic problem. Social studies was initiated in Uganda in 1975. Of 157 teachers participating in a 1984 social studies seminar, 56% did not know that social studies was supposed to be different from history, geography, and civics. Of 60 teacher-college lecturers surveyed the same year, 75% claimed "complete ignorance" of social studies. They regarded it as "a vague and undeveloped subject that had no experts to explain all that it is about" (p. 4).

Odada also reviewed 29 Ugandan research studies on social studies undertaken by students at Makerere University, Gaba Teacher College, and Canon Apolo Teacher College from 1985–1987. In 24 of the 29 reports, the researchers concluded that the social studies teachers were totally untrained or inadequately trained in social studies. It should be noted that these reports did not mention Uganda's political turmoil during the previous 13 years and its effects on education. One can only hypothesize as to what degree civil strife has constrained the development of social studies there.

Ghana. Social studies was initiated in Ghana in 1969. In 1976 all teacher-training institutions were told to prepare their students to teach (integrated) social studies instead of the separate subjects of history and geography. Tamakloe (1988) recently examined the status of social studies in the nation's teacher-training institutions. He found that, in 74% of the institutions, the separate subjects of history, geography, and civics were taught instead of integrated social studies. When asked to rate the importance of different subjects in Ghana's teacher education programs, the heads of the teacher-training colleges ranked social studies in the lower third, just above physical education and home science. When asked why social studies was so unimportant, the heads ascribed the situation to the lack of competent social studies lecturers. Lecturers trained in history or geography did not want to teach social studies, despite the fact that their graduates were supposed to teach it in the nation's primary and junior secondary schools.

Kenya. When African education ministries decided to adopt social studies, they also made decisions as to where to begin. Some nations first changed the primary-school syllabus. Others began with the primary teacher colleges. Kenya initiated social studies in the late 1970s with pilot testing at the primary level and the commencement of a master's program in social studies at Kenyatta University College (KUC). The master's program was designed to prepare the lecturers who would eventually teach courses in social studies in the nation's primary teacher colleges. However, social studies did not replace the separate subjects of geography and history in the primary teacher colleges until 1986.

From 1980 to 1986, several studies by KUC master's students documented the transition to social studies In his inquiry into the status of social studies in Kenya, Shiundu (1980) found primary school pupils' attitudes generally positive toward social studies, despite its low status in the educational system, lack of support in the community, and inadequate teacher preparation. Osindi (1982) tried to identify the limitations on effective social studies instruction in Kissi District. He concluded that untrained teachers and lack of inservice education were the major limiting factors. Most teachers and school administrators simply did not understand how to teach social studies. Paradoxically, the teach-

ers said that they enjoyed teaching social studies. Kabau (1983) explored the instructional problems of teachers piloting social studies in the Central Province and found the teachers to be unprepared and their attitudes unfavorable to social studies. Lijembe (1983) surveyed 10 schools in Kakamega district and concluded that inadequate training in social studies was a major problem. Makumba (1983) examined the preparedness of primary school staffs in Kakamega District to implement social studies. He characterized the learning environment as not conducive to achieving the objectives of social studies. However, teachers said they would welcome the new social studies.

In an evaluation of the pilot testing of social studies, the Kenya Institute of Education (1983) found teachers were in critical need of inservice education; 61% of the qualified teachers and 91% of the unqualified teachers (teachers who did not have teaching certificates) were not familiar with the philosophy of the social studies program they were in charge of implementing. In spite of their lack of understanding, over 72% said they enjoyed teaching social studies and wanted to continue doing so the next year.

Merryfield (1986a, 1986b) observed social studies instruction in Kenya in the last year of the pilot testing before national implementation. Most social studies teachers learned about the social studies approach on the job from other teachers. Teacher attitudes were supportive of social studies goals despite numerous complaints over lack of training and the quality of instructional materials.

Merryfield also interviewed college lecturers who were avidly against the implementation of social studies only a few months before it was to be introduced in all the teachers colleges. The teacher educators perceived their jobs to be threatened by social studies, as they thought they knew nothing about it and could not teach it.

These studies demonstrate some of the realities of teacher education in social studies in Kenya. Numerous other studies across Africa have painted a picture of social studies teachers who have inadequate training in its rationale, methods, and content (Adejunmobi, 1981; R. Adekeye, 1979; Dahunsi, 1979; Dondo, Krystall, & Thomas, 1974; Enaohwo, 1982; Funtua 1979, 1980; Lolo, 1977; Obebe, 1981; Yahaya, 1979). Records of ASSP meetings, seminars, and evaluations from 1974 to 1985 document the critical need for effective social studies training for both teacher educators and teachers (ASSP, 1985; Dondo, Krystall & Thomas, 1974).

Attitudes Toward Social Studies. It is interesting to note that, along with this dismal picture of untrained teachers, there is some evidence that social studies is relatively popular with both students and teachers. In addition to the Kenyan studies cited above, Adejunmobi (1976) surveyed 1,143 Nigerian secondary school students on their perceptions of social studies versus history courses in the lower secondary curriculum. The students overwhelmingly preferred social studies because it provided "total human understanding," involved "problem-solving through subject fusion," and led to "community understanding" (p. 381). Adejunmobi noted that the results were especially impressive because most of the social studies teachers had not been specifically trained in social studies.

In another Nigerian study, Amodu (1984) found a strong positive correlation between students' attitudes and achievement in social studies.

Teaching Methods. Another research question involves the relationship between teacher education and instructional methods. A number of studies have found that social studies teachers use the same expository, teacher-centered methods characteristic of history and geography teachers. Salawu (1982) observed that social studies teachers in secondary schools in Ibadan, Nigeria, relied on rote memorization as their major teaching method. Yahaya (1979) found that social studies teachers in metropolitan Kano State, Nigeria, consistently taught by lecture and recall questions, even though 60% had been through social studies orientation courses organized by the Kano Inservice Training Center. Ogundare (1981) questioned 1,619 teachers from the Oyo and Ondo local government areas of Nigeria as they were taking an extensive inservice course for an Associateship Certificate in Education at Oyo State College. He found that few had any basic skills in inquiry methods of teaching, and he concluded that they would not be able to teach using the investigation-oriented methods advocated in social studies. In his evaluation of a social studies program in Kano State, Nigeria, Guri (1979) concluded that the social studies teachers did relatively well at teaching for the recall of information but were unable to teach higher order skills. In Esiwe's (1974) study of social studies instruction in Zaria, Nigeria, 77% of the social studies teachers did not teach according to the prescribed methods.

Ayo and Fwa (1984) questioned both teachers and students in the Jos and Misau areas of Nigeria on instructional methods. The teachers claimed their instruction was divided equally between dramatization (role playing), group work, lecture, inquiry, and field trips. However, their students classified 45% of the instruction as lecture, 22.5% as reading from the text, 16% as written assignments, 9.5% as dramatization, and 6% as field trips. Observational data supported the conclusion that the most frequently used teaching method was lecture. Questions predominantly called for recall answers. There was no evidence of inquiry methods.

On the other hand, Funtua (1979) studied 118 National Certificate Examination (the basic teaching certificate) student teachers in Nigeria and found there were differences in teaching methods depending on where the students had received their social studies training and the length of time their instructors had actually spent on teaching methods. In another Nigerian study, Funtua (1980) observed 20 teachers who had training in social studies and 20 who had not. He found the teachers with training did use the prescribed social studies methods, whereas the other teachers taught with the standard methods of history or geography.

Merryfield (1986a) carried out a direct comparison of classroom instruction in social studies with that in history, geography, and civics in Kenya. In 6 months of observations she found little difference in teaching methods, although the social studies teachers occasionally asked inquiry-based questions. The greatest difference was that the social studies teachers consistently related content to the experiences and environment of their students, an instructional strategy central to social studies in Africa.

There is general consensus that the methods used to teach social studies are primarily teacher lecture, teacher question, and student answer (sometimes called discussion) with occasional role playing (dramatization) and field trips for observation (Adeniyi, 1982; Ayo & Fwa, 1984; Kenya Institute of Education, 1983; Makumba, 1983; Merryfield, 1986a, 1986b; Obebe, 1981; Ogundare, 1981; Salawu, 1982; Yahaya, 1979) However, most of these studies have focused on either untrained teachers or populations in which trained and untrained teachers are not differentiated. There certainly needs to be more work in the vein of Funtua's (1979), in which the instruction of graduates from different social studies programs was monitored over a period of time.

Inadequate Instructional Materials are a Major Obstacle to Effective Social Studies Instruction

The first instructional materials for social studies in Africa developed from two experimental projects in Nigeria in the early 1960s. Aiyetoro Comprehensive High School produced the first textbooks for secondary school social studies. The Northern Nigerian Teacher Education Project developed and tested the first materials for teacher education. At the Mombasa Conference of 1968, these were the state-of-the-art of social studies curriculum development in Africa.

Over the next 20 years the adoption of social studies became synonymous with the development of new syllabi (the scope and sequence of courses), teacher guides (instructional methods and content to help teachers teach the syllabi), student texts, and other teaching aids and resources. Some countries blessed with social studies expertise developed methods books and content books for teacher education programs at a variety of levels (certification, diploma, degree). Unfortunately, most countries moved more quickly in telling teachers to teach social studies than in providing them the instructional materials with which to teach. From the beginning of the African social studies movement until now, teachers have consistently complained about the quantity and quality of materials (African Social Studies Programme, 1985; Dondo et al., 1974). In almost every study in this review, the problem of inadequate instructional materials has surfaced.

There is wide variance among the ASSP countries in the quantity and quality of social studies materials. Table 53–1 lists the materials available in selected countries. It is important to note that, because a country has a Standard 4 social studies book, it does not necessarily follow that all schools in that country have the book or that all students in a Standard 4 class have a copy. Publication and dissemination are two separate steps.

In Merryfield's (1986b) comparison of social studies in Malawi and Nigeria, she described instructional materials in primary schools and teacher colleges. In Malawi, no primary schools had classroom sets of geography, history, or civics books (social studies is not an integrated subject in Malawi). In most schools there was one copy of a primary history or geography textbook that the teacher used as a reference. Some teachers used their own primary school notebooks (notes they had written as primary school students) as their only source of information. Textbooks for students were nonexistent at the primary teacher colleges. Even paper was in short supply. Consequently, the instructional materials with which graduates left teacher colleges were usually notes taken from courses. Some primary schools did have secondary texts that the teachers used for reference when preparing lectures. However, most of the books were 15–30 years old. Some presented a colonial view of Africa. In reports of other Malawian studies (Hara, 1983; Misoya, 1982), these problems have been pointed to as serious constraints on effective teaching.

In Nigeria, there are many social studies textbooks at all levels. Because of Nigeria's huge market, international as well as Nigerian publishers are anxious to have textbooks for sale in every subject. However, students may not have textbooks because of economic problems in the state, community, or family. The oil bust of the 1980s did affect outlays for education, including the quantity of books in the hands of students. Unfortunately, the wide selection of books is countered by lack of quality control, as authors and publishers are more interested in making money than in improving social studies (Adejunmobi, 1981).

Most Nigerian teachers and teacher educators do have some professional books and references from which to teach (Merryfield, 1986b). Whether they have suitable resources for teaching by inquiry methods is another question. Teaching materials needed for inquiry are sometimes nonexistent, usually not available in the local language, and relatively expensive when available (Onyabe, 1979). When the reference materials, newspapers, and media packets for inquiry teaching are unavailable, the teacher usually follows the traditional approach (Lafene, 1977). A number of studies (Dahunsi, 1979; Dondo et al., 1974; Lijembe, 1983; Okoh, 1979; Oshungbohun, 1984) have found that inadequate materials limit effective social studies instruction in Africa. Even when materials are available, Ayanaba (1975) noted, teachers need guidance in how to use them.

Textbook Evaluations. Few studies have been focused on evaluating social studies materials. Ekpunobi (1983) reviewed some Nigerian social studies textbooks for ethnic stereotypes, an important concern in a culturally diverse nation that has adopted social studies as a means towards national integration. She found numerous examples of stereotypical information presented as facts.

A study by Morrow (1985) included some textbook evaluation. Morrow cataloged resources available for the teaching of history in 10 of Malawi's secondary schools. The schools selected were representative of the types (district, government, mission, prestige) of schools in Malawi. He found a very uneven availability of resources across schools; some schools had no texts or any materials for required courses, but others had texts, maps, a good library, and teaching aids such as overhead projectors. Most texts dated from the late 1960s when the syllabus was originally developed. Although the texts have been revised and many other texts published since, the schools continued to use the older books. Morrow identified some of these books as portraying a white settler's view of history.

The Development of Social Studies is Inhibited by the Force of Tradition and Restraints on African Educational Systems

In addition to the three prior generalizations, there are a number of other constraints on the development and diffusion of social studies in Africa. They appear in the findings or recommendations of a number of studies.

Examinations. Inherited from colonial education, examinations are instruments of selection in systems of limited educational opportunity. Usually children take their first examination at the end of lower primary school, the third to fifth year of school. These examinations usually focus on English, another national language, and mathematics.

All of the countries included in this chapter have primary school leaving exams that are given at the end of 6 to 9 years of primary school to select the students who will go on to secondary school. Although some African countries are moving toward universal junior secondary education (Botswana, for example), the vast majority (approximately 83%) of young people in ASSP countries do not receive more than a primary education. Approximately 17% of the secondary age children in ASSP countries actually attend secondary schools. The percentages range from a low of 3% in Tanzania to a high of 39% in Zimbabwe. The examinations, therefore, are of critical importance because the economic mobility of a family often depends on whether or not a child acquires a postprimary certificate or diploma.

The secondary schools also have examinations, sometimes at the end of junior secondary (around the 9th or 10th year of schooling) and always at the end of secondary schooling (usually 12 years). Those students with the highest scores are given places at the university; the next highest scorers find places in polytechnics, teacher colleges, and other institutions of higher learning. Less than 2% of the college-age group in ASSP countries attend tertiary education institutions compared with 57% in the United States (World Bank, 1987).

Examinations affect social studies in a number of ways. Traditionally, geography, economics, political science, and history exams have assessed the recall of information, of the facts of history and the social sciences. Social studies exams are not recognizably different. Unfortunately, the exams are often those developed for the old curriculum and are incongruent with those objectives that differentiate social studies from the social sciences (Dondo et al., 1974; Salawu, 1982). Because schools and teachers are evaluated mainly by examination results, teachers teach directly for what they think will be on the exams (Merryfield, 1986b).

In his study of social studies in Ghana's primary teacher colleges, Tamakloe (1988) accounted for the low status of social studies instruction by the lack of an external examination in social studies. Although students were required to pass national examinations in English, mathematics, and a number of other subjects to be certified, they did not take an examination in social studies. Consequently neither students nor lecturers were concerned about the subject.

The same phenomenon sometimes occurs with social studies in primary schools. Merryfield (1986b) observed that many Malawian teachers in standards 1–4 did not teach history and geography when it was scheduled on the timetable. Instead, they used those periods to teach extra classes of English and mathematics because those subjects were the ones the children had to pass on their lower primary exam.

Another problem comes from the superior status of the secondary exams over the primary exams. Many African Social Studies Programme countries have social studies at the primary and junior secondary levels but then examine on geography, history, economics, and other social science subjects at the end of the secondary level. Teachers, administrators, parents, and students take this sequence as a sign that social studies is somehow inferior, not of real significance because a student must pass the examinations on the separate subjects to complete secondary school. Because the secondary exams do not test attitudes, inquiry, or problem-solving abilities, how can those outcomes be important? Why should even a primary teacher waste time with field trips or group work when what really matters are the facts tested on the secondary school leaving exam? For these and other reasons, social studies instruction is constrained by examinations (A. Adekeye, 1982; Makumba, 1983; Osindi, 1982; Salawu, 1982; Sunal, Gaba, & Osa, 1987).

Placement of Social Studies Graduates. After graduation from teacher colleges or universities, most teachers or teacher educators are placed in schools or teacher colleges by ministries of education. Unfortunately for the development of social studies, many of those persons who have received extensive training never teach or, if they teach, it is not social studies. DuBey (1983) carried out a follow-up study of the 315 graduates of ABU's BEd in Social Studies program from 1977 to 1982. The program was designed to train teacher educators who would then train primary teachers. Of all graduates, only 49.3% were still teaching. The others were in school administration, in the ministry or had left education for politics, business, or public service. Of those still teaching, 77% were teaching social studies. The others were teaching education, English, history, and religious knowledge. Only 23% of the graduates were involved in the training of teachers, the goal of the BEd program.

Other authors have remarked on the detrimental effect on dissemination because persons educated in social studies are not placed in social studies positions (Ate, Akai, Bamindah, Lele, & Okai, 1983; Merryfield, 1986b). The problem grew out of the shortage of educated people in times of great educational expansion. The declaration of universal primary education in Nigeria in 1976 thrust many skilled teachers into administrative posts (Adejunmobi, 1981; Obebe, 1981). Social studies suffers more than other subjects in times of expansion because it has fewer trained teachers to begin with.

The Question of Language. Language affects social studies instruction in a number of ways. In most countries, social studies is taught in the students' mother tongue at the lower primary level. However, few countries have had the resources to translate textbooks into local languages. Teachers are placed in the position of teaching about the local community from an English-language textbook. The difficulty of translating cultural norms or traditions into English creates a confusing situation for both teachers and students (Adejunmobi, 1981). The low level of the spoken English of most school children also affects social studies. Nine-year-olds who are to be taught such concepts as manufacturing or urbanization often have English vocabularies that are inadequate for such learning. Examinations are in English in most of the ASSP countries, and social studies examinations are as much tests of English as they are tests of social studies (Ogunsanya, 1982).

The research on social studies in Africa during its formative years demonstrates the struggle of a new subject to achieve its own identity. Although the constraints on the development of social studies are considerable, there is evidence that social studies is gaining support and can offer a more relevant education than the subjects it has replaced.

WHAT RESEARCH IS NEEDED ON SOCIAL STUDIES IN AFRICA?

There has been so little research carried out on social studies in Africa that research is needed in every facet of social studies instruction. Although many research questions are similar to those asked in other parts of the world, the African context of limited resources and expertise necessitates the setting of priorities. The questions outlined below indicate some critical areas for inquiry.

To What Degree Do Existing Social Studies Programs Actually Address Development Goals?

In the process of initiating social studies to replace the separate subjects of history, geography, and civics, ministries have identified national development goals for social studies. Building a national consciousness, developing pride in the local community, addressing environmental problems, and developing problem-solving skills are examples of such goals. The degree to which such long-range goals have been reflected in the development and dissemination of social studies syllabi and instructional materials is an important question that could be investigated through examination of print materials (national development plans, syllabi, instructional materials), observation of planning, instruction, and testing, and interviews of stakeholders at the different points of dissemination (from ministers of education, curriculum developers, teacher educators, inspectors, school administrators, classroom teachers, to students and their parents). Determination of the goals actually addressed in social studies, and the inconsistencies with national goals could contribute to a more focused approach to the conceptualization and implementation of social studies in Africa.

How Do Social Studies Teachers Make Their Instructional Decisions?

As elsewhere in the world, teachers are the key players in the adoption of social studies. Although African educational systems are highly centralized with national syllabi and examinations, it is still the teacher who decides what is taught and how it is taught. Research is needed on the effects of such factors as different teacher education programs, instructional materials, exams, size of classes, community norms, and teacher involvement in curriculum planning on teachers' decisions about what knowledge, skills and attitudes they teach, how they interact with their students, and how they use or make instructional materials. Along with case studies of effective and ineffective teachers, experiments are needed with different types of teacher education programs, instructional materials, inservice education programs, class sizes, exams, and levels of teacher involvement in curriculum planning to determine the degree to which these factors influence teachers' instructional decisions.

How Do Students Use What they Learn in Social Studies?

The universal measure of what students learn in social studies in Africa is the national examination. Such examinations are usually made up of multiple-choice items that test factual knowledge, and rarely go beyond recall to assess the analysis, synthesis, or application of knowledge. If social studies is to contribute to the nation-building goals of Africa, students need to use what they learn in everyday living. Tests are needed to assess students' application of major concepts and generalizations from social studies to their nation, local community, their families, and themselves. For example, can they evaluate what deforestation would mean to them and their community if it were to happen at a specified rate for 20 years? The results from such exams could be used by ministries to identify needed projects in syllabus revision, teacher education, and materials development.

Such research questions ought to be examined in cross-national, comparative studies to evaluate the role of cultural norms and national settings in the diffusion of social studies. The research will, however, have the desired impacts only if better channels of communication are developed across national borders through collaborative research and social studies publications and conferences to disseminate findings both within and across African nations.

WHAT ARE METHODOLOGICAL ISSUES FOR RESEARCH ON SOCIAL STUDIES IN AFRICA

Methodological issues in social studies research within Africa include the problems of cross-cultural inquiry as well as the ambiguities and sensitivities that are the nature of social studies (Merryfield, 1985). Together, they comprise serious obstacles for even the experienced researcher. Although some Africans may carry out research totally within their own culture, most researchers, including all foreigners, will cross cultures. This section discusses some of the more common methodological problems these researchers face.

Cultural Differences

Cultural differences are often fundamental differences in the ways in which people view the world. Different realities and lack of shared assumptions lead to misperceptions, misunderstandings, worthless data, and false findings. Experience gained working in one culture does not necessarily apply to another culture, as each may be unique in some ways. Cultural differences relevant to research on social studies include beliefs and values, styles of interaction, sense of time, infrastructure (in, e.g., education, communications, transportation) and language.

Cultures may have beliefs or values that are contradictory to the goals or assumptions of social studies. For example, most African cultures do not encourage children and young people to ask questions or make decisions on their own. Therefore, research into why teachers are not using inquiry methods must include some attention to cultural values or a major factor influencing instruction will be missed. Cultural norms related to the family, work, schooling, women, religion, and views of the past must be understood as factors that affect the conceptualization and implementation of social studies.

Styles of interaction differ considerably across cultures. Although it is acceptable behavior in the United States to approach a stranger and ask personal or trivial questions, in many African cultures the arrival of a stranger triggers caution and suspicion. The head (principal) and teachers of a school may be told that a researcher wants to observe classes for some innocuous reason; but they will usually believe that a person with official entry (the only way to gain access to schools in most countries) has the power to ruin them and may well do so. Consequently, respondents will often give answers or teach in ways that they think the researcher wants; or, they may be so noncommittal that the data are totally inaccurate. Furthermore, the naive or inexperienced researcher may not even recognize what is happening. In many cultures, the age, sex, and position of the researcher may prohibit effective interaction. A young, unmarried woman without a degree will probably receive much less help (and data) from a principal of a teacher college than would an older man who is a full professor. Since collecting data is often dependent upon personal interaction, a researcher has to learn new contexts with each culture.

Cultural perceptions of time affect the conceptualization and diffusion of social studies. If it takes 3 years to develop a 40-page teacher's guide, who is to say whether that time frame is acceptable? Should cultural variables be taken into account when students complain about the time it takes to write exams or teachers disagree over the time it takes to teach about community customs? Without an understanding of the cultural context of time, researchers may impose their own perceptions and obfuscate their findings.

Differences in educational infrastructure can be mind-boggling for a researcher with no previous experience in Africa. Such basic research resources as records, research assistants, and gatekeepers reflect cultural differences. Ministry records of teacher education programs may be nonexistent or stacked in a room with termites feasting on them. School enrollment records may be grossly inflated for economic gain or political reasons. The paucity of educated people may occasionally lead to research assistants who collect data unsystematically because they see no reason to go to a school six miles away when there is one close by. African bureaucracies sometimes take substantial time in granting research permits, visas, or permission to visit particular institutions. Three months of a 12-month research grant may be taken up in gaining the proper signatures for a research permit. Then the transportation infrastructure may stall research further as the rainy season makes two-thirds of the country's roads impassable for another three months.

Language is the ultimate cross-cultural problem. Even though most educated Africans in the ASSP countries speak English, there are different cultural interpretations and connotations of words basic to social studies research, such as citizenship education, political participation, cultural diversity, or economic education. If researchers use children or their parents as respondents, fluency in the local language or translation is necessary. Few Americans or Europeans speak an African language. Finding reliable translators for a national study can be a major research problem. In one Kenyan study of primary school social studies (Merryfield, 1986b), five different translators were required because the study involved observations of standard 1–4 instruction in areas where the local languages were Luo, Nandi, Luyia, Kikuyu, and Swahili. Translation of instruments involves serious linguistic problems as synonyms may not be available in some languages.

Application of Western Methods of Research in African Contexts

The literature on cross-cultural inquiry is replete with the problems of applying methodology derived in the West to African settings (Hamnett & Brislin, 1980; Kumar, 1979; O'Barr, Spain, & Tessler, 1973; Patton, 1985; Triandis & Berry, 1980). The problems range from logistics for survey research to allegations of cultural imperialism. Major questions arise from a priori designs, standardized measures, the assumptions of the scientific paradigm, and ethical problems.

The researcher entering another culture often has problems with the a priori design for a study because important variables may not be known at the outset and contextual factors that shape social studies instruction may be ignored. For example, a researcher learns that the diffusion of social studies from teacher education institutions to primary schools in an important research problem in Africa. An instrument is developed and used to collect data on teaching methods and content in teacher colleges and primary schools in one nation, as well as to replicate the study in in another African nation. The researcher enters the second nation under the assumption that the the data collected with the instrument will be comparable. However, the context for social studies in the second nation is quite different. There are no teacher education programs in social studies for primary teachers. Practicing social studies teachers have materials but no training in social studies. The problem that was important in the first nation is not so in the second. The a priori design to compare two African countries on the diffusion of teacher education can be forced by the researcher, but the findings will be of dubious worth.

Problems exist with survey methods and questionnaires in Africa as people may not understand or appreciate the concepts of anonymity or segmented contacts. Head teachers may be used to answering all questions for teachers in their

schools and be humiliated or angry when the researcher insists on speaking with individual teachers in private. Questionnaires sent to all teachers in a school may be returned with identical answers as the head teacher has told the teachers what to say.

The belief systems of many African societies are contrary to the culture of the scientific method. The assumptions that predictability and control are both possible and desirable are not common to African societies. Is it ethical to base research on assumptions with which the research population themselves disagree? One reason it is becoming increasingly difficult for foreigners to get permission to do research in many African countries is because researchers from the West have used African peoples for data collection without consideration for local values or the research needs of the country.

Ethics in conducting research in cross-cultural contexts is extraordinarily complex because two sets, if not more, of values and expectations are involved. For example, is it ethical to spend a $30,000 research grant to duplicate an American study of the role of social studies in political socialization when the sites of the study, 20 primary schools in an African country, are so poor that students have no books and teachers have not been paid in three months? Or, what if in the process of exploring the use of instructional materials in social studies, the researcher comes across evidence that a ministry official has been bribed by a publisher to get exclusive rights to sell a certain set of texts to all schools despite their poor quality? What should or can the researcher do?

In some African cultures norms of confidentiality do not exist, and the researcher may not be able to hide or protect sources. Following one study, teacher centers listed in the research report as having staffs who suggested procedural changes for social studies inservices workshops were closed, and their staffs blacklisted. Moral dilemmas often arise because the researcher makes unwarranted assumptions based on previous experience without taking the effort to learn whether they are culturally appropriate.

Possible Solutions to Methodological Problems

Three suggestions for the researcher who is entering a new culture for research are (a) learn as much about that culture as possible, including the language, before conceptualizing the study, (b) use a variety of strategies and sources, and (c) involve local people in the process of inquiry.

It is important to have some grasp of cultural norms, taboos, and expectations in order to ease entry and gain acceptance. One way to identify a research problem is to begin the study with general data collection about the development of social studies and the concerns and issues of those people involved in its diffusion. The problem will be grounded in the realities of social studies in that country, and the research will contribute to a real problem as opposed to an imposed problem. The flexibility of an emerging research design can lead to more valid findings.

Multiple data-collection strategies, such as interviews, observations, documentary analysis, and unobtrusive measures, as well as multiple data sources from all stakeholding audiences, can provide triangulation of data and findings and make it more likely that the study will be worthwhile. Open-ended questionnaires tested with a small sample can be an important first step in designing survey instruments.

Local people can provide insight and feedback that is invaluable to the researcher. The novice researcher can benefit from selecting an informal advisory council of local people who are involved in social studies in different ways (such as a curriculum developer, a teacher, an inspector, a student, a researcher). They can advise the researcher on other people to talk to in

generating possible research topics, identify potential problems, recommend data collection strategies, help the researcher to gain access or clearances, review preliminary findings, and legitimate the data collection in the eyes of other people important to the study.

Research on social studies in Africa is a challenge. Potentially, there is no more powerful subject in the African curriculum than social studies. Much work on many problems is desperately needed. The contributions that researchers may make include shaping the development of social studies and perhaps the future for millions of African children.

References

Adejunmobi, S. A. (1976). The relative popularity of social studies and history in the lower classes of Oyo state secondary school. *West African Journal of Education, 22*(3), 377–388.

Adejunmobi, S. A. (1981). Problems and issues in the teaching of social studies with particular reference to teacher training colleges. In Nigerian Educational Research Council (Ed.), *The concept and scope of social studies education* (pp. 54–60). Ibadan: Onibonoje.

Adekeye, A. (1982). *Teaching social studies in Nigerian colleges.* Ife, Nigeria: University of Ife Press.

Adekeye, R. (1979). *The problems of teaching social studies in primary institutions in the Zaria local government area.* Unpublished bachelor's thesis, Ahmadu Bello University, Zaria, Nigeria.

Adeniyi, O. (1982). *Attitudes of students towards social studies in Ilorin local government area Kware State.* Unpublished master's thesis, Ahmadu Bello University, Zaria, Nigeria.

Adeyemi, M. B. (1985). *Secondary school teachers' perceptions of the instructional goals of social studies in Oyo State of Nigeria.* Unpublished doctoral dissertation, Indiana University.

Adeyemi, M. B. (1987). *A replication of Barth's cross cultural study on the preferences of teacher-candidates toward social studies.* Unpublished manuscript.

Adeyoyin, F. A. (1981). *The dynamics of teaching social studies at the grade two teachers' college level in Lagos State.* Unpublished doctoral dissertation, University of Lagos, Lagos, Nigeria.

African Social Studies Programme. (1985). *Report of the seminar of the coordinating committee of the ASSP.* Nairobi, Kenya: Author.

Amodu, L. (1984). *The relationship between pupil attitude and achievement in secondary school social studies education.* Unpublished master's thesis, University of Lagos, Lagos, Nigeria.

Ate, J., Akai, A., Bamindah, N., Lele, I., & Okai, A. (1983). *Evaluation of the success of the B.Ed (social studies) programme: A follow-up of graduates and their present jobs.* Unpublished bachelor's thesis, Admadu Bello University, Zaria, Nigeria.

Ayanaba, M. H. (1975). *The relationship of curriculum guidance and teacher effectiveness in primary school social studies.* Unpublished master's thesis, University of Ibadan, Ibadan, Nigeria.

Ayo, E., & Fwa, P. C. (1984). *Evaluation of learning outcomes in social studies in Jos and Misau areas of Nigeria.* Unpublished bachelor's thesis, Ahmadu Bello University, Zaria, Nigeria.

Barth, J. L. (1986). A comparison of Nigerian and Egyptian university students' responses to the Barth/Shermis Social Studies Preference Scale. *African Social Studies Forum, 1*(1), 24–32.

Barth, J. L., & Norris, W. R. (1976). A study examining the preferences of teacher candidates from different cultures toward social studies. *Nigeria Educational Forum, 2*(2), 53–58.

Dahunsi, A. (1979). *A survey of social studies resources in public and private schools in Ibadan, Ono state.* Unpublished masters' thesis, University of Ibadan, Ibadan, Nigeria.

Dondo, J. M. C., Krystall, A., & Thomas, D. (1974). *Report of an evaluation of the African Social Studies Programme.* Nairobi: African Social Studies Programme.

DuBey, O. C. (1983, September). *Teacher education in social studies: The problem of significant others.* Paper presented at the conference of the National Curriculum Association, University of Jos, Jos, Nigeria.

Ekpunobi, E. C. (1983, March). *Conceptualization, stereotypism and national integration in Nigerian social studies materials.* Paper presented at the Social Studies of Nigeria National Annual Conference.

Enaohwo, J. O. (1982). Staff constraints to the teaching of social studies in Nigerian secondary schools. In E. N. E. Udoh (Ed.), *Social studies for the eighties* (Report of the 1981 Annual Seminar of the Social Studies Association of Nigeria), pp. 77–86.

Esiwe, H. O. D. (1974). *The teaching of the social studies in Zaria town of North Central state.* Unpublished PGDE dissertation, Ahmadu Bello University, Zaria, Nigeria.

Funtua, L. I. (1979). *Towards formulating NCE social studies programme.* Unpublished master's thesis, Ahmadu Bello University, Zaria, Nigeria.

Funtua, L. I. (1980). Lack of trained personnel to teach social studies, especially at teachers' colleges. In Nigerian Educational Research Council (Ed.), *Social studies: Teaching issues and problems* (pp. 45–53). Benin, Nigeria: Ethiope.

Guri, U. A. (1979). *A product evaluation of the social studies programme in Kano state teacher training colleges.* Unpublished master's thesis, Ahmadu Bello University, Zaria, Nigeria.

Hamnett, M. P. & Brislin, R. W. (1980). *Research in culture learning.* Honolulu: East-West Center.

Hara, U. J. L. (1983). *The teaching of social studies in the senior primary schools in Malawi.* Unpublished thesis for a diploma in educational studies, University of Newcastle upon Tyne.

Kabau, I. N. (1983). *Teaching of social studies: Instructional problems facing teachers in the pilot primary schools of Central Province of Kenya.* Unpublished master's thesis, University of Nairobi.

Kenya Institute of Education. (1983). *Primary education project: Social studies evaluation* (Rep. No. 1). Nairobi: Author.

Kumar, K., (Ed.). (1979). *Bonds without bondage: explorations in transcultural interactions.* Honolulu: University Press of Hawaii.

Lafene, J. E. (1977). *Pioneering a social studies course in an ATC.* Paper presented at the National Social Studies Conference, Zaria, Nigeria.

Lijembe, Z. A. (1983). *Leading problems of teaching the traditional social studies programme in primary schools in Kakamega as conceived by teachers.* Unpublished master's thesis, University of Nairobi.

Lolo, D. (1977). *The problems of teaching social studies in upper classes of some selected primary schools in Kaduna Capital Territory.* Unpublished bachelor's thesis, Ahmadu Bello University, Zaria, Nigeria.

Makumba, P. (1983). *The degree of preparedness of the Kenyan primary schools in Kakamega District to receive and implement the new social studies programme.* Unpublished master's thesis, University of Nairobi.

Merryfield, M. M. (1985). The challenge of cross-cultural evaluation: Some views from the field. In Michael Quinn Patton (Ed.), *Culture and evaluation* (pp. 3–17). San Francisco: Jossey-Bass.

Merryfield, M. M. (1986a). Curricular reform in Kenyan primary schools: A comparison of classroom instruction in social studies with geography, history, and civics. *Kenya Journal of Education, 3*(1), 64–84.

Merryfield, M. M. (1986b). *Social studies education and national development in selected African nations.* Unpublished doctoral dissertation, Indiana University.

Misoya, D. E. (1982). *The teaching of environmental studies in primary schools in Malawi.* Unpublished thesis for a diploma in educational studies, University of Newcastle upon Tyne.

Morrow, S. (1985). *Teaching history in Malawi's secondary schools: the problem of resources* (Paper No. 14, History Seminar Series). Zombia, Malawi: University of Malawi, Chancellor College, History Department.

O'Barr, W. M., Spain, D. H., & Tessler, M. A. (Eds.). (1973). *Survey research in Africa.* Evanston, IL: Northwestern University Press.

Obebe, B. J. (1981). *An assessment of knowledge of social studies content and method of graduating elementary teachers (grade II) of Lagos and Ondo states, Nigeria.* Unpublished doctoral dissertation, Columbia University Teachers College, New York.

Odada, M. (1988). *The state of social studies education, Uganda.* Unpublished paper written for the African Social Studies Programme.

Ogundare, S. F. (1981). *Investigation-oriented instructional approaches in the Nigerian primary school social studies.* Paper presented at the conference of the Curriculum Organization of Nigeria, University of Jos.

Ogunsanya, M. (1982). Cognitive responses of pupils to the language of teaching social studies in primary schools in Oyo state. In N. E. Udoh (Ed.), *Social Studies for the Eighties* (Report of the 1981 Annual Seminar of the Social Studies Association of Nigeria), pp. 142–154.

Okoh, G. A. (1979). *Obstacles surrounding the teaching of integrated social studies in Ife Division secondary schools.* Unpublished master's thesis, University of Ife, Ile-Ife, Nigeria.

Onyabe, V. O. (1979). Social studies in Nigeria. In H. D. Mehlinger & J. L. Tucker (Eds.), *Teaching social studies in other nations* (pp. 59–75). Washington, DC: National Council for the Social Studies.

Orimoloye, P. (1983). *Social studies educators' perspectives on citizenship education in primary and secondary schools in Oyo State, Nigeria.* Unpublished doctoral dissertation, Michigan State University.

Oshungbohun, M. O. (1984). *A critical analysis of instructional resources for the teaching of secondary social studies in selected secondary schools in Lagos State, Nigeria.* Unpublished master's thesis, University of Lagos, Lagos, Nigeria.

Osindi, A. O. (1982). *Limitations for effective social studies teaching in the Kissi primary schools.* Unpublished master's thesis, University of Nairobi.

Patton, M. Q. (Ed.). (1985). *Culture and evaluation.* San Francisco: Jossey-Bass.

Salawu, A. (1982). *An investigation into the problems of teaching social studies in secondary grammar schools in Ibadan, Oyo, state.* Unpublished master's thesis, University of Ibadan, Ibadan, Nigeria.

Shiundu, J. (1980). *The status of social studies in primary education in Kenya: Implications for the new integrated social studies programme.* Unpublished master's thesis, University of Nairobi.

Sunal, C. S., Gaba, B. B., & Osa, O. (1987). Citizenship education in the primary school: Perceptions of Nigerian teachers. *Theory and Research in Social Education, 15*(2), 115–131.

Tamakloe, E. K. (1988). *A survey of the teaching of social studies in teacher training colleges in Ghana.* Unpublished manuscript.

Triandis, H. C., & Berry, J. W. (Eds.). (1980). *Handbook of cross-cultural psychology: Vol. 2. Methodology.* Boston: Allyn & Bacon.

White, C. S. (1982). A validation study of the Barth-Shermis Social Studies Preference Scale. *Theory and Research in Social Education, 10*(2), 1–20.

World Bank. (1987). *World development report 1987.* Washington, DC: Author.

Yahaya, S. (1979). *Attitudes of teachers towards social studies in Kano municipal area schools of Kano state.* Unpublished bachelor's thesis, Ahmadu Bello University Zaria, Nigeria.

INDEXES

SUBJECT INDEX